CHILD
DEVELOPMENT

Thirteenth Edition

JOHN W. SANTROCK
University of Texas at Dallas

Mc Graw Hill

Connect
Learn
Succeed™

The McGraw·Hill Companies

Connect
Learn
Succeed™

Published by McGraw-Hill, an imprint of The McGraw-Hill Companies, Inc., 1221 Avenue of the
Americas, New York, NY 10020. Copyright © 2011, 2009, 2007, 2004, 2001, 1996, 1992, 1989, 1987,
1982. All rights reserved. No part of this publication may be reproduced or distributed in any form or
by any means, or stored in a database or retrieval system, without the prior written consent of The
McGraw-Hill Companies, Inc., including, but not limited to, in any network or other electronic
storage or transmission, or broadcast for distance learning.

This book is printed on acid-free paper.

1 2 3 4 5 6 7 8 9 0 QDQ/QDQ 9 8 7 6 5 4 3 2 1 0

ISBN: 978-0-07-353208-0
MHID: 0-07-353208-8

Vice President Editorial: *Michael Ryan*
Publisher: *Mike Sugarman*
Senior Sponsoring Editor: *Allison McNamara*
Executive Marketing Manager: *Julia Flohr*
Marketing Manager: *Yasuko Okada*
Director of Development: *Dawn Groundwater*
Senior Developmental Editor: *Cara Labell*
Senior Project Manager: *Holly Irish*
Production Service: *Aaron Downey, Matrix Productions*
Manuscript Editor: *Janet Tilden*
Design Manager: *Laurie Entringer*
Text Designer: *Pam Verros*
Cover Designer: *Laurie Entringer*
Art Manager: *Robin Mouat*
Buyer II: *Tandra Jorgensen*
Composition: *9.5/12 Meridien Roman by Aptara®, Inc.*
Printing: *45# Pub Matte, Quad/Graphics, Dubuque, IA*

Credits: The credits section for this book begins on page 573 and is considered an extension of
the copyright page.

Library of Congress Cataloging-in-Publication Data
Santrock, John W.
    Child development : an introduction / John Santrock. — 13th ed.
        p. cm.
    Includes bibliographical references and index.
    ISBN 978-0-07-353208-0 (hardback)
  1. Child development. 2. Child psychology. I. Title.
    RJ131.S264 2010
    618.92—dc22

                                                                2010036055

The Internet addresses listed in the text were accurate at the time of publication. The inclusion of
a Web site does not indicate an endorsement by the authors or McGraw-Hill, and McGraw-Hill
does not guarantee the accuracy of the information presented at these sites.

www.mhhe.com

caring *connections*

The Quantum Opportunities Program

A downward trajectory is not inevitable for youth living in poverty (Carnegie Council on Adolescent Development, 1995). One potential positive path out of poverty for such youth is to become involved with a caring mentor. The Quantum Opportunities program, funded by the Ford Foundation, was a four-year, year-round mentoring effort (Carnegie Council on Adolescent Development, 1995). The students involved in this program were entering the ninth grade at a high school with high rates of poverty, were members of ethnic minority groups, and came from families that received public assistance. Each day for four years, mentors provided sustained support, guidance, and concrete assistance to their students.

The Quantum program required students to participate in (1) academic-related activities outside school hours, including reading, writing, math, science, and social studies; peer tutoring, and computer skills training; (2) community service projects, including tutoring elementary school students, cleaning up the neighborhood, and volunteering in hospitals, nursing homes, and libraries; and (3) cultural enrichment and personal development activities, including life skills training, college preparation, and job planning. In exchange for their commitment to the program, students were offered financial incentives that encouraged participation, completion, and long-range planning. A stipend of $1.33 was given to students for each hour they participated in these activities. For every 100 hours of education, ser-

Children participating in the Quantum Opportunities program at the Carver Center in Washington, DC.

vice, or development activities, students received a bonus of $100. The average cost per participant was $10,600 for the four years, which is one-half the cost of one year in prison.

An evaluation of the Quantum project compared the mentored students with a nonmentored control group. Sixty-three percent of the mentored students graduated from high school, but only 42 percent of the control group did; 42 percent of the mentored students were enrolled in college, but only 16 percent of the control group were. Furthermore, control-group students were twice as likely as the mentored students to receive food stamps or welfare, and they had more arrests. Such programs clearly have the potential to overcome the intergenerational transmission of poverty and its negative outcomes. While the original Quantum Opportunities program no longer exists, the Eisenhower Foundation (2010) recently began replicating the Quantum program in Alabama, South Carolina, New Hampshire, Virginia, Mississippi, Oregon, Maryland, and Washington, DC.

These research results confirm what we learned in Chapter 16: the most effective programs to discourage dropping out of high school provide tutoring and mentoring, emphasize the creation of caring environments and relationships, and offer community-service opportunities. This research also reinforces the philosophy that goal-setting (such as planning for college and/or a career) is an integral part of achievement.

connecting with careers

Rodney Hammond, Health Psychologist

In describing his college experiences, Rodney Hammond recalls, "When I started as an undergraduate at the University of Illinois at Champaign-Urbana, I hadn't decided on my major. But to help finance my education, I took a part-time job in a child development research program sponsored by the psychology department. There, I observed inner-city children in settings designed to enhance their learning. I saw firsthand the contribution psychology can make, and I knew I wanted to be a psychologist" (American Psychological Association, 2003, p. 26).

Rodney Hammond went on to obtain a doctorate in school and community psychology with a focus on children's development. For a number of years, he trained clinical psychologists at Wright State University in Ohio and directed a program to reduce violence in ethnic minority youth. There, he and his associates taught at-risk

Rodney Hammond, talking with an adolescent about strategies for coping with stress and avoiding risk-taking behaviors.

youth how to use social skills to effectively manage conflict and to recognize situations that could lead to violence. Today, Hammond is Director of Violence Prevention at the Centers for Disease Control and Prevention in Atlanta. Hammond says that if you are interested in people and problem solving, psychology is a wonderful way to put these together. (Source: American Psychological Association, 2003, pp. 26–27.)

64% of developmental psychology instructors state that fostering critical thinking is a top goal of their course.

Reflect *Your Own Personal Journey of Life*

- If and when you become a parent, how would you evaluate the benefits and drawbacks of allowing your 7-year-old to play for a soccer team in a competitive league in your town or city?

> *Child Development* helps students develop understandings of the applications of developmental psychology through examples in the text, *Caring Connections* and *Career Connections*. They are also prompted to think about how psychology applies to their own lives through *Reflect: Your Personal Journey of Life* questions.

WITHDRAWN

With special appreciation to
my wife, Mary Jo; my children, Tracy and Jennifer;
and my grandchildren, Jordan, Alex, and Luke

about the author

John W. Santrock

John Santrock received his Ph.D. from the University of Minnesota in 1973. He taught at the University of Charleston and the University of Georgia before joining the program in Psychology and Human Development at the University of Texas at Dallas, where he currently teaches a number of undergraduate courses.

John Santrock (center) teaching an undergraduate psychology course.

John has been a member of the editorial boards of *Child Development* and *Developmental Psychology*. His research on father custody is widely cited and used in expert witness testimony to promote flexibility and alternative considerations in custody disputes. John also has authored these exceptional McGraw-Hill texts: *Psychology* (7th edition), *Children* (11th edition), *Adolescence* (13th edition), *Life-Span Development* (13th edition), and *Educational Psychology* (5th edition).

For many years John was involved in tennis as a player, a teaching professional, and a coach of professional tennis players. He has been married for more than 35 years to his wife, Mary Jo, who is a Realtor. He has two daughters—Tracy, who also is a Realtor, and Jennifer, who is a medical sales specialist He has one granddaughter, Jordan, age 19, and two grandsons, Alex, age 6, and Luke, age 4. In the last decade, John also has spent time painting expressionist art.

brief contents

contents

SECTION 3   COGNITION AND LANGUAGE   168

SECTION 4 SOCIOEMOTIONAL DEVELOPMENT 286

SECTION 5   **SOCIAL CONTEXTS OF DEVELOPMENT   392**

expert consultants

Children's development has become an enormous, complex field, and no single author, or even several authors, can possibly keep up with all of the rapidly changing content in the many different areas of child development. To solve this problem, author John Santrock sought the input of leading experts about content in all age periods of human development. These experts provided detailed evaluations and recommendations in their area(s) of expertise. Their biographies and photographs follow.

Kirby Deater-Deckard Kirby Deater-Deckard is a leading expert on biological foundations of development, heredity-environment interaction, and parenting. He currently is a professor and the director of graduate programs in psychology at Virginia Polytechnic Institute and State University. Earlier he was a professor at the University of Oregon. Dr. Deater-Deckard obtained his Ph.D. from the University of Virginia. His research focuses on the development of individual differences in childhood and adolescence, with emphasis on gene-environment processes and parenting. He has written papers and book chapters in the areas of developmental psychology and psychopathology, co-edited *Gene-Environment Processes in Social Behaviors and Relationships* and *Immigrant Families*, and authored *Parenting Stress*. Dr. Deater-Deckard is currently on the editorial boards of a number of research journals, including *Infant and Child Development, Journal of Family Psychology,* and *Parenting: Science and Practice*. He also currently is the recipient of an NICHD grant to study maternal self-regulation and harsh parenting.

"The narrative is comprehensive with respect to evolutionary and genetic perspectives. The perspective is balanced, with fair presentation and treatment of the key areas. Inclusion of G × E, G × G, and epigenetic perspectives is cutting edge and important. . . . The language and use of examples is pitched just right and is highly accurate without sacrificing simplicity. A wide range of undergraduates will be able to understand this chapter [Chapter 2, "Biological Beginnings"], including those who are biology phobic." —**Kirby Deater-Deckhard,** *Virginia Tech*

Tiffany Field Tiffany Field is one of the world's leading experts on prenatal development, birth, and infant development. She currently is director of the Touch Research Institute (which she founded in 1992) in the Department of Pediatrics at the University of Miami School of Medicine. Dr. Field obtained her Ph.D. from the University of Massachusetts, Amherst. She has been awarded the Boyd McCandless Distinguished Young Scientist Award from the American Psychological Association, an NIMH Research Scientist Development Award, and an NIH Senior Research Scientist Award (1991–present). Dr. Field has served as an associate editor of *Infant Mental Health Journal* and on the editorial boards for *Child Development, Developmental Psychology,* and a number of other leading research journals. She has published over 400 journal articles and more than 20 books, including *The Amazing Infant* (2005) and *Massage Therapy* (2005). Her pioneering research on massage therapy is now widely practiced in NICU units to enhance the growth and development of preterm infants. Earlier in her career she founded preschool programs at the University of Miami School of Medicine and the University of Miami Coral Gables campus.

"The chapter on prenatal development and birth [Chapter 3] by John Santrock is a nice update to the twelfth edition. I think this is a great chapter." —**Tiffany Field,** *University of Miami*

Scott Johnson Scott Johnson is one of the world's leading experts on perceptual and cognitive development in infancy. He currently is a professor of psychology at UCLA. Dr. Johnson obtained his Ph.D. from Arizona State University and then did postdoctoral work in the Center for Visual Science at the University of Rochester. His research examines perceptual, cognitive, social, cortical, and motor development, with a focus on visual attention, electrophysiology, and learning mechanisms. Dr. Johnson is currently an associate editor of the journal *Cognition* and has served on the editorial boards of *Infancy, Infant Behavior & Development, Developmental Psychology, British Journal of Developmental Psychology,* and *Frontiers in Neuroscience*. His most recent edited book is *Neoconstructivism: The New Science of Cognitive Development* (2010, in press). Previous co-edited books include *Neurobiology of Infant Vision* and *Prenatal Development of Postnatal Functions*.

"I think the chapter [Chapter 5, "Motor, Sensory, and Perceptual Development"] does an admirable job sorting out a very complex picture. The focus on dynamic systems and ecological theories was just right, in my view. Each theory was described well and at a level consistent with the descriptions of empirical work. I liked how the nature-nurture question was brought in toward the end to provide additional context." —**Scott Johnson,** *UCLA*

Joan Grusec Joan Grusec is one of the world's leading experts on family processes and on emotional development. She currently is professor of psychology at the University of Toronto. Dr. Grusec obtained her Ph.D. from Stanford University. Her longstanding research interests have focused on the influence of parenting on children's socialization, determinants of parenting practices, and emotional development. Dr. Grusec has co-edited (with Leon Kuczynski) *Parenting and Children's Internalization of Values* and co-edited (with Paul Hastings) *Handbook of Socialization*. She also co-authored (with Daphne Bugental) the chapter "Socialization Processes" in the most recent edition of *Handbook of Child Psychology*. In the forthcoming *Annual Review of Psychology* for 2011 (Vol 62), she wrote a chapter titled "Socialization Processes in the Family: Social and Emotional Development." In addition, she has been an associate editor of *Developmental Psychology*.

"What is very evident in this chapter [Chapter 10, "Emotional Development"] is the author's knowledge of the developmental literature and his awareness of issues and challenges in understanding emotional development. This comes across very clearly. In addition, the writing is engaging and ideas are clearly presented. . . . I do have very great admiration for John Santrock's ability to reduce the complexity of emotional development to a very readable state without oversimplifying the issues, as well as enforcing for students that all assertions must be based on good research evidence." —**Joan Grusec,** *University of Toronto*

 **Velma LaPoint** Velma LaPoint is a leading expert on diversity and children's development. She currently is professor of child development in the Department of Human Development and Psychoeducational Studies, School of Education, at Howard University in Washington, DC. Dr. LaPoint teaches undergraduate and graduate students courses on diverse youth, youth placed at risk, youth and consumer culture, and social policies influencing youth and family development. Her research focuses on (a) school reform, academic achievement, and college/career readiness with a focus on science, technology, engineering, and mathematics (STEM) careers among diverse African American public school students; (b) parenting strategies and child academic achievement/social competence among diverse African American families; and (c) a culturally responsive weight management intervention project for African American female college freshman students. Dr. LaPoint has authored/co-authored journal articles, book chapters, and other reports in *New Directions in Evaluation, Journal of Black Psychology, Encyclopedia of Cross Cultural School Psychology, Monographs of the Society for Research in Child Development,* and *National Association of Secondary School Principals.* She has provided commentary on youth development issues to venues such as *The New York Times, Washington Post, Boston Globe,* and *Christian Science Monitor.*

"Dr. Santrock's exciting updated textbook has new information on child development research, policy, practice, and advocacy. Diversity of topics and photographs is represented in areas such as socioeconomic status, ethnicity, race, gender, sexual orientation, religion, and geographical space nationally and globally. The textbook comes 'alive for students as a learning tool' in its narratives and photographs. Dr. Santrock's text has a competitive advantage over many other college textbooks as a learning tool in the ever-changing world of educational media." —**Velma LaPoint,** *Howard University*

 **Jeffrey Lochman** Jeffrey Lochman is a leading expert on perceptual and cognitive development. He currently is a professor of psychology at Tulane University in New Orleans and formerly was department chair there. Dr. Lachman received his Ph.D. in child psychology from the Institute of Child Development at University of Minnesota. His research focuses on perception-action development and early cognition. He is currently editor of the leading journal, *Child Development,* has also served on the editorial boards of *Developmental Psychology,* and has been a member of the National Institutes of Health Motor Function, Speech and Rehabilitation Study Section. His research has been funded by the National Science Foundation and the National Institutes of Health.

"This is a well-written overview of motor, sensory, and perceptual development, which introduces students to key developmental milestones and theoretical perspectives in this field. Strengths of the chapter include the clear exposition of material, its theoretical focus, and the ways in which theory is integrated with findings and practice. . . . I believe students will receive an excellent introduction to contemporary research and theory on motor and perceptual development by reading this chapter [Chapter 5, "Motor, Sensory, and Perceptual Development"]." —**Jeffrey Lochman,** *Tulane University*

 **Celia Brownell** Celia Brownell is a leading expert on early socioemotional development. She currently is a professor in the Department of Psychology at the University of Pittsburgh. She obtained her Ph.D. from the Institute of Child Development at the University of Minnesota. Her research explores the early development of cooperation, sharing, and empathic responsiveness, with a special interest in prosocial behavior among infant peers. Dr. Brownell currently is an associate editor of *Infancy,* the official journal of the International Society for Infant Studies, and is on the editorial boards of *Child Development and Social Development.* She co-edited the recent volume of *Socioemotional Development in the Toddler Years: Transitions and Transformations.* Dr. Brownell has also been one of the investigators on the long-running NICHD Study of Early Child Care and Youth Development.

"These chapters are impressively up to date, reflecting new looks in each of the areas, from the neuroscience of emotional development, to cultural contexts as contributors to patterns of childrearing and family functioning, to adolescent romantic relationships and bullying/victimization. The new research is highly relevant to the text material and central to the field of child development. As a researcher-active instructor, I very much appreciate the frequent use of concrete research examples to make particular points and to illustrate how developmental science is actually done. The use of research experts is laudable, and choice of experts is excellent—they are all leading figures in their respective areas." —**Celia Brownell,** *University of Pittsburgh*

 **Catherine McBride-Chang** Catherine McBride-Chang is a leading expert on language development. She is currently a professor and director of the Developmental Centre at The Chinese University of Hong Kong. She obtained her Ph.D. in developmental psychology from the University of Southern California and was a postdoctoral fellow in the psychology department at Florida State University. Dr. McBride-Chang's research especially focuses on literacy development across cultures. She is the author of more than 100 peer-reviewed articles and two books. She also currently is an associate editor of *Developmental Psychology* and *Journal of Research in Reading.* A Fellow of the Association for Psychological Science, she serves on the editorial boards of six other education and psychology journals.

"I think you have covered all the bases and have some nice features in this text. It is quite comprehensive and useful." —**Catherine McBride-Chang,** *Chinese University of Hong Kong*

 **Shelly Hymel** Shelley Hymel is a leading expert on socioemotional development and peer relations. She currently is a professor in the Faculty of Education at the University of British Columbia. Among her many current activities are being a member of the management committee of the Human Early Learning Partnership (an interdisciplinary research unit aimed at optimizing children's development through early intervention), serving as one of the team leaders for PREVNet (a National Centre of Excellence New Initiative focused on promoting relationships and eliminating violence), and being a regional hub director for the Canadian Prevention Science Knowledge Cluster (funded by the Social Sciences and Humanities Research Council of Canada). In collaboration with Dr. S. Swearer, she has established the Bullying Research Network (BRNET), and has co-edited a unique knowledge translation effort—a peer-reviewed special issue of the online magazine www.education.com. Dr. Hymel has published extensively in the area of socioemotional development and peer relations (both nationally and internationally) and works regularly with children and youth experiencing social difficulties, as well as with schools and school districts that want to address the social aspects of learning.

"There is much to commend here. I like the structure of the book with clearly stated goals, "research interludes," and an ongoing consideration of applications as well as a focus on culture and diversity. . . . Major areas of inquiry within the research literature are considered and well summarized." —**Shelley Hymel,** *University of British Columbia*

 **Cynthia Stifter** Cynthia Stifter is a leading expert on temperament, self-regulation, and family processes. She currently is a professor of Human Development at the Pennsylvania State University. She obtained her Ph.D. from the University of Maryland. Her research focuses on how the temperament dimensions of approach and withdrawal in infancy interact with physiology, parental responsivity, and self-regulation to predict behavior problems. Dr. Stifter is currently conducting research relating temperament and parenting to rapid weight gain in infancy and on the role of positive affect in the physical health of young children. She has authored numerous publications on infant, toddler, and preschool development, including the subjects such as the emergence of emotion self-regulation, the effect of emotion regulation on behavioral control, emotion socialization skills of parents and child care workers, and the psychobiology of temperament. Dr. Stifter is currently an associate editor of *Child Development*, and has served on a number of other editorial boards and grant review panels.

"I liked the organization of the chapter [Chapter 10, "Emotional Development"]. I felt that John Santrock covered the most salient points in this developmental area and used current research to emphasize the importance of these concepts/points." —**Cynthia Stifter,** *Pennsylvania State University*

Making Connections . . . From My Classroom to *Child Development* to You

Having taught two or more undergraduate courses in developmental psychology—child development, adolescence, and life-span development—every year across four decades, I'm always looking for ways to improve my course and *Child Development*. Just as McGraw-Hill looks to those who teach the child development course for input, each year I ask the students in my undergraduate developmental courses to tell me what they like about the course and the text, and what they think could be improved. What have my students told me lately about my course and text? Students said that highlighting connections among the different aspects of children's development would help them to better understand the concepts. As I thought about this, it became clear that a *connections* theme would provide a systematic, integrative approach to the course material. I used this theme to shape my current goals for my course, which, in turn, influence the main goals of this text, as follows:

1. **Connecting with today's students** To help students *learn* about child development more effectively
2. **Connecting research to what we know about children's development** To provide students with the best and most recent *theory and research* in the world today about each of the periods of child development
3. **Connecting development processes** To guide students in making *developmental connections* across different points in child development
4. **Connecting development to real life** To help students understand ways to *apply* content about child development to the real world and improve people's lives, and to motivate students to think deeply about *their own personal journey through life* and better understand who they were, are, and will be

Connecting with Today's Students

My students often report development courses to be challenging due to the amount of material covered. To help today's students focus on the key ideas, the Learning Goals System I developed for *Child Development* provides extensive learning connections throughout the chapters. The learning system connects the chapter-opening outline, learning goals for the chapter, mini–chapter maps that open each main section of the chapter, **Review, Connect, and Reflect** at the end of each main section, and the chapter summary at the end of each chapter.

The learning system keeps the key ideas in front of the student from the beginning to the end of the chapter. The main headings of each chapter correspond to the learning goals, which are presented in the chapter-opening spread. Mini–chapter maps that link up with the learning goals are presented at the beginning of each major section in the chapter.

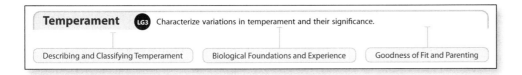

Then, at the end of each main section of a chapter, the learning goal is repeated in **Review, Connect, and Reflect,** which prompts students to review the key topics in the section, connect these topics to existing knowledge, and relate what they learned to their own personal journey through life. **Reach Your Learning Goals,** at the end of the chapter, guides students through the bulleted

Emotional Development

Exploring Emotion	**LG1** Discuss basic aspects of emotion.
What Are Emotions?	• Emotion is feeling, or affect, that occurs when people are engaged in interactions that are important to them, especially those that influence their well-being. Emotions can be classified as positive or negative. Darwin described the evolutionary basis of emotions, and today psychologists stress that emotions, especially facial expressions of emotions, have a biological foundation. Facial expressions of emotion are similar across cultures, but display rules are not culturally universal. Biological evolution endowed humans to be emotional, but culture and relationships with others provide diversity in emotional experiences.
A Functionalist View of Emotions	• The functionalist view of emotion emphasizes the importance of contexts and relationships in emotion. For example, when parents induce a positive mood in their child, the child is more likely to follow the parents' directions. In this view, goals are involved in emotions in a variety of ways, and the goal's specific nature can affect the individual's experience of a given emotion.
Emotional Competence	• Saarni argues that becoming emotionally competent involves developing a number of skills such as being aware of one's emotional states, discerning others' emotions, adaptively coping with negative emotions, and understanding the role of emotions in relationships.

chapter review, connecting with the chapter outline/learning goals at the beginning of the chapter and the *Review, Connect, and Reflect* material at the end of major chapter sections.

Connecting Research to What We Know about Children's Development

Over the years, it has been important for me to include the most up-to-date research available. I continue this tradition in this 13th edition by looking closely at specific areas of research, involving experts in related fields, and updating research throughout. **Connections Through Research,** formerly called *Research*

connecting through research

How Does Theory of Mind Differ in Children with Autism?

Approximately 1 in 150 children is estimated to have some sort of autism spectrum disorder (National Autism Association, 2010). Autism can usually be diagnosed by the age of 3 years, and sometimes earlier. Children with autism show a number of behaviors different from children their age, including deficits in social interaction and communication as well as repetitive behaviors or interests. They often show indifference toward others, in many instances preferring to be alone and showing more interest in objects than people. It now is accepted that autism is linked to genetic and brain abnormalities (Deeley & Murphy, 2009; Glessner & others, 2009).

Children and adults with autism have difficulty in social interactions. These deficits are generally greater than deficits in children the same mental age with mental retardation (Baron-Cohen, 2009, 2011). Researchers have found that children with autism have difficulty in developing a theory of mind, especially in understanding others' beliefs and emotions (Bertoglio & Hendren, 2009; Peterson & others, 2009). Although children with autism tend to do poorly reasoning in false-belief tasks (Peterson, 2005), they can perform much better on reasoning tasks requiring an understanding of physical causality.

In relation to theory of mind, however, it is important to consider the effects of individual variations in the abilities of children with autism (Harris, 2006). Children with autism are not a homogeneous group, and some have less severe social and communication problems than others. Thus, it is not surprising that children who have less severe forms of autism do better than those who have more severe forms of the disorder on some theory of mind tasks. For example, higher-functioning children with autism show reasonable progress in understanding others' desires (Harris, 2006). A further important consideration in thinking about autism and theory of mind is that children with autism might have

A young boy with autism. *What are some characteristics of children who are autistic? What are some deficits in their theory of mind?*

difficulty in understanding others' beliefs and emotions not solely due to theory of mind deficits but to other aspects of cognition such as problems in focusing attention or some general intellectual impairment (Renner, Grofer Klinger, & Klinger, 2006). Some recent theories of autism suggest that weaknesses in executive functioning may be related to the problems experienced by those with autism in performing theory of mind tasks. Other theories have pointed out that typically developing individuals process information by extracting the big picture, whereas those with autism process information in a very detailed, almost obsessive way. It may be that in autism, a number of different but related deficits lead to social cognitive deficits (Rajendran & Mitchell, 2007).

in Child Development, describes a study or program to illustrate how research in child development is conducted and how it influences our understanding of the discipline. Topics range from "Do Children Conceived Through In Vitro Fertilization Show Significantly Different Outcomes in Adolescence?" (Chapter 2) to "How Can We Study Newborns' Perception?" (Chapter 5) to "How Does Theory of Mind Differ in Children with Autism?" (Chapter 7).

The tradition of obtaining detailed, extensive input from a number of leading experts in different areas of child development also continues in this edition. Biographies and photographs of the leading experts in the field of child development appear on pages xiii to xv and the chapter-by-chapter highlights of new research content will be described shortly. Finally, the research discussions have been updated in every period and topic. I expended every effort to make this edition of *Child Development* as contemporary and up-to-date as possible. To that end, there are more than 800 citations from 2009, 2010, and 2011 in the text.

Connecting Development Processes

Too often we forget or fail to notice the many connections from one point in child development to another. I have substantially increased these connections made in the text narrative. I also created two new features to help students connect topics across the stages of child development. *Developmental Connections,* which appears multiple times in each chapter, points readers to where the topic is discussed in a previous, current, or subsequent chapter. This feature highlights links across topics of development *and* connections among biological, cognitive, and socioemotional processes. The key developmental processes are typically discussed in isolation from each other, and so students often fail to see their connections. Included in *Developmental Connections* is a brief description of the backward or forward connection. For example, consider the rapidly increasing interest in the field of developmental cognitive neuroscience that focuses on connections among development, cognitive processes, and the brain. This topic is initially presented in Chapter 1, "Introduction," and then highlighted again in various chapters, especially Chapter 4, "Physical Development and Health."

Furthermore, a new *Connect* question has been added to the section of self-reviews—*Review, Connect, and Reflect*—so students can practice making connections among topics. For example, in Chapter 9, students are asked to connect what they learned in Chapter 5 about the effect of culture on motor development to what they just read in Chapter 8 about how different cultures have different concepts of intelligence.

Connecting Development to Real Life

In addition to helping students make research and developmental connections, *Child Development* shows the important connections among the concepts discussed and the real world. In recent years, students in my development course have increasingly told me that they want more of this type of information. In this edition, real-life connections are explicitly made in the chapter-opening vignette, *Caring Connections,* the coverage of diversity, and *Connecting With Careers.*

Each chapter begins with a story designed to increase students' interest and motivation to read the chapter. *Caring Connections,* formerly called *Caring for Children,* provides applied information about parenting, education, or health and well-being related to topics ranging from "From Waterbirth to Music Therapy" (Chapter 3), to "Parents, Coaches, and Children's Sports" (Chapter 5), to "Guiding Children's Creativity" (Chapter 8). As will be seen later in the chapter-by-chapter changes, I created a number of new *Caring Connections* interludes for this edition, as well as significantly updated and expanded applied topics in many areas of child development.

---

developmental **connection**

Biological Processes. Can specific genes be linked to specific environmental experience? Chapter 2, p. 69

---

developmental **connection**

Research Methods. How does a correlational study differ from an experimental study? Chapter 1, pp. 34–35

Connect

- In this section you learned that different cultures have different concepts of intelligence, and in Chapter 5 you learned about culture's effect on motor development. What do these findings have in common?

caring *connections*

Parents, Coaches, and Children's Sports

If parents do not become overinvolved in their children's sports participation, they can help their children build physical skills and emotional maturity—for example, by discussing how to deal with a difficult coach, how to cope with a tough loss, and how to put in perspective a poorly played game. Parents should monitor their children as they participate in sports for signs of developing stress. If the problems appear to be beyond the intuitive skills of a volunteer coach or parent, consultation with a counselor or clinician may be needed. Also, the parent should be sensitive to whether a particular sport is the best one for the child and whether the child can handle its competitive pressures.

Here are some guidelines that can benefit parents and coaches of children in sports (Women's Sports Foundation, 2001):

Do:

- Make sports fun; the more children enjoy sports, the more they will want to play.
- Remember that it is okay for children to make mistakes; it means they are trying.
- Allow children to ask questions about the sport, and discuss the sport in a calm, supportive manner.
- Show respect for the child's sports participation.
- Be positive and convince the child that he or she is making a good effort.
- Be a positive role model for the child in sports.

Don't:

- Yell or scream at the child.
- Condemn the child for poor play or continue to bring up failures long after they happen.
- Point out the child's errors in front of others.
- Expect the child to learn something immediately.
- Expect the child to become a pro.
- Ridicule or make fun of the child.
- Compare the child to siblings or to more talented children.
- Make sports all work and no fun.

What specific negative outcomes of sports involvement discussed earlier might these guidelines help to counteract?

What are some of the possible positive and negative aspects of children's participation in sports? What are some guidelines that can benefit parents and coaches of children in sports?

Child Development puts a strong emphasis on diversity. For a number of editions, this text has benefited from having one or more leading experts on diversity to ensure that it provides students with current, accurate, sensitive information related to diversity in children's development. The diversity expert for this edition of *Child Development* is Velma LaPoint, a professor at Howard University.

connecting with diversity

The Increased Diversity of Adopted Children and Adoptive Parents

A number of changes have characterized adoptive children and adoptive parents in the last three to four decades (Brodzinsky & Pinderhughes, 2002). In the first half of the 20th century, most U.S. adopted children were healthy, non-Latino White infants who were adopted at birth or soon after; however, in recent decades as abortion became legal and contraception increased, fewer of these infants became available for adoption. Increasingly, U.S. couples adopted a much wider diversity of children—from other countries, from other ethnic groups, children with physical and/or mental problems, and children who had been neglected or abused.

Changes also have characterized adoptive parents in the last three to four decades (Brodzinsky & Pindehughes, 2002). In the first half of the 20th century, most adoptive parents were from non-Latino White middle or upper socioeconomic status backgrounds who were married and did not have any type of disability. However, in recent decades, increased diversity has characterized adoptive parents. Many adoption agencies today have no income requirements for adoptive parents and now allow adults from a wide range of backgrounds to adopt children, including single adults, gay male and lesbian adults, and older adults.

Many fertile adults adopt children, but many more adoptive individuals are infertile. Based on what you read prior to this interlude, why might an infertile couple or individual decide to adopt rather than undergo reproductive technology procedures?

An increasing number of Hollywood celebrities are adopting children from developing countries. Actress Angelina Jolie (above) carries her adopted daughter Zahara with adopted sons Maddox and Pax walking beside them.

Diversity is discussed in every chapter, and Chapter 17, "Culture and Diversity," includes extensive material on the subject. Further, **Diversity Connections,** formerly called *Connecting With Diversity,* appears throughout the text, focusing on a diversity topic related to the material at that point in the chapter. Topics range from "The Increased Diversity of Adopted Children and Adoptive Parents" (Chapter 2) to "Cultural Variations in Guiding Infants' Motor Development" (Chapter 5) to "The Contexts of Ethnic Identity Development" (Chapter 11).

Next, **Connecting With Careers,** formerly called *Careers in Child Development,* profiles careers ranging from genetic counselor (Chapter 2) to toy designer (Chapter 7) to supervisor of gifted and talented education (Chapter 8), all of which require a knowledge of child development. The careers highlighted extend from the Careers Appendix in Chapter 1, which provides a comprehensive overview of careers to show students where knowledge of child development could lead them.

Finally, part of applying knowledge of child development to the real world is understanding how it impacts oneself. Accordingly, one of the goals of my child development course and this text is to motivate students to think deeply about their own journey of life. In reflecting about ways to encourage students to make personal connections to content in the text, I added a **Reflect: Your Own Personal Journey of Life** prompt in the end-of-section review. This question asks students to reflect on some aspect of the discussion in the section they have just read and connect it to their own life. For example, in Chapter 1, related to a discussion of the early-later experience issue in development in the section, students are asked,

Can you identify an early experience that you believe contributed in important ways to your development?

Can you identify a recent or current (later) experience that you think had (is having) a strong influence on your development?

Chapter-by-Chapter Changes

Following are the main chapter-by-chapter changes that were made in this new edition of *Child Development*.

Chapter 1: Introduction

- Extensive editing for improved student understanding
- New description of the life of 17-year-old Dolly Akter and her efforts to improve the lives of females in the slum where she lives in Dhaka, Bangladesh
- Expanded discussion of poverty and children, including updated statistics on the percentage of U.S. children under 18 years of age living in poverty (Federal Interagency Forum on Child and Family Statistics, 2008)
- Updated information about the Minnesota Family Investment Program (2009) including coverage of a current study that is examining the influence of specific family services on families at high risk for engaging in child maltreatment
- New section, "Biological, Cognitive, and Socioemotional Processes" (Diamond, 2009; Diamond, Casey, & Munakata, 2011)
- New description of the rapidly emerging fields of developmental cognitive neuroscience and developmental social neuroscience to illustrate the interface of biological, cognitive, and socioemotional processes (Diamond, Casey, & Munakata, 2011; Johnson, 2009)
- At the request of a number of instructors, reduction of material on Freud's theory
- New *Caring Connections* interlude: "Strategies for Parenting, Educating, and Interacting with Children Based on Erikson's Theory"
- Expanded coverage of Bronfenbrenner's contributions (Gauvain & Parke, 2010)

Chapter 2: Biological Beginnings

- Extensive updating of citations and research
- Inclusion of changes based on leading expert Kirby Deater-Deakard's recommendations
- Expanded discussion of criticisms of evolutionary psychology to include it being on a time scale that does not allow its empirical study
- New introductory material connecting the discussion of evolution and genetics
- New coverage of susceptibility and longevity genes (Marques, Markus, & Morris, 2010; Tacutu, Budovsky, & Fraifeld, 2010)
- New material on the concept of gene-gene interaction (Chen & others, 2009; Jylhava & others, 2009)
- Coverage of a recent within-family design of families with a biological child and an adopted child indicating only a slight trend in more externalized problems for adopted children (Glover & others, 2009)
- Description of epigenetic research on early rearing experiences and their alteration of gene expression with that expression being linked to later behavior (Pauli-Pott & others, 2009)
- Inclusion of information based on a recent research review of the main risk factors in the future health of babies born through assisted reproduction techniques (Basatemur & Sutcliffe, 2008)
- Updated and expanded discussion of heredity-environment interaction (Barry, Kochanska, & Philibert, 2008; Shen, 2009)
- New section and coverage of the concept of G × E, which involves the interaction of a specific measured variation in the DNA sequence and a specific

measured aspect of the environment (Cheok & others, 2009; Diamond, 2009; Risch & others, 2009)

- Discussion of a recent G × E interaction study on the gene 5-HTTLPR and how the short version of the gene likely serves a protective function in children's parental loss (Caspers & others, 2009)
- New coverage of the field of *pharmacogenetics* and how it reflects G × E. (Berlin, Paul, & Vesell, 2009; Lima & others, 2009)
- New final paragraph on the interaction of heredity and environment with a connection to the discussion of development as a co-construction of biology, culture, and the individual

Chapter 3: Prenatal Development and Birth

- Coverage of recent research indicating that both maternal diabetes and obesity place the fetus at risk for developing neural tube defects (McQuire, Dyson, & Renfrew, 2010; Yazdy & others, 2010)
- New description of the field of behavioral teratology
- New commentary about male fetuses being affected far more by teratogens than female fetuses
- New discussion of the effects of antidepressant use by pregnant women on their offspring, including recent research (Simoncelli, Martin, & Beard, 2010; Yonkers & others, 2009)
- Updated research on low-dose aspirin during pregnancy and child outcomes (Marret & others, 2010)
- Description of recent research on impaired memory development in children with FASD (Pei & others, 2008)
- Addition of cardiovascular problems to the list of problems of offspring whose mothers smoked during pregnancy (Feng & others, 2010)
- Description of recent research on maternal smoking and inattention/ hyperactivity in children (Knopik, 2009; Pinkhardt & others, 2009)
- Discussion of a recent study indicating that children with FASD have impaired math skills that are linked to a number of brain regions (Lebel & others, 2010)
- Inclusion of recent research on cocaine use during pregnancy and children's deficits in behavioral self-regulation and sustained attention (Ackerman, Riggins, & Black, 2010)
- Coverage of a recent study linking prenatal cocaine exposure to an increased likelihood of being in special education and receiving support services (Levine & others, 2008)
- Description of recent research on prenatal methamphetamine exposure and memory deficits in children (Lu & others, 2009)
- Updated and expanded material on the offspring of diabetic mothers (Eriksson, 2009; Gluck & others, 2009)
- New discussion of a recent study on maternal depression and its link to negative prenatal and birth outcomes (Diego & others, 2009)
- Coverage of recent research on the positive effects of massage therapy in reducing pain in pregnant women, alleviating prenatal depression in both parents, and improving their relationship (Field & others, 2008)
- Discussion of recent research on a home visitation program that reduced the incidence of low birth weight infants (Lee & others, 2009)
- Description of a recent study indicating positive benefits in Centering Pregnancy groups (Klima & others, 2009)
- Updated figures on the increasing number of preterm births in the United States (National Center for Health Statistics, 2009)

- Discussion of a recent research study indicating that exercise in pregnancy was linked to reduced risk of preterm birth (Hegaard & others, 2008)
- Updated research on hypnosis and childbirth (Abasi & others, 2010)
- Coverage of a recent study of the NNNS at 1 month of age and its ability to predict certain developmental outcomes at 4.5 years of age (Liu & others, 2010)
- Significant updating of research on the role of progestin in preventing preterm births, indicating the conditions under which progestin is most successful (da Fonseca & others, 2009; Norman & others, 2009; Rode & others, 2009)
- Discussion of a recent study on the percent of women with postpartum depression who seek help for their depression (McGarry & others, 2009)
- Coverage of a recent research review of the interaction difficulties of depressed mothers and their infants (Field, 2010)
- New *Connecting with Careers* profile: "Diane Sanford, Clinical Psychologist and Postpartum Expert
- Updated coverage of fathers' adjustment during the postpartum period (Dietz & others, 2009; Smith & Howard, 2008)
- Discussion of a recent study linking paternal postpartum depression with children's psychological disorders seven years later (Ramchandani & others, 2008)

Chapter 4: Physical Development and Health

- New discussion of precocious puberty (Blakemore, Berenbaum, & Liben, 2009)
- Inclusion of recent information on a longitudinal study of the sequence of pubertal events in boys and girls (Susman & others, 2009)
- Inclusion of recent information that early maturing girls are less likely to graduate from high school and more likely to cohabit and marry earlier (Cavanagh, 2009)
- Updated coverage of the development of the brain based on expert consultant Martha Ann Bell's feedback
- New material on which individuals are most often the perpetrators of shaken baby syndrome (National Center for Shaken Baby Syndrome, 2009)
- Description of a recent study on right hemisphere dominance of language in children with perinatal brain damage to the left hemisphere (Guzzetta & others, 2008)
- Coverage of a recent meta-analysis that found no hemispheric specialization in creative thinking (Mihov, Denizer, & Forster, 2010)
- New material on Mark Johnson and his colleagues' (2009) view of the powerful neural leadership and organizational role of the prefrontal cortex during development
- Expanded coverage of the pruning of synapses and what this means by the end of adolescence (Kuhn, 2009)
- New description of how the information about changes in the adolescent brain reflect the rapidly emerging field of social developmental neuroscience (Johnson, 2009)
- Description of results from two studies on shared sleeping in African American and non-Latino White families (Fu & others, 2008; Hauck & others, 2008)
- Coverage of a recent study indicating that more than one-fourth of U.S. mothers did not use the recommended supine position for infant sleep (Hauck & others, 2008)
- Coverage of a recent study indicating that infants who sleep in bedrooms with a fan have a lower risk of SIDS (Coleman-Phox, Odouli, & Li, 2008)
- Inclusion of recent research on bedtime sleep resistance and problem behaviors in children (Carvalho Bos & others, 2008)

- Discussion of a recent study linking sleep problems from 3 to 8 years of age with the early onset of drug use and depression in adolescence (Wong, Brower, & Zucker, 2009)
- New material on a link between short sleep duration and being overweight in childhood (Nielsen, Danielson, & Sorensen, 2010; Nixon & others, 2008)
- Coverage of a recent study linking young children's exposure to second-hand smoke to sleep problems, including sleep-disordered breathing (Yolton & others, 2010)
- Much expanded and updated coverage of lead poisoning in children and its outcomes (Bellinger, 2008; Canfield & Jusko, 2008)
- New section on cardiovascular disease in children, including information about a recent national study indicating an increase in the percentage of U.S. children and adolescents with elevated blood pressure (Ostchega & others, 2009)
- Discussion of a recent research review that found no link between breast feeding and the quality of the mother-infant relationship (Jansen, de Weerth, & Riksen-Walraven, 2008)
- Inclusion of information from a recent research review on breast feeding (Ip & others, 2009)
- New coverage of a recent study child health and nutrition programs in Haiti that helped reduce the impact of economic hardship on stunting of children's growth (Donegan & others, 2010)
- Discussion of a recent study that illustrates the influence of malnutrition on young children's cognitive development (Kar, Rao, & Chandramouli, 2008)
- New *Caring Connections* interlude: "Improving the Nutrition of Infants and Young Children Living in Low-Income Families"
- Recent information about changes in the WIC program for 2009 (Food & Nutrition, Service, 2009)
- Inclusion of recent research on the changes and effectiveness of various aspects of the WIC program (Black & others, 2009; Heinig & others, 2009; Olson & others, 2009a, b)
- Coverage of a recent large-scale U.S. study indicating a higher percentage of being overweight or obese for African American and Latino children than non-Latino White children (Benson, Baer, & Kaelber, 2009)
- New *Connecting with Careers* profile: "T. Berry Brazelton, Pediatrician"
- Coverage of a recent national study of trends in children's meals eaten outside the home and the percentage of children's meals that exceed the recommended amount of saturated fat and trans fat (Center for Science in the Public Interest, 2008)
- Inclusion of a recent study that found children's weight at five years of age was significantly related to their weight at nine years of age (Gardner & others, 2009)
- Discussion of a recent study on developmental changes in the percentage of overweight children from 4 to 11 years of age depending on whether they have lean or obese parents (Semmler & others, 2009)
- Description of a recent study of preschool children's percentage of time spent in sedentary behavior and light to vigorous physical activity (Brown & others, 2009)
- Coverage of a recent study that revealed a positive role of aerobic exercise fitness on 9-year-old girls' performance on a cognitive control task that required them to inhibit irrelevant responses to obtain correct solutions (Hillman & others, 2009)

Chapter 5: Motor, Sensory, and Perceptual Development
- Coverage of a recent study illustrating the influence of visual information on 3-day-old infants' stepping actions (Barbu-Roth & others, 2009)

- Updated coverage of cultural variation in infant motor development (Adolph, Karasik, & Tamis-LeMonda, 2010)
- Much expanded discussion of sports in children's development (Theokas, 2009)
- Coverage of a recent study of infants' eye movements while watching an animated film indicating an increase in focusing on faces from 3 to 9 months of age and a decrease in looking at salient background stimuli (Frank & Johnson, 2009)
- Inclusion of recent information about the development of sophisticated eye-tracking equipment to study infant perception, including new Figure 5.8 of an infant in a study using eye-tracking equipment (Franchak & others, 2010)
- Deletion of figure on eye tracking (Banks & Salapatek, 1983) because it was done a number of years ago with rudimentary equipment and does not accurately portray newborns' eye movements
- Coverage of a recent studying indicating that young infants looked longest at reddish hues and shortest at greenish hues (Franklin & others, 2010)
- New section on the perception of occluded objects
- New material on the age at which infants develop the ability to perceive that occluded objects are complete
- Discussion of Scott Johnson's (2009, 2010a, b) view on why infants are able to develop the ability to perceive occluded objects as complete
- New description of a recent study by Bennett Bertenthal and his colleagues (2007) on infants' predictive tracking of briefly occluded moving objects, including new Figure 5.9
- New commentary about critics of the visual cliff concluding that it likely is a better test of social referencing and fear of heights than depth perception
- New main section—"Nature, Nurture, and Perceptual Development"—that examines nativist and empiricist views of perception (Aslin, 2009; Johnson, 2009, 2010a, b; Slater & others, 2010)
- Updated and expanded coverage of perceptual-motor coupling, including how infants develop new perceptual-motor couplings

Chapter 6: Cognitive Developmental Approaches

- New section on the nature-nurture issue in infant cognitive development
- New discussion of Elizbeth Spelke's (2000, 2003; Spelke & Kinzler, 2007; 2009) core knowledge approach
- New coverage of the intriguing question of whether young infants have a sense of number, including a new Figure 6.5
- Description of a recent study on the area of the brain activated when 3-month-old infants were observing changes in the number of objects compared to changes in the type of objects (Izard, Dehaene-Lambertz, & Dehaene, 2008)
- New discussion of Baillargeon's (2008; Baillargeon & others, 2009) innate bias view as expressed in the principle of persistence
- Inclusion of criticism of Spelke's core knowledge approach by Mark Johnson (2008)
- Expanded and updated conclusion to what are the focus and most difficult tasks infant researchers face in determining the influence of nature and nurture (Aslin, 2009)
- Description of recent research indicating that rather than perceiving themselves to be invulnerable, adolescents see themselves as vulnerable, with some studies even indicating that adolescents envision that they are vulnerable to experiencing a premature death (de Bruen, Parker, & Fischoff, 2007; Fischhoff & others, 2010 Jamieson & Romer, 2007; Reyna & Fisher, 2008)

- Coverage of recent research on the effectiveness of the Tools of the Mind curriculum to improve at-risk young children's self-regulatory and cognitive control skills (Diamond & others, 2007)

Chapter 7: Information Processing

- New Figure 7.7 that summarizes research on how long infants of different ages can remember information (Bauer, 2009a)
- Discussion of a recent study that linked children's attention problems at 54 months of age with a lower level of social skills in peer relations in the first and third grades (NICHD Early Child Care Research Network, 2009)
- New material on using computer exercises to improve children's attention (Jaeggi, Berman, & Jonides, 2009; Tang & Posner, 2009)
- New section on changes in attention during adolescence
- New discussion of multitasking and its possible harmful effects on adolescents' allocation of attention, especially when they engage in a challenging task (Bauerlein, 2008; Begley & Inerlandi, 2008)
- New coverage of three recent studies of working memory that illustrate how important and wide ranging working memory capacity is for children's cognitive development and achievement (Andersson, 2010; Asian, Zellner, & Bauml, 2010; Welsh & others, 2010)
- New section on changes in memory during adolescence
- Description of a recent study on young children's narrative ability and resistance to suggestion (Kulkofsky & Klemfuss, 2008)
- Expanded coverage of strategies for improving children's memory skills, including memory development expert Patricia Bauer's (2009b) emphasis on the importance of consolidation and reconsolidation in memory through variation on an instructional theme and linking often
- New material on Peter Ornstein and his colleagues' view (Ornstein, Coffman, & Grammar, 2009; Ornstein & others, 2010) that it is important for instructors to embed memory-relevant language in their teaching
- Expanded discussion of concept formation and categorization in infancy and a new final summary statement about the infant's remarkable degree of learning power (Diamond, Casey, & Munakata, 2011; Mandler, 2004, 2009; Quinn, 2011)
- New *Connecting Through Research* interlude, "How Does Theory of Mind Differ in Children with Autism?"
- New discussion of Ellen Langer's concept of mindfulness and its importance in critical thinking
- New section on changes in thinking during adolescence
- New material on how social contexts, especially the presence of peers, influence adolescent decision making (Steinberg, 2008)
- New discussion of the dual-process model of adolescent decision making
- New section on changes in metacognition in adolescence (Kuhn, 2008, 2009)

Chapter 8: Intelligence

- New description of Gardner's consideration of possibly adding a ninth type of intelligence—existentialist—to his list of multiple intelligences
- New section, "The Neuroscience of Intelligence" (Haier, 2009; Neubauer & Fink, 2009)
- Discussion of the link between overall brain size and intelligence (Luders & others, 2009)
- Coverage of recent research on a distributed neural network that involves the frontal and parietal lobes and the neural network's link to intelligence (Colom & others, 2009; Dreary, Penke, & Johnson, 2010; Glascher & others, 2010)

- New material on the role of neurological speed in intelligence (Waiter & others, 2009)
- Coverage of a recent analysis indicating that the Flynn effect may be due to improvements in prenatal and early postnatal nutrition (Flynn, 2007)
- New conclusion added to the section on heredity/environment and intelligence and tied the conclusion to the nature-nurture issue first discussed in Chapter 1
- Discussion of a recent study linking selective attention to novelty at 6 to 12 months of age with intelligence at 21 years of age (Fagan, Holland, & Wheeler, 2007)
- Coverage of a recent longitudinal study on the stability of intelligence from 12 months to 4 years of age (Blaga & others, 2009)
- Expanded and updated coverage of predicting children's intelligence from assessment of habituation in early infancy (Domsch, Lohaus, & Thomas, 2009)
- New section, "Nature-Nurture," in the discussion of "Children Who Are Gifted"
- New discussion of John Colombo and his colleagues' (2004, 2009) research on attempting to predict from infancy which children will have high cognitive ability as children
- New material on developmental changes in giftedness in childhood and adolescence with increased emphasis on domain-specific giftedness (Keating, 2009; Sternberg, 2010e)
- Inclusion of commentary by Bill Gates about domain-specific giftedness
- New material on the reason that children who are gifted don't always become adults who are gifted

Chapter 9: Language Development

- Modifications and updates of the discussion of language development based on comments by leading experts Catherine McBride-Chang, Barbara Pan and Gigliana Melzi
- Expanded definition of language to include words used by a community and the rules for combining and using them appropriately
- Discussion of recent research on differences in early gesture as explanations for SES disparities in child vocabulary at school entry (Rowe & Goldin-Meadow, 2009)
- Expanded discussion of emergent literacy skills in young children including a recent study linking maternal education with emergent literacy skills (Korat, 2009)
- Coverage of a recent study of key factors in young children's early literacy experiences in low-income families (Rodriquez & others, 2009)
- Coverage of a recent research review indicating that bilingual children have lower formal language proficiency than monolingual children (Bialystok & Craik, 2010)
- Description of a recent longitudinal study linking early home environment with early language skills, which in turn predicted school readiness (Forget-Dubois & others, 2009)
- New discussion of variations in early literacy across countries, including comparisons of children's learning of English and Chinese (McBride & others, 2008)
- Coverage of a recent study linking maternal sensitivity and negative intrusiveness to young children's language development (Pungello & others, 2009)

- Expanded material on why children in low-income families may have difficulty in language development
- New material on shared book reading and its benefits for infants and toddlers (Barbarin & Aikens, 2009; Raikes & others, 2006)
- Coverage of a recent study of 4-year-olds that revealed peers' expressive language abilities were positively linked to the 4-year-olds' receptive and expressive language development (Mashburn & others, 2009)
- New discussion of cultural variations in language support (Ochs & Schieffelin, 2008; Schieffelin, 2005)
- New description of a recent study of the contribution of infants' information processing skills to the growth of language development in early childhood (Rose, Feldman, & Jankowski, 2009)
- New material on joint attention in infancy being linked to vocabulary development in childhood (Colombo & others, 2009)
- More detailed information about the genetic basis of Williams syndrome (Haas & others, 2009)

Chapter 10: Emotional Development

- Reorganization of the discussion of emotional development into these categories based on expert Susan Denham's recommendation: expressing emotions, understanding emotions, and regulating emotions
- Added commentary about the importance of the communication aspect of emotion, especially in infancy (Campos, 2009)
- Expanded coverage of the onset of emotions in infancy, including Jerome Kagan's (2010) recent conclusion that emotions such as guilt, pride, despair, shame, and jealousy, which require thought, cannot be experienced in the first year because of the structural immaturity of the infant's brain
- New material on the importance of smiling in infancy as a means of developing a new social skill and being a key social signal (Campos, 2009)
- New discussion of anticipatory smiling in infancy and its link to social competence in early childhood (Parlade & others, 2009)
- Revised definition of temperament to include individual differences in emotions based on the view of leading expert Joseph Campos (2009)
- Expanded discussion of advances in young children's understanding of emotions (Cole & others, 2009)
- Coverage of a recent meta-analysis indicating that emotion knowledge was positively linked to 3- to 5-year-olds' social competence and negatively related to their internalizing and externalizing problems (Trentacosta & Fine, 2009)
- Discussion of a recent study linking young children's emotion understanding with their prosocial behavior (Ensor, Spencer, & Hughes, 2010)
- New discussion of a research that links specific components of parenting to specific emotions in young children (Davidoff & Grusec, 2006; Grusec, 2011; Grusec & Davidoff, 2010)
- Updated and expanded coverage of children's outcomes following a disaster (Kar, 2009)
- Updated coverage of temperament based on feedback from leading expert John Bates
- Discussion of a recent study of effortful control and children's adjustment problems in China and the United States (Zhou, Lengua, & Yang, 2009)
- Description of a recent study indicating an interaction between temperament style and the type of child care young children experience (Pluess & Belsky, 2009)

- New material on the importance of considering the multiple temperament dimensions of children rather than classifying them on a single dimension (Bates, 2008)
- New discussion of developmental changes in temperament characteristics and the importance of considering the individual differences that emerge from these developmental changes (Bates, 2008; Rothbart & Gartstein, 2008)
- Coverage of a recent meta-analysis of studies using the still-face paradigm and links between affect and secure attachment (Mesman, van IJzendoorn, & Bakersman-Kranenburg, 2009)
- Added commentary about the importance of locomotion for the development of independence in the infant and toddler years (Campos, 2009)
- Description of a recent study linking security of attachment at 24 and 36 months to the child's social problem solving skills at 54 months (Raike & Thompson, 2009)
- Discussion of a recent study of maternal sensitive parenting and infant attachment security (Finger & others, 2009)
- Coverage of a recent meta-analysis linking three types of insecure attachment to externalizing problems (Fearon & others, 2010)
- Added information about the link of maternal sensitivity to secure infant attachment not being especially strong (Campos, 2009)
- Description of recent research indicating a gene × environment interaction between disorganized attachment, the short version of the serontonin transporter gene—5-HTTLPR—and a low level of maternal responsiveness (Spangler & others, 2009)
- Important new section: "Developmental Social Neuroscience and Attachment," including recent theory and views on the role of the brain neuroanatomy, neurotransmitters, and hormones in the development of mother-infant attachment (Bales & Carter, 2009; De Haan & Gunnar, 2009; Gonzales, Atkinson, & Fleming, 2009)
- New Figure 10.10 that shows likely key brain structures in infant-mother attachment
- Much expanded discussion of fathers and mothers as caregivers
- New coverage of the Aka pygmy culture, where fathers are as involved in infant caregiving as much as mothers are (Hewlett, 2000: Hewlett & McFarland, 2010)
- Description of a recent study of multiple child-care arrangements and young children's behavioral outcomes (Morrissey, 2009)
- Expanded and updated material on the important role of sensitive parenting in child outcomes for children in child care (Friedman, Milhuish, & Hill, 2010; Thompson, 2009d)
- Inclusion of the following important point about the NICHD SECC research: findings consistently show that family factors are considerably stronger and more consistent predictors of a wide variety of child outcomes than are child care experiences (quality, quantity, type)

Chapter 11: The Self and Identity

- New coverage of cultural variations in toddlers' mirror self-recognition and information about physical self-recognition as possibly being more important in toddlers from Western than non-Western cultures (Keller & others, 2005; Thompson & Virmani, 2010)
- Inclusion of recent research on the early appearance of infants' conscious awareness of their bodies, which doesn't emerge until the second year (Brownell & others, 2009)

- Description of recent research on young children's understanding of joint commitments (Grafenhain & others, 2009)
- New coverage of leading expert Ross Thompson's (2009f) commentary about how current research on theory of mind and young children's social understanding is so dissonant with Piaget's egocentrism concept
- Description of a recent study that revealed adolescent males had higher self-esteem than adolescent females (McLean & Breen, 2009)
- New discussion of William Damon's (2008) book *The Path to Purpose* and his views on why too many of today's youths are struggling to find a path to a positive identity
- Expanded and updated description of why college often stimulates a greater integration of identity at a higher level (Phinney, 2008)
- Coverage of a recent meta-analysis of 127 studies focused on developmental changes in Marcia's identity statuses (Francis, Fraser, & Marcia, 2010)
- Description of a recent longitudinal study of ethnic identity resolution and proactive coping with discrimination (Umana-Taylor & others, 2008)
- Coverage of a recent study indicating the importance of exploration in ethnic identity development (Whitehead & others, 2009)
- Discussion of a recent study of Latino youth indicating a link between growth in identity exploration and an increase in self-esteem (Umana-Taylor, Gonzales-Backen, & Guimond, 2009)
- New **Connecting with Diversity** interlude: "The Contexts of Ethnic Identity Development," including recent research by Niobe Way and her colleagues (2008)

Chapter 12: Gender

- New major opening section: "What Is Gender?"
- Updated and expanded discussion of gender identity (Blakemore, Berenbaum, & Liben, 2009; Egan & Perry, 2001)
- Inclusion of a recent study on developmental changes in sex-typed behavior (Golombok & others, 2008)
- New discussion of a recent longitudinal study of the acquisition of gender labels in infancy and their link to sex-typed play (Zosuls & others, 2009)
- Coverage of a recent longitudinal study on a decline in male- and female-typed activities from 7 to 19 years of age (McHale & others, 2009)
- Coverage of a recent study linking higher prenatal testosterone levels to increased male-typical play in 6- to 10-year-old boys and girls (Auyeung & others, 2009)
- Expanded and updated discussion of gender differences in mothers' and fathers' parenting interactions with their children and adolescents (Galambos, Berenbaum, & McHale, 2009)
- Coverage of recent large-scale assessment of a gender difference in writing (National Assessment of Educational Progress, 2007) and lack of a difference in math (Hyde & others, 2008)
- New commentary about boys' having more rigid gender stereotypes than girls (Blakemore, Berenbaum, & Liben, 2009)
- Coverage of a recent study of 3- to 10-year-old boys' and girls' gender stereotyping (Miller & others, 2009)
- New summary of sex differences in the brain emphasizing caution in interpreting differences (Blakemore, Berenbaum, & Liben, 2009)
- New material on a lack of gender differences in overall intelligence but differences in some cognitive areas (Blakemore, Berenbaum, & Liben, 2009; Galambos, Berenbaum, & McHale, 2009)

- Description of how there is still gender disparity in math, science, and technology careers despite girls' school achievement gains in math and science (Watt, 2008; Watt & Eccles, 2008)
- Coverage of a recent study of same-sex education and its benefits for girls (Kessels & Hannover, 2008)
- Discussion of a recent study indicating that relational aggression increases in middle and late childhood (Dishion & Piehler, 2009)
- Inclusion of information from a recent research review that girls engage in more relational aggression than boys in adolescence but not in childhood (Smith, Rose, & Schwartz-Mette, 2009)
- Description of a recent study linking parents' psychological control to a higher incidence of relational aggression in their children (Kuppens & others, 2009)
- Updated description of gender differences in emotion (Blakemore, Berenbaum, & Liben, 2009)

Chapter 13: Moral Development

- Revision of the description of Kohlberg's theory based on leading expert John Gibbs' feedback
- New information about how most young adolescents around the world use moral judgment of mutuality (stage 3) that makes intimate friendships possible (Gibbs, 2009)
- New coverage of forgiveness as an aspect of prosocial behavior
- New discussion of gratitude, including a recent study of its link with a number of positive aspects of adolescent development (Froh, Yurkewicz, & Kashdan, 2009)
- Coverage of a recent study on African American and Latino adolescents' beliefs about the importance of service learning in keeping adolescents from dropping out of school (Bridgeland, DiIulio, & Wulsin, 2008)
- Inclusion of information about the prosocial and service learning contributions of Nina Vasan, "Superstar Volunteer and Fundraiser"
- New discussion of a recent national survey of almost 30,000 high school students regarding cheating (Josephson Institute of Ethics, 2008)
- Coverage of a recent study linking parents' lack of knowledge of their young adolescents' whereabouts and the adolescents' engagement in delinquency later in adolescence (Lahey & others, 2008)
- Discussion of a recent study implicating harsh discipline of children at 8 to 10 years of age as a predictor of which adolescent delinquents would persist in criminal activity after age 21 (Farrington, Ttofi, & Coid, 2009)
- Coverage of a recent longitudinal experimental study involving parenting intervention with divorced mothers and sons and a subsequent lower level of delinquency (Forgatch & others, 2009)
- Description of a recent study on the positive role of academic achievement in reducing the likelihood of becoming a juvenile delinquent (Loeber & others, 2008)
- New material on gender differences in religion in adolescence (King & Roeser, 2009; Smith & Denton, 2005)
- Updated and expanded coverage of links between cognitive changes and adolescents' religious and spiritual development (Good & Willoughby, 2008)

Chapter 14: Families

- Discussion of a recent study linking maternal scaffolding and young children's reasoning skills (Stright, Herr, & Neitzel, 2009)

- New main section on multiple developmental trajectories and the changing trajectory of parenthood timing (Parke & Buriel, 2006; Parke & others, 2008)
- New main section, "Domain Specific Socialization," which describes five domain-specific socialization practices involving parenting and their links to specific child outcomes (Grusec & Davidov, 2010)
- New section, "Further Thoughts on Parenting Styles," including material on caution in interpreting studies of parenting styles and children's development especially because they are correlational in nature and the interest in unpacking components of parenting styles
- Coverage of a recent study of mothers' use of physical punishment in six countries and its link to their children's aggression (Gershoff & others, 2010)
- Expanded discussion of the effects of punishment on children, including the current conclusion of some experts that adequate research evidence has not yet been obtained about the effects of abusive physical punishment and mild physical punishment
- Conclusions regarding punishment research that if physical punishment is used it needs to be mild, infrequent, age-appropriate, and used in the context of a positive parent-child relationship (Grusec, 2011)
- Updated child maltreatment statistics in the United States (U.S. Department of Health and Human Services, 2008)
- New material on adolescent outcomes of child abuse and neglect (Wekerle & others, 2009)
- Discussion of a recent study linking child maltreatment with financial and employment-related difficulties in adulthood (Zielinski, 2009)
- Inclusion of information about greater protection and monitoring of daughters than of sons in Latino families compared to non-Latino White families (Allen & others, 2008)
- Discussion of a recent longitudinal study of secure attachment in adolescence and outcomes in emerging adulthood (Allen & others, 2009)
- Description of a recent study of parent-adolescent conflict in Latino families (Crean, 2008)
- New section on intergenerational relationships and how they influence adolescent development
- New description of how females' relationships across generations are closer than males' (Etaugh & Bridges, 2010; Merrill, 2009)
- Coverage of a recent intergenerational study of divorce and secure attachment (Crowell, Treboux, & Brockmeyer, 2009)
- Discussion of recent study on the intergenerational transmission of smoking (Chassin & others, 2008)
- Description of developmental changes in sibling relationships from childhood to adolescence (East, 2009)
- Expanded and updated material on the positive and negative aspects of adolescent sibling relationships (East, 2009)
- New discussion of E. Mark Cummings and his colleagues' (Cummings, El-Sheikh, & Kouros, 2009; Cummings & Merrilees,2009) emotional security theory and its focus on the type of marital conflict that is negative for children's development

Chapter 15: Peers
- New discussion of the early development of friendships during the preschool years (Howes, 2009)
- Updated and expanded discussion of the connected worlds of parent-child and peer relations (Hartup, 2009; Ross & Howe, 2009)

- Description of a recent study on parenting behaviors that are linked to children's social competence and social acceptance (McDowell & Parke, 2009)
- Enhanced and updated discussion of why pretend play is an important aspect of early childhood development (Copland & Arbeau, 2009)
- Expanded and updated material on social play as the main context for most young children's interactions with peers (Copland & Arbeau, 2009)
- New section on contextual influences on peer relations (Brown & Dietz, 2009; Brown & others, 2008; Prinstein & Dodge, 2008)
- New section on individual difference factors in peer relations (Brown & Dietz, 2009; Brown & others, 2008)
- Inclusion of a recent study of rejected children and classroom participation (Ladd, Herald-Brown, & Reiser, 2008)
- Description of three recent suicides in middle and late childhood and early adolescence that likely were influenced by bullying (Meyers, 2010)
- New emphasis on the importance of contexts in the study of bullying (Salmivalli & others, 2009; Schwartz & others, 2010)
- Coverage of two recent studies of bullies' popularity in the peer group (Veenstra & others, 2010; Wivliet & others, 2010)
- Description of a recent study on peer victimization and the extent of its link to lower academic achievement (Nakamoto & Schwartz, 2010)
- Coverage of recent assessment of a decrease in bullying in the Steps to Respect antibullying program (Frey & others, 2009)
- Expanded and updated material on which adolescents are most likely to conform to their peers (Prinstein, 2007; Prinstein & Dodge, 2008; Prinstein & others, 2009)
- New discussion of the talk-featured, gossip aspect of friendship in adolescence (Buhrmester & Chong, 2009)
- New coverage of three stages in the development of romantic relationships in adolescence (Connolly & McIsaac, 2009)
- New material on the percentage of adolescents who are early and late bloomers in developing romantic relationships (Connolly & McIsaac, 2009)
- Coverage of a recent study of adolescents' romantic experience and links to various aspects of adjustment (Furman, Lo, & Ho, 2009)
- Discussion of two recent studies of adolescent girls' romantic involvement and its link to co-rumination, depressive symptoms, and emotionally unavailable parents (Starr & Davila, 2009; Steinberg & Davila, 2008)

Chapter 16: Schools and Achievement

- Updated coverage of developmentally appropriate practice, including a new figure (NAEYC, 2009)
- Expanded and updated discussion of the characteristics and goals of developmental appropriate education (Barbarin & Miller, 2009; Ritchie, Maxwell, & Bredekamp, 2009)
- New discussion of the Early Head Start program (Administration for Children & Families, 2008)
- New coverage of recent studies of the influence of Project Head Start on children's cognitive, language, and math skills and achievement (Hindman & others, 2010; Puma & others, 2010)
- New main section, "Extracurricular Activities," which highlights the positive aspects of these activities on adolescent development (Barber, Stone, & Eccles, 2010; Mahoney, Parente, & Zigler, 2010)

- Description of a recent study linking chronic poverty to adverse cognitive development outcomes in children (Najman & others, 2009)
- New discussion of dysgraphia
- Description of a recent study of gender differences in handwriting impairment (Berninger & others, 2009)
- New coverage of dyscalculia
- New coverage of neurotransmitters such as serotonin and dopamine and their possible link to ADHD (Levy, 2009; Rondou & others, 2010; Zhou & others, 2010)
- New section on emotional and behavioral disorders (Gargiulo, 2009; Kaufmann & Landrum, 2009)
- Significantly updated and expanded discussion of autism spectrum disorders (Anderson & others, 2009; Gong & others, 2009)
- New information about the recent increase in the estimate of the number of children with autistic spectrum disorders
- Expanded discussion of gender and autism, including Baron Cohen's (2008) argument that autism reflects an extreme male brain
- New material on recent research using animated faces and emotions to improve autistic children's ability to recognize faces, including new Figure 16.5 (Baron-Cohen & others, 2007)
- Description of a recent meta-analysis indicating that behavior management treatments are effective in reducing the effects of ADHD (Fabiano, 2009)
- New material on Ryan and Deci's (2009) description of autonomy-supportive teachers who create circumstances for students to engage in self-determination
- Coverage of a longitudinal study linking children's intrinsic motivation in math and science from 9 to 17 years of age to their parents' motivational practices (Gottfried & others, 2009)
- New main section, "Cognitive Processes," in the discussion of achievement
- Recent research and ideas about improving students' growth mindset by teaching them about the brain's plasticity and changes in the brain when you put considerable effort into learning (Blackwell & others, 2007; Dweck & Masters, 2009)
- New section, "Purpose," which focuses on the importance of purpose in achieving and the low percentage of parents and teachers who engage students in discussions of their purpose (Damon, 2008)
- Description of a recent study linking chronic poverty to adverse cognitive development outcomes in children (Najman & others, 2009)
- New discussion of the recent results from the large-scale international assessment of fourth-grade students' math and science scores with a focus on how U.S. students compare to students in other countries (TIMMS, 2008)

Chapter 17: Culture and Diversity

- New discussion of a recent cross-cultural comparison of U.S. and Chinese seventh- and eighth-graders' academic and motivational behavior (Yang & Pomerantz, 2009)
- New material on the adjustment problems of children and adolescents from affluent families (Ansary & Luthar, 2009; Luthar & Goldstein, 2008)
- New discussion of how adolescents in poverty likely are more aware of their social disadvantage and its associated stigma than are younger children (McLoyd & others, 2009)
- Coverage of a 12-year longitudinal study of SES and ethnic group influences on adolescents' and emerging adults' educational and occupational expectations

that illustrates the importance of controlling for SES in studies of ethnic minority children and youth (Mello, 2009)

- Description of a recent study of adolescents' perceived racial discrimination and its link to the broader society's negative views of African Americans (Seaton, Yip, & Sellers, 2009)

- Updated material on the dramatic increase in media multi-tasking by children and youth and how, if this is factored into statistics on media use, children and adolescents now use electronic media an average of eight hours per day (Roberts, Henrikson, & Foehr, 2009; Roberts & Foehr, 2008)

- Coverage of three recent studies by Douglas Gentile and his colleagues (2009) that illustrate a link between playing prosocial video games and an increase in prosocial behavior

- New description of the link between a high level of TV viewing and obesity in children and adolescents (Escobar-Chaves & Anderson, 2008)

- Coverage of a recent classroom-based intervention that was successful in reducing the amount of time children watched violent TV and in decreasing their identification with TV superheroes (Rosenkoetter, Rosenkoetter, & Acock, 2009)

- Description of a recent study linking media violence exposure to an increase in relational aggression in children (Gentile, Mathieson, & Crick, 2010)

- New discussion of TV/videos and infant cognitive and language development, including recent research (Christakis & others, 2009; Okuam & Tanimura, 2009; Zimmerman, Christakis, & Meltzoff, 2007)

- Coverage of a recent study linking of early TV exposure and subsequent attention problems (Cheng & others, 2010)

- Description of a recent survey of the significant threat minors encounter with both online and offline bullying (Palfrey & others, 2009)

- Discussion of recent research on adolescent self-disclosure on the Internet and which gender benefits more from self-disclosing with friends on the Internet (Schouten, Valkenburg, & Peter, 2007; Valkenburg & Peter, 2009)

- Description of a recent study of the sequence of using various electronic communication technologies by college females and males (Yang & Brown, 2009)

- Coverage of a recent study of pubertal timing and what adolescent boys do online (Skoog, Stattin, & Kerr, 2009)

- Expanded and updated coverage of the increase of adolescents' and emerging adults' reliance on digital mediation of their social environment (Roberts, Henrikson, & Foehr, 2009)

- Discussion of a recent study indicating that many parents do not monitor their adolescents' online activities (Rosen, Cheever, & Carrier, 2008)

- Description of recent research linking friendship and behavioral adjustment in early adolescence to emerging adults' communication on social networking sites (Mikami & others, 2010)

Resources

The resources listed here may accompany *Child Development*, 13th edition. Please contact your McGraw-Hill representative for details concerning policies, prices, and availability.

For the Instructor

The Online Learning Center   The instructor side of the Online Learning Center at www.mhhe.com/santrockcd13e contains the *Instructor's Manual*, Test Bank files, PowerPoint slides, CPS questions, Image Gallery, and other valuable material to help you design and enhance your course. Ask your local McGraw-Hill representative for your password.

Instructor's Manual   *by Ralph Carlini, University of Massachusetts–Dartmouth.* Each chapter of the *Instructor's Manual* is introduced by a Resources Overview. This fully integrated tool helps instructors more easily locate and choose among the many resources available for the course by linking each element of the *Instructor's Manual* to a particular teaching topic within the chapter. These elements include lecture suggestions, classroom activities, personal applications, research project ideas, video suggestions, and handouts.

Test Bank and Computerized Test Bank   *by Diane Powers, Iowa Central Community College.* By increasing the rigor of the Test Bank development process, McGraw-Hill aims to raise the bar for student assessment. Over 2,000 multiple-choice and over 50 essay and short answer questions were prepared to test factual, applied, and conceptual understanding and are keyed to Bloom's taxonomy, difficulty level, and page reference. The test bank is compatible with McGraw-Hill's computerized testing program EZ Test, and most Course Management systems.

PowerPoint Slides   *by Len Mendola, Adelphia University.* These presentations cover the key points of each chapter and include charts and graphs from the text. They can be used as is, or you may modify them to meet your specific needs.

CPS Questions   *by Alisha Janowsky, University of Central Florida.* These questions, formatted for use with the interactive Classroom Performance System, are organized by chapter and designed to test factual, applied, and conceptual understanding.

McGraw-Hill's Visual Asset Database for Lifespan Development ("VAD")

McGraw-Hill's Visual Assets Database for Lifespan Development (VAD 2.0) (www .mhhe.com/vad) is an on-line database of videos for use in the developmental psychology classroom, created specifically for instructors. You can customize classroom presentations by downloading the videos to your computer and showing the videos on their own or inserting them into your course cartridge or PowerPoint presentations. All of the videos are available with or without captions. Ask your McGraw-Hill representative for access information.

Create   Craft your teaching resources to match the way you teach! With McGraw-Hill Create, www.mcgrawhillcreate.com, you can easily rearrange chapters, combine material from other content sources, and quickly upload content you have written like your course syllabus or teaching notes. Find the content you need in Create by searching through thousands of leading McGraw-Hill textbooks. Arrange your book to fit your teaching style. Create even allows you to personalize your book's appearance by selecting the cover and adding your name, school, and course information. Order a Create book and you'll receive a complimentary print review copy in 3–5 business days or a complimentary electronic review copy (eComp) via email in about one hour. Go to www.mcgrawhillcreate.com today and register. Experience how McGraw-Hill Create empowers you to teach your students your way.

Blackboard   McGraw-Hill Higher Education and Blackboard have teamed up. What does this mean for you?
1. **Your life, simplified.** Now you and your students can access McGraw-Hill's Connect™ and Create™ right from within your Blackboard course—all with one single sign-on. Say goodbye to the days of logging in to multiple applications.
2. **Deep integration of content and tools.** Not only do you get single sign-on with Connect™ and Create™, you also get deep integration of McGraw-Hill

content and content engines right in Blackboard. Whether you're choosing a book for your course or building Connect™ assignments, all the tools you need are right where you want them—inside of Blackboard.

3. **Seamless Gradebooks.** Are you tired of keeping multiple gradebooks and manually synchronizing grades into Blackboard? We thought so. When a student completes an integrated Connect™ assignment, the grade for that assignment automatically (and instantly) feeds your Blackboard grade center.

4. **A solution for everyone.** Whether your institution is already using Blackboard or you just want to try Blackboard on your own, we have a solution for you. McGraw-Hill and Blackboard can now offer you easy access to industry leading technology and content, whether your campus hosts it, or we do. Be sure to ask your local McGraw-Hill representative for details.

Tegrity Tegrity Campus is a service that makes class time available all the time by automatically capturing every lecture in a searchable format for students to review when they study and complete assignments. With a simple one-click start and stop process, you capture all computer screens and corresponding audio. Students replay any part of any class with easy-to-use browser-based viewing on a PC or Mac. Educators know that the more students can see, hear, and experience class resources, the better they learn. With Tegrity Campus, students quickly recall key moments by using Tegrity Campus's unique search feature. This search helps students efficiently find what they need, when they need it across an entire semester of class recordings. Help turn all your students' study time into learning moments immediately supported by your lecture.

Student Resources

Online Learning Center (OLC)   This companion Web site, at www.mhhe.com/santrockcd13e offers a variety of student resources. *Multiple Choice* and *True/False quizzes* reinforce key principles and cover all the major concepts discussed throughout the text. Entirely different from the test items in the Test Bank, these quiz questions, Web links, and Taking it to the Net exercises and activities written by Elaine Cassell, Lord Fairfax Community College, assess students but also help them learn. Key terms from the text are presented as *Flashcards,* as well as in a *Glossary* of terms. *Decision Making Scenarios* present students with the opportunity to apply the information in the chapter to realistic situations, and see what effects their decisions have.

Annual Editions: Child Growth and Development 10/11   This reader is a collection of articles on topics related to the latest research and thinking in child development. Annual Editions are updated regularly and include useful features such as a topic guide, an annotated table of contents, unit overviews, and a topical index.

Taking Sides: Clashing Views in Childhood and Society   Current controversial issues are presented in a debate-style format designed to stimulate student interest and develop critical-thinking skills. Each issue is thoughtfully framed with an issue summary, an issue introduction, and a postscript.

CourseSmart   Here is a new way to find and buy eTextbooks. At CourseSmart you can save up to 50 percent off the cost of a print textbook, reduce your impact on the environment, and gain access to powerful Web tools for learning. CourseSmart has the largest selection of eTextbooks available anywhere, offering thousands of the most commonly adopted textbooks from a wide variety of higher education publishers. CourseSmart eTextbooks are available in one standard online reader with full-text search, notes and highlighting capabilities, and e-mail tools for sharing notes between classmates. For further details, contact your sales representative or go to **www.coursemart.com.**

ACKNOWLEDGMENTS

I very much appreciate the support and guidance provided to me by many people at McGraw-Hill. Beth Mejia, executive publisher, has done a marvelous job of directing and monitoring the development and publication of this text. Mike Sugarman, publisher, has brought a wealth of publishing knowledge and vision to bear on improving my texts. I have also considerably benefited from the expertise of my new executive editor in psychology, Krista Bettino. Cara Labell, senior developmental editor, has done an excellent job in organizing and monitoring numerous editorial matters in this new edition. Megan Stotts, editorial coordinator, has once again done a competent job of obtaining reviewers and handling many editioral chores. Yasuka Okada and Julia Flohr, marketing managers, have contributed in numerous positive ways to this book. Laurie Entringer created a beautiful cover and Pam Verros created a beautiful design for the text. Holly Irish, Project Manager, did a terrific job in coordinating the book's production. I've also especially enjoyed working with Aaron Downey, senior production manager at Matrix Productions, through the production process.

I also want to thank my wife, Mary Jo, our children, Tracy and Jennifer, and my grandchildren, Jordan, Alex, and Luke, for their wonderful contributions to my life and for helping me to better understand the marvels and mysteries of children's development. Alex, age 6, and Luke, age 4, have been especially helpful in reacquainting me with first-hand information about the marvels and intricacies of infants and young children.

Special thanks go to the many reviewers of 13th edition of this text. Their extensive contributions have made this a far better book.

Reviewers

I owe a special gratitude to the reviewers who provided detailed feedback about the book.

Expert Consultants

Child development has become an enormous, complex field and no single author can possibly be an expert in all areas of the field. To solve this problem, beginning with the sixth edition, I have sought the input of leading experts in many different areas of child development. This tradition continues in the thirteenth edition. The experts have provided me with detailed recommendations of new research to include. The panel of experts is literally a who's who in the field of child development. The experts' biographies and photographs appear on pages xiii–xv.

Previous Edition Expert Reviewers

Gustavo Carlo, *University of Nebraska;* **Beverly Goldfield,** *Rhode Island College;* **Diane Hughes,** *New York University;* **Michael Lewis,** *Rutgers University;* **Candice Mills,** *University of Texas at Dallas;* **Linda Smolak,** *Kenyon College;* **Robert J. Sternberg,** *Tufts University;* **Phyllis Bronstein,** *University of Vermont*

Previous Edition Reviewers

Kristine Anthis, *Southern Connecticut State University;* **Brein K. Ashdown,** *St. Louis University;* **Ruth L. Ault,** *Davidson College;* **Mary Ballard,** *Appalachian State University;* **William H. Barber,** *Midwestern State University;* **Marjorie M. Battaglia,** *George Mason University;* **Jann Belcher,** *Utah Valley State College;* **Wayne Benenson,** *Illinois State University;* **Michael Bergmire,** *Jefferson College;* **David Bernhardt,** *Carleton University;* **Kathryn Norcross Black,** *Purdue University;* **Elain Blakemore,** *Indiana University* **Susan Bland,** *Niagara County Community College;* **Bryan Bolea,** *Grand Valley State*

University; **Amy Booth**, *Northwestern University;* **Marc Bornstein**, *National Institute of Child Health and Human Development;* **Teresa Bossert-Braasch**, *McHenry County College;* **Megan E. Bradley**, *Frostburg State University;* **Albert Bramante**, *Union County College;* **Jo Ann Burnside**, *Richard J Daley College;* **Catherine Caldwell-Harris**, *Boston University;* **Maureen Callahan**, *Webster University;* **Victoria Candelora**, *Brevard Community College;* **D. Bruce Carter**, *Syracuse University;* **Elaine Cassel**, *Marymount University, Lord Fairfax Community; College;* **Lisa Caya**, *University of Wisconsin—LaCrosse;* **Steven Ceci**, *Cornell University;* **Theodore Chandler**, *Kent State University;* **Dante Cicchetti**, *University of Rochester;* **Audry E. Clark**, *California State University, Northridge;* **Debra E. Clark**, *SUNY—Cortland;* **Robert Cohen**, *The University of Memphis;* **John D. Coie**, *Duke University;* **Cynthia Garcia Coll**, *Wellesley College;* **W. Andrew Collins**, *University of Minnesota;* **Robert C. Coon**, *Louisiana State University;* **Roger W. Coulson**, *Iowa State University;* **William Curry**, *Wesleyan College;* **Fred Danner**, *University of Kentucky;* **Darlene DeMarie**, *University of South Florida;* **Marlene DeVoe**, *Saint Cloud State University;* **Denise M. DeZolt**, *Kent State University;* **K. Laurie Dickson**, *Northern Arizona University;* **Daniel D. DiSalvi**, *Kean College;* **Ruth Doyle**, *Casper College;* **Diane C. Draper**, *Iowa State University;* **Sean Duffy**, *Rutgers University;* **Jerry Dusek**, *Syracuse University;* **Beverly Brown Dupré**, *Southern University at New Orleans;* **Glen Elder, Jr.**, *University of North Carolina;* **Claire Etaugh**, *Bradley University;* **Karen Falcone**, *San Joaquin Delta College;* **Dennis T. Farrell**, *Luzerne County Community College;* **Saul Feinman**, *University of Wyoming;* **Gary Feng**, *Duke University;* **Tiffany Field**, *University of Miami;* **Oney Fitzpatrick, Jr.**, *Lamar University;* **Jane Goins Flanagan**, *Lamar University;* **Kate Fogarty**, *University of Florida—Gainesville;* **L. Sidney Fox**, *California State; University—Long Beach;* **Janet Frick**, *University of Georgia;* **Douglas Frye**, *University of Virginia;* **Dale Fryxell**, *Chamainde University;* **Janet A. Fuller**, *Mansfield University;* **Irma Galejs**, *Iowa State University;* **Mary Gauvain**, *University of California, Riverside;* **Eugene Geist**, *Ohio University;* **John Gibbs**, *Ohio State University;* **Colleen Gift**, *Highland Community College;* **Margaret S. Gill**, *Kutztown University;* **Hill Goldsmith**, *University of Wisconsin—Madison;* **Cynthia Graber**, *Columbia University;* **Nira Grannott**, *University of Texas at Dallas;* **Stephen B. Graves**, *University of South Florida;* **Donald E. Guenther**, *Kent State University;* **Julia Guttmann**, *Iowa Wesleyan College;* **Renee Ha**, *University of Washington;* **Robert A. Haaf**, *University of Toledo;* **Craig Hart**, *Brigham Young University;* **Susan Harter**, *University of Denver;* **Robin Harwood**, *Texas Tech University;* **Elizabeth Hasson**, *Westchester University;* **Rebecca Heikkinen**, *Kent State University;* **Joyce Hemphill**, *University of Wisconsin;* **Shirley-Anne Hensch**, *University of Wisconsin;* **Stanley Henson**, *Arkansas Technical University;* **Alice Honig**, *Syracuse University;* **Cynthia Hudley**, *University of California—Santa Barbara;* **Stephen Hupp**, *Southern Illinois University—Edwardsville;* **Vera John-Steiner**, *University of New Mexico;* **Helen L. Johnson**, *Queens College;* **Kathy E. Johnson**, *Indiana University—Purdue University; Indianapolis;* **Seth Kalichman**, *Loyola University;* **Kenneth Kallio**, *SUNY—Geneseo;* **Maria Kalpidou**, *Assumption College;* **Daniel W. Kee**, *California State University—Fullerton;* **Christy Kimpo**, *University of Washington;* **Melvyn B. King**, *SUNY—Cortland;* **Claire Kopp**, *UCLA;* **Deanna Kuhn**, *Columbia University;* **John Kulig**, *Northern Illinois University;* **Janice Kupersmidt**, *University of North Carolina;* **Michael Lamb**, *National Institute of Child Health and Human Development;* **Daniel K. Lapsley**, *University of Notre Dame;* **David B. Liberman**, *University of Houston;* **Robert Lickliter**, *Florida International University;* **Hsin-Hui Lin**, *University of Houston—Victoria;* **Marianna Footo Linz**, *Marshall University;* **Gretchen S. Lovas**, *Susquehanna University;* **Pamela Ludemann**, *Framingham State College;* **Kevin MacDonald**, *California State University—Long Beach;* **Virginia A. Marchman**, *University of Texas at Dallas;* **Saramma T. Mathew**, *Troy State University;* **Barbara McCombs**, *University of Denver;* **Dottie McCrossen**, *University of Ottawa;* **Sheryll Mennicke**, *Concordia College, St. Paul;* **Carolyn Meyer**, *Lake Sumter Community College;* **Dalton Miller-Jones**, *NE Foundation for Children;* **Marilyn Moore**, *Illinois State University;* **Carrie Mori**, *Boise State University;* **Brad Morris**, *Grand Valley State University;* **Winnie Mucherah**, *Ball State University;* **John P. Murray**, *Kansas State University;* **Dara**

Musher-Eizenman, *Bowling Green State University;* **José E. Nanes,** *University of Minnesota;* **Sherry J. Neal,** *Oklahoma City Community Center;* **Larry Nucci,** *University of Illinois at Chicago;* **Daniel J. O'Neill,** *Briston Community College;* **Randall E. Osborne,** *Southwest Texas State University;* **Margaret Owen,** *University of Texas at Dallas;* **Robert Pasnak,** *George Mason University;* **Barbara Aldis Patton,** *University of Houston—Victoria;* **Judy Payne,** *Murray State University;* **Elizabeth Pemberton,** *University of Delaware;* **Herb Pick,** *University of Minnesota;* **Kathy Lee Pillow,** *Arkansas State University, Beebe;* **Nan Ratner,** *University of Maryland;* **Brenda Reimer,** *Southern Missouri State University;* **John Reiser,** *Vanderbilt University;* **Cynthia Rickert,** *Dominican College;* **Cosby Steele Rogers,** *Virginia Polytechnic Institute and State University;* **Kimberly A. Gordon Rouse,** *Ohio State University;* **Jaynati Roy,** *Southern Connecticut State University;* **Kenneth Rubin,** *University of Maryland;* **Donna Ruiz,** *University of Cincinnati;* **Alan Russell,** *Flinders University;* **Carolyn Saarni,** *Sonoma State University;* **Douglas B. Sawin,** *University of Texas, Austin;* **Krista Schoenfeld,** *Colby Community College;* **Ed Scholwinski,** *Southwest Texas State University;* **Dale Schunk,** *Purdue University;* **Bill M. Seay,** *Louisiana State University;* **Matthew J. Sharps,** *California State University, Fresno;* **Marilyn Shea,** *University of Maine, Farmington;* **Susan Shonk,** *SUNY—College of Brockport;* **Susan Siaw,** *California Polytechnic Institute—Pomona;* **Robert Siegler,** *Carnegie Mellon University;* **Evelyn D. Silva,** *Cosumnes River College;* **Mildred D. Similton,** *Pfeiffer University;* **Dorothy Justus Sluss,** *Virginia Polytechnic Institute and State University;* **Janet Spence,** *University of Texas—Austin;* **Melanie Spence,** *University of Texas—Dallas;* **Richard Sprott,** *California State University, East Bay;* **Mark S. Strauss,** *University of Pittsburgh;* **Margaret Szewczyk,** *University of Chicago;* **Ross Thompson,** *University of California—Davis;* **Donna J. Tyler Thompson,** *Midland College;* **Marion K. Underwood,** *University of Texas—Dallas;* **Margot Underwood,** *College of DuPage;* **Cherie Valeithian,** *Kent State University;* **Jaan Valsiner,** *Clark University;* **Robin Yaure,** *Pennsylvania State—Mont Alto;* **Kourtney Valliancourt,** *New Mexico State University;* **Elizabeth Vera,** *Loyola University—Chicago;* **Lawrence Walker,** *University of British Columbia;* **Kimberlee L. Whaley,** *Ohio State University;* **Belinda M. Wholeben,** *Northern Illinois University;* **Frederic Wynn,** *County College of Morris.*

CHILD
DEVELOPMENT

In every child who is born, under no matter what circumstances, and of no matter what parents, the potentiality of the human race is born again.

—**JAMES AGEE**
American Writer, 20th Century

The Nature of Child Development

Examining the shape of childhood allows us to understand it better. Every childhood is distinct, the first chapter of a new biography in the world. This book is about children's development, its universal features, its individual variations, its nature at the beginning of the twenty-first century. *Child Development* is about the rhythm and meaning of children's lives, about turning mystery into understanding, and about weaving together a portrait of who each of us was, is, and will be. In Section 1, you will read one chapter: "Introduction" (Chapter 1).

chapter 1 INTRODUCTION

Ted Kaczynski sprinted through high school, not bothering with his junior year and making only passing efforts at social contact. Off to Harvard at age 16, Kaczynski was a loner during his college years. One of his roommates at Harvard said that he avoided people by quickly shuffling by them and slamming the door behind him. After obtaining his Ph.D. in mathematics at the University of Michigan, Kaczynski became a professor at the University of California at Berkeley. His colleagues there remember him as hiding from social circumstances—no friends, no allies, no networking.

After several years at Berkeley, Kaczynski resigned and moved to a rural area of Montana, where he lived as a hermit in a crude shack for 25 years. Town residents described him as a bearded eccentric. Kaczynski traced his own difficulties to growing up as a genius in a kid's body and sticking out like a sore thumb in his surroundings as a child. In 1996, he was arrested and charged as the notorious Unabomber, America's most wanted killer. Over the course of 17 years, Kaczynski had sent 16 mail bombs that left 23 people wounded or maimed, and 3 people dead. In 1998, he pleaded guilty to the offenses and was sentenced to life in prison.

A decade before Kaczynski mailed his first bomb, Alice Walker spent her days battling racism in Mississippi. She had recently won her first writing fellowship, but rather than use the money to follow her dream of moving to Senegal, Africa, she put herself into the heart and heat of the civil rights movement. Walker had grown up knowing the brutal effects of poverty and racism. Born in 1944, she was the eighth child of Georgia sharecroppers who earned $300 a year. When Walker was 8, her brother accidentally shot her in the left eye with a BB gun. Since her parents had no car, it took them a week to get her to a hospital. By the time she received medical care, she was blind in that eye, and it had developed a disfiguring layer of scar tissue. Despite the counts against her, Walker overcame pain and anger and went on to win a Pulitzer Prize for her book *The Color Purple*. She became not only a novelist but also an essayist, a poet, a short-story writer, and a social activist.

What leads one individual, so full of promise, to commit brutal acts of violence and another to turn poverty and trauma into a rich literary harvest? If you have ever wondered why people turn out the way they do, you have asked yourself the central question we will explore in this book.

Ted Kaczynski, the convicted Unabomber, traced his difficulties to growing up as a genius in a kid's body and not fitting in when he was a child.

Ted Kaczynski, about age 15–16.

Alice Walker won the Pulitzer Prize for her book *The Color Purple*. Like the characters in her book, Walker overcame pain and anger to triumph and celebrate the human spirit.

Alice Walker, about age 8.

preview

Why study children? Perhaps you are or will be a parent or teacher, and responsibility for children is or will be a part of your everyday life. The more you learn about children and the way researchers study them, the better you can guide them. Perhaps you hope to gain an understanding of your own history—as an infant, as a child, and as an adolescent. Perhaps you accidentally came across the course description and found it intriguing. Whatever your reasons, you will discover that the study of child development is provocative, intriguing, and informative. In this first chapter, we will explore historical views and the modern study of child development, consider why caring for children is so important, examine the nature of development, and outline how science helps us to understand it.

Child Development—Yesterday and Today

LG1 Discuss historical views and the modern era of child development.

Historical Views of Childhood

The Modern Study of Child Development

FIGURE **1.1**

HISTORICAL PERCEPTION OF CHILDREN. European paintings centuries ago often depicted children as miniature adults. *Do these artistic creations indicate that earlier Europeans did not view childhood as a distinct period?*

development The pattern of movement or change that begins at conception and continues through the life span.

original sin view Advocated during the Middle Ages, the belief that children were born into the world as evil beings and were basically bad.

tabula rasa view The idea, proposed by John Locke, that children are like a "blank tablet."

innate goodness view The idea, presented by Swiss-born French philosopher Jean-Jacques Rousseau, that children are inherently good.

What do we mean when we speak of an individual's development? **Development** is the pattern of change that begins at conception and continues through the life span. Most development involves growth, although it also includes decay. Anywhere you turn today, the development of children captures public attention. Historically, though, interest in the development of children has been uneven.

HISTORICAL VIEWS OF CHILDHOOD

Childhood has become such a distinct period that it is hard to imagine that it was not always thought of as markedly different from adulthood. However, in medieval Europe laws generally did not distinguish between child and adult offenses. After analyzing samples of art along with available publications, historian Philippe Ariès (1962) concluded that European societies prior to 1600 did not give any special status to children (see Figure 1.1).

Were children actually treated as miniature adults with no special status in medieval Europe? Ariès primarily sampled aristocratic, idealized subjects, which might have led to misperceptions. Childhood probably was recognized as a distinct phase of life more than Ariès believed, but his analysis helped to highlight cultural differences in how children are viewed and treated.

Throughout history, philosophers have speculated at length about the nature of children and how they should be reared. The ancient Egyptians, Greeks, and Romans held rich conceptions of children's development. More recently in European history, three influential philosophical views portrayed children in terms of original sin, tabula rasa, and innate goodness:

- In the **original sin view,** especially advocated during the Middle Ages, children were perceived as being born into the world as evil beings. The goal of child rearing was to provide salvation, to remove sin from the child's life.

- Toward the end of the 17th century, the **tabula rasa view** was proposed by English philosopher John Locke. He argued that children are not innately bad but, instead, start out like a "blank tablet." Locke believed that childhood experiences are important in determining adult characteristics. He advised parents to spend time with their children and to help them become contributing members of society.

- In the 18th century, the **innate goodness view** was presented by Swiss-born French philosopher Jean-Jacques Rousseau. He stressed that children are inherently good. Because children are basically good, said Rousseau, they should be permitted to grow naturally, with little parental monitoring or constraint.

Today, the Western view of children holds that childhood is a highly eventful and unique period of life that lays an important foundation for the adult years and is markedly different from them. Most current approaches to childhood identify distinct periods in which children master specific skills and tasks that prepare them for adulthood. Childhood is no longer seen as an inconvenient waiting period during which adults must suffer the incompetencies of the young. Instead, we protect children from the stresses and responsibilities of adult work through strict child labor laws. We handle their crimes in a special system of juvenile justice. We also have provisions for helping children when families fail. In short, we now value childhood as a special time of growth and change, and we invest great resources in caring for and educating children.

> Children are the legacy we leave for the time we will not live to see.
>
> —**Aristotle**
> *Greek Philosopher, 4th Century* B.C.

THE MODERN STUDY OF CHILD DEVELOPMENT

The modern era of studying children began with some important developments in the late 1800s (Cairns & Cairns, 2006). Since then, the study of child development has evolved into a sophisticated science with major theories, as well as elegant techniques and methods of study that help organize our thinking about children's development. This new era began during the last quarter of the 19th century when a major shift took place—from a strictly philosophical approach to human psychology to an approach that includes systematic observation and experimentation.

Most of the influential early psychologists were trained either in the natural sciences, such as biology or medicine, or in philosophy. The natural scientists valued experiments and reliable observations; after all, experiments and systematic observation had advanced knowledge in physics, chemistry, and biology. But these scientists were not at all sure that people, much less children or infants, could be studied in this way. Their hesitation was due, in part, to a lack of examples to follow in studying children. In addition, philosophers of the time debated, on both intellectual and ethical grounds, whether the methods of science were appropriate for studying people.

The deadlock was broken when some daring thinkers began to try new methods of studying infants, children, and adolescents. For example, near the turn of the century, French psychologist Alfred Binet invented many tasks to assess attention and memory. He used them to study his own daughters, other normal children, children with mental retardation, children who were gifted, and adults. Eventually, he collaborated in the development of the first modern test of intelligence (the Binet test). At about the same time, G. Stanley Hall pioneered the use of questionnaires with large groups of children.

Later, during the 1920s, many child development research centers were created and their professional staffs began to observe and chart a myriad of behaviors in infants and children. Research centers at the Universities of Minnesota, Iowa, California at Berkeley, Columbia, and Toronto became famous for their investigations of children's play, friendship patterns, fears, aggression and conflict, and sociability. This work became closely associated with the so-called child study movement, and a new organization, the Society for Research in Child Development, was formed at about the same time.

Another ardent observer of children was Arnold Gesell. With his photographic dome (shown in Figure 1.2), Gesell (1928) could systematically observe children's behavior without interrupting them. He strove for precision in charting what a child is like at specific ages.

Gesell not only developed sophisticated strategies for studying children but also held provocative views on children's development. His views were strongly influenced by Charles Darwin's evolutionary theory (Darwin had made the scientific study of children respectable when he developed a baby journal for recording systematic

FIGURE 1.2

GESELL'S PHOTOGRAPHIC DOME. Cameras rode on metal tracks at the top of the dome and were moved as needed to record the child's activities. Others could observe from outside the dome without being seen by the child.

observations of children). Gesell argued that certain characteristics of children simply "bloom" with age because of a biological, maturational blueprint.

Evolutionary theory also influenced G. Stanley Hall. Hall (1904) argued that child development follows a natural evolutionary course that can be revealed by child study. He theorized that child development unfolds in stages, with distinct motives and capabilities at each stage. Later in the chapter, you will see that today there is considerable debate about how strongly children's development is determined by biology and by environment, and the extent to which development occurs in stages.

The direct study of children, in which investigators directly observe children's behavior, conduct experiments, and obtain information about children by questioning their parents and teachers, had an auspicious start in the work of these child study experts. The flow of information about children, based on direct study, has only increased since that time. Methodological advances in observation, as well as the introduction of experimentation and the development of major theories, characterize the achievements of the modern era. Later in this chapter, we will spend considerable time describing the major theories and research methods of the field of child development today.

Review Connect Reflect

LG1 Discuss historical views and the modern era of child development.

Review

- What is development? How has childhood been perceived through history?
- What are the key characteristics of the modern study of child development?

Connect

- Think back to the story that opened this chapter. How would you interpret the development of Ted Kaczynski and Alice Walker using the original sin, tabula rasa, and innate goodness views?

Reflect *Your Own Personal Journey of Life*

- Now that you have studied historical views of childhood, think about how your own personal development might have been different if you had been born at a different time in history. How do you think your development might have been affected if you had been born 100 years ago? Fifty years ago?

Caring for Children

LG2 Identify five areas in which children's lives need to be improved, and explain the roles of resilience and social policy in children's development.

Improving the Lives of Children

Resilience, Social Policy, and Children's Development

Caring for children is an important theme of this text. To understand why caring for children is so important, we will explore why it is beneficial to study children's development, identify some areas in which children's lives need to be improved, and explore the roles of resilience and social policy in children's development.

> We reach backward to our parents and forward to our children to a future we will never see, but about which we need to care.
>
> —CARL JUNG
> *Swiss Psychoanalyst, 20th Century*

IMPROVING THE LIVES OF CHILDREN

If you were to pick up a newspaper or magazine in any U.S. town or city, you might see headlines like these: "Political Leanings May Be Written in the Genes," "Mother Accused of Tossing Children into Bay," "Gender Gap Widens," and "FDA Warns About ADHD Drug." Researchers are examining these and many other topics of contemporary concern. The roles that health and well-being, parenting,

Luis Vargas, Clinical Child Psychologist

Luis Vargas is Director of the Clinical Child Psychology Internship Program and a professor in child and adolescent psychiatry at the University of New Mexico School of Medicine. He obtained an undergraduate degree in psychology from Trinity University in Texas and a Ph.D. in clinical psychology at the University of Nebraska–Lincoln.

Vargas' work includes assessing and treating children, adolescents, and their families, especially when a child or adolescent has a serious mental disorder. Vargas also trains mental health professionals to provide culturally responsive and developmentally appropriate mental health services. In addition, he is interested in cultural and assessment issues with children, adolescents, and their families.

Vargas' clinical work is heavily influenced by contextual and ecological theories of development (which we will discuss later in this chapter). His first undergraduate course in human development, and subsequent courses in development, contributed to his decision to pursue a career in clinical child psychology.

Following this chapter you can read about many careers in child development, including more about the field of child clinical psychology. Also, at appropriate places throughout the book we will provide profiles of individuals in various child development careers.

Luis Vargas (*left*) conducting a child therapy session.

For more information about what clinical psychologists do, see page 45 in the Careers in Child Development appendix that directly follows this chapter.

education, and sociocultural contexts play in child development, as well as how social policy is related to these issues, are a particular focus of this textbook.

Health and Well-Being   Does a pregnant woman endanger her fetus if she has a few beers a week? How does a poor diet affect a child's ability to learn? Are children exercising less today than in the past? What roles do parents and peers play in whether adolescents abuse drugs? Throughout this text, we will discuss many questions like these regarding health and well-being.

Health professionals today recognize the roles played by lifestyles and psychological states in determining health and well-being (Hahn, Payne, & Lucas, 2011; Sparling & Redican, 2011). In every chapter of this book, issues of health and well-being are integrated into our discussion.

Clinical psychologists are among the health professionals who help people improve their well-being. In *Connecting With Careers,* you can read about clinical psychologist Luis Vargas, who helps adolescents with problems. A *Careers* Appendix that follows Chapter 1 describes the education and training required to become a clinical psychologist or to pursue other careers in child development.

Parenting   Can two gay men raise a healthy family? Are children harmed if both parents work outside the home? Does spanking have negative consequences for a child's development? How damaging is divorce to children's development? Controversial answers to questions like these reflect pressures on the contemporary family

Children learn to love when they are loved

(Patterson, 2009). We'll examine these questions and others that provide a context for understanding factors that influence parents' lives and their effectiveness in raising their children. How parents, as well as other adults, can make a positive difference in children's lives is another major theme of this book.

You might be a parent someday or might already be one. You should take seriously the importance of rearing your children, because they are the future of our society. Good parenting takes considerable time. If you plan to become a parent, commit yourself day after day, week after week, month after month, and year after year to providing your children with a warm, supportive, safe, and stimulating environment that will make them feel secure and allow them to reach their full potential as human beings. The poster on this page that states "Children learn to love when they are loved" reflects this theme.

Understanding the nature of children's development can help you become a better parent. Many parents learn parenting practices from their parents. Unfortunately, when parenting practices and child-care strategies are passed from one generation to the next, both desirable and undesirable ones are usually perpetuated. This book and your instructor's lectures in this course can help you become more knowledgeable about children's development and sort through the practices in your own upbringing to identify which ones you should continue with your own children and which ones you should abandon.

Education   There is widespread agreement that something needs to be done to improve the education of our nation's children (Johnson & others, 2011; McCombs, 2010). Among the questions involved in improving schools are: Are U.S. schools teaching children to be immoral? Are schools failing to teach students how to read and write and calculate adequately? Should there be more accountability in schools, with adequacy of student learning and teaching assessed by formal tests? Should schools challenge students more? Should schools focus only on developing children's knowledge and cognitive skills, or should they pay more attention to the whole child and consider the child's socioemotional and physical development as well? In this text, we will examine such questions about the state of education in the United States and consider recent research on solutions to educational problems (Nieto, 2010; Suarez-Orosco & Suarez-Orosco, 2010).

Ah! What would the
world be to us
If the children were no more?
We should dread the desert behind us
Worse than the dark before.

—HENRY WADSWORTH LONGFELLOW
American Poet, 19th Century

context The settings, influenced by historical, economic, social, and cultural factors, in which development occurs.

culture The behavior patterns, beliefs, and all other products of a group that are passed on from generation to generation.

cross-cultural studies Comparisons of one culture with one or more other cultures. These provide information about the degree to which children's development is similar, or universal, across cultures, and to the degree to which it is culture-specific.

ethnicity A characteristic based on cultural heritage, nationality, race, religion, and language.

socioeconomic status (SES) Categorization based on a person's occupational, educational, and economic characteristics.

gender The characteristics of people as males and females.

Marian Wright Edelman, president of the Children's Defense Fund (shown here interacting with young children), has been a tireless advocate of children's rights and has been instrumental in calling attention to the needs of children. *What are some of these needs?*

Sociocultural Contexts and Diversity   Health and well-being, parenting, and education—like development itself—are all shaped by their sociocultural context (Cole & Cagigas, 2010; Shiraev & Levy, 2010). The term **context** refers to the settings in which development occurs. These settings are influenced by historical, economic, social, and cultural factors. Four contexts to which we will pay special attention in this text are culture, ethnicity, socioeconomic status, and gender.

Culture encompasses the behavior patterns, beliefs, and all other products of a particular group of people that are passed on from generation to generation. Culture results from the interaction of people over many years. A cultural group can be as large as the United States or as small as an isolated Appalachian town. Whatever its size, the group's culture influences the behavior of its members (Goodnow, 2010; Hall, 2010; Kitayama, 2011). **Cross-cultural studies** compare aspects of two or more cultures. The comparison provides information about the degree to which development is similar, or universal, across cultures, or is instead culture-specific (Larson, Wilson, & Rickman, 2009; Shiraev & Levy, 2010).

Ethnicity (the word *ethnic* comes from the Greek word for "nation") is rooted in cultural heritage, nationality, race, religion, and language. African Americans, Latinos, Asian Americans, Native Americans, Polish Americans, and Italian Americans are a few examples of ethnic groups. Diversity exists within each ethnic group (Banks, 2010; Spring, 2010). Contrary to stereotypes, not all African Americans live in low-income circumstances; not all Latinos are Catholics; not all Asian Americans are high school math whizzes (Florence, 2010).

Socioeconomic status (SES) refers to a person's position within society based on occupational, educational, and economic characteristics. Socioeconomic status implies certain inequalities. Generally, members of a society have (1) occupations that vary in prestige, and some individuals have more access than others to higher-status occupations; (2) different levels of educational attainment, and some individuals have more access than others to better education; (3) different economic resources; and (4) different levels of power to influence a community's institutions. These differences in the ability to control resources and to participate in society's rewards produce unequal opportunities (Huston & Bentley, 2010; McLoyd & others, 2009).

Gender   Gender is another key dimension of children's development (Best, 2010; Martin & Ruble, 2010). **Gender** refers to the characteristics of people as males and females. How you view yourself, your relationships with other people, your life and your goals is shaped to a great extent by whether you are male or female and how your culture defines what is appropriate behavior for males and females.

In the United States, the sociocultural context has become increasingly diverse in recent years (Banks, 2010; Tamis-LeMonda & Fadden, 2010). Its population includes a greater variety of cultures and ethnic groups than ever before. This changing demographic tapestry promises not only the richness that diversity produces but also difficult challenges in extending the American dream to all individuals (Huston & Bentley, 2010; McLoyd & others, 2009). We will discuss sociocultural contexts and diversity in each chapter. In addition, *Connecting With Diversity*, which highlights an issue related to diversity, appears in every chapter. The *Connecting With Diversity* in this chapter focuses on gender, families, and children's development around the world.

RESILIENCE, SOCIAL POLICY, AND CHILDREN'S DEVELOPMENT

Some children develop confidence in their abilities despite negative stereotypes about their gender or their ethnic group, and some children triumph over poverty or other adversities. They show *resilience* (Gutman, 2008). Think back to the chapter-opening story about Alice Walker. In spite of racism, poverty, low socioeconomic status, and a disfiguring eye injury, she went on to become a successful author and champion for equality.

Inderjeet Poolust, 5, from India celebrates being one of 27 school children who recently became a U.S. citizen at an induction ceremony in Queens, New York.

developmental connection

Peers. Peers especially play an important role in gender development during childhood. Chapter 12, p. 350

Muslim school in Middle East with boys only.

Gender, Families, and Children's Development

Around the world, the experiences of male and female children and adolescents continue to be quite different (Best, 2010; UNICEF, 2009, 2010). One analysis found that a higher percentage of girls than boys around the world have never had any education (UNICEF, 2004) (see Figure 1.3). The countries with the fewest females being educated are in Africa, where in some areas, girls and women are receiving no education at all. Canada, the United States, and Russia have the highest percentages of educated women. In developing countries, 67 percent of women over the age of 25 (compared with 50 percent of men) have never been to school. At the beginning of the 21st century, 80 million more boys than girls were in primary and secondary educational settings around the world (United Nations, 2002).

A special cross-cultural concern is the educational and psychological conditions of women around the world (UNICEF, 2009, 2010). Inadequate educational opportunities, violence, and mental health issues are just some of the problems faced by many women.

In many countries, adolescent females have less freedom to pursue a variety of careers and engage in various leisure acts than males (Helgeson, 2009). Gender differences in sexual expression are widespread, especially in India, Southeast Asia, Latin America, and Arab countries, where there are far more restrictions on the sexual activity of adolescent females than males. In certain areas around the world, these gender differences do appear to be narrowing over time. In some countries, educational and career opportunities for women are expanding, and in some parts of the world control over adolescent girls' romantic and sexual relationships is weakening. However, in many countries females still experience considerable discrimination, and much work is needed to bridge the gap between the rights of males and females.

Consider Dhaka, Bangladesh, where sewers overflow, garbage rots in the streets, and children are undernourished. Nearly two-thirds of the young women in Bangladesh get married before they are 18. Doly Akter, age 17, who lives in a slum in Dhaka, recently created an organization supported by UNICEF in which girls go door-to-door to monitor the hygiene habits of households in their neighborhood. The girls' monitoring has led to improved hygiene and health in the families. Also, the organization Doly formed has managed to stop several child marriages by meeting with parents and convincing them that early marriage is not in their daughter's best interests. When talking with parents in their neighborhoods, the girls in the organization emphasize how staying in school will improve their daughter's future. Doly says the girls in her organization are far more aware of their rights than their mothers were (UNICEF, 2007).

In addition to sociocultural contexts and diversity, this interlude also covers the other topics introduced in this section of the chapter. *What health and well-being, parenting, and educational problems and interventions have affected the development of females worldwide?*

FIGURE **1.3**

PERCENTAGE OF CHILDREN 7 TO 18 YEARS OF AGE AROUND THE WORLD WHO HAVE NEVER BEEN TO SCHOOL OF ANY KIND. When UNICEF(2004) surveyed the education that children around the world are receiving, it found that far more girls than boys receive no formal schooling at all.

Doly Akter.

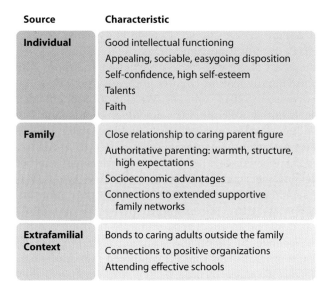

Source	Characteristic
Individual	Good intellectual functioning
	Appealing, sociable, easygoing disposition
	Self-confidence, high self-esteem
	Talents
	Faith
Family	Close relationship to caring parent figure
	Authoritative parenting: warmth, structure, high expectations
	Socioeconomic advantages
	Connections to extended supportive family networks
Extrafamilial Context	Bonds to caring adults outside the family
	Connections to positive organizations
	Attending effective schools

FIGURE **1.4**

CHARACTERISTICS OF RESILIENT CHILDREN AND THEIR CONTEXTS

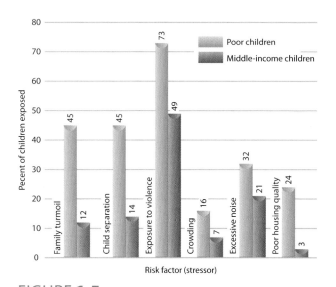

FIGURE **1.5**

EXPOSURE TO SIX STRESSORS AMONG POOR AND MIDDLE-INCOME CHILDREN. One study analyzed the exposure to six stressors among poor children and middle-income children (Evans & English, 2002). Poor children were much more likely to face each of these stressors.

Are there certain characteristics that make children like Alice Walker resilient? Are there other characteristics that make children lash out against society, like Ted Kaczynski, who became a killer despite his intelligence and education? After analyzing research on this topic, Ann Masten and her colleagues (2006, 2009a, b; Masten, Burt, & Coatsworth, 2006; Masten & others, 2009a, b) concluded that a number of individual factors influence resiliency, such as good intellectual functioning. In addition, as Figure 1.4 shows, their families and resources outside the children's families tend to show certain features. For example, resilient children are likely to have a close relationship to a caring parent figure and bonds to caring adults outside the family.

Should governments also take action to improve the contexts of children's development and aid their resilience? **Social policy** is a government's course of action designed to promote the welfare of its citizens. The shape and scope of social policy related to children are tied to the political system. The values held by citizens and elected officials, the nation's economic strengths and weaknesses, and partisan politics all influence the policy agenda.

Out of concern that policymakers are doing too little to protect the well-being of children, researchers increasingly are undertaking studies that they hope will lead to wise and effective decision making about social policy (Balsano, Theokas, & Bobek, 2009; Meece & Schaefer, 2010).

Children who grow up in poverty represent a special concern (McLoyd & others, 2009; Tamis-LeMonda & McFadden, 2010). In 2006, approximately 17.4 percent of U.S. children were living in families with incomes below the poverty line (Federal Interagency Forum on Child and Family Statistics, 2008).This is an increase from 2001 (16.2 percent) but down from a peak of 22.7 percent in 1993. As indicated in Figure 1.5, one study found that a higher percentage of U.S. children in poor families than in middle-income families were exposed to family turmoil, separation from a parent, violence, crowding, excessive noise, and poor housing (Evans & English, 2002). A recent study also revealed that the more years children spent living in poverty, the more their physiological indices of stress were elevated (Evans & Kim, 2007).

social policy A government's course of action designed to promote the welfare of its citizens.

The U.S. figure of 17.4 percent of children living in poverty is much higher than those from other industrialized nations. For example, Canada has a child poverty rate of 9 percent and Sweden has a rate of 2 percent.

What can we do to lessen the effect of these stressors on children and those who care for them? Strategies for improving the lives of children include improving social policy for families (Phillips & Lowenstein, 2011; Sandler, Wolchik, & Schoenfelder, 2011). In the United States, the national government, state governments, and city governments all play a role in influencing the well-being of children. When families fail or seriously endanger a child's well-being, governments often step in to help.

At the national and state levels, policymakers for decades have debated whether helping poor parents ends up helping their children as well. Researchers are providing some answers by examining the effects of specific policies (Brooks-Gunn, Johnson, & Leventhal, 2010; Huston & Bentley, 2010). For example, the Minnesota Family Investment Program (MFIP) was designed in the 1990s primarily to influence the behavior of adults—specifically, to move adults off the welfare rolls and into paid employment. A key element of the program was that it guaranteed that adults participating in the program would receive more income if they worked than if they did not. When the adults' income rose, how did that affect their children? A study of the effects of MFIP found that increases in the incomes of working poor parents were linked with benefits for their children (Gennetian & Miller, 2002). The children's achievement in school improved, and their behavior problems decreased. A current MFIP study is examining the influence of specific services on low-income families at risk for child maltreatment and other negative outcomes for children (Minnesota Family Investment Program, 2009).

Developmental psychologists and other researchers have examined the effects of many other government policies. They are seeking ways to help families living in poverty improve their well-being, and they have offered many suggestions for improving government policies (Huston & Bentley, 2010; Mahoney, Parente, & Zigler, 2010; Sandler, Wolchik, & Schoenfelder, 2011).

developmental **connection**

Socioeconomic Status. An increasing number of studies are showing that positive outcomes can be achieved through intervention in the lives of children living in poverty. Chapter 17, pp. 492–493

Review Connect Reflect

LG2 Identify five areas in which children's lives need to be improved, and explain the roles of resilience and social policy in children's development.

Review

- What are several aspects of children's development that need to be improved?
- What characterizes resilience in children's development? What is social policy, and how can it influence children's lives?

Connect

- How is the concept of resilience related to the story you read at the beginning of this chapter?

Reflect *Your Own Personal Journey of Life*

- Imagine what your development as a child would have been like in a culture that offered choices that were fewer or distinctively different from your own. How might your development have been different if your family had been significantly richer or poorer than it was as you were growing up?

Developmental Processes, Periods, and Issues

LG3 Discuss the most important processes, periods, and issues in development.

Biological, Cognitive, and Socioemotional Processes

Periods of Development

Issues in Development

Each of us develops in certain ways like *all* other individuals, like *some* other individuals, and like *no* other individuals. Most of the time, our attention is directed to a person's uniqueness, but psychologists who study development are drawn to both our shared characteristics and those that make us unique. As humans, we all have traveled some common paths. Each of us—Leonardo da Vinci, Joan of Arc, George Washington, Martin Luther King, Jr., and you—walked at about the age of 1, engaged in fantasy play as a young child, and became more independent as a youth. What shapes this common path of human development, and what are its milestones?

BIOLOGICAL, COGNITIVE, AND SOCIOEMOTIONAL PROCESSES

The pattern of human development is created by the interplay of three key processes. They are biological, cognitive, and socioemotional in nature.

Biological Processes   **Biological processes** produce changes in an individual's body. Genes inherited from parents, the development of the brain, height and weight gains, development of motor skills, and the hormonal changes of puberty all reflect the role of biological processes in development.

Cognitive Processes   **Cognitive processes** refer to changes in an individual's thought, intelligence, and language. The tasks of watching a mobile swinging above a crib, putting together a two-word sentence, memorizing a poem, solving a math problem, and imagining what it would be like to be a movie star all involve cognitive processes.

Socioemotional Processes   **Socioemotional processes** involve changes in an individual's relationships with other people, changes in emotions, and changes in personality. An infant's smile in response to her mother's touch, a child's attack on a playmate, another's development of assertiveness, and an adolescent's joy at the senior prom all reflect socioemotional development.

Connecting Biological, Cognitive, and Socioemotional Processes   Biological, cognitive, and socioemotional processes are inextricably intertwined (Diamond, 2009; Diamond, Casey, & Munakata, 2011). Consider a baby smiling in response to a parent's touch. This response depends on biological processes (the physical nature of touch and responsiveness to it), cognitive processes (the ability to understand intentional acts), and socioemotional processes (the act of smiling often reflects a positive emotional feeling, and smiling helps to connect us in positive ways with other human beings). Nowhere is the connection across biological, cognitive, and socioemotional processes more obvious than in two rapidly emerging fields:

- *developmental cognitive neuroscience*, which explores links between development, cognitive processes, and the brain (Diamond, Casey, & Munakata, 2011)
- *developmental social neuroscience*, which examines connections between development, socioemotional processes, and the brain (Calkins & Bell, 2010; de Haan & Gunnar, 2009; Johnson & others, 2009)

PEANUTS © United Features Syndicate, Inc.

biological processes Changes in an individual's body.

cognitive processes Changes in an individual's thinking, intelligence, and language.

socioemotional processes Changes in an individual's relationships with other people, emotions, and personality.

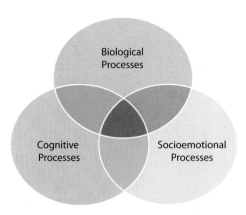

FIGURE 1.6

CHANGES IN DEVELOPMENT ARE THE RESULT OF BIOLOGICAL, COGNITIVE, AND SOCIOEMOTIONAL PROCESSES. The processes interact as individuals develop.

"This is the path to adulthood. You're here."

© The New Yorker Collection, 2001, Robert Weber from cartoonbank.com All rights reserved.

prenatal period The time from conception to birth.

infancy The developmental period that extends from birth to about 18 to 24 months.

early childhood The developmental period that extends from the end of infancy to about 5 or 6 years of age, sometimes called the preschool years.

middle and late childhood The developmental period that extends from about 6 to 11 years of age, sometimes called the elementary school years.

adolescence The developmental period of transition from childhood to early adulthood, entered at approximately 10 to 12 years of age and ending at 18 or 19 years of age.

In many instances, biological, cognitive, and socioemotional processes are bidirectional. For example, biological processes can influence cognitive processes and vice versa. Thus, although usually we will study the different processes of development (biological, cognitive, and socioemotional) in separate locations, keep in mind that we are talking about the development of an integrated individual with a mind and body that are interdependent (see Figure 1.6).

In many places throughout the book we will call attention to connections between biological, cognitive, and socioemotional processes. A feature titled Developmental Connections appears multiple times in each chapter to highlight these as well as other content connections earlier or later in the text.

In Connecting Across Content, you will see a backward-connecting arrow indicating chapter(s) where the topic has been discussed previously, or a forward-connecting arrow indicating chapter(s) where the topic will appear again. Included in the Developmental Connections feature is a brief description of the backward or forward connection.

PERIODS OF DEVELOPMENT

For purposes of organization and understanding, a child's development is commonly described in terms of periods that correspond to approximate age ranges. The most widely used classification of developmental periods describes a child's development in terms of the following sequence: the prenatal period, infancy, early childhood, middle and late childhood, and adolescence.

The **prenatal period** is the time from conception to birth, roughly a nine-month period. During this amazing time, a single cell grows into an organism, complete with a brain and behavioral capabilities.

Infancy is the developmental period that extends from birth to about 18 to 24 months of age. Infancy is a time of extreme dependence on adults. Many psychological activities are just beginning—the abilities to speak, to coordinate sensations and physical actions, to think with symbols, and to imitate and learn from others.

Early childhood is the developmental period that extends from the end of infancy to about 5 or 6 years of age; sometimes this period is called the preschool years. During this time, young children learn to become more self-sufficient and to care for themselves, they develop school readiness skills (following instructions, identifying letters), and they spend many hours in play and with peers. First grade typically marks the end of this period.

Middle and late childhood is the developmental period that extends between about 6 and 11 years of age; sometimes this period is referred to as the elementary school years. Children master the fundamental skills of reading, writing, and arithmetic, and they are formally exposed to the larger world and its culture. Achievement becomes a more central theme of the child's world, and self-control increases.

Adolescence is the developmental period of transition from childhood to early adulthood, entered at approximately 10 to 12 years of age and ending at about 18 to 19 years of age. Adolescence begins with rapid physical changes—dramatic gains in height and weight; changes in body contour; and the development of sexual characteristics such as enlargement of the breasts, growth of pubic and facial hair, and deepening of the voice. The pursuit of independence and an identity are prominent features of this period of development. More and more time is spent outside the family. Thought becomes more abstract, idealistic, and logical.

Today, developmentalists do not believe that change ends with adolescence (Depp, Vahia, & Jeste, 2010; Schaie, 2010, 2011). They describe development as a lifelong process. However, the purpose of this text is to describe the changes in development that take place from conception through adolescence. All of these periods of development are produced by the interplay of biological, cognitive, and socioemotional processes (see Figure 1.7).

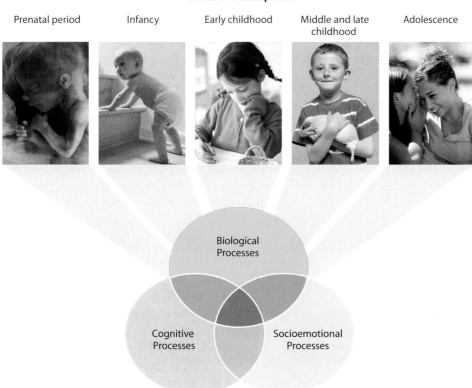

Periods of Development

Prenatal period   Infancy   Early childhood   Middle and late childhood   Adolescence

Biological Processes

Cognitive Processes   Socioemotional Processes

Processes of Development

FIGURE **1.7**

PROCESSES AND PERIODS OF DEVELOPMENT. Development moves through the prenatal, infancy, early childhood, middle and late childhood, and adolescence periods. These periods of development are the result of biological, cognitive, and socioemotional processes.

ISSUES IN DEVELOPMENT

Was Ted Kaczynski born a killer, or did his life turn him into one? Kaczynski himself thought that his childhood was the root of his troubles. He grew up as a genius in a boy's body and never fit in with other children. Did his early experiences determine his later life? Is your own journey through life marked out ahead of time, or can your experiences change your path? Are experiences that occur early in your journey more important than later ones? Is your journey like taking an elevator up a skyscraper with distinct stops along the way, or more like a cruise down a river with smoother ebbs and flows? These questions point to three issues about the nature of development: the roles played by nature and nurture, stability and change, and continuity and discontinuity.

Nature and Nurture   The **nature-nurture issue** involves the debate about whether development is primarily influenced by nature or by nurture (Goodnow, 2010; Kagan, 2010). *Nature* refers to an organism's biological inheritance, *nurture* to its environmental experiences. Almost no one today argues that development can be explained by nature alone or by nurture alone. But some ("nature" proponents) claim that the most important influence on development is biological inheritance, and others ("nurture" proponents) claim that environmental experiences are the most important influence.

According to the nature proponents, just as a sunflower grows in an orderly way—unless it is defeated by an unfriendly environment—so does a person. The range of environments can be vast, but evolutionary and genetic foundations

nature-nurture issue Debate about whether development is primarily influenced by nature or nurture. The "nature" proponents claim biological inheritance is the most important influence on development; the "nurture" proponents claim that environmental experiences are the most important.

developmental **connection**

Biological Processes. Can specific genes be linked to specific environmental experience? Chapter 2, p. 69

Continuity

Discontinuity

FIGURE **1.8**

CONTINUITY AND DISCONTINUITY IN

DEVELOPMENT. Is human development more like that of a seedling gradually growing into a giant oak or more like that of a caterpillar suddenly becoming a butterfly?

continuity-discontinuity issue Question about whether development involves gradual, cumulative change (continuity) or distinct stages (discontinuity).

early-later experience issue Controversy regarding the degree to which early experiences (especially during infancy) or later experiences are the key determinants of children's development.

produce commonalities in growth and development (Cosmides, 2011; Goldsmith, 2011; Mader, 2011). We walk before we talk, speak one word before two words, grow rapidly in infancy and less so in early childhood, and experience a rush of sexual hormones in puberty. Extreme environments—those that are psychologically barren or hostile—can stunt development, but nature proponents emphasize the influence of tendencies that are genetically wired into humans (Brooker, 2011; Raven, 2011).

By contrast, other psychologists emphasize the importance of nurture, or environmental experiences, to development (Gauvain & Parke, 2010; Grusec, 2011; Kopp, 2011). Experiences run the gamut from the individual's biological environment (nutrition, medical care, drugs, and physical accidents) to the social environment (family, peers, schools, community, media, and culture). For example, a child's diet can affect how tall the child grows and even how effectively the child can think and solve problems. Despite their genetic wiring, a child born and raised in a poor village in Bangladesh and a child in the suburbs of Denver are likely to have different skills, different ways of thinking about the world, and different ways of relating to people.

Continuity and Discontinuity Think about your own development for a moment. Did you become the person you are gradually, like the seedling that slowly, cumulatively grows into a giant oak? Or did you experience sudden, distinct changes, like the caterpillar that changes into a butterfly (see Figure 1.8)?

The **continuity-discontinuity issue** focuses on the extent to which development involves gradual, cumulative change (continuity) or distinct stages (discontinuity). For the most part, developmentalists who emphasize nurture usually describe development as a gradual, continuous process, like the seedling's growth into an oak. Those who emphasize nature often describe development as a series of distinct stages, like the change from caterpillar to butterfly.

Consider continuity first. As the oak grows from seedling to giant oak, it becomes more oak—its development is continuous. Similarly, a child's first word, though seemingly an abrupt, discontinuous event, is actually the result of weeks and months of growth and practice. Puberty, another seemingly abrupt, discontinuous occurrence, is actually a gradual process occurring over several years.

Viewed in terms of discontinuity, each person is described as passing through a sequence of stages in which change is qualitatively rather than quantitatively different. As the caterpillar changes to a butterfly, it does not become more caterpillar but a different kind of organism—its development is discontinuous. Similarly, at some point a child moves from not being able to think abstractly about the world to being able to do so. This change is a qualitative, discontinuous change in development, not a quantitative, continuous change.

Early and Later Experience The **early-later experience issue** focuses on the degree to which early experiences (especially in infancy) or later experiences are the key determinants of the child's development. That is, if infants experience harmful circumstances, can those experiences be overcome by later, positive ones? Or are the early experiences so critical—possibly because they are the infant's first, prototypical experiences—that they cannot be overridden by a later, better environment? To those who emphasize early experiences, life is an unbroken trail on which a psychological quality can be traced back to its origin (Kagan, 1992, 2000). In contrast, to those who emphasize later experiences, development is like a river, continually ebbing and flowing.

The early-later experience issue has a long history and continues to be hotly debated among developmentalists (Kagan, 2010; McElwain, 2009). Plato was sure that infants who were rocked frequently became better athletes. Nineteenth-century New England ministers told parents in Sunday afternoon sermons that the way they handled their infants would determine their children's later character. Some developmentalists argue that unless infants and young children experience warm, nurturing care, their development will never quite be optimal (Finger & others, 2009).

In contrast, later-experience advocates argue that children are malleable throughout development and that later sensitive caregiving is just as important as earlier sensitive caregiving. A number of developmentalists stress that too little attention has been given to later experiences in development (Baltes & Smith, 2008; Schaie, 2010, 2011; Scheibe & Carstensen, 2010; Staudinger & Gluck, 2011). They accept that early experiences are important contributors to development, but assert that they are no more important than later experiences. Jerome Kagan (2000, 2010) points out that even children who show the qualities of an inhibited temperament, which is linked to heredity, have the capacity to change their behavior. In his research, almost one-third of a group of children who had an inhibited temperament at 2 years of age were not unusually shy or fearful when they were 4 years of age (Kagan & Snidman, 1991).

What is the nature of the early and later experience issue?

People in Western cultures, especially those influenced by Freudian theory, have tended to support the idea that early experiences are more important than later experiences (Lamb & Sternberg, 1992). The majority of people in the world do not share this belief. For example, people in many Asian countries believe that experiences occurring after about 6 or 7 years of age are more important to development than are earlier experiences. This stance stems from the long-standing belief in Eastern cultures that children's reasoning skills begin to develop in important ways during middle childhood.

Evaluating the Developmental Issues   Most developmentalists recognize that it is unwise to take an extreme position on the issues of nature and nurture, continuity and discontinuity, and early and later experiences. Development is not all nature or all nurture, not all continuity or all discontinuity, and not all early or later experiences. Nature and nurture, continuity and discontinuity, and early and later experiences all play a part in development through the human life span. Along with this consensus, there is still spirited debate about how strongly development is influenced by each of these factors (Blakemore, Berenbaum, & Liben, 2009; Kagan, 2010). Are girls less likely to do well in math mostly because of inherited characteristics or because of society's expectations and because of how girls are raised? Can enriched experiences during adolescence remove deficits resulting from poverty, neglect, and poor schooling during childhood? The answers also have a bearing on social policy decisions about children and adolescents, and consequently on each of our lives.

Review *Connect* Reflect

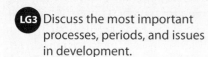 Discuss the most important processes, periods, and issues in development.

Review

- What are biological, cognitive, and socioemotional processes?
- What are the main periods of development?
- What are three important issues in development?

Connect

- Based on what you read earlier in this chapter, what do you think Ted Kaczynski would have to say about the early-later experience issue?

Reflect *Your Own Personal Journey of Life*

- Can you identify an early experience that you believe contributed in important ways to your development? Can you identify a recent or current (later) experience that you think had (or is having) a strong influence on your development?

The Science of Child Development

LG4 Summarize why research is important in child development, the main theories in child development, and research methods, designs, and challenges.

The Importance of Research | Research Methods for Collecting Data | Challenges in Child Development Research

Theories of Child Development | Research Designs

Science refines everyday thinking.

—ALBERT EINSTEIN

German-born American Physicist, 20th Century

Some people have difficulty thinking of child development as a science like physics, chemistry, and biology. Can a discipline that studies how parents nurture children, how peers interact, the ways in which children's thinking develops over time, and whether watching TV hour after hour is linked with being overweight, be equated with disciplines that study the molecular structure of a compound and how gravity works? Is child development really a science?

A child and his mentor in the One on One Mentoring program in Hennepin County, Minnesota. *If a researcher wanted to study the effects of the mentoring program on children's academic achievement by following the scientific method, what steps would the researcher take in setting up the study?*

THE IMPORTANCE OF RESEARCH

The answer to the last question is "yes." Science is defined not by *what* it investigates, but by *how* it investigates. Whether you're studying photosynthesis, butterflies, Saturn's moons, or children's development, it is the way you study that makes the approach scientific or not. How can we determine, for example, whether special care can repair the harm inflicted by child neglect or whether mentoring can improve children's achievement in school?

Scientific research provides the best answers to such questions. *Scientific research* is objective, systematic, and testable. It reduces the likelihood that information will be based on personal beliefs, opinions, and feelings (Graziano & Raulin, 2010; Smith & Davis, 2010; Stangor, 2011). In conducting research, child development researchers use the **scientific method,** a four-step process: (1) conceptualize a process or problem to be studied, (2) collect research information (data), (3) analyze data, and (4) draw conclusions.

THEORIES OF CHILD DEVELOPMENT

Theorizing is part of the scientific study of children's development. In the scientific method just described, theories often guide the conceptualization of a process or problem to be studied. A **theory** is an interrelated, coherent set of ideas that helps to explain and to make predictions. For example, a theory on mentoring might attempt to explain and predict why sustained support, guidance, and concrete experience make a difference in the lives of children from impoverished backgrounds. The theory might focus on children's opportunities to model the behavior and strategies of mentors, or it might focus on the effects of individual attention, which might be missing in the children's lives. A **hypothesis** is a specific, testable assumption or prediction. A hypothesis is often written as an *if-then* statement. In our example, a sample hypothesis might be: If children from impoverished backgrounds are given individual attention by mentors, the children will spend more time studying and earn higher grades. Testing a hypothesis can inform researchers whether a theory is likely to be accurate.

Wide-ranging theories make understanding children's development a challenging undertaking. This section outlines key aspects of five theoretical orientations to development: psychoanalytic, cognitive, behavioral and social cognitive, ethological,

scientific method An approach that can be used to obtain accurate information by carrying out four steps: (1) conceptualize the problem, (2) collect data, (3) draw conclusions, and (4) revise research conclusions and theory.

theory An interrelated, coherent set of ideas that helps to explain and make predictions.

hypotheses Specific assumptions and predictions that can be tested to determine their accuracy.

Oral Stage	**Anal Stage**	**Phallic Stage**	**Latency Stage**	**Genital Stage**
Infant's pleasure centers on the mouth.	Child's pleasure focuses on the anus.	Child's pleasure focuses on the genitals.	Child represses sexual interest and develops social and intellectual skills.	A time of sexual reawakening; source of sexual pleasure becomes someone outside the family.
Birth to 1½ Years	**1½ to 3 Years**	**3 to 6 Years**	**6 Years to Puberty**	**Puberty Onward**

FIGURE **1.9**
FREUDIAN STAGES

and ecological. Each contributes an important piece to the puzzle of understanding children's development. Although the theories disagree about certain aspects of development, many of their ideas are complementary rather than contradictory. Together they let us see the total landscape of children's development in all its richness.

Psychoanalytic Theories   **Psychoanalytic theories** describe development as primarily unconscious (beyond awareness) and heavily colored by emotion. Psychoanalytic theorists emphasize that behavior is merely a surface characteristic and that a true understanding of development requires analyzing the symbolic meanings of behavior and the deep inner workings of the mind. Psychoanalytic theorists also stress that early experiences with parents extensively shape development. These characteristics are highlighted in the psychoanalytic theory of Sigmund Freud (1856–1939).

Freud's Theory   As Freud listened to, probed, and analyzed his patients, he became convinced that their problems were the result of experiences early in life. He thought that as children grow up, their focus of pleasure and sexual impulses shifts from the mouth to the anus and eventually to the genitals. As a result, we go through five stages of psychosexual development: oral, anal, phallic, latency, and genital (see Figure 1.9). Our adult personality, Freud (1917) claimed, is determined by the way we resolve conflicts between sources of pleasure at each stage and the demands of reality.

Freud's theory has been significantly revised by a number of psychoanalytic theorists. Many of today's psychoanalytic theorists maintain that Freud overemphasized sexual instincts; they place more emphasis on cultural experiences as determinants of an individual's development. Unconscious thought remains a central theme, but thought plays a greater role than Freud envisioned. Next, we will outline the ideas of an important revisionist of Freud's ideas—Erik Erikson.

Erikson's Psychosocial Theory   Erik Erikson (1902–1994) recognized Freud's contributions but believed that Freud misjudged some important dimensions of human development. For one thing, Erikson (1950, 1968) said we develop in psychosocial stages, rather than in psychosexual stages, as Freud maintained. According to Freud, the primary motivation for human behavior is sexual in nature; according to Erikson, it is social and reflects a desire to affiliate with other people. According to Freud, our basic personality is shaped in the first five years of life; according to Erikson, developmental change occurs throughout the life span. Thus, in terms of the early-versus-later-experience issue described earlier in the chapter, Freud viewed early experience as far more important than later experiences, whereas Erikson emphasized the importance of both early and later experiences.

In **Erikson's theory,** eight stages of development unfold as we go through life (see Figure 1.10). At each stage, a unique developmental task confronts individuals with a crisis that must be resolved. According to Erikson, this crisis is not a catastrophe but a turning point marked by both increased vulnerability and enhanced potential. The more successfully an individual resolves the crises, the healthier development will be.

Trust versus mistrust is Erikson's first psychosocial stage, which is experienced in the first year of life. Trust in infancy sets the stage for a lifelong expectation

Sigmund Freud, the pioneering architect of psychoanalytic theory. *What are some characteristics of Freud's theory?*

psychoanalytic theories Theories that describe development as primarily unconscious and heavily colored by emotion. Behavior is merely a surface characteristic, and the symbolic workings of the mind have to be analyzed to understand behavior. Early experiences with parents are emphasized.

Erikson's theory Description of eight stages of human development. Each stage consists of a unique developmental task that confronts individuals with a crisis that must be resolved.

Erikson's Stages	Developmental Period
Integrity versus despair	Late adulthood (60s onward)
Generativity versus stagnation	Middle adulthood (40s, 50s)
Intimacy versus isolation	Early adulthood (20s, 30s)
Identity versus identity confusion	Adolescence (10 to 20 years)
Industry versus inferiority	Middle and late childhood (elementary school years, 6 years to puberty)
Initiative versus guilt	Early childhood (preschool years, 3 to 5 years)
Autonomy versus shame and doubt	Infancy (1 to 3 years)
Trust versus mistrust	Infancy (first year)

FIGURE 1.10

ERIKSON'S EIGHT LIFE-SPAN STAGES

developmental **connection**

Culture and Ethnicity. What characterizes an adolescent's ethnic identity? Chapter 11, p. 339

Erik Erikson with his wife, Joan, an artist. Erikson generated one of the most important developmental theories of the twentieth century. *Which stage of Erikson's theory are you in? Does Erikson's description of this stage characterize you?*

that the world will be a good and pleasant place to live.

Autonomy versus shame and doubt is Erikson's second stage. This stage occurs in late infancy and toddlerhood (1 to 3 years). After gaining trust in their caregivers, infants begin to discover that their behavior is their own. They start to assert their sense of independence or autonomy. They realize their will. If infants and toddlers are restrained too much or punished too harshly, they are likely to develop a sense of shame and doubt.

Initiative versus guilt, Erikson's third stage of development, occurs during the preschool years. As preschool children encounter a widening social world, they face new challenges that require active, purposeful, responsible behavior. Feelings of guilt may arise, though, if the child is irresponsible and is made to feel too anxious.

Industry versus inferiority is Erikson's fourth developmental stage, occurring approximately in the elementary school years. Children now need to direct their energy toward mastering knowledge and intellectual skills. The negative outcome is that the child may develop a sense of inferiority—feeling incompetent and unproductive.

During the adolescent years, individuals face finding out who they are, what they are all about, and where they are going in life. This is Erikson's fifth developmental stage, *identity versus identity confusion*. If adolescents explore roles in a healthy manner and arrive at a positive path to follow in life, then they achieve a positive identity; if not, identity confusion reigns.

Intimacy versus isolation is Erikson's sixth developmental stage, which individuals experience during the early adulthood years. At this time, individuals face the developmental task of forming intimate relationships. If young adults form healthy friendships and an intimate relationship with another, intimacy will be achieved; if not, isolation will result.

Generativity versus stagnation, Erikson's seventh developmental stage, occurs during middle adulthood. By generativity Erikson means primarily a concern for helping the younger generation to develop and lead useful lives. The feeling of having done nothing to help the next generation is stagnation.

Integrity versus despair is Erikson's eighth and final stage of development, which individuals experience in late adulthood. During this stage, a person reflects on the past. If the person's life review reveals a life well spent, integrity will be achieved; if not, the retrospective glances likely will yield doubt or gloom—the despair Erikson described.

We will discuss Erikson's theory again in the chapters on socioemotional development. In *Caring Connections* you can read about some effective strategies for improving the lives of children based on Erikson's view.

Evaluating Psychoanalytic Theories Contributions of psychoanalytic theories include an emphasis on a developmental framework, family relationships, and unconscious aspects of the mind. Criticisms include a lack of scientific support, too much emphasis on sexual underpinnings (Freud's theory), too much credit given to the unconscious mind, and an image of children that is too negative (Freud's theory).

caring *connections*

Strategies for Parenting, Educating, and Interacting with Children Based on Erikson's Theory

Parents, child care specialists, teachers, counselors, youth workers, and other adults can adopt positive strategies for interacting with children based on Erikson's theory. These strategies include the following:

1. ***Nurture infants and develop their trust, then encourage and monitor toddlers' autonomy.*** Because infants depend on others for their needs, it is critical for caregivers to consistently provide positive, attentive care for infants. Infants who experience consistently positive care feel safe and secure, sensing that people are reliable and loving, which leads them to develop trust in the world. Caregivers who neglect or abuse infants are likely to have infants who develop a sense of mistrust in their world. After having developed a sense of trust in their world, children moving from infancy into the toddler years should be given the freedom to explore it. Toddlers whose caregivers are too restrictive or harsh are likely to develop shame and doubt, sensing that they can't adequately do things on their own. As toddlers gain more independence, caregivers need to monitor their exploration and curiosity because there are many things that can harm them, such as running into the street and touching a hot stove.

2. ***Encourage initiative in young children.*** Children should be given a great deal of freedom to explore their world. They should be allowed to choose some of the activities they engage in. If their requests for doing certain activities are reasonable, the requests should be honored. Children need to be provided exciting materials that will stimulate their imagination. Young children at this stage love to play. It not only benefits their socioemotional development but also serves as an important medium for their cognitive growth. Criticism should be kept to a minimum so that children will not develop high levels of guilt and anxiety. Young children are going to make lots of mistakes and have lots of spills. They need good models far more than harsh critics. Their activities and environment should be structured for successes rather than failures by giving them developmentally appropriate tasks. For example, young children get frustrated when they have to sit for long periods of time and do academic paper-and-pencil tasks.

3. ***Promote industry in elementary school children.*** It was Erikson's hope that teachers could provide an atmosphere in which children would become passionate about learning. In Erikson's words, teachers should mildly but firmly coerce children into the adventure of finding out that they can learn to accomplish things that they themselves would never have thought they could do. In elementary school, children thirst to know. Most arrive at elementary school steeped in curiosity and a motivation to master tasks. In Erikson's view, it is important for teachers to nourish this motivation for mastery and curiosity. Teachers need to challenge students without overwhelming them; be firm in requiring students to be productive, but not be overly critical; and especially be tolerant of honest mis-

What are some applications of Erikson's theory for effective parenting?

takes and make sure that every student has opportunities for many successes.

4. ***Stimulate identity exploration in adolescence.*** It is important to recognize that the adolescent's identity is multidimensional. Aspects include vocational goals; intellectual achievement; and interests in hobbies, sports, music, and other areas. Adolescents can be asked to write essays about such dimensions, exploring who they are and what they want to do with their lives. They should be encouraged to think independently and to freely express their views, which stimulates their self-exploration. Adolescents can also be encouraged to listen to debates on political and ideological issues, which stimulates them to examine different perspectives. Another good strategy is to encourage adolescents to talk with a school counselor about career options as well as other aspects of their identity. Teachers can invite people in different careers to come into the classroom and talk with their students about their work, regardless of students' grade levels.

In each of the strategies above, identify what Erikson called the "vulnerability" and the "potential" with which the adult is trying to help the child.

Sensorimotor Stage	**Preoperational Stage**	**Concrete Operational Stage**	**Formal Operational Stage**
The infant constructs an understanding of the world by coordinating sensory experiences with physical actions. An infant progresses from reflexive, instinctual action at birth to the beginning of symbolic thought toward the end of the stage.	The child begins to represent the world with words and images. These words and images reflect increased symbolic thinking and go beyond the connection of sensory information and physical action.	The child can now reason logically about concrete events and classify objects into different sets.	The adolescent reasons in more abstract, idealistic, and logical ways.
Birth to 2 Years of Age	**2 to 7 Years of Age**	**7 to 11 Years of Age**	**11 Years of Age Through Adulthood**

FIGURE **1.11**
PIAGET'S FOUR STAGES OF COGNITIVE DEVELOPMENT

> One's children's children's children.
> Look back to us as we look to you; we are related by our imaginations. If we are able to touch, it is because we have imagined each other's existence, our dreams running back and forth along a cable from age to age.
>
> —ROGER ROSENBLATT
> *American Writer, 20th Century*

Piaget's theory Theory stating that children actively construct their understanding of the world and go through four stages of cognitive development.

Cognitive Theories Whereas psychoanalytic theories stress the importance of the unconscious, cognitive theories emphasize conscious thoughts. Three important cognitive theories are Piaget's cognitive developmental theory, Vygotsky's sociocultural cognitive theory, and information-processing theory.

Piaget's Cognitive Developmental Theory **Piaget's theory** states that children actively construct their understanding of the world and go through four stages of cognitive development. Two processes underlie the four stages of development in Piaget's theory: organization and adaptation. To make sense of our world, we organize our experiences. For example, we separate important ideas from less important ideas, and we connect one idea to another. In addition to organizing our observations and experiences, we *adapt*, adjusting to new environmental demands (Byrnes, 2008).

Piaget (1954) also held that we go through four stages in understanding the world (see Figure 1.11). Each stage is age-related and consists of a distinct way of thinking, a *different* way of understanding the world. Thus, according to Piaget, the child's cognition is *qualitatively* different in one stage compared with another. What are Piaget's four stages of cognitive development like?

The *sensorimotor stage*, which lasts from birth to about 2 years of age, is the first Piagetian stage. In this stage, infants construct an understanding of the world by coordinating sensory experiences (such as seeing and hearing) with physical, motoric actions—hence the term *sensorimotor*.

The *preoperational stage*, which lasts from approximately 2 to 7 years of age, is Piaget's second stage. In this stage, children begin to go beyond simply connecting sensory information with physical action and represent the world with words, images, and drawings. However, according to Piaget, preschool children still lack the ability to perform what he calls *operations*, which are internalized mental actions that allow children to do mentally what they previously could only do physically. For example, if you imagine putting two sticks together to see whether they would be as long as another stick, without actually moving the sticks, you are performing a concrete operation.

The *concrete operational stage*, which lasts from approximately 7 to 11 years of age, is the third Piagetian stage. In this stage, children can perform operations that involve objects, and they can reason logically as long as reasoning can be applied to specific or concrete examples. For instance, concrete operational thinkers cannot imagine the steps necessary to complete an algebraic equation, which is too abstract for thinking at this stage of development.

The *formal operational stage*, which appears between the ages of 11 and 15 and continues through adulthood, is Piaget's fourth and final stage. In this stage, individuals move beyond concrete experiences and think in abstract and more logical terms. As part of thinking more abstractly, adolescents develop images of ideal circumstances. They might think about what an ideal parent is like and compare their parents to this ideal standard. They begin to entertain possibilities for the future and are fascinated with what they can be. In solving problems, they become more systematic, developing hypotheses about why something is happening the way it is and then testing these hypotheses.

The preceding discussion is a brief introduction to Piaget's theory. It is provided here, along with other theories, to give you a broad understanding. In Chapter 6, "Cognitive Developmental Approaches," we will return to Piaget and examine his theory in more depth.

Jean Piaget, the famous Swiss developmental psychologist, changed the way we think about the development of children's minds. *What are some key ideas in Piaget's theory?*

developmental connection

Cognitive Theory. We owe to Piaget the entire field of children's cognitive development, but a number of criticisms of his theory have been made. Chapter 6, p. 189

Vygotsky's Sociocultural Cognitive Theory   Like Piaget, the Russian developmentalist Lev Vygotsky (1896–1934) argued that children actively construct their knowledge. However, Vygotsky (1962) gave social interaction and culture far more important roles in cognitive development than Piaget did. **Vygotsky's theory** is a sociocultural cognitive theory that emphasizes how culture and social interaction guide cognitive development.

Vygotsky portrayed the child's development as inseparable from social and cultural activities (Gauvain & Parke, 2010; Holzman, 2009). He argued that development of memory, attention, and reasoning involves learning to use the inventions of society, such as language, mathematical systems, and memory strategies. Thus, in one culture, children might learn to count with the help of a computer; in another, they might learn by using beads. According to Vygotsky, children's social interaction with more-skilled adults and peers is indispensable to their cognitive development. Through this interaction, they learn to use the tools that will help them adapt and be successful in their culture. For example, if you regularly help children learn how to read, you not only advance their reading skills but also communicate to them that reading is an important activity in their culture.

Vygotsky's theory has stimulated considerable interest in the view that knowledge is *situated* and *collaborative* (Gauvain & Parke, 2010). In this view, knowledge is not generated from within the individual but rather is constructed through interaction with other people and objects in the culture, such as books. This suggests that knowledge can best be advanced through interaction with others in cooperative activities.

Vygotsky's theory, like Piaget's, remained virtually unknown to American psychologists until the 1960s, but eventually both became influential among educators as well as psychologists. We will further examine Vygotsky's theory in Chapter 6.

There is considerable interest today in Lev Vygotsky's sociocultural cognitive theory of child development. *What were Vygotsky's basic ideas about children's development?*

Vygotsky's theory A sociocultural cognitive theory that emphasizes how culture and social interaction guide cognitive development.

------→

developmental **connection**

Education. Applications of Vygotsky's theory to children's education have been made in recent years. Chapter 6, pp. 192–193

←-------

The Information-Processing Theory Early computers may be the best candidates for the title of "founding fathers" of information-processing theory. Although many factors stimulated the growth of this theory, none was more important than the computer. Psychologists began to wonder if the logical operations carried out by computers might tell us something about how the human mind works. They drew analogies between a computer's hardware and the brain and between computer software and cognition.

This line of thinking helped to generate **information-processing theory,** which emphasizes that individuals manipulate information, monitor it, and strategize about it. Unlike Piaget's theory but like Vygotsky's theory, information-processing theory does not describe development as happening in stages. Instead, according to this theory, individuals develop a gradually increasing capacity for processing information, which allows them to acquire increasingly complex knowledge and skills (Sternberg, 2010a, b).

Robert Siegler (2006), a leading expert on children's information processing, states that thinking is information processing. In other words, when individuals perceive, encode, represent, store, and retrieve information, they are thinking. Siegler emphasizes that an important aspect of development is learning good strategies for processing information. For example, becoming a better reader might involve learning to monitor the key themes of the material being read.

Evaluating the Cognitive Theories Contributions of cognitive theories include a positive view of development and an emphasis on the active construction of understanding. Criticisms include skepticism about the pureness of Piaget's stages and assertions that too little attention is paid to individual variations.

Behavioral and Social Cognitive Theories At about the same time that Freud was interpreting patients' unconscious minds through their early childhood experiences, Ivan Pavlov and John B. Watson were conducting detailed observations of behavior in controlled laboratory settings. Their work provided the foundations of *behaviorism*, which essentially holds that we can study scientifically only what can be directly observed and measured. Out of the behavioral tradition grew the belief that development is observable behavior that can be learned through experience with the environment (Chance, 2009). In terms of the continuity-discontinuity issue discussed earlier in this chapter, the behavioral and social cognitive theories emphasize continuity in development and argue that development does not occur in stages. The three versions of the behavioral approach that we will explore are Pavlov's classical conditioning, Skinner's operant conditioning, and Bandura's social cognitive theory.

Pavlov's Classical Conditioning In the early 1900s, the Russian physiologist Ivan Pavlov (1927) knew that dogs salivate when they taste food. He became curious when he observed that dogs also salivate to various sights and sounds before eating their food. For example, when an individual paired the ringing of a bell with the food, the bell ringing subsequently elicited salivation from the dogs when it was presented by itself. With this experiment, Pavlov discovered the principle of *classical conditioning,* in which a neutral stimulus (in our example, hearing a bell ring) acquires the ability to produce a response originally produced by another stimulus (in our example, tasting food).

In the early twentieth century, John Watson and Rosalie Rayner (1920) demonstrated that classical conditioning occurs in human beings. He showed an infant named Albert a white rat to see if he was afraid of it. He was not. As Albert played with the rat, a loud noise was sounded behind his head. As you might imagine, the noise caused little Albert to cry. After several pairings of the loud noise and the white rat, Albert began to cry at the sight of the rat even when the noise was not sounded. Albert had been classically conditioned to fear the rat. Similarly, many of our fears may result from classical conditioning: fear of the dentist may be learned from a painful experience, fear of driving from being in an automobile accident, fear of heights from falling off a highchair when we were infants, and fear of dogs from being bitten.

information-processing theory Emphasizes that individuals manipulate information, monitor it, and strategize about it. Central to this theory are the processes of memory and thinking.

social cognitive theory The view of psychologists who emphasize behavior, environment, and cognition as the key factors in development.

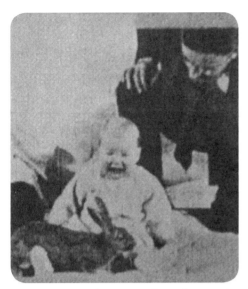

In 1920, Watson and Rayner conditioned 11-month-old Albert to fear a white rat by pairing the rat with a loud noise. When little Albert was subsequently presented with other stimuli similar to the white rat, such as the rabbit shown here with little Albert, he was afraid of them, too. This illustrates the principle of stimulus generalization in classical conditioning.

B. F. Skinner was a tinkerer who liked to make new gadgets. The younger of his two daughters, Deborah, was raised in Skinner's enclosed Air-Crib, which he invented because he wanted to control her environment completely. The Air-Crib was sound-proofed and temperature-controlled. Debbie, shown here as a child with her parents, is currently a successful artist, is married, and lives in London. *What do you think about Skinner's Air-Crib?*

Skinner's Operant Conditioning   Classical conditioning may explain how we develop many involuntary responses such as fears, but B. F. Skinner argued that a second type of conditioning accounts for the development of other types of behavior. According to Skinner (1938), through *operant conditioning* the consequences of a behavior produce changes in the probability of the behavior's occurrence. A behavior followed by a rewarding stimulus is more likely to recur, whereas a behavior followed by a punishing stimulus is less likely to recur. For example, when a person smiles at a child after the child has done something, the child is more likely to engage in the activity than if the person gives the child a nasty look.

According to Skinner, such rewards and punishments shape development. For example, Skinner's approach argues that shy people learned to be shy as a result of experiences they had while growing up. It follows that modifications in an environment can help a shy person become more socially oriented. Also, for Skinner the key aspect of development is behavior, not thoughts and feelings. He emphasized that development consists of the pattern of behavioral changes that are brought about by rewards and punishments.

Bandura's Social Cognitive Theory   Some psychologists agree with the behaviorists' notion that development is learned and is influenced strongly by environmental interactions. However, unlike Skinner, they argue that cognition is also important in understanding development. **Social cognitive theory** holds that behavior, environment, and cognition are the key factors in development.

American psychologist Albert Bandura (1925–) is the leading architect of social cognitive theory. Bandura (2001, 2007, 2009, 2010a, b) emphasizes that cognitive processes have important links with the environment and behavior. His early research program focused heavily on *observational learning* (also called *imitation* or *modeling*), which is learning that occurs through observing what others do. For example, a young boy might observe his father yelling in anger and treating other people with hostility; with his peers, the young boy later acts very aggressively, showing the same characteristics his father displayed. A girl might adopt the dominant and sarcastic style of her teacher, saying to her younger brother, "You are so slow. How can you do this work so slowly?" Social cognitive theorists stress that people acquire a wide

Albert Bandura has been one of the leading architects of social cognitive theory. *How does Bandura's theory differ from Skinner's?*

developmental **connection**

Theories. Bandura emphasizes that self-efficacy is a key person/cognitive factor in children's achievement. Chapter 16, p. 476

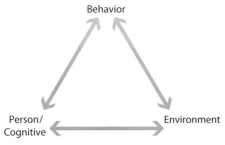

Behavior

Person/
Cognitive ⟷ Environment

FIGURE **1.12**

BANDURA'S SOCIAL COGNITIVE MODEL. The arrows illustrate how relations between behavior, person/cognition, and environment are reciprocal rather than unidirectional.

developmental **connection**

Attachment. Human babies go through a series of phases in developing an attachment to a caregiver. Chapter 10, p. 309

ethology Stresses that behavior is strongly influenced by biology, is tied to evolution, and is characterized by critical or sensitive periods.

range of behaviors, thoughts, and feelings through observing others' behavior and that these observations form an important part of children's development.

What is *cognitive* about observational learning, in Bandura's view? He proposes that people cognitively represent the behavior of others and then sometimes adopt this behavior themselves.

Bandura's (2001, 2007, 2009, 2010a, b) most recent model of learning and development includes three elements: behavior, the person/cognition, and the environment. An individual's confidence that he or she can control his or her success is an example of a person factor; strategies are an example of a cognitive factor. As shown in Figure 1.12, behavior, person/cognition, and environmental factors operate interactively. Behavior can influence person factors and vice versa. Cognitive activities can influence the environment. The environment can change the person's cognition, and so on.

Evaluating the Behavioral and Social Cognitive Theories Contributions of the behavioral and social cognitive theories include an emphasis on scientific research and environmental determinants of behavior, and in Bandura's social cognitive theory reciprocal links between the environment, behavior, and person/cognitive factors. Criticisms include too little emphasis on cognition in Skinner's view and giving inadequate attention to developmental changes and biological foundations.

Behavioral and social cognitive theories emphasize the importance of environmental experiences in human development. Next we turn our attention to a theory that underscores the importance of the biological foundations of development—ethological theory.

Ethological Theory American developmental psychologists began to pay attention to the biological bases of development during the mid-20th century thanks to the work of European zoologists who pioneered the field of ethology. **Ethology** stresses that behavior is strongly influenced by biology, is tied to evolution, and is characterized by critical or sensitive periods. These are specific time frames during which, according to ethologists, the presence or absence of certain experiences has a long-lasting influence on individuals.

European zoologist Konrad Lorenz (1903–1989) helped bring ethology to prominence. In his best-known experiment, Lorenz (1965) studied the behavior of greylag geese, which will follow their mothers as soon as they hatch.

In a remarkable set of experiments, Lorenz separated the eggs laid by one goose into two groups. One group he returned to the goose to be hatched by her. The other group was hatched in an incubator. The goslings in the first group performed as predicted. They followed their mother as soon as they hatched. However, those in the second group, which saw Lorenz when they first hatched, followed him everywhere, as though he were their mother. Lorenz marked the goslings and then placed both groups under a box. Mother goose and "mother" Lorenz stood aside as

Konrad Lorenz, a pioneering student of animal behavior, is followed through the water by three imprinted greylag geese. Describe Lorenz's experiment with the geese. *Do you think his experiment would have the same results with human babies? Explain.*

the box lifted. Each group of goslings went directly to its "mother." Lorenz called this process *imprinting*—rapid, innate learning within a limited, critical period of time that involves attachment to the first moving object seen.

At first, ethological research and theory had little or nothing to say about the nature of social relationships across the *human* life span, and the theory stimulated few studies involving people. Ethologists' viewpoint that normal development requires that certain behaviors emerge during a *critical period*, a fixed time period very early in development, seemed to be overstated. However, John Bowlby's work (1969, 1989) illustrated an important application of ethological theory to human development. Bowlby argued that attachment to a caregiver over the first year of life has important consequences throughout the life span. In his view, if this attachment is positive and secure, the infant will likely develop positively in childhood and adulthood. If the attachment is negative and insecure, children's development will likely not be optimal. Thus, in this view the first year of life is a *sensitive period* for the development of social relationships. In Chapter 10, "Emotional Development," we will explore the concept of infant attachment in greater detail.

Evaluating Ethological Theory Contributions of ethological theory include a focus on the biological and evolutionary basis of development, and the use of careful observations in naturalistic settings. Critics assert that too much emphasis is placed on biological foundations and that the critical and sensitive period concepts might be too rigid.

Another theory that emphasizes the biological aspects of human development—evolutionary psychology—will be presented in Chapter 2, "Biological Beginnings," along with views on the role of heredity in development.

Ecological Theory Whereas ethological theory stresses biological factors, ecological theory emphasizes environmental factors. One ecological theory that has important implications for understanding children's development was created by Urie Bronfenbrenner (1917–2005).

Bronfenbrenner's ecological theory (1986, 2000, 2004; Bronfenbrenner & Morris, 1998, 2006) holds that development reflects the influence of several environmental systems. The theory identifies five environmental systems (see Figure 1.13):

- *Microsystem:* The setting in which the individual lives. These contexts include the person's family, peers, school, neighborhood, and work. It is within the microsystem that the most direct interactions with social agents take place—with parents, peers, and teachers, for example.

- *Mesosystem:* Relations between microsystems or connections between contexts. Examples are the relationships between family experiences and school experiences, school experiences and church experiences, and family experiences and peer experiences. For example, children whose parents have rejected them may have difficulty developing positive relationships with teachers.

- *Exosystem:* Links between a social setting in which the individual does not have an active role and the individual's immediate context. For example, a husband's or child's experience at home may be influenced by a mother's experiences at work. The mother might receive a promotion that requires

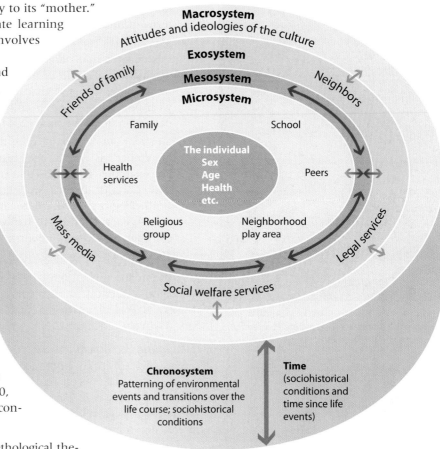

FIGURE **1.13**

BRONFENBRENNER'S ECOLOGICAL THEORY OF DEVELOPMENT. Bronfenbrenner's ecological theory consists of five environmental systems: microsystem, mesosystem, exosystem, macrosystem, and chronosystem.

Bronfenbrenner's ecological theory An environmental systems theory that focuses on five environmental systems: microsystem, mesosystem, exosystem, macrosystem, and chronosystem.

Urie Bronfenbrenner developed ecological theory, a perspective that is receiving increased attention. *What is the nature of ecological theory?*

more travel, which might increase conflict with the husband and change patterns of interaction with the child.

- *Macrosystem:* The culture in which individuals live. Remember from earlier in this chapter that *culture* refers to the behavior patterns, beliefs, and all other products of a group of people that are passed on from generation to generation. Remember also that cross-cultural studies—comparisons of one culture with one or more other cultures—provide information about the generality of development (Kitayama, 2011; Shiraev & Levy, 2010).

- *Chronosystem:* The patterning of environmental events and transitions over the life course, as well as sociohistorical circumstances (Schaie, 2009, 2010, 2011). For example, divorce is one transition. Researchers have found that the negative effects of divorce on children often peak in the first year after the divorce (Hetherington, 1993, 2006). By two years after the divorce, family interaction is less chaotic and more stable. As an example of sociohistorical circumstances, consider how career opportunities for women have increased during the last 30 years.

Bronfenbrenner (2000, 2004; Bronfenbrenner & Morris, 1998, 2006) has added biological influences to his theory and now describes it as a *bioecological* theory. Nonetheless, ecological, environmental contexts still predominate in Bronfenbrenner's theory (Gauvain & Parke, 2010).

Evaluating Ecological Theory   Contributions of ecological theory include a systematic examination of macro and micro dimensions of environmental systems, and attention to connections between environmental systems. A further contribution of Bronfenbrenner's theory is its emphasis on a range of social contexts beyond the family, such as neighborhood, religious organization, school, and workplace, as influential in children's development (Gauvain & Parke, 2010). Criticisms include giving inadequate attention to biological factors, as well as placing too little emphasis on cognitive factors.

An Eclectic Theoretical Orientation   No single theory described in this chapter can explain entirely the rich complexity of children's development, but each has contributed to our understanding of development. Psychoanalytic theory best explains the unconscious mind. Erikson's theory best describes the changes that occur in adult development. Piaget's, Vygotsky's, and the information-processing views provide the most complete description of cognitive development. The behavioral and social cognitive and ecological theories have been the most adept at examining the environmental determinants of development. The ethological theories have highlighted biology's role and the importance of sensitive periods in development.

In short, although theories are helpful guides, relying on a single theory to explain development is probably a mistake. This book instead takes an **eclectic theoretical orientation,** which does not follow any one theoretical approach but rather selects from each theory whatever is considered its best features. In this way, you can view the study of development as it actually exists—with different theorists making different assumptions, stressing different empirical problems, and using different strategies to discover information. Figure 1.14 compares the main theoretical perspectives in terms of how they view important issues in children's development.

RESEARCH METHODS FOR COLLECTING DATA

If they follow an eclectic orientation, how do scholars and researchers determine that one feature of a theory is somehow better than another? The scientific method discussed earlier in this chapter provides the guide. Recall that the steps in the scientific method involve conceptualizing the problem, collecting data, drawing conclusions, and revising research conclusions and theories. Through scientific research, the features of theories can be tested and refined.

Whether we are interested in studying attachment in infants, the cognitive skills of children, or peer relations among adolescents, we can choose from several ways

eclectic theoretical orientation An orientation that does not follow any one theoretical approach but rather selects from each theory whatever is considered its best aspects.

	Nature and nurture	Early and later experience	Continuity and discontinuity
Psychoanalytic	Freud's biological determinism interacting with early family experiences; Erikson's more balanced biological/cultural interaction perspective	Early experiences in the family very important influences	Emphasis on discontinuity between stages
Cognitive	Piaget's emphasis on interaction and adaptation; environment provides the setting for cognitive structures to develop. Vygotsky's theory involves interaction of nature and nurture with strong emphasis on culture. The information-processing approach has not addressed this issue extensively; mainly emphasizes biological/environment interaction.	Childhood experiences important influences	Discontinuity between stages in Piaget's theory; no stages in Vygotsky's theory or the information-processing approach
Behavioral and Social Cognitive	Environment viewed as the main influence on development	Experiences important at all points in development	Continuity with no stages
Ethological	Strong biological view	Early experience very important, which can contribute to change early in development; after early critical or sensitive period has passed, stability likely to occur	Discontinuity because of early critical or sensitive period; no stages
Ecological	Strong environmental view	Experiences involving the five environmental systems important at all points in development	No stages but little attention to the issue

FIGURE 1.14

A COMPARISON OF THEORIES AND ISSUES IN CHILD DEVELOPMENT

of collecting data. Here we outline the measures most often used, looking at the advantages and disadvantages of each.

Observation Scientific observation requires an important set of skills (Christensen, Johnson, & Turner, 2011). Unless we are trained observers and practice our skills regularly, we might not know what to look for, we might not remember what we saw, we might not realize that what we are looking for is changing from one moment to the next, and we might not communicate our observations effectively.

For observations to be effective, they have to be systematic. We have to have some idea of what we are looking for. We have to know whom we are observing, when and where we will observe, how the observations will be made, and how they will be recorded.

Where should we make our observations? We have two choices: the laboratory and the everyday world.

When we observe scientifically, we often need to control certain factors that determine behavior but are not the focus of our inquiry (Babble, 2011). For this

What are some important strategies in conducting observational research with children?

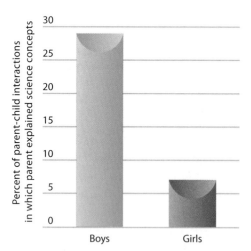

FIGURE **1.15**

PARENTS' EXPLANATIONS OF SCIENCE TO SONS AND DAUGHTERS AT A SCIENCE MUSEUM. In a naturalistic observation study at a children's science museum, parents were more than three times more likely to explain science to boys than to girls (Crowley & others, 2001). The gender difference occurred regardless of whether the father, the mother, or both parents were with the child, although the gender difference was greatest for fathers' science explanations to sons and daughters.

laboratory A controlled setting from which many of the complex factors of the "real world" have been removed.

naturalistic observation Behavioral observation that takes place in real-world settings.

standardized test A test with uniform procedures for administration and scoring. Many standardized tests allow a person's performance to be compared with the performance of other individuals.

reason, some research in life-span development is conducted in a **laboratory,** a controlled setting from which many of the complex factors of the "real world" have been removed. For example, suppose you want to observe how children react when they see other people behave aggressively. If you observe children in their homes or schools, you have no control over how much aggression the children observe, what kind of aggression they see, which people they see acting aggressively, or how other people treat the children. In contrast, if you observe the children in a laboratory, you can control these and other factors and therefore have more confidence about how to interpret your observations.

Laboratory research does have some drawbacks, however, including the following:

- It is almost impossible to conduct research without letting participants know they are being studied.
- The laboratory setting is unnatural and therefore can cause the participants to behave unnaturally.
- People who are willing to come to a university laboratory may not fairly represent groups from diverse cultural backgrounds.
- People who are unfamiliar with university settings and with the idea of "helping science" may be intimidated by the laboratory setting.
- Some aspects of children's development are difficult, if not impossible, to examine in the laboratory.
- Laboratory studies of certain types of stress may even be unethical.

Naturalistic observation provides insights that we sometimes cannot achieve in the laboratory. **Naturalistic observation** means observing behavior in real-world settings, making no effort to manipulate or control the situation. Child development researchers conduct naturalistic observations in homes, child-care centers, schools, neighborhoods, malls, and other contexts.

Naturalistic observation was used in one study that focused on conversations in a children's science museum (Crowley & others, 2001). Parents were more than three times as likely to engage boys than girls in explanatory talk while visiting exhibits at the science museum, suggesting a gender bias that encourages boys more than girls to be interested in science (see Figure 1.15). In another study, Mexican American parents who had completed high school used more explanations with their children when visiting a science museum than Mexican American parents who had not completed high school (Tenenbaum & others, 2002).

Survey and Interview Sometimes the best and quickest way to get information about people is to ask them for it. One technique is to interview them directly. A related method is the survey (sometimes referred to as a questionnaire), which is especially useful when information from many people is needed (Nardi, 2006). A standard set of questions is used to obtain people's self-reported attitudes or beliefs about a particular topic. In a good survey, the questions are clear and unbiased, allowing respondents to answer unambiguously.

Surveys and interviews can be used to study a wide range of topics, from religious beliefs to sexual habits to attitudes about gun control to beliefs about how to improve schools. Surveys and interviews today are conducted in person, over the telephone, and over the Internet.

One problem with surveys and interviews is the tendency for participants to answer questions in a way that they think is socially acceptable or desirable rather than telling what they truly think or feel (Creswell, 2008). For example, on a survey or in an interview some individuals might say that they do not take drugs even though they do.

Standardized Test A **standardized test** has uniform procedures for administration and scoring. Many standardized tests allow a person's performance to be compared with the performance of other individuals, thus providing information about individual differences among people (Drummond & Jones, 2010). One example is the Stanford-Binet intelligence test, which is described in Chapter 8, "Intelligence." Your score on the Stanford-Binet test shows how your performance compares with that of thousands of other people who have taken the test.

Standardized tests have three key weaknesses. First, they do not always predict behavior in nontest situations. Second, standardized tests are based on the belief that a person's behavior is consistent and stable, yet personality and intelligence—two primary targets of standardized testing—can vary with the situation. For example, individuals may perform poorly on a standardized intelligence test in an office setting but score much higher at home, where they are less anxious. This criticism is especially relevant for members of minority groups, some of whom have been inaccurately classified as mentally retarded on the basis of their scores on intelligence tests. A third weakness of standardized tests is that many psychological tests developed in Western cultures might not be appropriate in other cultures (Hall, 2010). The experiences of people in differing cultures may lead them to interpret and respond to questions differently.

Case Study   A **case study** is an in-depth look at a single individual. Case studies are performed mainly by mental health professionals when, for either practical or ethical reasons, the unique aspects of an individual's life cannot be duplicated and tested in other ways. A case study provides information about one person's fears, hopes, fantasies, traumatic experiences, upbringing, family relationships, health, or anything that helps the psychologist understand the person's mind and behavior. In later chapters, we discuss vivid case studies, such as that of Michael Rehbein, who had much of the left side of his brain removed at 7 years of age to end severe epileptic seizures.

Case histories provide dramatic, in-depth portrayals of people's lives, but remember that we must be cautious when generalizing from this information (McMillan & Wergin, 2010). The subject of a case study is unique, with a genetic makeup and personal history that no one else shares. In addition, case studies involve judgments of unknown reliability. Psychologists who conduct case studies rarely check to see if other psychologists agree with their observations.

Physiological Measures   Researchers are increasingly using physiological measures when they study children's development (Nelson, 2011). For example, as puberty unfolds, the blood levels of certain hormones increase. To determine the nature of these hormonal changes, researchers take blood samples from willing adolescents (Susman & Dorn, 2009).

Another physiological measure that is increasingly being used is neuroimaging, especially functional magnetic resonance imaging (fMRI), in which electromagnetic waves are used to construct images of a person's brain tissue and biochemical activity (see Figure 1.16). We will have much more to say about neuroimaging and other physiological measures at various points in this book.

RESEARCH DESIGNS

Suppose you want to find out whether the children of permissive parents are more likely than other children to be rude and unruly. The data-collection method that researchers choose often depends on the goal of their research. The goal may be simply to describe a phenomenon, or it may be to describe relationships between phenomena, or to determine the causes or effects of a phenomenon.

Perhaps you decide that you need to observe both permissive and strict parents with their children and compare them. How would you do that? In addition to choosing a method for collecting data, you would need to select a research design. There are three main types of research designs: descriptive, correlational, and experimental.

Mahatma Gandhi was the spiritual leader of India in the middle of the twentieth century. Erik Erikson conducted an extensive case study of his life to determine what contributed to his identity development. *What are some limitations of the case study approach?*

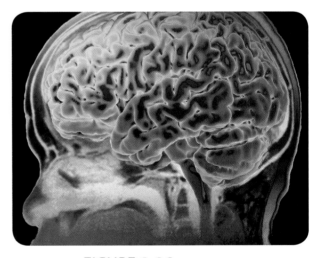

FIGURE **1.16**
MAGNETIC RESONANCE IMAGING

case study An in-depth look at a single individual.

Observed Correlation: As permissive parenting increases, childrens' self-control decreases.

Possible explanations for this observed correlation

| Permissive parenting | causes → | Childrens' lack of self-control |

| Childrens' lack of self-control | causes → | Permissive parenting |

| A third factor such as genetic tendencies or poverty | causes both → | Permissive parenting and childrens' lack of self-control |

An observed correlation between two events cannot be used to conclude that one event causes the second event. Other possibilities are that the second event causes the first event or that a third event causes the correlation between the first two events.

FIGURE **1.17**
POSSIBLE EXPLANATIONS OF CORRELATIONAL DATA

descriptive research Research that involves observing and recording behavior.

correlational research Research in which the goal is to describe the strength of the relationship between two or more events or characteristics.

correlation coefficient A number based on statistical analysis that is used to describe the degree of association between two variables.

experiment A carefully regulated procedure in which one or more of the factors believed to influence the behavior being studied are manipulated while all other factors are held constant.

Descriptive Research   All of the data-collection methods that we have discussed can be used in **descriptive research,** which aims to observe and record behavior. For example, a researcher might observe the extent to which people behave altruistically or aggressively toward each other. By itself, descriptive research cannot prove what causes a specific phenomenon, but it can yield important information about people's behavior (Leedy & Ormrod, 2010).

Correlational Research   In contrast with descriptive research, correlational research goes beyond describing phenomena and provides information that helps predict how people will behave. In **correlational research,** the goal is to describe the strength of the relationship between two or more events or characteristics. The more strongly the two events are correlated (or related or associated), the more effectively we can predict one event from the other (McMillan & Wergin, 2010).

For example, to determine whether children of permissive parents have less self-control than other children, you would need to carefully record observations of parents' permissiveness and their children's self-control. The data could then be analyzed statistically to yield a numerical measure, called a **correlation coefficient,** a number based on a statistical analysis that is used to describe the degree of association between two variables. The correlation coefficient ranges from −1.00 to +1.00. A negative number means an inverse relation. For example, researchers often find a negative correlation between permissive parenting and children's self-control. By contrast, they often find a positive correlation between parental monitoring of children and children's self-control.

The higher the correlation coefficient (whether positive or negative), the stronger the association between the two variables. A correlation of 0 means that there is no association between the variables. A correlation of −.40 is stronger than a correlation of +.20 because we disregard whether the correlation is positive or negative in determining the strength of the correlation.

A caution is in order, however. Correlation does not equal causation (Heiman, 2011; Kiess & Green, 2010). The correlational finding just mentioned does not mean that permissive parenting necessarily causes low self-control in children. It might mean that a child's lack of self-control caused the parents to simply give up trying to control the child. It might also mean that other factors, such as heredity or poverty, caused the correlation between permissive parenting and low self-control in children. Figure 1.17 illustrates these possible interpretations of correlational data.

Throughout this book you will read about numerous correlational research studies. Keep in mind how easy (and misleading) it can be to assume causality when two events or characteristics merely are correlated (Howell, 2010).

Experimental Research   To study causality, researchers turn to experimental research. An **experiment** is a carefully regulated procedure in which one or more factors believed to influence the behavior being studied are manipulated while all other factors are held constant. If the behavior under study changes when a factor is manipulated, we say that the manipulated factor has caused the behavior to change. In other words, the experiment has demonstrated cause and effect. The cause is the factor that was manipulated. The effect is the behavior that changed because of the manipulation. Nonexperimental research methods (descriptive and correlational research) cannot establish cause and effect because they do not involve manipulating factors in a controlled way (Mitchell & Jolley, 2010).

Independent and Dependent Variables   Experiments include two types of changeable factors, or variables: independent and dependent. An independent variable is a manipulated, influential, experimental factor. It is a potential cause. The label *independent* is used because this variable can be manipulated independently of other factors to determine its effect. One experiment may include several independent variables.

A dependent variable is a factor that can change in an experiment, in response to changes in the independent variable. As researchers manipulate the independent variable, they measure the dependent variable for any resulting effect.

For example, suppose that you conducted a study to determine whether aerobic exercise by pregnant women changes the breathing and sleeping patterns of their newborn babies. You might require one group of pregnant women to engage in a certain amount of exercise each week; the amount of exercise is thus the independent variable. When the infants are born, you would observe and measure their breathing and sleeping patterns. These patterns are the dependent variable, the factor that changes as the result of your manipulation.

Experimental and Control Groups   Experiments can involve one or more experimental groups and one or more control groups. An experimental group is a group whose experience is manipulated. A control group is a comparison group that is as much like the experimental group as possible and that is treated in every way like the experimental group except for the manipulated factor (independent variable). The control group serves as a baseline against which the effects of the manipulated condition can be compared.

Random assignment is an important principle for deciding whether each participant will be placed in the experimental group or in the control group. Random assignment means that researchers assign participants to experimental and control groups by chance. It reduces the likelihood that the experiment's results will be due to any preexisting differences between groups (Graziano & Raulin, 2010). In the example of the effects of aerobic exercise by pregnant women on the breathing and sleeping patterns of their newborns, you would randomly assign half of the pregnant women to engage in aerobic exercise over a period of weeks (the experimental group) and the other half to not exercise over the same number of weeks (the control group). Figure 1.18 illustrates the nature of experimental research.

Time Span of Research   Researchers in child development have a special concern with studies that focus on the relationship between age and some other variable. To do this, they study different individuals of different ages and compare them, or they study the same individuals as they age over time.

Cross-Sectional Approach   The **cross-sectional approach** is a research strategy in which individuals of different ages are compared at one time. A typical cross-sectional study might include a group of 5-year-olds, 8-year-olds, and 11-year-olds. The groups can be compared with respect to a variety of dependent variables: IQ, memory, peer relations, attachment to parents, hormonal changes, and so on. All of this can be accomplished in a short time. In some studies, data are collected in

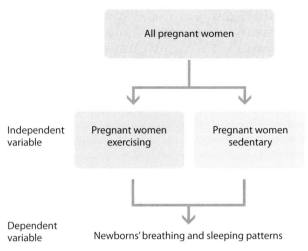

Independent variable

Dependent variable

FIGURE **1.18**

PRINCIPLES OF EXPERIMENTAL RESEARCH. Imagine that you decide to conduct an experimental study of the effects of aerobic exercise by pregnant women on their newborns' breathing and sleeping patterns. You would randomly assign pregnant women to experimental and control groups. The experimental-group women would engage in aerobic exercise over a specified number of sessions and weeks. The control group would not. Then, when the infants are born, you would assess their breathing and sleeping patterns. If the breathing and sleeping patterns of newborns whose mothers were in the experimental group are more positive than those of the control group, you would conclude that aerobic exercise caused the positive effects.

cross-sectional approach A research strategy in which individuals of different ages are compared at the same point in time.

FIGURE **1.19**

CONNECTIONS OF RESEARCH METHODS TO THEORIES

Research Method	Theory
Observation	• All theories emphasize some form of observation. • Behavioral and social cognitive theories place the strongest emphasis on laboratory observation. • Ethological theory places the strongest emphasis on naturalistic observation.
Interview/survey	• Psychoanalytic and cognitive studies (Piaget, Vygotsky) often use interviews. • Behavioral, social cognitive, and ethological theories are the least likely to use surveys or interviews.
Standardized test	• None of the theories discussed emphasize the use of this method.
Correlational research	• All of the theories use this research method, although psychoanalytic theories are the least likely to use it.
Experimental research	• The behavioral and social cognitive theories and the information-processing theories are the most likely to use the experimental method. • Psychoanalytic theories are the least likely to use it.
Cross-sectional/longitudinal methods	• No theory described uses these methods more than any other.

a single day. Even in large-scale cross-sectional studies with hundreds of participants, data collection does not usually take longer than several months to complete.

The main advantage of the cross-sectional study is that researchers don't have to wait for children to grow older. Despite its efficiency, the cross-sectional approach has its drawbacks. It gives no information about how individual children change or about the stability of their characteristics. It can obscure the increases and decreases of development—the hills and valleys of growth and development.

Longitudinal Approach   The **longitudinal approach** is a research strategy in which the same individuals are studied over a period of time, usually several years or more. For example, if a study of self-esteem were conducted longitudinally, the same children might be assessed three times—at 5, 8, and 11 years of age, for example. Some longitudinal studies take place over shorter time frames, even just a year or so.

Longitudinal studies provide a wealth of information about important issues such as stability and change in development and the influence of early experience on later development, but they are not without problems (Gibbons, Hedeker, & DuToit, 2010). They are expensive and time-consuming. Also, the longer the study lasts, the greater the number of participants who drop out. For example, children's families may move, get sick, lose interest, and so forth. Those who remain in the study may be dissimilar to those who drop out, biasing the results. Those individuals who remain in a longitudinal study over a number of years may be more compulsive and conformity-oriented than average, for example, or they might lead more stable lives.

Theories are often linked with a particular research method or methods. Therefore, methods that researchers use are associated with their particular theoretical approaches. Figure 1.19 illustrates connections between research methods and theories.

So far we have discussed many aspects of scientific research in child development, but where can you read about this research firsthand? Read *Connecting Through Research* to find out.

longitudinal approach A research strategy in which the same individuals are studied over a period of time, usually several years.

connecting through research

Where Is Child Development Research Published?

Regardless of whether you pursue a career in child development, psychology, or some related scientific field, you can benefit by learning about the journal process. As a student you might be required to look up original research in journals. As a parent, teacher, or nurse you might want to consult journals to obtain information that will help you understand and work more effectively with people. And as an inquiring person, you might look up information in journals after you have heard or read something that piqued your curiosity.

A journal publishes scholarly and academic information, usually in a specific domain such as physics, math, sociology, or our current interest, child development. Scholars in these fields publish most of their research in journals, which are the source of core information in virtually every academic discipline.

An increasing number of journals publish information about child development. Among the leading journals in child development are *Developmental Psychology, Child Development, Developmental Psychopathology, Pediatrics, Pediatric Nursing, Infant Behavior and Development, Journal of Research on Adolescence, Human Development,* and many others. Also, a number of journals that do not focus solely on development include articles on various aspects of human development. These journals include *Journal of Educational Psychology, Sex Roles, Journal of Cross-Cultural Research, Journal of Marriage and the Family, Exceptional Children,* and *Journal of Consulting and Clinical Psychology.*

Every journal has a board of experts who evaluate articles submitted for publication. Each submitted paper is accepted or rejected on the basis of factors such as its contribution to the field, methodological excellence, and clarity of writing. Some of the most prestigious journals reject as many as 80 to 90 percent of the articles submitted.

Journal articles are usually written for other professionals in the specialized field of the journal's focus; therefore, they often contain technical language and terms specific to the discipline that are difficult for nonprofessionals to understand. They usually consist of the follow-

Research journals are the core of information in virtually every academic discipline. Those shown here are among the increasing number of research journals that publish information about child development. *What are the main parts of a research article that presents findings from original research?*

ing elements: abstract, introduction, method, results, discussion, and references.

The *abstract* is a brief summary that appears at the beginning of the article. The abstract lets readers quickly determine whether the article is relevant to their interests. The *introduction* introduces the problem or issue that is being studied. It includes a concise review of research relevant to the topic, theoretical ties, and one or more hypotheses to be tested. The *method* section consists of a clear description of the subjects evaluated in the study, the measures used, and the procedures that were followed. The method section should be sufficiently clear and detailed so that reading it could allow another researcher to repeat or replicate the study. The *results* section reports the analysis of the data collected. In most cases, the results section includes statistical analyses that are difficult for nonprofessionals to understand. The *discussion* section describes the author's conclusions, inferences, and interpretation of what was found. Statements are usually made about whether the hypotheses presented in the introduction were supported, limitations of the study, and suggestions for future research. The last part of the journal article, called *references,* includes bibliographic information for each source cited in the article. The references section is often a good resource for finding other articles relevant to a topic that interests you.

Where do you find journals such as those we have described? Your college or university library likely has some of them, and some public libraries also carry journals. Online resources such as PsycINFO, which can facilitate the search for journal articles, are available to students on many campuses.

The research published in the journals mentioned above shapes our lives. It not only informs the work of other child development researchers, but it also informs the practices of law and policy makers, physicians, educators, parents, and many others. In fact, much of what you will find that is new in this edition of this textbook comes directly from research that can be found in the journals mentioned above.

CHALLENGES IN CHILD DEVELOPMENT RESEARCH

The scientific foundation of research in child development helps to minimize the effect of research bias and maximize the objectivity of the results. Still, subtle challenges remain for each researcher to resolve. One is to ensure that research is conducted in an ethical way; another is to recognize, and try to overcome, deeply buried personal biases.

Conducting Ethical Research   The explosion in technology has forced society to grapple with looming ethical questions that were unimaginable only a few decades ago. The same line of research that enables previously sterile couples to have children might someday let prospective parents "call up and order" the characteristics they prefer in their children or tip the balance of males and females in the world. For example, should embryos left over from procedures for increasing fertility be saved or discarded? Should people with inheritable fatal diseases (such as Huntington's disease) be discouraged from having their own biological children?

Researchers also face ethical questions both new and old. They have a responsibility to anticipate the personal problems their research might cause and to at least inform the participants of the possible fallout. Safeguarding the rights of research participants is a challenge because the potential harm is not always obvious (Fisher, 2009).

Ethics in research may affect you personally if you ever serve as a participant in a study. In that event, you need to know your rights as a participant and the responsibilities of researchers to assure that these rights are safeguarded.

If you ever become a researcher in child development yourself, you will need an even deeper understanding of ethics. Even if you only carry out experimental projects in psychology courses, you must consider the rights of the participants in those projects.

Today, proposed research at colleges and universities must pass the scrutiny of a research ethics committee before the research can be initiated. In addition, the American Psychological Association (APA) has developed ethics guidelines for its members. The APA code of ethics instructs psychologists to protect their participants from mental and physical harm. The participants' best interests need to be kept foremost in the researcher's mind (Fisher, 2009; Jackson, 2008). APA's guidelines address four important issues: informed consent, confidentiality, debriefing, and deception.

- *Informed consent*. All participants must know what their participation will involve and what risks might develop. For example, participants in a study on dating should be told beforehand that a questionnaire might stimulate thoughts about issues in their relationship that they had not considered. Participants also should be informed that in some instances a discussion of the issues might improve their relationship, but in others it might worsen the relationship and even end it. Even after informed consent is given, participants must retain the right to withdraw from the study at any time and for any reason.

- *Confidentiality*. Researchers are responsible for keeping all of the data they gather on individuals completely confidential and, when possible, completely anonymous.

- *Debriefing*. After the study has been completed, participants should be informed of its purpose and the methods that were used. In most cases, the experimenter also can inform participants in a general manner beforehand about the purpose of the research without leading participants to behave in a way they think that the experimenter is expecting. When preliminary information about the study is likely to affect the results, participants can at least be debriefed after the study has been completed.

- *Deception*. This is an ethical issue that researchers debate extensively. In some circumstances, telling the participants beforehand what the research study is

Pam Reid, Educational and Developmental Psychologist

When she was a child, Pam Reid liked to play with chemistry sets. Reid majored in chemistry during college and wanted to become a doctor. However, when some of her friends signed up for a psychology class as an elective, she also decided to take the course. She was intrigued by learning about how people think, behave, and develop—so much so that she changed her major to psychology. Reid went on to obtain her Ph.D. in psychology (American Psychological Association, 2003, p. 16).

For a number of years Reid was a professor of education and psychology at the University of Michigan, where she also was a research scientist at the Institute for Research on Women and Gender. Her main focus has been on how children and adolescents develop social skills, with a special interest in the development of African American girls (Reid & Zalk, 2001). In 2004, Reid became provost and executive vice-president at Roosevelt University in Chicago.

Pam Reid (*center*) with students at Saint Joseph College in Hartford, Connecticut, where she is the president of the college.

For more information about what professors, researchers, and educational psychologists do, see pages 44–45 in the Careers in Child Development appendix immediately following this chapter.

about substantially alters the participants' behavior and invalidates the researcher's data. In all cases of deception, however, the psychologist must ensure that the deception will not harm the participants and that the participants will be told the complete nature of the study (debriefed) as soon as possible after the study is completed.

Minimizing Bias   Studies of children's development are most useful when they are conducted without bias or prejudice toward any particular group of people. Of special concern is bias based on gender and bias based on culture or ethnicity.

Gender Bias   For most of its existence, our society has had a strong gender bias, a preconceived notion about the abilities of males and females that prevented individuals from pursuing their own interests and achieving their full potential (Etaugh & Bridges, 2010). Gender bias also has had a less obvious effect within the field of child development. For example, it is not unusual for conclusions to be drawn about females' attitudes and behaviors from research conducted with males as the only participants.

Furthermore, when researchers find gender differences, their reports sometimes magnify those differences (Denmark & others, 1988). For example, a researcher might report that 74 percent of the boys in a study had high achievement expectations versus only 67 percent of the girls and go on to talk about the differences in some detail. In reality, this might be a rather small difference. It also might disappear if the study was repeated, or the study might have methodological problems that don't allow such strong interpretations.

Pam Reid is a leading researcher who studies gender and ethnic bias in development. To read about Pam's interests, see *Connecting With Careers*.

Cultural and Ethnic Bias   The realization that research on children's development needs to include more children from diverse ethnic groups has also been building

Look at these two photographs, one of all White male children, the other of a diverse group of girls and boys from different ethnic groups, including some non-Latino White children. Consider a topic in child development, such as parenting, cultural values, or independence seeking. *If you were conducting research on this topic, might the results of the study be different depending on whether the participants in your study were the children in the left or right photograph?*

(Ceballo, Huerta, & Ngo, 2010; Rowley, Kurtz-Costes, & Cooper, 2010). Historically, children from ethnic minority groups (African American, Latino, Asian American, and Native American) were excluded from most research in the United States and simply thought of as variations from the norm or average. If minority children were included in samples and their scores didn't fit the norm, they were viewed as confounds or "noise" in data and discounted. Given the fact that children from diverse ethnic groups were excluded from research on child development for so long, we might reasonably conclude that children's real lives are perhaps more varied than research data have indicated in the past.

Researchers also have tended to overgeneralize about ethnic groups (Banks, 2010; Liu & others, 2009). **Ethnic gloss** is using an ethnic label such as *African American* or *Latino* in a superficial way that portrays an ethnic group as being more homogeneous than it really is (Trimble, 1988). For example, a researcher might describe a research sample like this: "The participants were 60 Latinos." A more complete description of the Latino group might be something like this: "The 60 Latino participants were Mexican Americans from low-income neighborhoods in the southwestern area of Los Angeles. Thirty-six were from homes in which Spanish is the dominant language spoken, 24 from homes in which English is the main language spoken. Thirty were born in the United States, 30 in Mexico. Twenty-eight described themselves as Mexican American, 14 as Mexican, 9 as American, 6 as Chicano, and 3 as Latino." Ethnic gloss can cause researchers to obtain samples of ethnic groups that are not representative of the group's diversity, which can lead to overgeneralization and stereotyping.

Research on ethnic minority children and their families has not been given adequate attention, especially in light of their significant rate of growth within the U.S. population (Tamis-Lemonda & McFadden, 2010). Until recently, ethnic minority families were combined in the category "minority," which masks important differences among ethnic groups as well as diversity within an ethnic group. At present and in the foreseeable future, the growth of minority families in the United States will be mainly due to the immigration of Latino and Asian families. Researchers need to take into account their acculturation level and generational status of parents and children, and how both factors influence family processes and child outcomes (Bornstein & Cote, 2010). More attention also needs to be given to biculturalism because the complexity of diversity means that some children of color identify with two or more ethnic groups (Levine & McClosky, 2009).

ethnic gloss Use of an ethnic label such as *African American* or *Latino* in a superficial way that portrays an ethnic group as being more homogeneous than it really is.

Review *Connect* Reflect

 LG4 Summarize why research is important in child development, the main theories of child development, and research methods, designs, and challenges.

Review

- What is scientific research, what is it based on, and why is scientific research on child development important?
- What are the main theories of child development?
- What are the main research methods for collecting data about children's development?
- What types of research designs do child development researchers use?
- What are some research challenges in studying children's development?

Connect

- Which of the research methods for collecting data would be appropriate or inappropriate for studying Erikson's stage of trust versus mistrust? Why?

Reflect *Your Own Personal Journey of Life*

- Which of the theories of child development do you think best explains your own development? Why?

reach your learning goals

Child Development—Yesterday and Today

 LG1 Discuss historical views and the modern era of child development.

Historical Views of Childhood

The Modern Study of Child Development

- Development is the pattern of change that begins at conception and continues through the life span; usually involves growth although it also involves decay. The history of interest in children is long and rich. Prior to the nineteenth century, philosophical views of childhood were prominent, including the notions of original sin, tabula rasa, and innate goodness.

- Today, we conceive of childhood as an important time of development. The modern era of studying children spans a little more than a century, an era in which the study of child development has become a sophisticated science. Methodological advances in observation as well as the introduction of experimentation and the development of major theories characterize the achievements of the modern era.

Caring for Children

 LG2 Identify five areas in which children's lives need to be improved, and explain the roles of resilience and social policy in children's development.

Improving the Lives of Children

- Health and well-being is an important area in which children's lives can be improved. Today, many children in the United States and around the world need improved health care. We now recognize the importance of lifestyles and psychological states in promoting health and well-being. Parenting is an important influence on children's development. One-parent families, working parents, and child care are among the family issues that influence children's well-being. Education can also contribute to children's health and well-being. There is widespread concern that the education of children needs to be more effective, and there are many views in contemporary education about ways to improve schools.

| Resilience, Social Policy, and Children's Development | • Some children triumph over adversity—they are resilient. Researchers have found that resilient children are likely to have a close relationship with a parent figure and bonds with caring people outside the family. Social policy is a government's course of action designed to promote the welfare of its citizens. The poor conditions of life for a significant percentage of U.S. children, and the lack of attention to prevention of these poor conditions, point to the need for revised social policies. |

Developmental Processes, Periods, and Issues

 Discuss the most important processes, periods, and issues in development.

Biological, Cognitive, and Socioemotional Processes

• Three key processes of development are biological, cognitive, and socioemotional. Biological processes (such as genes inherited from parents) involve changes in an individual's body. Cognitive processes (such as thinking) consist of changes in an individual's thought, intelligence, and language. Socioemotional processes (such as smiling) include changes in an individual's relationships with others, in emotions, and in personality.

Periods of Development

• Childhood's five main developmental periods are (1) prenatal, from conception to birth, (2) infancy, from birth to 18 to 24 months, (3) early childhood, from the end of infancy to about 5 or 6 years of age, (4) middle and late childhood, from about 6 to 11 years of age, and (5) adolescence, which begins at about 10 or 12 and ends at about 18 or 19 years of age.

Issues in Development

• The nature-nurture issue focuses on the extent to which development is mainly influenced by nature (biological inheritance) or nurture (environmental experience). Some developmentalists describe development as continuous (gradual, cumulative change), while others describe it as discontinuous (a sequence of distinct stages). The early-later experience issue focuses on whether early experiences (especially in infancy) are more important in development than later experiences. Most developmentalists recognize that extreme positions on the nature-nurture, continuity-discontinuity, and early-later experience issues are not supported by research. Despite this consensus, they continue to debate the degree to which each position influences children's development.

The Science of Child Development

 Summarize why research is important in child development, the main theories of child development, and research methods, designs, and challenges.

The Importance of Research

• Scientific research is objective, systematic, and testable. Scientific research is based on the scientific method, which includes these steps: conceptualize the problem, collect data, draw conclusions, and revise theory. Scientific research on child development reduces the likelihood that the information gathered is based on personal beliefs, opinions, and feelings.

Theories of Child Development

• Psychoanalytic theories describe development as primarily unconscious and as heavily colored by emotion. The two main psychoanalytic theories in developmental psychology are Freud's and Erikson's. Freud also proposed that individuals go through five psychosexual stages—oral, anal, phallic, latency, and genital. Erikson's theory emphasizes eight psychosocial stages of development. The three main cognitive theories are Piaget's cognitive developmental theory, Vygotsky's sociocultural theory, and information-processing theory. Cognitive theories emphasize conscious thoughts. In Piaget's theory, children go through four cognitive stages: sensorimotor, preoperational, concrete operational, and formal operational. Vygotsky's sociocultural cognitive theory emphasizes how culture and social interaction guide cognitive development. The information-processing theory emphasizes that individuals manipulate information, monitor it, and strategize about it. Three versions of the behavioral and social cognitive theories are Pavlov's classical conditioning, Skinner's operant conditioning, and Bandura's social cognitive theory. Ethology stresses that behavior is strongly influenced by biology, is tied to evolution, and is characterized by critical or sensitive periods. Ecological theory is Bronfenbrenner's environmental systems view of development. It consists of five environmental systems: microsystem, mesosystem, exosystem, macrosystem, and chronosystem. An eclectic theoretical orientation does not follow any one theoretical approach, but rather selects from each theory whatever is considered the best in it.

- Research methods for collecting data about child development include observation (in a laboratory or a naturalistic setting), survey (questionnaire) or interview, standardized test, case study, and physiological measures.

- Descriptive research aims to observe and record behavior. In correlational research, the goal is to describe the strength of the relationship between two or more events or characteristics. Experimental research involves conducting an experiment, which can determine cause and effect. An independent variable is the manipulated, influential, experimental factor. A dependent variable is a factor that can change in an experiment, in response to changes in the independent variable. Experiments can involve one or more experimental groups and control groups. In random assignment, researchers assign participants to experimental and control groups by chance. When researchers decide about the time span of their research, they can conduct cross-sectional or longitudinal studies.

- Researchers' ethical responsibilities include seeking participants' informed consent, ensuring their confidentiality, debriefing them about the purpose and potential personal consequences of participating, and avoiding unnecessary deception of participants. Researchers need to guard against gender, cultural, and ethnic bias in research. Every effort should be made to make research equitable for both females and males. Individuals from varied ethnic backgrounds need to be included as participants in child research, and overgeneralization about diverse members within a group must be avoided.

Research Methods for Collecting Data

Research Designs

Challenges in Child Development Research

key terms

development 6
original sin view 6
tabula rasa view 6
innate goodness view 6
context 11
culture 11
cross-cultural studies 11
ethnicity 11
socioeconomic status (SES) 11
gender 11
social policy 13
biological processes 15
cognitive processes 15

socioemotional processes 15
prenatal period 16
infancy 16
early childhood 16
middle and late childhood 16
adolescence 16
nature-nurture issue 17
continuity-discontinuity issue 18
early-later experience issue 18
scientific method 20

theory 20
hypothesis 20
psychoanalytic theories 21
Erikson's theory 21
Piaget's theory 24
Vygotsky's theory 25
information-processing theory 26
social cognitive theory 27
ethology 28
Bronfenbrenner's ecological theory 29
eclectic theoretical orientation 30

laboratory 32
naturalistic observation 32
standardized test 32
case study 33
descriptive research 34
correlational research 34
correlation coefficient 34
experiment 34
cross-sectional approach 35
longitudinal approach 36
ethnic gloss 40

key people

Philippe Ariès 6
John Locke 6
Jean-Jacques Rousseau 6
Alfred Binet 7
G. Stanley Hall 7

Arnold Gesell 7
Ann Masten 13
Jerome Kagan 19
Sigmund Freud 21
Erik Erikson 21

Jean Piaget 25
Lev Vygotsky 25
Robert Siegler 26
Ivan Pavlov 26
John Watson 26

Rosalie Raynor 26
B. F. Skinner 27
Albert Bandura 27
Konrad Lorenz 28
Urie Bronfenbrenner 29

appendix

Careers in Child Development

Each of us wants to find a rewarding career and enjoy the work we do. The field of child development offers an amazing breadth of career options that can provide extremely satisfying work.

If you decide to pursue a career in child development, what career options are available to you? There are many. College and university professors teach courses in areas of child development, education, family development, nursing, and medicine. Teachers impart knowledge, understanding, and skills to children and adolescents. Counselors, clinical psychologists, nurses, and physicians help parents and children of all ages to cope more effectively with their lives and well-being. Various professionals work with families to improve the quality of family functioning.

Although an advanced degree is not absolutely necessary in some areas of child development, you usually can expand your opportunities (and income) considerably by obtaining a graduate degree. Many careers in child development pay reasonably well. For example, psychologists earn well above the median salary in the United States. Also, by working in the field of child development you can guide people in improving their lives, understand yourself and others better, possibly advance the state of knowledge in the field, and have an enjoyable time while you are doing these things.

If you are considering a career in child development, would you prefer to work with infants, children, adolescents, parents or a combination of these? As you go through this term, try to spend some time with children of different ages. Observe their behavior. Talk with them about their lives. Think about whether you would like to work with children of this age in your life's work.

Another important aspect of exploring careers is to talk with people who work in various jobs. For example, if you have some interest in becoming a school counselor, call a school, ask to speak with a counselor, and set up an appointment to discuss the counselor's career and work.

Something else that should benefit you is to work in one or more jobs related to your career interests while you are in college. Many colleges and universities have internships or work experiences for students who major in fields such as child development. In some instances, these jobs earn course credit or pay; in others, they are strictly on a volunteer basis. Take advantage of these opportunities. They can provide you with valuable experiences to help you decide whether this is the right career for you, and they can help you get into graduate school if you decide that you want to go.

In the upcoming sections, we will profile careers in four areas: education and research; clinical and counseling; medical, nursing, and physical development; and families and relationships. We have provided page numbers after some entries telling you where within the text you can find *Connecting With Careers*, the career profiles of people who hold some of these positions. These are not the only career options in child development, but they should provide you with an idea of the range of opportunities available and information about some of the main career avenues you might pursue. In profiling these careers, we will address the amount of education required, the type of training involved, and the nature of the work.

Education and Research

Numerous career opportunities in child development involve education or research. These positions range from college professor to child-care director to school psychologist.

College/University Professor

Courses in child development are taught in many programs and schools in colleges and universities, including psychology, education, nursing, child and family studies, social work, and medicine. The work that college professors do includes teaching courses at the undergraduate or graduate level (or both), conducting research in a specific area, advising students and/or directing their research, and serving on college or university committees. Some college instructors do not conduct research as part of their job but instead focus mainly on teaching. Research is most likely to be part of the job description at universities with master's and Ph.D. programs. A Ph.D. or master's degree almost always is required to teach in some area of child development in a college or university. Obtaining a doctoral degree usually takes four to six years of graduate work. A master's degree requires approximately two years of graduate work. The training involves taking graduate courses, learning to conduct research, and attending and presenting papers at professional meetings. Many graduate students work as teaching or research assistants for professors in an apprenticeship relationship that helps them to become competent teachers and researchers.

If you are interested in becoming a college or university professor, you might want to make an appointment with your instructor in this class on child development to learn more about his or her profession and work. **Read a profile of a professor on p. 495.**

Researcher

Some individuals in the field of child development work in research positions. In most instances, they have either a master's or Ph.D. in some area of child development. The researchers might work at a university, perhaps in a university professor's research program, in government at agencies such as the National Institute of Mental Health, or in private industry. Individuals who have full-time research positions in child development generate innovative research ideas, plan studies, carry out the research by collecting data, analyze the data, and then interpret it. Then they will usually attempt to publish the research in a scientific journal. A researcher often works in a collaborative manner with other researchers on a project and may present the research at scientific meetings. One researcher might spend much of his or her time in a laboratory while another researcher might work out in the field, such as in schools, hospitals, and so on.

Elementary School Teacher

The work of an elementary or secondary school teacher involves teaching in one or more subject areas, preparing the curriculum, giving tests, assigning grades, monitoring students' progress, conducting parent-teacher conferences, and attending in-service workshops. Becoming an elementary or secondary school teacher requires a minimum of an undergraduate degree. The training involves taking a wide range of courses with a major or concentration in education as well as completing a supervised practice-teaching internship. **Read a profile of an elementary school teacher on p. 275.**

Exceptional Children (Special Education) Teacher

A teacher of exceptional children spends concentrated time with individual children who have a disability or are gifted. Among the children a teacher of exceptional children might work with are children with learning disabilities, ADHD (attention deficit hyperactivity disorder), mental retardation, or a physical disability such as cerebral palsy. Some of this work will usually be done outside of the student's regular classroom, and some of it will be carried out when the student is in the regular classroom. A teacher of exceptional children works closely with the student's regular classroom teacher and parents to create the best educational program for the student. Becoming a teacher of exceptional children requires a minimum of an undergraduate degree. The training consists of taking a wide range of courses in education and a concentration of courses in educating children with disabilities or children who are gifted. Teachers of exceptional children often continue their education after obtaining their undergraduate degree and attain a master's degree.

Early Childhood Educator

Early childhood educators work on college faculties and have a minimum of a master's degree in their field. In graduate school, they take courses in early childhood education and receive supervisory training in child-care or early childhood programs. Early childhood educators usually teach in community colleges that award an associate degree in early childhood education.

Preschool/Kindergarten Teacher

Preschool teachers teach mainly 4-year-old children, and kindergarten teachers primarily teach 5-year-old children. They usually have an undergraduate degree in education, specializing in early childhood education. State certification to become a preschool or kindergarten teacher usually is required.

Family and Consumer Science Educator

Family and consumer science educators may specialize in early childhood education or instruct middle and high school students about topics such as nutrition, interpersonal relationships, human sexuality, parenting, and human development. Hundreds of colleges and universities throughout the United States offer two- and four-year degree programs in family and consumer science. These programs usually include an internship requirement. Additional education courses may be needed to obtain a teaching certificate. Some family and consumer educators go on to graduate school for further training, which provides a background for possible jobs in college teaching or research.

Educational Psychologist

An educational psychologist most often teaches in a college or university and conducts research in areas of educational psychology such as learning, motivation, classroom management, and assessment. Most educational psychologists have a doctorate in education, which takes four to six years of graduate work. They help to train students who will take various positions in education, including educational psychology, school psychology, and teaching.

School Psychologist

School psychologists focus on improving the psychological and intellectual well-being of elementary and secondary school students. They may work in a centralized office in a school district or in one or more schools. They give psychological tests, interview students and their parents, consult with teachers, and may provide counseling to students and their families.

School psychologists usually have a master's or doctoral degree in school psychology. In graduate school, they take courses in counseling, assessment, learning, and other areas of education and psychology.

Clinical and Counseling

A wide variety of clinical and counseling jobs are linked with child development. These range from child clinical psychologist to adolescent drug counselor.

Clinical Psychologist

Clinical psychologists seek to help people with psychological problems. They work in a variety of settings, including colleges and universities, clinics, medical schools, and private practice. Some clinical psychologists only conduct psychotherapy, others do psychological assessment and psychotherapy, and some also do research. Clinical psychologists may specialize in a particular age group, such as children (child clinical psychologist).

Clinical psychologists have either a Ph.D. (which involves clinical and research training) or a Psy.D. degree (which only involves clinical training). This graduate training usually takes five to seven years and includes courses in clinical psychology and a one-year supervised internship in an accredited setting toward the end of the training. In most cases, they must pass a test to become licensed in a state and to call themselves clinical psychologists. **Read a profile of a clinical child psychologist on p. 19.**

Psychiatrist

Like clinical psychologists, psychiatrists might specialize in working with children (child psychiatry) or adolescents (adolescent psychiatry). Psychiatrists might work in medical schools in teaching and research roles, in a medical clinic, or in private practice. In addition to administering drugs to help improve the lives of people with psychological problems, psychiatrists also may conduct psychotherapy. Psychiatrists obtain a medical degree and then do a residency in psychiatry. Medical school takes approximately four years, and the psychiatry residency another three to four years. Unlike psychologists (who do not go to medical school) in most states, psychiatrists can administer drugs to clients.

Counseling Psychologist

Counseling psychologists work in the same settings as clinical psychologists, and may do psychotherapy, teach, or conduct research. In many instances, however, counseling psychologists do not work with individuals who have a severe mental disorder. A counseling psychologist might specialize in working with children, adolescents, and/or families.

Counseling psychologists go through much of the same training as clinical psychologists, although in a graduate program in counseling rather than clinical psychology. Counseling psychologists have either a master's degree or a doctoral degree. They also must go through a licensing procedure. One type of master's degree in counseling leads to the designation of licensed professional counselor.

School Counselor

School counselors help to identify students' abilities and interests, guide students in developing academic plans, and explore career options with students. They may help students cope with adjustment problems. They may work with students individually, in small groups, or even in a classroom. They often consult with parents, teachers, and school administrators when trying to help students with their problems.

High school counselors advise students on choosing a major, satisfying admissions requirements for college, taking entrance exams, applying for financial aid, and pursuing appropriate vocational and technical training. Elementary school counselors are mainly involved in counseling students about social and personal problems. They may observe children in the classroom and at play as part of their work. School counselors usually have a master's degree in counseling.

Social Worker

Social workers often are involved in helping children and adults with social or economic problems. They may investigate, evaluate, and attempt to rectify reported cases of abuse, neglect, endangerment, or domestic disputes. They can intervene in families if necessary and provide counseling and referral services to children and families.

Social workers have a minimum of an undergraduate degree from a school of social work that includes coursework in various areas of sociology and psychology. Some social workers also have a master's or doctoral degree. They often work for publicly funded agencies at the city, state, or national level, although increasingly they work in the private sector in areas such as drug rehabilitation and family counseling.

In some cases, social workers specialize in a certain area, as is true of a medical social worker, who has a master's degree in social work (MSW). This involves graduate coursework and supervised clinical experiences in medical settings. A medical social worker might coordinate a variety of support services to people with severe or long-term disabilities. Family care social workers often work with families who need support services.

Drug Counselor

Drug counselors provide counseling to children and adults with drug abuse problems. They may work on an individual basis with a substance abuser or conduct group therapy sessions. They may work in private practice, with a state or federal government agency, with a company, or in a hospital setting. Some drug counselors specialize in working with adolescents or families. Most states provide a certification procedure for obtaining a license to practice drug counseling.

At a minimum, drug counselors go through an associate's or certificate program. Many have an undergraduate degree in substance-abuse counseling, and some have master's and doctoral degrees.

Medical, Nursing, and Physical Development

This third main area of careers in child development includes a wide range of careers in the medical and nursing areas, as well as jobs that focus on improving some aspect of the child's physical development.

Obstetrician/Gynecologist

An obstetrician/gynecologist prescribes prenatal and postnatal care and performs deliveries in maternity cases. The individual also treats diseases and injuries of the female reproductive system. Obstetricians may work in private practice, in a medical clinic, a hospital, or in a medical school. Becoming an obstetrician/ gynecologist requires a medical degree plus three to five years of residency in obstetrics/ gynecology.

Pediatrician

A pediatrician monitors infants' and children's health, works to prevent disease or injury, helps children attain optimal health, and treats children with health problems. Pediatricians may work in private practice, in a medical clinic, in a hospital, or in a medical school. As medical doctors, they can administer drugs to children and may counsel parents and children on ways to improve children's health. Many pediatricians on the faculties of medical schools also teach and conduct research on children's health and diseases. Pediatricians have attained a medical degree and completed a three- to five-year residency in pediatrics.

Neonatal Nurse

A neonatal nurse is involved in the delivery of care to newborn infants. The neonatal nurse may work to improve the health and well-being of infants born under normal circumstances or be involved in the delivery of care to premature and critically ill neonates.

A minimum of an undergraduate degree in nursing with a specialization in the newborn is required. This training involves coursework in nursing and the biological sciences, as well as supervisory clinical experiences.

Nurse-Midwife

A nurse-midwife formulates and provides comprehensive care to selected maternity patients, cares for the expectant mother as she prepares to give birth and guides her through the birth process, and cares for the postpartum patient. The nurse-midwife also may provide care to the newborn, counsel parents on the infant's development and parenting, and provide guidance about health practices. Becoming a nurse-midwife generally requires an undergraduate degree from a school of nursing. A nurse-midwife most often works in a hospital setting. **Read the profile of a perinatal nurse on p. 93.**

Pediatric Nurse

Pediatric nurses have a degree in nursing that takes from two to five years to complete. Some also may obtain a master's or doctoral degree in pediatric nursing. Pediatric nurses take courses in biological sciences, nursing care, and pediatrics, usually in a school of nursing. They also undergo supervised clinical experiences in medical settings. They monitor infants' and children's health, work to prevent disease or injury, and help children attain optimal health. They may work in hospitals, schools of nursing, or with pediatricians in private practice or at a medical clinic. **Read a profile of a pediatric nurse on p. 135.**

Audiologist

An audiologist has a minimum of an undergraduate degree in hearing science. This includes courses and supervisory training. Audiologists assess and identify the presence and severity of hearing loss, as well as problems in balance. Some audiologists also go on to obtain a master's and/or doctoral degree. They may work in a medical clinic, with a physician in private practice, in a hospital, or in a medical school.

Speech Therapist

Speech therapists are health-care professionals who are trained to identify, assess, and treat speech and language problems. They may work with physicians, psychologists, social workers, and other health-care professionals as a team to help individuals with physical or psychological problems that include speech and language problems. Speech pathologists have a minimum of an undergraduate degree in speech and hearing science or communication disorders. They may work in private practice, in hospitals and medical schools, or in government agencies with individuals of any age. Some specialize in working with children or with a particular type of speech disorder. **Read a profile of a speech pathologist on p. 267.**

Genetic Counselor

Genetic counselors work as members of a health care team, providing information and support to families who have members with birth defects or genetic disorders and to families who may be at risk for a variety of inherited conditions. They identify families at risk and provide supportive counseling. They serve as educators and resource people for other health care professionals and the public. Almost half work in university medical centers and another one-fourth work in private hospital settings.

Most genetic counselors enter the field after majoring in undergraduate school in such disciplines as biology, genetics, psychology, nursing, public health, and social work. They have specialized graduate degrees and experience in medical genetics and counseling. **Read a profile of a genetic counselor on p. 62.**

Families and Relationships

A number of careers are available for working with families and relationship problems. These range from being a child welfare worker to a marriage and family therapist.

Child Welfare Worker

A child welfare worker is employed by the child protective services unit of each state. The child welfare worker protects the child's rights,

Katherine Duchen Smith, Nurse and Child-Care Health Consultant

Katherine Duchen Smith has a master's degree in nursing and works as a child-care health consultant. She lives in Fort Collins, Colorado, and in 2004 was appointed as the public relations chair of the National Association of Pediatric Nurse Practitioners (NAPNAP), which has more than 6,000 members.

Smith provides health consultation and educational services to child-care centers, private schools, and hospitals. She also teaches in the Regis University Family Nurse Practitioner Program. Smith developed an interest in outreach and public-relations activities during her five-year term as a board member for the Fort Collins Poudre Valley Hospital System. Later, she became the organization's outreach consultant.

As child-care health consultants, nurses might provide telephone consultation and link children, families, or staff with primary care providers. In underserved areas, they might also be asked to administer immunizations, help chronically ill children access specialty care, or develop a comprehensive health promotion or injury prevention program for caregivers and families.

Katherine Duchen Smith (*left*), nurse and child-care health consultant, at a child-care center where she is a consultant.

evaluates any maltreatment the child might experience, and may have the child removed from the home if necessary. A child social worker has a minimum of an undergraduate degree in social work.

Child Life Specialist

Child life specialists work with children and their families when the child needs to be hospitalized. They monitor the child patient's activities, seek to reduce the child's stress, help the child cope effectively, and assist the child in enjoying the hospital experience as much as possible. Child life specialists may provide parent education and develop individualized treatment plans based on an assessment of the child's development, temperament, medical plan, and available social supports.

Child life specialists have an undergraduate degree. As undergraduates, they take courses in child development and education and usually take additional courses in a child life program.

Marriage and Family Therapist

Marriage and family therapists work on the principle that many individuals who have psychological problems benefit when psychotherapy is provided in the context of a marital or family relationship. Marriage and family therapists may provide marital therapy, couples therapy to individuals in a relationship who are not married, and family therapy to two or more members of a family.

Marriage and family therapists have a master's or doctoral degree. They go through a

training program in graduate school similar to that of a clinical psychologist but with the focus on marital and family relationships. To practice marital and family therapy in most states, it is necessary to go through a licensing procedure.

These are only a handful of careers that require knowledge of developmental psychology. *Connecting With Careers* throughout this text highlight additional careers, including toy designer (p. 219), infant assessment specialist (p. 247), supervisor of gifted and talented education (p. 252), bilingual education teacher (p. 275), child-care director (p. 316), health psychologist (p. 386), and director of children's services. *What other careers can you think of that require knowledge of children's development?*

What endless questions vex the thought, of whence and whither, when and how.

—SIR RICHARD BURTON
British Explorer, 19th Century

Biological Processes, Physical Development, and Perceptual Development

The rhythm and meaning of life involve beginnings, with questions raised about how, from so simple a beginning, complex forms develop, grow, and mature. What was this organism, what is this organism, and what will this organism be? In Section 2, you will read four chapters: "Biological Beginnings" (Chapter 2), "Prenatal Development and Birth" (Chapter 3), "Physical Development and Health" (Chapter 4), and "Motor, Sensory, and Perceptual Development" (Chapter 5).

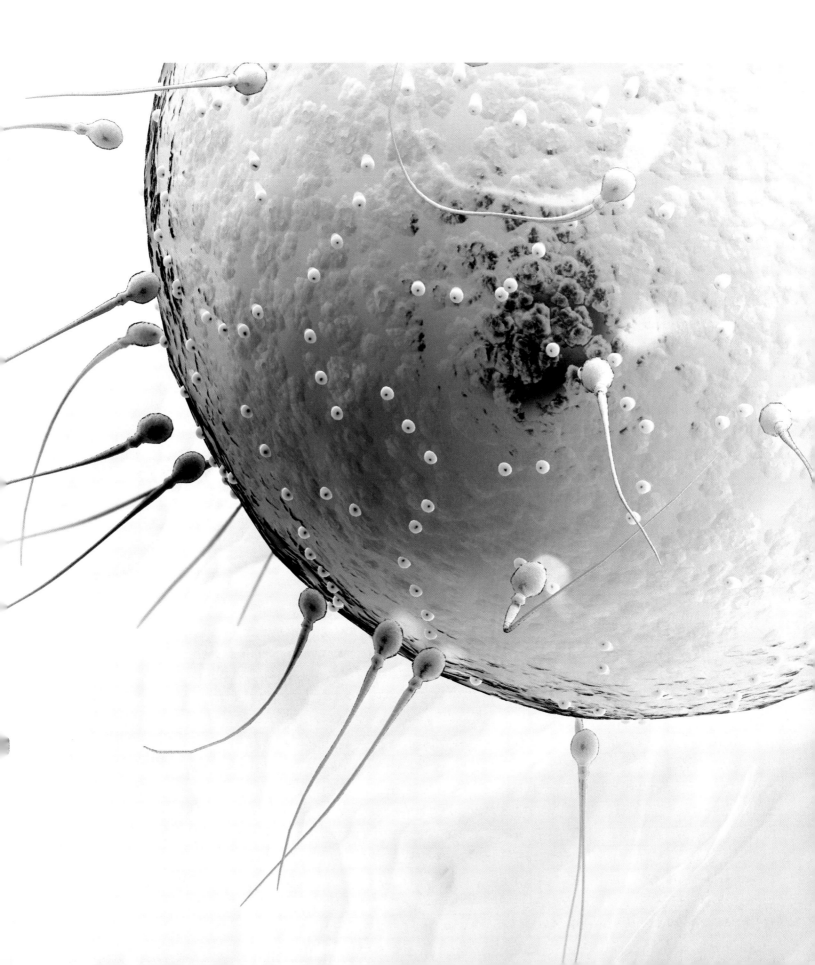

chapter 2   BIOLOGICAL BEGINNINGS

Jim Springer and Jim Lewis are identical twins. They were separated at 4 weeks of age and did not see each other again until they were 39 years old. Both worked as part-time deputy sheriffs, vacationed in Florida, drove Chevrolets, had dogs named Toy, and married and divorced women named Betty. One twin named his son James Allan, and the other named his son James Alan. Both liked math but not spelling, enjoyed carpentry and mechanical drawing, chewed their fingernails down to the nubs, had almost identical drinking and smoking habits, had hemorrhoids, put on 10 pounds at about the same point in development, first suffered headaches at the age of 18, and had similar sleep patterns.

Jim and Jim do have some differences. One wears his hair over his forehead; the other slicks it back and has sideburns. One expresses himself best orally; the other is more proficient in writing. But, for the most part, their profiles are remarkably similar.

Jim Lewis (*left*) and Jim Springer (*right*).

Another pair of identical twins, Daphne and Barbara, are called the "giggle sisters" because, after being reunited, they were always making each other laugh. A thorough search of their adoptive families' histories revealed no gigglers. The giggle sisters ignored stress, avoided conflict and controversy whenever possible, and showed no interest in politics.

Jim and Jim and the giggle sisters were part of the Minnesota Study of Twins Reared Apart, directed by Thomas Bouchard and his colleagues. The study brings identical twins (identical genetically because they come from the same fertilized egg) and fraternal twins (who come from different fertilized eggs) from all over the world to Minneapolis to investigate their lives. There the twins complete personality and intelligence tests, and they provide detailed medical histories, including information about diet and smoking, exercise habits, chest X-rays, heart stress tests, and EEGs. The twins are asked more than 15,000 questions about their family and childhood, personal interests, vocational orientation, values, and aesthetic judgments (Bouchard & others, 1990).

When genetically identical twins who were separated as infants show such striking similarities in their tastes and habits and choices, can we conclude that their genes must have caused the development of those tastes and habits and choices? Other possible causes need to be considered. The twins shared not only the same genes but also some experiences. Some of the separated twins lived together for several months prior to their adoption; some of the twins had been reunited prior to testing (in some cases, many years earlier); adoption agencies often place twins in similar homes; and even strangers who spend several hours together and start comparing their lives are likely to come up with some coincidental similarities (Joseph, 2006). The Minnesota study of identical twins points to both the importance of the genetic basis of human development and the need for further research on genetic and environmental factors (Lykken, 2001).

preview

The examples of Jim and Jim and the giggle sisters stimulate us to think about our genetic heritage and the biological foundations of our existence. However, organisms are not like billiard balls, moved by simple external forces to predictable positions on life's table. Environmental experiences and biological foundations work together to make us who we are. Our coverage of life's biological beginnings focuses on evolution, genetic foundations, challenges and choices regarding reproduction, and the interaction of heredity and environment.

The Evolutionary Perspective LG1 Discuss the evolutionary perspective on child development.

| Natural Selection and Adaptive Behavior | Evolutionary Psychology |

In evolutionary time, humans are relative newcomers to Earth. As our earliest ancestors left the forest to feed on the savannahs, and then to form hunting societies on the open plains, their minds and behaviors changed, and they eventually established humans as the dominant species on Earth. How did this evolution come about?

NATURAL SELECTION AND ADAPTIVE BEHAVIOR

Natural selection is the evolutionary process by which those individuals of a species that are best adapted are the ones that survive and reproduce. To understand what this means, let's return to the middle of the 19th century, when the British naturalist Charles Darwin was traveling around the world, observing many different species of animals in their natural surroundings. Darwin, who published his observations and thoughts in *On the Origin of Species* (1859), noted that most organisms reproduce at rates that would cause enormous increases in the population of most species and yet populations remain nearly constant. He reasoned that an intense, constant struggle for food, water, and resources must occur among the many young born each generation, because many of the young do not survive. Those that do survive and reproduce pass on their characteristics to the next generation. Darwin argued that these survivors are better *adapted* to their world than are the nonsurvivors (Brooker, 2011; Raven, 2011). The best-adapted individuals survive to leave the most offspring. Over the course of many generations, organisms with the characteristics needed for survival make up an increasing percentage of the population. Over many, many generations, this could produce a gradual modification of the whole population. If environmental conditions change, however, other characteristics might become favored by natural selection, moving the species in a different direction (Mader, 2011).

All organisms must adapt to particular places, climates, food sources, and ways of life (Audesirk, Audesirk, & Byers, 2011). An eagle's claws are a physical adaptation that facilitates predation. *Adaptive behavior* is behavior that promotes an organism's survival in the natural habitat (Johnson & Losos, 2010). For example, attachment between a caregiver and a baby ensures the infant's closeness to a caregiver for feeding and protection from danger, thus increasing the infant's chances of survival.

There are one hundred and ninety-three living species of monkeys and apes. One hundred and ninety-two of them are covered with hair. The exception is the naked ape, self-named *Homo sapiens*.

—**DESMOND MORRIS**
British Zoologist, 20th Century

evolutionary psychology Branch of psychology that emphasizes the importance of adaptation, reproduction, and "survival of the fittest" in shaping behavior.

EVOLUTIONARY PSYCHOLOGY

Although Darwin introduced the theory of evolution by natural selection in 1859, his ideas only recently have become a popular framework for explaining behavior. Psychology's newest approach, **evolutionary psychology,** emphasizes the importance of adaptation, reproduction, and "survival of the fittest" in shaping behavior. "Fit" in this sense refers to the ability to bear offspring that survive long enough to bear offspring of their own. In this view, natural selection favors behaviors that increase reproductive success—the ability to pass genes to the next generation (Confer & others, 2010; Cosmides, 2011).

David Buss (1995, 2004, 2008) has been especially influential in stimulating new interest in how evolution can explain human behavior. He reasons that just as evolution shapes our physical features, such as body shape and height, it also pervasively influences how we make decisions, how aggressive we are, our fears, and our mating patterns. For example, assume that our ancestors were hunters and gatherers on the plains and that men did most of the hunting and women stayed close to home gathering seeds and plants for food. If you have to travel some distance from your home in an effort to find and slay a fleeing animal, you need not only certain physical traits but also the ability for certain types of spatial thinking. Men born with these traits would be more likely than men without them to survive, to bring home lots of food, and to be considered attractive mates—and thus to reproduce and pass on these characteristics to their children. In other words, these traits would provide a reproductive advantage for males. Over many generations, men with good spatial thinking skills might become more numerous in the population. Critics point out that this scenario might or might not have actually happened.

How does the attachment of this Vietnamese baby to its mother reflect the evolutionary process of adaptive behavior?

Evolutionary Developmental Psychology   Recently, interest has grown in using the concepts of evolutionary psychology to understand human development (Bjorklund, 2007; Greve & Bjorklund, 2009). Here we discuss some ideas proposed by evolutionary developmental psychologists (Bjorklund & Pellegrini, 2002).

An extended childhood period evolved because humans require time to develop a large brain and learn the complexity of human societies. Humans take longer to become reproductively mature than any other mammal (see Figure 2.1). During this extended childhood period, they develop a large brain and the experiences needed to become competent adults in a complex society.

Many evolved psychological mechanisms are domain-specific—that is, the mechanisms apply only to a specific aspect of a person's makeup. Information processing is one example. According to evolutionary psychology, the mind is not a general-purpose device that can be applied equally to a vast array of problems. Instead, as our ancestors dealt with certain recurring problems, such as hunting and finding shelter, specialized modules evolved that process information related to those problems—for example, a module for physical knowledge for tracking animals, a module for mathematical knowledge for trading, and a module for language.

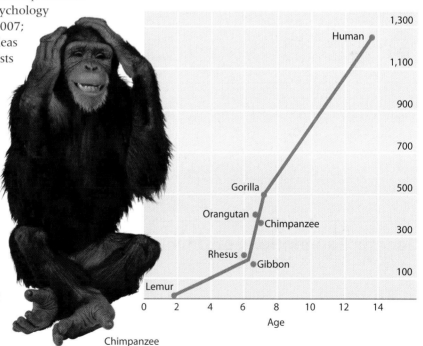

FIGURE **2.1**

THE BRAIN SIZES OF VARIOUS PRIMATES AND HUMANS IN RELATION TO THE LENGTH OF THE CHILDHOOD PERIOD. Compared with other primates, humans have both a larger brain and a longer childhood period. *What conclusions can you draw from the relationship indicated by this graph?*

Children in all cultures are interested in the tools that adults in their cultures use. For example, this 11-month-old boy from the Efe culture in the Democratic Republic of the Congo in Africa is trying to cut a papaya with an *apopau* (a smaller version of a machete). *Might the infant's behavior be evolutionary-based or be due to both biological and environmental conditions?*

Evolved mechanisms are not always adaptive in contemporary society. Some behaviors that were adaptive for our prehistoric ancestors may not serve us well today. For example, the food-scarce environment of our ancestors likely led to humans' propensity to gorge when food is available and to crave high-caloric foods, a trait that might lead to an epidemic of obesity when food is plentiful.

Evaluating Evolutionary Psychology   Although the popular press gives a lot of attention to the ideas of evolutionary psychology, it remains just one theoretical approach. Like the theories described in Chapter 1, it has limitations, weaknesses, and critics. Albert Bandura (1998), whose social cognitive theory was described in Chapter 1, acknowledges the important influence of evolution on human adaptation. However, he rejects what he calls "one-sided evolutionism," which sees social behavior as the product of evolved biology. An alternative is a bidirectional view, in which environmental and biological conditions influence each other. In this view, evolutionary pressures created changes in biological structures that allowed the use of tools, which enabled our ancestors to manipulate the environment, constructing new environmental conditions. In turn, environmental innovations produced new selection pressures that led to the evolution of specialized biological systems for consciousness, thought, and language.

In other words, evolution gave us bodily structures and biological potentialities; it does not dictate behavior. People have used their biological capacities to produce diverse cultures—aggressive and pacific, egalitarian and autocratic. As American scientist Stephen Jay Gould (1981) concluded, in most domains of human functioning, biology allows a broad range of cultural possibilities.

The "big picture" idea of natural selection leading to the development of human traits and behaviors is difficult to refute or test because it is on a time scale that does not lend itself to empirical study. Thus, studying specific genes in humans and other species—and their links to traits and behaviors—may be the best approach for testing ideas coming out of the evolutionary psychology perspective.

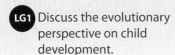

Review *Connect* Reflect

LG1 Discuss the evolutionary perspective on child development.

Review

- How can natural selection and adaptive behavior be defined?
- What is evolutionary psychology? What are some basic ideas about human development proposed by evolutionary psychologists? How might evolutionary influences have different effects at different points in the life span? How can evolutionary psychology be evaluated?

Connect

- In Chapter 1, you learned about how different developmental processes interact. How was that principle reinforced by the information in this section?

Reflect *Your Own Personal Journey of Life*

- Which do you think is more persuasive in explaining your development: the views of evolutionary psychologists or those of their critics? Why?

Genetic Foundations of Development

LG2 Describe what genes are and how they influence children's development.

The Collaborative Gene

Genes and Chromosomes

Genetic Principles

Chromosomal and Gene-Linked Abnormalities

Genetic influences on behavior evolved over time and across many species. The many traits and characteristics that are genetically influenced have a long evolutionary history that is retained in our DNA. Our DNA is not just inherited from

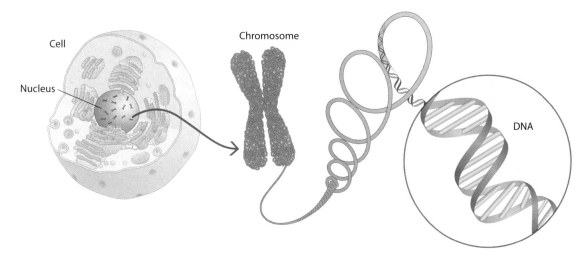

FIGURE **2.2**

CELLS, CHROMOSOMES, DNA, AND GENES. (*Left*) The body contains trillions of cells. Each cell contains a central structure, the nucleus. (*Middle*) Chromosomes are threadlike structures located in the nucleus of the cell. Chromosomes are composed of DNA. (*Right*) DNA has the structure of a spiral staircase. A gene is a segment of DNA.

our parents; it's what we as a species have inherited from other species that came before our own.

How are characteristics that suit a species for survival transmitted from one generation to the next? Darwin could not answer this question because genes and the principles of genetics had not yet been discovered. Each of us carries a human "genetic code" that we inherited from our parents. Because a fertilized egg carries this human code, a fertilized human egg cannot grow into an egret, eagle, or elephant.

THE COLLABORATIVE GENE

Each of us began life as a single cell weighing about one twenty-millionth of an ounce! This tiny piece of matter housed our entire genetic code—instructions that orchestrated growth from that single cell to a person made of trillions of cells, each containing a replica of the original code. That code is carried by our genes (Mader, 2010). What are genes and what do they do? For the answer, we need to look into our cells.

The nucleus of each human cell contains **chromosomes,** which are threadlike structures made up of deoxyribonucleic acid, or DNA. **DNA** is a complex molecule that has a double helix shape (like a spiral staircase) and contains genetic information. **Genes,** the units of hereditary information, are short segments of DNA, as you can see in Figure 2.2. They direct cells to reproduce themselves and to assemble proteins. Proteins, in turn, are the building blocks of cells as well as the regulators that direct the body's processes (Freeman, 2011).

Each gene has its own location, its own designated place on a particular chromosome. Today, there is a great deal of enthusiasm about efforts to discover the specific locations of genes that are linked to certain functions (Lewis, 2010). An important step in this direction is the Human Genome Project's efforts to map the human genome—the complete set of developmental instructions for creating proteins that initiate the making of a human organism (Willey, Sherwood, & Wolverton, 2011).

One of the big surprises of the Human Genome Project was an early report indicating that humans have only about 30,000 genes (U.S. Department of Energy, 2001). More recently, the number of human genes has been revised further downward to approximately 20,500 (Science Daily, 2008). Scientists had thought that humans had as many as 100,000 or more genes. They had also maintained that each gene programmed just one protein. In fact, humans have far more proteins

chromosomes Threadlike structures that come in 23 pairs, with one member of each pair coming from each parent. Chromosomes contain the genetic substance DNA.

DNA A complex molecule that contains genetic information.

genes Units of hereditary information composed of DNA. Genes direct cells to reproduce themselves and manufacture the proteins that maintain life.

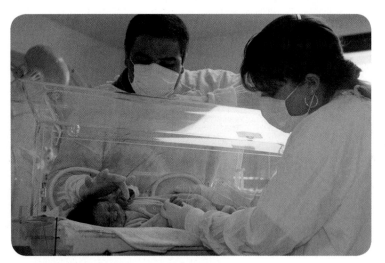

A positive result from the Human Genome Project. Shortly after Andrew Gobea was born (*above*), his cells were genetically altered to prevent his immune system from failing.

than they have genes, so there cannot be a one-to-one correspondence between genes and proteins (Commoner, 2002). Each gene is not translated, in automaton like fashion, into one and only one protein. A gene does not act independently, as developmental psychologist David Moore (2001) emphasized by titling his book *The Dependent Gene*.

Rather than being a group of independent genes, the human genome consists of many genes that collaborate both with each other and with nongenetic factors inside and outside the body. The collaboration operates at many points. For example, the cellular machinery mixes, matches, and links small pieces of DNA to reproduce the genes—and that machinery is influenced by what is going on around it.

Whether a gene is turned "on," working to assemble proteins, is also a matter of collaboration. The activity of genes (genetic expression) is affected by their environment (Gottlieb, 2007). For example, hormones that circulate in the blood make their way into the cell where they can turn genes "on" and "off." And the flow of hormones can be affected by environmental conditions, such as light, day length, nutrition, and behavior. Numerous studies have shown that external events outside of the original cell and the person, as well as events inside the cell, can excite or inhibit gene expression (Gottlieb, Wahlsten, & Lickliter, 2006). For example, one recent study revealed that an increase in the concentration of stress hormones such as cortisol produced a fivefold increase in DNA damage (Flint & others, 2007). Other research has shown that experiences early in development can alter gene expression and this expression is related to later behavior (Francis & others, 2003).

In short, a single gene is rarely the source of a protein's genetic information, much less of an inherited trait (Gottlieb, 2007).

GENES AND CHROMOSOMES

Genes are not only collaborative, they are enduring. How do the genes manage to get passed from generation to generation and end up in all of the trillion cells in the body? Three processes explain the heart of the story: mitosis, meiosis, and fertilization.

Mitosis, Meiosis, and Fertilization Every cell in your body, except the sperm and egg, has 46 chromosomes arranged in 23 pairs. These cells reproduce by a process called **mitosis.** During mitosis, the cell's nucleus—including the chromosomes—duplicates itself and the cell divides. Two new cells are formed, each containing the same DNA as the original cell, arranged in the same 23 pairs of chromosomes.

mitosis Cellular reproduction in which the cell's nucleus duplicates itself with two new cells being formed, each containing the same DNA as the parent cell, arranged in the same 23 pairs of chromosomes.

meiosis A specialized form of cell division that forms eggs and sperm (or gametes).

fertilization A stage in reproduction whereby an egg and a sperm fuse to create a single cell, called a zygote.

zygote A single cell formed through fertilization.

genotype A person's genetic heritage; the actual genetic material.

phenotype The way an individual's genotype is expressed in observed and measurable characteristics.

Calvin and Hobbes

by Bill Watterson

However, a different type of cell division—**meiosis**—forms eggs and sperm (or gametes). During meiosis, a cell of the testes (in men) or ovaries (in women) duplicates its chromosomes but then divides twice, thus forming four cells, each of which has only half of the genetic material of the parent cell (Klug & others, 2010; Mader, 2011). By the end of meiosis, each egg or sperm has 23 unpaired chromosomes.

During **fertilization,** an egg and a sperm fuse to create a single cell, called a **zygote** (see Figure 2.3). In the zygote, the 23 unpaired chromosomes from the egg and the 23 unpaired chromosomes from the sperm combine to form one set of 23 paired chromosomes—one chromosome of each pair from the mother's egg and the other from the father's sperm. In this manner, each parent contributes half of the offspring's genetic material.

Figure 2.4 shows 23 paired chromosomes of a male and a female. The members of each pair of chromosomes are both similar and different: Each chromosome in the pair contains varying forms of the same genes, at the same location on the chromosome. A gene for hair color, for example, is located on both members of one pair of chromosomes, in the same location on each. However, one of those chromosomes might carry the gene for blond hair; the other chromosome in the pair might carry the gene for brown hair.

Do you notice any obvious differences between the chromosomes of the male and the chromosomes of the female in Figure 2.4? The difference lies in the 23rd pair. Ordinarily, in females this pair consists of two chromosomes called X chromosomes; in males the 23rd pair consists of an X and a Y chromosome. The presence of a Y chromosome is what makes a person male rather than female.

Sources of Variability

Combining the genes of two parents in their offspring increases genetic variability in the population, which is valuable for a species because it provides more characteristics for natural selection to operate on (Starr, 2011). In fact, the human genetic process creates several important sources of variability.

First, the chromosomes in the zygote are not exact copies of those in the mother's ovaries and the father's testes. During the formation of the sperm and egg in meiosis, the members of each pair of chromosomes are separated, but which chromosome in the pair goes to the gamete is a matter of chance. In addition, before the pairs separate, pieces of the two chromosomes in each pair are exchanged, creating a new combination of genes on each chromosome (Mader, 2011). Thus, when chromosomes from the mother's egg and the father's sperm are brought together in the zygote, the result is a truly unique combination of genes.

If each zygote is unique, how do identical twins like those discussed in the opening of the chapter exist? *Identical twins* (also called monozygotic twins) develop from a single zygote that splits into two genetically identical replicas, each of which becomes a person. *Fraternal twins* (called dizygotic twins) develop from separate eggs and separate sperm, making them genetically no more similar than ordinary siblings.

Another source of variability comes from DNA (Brooker, 2011). Chances, a mistake by cellular machinery, or damage from an environmental agent such as radiation may produce a *mutated gene*, which is a permanently altered segment of DNA.

Even when their genes are identical, however, people vary. The difference between genotypes and phenotypes helps us to understand this source of variability. All of a person's genetic material makes up his or her **genotype.** However, not all of the genetic material is apparent in our observed and measurable characteristics. A **phenotype** consists of observable characteristics. Phenotypes include physical characteristics (such as height, weight, and hair color) and psychological characteristics (such as personality and intelligence).

For each genotype, a range of phenotypes can be expressed, providing another source of variability (Gottlieb, 2007). An individual can inherit the genetic potential to grow very large, for example, but good nutrition, among other things, will be essential to achieving that potential.

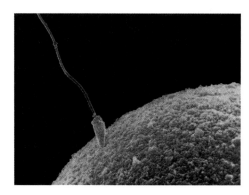

FIGURE **2.3**

A SINGLE SPERM PENETRATING AN EGG AT THE POINT OF FERTILIZATION

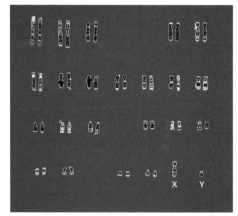

(a)

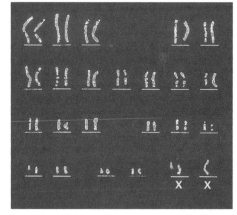

(b)

FIGURE **2.4**

THE GENETIC DIFFERENCE BETWEEN MALES AND FEMALES. Set (*a*) shows the chromosome structure of a male, and set (*b*) shows the chromosome structure of a female. The last pair of 23 pairs of chromosomes is in the bottom right box of each set. Notice that the Y chromosome of the male is smaller than the X chromosome of the female. To obtain this kind of chromosomal picture, a cell is removed from a person's body, usually from the inside of the mouth. The chromosomes are stained by chemical treatment, magnified extensively, and then photographed.

GENETIC PRINCIPLES

What determines how a genotype is expressed to create a particular phenotype? Much is unknown about the answer to this question (Starr, 2011). However, a number of genetic principles have been discovered, among them those of dominant-recessive genes, sex-linked genes, genetic imprinting, and polygenically determined characteristics.

Dominant-Recessive Genes Principle   In some cases, one gene of a pair always exerts its effects; it is *dominant*, overriding the potential influence of the other gene, called the recessive gene. This is the *dominant-recessive genes principle*. A recessive gene exerts its influence only if the two genes of a pair are both recessive. If you inherit a recessive gene for a trait from each of your parents, you will show the trait. If you inherit a recessive gene from only one parent, you may never know you carry the gene. Brown hair, farsightedness, and dimples rule over blond hair, nearsightedness, and freckles in the world of dominant-recessive genes.

Can two brown-haired parents have a blond-haired child? Yes, they can. Suppose that each parent has a dominant gene for brown hair and a recessive gene for blond hair. Since dominant genes override recessive genes, the parents have brown hair, but both are carriers of blondness and pass on their recessive genes for blond hair. With no dominant gene to override them, the recessive genes can make the child's hair blond.

Sex-Linked Genes   Most mutated genes are recessive. When a mutated gene is carried on the X chromosome, the result is called *X-linked inheritance*. The implications for males may be very different from those for females (Petersen, Wang, & Willems, 2008). Remember that males have only one X chromosome. Thus, if there is an altered, disease-creating gene on the X chromosome, males have no "backup" copy to counter the harmful gene and therefore may carry an X-linked disease. However, females have a second X chromosome, which is likely to be unchanged. As a result, they are not likely to have the X-linked disease. Thus, most individuals who have X-linked diseases are males. Females who have one changed copy of the X gene are known as "carriers," and they usually do not show any signs of the X-linked disease. Fragile-X syndrome, which we will discuss later in the chapter, is an example of an X-linked inheritance disease (Rogaev & others, 2009).

Genetic Imprinting   Genetic imprinting occurs when the expression of a gene has different effects depending on whether the mother or the father passed on the gene (Zaitoun & others, 2010). A chemical process "silences" one member of the gene pair. For example, as a result of imprinting, only the maternally derived copy of the Expressed gene might be active, while the paternally derived copy of the same Expressed gene is silenced—or vice versa. Only a small percentage of human genes appear to undergo imprinting, but it is a normal and important aspect of development (Koerner & Barlow, 2010). When imprinting goes awry, development is disturbed, as in the case of Beckwith-Wiedemann syndrome, a growth disorder, and Wilms tumor, a type of cancer (Hartwig & others, 2010).

Genetic transmission is usually more complex than the simple examples we have examined thus far (Fry, 2009). Few characteristics reflect the influence of only a single gene or pair of genes. Most are determined by the interaction of many different genes; they are said to be polygenically determined. Even a simple characteristic such as height, for example, reflects the interaction of many genes, as well as the influence of the environment. Most diseases, such as cancer and diabetes, develop as a consequence of complex gene interactions and environmental factors (Ekeblad, 2010; Vimaleswaran & Loos, 2010).

The term *gene-gene interaction* is increasingly used to describe studies that focus on the interdependence of two or more genes in influencing characteristics, behavior,

Name	Description	Treatment	Incidence
Down syndrome	An extra chromosome causes mild to severe retardation and physical abnormalities.	Surgery, early intervention, infant stimulation, and special learning programs	1 in 1,900 births at age 20 1 in 300 births at age 35 1 in 30 births at age 45
Klinefelter syndrome (XXY)	An extra X chromosome causes physical abnormalities.	Hormone therapy can be effective	1 in 600 male births
Fragile X syndrome	An abnormality in the X chromosome can cause mental retardation, learning disabilities, or short attention span.	Special education, speech and language therapy	More common in males than in females
Turner syndrome (XO)	A missing X chromosome in females can cause mental retardation and sexual underdevelopment.	Hormone therapy in childhood and puberty	1 in 2,500 female births
XYY syndrome	An extra Y chromosome can cause above-average height.	No special treatment required	1 in 1,000 male births

FIGURE **2.5**

SOME CHROMOSOMAL ABNORMALITIES. The treatments for these abnormalities do not necessarily erase the problem but may improve the individual's adaptive behavior and quality of life.

diseases, and development (Costanzo & others, 2010). For example, recent studies have documented gene-gene interaction in cancer (Chen & others, 2009) and cardiovascular disease (Jylhava & others, 2009).

developmental connection

Conditions, Diseases, and Disorders. Mental retardation can be classified in several ways. Chapter 8, p. 249

CHROMOSOMAL AND GENE-LINKED ABNORMALITIES

Sometimes abnormalities characterize the genetic process. Some of these abnormalities involve whole chromosomes that do not separate properly during meiosis. Other abnormalities are produced by harmful genes.

Chromosomal Abnormalities   When a gamete is formed, sometimes the male's sperm and/or the female's ovum do not have their normal set of 23 chromosomes. The most notable examples involve Down syndrome and abnormalities of the sex chromosomes (see Figure 2.5).

Down Syndrome   An individual with **Down syndrome** has a round face, a flattened skull, an extra fold of skin over the eyelids, a protruding tongue, short limbs, and retardation of motor and mental abilities (Fidler, 2008). The syndrome is caused by the presence of an extra copy of chromosome 21. It is not known why the extra chromosome is present, but the health of the male sperm or female ovum may be involved.

Down syndrome appears approximately once in every 700 live births. Women between the ages of 16 and 34 are less likely to give birth to a child with Down syndrome than are younger or older women. African American children are rarely born with Down syndrome.

Sex-Linked Chromosomal Abnormalities   Recall that a newborn normally has either an X and a Y chromosome, or two X chromosomes. Human embryos must possess at least one X chromosome to be viable. The most common sex-linked chromosomal abnormalities involve the presence of an extra chromosome (either an X or Y) or the absence of one X chromosome in females.

These athletes, several of whom have Down syndrome, are participating in a Special Olympics competition. Notice the distinctive facial features of the individuals with Down syndrome, such as a round face and a flattened skull. *What causes Down syndrome?*

Down syndrome A chromosomally transmitted form of mental retardation, caused by the presence of an extra copy of chromosome 21.

Klinefelter syndrome is a genetic disorder in which males have an extra X chromosome, making them XXY instead of XY. Males with this disorder have undeveloped testes, and they usually have enlarged breasts and become tall (Ross & others, 2008). Klinefelter syndrome occurs approximately once in every 600 live male births.

Fragile X syndrome is a genetic disorder that results from an abnormality in the X chromosome, which becomes constricted and often breaks (Penagarikano, Mulle, & Warren, 2007). Mental deficiency often is an outcome, but it may take the form of mental retardation, a learning disability, or a short attention span. A recent study revealed that boys with fragile X syndrome were characterized by cognitive deficits in inhibition, memory, and planning (Hooper & others, 2008). This disorder occurs more frequently in males than in females, possibly because the second X chromosome in females negates the effects of the other abnormal X chromosome (Gomez-Raposo & others, 2010).

Turner syndrome is a chromosomal disorder in females in which either an X chromosome is missing, making the person XO instead of XX, or part of one X chromosome is deleted. Females with Turner syndrome are short in stature and have a webbed neck. They might be infertile and have difficulty in mathematics, but their verbal ability is often quite good (Murphy & Mazzocco, 2008). Turner syndrome occurs in approximately 1 of every 2,500 live female births.

The **XYY syndrome** is a chromosomal disorder in which the male has an extra Y chromosome (Isen & Baker, 2008). Early interest in this syndrome focused on the belief that the extra Y chromosome found in some males contributed to aggression and violence. However, researchers subsequently found that XYY males are no more likely to commit crimes than are XY males (Witkin & others, 1976).

Gene-Linked Abnormalities Abnormalities can be produced not only by an uneven number of chromosomes, but also by harmful genes (Presson & Jenner, 2008). More than 7,000 such genetic disorders have been identified, although most of them are rare.

Phenylketonuria (PKU) is a genetic disorder in which the individual cannot properly metabolize phenylalanine, an amino acid. It results from a recessive gene and occurs about once in every 10,000 to 20,000 live births. Today, phenylketonuria is easily detected, and it is treated by a diet that prevents an excess accumulation of phenylalanine. If phenylketonuria is left untreated, however, excess phenylalanine builds up in the child, producing mental retardation and hyperactivity. Phenylketonuria accounts for approximately 1 percent of institutionalized individuals who are mentally retarded, and it occurs primarily in Whites.

The story of phenylketonuria has important implications for the nature-nurture issue. Although phenylketonuria is a genetic disorder (nature), how or whether a gene's influence in phenylketonuria is played out depends on environmental influences since the disorder can be treated (nurture) (van Spronsen & Enns, 2010). That is, the presence of a genetic defect does not inevitably lead to the development of the disorder if the individual develops in the right environment (one free of phenylalanine) (Grosse, 2010). This is one example of the important principle of heredity-environment interaction. Under one environmental condition (phenylalanine in the diet), mental retardation results, but when other nutrients replace phenylalanine, intelligence develops in the normal range. The same genotype has different outcomes depending on the environment (in this case, the nutritional environment).

Sickle-cell anemia, which occurs most often in African Americans, is a genetic disorder that impairs the body's red blood cells. Red blood cells carry oxygen to the body's cells and are usually shaped like disks. In sickle-cell anemia, a recessive gene causes the red blood cell to become a hook-shaped "sickle" that cannot carry oxygen properly and dies quickly. As a result, the body's cells do not receive adequate oxygen, causing anemia and early death (Benson & Therrell, 2010). About 1 in 400 African American babies is affected by sickle-cell anemia. One in 10 African Americans is a carrier, as is 1 in 20 Latin Americans. A National Institutes of Health (2008) panel recently concluded that the only FDA-approved drug (hydroxyurea)

Klinefelter syndrome A chromosomal disorder in which males have an extra X chromosome, making them XXY instead of XY.

fragile X syndrome A genetic disorder involving an abnormality in the X chromosome, which becomes constricted and often breaks.

Turner syndrome A chromosome disorder in females in which either an X chromosome is missing, making the person XO instead of XX, or the second X chromosome is partially deleted.

XYY syndrome A chromosomal disorder in which males have an extra Y chromosome.

phenylketonuria (PKU) A genetic disorder in which an individual cannot properly metabolize an amino acid. PKU is now easily detected but, if left untreated, results in mental retardation and hyperactivity.

sickle-cell anemia A genetic disorder that affects the red blood cells and occurs most often in people of African descent.

Name	Description	Treatment	Incidence
Cystic fibrosis	Glandular dysfunction that interferes with mucus production; breathing and digestion are hampered, resulting in a shortened life span.	Physical and oxygen therapy, synthetic enzymes, and antibiotics; most individuals live to middle age.	1 in 2,000 births
Diabetes	Body does not produce enough insulin, which causes abnormal metabolism of sugar.	Early onset can be fatal unless treated with insulin.	1 in 2,500 births
Hemophilia	Delayed blood clotting causes internal and external bleeding.	Blood transfusions/injections can reduce or prevent damage due to internal bleeding.	1 in 10,000 males
Huntington disease	Central nervous system deteriorates, producing problems in muscle coordination and mental deterioration.	Does not usually appear until age 35 or older; death likely 10 to 20 years after symptoms appear.	1 in 20,000 births
Phenyketonuria (PKU)	Metabolic dosorder that, left untreated, causes mental retardation.	Special diet can result in average intelligence and normal life span.	1 in 10,000 to 1 in 20,000 births
Sickle-cell anemia	Blood disorder that limits the body's oxygen supply; it can cause joint swelling, as well as heart and kidney failure.	Penicillin, medication for pain, antibiotics, and blood transfusions.	1 in 400 African American children (lower among other groups)
Spina bifida	Neural tube disorder that causes brain and spine abnormalities.	Corrective surgery at birth, orthopedic devices, and physical/medical therapy.	2 in 1,000 births
Tay-Sachs disease	Deceleration of mental and physical development caused by an accumulation of lipids in the nervous system.	Medication and special diet are used, but death is likely by 5 years of age.	1 in 30 American Jews is a carrier.

FIGURE **2.6**
SOME GENE-LINKED ABNORMALITIES

to treat sickle-cell anemia in adolescents and adults has been underutilized. Research is currently being conducted in a study named Baby HUG to determine if the drug works with babies.

Other diseases that result from genetic abnormalities include cystic fibrosis, diabetes, hemophilia, Huntington disease, spina bifida, and Tay-Sachs disease (Velagaleti & O'Donnell, 2010; Viet & Schmidt, 2010). Figure 2.6 provides further information about these diseases. Someday, scientists may be able to identify why these and other genetic abnormalities occur and discover how to cure them.

Dealing with Genetic Abnormalities   Every individual carries DNA variations that might predispose the person to serious physical disease or mental disorder. But not all individuals who carry a genetic disorder display the disorder. Other genes or developmental events sometimes compensate for genetic abnormalities (Gottlieb, Wahlsten, & Lickliter, 2006). For example, recall the earlier example of phenylketonuria: Even though individuals might carry the genetic disorder of phenylketonuria, it is not expressed when phenylalanine is replaced by other nutrients in their diet.

Thus, genes are not destiny, but genes that are missing, nonfunctional, or mutated can be associated with disorders (Zaghloul & Katsanis, 2010). Identifying such genetic flaws could enable doctors to predict an individual's risks, recommend healthy practices, and prescribe the safest and most effective drugs (Wider, Foroud, & Wszolek, 2010). A decade or two from now, parents of a newborn baby may be able to leave the hospital with a full genome analysis of their offspring that reveals disease risks.

However, this knowledge might bring important costs as well as benefits. Who would have access to a person's genetic profile? An individual's ability to land and hold jobs or obtain insurance might be threatened if it is known that he or she is considered at risk for some disease. For example, should an

During a physical examination for a college football tryout, Jerry Hubbard, 32, learned that he carried the gene for sickle-cell anemia. Daughter Sara is healthy, but daughter Avery (in the print dress) has sickle-cell anemia. *If you were a genetic counselor, would you recommend that this family have more children? Explain.*

Holly Ishmael, Genetic Counselor

Holly Ishmael is a genetic counselor at Children's Mercy Hospital in Kansas City. She obtained an undergraduate degree in psychology and a master's degree in genetic counseling from Sarah Lawrence College.

Genetic counselors like Ishmael work as members of a health care team, providing information and support to families with birth defects or genetic disorders. They identify families at risk by analyzing inheritance patterns, and they explore options with the family. Some genetic counselors, like Ishmael, become specialists in prenatal and pediatric genetics; others specialize in cancer genetics or psychiatric genetic disorders.

Ishmael says, "Genetic counseling is a perfect combination for people who want to do something science-oriented, but need human contact and don't want to spend all of their time in a lab or have their nose in a book" (Rizzo, 1999, p. 3).

Genetic counselors have specialized graduate degrees in the areas of medical genetics and counseling. They enter graduate school with undergraduate backgrounds from a variety of disciplines, including biology, genetics, psychology, public health, and social work. There are approximately 30 graduate genetic counseling programs in the United States. If you are interested in this profession, you can obtain

Holly Ishmael (*left*) in a genetic counseling session.

further information from the National Society of Genetic Counselors at www.nsgc.org.

For more information about what genetic counselors do, see page 46 in the Careers in Child Development appendix immediately preceding this chapter.

airline pilot or a neurosurgeon who is predisposed to develop a disorder that makes one's hands shake be required to leave that job early?

Genetic counselors, usually physicians or biologists who are well-versed in the field of medical genetics, understand the kinds of problems just described, the odds of encountering them, and helpful strategies for offsetting some of their effects (Boks & others, 2010; Sivell & others, 2008). To read about the career and work of a genetic counselor, see *Connecting With Careers*.

Review *Connect* Reflect

LG2 Describe what genes are and how they influence children's development.

Review

- What are genes?
- How are genes passed on?
- What basic principles describe how genes interact?
- What are some chromosome and gene-linked abnormalities?

Connect

- Explain how environment interacts with genes in gene-linked abnormalities.

Reflect *Your Own Personal Journey of Life*

- Would you want to be able to access a full genome analysis of yourself or your offspring? Why or why not?

Reproductive Challenges and Choices

LG3 Identify some important reproductive challenges and choices.

Prenatal Diagnostic Tests	Infertility and Reproductive Technology	Adoption

The facts and principles we have discussed regarding meiosis, genetics, and genetic abnormalities are a small part of the recent explosion of knowledge about human biology. This knowledge not only helps us understand human development but also opens up many new choices to prospective parents—choices that can also raise ethical questions.

PRENATAL DIAGNOSTIC TESTS

One choice open to prospective mothers is the option to undergo prenatal testing. A number of tests can indicate whether a fetus is developing normally, including ultrasound sonography, fetal MRI, chorionic villus sampling, amniocentesis, maternal blood screening, and noninvasive prenatal diagnosis (Lenzi & Johnson, 2008).

An ultrasound test is often conducted seven weeks into a pregnancy and at various times later in pregnancy (Cignini & others, 2010). *Ultrasound sonography* is a prenatal medical procedure in which high-frequency sound waves are directed into the pregnant woman's abdomen. The echo from the sounds is transformed into a visual representation of the fetus's inner structures. This technique can detect many structural abnormalities in the fetus, including microencephaly, a form of mental retardation involving an abnormally small brain; it can also determine the number of fetuses and give clues to the baby's sex (Gerards & others, 2008). There is virtually no risk to the woman or fetus in this test.

The development of brain-imaging techniques has led to increasing use of *fetal MRI* to diagnose fetal malformations (Daltro & others, 2010; Duczkowska & others, 2010) (see Figure 2.7). *MRI* stands for magnetic resonance imaging and uses a powerful magnet and radio images to generate detailed images of the body's organs and structures. Currently, ultrasound is still the first choice in fetal screening, but fetal MRI can provide more detailed images than ultrasound. In many instances, ultrasound will indicate a possible abnormality and then fetal MRI will be used to obtain a clearer, more detailed image (Obenauer & Maestre, 2008). Among the fetal malformations that fetal MRI may be able to detect better than ultrasound sonography are certain abnormalities of the central nervous system, chest, gastrointestinal tract, genital/urinary system, and placenta (Baysinger, 2010; Panigraphy, Borzaga, & Blumi, 2010; Weston, 2010).

At some point between the 10th and 12th weeks of pregnancy, chorionic villus sampling may be used to detect genetic defects and chromosomal abnormalities such as those discussed in the previous section. *Chorionic villus sampling (CVS)* is a prenatal medical procedure in which a small sample of the placenta (the vascular organ that links the fetus to the mother's uterus) is removed. Diagnosis takes about 10 days. There is a small risk of limb deformity when CVS is used.

Between the 15th and 18th weeks of pregnancy, amniocentesis may be performed. *Amniocentesis* is a prenatal medical procedure in which a sample of amniotic fluid is withdrawn by syringe and tested for chromosomal or metabolic disorders (Nagel & others, 2007). The amnionic fluid is found within the amnion, a thin sac in which the embryo is suspended. Ultrasound sonography is often used during amniocentesis so that the syringe can be placed precisely. The later in the pregnancy amniocentesis is performed, the better its diagnostic potential. The earlier it is performed, the more useful it is in deciding how to handle a pregnancy. It may take two weeks for enough cells to grow and amniocentesis test results to be obtained. Amniocentesis brings a small risk of miscarriage: about 1 woman in every 200 to 300 miscarries after the procedure.

A 6-month-old infant poses with the ultrasound sonography record taken four months into the baby's prenatal development. *What is ultrasound sonography?*

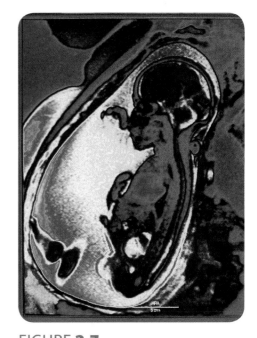

FIGURE **2.7**

A FETAL MRI, WHICH IS INCREASINGLY BEING USED IN PRENATAL DIAGNOSIS OF FETAL MALFORMATIONS

developmental **connection**

Biological Processes. Discover what the development of the fetus is like at the time chorionic villus sampling and amniocentesis can be used. Chapter 3, Fig. 3.3, p. 81

Both amniocentesis and chorionic villus sampling provide valuable information about the presence of birth defects, but they also raise difficult issues for parents about whether an abortion should be obtained if birth defects are present (Quadrelli & others, 2007; Zhang & others, 2010). Chorionic villus sampling allows parents to make a decision sooner, near the end of the first 12 weeks of pregnancy, when abortion is safer and less traumatic than later. Although earlier reports indicated that chorionic villus sampling brings a slightly higher risk of pregnancy loss than amniocentesis, a recent U.S. study of more than 40,000 pregnancies found that loss rates for CVS decreased over the period from 1998 to 2003 and that there is no longer a difference in pregnancy loss risk between CVS and amniocentesis (Caughey, Hopkins, & Norton, 2006).

During the 16th to 18th weeks of pregnancy, maternal blood screening may be performed. *Maternal blood screening* identifies pregnancies that have an elevated risk for birth defects such as spina bifida (a defect in the spinal cord) and Down syndrome (Bustamante-Aragones & others, 2010). The current blood test is called the *triple screen* because it measures three substances in the mother's blood. After an abnormal triple screen result, the next step is usually an ultrasound examination. If an ultrasound does not explain the abnormal triple screen results, amniocentesis is typically used.

Noninvasive prenatal diagnosis (NIPD) is increasingly being explored as an alternative to procedures such as chorionic villus sampling and amniocentesis (Susman & others, 2010). At this point, NIPD has mainly focused on the isolation and examination of fetal cells circulating in the mother's blood and analysis of cell-free fetal DNA in maternal plasma (Prakash, Powell, & Geva, 2010).

Researchers already have used NIPD to successfully test for genes inherited from a father that cause cystic fibrosis and Huntington disease. They also are exploring the potential for using NIPD to identify a baby's sex as early as five weeks after conception and to diagnose Down syndrome (Avent & others, 2008). Being able to detect an offspring's sex and various diseases and defects so early raises ethical concerns about couples' motivation to terminate a pregnancy (Benn & Chapman, 2010).

INFERTILITY AND REPRODUCTIVE TECHNOLOGY

Recent advances in biological knowledge have also opened up many choices for infertile people. Approximately 10 to 15 percent of couples in the United States experience infertility, which is defined as the inability to conceive a child after 12 months of regular intercourse without contraception. The cause of infertility can rest with the woman or the man (Verhaak & others, 2010; Walsh, Pera, & Turek, 2010). The woman may not be ovulating (releasing eggs to be fertilized), she may be producing abnormal ova, her fallopian tubes by which ova normally reach the womb may be blocked, or she may have a disease that prevents implantation of the embryo into the uterus. The man may produce too few sperm, the sperm may lack motility (the ability to move adequately), or he may have a blocked passageway (Kini & others, 2010).

In the United States, more than 2 million couples seek help for infertility every year. In some cases of infertility, surgery may correct the cause; in others, hormone-based drugs may improve the probability of having a child. Of the 2 million couples who seek help for infertility every year, about 40,000 try high-tech assisted reproduction. By far the most common technique used is *in vitro fertilization (IVF)*, in which eggs and sperm are combined in a laboratory dish. If any eggs are successfully fertilized, one or more of the resulting fertilized eggs is transferred into the woman's uterus. A national study in the United States by the Centers for Disease Control and Prevention (2006) found the success rate of IVF depends on the mother's age (see Figure 2.8).

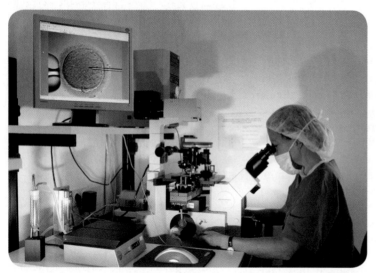

A technician using a micro-needle to inject human sperm into a human egg cell as part of an in vitro fertilization procedure. The injected sperm fertilizes the egg, and the resulting zygote is then grown in the laboratory until it reaches an early stage of embryonic development. Then it is implanted in the uterus.

The creation of families by means of the new reproductive technologies raises important questions about the physical and psychological consequences for children (Steel & Sutcliff, 2010; Wisborg, Ingerslev, & Henriksen, 2010). One result of fertility treatments is an increase in multiple births (Jones, 2007). Twenty-five to 30 percent of pregnancies achieved by fertility treatments—including in vitro fertilization—now result in multiple births. A recent *meta-analysis* (a statistical technique that combines the results of multiple studies to determine the strength of the effect) revealed that twins conceived through in-vitro fertilization have a slightly increased risk of low birth weight (McDonald & others, 2010), and another meta-analysis found that in-vitro fertilization singletons have a significant risk of low birth weight (McDonald & others, 2009). To read about a study that addresses longer-term consequences of in-vitro fertilization, see *Connecting Through Research*.

ADOPTION

Although surgery and fertility drugs can sometimes solve the infertility problem, another choice is to adopt a child (Bernard & Dozier, 2008; Cohen & others, 2008). Adoption is the social and legal process by which a parent-child relationship is established between persons unrelated at birth. As discussed in *Connecting With Diversity*, an increase in diversity has characterized the adoption of children in the United States in recent years.

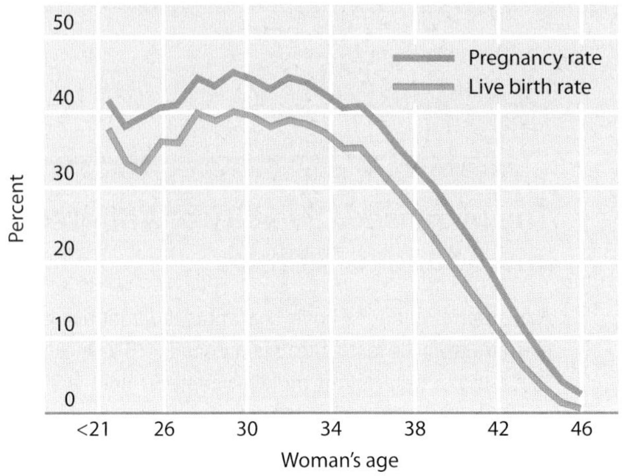

FIGURE **2.8**

SUCCESS RATES OF IN VITRO FERTILIZATION VARY ACCORDING TO THE WOMAN'S AGE

connecting through research

Do Children Conceived Through In Vitro Fertilization Show Significantly Different Developmental Outcomes in Adolescence?

A longitudinal study examined 34 in vitro fertilization families, 49 adoptive families, and 38 families with a naturally conceived child (Golombok, MacCallum, & Goodman, 2001). Each type of family included a similar portion of boys and girls. Also, the age of the young adolescents did not differ according to family type (mean age of 11 years, 11 months).

Children's socioemotional development was assessed by (1) interviewing the mother and obtaining detailed descriptions of any problems the child might have; (2) administering a Strengths and Difficulties questionnaire to the child's mother and teacher; and (3) administering the Social Adjustment Inventory for Children and Adolescents, which examines functioning in school, peer relationships, and self-esteem.

No significant differences between the children from the in vitro fertilization, adoptive, and naturally conceiving families were found. The results from the Social Adjustment Inventory for Children and Adolescents are shown in Figure 2.9. Another study also revealed no psychological differences between IVF babies and those not conceived by IVF, but more research is needed to reach firm conclusions in this area (Goldbeck & others, 2008).

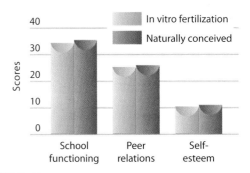

FIGURE **2.9**

SOCIOEMOTIONAL FUNCTIONING OF CHILDREN CONCEIVED THROUGH IN VITRO FERTILIZATION OR NATURALLY CONCEIVED.
This graph shows the results of a study that compared the socioemotional functioning of young adolescents who had either been conceived through in vitro fertilization (IVF) or naturally conceived (Golombok, MacCallum, & Goodman, 2001). For each type of family, the study included a similar portion of boys and girls and children of similar age (mean age of 11 years, 11 months). Although the means for the naturally conceived group were slightly higher, this is likely due to chance: there were no significant differences between the groups.

The Increased Diversity of Adopted Children and Adoptive Parents

A number of changes have characterized adoptive children and adoptive parents in the last three to four decades (Brodzinsky & Pinderhughes, 2002). In the first half of the 20th century, most U.S. adopted children were healthy, non-Latino White infants who were adopted at birth or soon after; however, in recent decades as abortion became legal and contraception increased, fewer of these infants became available for adoption. Increasingly, U.S. couples adopted a much wider diversity of children—from other countries, from other ethnic groups, children with physical and/or mental problems, and children who had been neglected or abused.

Changes also have characterized adoptive parents in the last three to four decades (Brodzinsky & Pindehughes, 2002). In the first half of the 20th century, most adoptive parents were from non-Latino White middle or upper socioeconomic status backgrounds who were married and did not have any type of disability. However, in recent decades, increased diversity has characterized adoptive parents. Many adoption agencies today have no income requirements for adoptive parents and now allow adults from a wide range of backgrounds to adopt children, including single adults, gay male and lesbian adults, and older adults.

Many fertile adults adopt children, but many more adoptive individuals are infertile. Based on what you read prior to this interlude, why might an infertile couple or individual decide to adopt rather than undergo reproductive technology procedures?

An increasing number of Hollywood celebrities are adopting children from developing countries. Actress Angelina Jolie (*above*) carries her adopted daughter Zahara with adopted sons Maddox and Pax walking beside them.

How do adopted children fare after they are adopted? Children who are adopted very early in their lives are more likely to have positive outcomes than children adopted later in life. In one study, the later adoption occurred, the more problems the adoptees had. Infant adoptees had the fewest adjustment difficulties; those adopted after they were 10 years of age had the most problems (Sharma, McGue, & Benson, 1996).

In general, adopted children and adolescents are more likely to experience psychological and school-related problems than nonadopted children (Keyes & others, 2008). For example, a recent meta-analysis (a statistical procedure that combines the results of a number of studies) revealed that adoptees were far more likely to be using mental health services than their nonadopted counterparts (Juffer & van Ijzendoorn, 2005). Adopted children also showed more behavior problems than nonadoptees, but this difference was small. A recent large-scale study found that adopted children are more likely to have a learning disability than nonadopted children (Altarac & Saroha, 2007).

Research that contrasts adopted and nonadopted adolescents has also found positive characteristics among the adopted adolescents. For example, in one study, although adopted adolescents were more likely than nonadopted adolescents to use illicit drugs and to engage in delinquent behavior, the adopted adolescents were also less likely to be withdrawn and engaged in more prosocial behavior, such as being altruistic, caring, and supportive of others (Sharma, McGue, & Benson, 1996).

However, the vast majority of adopted children (including those adopted at older ages, transracially, and across national borders) adjust effectively, and their parents report considerable satisfaction with their decision to adopt (Brodzinsky & Pinder-hughes, 2002; Castle & others, 2010). In a national study, there were no differences in the antisocial behavior of adopted and nonadopted U.S. young adults (Grotevant & others, 2006). A recent research review of 88 studies also revealed no difference in the self-esteem of adopted and nonadopted children, as well as no differences between transracial and same-race adoptees (Juffer & van Ijzendoorn, 2007).

Most studies of adopted and non-adopted children compare different families (adoptive and non-adoptive). In a recent study, a different strategy was followed: families were studied who had a biological child of their own as well as a child they had adopted (Glover & others, 2010). Findings similar to studies of between-family comparisons occurred with only a slight (but non-significant) trend for adopted children to show more internalized (such as depression) and externalized problems (such as antisocial behavior).

In other comparisons, adopted children fare much better than children raised in long-term foster care or in an institutional environment (Bernard & Dozier, 2008). A recent study of infants in China revealed that their cognitive development improved 2 to 6 months following their adoption from foster homes and institutions (van den Dries & others, 2010).

In sum, the changes in adoption practice over the last several decades make it difficult to generalize about the average adopted child or average adoptive parent. To read more about adoption, see *Caring Connections* in which we discuss effective parenting strategies with adopted children.

caring *connections*

Parenting Adopted Children

Many of the keys to effectively parenting adopted children are no different from those for effectively parenting biological children: Be supportive and caring, be involved and monitor the child's behavior and whereabouts, be a good communicator, and help the child learn to develop self-control. However, parents of adopted children face some unique circumstances (Fontenot, 2007). They need to recognize the differences involved in adoptive family life, communicate about these differences, show respect for the birth family, and support the child's search for self and identity.

Following are some of the problems parents face when their adopted children are at different points in development and some recommendations for how to handle these problems (Brodzinsky & Pinderhughes, 2002):

- **Infancy.** Researchers have found few differences in the attachment that adopted and nonadopted infants form with their parents. However, at-

What are some strategies for parenting adopted children at different points in their development?

tachment can become problematic if parents have unresolved fertility issues or the child does not meet the parents' expectations. Counselors can help prospective adoptive parents develop realistic expectations.

- **Early childhood.** Because many children begin to ask where they came from when they are about 4 to 6 years old, this is a natural time to begin to talk in simple ways to children about their adoption status (Warshak, 2007). Some parents (although not as many as in the past) decide not to tell their children about the adoption. This secrecy may create psychological risks for the child if he or she later finds out about the adoption.

- **Middle and late childhood.** During the elementary school years, children begin to show more interest in their origins and may ask questions

(continued)

caring *connections*

(continued)

related to where they came from, what their parents looked like, and why their parents abandoned them. As they grow older, children may develop mixed feelings about being adopted and question their adoptive parents' explanations. It is important for adoptive parents to recognize that this ambivalence is normal. Also, problems may arise from the desire of adoptive parents to make life too perfect for the adoptive child and to present a perfect image of themselves to the child. The result too often is that adopted children feel that they cannot release any angry feelings or openly discuss problems.

- **Adolescence.** Adolescents are likely to develop more abstract and logical thinking processes, to focus their attention on their bodies, and to search for an identity. These characteristics provide the foundation for adopted adolescents to reflect on their adoption status in more complex ways, such as focusing on physical differences between themselves and their adoptive parents. As they explore their identity, adopted adolescents may have difficulty incorporating their adopted status into their identity in positive ways. It is important for adoptive parents to understand the complexity of the adopted adolescent's identity exploration and be patient with the adolescent's lengthy identity search.

According to the information presented in this box and in the text that precedes it, how can mental health professionals help both adopting parents and adopted children?

Review *Connect* Reflect

 LG3 Identify some important reproductive challenges and choices.

Review

- What are some common prenatal diagnostic tests?
- What are some techniques that help infertile people to have children?
- How does adoption affect children's development?

Connect

- In Chapter 1, you learned about different methods for collecting data. How would you characterize the methods used in prenatal diagnostic testing?

Reflect *Your Own Personal Journey of Life*

- If you were an adult who could not have children, would you want to adopt a child? Why or why not?

Heredity and Environment Interaction: The Nature-Nurture Debate

 LG4 Explain some of the ways that heredity and environment interact to produce individual differences in development.

Behavior Genetics

Shared and Nonshared Environmental Experiences

Conclusions About Heredity-Environment Interaction

Heredity-Environment Correlations

The Epigenetic View and Heredity × Environment (H × E) Interaction

Is it possible to untangle the influence of heredity from that of environment and discover the role of each in producing individual differences in development? When heredity and environment interact, how does heredity influence the environment, and vice versa?

BEHAVIOR GENETICS

Behavior genetics is the field that seeks to discover the influence of heredity and environment on individual differences in human traits and development (Kandler, Riemann, & Kampfe, 2009). Note that behavior genetics does not determine the extent to which genetics or the environment affects an individual's traits. Instead, behavior geneticists try to figure out what is responsible for the differences among people—that is, to what extent people differ because of differences in genes, environment, or a combination of these (Silberg, Maes, & Eaves, 2010). To study the influence of heredity on behavior, behavior geneticists often use either twins or adoption situations (Goldsmith, 2011; Mustelin & others, 2009).

In the most common **twin study,** the behavioral similarity of identical twins (who are genetically identical) is compared with the behavioral similarity of fraternal twins. Recall that although fraternal twins share the same womb, they are no more genetically alike than any other brothers or sisters. Thus, by comparing groups of identical and fraternal twins, behavior geneticists capitalize on the basic knowledge that identical twins are more similar genetically than are fraternal twins (Isen & others, 2009; Loehlin, 2010). For example, one study found that conduct problems were more prevalent in identical twins than fraternal twins; the researchers concluded that the study demonstrated an important role for heredity in conduct problems (Scourfield & others, 2004).

However, several issues complicate interpretation of twin studies. For example, perhaps the environments of identical twins are more similar than the environments of fraternal twins. Adults might stress the similarities of identical twins more than those of fraternal twins, and identical twins might perceive themselves as a "set" and play together more than fraternal twins do. If so, the influence of the environment on the observed similarities between identical and fraternal twins might be very significant.

In an **adoption study,** investigators seek to discover whether the behavior and psychological characteristics of adopted children are more like those of their adoptive parents, who have provided a home environment, or more like those of their biological parents, who have contributed their heredity (Loehlin, Horn, & Ernst, 2007). Another form of the adoption study compares adoptive and biological siblings.

HEREDITY-ENVIRONMENT CORRELATIONS

The difficulties that researchers encounter when they interpret the results of twin studies and adoption studies reflect the complexities of heredity-environment interaction. Some of these interactions are *heredity-environment correlations,* which means that individuals' genes may influence the types of environments to which they are exposed. In a sense, individuals "inherit" environments that may be related or linked to genetic "propensities." Behavior geneticist Sandra Scarr (1993) described three ways that heredity and environment are correlated (see Figure 2.10):

- **Passive genotype-environment correlations** occur because biological parents, who are genetically related to the child, provide a rearing environment for the child. For example, the parents might have a genetic predisposition to be intelligent and read skillfully. Because they read well and enjoy reading, they provide their children with books to read. The likely outcome is that their children, given their own inherited predispositions from their parents and their book-filled environment, will become skilled readers.
- **Evocative genotype-environment correlations** occur because a child's characteristics elicit certain types of environments. For example, active, smiling children receive more social stimulation than passive, quiet children do. Cooperative, attentive children evoke more pleasant and instructional responses from the adults around them than uncooperative, distractible children do.

Twin studies compare identical twins with fraternal twins. Identical twins develop from a single fertilized egg that splits into two genetically identical organisms. Fraternal twins develop from separate eggs, making them genetically no more similar than nontwin siblings. *What is the nature of the twin study method?*

behavior genetics The field that seeks to discover the influence of heredity and environment on individuals differences in human traits and development.

twin study A study in which the behavioral similarity of identical twins is compared with the behavioral similarity of fraternal twins.

adoption study A study in which investigators seek to discover whether, in behavior and psychological characteristics, adopted children are more like their adoptive parents, who provided a home environment, or more like their biological parents, who contributed their heredity. Another form of the adoption study is one that compares adoptive and biological siblings.

passive genotype-environment correlations Correlations that exist when the natural parents, who are genetically related to the child, provide a rearing environment for the child.

evocative genotype-environment correlations Correlations that exist when the child's genotype elicits certain types of physical and social environments.

Heredity-Environment Correlation	Description	Examples
Passive	Children inherit genetic tendencies from their parents, and parents also provide an environment that matches their own genetic tendencies.	Musically inclined parents usually have musically inclined children and are likely to provide an environment rich in music for their children.
Evocative	The child's genetic tendencies elicit stimulation from the environment that supports a particular trait. Thus, genes evoke environmental support.	A happy, outgoing child elicits smiles and friendly responses from others.
Active (niche-picking)	Children actively seek out "niches" in their environment that reflect their own interests and talents and are thus in accord with their genotype.	Libraries, sports fields, and a store with musical instruments are examples of environmental niches children might seek out if they have intellectual interests in books, talent in sports, or musical talents, respectively.

FIGURE **2.10**

EXPLORING HEREDITY-ENVIRONMENT CORRELATIONS

active (niche-picking) genotype-environment correlations Correlations that exist when children seek out environments they find compatible and stimulating.

shared environmental experiences Siblings' common environmental experiences, such as their parents' personalities and intellectual orientation, the family's socioeconomic status, and the neighborhood in which they live.

nonshared environmental experiences The child's own unique experiences, both within the family and outside the family, that are not shared by another sibling. Thus, experiences occurring within the family can be part of the "nonshared environment."

- **Active (niche-picking) genotype-environment correlations** occur when children seek out environments that they find compatible and stimulating. *Niche-picking* refers to finding a setting that is suited to one's abilities. Children select from their surrounding environment some aspect that they respond to, learn about, or ignore. Their active selections of environments are related to their particular genotype. For example, outgoing children tend to seek out social contexts in which to interact with people, whereas shy children don't. Children who are musically inclined are likely to select musical environments in which they can successfully perform their skills. How these "tendencies" come about will be discussed shortly under the topic of the epigenetic view.

Scarr observes that the relative importance of the three genotype-environment correlations changes as children develop from infancy through adolescence. In infancy, much of the environment that children experience is provided by adults. Thus, passive genotype-environment correlations are more common in the lives of infants and young children than they are for older children and adolescents who can extend their experiences beyond the family's influence and create their environments to a greater degree.

SHARED AND NONSHARED ENVIRONMENTAL EXPERIENCES

Behavior geneticists have argued that to understand the environment's role in differences between people, we should distinguish between shared and nonshared environments. That is, we should consider experiences that children share in common with other children living in the same home, and experiences that are not shared (Burt, McGue, & Iacono, 2010; Cerda & others, 2010).

Shared environmental experiences are siblings' common experiences, such as their parents' personalities or intellectual orientation, the family's socioeconomic status, and the neighborhood in which they live. By contrast, **nonshared environmental experiences** are a child's unique experiences, both within the family and outside the family, that are not shared with a sibling. Even experiences occurring within the family can be part of the "nonshared environment." For example, parents often interact differently with each sibling, and siblings interact differently with parents. Siblings often have different peer groups, different friends, and different teachers at school.

Behavior geneticist Robert Plomin (2004) has found that shared environment accounts for little of the variation in children's personality or interests. In other words, even though two children live under the same roof with the same parents, their personalities are often very different. Further, Plomin argues that heredity influences the nonshared environments of siblings through the heredity-environment correlations we described earlier. For example, a child who has inherited a genetic tendency to be athletic is likely to spend more time in environments related to sports, and a child who has inherited a tendency to be musically inclined is more likely to spend time in environments related to music.

What are the implications of Plomin's interpretation of the role of shared and nonshared environments in development? In the *Nurture Assumption*, Judith Harris (1998, 2009) argued that what parents do does not make a difference in their children's and adolescents' behavior. Yell at them. Hug them. Read to them. Ignore them. Harris says it won't influence how they turn out. She argues that genes and peers are far more important than parents in children's and adolescents' development.

Genes and peers do matter, but Harris' descriptions of peer influences do not take into account the complexity of peer contexts and developmental trajectories (Hartup, 2009). In addition, Harris is wrong in saying that parents don't matter. For example, in the early childhood years parents play an important role in selecting children's peers and indirectly influencing children's development (Baumrind, 1999). A large volume of parenting literature with many research studies documents the importance of parents in children's development (Meaney, 2010; Schultz & others, 2009). We will discuss parents' important roles throughout this book.

Tennis stars Venus and Serena Williams. *What might be some shared and nonshared environmental experiences they had while they were growing up that contributed to their tennis stardom?*

THE EPIGENETIC VIEW AND GENE × ENVIRONMENT (G × E) INTERACTION

Critics argue that the concept of heredity-environment correlation gives heredity too much of a one-sided influence in determining development because it does not consider the role of prior environmental influences in shaping the correlation itself (Gottlieb, 2007). However, earlier in the chapter we discussed how genes are collaborative, not determining an individual's traits in an independent manner but rather interacting with the environment.

The Epigenetic View In line with the concept of a collaborative gene, Gilbert Gottlieb (2007) emphasizes the **epigenetic view,** which states that development is the result of an ongoing, bidirectional interchange between heredity and the environment. Figure 2.11 compares the heredity-environment correlation and epigenetic views of development.

Let's look at an example that reflects the epigenetic view. A baby inherits genes from both parents at conception. During prenatal development, toxins, nutrition, and stress can influence some genes to stop functioning while others become stronger or weaker. During infancy, the same environmental experiences such as toxins, nutrition, stress, learning, and encouragement continue to modify genetic activity and the activity of the nervous system that directly underlies behavior. Heredity and environment operate together—or collaborate—to produce a person's intelligence, temperament, height, weight, ability to pitch a baseball, ability to read, and so on (Gottlieb, 2007; Meaney, 2010).

Gene × Environment (G × E) Interaction An increasing number of studies are exploring how the interaction of heredity and environment influence development, including interactions that involve specific DNA sequences (Caspi & others, 2010; Keers & others, 2010; Pauli-Pott & others, 2009; Shen, 2009; Wright & Christiani, 2010). One research study found that individuals who have a short version of a genotype labeled 5-HTTLPR (a gene involving the neurotransmitter serotonin) have an elevated risk of developing depression only if they also have stressful lives (Caspi & others, 2003). Thus, the specific gene did not link directly to the development of depression, but rather interacted with environmental exposure to stress to predict

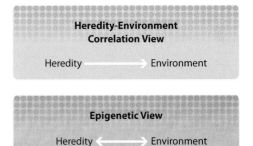

FIGURE **2.11**

COMPARISON OF THE HEREDITY-ENVIRONMENT CORRELATION AND EPIGENETIC VIEWS

epigenetic view Emphasizes that development is the result of an ongoing, bidirectional interchange between heredity and environment.

developmental **connection**

Biological Processes. A recent study revealed links between infant attachment, responsive parenting, and the short/long version of the 5-HTTLPR gene. Chapter 10, pp. 311–312

developmental **connection**

Nature vs. Nurture. The nature and nurture issue is one of the main issues in the study of life-span development. Chapter 1, p. 17

gene × environment (G × E) interaction The interaction of a specific measured variation in the DNA and a specific measured aspect of the environment

whether individuals would develop depression; however, some studies have not replicated this finding (Goldman & others, 2010; Risch & others, 2009). In a recent study, adults who experienced parental loss as young children were more likely to have unresolved attachment as adults only when they had the short version of the 5-HTTLPR gene (Caspers & others, 2009). The long version of the serotonin transporter gene apparently provided some protection and ability to cope better with parental loss.

The type of research just described is referred to as **gene × environment (G × E) interaction**—the interaction of a specific, measured variation in the DNA and a specific, measured aspect of the environment (Caspi & others, 2010; Seabrook & Avison, 2010). The field of *pharmacogenetics* is the study of gene-environment interaction involving the individual's genotype and drug treatment (the environment factor) (Cheok & others, 2009; Keers & others, 2010). The goal of many pharmacogenetic studies is to discover whether certain drugs are safer or more dangerous to use if the individual's genotype is known (Berlin, Paul, & Vesell, 2009; Lima & others, 2009).

CONCLUSIONS ABOUT HEREDITY-ENVIRONMENT INTERACTION

If an attractive, popular, intelligent girl is elected president of her senior class in high school, is her success due to heredity or to environment? Of course, the answer is both.

The relative contributions of heredity and environment are not additive. That is, we can't say that such-and-such a percentage of nature and such-and-such a percentage of experience make us who we are. Nor is it accurate to say that full genetic expression happens once, around conception or birth, after which we carry our genetic legacy into the world to see how far it takes us. Genes produce proteins throughout the life span, in many different environments. Or they don't produce these proteins, depending in part on how harsh or nourishing those environments are.

The emerging view is that complex behaviors have some genetic loading that gives people a propensity for a particular developmental trajectory (Goldsmith, 2011; Guo & Tillman, 2009). However, the actual development requires more: an environment. And that environment is complex, just like the mixture of genes we inherit (Duncan, Ziol-Guest, & Kalil, 2010; Gauvain & Parke, 2010). Environmental influences range from the things we lump together under "nurture" (such as parenting, family dynamics, schooling, and neighborhood quality) to biological encounters (such as viruses, birth complications, and even biological events in cells).

Imagine for a moment that there is a cluster of genes somehow associated with youth violence (this example is hypothetical because we don't know of any such combination). The adolescent who carries this genetic mixture might experience a world of loving parents, regular nutritious meals, lots of books, and a series of masterful teachers. Or the adolescent's world might include parental neglect, a neighborhood in which gunshots and crime are everyday occurrences, and inadequate schooling. In which of these environments are the adolescent's genes likely to manufacture the biological underpinnings of criminality?

If heredity and environment interact to determine the course of development, is that all there is to answering the question of what causes development? Are children completely at the mercy of their genes and environment as they develop? Genetic heritage and environmental experiences are pervasive influences on development (Sameroff, 2010; Wermter & others, 2010). But children's development is not solely the outcome of their heredity and environment; children also can author a unique developmental path by changing their environment. As one psychologist recently concluded:

> In reality, we are both the creatures and creators of our worlds. We are . . . the products of our genes and environments. Nevertheless, . . . the stream of causation that shapes the future runs through our present choices . . . Mind matters . . . Our hopes, goals, and expectations influence our future. (Myers, 2010, p.168)

Review *Connect* Reflect

LG4 Explain some of the ways that heredity and environment interact to produce individual differences in development.

Review

- What is behavior genetics?
- What are three types of heredity-environment correlations?
- What is meant by the concepts of shared and nonshared environmental experiences?
- What is the epigenetic view of development? What characterizes gene × environment (G × E) interaction?
- What conclusions can be reached about heredity-environment interaction?

Connect

- Of passive, evocative, and active genotype-environment correlations, which is the best explanation for the similarities discovered between the twins discussed in the story that opened this chapter?

Reflect *Your Own Personal Journey of Life*

- Imagine that someone tells you that he or she has analyzed your genetic background and environmental experiences and reached the conclusion that the environment you grew up in as a child definitely had little influence on your intelligence. What would you say about this analysis?

---

reach your **learning goals**

Biological Beginnings

The Evolutionary Perspective

 LG1 Discuss the evolutionary perspective on child development.

Natural Selection and Adaptive Behavior

- Natural selection is the process by which those individuals of a species that are best adapted to the environment survive and reproduce. Darwin proposed that natural selection fuels evolution. In evolutionary theory, adaptive behavior is behavior that promotes the organism's survival in a natural habitat.

Evolutionary Psychology

- Evolutionary psychology holds that adaptation, reproduction, and "survival of the fittest" are important in shaping behavior. Ideas proposed by evolutionary developmental psychology include the view that an extended childhood period is needed to develop a large brain and learn the complexity of human social communities. Like other theoretical approaches to development, evolutionary psychology has limitations. Bandura rejects "one-sided evolutionism" and argues for a bidirectional link between biology and environment. Biology allows for a broad range of cultural possibilities.

Genetic Foundations of Development

LG2 Describe what genes are and how they influence children's development.

The Collaborative Gene

- Short segments of DNA constitute genes, the units of hereditary information that direct cells to reproduce and manufacture proteins. Genes act collaboratively, not independently.

Genes and Chromosomes

- Genes are passed on to new cells when chromosomes are duplicated during the process of mitosis and meiosis, which are two ways in which new cells are formed. When an egg and a sperm unite in the fertilization process, the resulting zygote contains the genes from the chromosomes in the father's sperm and the mother's egg. Despite this transmission of genes from generation to generation, variability is created in several ways, including the exchange of chromosomal segments during meiosis, mutations, and environmental influences.

Genetic Principles

- Genetic principles include those involving dominant-recessive genes, sex-linked genes, genetic imprinting, and polygenic inheritance.

Chromosome and Gene-Linked Abnormalities

- Chromosome abnormalities produce Down syndrome, which is caused by the presence of an extra copy of chromosome 21, as well as sex-linked chromosomal abnormalities such as Klinefelter syndrome, fragile X syndrome, Turner syndrome, and XYY syndrome. Gene-linked abnormalities involve harmful genes. Gene-linked disorders include phenylketonuria (PKU) and sickle-cell anemia. Genetic counseling offers couples information about their risk of having a child with inherited abnormalities.

Reproductive Challenges and Choices

LG3 Identify some important reproductive challenges and choices.

Prenatal Diagnostic Tests

- Ultrasound sonography, fetal MRI, chorionic villus sampling, amniocentesis, and maternal blood screening are used to determine whether a fetus is developing normally. Noninvasive prenatal diagnosis is increasingly being explored.

Infertility and Reproductive Technology

- Approximately 10 to 15 percent of U.S. couples have infertility problems, some of which can be corrected through surgery or fertility drugs. An additional option is in vitro fertilization.

Adoption

- Although adopted children and adolescents have more problems than their non-adopted counterparts, the vast majority of adopted children adapt effectively. When adoption occurs very early in development, the outcomes for the child are improved. Because of the dramatic changes that occurred in adoption in recent decades, it is difficult to generalize about the average adopted child or average adoptive family.

Heredity and Environment Interaction: The Nature-Nurture Debate

LG4 Explain some of the ways that heredity and environment interact to produce individual differences in development.

Behavior Genetics

- Behavior genetics is the field concerned with the influence of heredity and environment on individual differences in human traits and development. Methods used by behavior geneticists include twin studies and adoption studies.

Heredity-Environment Correlations

- In Scarr's heredity-environment correlations view, heredity directs the types of environments that children experience. She describes three genotype-environment correlations: passive, evocative, and active (niche-picking). Scarr argues that the relative importance of these three genotype-environment correlations changes as children develop.

Shared and Nonshared Environmental Experiences

- Shared environmental experiences refer to siblings' common experiences, such as their parents' personalities and intellectual orientation, the family's socioeconomic status, and the neighborhood in which they live. Nonshared environmental experiences involve the child's unique experiences, both within a family and outside a family, that are not shared with a sibling. Many behavior geneticists argue that differences in the development of siblings are due to nonshared environmental experiences (and heredity) rather than shared environmental experiences.

The Epigenetic View and Gene × Environment (G × E) Interaction

- The epigenetic view emphasizes that development is the result of an ongoing, bidirectional interchange between heredity and environment. Gene × environment interaction involves the interaction of a specific, measured variation in the DNA and a specific, measured aspect of the environment. An increasing number of G × E studies are being conducted.

- Complex behaviors have some genetic loading that gives people a propensity for a particular developmental trajectory. However, actual development also requires an environment, and that environment is complex. The interaction of heredity and environment is extensive. Much remains to be discovered about the specific ways that heredity and environment interact to influence development. Although heredity and environment are pervasive influences on development, humans can author a unique developmental path by changing their environment.

key terms

key people

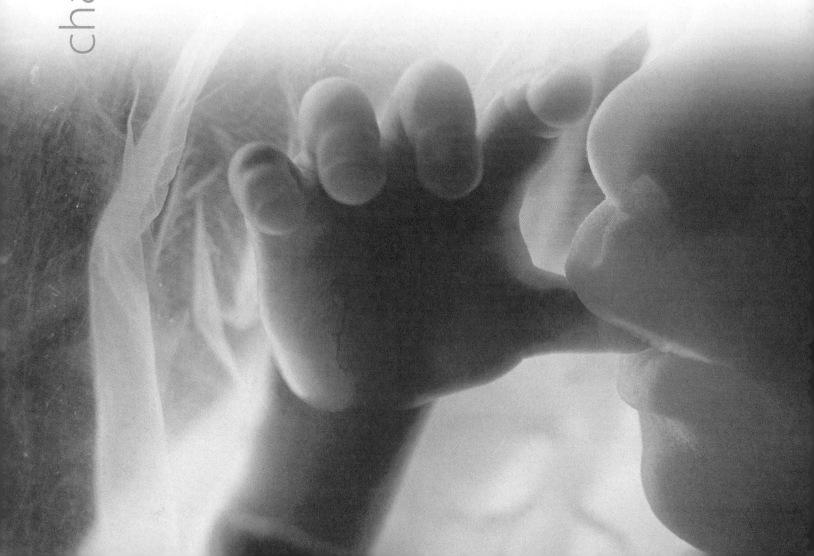

chapter **3**

chapter **outline**

PRENATAL DEVELOPMENT AND BIRTH

Diana and Roger married when he was 38 and she was 34. Both worked full-time and were excited when Diana became pregnant. Two months later, Diana began to have some unusual pains and bleeding. Just two months into her pregnancy she had lost the baby. Diana thought deeply about why she was unable to carry the baby to full term. It was about the time she became pregnant that the federal government began to warn that eating certain types of fish with a high mercury content during pregnancy on a regular basis can cause a miscarriage. Now she eliminated these fish from her diet.

Six months later, Diana became pregnant again. She and Roger read about pregnancy and signed up for birth preparation classes. Each Friday night for eight weeks they practiced simulated contractions. They talked about what kind of parents they wanted to be and discussed how their lives would change after the baby was born. When they found out that their offspring was going to be a boy, they gave him a nickname: Mr. Littles.

This time, Diana's pregnancy went well, and Alex, also known as Mr. Littles, was born. During the birth, however, Diana's heart rate dropped precipitously, and she was given a stimulant to raise it. Apparently the stimulant also increased Alex's heart rate and breathing to a dangerous point, and he had to be placed in a neo-natal intensive care unit (NICU).

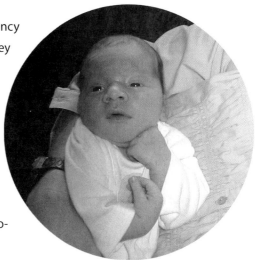

Alex, also known as "Mr. Littles."

Several times a day, Diana and Roger visited Alex in the NICU. A number of babies in the NICU who had a very low birth weight had been in intensive care for weeks, and some of these babies were not doing well. Fortunately, Alex was in better health. After several days in the NICU, his parents were permitted to take home a very healthy Alex.

preview

This chapter chronicles the truly remarkable developments from conception through birth. We will look at normal development as well as hazards to normal development (such as mercury, mentioned in the preceding story). We will outline the birth process and the tests used to assess the newborn. We will examine the physical, emotional, and psychological adjustments that a mother goes through during the time following birth, the postpartum period. And we will end by comparing theories on parent-infant bonding.

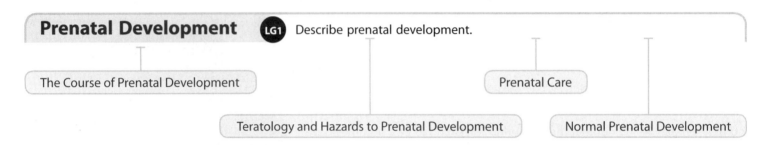

Prenatal Development   LG1 Describe prenatal development.

- The Course of Prenatal Development
- Teratology and Hazards to Prenatal Development
- Prenatal Care
- Normal Prenatal Development

Imagine how Alex ("Mr. Littles") came to be. Out of thousands of eggs and millions of sperm, one egg and one sperm united to produce him. Had the union of sperm and egg come a day or even an hour earlier or later, he might have been very different—maybe even of the opposite sex. *Conception* occurs when a single sperm cell from the male unites with an ovum (egg) in the female's fallopian tube in a process called fertilization. Over the next few months, the genetic code discussed in Chapter 2 directs a series of changes in the fertilized egg, but many events and hazards will influence how that egg develops and becomes tiny Alex.

THE COURSE OF PRENATAL DEVELOPMENT

Typical prenatal development begins with fertilization and ends with birth, lasting between 266 and 280 days (from 38 to 40 weeks). It can be divided into three periods: germinal, embryonic, and fetal.

The Germinal Period   The **germinal period** is the period of prenatal development that takes place in the first two weeks after conception. It includes the creation of the fertilized egg, called a zygote, followed by cell division and attachment of the zygote to the uterine wall.

Rapid cell division by the zygote continues throughout the germinal period (recall from Chapter 2 that this cell division occurs through a process called *mitosis*). By approximately one week after conception, the differentiation of these cells—their specialization for different tasks—has already begun. At this stage, the group of cells, now called the **blastocyst,** consists of an inner mass of cells that will eventually develop into the embryo, and the **trophoblast,** an outer layer of cells that later provides nutrition and support for the embryo. *Implantation*, the attachment of the zygote to the uterine wall, takes place about 11 to 15 days after conception. Figure 3.1 illustrates some of the most significant developments during the germinal period.

The Embryonic Period   The **embryonic period** is the period of prenatal development that occurs from two to eight weeks after conception. During the embryonic period, the rate of cell differentiation intensifies, support systems for cells form, and organs appear.

This period begins as the blastocyst attaches to the uterine wall. The mass of cells is now called an *embryo,* and three layers of cells form. The embryo's *endoderm* is the inner layer of cells, which will develop into the digestive and respiratory systems.

germinal period The period of prenatal development that takes place in the first two weeks after conception. It includes the creation of the zygote, continued cell division, and the attachment of the zygote to the uterine wall.

blastocyst The inner layer of cells that develops during the germinal period. These cells later develop into the embryo.

trophoblast The outer layer of cells that develops in the germinal period. These cells provide nutrition and support for the embryo.

embryonic period The period of prenatal development that occurs two to eight weeks after conception. During the embryonic period, the rate of cell differentiation intensifies, support systems for the cells form, and organs appear.

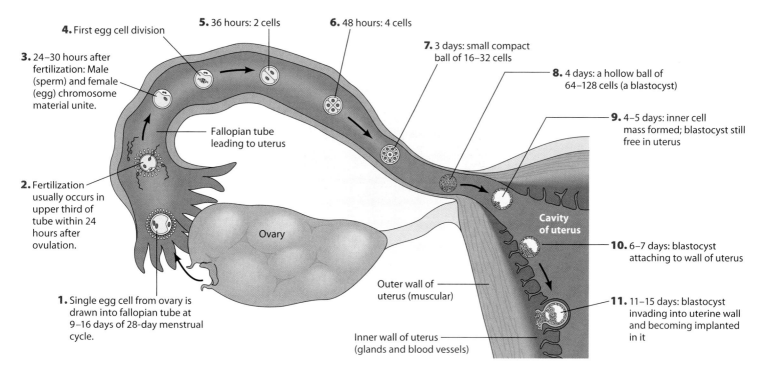

4. First egg cell division

5. 36 hours: 2 cells

6. 48 hours: 4 cells

3. 24–30 hours after fertilization: Male (sperm) and female (egg) chromosome material unite.

7. 3 days: small compact ball of 16–32 cells

8. 4 days: a hollow ball of 64–128 cells (a blastocyst)

Fallopian tube leading to uterus

9. 4–5 days: inner cell mass formed; blastocyst still free in uterus

2. Fertilization usually occurs in upper third of tube within 24 hours after ovulation.

Ovary

Cavity of uterus

10. 6–7 days: blastocyst attaching to wall of uterus

Outer wall of uterus (muscular)

1. Single egg cell from ovary is drawn into fallopian tube at 9–16 days of 28-day menstrual cycle.

11. 11–15 days: blastocyst invading into uterine wall and becoming implanted in it

Inner wall of uterus (glands and blood vessels)

FIGURE **3.1**

SIGNIFICANT DEVELOPMENTS IN THE GERMINAL PERIOD. Just one week after conception, cells of the blastocyst have already begun specializing. The germination period ends when the blastocyst attaches to the uterine wall. *Which of the steps shown in the drawing occur in the laboratory when IVF (described in Chapter 2) is used?*

The *mesoderm* is the middle layer, which will become the circulatory system, bones, muscles, excretory system, and reproductive system. The *ectoderm* is the outermost layer, which will become the nervous system and brain, sensory receptors (ears, nose, and eyes, for example), and skin parts (hair and nails, for example). Every body part eventually develops from these three layers. The endoderm primarily produces internal body parts, the mesoderm primarily produces parts that surround the internal areas, and the ectoderm primarily produces surface parts.

As the embryo's three layers form, life-support systems for the embryo develop rapidly. These life-support systems include the amnion, the umbilical cord (both of which develop from the fertilized egg, not the mother's body), and the placenta. The **amnion** is like a bag or an envelope and contains a clear fluid in which the developing embryo floats. The amniotic fluid provides an environment that is temperature and humidity controlled, as well as shockproof. The **umbilical cord** contains two arteries and one vein, and connects the baby to the placenta. The **placenta** consists of a disk-shaped group of tissues in which small blood vessels from the mother and the offspring intertwine but do not join.

Figure 3.2 illustrates the placenta, the umbilical cord, and the blood flow in the expectant mother and developing organism. Very small molecules—oxygen, water, salt, food from the mother's blood, as well as carbon dioxide and digestive wastes from the offspring's blood—pass back and forth between the mother and embryo or fetus (Wick & others, 2010). Large molecules cannot pass through the placental wall; these include red blood cells and harmful substances, such as most bacteria and maternal wastes. The mechanisms that govern the transfer of substances across the placental barrier are complex and are still not entirely understood (Barta & Drugan, 2010; Cetin & Alvino, 2009).

By the time most women know they are pregnant, the major organs have begun to form. **Organogenesis** is the name given to the process of organ formation during the first two months of prenatal development. While they are being formed, the organs are especially vulnerable to environmental changes (Rojas & others, 2010; Torchinsky & Toder, 2010). In the third week after conception, the neural tube that eventually becomes the spinal cord forms. At about 21 days, eyes begin to appear, and at 24 days the cells for the heart begin to differentiate. During the fourth week, the urogenital system becomes apparent, and arm and leg buds emerge. Four chambers of the heart take shape, and blood vessels appear. From the fifth to the eighth

amnion Prenatal life-support system that is a bag or envelope that contains a clear fluid in which the developing embryo floats.

umbilical cord A life-support system that contains two arteries and one vein and connects the baby to the placenta.

placenta A life-support system that consists of a disk-shaped group of tissues in which small blood vessels from the mother and offspring intertwine.

organogenesis Organ formation that takes place during the first two months of prenatal development.

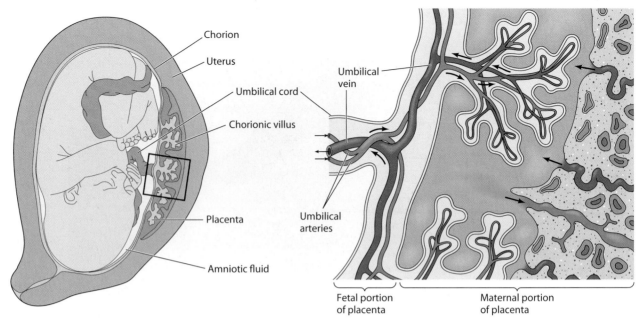

Chorion
Uterus
Umbilical cord
Chorionic villus
Placenta
Amniotic fluid

Umbilical vein
Umbilical arteries

Fetal portion of placenta
Maternal portion of placenta

FIGURE 3.2

THE PLACENTA AND THE UMBILICAL CORD. The area bound by the square in the right half of the illustration is enlarged. Arrows indicate the direction of blood flow. Maternal blood flows through the uterine arteries to the spaces housing the placenta, and it returns through the uterine veins to the maternal circulation. Fetal blood flows through the umbilical arteries into the capillaries of the placenta and returns through the umbilical vein to the fetal circulation. The exchange of materials takes place across the layer separating the maternal and fetal blood supplies, so the bloods never come into contact. *What is known about how the placental barrier works and its importance?*

week, arms and legs differentiate further; at this time, the face starts to form but still is not very recognizable. The intestinal tract develops and the facial structures fuse. At eight weeks, the developing organism weighs about 1/30 ounce and is just over 1 inch long.

The Fetal Period   The **fetal period,** lasting about seven months, is the prenatal period between two months after conception and birth in typical pregnancies. Growth and development continue their dramatic course during this time.

Three months after conception, the fetus is about 3 inches long and weighs about 3 ounces. It has become active, moving its arms and legs, opening and closing its mouth, and moving its head. The face, forehead, eyelids, nose, and chin are distinguishable, as are the upper arms, lower arms, hands, and lower limbs. In most cases, the genitals can be identified as male or female. By the end of the fourth month of pregnancy, the fetus has grown to 6 inches in length and weighs 4 to 7 ounces. At this time, a growth spurt occurs in the body's lower parts. For the first time, the mother can feel arm and leg movements.

By the end of the fifth month, the fetus is about 12 inches long and weighs close to a pound. Structures of the skin have formed—toenails and fingernails, for example. The fetus is more active, showing a preference for a particular position in the womb. By the end of the sixth month, the fetus is about 14 inches long and has gained another half pound to a pound. The eyes and eyelids are completely formed, and a fine layer of hair covers the head. A grasping reflex is present and irregular breathing movements occur.

As early as six months of pregnancy (about 24 to 25 weeks after conception), the fetus for the first time has a chance of surviving outside of the womb—that is, it is *viable.* Infants who are born early, or between 24 and 37 weeks of pregnancy, usually need help breathing because their lungs are not yet fully mature. By the end of the seventh month, the fetus is about 16 inches long and weighs about 3 pounds.

During the last two months of prenatal development, fatty tissues develop, and the functioning of various organ systems—heart and kidneys, for example—steps

> The history of man for nine months preceding his birth would, probably, be far more interesting, and contain events of greater moment than all three score and ten years that follow it.
>
> —SAMUEL TAYLOR COLERIDGE
> *English Poet, Essayist, 19th Century*

fetal period The period from two months after conception until birth, lasting about seven months in typical pregnancies.

First trimester (first 3 months)

Conception to 4 weeks

- Is less than $1/10$ inch long
- Beginning development of spinal cord, nervous system, gastrointestinal system, heart, and lungs
- Amniotic sac envelopes the preliminary tissues of entire body
- Is called a "zygote"

8 weeks

- Is just over 1 inch long
- Face is forming with rudimentary eyes, ears, mouth, and tooth buds
- Arms and legs are moving
- Brain is forming
- Fetal heartbeat is detectable with ultrasound
- Is called an "embryo"

12 weeks

- Is about 3 inches long and weighs about 1 ounce
- Can move arms, legs, fingers, and toes
- Fingerprints are present
- Can smile, frown, suck, and swallow
- Sex is distinguishable
- Can urinate
- Is called a "fetus"

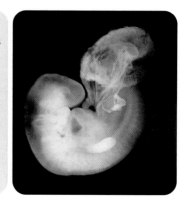

Second trimester (middle 3 months)

16 weeks

- Is about 6 inches long and weighs about 4 to 7 ounces
- Heartbeat is strong
- Skin is thin, transparent
- Downy hair (lanugo) covers body
- Fingernails and toenails are forming
- Has coordinated movements; is able to roll over in amniotic fluid

20 weeks

- Is about 12 inches long and weighs close to 1 pound
- Heartbeat is audible with ordinary stethoscope
- Sucks thumb
- Hiccups
- Hair, eyelashes, eyebrows are present

24 weeks

- Is about 14 inches long and weighs 1 to $1/2$ pounds
- Skin is wrinkled and covered with protective coating (vernix caseosa)
- Eyes are open
- Waste matter is collected in bowel
- Has strong grip

Third trimester (last 3 months)

28 weeks

- Is about 16 inches long and weighs about 3 pounds
- Is adding body fat
- Is very active
- Rudimentary breathing movements are present

32 weeks

- Is $16 1/2$ to 18 inches long and weighs 4 to 5 pounds
- Has periods of sleep and wakefulness
- Responds to sounds
- May assume the birth position
- Bones of head are soft and flexible
- Iron is being stored in liver

36 to 38 weeks

- Is 19 to 20 inches long and weighs 6 to $7 1/2$ pounds
- Skin is less wrinkled
- Vernix caseosa is thick
- Lanugo is mostly gone
- Is less active
- Is gaining immunities from mother

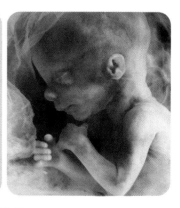

FIGURE **3.3**

THE THREE TRIMESTERS OF PRENATAL DEVELOPMENT. Both the germinal and embryonic periods occur during the first trimester. The end of the first trimester as well as the second and third trimesters are part of the fetal period.

up. During the eighth and ninth months, the fetus grows longer and gains substantial weight—about another 4 pounds. At birth, the average American baby weighs 7½ pounds and is about 20 inches long.

Figure 3.3 gives an overview of the main events during prenatal development. Notice that instead of describing development in terms of germinal, embryonic, and fetal periods, Figure 3.3 divides prenatal development into equal periods of three months, called *trimesters*. Remember that the three trimesters are not the same as the three prenatal periods we have discussed. The germinal and embryonic periods occur in the first trimester. The fetal period begins toward the end of the first trimester and continues through the second and third trimesters. Viability (the possibility of surviving outside the womb) occurs at the very end of the second trimester.

The Brain   One of the most remarkable aspects of the prenatal period is the development of the brain (Nelson, 2011). By the time babies are born, they have approximately 100 billion **neurons,** or nerve cells, which handle information processing at the cellular level in the brain. During prenatal development, neurons spend time

neurons Nerve cells, which handle information processing at the cellular level in the brain.

Yelyi Nordone, 12, of New York City, recently cast her line out into the pond during Camp Spifida at Camp Victory, near Millville, Pennsylvania. Camp Spifida is a week-long residential camp for children with spina bifida.

developmental **connection**

Brain Development. At birth, the brain's weight is approximately 25 percent of its adult weight. Chapter 4, p. 116

FIGURE **3.4**

EARLY FORMATION OF THE NERVOUS SYSTEM. The photograph shows the primitive, tubular appearance of the nervous system at six weeks in the human embryo.

moving to the right locations and are starting to become connected. The basic architecture of the human brain is assembled during the first two trimesters of prenatal development. In typical development, the third trimester of prenatal development and the first two years of postnatal life are characterized by connectivity and functioning of neurons (Moulson & Nelson, 2008).

As the human embryo develops inside its mother's womb, the nervous system begins forming as a long, hollow tube located on the embryo's back. This pear-shaped *neural tube*, which forms at about 18 to 24 days after conception, develops out of the ectoderm. The tube closes at the top and bottom at about 24 days after conception. Figure 3.4 shows that the nervous system still has a tubular appearance six weeks after conception.

Two birth defects related to a failure of the neural tube to close are anencephaly and spina bifida. The highest regions of the brain fail to develop when fetuses have anencephaly or when the head end of the neural tube fails to close. Such infants die in the womb, during childbirth, or shortly after birth (Levene & Chervenak, 2009). Spina bifida results in varying degrees of paralysis of the lower limbs. Individuals with spina bifida usually need assistive devices such as crutches, braces, or wheelchairs. A strategy that can help to prevent neural tube defects is for women to take adequate amounts of the B vitamin folic acid, a topic we will discuss later in the chapter (Bell & Oakley, 2009; Rasmussen & Clemmenson, 2010; Shookoff & Ian Gallicano, 2010). And both maternal diabetes and obesity place the fetus at risk for developing neural tube defects (McGuire, Dyson, & Renfrew, 2010; Yazdy & others, 2010).

In a normal pregnancy, once the neural tube has closed, a massive proliferation of new immature neurons begins to takes place at about the fifth prenatal week and continues throughout the remainder of the prenatal period. The generation of new neurons is called *neurogenesis* (Kronenberg & others, 2010). At the peak of neurogenesis, it is estimated that as many as 200,000 neurons are being generated every minute.

At approximately 6 to 24 weeks after conception, *neuronal migration* occurs (Nelson, 2011). This involves cells moving outward from their point of origin to their appropriate locations and creating the different levels, structures, and regions of the brain (Cozzi & others, 2010; Kuriyama & Mayor, 2009). Once a cell has migrated to its target destination, it must mature and develop a more complex structure.

At about the 23rd prenatal week, connections between neurons begin to occur, a process that continues postnatally (Moulson & Nelson, 2008). We will have much more to say about the structure of neurons, their connectivity, and the development of the infant brain in Chapter 4.

TERATOLOGY AND HAZARDS TO PRENATAL DEVELOPMENT

For Alex, the baby discussed at the opening of this chapter, the course of prenatal development went smoothly. His mother's womb protected him as he developed. Despite this protection, the environment can affect the embryo or fetus in many well-documented ways.

General Principles   A **teratogen** is any agent that can potentially cause a birth defect or negatively alter cognitive and behavioral outcomes. (The word comes from the Greek word *tera*, meaning "monster.") So many teratogens exist that practically every fetus is exposed to at least some teratogens. For this reason, it is difficult to determine which teratogen causes which problem. In addition, it may take a long time for the effects of a teratogen to show up. Only about half of all potential effects appear at birth.

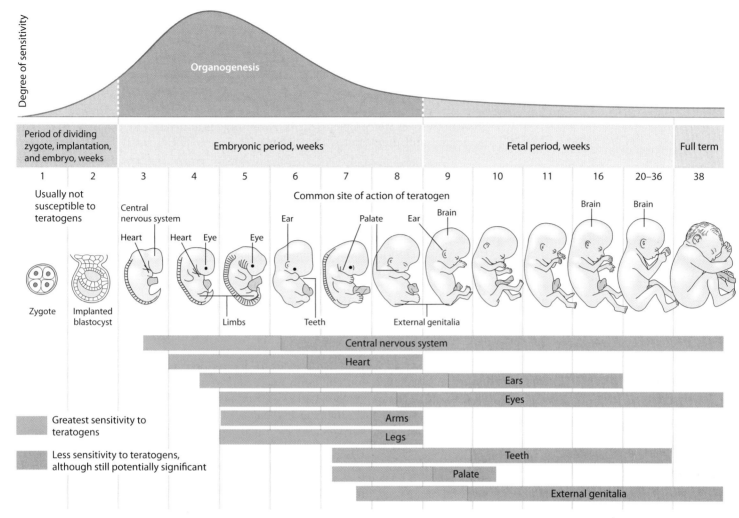

FIGURE 3.5

TERATOGENS AND THE TIMING OF THEIR EFFECTS ON PRENATAL DEVELOPMENT.
The danger of structural defects caused by teratogens is greatest early in embryonic development. The period of organogenesis (red color) lasts for about six weeks. Later assaults by teratogens (blue-green color) mainly occur in the fetal period and instead of causing structural damage are more likely to stunt growth or cause problems of organ function.

The field of study that investigates the causes of birth defects is called *teratology*. Some exposures to teratogens do not cause physical birth defects but can alter the developing brain and influence cognitive and behavioral functioning, in which case the field of study is called *behavioral teratology*.

The dose, genetic susceptibility, and the time of exposure to a particular teratogen influence both the severity of the damage to an embryo or fetus and the type of defect:

- **Dose.** The dose effect is rather obvious—the greater the dose of an agent, such as a drug, the greater the effect.

- **Genetic susceptibility.** The type or severity of abnormalities caused by a teratogen is linked to the genotype of the pregnant woman and the genotype of the embryo or fetus (Lidral & Murray, 2005). For example, how a mother metabolizes a particular drug can influence the degree to which the drug effects are transmitted to the embryo or fetus. The extent to which an embryo or fetus is vulnerable to a teratogen may also depend on its genotype (Marinucci & others, 2009). Also, for unknown reasons, male fetuses are far more likely to be affected by teratogens than female fetuses.

- **Time of exposure.** Teratogens do more damage when they occur at some points in development than at others (Weiner & Buhimschi, 2009). Damage during the germinal period may even prevent implantation. In general, the embryonic period is more vulnerable than the fetal period.

Figure 3.5 summarizes additional information about the effects of time of exposure to a teratogen. The probability of a structural defect is greatest early in the

teratogen From the Greek word *tera*, meaning "monster." Any agent that causes a birth defect. The field of study that investigates the causes of birth defects is called teratology.

embryonic period, when organs are being formed (Hill, 2007). Each body structure has its own critical period of formation. Recall from Chapter 1 that a *critical period* is a fixed time period very early in development during which certain experiences or events can have a long-lasting effect on development. The critical period for the nervous system (week 3) is earlier than for arms and legs (weeks 4 and 5).

After organogenesis is complete, teratogens are less likely to cause anatomical defects. Instead, exposure during the fetal period is more likely instead to stunt growth or to create problems in the way organs function. To examine some key teratogens and their effects, let's begin with drugs.

Prescription and Nonprescription Drugs Many U.S. women are given prescriptions for drugs while they are pregnant—especially antibiotics, analgesics, and asthma medications. Prescription as well as nonprescription drugs, however, may have effects on the embryo or fetus that the women never imagine (Weiner & Buhimschi, 2009).

Prescription drugs that can function as teratogens include antibiotics, such as streptomycin and tetracycline; some antidepressants; certain hormones, such as progestin and synthetic estrogen; and Accutane (which often is prescribed for acne) (Bayraktar & others, 2010; Teichert & others, 2010).

Antidepressant use by pregnant women has been extensively studied (Pedersen & others, 2009; Reis & Kallen, 2010; Simoncelli, Martin, & Berard, 2010). A recent study revealed that the offspring of pregnant women who redeemed prescriptions for more than one type of SSRI (selective serotonin reuptake inhibitor) early in pregnancy had an increased risk of heart defects (Pedersen & others, 2009). In this study, negative effects on children's heart functioning increased when their mothers took two SSRIs early in pregnancy—sertraline and citalopram. However, a recent research review by the American Psychiatric Association and the American College of Obstetricians and Gynecologists indicated that although some studies have found negative outcomes for antidepressant use during pregnancy, failure to control for various factors that can influence birth outcomes, such as maternal illness or problematic health behaviors, make it difficult to draw conclusions about a link between prenatal antidepressant use and birth outcomes (Yonkers & others, 2009). Later in the chapter, we will further discuss depression during pregnancy.

Nonprescription drugs that can be harmful include diet pills and high dosages of aspirin (Norgard & others, 2006). However, recent research indicated that low doses of aspirin pose no harm for the fetus but that high doses can contribute to maternal and fetal bleeding (James, Brancazio, & Price, 2008; Marret & others, 2010).

Psychoactive Drugs *Psychoactive drugs* are drugs that act on the nervous system to alter states of consciousness, modify perceptions, and change moods. Examples include caffeine, alcohol, and nicotine, as well as illicit drugs such as cocaine, methamphetamine, marijuana, and heroin.

Caffeine People often consume caffeine by drinking coffee, tea, or colas, or by eating chocolate. A recent study revealed that pregnant women who consumed 200 or more milligrams of caffeine a day had an increased risk of miscarriage (Weng, Odouli, & Li, 2008). Taking into account such results, the Food and Drug Administration recommends that pregnant women either not consume caffeine or consume it only sparingly.

Alcohol Heavy drinking by pregnant women can be devastating to offspring. **Fetal alcohol spectrum disorders (FASD)** are a cluster of abnormalities and problems that appear in the offspring of mothers who drink alcohol heavily during pregnancy. The abnormalities include facial deformities and defective limbs, face, and heart (Klingenberg & others, 2010). Most children with FASD have learning problems and many are below average in intelligence, while some are mentally retarded (Caley & others, 2008). Recent studies revealed that children and adults with FASD have impaired memory development (Coles & others, 2010; Pei & others, 2008). Another recent study found that children with FASD have impaired math ability linked to

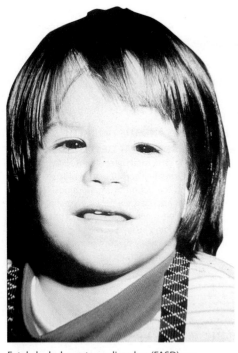

Fetal alcohol spectrum disorders (FASD) are characterized by a number of physical abnormalities and learning problems. Notice the wide-set eyes, flat cheekbones, and thin upper lip in this child with FASD.

fetal alcohol spectrum disorders (FASD) A cluster of abnormalities and problems that appear in the offspring of mothers who drink alcohol heavily during pregnancy.

multiple regions of the brain (Lebel & others, 2010). Although many mothers of FASD infants are heavy drinkers, many mothers who are heavy drinkers do not have children with FASD or have one child with FASD and other children who do not have it.

What are some guidelines for alcohol use during pregnancy? Even drinking just one or two servings of beer or wine or one serving of hard liquor a few days a week can have negative effects on the fetus, although it is generally agreed that this level of alcohol use will not cause fetal alcohol syndrome. The U.S. Surgeon General recommends that *no* alcohol be consumed during pregnancy. And research suggests that it may not be wise to consume alcohol at the time of conception. One study revealed that alcohol intake by both men and women during the weeks of conception increased the risk of early pregnancy loss (Henriksen & others, 2004).

Nicotine   Cigarette smoking by pregnant women can also adversely influence prenatal development, birth, and postnatal development (Blood-Siegfried & Rende, 2010). Preterm births and low birth weights, fetal and neonatal deaths, respiratory problems, sudden infant death syndrome (SIDS, also known as crib death), and cardiovascular problems are all more common among the offspring of mothers who smoked during pregnancy (Feng & others, 2010; Lazic & others, 2010). Maternal smoking during pregnancy also has been identified as a risk factor for the development of attention deficit hyperactivity disorder in offspring (Knopik, 2009; Pinkhardt & others, 2009). A recent research review also indicated that environmental tobacco smoke was linked to increased risk of low birth weight in offspring (Leonardi-Bee & others, 2008).

Cocaine   Does cocaine use during pregnancy harm the developing embryo and fetus? The most consistent finding is that cocaine exposure during prenatal development is associated with reduced birth weight, length, and head circumference (Smith & others, 2001). Also, in other studies, prenatal cocaine exposure has been linked to lower arousal, less effective self-regulation, higher excitability, and lower quality of reflexes at 1 month of age (Lester & others, 2002); to impaired motor development at 2 years of age and a slower rate of growth through 10 years of age (Richardson, Goldschmidt, & Willford, 2008); to deficits in behavioral self-regulation (Ackerman, Riggins, & Black, 2010) to impaired language development and information processing (Beeghly & others, 2006), including attention deficits (especially in sustained attention) in preschool and elementary school children (Accornero & others, 2006; Ackerman, Riggins, & Black, 2010); and to increased likelihood of being in a special education program that involves support services (Levine & others, 2008).

Some researchers argue that these findings should be interpreted cautiously (Accornero & others, 2006). Why? Because other factors in the lives of pregnant women who use cocaine (such as poverty, malnutrition, and other substance abuse) often cannot be ruled out as possible contributors to the problems found in their children (Hurt & others, 2005). For example, cocaine users are more likely than nonusers to smoke cigarettes, use marijuana, drink alcohol, and take amphetamines.

Despite these cautions, the weight of research evidence indicates that children born to mothers who use cocaine are likely to have neurological, medical, and cognitive deficits (Field, 2007; Mayer & Zhang, 2009). Cocaine use by pregnant women is never recommended.

Methamphetamine   Methamphetamine, like cocaine, is a stimulant, speeding up an individual's nervous system. Babies born to mothers who use methamphetamine, or "meth," during pregnancy are at risk for a number of problems, including higher rates of infant mortality, low birth weight, and developmental and behavioral problems. A recent study also found memory deficits in children whose mothers used methamphetamine during pregnancy (Lu & others, 2009).

What are some links between expectant mothers' drinking and cigarette smoking and outcomes for their offspring?

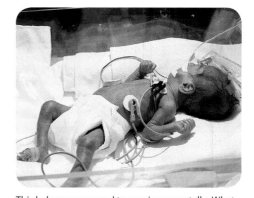

This baby was exposed to cocaine prenatally. *What are some of the possible effects on development of being exposed to cocaine prenatally?*

Marijuana   An increasing number of studies find that marijuana use by pregnant women also has negative outcomes for offspring. For example, a recent study found that prenatal marijuana exposure was related to lower intelligence in children (Goldschmidt & others, 2008). Another study indicated that prenatal exposure to marijuana was linked to marijuana use at 14 years of age (Day, Goldschmidt, & Thomas, 2006). In sum, marijuana use is not recommended for pregnant women.

Heroin   It is well documented that infants whose mothers are addicted to heroin show several behavioral difficulties at birth (Steinhausen, Blattmann, & Pfund, 2007). The difficulties include withdrawal symptoms, such as tremors, irritability, abnormal crying, disturbed sleep, and impaired motor control. Many still show behavioral problems at their first birthday, and attention deficits may appear later in development. The most common treatment for heroin addiction, methadone, is associated with very severe withdrawal symptoms in newborns (Binder & Vavrinkova, 2008).

An explosion at the Chernobyl nuclear power plant in the Ukraine produced radioactive contamination that spread to surrounding areas. Thousands of infants were born with health problems and deformities as a result of the nuclear contamination, including this boy whose arm did not form. *Other than radioactive contamination, what are some other types of environmental hazards to prenatal development?*

Incompatible Blood Types   Incompatibility between the mother's and father's blood type poses another risk to prenatal development. Blood types are created by differences in the surface structure of red blood cells. One type of difference in the surface of red blood cells creates the familiar blood groups—A, B, O, and AB. A second difference creates what is called Rh-positive and Rh-negative blood. If a surface marker, called the *Rh-factor*, is present in an individual's red blood cells, the person is said to be Rh-positive; if the Rh-marker is not present, the person is said to be Rh-negative. If a pregnant woman is Rh-negative and her partner is Rh-positive, the fetus may be Rh-positive. If the fetus' blood is Rh-positive and the mother's is Rh-negative, the mother's immune system may produce antibodies that will attack the fetus. This can result in any number of problems, including miscarriage or stillbirth, anemia, jaundice, heart defects, brain damage, or death soon after birth (Moise, 2005).

Generally, the first Rh-positive baby of an Rh-negative mother is not at risk, but with each subsequent pregnancy the risk increases. A vaccine (RhoGAM) may be given to the mother within three days of the first child's birth to prevent her body from making antibodies that will attack any future Rh-positive fetuses in subsequent pregnancies. Also, babies affected by Rh incompatibility can be given blood transfusions before or right after birth (Flegal, 2007).

Environmental Hazards   Many aspects of our modern industrial world can endanger the embryo or fetus. Some specific hazards to the embryo or fetus include radiation, toxic wastes, and other chemical pollutants (O'Connor & Roy, 2008).

X-ray radiation can affect the developing embryo or fetus, especially in the first several weeks after conception, when women do not yet know they are pregnant (Urbano & Tait, 2004). Women and their physicians should weigh the risk of an X-ray when an actual or potential pregnancy is involved (Baysinger, 2010; Menias & others, 2007). However, a routine diagnostic X-ray of a body area other than the abdomen, with the woman's abdomen protected by a lead apron, is generally considered safe (Brent, 2009).

Environmental pollutants and toxic wastes are also sources of danger to unborn children. Among the dangerous pollutants are carbon monoxide, mercury, and lead, as well as certain fertilizers and pesticides.

Maternal Diseases   Maternal diseases and infections can produce defects in offspring by crossing the placental barrier, or they can cause damage during birth. Rubella (German measles) is one disease that can cause prenatal defects. Women who plan to have children should have a blood test before they become pregnant to determine whether they are immune to the disease (Coonrod & others, 2008).

Syphilis (a sexually transmitted infection) is more damaging later in prenatal development—four months or more after conception. Damage includes eye lesions, which can cause blindness, and skin lesions.

Another infection that has received widespread attention is genital herpes. Newborns contract this virus when they are delivered through the birth canal of a mother with genital herpes (Hollier & Wendel, 2008). About one-third of babies delivered through an infected birth canal die; another one-fourth become brain damaged. If an active case of genital herpes is detected in a pregnant woman close to her delivery date, a cesarean section can be performed (in which the infant is delivered through an incision in the mother's abdomen) to keep the virus from infecting the newborn (Sellner & others, 2009).

AIDS is a sexually transmitted infection that is caused by the human immunodeficiency virus (HIV), which destroys the body's immune system. A mother can infect her offspring with HIV/AIDS in three ways: (1) during gestation across the placenta, (2) during delivery through contact with maternal blood or fluids, and (3) postpartum (after birth) through breast feeding. The transmission of AIDS through breast feeding is especially a problem in many developing countries (UNICEF, 2010). Babies born to HIV-infected mothers can be (1) infected and symptomatic (show HIV symptoms), (2) infected but asymptomatic (not show HIV symptoms), or (3) not infected at all. An infant who is infected and asymptomatic may still develop HIV symptoms until 15 months of age.

The more widespread disease of diabetes, characterized by high levels of sugar in the blood, also affects offspring (Huda & others, 2010; Oostdam & others, 2009; Most & others, 2009). A recent large-scale study revealed that twice as many women and five times as many adolescents giving birth had diabetes in 2005 as in 1999 (Lawrence & others, 2008).

A research review indicated that newborns with physical defects are more likely to have diabetic mothers (Eriksson, 2009). Women who have gestational diabetes also may deliver very large infants (weighing 10 pounds or more), and these infants are at risk for diabetes themselves (Gluck & others, 2009).

Other Parental Factors   So far we have discussed a number of drugs, environmental hazards, maternal diseases, and incompatible blood types that can harm the embryo or fetus. Here we will explore other characteristics of the mother and father that can affect prenatal and child development, including nutrition, age, and emotional states and stress.

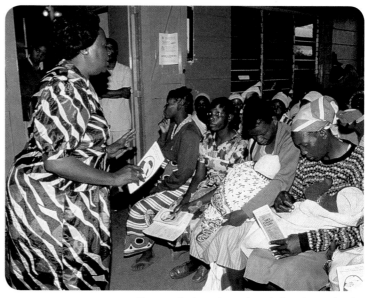

Because the fetus depends entirely on its mother for nutrition, it is important for the pregnant woman to have good nutritional habits. In Kenya, this government clinic provides pregnant women with information about how their diet can influence the health of their fetus and offspring. *What might the information about diet be like?*

Maternal Diet and Nutrition   A developing embryo or fetus depends completely on its mother for nutrition, which comes from the mother's blood (Shapira, 2008). The nutritional status of the embryo or fetus is determined by the mother's total caloric intake and by her intake of proteins, vitamins, and minerals. Children born to malnourished mothers are more likely than other children to be malformed.

Being overweight before and during pregnancy can also put the embryo or fetus at risk, and an increasing number of pregnant women in the United States are overweight (Griffiths & others, 2010; Sullivan & others, 2010). A recent research review concluded that obesity during pregnancy is linked to increased maternal risks of infertility, hypertensive disorders, diabetes, and delivery by Caesarean section (Arendas, Qui, & Gruslin, 2008). In this review, obesity during pregnancy was associated with the following increased risks to the fetus: macrosomia (newborn with excessive birth weight), intrauterine fetal death, stillbirth, and admission to the neonatal intensive care unit (NICU).

One aspect of maternal nutrition that is important for normal prenatal development is consumption of folic acid, a B-complex vitamin (Rasmussen & Clemmensen,

developmental **connection**

Nutrition and Weight. What are some key factors that influence whether children become obese? Chapter 4, p. 133

What are some of the risks for infants born to adolescent mothers?

2010). A recent study of more than 34,000 women indicated that taking folic acid either alone or as part of a multivitamin for at least one year prior to conceiving was linked with a 70 percent lower risk of delivering from 20 to 28 weeks and a 50 percent lower risk of delivering between 28 and 32 weeks (Bukowski & others, 2008). Another recent study revealed that toddlers of mothers who did not use folic acid supplements in the first trimester of pregnancy had more behavior problems (Roza & others, 2010). Also, as indicated earlier in the chapter, a lack of folic acid is related to neural tube defects in offspring, such as spina bifida (a defect in the spinal cord) (Levene & Chervenak, 2009; Shookhoff & Ian Gallicano, 2010). The U.S. Department of Health and Human Services (2009) recommends that pregnant women consume a minimum of 400 micrograms of folic acid per day (about twice the amount the average woman gets in one day). Orange juice and spinach are examples of foods rich in folic acid.

Eating fish is often recommended as part of a healthy diet, but pollution has made many fish a risky choice for pregnant women. Some fish contain high levels of mercury, which is released into the air both naturally and by industrial pollution (Genuis, 2009). When mercury falls into the water it can become toxic and accumulate in large fish, such as shark, swordfish, king mackerel, and some species of large tuna (Mayo Clinic, 2009; Ramon & others, 2009). Mercury is easily transferred across the placenta, and the embryo's developing brain and nervous system are highly sensitive to the metal. Researchers have found that prenatal mercury exposure is linked to adverse outcomes, including miscarriage, preterm birth, and lower intelligence (Triche & Hossain, 2007; Xue & others, 2007).

Maternal Age   When possible harmful effects on the fetus and infant are considered, two maternal ages are of special interest: adolescence and 35 years and older (Malizia, Hacker, & Penzias, 2009). The mortality rate of infants born to adolescent mothers is double that of infants born to mothers in their twenties. Adequate prenatal care decreases the probability that a child born to an adolescent girl will have physical problems. However, among women in all age groups adolescents are the least likely to obtain prenatal assistance from clinics and health services.

Maternal age is also linked to the risk that a child will have Down syndrome (Allen & others, 2009; Ghosh & others, 2010). As discussed in Chapter 2, an individual with *Down syndrome* has distinctive facial characteristics, short limbs, and retardation of motor and mental abilities. A baby with Down syndrome rarely is born to a mother 16 to 34 years of age. However, when the mother reaches 40 years of age, the probability is slightly over 1 in 100 that a baby born to her will have Down syndrome, and by age 50 it is almost 1 in 10. When mothers are 35 years and older, risks also increase for low birth weight, for preterm delivery, and for fetal death (Mbugua Gitau, & others, 2009).

We still have much to learn about the role of the mother's age in pregnancy and childbirth. As women remain active, exercise regularly, and are careful about their nutrition, their reproductive systems may remain healthier at older ages than was thought possible in the past.

Emotional States and Stress   When a pregnant woman experiences intense fears, anxieties, and other emotions or negative mood states, physiological changes occur that may affect her fetus (Entringer & others, 2009; Leung & others, 2010). A mother's stress may also influence the fetus indirectly by increasing the likelihood that the mother will engage in unhealthy behaviors, such as taking drugs and engaging in poor prenatal care.

High maternal anxiety and stress during pregnancy can have long-term consequences for the offspring. A recent research review indicated that pregnant women with high levels of stress are at increased risk for having a child with emotional or cognitive problems, attention deficit hyperactivity disorder (ADHD), and language delay (Taige & others, 2007).

Might maternal depression also have an adverse effect on prenatal development and birth? A recent study revealed maternal depression was linked to preterm birth and slower prenatal growth rates (Diego & others, 2009). In this study, mothers who were depressed had elevated cortisol levels, which likely contributed to the negative outcomes for the fetus and newborn.

Paternal Factors   So far, we have discussed how characteristics of the mother—such as drug use, disease, diet and nutrition, age, and emotional states—can influence prenatal development and the development of the child. Might there also be some paternal risk factors? Indeed, there are several. Men's exposure to lead, radiation, certain pesticides, and petrochemicals may cause abnormalities in sperm that lead to miscarriage or diseases, such as childhood cancer (Cordier, 2008). The father's smoking during the mother's pregnancy also can cause problems for the offspring. In one study, heavy paternal smoking was associated with the risk of early pregnancy loss (Venners & others, 2004). This negative outcome may be related to secondhand smoke.

In one study, in China, the longer fathers smoked the greater the risk that their children would develop cancer (Ji & others, 1997). *What are some other paternal factors that can influence the development of the fetus and the child?*

PRENATAL CARE

Although prenatal care varies enormously, it usually involves a defined schedule of visits for medical care, which typically includes screening for manageable conditions and treatable diseases that can affect the baby or the mother (Lu & Lu, 2008). In addition to medical care, prenatal programs often include comprehensive educational, social, and nutritional services.

Does prenatal care matter? Information about pregnancy, labor, delivery, and caring for the newborn can be especially valuable for first-time mothers (Lowdermilk, Perry, & Cashion, 2010; Murray & McKinney, 2010). Prenatal care is also very important for women in poverty because it links them with other social services (Mattson & Smith, 2011; Perry & others, 2010).

An innovative program that is rapidly expanding in the United States is CenteringPregnancy (Steming, 2008). This program is relationship-centered and provides complete prenatal care in a group setting. CenteringPregnancy replaces traditional 15-minute physician visits with 90-minute peer group support settings and self-examination led by a physician or certified nurse-midwife. Groups of up to 10 women (and often their partners) meet regularly beginning at 12 to 16 weeks of pregnancy. The sessions emphasize empowering women to play an active role in experiencing a positive pregnancy. A recent study revealed that CenteringPregnancy groups made more prenatal visits, had higher breast feeding rates, and were more satisfied with their prenatal care than women in individual care (Klima & others, 2009).

Some prenatal programs for parents focus on home visitation (Eckenrode & others, 2010; Lee & others, 2009). Research evaluations indicate that the Nurse Family Partnership created by David Olds and his colleagues (2004, 2007) has been successful. The Nurse Family Partnership involves home visits by trained nurses beginning in the second or third trimester of prenatal development. The extensive program consists of approximately 50 home visits starting with the prenatal period and continuing through two years of age. The home visits focus on the mother's health, access to health care, parenting, and improvement of the mother's life by providing guidance in education, work, and relationships. Research revealed that the Nurse Family Partnership has numerous positive outcomes including fewer pregnancies, better work circumstances, and stability in relationship partners for the mother, and improved academic success and social development for the child (Olds & others, 2004, 2007). In another home visitation program, high-risk pregnant women and adolescents, many living in poverty conditions, were provided with biweekly home visitation services that encouraged healthy prenatal behavior, social support, and links to medical and other community services (Lee & others, 2009). Compared with a control group of pregnant women and adolescents who did not receive the home visits, the home visitation group gave birth to fewer low birth weight infants.

A Centering Pregnancy program in St. Louis Park, Minnesota. This rapidly expanding program alters routine prenatal care by bringing women out of exam rooms and into relationship-oriented groups.

Normal Prenatal Development Much of our discussion so far in this chapter has focused on what can go wrong with prenatal development. Prospective parents should take steps to avoid the vulnerabilities to fetal development that we have described. But it is important to keep in mind that most of the time, prenatal development does not go awry, and development occurs along the positive path that we described at the beginning of the chapter.

Review Connect Reflect

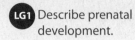 Describe prenatal development.

Review

- What is the course of prenatal development?
- What is teratology, and what are some of the main hazards to prenatal development?
- What are some good prenatal care strategies?
- Why is it important to take a positive approach to prenatal development?

Connect

- In Chapter 2, we discussed chromosomal and gene-linked abnormalities that can affect prenatal development. How are the symptoms of the related conditions or risks similar or different from those caused by teratogens or other hazards?

Reflect *Your Own Personal Journey of Life*

- If you are a woman, imagine that you have just found out that you are pregnant. What health-enhancing strategies will you follow during the prenatal period? For men, imagine that you are the partner of a woman who has just found out she is pregnant. What will be your role in increasing the likelihood that the prenatal period will go smoothly?

Birth LG2 Discuss the birth process.

The Birth Process   Assessing the Newborn   Preterm and Low Birth Weight Infants

Nature writes the basic script for how birth occurs, but parents make important choices about conditions surrounding birth. We look first at the sequence of physical steps that take place when a child is born.

THE BIRTH PROCESS

The birth process occurs in stages, occurs in different contexts, and in most cases involves one or more attendants.

Stages of Birth   The birth process occurs in three stages. The first stage is the longest of the three. Uterine contractions are 15 to 20 minutes apart at the beginning and last up to a minute each. These contractions cause the woman's cervix to stretch and open. As the first stage progresses, the contractions come closer together, appearing every two to five minutes. Their intensity increases. By the end of the first birth stage, contractions dilate the cervix to an opening of about 10 centimeters (4 inches), so that the baby can move from the uterus into the birth canal. For a woman having her first child, the first stage lasts an average of 6 to 12 hours; for subsequent children, this stage typically is much shorter.

The second birth stage begins when the baby's head starts to move through the cervix and the birth canal. It terminates when the baby emerges completely from the mother's body. With each contraction, the mother bears down hard to push the baby out of her body. By the time the baby's head is out of the mother's body, the contractions come almost every minute and last for about a minute each. This stage typically lasts approximately 45 minutes to an hour.

Afterbirth is the third stage, at which time the placenta, umbilical cord, and other membranes are detached and expelled. This final stage is the shortest of the three birth stages, lasting only minutes.

> There was a star danced, and under that I was born.
>
> —**William Shakespeare**
> *English Playwright, 17th Century*

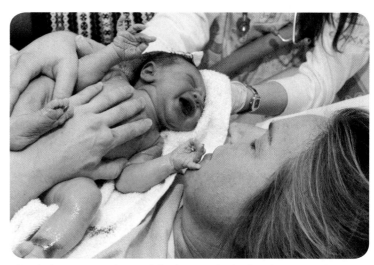

After the long journey of prenatal development, birth takes place. During birth the baby is on a threshold between two worlds. *What is the fetus/newborn transition like?*

Childbirth Setting and Attendants   In the United States, 99 percent of births take place in hospitals, a figure that has remained constant for several decades (Martin & others, 2005). The people who help a mother during birth vary across cultures. In U.S. hospitals, it has become the norm for fathers or birth coaches to be with the mother throughout labor and delivery. In the East African Nigoni culture, men are completely excluded from the childbirth process. When a woman is ready to give birth, female relatives move into the woman's hut and the husband leaves, taking his belongings (clothes, tools, weapons, and so on) with him. He is not permitted to return until after the baby is born. In some cultures, childbirth is an open, community affair. For example, in the Pukapukan culture in the Pacific Islands, women give birth in a shelter that is open for villagers to observe.

Midwives   Midwifery is practiced in most countries throughout the world (Wickham, 2009). In Holland, more than 40 percent of babies are delivered by midwives rather than doctors. However, in 2003, 91 percent of U.S. births were attended by physicians, and only 8 percent of women who delivered a baby were attended by a *midwife* (Martin & others, 2005). Nonetheless, the 8 percent figure in 2003 represents a substantial increase from less than 1 percent of U.S. women attended by a midwife in 1975 (Martin & others, 2005). Ninety-five percent of the midwives who delivered babies in the United States in 2003 were certified nurse-midwives.

Doulas   In some countries, a doula attends a childbearing woman. *Doula* is a Greek word that means "a woman who helps." A **doula** is a caregiver who provides continuous physical, emotional, and educational support for the mother before, during, and after childbirth. Doulas remain with the parents throughout labor, assessing and

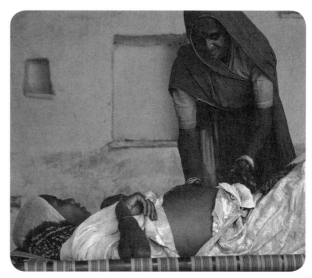

In India, a midwife checks on the size, position, and heartbeat of a fetus. Midwives deliver babies in many cultures around the world. *What are some cultural variations in prenatal care?*

afterbirth The third stage of birth, when the placenta, umbilical cord, and other membranes are detached and expelled.

doula A caregiver who provides continuous physical, emotional, and educational support for the mother before, during, and after childbirth.

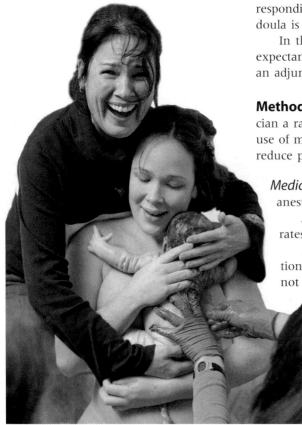

A doula assisting a birth. *What types of support do doulas provide?*

responding to the mother's needs. Researchers have found positive effects when a doula is present at the birth of a child (Berghella, Baxter, & Chauhan, 2008).

In the United States, most doulas work as independent providers hired by the expectant parents. Doulas typically function as part of a "birthing team," serving as an adjunct to the midwife or the hospital's obstetric staff.

Methods of Childbirth   U.S. hospitals often allow the mother and her obstetrician a range of options regarding their method of delivery. Key choices involve the use of medication, whether to use any of a number of nonmedicated techniques to reduce pain, and when to have a cesarean delivery.

Medication   Three basic kinds of drugs that are used for labor are analgesia, anesthesia, and oxytocin/pitocin.

Analgesia is used to relieve pain. Analgesics include tranquilizers, barbiturates, and narcotics (such as Demerol).

Anesthesia is used in late first-stage labor and during delivery to block sensation in an area of the body or to block consciousness. There is a trend toward not using general anesthesia, which blocks consciousness, in normal births because general anesthesia can be transmitted through the placenta to the fetus (Lieberman & others, 2005). An *epidural block* is regional anesthesia that numbs the woman's body from the waist down. Researchers are continuing to explore safer drug mixtures for use at lower doses to improve the effectiveness and safety of epidural anesthesia (Balaji, Dhillon, & Russell, 2009).

Oxytocin is a synthetic hormone that is used to stimulate contractions; pitocin is the most widely used oxytocin. The benefits and risks of oxytocin as a part of childbirth continue to be debated (Vasdev, 2008).

Predicting how a drug will affect an individual woman and her fetus is difficult (Lowdermilk, Perry, & Cashion, 2010; Smith, 2009). A particular drug might have only a minimal effect on one fetus yet have a much stronger effect on another. The drug's dosage also is a factor. Stronger doses of tranquilizers and narcotics given to decrease the mother's pain potentially have a more negative effect on the fetus than mild doses. It is important for the mother to assess her level of pain and have a voice in the decision of whether she should receive medication.

Natural and Prepared Childbirth   For a brief time not long ago, the idea of avoiding all medication during childbirth gained favor in the United States. Instead, many women chose to reduce the pain of childbirth through techniques known as natural childbirth and prepared childbirth. Today, at least some medication is used in the typical childbirth, but elements of natural childbirth and prepared childbirth remain popular (Oates & Abraham, 2010).

Natural childbirth is the method that aims to reduce the mother's pain by decreasing her fear through education about childbirth and by teaching her and her partner to use breathing methods and relaxation techniques during delivery.

French obstetrician Ferdinand Lamaze developed a method similar to natural childbirth that is known as **prepared childbirth,** or the Lamaze method. It includes a special breathing technique to control pushing in the final stages of labor, as well as more detailed education about anatomy and physiology. The Lamaze method has become very popular in the United States. The pregnant woman's partner usually serves as a coach who attends childbirth classes with her and helps her with her breathing and relaxation during delivery.

In sum, proponents of current prepared childbirth methods conclude that when information and support are provided, women *know* how to give birth. To read about one nurse whose research focuses on fatigue during childbearing and breathing exercises during labor, see the *Connecting With Careers* profile on Linda Pugh. And to read about the increased variety of techniques now being used to reduce stress and control pain during labor, see *Caring Connections*.

natural childbirth This method attempts to reduce the mother's pain by decreasing her fear through education about childbirth and relaxation techniques during delivery.

prepared childbirth Developed by French obstetrician Ferdinand Lamaze, this childbirth strategy is similar to natural childbirth but includes a special breathing technique to control pushing in the final stages of labor and a more detailed anatomy and physiology course.

Linda Pugh, Perinatal Nurse

Perinatal nurses work with childbearing women to support health and well-being during the childbearing experience. Linda Pugh, Ph.D., R.N.C., is a perinatal nurse on the faculty at The John Hopkins University School of Nursing. She is certified as an inpatient obstetric nurse and specializes in the care of women during labor and delivery. She teaches undergraduate and graduate students, educates professional nurses, and conducts research. In addition, Pugh consults with hospitals and organizations about women's health issues and topics we discuss in this chapter.

Her research interests include nursing interventions with low-income breast feeding women, discovering ways to prevent and ameliorate fatigue during childbearing, and using breathing exercises during labor.

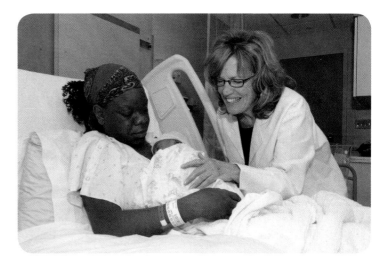

Linda Pugh (*right*) with a new mother and baby.

From Waterbirth to Music Therapy

The effort to reduce stress and control pain during labor has recently led to an increase in the use of some older and some newer nonmedicated techniques (Field, 2007; Kalder & others, 2010; Moleti, 2009; Simkin & Bolding, 2004). These include waterbirth, massage, acupuncture, hypnosis, and music therapy.

Waterbirth

Waterbirth involves giving birth in a tub of warm water. Some women go through labor in the water and get out for delivery; others remain in the water for delivery. The rationale for waterbirth is that the baby has been in an amniotic sac for many months and that delivery in a similar environment is likely to be less stressful for the baby and the mother (Meyer, Weible, & Woeber, 2010). Mothers get into the warm water when contractions become closer together and more intense. Getting into the water too soon can cause labor to slow or stop. Reviews of research have indicated mixed results for waterbirths (Cluett & Burns, 2009; Pinette, Wax, & Wilson, 2004; Thöni & Moroder, 2004). Waterbirth has been practiced more often in European countries such as Switzerland and Sweden in recent decades than in the United States, but it is increasingly being included in U.S. birth plans.

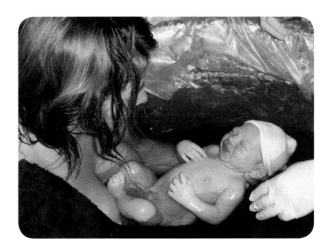

What characterizes the use of waterbirth in delivering a baby?

Massage

Massage is increasingly used prior to and during delivery (Field, 2007; Kimber & others, 2008; Stager 2009–2010). Researchers have found that

(continued)

caring *connections*

(continued)

massage can reduce pain and anxiety during labor (Chang, Chen, & Huang, 2006). A recent study revealed that massage therapy reduced pain during labor and delivery and alleviated prenatal depression in both parents while improving their relationship (Field & others, 2008).

Acupuncture

Acupuncture, the insertion of very fine needles into specific locations in the body, is used as a standard procedure to reduce the pain of childbirth in China, although only recently has it begun to be used in the United States for this purpose (Moleti, 2009). One study revealed that acupuncture resulted in less time spent in labor and a reduction in the need for oxytocin to augment labor (Gaudernack, Forbord, & Hole, 2006).

Hypnosis

Hypnosis, the induction of a psychological state of altered attention and awareness in which the individual is unusually responsive to suggestions, is also increasingly being used during childbirth (Wilcox, 2010). Some studies have indicated positive effects of hypnosis for reducing pain during childbirth (Abasi & others, 2009; Barabasz & Perez, 2007).

Music Therapy

Music therapy during childbirth, which involves the use of music to reduce stress and manage pain, is becoming more prevalent (Tagore, 2009). More research is needed to determine its effectiveness (Laopaiboon & others, 2009).

What are some reasons that natural childbirth methods such as these might be chosen instead of the use of medication?

What characterizes the transition from fetus to newborn?

Cesarean Delivery   Normally, the baby's head comes through the vagina first. But if the baby is in a **breech position,** the baby's buttocks are the first part to emerge from the vagina. In 1 of every 25 deliveries, the baby's head is still in the uterus when the rest of the body is out. Breech births can cause respiratory problems. As a result, if the baby is in a breech position, a surgical procedure known as a cesarean section, or a cesarean delivery, is usually performed. In a **cesarean delivery,** the baby is removed from the mother's uterus through an incision made in her abdomen (Lee, El-Sayed, & Gould, 2008). The benefits and risks of cesarean sections continue to be debated (Bangdiwala & others, 2010).

ASSESSING THE NEWBORN

Almost immediately after birth, after the baby and its parents have been introduced, a newborn is taken to be weighed, cleaned up, and tested for signs of developmental problems that might require urgent attention (Als & Butler, 2008; Therrells & others, 2010). The **Apgar Scale** is widely used to assess the health of newborns at one and five minutes after birth. The Apgar Scale evaluates infants' heart rate, respiratory effort, muscle tone, body color, and reflex irritability. An obstetrician or a nurse does the evaluation and gives the newborn a score, or reading, of 0, 1, or 2 on each of these five health signs (see Figure 3.6). A total score of 7 to 10 indicates that the newborn's condition is good. A score of 5 indicates there may be

Score	0	1	2
Heart rate	Absent	Slow—less than 100 beats per minute	Fast—100–140 beats per minute
Respiratory effort	No breathing for more than one minute	Irregular and slow	Good breathing with normal crying
Muscle tone	Limp and flaccid	Weak, inactive, but some flexion of extremities	Strong, active motion
Body color	Blue and pale	Body pink, but extremities blue	Entire body pink
Reflex irritability	No response	Grimace	Coughing, sneezing and crying

FIGURE **3.6**

THE APGAR SCALE. A newborn's score on the Apgar Scale indicates whether the baby has urgent medical problems. *What are some trends in the Apgar scores of U.S. babies?*

developmental difficulties. A score of 3 or below signals an emergency and indicates that the baby might not survive.

The Apgar Scale is especially good at assessing the newborn's ability to cope with the stress of delivery and the new environment (Oberlander & others, 2008; Reynolds & others, 2010). It also identifies high-risk infants who need resuscitation. For a more thorough assessment of the newborn, the Brazelton Neonatal Behavioral Assessment Scale or the Neonatal Intensive Care Unit Network Neurobehavioral Scale may be used.

The **Brazelton Neonatal Behavioral Assessment Scale (NBAS)** is typically performed within 24 to 36 hours after birth. It is also used as a sensitive index of neurological competence up to one month after birth for typical infants and as a measure in many studies of infant development (Mamtani, Patel, & Kulkarni, 2008). The NBAS assesses the newborn's neurological development, reflexes, and reactions to people and objects. Sixteen reflexes, such as sneezing, blinking, and rooting, are assessed, along with reactions to animate stimuli (such as a face and voice) and inanimate stimuli (such as a rattle). (We will have more to say about reflexes in Chapter 4, when we discuss motor development in infancy.)

An "offspring" of the NBAS, the **Neonatal Intensive Care Unit Network Neurobehavioral Scale (NNNS)** provides another assessment of the newborn's behavior, neurological and stress responses, and regulatory capacities (Brazelton, 2004; Lester, Tronick, & Brazelton, 2004). Whereas the NBAS was developed to assess normal, healthy, full-term infants, T. Berry Brazelton, along with Barry Lester and Edward Tronick, developed the NNNS to assess the "at-risk" infant. It is especially useful for evaluating preterm infants (although it may not be appropriate for those of less than 30 weeks' gestational age) and substance-exposed infants (Boukydis & Lester, 2008). A recent NNNS assessment (at one month of age) of preterm infants who were exposed to substance abuse prenatally revealed that the NNNS predicted

breech position The baby's position in the uterus that causes the buttocks to be the first part to emerge from the vagina.

cesarean delivery Removal of the baby from the mother's uterus through an incision made in her abdomen.

Apgar Scale A widely used method to assess the health of newborns at one and five minutes after birth. The Apgar Scale evaluates infants' heart rate, respiratory effort, muscle tone, body color, and reflex irritability.

Brazelton Neonatal Behavioral Assessment Scale (NBAS) A measure that is used in the first month of life to assess the newborn's neurological development, reflexes, and reactions to people and objects.

Neonatal Intensive Care Unit Network Neurobehavioral Scale (NNNS) An "offspring" of the NBAS, the NNNS provides an assessment of the "at-risk" newborn's behavior, neurological and stress responses, and regulatory capacities.

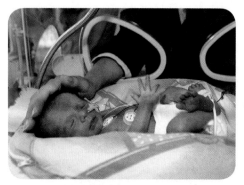

A "kilogram kid," weighing less than 2.3 pounds at birth. *What are some long-term outcomes for weighing so little at birth?*

certain developmental outcomes, such as neurological difficulties, IQ, and school readiness at 4.5 years of age (Liu & others, 2010).

PRETERM AND LOW BIRTH WEIGHT INFANTS

Different conditions that pose threats for newborns have been given different labels. We will examine these conditions and discuss interventions for improving outcomes of preterm infants.

Preterm and Small for Date Infants   Three related conditions pose threats to many newborns: low birth weight, preterm delivery, and being small for date. **Low birth weight infants** weigh less than 5½ pounds at birth. *Very low birth weight* newborns weigh under 3½ pounds, and *extremely low birth weight* newborns weigh under 2 pounds. **Preterm infants** are those born three weeks or more before the pregnancy has reached its full term—in other words, before the completion of 37 weeks of gestation (the time between fertilization and birth). **Small for date infants** (also called *small for gestational age infants*) are those whose birth weight is below normal when the length of the pregnancy is considered. They weigh less than 90 percent of all babies of the same gestational age. Small for date infants may be preterm or full term. One study found that small for date infants had more than a fourfold increased risk of death (Regev & others, 2003).

In 2006, 12.8 percent of U.S. infants were born preterm—a 36 percent increase since the 1980s (National Center for Health Statistics, 2008). The increase in preterm birth is likely due to several factors, including the increasing number of births to women 35 years and older, increasing rates of multiple births, increased management of maternal and fetal conditions (for example, inducing labor preterm if medical technology indicates it will increase the likelihood of survival), increased substance abuse (tobacco, alcohol), and increased stress (Goldenberg & Culhane, 2007). Ethnic variations characterize preterm birth (Balchin & Steer, 2007). For example, in 2006, the likelihood of being born preterm was 12.8 percent for all U.S. infants, but the rate was 18.5 percent for African American infants (National Center for Health Statistics, 2009).

Recently, there has been considerable interest in exploring the role that progestin might play in reducing preterm births (O'Brien & Lewis, 2009). Recent research reviews indicate that progestin is most effective in reducing preterm births when it is administered to women with a history of a previous spontaneous birth at less than 37 weeks (da Fonseca & others, 2009), to women who have a short cervical length of 15 mm or less (da Fonseca & others, 2009), and to women pregnant with a singleton rather than twins (Norman & others, 2009; Rode & others, 2009).

Might exercise during pregnancy reduce the likelihood of preterm birth? A recent study found that compared to sedentary pregnant women, women who engaged in light leisure time physical activity had a 24 percent reduced likelihood of preterm delivery, and those who participated in moderate to heavy leisure time physical activity had a 66 percent reduced risk of preterm delivery (Hegaard & others, 2008). Researchers also have found that yoga is positively linked to pregnancy outcomes (Narendran & others, 2005).

The incidence of low birth weight varies considerably from country to country. To read about cross-cultural variations in low birth weight, see *Connecting With Diversity*.

Consequences of Preterm Birth and Low Birth Weight   Although most preterm and low birth weight infants are healthy, as a group they experience more health and developmental problems than infants of normal birth weight (Minde & Zelkowitz, 2008). For preterm birth, the terms *extremely preterm* and *very preterm* are increasingly used (Smith, 2009). *Extremely preterm infants* are those born before the 28th week of pregnancy, and *very preterm infants* are those born before 33 weeks of

low birth weight infant Infant that weighs less than 5½ pounds at birth.

preterm infants Those born before the completion of 37 weeks of gestation (the time between fertilization and birth).

small for date infants Also called small for gestational age infants, these infants have birth weights that are below normal when the length of pregnancy is considered. Small for date infants may be preterm or full term.

kangaroo care Treatment for preterm infants that involves skin-to-skin contact.

Cross-Cultural Variations in the Incidence and Causes of Low Birth Weight

In some countries, such as India and Sudan, where poverty is rampant and the health and nutrition of mothers are poor, the percentage of low birth weight babies reaches as high as 31 percent (see Figure 3.7). In the United States, there has been an increase in low birth weight infants in the last two decades. The U.S. low birth weight rate of 8 percent in 2004 is considerably higher than that of many other developed countries (Hoyert & others, 2006). For example, only 4 percent of the infants born in Sweden, Finland, Norway, and Korea are low birth weight, and only 5 percent of those born in New Zealand, Australia, and France are low birth weight.

In both developed and developing countries, adolescents who give birth when their bodies have not fully matured are at risk for having low birth weight babies (Malamitsi-Puchner & Boutsikou, 2006). In the United States, the increase in the number of low birth weight infants has been attributed to drug use, poor nutrition, multiple births, reproductive technologies, and improved technology and prenatal care that result in more high-risk babies surviving (Chen & others, 2007). Nonetheless, poverty continues to be a major factor is preterm birth in the United States. Women living in poverty are more likely to be obese, have diabetes and hypertension, smoke cigarettes, and use illicit drugs, and they are less likely to receive regular prenatal care (Goldenberg & Nagahawatte, 2008).

In the preceding sentence, we learned that women living in poverty are less likely to receive regular prenatal care. *What did you learn earlier in the chapter about the benefits of regular prenatal care? Aside from women living in poverty, which other demographic group is not likely to receive adequate prenatal care?*

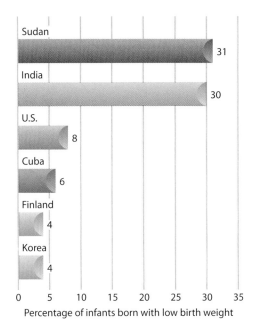

FIGURE 3.7

PERCENTAGE OF INFANTS BORN WITH LOW BIRTH WEIGHT IN SELECTED COUNTRIES

gestational age. Figure 3.8 shows the results of a recent Norwegian study indicating that the earlier preterm infants are born, the more likely they are to drop out of school (Swamy, Ostbye, & Skjaerven, 2008).

The number and severity of these problems increase when infants are born very early and as their birth weight decreases. Survival rates for infants who are born very early and very small have risen, but with this improved survival rate have come increases in rates of severe brain damage (Casey, 2008). Children born at low birth weights are more likely than their normal birth weight counterparts to develop a learning disability, attention deficit hyperactivity disorder, or breathing problem such as asthma (Espirito Santo, Portuguez, & Nunes, 2009). Approximately 50 percent of all low birth weight children are enrolled in special education programs.

Nurturing Low Birth Weight and Preterm Infants Two increasingly used interventions in the neonatal intensive care unit (NICU) are kangaroo care and massage therapy. **Kangaroo care** involves skin-to-skin contact in which the baby, wearing only a diaper, is held upright against the parent's bare chest, much as a baby kangaroo is carried inside its mother's pouch. Kangaroo care is typically practiced for two to three hours per day, skin-to-skin, over an extended time in early infancy.

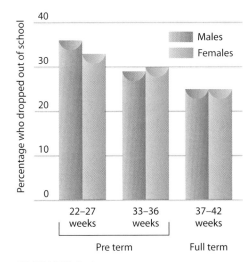

FIGURE 3.8

PERCENTAGE OF PRETERM AND FULL-TERM BIRTH INFANTS WHO DROPPED OUT OF SCHOOL

A new mother practicing kangaroo care. *What is kangaroo care?*

Why use kangaroo care with preterm infants? Preterm infants often have difficulty coordinating their breathing and heart rate, and the close physical contact with the parent provided by kangaroo care can help to stabilize the preterm infant's heartbeat, temperature, and breathing (Begum & others, 2008; Ludington-Hoe & Others, 2006; Nyqvist & others, 2010). Preterm infants who experience kangaroo care also gain more weight than their counterparts who are not given this care (Gathwala, Singh, & Balhara, 2008). A recent study also revealed that kangaroo care decreased pain responses in preterm infants (Johnston & others, 2009).

Many adults will attest to the therapeutic effects of receiving a massage. In fact, many will pay a premium to receive one at a spa on a regular basis. But can massage play a role in improving developmental outcomes for preterm infants? To find out, see *Connecting Through Research*.

connecting through research

How Does Massage Therapy Affect the Mood and Behavior of Babies?

Throughout history and in many cultures, caregivers have massaged infants. In Africa and Asia, infants are routinely massaged by parents or other family members for several months after birth. In the United States, interest in using touch and massage to improve the growth, health, and well-being of infants has been stimulated by the research of Tiffany Field (2001, 2007; Diego, Field, & Hernandez-Reif, 2008; Field, Diego, & Hernandez-Reif, 2008, 2010; Field & others, 2006; Hernandez-Reif, Diego, & Field, 2007), director of the Touch Research Institute at the University of Miami School of Medicine.

In a recent study, preterm infants in a neonatal intensive care unit (NICU) were randomly assigned to a massage therapy group or a con-

trol group (Hernandez-Reif, Diego, & Field, 2007). For five consecutive days, the preterm infants in the massage group were given three 15-minute moderate pressure massages. Behavioral observations of the following stress behaviors were made on the first and last days of the study: crying, grimacing, yawning, sneezing, jerky arm and leg movements, startles, and finger flaring. The various stress behaviors were summarized in a composite stress behavior index. As indicated in Figure 3.9, massage had a stress-reducing effect on the preterm infants,

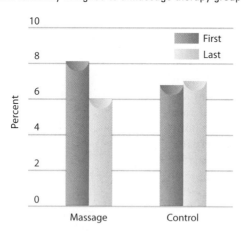

FIGURE **3.9**

PRETERM INFANTS SHOW REDUCED STRESS BEHAVIORS AND ACTIVITY AFTER FIVE DAYS OF MASSAGE THERAPY (HERNANDEZ-REIF, DIEGO, & FIELD, 2007)

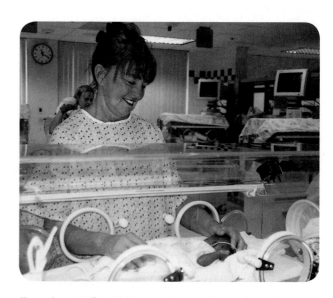

Shown here is Tiffany Field massaging a newborn infant. *What types of infants has massage therapy been shown to help?*

(continued)

(continued)

which is especially important because they encounter numerous stressors while they are hospitalized.

In another study, Field and her colleagues (2004) tested a more cost-effective massage strategy. They taught mothers how to massage their full-term infants rather than having health-care professionals do the massage. Beginning from day one of the newborn's life to the end of the first month, once a day before bedtime the mothers massaged the babies using either light or moderate pressure. Infants who were massaged with moderate pressure gained more weight, performed better on the orientation scale of the Brazelton, were less excitable and less depressed, and were less agitated during sleep.

Field has demonstrated the benefits of massage therapy for infants who face a variety of problems. For example, preterm infants exposed to cocaine in utero who received massage therapy gained weight and improved their scores on developmental tests (Wheeden & others, 1993). Another study investigated 1- to 3-month-old infants born to de-

pressed adolescent mothers (Field & others, 1996). The infants of depressed mothers who received massage therapy had lower stress—as well as improved emotionality, sociability, and soothability—compared with the nonmassaged infants of depressed mothers.

In a research review of massage therapy with preterm infants, Field and her colleagues (2004) concluded that the most consistent findings involve two positive results: (1) increased weight gain and (2) discharge from the hospital from three to six days earlier.

Infants are not the only ones who may benefit from massage therapy (Field, 2007). In other studies, Field and her colleagues have demonstrated the benefits of massage therapy with women in reducing labor pain (Field, Hernandez-Reif, Taylor, & others, 1997), with children who have asthma (Field, Henteleff, & others, 1998), with autistic children's attentiveness (Field, Lasko, & others, 1997), and with adolescents who have attention deficit hyperactivity disorder (Field, Quintino, & others, 1998).

Review Connect Reflect

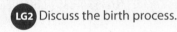 **LG2** Discuss the birth process.

Review

- What are the three main stages of birth? What are some different birth strategies? What is the transition from fetus to newborn like for the infant?
- What are three measures of neonatal health and responsiveness?
- What are the outcomes for children if they are born preterm or with a low birth weight?

Connect

- What correlations have been found between birth weight and country of birth, and what might the causes be?

Reflect *Your Own Personal Journey of Life*

- If you are a female who would like to have a baby, which birth strategy do you prefer? Why? If you are a male, how involved would you want to be in helping your partner through the birth of your baby? Explain.

The Postpartum Period

 LG3 Explain the changes that take place in the postpartum period.

| Physical Adjustments | Emotional and Psychological Adjustments | Bonding |

The weeks after childbirth present challenges for many new parents and their offspring. This is the **postpartum period,** the period after childbirth or delivery that lasts for about six weeks or until the mother's body has completed its adjustment and has returned to a nearly prepregnant state. It is a time when the woman adjusts, both physically and psychologically, to the process of childbearing.

postpartum period The period after childbirth when the mother adjusts, both physically and psychologically, to the process of childbirth. This period lasts about six weeks or until her body has completed its adjustment and returned to a near prepregnant state.

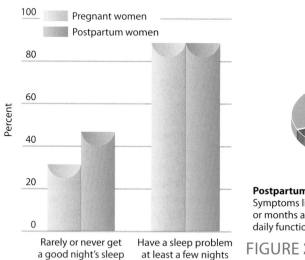

FIGURE **3.10**

SLEEP DEPRIVATION IN PREGNANT AND POSTPARTUM WOMEN

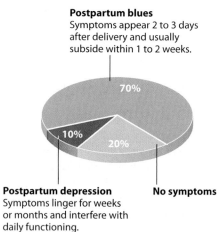

Postpartum blues
Symptoms appear 2 to 3 days after delivery and usually subside within 1 to 2 weeks.

Postpartum depression
Symptoms linger for weeks or months and interfere with daily functioning.

No symptoms

FIGURE **3.11**

POSTPARTUM BLUES AND POSTPARTUM DEPRESSION AMONG U.S. WOMEN. Some health professionals refer to the postpartum period as the "fourth trimester." Though the time span of the postpartum period does not necessarily cover three months, the term "fourth trimester" suggests continuity and the importance of the first several months after birth for the mother.

The postpartum period involves a great deal of adjustment and adaptation. The adjustments needed are physical, emotional, and psychological.

PHYSICAL ADJUSTMENTS

A woman's body makes numerous physical adjustments in the first days and weeks after childbirth (Smith, 2009). She may have a great deal of energy or feel exhausted and let down. Though these changes are normal, the fatigue can undermine the new mother's sense of well-being and confidence in her ability to cope with a new baby and a new family life (Runquist, 2007).

A concern is the loss of sleep that the primary caregiver experiences in the postpartum period (Gunderson & others, 2008). In the 2007 Sleep in America survey, a substantial percentage of women reported loss of sleep during pregnancy and in the postpartum period (National Sleep Foundation, 2007) (see Figure 3.10). The loss of sleep can contribute to stress, marital conflict, and impaired decision making (Meerlo, Sgoifo, & Suchecki, 2008).

After delivery, a mother's body undergoes sudden and dramatic changes in hormone production. When the placenta is delivered, estrogen and progesterone levels drop steeply and remain low until the ovaries start producing hormones again.

Involution is the process by which the uterus returns to its prepregnant size five or six weeks after birth. Immediately following birth, the uterus weighs 2 to 3 pounds. By the end of five or six weeks, the uterus weighs 2 to 3½ ounces. Nursing the baby helps contract the uterus at a rapid rate.

EMOTIONAL AND PSYCHOLOGICAL ADJUSTMENTS

Emotional fluctuations are common for mothers in the postpartum period. For some women, emotional fluctuations decrease within several weeks after the delivery, but other women experience more long-lasting mood swings.

As shown in Figure 3.11, about 70 percent of new mothers in the United States have what are called the postpartum blues. About two to three days after birth, they begin to feel depressed, anxious, and upset. These feelings may come and go for

postpartum depression Characteristic of women who have such strong feelings of sadness, anxiety, or despair that they have trouble coping with daily tasks during the postpartum period.

Diane Sanford, Clinical Psychologist and Postpartum Expert

Diane Sanford has a doctorate in clinical psychologist, and for many years she had a private practice that focused on marital and family relationships. But after she began collaborating with a psychiatrist whose clients included women with postpartum depression, Dr. Sanford, together with a women's health nurse, founded Women's Healthcare Partnership in St. Louis, Missouri, which specializes in women's adjustment during the postpartum period. Subsequently, they added a marriage and family relationships counselor and a social worker to their staff, and then later hired nurse educators, a dietician, and a fitness expert as consultants (Clay, 2001).

For more information about what clinical psychologists do, see page 45 in the Careers in Child Development appendix following Chapter 1.

Diane Sanford holding an infant of one of the mothers who comes to her for help in coping with postpartum issues.

several months after the birth, often peaking about three to five days after birth. Even without treatment, these feelings usually go away after one or two weeks.

However, some women develop **postpartum depression,** which involves a major depressive episode that typically occurs about four weeks after delivery. In other words, women with postpartum depression have such strong feelings of sadness, anxiety, or despair that for at least a two-week period they have trouble coping with their daily tasks. Without treatment, postpartum depression may become worse and last for many months (Nolen-Hoeksema, 2011). And many women with postpartum treatment don't seek help. For example, one recent study found that 15 percent of the women reported postpartum depression symptoms but less than half sought help (McGarry & others, 2009). Estimates indicate that 10 to 14 percent of new mothers experience postpartum depression.

Several antidepressant drugs are effective in treating postpartum depression and appear to be safe for breast feeding women (Logsdon, Wisner, & Hanusa, 2009). Psychotherapy, especially cognitive therapy, also is an effective treatment of postpartum depression for many women (Beck, 2006). Also, engaging in regular exercise may help in treating postpartum depression (Daley, Macarthur, & Winter, 2007).

Can a mother's postpartum depression affect the way she interacts with her infant? A recent research review concluded that the interaction difficulties of depressed mothers and their infants occur across cultures and socioeconomic status groups, and encompass less sensitivity of the mothers and less responsiveness on the part of their infants (Field, 2010). Several caregiving activities also are compromised, including feeding (especially breast feeding), sleep routines, and safety practices. To read about one individual who specializes in women's adjustment during the postpartum period, see *Connecting With Careers.*

Fathers also undergo considerable adjustment during the postpartum period, even when they work away from home all day. Many fathers feel that the baby

The postpartum period is a time of considerable adjustment and adaptation for both the mother and the father. Fathers can provide an important support system for mothers, especially in helping mothers care for young infants. *What kinds of tasks might the father of a newborn do to support the mother?*

A mother bonds with her infant moments after it is born. *How critical is bonding for the development of social competence later in childhood?*

developmental **connection**

Theories. Lorenz demonstrated the importance of bonding in graylag geese, but the first few days of life are unlikely to be a critical period for bonding in human infants. Chapter 1, p. 28

bonding The formation of a close connection, especially a physical bond, between parents and their newborn in the period shortly after birth.

comes first and gets all of the mother's attention; some feel that they have been replaced by the baby.

The father's support and caring can play a role in whether the mother develops postpartum depression (Dietz & others, 2009; Gao, Chan, & Mao, 2009). A recent study revealed that higher support by fathers was related to lower incidence of postpartum depression in women (Smith & Howard, 2008).

BONDING

A special component of the parent-infant relationship is **bonding,** the formation of a connection, especially a physical bond between parents and the newborn in the period shortly after birth. Sometimes hospitals seem determined to deter bonding. Drugs given to the mother to make her delivery less painful can make the mother drowsy, interfering with her ability to respond to and stimulate the newborn. Mothers and newborns are often separated shortly after delivery, and preterm infants are isolated from their mothers even more than full-term infants.

Do these practices do any harm? Some physicians believe that during the period shortly after birth, the parents and newborn need to form an emotional attachment as a foundation for optimal development in the years to come (Kennell, 2006; Kennell & McGrath, 1999). Is there evidence that close contact between mothers and infants in the first several days after birth is critical for optimal development later in life? Although some research supports this bonding hypothesis (Klaus & Kennell, 1976), a body of research challenges the significance of the first few days of life as a critical period (Bakeman & Brown, 1980; Rode & others, 1981). Indeed, the extreme form of the bonding hypothesis—that the newborn must have close contact with the mother in the first few days of life to develop optimally—simply is not true.

Nonetheless, the weakness of the bonding hypothesis should not be used as an excuse to keep motivated mothers from interacting with their newborns. Such contact brings pleasure to many mothers. In some mother-infant pairs—including preterm infants, adolescent mothers, and mothers from disadvantaged circumstances—early close contact may establish a climate for improved interaction after the mother and infant leave the hospital.

Many hospitals now offer a *rooming-in* arrangement, in which the baby remains in the mother's room most of the time during its hospital stay. However, if parents choose not to use this rooming-in arrangement, the weight of the research suggests that this decision will not harm the infant emotionally (Lamb, 1994).

Review Connect Reflect

LG3 Explain the changes that take place in the postpartum period.

Review

- What does the postpartum period involve? What physical adjustments does the woman's body make during this period?
- What emotional and psychological adjustments characterize the postpartum period?
- Is bonding critical for optimal development?

Connect

- How can exercise help pregnant women before delivery and women with postpartum depression after giving birth?

Reflect *Your Own Personal Journey of Life*

- If you are a female who plans to have children, what can you do to adjust effectively in the postpartum period? If you are the partner of a new mother, what can you do to help in the postpartum period?

Prenatal Development and Birth

Prenatal Development

LG1 Describe prenatal development.

The Course of Prenatal Development

- Prenatal development is divided into three periods: germinal (conception until 10 to 14 days later), which ends when the zygote (a fertilized egg) attaches to the uterine wall; embryonic (two to eight weeks after conception), during which the embryo differentiates into three layers, life-support systems develop, and organ systems form (organogenesis); and fetal (two months after conception until about nine months, or when the infant is born), a time when organ systems have matured to the point at which life can be sustained outside of the womb. The growth of the brain during prenatal development is nothing short of remarkable. By the time babies are born they have approximately 100 billion neurons, or nerve cells. Neurogenesis is the term that means the formation of new neurons. The nervous system begins with the formation of a neural tube at 18 to 24 days after conception. Proliferation and migration are two processes that characterize brain development in the prenatal period. The basic architecture of the brain is formed in the first two trimesters of prenatal development.

Teratology and Hazards to Prenatal Development

- Teratology is the field that investigates the causes of congenital (birth) defects. Any agent that causes birth defects is called a teratogen. The dose, genetic susceptibility, and time of exposure influence the severity of the damage to an unborn child and the type of defect that occurs. Prescription drugs that can be harmful include antibiotics, some antidepressants, certain hormones, and Accutane. Nonprescription drugs that can be harmful include diet pills and aspirin. Legal psychoactive drugs that are potentially harmful to prenatal development include caffeine, alcohol, and nicotine. Fetal alcohol spectrum disorders are a cluster of abnormalities that appear in offspring of mothers who drink heavily during pregnancy. Even when pregnant women drink moderately (one to two drinks a few days a week), negative effects on their offspring have been found. Cigarette smoking by pregnant women has serious adverse effects on prenatal and child development (such as low birth weight). Illegal psychoactive drugs that are potentially harmful to offspring include methamphetamine, marijuana, cocaine, and heroin. Incompatibility of the mother's and the father's blood types can also be harmful to the fetus. Environmental hazards include radiation, environmental pollutants, and toxic wastes. Syphilis, rubella (German measles), genital herpes, and AIDS are infectious diseases that can harm the fetus. Other parental factors include maternal diet and nutrition, age, emotional states and stress, and paternal factors. A developing fetus depends entirely on its mother for nutrition. Maternal age can negatively affect the offspring's development if the mother is an adolescent or over 35. High stress in the mother is linked with less than optimal prenatal and birth outcomes. Paternal factors that can adversely affect prenatal development include exposure to lead, radiation, certain pesticides, and petrochemicals.

Prenatal Care

- Prenatal care varies extensively but usually involves medical care services with a defined schedule of visits.

Normal Prenatal Development

- It is important to remember that, although things can and do go wrong during pregnancy, most of the time pregnancy and prenatal development go well.

Birth

LG2 Discuss the birth process.

The Birth Process

- Childbirth occurs in three stages. The first stage, which lasts about 6 to 12 hours for a woman having her first child, is the longest stage. The cervix dilates to about 10 centimeters (4 inches) at the end of the first stage. The second stage begins when the baby's head starts to move through the cervix and ends with the baby's complete emergence. The third stage involves the delivery of the placenta after birth. Childbirth strategies involve the childbirth setting and attendants. In many countries, a doula attends a childbearing woman. Methods of delivery include medicated, natural or prepared, and cesarean. Being born involves considerable stress for the baby, but the baby is well prepared and adapted to handle the stress. Anoxia—insufficient oxygen supply to the fetus/newborn—is a potential hazard.

Assessing the Newborn

- For many years, the Apgar Scale has been used to assess the health of newborn babies. The Brazelton Neonatal Behavioral Assessment Scale (NBAS) examines the newborn's neurological development, reflexes, and reactions to people. Recently, the Neonatal Intensive Care Unit Network Neurobehavioral Scale (NNNS) was created to assess at-risk infants.

Preterm and Low Birth Weight Infants

- Low birth weight infants weigh less than 5½ pounds, and they may be preterm (born before the completion of 37 weeks of gestation) or small for date (also called small for gestational age), which refers to infants whose birth weight is below normal when the length of pregnancy is considered. Small for date infants may be preterm or full term. Although most low birth weight and preterm infants are normal and healthy, as a group they experience more illness and developmental problems than normal birth weight infants. Kangaroo care and massage therapy have been shown to have benefits for preterm infants.

The Postpartum Period

 LG3 Explain the changes that take place in the postpartum period.

Physical Adjustments

- The postpartum period is the period after childbirth or delivery. The period lasts for about six weeks or until the woman's body has completed its adjustment. Physical adjustments in the postpartum period include fatigue, involution (the process by which the uterus returns to its prepregnant size five or six weeks after birth), and hormonal changes.

Emotional and Psychological Adjustments

- Emotional fluctuations on the part of the mother are common in this period, and they can vary greatly from one mother to the next. Postpartum depression characterizes women who have such strong feelings of sadness, anxiety, or despair that they have trouble coping with daily tasks in the postpartum period. Postpartum depression occurs in about 10 percent of new mothers. The father also goes through a postpartum adjustment.

Bonding

- Bonding is the formation of a close connection, especially a physical bond, between parents and the newborn shortly after birth. Early bonding has not been found to be critical in the development of a competent infant.

key terms

germinal period 78
blastocyst 78
trophoblast 78
embryonic period 78
amnion 79
umbilical cord 79
placenta 79
organogenesis 79
fetal period 80

neurons 81
teratogen 82
fetal alcohol spectrum
　disorders (FASD) 84
afterbirth 91
doula 91
natural childbirth 92
prepared childbirth 92
breech position 94

cesarean delivery 94
Apgar Scale 94
Brazelton Neonatal
　Behavioral Assessment
　Scale (NBAS) 95
Neonatal Intensive
　Care Unit Network
　Neurobehavioral Scale
　(NNNS) 95

low birth weight infants 96
preterm infants 96
small for date infants 96
kangaroo care 97
postpartum period 99
postpartum depression 101
bonding 102

key people

David Olds 89　　　　　Ferdinand Lamaze 92　　　　　T. Berry Brazelton 95　　　　　Tiffany Field 99

chapter 4

PHYSICAL DEVELOPMENT AND HEALTH

Angie, an elementary-school-aged girl, provided the following comments about losing weight:

When I was eight years old, I weighed 125 pounds. My clothes were the size that large teenage girls wear. I hated my body and my classmates teased me all the time. I was so overweight and out of shape that when I took a P.E. class my face would get red and I had trouble breathing. I was jealous of the kids who played sports and weren't overweight like I was.

I'm nine years old now and I've lost 30 pounds. I'm much happier and proud of myself. How did I lose the weight? My mom said she had finally decided enough was enough. She took me to a pediatrician who specializes in helping children lose weight and keep it off. The pediatrician counseled my mom about my eating and exercise habits, then had us join a group that he had created for overweight children and their parents. My mom and I go to the group once a week and we've now been participating in the program for six months. I no longer eat fast food meals and my mom is cooking more healthy meals. Now that I've lost weight, exercise is not as hard for me and I don't get teased by the kids at school. My mom's pretty happy too because she's lost 15 pounds herself since we've been in the counseling program.

Not all overweight children are as successful as Angie at reducing their weight. Indeed, being overweight in childhood has become a major national concern in the United States (Insel & Roth, 2010; Wardlaw & Smith, 2008). Later in the chapter, we will explore the causes and consequences of being overweight in childhood.

preview

Think about how much you changed physically as you grew up. You came into this life as a small being but grew very rapidly in infancy, more slowly in childhood, and once again more rapidly during puberty. In this chapter, we will explore changes in body growth, the brain, and sleep. We also will examine aspects of children's health.

Body Growth and Change **LG1** Discuss developmental changes in the body.

| Patterns of Growth | Infancy and Childhood | Adolescence |

In the journey of childhood, we go through many bodily changes. Let's begin by studying some basic patterns of growth and then turn to the bodily changes that occur from infancy through adolescence.

PATTERNS OF GROWTH

During prenatal development and early infancy, the head constitutes an extraordinarily large portion of the total body (see Figure 4.1). Gradually, the body's proportions change. Why? Growth is not random. Instead, it generally follows two patterns: the cephalocaudal pattern and the proximodistal pattern.

The **cephalocaudal pattern** is the sequence in which the fastest growth always occurs at the top—the head. Physical growth in size, weight, and feature differentiation gradually works its way down from the top to the bottom—for example, from neck to shoulders, to middle trunk, and so on. This same pattern occurs in the head area; the top parts of the head—the eyes and brain—grow faster than the lower parts, such as the jaw.

Sensory and motor development also generally proceed according to the cephalocaudal principle. For example, infants see objects before they can control

cephalocaudal pattern The sequence in which the fastest growth occurs at the top of the body—the head—with physical growth in size, weight, and feature differentiation gradually working from top to bottom.

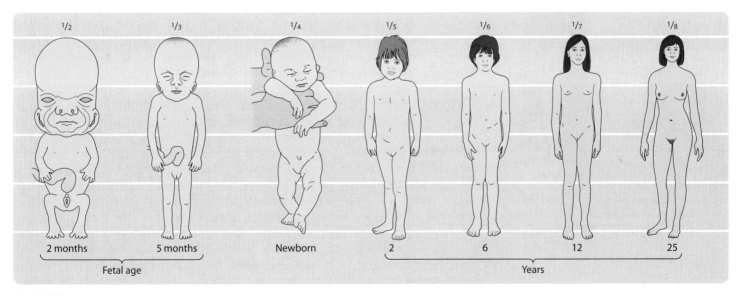

FIGURE **4.1**

CHANGES IN PROPORTIONS OF THE HUMAN BODY DURING GROWTH. As individuals develop from infancy through adulthood, one of the most noticeable physical changes is that the head becomes smaller in relation to the rest of the body. The fractions listed refer to head size as a proportion of total body length at different ages.

developmental connection

Dynamic Systems Theory. Sensory and motor development are coupled in many aspects of children's acquisition of skills. Chapter 5, pp. 164–165

their torso, and they can use their hands long before they can crawl or walk. However, one study found that infants reached for toys with their feet prior to using their hands (Galloway & Thelen, 2004). On average, infants first touched the toy with their feet when they were 12 weeks old and with their hands when they were 16 weeks old. We will have much more to say about sensory and motor development in Chapter 5.

The **proximodistal pattern** is the growth sequence that starts at the center of the body and moves toward the extremities. For example, muscle control of the truck and arms matures before control of the hands and fingers. Further, infants use their whole hand as a unit before they can control several fingers.

INFANCY AND CHILDHOOD

Height and weight increase rapidly in infancy (Lampl, 2008). Growth takes a slower course during the childhood years.

Infancy   The average North American newborn is 20 inches long and weighs 7½ pounds. Ninety-five percent of full-term newborns are 18 to 22 inches long and weigh between 5½ and 10 pounds.

In the first several days of life, most newborns lose 5 to 7 percent of their body weight. Once infants adjust to sucking, swallowing, and digesting, they grow rapidly, gaining an average of 5 to 6 ounces per week during the first month. They have doubled their birth weight by the age of 4 months and have nearly tripled it by their first birthday. Infants grow about one inch per month during the first year, reaching approximately 1½ times their birth length by their first birthday.

In the second year of life, infants' rate of growth slows considerably. By 2 years of age, infants weigh approximately 26 to 32 pounds, having gained a quarter to half a pound per month during the second year; at age 2 they have reached about one-fifth of their adult weight. The average 2-year-old is 32 to 35 inches tall, which is nearly one-half of adult height.

Early Childhood   As the preschool child grows older, the percentage of increase in height and weight decreases with each additional year (Darrah, Senthilselvan, & Magill-Evans, 2009). Girls are only slightly smaller and lighter than boys during these years. Both boys and girls slim down as the trunks of their bodies lengthen. Although their heads are still somewhat large for their bodies, by the end of the preschool years most children have lost their top-heavy look. Body fat declines slowly but steadily during the preschool years. Girls have more fatty tissue than boys; boys have more muscle tissue.

Growth patterns vary individually (Burns & others, 2009). Much of the variation is due to heredity, but environmental experiences are involved to some extent. A review of the height and weight of children around the world concluded that two important contributors to height differences are ethnic origin and nutrition (Meredith, 1978). Also, urban, middle-socioeconomic-status, and firstborn children were taller than rural, lower-socioeconomic-status, and later-born children. The children whose mothers smoked during pregnancy were half an inch shorter than the children whose mothers did not smoke during pregnancy. In the United States, African American children are taller than White children.

Why are some children unusually short? The culprits are congenital factors (genetic or prenatal problems), growth hormone deficiency, a physical problem that develops in childhood, or an emotional difficulty. When congenital growth problems are the cause of unusual shortness, often the child can be treated with hormones. Usually this treatment is directed at the pituitary, the body's master gland, located at the base of the brain. This gland secretes growth-related hormones. Physical problems during childhood that can stunt growth include malnutrition and chronic infections. However, if the problems are properly treated, normal growth usually is attained.

The bodies of 5-year-olds and 2-year-olds are different. Notice how the 5-year-old not only is taller and weighs more, but also has a longer trunk and legs than the 2-year-old. *What might be some other physical differences in 2- and 5-year-olds?*

proximodistal pattern The sequence in which growth starts at the center of the body and moves toward the extremities.

Middle and Late Childhood The period of middle and late childhood—from about 6 to 11 years of age—involves slow, consistent growth. This is a period of calm before the rapid growth spurt of adolescence.

During the elementary school years, children grow an average of 2 to 3 inches a year. At the age of 8 the average girl and the average boy are 4 feet 2 inches tall. During the middle and late childhood years, children gain about 5 to 7 pounds a year. The average 8-year-old girl and the average 8-year-old boy weigh 56 pounds (National Center for Health Statistics, 2000). The weight increase is due mainly to increases in the size of the skeletal and muscular systems, as well as the size of some body organs. Muscle mass and strength gradually increase as "baby fat" decreases in middle and late childhood (Hockenberry & Wilson, 2009).

The loose movements of early childhood give way to improved muscle tone in middle and late childhood. Children also double their strength capacity during these years. The increase in muscular strength is due to heredity and to exercise. Because they have more muscle cells, boys tend to be stronger than girls.

Changes in proportions are among the most pronounced physical changes in middle and late childhood. Head circumference, waist circumference, and leg length decrease in relation to body height (Kliegman & others, 2007). A less noticeable physical change is that bones continue to harden during middle and late childhood; still, they yield to pressure and pull more than mature bones.

What characterizes physical growth during middle and late childhood?

ADOLESCENCE

After slowing through childhood, growth surges during puberty. **Puberty** is a period of rapid physical maturation involving hormonal and bodily changes that occur primarily in early adolescence. The features and proportions of the body change as the individual becomes capable of reproducing. We will begin our exploration of puberty by describing its determinants and then examine important physical changes and psychological accompaniments of puberty.

Determinants of Puberty Puberty is not the same as adolescence. For virtually everyone, puberty has ended long before adolescence is over. Puberty is often thought of as the most important marker for the beginning of adolescence.

puberty A period of rapid physical maturation involving hormonal and bodily changes that take place primarily in early adolescence.

From *Penguin Dreams and Stranger Things*, by Berke Breathed. Copyright © 1985 by The Washington Post Company. By permission of Little, Brown & Company, Inc. and International Creative Management.

There are wide variations in the onset and progression of puberty. Puberty might begin as early as 10 years of age or as late as 13½ for boys. It might end as early as 13 years or as late as 17 years.

In fact, over the years the timing of puberty has changed. Imagine a 3-year-old girl with fully developed breasts or a boy just slightly older with a deep male voice. That is what toddlers would be like by the year 2250 if the age at which puberty arrives were to continue decreasing as it did for much of the twentieth century. For example, in Norway, **menarche**—a girl's first menstruation—now occurs at just over 13 years of age, compared with 17 years of age in the 1840s (Petersen, 1979). In the United States, where children mature up to a year earlier than in European countries, the average age of menarche dropped an average of two to four months per decade for much of the twentieth century, to about 12½ years today. Some researchers have found evidence that the age of puberty is still dropping for American girls; others suggest that the evidence is inconclusive or that the decline in age is slowing down (Herman-Giddens, 2007). The earlier onset of puberty is likely the result of improved health and nutrition (Herman-Giddens, 2007).

The normal range for the onset and progression of puberty is wide enough that, given two boys of the same chronological age, one might complete the pubertal sequence before the other one has begun it. For girls, the age range of menarche is even wider. It is considered within a normal range when it occurs between the ages of 9 and 15.

Precocious puberty is the term used to describe the very early onset and rapid progression of puberty. Judith Blakemore and her colleagues (2009, p. 58) recently described the following characteristics of precocious puberty. Precocious puberty is usually diagnosed when pubertal onset occurs before 8 years of age in girls and before 9 years of age in boys. Precocious puberty occurs approximately 10 times more often in girls than in boys. When precocious puberty occurs, it usually is treated by medically suppressing gonadotropic secretions, which temporarily stops pubertal change. The reasons for this treatment is that children who experience precocious puberty are ultimately likely to have short stature, early sexual capability, and the potential for engaging in age-inappropriate behavior (Blakemore, Berenbaum, & Liben, 2009).

Among the most important factors that influence the onset and sequence of puberty are heredity, hormones, weight, and body fat (Divall & Radovick, 2008).

Heredity   Puberty is not an environmental accident. It does not take place at 2 or 3 years of age, and it does not occur in the twenties. Programmed into the genes of every human being is a timing for the emergence of puberty. Nonetheless, within the boundaries of about 9 to 16 years of age, environmental factors such as health, weight, and stress can influence the onset and duration of puberty.

Hormones   Behind the first whisker in boys and the widening of hips in girls is a flood of hormones. **Hormones** are powerful chemical substances secreted by the endocrine glands and carried through the body by the bloodstream. In the case of puberty, the secretion of key hormones is controlled by the interaction of the hypothalamus, the pituitary gland, and the gonads (sex glands). The *hypothalamus* is a structure in the brain best known for monitoring eating, drinking, and sex. The *pituitary gland* is an important endocrine gland that controls growth and regulates other glands. The *gonads* are the sex glands—the testes in males, the ovaries in females.

The key hormonal changes involve two classes of hormones that have significantly different concentrations in males and females (Susman & Dorn, 2009). **Androgens** are the main class of male sex hormones. **Estrogens** are the main class of female hormones.

Testosterone is an androgen that is a key hormone in the development of puberty in boys. As the testosterone level rises during puberty, external genitals enlarge, height increases, and the voice changes. **Estradiol** is an estrogen that plays an important role in female pubertal development. As the estradiol level rises, breast development, uterine development, and skeletal changes occur. In one study,

menarche A girl's first menstruation.

precocious puberty Very early onset and rapid progression of puberty.

hormones Powerful chemical substances secreted by the endocrine glands and carried through the body by the bloodstream.

androgens The main class of male sex hormones.

estrogens The main class of female sex hormones.

testosterone An androgen that is a key hormone in boys' pubertal development.

estradiol An estrogen that is a key hormone in girls' pubertal development.

testosterone levels increased eighteenfold in boys but only twofold in girls across puberty; estradiol levels increased eightfold in girls but only twofold in boys across puberty (Nottleman & others, 1987) (see Figure 4.2).

Are there links between concentrations of hormones and adolescent behavior? Findings are inconsistent (Vermeersch & others, 2008). In any event, hormonal factors alone are not responsible for adolescent behavior (Graber, 2008). For example, one study found that social factors accounted for two to four times as much variance as hormonal factors in young adolescent girls' depression and anger (Brooks-Gunn & Warren, 1989). Hormones do not act independently; hormonal activity is influenced by many environmental factors, including parent-adolescent relationships. Stress, eating patterns, sexual activity, and depression can also activate or suppress various aspects of the hormone system (Susman & Dorn, 2009).

Growth Spurt Puberty ushers in the most rapid increases in growth since infancy. As indicated in Figure 4.3, the growth spurt associated with puberty occurs approximately two years earlier for girls than for boys. The mean beginning of the growth spurt in the United States today is 9 years of age for girls and 11 years of age for boys. Pubertal change peaks at an average of 11.5 years for girls and 13.5 years for boys. During their growth spurt, girls increase in height about 3.5 inches per year, boys about 4 inches.

Boys and girls who are shorter or taller than their peers before adolescence are likely to remain so during adolescence. At the beginning of adolescence, girls tend to be as tall as or taller than boys their age, but by the end of the middle school years most boys have caught up, or, in many cases, even surpassed girls in height. And although height in elementary school is a good predictor of height later in adolescence, as much as 30 percent of the height of individuals in late adolescence is unexplained by height in the elementary school years.

Sexual Maturation Think back to the onset of your puberty. Of the striking changes that were taking place in your body, what was the first change that occurred? Researchers have found that male pubertal characteristics develop in this order:

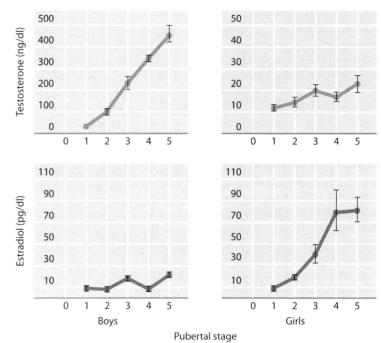

FIGURE **4.2**

HORMONE LEVELS BY SEX AND PUBERTAL STAGE FOR TESTOSTERONE AND ESTRADIOL. The five stages range from the early beginning of puberty (stage 1) to the most advanced stage of puberty (stage 5). Notice the significant increase in testosterone in boys and the significant increase in estradiol in girls.

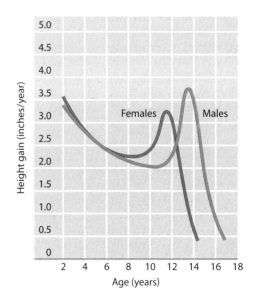

FIGURE **4.3**

PUBERTAL GROWTH SPURT. On the average, the peak of the growth spurt that characterizes pubertal change occurs two years earlier for girls (11½) than for boys (13½).

ZITS By Jerry Scott and Jim Borgman

© ZITS Partnership. King Features Syndicate.

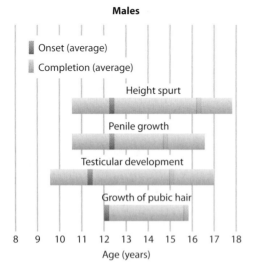

Males

■ Onset (average)
□ Completion (average)

Height spurt

Penile growth

Testicular development

Growth of pubic hair

8 9 10 11 12 13 14 15 16 17 18
Age (years)

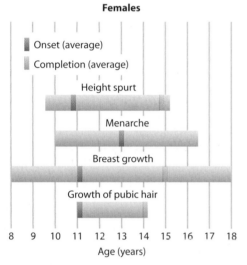

Females

■ Onset (average)
□ Completion (average)

Height spurt

Menarche

Breast growth

Growth of pubic hair

8 9 10 11 12 13 14 15 16 17 18
Age (years)

FIGURE **4.4**

NORMAL RANGE AND AVERAGE DEVELOPMENT OF SEXUAL CHARACTERISTICS IN MALES AND FEMALES

What gender differences characterize adolescents' body image? What might explain the differences?

increase in penis and testicle size, appearance of straight pubic hair, minor voice change, first ejaculation (which usually occurs through masturbation or a wet dream), appearance of pubic hair, onset of maximum body growth, growth of hair in armpits, more detectable voice changes, and growth of facial hair. Three of the most noticeable areas of sexual maturation in boys are penis elongation, testes development, and growth of facial hair. The normal range and average age of development in boys and girls for these sexual characteristics, along with height spurt, is shown in Figure 4.4.

What is the order of appearance of physical changes in females? First, on average the breasts enlarge and then pubic hair appears. These are two of the most noticeable aspects of female pubertal development. A recent longitudinal study revealed that on average, girls' breast development preceded their pubic hair development by about 2 months (Susman & Dorn, 2009). Later, hair appears in the armpits. As these changes occur, the female grows in height, and her hips become wider than her shoulders. Her first menstruation (menarche) occurs rather late in the pubertal cycle; it is considered normal if it occurs between the ages of 9 and 15. Initially, her menstrual cycles may be highly irregular. For the first several years, she might not ovulate during every menstrual cycle. Some girls do not become fertile until two years after their periods begin. Pubertal females do not experience voice changes comparable to those in pubertal males. By the end of puberty, the female's breasts have become more fully rounded.

Body Image   One psychological aspect of physical change in puberty is certain: Adolescents are preoccupied with their bodies and develop images of what their bodies are like (Mueller, 2009). Preoccupation with body image is strong throughout adolescence, but it is especially acute during early adolescence, a time when adolescents are more dissatisfied with their bodies than in late adolescence.

Gender differences characterize adolescents' perceptions of their bodies. In general, girls are less happy with their bodies and have more negative body images than boys throughout puberty (Bearman & others, 2006). As pubertal change proceeds, girls often become more dissatisfied with their bodies, probably because their body fat increases. In contrast, boys become more satisfied as they move through puberty, probably because their muscle mass increases.

Although we have described gender differences in the body images of adolescents, emphasizing that girls tend to have more negative body images than boys, keep in mind that there is considerable variation, with many adolescent girls having positive body images and many adolescent boys having negative body images. Further, a recent research review revealed an increase in body satisfaction for non-Latino White adolescent girls but not for African American adolescent girls (Grabe & Hyde, 2006).

Early and Late Maturation   Did you enter puberty early, late, or on time? When adolescents mature earlier or later than their peers, they often perceive themselves differently and their maturational timing is linked to their socioemotional development and whether they develop problems (Susman & Dorn, 2009). In the Berkeley Longitudinal Study conducted some years ago, early-maturing boys perceived themselves more positively and had more successful peer relations than did late-maturing boys (Jones, 1965). The findings for early-maturing girls were similar but not as strong as for boys. When the late-maturing boys were in their thirties, however, they had developed a more positive identity than the early-maturing boys had (Peskin, 1967). Perhaps the late-maturing boys had more time to explore life's options, or perhaps the early-maturing boys continued to focus on their physical status instead of paying attention to career development and achievement.

An increasing number of researchers have found that early maturation increases girls' vulnerability to a number of problems (Cavanagh, 2009; Ge & Natsuaki, 2010). Early-maturing girls are more likely to smoke, drink, be depressed, have an eating disorder, struggle for earlier independence from their parents, and have older friends; and their bodies are likely to elicit responses from males that lead to earlier dating and earlier sexual experiences (Wiesner & Ittel, 2002). For example, a recent study revealed that early-maturing girls were more likely to try cigarettes and alcohol without their parents' knowledge (Westling & others, 2008). And early-maturing girls are less likely to graduate from high school and tend to cohabit and marry earlier (Cavanagh, 2009). Apparently as a result of their social and cognitive immaturity, combined with early physical development, early-maturing girls are easily lured into problem behaviors, not recognizing the possible long-term effects of these on their development.

Review Connect Reflect

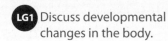 Discuss developmental changes in the body.

Review

- What are cephalocaudal and proximodistal patterns?
- How do height and weight change in infancy and childhood?
- What changes characterize puberty?

Connect

- Describe the influence of nature and nurture on the relationship between hormones and puberty.

Reflect *Your Own Personal Journey of Life*

- Did you experience puberty early, late, or on time? How do you think this affected your social relationships and development?

The Brain

LG2 Describe how the brain changes.

| Brain Physiology | Infancy | Childhood | Adolescence |

In every physical change we have described so far, the brain is involved in some way. Structures of the brain help to regulate not only behavior but also metabolism, the release of hormones, and other aspects of the body's physiology.

Until recently, little was known for certain about how the brain changes as children develop. Not long ago, scientists thought that our genes determined how our brains were "wired" and that unlike most cells, the cells in the brain responsible for processing information stopped dividing early in childhood. Whatever brain your heredity dealt you, you were essentially stuck with it. This view, however, turned out to be wrong. Instead, the brain has plasticity, and its development depends on context (Diamond, Casey, & Munakata, 2011; Nelson, 2011). What we do can change the development of our brain.

We described the amazing growth of the brain from conception to birth in Chapter 3. In this section, we initially will explore the basic structures and function of the brain, then examine developmental changes in the brain from infancy through adolescence.

developmental **connection**

Brain Development. How does the brain change from conception to birth? Chapter 3, pp. 81–82

developmental **connection**

Gender. How large are gender differences in the brain? Chapter 12, p. 354

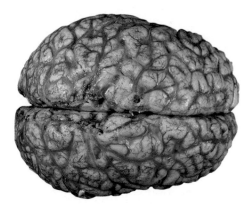

FIGURE **4.5**

THE HUMAN BRAIN'S HEMISPHERES. The two halves (hemispheres) of the human brain are clearly seen in this photograph.

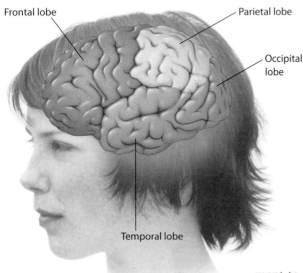

Frontal lobe

Parietal lobe

Occipital lobe

Temporal lobe

FIGURE **4.6**

THE BRAIN'S FOUR LOBES. Shown here are the locations of the brain's four lobes: frontal, occipital, temporal, and parietal.

lateralization Specialization of function in one hemisphere of the cerebral cortex or the other.

BRAIN PHYSIOLOGY

The brain includes a number of major structures. The key components of these structures are *neurons*, the nerve cells that handle information processing, which we initially described in Chapter 3.

Structure and Function   Looked at from above, the brain has two halves, or hemispheres (see Figure 4.5). The top portion of the brain, farthest from the spinal cord, is known as the *forebrain*. Its outer layer of cells, the cerebral cortex, covers it like a cap. The *cerebral cortex* is responsible for about 80 percent of the brain's volume and is critical in perception, thinking, language, and other important functions.

Each hemisphere of the cortex has four major areas, called *lobes*. Although the lobes usually work together, each has a somewhat different primary function (see Figure 4.6):

- *Frontal lobes* are involved in voluntary movement, thinking, personality, and intentionality or purpose.
- *Occipital lobes* function in vision.
- *Temporal lobes* have an active role in hearing, language processing, and memory.
- *Parietal lobes* play important roles in registering spatial location, attention, and motor control.

Deeper in the brain, beneath the cortex, lie other key structures. These include the hypothalamus and the pituitary gland as well as the *amygdala*, which plays an important role in emotions, and the *hippocampus*, which is especially active in memory and emotion.

Neurons   How do these structures work? As we indicated, the neurons process information. Figure 4.7 shows some important parts of the neuron, including the *axon* and *dendrites*. Basically, an axon sends electrical signals away from the central part of the neuron. At the end of the axon are terminal buttons, which release chemicals called *neurotransmitters* into *synapses*, which are tiny gaps between neurons' fibers. Chemical interactions in synapses connect axons and dendrites, allowing information to pass from neuron to neuron (Turrigiano, 2010). Think of the synapse as a river that blocks a road. A grocery truck arrives at one bank of the river, crosses by ferry, and continues its journey to market. Similarly, a message in the brain is "ferried" across the synapse by a neurotransmitter, which pours out information contained in chemicals when it reaches the other side of the river.

Most axons are covered by a myelin sheath, which is a layer of fat cells. The sheath helps impulses travel faster along the axon, increasing the speed with which information travels from neuron to neuron. The myelin sheath developed as the brain evolved. As brain size increased, it became necessary for information to travel faster over longer distances in the nervous system. We can compare the myelin sheath's development to the evolution of freeways as cities grew. A freeway is a shielded road, and it keeps fast-moving, long-distance traffic from getting snarled by slow local traffic.

Which neurons get which information? Clusters of neurons known as *neural circuits* work together to handle particular types of information. The brain is organized in many neural circuits. For example, one neural circuit is important in attention and working memory (the type of memory that holds information for a brief time and is like a "mental workbench" as we perform a task) (Krimer & Goldman-Rakic, 2001). This neural circuit uses the neurotransmitter dopamine and lies in the prefrontal cortex area of the frontal lobes.

To some extent, the type of information handled by neurons depends on whether they are in the left or right hemisphere of the cortex (Bortfeld, Fava, &

Boas, 2009; Iturria-Medina & others, 2010). Speech and grammar, for example, depend on activity in the left hemisphere in most people; humor and the use of metaphors depends on activity in the right hemisphere (Hamilton, Martin, & Burton, 2010; Hornickel, Skoe, & Kraus, 2008; Wolmetz, Poeppel, & Rapp, 2010). This specialization of function in one hemisphere of the cerebral cortex or the other is called **lateralization.** However, most neuroscientists agree that complex functions such as reading or performing music involve both hemispheres (Stroobant, Buijs, & Vingerhoets, 2009). Labeling people as "left-brained" because they are logical thinkers and "right-brained" because they are creative thinkers does not correspond to the way the brain's hemispheres work. Complex thinking in normal people is the outcome of communication between both hemispheres of the brain (Liegeois & others, 2008). For example, a recent meta-analysis revealed no hemispheric specialization in creative thinking (Mihov, Denzler, & Forster, 2010).

INFANCY

As we saw in Chapter 3, brain development occurs extensively during the prenatal period. The brain's development is also substantial during infancy and later (Diamond, Casey, & Munakata, 2011; Nelson, 2011).

Because the brain is still developing so rapidly in infancy, the infant's head should be protected from falls or other injuries and the baby should never be shaken. *Shaken baby syndrome,* which includes brain swelling and hemorrhaging, affects hundreds of babies in the United States each year (Croucher, 2010; Fanconi & Lips, 2010). A recent analysis found that fathers were the most frequent perpetrators of shaken baby syndrome, followed by child care providers and by a boyfriend of the victim's mother (National Center on Shaken Baby Syndrome, 2010).

Studying the brain's development in infancy is not as easy as it might seem. Even the latest brain-imaging technologies (described in Chapter 1) cannot make out fine details in adult brains and cannot be used with babies (Nelson, 2011). Positron-emission tomography (PET) scans pose a radiation risk to babies, and infants wriggle too much to allow technicians to capture accurate images using magnetic resonance imaging (MRI). However, researchers have been successful in using the electroencephalogram (EEG), a measure of the brain's electrical activity, to learn about the brain's development in infancy (Bell & Wolfe, 2007).

Among the researchers who are making strides in finding out more about the brain's development in infancy are Charles Nelson and his colleagues (2007, 2011; Fox, Levitt, & Nelson, 2010; Moulson & Nelson, 2008). In his research, Nelson attaches up to 128 electrodes to a baby's scalp (see Figure 4.8). He has found that even newborns produce distinctive brain waves that reveal they can distinguish their mother's voice from another woman's, even while they are asleep.

As an infant walks, talks, runs, shakes a rattle, smiles, and frowns, changes in its brain are occurring. Consider that the infant began life as a single cell and nine months later was born with a brain and nervous system that contained approximately 100 billion nerve cells, or neurons. What determines how those neurons are connected to communicate with each other?

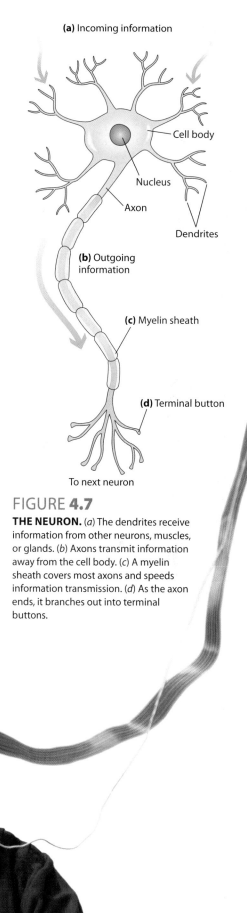

(a) Incoming information

Cell body

Nucleus

Axon

Dendrites

(b) Outgoing information

(c) Myelin sheath

(d) Terminal button

To next neuron

FIGURE **4.7**

THE NEURON. (*a*) The dendrites receive information from other neurons, muscles, or glands. (*b*) Axons transmit information away from the cell body. (*c*) A myelin sheath covers most axons and speeds information transmission. (*d*) As the axon ends, it branches out into terminal buttons.

FIGURE **4.8**

MEASURING THE ACTIVITY OF AN INFANT'S BRAIN. By attaching up to 128 electrodes to a baby's scalp to measure the brain's activity, Charles Nelson (2003, 2011; Nelson, Thomas, & de Haan, 2006) has found that even newborns produce distinctive brain waves that reveal they can distinguish their mother's voice from another woman's, even while they are asleep. *Why is it so difficult to measure infants' brain activity?*

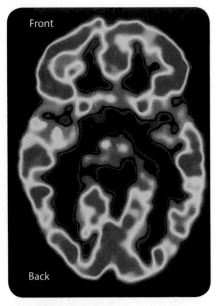

(a)

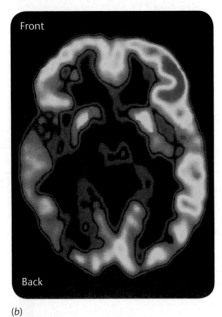

(b)

FIGURE **4.9**

EARLY DEPRIVATION AND BRAIN

ACTIVITY. These two photographs are PET (positron emission tomography) scans (which use radioactive tracers to image and analyze blood flow and metabolic activity in the body's organs) of the brains of (a) a normal child and (b) an institutionalized Romanian orphan who experienced substantial deprivation since birth. In PET scans, the highest to lowest brain activity is reflected in the colors of red, yellow, green, blue, and black, respectively. As can be seen, red and yellow show up to a much greater degree in the PET scan of the normal child than the deprived Romanian orphan.

Early Experience and the Brain Children who grow up in a deprived environment may also have depressed brain activity (Fox, Levitt, & Nelson, 2010; Pollack & others, 2010; Reeb & others, 2009). As shown in Figure 4.9, a child who grew up in the unresponsive and unstimulating environment of a Romanian orphanage showed considerably depressed brain activity compared with a normal child.

Are the effects of deprived environments irreversible? There is reason to think the answer is no. The brain demonstrates both flexibility and resilience. Consider 14-year-old Michael Rehbein. At age 7, he began to experience uncontrollable seizures—as many as 400 a day. Doctors said the only solution was to remove the left hemisphere of his brain where the seizures were occurring. Recovery was slow, but his right hemisphere began to reorganize and take over functions that normally occur in the brain's left hemisphere, including speech (see Figure 4.10). A recent study of 10 children who had experienced an arterial stroke perinatally (during or around birth) revealed that in 8 of the 10 the right hemisphere was dominant in processing language (Guzzetta & others, 2008).

Neuroscientists believe that what wires the brain—or rewires it, in the case of Michael Rehbein—is repeated experience. Each time a baby tries to touch an attractive object or gazes intently at a face, tiny bursts of electricity shoot through the brain, knitting together neurons into circuits. The results are some of the behavioral milestones we discuss in this chapter.

In sum, the infant's brain is waiting for experiences to determine how connections are made (Dalton & Bergenn, 2007). Before birth, it appears that genes mainly direct basic wiring patterns. Neurons grow and travel to distant places awaiting further instructions (Sheridan & Nelson, 2008). After birth, the inflowing stream of sights, sounds, smells, touches, language, and eye contact help shape the brain's neural connections (Diamond, Casey, & Munakata, 2011; Nelson, 2011).

Changing Neurons At birth, the newborn's brain is about 25 percent of its adult weight. By the second birthday, the brain is about 75 percent of its adult weight. Two key developments during these first two years involve the myelin sheath (the layer of fat cells that speeds up the electrical impulse along the axon) and connections between dendrites.

(b)

(a)

FIGURE **4.10**

PLASTICITY IN THE BRAIN'S HEMISPHERES.
(a) Michael Rehbein at 14 years of age. (b) Michael's right hemisphere (right) has reorganized to take over the language functions normally carried out by corresponding areas in the left hemisphere of an intact brain (left). However, the right hemisphere is not as efficient as the left, and more areas of the brain are recruited to process speech.

Myelination, the process of encasing axons with a myelin sheath, begins pre-natally and continues after birth (see Figure 4.11). As we indicated earlier, this process increases the speed of processing information. Myelination for visual pathways occurs rapidly after birth, being completed in the first six months. Auditory myelination is not completed until 4 or 5 years of age. Some aspects of myelination continue even into adolescence. Indeed, the most extensive changes in myelination in the frontal lobes occur during adolescence (Paus, 2009; Jackson-Newsom & Shelton, 2010).

Dramatic increases in dendrites and synapses (the tiny gaps between neurons across which neurotransmitters carry information) also characterize the development of the brain in the first two years of life (see Figure 4.12). Nearly twice as many of these connections are made as will ever be used (Huttenlocher & others, 1991; Huttenlocher & Dabholkar, 1997). The connections that are used become strengthened and survive; the unused ones are replaced by other pathways or disappear (Nelson, 2011). That is, connections are "pruned" (Faissner & others, 2010). Figure 4.13 vividly illustrates the growth and later pruning of synapses in the visual, auditory, and prefrontal cortex areas of the brain (Huttenlocher & Dabholkar, 1997).

As shown in Figure 4.13, "blooming and pruning" vary considerably by brain region in humans. For example, the peak synaptic overproduction in the area concerned with vision occurs about the fourth postnatal month, followed by a gradual pruning until the middle to end of the preschool years (Huttenlocher & Dabholkar, 1997). In areas of the brain involved in hearing and language, a similar, though somewhat later, course is detected. However, in the *prefrontal cortex* (the area of the brain where higher-level thinking and self-regulation occur), the peak of overproduction occurs at just after 3 years of age. Both heredity and environment are thought to influence synaptic overproduction and subsequent pruning.

Changing Structures   At birth, the hemispheres already have started to specialize: Newborns show greater electrical activity in the left hemisphere than in the right hemisphere when they are making or listening to speech sounds (Imada & others, 2007).

In general, some areas of the brain, such as the primary motor areas, develop earlier than others, such as the primary sensory areas. The frontal lobes are immature in the newborn. However, as neurons in the frontal lobes become myelinated and interconnected during the first year of life, infants develop an ability to regulate their physiological states, such as sleep, and gain more control over their reflexes. Cognitive skills that require deliberate thinking do not emerge until later in the first year (Bell & Fox, 1992; Bell & Morasch, 2007).

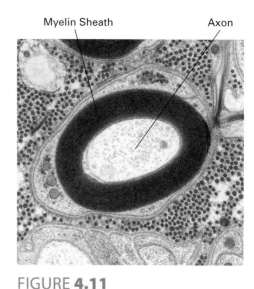

FIGURE **4.11**

A MYELINATED NERVE FIBER. The myelin sheath, shown in brown, encases the axon (white). This image was produced by an electron microscope that magnified the nerve fiber 12,000 times. *What role does myelination play in the brain's development?*

myelination The process of encasing axons with a myelin sheath that increases the speed of processing information.

FIGURE **4.12**

THE DEVELOPMENT OF DENDRITIC

SPREADING. Note the increase in connectedness between neurons over the course of the first two years of life.
Reprinted by permission of the publisher from *The Postnatal Development of the Human Cerebral Cortex, Volumes 1-VIII* by Jesse LeRoy Conel, Cambridge, Mass.: Harvard University Press, Copyright © 1939, 1941, 1947, 1951, 1955, 1959, 1963, 1967 by the President and Fellows of Harvard College. Copyright © renewed 1967, 1969, 1975, 1983, 1991.

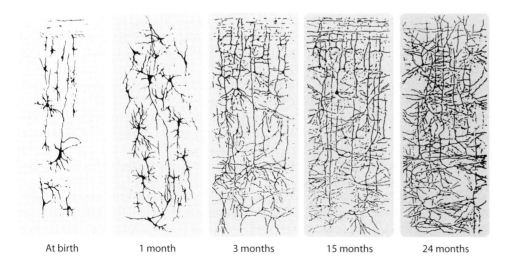

At birth   1 month   3 months   15 months   24 months

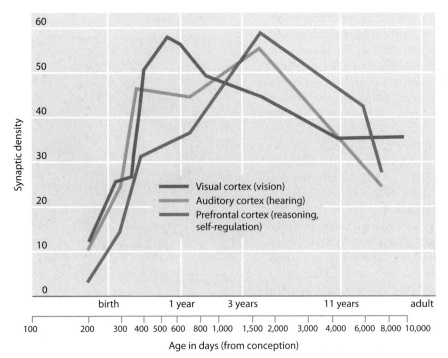

FIGURE **4.13**

SYNAPTIC DENSITY IN THE HUMAN BRAIN FROM INFANCY TO ADULTHOOD. The graph shows the dramatic increase and then pruning in synaptic density for three regions of the brain: visual cortex, auditory cortex, and prefrontal cortex. Synaptic density is believed to be an important indication of the extent of connectivity between neurons.

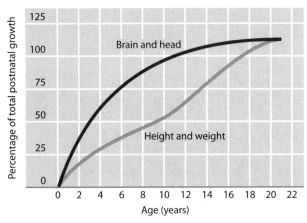

FIGURE **4.14**

GROWTH CURVES FOR THE HEAD AND BRAIN AND FOR HEIGHT AND WEIGHT. The more rapid growth of the brain and head can easily be seen. Height and weight advance more gradually over the first two decades of life.

developmental **connection**

Intelligence. Are some regions of the brain linked with children's intelligence more than others? Chapter 8, pp. 240–241

CHILDHOOD

The brain and other parts of the nervous system continue developing through childhood and adolescence. These changes enable children to plan their actions, to attend to stimuli more effectively, and to make considerable strides in language development.

During early childhood, the brain and head grow more rapidly than any other part of the body. Figure 4.14 shows how the growth curve for the head and brain advances more rapidly than the growth curve for height and weight. Some of the brain's increase in size is due to myelination and some is due to an increase in the number and size of dendrites. Some developmentalists conclude that myelination is important in the maturation of a number of abilities in children (Fair & Schlaggar, 2008). For example, myelination in the areas of the brain related to hand-eye coordination is not complete until about 4 years of age. A functional magnetic resonance imaging (fMRI) study of children (mean age, 4 years) found that those who were characterized by developmental delay of motor and cognitive milestones had significantly reduced levels of myelination (Pujol & others, 2004). Myelination in the areas of the brain related to focusing attention is not complete until middle or late childhood.

The brain in early childhood is not growing as rapidly as in infancy. However, the anatomical changes in the child's brain between the ages of 3 and 15 are dramatic. By repeatedly obtaining brain scans of the same children for up to four years, scientists have found that children's brains experience rapid, distinct bursts of growth (Gogtay & Thompson, 2010; Thompson & others, 2000). The amount of brain material in some areas can nearly double in as little as one year, followed by a drastic loss of tissue as unneeded cells are purged and the brain continues to reorganize itself. The overall size of the brain does not increase dramatically from 3 to 15. What does dramatically change are local patterns within the brain (Gogtay & Thompson, 2010; Thompson & others, 2000). From 3 to 6 years of age, the most rapid growth occurs in the frontal lobe areas involved in planning and organizing new actions and in maintaining attention to tasks (Diamond, Casey, & Munakata, 2011). From age 6 through puberty, the most dramatic growth takes place in the temporal and parietal lobes, especially in areas that play major roles in language and spatial relations.

Developmental neuroscientist Mark Johnson and his colleagues (2009) recently proposed that the prefrontal cortex likely orchestrates the functions of many other brain regions during development. As part of this neural leadership and organizational role, the prefrontal cortex may provide an advantage to neural connections and networks that include the prefrontal cortex. In the view of these researchers, the prefrontal cortex likely coordinates the best neural connections for solving a problem.

Links between the changing brain and children's cognitive development involve activation of brain areas, with some areas increasing in activation while others decrease (Diamond, Casey, & Munakata, 2011). One shift in activation that occurs as children develop in middle and late childhood is from diffuse, larger areas to more focal, smaller areas (Durston & others, 2006). This shift is characterized by synaptic pruning in which areas of the brain not being used lose synaptic connections and those being used show an increase in connections. In a recent study, researchers found less diffusion and more focal activation in the prefrontal cortex (the highest level of the frontal lobes) from 7 to 30 years of age (Durston & others, 2006). The activation change was accompanied by increased efficiency in cognitive performance, especially in *cognitive control*, which involves flexible and effective control in a number of areas. These areas include controlling attention, reducing interfering thoughts, inhibiting motor actions, and being flexible in switching between competing choices (Diamond, Casey, & Munakata, 2011).

ADOLESCENCE

Along with the rest of the body, the brain is changing during adolescence, but the study of adolescent brain development is in its infancy (Ernst & Mueller, 2008). As advances in technology take place, significant strides will also likely be made in charting developmental changes in the adolescent brain. What do we know now?

Earlier we indicated that connections between neurons become "pruned" as children and adolescents develop. The pruning means that the connections which are used strengthen and survive, while the unused ones are replaced by other pathways or disappear. What results from this pruning is that by the end of adolescence individuals have "fewer, more selective, more effective neuronal connections than they did as children" (Kuhn, 2009, p. 153). And this pruning indicates that the activities adolescents choose to engage in and not to engage in influence which neural connections will be strengthened and which will disappear.

Using fMRI brain scans, scientists have recently discovered that adolescents' brains undergo significant structural changes (Giedd & others, 2009). The **corpus callosum,** where fibers connect the brain's left and right hemispheres, thickens in adolescence; this improves adolescents' ability to process information. We just described advances in the development of the **prefrontal cortex**—the highest level of the frontal lobes involved in reasoning, decision making, and self-control. The prefrontal cortex doesn't finish maturing until the emerging adult years (approximately 18 to 25 years of age) or later, but the **amygdala**—the seat of emotions such as anger—matures earlier than the prefrontal cortex. Figure 4.15 shows the locations of the corpus callosum, prefrontal cortex, and amygdala. A recent study of 137 early adolescents revealed a positive link between the volume of the amygdala and the duration of adolescents' aggressive behavior during interactions with parents (Whittle & others, 2008).

Many of the changes in the adolescent brain that have been described involve the rapidly emerging field of *developmental social neuroscience*, which involves connections between development, the brain, and socioemotional processes (Bell, Greene, & Wolfe, 2010; Blakemore, 2010; de Haan & Gunnar, 2009). For example, consider leading researcher Charles Nelson's (2003) view that although adolescents are capable of very strong emotions, their prefrontal cortex hasn't developed to the point at which they can control these passions. It is as if their brain doesn't have the brakes to slow down their emotions. Or consider this interpretation of the development of emotion and cognition in adolescents: "early activation of strong 'turbo-charged' feelings with a relatively un-skilled set of 'driving skills' or cognitive abilities to modulate strong emotions and motivations" (Dahl, 2004, p. 18).

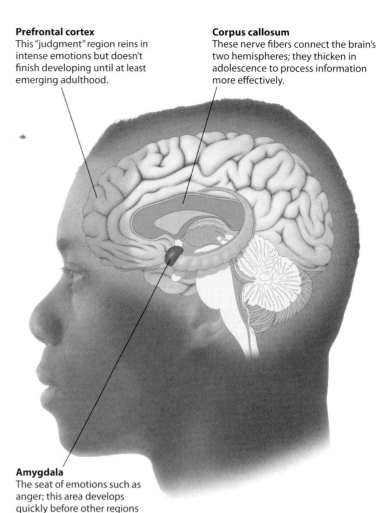

Prefrontal cortex
This "judgment" region reins in intense emotions but doesn't finish developing until at least emerging adulthood.

Corpus callosum
These nerve fibers connect the brain's two hemispheres; they thicken in adolescence to process information more effectively.

Amygdala
The seat of emotions such as anger; this area develops quickly before other regions that help to control it.

FIGURE **4.15**
CHANGES IN THE ADOLESCENT BRAIN

developmental **connection**

Brain Development. Developmental social neuroscience is a recently developed field that focuses on connections between development, socioemotional factors, and neuroscience. Chapter 1, p. 15

corpus callosum Brain area where fibers connect the brain's left and right hemispheres.

prefrontal cortex The highest level of the frontal lobes that is involved in reasoning, decision making, and self-control.

amygdala The seat of emotions in the brain.

developmental **connection**

Brain Development. How might developmental changes in the adolescent's brain be linked to adolescents' decision-making skills? Chapter 7, pp. 223–224

Of course, a major issue is which comes first: biological changes in the brain or experiences that stimulate these changes (Lerner, Boyd, & Du, 2009). Consider a recent study in which the prefrontal cortex thickened and more brain connections formed when adolescents resisted peer pressure (Paus & others, 2007). Scientists have yet to determine whether the brain changes come first or whether they result from experiences with peers, parents, and others. Once again, we encounter the nature/nurture issue that is so prominent in examining development.

Review *Connect* Reflect

 Describe how the brain changes.

Review

- What is the nature of brain physiology?
- How does the brain change in infancy?
- What characterizes the development of the brain in childhood?
- How does the brain change in adolescence, and how might this change be linked to adolescents' behavior?

Connect

- Both infancy and adolescence are times of significant change in the brain. Compare and contrast these changes.

Reflect *Your Own Personal Journey of Life*

- A parent tells you that his or her child is "left-brained" and that this aspect of the brain explains why the child does well in school. Is the parent likely to be providing an accurate explanation or probably off-base? Explain.

Sleep　LG3　Summarize how sleep patterns change as children and adolescents develop.

Infancy　　　Childhood　　　Adolescence

Sleep restores, replenishes, and rebuilds our brains and bodies. Some neuroscientists believe that sleep gives neurons that have been used while we are awake a chance to shut down and repair themselves (National Institute of Neurological Disorders and Stroke, 2009). How do sleeping patterns change during the childhood years?

INFANCY

How much do infants sleep? Are there any special problems that can develop regarding infants' sleep?

> Sleep that knits up the ravelled sleave of care . . . Balm of hurt minds, nature's second course. Chief nourisher in life's feast.
>
> —**William Shakespeare**
> *English Playwright, 17th Century*

The Sleep/Wake Cycle　When we were infants, sleep consumed more of our time than it does now (Miano & others, 2009). Newborns sleep 16 to 17 hours a day, although some sleep more and others less. The range is from a low of about 10 hours to a high of about 21 hours, although the longest period of sleep is not always between 11 P.M. and 7 A.M. Although total sleep remains somewhat consistent for young infants, their sleep during the day does not always follow a rhythmic pattern. An infant might change from sleeping several long bouts of 7 or 8 hours to three or four shorter sessions only several hours in duration. By about 1 month of age, most infants have begun to sleep longer at night. By 6 months of age, they usually have moved closer to adultlike sleep patterns, spending their longest span of sleep at night and their longest span of waking during the day (Sadeh, 2008).

The most common infant sleep-related problem reported by parents is night waking (The Hospital for Sick Children & others, 2010). Surveys indicate that 20 to 30 percent of infants have difficulty going to sleep at night and staying asleep all night (Sadeh, 2008). What factors are involved in infant night waking? Infant night-waking problems have consistently been linked to excessive parental involvement in sleep-related interactions with their infant (Sadeh, 2008). Also, a recent study of 9-month-old infants revealed that more time awake at night was linked to intrinsic factors such as daytime crying and fussing, and extrinsic factors such as being distressed when separated from the mother, breast feeding, and co-sleeping (DeLeon & Karraker, 2007).

Cultural variations influence infant sleeping patterns (Mindell & others, 2010a, b). For example, in the Kipsigis culture in Kenya, infants sleep with their mothers at night and are permitted to nurse on demand (Super & Harkness, 1997). During the day, they are strapped to their mothers' backs, accompanying them on daily rounds of chores and social activities. As a result, the Kipsigis infants do not sleep through the night until much later than American infants do. During the first eight months of postnatal life, Kipsigis infants rarely sleep longer than three hours at a stretch, even at night. This sleep pattern contrasts with that of American infants, many of whom begin to sleep up to eight hours a night by 8 months of age.

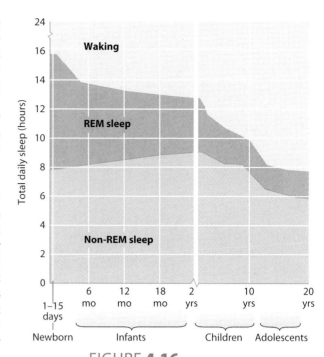

FIGURE **4.16**

DEVELOPMENTAL CHANGES IN REM AND NON-REM SLEEP

REM Sleep   In *REM sleep*, the eyes flutter beneath closed lids; in *non-REM sleep*, this type of eye movement does not occur and sleep is quieter. Figure 4.16 shows developmental changes in the average number of total hours spent in REM and non-REM sleep. By the time they reach adulthood, individuals spend about one-fifth of their night in REM sleep, and REM sleep usually appears about one hour after non-REM sleep. However, about half of an infant's sleep is REM sleep, and infants often begin their sleep cycle with REM sleep rather than non-REM sleep (Sadeh, 2008). A much greater amount of time is taken up by REM sleep in infancy than at any other point in the life span. By the time infants reach 3 months of age, the percentage of time they spend in REM sleep falls to about 40 percent, and REM sleep no longer begins their sleep cycle.

Why do infants spend so much time in REM sleep? Researchers are not certain. The large amount of REM sleep may provide infants with added self-stimulation, since they spend less time awake than do older children. REM sleep also might promote the brain's development in infancy (Graven, 2006).

When adults are awakened during REM sleep, they frequently report that they have been dreaming—but when they are awakened during non-REM sleep, they are much less likely to report they have been dreaming (Cartwright & others, 2006). Since infants spend more time than adults in REM sleep, can we conclude that they dream a lot? We don't know whether infants dream or not, because they don't have any way of reporting dreams.

Shared Sleeping   Sleeping arrangements for newborns vary from culture to culture (Mindell & others, 2010a, b). Sharing a bed with a mother is a common practice in many cultures, such as Guatemala and China, whereas in others, such as the United States and Great Britain, most newborns sleep in a crib, either in the same room as the parents or in a separate room. In some cultures, infants sleep with the mother until they are weaned, after which they sleep with siblings until middle and late childhood (Walker, 2006). Whatever the sleeping arrangements, it is recommended that the infant's bedding provide firm support and that cribs have side rails.

In the United States, sleeping in a crib in a separate room is the most frequent sleeping arrangement for an infant. In one cross-cultural study, American mothers said they have their infants sleep in a separate room to promote the infants' self-reliance and independence (Morelli & others, 1992). By contrast, Mayan mothers in rural Guatemala had infants sleep in their bed until the birth of a new sibling, at which time the infant would sleep with another family member or in a separate bed in the mother's room. The Mayan mothers believed that the co-sleeping arrangement with their infants enhanced the closeness of their relationship with the infants and were shocked when told that American mothers have their babies sleep alone.

Shared sleeping, or co-sleeping, is a controversial issue among experts (Adams, Good, & Defranco, 2009; Sadeh, 2008). According to some child experts, shared sleeping brings several benefits: It promotes breast feeding and a quicker response to the baby's cries, and it allows the mother to detect potentially dangerous breathing pauses in the baby (Pelayo & others, 2006). However, shared sleeping remains controversial, with some experts recommending it and others arguing against it (Mitchell, 2007; Newton & Vandeven, 2006). The American Academy of Pediatrics (AAP) Task Force on Infant Positioning and SIDS (2000) discourages shared sleeping. The Task Force concluded that bed sharing increases the risk that the sleeping mother will roll over onto her baby or increase the risk of sudden infant death syndrome (SIDS). Researchers have found that bed sharing is linked with a greater incidence of SIDS, especially when parents smoke (Alm & others, 2006; Bajanowski & others, 2007). Also, shared sleeping is more likely to place the infant at risk if the caregivers are impaired by alcohol, smoking, or overly tired (Baddock & others, 2007; Ostfeld & others, 2010). And recent studies indicate that African American mothers and their infants are more likely to bed share than non-Latino White mothers (Fu & others, 2008; Hauck & others, 2008).

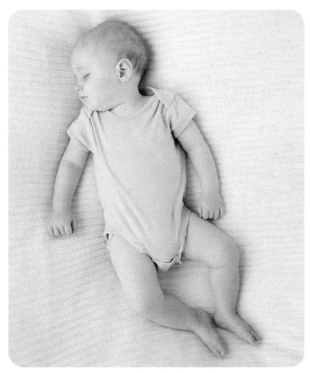

Is this a good sleep position for infants? Why or why not?

SIDS **Sudden infant death syndrome (SIDS)** is a condition that occurs when infants stop breathing, usually during the night, and die suddenly without an apparent cause. SIDS remains the leading cause of infant death in the United States, with nearly 3,000 infant deaths annually attributed to SIDS. Risk of SIDS is highest at 2 to 4 months of age (NICHD, 2010).

Since 1992, The American Academy of Pediatrics (AAP) has recommended that infants be placed to sleep on their backs to reduce the risk of SIDS, and the frequency of prone sleeping among U.S. infants has dropped dramatically (American Academy of Pediatrics Task Force on Infant Positioning and SIDS, 2000). Researchers have found that SIDS does indeed decrease when infants sleep on their backs rather than their stomachs or sides (Dwyer & Ponsonby, 2009; McMullen, Lipke, & LeMura, 2009). Among the reasons given for prone sleeping being a high risk factor for SIDS are that it impairs the infant's arousal from sleep and restricts the infant's ability to swallow effectively (Mitchell, 2009). A recent study revealed that at 3 months, 26 percent of U.S. mothers did not use the recommended supine position for their infants' nighttime sleep (Hauck & others, 2008).

In addition to sleeping in a prone position, researchers have found that the following are risk factors for SIDS:

- SIDS is less likely to occur in infants who use a pacifier when they go to sleep (Li & others, 2006).

- Low birth weight infants are 5 to 10 times more likely to die of SIDS than are their normal-weight counterparts (Horne & others, 2002).

- Infants whose siblings have died of SIDS are two to four times as likely to die of it (Lenoir, Mallet, & Calenda, 2000).

- Six percent of infants with *sleep apnea,* a temporary cessation of breathing in which the airway is completely blocked, usually for 10 seconds or longer, die of SIDS (McNamara & Sullivan, 2000).

- African American and Eskimo infants are four to six times more likely than all others to die of SIDS (Ige & Shelton, 2004; Kitsantas & Gaffney, 2010).

sudden infant death syndrome (SIDS) A condition that occurs when an infant stops breathing, usually during the night, and suddenly dies without an apparent cause.

- SIDS is more common in lower socioeconomic groups (Mitchell & others, 2000).
- SIDS is more common in infants who are passively exposed to cigarette smoke (Shea & Steiner, 2008).
- SIDS is more common if infants sleep in soft bedding (McGarvey & others, 2006).
- SIDS is less common when infants sleep in a bedroom with a fan. A recent study revealed that sleeping in a bedroom with a fan lowers an infant's risk of SIDS by 70 percent (Coleman-Phox, Odouli, & Li, 2008).
- SIDS occurs more often in infants with abnormal brain stem functioning involving the neurotransmitter serotonin (Kinney & others, 2009).

CHILDHOOD

Experts recommend that young children get 11 to 13 hours of sleep each night (National Sleep Foundation, 2010). Most young children sleep through the night and have one daytime nap.

Following is a sampling of recent research on factors linked to children's sleep problems. A national survey indicated that children are more likely to get inadequate amounts of sleep if they show depressive symptoms, have problems at school, have a father in poor health, live in a family characterized by frequent disagreements and heated arguments, and live in an unsafe neighborhood (Smaldone, Honig, & Byrne, 2007).

One estimate indicates that more than 40 percent of children experience a sleep problem at some point in their development (Boyle & Cropley, 2004). Among the sleep problems children can develop are narcolepsy (extreme daytime sleepiness), insomnia (difficulty going to sleep or staying asleep), and nightmares (Nevsimalova, 2009; Sadeh, 2008). A recent study revealed that children who had sleep problems from 3 to 8 years of age were more likely to develop adolescent problems, such as early onset of drug use and depression.

Not only is the amount of sleep children get important, but so is uninterrupted sleep. It can be challenging to get young children to go to sleep as they drag out their bedtime routine. A recent study found that bedtime resistance was associated with conduct problems or hyperactivity in children (Carvalho Bos & others, 2009). And recent research indicates that short sleep duration in children is linked with being overweight (Nielsen, Danielsen, & Sorensen, 2010; Nixon & others, 2008).

Helping the child slow down before bedtime often contributes to less resistance in going to bed. Reading the child a story, playing quietly with the child in the bath, or letting the child sit on the caregiver's lap while listening to music are quieting activities.

What are some links between children's sleep patterns and other aspects of development?

ADOLESCENCE

There has recently been a surge of interest in adolescent sleep patterns (Moseley & Gradisar, 2009; Noland & others, 2009). This interest focuses on the belief that many adolescents are not getting enough sleep, that there are physiological underpinnings to the desire of adolescents, especially older ones, to stay up later at night and sleep longer in the morning, and that these findings have implications for understanding when adolescents learn most effectively in school (Hansen & others, 2005). For example, a recent national survey found that 8 percent of middle school students and 14 percent of high school students are late for school or miss school because they oversleep (National Sleep Foundation, 2006). Also in this survey, 6 percent of middle school students and 28 percent of high school students fall asleep in U.S. schools on any given day.

Mary Carskadon (2002, 2004, 2005, 2006) has conducted a number of research studies on adolescent sleep patterns. She has found that adolescents sleep an average

In Mary Carskadon's sleep laboratory at Brown University, an adolescent girl's brain activity is being monitored. Carskadon (2005) says that in the morning, sleep-deprived adolescents'"brains are telling them it's night time . . . and the rest of the world is saying it's time to go to school" (p. 19).

of 9 hours and 25 minutes when given the opportunity to sleep as long as they like. Most adolescents get considerably less sleep than this, especially during the week. This creates a sleep debt, which adolescents often try to make up on the weekend. Carskadon also found that older adolescents are often more sleepy during the day than are younger adolescents and concluded that this was not because of factors such as academic work and social pressures. Rather, her research suggests that adolescents' biological clocks undergo a hormonal phase shift as they get older. This pushes the time of wakefulness to an hour later than when they were young adolescents. Carskadon found that this shift was caused by a delay in the nightly presence of the hormone *melatonin*, which is produced by the brain's pineal gland in preparation for the body to sleep. Melatonin is secreted at about 9:30 P.M. in younger adolescents but is produced approximately an hour later in older adolescents, which delays the onset of sleep.

Carskadon determined that early school starting times can result in grogginess and lack of attention in class and poor performance on tests. Based on this research, schools in Edina, Minnesota, made the decision to start classes at 8:30 A.M. instead of 7:25 A.M. Discipline problems and the number of students who report an illness or depression have dropped. Test scores in Edina have improved for high school students, but not for middle school students, which supports Carskadon's idea that older adolescents are more affected by earlier school start times than younger adolescents are.

Review Connect Reflect

LG3 Summarize how sleep patterns change as children and adolescents develop.

Review

- How can sleep be characterized in infancy?
- What changes occur in sleep during childhood?
- How does adolescence affect sleep?

Connect

- In this section, you learned that exposure to cigarette smoke can affect an infant's risk for SIDS. In Chapter 3, what did you learn about cigarette smoke's effect on fetal development?

Reflect *Your Own Personal Journey of Life*

- Did your sleep patterns start to change when you became an adolescent? Have they changed since you went through puberty? If so, how?

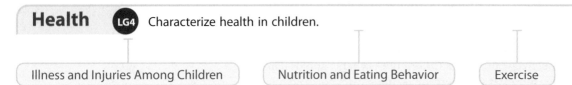

Health **LG4** Characterize health in children.

| Illness and Injuries Among Children | Nutrition and Eating Behavior | Exercise |

What are the major threats to children's health today? We will look first at the major illnesses and injuries experienced by children and adolescents before turning to less obvious threats to healthy development: poor nutrition and eating habits, and lack of exercise. The formation of healthy habits in childhood, such as eating foods low in fat and cholesterol and engaging in regular exercise, not only has immediate benefits but also contributes to the delay or prevention of premature disability and mortality in adulthood from heart disease, stroke, diabetes, and cancer.

ILLNESS AND INJURIES AMONG CHILDREN

In this section, we first examine broad patterns in the causes of illness and death among children and adolescents. Then, we turn to the difficulties faced by poor children in the United States and around the world.

Early Childhood   Young children's active and exploratory nature, coupled with being unaware of danger in many instances, often puts them in situations in which they are at risk for injuries. Most of the cuts, bumps, and bruises sustained by young children are minor, but some accidental injuries can produce serious impairment or even death. In the United States, motor vehicle accidents are the leading cause of death in young children, followed by cancer and cardiovascular disease (National Vital Statistics Report, 2004) (see Figure 4.17). In addition to motor vehicle accidents, other accidental deaths in children involve drowning, falls, burns, and poisoning (Lee & others, 2008).

Parental smoking is another major danger to children (Bolte, Fromme & the GME Study Group, 2009). Estimates indicate that approximately 22 percent of children and adolescents in the United States are exposed to tobacco smoke in the home. An increasing number of studies reach the conclusion that children are at risk for health problems when they live in homes in which a parent smokes (Carlsen & Carlsen, 2008; Chang, 2009). Children exposed to tobacco smoke in the home are more likely to develop wheezing symptoms and asthma than children in nonsmoking homes (Herrmann, King, & Weitzman, 2008). A recent study revealed that exposure to second-hand smoke was related to young children's sleep problems, including sleep-disordered breathing (Yolton & others, 2010).

An estimated 3 million U.S. children under 6 years of age are thought to be at risk for lead poisoning (Moya, Bearer, & Etzel, 2004). The negative effects of high lead levels in children's blood include lower intelligence, lower achievement, attention deficit hyperactivity disorder, and elevated blood pressure (Bellinger, 2008; Canfield & Jusko, 2008). Children in poverty face a higher risk for lead poisoning than children living in higher-socioeconomic conditions (Canfield & Jusko, 2008; Warniment, Tsang, & Galazka, 2010).

Middle and Late Childhood   For the most part, middle and late childhood is a time of excellent health (Van Dyck, 2007). Disease and death are less prevalent in this period than in early childhood and adolescence.

The most common cause of severe injury and death in middle and late childhood is motor vehicle accidents, either as a pedestrian or as a passenger (Frisbie, Hummer, & McKinnon, 2009). Using safety-belt restraints is important in reducing the severity of motor vehicle injuries.

Most accidents occur in or near the child's home or school. The most effective prevention strategy is to educate the child about the hazards of risk taking and improper use of equipment (Snowdon & others, 2008). Appropriate safety helmets, protective eye and mouth shields, and protective padding are recommended for children who engage in active sports.

Cancer   Children not only are vulnerable to injuries, they also may develop life-threatening diseases. Cancer is the second leading cause of death in children 5 to 14 years of age. Three percent of all children's deaths in this age period are due to

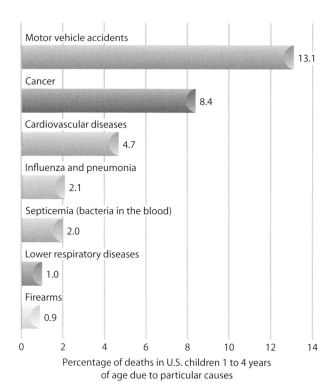

Percentage of deaths in U.S. children 1 to 4 years of age due to particular causes

FIGURE **4.17**

MAIN CAUSES OF DEATH IN CHILDREN 1 THROUGH 4 YEARS OF AGE. These figures show the percentage of deaths in U.S. children 1 to 4 years of age due to particular causes in 2002 (National Vital Statistics Reports, 2004).

cancer. Currently, 1 in every 330 children in the United States develops cancer before the age of 19. Moreover, the incidence of cancer in children is increasing (National Cancer Institute, 2009a).

Childhood cancers have a different profile from adult cancers. Cancers in adults attack mainly the lungs, colon, breast, prostate, and pancreas. In children, cancers mainly attack the white blood cells (leukemia), brain, bone, lymphatic system, muscles, kidneys, and nervous system (Eden, 2010; Kaatsch, 2010).

The most common cancer in children is leukemia, a cancer of the tissues that make blood cells (Chang, 2009; Stanulla & Schrappe, 2009). In leukemia, the bone marrow makes an abundance of white blood cells that don't function properly. They crowd out normal cells, making the child susceptible to bruising and infection.

Cardiovascular Disease   Cardiovascular disease is uncommon in children. Nonetheless, environmental experiences and behavior in the childhood years can sow the seeds for cardiovascular disease in adulthood. Many elementary-school-aged children already possess one or more of the risk factors for cardiovascular disease, such as hypertension and obesity (Urbina, 2008). A recent national study found that an increasing percentage of U.S. children and adolescents had elevated blood pressure from 1988 to 2006 (Ostchega & others, 2009). In this study, children who were obese were more likely to have elevated blood pressure. Further, one study revealed that high blood pressure goes undiagnosed in 75 percent of children with the disease (Hansen, Gunn, & Kaelber, 2007).

Health, Illness, and Poverty Among the World's Children   An estimated 7 percent of U.S. children receive no health care, and the vast majority of these children live in poverty. One approach to children's health aims to treat not only medical problems of the individual child but also the conditions of the entire family. In fact, some programs seek to identify children who are at risk for problems and then try to alter the risk factors in an effort to prevent illness and disease.

Poverty in the United States is dwarfed by poverty in developing countries around the world. Each year UNICEF produces a report entitled *The State of the World's Children*. In a recent report, UNICEF (2006) concluded that the under-5 mortality rate is the result of a wide range of factors, including the nutritional health and health knowledge of mothers, the level of immunization, dehydration, availability of maternal and child health services, income and food availability in the

What are some of the main causes of death in young children around the world?

family, availability of clean water and safe sanitation, and the overall safety of the child's environment.

Devastating effects on the health of young children occur in countries where poverty rates are high (UNICEF, 2009, 2010). The poor are the majority in nearly one of every five nations in the world (UNICEF, 2009). They often experience lives of hunger, malnutrition, illness, inadequate access to health care, unsafe water, and a lack of protection from harm (Horton, 2006).

In the last decade, there has been a dramatic increase in the number of young children who have died because HIV/AIDS was transmitted to them by their parents (UNICEF, 2009). Deaths in young children due to HIV/AIDS occur most frequently in countries with high rates of poverty and low levels of education. For example, uneducated people are four times more likely to believe that there is no way to avoid AIDS and three times more likely to be unaware that the virus can be transmitted from mother to child (UNICEF, 2006).

Many of the deaths of young children around the world can be prevented by a reduction in poverty and improvements in nutrition, sanitation, education, and health services (UNICEF, 2009, 2010).

NUTRITION AND EATING BEHAVIOR

Poverty influences health in part through its effects on nutrition. However, it is not just children living in low-income families who have health-related nutrition problems; across the spectrum of income levels, recent decades have seen a dramatic increase in the percent of U.S. children who are overweight.

Infancy   From birth to 1 year of age, human infants nearly triple their weight and increase their length by 50 percent. What do they need to sustain this growth?

Nutritional Needs and Eating Behavior   Individual differences among infants in terms of their nutrient reserves, body composition, growth rates, and activity patterns make it difficult to define actual nutrient needs (Burns & others, 2009; Schiff, 2011; Wardlaw & Smith, 2011). However, because parents need guidelines, nutritionists recommend that infants consume approximately 50 calories per day for each pound they weigh—more than twice an adult's requirement per pound.

A national study of more than 3,000 randomly selected 4- to 24-month-olds documented that many U.S. parents aren't feeding their babies enough fruits and vegetables, but are feeding them too much junk food (Fox & others, 2004). Up to one-third of the babies ate no vegetables and fruit but frequently ate French fries, and almost half of the 7- to 8-month-old babies were fed desserts, sweets, or sweetened drinks. By 15 months, French fries were the most common vegetable the babies ate.

Such poor dietary patterns early in development can result in more infants being overweight (Black & others, 2009; Hesketh & Campbell, 2010). The Centers for Disease Control and Prevention (2009) has a category of obesity for adults but does not have an obesity category for infants, children, and adolescents because of the stigma the label may bring. Rather, they have categories for being overweight or at risk for being overweight in childhood and adolescence. Children are considered overweight if they are above the 95th percentile in weight for their age and gender; they are labeled at-risk for being overweight if they are between the 85th and 95th percentiles.

One analysis revealed that in 1980, 3.4 percent of U.S. babies less than 6 months old were overweight, a percentage that increased to 5.9 percent in 2001 (Kim & others, 2006). As shown in Figure 4.18, as younger infants become older infants, an even greater percentage are overweight. Also in this study, in addition to the 5.9 percent of infants

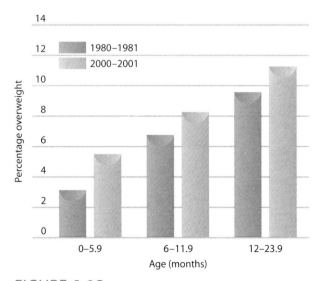

FIGURE **4.18**

PERCENTAGE OF OVERWEIGHT U.S. INFANTS IN 1980–1981 AND 2000–2001. *Note:* Infants above the 95th percentile for their age and gender on a weight-for-height index were categorized as overweight.

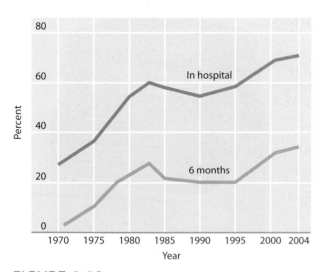

FIGURE 4.19

TRENDS IN BREAST FEEDING IN THE UNITED STATES: 1970–2004

Human milk or an alternative formula is a baby's source of nutrients for the first four to six months. The growing consensus is that breast feeding is better for the baby's health, although controversy still swirls about the issue of breast feeding versus bottle feeding. *Why is breast feeding strongly recommended by pediatricians?*

less than 6 months old who were overweight in 2001, another 11 percent were categorized as at risk for being overweight.

In addition to consuming too many French fries, sweetened drinks, and desserts, are there other factors that might explain this increase in overweight U.S. infants? A mother's weight gain during pregnancy and a mother's own high weight before pregnancy may be factors (McGuire, Dyson, & Renfrew, 2010; Murray & McKinney, 2010). One important factor seems to be whether an infant is breast fed or bottle fed. Breast fed infants have lower rates of weight gain than bottle fed infants by school age, and it is estimated that breast feeding reduces the risk of obesity by approximately 20 percent (Li & others, 2007).

Breast Versus Bottle Feeding For the first four to six months of life, human milk or an alternative formula is the baby's source of nutrients and energy. For years, debate has focused on whether breast feeding is better for the infant than bottle feeding. The growing consensus is that breast feeding is better for the baby's health (Lawrence, 2008; Thorley, 2009; Walker, 2010; Wilson, 2010). Since the 1970s, breast feeding by U.S. mothers has soared (see Figure 4.19). In 2004 more than two-thirds of U.S. mothers breast fed their newborns, and more than a third breast fed their 6-month-olds. The American Academy of Pediatrics (AAP) and the American Dietetic Association strongly endorse breast feeding throughout the infant's first year (AAP Work Group on Breastfeeding, 1997; James & Dobson, 2005).

What are some of the benefits of breast feeding? The following conclusions are based on the current status of research:

Evaluation of Outcomes for Child

- *Gastrointestinal infections.* Breast fed infants have fewer gastrointestinal infections (Garofalo, 2010; Pfluger & others, 2010).

- *Lower respiratory tract infections.* Breast fed infants have fewer infections of the lower respiratory tract (Ip & others, 2009).

- *Allergies.* A recent research review by the American Academy of Pediatrics indicated that there is no evidence that breast feeding reduces the risk of allergies in children (Greer & others, 2008). The research review also concluded that modest evidence exists for feeding hyperallergenic formulas to susceptible babies if they are not solely breast fed.

- *Asthma.* The recent research review by the American Academy of Pediatrics concluded that exclusive breast feeding for three months protects against wheezing in babies, but whether it prevents asthma in older children is unclear (Greer & others, 2008).

- *Otitis media.* Breast fed infants are less likely to develop this middle ear infection (Rovers, de Kok, & Schilder, 2006).

- *Atopic dermatitis.* Breast fed babies are less likely to have this chronic inflammation of the skin (Snijders & others, 2007). The recent research review by the American Academy of Pediatrics also concluded that for infants with a family history of allergies, breast feeding exclusively for at least four months is linked to a lower risk of skin rashes (Greer & others, 2008).

- *Overweight and obesity.* Consistent evidence indicates that breast fed infants are less likely to become overweight or obese in childhood, adolescence, and adulthood (Lamb & others, 2010; Moschonis, Grammatikaki, & Manios, 2008).

- *Diabetes.* Breast fed infants are less likely to develop type 1 diabetes in childhood (Ping & Hagopian, 2006) and type 2 diabetes in adulthood (Villegas & others, 2008).

- *SIDS.* Breast fed infants are less likely to experience SIDS (Alm, Lagercrantz, & Wennergren, 2006; Stuebe, 2009).

In recent large-scale research reviews, no conclusive evidence for the benefits of breast feeding was found for children's cognitive development and cardiovascular system (Agency for Healthcare Research and Quality, 2007; Ip & others, 2009).

Evaluation of Outcomes for Mother

- *Breast cancer.* Consistent evidence indicates a lower incidence of breast cancer in women who breast feed their infants (Akbari & others, 2010; Shema & others, 2007).
- *Ovarian cancer.* Evidence also reveals a reduction in ovarian cancer in women who breast feed their infants (Jordan & others, 2008; Stuebe & Schwartz, 2010).
- *Type 2 diabetes.* Some evidence suggests a small reduction in type 2 diabetes in women who breast feed their infants (Ip & others, 2009; Stuebe & Schwartz, 2010).

In recent large-scale research reviews, no conclusive evidence could be found for maternal benefits of breast feeding with regard to return to prepregnancy weight, osteoporosis, and postpartum depression (Agency for Healthcare Research and Quality, 2007; Ip & others, 2009). However, a recent study revealed that women who breast fed their infants had a lower incidence of metabolic syndrome (a disorder characterized by obesity, hypertension, and insulin resistance) in midlife (Ram & others, 2008).

Many health professionals have argued that breast feeding facilitates the development of an attachment bond between the mother and infant (Britton, Britton, & Gronwaldt, 2006; Wittig & Spatz, 2008). However, a recent research review found that the positive role of breast feeding on the mother-infant relationship is not supported by research (Jansen, de Weerth, & Riksen-Walraven, 2008). The review concluded that recommending breast feeding should not be based on its role in improving the mother-infant relationship but rather on its positive effects on infant and maternal health.

The AAP Work Group on Breastfeeding strongly endorses breast feeding throughout the first year of life (AAPWGB, 1997). Are there circumstances when mothers should not breast feed? Yes, a mother should not breast feed (1) when she is infected with HIV or some other infectious disease that can be transmitted through her milk, (2) if she has active tuberculosis, or (3) if she is taking any drug that may not be safe for the infant (Berlin, Paul, & Vesell, 2009; Buhimschi & Weiner, 2009; Gumbo & others, 2010; Oladokun & others, 2010).

Some women cannot breast feed their infants because of physical difficulties; others feel guilty if they terminate breast feeding early. Mothers may also worry that they are depriving their infants of important emotional and psychological benefits if they bottle feed rather than breast feed. Some researchers have found, however, that there are no psychological differences between breast fed and bottle fed infants (Ferguson, Harwood, & Shannon, 1987; Young, 1990).

A further issue in interpreting the benefits of breast feeding was underscored in recent large-scale research reviews (Agency for Healthcare Research and Quality, 2007; Ip & others, 2009). While highlighting a number of breast feeding benefits for children and mothers, the report issued a caution about breast feeding research: None of the findings imply causality. Breast versus bottle feeding studies are correlational rather than experimental, and women who breast feed are wealthier, older, more educated, and likely more health-conscious than their bottle feeding counterparts, which could explain why breast fed children are healthier.

developmental connection

Research Methods. How does a correlational study differ from an experimental study? Chapter 1, pp. 34–35

Malnutrition in Infancy Early weaning of infants from breast milk to inadequate sources of nutrients, such as unsuitable and unsanitary cow's milk formula, can cause protein deficiency and malnutrition in infants (Kramer, 2003). Something that looks like milk but is not, usually a form of tapioca or rice, is also often substituted for breast milk. In many of the world's developing countries, mothers used to breast feed their infants for at least two years. To become more modern, they stopped

The Stories of Latonya and Ramona: Breast and Bottle Feeding in Africa

Latonya is a newborn baby in Ghana. During her first days of life, she has been kept apart from her mother and bottle fed. Manufacturers of infant formula provide free or subsidized milk powder to the hospital where she was born. Her mother has been persuaded to bottle feed rather than breast feed Latonya. When her mother bottle feeds Latonya, she overdilutes the milk formula with unclean water. Latonya's feeding bottles have not been sterilized. Latonya becomes very sick, and she dies before her first birthday.

Ramona was born in Nigeria, where her family takes part in a "baby-friendly" program. In this program, babies are not separated from their mothers when they are born, and the mothers are encouraged to breast feed them. The mothers are told of the perils that bottle feeding can bring because of unsafe water and unsterilized bottles. They also are informed about the advantages of breast milk, which include its nutritious and hygienic qualities, its ability to immunize babies against common illnesses, and its role in reducing the mother's risk of breast and ovarian cancer. Ramona's mother is breast feeding her. At 1 year of age, Ramona is very healthy.

For many years, maternity units in hospitals favored bottle feeding and did not give mothers adequate information about the benefits of breast feeding. In recent years, the World Health Organization and UNICEF have tried to reverse the trend toward bottle feeding of infants in many impoverished countries. They instituted the "baby-friendly" program in many countries (Grant, 1993). They also persuaded the International Association of Infant Formula Manufacturers to stop marketing their baby formulas to hospitals in countries where the governments support the baby-friendly initiatives (Grant, 1997). For the hospitals themselves, costs actually were reduced as infant formula, feeding bottles, and separate nurseries become unnecessary. For example, baby-friendly Jose Fabella Memorial Hospital in the Philippines reported saving 8 percent of its annual budget.

The advantages of breast feeding in impoverished countries are substantial. However, these advantages must be balanced against the risk of passing HIV to the babies through breast milk if the mothers have the virus; the majority of mothers don't know that they are infected (Gumbo & others, 2010; Moorthy & others, 2009; Oladokun & others, 2010). In some areas of Africa, more than 30 percent of mothers have the human immunodeficiency virus (HIV).

In what ways does education play a role in the health decisions discussed in this interlude?

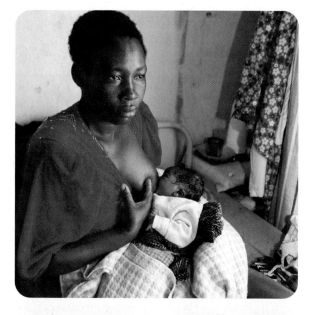

(*Top*) An HIV-infected mother breast feeding her baby in Nairobi, Africa. (*Bottom*) A Rwandan mother bottle feeding her baby. *What are some concerns about breast versus bottle feeding in impoverished African countries?*

breast feeding much earlier and replaced it with bottle feeding. Comparisons of breast fed and bottle fed infants in countries such as Afghanistan, Haiti, Ghana, and Chile document that the mortality rate of bottle fed infants is as much as five times that of breast fed infants (Grant, 1997). However, in the *Connecting With Diversity* interlude above, you can read about a recent concern regarding breast feeding.

Two life-threatening conditions that can result from malnutrition are marasmus and kwashiorkor. **Marasmus** is caused by a severe protein-calorie deficiency and results in a wasting away of body tissues in the infant's first year. The infant becomes grossly underweight and his or her muscles atrophy. **Kwashiorkor,** caused by severe protein deficiency, usually appears between 1 and 3 years of age. Children with kwashiorkor sometimes appear to be well fed even though they are not because the disease can cause the child's abdomen and feet to swell with water. Kwashiorkor causes a child's vital organs to collect the nutrients that are present and deprive other parts of the body of them. The child's hair becomes thin, brittle, and colorless, and the child's behavior often becomes listless.

Even if it is not fatal, severe and lengthy malnutrition is detrimental to physical, cognitive, and social development (de Onis & others, 2006; Ruel, 2010; Victoria & others, 2010). A recent study of Indian children documented the negative influence of chronic malnutrition on children's cognitive development. Children who had a history of chronic malnutrition performed more poorly on tests of attention and memory than their counterparts who were not malnourished (Kar, Rao, & Chandramouli, 2008).

Another study linked the diets of rural Guatemalan infants with their social development at the time they entered elementary school (Barrett, Radke-Yarrow, & Klein, 1982). Children whose mothers had been given nutritious supplements during pregnancy, and who themselves had been given more nutritious, high-calorie foods in their first two years of life, were more active, more involved, more helpful with their peers, less anxious, and happier than their counterparts who had not been given nutritional supplements. Also, a recent study found that two food-assisted maternal and child health nutrition programs (both emphasizing food provision, communication about behavior change, and preventive health services) helped to reduce the impact of economic hardship on stunting of children's growth in Haiti (Donegan & others, 2010). To read further about providing nutritional supplements to improve infants' and young children's nutrition, see *Caring Connections* on the next page.

Adequate early nutrition is an important aspect of healthy development (Schiff, 2011; Wardlaw & Smith, 2011). In addition to sound nutrition, children need a nurturing, supportive environment (Banta, 2010; Hewitt-Taylor, 2010). One individual who has stood out as an advocate of caring for children is T. Berry Brazelton, who is featured in the *Connecting With Careers* profile on page 133.

This Honduran child has kwashiorkor. Notice the telltale sign of kwashiorkor—a greatly expanded abdomen. *What are some other characteristics of kwashiorkor?*

Childhood   Poor nutrition in childhood can lead to a number of problems and occurs more frequently in low-income than in higher-income families (Ruel & others, 2008). A special concern is the increasing epidemic of overweight children.

Malnutrition Among Children in Low-Income Families   Malnutrition and even starvation are daily facts of life for children in many developing countries (UNICEF, 2009, 2010). Malnutrition also is a problem for U.S. children, with approximately 11 million preschool children experiencing malnutrition, placing their health at risk (Richter, 2004). One of the most common nutritional problems in early childhood is iron deficiency anemia, which results in chronic fatigue (Bartle, 2007). This problem results from the failure to eat adequate amounts of quality meats and dark green vegetables. Young children from low-income families are most likely to develop iron deficiency anemia (Shamah & Villalpando, 2006). A recent study revealed that preschool children with iron deficiency anemia were slower to display positive affect and to touch novel toys for the first time than their nonanemic counterparts (Lozoff & others, 2007).

Eating Behavior and Parental Feeding Styles   For most children in the United States, insufficient food is not the key problem. Instead, unhealthy eating habits and being overweight threaten their present and future health (Bolling & Daniels, 2008).

Children's eating behavior is strongly influenced by their caregivers' behavior (Black & Hurley, 2007; Ventura, Gromis, & Lohse, 2010). Children's eating behavior improves when caregivers eat with children on a predictable schedule, model eating

marasmus Severe malnutrition caused by an insufficient protein-calorie intake, resulting in a shrunken, elderly appearance.

kwashiorkor Severe malnutrition caused by a protein-deficient diet, causing the feet and abdomen to swell with water.

Improving the Nutrition of Infants and Young Children Living in Low-Income Families

Poor nutrition is a special concern in the lives of infants from low-income families. To address this problem in the United States, the WIC (Women, Infants, and Children) program provides federal grants to states for healthy supplemental foods, health care referrals, and nutrition education for women from low-income families beginning in pregnancy, and to infants and young children up to five years of age who are at nutritional risk (Food & Nutrition Service, 2009; WIC New York, 2009). WIC serves approximately 7,500,000 participants in the United States. In 2009, WIC made changes in the program to promote breast feeding and provide more nutritious food (Food & Nutrition Service, 2009; WIC New York, 2009):

- *Increase breast feeding.* WIC staff are being trained in lactation counseling and in most programs, peer counseling services are available to pregnant women and new mothers.
- *Provide food lower in fat content.* Only one percent or skim milk is available for children two years of age and older and women; low fat cheese and tofu are options.
- *Distribute food higher in fiber, and include more vegetables and fruits.* Vouchers provided to low-income families encourage the consumption of whole-grain cereals and breads, as well as more vegetable and fruits.
- *Have food available that is more culturally appropriate.* For example, brown rice or whole-grain tortillas can be substituted for whole-grain breads; calcium-set tofu or calcium-fortified soy milk can be substituted for cow's milk.

    An expanding research initiative is exploring ways to improve the WIC program and assess its influence on mothers, infants, and young children's nutrition and health (Black & others, 2009; Davis, Lazariu, & Sekhobo, 2010; Hannan & others, 2009; Heinig & others, 2009; Olson & others, 2010a, b; Sekhobo & others, 2010). A recent study revealed that a WIC program that introduced peer counseling services for pregnant

Participants in the WIC program. *What are some of the recent changes implemented in the WIC program in 2009?*

women increased breast feeding initiation by 27 percent (Olson & others, 2010a, b). Another recent study found that entry in the first trimester of pregnancy to the WIC program in Rhode Island reduced maternal cigarette smoking. Yet another study indicated that participating in WIC was linked with a lower risk for being overweight in young Mexican American children (Melgar-Quinonez & Kaiser, 2004).

Why would the WIC program provide lactation counseling as part of its services?

healthy food, make mealtimes pleasant occasions, and engage in certain feeding styles. Distractions from television, family arguments, and competing activities should be minimized so children can focus on eating. A sensitive/responsive caregiver feeding style is recommended, in which the caregiver is nurturant, provides clear information about what is expected, and responds appropriately to children's cues (Black & Hurley, 2007). Forceful and restrictive caregiver behaviors are not recommended. For example, a restrictive feeding style is linked to children being overweight (Black & Lozoff, 2008).

Overweight Children Being overweight has become a serious health problem in early childhood (Blake, 2011; Marcdante, Kliegman, & Behrman, 2011). A recent national study revealed that 45 percent of children's meals exceed recommendations

connecting with careers

T. Berry Brazelton, Pediatrician

T. Berry Brazelton is America's best-known pediatrician as a result of his numerous books, television appearances, and newspaper and magazine articles about parenting and children's health. He takes a family-centered approach to child development issues and communicates with parents in easy-to-understand ways.

Dr. Brazelton founded the Child Development Unit at Boston Children's Hospital and created the Brazelton Neonatal Behavioral Assessment Scale, a widely used measure of the newborn's health and well-being (described in Chapter 3). He also has conducted a number of research studies on infants and children and has been president of the Society for Research in Child Development, a leading research organization.

For more information about what pediatricians do, see page 46 in the Careers in Child Development appendix following Chapter 1.

T. Berry Brazelton, pediatrician, with a young child.

---

for saturated and trans fat, which can raise cholesterol levels and increase the risk of heart disease (Center for Science in the Public Interest, 2008). This study also found that one-third of children's daily caloric intake comes from restaurants, twice the percentage consumed away from home in the 1980s. Further, 93 percent of almost 1,500 possible choices at 13 major fast food chains exceeded 430 calories—one third of what the National Institute of Medicine recommends that 4- to 8-year old children consume in a day. Nearly every combination of children's meals at KFC, Taco Bell, Sonic, Jack in the Box, and Chick-fil-A were too high in calories.

The percentages of young children who are overweight or at risk for being overweight in the United States have increased dramatically in recent decades (see Figure 4.20), and these percentages are likely to grow unless changes are made in children's lifestyles (Sorte, Daeschel, & Amador, 2011; Thompson, Manore, & Vaughn, 2011). A recent study revealed that in the period from 2003 to 2006, 11 percent of U.S. 2- to 19-year-olds were obese, 16 percent were overweight, and 38 percent were at risk for being overweight (Ogden, Carroll, & Flegal, 2008). The good news from this large-scale study is that the percentages in these categories have started to level off rather than increase, as they had been doing in the last several decades.

Still, the levels of being overweight or at-risk for being overweight remain far too high (Donatelle, 2011; Frisco, 2009). Note that girls are more likely than boys to be overweight, and this gender difference occurs in many countries (Sweeting, 2008). In a recent large-scale U.S. study, African American and Latino children were more likely to be overweight or obese than non-Latino White children (Benson, Baer, & Kaelber, 2009).

It is not just in the United States that children are becoming more overweight. Recent surveys and policy prescriptions in Australia, mainland China, Hong Kong, and other countries indicate that children in many countries around the world are becoming more overweight (Chan, 2008; Li & others, 2009).

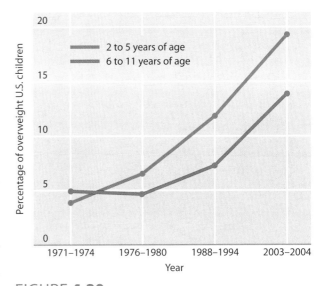

FIGURE **4.20**

THE INCREASE IN THE PERCENTAGE OF OVERWEIGHT CHILDREN IN THE UNITED STATES (CENTERS FOR DISEASE CONTROL AND PREVENTION, 2008B)

The risk for overweight children continuing to be overweight when they become older was documented in one study. In this study, children's weight at five years of age was significantly linked to their weight at nine years of age (Gardner & others, 2009). And another study revealed that the prevalence of being overweight remained stable from 4 to 11 years of age for children with lean parents but more than doubled across this time frame for children with obese parents (17 percent to 45 percent) (Semmler & others, 2009).

Being overweight in childhood is linked to being overweight in adulthood. One study revealed that girls who were overweight in childhood were 11 to 30 times more likely to be obese in adulthood than girls who were not overweight in childhood (Thompson & others, 2007).

The increase in overweight children in recent decades is cause for great concern because being overweight raises the risk of developing many medical and psychological problems (Jago & others, 2010; Oliver & others, 2010; Pott & others, 2009; Raghuveer, 2010). Overweight children are at risk for developing pulmonary problems, such as sleep apnea (which involves upper-airway obstruction), and hip problems (Goodwin & others, 2010). Diabetes, hypertension (high blood pressure), and elevated blood cholesterol levels also are common in children who are overweight (Viikari & others, 2009). Once considered rare, childhood hypertension has become increasingly common in overweight children (Amed & others, 2010). Social and psychological consequences of being overweight in childhood include low self-esteem, depression, and exclusion of obese children from peer groups (Gibson & others, 2008).

Both heredity and environment influence whether children will become overweight. Recent genetic analysis indicates that heredity is an important factor in children becoming overweight (Wardle & others, 2008). Overweight parents tend to have overweight children, even if they are not living in the same household (Wardlaw & Hampl, 2007). One study found that the greatest risk factor for being overweight at 9 years of age was having a parent who was overweight (Agras & others, 2004).

Environmental factors that influence whether children become overweight include availability of food (especially food high in fat content), use of energy-saving devices, lack of declining physical activity, lack of parental monitoring of children's eating habits, the context in which a child eats, and heavy TV watching (Byrd-Williams & others, 2008; Shoup & others, 2008). The American culture provides ample encouragement of overeating in children. Food is everywhere children go and easily accessed—in vending machines, fast-food restaurants, and so on (Rosenheck, 2008). Also, the portion size that children eat in meals in the United States has grown.

Many experts recommend a program that involves a combination of diet, exercise, and behavior modification to help children lose weight (Wittmeier, Mollar, & Kriellaars, 2008). As we learned in Angie's story at the beginning of the chapter, a combination of behavioral modification, a structured program, and positive parental involvement can be effective in helping overweight children.

Parents play an important role in preventing children from becoming overweight and helping them lose weight if they become overweight (Slawta & Deneui, 2009). They can encourage healthy eating habits in children by eating more family meals together, making healthy foods available, and not keeping sugar-sweetened beverages and other unhealthy foods in the home. They also can help reduce the likelihood their children will become overweight by reducing children's TV time, getting children involved in sports and other physical activities, and being healthy and physically active themselves.

In sum, healthy eating and an active rather than a sedentary lifestyle play important roles in children's development (Graham, Holt/Hale, & Parker, 2010; Roemmich & others, 2009; Stone & others, 2009). Pediatric nurses can influence

What are some concerns about overweight children?

Barbara Deloin, Pediatric Nurse

Barbara Deloin is a pediatric nurse in Denver, Colorado. She practices nursing in the Pediatric Oral Feeding Clinic and is involved in research as part of an irritable infant study for the Children's Hospital in Denver. She also is on the faculty of nursing at the Colorado Health Sciences Center. Deloin previously worked in San Diego where she was coordinator of the Child Health Program for the County of San Diego.

Her research interests focus on children with special health-care needs, especially high-risk infants and children, and promoting positive parent-child experiences. Deloin was elected president of the National Association of Pediatric Nurse Associates and Practitioners for the 2000–2001 term.

For more information about what pediatric nurses do, see page 46 in the Careers in Child Development appendix following Chapter 1.

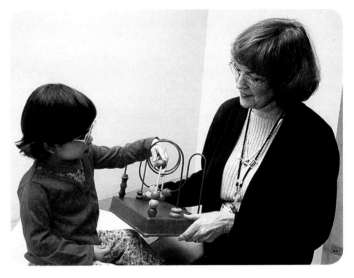

Barbara Deloin working with a child with special health care needs.

the health of children by providing advice to parents about ways to improve their children's eating habits and activity levels. To read about the work of one pediatric nurse, see the *Connecting With Careers* profile of Barbara Deloin.

EXERCISE

Because of their activity level and the development of large muscles, especially in the arms and legs, children need daily exercise (Graham, Holt/Hale, & Parker, 2010; Rink, 2009). However, children are not getting nearly enough exercise (Fahey, Insel, & Roth, 2011; Lumpkin, 2011). In one historical comparison, the percentage of children involved in daily physical education (P.E.) programs in schools decreased from 80 percent in 1969 to 20 percent in 1999 (Health Management Resources, 2001). Educators and policy makers in many other countries around the world, including China, Finland, and Great Britain, have become extremely concerned about the sedentary lifestyles of many children in their countries (Fogelholm, 2008).

Television watching is linked with low activity and obesity in children (Wells & others, 2008). A related concern is the dramatic increase in computer use by children. Researcher have found that the total time that children spend in front of a television or computer screen places them at risk for reduced activity and possible weight gain (Lajunen & others, 2007). A longitudinal study found that a higher incidence of watching TV in childhood and adolescence was linked with being overweight, being less physically fit, and having higher cholesterol levels at 26 years of age (Hancox, Milne, & Poulton, 2004).

Routine physical activity should be a daily occurrence for young children (Dowda & others, 2009). Guidelines recommend that preschool children engage in two hours of physical activity per day, divided into one hour of structured activity and one hour of unstructured free play (National Association for Sport and Physical Education, 2002). The child's life should be centered around activities, not meals.

What are some positive outcomes when young children exercise regularly?

Following are descriptions of three recent research studies that examine young children's exercise and activities:

- Observations of 3- to 5-year-old children during outdoor play at preschools revealed that the preschool children were mainly sedentary even when participating in outdoor play (Brown & others, 2009). In this study, throughout the day the preschoolers were sedentary 89 percent of the time, engaged in light activity 8 percent of the time, and participated in moderate to vigorous physical activity only 3 percent of the time.

- Preschool children's physical activity was enhanced by family members engaging in sports together and by parents' perception that it was safe for their children to play outside (Beets & Foley, 2008).

- Incorporation of a "move and learn" physical activity curriculum increased the activity level of 3- to 5-year-old children in a half-day preschool program (Trost, Fees, & Dzewaltowski, 2008).

Increasing children's exercise levels has positive outcomes (McGuigan & others, 2009). A recent study found that 45 minutes of moderate physical activity and 15 minutes of vigorous physical activity daily were related to decreased odds of children being overweight (Wittmeier, Mollar, & Kriellaars, 2008).

Parents and schools play important roles in children's exercise levels (Fahey, Insel, & Roth, 2011; Loprinzi & Trost, 2010). Growing up with parents who exercise regularly provides positive models of exercise for children (Crawford & others, 2010; Loprinzi & Trost, 2010). A recent study revealed that mothers were more likely than fathers to limit sedentary behavior in boys and girls (Edwardson & Gorely, 2010). In this study, fathers did have an influence on their sons' physical activity, but primarily through explicit modeling of physical activity, such as showing their sons how to shoot a basketball. Another recent study found that a school-based physical activity was successful in improving children's fitness and lowering their fat content (Kriemler & others, 2010).

Researchers also are finding that exercise is linked to children's cognitive development. For example, a recent research study revealed that aerobic exercise was linked to increases in an important cognitive activity—planning—in overweight 9-year-old children (Davis & others, 2007). In another recent study, 9-year-old girls who were more physically fit (as measured on a field test of aerobic capacity) showed better cognitive performance on a cognitive control task that involved inhibiting task-irrelevant information to obtain correct solutions than 9-year-old girls who were less physically fit (Hillman & others, 2009).

Boys and girls become less active as they reach and progress through adolescence (Merrick & others, 2005). A study of more than 3,000 U.S. adolescents found

In 2007, Texas became the first state to test students' physical fitness. The student shown here is performing the trunk lift. Other assessments include aerobic exercise, muscle strength, and body fat. Assessments will be done annually.

that 34 percent were in the lowest fitness category (Carnethon, Gulati, & Greenland, 2005). Another study revealed that physical fitness in adolescence was linked to physical fitness in adulthood (Mikkelsson & others, 2006).

Gender and ethnic differences in exercise participation rates are noteworthy, and they reflect the trend of decreasing exercise from early through late adolescence. A recent study revealed that 40 percent of female and 57 percent of male adolescents met U.S. guidelines for physical activity (Butcher & others, 2008). Also, as indicated in Figure 4.21, in the National Youth Risk Survey, non-Latino White boys exercised the most, African American girls the least (Eaton & others, 2006).

Here are some ways to get children and adolescents to exercise more:

- Improve physical fitness classes in schools.
- Offer more physical activity programs run by volunteers at school facilities.
- Have children plan community and school exercise activities that really interest them.
- Encourage families to focus on physical activity, and challenge parents to exercise more.

To find out how much activity most preschool students are currently getting, see *Connecting Through Research*.

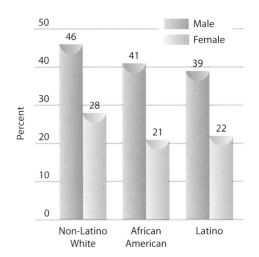

FIGURE 4.21

EXERCISE RATES OF U.S. HIGH SCHOOL STUDENTS: GENDER AND ETHNICITY.
Note: Data are for high school students who were physically active doing any kind of physical activity that increased their heart rate and made them breathe hard some of the time for a total of at least 60 minutes a day on five or more of the seven days preceding the survey.

connecting through research

Are Preschool Children Getting Enough Physical Activity?

One study examined the activity level of 281 3- to 5-year-olds in nine preschools (Pate & others, 2004). Each child wore an accelerometer (a small activity monitor) for four to five hours a day. Height and weight assessments of the children were made to calculate each child's body mass index (BMI).

Recently developed guidelines recommend that preschool children engage in two hours of physical activity per day, divided into one hour of structured activity and one hour of unstructured free play (National Association for Sport and Physical Education, 2002). In this study, the young children participated in an average of 7.7 minutes per hour of moderate to vigorous activity, usually in a block of time when they were outside. Over the course of eight hours of a preschool day, these children would get approximately one hour of moderate and vigorous physical activity, only about 50 percent of the amount recommended. The researchers concluded that young children are unlikely to engage in another hour per day of moderate and vigorous physical activity outside their eight hours spent in preschool and thus are not getting adequate opportunities for physical activity.

Gender and age differences characterized the preschool children's physical activity. Boys were more likely to engage in moderate or vigorous physical activity than girls. Four- and five-year-old children were more likely to be sedentary than three-year-old children.

The young children's physical activity also varied according to the particular preschool they attended. The extent to which they participated in moderate and vigorous physical activity ranged from 4.4 to 10.2 minutes per hour across the nine preschools. Thus, the policies and practices of particular preschools influence the extent to which children engage in physical activity. The researchers concluded that young children need more vigorous play and organized activities. Unfortunately, there is a trend toward reducing time for physical activity, especially eliminating recess, in U.S. elementary schools that is trickling down to kindergarten and preschool programs. This decrease is part of a larger trend that involves narrowing early childhood programs to focus on academic learning and moving away from more comprehensive programs that focus on the whole child (Hyson, Copple, & Jones, 2006).

Earlier, we discussed heredity and the influence of parents' health behaviors on their children's health behaviors. Here, we have identified preschool policies and practices as an environmental factor affecting children's health. As adolescents, they also will have to contend with the strong influences of their peers and the media on their health behaviors. These influences can have a compounding effect over time, so establishing healthy role models and environments for children early on is clearly important.

Review

- What are the key health problems facing children?
- What are some important aspects of children's nutrition and eating behavior?
- What role does exercise play in children's development?

Connect

- Nutrition was discussed earlier in the chapter as well. What did you learn about nutrition's effect on growth?

Reflect *Your Own Personal Journey of Life*

- What were your eating habits like as a child? In what ways are they similar to or different from your current eating habits? Do you think your early eating habits predicted whether you would have weight problems in adulthood?

reach your **learning goals**

Physical Development and Health

Body Growth and Change

LG1 Discuss developmental changes in the body.

Patterns of Growth

Infancy and Childhood

Adolescence

- Human growth follows cephalocaudal and proximodistal patterns. In a cephalocaudal pattern, the fastest growth occurs at the top—the head. Physical growth in size, weight, and feature differentiation occurs gradually, moves from the top to the bottom. In a proximodistal pattern, growth begins at the center of the body and then moves toward the extremities.

- Height and weight increase rapidly in infancy and then take a slower course during childhood. The average North American newborn is 20 inches long and weighs 7½ pounds. Infants grow about 1 inch per month during their first year. In early childhood, girls are only slightly smaller and lighter than boys. Growth is slow and consistent in middle and late childhood, and head circumference, waist circumference, and leg length decrease in relation to body height.

- Puberty is a rapid maturation involving hormonal and body changes that occur primarily in early adolescence. Puberty began to occur at younger ages during the twentieth century. There are wide individual variations in the age at which puberty begins. Heredity plays an important role in determining the onset of puberty. Key hormones involved in puberty are testosterone and estradiol. Rising testosterone levels in boys cause voice changes, enlargement of external genitals, and increased height. In girls, increased levels of estradiol influence breast and uterine development and skeletal change. Key physical changes of puberty include a growth spurt as well as sexual maturation. The growth spurt occurs an average of two years earlier for girls than for boys. Adolescents are preoccupied with their bodies and develop images of their bodies. Adolescent girls have more negative body images than adolescent boys. Early maturation favors boys during adolescence, but in adulthood late-maturing boys have a more successful identity. Early-maturing girls are vulnerable to a number of problems including eating disorders, smoking, and depression.

The Brain

Brain Physiology

Infancy

Childhood

Adolescence

LG2 Describe how the brain changes.

- Each hemisphere of the brain's cerebral cortex has four lobes (frontal, occipital, temporal, and parietal) with somewhat different primary functions. Neurons are nerve cells in the brain that process information. Communication between neurons occurs through the release of neurotransmitters at gaps called synapses. Communication is speeded by the myelin sheath that covers most axons. Clusters of neurons, known as neural circuits, work together to handle particular types of information. Specialization of functioning occurs in the brain's hemispheres, as in speech and grammar, but for the most part both hemispheres are involved in most complex functions, such as reading or performing music.

- Researchers have found that experience influences the brain's development. Early experiences are very important in brain development, and growing up in deprived environments can harm the brain. Myelination continues throughout the childhood years and even into adolescence for some brain areas such as the frontal lobes. Dramatic increases in dendritic and synaptic connections occur in infancy. These connections are overproduced and later pruned.

- During early childhood, the brain and head grow more rapidly than any other part of the body. Rapid, distinct bursts of growth occur in different areas of the brain between 3 and 15 years of age. One shift in brain activation in middle and late childhood is from diffuse, larger areas to more focal, smaller areas, especially in cognitive control.

- In adolescence, the corpus callosum thickens, and this improves information processing. Also, the amygdala, which is involved in emotions such as anger, develops earlier than the prefrontal cortex, which functions in reasoning and self-regulation. This gap in development may help to explain the increase in risk-taking behavior that characterizes adolescence.

Sleep

Infancy

Childhood

Adolescence

LG3 Summarize how sleep patterns change as children and adolescents develop.

- The typical newborn sleeps 16 to 17 hours a day. By 6 months of age, most infants have sleep patterns similar to those of adults. REM sleep occurs more in infancy than in childhood and adulthood. Sleeping arrangements vary across cultures, and there is controversy about shared sleeping. SIDS is a special concern in early infancy.

- Most young children sleep through the night and have one daytime nap. It is recommended that preschool children sleep 11 to 13 hours each night and 5- to 12-year-old children 10 to 12 hours each night. Among sleep problems that may develop are narcolepsy, insomnia, and nightmares. Sleep problems in childhood are linked to negative outcomes in other areas of children's development.

- Many adolescents stay up later than when they were children and are getting less sleep than they need. Research suggests that as adolescents get older, the hormone melatonin is released later at night, shifting the adolescent's biological clock. Inadequate sleep is linked to an unhealthy diet, low exercise level, depression, and ineffective stress management.

Health

Illness and Injuries Among Children

LG4 Characterize health in children.

- In recent decades, vaccines have greatly reduced the incidence of many diseases that once were responsible for the deaths of many young children. The disorders most likely to be fatal during early childhood today are birth defects, cancer, and heart disease. Motor vehicle accidents are the number one cause of death in

Nutrition and
Eating Behavior

Exercise

middle and late childhood, followed by cancer. Parental smoking is a major danger for young children. For the most part, middle and late childhood is a time of excellent health. Caregivers play an important role in preventing childhood injuries. A special concern is the health of children living in poverty here and abroad. Improvements are needed in sanitation, nutrition, education, and health services in addition to a reduction in poverty. In low-income countries, there has been a dramatic increase in the number of children who have died from HIV/AIDS that was transmitted to them by their parents.

• The importance of adequate energy intake consumed in a loving and supportive environment during infancy cannot be overstated. Breast feeding is increasingly recommended over bottle feeding. Marasmus and kwashiorkor are diseases caused by severe malnutrition. Concerns about nutrition in childhood focus on malnutrition, fat content in diet, and overweight children. The percentage of overweight children has increased dramatically in recent years. Being overweight increases a child's risk of developing many medical and psychological problems.

• Most children and adolescents are not getting nearly enough exercise. Boys and girls become less active as they reach and progress through adolescence. TV watching and computer time place children and adolescents at risk for lack of physical fitness and being overweight.

key terms

cephalocaudal pattern 107
proximodistal pattern 108
puberty 109
menarche 110
precocious puberty 110

hormones 110
androgens 110
estrogens 110
testosterone 110
estradiol 110

lateralization 115
myelination 117
corpus callosum 119
prefrontal cortex 119
amygdala 119

sudden infant death
 syndrome (SIDS) 122
marasmus 131
kwashiorkor 131

key people

Charles Nelson 115

Mark Johnson 118

chapter 5

MOTOR, SENSORY, AND PERCEPTUAL DEVELOPMENT

In 1950, the newly born Steveland Morris was placed in an incubator in which he was given too much oxygen. The result was permanent blindness. In 1962, as 12-year-old singer and musician Stevie Wonder, he began a career that has included such hits as "My Cherie Amour" and "Signed, Sealed, Delivered." At the beginning of the 21st century, his music is still perceived by some as "wondrous."

At age 12, Andrea Bocelli lost his sight in a soccer mishap. Today, now in his forties and after a brief career as a lawyer, Andrea has taken the music world by storm with his magnificent, classically trained voice.

Although Bocelli's and Stevie Wonder's accomplishments are great, imagine how very difficult it must have been for them as children to do many of the things we take for granted in sighted children. Yet children who lose one channel of sensation—such as vision—often compensate for the loss by enhancing their sensory skills in another area, such as hearing or touch. For example, researchers have found that blind individuals are more accurate at locating a sound source and have greater sensitivity to touch than sighted individuals (Forster, Eardley, & Eimer, 2007). In one study, blind children were more skillful than blindfolded sighted children at using hearing to detect walls (Ashmead & others, 1998). In this study, acoustic information was most useful when the blind children were within one meter of a wall—at which point, sound pressure increases.

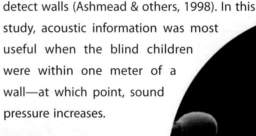

Two "sensations": Stevie Wonder (*left*) and Andrea Bocelli (*right*). *How have they adapted to life without sight?*

preview

Think about what is required for children to find their way around their environment, to play sports, or to create art. These activities require both active perception and precisely timed motor actions. Neither innate, automatic movements nor simple sensations are enough to let children do the things they do every day. How do children develop perceptual and motor abilities? In this chapter, we will focus first on the development of motor skills, then on sensory and perceptual development, and finally on the coupling of perceptual-motor skills.

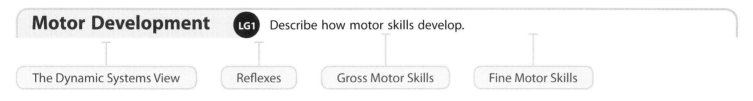

Motor Development — LG1 Describe how motor skills develop.

The Dynamic Systems View | Reflexes | Gross Motor Skills | Fine Motor Skills

Most adults are capable of coordinated, purposive actions of considerable skill, including driving a car, playing golf, and typing effectively on a computer keyboard. Some adults have extraordinary motor skills, such as those involved in winning an Olympic pole vault competition, performing heart surgery, painting a masterpiece, or in the case of Stevie Wonder, being extraordinarily talented at playing the piano. Look all you want at a newborn infant, and you will observe nothing even remotely approaching these skilled actions. How, then, do the motor behaviors of adults come about?

> A baby is the most complicated object made by unskilled labor.
>
> —ANONYMOUS

THE DYNAMIC SYSTEMS VIEW

Arnold Gesell (1934) thought his painstaking observations had revealed how people develop their motor skills. He had discovered that infants and children develop rolling, sitting, standing, and other motor skills in a fixed order and within specific time frames. These observations, said Gesell, show that motor development comes about through the unfolding of a genetic plan, or *maturation.*

Later studies, however, demonstrated that the sequence of developmental milestones is not as fixed as Gesell indicated and not due as much to heredity as Gesell argued (Adolph, Burger, & Leo, 2010; Adolph & Joh, 2009; Adolph, Karasik, & Tamis-LeMonda, 2010). In the last two decades, the study of motor development experienced a renaissance as psychologists developed new insights about *how* motor skills develop (Thelen & Smith, 1998, 2006). One increasingly influential theory is dynamic systems theory, proposed by Esther Thelen.

According to **dynamic systems theory,** infants assemble motor skills for perceiving and acting. Notice that perception and action are coupled, according to this theory (Thelen & Smith, 2006). To develop motor skills, infants must perceive something in the environment that motivates them to act and then use their perceptions to fine-tune their movements. Motor skills represent solutions to the infant's goals (Clearfield & others, 2009).

How is a motor skill developed, according to this theory? When infants are motivated to do something, they might create a new motor behavior. The new behavior is the result of many converging factors: the development of the nervous system, the body's physical properties and its possibilities for movement, the goal the child is motivated to reach, and the environmental support for the skill (von Hofsten, 2008). For example, babies learn to walk only when maturation of the nervous system allows them to control certain leg muscles, when their legs have grown enough to support their weight, and when they want to move.

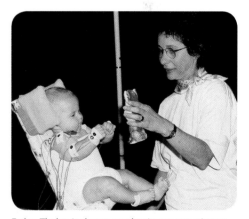

Esther Thelen is shown conducting an experiment to discover how infants learn to control their arms to reach and grasp for objects. A computer device is used to monitor the infant's arm movements and to track muscle patterns. Thelen's research is conducted from a dynamic systems perspective. *What is the nature of this perspective?*

dynamic systems theory A theory, proposed by Esther Thelen, that seeks to explain how motor behaviors are assembled for perceiving and acting.

How might dynamic systems theory explain the development of learning to walk?

developmental **connection**

Nature vs. Nurture. The epigenetic view states that development is an ongoing, bidirectional interchange between heredity and the environment. Chapter 2, p. 71

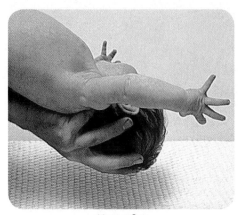

Moro reflex

The Moro reflex usually disappears around three months.

reflexes Built-in reactions to stimuli.

Mastering a motor skill requires the infant's active efforts to coordinate several components of the skill. Infants explore and select possible solutions to the demands of a new task; they assemble adaptive patterns by modifying their current movement patterns. The first step occurs when the infant is motivated by a new challenge—such as the desire to cross a room—and gets into the "ballpark" of the task demands by taking a couple of stumbling steps. Then, the infant "tunes" these movements to make them smoother and more effective. The tuning is achieved through repeated cycles of action and perception of the consequences of that action. According to the dynamic systems view, even universal milestones, such as crawling, reaching, and walking, are learned through this process of adaptation: infants modulate their movement patterns to fit a new task by exploring and selecting possible configurations (Adolph, Karasik, & Tamis-LeMonda, 2010; Spencer & others, 2009; Thelen & Smith, 2006).

To see how dynamic systems theory explains motor behavior, imagine that you offer a new toy to a baby named Gabriel (Thelen & others, 1993). There is no exact program that can tell Gabriel ahead of time how to move his arm and hand and fingers to grasp the toy. Gabriel must adapt to his goal—grasping the toy—and the context. From his sitting position, he must make split-second adjustments to extend his arm, holding his body steady so that his arm and torso don't plow into the toy. Muscles in his arm and shoulder contract and stretch in a host of combinations, exerting a variety of forces. He improvises a way to reach out with one arm and wrap his fingers around the toy.

Thus, according to dynamic systems theory, motor development is not a passive process in which genes dictate the unfolding of a sequence of skills over time. Rather, the infant actively puts together a skill to achieve a goal within the constraints set by the infant's body and environment. Nature and nurture, the infant and the environment, are all working together as part of an ever-changing system.

As we examine the course of motor development, we will describe how dynamic systems theory applies to some specific skills. First, though, let's examine how the story of motor development begins with reflexes.

REFLEXES

The newborn is not completely helpless. Among other things, it has some basic reflexes. For example, the newborn automatically holds its breath and contracts its throat to keep water out. **Reflexes** are built-in reactions to stimuli; they govern the newborn's movements, which are automatic and beyond the newborn's control. Reflexes are genetically carried survival mechanisms. They allow infants to respond adaptively to their environment before they have had an opportunity to learn.

The rooting and sucking reflexes are important examples. Both have survival value for newborn mammals, who must find a mother's breast to obtain nourishment. The **rooting reflex** occurs when the infant's cheek is stroked or the side of the mouth is touched. In response, the infant turns its head toward the side that was touched in an apparent effort to find something to suck. The **sucking reflex** occurs when newborns automatically suck an object placed in their mouth. This reflex enables newborns to get nourishment before they have associated a nipple with food; sucking also serves as a self-soothing or self-regulating mechanism.

Another example is the **Moro reflex,** which occurs in response to a sudden, intense noise or movement. When startled, the newborn arches its back, throws back its head, and flings out its arms and legs. Then the newborn rapidly closes its arms and legs. The Moro reflex is believed to be a way of grabbing for support while falling; it would have had survival value for our primate ancestors.

Reflex	Stimulation	Infant's Response	Developmental Pattern
Blinking	Flash of light, puff of air	Closes both eyes	Permanent
Babinski	Sole of foot stroked	Fans out toes, twists foot in	Disappears after 9 months to 1 year
Grasping	Palms touched	Grasps tightly	Weakens after 3 months, disappears after 1 year
Moro (startle)	Sudden stimulation, such as hearing loud noise or being dropped	Startles, arches back, throws head back, flings out arms and legs and then rapidly closes them to center of body	Disappears after 3 to 4 months
Rooting	Cheek stroked or side of mouth touched	Turns head, opens mouth, begins sucking	Disappears after 3 to 4 months
Stepping	Infant held above surface and feet lowered to touch surface	Moves feet as if to walk	Disappears after 3 to 4 months
Sucking	Object touching mouth	Sucks automatically	Disappears after 3 to 4 months
Swimming	Infant put face down in water	Makes coordinated swimming movements	Disappears after 6 to 7 months
Tonic neck	Infant placed on back	Forms fists with both hands and usually turns head to the right (sometimes called the "fencer's pose" because the infant looks like it is assuming a fencer's position)	Disappears after 2 months

FIGURE 5.1

INFANT REFLEXES. This chart describes some of the infant's reflexes.

Some reflexes—coughing, sneezing, blinking, shivering, and yawning, for example—persist throughout life. They are as important for the adult as they are for the infant. Other reflexes, though, disappear several months following birth, as the infant's brain matures, and voluntary control over many behaviors develops (Pedroso, 2008). The rooting and Moro reflexes, for example, tend to disappear when the infant is 3 to 4 months old.

The movements of some reflexes eventually become incorporated into more complex, voluntary actions. One important example is the **grasping reflex,** which occurs when something touches the infant's palms. The infant responds by grasping tightly. By the end of the third month, the grasping reflex diminishes, and the infant shows a more voluntary grasp. As its motor development becomes smoother, the infant will grasp objects, carefully manipulate them, and explore their qualities. An overview of the reflexes we have discussed, along with others, is given in Figure 5.1

Although reflexes are automatic and inborn, differences in reflexive behavior are soon apparent. For example, the sucking capabilities of newborns vary considerably. Some newborns are efficient at forcefully sucking and obtaining milk; others are not as adept and get tired before they are full. Most infants take several weeks to establish a sucking style that is coordinated with the way the mother is holding the infant, the way milk is coming out of the bottle or breast, and the infant's temperament (Blass, 2008).

Pediatrician T. Berry Brazelton (1956) observed how infants' sucking changed as they grew older. Over 85 percent of the infants engaged in considerable sucking behavior unrelated to feeding. They sucked their fingers, their fists, and pacifiers. By the age of 1 year, most had stopped the sucking behavior, but as many as 40 percent

rooting reflex A newborn's built-in reaction that occurs when the infant's cheek is stroked or the side of the mouth is touched. In response, the infant turns its head toward the side that was touched, in an apparent effort to find something to suck.

sucking reflex A newborn's built-in reaction of automatically sucking an object placed in its mouth. The sucking reflex enables the infant to get nourishment before it has associated a nipple with food.

Moro reflex A neonatal startle response that occurs in reaction to a sudden, intense noise or movement. When startled, the newborn arches its back, throws its head back, and flings out its arms and legs. Then the newborn rapidly closes its arms and legs to the center of the body.

grasping reflex A neonatal reflex that occurs when something touches the infant's palms. The infant responds by grasping tightly.

of children continued to suck their thumbs after starting school (Kessen, Haith, & Salapatek, 1970). Most developmentalists do not attach a great deal of significance to this behavior.

GROSS MOTOR SKILLS

Ask any parents about their baby, and sooner or later you are likely to hear about motor milestones, such as "Cassandra just learned to crawl," "Jesse is finally sitting alone," or "Angela took her first step last week." Parents proudly announce such milestones as their children transform themselves from babies unable to lift their heads to toddlers who grab things off the grocery store shelf, chase a cat, and participate actively in the family's social life (Thelen, 2000). These milestones are examples of **gross motor skills,** which are skills that involve large-muscle activities, such as moving one's arms and walking.

The Development of Posture   How do gross motor skills develop? As a foundation, these skills require postural control (Adolph & Joh, 2009). For example, to track moving objects, you must be able to control your head in order to stabilize your gaze; before you can walk, you must be able to balance on one leg.

Posture is more than just holding still and straight. Posture is a dynamic process that is linked with sensory information in the skin, joints, and muscles, which tell us where we are in space; in vestibular organs in the inner ear that regulate balance and equilibrium; and in vision and hearing (Thelen & Smith, 2006).

Newborn infants cannot voluntarily control their posture. Within a few weeks, though, they can hold their heads erect, and soon they can lift their heads while prone. By 2 months of age, babies can sit while supported on a lap or an infant seat, but they cannot sit independently until they are 6 or 7 months of age. Standing also develops gradually during the first year of life. By about 8 to 9 months of age, infants usually learn to pull themselves up and hold on to a chair, and they often can stand alone by about 10 to 12 months of age.

Learning to Walk   Locomotion and postural control are closely linked, especially in walking upright (Adolph & Joh, 2009). Babies need to master several key skills before they can walk alone.

Even young infants can make the alternating leg movements that are needed for walking. The neural pathways that control leg alternation are in place from a very early age, possibly even at birth or before. A recent study found that 3-day-old infants adapted their stepping pattern to visual input (Barbu-Roth & others, 2009). In this study, the very young infants took more steps when they saw a visual treadmill moving beneath their feet than their counterparts who saw a stationary image or an image that rotated. This study also illustrates the key concept of the coupling of perception and action in dynamic systems theory.

Infants also engage in frequent alternating kicking movements throughout the first six months of life when they are lying on their backs. Also, when 1- to 2-month-olds are supported and their feet are in contact with a motorized treadmill, they show well-coordinated, alternating steps.

Despite these early abilities, most infants do not learn to walk until about the time of their first birthday. If infants can produce forward stepping movements so early, why does it take them so long to learn to walk? The key skills in learning to walk appear to be stabilizing balance on one leg long enough to swing the other forward and shifting the weight without falling. These are difficult biomechanical problems to solve, and it takes infants about a year to do so.

When infants learn to walk, they typically take small steps because of their limited balance control and strength. However, a recent study revealed that infants occasionally take a few large steps that even exceed their leg length, and these large steps indicate increased balance and strength (Badaly & Adolph, 2008).

What are some developmental changes in posture during infancy?

gross motor skills Motor skills that involve large-muscle activities, such as moving one's arms and walking.

In learning to locomote, infants learn what kinds of places and surfaces are safe for locomotion (Adolph & Joh, 2009; Gill, Adolph, & Vereijken, 2009). Karen Adolph (1997) investigated how experienced and inexperienced crawling infants and walking infants go down steep slopes (see Figure 5.2). Newly crawling infants, who averaged about 8½ months in age, rather indiscriminately went down the steep slopes, often falling in the process (with their mothers next to the slope to catch them). After weeks of practice, the crawling babies became more adept at judging which slopes were too steep to crawl down and which ones they could navigate safely. New walkers also could not judge the safety of the slopes, but experienced walkers accurately matched their skills with the steepness of the slopes. They rarely fell downhill, either refusing to go down the steep slopes or going down backward in a cautious manner. Experienced walkers perceptually assessed the situation—looking, swaying, touching, and thinking before they moved down the slope. With experience, both the crawlers and the walkers learned to avoid the risky slopes where they would fall, integrating perceptual information with the development of a new motor behavior.

An important conclusion from Karen Adolph's (1997) study involves the *specificity of learning*—the idea that infants who have experience with one mode of locomotion (crawling, for example) don't seem to appreciate the dangers inherent in another mode of locomotion—risky walkways when they are making the transition to walking. Also in Adolph's (1997) research, we again see the importance of perceptual-motor coupling in the development of motor skills. Thus, practice is very important in the development of new motor skills (Adolph & Joh 2009; Adolph, Karasik, & Tamis-LeMonda, 2010).

Practice is especially important in learning to walk (Adolph & Joh, 2009). Infants and toddlers accumulate an immense number of experiences with balance and locomotion. For example, the average toddler traverses almost 40 football fields a day and has 15 falls per hour (Adolph, 2010). From the perspective of Karen Adolph and her colleagues (2003, p. 495):

> Thousands of daily walking steps, each step slightly different from the last because of variations in the terrain and the continually varying bio-mechanical constraints on the body, may help infants to identify the relevant combination of strength and balance required to improve their walking skills.

The First Year: Motor Development Milestones and Variations

Figure 5.3 summarizes important accomplishments in gross motor skills during the first year, culminating in the ability to walk easily. The timing of these milestones, especially the later ones, may vary by as much as two to four months, and experiences can modify the onset of these accomplishments (Eaton, 2008). For example, since 1992, when pediatricians began recommending that parents place their babies on their backs when they sleep, fewer babies crawled, and those who did crawled later (Davis & others, 1998). Also, some infants do not follow the standard sequence of motor accomplishments. For example, many American infants never crawl on their belly or on their hands and knees. They may discover an idiosyncratic form of locomotion before walking, such as rolling, or they might never locomote until they get upright (Adolph & Joh, 2009). In the African Mali tribe, most infants do not crawl (Bril, 1999).

According to Karen Adolph and Sarah Berger (2005), "The old-fashioned view that growth and motor development reflect merely the age-related output of maturation is, at best, incomplete. Rather, infants acquire new skills with the help of their caregivers in a real-world environment of objects, surfaces, and planes."

Development in the Second Year

The motor accomplishments of the first year bring increasing independence, allowing infants to explore their environment more extensively and to initiate interaction with others more readily. In the second year of life, toddlers become more motorically skilled and mobile. Motor activity during

Newly crawling infant

Experienced walker

FIGURE 5.2

THE ROLE OF EXPERIENCE IN CRAWLING AND WALKING INFANTS' JUDGMENTS OF WHETHER TO GO DOWN A SLOPE. Karen Adolph (1997) found that locomotor experience rather than age was the primary predictor of adaptive responding on slopes of varying steepness. Newly crawling and walking infants could not judge the safety of the various slopes. With experience, they learned to avoid slopes where they would fall. When expert crawlers began to walk, they again made mistakes and fell, even though they had judged the same slope accurately when crawling. Adolph referred to this as the *specificity of learning* because it does not transfer across crawling and walking.

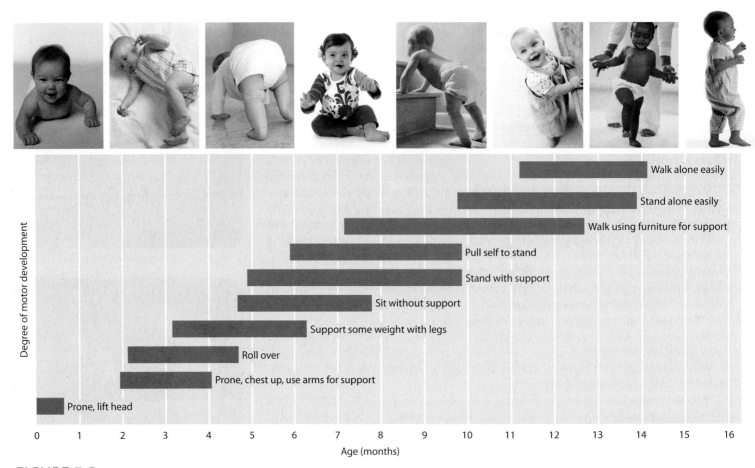

FIGURE **5.3**
MILESTONES IN GROSS MOTOR DEVELOPMENT

> The experiences of the first three years of life are almost entirely lost to us, and when we attempt to enter into a small child's world, we come as foreigners who have forgotten the landscape and no longer speak the native tongue.
>
> —SELMA FRAIBERG
> *Developmentalist and Child Advocate, 20th Century*

the second year is vital to the child's competent development, and few restrictions, except for safety, should be placed on their adventures.

By 13 to 18 months, toddlers can pull a toy attached to a string and use their hands and legs to climb up a number of steps. By 18 to 24 months, toddlers can walk quickly or run stiffly for a short distance, balance on their feet in a squatting position while playing with objects on the floor, walk backward without losing their balance, stand and kick a ball without falling, stand and throw a ball, and jump in place.

Can parents give their babies a head start on becoming physically fit and physically talented through structured exercise classes? Most infancy experts recommend against structured exercise classes for babies. But there are other ways of guiding infants' motor development. Caregivers in some cultures do handle babies vigorously, and this might advance motor development, as we discuss in *Connecting With Diversity*.

Childhood Our exploration of motor development in childhood begins with a focus on developmental changes in gross motor skills, and then we examine the role of sports in children's development.

Developmental Changes The preschool child no longer has to make an effort to stay upright and to move around. As children move their legs with more confidence and carry themselves more purposefully, moving around in the environment becomes more automatic.

At 3 years of age, children enjoy simple movements, such as hopping, jumping, and running back and forth, just for the sheer delight of performing these activities.

Cultural Variations in Guiding Infants' Motor Development

Mothers in developing countries tend to stimulate their infants' motor skills more than mothers in more modern countries (Hopkins, 1991). In many African, Indian, and Caribbean cultures, mothers massage and stretch their infants during daily baths (Adolph, Karasik, & Tamis-LeMonda, 2010). Jamaican and Mali mothers regularly massage their infants and stretch their arms and legs (Adolph, Karasik, & Tamis-LeMonda, 2010). Mothers in the Gusii culture of Kenya also encourage vigorous movement in their babies (Hopkins & Westra, 1988).

Do these cultural variations make a difference in the development of motor skills? When caregivers provide babies with physical guidance by physically handling them in special ways (such as stroking, massaging, or stretching) or by giving them opportunities for exercise, the infants often reach motor milestones earlier than infants whose caregivers have not provided these activities (Adolph, Karasik, & Tamis-LeMonda, 2010). For example, Jamaican mothers expect their infants to sit and walk alone 2 to 3 months earlier than English mothers do (Hopkins & Westra, 1990).

Nonetheless, even when infants' motor activity is restricted, many infants still reach the milestones of motor development at a normal age. For example, Algonquin infants in Quebec, Canada, spend much of their

(*Left*) In the Algonquin culture in Quebec, Canada, babies are strapped to a cradle board for much of their infancy. (*Right*) In Jamaica, mothers massage and stretch their infants' arms and legs. *To what extent do cultural variations in the activity infants engage in influence the time at which they reach motor milestones?*

first year strapped to a cradle board. Despite their inactivity, these infants still sit up, crawl, and walk within an age range similar to that of infants in cultures where they have had much greater opportunity for activity.

To help babies with their motor development, is stroking, massaging, or stretching their arms and legs a better or worse strategy than engaging them in a structured exercise class?

They take considerable pride in showing how they can run across a room and jump all of 6 inches. The run-and-jump will win no Olympic gold medals, but for the 3-year-old the activity is a source of pride.

At 4 years of age, children are still enjoying the same kind of activities, but they have become more adventurous. They scramble over low jungle gyms as they display their athletic prowess. Although they have been able to climb stairs with one foot on each step for some time, they are just beginning to be able to come down the same way.

At 5 years of age, children are even more adventuresome than they were at 4. It is not unusual for self-assured 5-year-olds to perform hair-raising stunts on practically any climbing object. They run hard and enjoy races with each other and their parents.

During middle and late childhood, children's motor development becomes much smoother and more coordinated than it was in early childhood. For example, only one child in a thousand can hit a tennis ball over the net at the age of 3, yet by the age of 10 or 11 most children can learn to play the sport. Running, climbing, skipping rope, swimming, bicycle riding, and skating are just a few of the many physical skills elementary school children can master. And, when mastered, these physical skills are a source of great pleasure and a sense of accomplishment. A recent

What are some developmental changes in children's motor development in early childhood and middle and late childhood?

study of 9-year-olds revealed that those who were more physically fit had a better mastery of motor skills (Haga, 2008). In gross motor skills involving large-muscle activity, boys usually outperform girls.

As children move through the elementary school years, they gain greater control over their bodies and can sit and pay attention for longer periods of time. However, elementary school children are far from being physically mature, and they need to be active. Elementary school children become more fatigued by long periods of sitting than by running, jumping, or bicycling (Rink, 2009). Physical action is essential for these children to refine their developing skills, such as batting a ball, skipping rope, or balancing on a beam. Children benefit from exercise breaks periodically during the school day on the order of 15 minutes every two hours (Keen, 2005). In sum, elementary school children should be engaged in active, rather than passive, activities.

Sports   Organized sports are one way of encouraging children to be active and to develop their motor skills. Schools and community agencies offer programs for children that involve baseball, soccer, football, basketball, swimming, gymnastics, and other sports. In the United States and most other countries, sports play a central role in children's lives.

Participation in sports can have positive and negative outcomes for children (Coatsworth & Conroy, 2009; Gaudreau, Amiot, & Vallerand, 2009). Researchers have found that participation in sports often confers a number of benefits for many children, including exercise, opportunities to develop a skill and learn how to compete, enhanced self-esteem, persistence, and a setting for developing peer relations and friendships (Theokas, 2009). Further, participating in sports reduces the likelihood that children will become obese (Sturm, 2005). For example, in one recent study, Mexican youth who did not participate in sports were more likely to be overweight or obese than those who participated (Salazar-Martinez & others, 2006). Another study also revealed that participation in sports for three hours per week or more beyond regular physical education classes was related to increased physical fitness and lower fat mass in 9-year-old boys (Ara & others, 2004).

However, sports also can bring pressure to achieve and win, physical injuries, a distraction from academic work, and unrealistic expectations for success as an athlete (Koutures & Gregory, 2010; Maffulli & others, 2010). High-pressure sports that involve championship play under the media spotlight cause special concern. Some psychologists argue that such activities put undue stress on children and teach them the wrong values—namely, a win-at-all-costs philosophy. Overly ambitious parents, coaches, and community boosters can unintentionally create a highly stressful atmosphere in children's sports (American Academy of Pediatrics Council on Sports Medicine and Fitness, McCambridge, & Stricker, 2008).

When the prestige of parents, an institution, or a community becomes the focus of the child's participation in sports, the danger of exploitation is clearly present. Programs oriented toward such purposes often require arduous training sessions over many months and years, frequently leading to sports specialization at too early an age. In such circumstances, adults often communicate the distorted view that the sport is the most important aspect of the child's life.

developmental **connection**

Education. Carol Dweck argues that a mastery orientation (focusing on the task and process of learning) produces more positive achievement outcomes than a performance orientation in which the outcome—winning—is the most important aspect of achieving. Chapter 16, p. 474

caring *connections*

Parents, Coaches, and Children's Sports

If parents do not become overinvolved in their children's sports participation, they can help their children build physical skills and emotional
maturity—for example, by discussing how to deal with a difficult coach,
how to cope with a tough loss, and how to put in perspective a poorly
played game. Parents should monitor their children as they participate
in sports for signs of developing stress. If the problems appear to be
beyond the intuitive skills of a volunteer coach or parent, consultation
with a counselor or clinician may be needed. Also, the parent should be
sensitive to whether a particular sport is the best one for the child and
whether the child can handle its competitive pressures.

Here are some guidelines that can benefit parents and coaches of
children in sports (Women's Sports Foundation, 2001):

Do:

- Make sports fun; the more children enjoy sports, the more they will
  want to play.
- Remember that it is okay for children to make mistakes; it means
  they are trying.
- Allow children to ask questions about the sport, and discuss the
  sport in a calm, supportive manner.
- Show respect for the child's sports participation.
- Be positive and convince the child that he or she is making a good effort.
- Be a positive role model for the child in sports.

Don't:

- Yell or scream at the child.
- Condemn the child for poor play or continue to bring up failures long
  after they happen.
- Point out the child's errors in front of others.
- Expect the child to learn something immediately.
- Expect the child to become a pro.
- Ridicule or make fun of the child.
- Compare the child to siblings or to more talented children.
- Make sports all work and no fun.

What are some of the possible positive and negative aspects of children's participation in sports? What are some guidelines that can benefit parents and coaches of children in sports?

*What specific negative outcomes of sports involvement dis-
cussed earlier might these guidelines help to counteract?*

In thinking about the influence of sports on children's development, it is
important to keep in mind that just participating in sports does not necessarily
lead to benefits for children (Theokas, 2009). It is the quality of the participation
experience that confers benefits. Also, in many research studies, the influence of
sports is considered in a general way, yet different sports have different characteristics, demands, and patterns of interaction with coaches, parents, and the community. The *Caring Connections* interlude examines the roles of parents and coaches
in children's sports.

A young girl using a pincer grip to pick up puzzle pieces.

FINE MOTOR SKILLS

Whereas gross motor skills involve large-muscle activity, **fine motor skills** involve finely tuned movements. Grasping a toy, using a spoon, buttoning a shirt, or doing anything that requires finger dexterity demonstrates fine motor skills.

Infancy Infants have hardly any control over fine motor skills at birth, but they do have many components of what will become finely coordinated arm, hand, and finger movements. The onset of reaching and grasping marks a significant achievement in infants' ability to interact with their surroundings (van Hof, van der Kamp, & Savelsbergh, 2008). During the first two years of life, infants refine how they reach and grasp (Needham, 2009). Initially, infants reach by moving their shoulders and elbows crudely, swinging toward an object. Later, when infants reach for an object they move their wrists, rotate their hands, and coordinate their thumb and forefinger. Infants do not have to see their own hands in order to reach for an object (Clifton & others, 1993). Cues from muscles, tendons, and joints, not sight of the limb, guide reaching by 4-month-old infants.

Infants refine their ability to grasp objects by developing two types of grasps. Initially, infants grip with the whole hand, which is called the *palmer grasp*. Later, toward the end of the first year, infants also grasp small objects with their thumb and forefinger, which is called the *pincer grip*. Their grasping system is very flexible. They vary their grip on an object depending on its size, shape, and texture, as well as the size of their own hands relative to the object's size. Infants grip small objects with their thumb and forefinger (and sometimes their middle finger too), whereas they grip large objects with all of the fingers of one hand or both hands.

Perceptual-motor coupling is necessary for the infant to coordinate grasping (Barrett, Traupman, & Needham, 2008). Which perceptual system the infant is most likely to use to coordinate grasping varies with age. Four-month-old infants rely greatly on touch to determine how they will grip an object; 8-month-olds are more likely to use vision as a guide (Newell & others, 1989). This developmental change is efficient because vision lets infants preshape their hands as they reach for an object.

Experience plays a role in reaching and grasping. In one study, three-month old infants participated in play sessions wearing "sticky mittens"— "mittens with palms that stuck to the edges of toys and allowed the infants to pick up the toys" (Needham, Barrett, & Peterman, 2002, p. 279) (see Figure 5.4). Infants who participated in sessions with the mittens grasped and manipulated objects earlier in their development than a control group of infants who did not receive the "mitten" experience. The experienced infants looked at the objects longer, swatted at them more during visual contact, and were more likely to mouth the objects.

Just as infants need to exercise their gross motor skills, they also need to exercise their fine motor skills (Needham, 2009). Especially when they can manage a pincer grip, infants delight in picking up small objects. Many develop the pincer grip and begin to crawl at about the same time, and infants at this time pick up virtually everything in sight, especially on the floor, and put the objects in their mouth. Thus, parents need to be vigilant in regularly monitoring what objects are within the infant's reach (Keen, 2005).

Childhood As children get older, their fine motor skills improve (Sveistrup & others, 2008). At 3 years of age, children have had the ability to pick up the tiniest objects between their thumb and forefinger for some time, but they are still somewhat clumsy at it. Three-year-olds can build surprisingly high block towers, each block placed with intense concentration but often not in a completely straight line. When 3-year-olds play with a form board or a simple puzzle, they are rather rough

FIGURE **5.4**

INFANTS' USE OF "STICKY MITTENS" TO EXPLORE OBJECTS. Amy Needham and her colleagues (2002) found that "sticky mittens" enhanced young infants' object exploration skills.

fine motor skills Motor skills that involve more finely tuned movements, such as finger dexterity.

in placing the pieces. When they try to position a piece in a hole, they often try to force the piece or pat it vigorously.

By 4 years of age, children's fine motor coordination is much more precise. Sometimes 4-year-old children have trouble building high towers with blocks because, in their desire to place each of the blocks perfectly, they upset those already stacked. By age 5, children's fine motor coordination has improved further. Hand, arm, and fingers all move together under better command of the eye. Mere towers no longer interest the 5-year-old, who now wants to build a house or a church, complete with steeple. (Adults may still need to be told what each finished project is meant to be.)

Increased myelination of the central nervous system is reflected in the improvement of fine motor skills during middle and late childhood. Recall from Chapter 4 that myelination involves the covering of the axon with a myelin sheath, a process that increases the speed with which information travels from neuron to neuron. By middle childhood, children can use their hands adroitly as tools. Six-year-olds can hammer, paste, tie shoes, and fasten clothes. By 7 years of age, children's hands have become steadier. At this age, children prefer a pencil to a crayon for printing, and reversal of letters is less common. Printing becomes smaller. At 8 to 10 years of age, children can use their hands independently with more ease and precision; children can now write rather than print words. Letter size becomes smaller and more even. At 10 to 12 years of age, children begin to show manipulative skills similar to the abilities of adults. The complex, intricate, and rapid movements needed to produce fine-quality crafts or to play a difficult piece on a musical instrument can be mastered. Girls usually outperform boys in fine motor skills.

Review Connect Reflect

LG1 Describe how motor skills develop.

Review

- What is the dynamic systems view of motor development?
- What are some reflexes of infants?
- How do gross motor skills develop?
- How do fine motor skills develop?

Connect

- In this section, you learned how infants explore their environment as they develop gross and fine motor skills. How does this experience affect infants' neural connections (discussed in Chapter 4)?

Reflect *Your Own Personal Journey of Life*

- If and when you become a parent, how would you evaluate the benefits and drawbacks of allowing your 7-year-old to play for a soccer team in a competitive league in your town or city?

Sensory and Perceptual Development

LG2 Outline the course of sensory and perceptual development.

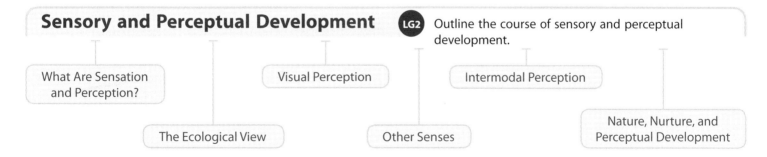

What Are Sensation and Perception?

Visual Perception

Intermodal Perception

The Ecological View

Other Senses

Nature, Nurture, and Perceptual Development

How do sensations and perceptions develop? Can a newborn see? If so, what can it perceive? What about the other senses—hearing, smell, taste, and touch? What are they like in the newborn, and how do they develop? Can an infant put together information from two modalities, such as sight and sound? What roles do nature and nurture play in perceptual development? These are among the intriguing questions that we will explore in this section.

How would you use the Gibsons' ecological theory of perception and the concept of affordance to explain the role that perception is playing in this toddler's activity?

WHAT ARE SENSATION AND PERCEPTION?

How does a newborn know that her mother's skin is soft rather than rough? How does a 5-year-old know what color his hair is? Infants and children "know" these things as a result of information that comes through the senses. Without vision, hearing, touch, taste, and smell, we would be isolated from the world; we would live in dark silence, a tasteless, colorless, feelingless void.

Sensation occurs when information interacts with sensory *receptors*—the eyes, ears, tongue, nostrils, and skin. The sensation of hearing occurs when waves of pulsating air are collected by the outer ear and transmitted through the bones of the inner ear to the auditory nerve. The sensation of vision occurs as rays of light contact the eyes, become focused on the retina, and are transmitted by the optic nerve to the visual centers of the brain.

Perception is the interpretation of what is sensed. The air waves that contact the ears might be interpreted as noise or as musical sounds, for example. The physical energy transmitted to the retina of the eye might be interpreted as a particular color, pattern, or shape, depending on how it is perceived.

THE ECOLOGICAL VIEW

In recent decades, much of the research on perceptual development in infancy has been guided by the ecological view of Eleanor and James J. Gibson (E. Gibson, 1969, 1989, 2001; J. Gibson, 1966, 1979). They argue that we do not have to take bits and pieces of data from sensations and build up representations of the world in our minds. Instead, our perceptual system can select from the rich information that the environment itself provides.

According to the Gibsons' **ecological view,** we directly perceive information that exists in the world around us. The view is called *ecological* "because it connects perceptual capabilities to information available in the world of the perceiver" (Kellman & Arterberry, 2006, p. 112). Thus, perception brings us into contact with the environment in order to interact with and adapt to it. Perception is designed for action. Perception gives people such information as when to duck, when to turn their bodies to get through a narrow passageway, and when to put their hands up to catch something.

In the Gibsons' view, objects have **affordances,** which are opportunities for interaction offered by objects that fit within our capabilities to perform activities. A pot may afford you something to cook with, and it may afford a toddler something to bang. Adults typically know when a chair is appropriate for sitting, when a surface is safe for walking, or when an object is within reach. We directly and accurately perceive these affordances by sensing information from the environment—the light or sound reflecting from the surfaces of the world—and from our own bodies through muscle receptors, joint receptors, and skin receptors, for example.

As we described earlier in the section on motor development, infants who were just learning to crawl or just learning to walk were less cautious when confronted with a steep slope than experienced crawlers or walkers were (Adolph, 1997). The more experienced crawlers and walkers perceived that a slope *affords* the possibility for not only faster locomotion but also for falling. Again, infants coupled perception and action to make a decision about what do in their environment. Through perceptual development, children become more efficient at discovering and using affordances.

Studying the infant's perception has not been an easy task. For instance, if newborns have limited communication abilities and are unable to tell us what they are seeing, hearing, smelling, and so on, how can we study their perception? *Connecting Through Research* describes some of the ingenious ways researchers study infants' perception.

sensation Reaction that occurs when information contacts sensory receptors—the eyes, ears, tongue, nostrils, and skin.

perception The interpretation of sensation.

ecological view The view, proposed by the Gibsons, that people directly perceive information in the world around them. Perception brings people in contact with the environment in order to interact with it and adapt to it.

affordances Opportunities for interaction offered by objects that are necessary to perform activities.

visual preference method A method developed by Fantz to determine whether infants can distinguish one stimulus from another by measuring the length of time they attend to different stimuli.

habituation Decreased responsiveness to a stimulus after repeated presentations of the stimulus.

dishabituation The recovery of a habituated response after a change in stimulation.

How Can We Study Newborns' Perception?

The creature has poor motor coordination and can move itself only with great difficulty. Although it cries when uncomfortable, it uses few other vocalizations. In fact, it sleeps most of the time, about 16 to 17 hours a day. You are curious about this creature and want to know more about what it can do. You think to yourself, "I wonder if it can see. How could I find out?"

You obviously have a communication problem with the creature. You must devise a way that will allow the creature to "tell" you that it can see. While examining the creature one day, you make an interesting discovery. When you move an object horizontally in front of the creature, its eyes follow the object's movement.

The creature's head movement suggests that it has at least some vision. In case you haven't already guessed, the creature you have been reading about is the human infant, and the role you played is that of a researcher interested in devising techniques to learn about the infant's visual perception. After years of work, scientists have developed research methods and tools sophisticated enough to examine the subtle abilities of infants and to interpret their complex actions (Bendersky & Sullivan, 2007).

Visual Preference Method

Robert Fantz (1963) was a pioneer in the study of infants' perception. Fantz made an important discovery that advanced the ability of researchers to investigate infants' visual perception: Infants look at different things for different lengths of time. Fantz placed infants in a "looking chamber," which had two visual displays on the ceiling above the in-

fant's head. An experimenter viewed the infant's eyes by looking through a peephole. If the infant was fixating on one of the displays, the experimenter could see the display's reflection in the infant's eyes. This allowed the experimenter to determine how long the infant looked at each display. Fantz (1963) found that infants only 2 days old look longer at patterned stimuli, such as faces and concentric circles, than at red, white, or yellow discs. Infants 2 to 3 weeks old preferred to look at patterns—a face, a piece of printed matter, or a bull's-eye—longer than at red, yellow, or white discs (see Figure 5.5). Fantz's research method—studying whether infants can distinguish one stimulus from another by measuring the length of time they attend to different stimuli—is referred to as the **visual preference method.**

Habituation and Dishabituation

Another way that researchers have studied infants' perception is to present a stimulus (such as a sight or a sound) a number of times. If the infant decreases its response to the stimulus after several presentations, this indicates that the infant is no longer interested in looking at the stimulus. If the researcher now presents a new stimulus, the infant's response will recover, indicating that the infant could discriminate between the old and new stimuli (Colombo & others, 2010; Snyder & Torrence, 2008).

Habituation is the name given to decreased responsiveness to a stimulus after repeated presentations of the stimulus. **Dishabituation** is the recovery of a habituated response after a change in stimulation.

(continued)

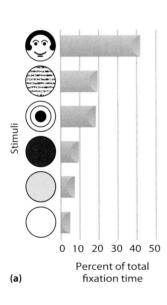

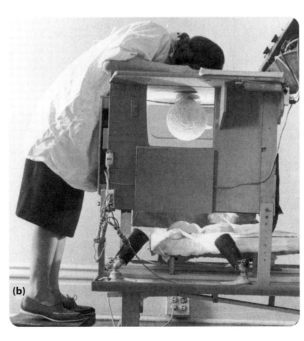

FIGURE **5.5**

FANTZ'S EXPERIMENT ON INFANTS' VISUAL PERCEPTION. (*a*) Infants 2 to 3 weeks old preferred to look at some stimuli more than others. In Fantz's experiment, infants preferred to look at patterns rather than at color or brightness. For example, they looked longer at a face, a piece of printed matter, or a bull's-eye than at red, yellow, or white discs. (*b*) Fantz used a "looking chamber" to study infants' perception of stimuli.

connecting through research

(continued)

Habituation

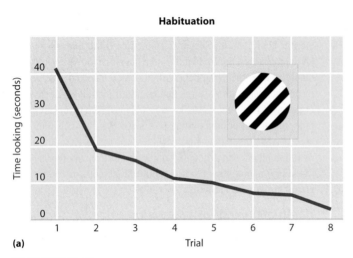

(a)

Dishabituation

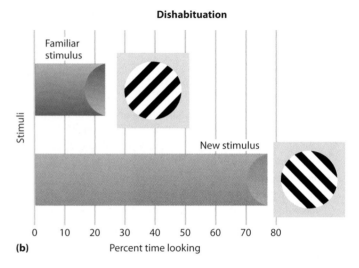

(b)

FIGURE **5.6**

HABITUATION AND DISHABITUATION. In the first part of one study, 7-hour-old newborns were shown the stimulus in (*a*). As indicated, the newborns looked at it an average of 41 seconds when it was first presented to them (Slater, Morison, & Somers, 1988). Over seven more presentations of the stimulus, they looked at it less and less. In the second part of the study, infants were presented with both the familiar stimulus to which they had just become habituated (*a*) and a new stimulus (shown in *b*, which was rotated 90 degrees). The newborns looked at the new stimulus three times as much as the familiar stimulus.

Newborn infants can habituate to repeated sights, sounds, smells, or touches (Rovee-Collier, 2004). Among the measures researchers use in habituation studies are sucking behavior (sucking stops when the young infant attends to a novel object), heart and respiration rates, and the length of time the infant looks at an object. Figure 5.6 shows the results of one study of habituation and dishabituation with newborns (Slater, Morison, & Somers, 1988).

High-Amplitude Sucking

To assess an infant's attention to sound, researchers often use a method called *high-amplitude sucking.* In this method, infants are given a nonnutritive nipple to suck, and the nipple is connected to a sound generating system. "Each suck causes a noise to be generated, and the infant learns quickly that sucking brings about this noise. At first, babies suck frequently, so the noise occurs often. Then, gradually, they lose interest in hearing repetitions of the same noise and begin to suck less frequently. At

FIGURE **5.7**

AN INFANT WEARING EYE-TRACKING HEADGEAR
Photo from Karen Adolph's laboratory at New York University.

this point, the experimenter changes the sound that is being generated. If the babies renew vigorous sucking, we infer that they have discriminated the sound change and are sucking more because they want to hear the interesting new sound" (Menn & Stoel-Gammon, 2009, p. 67).

The Orienting Response and Tracking

A technique that can be used to determine whether an infant can see or hear is the *orienting response,* which involves turning one's head toward a sight or sound. Another technique, *tracking,* consists of eye movements that follow (*track*) a moving object and can be used to evaluate an infant's early visual ability. Likewise, a startle response can be used as an indicator of an infant's reaction to a noise (Bendersky & Sullivan, 2007). Researchers increasingly are using sophisticated eye-tracking equipment to improve understanding of infant perception. Figure 5.7 shows an infant wearing an eye-tracking

(continued)

headgear in a recent study on visually guided motor behavior and social interaction (Franchak & others, 2010).

Equipment

Technology can facilitate the use of most methods for investigating the infant's perceptual abilities. Videotape equipment allows researchers to investigate elusive behaviors. High-speed computers make it possible to perform complex data analysis in minutes. Other equipment records respiration, heart rate, body movement, visual fixation, and sucking behavior, which provide clues to what the infant is perceiving.

For example, some researchers use equipment that detects whether a change in infants' respiration follows a change in the pitch of a sound. If so, it suggests that the infants heard the pitch change.

Scientists have had to be very creative when assessing the development of infants, discovering ways to "interview" them even though they cannot yet talk. Other segments of the population, such as adults who have suffered from a stroke, have trouble communicating verbally. What kinds of methods or equipment do you think researchers might use to evaluate their perception abilities?

VISUAL PERCEPTION

What do newborns see? How does visual perception develop in infancy? How does visual perception develop in childhood?

Infancy   Some important changes in visual perception with age can be traced to differences in how the eye itself functions over time. These changes in the eye's functioning influence, for example, how clearly we can see an object, whether we can differentiate its colors, at what distance, and in what light.

Visual Acuity   Psychologist William James (1890/1950) called the newborn's perceptual world a "blooming, buzzing confusion." More than a century later, we can safely say that he was wrong (Slater, Field, & Hernandez-Reif, 2007). Even the newborn perceives a world with some order. That world, however, is far different from the one perceived by the toddler or the adult.

Just how well can infants see? At birth, the nerves and muscles and lens of the eye are still developing. As a result, newborns cannot see small things that are far away. The newborn's vision is estimated to be 20/240 on the well-known Snellen chart used for eye examinations, which means that a newborn can see at 20 feet what a normal adult can see at 240 feet (Aslin & Lathrop, 2008). In other words, an object 20 feet away is only as clear to the newborn as it would be if it were 240 feet away from an adult with normal vision (20/20). By 6 months of age, though, on *average* vision is 20/40 (Aslin & Lathrop, 2008).

Face Perception   Infants show an interest in human faces soon after birth (Balas, 2010; Cashon, 2010; Quinn & others, 2009). Figure 5.8 shows a computer estimation of what a picture of a face looks like to an infant at different ages from a distance of about 6 inches. Infants spend more time looking at their mother's face than a stranger's face as early as 12 hours after being born (Bushnell, 2003). By 3 months of age, infants match voices to faces, distinguish between male and female faces, and discriminate between faces of their own ethnic group and those of other ethnic groups (Kelly & others, 2007, 2009; Pascalis & Kelly, 2008).

As infants develop, they change the way they gather information from the visual world, including human faces (Quinn & others, 2009). A recent study recorded eye movements of 3-, 6-, and 9-month old infants as they viewed clips from an animated

developmental **connection**

Research Methods. The still-face paradigm has been used to study face-to-face interaction between infants and caregivers. Chapter 10, p. 306

FIGURE **5.8**

VISUAL ACUITY DURING THE FIRST MONTHS OF LIFE. The four photographs represent a computer estimation of what a picture of a face looks like to a 1-month-old, 2-month-old, 3-month-old, and 1-year-old (which approximates the visual acuity of an adult).

film—*Charlie Brown's Christmas* (Frank & Johnson, 2009). From 3 to 9 months of age, infants gradually began focusing their attention more on the faces of the characters in the animated film and less on salient background stimuli.

Pattern Perception As we discussed in the *Connecting Through Research* interlude, young infants can perceive certain patterns. With the help of his "looking chamber," Robert Fantz (1963) revealed that even 2- to 3-week-old infants prefer to look at patterned displays rather than nonpatterned displays. For example, they prefer to look at a normal human face rather than one with scrambled features, and they prefer to look at a bull's-eye target or black-and-white stripes rather than a plain circle.

Color Vision The infant's color vision also improves (Kellman & Arterberry, 2006). By 8 weeks, and possibly as early as 4 weeks, infants can discriminate between some colors (Kelly, Borchert, & Teller, 1997). By 4 months of age, they have color preferences that mirror those of adults in some cases, preferring saturated colors such as royal blue over pale blue, for example (Bornstein, 1975). A recent study of 4- to 5-month-olds found that they looked longest at reddish hues and shortest at greenish hues (Franklin & others, 2010). In part, these changes in vision reflect maturation. Experience, however, is also necessary for vision to develop normally. For example, one study found that experience is necessary for normal color vision to develop (Sugita, 2004).

Perceptual Constancy Some perceptual accomplishments are especially intriguing because they indicate that the infant's perception goes beyond the information provided by the senses (Slater & others, 2010). This is the case in *perceptual constancy*, in which sensory stimulation is changing but perception of the physical world remains constant. If infants did not develop perceptual constancy, each time they saw an object at a different distance or in a different orientation, they would perceive it as a different object. Thus, the development of perceptual constancy allows infants to perceive their world as stable. Two types of perceptual constancy are size constancy and shape constancy.

Size constancy is the recognition that an object remains the same even though the retinal image of the object changes as you move toward or away from the object. The farther away from us an object is, the smaller is its image on our eyes. Thus, the size of an object on the retina is not sufficient to tell us its actual size. For example, you perceive a bicycle standing right in front of you as smaller than the car parked across the street, even though the bicycle casts a larger image on your eyes than the car does. When you move away from the bicycle, you do not

size constancy Recognition that an object remains the same even though the retinal image of the object changes.

perceive it to be shrinking even though its image on your retinas shrinks; you perceive its size as constant.

But what about babies? Do they have size constancy? Researchers have found that babies as young as 3 months of age show size constancy (Bower, 1966; Day & McKenzie, 1973). However, at 3 months of age, this ability is not full-blown. It continues to develop until 10 or 11 years of age (Kellman & Banks, 1998).

Shape constancy is the recognition that an object remains the same shape even though its orientation to us changes. Look around the room you are in right now. You likely see objects of varying shapes, such as tables and chairs. If you get up and walk around the room, you will see these objects from different sides and angles. Even though your retinal image of the objects changes as you walk and look, you will still perceive the objects as the same shape.

Do babies have shape constancy? As with size constancy, researchers have found that babies as young as 3 months of age have shape constancy (Bower, 1966; Day & McKenzie, 1973). Three-month-old infants, however, do not have shape constancy for irregularly shaped objects, such as tilted planes (Cook & Birch, 1984).

Perception of Occluded Objects   Look around the context where you are now. You likely see that some objects are partly occluded by other objects that are in front of them—possibly a desk behind a chair, some books behind a computer, or a car parked behind a tree. Do infants perceive an object as complete when it is occluded by an object in front of it?

In the first two months of postnatal development, infants don't perceive occluded objects as complete, instead only perceiving what is visible (Johnson, 2009). Beginning at about 2 months of age, infants develop the ability to perceive that occluded objects are whole (Slater, Field, & Hernandez-Reif, 2007). How does perceptual completion develop? In Scott Johnson's research (2004, 2009, 2010a, b; Johnson & others, 2000), learning, experience, and self-directed exploration via eye movements play key roles in the development of perceptual completion in young infants.

Many objects that are occluded appear and disappear behind closer objects, as when you are walking down the street and see cars appear and disappear behind buildings as they move or you move. Can infants predictively track briefly occluded moving objects? They develop the ability to track briefly occluded moving objects at about 3 to 5 months of age (Bertenthal, 2008). A recent study explored 5- to 9-month-old infants' ability to track moving objects that disappeared gradually behind an occluded partition, disappeared abruptly, or imploded (shrank quickly in size) (Bertenthal, Longo, & Kenny, 2007) (see Figure 5.9). In this study, the infants were more likely to accurately predict the path of the moving object when it disappeared gradually rather than when it disappeared abruptly or imploded.

Depth Perception   Might infants be able to perceive depth? To investigate this question, Eleanor Gibson and Richard Walk (1960) constructed in their laboratory a miniature cliff with a dropoff covered by glass. They placed infants on the edge of this visual cliff and had their mothers coax them to crawl onto the glass (see Figure 5.10). Most infants would not crawl out on the glass, choosing instead to remain on the shallow side, an indication that they could perceive depth, according to Gibson and Walk. However, critics point out that the visual cliff likely is a better test of social referencing and fear of heights than depth perception.

The 6- to 12-month-old infants in the visual cliff experiment had extensive visual experience. Do younger infants without this experience still perceive depth? Since younger infants do not crawl, this question is difficult to answer. Two- to 4-month-old infants show differences in heart rate when they are placed directly on the deep side of the visual cliff instead of on the shallow side (Campos, Langer, & Krowitz,

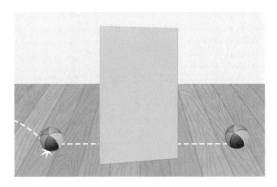

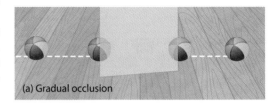

(a) Gradual occlusion

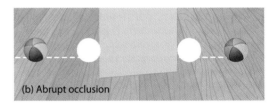

(b) Abrupt occlusion

(c) Implosion

FIGURE **5.9**

INFANTS' PREDICTIVE TRACKING OF A BRIEFLY OCCLUDED MOVING BALL. The top drawing shows a visual scene that infants experienced. At the beginning of each event, a multicolored ball bounded up and down with an accompanying bouncing sound, and then rolled across the floor until it disappeared behind the partition. The bottom drawing shows the three stimulus events the 5- to 9-month-old infants experienced: occlusion, disappearance, and implosion. (*a*) *Gradual Occlusion:* The ball gradually disappears behind the right side of the occluding partition located in the center of the display. (*b*) *Abrupt Disappearance:* The ball abruptly disappears when it reaches the location of the white circle and then abruptly reappears 2 seconds later at the location of the second white circle on the other side of the occluding partition. (*c*) *Implosion:* The rolling ball quickly decreases in size as it approaches the occluding partition and rapidly increases in size as it reappears on the other side of the occluding partition.

shape constancy Recognition that an object remains the same even though its orientation to the viewer changes.

FIGURE **5.10**

EXAMINING INFANTS' DEPTH PERCEPTION ON THE VISUAL CLIFF.
Eleanor Gibson and Richard Walk (1960) found that most infants would not crawl out on the glass, which, according to Gibson and Walk, indicated that they had depth perception. However, critics point out that the visual cliff is a better indication of the infant's social referencing and fear of heights than the infant's perception of depth.

1970). However, these differences might mean that young infants respond to differences in some visual characteristics of the deep and shallow cliffs, with no actual knowledge of depth. Although researchers do not know exactly how early in life infants can perceive depth, we do know that infants develop the ability to use binocular cues to discern depth by about 3 to 4 months of age.

Childhood   Children become increasingly efficient at detecting the boundaries between colors (such as red and orange) at 3 to 4 years of age (Gibson, 1969). When they are about 4 or 5 years old, most children's eye muscles are developed enough for them to move their eyes efficiently across a series of letters. Many preschool children are farsighted, unable to see close up as well as they can see far away. By the time they enter first grade, though, most children can focus their eyes and sustain their attention effectively on close-up objects.

After infancy, children's visual expectations about the physical world continue to develop. In one study, 2- to 4½-year-old children were given a task in which the goal was to find a toy ball that had been dropped through an opaque tube (Hood, 1995). As shown in Figure 5.11, if the ball is dropped into the tube at the top right, it will land in the box at the bottom left. However, in this task, most of the 2-year-olds, and even some of the 4-year-olds, persisted in searching in the box immediately beneath the dropping point. For them, gravity ruled, and they had failed to perceive the end location of the curved tube.

How do children learn to deal with situations like that in Figure 5.11, and how do they come to understand other laws of the physical world? These questions are addressed by studies of cognitive development, which we will discuss in Chapters 6 and 7.

OTHER SENSES

Other sensory systems besides vision also develop during infancy. We will explore development in hearing, touch and pain, smell, and taste.

Hearing   During the last two months of pregnancy, as the fetus nestles in its mother's womb, it can hear sounds such as the mother's voice, music, and so on (Kisilevsky & Hains, 2010; Kisilevsky & others, 2009). Two psychologists wanted to find out if a fetus that heard Dr. Seuss' classic story *The Cat in the Hat* while still in the mother's womb would prefer hearing the story after birth (DeCasper & Spence, 1986). During the last months of pregnancy, sixteen women read *The Cat in the Hat* to their fetuses. Then shortly after they were born, the mothers read either *The Cat in the Hat* or a story with a different rhyme and pace, *The King, the Mice and the Cheese* (which was not read to them during prenatal development). The infants sucked on a nipple in a different way when the mothers read the two stories, suggesting that the infants recognized the pattern and tone of *The Cat in the Hat* (see Figure 5.12). This study illustrates not only that a fetus can hear but also that it has a remarkable ability to learn even before birth.

FIGURE **5.11**

VISUAL EXPECTATIONS ABOUT THE PHYSICAL WORLD. When young children see a ball dropped into the tube, many of them will search for it immediately below the dropping point.

The fetus can also recognize the mother's voice, as one study demonstrated (Kisilevsky & others, 2004). Sixty third-trimester fetuses (mean gestational age, 38.4 weeks) were exposed to a tape recording either of their mother or of a female stranger reading a passage. The sounds of the tape were delivered through a loudspeaker held just above the mother's abdomen. Fetal heart rate increased in response to the mother's voice but decreased in response to the stranger's voice.

What kind of changes in hearing take place during infancy? They involve perception of a sound's loudness, pitch, and localization:

- *Loudness.* Immediately after birth, infants cannot hear soft sounds quite as well as adults can; a stimulus must be louder to be heard by a newborn than by an adult (Trehub & others, 1991). For example, an adult can hear a whisper from about 4 to 5 feet away, but a newborn requires that sounds be closer to a normal conversational level to be heard at that distance.

- *Pitch.* Infants are also less sensitive to the pitch of a sound than adults are. *Pitch* is the perception of the frequency of a sound. A soprano voice sounds high-pitched, a bass voice low-pitched. Infants are less sensitive to low-pitched sounds and are more likely to hear high-pitched sounds (Aslin, Jusczyk, & Pisoni, 1998). By 2 years of age, infants have considerably improved their ability to distinguish sounds with different pitches.

- *Localization.* Even newborns can determine the general location from which a sound is coming, but by 6 months of age, they are more proficient at *localizing* sounds or detecting their origins. Their ability to localize sounds continues to improve during the second year (Saffran, Werker, & Warner, 2006).

Touch and Pain   Do newborns respond to touch? Can they feel pain?

Newborns do respond to touch. A touch to the cheek produces a turning of the head; a touch to the lips produces sucking movements.

Newborns can also feel pain (Gunnar & Quevado, 2007). If and when you have a son and consider whether he should be circumcised, the issue of an infant's pain perception probably will become important to you. Circumcision is usually performed on young boys about the third day after birth. Will your young son experience pain if he is circumcised when he is 3 days old? An investigation by Megan Gunnar and her colleagues (1987) found that newborn infant males cried intensely during circumcision. The circumcised infant also displays amazing resiliency. Within several minutes after the surgery, they can nurse and interact in a normal manner with their mothers. And, if allowed to, the newly circumcised newborn drifts into a deep sleep, which seems to serve as a coping mechanism.

For many years, doctors performed operations on newborns without anesthesia. This practice was accepted because of the dangers of anesthesia and because of the

developmental **connection**

Biological Processes. Prenatal development is divided into three periods: germinal (first 2 weeks after conception), embryonic (2 to 8 weeks after conception), and fetal (begins at 2 months after conception and lasts for 7 months on average). Chapter 3, pp. 78–81

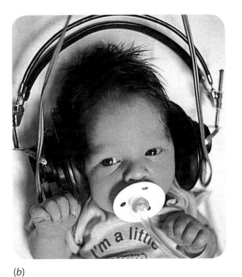

(a)   (b)

FIGURE **5.12**

HEARING IN THE WOMB. (a) Pregnant mothers read *The Cat in the Hat* to their fetuses during the last few months of pregnancy. (b) When they were born, the babies preferred listening to a recording of their mothers reading *The Cat in the Hat*—as evidenced by their sucking on a nipple—rather than another story, *The King, the Mice and the Cheese.*

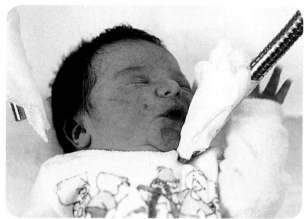

FIGURE **5.13**

NEWBORNS' PREFERENCE FOR THE SMELL OF THEIR MOTHER'S BREAST PAD. In the experiment by MacFarlane (1975), 6-day-old infants preferred to smell their mother's breast pad rather than a clean one that had never been used, but 2-day-old infants did not show this preference, indicating that this odor preference requires several days of experience to develop.

What is intermodal perception? Which two senses is this infant using to integrate information about the blocks?

intermodal perception The ability to relate and integrate information about two or more sensory modalities, such as vision and hearing.

supposition that newborns do not feel pain. As researchers demonstrated that newborns can feel pain, the practice of operating on newborns without anesthesia is being challenged. Anesthesia now is used in some circumcisions (Taddio, 2008).

Smell Newborns can differentiate odors (Doty & Shah, 2008). The expressions on their faces seem to indicate that they like the way vanilla and strawberry smell but do not like the way rotten eggs and fish smell (Steiner, 1979). In one investigation, 6-day-old infants who were breast fed showed a clear preference for smelling their mother's breast pad rather than a clean breast pad (MacFarlane, 1975) (see Figure 5.13). However, when they were 2 days old, they did not show this preference, indicating that they require several days of experience to recognize this odor.

Taste Sensitivity to taste might be present even before birth (Doty & Shah, 2008). When saccharin was added to the amniotic fluid of a near-term fetus, swallowing increased (Windle, 1940). In one study, even at only 2 hours of age, babies made different facial expressions when they tasted sweet, sour, and bitter solutions (Rosenstein & Oster, 1988) (see Figure 5.14). At about 4 months of age, infants begin to prefer salty tastes, which as newborns they had found to be aversive (Harris, Thomas, & Booth, 1990).

INTERMODAL PERCEPTION

Imagine yourself playing basketball or tennis. You are experiencing many visual inputs: the ball coming and going, other players moving around, and so on. However, you are experiencing many auditory inputs as well: the sound of the ball bouncing or being hit, the grunts and groans of the players, and so on. There is a good correspondence between much of the visual and auditory information: When you see the ball bounce, you hear a bouncing sound; when a player stretches to hit a ball, you hear a groan. When you look at and listen to what is going on, you do not experience just the sounds or just the sights—you put all these things together. You experience a unitary episode. This is **intermodal perception,** which involves integrating information from two or more sensory modalities, such as vision and hearing (Bremner & others, 2010; Walker & others, 2010).

Early, exploratory forms of intermodal perception exist even in newborns (Bahrick & Hollich, 2008). For example, newborns turn their eyes and their head toward the sound of a voice or rattle when the sound is maintained for several seconds (Clifton & others, 1981), but the newborn can localize a sound and look at an object only in a crude way (Bechtold, Bushnell, & Salapatek, 1979). These early forms of intermodal perception become sharpened with experience in the first year of life (Hollich, Newman, & Jusczyk, 2005). In one study, infants as young as 3 months old looked more at their mother when they also heard her voice and longer at their father when they also heard his voice (Spelke & Owsley, 1979). Thus, even young infants can coordinate visual-auditory information involving people.

Can young infants put vision and sound together as precisely as adults do? In the first six months, infants have difficulty connecting sensory input from different modes, but in the second half of the first year they show an increased ability to make this connection mentally.

The important ability to connect information about vision with information about touch also is evident early in infancy (Corbetta & Snapp-Childs, 2009). Coordination of vision and touch has been demonstrated in 2- to 3-month-olds (Streri, 1993).

Thus, babies are born into the world with some innate abilities to perceive relations among sensory modalities, but their intermodal abilities improve considerably through experience (Banks, 2005). As with all aspects of development, in perceptual development, nature and nurture interact and cooperate (Banks, 2005).

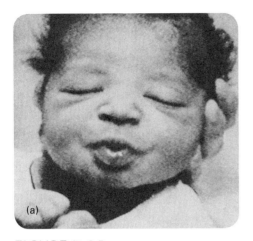
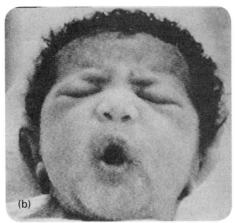
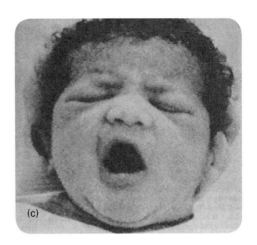

FIGURE **5.14**

NEWBORNS' FACIAL RESPONSES TO BASIC TASTES. Facial expression elicited by (*a*) a sweet solution, (*b*) a sour solution, and (*c*) a bitter solution.

NATURE, NURTURE, AND PERCEPTUAL DEVELOPMENT

Now that we have discussed many aspects of perceptual development, let's explore one of developmental psychology's key issues as it relates to perceptual development: the nature-nurture issue. There has been a long-standing interest in how strongly infants' perception is influenced by nature or nurture (Aslin, 2009; Johnson, 2009, 2010a, b; Slater & others, 2010). In the field of perceptual development, nature proponents are referred to as *nativists* and those who emphasize learning and experience are called *empiricists*.

In the nativist view, the ability to perceive the world in a competent, organized way is inborn or innate. At the beginning of our discussion of perceptual development, we examined the ecological view of the Gibsons because it has played such a pivotal role in guiding research in perceptual development. The Gibsons' ecological view leans toward a nativist explanation of perceptual development because it holds that perception is direct and evolved over time to allow the detection of size and shape constancy, a three-dimensional world, intermodal perception, and so on early in infancy. However, the Gibsons' view is not entirely nativist because they emphasized that "perceptual development involves distinctive features that are detected at different ages" (Slater & others, 2010).

The Gibsons' ecological view is quite different from Piaget's constructivist view, which reflects an empiricist approach to explaining perceptual development. According to Piaget, much of perceptual development in infancy must await the development of a sequence of cognitive stages for infants to construct more complex perceptual tasks. Thus, in Piaget's view, the ability to perceive size and shape constancy, a three-dimensional world, intermodal perception, and so on develops later in infancy than the Gibsons envision.

Today, it is clear that an extreme empiricist position on perceptual development is unwarranted. Much of early perception develops from innate (nature) foundations and the basic foundation of many perceptual abilities can be detected in newborns, whereas other abilities unfold maturationally (Arterberry, 2008). However, as infants develop, environmental experiences (nurture) refine or calibrate many perceptual functions and may be the driving force behind some functions (Amso & Johnson, 2010). The accumulation of experience with and knowledge about their perceptual world contributes to infants' ability to form coherent perceptions of people and things (Slater & others, 2010). Thus, a full portrait of perceptual development includes the influence of nature, nurture, and a developing sensitivity to information (Arterberry, 2008).

developmental **connection**

Cognitive Development. Piaget's theory states that children construct their understanding of the world and go through four stages of cognitive development. Chapter 1, pp. 24–25; Chapter 6, pp. 173–174

What roles do nature and nurture play in the infant's perceptual development?

Perceptual-Motor Coupling

LG3 Discuss the connections of perception and action.

As we come to the end of this chapter, we return to the important theme of perceptual-motor coupling. The distinction between perceiving and doing has been a time-honored tradition in psychology. However, a number of experts on perceptual and motor development question whether this distinction makes sense (Soska, Adolph, & Johnson, 2010; Thelen & Smith, 2006). The main thrust of research in Esther Thelen's dynamic systems approach is to explore how people assemble motor behaviors for perceiving and acting. The main theme of the ecological approach of Eleanor and James J. Gibson is to discover how perception guides action. Action can guide perception, and perception can guide action. Only by moving one's eyes, head, hands, and arms and by moving from one location to another can an individual fully experience his or her environment and learn how to adapt to it. Perception and action are coupled (Corbetta & Snapp-Childs, 2009; Kim & Johnson, 2010).

Babies, for example, continually coordinate their movements with perceptual information to learn how to maintain balance, reach for objects in space, and move across various surfaces and terrains (Adolph, Eppler, & Joh, 2010; Thelen & Smith, 2006). They are motivated to move by what they perceive. Consider the sight of an attractive toy across the room. In this situation, infants must perceive the current state of their bodies and learn how to use their limbs to reach the toy. Although their movements at first are awkward and uncoordinated, babies soon learn to select patterns that are appropriate for reaching their goals.

Equally important is the other part of the perception-action coupling. That is, action educates perception (Soska, Adolf, & Johnson, 2010; Thelen & Smith, 2006). For example, watching an object while exploring it manually helps infants to discriminate its texture, size, and hardness. Locomoting in the environment teaches babies about how objects and people look from different perspectives, or whether surfaces will support their weight.

How do infants develop new perceptual-motor couplings? Recall from our discussion earlier in this chapter that in the traditional view of Gesell, infants' perceptual-motor development is prescribed

How are perception and action coupled in children's development?

by a genetic plan to follow a fixed and sequential progression of stages in development. The genetic determination view has been replaced by the dynamic systems view that infants learn new perceptual-motor couplings by assembling skills for perceiving and acting. New perceptual-motor coupling is not passively accomplished; rather, the infant actively develops a skill to achieve a goal within the constraints set by the infant's body and the environment.

Children perceive in order to move and move in order to perceive. Perceptual and motor development do not occur in isolation from each other but instead are coupled.

Review *Connect* Reflect

LG3 Discuss the connection of perception and action.

Review

- How are perception and motor actions coupled in development?

Connect

- In this section, you learned that perceptual and motor development do not occur in isolation from each other but instead are coupled. How is this distinction similar to the distinction psychologists make when

speaking of nature and nurture when describing development?

Reflect *Your Own Personal Journey of Life*

- Think about your development as a child. Describe two examples, not given in the text, in which your perception guided your action. Then describe two examples, not given in the text, in which your action guided your perception.

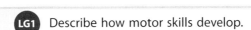

reach your **learning goals**

Motor, Sensory, and Perceptual Development

Motor Development

LG1 Describe how motor skills develop.

The Dynamic Systems View

- Thelen's dynamic systems theory describes the development of motor skills as the assembling of behaviors for perceiving and acting. Perception and action are coupled. According to this theory, the development of motor skills depends on the development of the nervous system, the body's physical properties and its movement possibilities, the goal the child is motivated to reach, and environmental support for the skill. In the dynamic systems view, motor development is far more complex than the result of a genetic blueprint; the infant or child actively puts together a skill in order to achieve a goal within constraints set by the body and the environment.

Reflexes

- Reflexes—built-in reactions to stimuli—govern the newborn's movements. They include the sucking, rooting, and Moro reflexes, all of which typically disappear after three to four months. Some reflexes, such as blinking and yawning, persist throughout life; components of other reflexes are incorporated into voluntary actions.

Gross Motor Skills

- Gross motor skills involve large-muscle activities. Key skills developed during infancy include control of posture and walking. Gross motor skills improve dramatically during the childhood years. Boys usually outperform girls in gross motor skills involving large-muscle activity.

| Fine Motor Skills | • Fine motor skills involve finely tuned movements. The onset of reaching and grasping marks a significant accomplishment. Fine motor skills continue to develop through the childhood years and by 4 years of age are much more precise. Children can use their hands as tools by middle childhood, and at 10 to 12 years of age start to show manipulative fine motor skills similar to those of adults. |

Sensory and Perceptual Development   Outline the course of sensory and perceptual development.

| What Are Sensation and Perception? | • Sensation occurs when information interacts with sensory receptors. Perception is the interpretation of sensation. |

| The Ecological View | • The Gibsons' ecological view states that people directly perceive information that exists in the world. Perception brings people in contact with the environment in order to interact and adapt to it. Affordances are opportunities for interaction offered by objects that are necessary to perform activities. Researchers have developed a number of methods to assess infants' perception, including the visual preference method (which Fantz used to determine young infants' interest in looking at patterned over nonpatterned displays), habituation and dishabituation, high-amplitude sucking, and tracking. |

| Visual Perception | • The infant's visual acuity increases dramatically in the first year of life. Infants show an interest in human faces soon after birth, and young infants systematically scan faces. Possibly by 4 weeks of age, infants can discriminate some colors. By 3 months of age, infants show size and shape constancy. At approximately 2 months of age, infants develop the ability to perceive that occluded objects are complete. In Gibson and Walk's classic study, infants as young as 6 months of age had depth perception. After infancy, children's visual expectations continue to develop, and further color differentiation occurs from 3 to 4 years of age. A number of children experience vision problems. |

| Other Senses | • The fetus can hear several weeks prior to birth. Developmental changes in the perception of loudness, pitch, and localization of sound occur during infancy. Newborns can respond to touch and feel pain. Newborns can differentiate odors, and sensitivity to taste may be present before birth. |

| Intermodal Perception | • Intermodal perception is the ability to relate and integrate information from two or more sensory modalities. Crude, exploratory forms of intermodal perception are present in newborns and become sharpened over the first year of life. |

| Nature, Nurture, and Perceptual Development | • With regard to the study of perception, nature advocates are referred to as nativists and nurture proponents are called empiricists. The Gibsons' ecological view that has guided much of perceptual development research leans toward a nativist approach but still allows for developmental changes in distinctive features. Piaget's constructivist view leans toward an empiricist approach, emphasizing that many perceptual accomplishments must await the development of cognitive stages in infancy. A strong empiricist approach is unwarranted. A full account of perceptual development includes the roles of nature, nurture, and increasing sensitivity to information. |

Perceptual-Motor Coupling **LG3** Discuss the connections of perception and action.

• Perception and action are coupled—individuals perceive in order to move and move in order to perceive. New perceptual-motor couplings do not occur as the result of genetic predetermination but rather because the infant actively assembles skills for perceiving and acting.

key terms

dynamic systems theory 143
reflexes 144
rooting reflex 144
sucking reflex 144
Moro reflex 144

grasping reflex 145
gross motor skills 146
fine motor skills 152
sensation 154
perception 154

ecological view 154
affordances 154
visual preference
  method 155
habituation 155

dishabituation 155
size constancy 158
shape constancy 159
intermodal perception 162

key people

Esther Thelen 143
T. Berry Brazelton 145
Karen Adolph 147

Rachel Clifton 152
Eleanor and James
  J. Gibson 154

Robert Fantz 155
William James 157
Scott Johnson 159

Richard Walk 159
Megan Gunnar 161

Learning is an ornament in prosperity, a refuge in adversity.

—ARISTOTLE
Greek Philosopher, 4th Century B.C.

Cognition and Language

Children thirst to know and understand. In their effort to know and understand, they construct their own ideas about the world around them. They are remarkable for their curiosity and their intelligence. In Section 3, you will read four chapters: "Cognitive Developmental Approaches" (Chapter 6), "Information Processing" (Chapter 7), "Intelligence" (Chapter 8), and "Language Development" (Chapter 9).

COGNITIVE DEVELOPMENTAL APPROACHES

Jean Piaget, the famous Swiss psychologist, was a meticulous observer of his three children—Laurent, Lucienne, and Jacqueline. His books on cognitive development are filled with these observations. Here are a few of Piaget's observations of his children in infancy (Piaget, 1952):

- At 21 days of age, "Laurent found his thumb after three attempts: prolonged sucking begins each time. But, once he has been placed on his back, he does not know how to coordinate the movement of the arms with that of the mouth and his hands draw back even when his lips are seeking them" (p. 27).

- During the third month, thumb sucking becomes less important to Laurent because of new visual and auditory interests. But, when he cries, his thumb goes to the rescue.

- Toward the end of Lucienne's fourth month, while she is lying in her crib, Piaget hangs a doll above her feet. Lucienne thrusts her feet at the doll and makes it move. "Afterward, she looks at her motionless foot for a second, then recommences. There is no visual control of her foot, for the movements are the same when Lucienne only looks at the doll or when I place the doll over her head. On the other hand, the tactile control of the foot is apparent: after the first shakes, Lucienne makes slow foot movements as though to grasp and explore" (p. 159).

- At 11 months, "Jacqueline is seated and shakes a little bell. She then pauses abruptly in order to delicately place the bell in front of her right foot; then she kicks hard. Unable to recapture it, she grasps a ball which she then places at the same spot in order to give it another kick" (p. 225).

- At 1 year, 2 months, "Jacqueline holds in her hands an object which is new to her: a round, flat box which she turns all over, shakes, (and) rubs against the bassinet. . . . She lets it go and tries to pick it up. But she only succeeds in touching it with her index finger, without grasping it. She nevertheless makes an attempt and presses on the edge. The box then tilts up and falls again" (p. 273). Jacqueline shows an interest in this result and studies the fallen box.

- At 1 year, 8 months, "Jacqueline arrives at a closed door with a blade of grass in each hand. She stretches out her right hand toward the [door] knob but sees that she cannot turn it without letting go of the grass. She puts the grass on the floor, opens the door, picks up the grass again, and enters. But when she wants to leave the room, things become complicated. She puts the grass on the floor and grasps the doorknob. But then she perceives that in pulling the door toward her she will simultaneously chase away the grass which she placed between the door and the threshold. She therefore picks it up in order to put it outside the door's zone of movement" (p. 339).

For Piaget, these observations reflect important changes in the infant's cognitive development. Later in the chapter, you will learn that Piaget argued that infants go through six substages of development and that the behaviors you have just read about characterize those substages.

preview

Cognitive developmental approaches place a special emphasis on how children actively construct their thinking. They also focus heavily on how thinking changes from one point in development to another. In this chapter, we will highlight the cognitive developmental approaches of Jean Piaget and Lev Vygotsky.

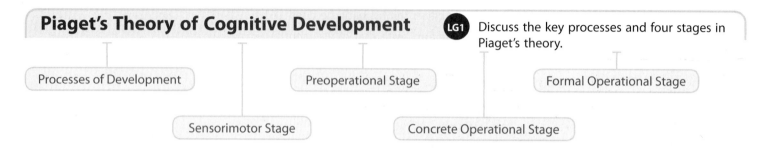

Piaget's Theory of Cognitive Development

LG1 Discuss the key processes and four stages in Piaget's theory.

Processes of Development

Sensorimotor Stage

Preoperational Stage

Concrete Operational Stage

Formal Operational Stage

> We are born capable of learning.
>
> —JEAN-JACQUES ROUSSEAU
> *Swiss-Born French Philosopher,*
> *18th Century*

Poet Nora Perry asked, "Who knows the thoughts of a child?" As much as anyone, Piaget knew. Through careful observations of his own three children—Laurent, Lucienne, and Jacqueline—and observations and interviews with other children, Piaget changed perceptions of the way children think about the world.

Piaget's theory is a general, unifying story of how biology and experience sculpt cognitive development. Piaget thought that, just as our physical bodies have structures that enable us to adapt to the world, we build mental structures that help us to adapt to the world. *Adaptation* involves adjusting to new environmental demands. Piaget stressed that children actively construct their own cognitive worlds; information is not just poured into their minds from the environment. He sought to discover how children at different points in their development think about the world and how systematic changes in their thinking occur.

PROCESSES OF DEVELOPMENT

What processes do children use as they construct their knowledge of the world? Piaget stressed that the following processes are especially important in this regard: schemes, assimilation, accommodation, organization, and equilibration.

In Piaget's view, what is a scheme? What schemes might this young infant be displaying?

Schemes Piaget (1954) said that as the child seeks to construct an understanding of the world, the developing brain creates **schemes.** These are actions or mental representations that organize knowledge. In Piaget's theory, behavioral schemes (physical activities) characterize infancy, and mental schemes (cognitive activities) develop in childhood (Lamb, Bornstein, & Teti, 2002). A baby's schemes are structured by simple actions that can be performed on objects, such as sucking, looking, and grasping. Older children have schemes that include strategies and plans for solving problems. For example, a 5-year-old might have a scheme that involves the strategy of classifying objects by size, shape, or color. By the time we have reached adulthood, we have constructed an enormous number of diverse schemes, ranging from driving a car to balancing a budget to achieving fairness.

Assimilation and Accommodation To explain how children use and adapt their schemes, Piaget proposed two concepts: assimilation and accommodation. Recall that **assimilation** occurs when children incorporate new information into their existing schemes. **Accommodation** occurs when children adjust their schemes to fit new information and experiences.

Think about a toddler who has learned the word *car* to identify the family's car. The toddler might call all moving vehicles on roads "cars," including motorcycles

schemes In Piaget's theory, actions or mental representations that organize knowledge.

assimilation Piagetian concept of the incorporation of new information into existing knowledge.

accommodation Piagetian concept of adjusting schemes to fit new information and experiences.

and trucks; the child has assimilated these objects into his or her existing scheme. But the child soon learns that motorcycles and trucks are not cars and then fine-tunes the category to exclude motorcycles and trucks, accommodating the scheme.

Assimilation and accommodation operate even in very young infants. Newborns reflexively suck everything that touches their lips; they assimilate all sorts of objects into their sucking scheme. By sucking different objects, they learn about their taste, texture, shape, and so on. After several months of experience, though, they construct their understanding of the world differently. Some objects, such as fingers and the mother's breast, can be sucked, and others, such as fuzzy blankets, should not be sucked. In other words, babies accommodate their sucking scheme.

Organization   To make sense out of their world, said Piaget, children cognitively organize their experiences. **Organization** in Piaget's theory is the grouping of isolated behaviors and thoughts into a higher-order system. Continual refinement of this organization is an inherent part of development. A boy who has only a vague idea about how to use a hammer may also have a vague idea about how to use other tools. After learning how to use each one, he relates these uses, grouping items into categories and organizing his knowledge.

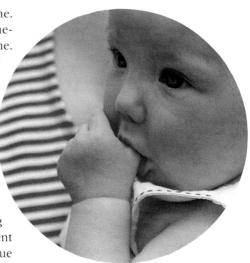

How might assimilation and accommodation be involved in infants' sucking?

Equilibration and Stages of Development   **Equilibration** is a mechanism that Piaget proposed to explain how children shift from one stage of thought to the next. The shift occurs as children experience cognitive conflict, or disequilibrium, in trying to understand the world. Eventually, they resolve the conflict and reach a balance, or equilibrium, of thought. Piaget argued that there is considerable movement between states of cognitive equilibrium and disequilibrium as assimilation and accommodation work in concert to produce cognitive change. For example, if a child believes that the amount of a liquid changes simply because the liquid is poured into a container with a different shape—for instance, from a container that is short and wide into a container that is tall and narrow—she might be puzzled by such issues as where the "extra" liquid came from and whether there is actually more liquid to drink. The child will eventually resolve these puzzles as her thought becomes more advanced. In the everyday world, the child is constantly faced with such counterexamples and inconsistencies.

Assimilation and accommodation always take the child to a higher ground. For Piaget, the motivation for change is an internal search for equilibrium. As old schemes are adjusted and new schemes are developed, the child organizes and reorganizes the old and new schemes. Eventually, the organization is fundamentally different from the old organization; it is a new way of thinking, a new stage. The result of these processes, according to Piaget, is that individuals go through four stages of development. A different way of understanding the world makes one stage more advanced than another. Cognition is *qualitatively* different in one stage compared with another. In other words, the way children reason at one stage is different from the way they reason at another stage.

Each of Piaget's stages is age-related and consists of distinct ways of thinking. Piaget identified four stages of cognitive development: sensorimotor, preoperational, concrete operational, and formal operational (see Figure 6.1).

SENSORIMOTOR STAGE

The **sensorimotor stage** lasts from birth to about 2 years of age. In this stage, infants construct an understanding of the world by coordinating sensory experiences (such as seeing and hearing) with physical, motoric actions—hence the term "sensorimotor." At the beginning of this stage, newborns have little more than reflexive patterns with which to work. At the end of the sensorimotor stage, 2-year-olds can produce complex sensorimotor patterns and use primitive symbols. We first will summarize Piaget's descriptions of how infants develop. Later we will consider criticisms of his views.

organization Piaget's concept of grouping isolated behaviors into a higher-order, more smoothly functioning cognitive system; the grouping or arranging of items into categories.

equilibration A mechanism that Piaget proposed to explain how children shift from one stage of thought to the next. The shift occurs as children experience cognitive conflict, or disequilibrium, in trying to understand the world. Eventually, they resolve the conflict and reach a balance, or equilibrium, of thought.

sensorimotor stage The first of Piaget's stages, which lasts from birth to about 2 years of age; infants construct an understanding of the world by coordinating sensory experiences (such as seeing and hearing) with motoric actions.

Sensorimotor Stage

Infants gain knowledge of the world from the physical actions they perform on it. Infants coordinate sensory experiences with these physical actions. An infant progresses from reflexive, instinctual action at birth to the beginning of symbolic thought toward the end of the stage.

Birth to 2 Years of Age

Preoperational Stage

The child begins to use mental representations to understand the world. Symbolic thinking, reflected in the use of words and images, is used in this mental representation, which goes beyond the connection of sensory information with physical action. However, there are some constraints on the child's thinking at this stage, such as egocentrism and centration.

2 to 7 Years of Age

Concrete Operational Stage

The child can now reason logically about concrete events, understands the concept of conservation, organizes objects into hierarchical classes (classification), and places objects in ordered series (seriation).

7 to 11 Years of Age

Formal Operational Stage

The adolescent reasons in more abstract, idealistic, and logical (hypothetical-deductive) ways.

11 Years of Age Through Adulthood

FIGURE **6.1**
PIAGET'S FOUR STAGES OF COGNITIVE DEVELOPMENT

Substages   Piaget divided the sensorimotor stage into six substages: (1) simple reflexes; (2) first habits and primary circular reactions; (3) secondary circular reactions; (4) coordination of secondary circular reactions; (5) tertiary circular reactions, novelty, and curiosity; and (6) internalization of schemes (see Figure 6.2).

1. *Simple reflexes*, the first sensorimotor substage, corresponds to the first month after birth. In this substage, sensation and action are coordinated primarily through reflexive behaviors, such as the rooting and sucking reflexes. Soon the infant produces behaviors that resemble reflexes in the absence of the usual stimulus for the reflex. For example, a newborn will suck a nipple or bottle only when it is placed directly in the baby's mouth or touched to the lips. But soon the infant might suck when a bottle or nipple is only nearby. The infant is initiating action and is actively structuring experiences in the first month of life.

2. *First habits and primary circular reactions* is the second sensorimotor substage, which develops between 1 and 4 months of age. In this substage, the infant coordinates sensation and two types of schemes: habits and primary circular reactions.

   • A *habit* is a scheme based on a reflex that has become completely separated from its eliciting stimulus. For example, infants in substage 1 suck when bottles are put to their lips or when they see a bottle. Infants in substage 2 might suck even when no bottle is present. A *circular reaction* is a repetitive action.

   • A *primary circular reaction* is a scheme based on the attempt to reproduce an event that initially occurred by chance. For example, suppose an infant accidentally sucks his fingers when they are placed near his mouth. Later, he searches for his fingers to suck them again, but the fingers do not cooperate because the infant cannot coordinate visual and manual actions.

Substage	Age	Description	Example
1 Simple reflexes	Birth to 1 month	Coordination of sensation and action through reflexive behaviors.	Rooting, sucking, and grasping reflexes; newborns suck reflexively when their lips are touched.
2 First habits and primary circular reactions	1 to 4 months	Coordination of sensation and two types of schemes: habits (reflex) and primary circular reactions (reproduction of an event that initially occurred by chance). Main focus is still on the infant's body.	Repeating a body sensation first experienced by chance (sucking thumb, for example); then infants might accommodate actions by sucking their thumb differently from how they suck on a nipple.
3 Secondary circular reactions	4 to 8 months	Infants become more object-oriented, moving beyond self-preoccupation; repeat actions that bring interesting or pleasurable results.	An infant coos to make a person stay near; as the person starts to leave, the infant coos again.
4 Coordination of secondary circular reactions	8 to 12 months	Coordination of vision and touch—hand-eye coordination; coordination of schemes and intentionality.	Infant manipulates a stick in order to bring an attractive toy within reach.
5 Tertiary circular reactions, novelty, and curiosity	12 to 18 months	Infants become intrigued by the many properties of objects and by the many things they can make happen to objects; they experiment with new behavior.	A block can be made to fall, spin, hit another object, and slide across the ground.
6 Internalization of schemes	18 to 24 months	Infants develop the ability to use primitive symbols and form enduring mental representations.	An infant who has never thrown a temper tantrum before sees a playmate throw a tantrum; the infant retains a memory of the event, then throws one himself the next day.

FIGURE **6.2**

PIAGET'S SIX SUBSTAGES OF SENSORIMOTOR DEVELOPMENT

Habits and circular reactions are stereotyped—that is, the infant repeats them the same way each time. During this substage, the infant's own body remains his or her center of attention. There is no outward pull by environmental events.

3. *Secondary circular reactions* is the third sensorimotor substage, which develops between 4 and 8 months of age. In this substage, the infant becomes more object-oriented, moving beyond preoccupation with the self. By chance, an infant might shake a rattle. The infant repeats this action for the sake of its fascination.

The infant also imitates some simple actions, such as the baby talk or burbling of adults, and some physical gestures. However, the baby imitates only actions that he or she is already able to produce. Although directed toward objects in the world, the infant's schemes are not intentional or goal-directed.

4. *Coordination of secondary circular reactions* is Piaget's fourth sensorimotor substage, which develops between 8 and 12 months of age. To progress into this substage, the infant must coordinate vision and touch, eye and hand. Actions become more outwardly directed. Significant changes during this substage involve the coordination of schemes and intentionality. Infants readily combine and recombine previously learned schemes in a coordinated way. They might look at an object and grasp it simultaneously, or they might visually inspect a toy, such as a rattle, and finger it simultaneously, exploring it tactilely. Actions are even more outwardly directed than before. Related to this coordination is the second achievement—the presence of intentionality. For example, infants might manipulate a stick in order to bring a desired toy within reach, or they might knock over one block to reach and play with another one.

5. *Tertiary circular reactions, novelty, and curiosity* is Piaget's fifth sensorimotor substage, which develops between 12 and 18 months of age. In this substage, infants become intrigued by the many properties of objects and by the many things that they can make happen to objects. A block can be made to fall, spin, hit another object, and slide across the ground. *Tertiary circular reactions* are schemes in which the infant purposely explores new possibilities with objects, continually doing new things to them and exploring the results.

This 17-month-old is in Piaget's stage of tertiary circular reactions. *What might the infant do to suggest that she is in this stage?*

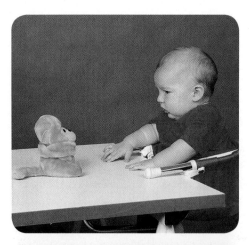

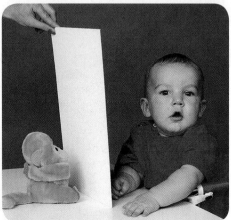

FIGURE **6.3**

OBJECT PERMANENCE. Piaget argued that object permanence is one of infancy's landmark cognitive accomplishments. For this 5-month-old boy, "out of sight" is literally out of mind. The infant looks at the toy monkey (*top*), but when his view of the toy is blocked (*bottom*), he does not search for it. Several months later, he will search for the hidden toy monkey, reflecting the presence of object permanence.

object permanence The Piagetian term for one of an infant's most important accomplishments: understanding that objects and events continue to exist even when they cannot directly be seen, heard, or touched.

A-not-B error Also called A–B̄ error, this occurs when infants make the mistake of selecting the familiar hiding place (A) rather than the new hiding place (B̄) as they progress into substage 4 in Piaget's sensorimotor stage.

Piaget says that this stage marks the starting point for human curiosity and interest in novelty.

6. *Internalization of schemes* is Piaget's sixth and final sensorimotor substage, which develops between 18 and 24 months of age. In this substage, the infant develops the ability to use primitive symbols. For Piaget, a *symbol* is an internalized sensory image or word that represents an event. Primitive symbols permit the infant to think about concrete events without directly acting them out or perceiving them. Moreover, symbols allow the infant to manipulate and transform the represented events in simple ways. In a favorite Piagetian example, Piaget's young daughter saw a matchbox being opened and closed. Later, she mimicked the event by opening and closing her mouth. This was an obvious expression of her image of the event.

Object Permanence   Imagine how chaotic and unpredictable your life would be if you could not distinguish between yourself and your world. This is what the life of a newborn must be like, according to Piaget. There is no differentiation between the self and world; objects have no separate, permanent existence.

By the end of the sensorimotor period, children understand that objects are both separate from the self and permanent. **Object permanence** is the understanding that objects and events continue to exist even when they cannot be seen, heard, or touched. Acquiring the sense of object permanence is one of the infant's most important accomplishments. According to Piaget, infants develop object permanence in a series of substages that correspond to the six substages of sensorimotor development.

How can anyone know whether an infant has developed a sense of object permanence? The principal way that object permanence is studied is by watching an infant's reaction when an interesting object disappears (see Figure 6.3). If infants search for the object, it is assumed that they believe it continues to exist.

Object permanence is just one of the basic concepts about the physical world developed by babies. To Piaget, children—even infants—are much like little scientists, examining the world to see how it works. But how can adult scientists determine what these "baby scientists" are finding out about the world and at what age they're finding it out? To answer this question, read the *Connecting Through Research* interlude that follows.

Evaluating Piaget's Sensorimotor Stage   Piaget opened up a new way of looking at infants with his view that their main task is to coordinate their sensory impressions with their motor activity. However, the infant's cognitive world is not as neatly packaged as Piaget portrayed it, and some of Piaget's explanations for the cause of cognitive changes in development are debated. In the past several decades, sophisticated experimental techniques have been devised to study infants, and there have been a large number of research studies on infant development. Much of the new research suggests that Piaget's view of sensorimotor development needs to be modified (Baillargeon & others, 2011; de Hevia & Spelke, 2010; Johnson, 2009, 2010a, b; Meltzoff, 2011; Quinn, 2011).

The A-not-B Error   One modification concerns Piaget's claim that certain processes are crucial in transitions from one stage to the next. The data do not always support his explanations. For example, in Piaget's theory, an important feature in the progression into substage 4, *coordination of secondary circular reactions*, is an infant's inclination to search for a hidden object in a familiar location rather than to look for the object in a new location. For example, if a toy is hidden twice, initially at location A and subsequently at location B̄, 8- to 12-month-old infants search correctly at location A initially. But when the toy is subsequently hidden at location B̄, they make the mistake of continuing to search for it at location A. **A-not-B error** (also called A-B̄ error) is the term used to describe this common mistake. Older infants are less likely to make the A-not-B error because their concept of object permanence is more complete.

How Do Researchers Determine Infants' Understanding of Object Permanence and Causality?

Two accomplishments of infants that Piaget examined were the development of object permanence and the child's understanding of causality. Let's examine two research studies that address these topics.

In both studies, Renée Baillargeon and her colleagues used a research method that involves *violation of expectations*. In this method, infants see an event happen as it normally would. Then, the event is changed in a way that violates what the infant expects to see. When infants look longer at the event that violates their expectations, it indicates they are surprised by it.

In one study focused on object permanence, researchers showed infants a toy car that moved down an inclined track, disappeared behind a screen, and then reemerged at the other end, still on the track (Baillargeon & DeVoe, 1991) (see Figure 6.4a). After this sequence was repeated several times, something different occurred: A toy mouse was placed *behind* the tracks but was hidden by the screen while the car rolled by (b). This was the "possible" event. Then, the researchers created an "impossible event": The toy mouse was placed *on* the tracks but was secretly removed after the screen was lowered so that the car seemed to go through the mouse (c). In this study, infants as young as 3½ months of age looked longer at the impossible event than at the possible event, indicating that they were surprised by it. Their surprise suggested that they remembered not only that the toy mouse still existed (object permanence) but its location.

Another study focused on infants' understanding of causality (Kotovsky & Baillargeon, 1994). In this research, a cylinder rolls down a ramp and hits a toy bug at the bottom of the ramp. By 5½ and 6½ months of age, after infants have seen how far the bug will be pushed by a medium-sized cylinder, their reactions indicate that they understand that the bug will roll farther if it is hit by a large cylinder than if it is hit by a small cylinder. Thus, by the middle of the first year of life infants understand that the size of a moving object determines how far it will move a stationary object that it collides with.

In Baillargeon's (2008; Baillargeon & others, 2009) view, infants have a pre-adapted, innate bias called the *principle of persistence* that explains their assumption that objects don't change their properties—including how solid they are, their location, their color, and their form—unless some external factor (a person who moves the object, for example) obviously intervenes. Shortly, we will revisit the extent to which nature and nurture are at work in the changes that take place in the infant's cognitive development.

The research findings discussed in this interlude and other research indicate that infants develop object permanence and causal reasoning much earlier than Piaget proposed (Baillargeon & others, 2009; Luo, Kaufman, & Baillargeon, 2009). Indeed, as you will see in the next section, a major theme of infant cognitive development today is that infants are more cognitively competent than Piaget envisioned.

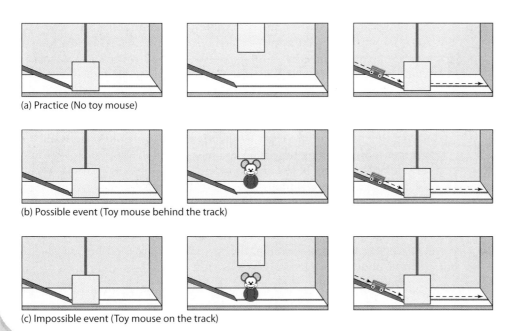

(a) Practice (No toy mouse)

(b) Possible event (Toy mouse behind the track)

(c) Impossible event (Toy mouse on the track)

FIGURE **6.4**

USING THE VIOLATION OF EXPECTATIONS METHOD TO STUDY OBJECT PERMANENCE IN INFANTS. If infants looked longer at (*c*) than at (*b*), researchers reasoned that the impossible event in (*c*) violated the infants' expectations and that they remembered that the toy mouse existed.

Researchers have found, however, that the A-not-B error does not show up consistently (Sophian, 1985). The evidence indicates that A-not-B errors are sensitive to the delay between hiding the object at B⁻ and the infant's attempt to find it (Diamond, 1985). Thus, the A-not-B error might be due to a failure in memory. Another explanation is that infants tend to repeat a previous motor behavior (Clearfield & others, 2006).

Perceptual Development and Expectations   A number of theorists, such as Eleanor Gibson (2001) and Elizabeth Spelke (1991; Spelke & Kinzler, 2009), argue that infants' perceptual abilities are highly developed very early in life. Spelke concludes that young infants interpret the world as having predictable occurrences. For example, in Chapter 4 we discussed research that demonstrated the presence of intermodal perception—the ability to coordinate information from two or more sensory modalities, such as vision and hearing—by 3½ months of age, much earlier than Piaget would have predicted (Spelke & Owsley, 1979).

Research also suggests that infants develop the ability to understand how the world works at a very early age (Baillargeon & others, 2009, 2011). For example, by the time they are 3 to 4 months of age, infants develop expectations about future events. What kinds of expectations do infants form? Experiments by Spelke (1991, 2000; Spelke & Hespos, 2001) have addressed these questions. She placed babies before a puppet stage and showed them a series of actions that are unexpected if you know how the physical world works—for example, one ball seemed to roll through a solid barrier, another seemed to leap between two platforms, and a third appeared to hang in midair (Spelke, 1979). Spelke measured and compared the babies' looking times for unexpected and expected actions. She concluded that, by 4 months of age, even though infants do not yet have the ability to talk about objects, move and manipulate objects, or even see objects with high resolution, they expect objects to be solid and continuous. However, at 4 months of age, infants do not expect an object to obey gravitational constraints (Spelke & others, 1992). Similarly, research by Renée Baillargeon and her colleagues (1995, 2004) documents that infants as young as 3 to 4 months expect objects to be *substantial* (in the sense that other objects cannot move through them) and *permanent* (in the sense that objects continue to exist when they are hidden).

However, some critics, such as Andrew Meltzoff (2008; Moore & Meltzoff, 2008), argue that Spelke's and Baillargeon's research relies on how long infants look at unexpected events and thus assesses infants' *perceptual expectations* about where and when objects will reappear rather than tapping their *knowledge* about where the objects are when they are out of sight. Meltzoff points out that whether infants act on their perception is an important aspect of assessing object permanence and states that it does not appear that young infants can act on the information. Thus, Meltzoff (2008) concludes, it is still unclear whether longer looking time is a valid measure of object permanence and how early infants develop object permanence.

By 6 to 8 months, infants have learned to perceive gravity and support—that an object hanging on the end of a table should fall, that ball-bearings will travel farther when rolled down a longer rather than a shorter ramp, and that cup handles will not fall when attached to a cup (Slater, Field, & Hernandez-Reif, 2007). As infants develop, their experiences and actions on objects help them to understand physical laws (Bremner, 2007).

The Nature/Nurture Issue   In considering the big issue of whether nature or nurture plays the more important role in infant development, Elizabeth Spelke (Spelke, 2000; Spelke & Kinzler, 2007, 2009) comes down clearly on the side of nature. Spelke endorses a **core knowledge approach,** which states that infants are born with domain-specific innate knowledge systems. Among these domain-specific knowledge systems are those involving space, number sense, object permanence, and language (which we will discuss later in this chapter). Strongly influenced by

developmental **connection**

Theories. Eleanor Gibson was a pioneer in crafting the ecological perception view of development. Chapter 5, pp. 159–160

A 4-month-old in Elizabeth Spelke's infant perception laboratory is tested to determine if she knows that an object in motion will not stop in midair. Spelke concluded that at 4 months babies don't expect objects like these balls to obey gravitational constraints, but that they do expect objects to be solid and continuous. Research by Spelke, Renée Baillargeon, and others suggest that infants develop an ability to understand how the world works earlier than Piaget envisioned. However, critics such as Andrew Meltzoff fault their research and conclude there is still controversy about how early some infant cognitive accomplishments occur.

core knowledge approach States that infants are born with domain-specific innate knowledge systems, such as those involving space, number sense, object permanence, and language.

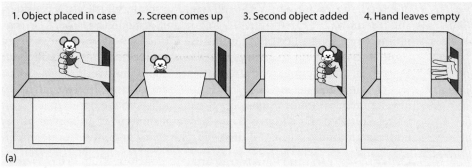

Original event

1. Object placed in case
2. Screen comes up
3. Second object added
4. Hand leaves empty

(a)

Test events

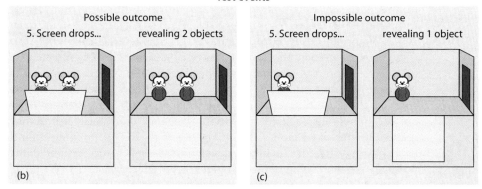

Possible outcome

5. Screen drops... revealing 2 objects

(b)

Impossible outcome

5. Screen drops... revealing 1 object

(c)

FIGURE 6.5

INFANTS' NUMBER SENSE. Shown here is one of the sequences in Karen Wynn's (1992) study of 5-month-old infants' number sense. The experimenter was hidden behind the display and manipulated the objects through a trap door in the wall of the display. Five-month-old infants who saw the impossible event (only one Mickey Mouse doll) looked longer at the event than their 5-month-old counterparts who saw the possible event (two dolls).

Reprinted by permission from Macmillan Publishers Ltd: *Nature,* 358, pp. 749–750, "Addition and Subtraction by Human Infants" by Karen Wynn. Copyright © 1992.

evolution, the core knowledge domains are theorized to be prewired to allow infants to make sense of their world. After all, Spelke asks, how could infants possibly grasp the complex world in which they live if they didn't come into the world equipped with core sets of knowledge? In this approach, the innate core knowledge domains form a foundation around which more mature cognitive functioning and learning develop. The core knowledge approach argues that Piaget greatly underestimated the cognitive abilities of infants, especially young infants.

An intriguing domain of core knowledge that has been investigated in young infants is whether they have a sense of number. Spelke concludes that they do. Using the violations of expectations method discussed in the Research on Child Development interlude, Karen Wynn (1992) conducted an early experiment on infants' sense of number (see Figure 6.5). Five-month-old infants were shown one or two Mickey Mouse dolls on a puppet stage. Then the experimenter hid the doll(s) behind a screen and visibly removed or added one. Next, when the screen was lifted, the infants looked longer when they saw the incorrect number of dolls. Spelke and her colleagues (de Hevia & Spelke, 2010; Hyde & Spelke, 2009; Izard & Spelke, 2010; Lipton & Spelke, 2004; Spelke & Kinsler, 2007; Xu, Spelke, & Goddard, 2005) have found that infants can distinguish between different numbers of objects, actions, and sounds. Efforts to find further support for infants' sense of number are extending to assessments of brain activity. For example, a recent study of 3-month-olds observing changes either in the identity of objects or the number of objects revealed that changes in the type of objects activated a region of the brain's temporal lobe, while changes in the number of objects activated an additional region of the parietal lobe (Izard, Dehaene-Lambertz, & Dehaene, 2008). In older children and adults, number sense activates the same region of the parietal lobe that was activated in the 3-month-old infants in this study.

Not everyone agrees with Spelke's conclusions about young infants' math skills (Cohen, 2002). One criticism is that infants in the number experiments are merely responding to changes in the display that violated their expectations.

In criticizing the core knowledge approach, British developmental psychologist Mark Johnston (2008) says that the infants Spelke assesses in her research already

developmental connection

Nature vs. Nurture. The nature-nurture issue involves the debate about whether development is primarily influenced by nature (biological inheritance) or nurture (environmental experiences). Chapter 1, pp. 17–18; Chapter 2, p. 72

What revisions in Piaget's theory of sensorimotor development do contemporary researchers conclude need to be made?

have accumulated hundreds, and in some cases even thousands, of hours of experience in grasping what the world is about, which gives considerable room for the environment's role in the development of infant cognition (Highfield, 2008). According to Johnston (2008), infants likely come into the world with "soft biases to perceive and attend to different aspects of the environment, and to learn about the world in particular ways." Although debate about the cause and course of infant cognitive development continues, most developmentalists today agree that Piaget underestimated the early cognitive accomplishments of infants and that both nature and nurture are involved in infants' cognitive development.

Conclusions   In sum, many researchers conclude that Piaget wasn't specific enough about how infants learn about their world and that infants, especially young infants, are more competent than Piaget thought (Baillargeon & others, 2011; Bauer, Larkina, & Deocampo, 2011; Diamond, Casey, & Munakata, 2011; Spelke & Kinzler, 2009). As they have examined the specific ways that infants learn, the field of infant cognition has become very specialized. Many researchers are at work on different questions, with no general theory emerging that can connect all of the different findings (Nelson, 1999). Their theories often are local theories, focused on specific research questions, rather than grand theories like Piaget's (Kuhn, 1998). If there is a unifying theme, it is that investigators in infant development seek to understand more precisely how developmental changes in cognition take place and to explore the big issue of nature and nurture (Aslin, 2009; Woodward & Needham, 2009). As they seek to identify more precisely the contributions of nature and nurture to infant development, researchers face the difficult task of determining whether the course of acquiring information, which is very rapid in some domains, is best accounted for by an innate set of biases (that is, core knowledge) or by the extensive input of environmental experiences to which the infant is exposed (Aslin, 2009).

PREOPERATIONAL STAGE

The cognitive world of the preschool child is creative, free, and fanciful. The imagination of preschool children works overtime, and their mental grasp of the world improves. Piaget described the preschool child's cognition as *preoperational*. What did he mean?

Because Piaget called this stage preoperational, it might sound unimportant. Not so. Preoperational thought is anything but a convenient waiting period for the next stage, concrete operational thought. However, the label *preoperational* emphasizes that the child does not yet perform **operations,** which are internalized actions that allow children to do mentally what they could formerly do only physically. Operations are reversible mental actions. Mentally adding and subtracting numbers are examples of operations. *Preoperational thought* is the beginning of the ability to reconstruct in thought what has been established in behavior.

The **preoperational stage,** which lasts from approximately 2 to 7 years of age, is the second Piagetian stage. In this stage, children begin to represent the world with words, images, and drawings. Symbolic thought goes beyond simple connections of sensory information and physical action. Stable concepts are formed, mental reasoning emerges, egocentrism is present, and magical beliefs are constructed. Preoperational thought can be divided into substages: the symbolic function substage and the intuitive thought substage.

The Symbolic Function Substage   The **symbolic function substage** is the first substage of preoperational thought, occurring roughly between the ages of 2 and 4. In this substage, the young child gains the ability to mentally represent an object that is not present. This ability vastly expands the child's mental world (Carlson &

operations Internalized actions that allow children to do mentally what before they had done only physically. Operations also are reversible mental actions.

preoperational stage The second Piagetian developmental stage, which lasts from about 2 to 7 years of age, when children begin to represent the world with words, images, and drawings.

symbolic function substage The first substage of preoperational thought, occurring roughly between the ages of 2 and 4. In this substage, the young child gains the ability to represent mentally an object that is not present.

egocentrism An important feature of preoperational thought: the inability to distinguish between one's own and someone else's perspective.

animism A facet of preoperational thought: the belief that inanimate objects have lifelike qualities and are capable of action.

Model of Mountains

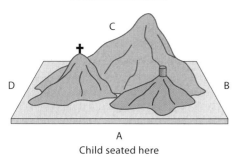

Child seated here

Photo 1
(View from A)

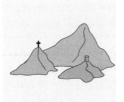

Photo 2
(View from B)

Photo 3
(View from C)

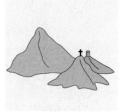

Photo 4
(View from D)

FIGURE **6.6**

THE THREE-MOUNTAINS TASK. The mountain model on the far left shows the child's perspective from view A, where he or she is sitting. The four squares represent photos showing the mountains from four different viewpoints of the model—A, B, C, and D. The experimenter asks the child to identify the photo in which the mountains look as they would from position B. To identify the photo correctly, the child has to take the perspective of a person sitting at spot B. Invariably, a child who thinks in a preoperational way cannot perform this task. When asked what a view of the mountains looks like from position B, the child selects Photo 1, taken from location A (the child's own view at the time) instead of Photo 2, the correct view.

Zelazo, 2008; Deloache, 2011). Young children use scribble designs to represent people, houses, cars, clouds, and so on; they begin to use language and engage in pretend play. However, although young children make distinct progress during this substage, their thought still has several important limitations, two of which are egocentrism and animism.

Egocentrism is the inability to distinguish between one's own perspective and someone else's perspective. The following telephone conversation between 4-year-old Mary, who is at home, and her father, who is at work, typifies Mary's egocentric thought:

Father: Mary, is Mommy there?

Mary: (Silently nods)

Father: Mary, may I speak to Mommy?

Mary: (Nods again silently)

Mary's response is egocentric in that she fails to consider her father's perspective before replying. A nonegocentric thinker would have responded verbally.

Piaget and Barbel Inhelder (1969) initially studied young children's egocentrism by devising the three-mountains task (see Figure 6.6). The child walks around the model of the mountains and becomes familiar with what the mountains look like from different perspectives, and she can see that there are different objects on the mountains. The child is then seated on one side of the table on which the mountains are placed. The experimenter moves a doll to different locations around the table, at each location asking the child to select from a series of photos the one photo that most accurately reflects the view the doll is seeing. Children in the preoperational stage often pick their own view rather than the doll's view. Preschool children frequently show perspective skills on some tasks but not others.

Animism, another limitation of preoperational thought, is the belief that inanimate objects have lifelike qualities and are capable of action (Gelman & Opfer, 2004; Opfer & Gelman, 2011). A young child might show animism by saying, "That tree pushed the leaf off, and it fell down" or "The sidewalk made me mad; it made me fall down." A young child who uses animism fails to distinguish the appropriate occasions for using human and nonhuman perspectives.

Possibly because young children are not very concerned about reality, their drawings are fanciful and inventive. Suns are blue, skies are yellow, and cars float on clouds in their symbolic, imaginative world. One 3½-year-old looked at a scribble he had just drawn and described it as a pelican kissing a seal (see Figure 6.7a). The symbolism is simple but strong, like abstractions found in some modern art. Twentieth-century Spanish artist Pablo Picasso commented, "I used to draw like Raphael but it has taken

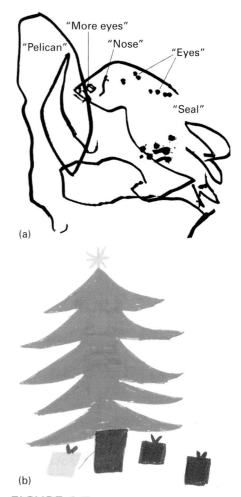

FIGURE **6.7**

THE SYMBOLIC DRAWINGS OF YOUNG CHILDREN. (*a*) A 3½-year-old's symbolic drawing. Halfway into this drawing, the 3½-year-old artist said it was "a pelican kissing a seal." (*b*) This 11-year-old's drawing is neater and more realistic but also less inventive.

"I still don't have all the answers, but I'm beginning to ask the right questions."
© New Yorker Collection 1989 Lee Lorenz from cartoonbank.com. All rights reserved. Reprinted with permission.

me a lifetime to draw like young children." In the elementary school years, a child's drawings become more realistic, neat, and precise (see Figure 6.7b). Suns are yellow, skies are blue, and cars travel on roads (Winner, 1986).

The Intuitive Thought Substage   The **intuitive thought substage** is the second substage of preoperational thought, occurring between approximately 4 and 7 years of age. In this substage, children begin to use primitive reasoning and want to know the answers to all sorts of questions. Consider 4-year-old Tommy, who is at the beginning of the intuitive thought substage. Although he is starting to develop his own ideas about the world he lives in, his ideas are still simple, and he is not very good at thinking things out. He has difficulty understanding events that he knows are taking place but which he cannot see. His fantasized thoughts bear little resemblance to reality. He cannot yet answer the question "What if?" in any reliable way. For example, he has only a vague idea of what would happen if a car were to hit him. He also has difficulty negotiating traffic because he cannot do the mental calculations necessary to estimate whether an approaching car will hit him when he crosses the road.

By the age of 5, children have just about exhausted the adults around them with "why" questions. The child's questions signal the emergence of interest in reasoning and in figuring out why things are the way they are. Following are some samples of the questions children ask during the questioning period of 4 to 6 years of age (Elkind, 1976):

"What makes you grow up?"

"What makes you stop growing?"

"Why does a lady have to be married to have a baby?"

"Who was the mother when everybody was a baby?"

"Why do leaves fall?"

"Why does the sun shine?"

Piaget called this substage *intuitive* because young children seem so sure about their knowledge and understanding yet are unaware of how they know what they know. That is, they know something but know it without the use of rational thinking.

Centration and the Limitations of Preoperational Thought   One limitation of preoperational thought is **centration,** a centering of attention on one characteristic to the exclusion of all others. Centration is most clearly evidenced in young children's lack of **conservation,** the awareness that altering an object's or a substance's appearance does not change its basic properties. For example, to adults, it is obvious that a certain amount of liquid stays the same, regardless of a container's shape. But this is not at all obvious to young children. Instead, they are struck by the height of the liquid in the container; they focus on that characteristic to the exclusion of others.

The situation that Piaget devised to study conservation is his most famous task. In the conservation task, a child is presented with two identical beakers, each filled to the same level with liquid (see Figure 6.8). The child is asked if these beakers have the same amount of liquid, and she usually says "yes." Then the liquid from one beaker is poured into a third beaker, which is taller and thinner than the first two. The child is then asked if the amount of liquid in the tall, thin beaker is equal to that which remains in one of the original beakers. Children who are less than 7 or 8 years old usually say "no" and justify their answers in terms of the differing height or width of the beakers. Older children usually answer "yes" and justify their answers appropriately ("If you poured the water back, the amount would still be the same").

In Piaget's theory, failing the conservation-of-liquid task is a sign that children are at the preoperational stage of cognitive development. The preoperational child fails to show conservation not only of liquid but also of number, matter, length, volume, and area. Figure 6.9 portrays several of these dimensions of conservation.

intuitive thought substage The second substage of preoperational thought, occurring between approximately 4 and 7 years of age, when children begin to use primitive reasoning.

centration Focusing attention on one characteristic to the exclusion of all others.

conservation The idea that altering an object's or substance's appearance does not change its basic properties.

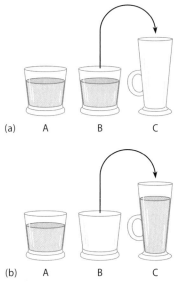

FIGURE 6.8

PIAGET'S CONSERVATION TASK. The beaker test is a well-known Piagetian task to determine whether a child can think operationally—that is, can mentally reverse actions and show conservation of the substance. (*a*) Two identical beakers are presented to the child. Then, the experimenter pours the liquid from B into C, which is taller and thinner than A or B. (*b*) The child is asked if these beakers (A and C) have the same amount of liquid. The preoperational child says "no." When asked to point to the beaker that has more liquid, the preoperational child points to the tall, thin beaker.

Children often vary in their performance on different conservation tasks. Thus, a child might be able to conserve volume but not number.

Some developmentalists do not believe Piaget was entirely correct in his estimate of when children's conservation skills emerge. For example, Rochel Gelman (1969) showed that when the child's attention to relevant aspects of the conservation task is improved, the child is more likely to conserve. Gelman has also demonstrated that attentional training on one dimension, such as number, improves the preschool child's performance on another dimension, such as mass. Thus, Gelman suggests that conservation appears earlier than Piaget thought and that attention is especially important in explaining conservation.

CONCRETE OPERATIONAL STAGE

The **concrete operational stage,** which lasts approximately from 7 to 11 years of age, is the third Piagetian stage. In this stage, logical reasoning replaces intuitive reasoning as long as the reasoning can be applied to specific or concrete examples.

concrete operational stage Piaget's third stage, which lasts from approximately 7 to 11 years of age, when children can perform concrete operations, and logical reasoning replaces intuitive reasoning as long as the reasoning can be applied to specific or concrete examples.

Type of Conservation	Initial Presentation	Manipulation	Preoperational Child's Answer
Number	Two identical rows of objects are shown to the child, who agrees they have the same number.	One row is lengthened and the child is asked whether one row now has more objects.	Yes, the longer row.
Matter	Two identical balls of clay are shown to the child. The child agrees that they are equal.	The experimenter changes the shape of one of the balls and asks the child whether they still contain equal amounts of clay.	No, the longer one has more.
Length	Two sticks are aligned in front of the child. The child agrees that they are the same length.	The experimenter moves one stick to the right, then asks the child if they are equal in length.	No, the one on the top is longer.

FIGURE **6.9**

SOME DIMENSIONS OF CONSERVATION: NUMBER, MATTER, AND LENGTH. *What characteristics of preoperational thought do children demonstrate when they fail these conservation tasks?*

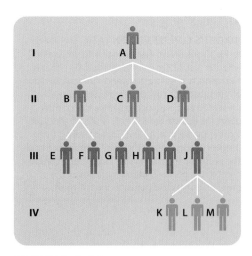

FIGURE **6.10**

CLASSIFICATION: AN IMPORTANT ABILITY IN CONCRETE OPERATIONAL THOUGHT. A family tree of four generations (*I to IV*): The preoperational child has trouble classifying the members of the four generations; the concrete operational child can classify the members vertically, horizontally, and obliquely (up and down and across). For example, the concrete operational child understands that a family member can be a son, a brother, and a father, all at the same time.

horizontal décalage Piaget's concept that similar abilities do not appear at the same time within a stage of development.

seriation The concrete operation that involves ordering stimuli along a quantitative dimension (such as length).

For instance, concrete operational thinkers cannot imagine the steps necessary to complete an algebraic equation, which is too abstract for thinking at this stage of development. Children at this stage can performs *concrete operations*, which are reversible mental actions on real, concrete objects.

Conservation The conservation tasks demonstrate a child's ability to perform concrete operations. In the test of reversibility of thought involving conservation of matter (shown in Figure 6.9), a child is presented with two identical balls of clay. An experimenter rolls one ball into a long, thin shape; the other remains in its original ball shape. The child is then asked if there is more clay in the ball or in the long, thin piece of clay. By the time children reach the age 7 or 8, most answer that the amount of clay is the same. To answer this problem correctly, children have to imagine the clay ball rolling back into a ball after it has been changed into a long, thin shape; they have mentally reversed the action on the ball.

Concrete operations allow children to coordinate several characteristics rather than focus on a single property of an object. In the clay example, a preoperational child is likely to focus on height or width; a concrete operational child coordinates information about both dimensions. Conservation involves recognition that the length, number, mass, quantity, area, weight, and volume of objects and substances are not changed by transformations that merely alter their appearance.

Children do not conserve all quantities or conserve on all tasks simultaneously. The order of their mastery is number, length, liquid quantity, mass, weight, and volume. **Horizontal décalage** is Piaget's concept that similar abilities do not appear at the same time within a stage of development. During the concrete operational stage, conservation of number usually appears first and conservation of volume last. Also, an 8-year-old child may know that a long stick of clay can be rolled back into a ball but not understand that the ball and the stick weigh the same. At about 9 years of age, the child recognizes that they weigh the same, and eventually, at about 11 to 12 years of age, the child understands that the clay's volume is unchanged by rearranging it. Children initially master tasks in which the dimensions are more salient and visible, only later mastering those not as visually apparent, such as volume.

Classification Many of the concrete operations identified by Piaget involve the ways children reason about the properties of objects. One important skill that characterizes children in the concrete operational stage is the ability to classify things and to consider their relationships. Specifically, concrete operational children can understand (1) the interrelationships among sets and subsets, (2) seriation, and (3) transitivity.

The ability of the concrete operational child to divide things into sets and subsets and understand their relationships is illustrated by a family tree of four generations (Furth & Wachs, 1975) (see Figure 6.10). This family tree suggests that the grandfather (A) has three children (B, C, and D), each of whom has two children (E through J), and that one of these children (J) has three children (K, L, and M). The concrete operational child understands that person J can, at the same time, be father, brother, and grandson. A child who comprehends this classification system can move up and down a level (vertically), across a level (horizontally), and up and down and across (obliquely) within the system.

Seriation is the ordering of stimuli along a quantitative dimension (such as length). To see if children can serialize, a teacher might haphazardly place eight sticks of varying lengths on a table. The teacher then asks the children to order the sticks by length. Many young children put the sticks into two or three small groups of "big" sticks or "little" sticks, rather than a correct ordering of all eight sticks. Or they line up the tops of the sticks but ignore the bottoms. The concrete operational thinker simultaneously understands that each stick must be longer than the one that precedes it and shorter than the one that follows it.

Transitivity involves the ability to reason about and logically combine relationships. If a relation holds between a first object and a second object, and also holds between the second object and a third object, then it also holds between the first and third objects. For example, consider three sticks (A, B, and C) of differing lengths. A is the longest, B is intermediate in length, and C is the shortest. Does the child understand that if A is longer than B, and B is longer than C, then A is longer than C? In Piaget's theory, concrete operational thinkers do; preoperational thinkers do not.

FORMAL OPERATIONAL STAGE

So far we have studied the first three of Piaget's stages of cognitive development: sensorimotor, preoperational, and concrete operational. What are the characteristics of the fourth stage?

The **formal operational stage,** which appears between 11 and 15 years of age, is the fourth and final Piagetian stage. In this stage, individuals move beyond concrete experiences and think in abstract and more logical ways. As part of thinking more abstractly, adolescents develop images of ideal circumstances. They might think about what an ideal parent is like and compare their parents to their ideal standards. They begin to entertain possibilities for the future and are fascinated with what they might become. In solving problems, formal operational thinkers are more systematic and use logical reasoning.

Abstract, Idealistic, and Logical Thinking The abstract quality of the adolescent's thought at the formal operational level is evident in the adolescent's verbal problem-solving ability. The concrete operational thinker needs to see the concrete elements A, B, and C to be able to make the logical inference that if A = B and B = C, then A = C. The formal operational thinker can solve this problem merely through verbal presentation.

Another indication of the abstract quality of adolescents' thought is their increased tendency to think about thought itself. One adolescent commented, "I began thinking about why I was thinking about what I was. Then I began thinking about why I was thinking about what I was thinking about what I was." If this sounds abstract, it is, and it characterizes the adolescent's enhanced focus on thought and its abstract qualities.

Accompanying the abstract thought of adolescence is thought full of idealism and possibilities. While children frequently think in concrete ways, or in terms of what is real and limited, adolescents begin to engage in extended speculation about ideal characteristics—qualities they desire in themselves and in others. Such thoughts often lead adolescents to compare themselves with others in regard to ideal standards. And the thoughts of adolescents are often fantasy flights into future possibilities. It is not unusual for the adolescent to become impatient with these newfound ideal standards and to become perplexed over which of many ideal standards to adopt.

As adolescents are learning to think more abstractly and idealistically, they are also learning to think more logically. Children are likely to solve problems in a trial-and-error fashion. Adolescents begin to think more as a scientist thinks, devising plans to solve problems and systematically testing solutions. They use **hypothetical-deductive reasoning,** which means that they develop hypotheses, or best guesses,

Might adolescents' ability to reason hypothetically and to evaluate what is ideal versus what is real lead them to engage in demonstrations, such as this protest related to better ethnic relations? What other causes might be attractive to adolescents' newfound cognitive abilities of hypothetical-deductive reasoning and idealistic thinking?

transitivity Principle that says if a relation holds between a first object and a second object, and holds between the second object and a third object, then it holds between the first object and the third object. Piaget argued that an understanding of transitivity is characteristic of concrete operational thought.

formal operational stage Piaget's fourth and final stage, which occurs between the ages of 11 and 15, when individuals move beyond concrete experiences and think in more abstract and logical ways.

hypothetical-deductive reasoning Piaget's formal operational concept that adolescents have the cognitive ability to develop hypotheses about ways to solve problems and can systematically deduce which is the best path to follow in solving the problem.

and systematically deduce, or conclude, which is the best path to follow in solving the problem.

Assimilation (incorporating new information into existing knowledge) dominates the initial development of formal operational thought, and these thinkers perceive the world subjectively and idealistically. Later in adolescence, as intellectual balance is restored, these individuals accommodate to the cognitive upheaval that has occurred (they adjust to the new information).

Some of Piaget's ideas on formal operational thought are being challenged (Kuhn, 2009). There is much more individual variation in formal operational thought than Piaget envisioned. Only about one in three young adolescents is a formal operational thinker. Many American adults never become formal operational thinkers, and neither do many adults in other cultures.

Adolescent Egocentrism In addition to thinking more logically, abstractly, and idealistically—characteristics of Piaget's formal operational thought stage—in what other ways do adolescents change cognitively? David Elkind (1978) has described how adolescent egocentrism governs the way that adolescents think about social matters. **Adolescent egocentrism** is the heightened self-consciousness of adolescents, which is reflected in their belief that others are as interested in them as they are in themselves, and in their sense of personal uniqueness and invincibility. Elkind proposes that adolescent egocentrism can be dissected into two types of social thinking—imaginary audience and personal fable.

The **imaginary audience** refers to the aspect of adolescent egocentrism that involves attention-getting behavior—the attempt to be noticed, visible, and "onstage." An adolescent boy might think that others are as aware of a few hairs that are out of place as he is. An adolescent girl walks into her classroom and thinks that all eyes are riveted on her complexion. Adolescents especially sense that they are "onstage" in early adolescence, believing they are the main actors and all others are the audience.

According to Elkind, the **personal fable** is the part of adolescent egocentrism that involves an adolescent's sense of personal uniqueness and invincibility. Adolescents' sense of personal uniqueness makes them feel that no one can understand how they really feel. For example, an adolescent girl thinks that her mother cannot possibly sense the hurt she feels because her boyfriend has broken up with her. As part of their effort to retain a sense of personal uniqueness, adolescents might craft stories about themselves that are filled with fantasy, immersing themselves in a world that is far removed from reality. Personal fables frequently show up in adolescent diaries.

Adolescents also often show a sense of invincibility—feeling that although others might be vulnerable to tragedies, such as a terrible car wreck, these things won't happen to them. Some developmentalists believe that the sense of uniqueness and invincibility that egocentrism generates is responsible for some of the seemingly reckless behavior of adolescents, including drag racing, drug use, suicide, and failure to use contraceptives during intercourse (Alberts, Elkind, & Ginsberg, 2007). For example, one study found that eleventh- and twelfth-grade females who were high in adolescent egocentrism were more likely to say they would not get pregnant from engaging in sex without contraception than were their counterparts who were low in adolescent egocentrism (Arnett, 1990).

Reason to question the accuracy of the invulnerability aspect of the personal fable is provided by research that reveals many adolescents don't consider themselves invulnerable (Bruine de Bruin, Parker, & Fischhoff, 2007). Indeed, some research studies suggest that, rather than perceiving themselves to be invulnerable, most adolescents tend to portray themselves as vulnerable to experiencing a premature death (Fischhoff & others, 2010; Jamieson & Romer, 2008; Reyna & Rivers, 2008). In recent research, 12- to 18-year-olds were asked about their chance of dying in the next year and prior to age 20; the adolescents greatly overestimated their chance of dying (Fischhoff & others, 2010).

Many adolescent girls spend long hours in front of the mirror, depleting cans of hairspray, tubes of lipstick, and jars of cosmetics. *How might this behavior be related to changes in adolescent cognitive and physical development?*

adolescent egocentrism The heightened self-consciousness of adolescents, which is reflected in adolescents' beliefs that others are as interested in them as they are in themselves, and in adolescents' sense of personal uniqueness and invulnerability.

imaginary audience The aspect of adolescent egocentrism that involves attention-getting behavior motivated by a desire to be noticed, visible, and "onstage."

personal fable The part of adolescent egocentrism that involves an adolescent's sense of uniqueness and invincibility.

Applying and Evaluating Piaget's Theory

LG2 Apply Piaget's theory to education and evaluate his theory.

Piaget and Education

Evaluating Piaget's Theory

What are some applications of Piaget's theory to education? What are the main contributions and criticisms of Piaget's theory?

PIAGET AND EDUCATION

Piaget was not an educator, but he provided a sound conceptual framework for viewing learning and education. Following are some ideas in Piaget's theory that can be applied to teaching children (Elkind, 1976; Heuwinkel, 1996):

1. *Take a constructivist approach.* Piaget emphasized that children learn best when they are active and seek solutions for themselves. Piaget opposed teaching methods that treat children as passive receptacles. The educational implication of Piaget's view is that, in all subjects, students learn best by making discoveries, reflecting on them, and discussing them, rather than blindly imitating the teacher or doing things by rote.

2. *Facilitate, rather than direct, learning.* Effective teachers design situations that allow students to learn by doing. These situations promote students' thinking and discovery. Effective teachers listen, watch, and question students, to help them gain better understanding. They don't just examine what students think and the product of their learning. Rather, they carefully observe students and find out how they think, pose relevant questions to stimulate their thinking, and ask them to explain their answers.

3. *Consider the child's knowledge and level of thinking.* Students do not come to class with empty minds. They have many ideas about the physical and natural world. They have concepts of space, time, quantity, and causality.

What are some educational strategies that can be derived from Piaget's theory?

These ideas differ from the ideas of adults. Teachers need to interpret what a student is saying and respond in a way that is not too far from the student's level. Also, Piaget suggested that it is important to examine children's mistakes in thinking, not just what they get correct, to help guide them to a higher level of understanding.

4. *Use ongoing assessment.* Individually constructed meanings cannot be measured by standardized tests. Math and language portfolios (which contain work in progress as well as finished products), individual conferences in which students discuss their thinking strategies, and students' written and verbal explanations of their reasoning can be used to evaluate progress.

5. *Promote the student's intellectual health.* When Piaget came to lecture in the United States, he was asked, "What can I do to get my child to a higher cognitive stage sooner?" He was asked this question so often here compared with other countries that he called it the American question. For Piaget, children's learning should occur naturally. Children should not be pushed and pressured into achieving too much too early in their development, before they are maturationally ready. Some parents spend long hours every day holding up large flash cards with words on them to improve their baby's vocabulary. In the Piagetian view, this is not the best way for infants to learn. It places too much emphasis on speeding up intellectual development, involves passive learning, and will not work.

6. *Turn the classroom into a setting of exploration and discovery.* What do actual classrooms look like when the teachers adopt Piaget's views? Several first- and second-grade math classrooms provide some examples (Kamii, 1985, 1989). The teachers emphasize students' own exploration and discovery. The classrooms are less structured than what we think of as a typical classroom. Workbooks and predetermined assignments are not used. Rather, the teachers observe the students' interests and natural participation in activities to determine the course of learning. For example, a math lesson might be constructed around counting the day's lunch money or dividing supplies among students. Often, games are used to stimulate mathematical thinking. For example, a version of dominoes teaches children about even-numbered combinations; a variation on tic-tac-toe replaces *X*s and *O*s with numbers. Teachers encourage peer interaction during the lessons and games because students' different viewpoints can contribute to advances in thinking.

EVALUATING PIAGET'S THEORY

What were Piaget's main contributions? Has his theory withstood the test of time?

Contributions   Piaget was a giant in the field of developmental psychology, the founder of the present field of children's cognitive development. Psychologists owe him for a long list of masterful concepts of enduring power and fascination: assimilation, accommodation, object permanence, egocentrism, conservation, and others (Carpendale, Muller, & Bibok, 2008). Psychologists also owe him for the current vision of children as active, constructive thinkers. And they are indebted to him for creating a theory that generated a huge volume of research on children's cognitive development.

Piaget also was a genius when it came to observing children. His careful observations demonstrated inventive ways to discover how children act on and adapt to their world. Piaget showed us some important things to look for in cognitive development, such as the shift from preoperational to concrete operational thinking. He also showed us how children need to make their experiences fit their schemes (cognitive frameworks) yet simultaneously adapt their schemes to experience. Piaget also revealed how cognitive change is likely to occur if the context is structured to allow gradual movement to the next higher level. Concepts do not emerge suddenly,

neo-Piagetians Developmentalists who have elaborated on Piaget's theory, believing that children's cognitive development is more specific in many respects than Piaget thought and giving more emphasis to how children use memory, attention, and strategies to process information.

full-blown, but instead develop through a series of partial accomplishments that lead to increasingly comprehensive understanding (Diamond, Casey, & Munakata, 2011; Quinn, 2011).

Criticisms   Piaget's theory has not gone unchallenged. Questions are raised about estimates of children's competence at different developmental levels, stages, the training of children to reason at higher levels, and culture and education.

Estimates of Children's Competence   Some cognitive abilities emerge earlier than Piaget thought (Bauer & others, 2011; Carpenter, 2011; Miller, 2011). For example, as previously noted, some aspects of object permanence emerge earlier than he proposed. Even 2-year-olds are nonegocentric in some contexts. When they realize that another person will not see an object, they investigate whether the person is blindfolded or looking in a different direction. Some understanding of the conservation of number has been demonstrated as early as age 3, although Piaget did not think it emerged until 7. Young children are not as uniformly "pre" this and "pre" that (precausal, preoperational) as Piaget thought.

Cognitive abilities also can emerge later than Piaget thought (Kuhn, 2009). Many adolescents still think in concrete operational ways or are just beginning to master formal operations. Even many adults are not formal operational thinkers. In sum, recent theoretical revisions highlight more cognitive competencies of infants and young children and more cognitive shortcomings of adolescents and adults.

Stages   Piaget conceived of stages as unitary structures of thought. Thus, his theory assumes developmental synchrony—that is, various aspects of a stage should emerge at the same time. However, some concrete operational concepts do not appear in synchrony. For example, children do not learn to conserve at the same time that they learn to cross-classify. Thus, most contemporary developmentalists agree that children's cognitive development is not as stage-like as Piaget thought (Kuhn, 2009).

Effects of Training   Some children who are at one cognitive stage (such as preoperational) can be trained to reason at a higher cognitive stage (such as concrete operational). This poses a problem for Piaget's theory. He argued that such training is only superficial and ineffective, unless the child is at a maturational transition point between the stages (Gelman & Williams, 1998).

Culture and Education   Culture and education exert stronger influences on children's development than Piaget reasoned (Holzman, 2009). For example, the age at which children acquire conservation skills is related to how much practice their culture provides in these skills. Among Wolof children in the West African nation of Senegal, only 50 percent of the 10- to 13-year-olds understood the principle of conservation (Greenfield, 1966). Comparable studies among cultures in central Australia, New Guinea (an island north of Australia), the Amazon jungle region of Brazil, and rural Sardinia (an island off the coast of Italy) yielded similar results (Dasen, 1977). An outstanding teacher and instruction in the logic of math and science can promote the development of concrete and formal operational thought.

The Neo-Piagetian Approach   **Neo-Piagetians** argue that Piaget got some things right but that his theory needs considerable revision. They give more emphasis to how children use attention, memory, and strategies to process information (Case, 1987, 1999; Morra & others, 2007). They especially believe that a more accurate

Jean Piaget, the main architect of the field of cognitive development, at age 27.

An outstanding teacher and education in the logic of science and mathematics are important cultural experiences that promote the development of operational thought. *Might Piaget have underestimated the roles of culture and schooling in children's cognitive development?*

portrayal of children's thinking requires attention to children's strategies, the speed at which children process information, the particular task involved, and the division of problems into smaller, more precise steps (Demetriou, 2001). In Chapter 7 we will discuss these aspects of children's thought.

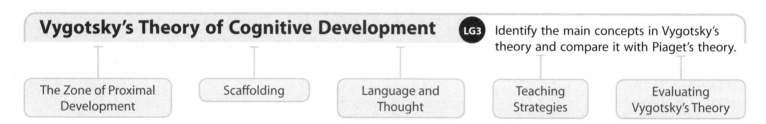

Review *Connect* Reflect

LG2 Apply Piaget's theory to education and evaluate his theory.

Review
- How can Piaget's theory be applied to educating children?
- What are some key contributions and criticisms of Piaget's theory?

Connect
- In this section, you learned that culture exerts a strong influence on cognitive development. In Chapter 5, what did we

learn about the influence of different cultural practices on infants' motor skills?

Reflect *Your Own Personal Journey of Life*
- How might thinking in formal operational ways rather than concrete operational ways help you to develop better study skills?

Vygotsky's Theory of Cognitive Development

LG3 Identify the main concepts in Vygotsky's theory and compare it with Piaget's theory.

| The Zone of Proximal Development | Scaffolding | Language and Thought | Teaching Strategies | Evaluating Vygotsky's Theory |

Piaget's theory is a major developmental theory. Another developmental theory that focuses on children's cognition is Vygotsky's theory. Like Piaget, Vygotsky (1962) emphasized that children actively construct their knowledge and understanding. In Piaget's theory, children develop ways of thinking and understanding by their actions and interactions with the physical world. In Vygtosky's theory, children are more often described as social creatures than in Piaget's theory. They develop their ways of thinking and understanding primarily through social interaction (Daniels, 2011; Gredler, 2009). Their cognitive development depends on the tools provided by society, and their minds are shaped by the cultural context in which they live (Gauvain & Parke, 2010; Holzman, 2009).

We briefly described Vygotsky's theory in Chapter 1. Here we take a closer look at his ideas about how children learn and his view of the role of language in cognitive development.

THE ZONE OF PROXIMAL DEVELOPMENT

Vygotsky's belief in the importance of social influences, especially instruction, on children's cognitive development is reflected in his concept of the zone of proximal development. **Zone of proximal development (ZPD)** is Vygotsky's term for the range of tasks that are too difficult for the child to master alone but that can be learned with guidance and assistance of adults or more-skilled children. Thus, the lower limit of the ZPD is the level of skill reached by the child working independently. The upper limit is the level of additional responsibility the child can accept with the assistance of an able instructor (see Figure 6.11). The ZPD captures the child's cognitive skills that are in the process of maturing and can be accomplished only with the assistance of a more-skilled person (Alvarez & del Rio, 2007). Vygotsky (1962) called these the "buds" or "flowers" of development, to distinguish them from the "fruits" of development, which the child already can accomplish independently.

zone of proximal development (ZPD) Vygotsky's term for tasks that are too difficult for children to master alone but can be mastered with assistance from adults or more-skilled children.

scaffolding In cognitive development, Vygotsky used this term to describe the practice of changing the level of support provided over the course of a teaching session, with the more-skilled person adjusting guidance to fit the child's current performance level.

Vygotsky's concept of the zone of proximal development—that children learn by interacting with more experienced adults and peers, who help them think beyond the "zone" in which they would be able to perform without assistance—has been applied primarily to academic learning. Barbara Rogoff (1990, 2003; Rogoff & others, 2007) argues that many of Vygotsky's ideas, including the zone of proximal development, are important in understanding children's development beyond the classroom in everyday interactions with adults and peers. To read further about Rogoff's ideas, see *Connecting With Diversity* on the next page.

SCAFFOLDING

Closely linked to the idea of the ZPD is the concept of scaffolding. **Scaffolding** means changing the level of support. Over the course of a teaching session, a more-skilled person (a teacher or advanced peer) adjusts the amount of guidance to fit the child's current performance (Daniels, 2007, 2011). When the student is learning a new task, the skilled person may use direct instruction. As the student's competence increases, less guidance is given.

Dialogue is an important tool of scaffolding in the zone of proximal development (Tappan, 1998). Vygotsky viewed children as having rich but unsystematic, disorganized, and spontaneous concepts. In a dialogue, these concepts meet with the skilled helper's more systematic, logical, and rational concepts. As a result, the child's concepts become more systematic, logical, and rational. For example, a dialogue might take place between a teacher and a child when the teacher uses scaffolding to help a child understand a concept like "transportation."

LANGUAGE AND THOUGHT

The use of dialogue as a tool for scaffolding is only one example of the important role of language in a child's development. According to Vygotsky, children use speech not only for social communication, but also to help them solve tasks. Vygotsky (1962) further concluded that young children use language to plan, guide, and monitor their behavior. This use of language for self-regulation is called *private speech.* For Piaget private speech is egocentric and immature, but for Vygotsky it is an important tool of thought during the early childhood years (John-Steiner, 2007; Wertsch, 2007).

Vygotsky said that language and thought initially develop independently of each other and then merge. He emphasized that all mental functions have external, or social, origins. Children must use language to communicate with others before they can focus inward on their own thoughts. Children also must communicate externally and use language for a long period of time before they can make the transition from external to internal speech. This transition period occurs between 3 and 7 years of age and involves talking to oneself. After a while, the self-talk becomes second nature to children, and they can act without verbalizing. When this occurs, children have internalized their egocentric speech in the form of *inner speech*, which becomes their thoughts.

Vygotsky reasoned that children who use a lot of private speech are more socially competent than those who don't. He argued that private speech represents an early transition in becoming more socially communicative. For Vygotsky, when young children talk to themselves, they are using language to govern their behavior and guide themselves. For example, a child working on a puzzle might say to herself, "Which pieces should I put together first? I'll try those green ones first. Now I need some blue ones. No, that blue one doesn't fit there. I'll try it over here."

Piaget stressed that self-talk is egocentric and reflects immaturity. However, researchers have found support for Vygotsky's view that private speech plays a positive role in children's development (Winsler, Carlton, & Barry, 2000). Researchers have found that children use private speech more when tasks are difficult, when they have made a mistake, and when they are not sure how to proceed (Berk, 1994).

Upper limit

Level of additional responsibility child can accept with assistance of an able instructor

Zone of proximal development (ZPD)

Lower limit

Level of problem solving reached on these tasks by child working alone

FIGURE **6.11**

VYGOTSKY'S ZONE OF PROXIMAL DEVELOPMENT. Vygotsky's zone of proximal development has a lower limit and an upper limit. Tasks in the ZPD are too difficult for the child to perform alone. They require assistance from an adult or a more-skilled child. As children experience the verbal instruction or demonstration, they organize the information in their existing mental structures so that they can eventually perform the skill or task alone.

developmental **connection**

Parenting. Scaffolding also is an effective strategy for parents to adopt in interacting with their infants. Chapter 14, p. 396

developmental **connection**

Language. In thinking about links between language and cognition, we might ask: (1) Is language necessary for cognition? and (2) Is cognition necessary for language? Chapter 9, pp. 282–283

Guided Participation and Cultural Contexts

According to Rogoff, children serve a sort of apprenticeship in thinking through *guided participation* in social and cultural activities. Guided participation may occur, for example, when adults and children share activities.

Parents can broaden or limit children's opportunities through their decisions about how much and when to expose children to books, television, and child care. They may give children opportunities to learn about cultural traditions and practices through their routines and play. For example, in the Zambian culture of Chewa, children play numerous games, such as "hide-and-seek, guessing games, complex sand drawing games, imaginative games representing local work and family routines, skill games like jacks and a rule game requiring considerable strategic planning and numerical calculations, and constructing models of wire or clay" (Rogoff, 2003, p. 297). In addition, through observational learning, or as Rogoff calls it, learning by "osmosis," children adopt values, skills, and mannerisms by simply watching and listening to peers and adults.

Guided participation is widely used around the world, but cultures may differ in the goals of development—what content is to be learned— and the means for providing guided participation (Rogoff & others, 2007). Around the world, caregivers and children arrange children's activities and revise children's responsibilities as they gain skill and knowledge. With guidance, children participate in cultural activities that socialize them into skilled activities. For example, Mayan mothers in Guatemala

At about 7 years of age, Mayan girls in Guatemala are assisted in beginning to learn to weave a simple belt, with the loom already set up for them. The young girl shown here is American developmental psychologist Barbara Rogoff's daughter, being taught to weave by a Mayan woman. *What are some other ways that children learn through guided participation?*

help their daughters learn to weave through guided participation. Throughout the world, learning occurs, not just by studying or by attending classes, but also through interaction with knowledgeable people.

How does Rogoff's concept of guided participation relate to Vygotsky's concept of the zone of proximal development?

They also have revealed that children who use private speech are more attentive and improve their performance more than children who do not use private speech (Berk & Spuhl, 1995).

TEACHING STRATEGIES

Vygotsky's theory has been embraced by many teachers and has been successfully applied to education (Daniels, 2011; Gredler, 2009; Holzman, 2009; Shayer & Adhami, 2010). Here are some ways Vygotsky's theory can be incorporated in classrooms:

1. *Assess the child's ZPD.* Like Piaget, Vygotsky did not think that formal, standardized tests are the best way to assess children's learning. Rather, Vygotsky argued that assessment should focus on determining the child's zone of proximal development. The skilled helper presents the child with tasks of varying difficulty to determine the best level at which to begin instruction.

2. *Use the child's ZPD in teaching.* Teaching should begin toward the zone's upper limit, so that the child can reach the goal with help and move to a higher level of skill and knowledge. Offer just enough assistance. You might ask, "What can I do to help you?" Or simply observe the child's intentions and attempts and provide support when needed. When the

Lev Vygotsky (1896–1934), shown here with his daughter, believed that children's cognitive development is advanced through social interaction with skilled individuals embedded in a sociocultural backdrop.

Donene Polson, Elementary School Teacher

Donene Polson teaches at Washington Elementary School in Salt Lake City, Utah. Washington is an innovative school that emphasizes the importance of people learning together as a community of learners. Children as well as adults plan learning activities. Throughout the school day, children work in small groups.

Polson says that she loves working in a school in which students, teachers, and parents work together as a community to help children learn. Before the school year begins, Polson meets with parents at the family's home to prepare for the upcoming year, get acquainted, and establish schedules to determine when parents can contribute to classroom instruction. At monthly parent-teacher meetings, Polson and the parents plan the curriculum and discuss how children's learning is progressing. They brainstorm about resources in the community that can be used effectively to promote children's learning.

For more information about what elementary school teachers do, see page 44 in the Careers in Child Development appendix following Chapter 1.

child hesitates, offer encouragement. And encourage the child to practice the skill. You may watch and appreciate the child's practice or offer support when the child forgets what to do.

3. *Use more-skilled peers as teachers.* Remember that it is not just adults who are important in helping children learn. Children also benefit from the support and guidance of more-skilled children (John-Steiner, 2007).

4. *Monitor and encourage children's use of private speech.* Be aware of the developmental change from externally talking to oneself when solving a problem during the preschool years to privately talking to oneself in the early elementary school years. In the elementary school years, encourage children to internalize and self-regulate their talk to themselves.

5. *Place instruction in a meaningful context.* Educators today are moving away from abstract presentations of material, instead providing students with opportunities to experience learning in real-world settings. For example, instead of just memorizing math formulas, students work on math problems with real-world implications.

How can Vygotsky's ideas be applied to educating children?

6. *Transform the classroom with Vygotskian ideas.* What does a Vygotskian classroom look like? The Kamehameha Elementary Education Program (KEEP) is based on Vygotsky's theory (Tharp, 1994). The ZPD is the key element of instruction in this program and many of the learning activities take place in small groups. All children spend at least 20 minutes each morning in a setting called "Center One." In this context, scaffolding is used to improve children's literary skills. The instructor asks questions, responds to students' queries, and builds on the ideas that students generate. Thousands of children from low-income families have attended KEEP public schools—in Hawaii, on an Arizona Navajo Indian reservation, and in Los Angeles. Compared with a control group of non-KEEP children, the KEEP children participated more actively in classroom discussion, were more attentive in class, and had higher levels of reading achievement (Tharp & Gallimore, 1988).

To read about the work of a teacher who applies Vygotsky's theory to her teaching, see the *Connecting With Careers* profile. The *Caring Connections* interlude further explores the implications of Vygotsky's theory for children's education.

caring *connections*

Tools of the Mind

Tools of the Mind is an early childhood education curriculum that emphasizes children's development of self-regulation and the cognitive foundations of literacy (Hyson, Copple, & Jones, 2006). The curriculum was created by Elena Bodrova and Deborah Leong (2007) and has been implemented in more than 200 classrooms. Most of the children in the Tools of the Mind programs are at risk because of their living circumstances, which in many instances involve poverty and other difficult conditions such as being homeless and having parents with drug problems.

Tools of the Mind is grounded in Vygotsky's (1962) theory, with special attention given to cultural tools and developing self-regulation, the zone of proximal development, scaffolding, private speech, shared activity, and play as important activity. In a Tools of the Mind classroom, dramatic play has a central role. Teachers guide children in creating themes that are based on the children's interests, such as treasure hunt, store, hospital, and restaurant. Teachers also incorporate field trips, visitor presentations, videos, and books in the development of children's play. They help children develop a play plan, which increases the maturity of their play. Play plans describe what the children expect to do during the play period, including the imaginary context, roles, and props to be used. The play plans increase the quality of their play and self-regulation.

Scaffolding writing is another important theme in the Tools of the Mind classroom. Teachers guide children in planning their own message by drawing a line to stand for each word the child says. Children then repeat the message, pointing to each line as they say the word. Next, the child writes on the lines, trying to represent each word with some letters or symbols. Figure 6.12 shows how the scaffolding writing process improved a 5-year-old child's writing over the course of two months.

Research assessments of children's writing in Tools of the Mind classrooms revealed that they have more advanced writing skills than children in other early childhood programs (Bodrova & Leong, 2007) (see Figure 6.12). For example, they write more complex messages, use more words, spell more accurately, show better letter recognition, and have a better understanding of the concept of a sentence.

A recent study assessed the effects of the Tools of the Mind curriculum on at-risk preschool children (Diamond & others, 2007). The results indicated that the Tools of the Mind curriculum improved the self-regulatory and cognitive control skills (such as resisting distractions and temptations) of the at-risk children. Other research on the Tools of the Mind curriculum also has found that it improves young children's cognitive skills (Barnett & others, 2006; Saifer, 2007).

Earlier in this section of the chapter, we outlined strategies for incorporating Vygotsky's theory into teaching. Revisit that list and explain how the Tools of the Mind curriculum uses those strategies.

(a) Five-year-old Aaron's independent journal writing prior to the scaffolded writing technique.

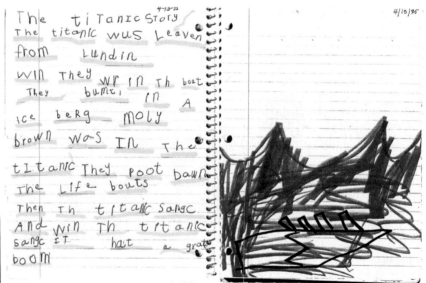

(b) Aaron's journal two months after using the scaffolded writing technique.

FIGURE **6.12**

WRITING PROGRESS OF A 5-YEAR-OLD BOY OVER TWO MONTHS USING THE SCAFFOLDING WRITING PROCESS IN TOOLS OF THE MIND

	Vygotsky		Piaget
Sociocultural Context	Strong emphasis		Little emphasis	
Constructivism	Social constructivist		Cognitive constructivist
Stages	No general stages of development proposed		Strong emphasis on stages (sensorimotor, preoperational, concrete operational, and formal operational)
Key Processes	Zone of proximal development, language, dialogue, tools of the culture		Schema, assimilation, accommodation, operations, conservation, classification
Role of Language	A major role; language plays a powerful role in shaping thought		Language has a minimal role; cognition primarily directs language
View on Education	Education plays a central role, helping children learn the tools of the culture		Education merely refines the child's cognitive skills that have already emerged
Teaching Implications	Teacher is a facilitator and guide, not a director; establish many opportunities for children to learn with the teacher and more-skilled peers		Also views teacher as a facilitator and guide, not a director; provide support for children to explore their world and discover knowledge

FIGURE 6.13

COMPARISON OF VYGOTSKY'S AND PIAGET'S THEORIES

EVALUATING VYGOTSKY'S THEORY

Even though their theories were proposed at about the same time, most of the world learned about Vygotsky's theory later than they learned about Piaget's theory, so Vygotsky's theory has not yet been evaluated as thoroughly. Vygotsky's view of the importance of sociocultural influences on children's development fits with the current belief that it is important to evaluate the contextual factors in learning (Daniels, 2011; Gauvain & Parke, 2010; Holzman, 2009).

We already have mentioned several distinctions between Vygotsky's and Piaget's theories, such as Vygotsky's emphasis on the importance of inner speech in development and Piaget's view that such speech is immature. Although both theories are constructivist, Vygotsky's is a **social constructivist approach,** which emphasizes the social contexts of learning and the construction of knowledge through social interaction.

In moving from Piaget to Vygotsky, the conceptual shift is from the individual to collaboration, social interaction, and sociocultural activity (Halford, 2008). The end point of cognitive development for Piaget is formal operational thought. For Vygotsky, the endpoint can differ, depending on which skills are considered to be the most important in a particular culture. For Piaget, children construct knowledge by transforming, organizing, and reorganizing previous knowledge. For Vygotsky, children construct knowledge through social interaction (Rogoff & others, 2007). The implication of Piaget's theory for teaching is that children need support to explore their world and discover knowledge. The main implication of Vygotsky's theory for teaching is that students need many opportunities to learn with their teachers and more-skilled peers. In both Piaget's and Vygotsky's theories, teachers serve as facilitators and guides, rather than as directors and molders of learning. Figure 6.13 compares Vygotsky's and Piaget's theories.

Criticisms of Vygotsky's theory also have surfaced (Karpov, 2006). Some critics point out that Vygotsky was not specific enough about age-related changes (Gauvain, 2008). Another criticism asserts that Vygotsky does not adequately describe how changes in socioemotional capabilities contribute to cognitive development (Gauvain, 2008). Yet another criticism is that he overemphasized the role of language in thinking. Also, his emphasis on collaboration and guidance has potential pitfalls. Might

developmental **connection**

Education. Whether to follow a constructivist or direct instruction approach is a major issue for teachers. Chapter 16, pp. 454–455

social constructivist approach An emphasis on the social contexts of learning and the construction of knowledge through social interaction. Vygotsky's theory reflects this approach.

facilitators be too helpful in some cases, as when a parent becomes too overbearing and controlling? Further, some children might become lazy and expect help when they might have learned more by doing something on their own.

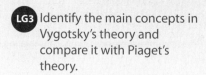

Revie... onnect Reflect

LG3 Identify the main concepts in Vygotsky's theory and compare it with Piaget's theory.

Review

- What is the zone of proximal development?
- What is scaffolding?
- How did Vygotsky view language and thought?
- How can Vygotsky's theory be applied to education?
- What are some similarities and differences between Vygotsky's and Piaget's theories?
- What are some criticisms of Vygotsky's theory?

Connect

- Compare the strategies that were laid out in the section for using Piaget's theories in teaching to those for applying Vygotsky's theories in teaching. What are the similarities? Differences?

Reflect *Your Own Personal Journey of Life*

- Which theory—Piaget's or Vygotsky's—do you think is more effective in explaining your own cognitive development as a child?

reach your **learning goals**

Cognitive Developmental Approaches

Piaget's Theory of Cognitive Development

 LG1 Discuss the key processes and four stages in Piaget's theory.

Processes of Development

- According to Piaget's theory, children construct their own cognitive worlds, building mental structures to adapt to their world. Schemes are actions or mental representations that organize knowledge. Behavioral schemes (physical activities) characterize infancy, and mental schemes (cognitive activities) develop in childhood. Adaptation involves assimilation and accommodation. Assimilation occurs when children incorporate new information into their existing schemes. Accommodation refers to children's adjustment of their schemes to fit new information and experiences. Through organization, children group isolated behaviors into a higher-order, more smoothly functioning cognitive system. Equilibration is a mechanism Piaget proposed to explain how children shift from one cognitive stage to the next. As children experience cognitive conflict in trying to understand the world, they seek equilibrium. The result is equilibration, which brings the child to a new stage of thought. According to Piaget, there are four qualitatively different stages of thought: sensorimotor, preoperational, concrete operational, and formal operational.

Sensorimotor Stage

- In sensorimotor thought, the first of Piaget's four stages, the infant organizes and coordinates sensory experiences (such as seeing and hearing) with physical movements. This stage lasts from birth to about 2 years of age and is nonsymbolic throughout, according to Piaget. Sensorimotor thought has six substages: simple reflexes; first habits and primary circular reactions; secondary circular reactions; coordination of secondary circular reactions; tertiary circular reactions, novelty, and curiosity; and internalization of schemes. One key aspect of this stage is object permanence, the ability to understand that objects continue to exist even though the infant is no longer observing them. Another aspect involves infants' understanding of cause and effect. In the past two decades, revisions of Piaget's view have been proposed based on research. For example, researchers have found that a stable and differentiated perceptual world is established earlier than Piaget envisioned. However, controversy surrounds the question of when object permanence emerges. The nature-nurture issue is a key aspect of infant cognitive development. Spelke's core knowledge approach is a strong naturist view. Most developmentalists conclude that nature and nurture are both important in infant cognitive development.

Preoperational Stage

- Preoperational thought is the beginning of the ability to reconstruct at the level of thought what has been established in behavior. It involves a transition from a primitive to a more sophisticated use of symbols. In preoperational thought, the child does not yet think in an operational way. The symbolic function substage occurs roughly from 2 to 4 years of age and is characterized by symbolic thought, egocentrism, and animism. The intuitive thought substage stretches from about 4 to 7 years of age. It is called intuitive because children seem sure about their knowledge yet are unaware of how they know what they know. The preoperational child lacks conservation and asks a barrage of questions.

Concrete Operational Stage

- Concrete operational thought occurs roughly from 7 to 11 years of age. During this stage, children can perform concrete operations, think logically about concrete objects, classify things, and reason about relationships among classes of things. Concrete thought is not as abstract as formal operational thought.

Formal Operational Stage

- Formal operational thought appears between 11 and 15 years of age. Formal operational thought is more abstract, idealistic, and logical than concrete operational thought. Piaget maintains that adolescents become capable of engaging in hypothetical-deductive reasoning. But Piaget did not give adequate attention to individual variation in adolescent thinking. Many young adolescents do not think in hypothetical-deductive ways but rather are consolidating their concrete operational thinking. In addition, according to Elkind, adolescents develop a special kind of egocentrism that involves an imaginary audience and a personal fable about being unique and invulnerable. However, recent research questions the accuracy of the invulnerability aspect of the personal fable.

Applying and Evaluating Piaget's Theory

 Apply Piaget's theory to education and evaluate his theory.

Piaget and Education

- Piaget was not an educator, but his constructivist views have been applied to teaching. These applications include an emphasis on facilitating rather than directing learning, considering the child's level of knowledge, using ongoing assessment, promoting the student's intellectual health, and turning the classroom into a setting of exploration and discovery.

Evaluating Piaget's Theory

- We owe to Piaget the field of cognitive development. He was a genius at observing children, and he gave us a number of masterful concepts such as assimilation, accommodation, object permanence, and egocentrism. Critics question his estimates of competence at different developmental levels, his stage concept, and other ideas. Neo-Piagetians, who emphasize the importance of information processing, stress that children's cognition is more specific than Piaget thought.

Vygotsky's Theory of Cognitive Development

 Identify the main concepts in Vygotsky's theory and compare it with Piaget's theory.

The Zone of Proximal Development

- Zone of proximal development (ZPD) is Vygotsky's term for the range of tasks that are too difficult for children to master alone but can be learned with the guidance and assistance of adults or more-skilled peers.

Scaffolding

- Scaffolding is a teaching technique in which a more-skilled person adjusts the level of guidance to fit the child's current performance level. Dialogue is an important aspect of scaffolding.

- Vygotsky stressed that language plays a key role in cognition. Language and thought initially develop independently, but then children internalize their egocentric speech in the form of inner speech, which becomes their thoughts. This transition to inner speech occurs between 3 and 7 years of age.

- Applications of Vygotsky's ideas to education include using the child's ZPD and scaffolding, using more-skilled peers as teachers, monitoring and encouraging children's use of private speech, and accurately assessing the ZPD. These practices can transform the classroom and establish a meaningful context for instruction.

- Like Piaget, Vygotsky emphasized that children actively construct their understanding of the world. Unlike Piaget, he did not propose stages of cognitive development, and he emphasized that children construct knowledge through social interaction. According to Vygotsky's theory, children depend on tools provided by the culture, which determines which skills they will develop. Vygotsky's view contrasts with Piaget's view that young children's speech is immature and egocentric. Critics of Vygotsky's theory assert that it lacks specificity about age-related changes and overemphasizes the role of language in thinking.

key terms

schemes 172
assimilation 172
accommodation 172
organization 173
equilibration 173
sensorimotor stage 173
object permanence 176
A-not-B error 176
core knowledge
   approach 178

operations 180
preoperational stage 180
symbolic function
   substage 180
egocentrism 181
animism 181
intuitive thought
   substage 182
centration 182
conservation 182

concrete operational
   stage 183
horizontal décalage 184
seriation 184
transitivity 185
formal operational stage 185
hypothetical-deductive
   reasoning 185
adolescent egocentrism 186
imaginary audience 186

personal fable 186
neo-Piagetians 189
zone of proximal
   development (ZPD) 190
scaffolding 191
social constructivist
   approach 195

key people

Jean Piaget 171
Renée Baillargeon 177

Andrew Meltzoff 178
Karen Wynn 179

Barbel Inhelder 181
Rochel Gelman 183

David Elkind 186
Lev Vygotsky 190

chapter 7 INFORMATION PROCESSING

Laura Bickford is a master teacher who chairs the English Department at Nordoff High School in Ojai, California. She recently spoke about how she encourages her students to think:

I believe the call to teach is a call to teach students how to think. In encouraging critical thinking, literature itself does a good bit of work for us but we still have to be guides. We have to ask good questions. We have to show students the value in asking their own questions, in having discussions and conversations. In addition to reading and discussing literature, the best way to move students to think critically is to have them write. We write all the time in a variety of modes: journals, formal essays, letters, factual reports, news articles, speeches, or other formal oral presentations. We have to show students where they merely scratch the surface in their thinking and writing. I call these moments "hits and runs." When I see this "hit and run" effort, I draw a window on the paper. I tell them it is a "window of opportunity" to go deeper, elaborate, and clarify. Many students don't do this kind of thinking until they are prodded to do so.

I also ask them to keep reading logs so they can observe their own thinking as it happens. In addition, I ask students to comment on their own learning by way of grading themselves. This year a student gave me one of the most insightful lines about her growth as a reader I have ever seen from a student. She wrote, "I no longer think in a monotone when I'm reading." I don't know if she grasps the magnitude of that thought or how it came to be that she made that change. It is magic when students see themselves growing like this.

Laura Bickford, working with students writing papers.

preview

What do children notice in the environment? What do they remember? And how do they think about it? These questions illustrate the information-processing approach. Using this approach, researchers usually do not describe children as being in one stage of cognitive development or another. But they do describe and analyze how the speed of processing information, attention, memory, thinking, and metacognition change over time.

What are some of the basic ideas in the information-processing approach? How is it similar to and different from the cognitive developmental approaches we described in Chapter 6?

THE INFORMATION-PROCESSING APPROACH TO DEVELOPMENT

The information-processing approach shares a basic characteristic with the theories of cognitive development that were discussed in Chapter 6. Like those theories, the information-processing approach rejected the behavioral approach that dominated psychology during the first half of the twentieth century. As we discussed in Chapter 1, the behaviorists argued that to explain behavior it is important to examine associations between stimuli and behavior. In contrast, the theories of Piaget and Vygotsky (described in Chapter 6) and the information-processing approach focus on how children think.

The **information-processing approach** analyzes how children manipulate information, monitor it, and create strategies for handling it (Halford & Andrews, 2011; Martinez, 2009; Siegler, 2006; Sternberg, 2009). A computer metaphor can illustrate how the information-processing approach can be applied to development. A computer's information processing is *limited* by its hardware and software. The hardware limitations include the amount of data the computer can process—its capacity—and speed. The software limits the kind of data that can be used as input and the ways that data can be manipulated; word processing doesn't handle music, for example. Similarly, children's information processing may be limited by capacity and speed as well as by their ability to manipulate information—in other words, their ability to apply appropriate strategies to acquire and use knowledge. In the information-processing approach, children's cognitive development results from their ability to overcome processing limitations by increasingly executing basic operations, expanding information-processing capacity, and acquiring new knowledge and strategies.

COGNITIVE RESOURCES: CAPACITY AND SPEED OF PROCESSING INFORMATION

Developmental changes in information processing are likely influenced by increases in both capacity and speed of processing (Frye, 2004). These two characteristics are often referred to as *cognitive resources,* which are proposed to have an important influence on memory and problem solving.

Both biology and experience contribute to growth in cognitive resources (Goldstein, 2011; Reed, 2010). Think about how much faster you can process information in your native language than a second language. The changes in the brain we described in Chapter 4 provide a biological foundation for increased cognitive

> **developmental connection**
>
> **Theories.** In Skinner's behavioral view, it is external rewards and punishment that determine behavior, not thoughts. Chapter 1, p. 27

> The mind is an enchanting thing.
>
> —**MARIANNE MOORE**
> *American Poet, 20th Century*

information-processing approach An approach that focuses on the ways children process information about their world—how they manipulate information, monitor it, and create strategies to deal with it.

How does speed of processing information change during the childhood and adolescent years?

resources (Nelson, 2011). Important biological developments occur both in brain structures, such as changes in the frontal lobes, and at the level of neurons, such as the blooming and pruning of connections between neurons. Also, as we discussed in Chapter 4, myelination (the process in which the axon is covered with a myelin sheath) increases the speed of electrical impulses in the brain. Myelination continues through childhood and adolescence (Paus, 2009).

Most information-processing psychologists argue that an increase in capacity also improves processing of information (Halford & Andrews, 2011; Mayer, 2008). For example, as children's information-processing capacity increases, they likely can hold in mind several dimensions of a topic or problem simultaneously, whereas younger children are more prone to focus on only one dimension.

What is the role of processing speed? How quickly children can process information often influences what they can do with that information. If an adolescent is trying to add up mentally the cost of items he or she is buying at the grocery store, the adolescent needs to be able to compute the sum before he or she has forgotten the price of the individual items. Children's speed in processing information is linked with their competence in thinking (Bjorklund, 2005). For example, the speed with which children can articulate a series of words affects how many words they can remember. Generally, fast processing is linked with good performance on cognitive tasks. However, some compensation for slower processing speed can be achieved by creating effective strategies.

Researchers have devised a number of ways to assess processing speed. For example, it can be assessed through a *reaction-time task* in which individuals are asked to push a button as soon as they see a stimulus such as a light. Or individuals might be asked to match letters or match numbers with symbols on a computer screen.

There is abundant evidence that the speed with which such tasks are completed improves dramatically across the childhood years (Hommel, Li, & Li, 2004; Kail, 2007; Kuhn, 2009). For example, a recent study of 8- to 13-year-old children revealed that processing speed increased with age, and furthermore, that the developmental change in processing speed preceded an increase in working memory capacity (Kail, 2007).

MECHANISMS OF CHANGE

According to Robert Siegler (1998), three mechanisms work together to create changes in children's cognitive skills: encoding, automaticity, and strategy construction.

Encoding is the process by which information gets into memory. Changes in children's cognitive skills depend on increased skill at encoding relevant information and ignoring irrelevant information. For example, to a 4-year-old, an *s* in cursive writing is a shape very different from an *s* that is printed. But a 10-year-old has learned to encode the relevant fact that both are the letter *s* and to ignore the irrelevant differences in their shape.

Automaticity refers to the ability to process information with little or no effort. Practice allows children to encode increasing amounts of information automatically. For example, once children have learned to read well, they do not think about each letter in a word as a letter; instead, they encode whole words. Once a task is automatic, it does not require conscious effort. As a result, as information processing becomes more automatic, we can complete tasks more quickly and handle more than one task at a time. If you did not

What are some important mechanisms of change in the development of children's information processing?

encode words automatically but instead read this page by focusing your attention on each letter in each word, imagine how long it would take you to read it.

Strategy construction is the creation of new procedures for processing information. For example, children's reading benefits when they develop the strategy of stopping periodically to take stock of what they have read so far (Pressley, 2007).

In addition, Siegler (2006) argues that children's information processing is characterized by *self-modification*. That is, children learn to use what they have learned in previous circumstances to adapt their responses to a new situation. Part of this self-modification draws on **metacognition,** which means knowing about knowing (Flavell, 2004). One example of metacognition is what children know about the best ways to remember what they have read. Do they know that they will remember what they have read better if they can relate it to their own lives in some way? Thus, in Siegler's application of the information-processing approach to development, children play an active role in their cognitive development.

COMPARISONS WITH PIAGET'S THEORY

How does the information-processing approach compare with Piaget's theory? According to Piaget (as discussed in Chapter 6), children actively construct their knowledge and understanding of the world. Their thinking develops in distinct stages. At each stage, children develop qualitatively different types of mental structures (or schemes) that allow them to think about the world in new ways.

Like Piaget's theory, some versions of the information-processing approach are constructivist; they see children as directing their own cognitive development. And like Piaget, information-processing psychologists identify cognitive capabilities and limitations at various points in development. They describe ways in which individuals do and do not understand important concepts at different points in life and try to explain how more advanced understanding grows out of a less advanced version. They emphasize the impact that existing understanding has on the ability to acquire a new understanding of something.

Unlike Piaget, however, developmentalists who take an information-processing approach do not see development as occurring abruptly in distinct stages with a brief transition period from one stage to the next. Instead, according to the information-processing approach, individuals develop a gradually increasing capacity to process information, which allows them to acquire increasingly complex knowledge and skills (Halford & Andrews, 2011; Sternberg, 2009). Compared with Piaget, the information-processing approach also focuses on more precise analysis of change and on the contributions made by ongoing cognitive activity—such as encoding and strategies—to that change.

developmental **connection**

Cognitive Theory. Piaget theorized that cognitive development occurs in four stages: sensorimotor, preoperational, concrete operational, and formal operational. Chapter 6, p. 174

encoding The mechanism by which information gets into memory.

automaticity The ability to process information with little or no effort.

strategy construction Creation of new procedures for processing information.

metacognition Cognition about cognition, or "knowing about knowing."

Review *Connect* Reflect

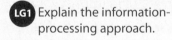 Explain the information-processing approach.

Review

- What is the information-processing approach to development?
- How do capacity and processing speed change developmentally?
- What are three important mechanisms of change involved in information processing?
- How can the information-processing approach be compared to Piaget's theory?

Connect

- In this section, we learned that changes in the brain are linked to advances in information processing. What did you learn about changes in brain structure and the cognitive abilities of infants, 15-year-olds, and 20-year-olds in Chapter 4?

Reflect *Your Own Personal Journey of Life*

- In terms of your ability to learn, think about your early childhood, elementary, and middle school years. Describe a task on which you were faster in processing information in elementary school than in preschool, and then describe a task on which you were faster in processing information in middle school than in elementary school.

The world holds a lot of information to perceive. Right now, you are perceiving the letters and words that make up this sentence. Now look around you and pick out something to look at other than this book. After that, curl up the toes on your right foot. In each of these circumstances, you engaged in the process of paying attention. What is attention, and what effect does it have on processing information? How does attention change with age?

WHAT IS ATTENTION?

Attention is the focusing of mental resources. Attention improves cognitive processing for many tasks, from grabbing a toy to hitting a baseball or adding numbers. At any one time, though, children, like adults, can pay attention to only a limited amount of information. They allocate their attention in different ways. Psychologists have labeled these types of allocation as selective attention, divided attention, sustained attention, and executive attention.

- **Selective attention** is focusing on a specific aspect of experience that is relevant while ignoring others that are irrelevant. Focusing on one voice among many in a crowded room or a noisy restaurant is an example of selective attention. When you switched your attention to the toes on your right foot, you were engaging in selective attention.

- **Divided attention** involves concentrating on more than one activity at the same time. If you are listening to music or the television while you are reading this, you are engaging in divided attention.

- **Sustained attention** is the ability to maintain attention to a selected stimulus for a prolonged period of time. Sustained attention is also called *focused attention* and *vigilance*.

- **Executive attention** involves action planning, allocating attention to goals, error detection and compensation, monitoring progress on tasks, and dealing with novel or difficult circumstances.

What are some different ways that children allocate their attention?

INFANCY

How effectively can infants attend to something? Even newborns can detect a contour and fixate on it. Older infants scan patterns more thoroughly. By 4 months, infants can selectively attend to an object.

Orienting/Investigative Progress Attention in the first year of life is dominated by an *orienting/investigative process* (Posner & Rothbart, 2007). This process involves directing attention to potentially important locations in the environment (that is, *where*) and recognizing objects and their features (such as color and form) (that is, *what*) (Courage & Richards, 2008). From 3 to 9 months of age, infants can deploy their attention more flexibly and quickly. Another important type of attention is *sustained attention*, also referred to as *focused attention* (Courage & Richards, 2008). New stimuli typically elicit an orienting response followed by sustained attention. It is sustained attention that allows infants to learn about and remember characteristics of a stimulus as it becomes familiar. Researchers have found that infants as young as 3 months of age can engage in 5 to 10 seconds of sustained attention.

attention Concentrating and focusing mental resources.

selective attention Focusing on a specific aspect of experience that is relevant while ignoring others that are irrelevant.

divided attention Concentrating on more than one activity at the same time.

sustained attention The ability to maintain attention to a selected stimulus for a prolonged period of time. Sustained attention is also called *focused attention* and *vigilance*.

executive attention Involves action planning, allocating attention to goals, error detection and compensation, monitoring progress on tasks, and dealing with novel or difficult circumstances.

joint attention Individuals focusing on the same object or event; requires the ability to track another's behavior, one person directing another's attention, and reciprocal interaction.

From this age through the second year, the length of sustained attention increases (Courage & Richards, 2008).

Habituation and Dishabituation   Closely linked with attention are the processes of habituation and dishabituation that we discussed in Chapter 5 (Kavsek, 2009). Recall that if a stimulus—a sight or sound—is presented to infants several times in a row, they usually pay less attention to it each time. This suggests they are bored with it. This is the process of *habituation*—decreased responsiveness to a stimulus after repeated presentations of the stimulus. *Dishabituation* is the recovery of a habituated response after a change in stimulation.

Infants' attention is so strongly governed by novelty and habituation that when an object becomes familiar, attention becomes shorter, making infants more vulnerable to distraction (Amos & Johnson, 2006). Researchers study habituation to determine the extent to which infants can see, hear, smell, taste, and experience touch (Slater, Field, & Hernandez-Reif, 2007).

Parents can use knowledge of habituation and dishabituation to improve interaction with their infant. If parents keep repeating the same form of stimulation, the infant will stop responding. It is important for parents to do novel things and to repeat them often until the infant stops responding. Wise parents sense when the infant shows interest and know that many repetitions of the stimulus may be necessary for the infant to process the information. The parents stop or change their behavior when the infant redirects attention (Rosenblith, 1992).

Joint Attention   Another aspect of attention that is an important aspect of infant development is **joint attention**, in which individuals focus on the same object or event. Joint attention requires (1) an ability to track another's behavior, such as following someone's gaze; (2) one person directing another's attention; and (3) reciprocal interaction. Early in infancy, joint attention usually involves a caregiver pointing or using words to direct an infant's attention. Emerging forms of joint attention occur at about 7 to 8 months, but it is not until toward the end of the first year that joint attention skills are frequently observed (Liszkowski, 2007). In a study conducted by Rechele Brooks and Andrew Meltzoff (2005), at 10 to 11 months of age infants first began engaging in "gaze following," looking where another person has just looked (see Figure 7.1). And by their first birthday, infants have begun to direct adults to objects that capture their interest (Heimann & others, 2006).

Joint attention plays important roles in many aspects of infant development and considerably increases infants' ability to learn from other people (Flom & Pick, 2007). Nowhere is this more apparent than in observations of interchanges between caregivers and infants as infants are learning language (Meltzoff & Brooks, 2006). When caregivers and infants frequently engage in joint attention, infants say their first word

---→

developmental connection

Research Methods. Among the measures researchers use in habituation studies are sucking behavior, heart and respiration rates, and how long an infant looks at an object. Chapter 5, pp. 155–156

◀---

This young infant's attention is riveted on the red block that has just been placed in front of him. His attention to the block will be strongly regulated by the processes of habituation and dishabituation. *What characterizes these processes?*

A father and his infant son engaging in joint attention. *What about this photograph tells you that joint attention is occurring? Why is joint attention an important aspect of infant development?*

(a)   (b)

FIGURE **7.1**

GAZE FOLLOWING IN INFANCY. Researcher Rechele Brooks shifts her eyes from the infant to a toy in the foreground (a). The infant then follows her eye movement to the toy (b). Brooks and colleague Andrew Meltzoff (2005) found that infants begin to engage in this kind of behavior called "gaze following" at 10 to 11 months of age. *Why might gaze following be an important accomplishment for an infant?*

earlier and develop a larger vocabulary (Carpenter, Nagell, & Tomasello, 1998; Flom & Pick, 2003). In one study, infants' initiation of joint attention was linked to their receptive and expressive language at 3 years of age (Ulvund & Smith, 1996).

CHILDHOOD

Although the infant's attention is related to cognitive development in early childhood, there are some important developmental changes in attention during early childhood. The toddler wanders around, shifts attention from one activity to another, and seems to spend little time focused on any one object or event. In contrast, the preschool child might watch television for a half-hour at a time (Giavecchio, 2001). One study that observed 99 families in their homes for 4,672 hours found that visual attention to television dramatically increased during the preschool years (Anderson & others, 1985).

Young children especially make advances in two aspects of attention—executive attention and sustained attention. Mary Rothbart and Maria Gartstein (2008, p. 332) described why advances in executive and sustained attention are so important in early childhood:

> The development of the . . . executive attention system supports the rapid increases in effortful control in the toddler and preschool years. Increases in attention are due, in part, to advances in comprehension and language development. As children are better able to understand their environment, this increased appreciation of their surroundings helps them to sustain attention for longer periods of time.

In Central European countries, such as Hungary, kindergarten children participate in exercises designed to improve their attention (Mills & Mills, 2000; Posner & Rothbart, 2007). For example, in one eye-contact exercise, the teacher sits in the center of a circle of children, and each child is required to catch the teacher's eye before being permitted to leave the group. In other exercises created to improve attention, teachers have children participate in stop-go activities during which they have to listen for a specific signal, such as drumbeat or an exact number of rhythmic beats, before stopping the activity.

Computer exercises also recently have been developed to improve children's attention (Jaeggi, Berman, & Jonides, 2009; Tang & Posner, 2009). For example, one study revealed that five days of computer exercises that involved learning how to use a joystick, working memory, and the resolution of conflict improved the attention of 4- to 6-year-old children (Rueda, Posner, & Rothbart, 2005).

Control over attention shows important changes during middle and late childhood (Posner & Rothbart, 2007). External stimuli are likely to determine the target of the preschooler's attention; what is salient, or obvious, grabs the preschooler's attention. For example, suppose a flashy, attractive clown presents the directions for solving a problem. Preschool children are likely to pay attention to the clown and ignore the directions, because they are influenced strongly by the salient features of the environment. After the age of 6 or 7, children pay more attention to features relevant to performing a task or solving a problem, such as the directions. Thus, instead of being controlled by the most striking stimuli in their environment, older children can direct their attention to more important stimuli. This change reflects a shift to *cognitive control* of attention, so that children act less impulsively and reflect more. Recall from Chapter 4 that the increase in cognitive control during the elementary school years is linked to changes in the brain, especially more focal activation in the prefrontal cortex (Durston & others, 2006).

What are some advances in children's attention as they go through early childhood and middle and late childhood?

developmental **connection**

Brain Development. One shift in activation of some areas of the brain more than others in middle and late childhood is from diffuse, large areas to more focused, smaller areas, which especially involves more focal activation in the prefrontal cortex. Chapter 4, p. 118

Preschool children's ability to control and sustain their attention is related to school readiness (Posner & Rothbart, 2007). For example, a study of more than 1,000 children revealed that their ability to sustain their attention at 54 months of age was linked to their school readiness (which included achievement and language skills) (NICHD Early Child Care Research Network, 2005). And in a recent study, children whose parents and teachers rated them higher on a scale of having attention problems at 54 months of age had a higher level of social skills in peer relations in the first and third grades than their counterparts who were rated lower on the attention problems scale at 54 months of age (NICHD Early Child Care Research Network, 2009).

ADOLESCENCE

Adolescents typically have better attentional skills than children do, although there are wide individual differences in how effectively adolescents deploy their attention. Sustained and executive attention are very important aspects of adolescent cognitive development. As adolescents are required to engage in larger, increasingly complex tasks that require longer time frames to complete, their ability to sustain attention is critical for succeeding on the tasks. An increase in executive attention supports the rapid increase in effortful control required to effectively engage in these complex academic tasks (Rothbart & Gartstein, 2008).

One trend involving divided attention is adolescents' multi-tasking, which in some cases involves dividing attention not just between two activities, but even among three or more (Bauerlein, 2008). A major influence on the increase in multi-tasking is availability of multiple electronic media. Many adolescents have a range of electronic media at their disposal. It is not unusual for adolescents to simultaneously divide their attention among working on homework, engaging in an instant messaging conversation, surfing the Web, and looking at an iTunes playlist. And a national survey revealed that 50 percent of adolescents made and answered phone calls while driving, and 13 percent (approximately 1.7 million) wrote and/or read text messages while driving (Allstate Foundation, 2005).

Is this multi-tasking beneficial or distracting? Multi-tasking expands the information adolescents attend to and forces the brain to share processing resources, which can distract the adolescent's attention from what might be most important at the moment (Begley & Interlandi, 2008). And, if the key task is at all complex and challenging, such as trying to figure out how to solve a homework problem, multi-tasking considerably reduces attention to the key task (Myers, 2008).

Is multi-tasking beneficial or distracting for adolescents?

developmental connection

Media. A recent study revealed that when media multitasking is taken into account, 8- to 18-year-olds use media an average of 8 hours a day, rather than just 6 hours a day (Robert & Foehr, 2008). Chapter 17, p. 500

Review Connect Reflect

LG2 Define attention and outline its developmental changes.

Review

- What is attention? What are four ways in which children can allocate attention?
- How does attention develop in infancy?
- How does attention develop in childhood?
- What are some characteristics of attention in adolescence?

Connect

- In this section, you learned about joint attention. How might a child's ability to engage in joint attention be important in the successful implementation of a zone of proximal development teaching strategy?

Reflect Your Own Personal Journey of Life

- Imagine that you are an elementary school teacher. Devise some strategies to help children pay attention in class.

Twentieth-century American playwright Tennessee Williams once commented that life is all memory except for that one present moment that goes by so quickly that you can hardly catch it going. But just what do we do when we remember something, and how does our ability to remember develop?

WHAT IS MEMORY?

Memory is the retention of information over time. Without memory you would not be able to connect what happened to you yesterday with what is going on in your life today. Human memory is truly remarkable when you consider how much information we put into our memories and how much we must retrieve to perform all of life's activities.

Processes and Types of Memory   Researchers study how information is initially placed or encoded into memory, how it is retained or stored after being encoded, and how it is found or retrieved for a certain purpose later (see Figure 7.2). Encoding, storage, and retrieval are the basic processes required for memory. Failures can occur in any of these processes. Some part of an event might not be encoded, the mental representation of the event might not be stored, or even if the memory exists, you might not be able to retrieve it.

Examining the storage process led psychologists to classify memories based on their permanence. **Short-term memory** is a memory system with a limited capacity in which information is usually retained for up to 15 to 30 seconds unless strategies are used to retain it longer. **Long-term memory** is a relatively permanent and unlimited type of memory. People are usually referring to long-term memory when they talk about "memory." When you remember the type of games you enjoyed playing as a child or the details of your first date, you are drawing on your long-term memory. But when you remember the word you just read a few seconds ago, you are using short-term memory.

When psychologists first analyzed short-term memory, they described it as if it were a passive storehouse with shelves to store information until it is moved to long-term memory. But we do many things with the information stored in short-term memory. For example, the words in this sentence are part of your short-term memory, and you are manipulating them to form a meaningful whole.

The concept of working memory acknowledges the importance of our manipulations of the information in short-term memory. **Working memory** is a kind of mental "workbench" where individuals manipulate and assemble information when

"Can we hurry up and get to the test? My short-term memory is better than my long-term memory."
© Wm Hoest Enterprises, Inc. Reprinted courtesy of Bunny Hoest.

memory Retention of information over time.

short-term memory Limited-capacity memory system in which information is usually retained for up to 30 seconds, assuming there is no rehearsal of the information. Using rehearsal, individuals can keep the information in short-term memory longer.

long-term memory A relatively permanent and unlimited type of memory.

working memory A mental "workbench" where individuals manipulate and assemble information when making decisions, solving problems, and comprehending written and spoken language.

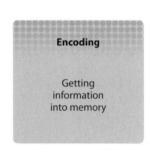

Encoding

Getting information into memory

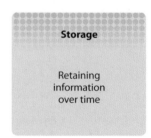

Storage

Retaining information over time

Retrieval

Taking information out of storage

FIGURE **7.2**

PROCESSING INFORMATION IN MEMORY. As you read about the many aspects of memory in this chapter, think about the organization of memory in terms of these three main activities.

they make decisions, solve problems, and comprehend written and spoken language (Baddeley, 1990, 2001, 2007). Many psychologists prefer the term *working memory* over *short-term memory* to describe how memory works.

Figure 7.3 shows Alan Baddeley's model of working memory. Notice that it includes two short-term stores—one for speech and one for visual and spatial information—as well as a *central executive*. It is the job of the central executive to monitor and control the system—determining what information is stored, relating information from long-term memory to the information in the short-term stores, and moving information into long-term memory.

Working memory is linked to many aspects of children's development (Ang & Lee, 2010; Alloway, Gathercole, & Elliott, 2010; Cowan & Alloway, 2009; Reznick, 2009). For example, children who have better working memory are more advanced in reading comprehension, math skills, and problem solving than their counterparts with less effective working memory (Dyck & Piek, 2010; Locascio & others, 2010).

The following three recent studies illustrate the importance of working memory in young children's cognitive development:

- Working memory and attention control predicted growth in emergent literacy and number skills in young children in low-income families (Welsh & others, 2010).

- Working memory capacity at 9 to 10 years of age predicted foreign language comprehension two years later at 11 to 12 years of age (Andersson, 2010).

- Working memory capacity predicted how many items on a to-be-remembered list that fourth-grade children forgot (Asian, Zellner, & Bauml, 2010).

Constructing Memories   Memory is not like a tape recorder or a camera or even like computer memory; we don't store and retrieve bits of data in computer-like fashion (Schachter, 2001). Children and adults construct and reconstruct their memories.

Schema Theory   According to **schema theory,** people mold memories to fit information that already exists in their minds. This process is guided by **schemas,** which are mental frameworks that organize concepts and information. Suppose a football fan and a visitor from a country where the sport isn't played are eating at a restaurant and overhear a conversation about last night's game. Because the visitor doesn't have a schema for information about football, he or she is more likely than the fan to mishear what is said. Perhaps the visitor will interpret the conversation in terms of a schema for another sport, constructing a false memory of the conversation.

Schemas influence the way we encode, make inferences about, and retrieve information. We reconstruct the past rather than take an exact photograph of it, and the mind can distort an event as it encodes and stores impressions of it. Often when we retrieve information, we fill in the gaps with fragmented memories.

Fuzzy Trace Theory   Another variation of how individuals reconstruct their memories has been proposed by Charles Brainerd and Valerie Reyna (2004; Reyna & Brainerd, 1995). **Fuzzy trace theory** states that when individuals encode information, they create two types of memory representations: (1) a *verbatim memory trace*, which consists of precise details; and (2) a *fuzzy trace, or gist*, which is the central idea of the information. For example, consider a child who is presented with information about a pet store that has 10 birds, 6 cats, 8 dogs, and 7 rabbits. Then the child is asked two types of questions: (1) verbatim questions, such as "How many cats are

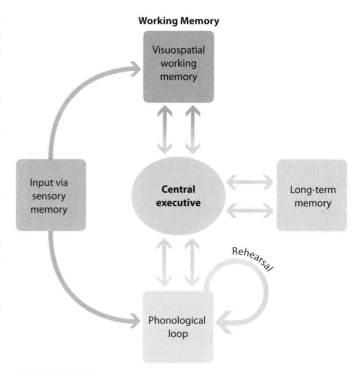

Working Memory

FIGURE **7.3**

WORKING MEMORY. In Baddeley's working memory model, working memory is like a mental workbench where a great deal of information processing is carried out. Working memory consists of three main components: the phonological loop and visuospatial working memory serve as assistants, helping the central executive do its work. Input from sensory memory goes to the phonological loop, where information about speech is stored and rehearsal takes place, and visuospatial working memory, where visual and spatial information, including imagery, are stored. Working memory is a limited-capacity system, and information is stored there for only a brief time. Working memory interacts with long-term memory, using information from long-term memory in its work and transmitting information to long-term memory for longer storage.

developmental **connection**

Gender. Gender schema theory emphasizes children's gender schemas that organize the world in terms of male and female. Chapter 12, pp. 350–351

schema theory States that when people reconstruct information, they fit it into information that already exists in their minds.

schemas Mental frameworks that organize concepts and information.

fuzzy trace theory States that memory is best understood by considering two types of memory representations: (1) verbatim memory trace; and (2) fuzzy trace, or gist. According to this theory, older children's better memory is attributed to the fuzzy traces created by extracting the gist of information.

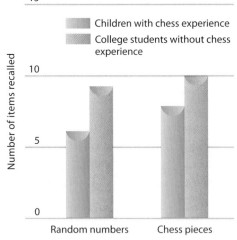

15

10

Number of items recalled

5

0

Children with chess experience
College students without chess experience

Random numbers   Chess pieces

FIGURE **7.4**
MEMORY FOR NUMBERS AND CHESS PIECES

FIGURE **7.5**

THE TECHNIQUE USED IN ROVEE-COLLIER'S INVESTIGATION OF INFANT MEMORY. In Rovee-Collier's experiment, operant conditioning was used to demonstrate that infants as young as 2½ months of age can retain information from the experience of being conditioned.

implicit memory Memory without conscious recollection; memory of skills and routine procedures that are performed automatically.

explicit memory Conscious memory of facts and experiences.

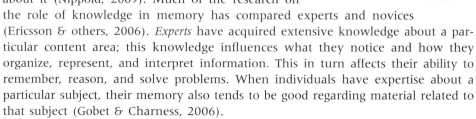

in the pet store, 6 or 8?" and (2) gist questions, such as "Are there more cats or more dogs in the pet store?" Researchers have found that preschool children tend to remember verbatim information more than gist information, but elementary-school-aged children are more likely to remember gist information (Brainerd & Gordon, 1994). The increased use of gist by elementary-school-aged children accounts for their improved memory because fuzzy traces are less likely to be forgotten than verbatim traces (Reyna & Rivers, 2008).

Content Knowledge and Expertise   Our ability to remember new information about a subject depends considerably on what we already know about it (Nippold, 2009). Much of the research on the role of knowledge in memory has compared experts and novices (Ericsson & others, 2006). *Experts* have acquired extensive knowledge about a particular content area; this knowledge influences what they notice and how they organize, represent, and interpret information. This in turn affects their ability to remember, reason, and solve problems. When individuals have expertise about a particular subject, their memory also tends to be good regarding material related to that subject (Gobet & Charness, 2006).

For example, one study found that 10- and 11-year-olds who were experienced chess players ("experts") were able to remember more information about chess pieces than college students who were not chess players ("novices") (Chi, 1978) (see Figure 7.4). In contrast, when the college students were presented with other stimuli, they were able to remember them better than the children were. Thus, the children's expertise in chess gave them superior memories, but only in chess.

There are developmental changes in expertise. Older children usually have more expertise about a subject than younger children do, which can contribute to their better memory for the subject.

In their study of memory, researchers have not extensively examined the roles that sociocultural factors might play. In *Connecting With Diversity*, we will explore culture's role in children's memory.

We have examined a number of basic processes that are important in understanding children's memory. In several places, we have described developmental changes in these processes. Let's now further explore how memory changes from infancy through childhood.

INFANCY

Popular child-rearing expert Penelope Leach (1990) told parents that 6- to 8-month-old babies cannot hold in their mind a picture of their mother or father. Child development researchers, however, have revealed that infants as young as 3 months of age show a limited type of memory (Courage, Howe, & Squires, 2004).

First Memories   Carolyn Rovee-Collier (1987, 2007; Rovee-Collier & Cuevas, 2009) has conducted research demonstrating that infants can remember perceptual-motor information. In a characteristic experiment, she places a baby in a crib underneath an elaborate mobile and ties one end of a ribbon to the baby's ankle and the other end to the mobile. The baby kicks and makes the mobile move (see Figure 7.5). Weeks later, the baby is returned to the crib, but its foot is not tied to the mobile. The baby kicks, apparently trying to make the mobile move. However, if the mobile's makeup is changed even slightly, the baby doesn't kick. If the mobile is then restored to being exactly as it was when the baby's ankle was originally tied to it, the baby will begin kicking again. According to Rovee-Collier, even by 2½ months the baby's memory is incredibly detailed.

Culture and Children's Memory

A culture sensitizes its members to certain objects, events, and strategies, which in turn can influence the nature of memory (Fivush, 2009). In schema theory, a child's background, which is encoded in schemas, is revealed in the way the child reconstructs a story. This effect of cultural background on memory is called the *cultural-specificity hypothesis*. It states that cultural experiences determine what is relevant in a person's life and, thus, what the person is likely to remember. For example, imagine a child living on a remote island in the Pacific Ocean whose parents make their livelihood by fishing. The child's memory about how weather affects fishing is likely to be highly developed. By contrast, a Pacific Islander child might be hard-pressed to encode and recall the details of a major league baseball team.

Cultures may vary in the strategies that children use to remember information, and these cultural variations are usually due to schooling (Cole, 2006). Children who have experienced schooling are more likely to cluster items together in meaningful ways, which helps them to remember the items. Schooling provides children with specialized information-processing tasks, such as committing large amounts of information to memory in a short time frame and using logical reasoning, that may generate specialized memory strategies. However, there is no evidence that schooling increases memory capacity per se; rather, it influences the strategies for remembering (Cole, 2006).

Scripts are schemas for an event. In one study, adolescents in the United States and Mexico remembered according to script-based knowledge (Harris, Schoen, & Hensley, 1992). In line with common practices in their respective cultures, adolescents in the United States remembered information about a dating script better when no chaperone was present on a date, whereas adolescents in Mexico remembered the information better when a chaperone was present.

American children, especially American girls, describe autobiographical narratives

> that are longer, more detailed, more specific, and more 'personal' (both in terms of mention of self, and mention of internal states), than narratives by

Senegalese students attend a lesson in the town of Fatick, Senegal. *How might their schooling influence their memory?*

children from China and Korea. The pattern is consistent with expectations derived from the finding that in their conversations about past events, American mothers and their children are more elaborative and more focused on autonomous themes . . . and that Korean mothers and their children have less frequent and less detailed conversations about the past. . . . (Bauer, 2006, p. 411)

Possibly the more elaborated content of American children's narratives contributes to the earlier first memories researchers have found in American adults (Han, Leichtman, & Wang,1998).

How might guided participation, which is used in many different cultures (as discussed in Chapter 6), support the influence of culture on memory?

How well can infants remember? Some researchers such as Rovee-Collier have concluded that infants as young as 2 to 6 months of age can remember some experiences through 1½ to 2 years of age (Rovee-Collier, 2007, 2009). However, critics such as Jean Mandler (2000), a leading expert on infant cognition, argue that the infants in Rovee-Collier's experiments are displaying only implicit memory. **Implicit memory** refers to memory without conscious recollection—memories of skills and routine procedures that are performed automatically, such as riding a bicycle. In contrast, **explicit memory** refers to the conscious memory of facts and experiences.

developmental **connection**

Culture and Ethnicity. Culture encompasses the behavior patterns, beliefs, and all other products of a particular group of people that are passed on from generation to generation. Chapter 14, p. 420

Age Group	Length of Delay
6-month-olds	24 hours
9-month-olds	1 month
10–11-month-olds	3 months
13–14-month-olds	4–6 months
20-month-olds	12 months

FIGURE 7.6

AGE-RELATED CHANGES IN THE LENGTH OF TIME OVER WHICH MEMORY OCCURS.
Source: Bauer (2009a).

When people think about memory, they are usually referring to explicit memory. Most researchers find that babies do not show explicit memory until the second half of the first year (Bauer, 2007, 2009a; Bayer, Larkina, & Deocampo, 2011). Then, explicit memory improves substantially during the second year of life (Bauer, 2007, 2009a; Bauer, Larkina, & Deocampo, 2011). In one longitudinal study, infants were assessed several times during their second year (Bauer & others, 2000). Older infants showed more accurate memory and required fewer prompts to demonstrate their memory than younger infants. Figure 7.6 summarizes how long researchers have found infants of different ages can remember information (Bauer, 2009a). As indicated in Figure 7.6, researchers have documented that 6-month-olds can remember information for 24 hours, but by 20 months of age infants can remember information they encountered 12 months earlier.

What changes in the brain are linked to infants' memory development? From about 6 to 12 months of age, the maturation of the hippocampus and the surrounding cerebral cortex, especially the frontal lobes, makes the emergence of explicit memory possible (Bower, Larkina, & Deocampo, 2011; Nelson, 2011) (see Figure 7.7). Explicit memory continues to improve in the second year, as these brain structures further mature and connections between them increase. Less is known about the areas of the brain involved in implicit memory in infancy.

Infantile Amnesia Let's examine another aspect of memory. Do you remember your third birthday party? Probably not. Most adults can remember little, if anything, from the first three years of their life. This is called *infantile,* or *childhood, amnesia.* The few reported adult memories of life at age 2 or 3 are at best very sketchy (Howe, Courage, & Rooksby, 2009; Newcombe, 2007). Elementary school children also do not remember much of their early childhood years (Lie & Newcombe, 1999).

What is the cause of infantile amnesia? One reason older children and adults have difficulty recalling events from their infant and early child years is that during these early years the prefrontal lobes of the brain are immature; this area of the brain is believed to play an important role in storing memories of events (Boyer & Diamond, 1992).

In sum, most of young infants' conscious memories appear to be rather fragile and short-lived, although their implicit memory of perceptual-motor actions can be substantial (Bauer, 2007, 2009a; Mandler, 2004). By the end of the second year, long-term memory is more substantial and reliable (Bauer, 2009a; Bauer, Larkina, & Deocampo, 2011).

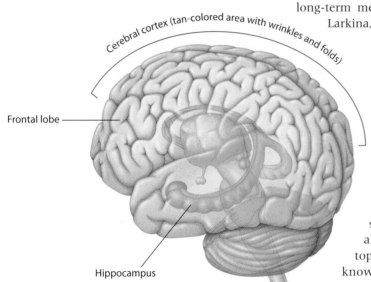

Cerebral cortex (tan-colored area with wrinkles and folds)

Frontal lobe

Hippocampus

FIGURE 7.7

KEY BRAIN STRUCTURES INVOLVED IN MEMORY DEVELOPMENT IN INFANCY

CHILDHOOD

Children's memory improves considerably after infancy. Sometimes the long-term memories of preschoolers seem erratic, but young children can remember a great deal of information if they are given appropriate cues and prompts.

One reason children remember less than adults is that they are far less expert in most areas, but their growing knowledge is one likely source of their memory improvement. For example, a child's ability to recount what she has seen on a trip to the library depends greatly on what she already knows about libraries, such as where books on certain topics are located, how to check out books, and so on. If a child knows little about libraries, she will have a much more difficult time recounting what she saw there.

Fuzzy trace theory suggests another way in which memory develops during childhood. Recall from our earlier discussion that young children tend to encode, store, and retrieve verbatim traces, whereas elementary-school-aged children begin to use gist more. The increased use of gist likely produces more enduring memory traces of information. Other sources of improvement in children's memory include changes in memory span and their use of strategies.

Memory Span Unlike long-term memory, short-term memory has a very limited capacity. One method of assessing that capacity is the *memory-span task.* You simply hear a short list of stimuli—usually digits—presented at a rapid pace (one per second, for example). Then you are asked to repeat the digits.

Research with the memory-span task suggests that short-term memory increases during childhood. For example, in one investigation, memory span increased from about two digits in 2-year-old children to about five digits in 7-year-old children. Between 7 and 12 years of age, memory span increased by only one and a half digits (Dempster, 1981) (see Figure 7.8). Keep in mind, though, that individuals have different memory spans.

Why does memory span change with age? Speed of processing information is important, especially the speed with which memory items can be identified. For example, one study tested children on their speed at repeating words presented orally (Case, Kurland, & Goldberg, 1982). Speed of repetition was a powerful predictor of memory span. Indeed, when the speed of repetition was controlled, the 6-year-olds' memory spans were equal to those of young adults. Rehearsal of information is also important; older children rehearse the digits more than younger children.

Strategies Rehearsal is just one of the strategies that can sometimes aid memory, although rehearsal is a better strategy for short-term memory than long-term memory. Following are some strategies that benefit children's long-term retention of information.

Organization If children organize information when they encode it, their memory benefits. Consider this demonstration: Recall the 12 months of the year as quickly as you can. How long did it take you? What was the order of your recall? You probably answered something like "a few seconds" and "in chronological order." Now try to remember the months of the year in alphabetical order. Did you make any errors? How long did it take you? It should be obvious that your memory for the months of the year is organized in a particular way.

Organizing is a strategy that older children (and adults) typically use, and it helps them to remember information. Preschool children usually don't use strategies like organization; in middle and late childhood they are more likely to use organization when they need to remember something (Flavell, Miller, & Miller, 2002).

Elaboration Another important strategy is elaboration, which involves engaging in more extensive processing of information. When individuals engage in elaboration, their memory benefits (Kellogg, 2007). Thinking of examples is a good way to elaborate information. For example, self-reference is an effective way to elaborate information. Thinking about personal associations with information makes the information more meaningful and helps children to remember it.

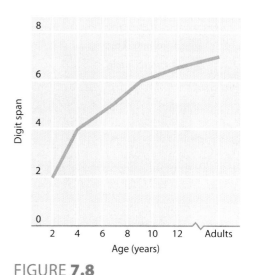

FIGURE **7.8**

DEVELOPMENTAL CHANGES IN MEMORY SPAN. In one study, memory span increased by about three digits from 2 years of age to 7 years of age (Dempster, 1981). By 12 years of age, memory span had increased on average another one and a half digits.

Frank and Ernest

FRANK & ERNEST © Thaves/Dist. by United Features Syndicate, Inc.

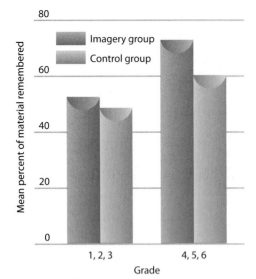

FIGURE 7.9

IMAGERY AND MEMORY OF VERBAL INFORMATION. Imagery improved older elementary-school-aged children's memory for sentences more than younger elementary-school-aged children's memory for sentences.

The use of elaboration changes developmentally (Pressley, 2003; Schneider, 2011). Adolescents are more likely than children to use elaboration spontaneously. Elementary-school-aged children can be taught to use elaboration strategies on a learning task, but they will be less likely than adolescents to use the strategies on other learning tasks in the future. Nonetheless, verbal elaboration can be an effective strategy even for young elementary-school-aged children.

Imagery Creating mental images is another strategy for improving memory. However, using imagery to remember verbal information works better for older children than for younger children (Schneider, 2004, 2011). In one study, 20 sentences were presented to first- through sixth-grade children to remember—such as "The angry bird shouted at the white dog" and "The policeman painted the circus tent on a windy day" (Pressley & others, 1987). Children were randomly assigned to an imagery condition (in which they were told to make a picture in their head for each sentence) and a control condition (in which they were told just to try hard). Figure 7.9 shows that the imagery instructions helped older elementary-school-aged children (grades 4 through 6) but was not nearly as helpful to the younger elementary-school-aged children (grades 1 through 3). However, mental imagery can help young schoolchildren to remember pictures (Schneider, 2004, 2011; Schneider & Pressley, 1997).

Teaching Strategies So far we have described several important strategies adults can adopt when guiding children to remember information more effectively over the long term. These strategies include guiding children to organize information, elaborate the information, and develop images of the information. Another good strategy is to encourage children to understand the material that needs to be remembered rather than rotely memorizing it. Two other strategies adults can use to guide children's retention of memory were recently proposed:

- *Repeat with variation on the instructional information and link early and often.* These are memory development research expert Patricia Bauer's (2009) recommendations to improve children's consolidation and reconsolidation of the information they are learning. Variations on a lesson theme increase the number of associations in memory storage, and linking expands the network of associations in memory storage; both strategies expand the routes for retrieving information from storage.

- *Embed memory-relevant language when instructing children.* Teachers vary considerably in how much they use memory-relevant language that encourages students to remember information. In recent research that involved extensive observations of a number of first-grade teachers in the classroom, Peter Ornstein & his colleagues (Ornstein, Coffman, & Grammer, 2007, 2009; Ornstein & others, 2010) found that in the time segments observed, the teachers rarely used strategy suggestions or metacognitive (thinking about thinking) questions. In this research, when lower-achieving students were placed in classrooms in which teachers were categorized as "high-mnemonic teachers" who frequently embedded memory-relevant information in their teaching, their achievement increased (Ornstein, Coffman, & Grammer, 2007).

Reconstructive Memory and Children as Eyewitnesses Children's memories, like those of adults, are constructive and reconstructive. Children have schemas for all sorts of information, and these schemas affect how they encode, store, and retrieve memories. If a teacher tells her class a story about two men and two women who were involved in a train crash in France, students won't remember every detail of the story and will reconstruct the story, putting their own individual stamp on it. One student might reconstruct the story by saying the characters died in a plane crash, another might describe three men and three women, another might say the crash was in Germany, and so on.

Reconstruction and distortion are nowhere more apparent than in clashing testimony given by eyewitnesses at trials. A special concern is susceptibility to suggestion and how this can alter memory (Bruck, Ceci, & Principe, 2006; Paz-Alonso & others, 2009; Pipe & Salmon, 2009). Consider a study of individuals who had visited Disneyland (Pickrell & Loftus, 2001). Four groups of participants read ads and answered questionnaires about a trip to Disneyland. One group saw an ad that mentioned no cartoon characters; the second read the same ad and saw a four-foot-tall cardboard figure of Bugs Bunny; the third read a fake ad for Disneyland with Bugs Bunny on it; and the fourth saw the same fake ad along with cardboard Bugs. Participants were asked whether they had ever met Bugs Bunny at Disneyland. Less than 10 percent of those in the first two groups reported having met Bugs Bunny at Disneyland, but approximately 30 to 40 percent of the third and fourth groups remembered meeting Bugs there. People were persuaded they had met Bugs Bunny at Disneyland, even though Bugs is a Warner Brothers character who would never appear at a Disney theme park.

The following conclusions about children as eyewitnesses indicate that a number of factors can influence the accuracy of a young child's memory (Bruck & Ceci, 1999):

- *There are age differences in children's susceptibility to suggestion.* Preschoolers are the most suggestible age group in comparison with older children and adults (Ceci, Papierno, & Kulkofsky, 2007). For example, preschool children are more susceptible to believing misleading or incorrect information given after an event (Ghetti & Alexander, 2004). Despite these age differences, there is still concern about the reaction of older children when they are subjected to suggestive interviews (Poole & Lindsay, 1996).

- *There are individual differences in susceptibility.* Some preschoolers are highly resistant to interviewers' suggestions, whereas others immediately succumb to the slightest suggestion. A recent study revealed that preschool children's ability to produce a high-quality narrative was linked to their resistance to suggestion (Kulkofsky & Klemfuss, 2008).

- *Interviewing techniques can produce substantial distortions in children's reports about highly salient events.* Children are suggestible not just about peripheral details but also about the central aspects of an event (Bruck, Ceci, & Hembrooke, 1998). When children do accurately recall information about an event, the interviewer often has a neutral tone, there is limited use of misleading questions, and there is an absence of any motivation for the child to make a false report (Bruck & Ceci, 1999).

In sum, whether a young child's eyewitness testimony is accurate may depend on a number of factors such as the type, number, and intensity of the suggestive techniques the child has experienced (Melinder & others, 2010).

ADOLESCENCE

There has been little research on memory changes in adolescence. As you saw in Figure 7.8, memory span (which is a measure of short-term memory) increases during adolescence. There also is evidence that working memory increases during adolescence. In one study, the performances of individuals from 6 to 57 years of age were examined on both verbal and visuospatial working memory tasks (Swanson, 1999). As shown in Figure 7.10, working memory increased substantially from 8 through 24 years of age no matter what the task. Thus, the adolescent years are likely to be an important developmental period for improvement in working memory. Note that working memory continues to improve through the transition to adulthood and beyond.

Four-year-old Jennifer Royal was the only eyewitness to one of her playmates being shot to death. She was allowed to testify in open court, and the clarity of her statements helped to convict the gunman. *What are some issues involved in whether young children should be allowed to testify in court?*

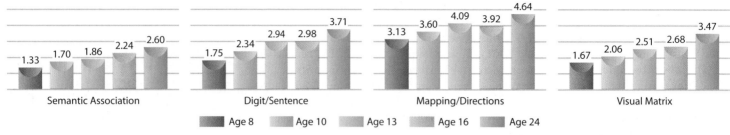

Verbal tasks

Semantic Association

Age	Score
8	1.33
10	1.70
13	1.86
16	2.24
24	2.60

Digit/Sentence

Age	Score
8	1.75
10	2.34
13	2.94
16	2.98
24	3.71

Visuospatial tasks

Mapping/Directions

Age	Score
8	3.13
10	3.60
13	4.09
16	3.92
24	4.64

Visual Matrix

Age	Score
8	1.67
10	2.06
13	2.51
16	2.68
24	3.47

■ Age 8 ■ Age 10 ■ Age 13 ■ Age 16 ■ Age 24

FIGURE **7.10**

DEVELOPMENTAL CHANGES IN WORKING MEMORY. *Note:* The scores shown here are the means for each age group, and the age also represents a mean age. Higher scores reflect superior working memory performance.

Review *Connect* Reflect

LG3 Describe what memory is and how it changes.

Review

- What is memory? What are some important processes and types of memory?
- How does memory develop in infancy?
- How does memory change in childhood?
- How does memory change in adolescence?

Connect

- In this section, we learned about *schemas* as they relate to memory. How is this concept similar to or different from the concept of *schemes,* as related to Piaget's theory of development discussed in Chapter 6?

Reflect *Your Own Personal Journey of Life*

- What is your earliest memory? Why do you think you can remember this particular situation?

Thinking **LG4** Characterize thinking and its developmental changes.

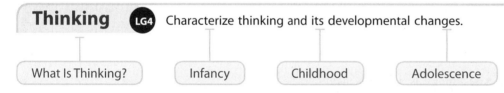

What Is Thinking? Infancy Childhood Adolescence

Attention and memory are often steps toward another level of information processing—thinking. What is thinking? How does it change developmentally? What is children's scientific thinking like, and how do they solve problems? Let's explore these questions.

WHAT IS THINKING?

Thinking involves manipulating and transforming information in memory; it is the job of the central executive in Baddeley's model of working memory shown in Figure 7.4. We think in order to reason, reflect, evaluate ideas, solve problems, and make decisions. Let's explore how thinking changes developmentally, beginning with infancy.

INFANCY

Interest in thinking during infancy has especially focused on concept formation and categorization (Cohen, 2009; Mandler, 2009; Oakes & Rakison, 2009; Quinn, 2011). To understand what concepts are, we first have to define *categories:* they group objects,

"For God's sake, think! Why is he being so nice to you?"
Copyright © The New Yorker Collection, 1998, Sam Gross from cartoonbank.com. All rights reserved.

thinking Manipulating and transforming information in memory, usually to form concepts, reason, think critically, and solve problems.

events, and characteristics on the basis of common properties. *Concepts* are ideas about what categories represent, or said another way, the sort of thing we think category members are. Concepts and categories help us to simplify and summarize information. Without concepts, you would see each object and event as unique; you would not be able to make any generalizations.

Do infants form concepts? Yes, they do, although we do not know just how early concept formation begins (Mandler, 2009). Using habituation experiments like those described earlier in the chapter, some researchers have found that infants as young as 3 months of age can group together objects with similar appearances (Quinn, 2009a, b; 2011). This research capitalizes on the knowledge that infants are more likely to look at a novel object than a familiar object. For example, in a characteristic study, young infants are shown a series of photographs of different types of cats in pairs (Quinn & Eimas, 1996). As they are shown more pictures of cats, they habituate to the animals, looking at them less and less. Then, after seeing a series of cats paired in photographs, when they are shown a photograph of a cat paired with a photogaph of a dog, they look longer at the dog, indicating an ability to group together objects characterized by similar properties.

Jean Mandler (2004, 2009) argues that these early categorizations are best described as *perceptual categorization*. That is, the categorizations are based on similar perceptual features of objects, such as size, color, and movement, as well as parts of objects, such as legs for animals. Mandler (2004) concludes that it is not until about 7 to 9 months of age that infants form *conceptual* categories rather than just making perceptual discriminations between different categories. In one study of 9- to 11-month-olds, infants classified birds as animals and airplanes as vehicles even though the objects were perceptually similar—airplanes and birds with their wings spread (Mandler & McDonough, 1993) (see Figure 7.11).

Further advances in categorization occur in the second year of life (Booth, 2006; Booth & Ware, 2010). Many infants' "first concepts are broad and global in nature, such as 'animal' or 'indoor thing.' Gradually, over the first two years these broad concepts become more differentiated into concepts such as 'land animal,' then 'dog,' or to 'furniture,' then 'chair'" (Mandler, 2010). Also in the second year, infants often categorize objects on the basis of their shape (Landau, Smith, & Jones, 1998).

Do some very young children develop an intense, passionate interest in a particular category of objects or activities? A recent study confirmed that they do (DeLoache, Simcock, & Macari, 2007). A striking finding was the large gender difference in categories, with an intense interest in particular categories stronger for boys than girls. Categorization of boys' intense interests focused on vehicles, trains, machines, dinosaurs, and balls; girls' intense interests were more likely to involve dress-ups and books/reading (see Figure 7.12). When your author's grandson Alex was 18 to 24 months old, he already had developed an intense, passionate interest in the category of vehicles. For example, at this age, he categorized vehicles into such subcategories as cars, trucks, earth-moving equipment, and buses. In addition to common classifications of cars into police cars, jeeps, taxis, and such, and trucks into firetrucks, dump trucks, and the like, his categorical knowledge of earth-moving equipment included bulldozers and excavators, and he categorized buses into school buses, London buses, and funky Malta buses (retro buses on the island of Malta). Later, at 2 to 3 years of age, Alex developed an intense, passionate interest in categorizing dinosaurs.

In sum, the infant's advances in processing information—through attention, memory, imitation, and concept formation—is much richer, more gradual and less stage-like, and occurs earlier than was envisioned by earlier theorists, such as Piaget (Diamond, Casey, & Munakata, 2011;

FIGURE **7.11**

CATEGORIZATION IN 9-TO 11-MONTH-OLDS. These are the stimuli used in the study that indicated 9- to 11-month-old infants categorized birds as animals and airplanes as vehicles even though the objects were perceptually similar (Mandler & McDonough, 1993).

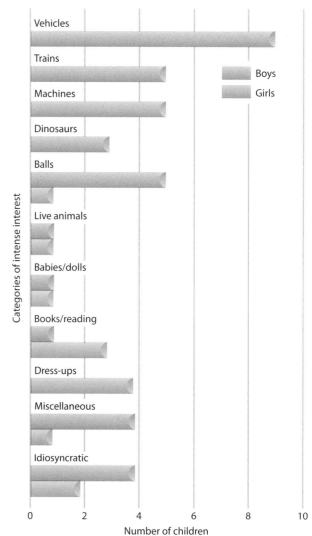

FIGURE **7.12**

CATEGORIZATION OF BOYS' AND GIRLS' INTENSE INTERESTS

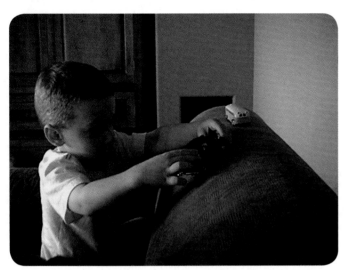

The author's grandson Alex at 2 years of age showing his intense, passionate interest in the category of vehicles while playing with a London taxi and a funky Malta bus.

Meltzoff, 2011; Quinn, 2011). As leading infant researcher Jean Mandler (2004) concluded, "The human infant shows a remarkable degree of learning power and complexity in what is being learned and in the way it is represented" (p. 304).

CHILDHOOD

To explore thinking in childhood, we will examine three important types of thinking: critical thinking, scientific thinking, and problem solving.

Currently, there is considerable interest among psychologists and educators in critical thinking (Bonney & Sternberg, 2010; Gruenfeld, 2010; Fraser-Abder, 2010). **Critical thinking** involves thinking reflectively and productively, and evaluating evidence. If you think critically, you will do the following:

- Ask not only what happened but how and why.
- Examine supposed "facts" to determine whether there is evidence to support them.
- Argue in a reasoned way rather than through emotions.
- Recognize that there is sometimes more than one good answer or explanation.
- Compare various answers and judge which is the best answer.
- Evaluate what other people say rather than immediately accepting it as the truth.
- Ask questions and speculate beyond what is known to create new ideas and new information.

According to Ellen Langer (2005), **mindfulness**—being alert, mentally present, and cognitively flexible while going through life's everyday activities and tasks—is an important aspect of thinking critically. Mindful children and adults maintain an active awareness of the circumstances in their life and are motivated to find the best solutions to tasks. Mindful individuals create new ideas, are open to new information, and can operate from more than one perspective. By contrast, mindless individuals are entrapped in old ideas, engage in automatic behavior, and operate from a single perspective.

In the view of critics such as Jacqueline and Martin Brooks (1993, 2001), few schools teach students to think critically. Schools push students to give a single correct answer rather than encouraging them to come up with new ideas and rethink conclusions. Too often teachers ask students to recite, define, describe, state, and list rather than to analyze, infer, connect, synthesize, criticize, create, evaluate, think, and rethink. As a result, many schools graduate students who think superficially, staying on the surface of problems rather than becoming deeply engaged in meaningful thinking.

One way to encourage students to think critically is to present them with controversial topics or both sides of an issue to discuss (Osborne, 2010). Some teachers shy away from having students debate issues because arguments supposedly are not "polite" or "nice" (Winn, 2004). But debates can motivate students to delve more deeply into a topic and examine issues, especially if teachers refrain from stating their own views so that students feel free to explore multiple perspectives.

critical thinking Thinking reflectively and productively, and evaluating the evidence.

mindfulness Being alert, mentally present, and cognitively flexible while going through life's everyday activities and tasks.

To read about one developmental psychologist who used her training in cognitive development to pursue a career in an applied area, see the *Connecting With Careers* profile.

Scientific Thinking   Some aspects of thinking are specific to a particular domain, such as mathematics, science, or reading. We will explore reading in Chapter 9, "Language Development." Here we will examine scientific thinking by children.

Helen Schwe, Developmental Psychologist and Toy Designer

Helen Schwe obtained a Ph.D. from Stanford University in developmental psychology, but she now spends her days talking with computer engineers and designing "smart" toys for children. Smart toys are designed to improve children's problem-solving and symbolic thinking skills.

When she was a graduate student, Schwe worked part-time for Hasbro toys, testing its children's software on preschoolers. Her first job after graduate school was with Zowie Entertainment, which was subsequently bought by LEGO. According to Schwe, "Even in a toy's most primitive stage of development, . . . you see children's creativity in responding to challenges, their satisfaction when a problem is solved or simply their delight when they are having fun" (Schlegel, 2000, p. 50). In addition to conducting experiments and focus groups at different stages of a toy's development, Schwe also assesses the age appropriateness of a toy. Most of her current work focuses on 3- to 5-year-old children. (Source: Schlegel, 2000, pp. 50–51)

Helen Schwe, a developmental psychologist, with some of the toys she designed for her current work on teaching foreign languages to children.

For more information about what researchers do, see page 44 in the Careers in Child Development appendix following Chapter 1.

Like scientists, children ask fundamental questions about reality and seek answers to problems that seem utterly trivial or unanswerable to other people (such as, Why is the sky blue?). Do children generate hypotheses, perform experiments, and reach conclusions about their data in ways resembling those of scientists?

Scientific reasoning often is aimed at identifying causal relationships. Like scientists, children place a great deal of emphasis on causal mechanisms (Martin & others, 2005). Their understanding of how events are caused weighs more heavily in their causal inferences than even such strong influences as whether the cause happened immediately before the effect.

There also are important differences between the reasoning of children and the reasoning of scientists (Abruscato & DeRosa, 2010). Children are more influenced by happenstance events than by an overall pattern, and children tend to maintain their old theories regardless of the evidence (Kuhn, Schauble, & Garcia-Mila, 1992). Children might go through mental gymnastics trying to reconcile seemingly contradictory new information with their existing beliefs. For example, after learning about the solar system, children sometimes conclude that there are two Earths, the seemingly flat world in which they live and the round ball floating in space that their teacher described.

Children also have difficulty designing experiments that can distinguish among alternative causes (Kuhn, 2011; Kuhn & others, 2008). Instead, they tend to bias the experiments in favor of whatever hypothesis they began with. Sometimes they see the results as supporting their original hypothesis even when the results directly contradict it (Schauble, 1996). Thus, although there are important similarities between

Pete Karpyk, who teaches chemistry in Weirton, West Virginia, uses an extensive array of activities that bring science alive for students. Here he has shrink-wrapped himself to demonstrate the effects of air pressure. He has some students give chemistry demonstrations at elementary schools and has discovered that in some cases students who don't do well on tests excel when they teach children. He also adapts his teaching based on feedback from former students and incorporates questions from their college chemistry tests as bonus questions on the tests he gives his high school students. (Source: Wong Briggs, 2005. p. 6D).

children and scientists, in their basic curiosity and in the kinds of questions they ask, there are also important differences in the degree to which they can separate theory and evidence and in their ability to design conclusive experiments (Lehrer & Schauble, 2006).

Too often, the skills scientists use, such as careful observation, graphing, self-regulatory thinking, and knowing when and how to apply one's knowledge to solve problems, are not routinely taught in schools. Children have many concepts that are incompatible with science and reality. Good teachers perceive and understand a child's underlying scientific concepts, then use the concepts as a scaffold for learning (Kuhn, 2011; Magnusson & Palinscar, 2005). Effective science teaching helps children distinguish between fruitful errors and misconceptions, and detect plainly wrong ideas that need to be replaced by more accurate conceptions (van der Broek, 2010).

Solving Problems   Children face many problems, both in school and out of school. *Problem solving* involves finding an appropriate way to attain a goal. Let's examine two ways children solve problems—by applying rules and by using analogies—and then consider some ways to help children learn effective strategies for solving problems.

Using Rules to Solve Problems   During early childhood, the relatively stimulus-driven toddler is transformed into a child capable of flexible, goal-directed problem solving (Zelazo & Muller, 2004). One element in this change is children's developing ability to form representations of reality.

For example, because they lack a concept of perspectives, 3- to 4-year-olds cannot understand that a single stimulus can be redescribed in a different, incompatible way (Perner & others, 2002). Consider a problem in which children must sort stimuli using the rule of *color.* In the course of the color sorting, a child may describe a red rabbit as a *red one* to solve the problem. However, in a subsequent task, the child may need to discover a rule that describes the rabbit as just a *rabbit* to solve the problem. If 3- to 4-year-olds fail to understand that it is possible to provide multiple descriptions of the same stimulus, they persist in describing the stimulus as a red rabbit. In other words, the 3- to 4-year-olds show representational inflexibility. Researchers have found that at about 4 years of age, children acquire the concept of perspectives, which allows them to appreciate that a single thing can be described in different ways (Frye, 1999).

With age, children also learn better rules to apply to problems (Williamson, Jaswal, & Meltzoff, 2010). Figure 7.13 provides an example; it shows the balance scale problem that has been used to examine children's use of rules in solving problems. The scale includes a fulcrum and an arm that can rotate around it. The arm can tip left or right or remain level, depending on how weights (metal disks with

FIGURE **7.13**

THE TYPE OF BALANCE SCALE USED BY SIEGLER (1976). Weights could be placed on pegs on each side of the fulcrum; the torque (the weight on each side times the distance of that weight from the fulcrum) determined which side would go down.

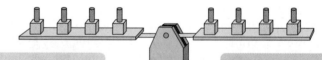

Rule I. If the weight is the same on both sides, predict that the scale will balance. If the weight differs, predict that the side with more weight will go down.

Rule II. If the weight is greater on one side, say that that side will go down. If the weights on the two sides are equal, choose the side on which the weight is farther from the fulcrum.

Balance scale apparatus

Rule III. Act as in Rule II, except that if one side has more weight and the weight on the other side is farther from the fulcrum, then guess.

Rule IV. Proceed as in Rule III, unless one side has more weight and the other more distance. In that case, calculate torques by multiplying weight times distance on each side. Then predict that the side with the greater torque will go down.

holes in the center) are arranged on the pegs in each side of the fulcrum. The child's task is to look at the configuration of weights on the pegs in each problem and then predict whether the left side will go down, the right side will go down, or the arm will balance.

Robert Siegler (1976) hypothesized that children would use one of the four rules listed in Figure 7.13. He reasoned that presenting problems on which different rules would generate different outcomes would allow assessment of each child's rules. Through a child's pattern of correct answers and errors on a set of such problems, that child's underlying rule could be inferred.

What were the results? Almost all 5-year-olds used Rule I, in which the child considers only the weight on the scales. Almost all 9-year-olds used either Rule II or Rule III, which takes both weight and distance into account, or Rule III, which calls for guessing when the weight and distance dimensions would give conflicting information. Both 13-year-olds and 17-year-olds generally used Rule III.

In other words, the older children performed better at solving the problems because they used a better rule. But even 5-year-old children can be trained to use Rule III if they are taught to pay attention to differences in distance. As children learn more about what is relevant to a problem, and learn to encode the relevant information, their ability to use rules in problem solving improves.

Interestingly, despite the 17-year-olds' having studied balance scales in their physics course, almost none of them used the only rule that generated consistently correct answers, Rule IV. Discussions with their teachers revealed why: The balance scale the students had studied was a pan balance, on which small pans could be hung from various locations along the arm, rather than an arm balance, with pegs extending upward. Retesting the children showed that most could consistently solve the problems when the familiar pan balance was used. This example illustrates a set of lessons that frequently emerge from studies of problem solving—learning is often quite narrow, generalization beyond one's existing knowledge is difficult, and even analogies that seem straightforward are often missed.

Using Analogies to Solve Problems An *analogy* involves correspondence in some respects between things that are dissimilar. Even very young children can draw reasonable analogies under some circumstances and use them to solve problems (Freeman & Gehl, 1995). Under other circumstances, even college students fail to draw seemingly obvious analogies (as in the high school students' difficulty in extrapolating from the familiar pan balance to the unfamiliar arm balance).

In one effort to discover developmental changes in young children's analogical problem solving, Judy DeLoache (1989) created a situation in which 2½- and 3-year-olds were shown a small toy hidden within a scale model of a room. The child was then asked to find the toy in a real room that was a bigger version of the scale model. If the toy was hidden under the armchair in the scale model, it was also hidden under the armchair in the real room. Considerable development occurred between 2½ and 3 years of age on this task. Thirty-month-old children rarely could solve the problem, but most 36-month-old children could.

Why was the task so difficult for the 2½-year-olds? Their problem was not an inability to understand that a symbol can represent another situation. Shown line drawings or photographs of the larger room, 2½-year-olds had no difficulty finding the object. Instead, the difficulty seemed to come from the toddlers' simultaneously viewing the scale model as a symbol of the larger room and as an object in itself. When children were allowed to play with the scale model before using it as a symbol, their performance worsened, presumably because playing with it made them think of it more as an object in itself. Conversely, when the scale model was placed in a glass case, where the children could not handle it at all, more children used it successfully to find the object hidden in the larger room. The general lesson is that young children can use a variety of tools to draw analogies, but they easily can forget that an object is being used as a symbol of something else and instead treat it as an object in its own right (DeLoache, 2004).

Judy DeLoache (*left*) has conducted research that focuses on young children's developing cognitive abilities. She has demonstrated that children's symbolic representation between 2½ and 3 years of age enables them to find a toy in a real room that is a much bigger version of the scale model.

Helping Children Learn Strategies

In Michael Pressley's view (Pressley, 2003, 2007; Pressley & Hilden, 2006), the key to education is helping students learn a rich repertoire of strategies for solving problems. Pressley argues that when children are given instruction about effective strategies, they often can apply strategies that they had not used on their own. Pressley emphasizes that children benefit when the teacher (1) models the appropriate strategy, (2) verbalizes the steps in the strategy, and (3) guides the children to practice the strategy and supports their practice with feedback. "Practice" means that children use the strategy over and over until they perform it automatically. To execute strategies effectively, they need to have the strategies in long-term memory, and extensive practice makes this possible.

Just having children learn a new strategy is usually not enough for them to continue to use it and to transfer the strategy to new situations. Children need to be motivated to learn and to use the strategies. For effective maintenance and transfer, children should be encouraged to monitor the effectiveness of the new strategy by comparing their performance on tests and other assessments.

Let's examine an example of effective strategy instruction. Good readers extract the main ideas from text and summarize them. In contrast, novice readers (for example, most children) usually don't store the main ideas of what they read. One intervention based on what is known about the summarizing strategies of good readers consisted of instructing children to (1) skim over trivial information, (2) ignore redundant information, (3) replace less inclusive terms with more inclusive ones, (4) use a more inclusive action term to combine a series of events, (5) choose a topic sentence, and (6) create a topic sentence if none is given (Brown & Day, 1983). Instructing elementary school students to use these summarizing strategies improves their reading performance (Rinehart, Stahl, & Erickson, 1986).

Pressley and his colleagues (Pressley & Harris, 2006; Pressley & Hilden, 2006; Pressley & others, 2001, 2003, 2004; 2007) have spent considerable time in recent years observing the use of strategy instruction

What are some effective ways that teachers can help students learn to develop a rich repertoire of strategies for solving problems?

by teachers and strategy use by students in elementary and secondary school classrooms. They conclude that teachers' use of strategy instruction is far less complete and intense than what is needed for students to learn how to use strategies effectively. They argue that education needs to be restructured so that students are provided with more opportunities to become competent strategic learners.

How do the research findings of Peter Ornstein and his colleagues regarding teachers' use of strategy suggestions or metacognitive questions in the classroom (mentioned earlier in this chapter) compare with Pressley and his colleagues' findings about teaching strategies?

Using Strategies to Solve Problems Good thinkers routinely use strategies and effective planning to solve problems (Bjorklund, Dukes, & Brown, 2009). Do children use one strategy or multiple strategies in problem solving? They often use more than one strategy (Pressley, 2007).

Most children benefit from generating a variety of alternative strategies and experimenting with different approaches to a problem, discovering what works well, when, and where. This is especially true for children from the middle elementary school grades on, although some cognitive psychologists stress that even young children should be encouraged to practice varying strategies (Siegler & Alibali, 2005). To read further about guiding children to learn effective strategies, see the *Caring Connections* interlude.

ADOLESCENCE

Two important aspects of thinking in adolescence are critical thinking and decision making. The ability to think critically and make competent decisions increases in adolescence. However, adolescents don't always deploy these important advances in cognitive skills in real-world contexts, especially in emotionally tense situations and in the presence of peer pressure.

Critical Thinking In one study of fifth-, eighth-, and eleventh-graders, critical thinking increased with age, but still occurred only in 43 percent of eleventh-graders. Many adolescents showed self-serving biases in their thinking.

Adolescence is an important transitional period in the development of critical thinking (Keating, 1990). Among the cognitive changes that allow improved critical thinking during this period are the following:

- Increased speed, automaticity, and capacity of information processing, which free cognitive resources for other purposes
- Greater breadth of content knowledge in a variety of domains
- Increased ability to construct new combinations of knowledge
- A greater range and more spontaneous use of strategies and procedures for obtaining and applying knowledge, such as planning, considering the alternatives, and cognitive monitoring

Although adolescence is an important period in the development of critical-thinking skills, if a solid basis of fundamental skills (such as literacy and math skills) was not developed during childhood, critical-thinking skills are unlikely to develop adequately in adolescence.

Decision Making Adolescence is a time of increased decision making: which friends to choose; which person to date; whether to have sex, buy a car, go to college, and so on (Sunstein, 2008). How competent are adolescents at making decisions? Older adolescents are described as more competent than younger adolescents, who in turn are more competent than children (Keating, 1990). Compared with children, young adolescents are more likely to generate different options, examine a situation from a variety of perspectives, anticipate the consequences of decisions, and consider the credibility of sources.

How do emotions and social contexts influence adolescents' decision making?

Most people make better decisions when they are calm rather than emotionally aroused. That may be especially true for adolescents, who have a tendency to be emotionally intense. The same adolescent who makes a wise decision when calm may make an unwise decision when emotionally aroused (Paus, 2009; Steinberg, 2009). In the heat of the moment, emotions may overwhelm decision-making ability.

The social context plays a key role in adolescent decision making. For example, adolescents' willingness to make risky decisions is more likely to occur in contexts where substances and other temptations are readily available (Reyna & Rivers, 2008). Recent research reveals that the presence of peers in risk-taking situations increases the likelihood that adolescents will make risky decisions (Steinberg, 2008).

Adolescents need more opportunities to practice and discuss realistic decision making. Many real-world decisions on matters such as sex, drugs, and daredevil driving occur in an atmosphere of stress that includes time constraints and emotional involvement. One strategy for improving adolescent decision making is to provide more opportunities for them to engage in role playing and peer group problem solving.

One proposal to explain adolescent decision making is the **dual-process model,** which states that decision making is influenced by two cognitive systems, one analytical and one experiential, which compete with each other (Klacyznski, 2001; Reyna & Farley, 2006). The dual-process model emphasizes that it is the experiential system—monitoring and managing actual experiences—that benefits adolescents' decision making, not the analytical system. In this view, adolescents don't benefit from engaging in reflective, detailed, higher-level cognitive analysis about a decision, especially in high-risk, real-world contexts. In such contexts, adolescents need to know that some circumstances are so dangerous that they must be avoided at all costs (Mills, Reyna, & Estrada, 2008). However, some experts on adolescent cognition argue that in many cases adolescents benefit from both analytical and experiential systems (Kuhn, 2009).

dual-process model States that decision-making is influenced by two systems, one analytical and one experiential, that compete with each other. In this model, it is the experiential system—monitoring and managing actual experiences—that benefits adolescent decision making.

Review *Connect* Reflect

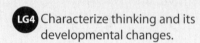 Characterize thinking and its developmental changes.

Review

- What is thinking?
- How does thinking develop in infancy?
- Can children engage in critical and scientific thinking? What are some ways that children solve problems?
- What are some important aspects of thinking in adolescence?

Connect

- In this section, you learned about a study that found a difference between boys' and girls' interests in particular categories of objects or activities. Why do researchers need to be careful about making conclusions regarding gender based on their findings?

Reflect *Your Own Personal Journey of Life*

- How good was your decision making in adolescence? What factors do you think contributed to whether you made good decisions during adolescence?

Metacognition LG5 Define metacognition and summarize its developmental changes.

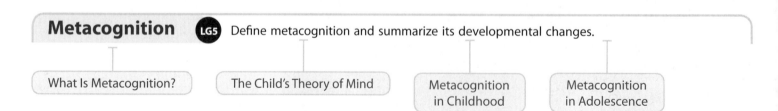

| What Is Metacognition? | The Child's Theory of Mind | Metacognition in Childhood | Metacognition in Adolescence |

As discussed earlier in this chapter, *metacognition* is cognition about cognition, or "knowing about knowing" (Flavell, 2004). It is a function of the central executive in Baddeley's model (see Figure 7.3).

WHAT IS METACOGNITION?

Metacognition helps children to perform many cognitive tasks more effectively (Efklides, 2009; Flavell, 2004). In one study, students were taught metacognitive skills to help them solve math problems (Cardelle-Elawar, 1992). In each of 30 daily lessons involving math story problems, a teacher guided low-achieving students to recognize when they did not know the meaning of a word, did not have all of the information necessary to solve a problem, did not know how to subdivide the problem into specific steps, or did not know how to carry out a computation. After the 30 daily lessons, the students who were given this metacognitive training had better math achievement and attitudes toward math.

Metacognition can take many forms. It includes knowledge about when and where to use particular strategies for learning or for solving problems. **Metamemory,** individuals' knowledge about memory, is an especially important form of metacognition. Metamemory includes general knowledge about memory, such as knowing that recognition tests (such as multiple-choice questions) are easier than recall tests (such as essay questions). It also encompasses knowledge about one's own memory, such as knowing whether you have studied enough for an upcoming test.

Cognitive developmentalist John Flavell (*left*) is a pioneer in providing insights about children's thinking. Among his many contributions are establishing the field of metacognition and conducting numerous studies in this area, including matamemory and theory of mind studies.

THE CHILD'S THEORY OF MIND

Even young children are curious about the nature of the human mind (Gelman, 2009). They have a **theory of mind,** which refers to awareness of one's own mental processes and the mental processes of others. Studies of theory of mind view the child as "a thinker who is trying to explain, predict, and understand people's thoughts, feelings, and utterances" (Harris, 2006, p. 847).

Developmental Changes Children's theory of mind changes as they develop through childhood (Doherty, 2009; Gelman, 2009; Wellman, 2011). Some changes occur quite early in development, as we see next.

From 18 months to 3 years of age, children begin to understand three mental states:

- *Perceptions.* By 2 years of age, children recognize that another person will see what's in front of her own eyes instead of what's in front of the child's eyes (Lempers, Flavell, & Flavell, 1977), and by 3 years of age, they realize that looking leads to knowing what's inside a container (Pratt & Bryant, 1990).

- *Emotions.* The child can distinguish between positive (for example, happy) and negative (sad, for example) emotions. A child might say, "Tommy feels bad."

- *Desires.* All humans have some sort of desires. But when do children begin to recognize that someone else's desires may differ from their own? Toddlers recognize that if people want something, they will try to get it. For instance, a child might say, "I want my mommy."

Two- to 3-year-olds understand the way that desires are related to actions and to simple emotions. For example, they understand that people will search for what they want and that if they obtain it, they are likely to feel happy, but if they don't they will keep searching for it and are likely to feel sad or angry (Wellman & Woolley, 1990). Children also refer to desires earlier and more frequently than they refer to cognitive states such as thinking and knowing (Bartsch & Wellman, 1995).

One of the landmark developments in understanding others' desires is recognizing that someone else may have different desires from one's own (Doherty, 2009; Wellman, 2011). Eighteen-month-olds understand that their own food preferences may not match the preferences of others—they will give an adult the food to which she says "Yummy!" even if the food is something that the infants detest (Repacholi & Gopnik, 1997). As they get older, they can verbalize that they themselves do not like something but an adult might (Flavell & others, 1992).

Between the ages of 3 and 5, children come to understand that the mind can represent objects and events accurately or inaccurately. The realization that people

metamemory Knowledge about memory.

theory of mind Awareness of one's own mental processes and the mental processes of others.

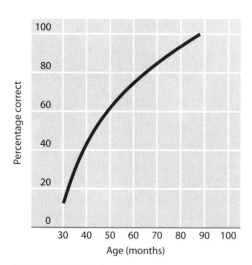

FIGURE **7.14**

**DEVELOPMENTAL CHANGES IN FALSE-
BELIEF PERFORMANCE.** False-belief
performance dramatically increases from 2½ years
of age through the middle of the elementary school
years. In a summary of the results of many studies,
2½-year-olds gave incorrect responses about
80 percent of the time (Wellman, Cross, & Watson,
2001). At 3 years, 8 months, they were correct about
50 percent of the time, and after that, gave
increasingly correct responses.

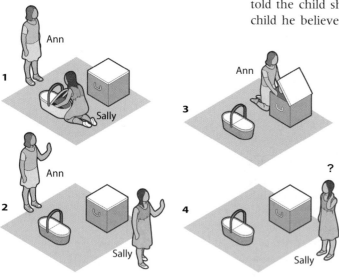

FIGURE **7.15**

THE SALLY AND ANN FALSE-BELIEF TASK. In the false-belief task, the
skit above in which Sally has a basket and Ann has a box is shown to children.
Sally places a toy in her basket and then leaves. While Sally is gone and can't
watch, Ann removes the toy from Sally's basket and places it in her box. Sally
then comes back and the children are asked where they think Sally will look for
her toy. Children are said to "pass" the false-belief task if they understand that
Sally looks in her basket first before realizing the toy isn't there.

can have *false beliefs*—beliefs that are not true—develops in a majority of children
by the time they are 5 years old (Wellman, Cross, & Watson, 2001) (see Figure 7.14).
This point is often described as a pivotal one in understanding the mind—recognizing
that beliefs are not just mapped directly into the mind from the surrounding
world, but also that different people can have different, and sometimes incorrect,
beliefs (Gelman, 2009). In a classic false-belief task, young children were shown a
Band-Aids box and asked what was inside (Jenkins & Astington, 1996). To the
children's surprise, the box actually contained pencils. When asked what a child
who had never seen the box would think was inside, 3-year-olds typically responded,
"Pencils." However, the 4- and 5-year-olds, grinning at the anticipation of the false
beliefs of other children who had not seen what was inside the box, were more
likely to say "Band-Aids."

In a similar task, children are told a story about Sally and Anne: Sally places a
toy in a basket and then leaves the room (see Figure 7.15). In her absence, Anne
takes the toy from the basket and places it in a box. Children are asked where Sally
will look for the toy when she returns. The major finding is that 3-year-olds tend
to fail false-belief tasks, saying that Sally will look in the box (even though Sally
could not know that the toy has moved to this new location). Four-year-olds and
older children tend to pass the task, correctly saying that Sally will have a "false
belief"—she will think the object is in the basket, even though that belief is now
false. The conclusion from these studies is that children younger than 4 years old
do not understand that it is possible to have a false belief.

It is only beyond the preschool years—at approximately 5 to 7 years of age—that
children have a deepening appreciation of the mind itself rather than just an understanding of mental states (Wellman, 2011). For example, they begin to recognize
that people's behaviors do not necessarily reflect their thoughts and feelings (Flavell,
Green, & Flavell, 1993). Not until middle and late childhood do children see the
mind as an active constructor of knowledge or a processing center (Flavell, Green,
& Flavell, 1998) and move from understanding that beliefs can be false to realizing
that the same event can be open to multiple interpretations (Carpendale & Chandler,
1996). For example, in one study, children saw an ambiguous line drawing (for
example, a drawing that could be seen as either a duck or a rabbit); one puppet
told the child she believed the drawing was a duck while another puppet told the
child he believed the drawing was a rabbit (see Figure 7.16). Before the age of 7,
children said that there was one right answer, and it was not
okay for both puppets to have different opinions.

While most research on children's theory of mind focuses on
children around or before their preschool years, at 7 years of age
and beyond there are important developments in the ability to
understand the beliefs and thoughts of others. Although understanding that people may have different interpretations is important, it is also necessary to recognize that some interpretations
and beliefs may still be evaluated on the basis of the merits of
arguments and evidence (Kuhn, Cheney, & Weinstock, 2000). In
early adolescence, children begin to understand that people can
have ambivalent feelings (Flavell & Miller, 1998). They start to
recognize that the same person can feel both happy and sad
about the same event. They also engage in more recursive thinking: thinking about what other people are thinking about.

Individual Differences As in other developmental research,
there are individual differences in the ages when children reach
certain milestones in their theory of mind. For example, children
who talk with their parents about feelings frequently as 2-year-
olds show better performance on theory of mind tasks (Ruffman,
Slade, & Crowe, 2002), as do children who frequently engage in
pretend play (Harris, 2000).

How Does Theory of Mind Differ in Children with Autism?

Approximately 1 in 150 children is estimated to have some sort of autism spectrum disorder (National Autism Association, 2010). Autism can usually be diagnosed by the age of 3 years, and sometimes earlier. Children with autism show a number of behaviors different from children their age, including deficits in social interaction and communication as well as repetitive behaviors or interests. They often show indifference toward others, in many instances preferring to be alone and showing more interest in objects than people. It now is accepted that autism is linked to genetic and brain abnormalities (Deeley & Murphy, 2009; Glessner & others, 2009).

Children and adults with autism have difficulty in social interactions. These deficits are generally greater than deficits in children the same mental age with mental retardation (Baron-Cohen, 2009, 2011). Researchers have found that children with autism have difficulty in developing a theory of mind, especially in understanding others' beliefs and emotions (Bertoglio & Hendren, 2009; Peterson & others, 2009). Although children with autism tend to do poorly reasoning in false-belief tasks (Peterson, 2005), they can perform much better on reasoning tasks requiring an understanding of physical causality.

In relation to theory of mind, however, it is important to consider the effects of individual variations in the abilities of children with autism (Harris, 2006). Children with autism are not a homogeneous group, and some have less severe social and communication problems than others. Thus, it is not surprising that children who have less severe forms of autism do better than those who have more severe forms of the disorder on some theory of mind tasks. For example, higher-functioning children with autism show reasonable progress in understanding others' desires (Harris, 2006). A further important consideration in thinking about autism and theory of mind is that children with autism might have

A young boy with autism. *What are some characteristics of children who are autistic? What are some deficits in their theory of mind?*

difficulty in understanding others' beliefs and emotions not solely due to theory of mind deficits but to other aspects of cognition such as problems in focusing attention or some general intellectual impairment (Renner, Grofer Klinger, & Klinger, 2006). Some recent theories of autism suggest that weaknesses in executive functioning may be related to the problems experienced by those with autism in performing theory of mind tasks. Other theories have pointed out that typically developing individuals process information by extracting the big picture, whereas those with autism process information in a very detailed, almost obsessive way. It may be that in autism, a number of different but related deficits lead to social cognitive deficits (Rajendran & Mitchell, 2007).

Executive function, which describes several functions (such as inhibition and planning) that are important for flexible, future-oriented behavior, also may be connected to theory of mind development (Doherty, 2009; Pellicano, 2010). For example, in one executive function task, children are asked to say the word "night" when they see a picture of a sun, and the word "day" when they see a picture of a moon and stars. Children who perform better at executive function tasks seem also to have a better understanding of theory of mind (Sabbagh & others, 2006).

Another individual difference in understanding the mind involves autism (Doherty, 2009). To learn how theory of mind differs in children with autism, see *Connecting Through Research*.

METACOGNITION IN CHILDHOOD

By 5 or 6 years of age, children usually know that familiar items are easier to learn than unfamiliar ones, that short lists are easier than long ones, that recognition is

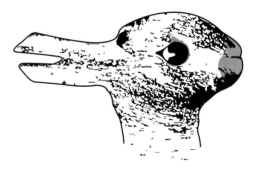

FIGURE 7.16
AMBIGUOUS LINE DRAWING

easier than recall, and that forgetting becomes more likely over time (Lyon & Flavell, 1993). However, in other ways young children's metamemory is limited. They don't understand that related items are easier to remember than unrelated ones or that remembering the gist of a story is easier than remembering information verbatim (Kreutzer & Flavell, 1975). By fifth grade, students understand that gist recall is easier than verbatim recall.

Preschool children also have an inflated opinion of their memory abilities. For example, in one study, a majority of preschool children predicted that they would be able to recall all 10 items of a list of 10 items. When tested, none of the young children managed this feat (Flavell, Friedrichs, & Hoyt, 1970). As they move through the elementary school years, children give more realistic evaluations of their memory skills (Schneider & Pressley, 1997).

Preschool children also have little appreciation for the importance of cues to memory, such as "It helps when you can think of an example of it." By 7 or 8 years of age, children better appreciate the importance of cueing for memory. In general, children's understanding of their memory abilities and their skill in evaluating their performance on memory tasks is relatively poor at the beginning of the elementary school years but improves considerably by 11 to 12 years of age (Bjorklund & Rosenbaum, 2000).

METACOGNITION IN ADOLESCENCE

Important changes in metacognition take place during adolescence (Kuhn, 2008, 2009). Compared with when they were children, adolescents have an increased capacity to monitor and manage cognitive resources to effectively meet the demands of a learning task. This increased metacognitive ability results in cognitive functioning and learning becoming more effective.

An important aspect of cognitive functioning and learning is determining how much attention will be allocated to an available resource. Evidence is accumulating that adolescents have a better understanding of how to effectively deploy their attention to different aspects of a task than children do (Kuhn, 2009). Further, adolescents have a better meta-level understanding of strategies—that is, knowing the best strategy to use and when to use it in performing a learning task.

Keep in mind, though, that there is considerable individual variation in adolescents' metacognition. Indeed, some experts argue that individual variation in metacognition becomes much more pronounced in adolescence than in childhood (Kuhn, 2008, 2009). Thus, some adolescents are quite good at using metacognition to improve their learning, others far less effective.

Review *Connect* Reflect

 LG5 Define metacognition and summarize its developmental changes.

Review

- What is metacognition?
- What is theory of mind? How does children's theory of mind change developmentally?
- How does metacognition change during childhood?

Connect

- Compare the classic false-belief task study you learned about in this section with what you learned about A-not-B error studies in Chapter 6. What is similar and what is different about these studies and what they are assessing?

Reflect *Your Own Personal Journey of Life*

- Do you remember your teachers ever instructing you in ways to improve your use of metacognition—that is, your "knowing about knowing" and "thinking about thinking," when you were in elementary and secondary school? To help you to think further about this question, connect the discussion of metacognition that you just read with the discussion of strategies earlier in the chapter.

Information Processing

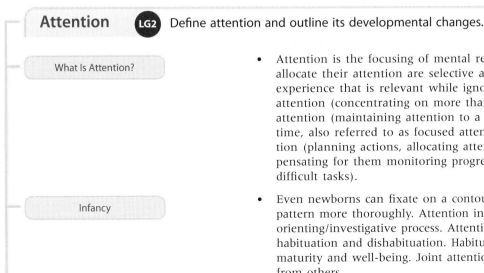

The Information-Processing Approach LG1 Explain the information-processing approach.

The Information-Processing Approach to Development

- The information-processing approach analyzes how individuals manipulate information, monitor it, and create strategies for handling it. Attention, memory, and thinking are involved in effective information processing. The computer has served as a model for how humans process information. In the information-processing approach, children's cognitive development results from their ability to overcome processing limitations by increasingly executing basic operations, expanding information-processing capacity, and acquiring new knowledge and strategies.

Cognitive Resources: Capacity and Speed of Processing Information

- Capacity and speed of processing information, often referred to as cognitive resources, increase across childhood and adolescence. Changes in the brain serve as biological foundations for developmental changes in cognitive resources. In terms of capacity, the increase is reflected in older children being able to hold in mind several dimensions of a topic simultaneously. A reaction-time task has often been used to assess speed of processing. Processing speed continues to improve in early adolescence.

Mechanisms of Change

- According to Siegler, three important mechanisms of change are encoding (how information gets into memory), automaticity (ability to process information with little or no effort), and strategy construction (creation of new procedures for processing information). Children's information processing is characterized by self-modification, and an important aspect of this self-modification involves metacognition—that is, knowing about knowing.

Comparisons with Piaget's Theory

- Unlike Piaget, the information-processing approach does not see development as occurring in distinct stages. Instead, this approach holds that individuals develop a gradually increasing capacity for processing information, which allows them to develop increasingly complex knowledge and skills. Like Piaget's theory, some versions of the information-processing approach are constructivist—they see children directing their own cognitive development.

Attention LG2 Define attention and outline its developmental changes.

What Is Attention?

- Attention is the focusing of mental resources. Four ways that children can allocate their attention are selective attention (focusing on a specific aspect of experience that is relevant while ignoring others that are irrelevant); divided attention (concentrating on more than one activity at the same time); sustained attention (maintaining attention to a selected stimulus for a prolonged period of time, also referred to as focused attention and vigilance); and executive attention (planning actions, allocating attention to goals, detecting errors and compensating for them monitoring progress on tasks, and dealing with novel or difficult tasks).

Infancy

- Even newborns can fixate on a contour, but as infants get older they can scan a pattern more thoroughly. Attention in the first year of life is dominated by the orienting/investigative process. Attention in infancy is often studied through habituation and dishabituation. Habituation can provide a measure of an infant's maturity and well-being. Joint attention increases an infant's ability to learn from others.

Childhood	• Salient stimuli tend to capture the attention of the preschooler. After 6 or 7 years of age, there is a shift to more cognitive control of attention. Young children especially make advances in executive and sustained attention. Selective attention also improves through childhood. Children's attentional skills are increasingly being found to predict later cognitive competencies, such as school readiness.
Adolescence	• Adolescents typically have better attentional skills than children do, although there are wide individual differences in how effectively adolescents deploy their attention. Sustained attention and executive attention are especially important as adolescents are required to work on increasingly complex tasks that take longer to complete. Multi-tasking is an example of divided attention, and it can harm adolescents' attention when they are engaging in a challenging task.

Memory **LG3** Describe what memory is and how it changes.

What Is Memory?	• Memory is the retention of information over time. Psychologists study the processes of memory: how information is initially placed or encoded into memory, how it is retained or stored, and how it is found or retrieved for a certain purpose later. Short-term memory involves retaining information for up to 30 seconds, assuming there is no rehearsal of the information. Long-term memory is a relatively permanent and unlimited type of memory. Working memory is a kind of "mental workbench" where individuals manipulate and assemble information when they make decisions, solve problems, and comprehend written and spoken language. Many contemporary psychologists prefer the term *working memory* over *short-term memory*. Working memory is linked to children's reading comprehension and problem solving. People construct and reconstruct their memories. Schema theory states that people mold memories to fit the information that already exists in their minds. Fuzzy trace theory states that memory is best understood by considering two types of memory representation: (1) verbatim memory trace, and (2) fuzzy trace, or gist. According to this theory, older children's better memory is attributed to the fuzzy traces created by extracting the gist of information. Children's ability to remember new information about a subject depends extensively on what they already know about it. The contribution of content knowledge is especially relevant in the memory of experts. Experts have a number of characteristics that can explain why they solve problems better than novices do.
Infancy	• Infants as young as 2 to 3 months of age display implicit memory, which is memory without conscious recollection, as in memory of perceptual-motor skills. However, many experts stress that explicit memory, which is the conscious memory of facts and experiences, does not emerge until the second half of the first year of life. Older children and adults remember little if anything from the first three years of their lives.
Childhood	• Young children can remember a great deal of information if they are given appropriate cues and prompts. One method of assessing short-term memory is with a memory-span task, on which there are substantial developmental changes through the childhood years. Children's memory improves in the elementary school years as they begin to use gist more, acquire more content knowledge and expertise, develop large memory spans, and use more effective strategies. Organization, elaboration, and imagery are important memory strategies. Current research focuses on how accurate children's long-term memories are and the implications of this accuracy for children as eyewitnesses.
Adolescence	• Short-term memory, as assessed in memory span, increases during adolescence. Working memory also increases in adolescence.

Thinking **LG4** Characterize thinking and its developmental changes.

What Is Thinking?

- Thinking involves manipulating and transforming information in memory. We can think about the past, reality, and fantasy. Thinking helps us reason, reflect, evaluate, solve problems, and make decisions.

Infancy

- Studies of thinking in infancy focus on concept formation and categorization. Concepts are categories that group objects, events, and characteristics on the basis of common properties. Infants form concepts early in their development, with perceptual categorization appearing as early as 3 months of age. Mandler argues that it is not until about 7 to 9 months of age that infants form conceptual categories. Infants' first concepts are broad. Over the first two years of life, these broad concepts gradually become more differentiated.

Childhood

- Critical thinking involves thinking reflectively and productively, and evaluating the evidence. Mindfulness is an important aspect of critical thinking. A lack of emphasis on critical thinking in schools is a special concern. Children and scientists think alike in some ways, but not alike in others. Problem solving relies on the use of strategies, rules, and analogies. Even young children can use analogies to solve problems in some circumstances.

Adolescence

- Two important aspects of adolescent thinking are critical thinking and decision making. Adolescence is an important transitional period in critical thinking because of cognitive changes such as increased speed, automaticity, and capacity of information processing; broadening of content knowledge; increased ability to construct new combinations of knowledge; and a greater range and spontaneous use of strategies. Older adolescents make better decisions than younger adolescents, who in turn are better at this than children are. Being able to make competent decisions, however, does not mean actually making them in everyday life, where breadth of experience comes into play. Adolescents often make better decisions when they are calm than when they are emotionally aroused. Social contexts, especially the presence of peers, influence adolescent decision making. The dual-process model has been advanced to explain the nature of adolescent decision making.

Metacognition **LG5** Define metacognition and summarize its developmental changes.

What Is Metacognition?

The Child's Theory of Mind

- Metacognition is cognition about cognition, or knowing about knowing.

- Theory of mind refers to a child's awareness of his or her own mental processes and the mental processes of others. Young children are curious about the human mind, and this has been studied under the topic of theory of mind. A number of developmental changes characterize children's theory of mind. For example, by 5 years of age most children realize that people can have false beliefs—beliefs that are untrue. Individual variations also are involved in theory of mind. For example, autistic children have difficulty in developing a theory of mind.

Metacognition in Childhood

- Metamemory improves in middle and late childhood. As children progress through the elementary school years, they make more realistic judgments about their memory skills and increasingly understand the importance of memory cues.

Metacognition in Adolescence

- Adolescents have an increased capacity to monitor and manage resources to effectively meet the demands of a learning task, although there is considerable individual variation in metacognition during adolescence.

key terms

key people

chapter 8 INTELLIGENCE

Shiffy Landa, a first-grade teacher at H. F. Epstein Hebrew Academy in St. Louis, Missouri, uses the multiple-intelligences approach of Howard Gardner (1983, 1993) in her classroom. Gardner argues that there is not just one general type of intelligence but at least eight specific types.

Landa (2000, pp. 6–8) believes that the multiple-intelligences approach is the best way to reach children because they have many different kinds of abilities. In Landa's words,

> My role as a teacher is quite different from the way it was just a few years ago. No longer do I stand in front of the room and lecture to my students. I consider my role to be one of a facilitator rather than a frontal teacher. The desks in my room are not all neatly lined up in straight rows . . . students are busily working in centers in cooperative learning groups, which gives them the opportunity to develop their interpersonal intelligences.

Landa explains that students use their "body-kinesthetic intelligence to form the shapes of the letters as they learn to write. . . . They also use this intelligence to move the sounds of the vowels that they are learning, blending them together with letters, as they begin to read."

Landa believes that "intrapersonal intelligence is an intelligence that often is neglected in the traditional classroom." In her classroom, students "complete their own evaluation sheets after they have concluded their work at the centers. They evaluate their work and create their own portfolios," in which they keep their work so they can see their progress.

As she was implementing the multiple-intelligences approach in her classroom, Landa recognized that she needed to educate parents about it. She created a parent education class called The Parent-Teacher Connection, which meets periodically to view videos, talk about multiple intelligences, and discuss how they are being introduced in the classroom. She also sends a weekly newsletter to parents, informing them about the week's multiple-intelligences activities and students' progress.

preview

Shiffy Landa's classroom techniques build on Howard Gardner's multiple-intelligences theory, one of the theories of intelligence that we will explore in this chapter. You will see that there is spirited debate about whether people have a general intelligence or a number of specific intelligences. The concept of intelligence also has generated other controversies, including whether intelligence is more strongly influenced by heredity or by environment, whether there is cultural bias in intelligence testing, and whether intelligence tests are misused. We will explore these controversies in this chapter, and we will trace the development of intelligence from infancy through adolescence. Finally, we will look at the extremes of intelligence and creativity.

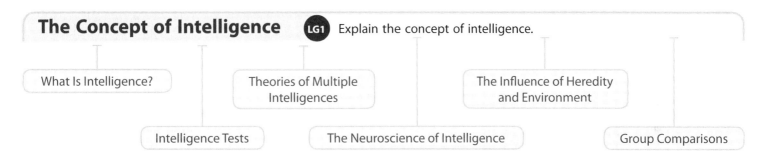

The Concept of Intelligence   **LG1**   Explain the concept of intelligence.

- What Is Intelligence?
- Theories of Multiple Intelligences
- The Influence of Heredity and Environment
- Intelligence Tests
- The Neuroscience of Intelligence
- Group Comparisons

Intelligence is one of our most prized attributes. However, even the most intelligent people do not agree on how to define it and how to measure it.

WHAT IS INTELLIGENCE?

What does the term *intelligence* mean to psychologists? Some experts describe intelligence as the ability to solve problems. Others describe it as the capacity to adapt and learn from experience. Still others argue that intelligence includes characteristics such as creativity and interpersonal skills.

The problem with intelligence is that, unlike height, weight, and age, intelligence cannot be directly measured. We can't peel back a person's scalp and see how much intelligence he or she has. We can evaluate intelligence only *indirectly* by studying and comparing the intelligent acts that people perform.

The primary components of intelligence are similar to the cognitive processes of memory and thinking that we discussed in Chapter 7. The differences in how these cognitive processes are described, and how we will discuss intelligence, lie in the concepts of individual differences and assessment. *Individual differences* are the stable, consistent ways in which people differ from one another. Individual differences in intelligence generally have been measured by intelligence tests designed to tell us whether a person can reason better than others who have taken the test.

We will use as our definition of **intelligence** the ability to solve problems and to adapt and learn from experiences. But even this broad definition doesn't satisfy everyone. As you will see shortly, Howard Gardner proposes that musical skills should be considered part of intelligence. Also, a definition of intelligence based on a theory such as Vygotsky's, which we discussed in Chapter 6, would have to include the ability to use the tools of the culture with help from more-skilled individuals. Because intelligence is such an abstract, broad concept, it is not surprising that there are different ways to define it.

> As many people, as many minds, each in his own way.
>
> —**TERENCE**
> *Roman Playwright, 2nd Century B.C.*

developmental connection

Information Processing. The information processing approach emphasizes how children manipulate, monitor, and create strategies for handling information. Chapter 7, p. 201

intelligence The ability to solve problems and to adapt to and learn from experiences.

Alfred Binet constructed the first intelligence test after being asked to create a measure to determine which children could benefit from instruction in France's schools and which could not.

INTELLIGENCE TESTS

The two main intelligence tests that are administered to children on an individual basis today are the Stanford-Binet test and the Wechsler scales. As you will see next, an early version of the Binet was the first intelligence test to be devised.

The Binet Tests In 1904, the French Ministry of Education asked psychologist Alfred Binet to devise a method of identifying children who were unable to learn in school. School officials wanted to reduce crowding by placing in special schools students who did not benefit from regular classroom teaching. Binet and his student Theophile Simon developed an intelligence test to meet this request. The test is called the 1905 Scale. It consisted of 30 questions, ranging from the ability to touch one's ear to the abilities to draw designs from memory and define abstract concepts.

Binet developed the concept of **mental age (MA),** an individual's level of mental development relative to others. In 1912, William Stern created the concept of **intelligence quotient (IQ),** which refers to a person's mental age divided by chronological age (CA), multiplied by 100. That is, $IQ = MA/CA \times 100$.

If mental age is the same as chronological age, then the person's IQ is 100. If mental age is above chronological age, then IQ is more than 100. For example, a 6-year-old with a mental age of 8 would have an IQ of 133. If mental age is below chronological age, then IQ is less than 100. For example, a 6-year-old with a mental age of 5 would have an IQ of 83.

The Binet test has been revised many times to incorporate advances in the understanding of intelligence and intelligence testing. These revisions are called the *Stanford-Binet tests* (because the revisions were made at Stanford University). By administering the test to large numbers of people of different ages from different backgrounds, researchers have found that scores on a Stanford-Binet test approximate a normal distribution (see Figure 8.1). A **normal distribution** is symmetrical, with a majority of the scores falling in the middle of the possible range of scores and few scores appearing toward the extremes of the range.

The current Stanford-Binet test is administered individually to people aged 2 through adult. It includes a variety of items, some of which require verbal responses, others nonverbal responses. For example, items that reflect a typical 6-year-old's level of performance on the test include the verbal ability to define at least six words, such as *orange* and *envelope*, as well as the nonverbal ability to trace a path through a maze. Items that reflect an average adult's level of performance include defining such words as *disproportionate* and *regard*, explaining a proverb, and comparing idleness and laziness.

The fourth edition of the Stanford-Binet was published in 1985. One important addition to this version was the analysis of the individual's responses in terms of four functions: verbal reasoning, quantitative reasoning, abstract visual reasoning,

mental age (MA) An individual's level of mental development relative to others.

intelligence quotient (IQ) An individual's mental age divided by chronological age and multiplied by 100; devised in 1912 by William Stern.

normal distribution A symmetrical distribution with a majority of the cases falling in the middle of the possible range of scores and few scores appearing toward the extremes of the range.

FIGURE **8.1**

THE NORMAL CURVE AND STANDARD-BINET IQ SCORES. The distribution of IQ scores approximates a normal curve. Most of the population falls in the middle range of scores. Notice that extremely high and extremely low scores are very rare. Slightly more than two-thirds of the scores fall between 84 and 116. Only about 1 in 50 individuals has an IQ of more than 132, and only about 1 in 50 individuals has an IQ of less than 68.

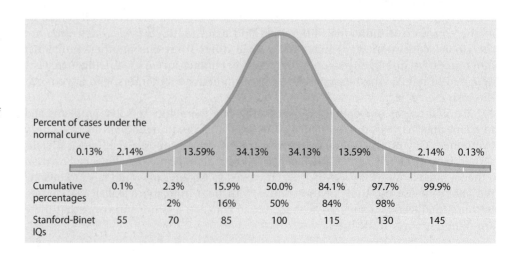

Percent of cases under the normal curve							
0.13%	2.14%	13.59%	34.13%	34.13%	13.59%	2.14%	0.13%
Cumulative percentages	0.1%	2.3%	15.9%	50.0%	84.1%	97.7%	99.9%
		2%	16%	50%	84%	98%	
Stanford-Binet IQs	55	70	85	100	115	130	145

and short-term memory. A general composite score is still obtained to reflect overall intelligence. The Stanford-Binet continues to be one of the most widely used tests to assess students' intelligence (Neukrug & Fawcett, 2010).

The Wechsler Scales   Another set of tests widely used to assess students' intelligence is called the *Wechsler scales,* developed by psychologist David Wechsler. They include the Wechsler Preschool and Primary Scale of Intelligence–Third Edition (WPPSI-III) to test children from 2 years 6 months to 7 years 3 months of age; the Wechsler Intelligence Scale for Children–Fourth Edition (WISC-IV) for children and adolescents 6 to 16 years of age; and the Wechsler Adult Intelligence Scale–Third Edition (WAIS-III).

The Wechsler scales not only provide an overall IQ score and scores on a number of subtests but also yield several composite indexes (for example, the Verbal Comprehension Index, the Working Memory Index, and the Processing Speed Index). The subtest and composite scores allows the examiner to quickly determine the areas in which the child is strong or weak. Three of the Wechsler subscales are shown in Figure 8.2.

Intelligence tests such as the Stanford-Binet and Wechsler are given on an individual basis. A psychologist approaches an individual assessment of intelligence as a structured interaction between the examiner and the child. This provides the psychologist with an opportunity to sample the child's behavior. During the testing, the examiner observes the ease with which rapport is established, the child's enthusiasm and interest, whether anxiety interferes with the child's performance, and the child's degree of tolerance for frustration.

The Use and Misuse of Intelligence Tests   Intelligence tests have real-world applications as predictors of school and job success (Brody, 2007). For example, scores on tests of general intelligence are substantially correlated with school grades and achievement test performance, both at the time of the test and years later (Brody, 2007). IQ in the sixth grade correlates about .60 with the number of years of education the individual will eventually obtain (Jencks, 1979). Intelligence tests also are moderately correlated with work performance (Lubinski, 2000).

Despite the links between IQ and academic achievement and occupational success, it is important to keep in mind that many other factors contribute to success in school and work. These include the motivation to succeed, physical and mental health, and social skills (Sternberg, 2009a).

The single number provided by many IQ tests can easily lead to false expectations about an individual (Rosnow & Rosenthal, 1996). Sweeping generalizations are too often made on the basis of an IQ score. IQ scores are misused and can become self-fulfilling prophecies (Weinstein, 2004).

To be effective, information about a child's performance on an intelligence test should be used in conjunction with other information about the child. For example, an intelligence test alone should not determine whether a child is placed in a special education or gifted class. The child's developmental history, medical background, performance in school, social competencies, and family experiences should be taken into account, too.

THEORIES OF MULTIPLE INTELLIGENCES

Is it more appropriate to think of a child's intelligence as a general ability or as a number of specific abilities? Psychologists have thought about this question since early in the twentieth century and continue to debate the issue.

Verbal Subscales

Similarities

A child must think logically and abstractly to answer a number of questions about how things might be similar.

Example: "In what way are a lion and a tiger alike?"

Comprehension

This subscale is designed to measure an individual's judgment and common sense.

Example: "What is the advantage of keeping money in a bank?"

Nonverbal Subscales

Block Design

A child must assemble a set of multicolored blocks to match designs that the examiner shows.
Visual-motor coordination, perceptual organization, and the ability to visualize spatially are assessed.

Example: "Use the four blocks on the left to make the pattern on the right."

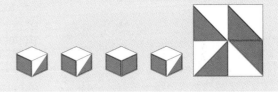

FIGURE **8.2**

SAMPLE SUBSCALES OF THE WECHSLER INTELLIGENCE SCALE FOR CHILDREN–FOURTH EDITION (WISC-IV). Simulated items similar to those in the *Wechsler Intelligence Scale for Children–* Fourth Edition (*WISC-IV*). Copyright © 2003 by NCS Pearson, Inc. Reproduced with permission. All rights reserved. *"Wechsler Intelligence Scale for Children" and "WISC"* are trademarks, in the US and/or other countries, of Pearson Education, Inc. or its affiliates.

"How are her scores?"
© Edward Koren/The New Yorker Collection/
www.cartoonbank.com

Robert J. Sternberg, who developed the triarchic theory of intelligence.

"You're wise, but you lack tree smarts."
© Donald Reilly/The New Yorker Collection/
www. cartoonbank.com

triarchic theory of intelligence Sternberg's theory that intelligence comes in three forms: analytical, creative, and practical.

Sternberg's Triarchic Theory According to Robert J. Sternberg's (1986, 2004, 2008, 2009b, d; 2010, c, d) **triarchic theory of intelligence,** intelligence comes in three forms: analytical, creative, and practical. *Analytical intelligence* involves the ability to analyze, judge, evaluate, compare, and contrast. *Creative intelligence* consists of the ability to create, design, invent, originate, and imagine. *Practical intelligence* focuses on the ability to use, apply, implement, and put into practice.

Sternberg (2009b, d; 2010c, d) says that students with different triarchic patterns look different in school. Students with high analytic ability tend to be favored in conventional schools. They often do well in classes in which the teacher lectures and gives objective tests. These students typically get good grades, do well on traditional IQ tests and the SAT, and later gain admission to competitive colleges.

Students high in creative intelligence often are not in the top rung of their class. Creatively intelligent students might not conform to teachers' expectations about how assignments should be done. They give unique answers, for which they might get reprimanded or marked down.

Like students high in creative intelligence, students who are practically intelligent often do not relate well to the demands of school. However, these students frequently do well outside the classroom's walls. Their social skills and common sense may allow them to become successful managers or entrepreneurs, despite undistinguished school records.

Sternberg (2004, 2010c, d) stresses that few tasks are purely analytic, creative, or practical. Most tasks require some combination of these skills. For example, when students write a book report, they might analyze the book's main themes, generate new ideas about how the book could have been written better, and think about how the book's themes can be applied to people's lives. Sternberg argues that it is important for classroom instruction to give students opportunities to learn through all three types of intelligence.

Sternberg (1998, 2009e, f) argues that wisdom is linked to both practical and academic intelligence. In his view, academic intelligence is a necessary but in many cases insufficient requirement for wisdom. Practical knowledge about the realities of life also is needed for wisdom. For Sternberg, balance between self-interest, the interests of others, and contexts produces a common good. Thus, wise individuals don't just look out for themselves—they also need to consider others' needs and perspectives, as well as the particular context involved. Sternberg assesses wisdom by presenting problems that require solutions highlighting various intrapersonal, interpersonal, and contextual interests. He also emphasizes that such aspects of wisdom should be taught in schools (Sternberg, 2009f; Sternberg, Jarvin, & Reznitskaya, 2009).

Gardner's Eight Frames of Mind As we indicated in the introduction to this chapter, Howard Gardner (1983, 1993, 2002) says there are many specific types of intelligence, or frames of mind. They are described here along with examples of the occupations in which they are reflected as strengths (Campbell, Campbell, & Dickinson, 2004):

- *Verbal skills:* The ability to think in words and to use language to express meaning. Occupations: Authors, journalists, speakers.
- *Mathematical skills*: The ability to carry out mathematical operations. Occupations: Scientists, engineers, accountants.
- *Spatial skills*: The ability to think three-dimensionally. Occupations: Architects, artists, sailors.
- *Bodily-kinesthetic skills*: The ability to manipulate objects and be physically adept. Occupations: Surgeons, craftspeople, dancers, athletes.
- *Musical skills*: A sensitivity to pitch, melody, rhythm, and tone. Occupations: Composers, musicians, and music therapists.
- *Intrapersonal skills*: The ability to understand oneself and effectively direct one's life. Occupations: Theologians, psychologists.

- *Interpersonal skills*: The ability to understand and effectively interact with others.
  Occupations: Successful teachers, mental health professionals.
- *Naturalist skills*: The ability to observe patterns in nature and understand natural and human-made systems.
  Occupations: Farmers, botanists, ecologists, landscapers.

Recently, Gardner has considered adding a ninth type of intelligence to his list of multiple intelligences—*existentialist*, which involves exploring and finding meaning in life, especially regarding questions about life, death, and existence.

Gardner argues that each form of intelligence can be destroyed by a different pattern of brain damage, that each involves unique cognitive skills, and that each shows up in unique ways in both the gifted and idiot savants (individuals who have mental retardation but have an exceptional talent in a particular domain, such as drawing, music, or numerical computation).

Let's look at a school that used Gardner's multiple intelligences as a foundation of its instruction. The Key School, a K–6 elementary school in Indianapolis, immerses students in activities involving a range of skills that closely correlate with Gardner's eight intelligences (Goleman, Kaufman, & Ray, 1993). Each day every student is exposed to materials designed to stimulate a range of human abilities, including art, music, language skills, math skills, and physical games. In addition, students devote attention to understanding themselves and others.

The Key School's goal is to allow students to discover their natural curiosity and talent, then let them explore these domains. Gardner underscores that if teachers give students opportunities to use their bodies, imaginations, and different senses, almost every student finds that he or she is good at something. Even students who are not outstanding in any single area will still find that they have relative strengths.

Children in the Key School form "pods" in which they pursue activities of special interest to them. Every day, each child can choose from activities that draw on Gardner's eight frames of mind. The school has pods that range from gardening to architecture to gliding to dancing.

Emotional Intelligence Both Gardner's and Sternberg's theories include one or more categories related to the ability to understand one's self and others and to get along in the world. In Gardner's theory, the categories are called interpersonal intelligence and intrapersonal intelligence; in Sternberg's theory, practical intelligence. Other theorists who emphasize interpersonal, intrapersonal, and practical aspects of intelligence focus on what is called *emotional intelligence*, which was popularized by Daniel Goleman (1995) in his book *Emotional Intelligence*.

The concept of emotional intelligence was initially developed by Peter Salovey and John Mayer (1990). They conceptualize **emotional intelligence** as the ability to perceive and express emotion accurately and adaptively (such as taking the perspective of others), to understand emotion and emotional knowledge (such as understanding the roles that emotions play in friendship and other relationships), to use feelings to facilitate thought (such as being in a positive mood, which is linked to creative thinking), and to manage emotions in oneself and others (such as being able to control one's anger).

There continues to be considerable interest in the concept of emotional intelligence (Rode & others, 2008). Critics argue that emotional intelligence broadens the concept of intelligence too far and has not been adequately assessed and researched (Matthews, Zeidner, & Roberts, 2006).

Do Children Have One Intelligence or Many Intelligences? Figure 8.3 compares the views of Gardner, Sternberg, and Salovey/Mayer. Notice that Gardner includes a number of types of intelligence not addressed by the other views, and

Gardner	Sternberg	Salovey/Mayer
Verbal Mathematical	Analytical	
Spatial Movement Musical	Creative	
Interpersonal Intrapersonal	Practical	Emotional
Naturalistic		

FIGURE 8.3

COMPARING STERNBERG'S, GARDNER'S, AND SALOVEY/MAYER'S INTELLIGENCES

emotional intelligence The ability to perceive and express emotion accurately and adaptively, to understand emotion and emotional knowledge, to use feelings to facilitate thought, and to manage emotions in oneself and others.

that Sternberg is unique in emphasizing creative intelligence. These theories of multiple intelligences have much to offer. They have stimulated us to think more broadly about what makes up people's intelligence and competence (Moran & Gardner, 2006). And they have motivated educators to develop programs that instruct students in different domains (Winner, 2006).

Theories of multiple intelligences have critics (Jensen, 2008) who conclude that the research base to support these theories has not yet developed. In particular, some argue that Gardner's classification seems arbitrary. For example, if musical skills represent a type of intelligence, why don't we also refer to chess intelligence, prizefighter intelligence, and so on?

A number of psychologists still support the concept of g (general intelligence) (Jensen, 2008; Johnson, te Nijenhuis, & Bouchard, 2008). For example, one expert on intelligence, Nathan Brody (2007), argues that people who excel at one type of intellectual task are likely to excel at other intellectual tasks. Thus, individuals who do well at memorizing lists of digits are also likely to be good at solving verbal problems and spatial layout problems. This general intelligence includes abstract reasoning or thinking, the capacity to acquire knowledge, and problem-solving ability (Carroll, 1993).

Advocates of the concept of general intelligence point to its success in predicting school and job performance (Deary & others, 2007). For example, scores on tests of general intelligence are substantially correlated with school grades and achievement test performance, both at the time of the test and years later (Strenze, 2007). And intelligence tests are moderately correlated with job performance (Lubinski, 2000). Individuals with higher scores on tests designed to measure general intelligence tend to get higher-paying, more prestigious jobs (Strenze, 2007). However, general IQ tests predict only about one-fourth of the variation in job success, with most variation being attributable to other factors such as motivation and education (Wagner & Sternberg, 1986).

Some experts who argue for the existence of general intelligence conclude that individuals also have specific intellectual abilities (Brody, 2007). In sum, controversy still characterizes whether it is more accurate to conceptualize intelligence as a general ability, specific abilities, or both (Brody, 2007; Horn, 2007; Sternberg, 2009a, b; 2010c, d). Sternberg (2009a, b; 2010c, d) actually accepts that there is a g for the kinds of analytical tasks that traditional IQ tests assess but thinks that the range of tasks those tests measure is far too narrow.

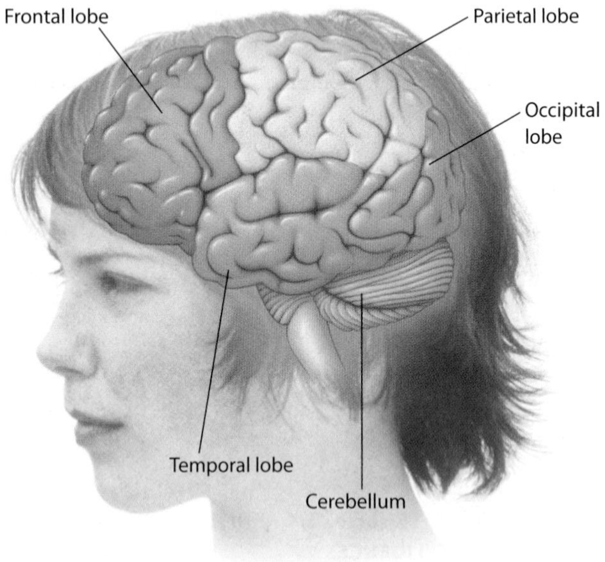

THE NEUROSCIENCE OF INTELLIGENCE

In the current era of extensive research on the brain, interest in the neuroscience underpinnings of intelligence has increased (Brans & others, 2010; Glascher & others, 2010; Haier, 2009; Neubauer & Fink, 2009). Among the questions asked about the brain's role in intelligence are the following: Is having a big brain linked to higher intelligence? Is intelligence located in certain brain regions? Is intelligence related to how fast the brain processes information?

Are individuals with a big brain more intelligent than those with a smaller brain? Recent studies using MRI scans to assess total brain volume indicate a moderate correlation (about +.3 to +.4) between brain size and intelligence (Carey, 2007; Luders & others, 2009).

Might intelligence be linked to specific regions of the brain? Early consensus was that the frontal lobes are the likely location of intelligence. However, researchers recently have found that intelligence is distributed more widely across brain regions (Haier, 2009; Karama & others, 2009; Luders & others, 2009). The most prominent finding from brain imaging studies is that a distributed neural network involving the frontal and parietal lobes is related to higher intelligence (Colom, Jung, & Haier, 2007; Colom & others, 2009; Deary, Penke, & Johnson, 2010; Glascher & others, 2010) (see Figure 8.4). Albert Einstein's total brain

---- →

developmental **connection**

Brain Development. The frontal lobes continue to develop through the adolescent and emerging adult years. Chapter 4, p. 119

← ----

FIGURE **8.4**

INTELLIGENCE AND THE BRAIN. Researchers have found that a higher level of intelligence is linked to a distributed neural network in the frontal and parietal lobes. To a lesser extent than the frontal/parietal network, the temporal and occipital lobes, as well as the cerebelllum, also have been found to have links to intelligence. The current consensus is that intelligence is likely to be distributed across brain regions rather than being localized in a specific region, such as the frontal lobes.

size was average, but a region of his brain's parietal lobe that is very active in processing math and spatial information was 15 percent larger than average (Witelson, Kigar, & Harvey, 1999). Other brain regions that have been linked to higher intelligence (although at a lower level of significance than the frontal/parietal lobe network) include the temporal and occipital lobes, as well as the cerebellum (Luders & others, 2009).

Examining the neuroscience of intelligence has also led to study of the role that neurological speed might play in intelligence (Waiter & others, 2009). Research results have not been consistent for this possible link, although one recent study did find that speed of neurological functioning was faster for intellectually gifted children than for children with average intelligence (Liu & others, 2007).

As the technology to study the brain's functioning continues to advance in coming decades, we are likely to see more specific conclusions about the brain's role in intelligence. As this research proceeds, keep in mind that both heredity and environment likely contribute to links between the brain and intelligence, including the connections we discussed between brain size and intelligence.

THE INFLUENCE OF HEREDITY AND ENVIRONMENT

We have seen that intelligence is a slippery concept with competing definitions, tests, and theories. It is not surprising, therefore, that attempts to understand the concept of intelligence are filled with controversy. One of the most controversial areas in the study of intelligence centers on the extent to which intelligence is influenced by genetics and the extent to which it is influenced by environment (Davis, Arden, & Plomin, 2008; Ruano & others, 2010; Sternberg, 2009a). In Chapter 2, we indicated how difficult it is to tease apart these influences, but that has not kept psychologists from trying to unravel them.

Genetic Influences To what degree do our genes make us smart? A research review found that the difference in the average correlations for identical and fraternal twins was not very high, only .15, (Grigorenko, 2000) (see Figure 8.5).

Adoption studies are also used in attempts to analyze the relative importance of heredity in intelligence (Plomin, DeFries, & Fulker, 2007). In most *adoption studies,* researchers determine whether the behavior of adopted children is more like that of their biological parents or their adoptive parents. In two studies, the educational levels attained by biological parents were better predictors of children's IQ scores than were the IQs of the children's adoptive parents (Petrill & Deater-Deckard, 2004; Scarr & Weinberg, 1983). But studies of adoption also document the influence of environments. For example, moving children into an adoptive family with a better environment than the child had in the past increased the children's IQs by an average of 12 points (Lucurto, 1990).

How strong is the effect of heredity on intelligence? The concept of heritability attempts to tease apart the effects of heredity and environment in a population. **Heritability** is the fraction of the variance within a population that is attributed to genetics. The heritability index is computed using correlational techniques. Thus, the highest degree of heritabilty is 1.00, and correlations of .70 and above suggest a strong genetic influence. A committee of respected researchers convened by the American Psychological Association concluded that by late adolescence, the heritability of intelligence is about .75, which reflects a strong genetic influence (Neisser & others, 1996).

A key point to keep in mind about heritability is that it refers to a specific group (population), *not* to individuals. Researchers use the concept of heritability to try to describe why people differ. Heritability says nothing about why a single individual, like yourself, has a certain intelligence. Nor does heritability say anything about differences *between* groups.

Most research on heredity and environment does not include environments that differ radically. Thus, it is not surprising that many genetic studies show environment to be a fairly weak influence on intelligence.

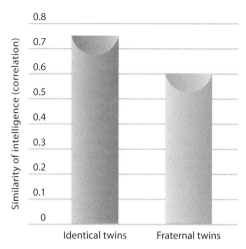

FIGURE **8.5**

CORRELATION BETWEEN INTELLIGENCE TEST SCORES AND TWIN STATUS. The graph represents a summary of research findings that have compared the intelligence test scores of identical and fraternal twins. An approximate .15 difference has been found, with a higher correlation for identical twins (.75) and a lower correlation for fraternal twins (.60).

developmental **connection**

Nature vs. Nurture. The epigenetic view emphasizes that development is an ongoing, bidirectional interchange between heredity and environment. Chapter 2, p. 71

heritability The fraction of the variance in a population that is attributed to genetics.

FIGURE **8.6**

THE INCREASE IN IQ SCORES FROM 1932 TO 1997. As measured by the Stanford-Binet intelligence test, American children seem to be getting smarter. Scores of a group tested in 1932 fell along a bell-shaped curve with half below 100 and half above. Studies show that if children took that same test today, half would score above 120 on the 1932 scale. Very few of them would score in the "intellectually deficient" end, on the left side, and about one-fourth would rank in the "very superior" range.

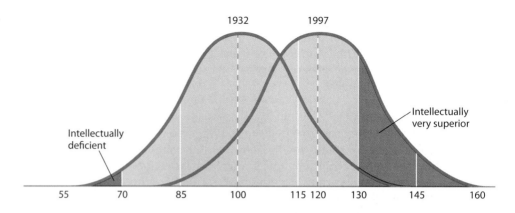

The heritability index has several flaws. It is only as good as the data that are entered into its analysis and the interpretations made from it. The data are virtually all from traditional IQ tests, which some experts believe are not always the best indicator of intelligence (Gardner, 2002; Sternberg, 2009a). Also, the heritability index assumes that we can treat genetic and environmental influences as factors that can be separated, with each part contributing a distinct amount of influence. As we discussed in Chapter 2, genes and the environment always work together. Genes always exist in an environment, and the environment shapes their activity.

Environmental Influences   Most experts today agree that the environment also plays an important role in intelligence (Campbell, 2007; Sternberg, 2010c, d; Zhang & Sternberg, 2011). This means that improving children's environments can raise their intelligence (Irvine & Berry, 2010; Tong & others, 2007). One argument for the importance of environment in intelligence involves the increasing scores on IQ tests around the world. Scores on these tests have been increasing so fast that a high percentage of people regarded as having average intelligence in the early 1900s would be considered below average in intelligence today (Flynn, 1999, 2007a, b) (see Figure 8.6). If a representative sample of today's children took the Stanford-Binet test used in 1932, about one-fourth would be defined as very superior, a label usually accorded to less than 3 percent of the population. Because the increase has taken place in a relatively short period of time, it can't be due to heredity. Rather, it might result from environmental factors such as increased exposure to information and education. A recent analysis indicated that the substantial increase in intelligence scores in recent years may be due to prenatal and early postnatal nutrition (Lynn, 2009). This worldwide increase in intelligence test scores over a short time frame is called the *Flynn effect*, after the researcher who discovered it, James Flynn (1999, 2007a, b).

Studies of schooling also reveal effects on intelligence (Ceci & Gilstrap, 2000; Gustafsson, 2007). The biggest effects occurred when large groups of children were deprived of formal education for an extended period, resulting in lower intelligence. In one study, the intellectual functioning of ethnic Indian children in South Africa, whose schooling was delayed by four years because of the unavailability of teachers, was investigated (Ramphal, 1962). Compared with children in nearby villages who had teachers, the Indian children whose entry into school was delayed by four years experienced a drop of 5 IQ points for each year of delay.

Researchers increasingly are interested in manipulating the early environment of children who are at risk for impoverished intelligence (Campbell, 2007; Sternberg, 2009a). The emphasis is on prevention rather than remediation. Many low-income parents have difficulty providing an intellectually stimulating environment for their children. Programs that educate parents to be more sensitive caregivers and better teachers, as well as support services such as quality child-care programs, can enhance a child's intellectual development.

Students in an elementary school in South Africa. *How might schooling influence the development of children's intelligence?*

The Abecedarian Project

In the Abecedarian Intervention program at the University of North Carolina at Chapel Hill, conducted by Craig Ramey and his colleagues (Ramey & Campbell, 1984; Ramey & Ramey, 1998; Ramey, Ramey, & Lanzi, 2006), 111 young children from low-income, poorly educated families were randomly assigned to either an intervention group, which received full-time, year-round child care along with medical and social work services, or a control group, which received medical and social benefits but no child care. The child-care program included game-like learning activities aimed at improving language, motor, social, and cognitive skills.

The success of the program in improving IQ was evident by the time the children were 3 years of age. At that age, the experimental group showed normal IQs averaging 101, a 17-point advantage over the control group. Recent follow-up results suggest that the effects are long-lasting. More than a decade later at 15, children from the intervention group maintained an IQ advantage of 5 points over the control-group children (97.7 to 92.6) (Campbell & others, 2001; Ramey, Ramey, & Lanzi, 2001). They also did better on standardized tests of reading and math and were less likely to be held back a year in school. Also, the greatest IQ gains were made by the children whose mothers had especially low IQs—below 70. At age 15, these children showed a 10-point IQ advantage over a group of children whose mothers' IQs were below 70 but who had not experienced the child-care intervention.

The results of the Abecedarian Intervention program are not unprecedented. A review of the research on early interventions reached the following conclusions (Brooks-Gunn, 2003):

- High-quality center-based interventions are associated with increases in children's intelligence and school achievement.
- Early interventions are most successful with poor children and children whose parents have little education.
- The positive benefits continue through adolescence but are stronger in early childhood and at the beginning of elementary school.
- The programs that are continued into middle and late childhood have the best long-term results.

What can we learn from research on the influence of early intervention on intelligence? To find out, see *Connecting Through Research*.

Revisiting the Nature/Nurture Issue In sum, there is a consensus among psychologists that both heredity and environment influence intelligence (Grigorenko & Takanishi, 2010). This consensus reflects the nature/nurture issue that was highlighted in Chapter 1. Recall that the nature/nurture issue focuses on the extent to which development is influenced by nature (heredity) and nurture (environment). Although psychologists agree that intelligence is the product of both nature and nurture, there is still disagreement about how strongly each factor influences intelligence (Deary, Penke, & Johnson, 2010; Sternberg, 2009a; Wadsworth, Olson, & Defries, 2010).

The highest-risk children often benefit the most cognitively when they experience early interventions.

—Craig Ramey
Contemporary Psychologist, Georgetown University

GROUP COMPARISONS

For decades, many controversies surrounding intelligence tests have grown from the tendency to compare one group with another. Many people keep asking whether their culture or ethnic group is more intelligent than others.

Cross-Cultural Comparisons Cultures vary in the way they describe what it means to be intelligent (Sternberg, 2009e; Zhang & Sternberg, 2011). People in Western cultures tend to view intelligence in terms of reasoning and thinking skills, whereas people in Eastern cultures see intelligence as a way for members of a community to successfully engage in social roles (Nisbett, 2003). One study found that Taiwanese-Chinese conceptions of intelligence emphasize understanding and relating to others, including knowing when to show and when not to show one's intelligence (Yang & Sternberg, 1997).

The intelligence of the Iatmul people of Papua New Guinea involves the ability to remember the names of many clans.

On the 680 Caroline Islands in the Pacific Ocean east of the Philippines, the intelligence of their inhabitants includes the ability to navigate by the stars. *Why might it be difficult to create a culture-fair intelligence test for the Iatmul children, Caroline Islands children, and U.S. children?*

culture-fair tests Intelligence tests that aim to avoid cultural bias.

Robert Serpell (1974, 1982, 2000) has studied concepts of intelligence in rural African communities since the 1970s. He has found that people in rural African communities, especially those in which Western schooling is not common, tend to blur the distinction between being intelligent and being socially competent. In rural Zambia, for example, the concept of intelligence involves being both clever and responsible. In one study in the Luo culture of rural Kenya, children who scored highly on a test of knowledge about medicinal herbs—a measure of practical intelligence—tended to score poorly on tests of academic intelligence (Sternberg & others, 2001). These results indicated that practical and academic intelligence can develop independently and may even conflict with each other. They also suggest that the values of a culture may influence the direction in which a child develops. In a cross-cultural context, then, intelligence depends a great deal on environment (Matsumoto & Juang, 2008; Shiraev & Levy, 2009).

Cultural Bias in Testing Many of the early intelligence tests were culturally biased, favoring people who were from urban rather than rural environments, of middle socioeconomic status rather than lower socioeconomic status, and White rather than African American (Miller-Jones, 1989; Provenzo, 2002). For example, one question on an early test asked what you should do if you find a 3-year-old child in the street. The correct answer was "call the police." But children from inner-city families who perceive the police as adversaries are unlikely to choose this answer. Similarly, children from rural areas might not choose this answer if there is no police force nearby. Such questions clearly do not measure the knowledge necessary to adapt to one's environment or to be "intelligent" in an inner-city neighborhood or in rural America (Scarr, 1984). Also, members of minority groups who do not speak English or who speak nonstandard English are at a disadvantage in trying to understand questions framed in standard English (Gibbs & Huang, 1989).

Connecting With Diversity examines some of the ways intelligence testing can be culturally biased.

Psychologists have developed **culture-fair tests,** which are intelligence tests that aim to avoid cultural bias. Two types of culture-fair tests have been developed. The first includes questions that are familiar to people from all socioeconomic and ethnic backgrounds. For example, a child might be asked how a bird and a dog are different, on the assumption that virtually all children are familiar with birds and dogs. The second type of culture-fair test contains no verbal questions. Figure 8.7 shows a sample question from Raven's Progressive Matrices tests. Even though tests such as Raven's Progressive Matrices are designed to be culture-fair, people with more education still score higher than those with less education (Greenfield, 2003).

Why is it so hard to create culture-fair tests? Most tests tend to reflect what the dominant culture thinks is important (Shiraev & Levy, 2006). If tests have time limits, that will bias the test against groups that are not concerned with time. If languages differ, the same words might have different meanings for different language groups. Even pictures can produce bias because some cultures have less experience with drawings and photographs (Anastasi & Urbina, 1997). Within the same culture, different groups could have different attitudes, values, and motivation, and this could affect their performance on intelligence tests. Items that ask why buildings should be made of brick are biased against children with little or no experience with brick houses. Questions about railroads, furnaces, seasons of the year, distances

Larry P.: Intelligent, But Not on Intelligence Tests

Larry P. is African American and poor. When he was 6 years old, he was placed in a class for the "educable mentally retarded" (EMR), which to school psychologists means that Larry learned much more slowly than average children. The primary reason Larry was placed in the EMR class was his very low score of 64 on an intelligence test.

Is there a possibility that the intelligence test Larry was given was culturally biased? Psychologists still debate this issue. A major class-action suit challenged the use of standardized IQ tests to place African American elementary school students in EMR classes. The initial lawsuit, filed on behalf of Larry P., claimed that the IQ test he took underestimated his true learning ability. The lawyers for Larry P. argued that IQ tests place too much emphasis on verbal skills and fail to account for the backgrounds of African American children. Therefore, it was argued, Larry was incorrectly labeled mentally retarded and might forever be saddled with that stigma.

As part of the lengthy court battle involving Larry P., six African American EMR students were independently retested by members of the Bay Association of Black Psychologists in California. The psychologists made sure they established good rapport with the students and made special efforts to overcome the students' defeatism and distraction. For example, items were reworded in terms more consistent with the children's social background, and recognition was given to non-

standard answers that showed a logical, intelligent approach to problems. This testing approach produced scores of 79 to 104—17 to 38 points higher than the scores the students received when initially tested by school psychologists. In every case, the retest scores were above the ceiling for placement in an EMR class.

What was the state's argument for using intelligence tests as one criterion for placing children in EMR classes? Testimony by intelligence-testing experts supported the *predictive validity* (using a measure, such as an intelligence test, to predict performance on another measure, such as grades in school) of IQ for different ethnic groups. In Larry's case, the judge ruled that IQ tests are biased and that their use discriminates against ethnic minorities. IQ tests cannot be used now in California to place children in EMR classes. The decision in favor of Larry P. was upheld by an appeals panel. However, in another court case, *Pace v. Hannon* in Illinois, a judge ruled that IQ tests are not culturally biased.

How do the decisions regarding intelligence testing for school placement in California and Illinois reflect differences in social policy, a topic discussed in Chapter 1?

between cities, and so on can be biased against groups who have less experience than others with these contexts. Because of such difficulties in creating culture-fair tests, Robert Sternberg and his colleagues (Sternberg, 2009e; Sternberg & Grigorenko, 2008; Zhang & Sternberg, 2011) conclude that there are no culture-fair tests, but only *culture-reduced* tests.

Ethnic Comparisons In the United States, children from African American and Latino families score below children from White families on standardized intelligence tests. On average, African American schoolchildren score 10 to 15 points lower on standardized intelligence tests than White American schoolchildren (Brody, 2000; Lynn, 1996). These are *average scores,* however. About 15 to 25 percent of African American schoolchildren score higher than half of White schoolchildren, and many Whites score lower than most African Americans. This is true because the distribution of scores for African Americans and Whites overlap.

As African Americans have gained social, economic, and educational opportunities, the gap between scores of African Americans and Whites on standardized intelligence tests has begun to narrow (Ogbu & Stern, 2001). This narrowing is especially apparent at the college level, where African American and White students often experience more similar environments than they did during the elementary and high school years (Myerson & others, 1998). Also, when children from disadvantaged African American families are adopted into more-advantaged middle-socioeconomic-status families, their scores on intelligence tests more closely resemble national averages for middle-socioeconomic-status children than those for lower-socioeconomic-status children (Scarr & Weinberg, 1983).

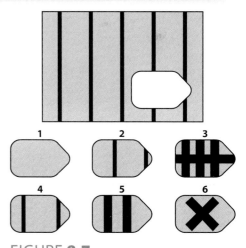

FIGURE **8.7**

SAMPLE ITEM FROM RAVEN'S PROGRESSIVE MATRICES TESTS. Individuals are presented with a matrix arrangement of symbols, such as the one at the top of this figure, and must then complete the matrix by selecting the appropriate missing symbol from a group of symbols, such as the ones at the bottom. Simulated items similar to those in *Raven's Progressive Matrices.* Copyright © 1998 by NCS Pearson, Inc. Reproduced by permission. All rights reserved. "Raven's Progressive Matrices" is a trademark, in the US and/or other countries, of Pearson Education, Inc. or its affiliates.

One potential influence on intelligence test performance is **stereotype threat,** the anxiety that one's behavior might confirm a negative stereotype about one's group (Hollis-Sawyer & Sawyer, 2008; Steele & Aronson, 2004). For example, when African Americans take an intelligence test, they may experience anxiety about confirming the old stereotype that Blacks are "intellectually inferior." Some studies have confirmed the existence of stereotype threat (Beilock, Rydell, & McConnell, 2007; Kellow & Jones, 2008). For example, African American students do more poorly on standardized tests if they perceive that they are being evaluated. If they think the test doesn't count, they perform as well as White students (Aronson, 2002). However, critics argue that the extent to which stereotype threat explains the testing gap has been exaggerated (Sackett, Hardison, & Cullen, 2005).

How might stereotype threat be involved in ethnic minority students' performance on standardized tests?

Review *Connect* Reflect

 LG1 Explain the concept of intelligence.

Review

- What is intelligence?
- What are the main individual tests of intelligence?
- What theories of multiple intelligences have been developed? Do people have one intelligence or many intelligences?
- What are some links between the brain and intelligence?
- What evidence indicates that heredity influences IQ scores? What evidence indicates that environment influences IQ scores?
- What is known about the intelligence of people from different cultures and ethnic groups?

Connect

- In this section you learned that different cultures have different concepts of intelligence, and in Chapter 5 you learned about culture's effect on motor development. What do these findings have in common?

Reflect *Your Own Personal Journey of Life*

- A CD-ROM is being sold to parents for testing their child's IQ. Several parents tell you that they purchased the CD-ROM and assessed their children's IQs. Why might you be skeptical about giving your children an IQ test and interpreting the results yourself?

The Development of Intelligence 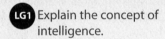 **LG2** Discuss the development of intelligence.

Tests of Infant Intelligence

Stability and Change in Intelligence Through Adolescence

How can the intelligence of infants be assessed? Is intelligence stable through childhood? These are some of the questions we will explore as we examine the development of intelligence.

TESTS OF INFANT INTELLIGENCE

The infant-testing movement grew out of the tradition of IQ testing. However, tests that assess infants are necessarily less verbal than IQ tests for older children. Tests for infants contain far more items related to perceptual-motor development. They

Toosje Thyssen Van Beveren, Infant Assessment Specialist

Toosje Thyssen Van Beveren is a developmental psychologist at the University of Texas Medical Center in Dallas. She has a master's degree in child clinical psychology and a Ph.D. in human development. Currently, Van Beveren is involved in a 12-week program called New Connections, which is a comprehensive intervention for young children who were affected by substance abuse prenatally and for their caregivers.

In the New Connections program, Van Beveren assesses infants' developmental status and progress. She might refer the infants to a speech, physical, or occupational therapist and monitor the infants' services and progress. Van Beveren trains the program staff and encourages them to use the exercises she recommends. She also discusses the child's problems with the primary caregivers, suggests activities, and assists them in enrolling infants in appropriate programs.

During her graduate work at the University of Texas at Dallas, Van Beveren was author John Santrock's teaching assistant in his undergraduate course on life-span development for four years. As a teaching assistant, she attended classes, graded exams, counseled students, and occasionally gave lectures. Each semester, Van Beveren returns to give a lecture on prenatal development and infancy. She also teaches part-time in the psychology department at UT–Dallas. In Van Beveren's words,

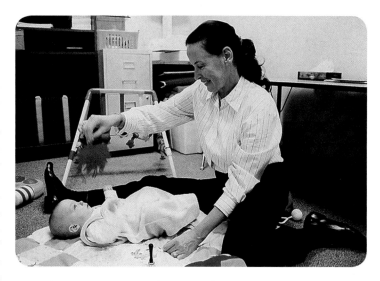

Toosje Thyssen Van Beveren conducting an infant assessment.

"My days are busy and full. The work is often challenging. There are some disappointments, but mostly the work is enormously gratifying."

For more information about what child life specialists do, see page 47 in the Careers in Child Development appendix following Chapter 1.

also include measures of social interaction. To read about the work of one infant assessment specialist, see *Connecting With Careers*.

The most important early contributor to the testing of infants was Arnold Gesell (1934). He developed a measure that helped sort out potentially normal babies from abnormal ones. This was especially useful to adoption agencies, which had large numbers of babies awaiting placement. Gesell's examination was used widely for many years and still is frequently employed by pediatricians to distinguish between normal and abnormal infants. The current version of the Gesell test has four categories of behavior: motor, language, adaptive, and personal-social. The **developmental quotient (DQ)** combines subscores in these categories to provide an overall score.

The widely used **Bayley Scales of Infant Development** were developed by Nancy Bayley (1969) to assess infant behavior and predict later development. The current version, Bayley-III, has five scales: cognitive, language, motor, socioemotional, and adaptive (Bayley, 2006). The first three scales are administered directly to the infant; the latter two are questionnaires given to the caregiver. The Bayley-III also is more appropriate for use in clinical settings than the two previous editions (Lennon & others, 2008).

How should a 6-month-old perform on the Bayley cognitive scale? The 6-month-old infant should be able to vocalize pleasure and displeasure, persistently search for objects that are just out of immediate reach, and approach a mirror that

stereotype threat Anxiexy that one's behavior might confirm a stereotype about one's group.

developmental quotient (DQ) An overall developmental score that combines subscores on motor, language, adaptive, and personal-social domains in the Gesell assessment of infants.

Bayley Scales of Infant Development Initially created by Nancy Bayley, these scales are widely used in assessing infant development. The current version has five scales: cognitive, language, motor, socioemotional, and adaptive.

Items used in the Bayley Scales of Infant Development.

is placed in front of the infant by the examiner. By 12 months of age, the infant should be able to inhibit behavior when commanded to do so, imitate words the examiner says (such as *Mama*), and respond to simple requests (such as "Take a drink").

The explosion of interest in infant development has produced many new measures, especially tasks that evaluate the ways infants process information (Fagan, Holland, & Wheeler, 2007; Rose, Feldman, & Wallace, 1992). The Fagan Test of Infant Intelligence is increasingly being used (Fagan, 1992). This test focuses on the infant's ability to process information by encoding the attributes of objects, detecting similarities and differences between objects, forming mental representations, and retrieving these representations. For example, it estimates intelligence by comparing the amount of time babies look at a new object with the amount of time they spend looking at a familiar object.

Unlike the Gesell and Bayley scales, the Fagan test is correlated with measures of intelligence in older children. In fact, evidence is accumulating that measures of habituation and dishabituation are linked to intelligence in childhood, adolescence, and even adulthood. For example, one study revealed that habituation assessed at 3 or 6 months of age was linked to verbal skills and intelligence assessed at 32 months of age. And in a recent study, selective attention to novelty at 6 to 12 months correlated positively with intelligence at 21 years of age (Fagan, Holland, & Wheeler, 2007). It is important, however, not to go too far and think that connections between cognitive development in early infancy and later cognitive development are so strong that no discontinuity takes place. As we discussed in Chapters 7 and 8, some important changes in cognitive development occur after infancy.

developmental **connection**

Information Processing. Habituation and dishabituation are important aspects of attention in infancy. Chapter 7, p. 205

STABILITY AND CHANGE IN INTELLIGENCE THROUGH ADOLESCENCE

A recent longitudinal study examined the intelligence of 200 children from 12 months (using the Bayley scales) to 4 years of age (using the Stanford-Binet test) (Blaga & others, 2009). The results indicated considerable stability from late infancy through the preschool years.

An early study examined correlations between IQ at a number of different ages (Honzik, MacFarlane, & Allen, 1948). There was a strong relation between IQ scores obtained at the ages of 6, 8, and 9 and IQ scores obtained at the age of 10. For example, the correlation between IQ at the age of 8 and IQ at the age of 10 was .88. The correlation between IQ at the age of 9 and IQ at the age of 10 was .90. These figures show a very close relationship between IQ scores obtained in these years. The correlation between IQ in the preadolescent years and IQ at the age of 18 was slightly lower but was still statistically significant. For example, the correlation between IQ at the age of 10 and IQ at the age of 18 was .70.

What has been said so far about the stability of intelligence has been based on measures of groups of individuals. The stability of intelligence also can be evaluated through studies of individuals. Robert McCall and his associates (McCall, Appelbaum, & Hogarty, 1973) studied 140 children between the ages of 2½ and 17. They found that the average range of IQ scores was more than 28 points. The scores of one out of three children changed by as much as 40 points.

What can we conclude about stability and changes in intelligence during childhood? Intelligence test scores can fluctuate dramatically across the childhood years. Intelligence is not as stable as the original intelligence theorists envisioned. Children are adaptive beings. They have the capacity for intellectual change, but they do not become entirely new intelligent beings. In a sense, children's intelligence changes but remains connected with early points in development.

Review Connect Reflect

Review

- How is intelligence assessed during infancy?
- How much does intelligence change through childhood and adolescence?

Connect

- In this section, you learned about research on the development of intelligence. Referring back to Chapter 1, identify which research methods and designs were used in these research studies and describe their pros and cons relative to their subject matter.

Reflect *Your Own Personal Journey of Life*

- As a parent, would you want to have your infant's intelligence tested? Why or why not?

The Extremes of Intelligence and Creativity

 LG3 Describe the characteristics of mental retardation, giftedness, and creativity.

Mental Retardation   Giftedness   Creativity

Mental retardation and intellectual giftedness are the extremes of intelligence. Often intelligence tests are used to identify exceptional individuals. After discussing mental retardation and giftedness, we'll explore how creativity differs from intelligence.

MENTAL RETARDATION

The most distinctive feature of mental retardation is inadequate intellectual functioning. Long before formal tests were developed to assess intelligence, individuals with mental retardation were identified by a lack of age-appropriate skills in learning and caring for themselves. Once intelligence tests were developed, they were used to identify degrees of mental retardation. But of two individuals with mental retardation having the same low IQ, one might be married, employed, and involved in the community while the other requires constant supervision in an institution. Such differences in social competence led psychologists to include deficits in adaptive behavior in their definition of mental retardation.

Mental retardation is a condition of limited mental ability in which the individual (1) has a low IQ, usually below 70 on a traditional intelligence test; (2) has difficulty adapting to everyday life; and (3) first exhibits these characteristics by age 18. The age limit is included in the definition of mental retardation because, for example, we don't usually think of a college student who suffers massive brain damage in a car accident, resulting in an IQ of 60, as being "mentally retarded." The low IQ and low adaptiveness should be evident in childhood, not after normal functioning is interrupted by damage of some form. About 5 million Americans fit this definition of mental retardation.

Mental retardation can be classified in several ways (Hallahan, Kaufmann, & Pullen, 2009). Most school systems use the classifications shown in Figure 8.8. It uses IQ scores to categorize retardation as mild, moderate, severe, or profound.

Note that a large majority of individuals diagnosed with mental retardation fit into the mild category. However, these categories are not perfect predictors of functioning. The American Association on Mental Retardation (1992) developed a different classification based on the degree of support required for a person with mental retardation to function at the highest level. These categories of support are: intermittent (supports given as needed), limited (supports are intense over time),

Type of Mental Retardation	IQ Range	Percentage
Mild	55–70	89
Moderate	40–54	6
Severe	25–39	4
Profound	Below 25	1

FIGURE 8.8

CLASSIFICATION OF MENTAL RETARDATION BASED ON IQ

mental retardation A condition of limited mental ability in which the individual (1) has a low IQ, usually below 70 on a traditional intelligence test; (2) has difficulty adapting to everyday life; and (3) has an onset of these characteristics by age 18.

This young boy has Down syndrome. *What causes a child to develop Down syndrome? In what major classification of mental retardation does the condition fall?*

At 2 years of age, art prodigy Alexandra Nechita colored in coloring books for hours and also took up pen and ink. She had no interest in dolls or friends. By age 5 she was using watercolors. Once she started school, she would start painting as soon as she got home. At the age of 8, in 1994, she saw the first public exhibit of her work. In succeeding years, working quickly and impulsively on canvases as large as 5 feet by 9 feet, she has completed hundreds of paintings, some of which sell for close to $100,000 apiece. As a teenager, she continues to paint—relentlessly and passionately. It is, she says, what she loves to do. *What are some characteristics of children who are gifted?*

extensive (supports needed are regular, typically every day), and pervasive (supports are constant, intense, and are needed in all settings).

Some cases of mental retardation have an organic cause. *Organic retardation* is mental retardation caused by a genetic disorder or by brain damage. Down syndrome is one form of organic mental retardation. As discussed in Chapter 2, it occurs when an extra chromosome is present.

Other causes of organic retardation include fragile X syndrome, an abnormality in the X chromosome that was discussed in Chapter 2; prenatal malformation; metabolic disorders; and diseases that affect the brain. Most people who suffer from organic retardation have IQs between 0 and 50.

When no evidence of organic brain damage can be found, cases of mental retardation are labeled *cultural-familial retardation.* Individuals with this type of retardation have IQs between 55 and 70. Psychologists suspect that these mental deficits often result from growing up in a below-average intellectual environment. Children who are familially retarded can be identified in schools, where they often fail, need tangible rewards (candy rather than praise), and are highly sensitive to what others expect of them. However, as adults, individuals who are familially retarded are usually unnoticed, perhaps because adult settings don't tax their cognitive skills as sorely. It may also be that individuals who are familially retarded increase their intelligence as they move toward adulthood.

GIFTEDNESS

There have always been people whose abilities and accomplishments have outshined others'—the whiz kid in class, the star athlete, the natural musician. People who are **gifted** have above-average intelligence (an IQ of 130 or higher) and/or superior talent for something. When it comes to programs for the gifted, most school systems select children who have intellectual superiority and academic aptitude, whereas children who are talented in the visual and performing arts (arts, drama, dance), who are skilled athletes, or who possess other special aptitudes tend to be overlooked (Horowitz, 2009; Winner, 2009).

What are the characteristics of children who are gifted? Despite speculation that giftedness is linked with having a mental disorder, no connection between giftedness and mental disorder has been found. Similarly, the idea that gifted children are maladjusted is a myth, as Lewis Terman (1925) found when he conducted an extensive study of 1,500 children whose Stanford-Binet IQs averaged 150. The children in Terman's study were socially well adjusted, and many went on to become successful doctors, lawyers, professors, and scientists. Studies support the conclusion that gifted people tend to be more mature than others, have fewer emotional problems than average, and grow up in a positive family climate (Davidson, 2000; Feldman, 2001).

Ellen Winner (1996) described three criteria that characterize gifted children, whether in art, music, or academic domains:

1. *Precocity.* Gifted children are precocious. They begin to master an area earlier than their peers. Learning in their domain is more effortless for them than for ordinary children. In most instances, these gifted children are precocious because they have an inborn high ability in a particular domain or domains.

2. *Marching to their own drummer.* Gifted children learn in a qualitatively different way from ordinary children. One way that they march to a different drummer is that they need minimal help, or scaffolding, from adults to learn. In many instances, they resist any kind of explicit instruction. They often make discoveries on their own and solve problems in unique ways.

3. *A passion to master.* Gifted children are driven to understand the domain in which they have high ability. They display an intense, obsessive interest and an ability to focus. They motivate themselves, says Winner, and do not need to be "pushed" by their parents.

Nature/Nurture Is giftedness a product of heredity or environment? Likely both (Sternberg, 2009b). Individuals who are gifted recall that they had signs of high ability in a particular area at a very young age, prior to or at the beginning of formal training (Howe & others, 1995). This suggests the importance of innate ability in giftedness. However, researchers have also found that individuals with world-class status in the arts, mathematics, science, and sports all report strong family support and years of training and practice (Bloom, 1985). Deliberate practice is an important characteristic of individuals who become experts in a particular domain. For example, in one study, the best musicians engaged in twice as much deliberate practice over their lives as did the least successful ones (Ericsson, Krampe, & Tesch-Romer, 1993).

Developmental Changes and Domain-Specific Giftedness

Can we predict from infancy who will be gifted as children, adolescents, and adults? John Colombo and his colleagues (2004, 2009) have found that measures of infant attention and habituation are not good predictors of high cognitive ability later in development. However, they have discovered a link between assessment with the Home Observation for Measure of the Environment at 18 months of age and high cognitive ability in the preschool years. The best predictor at 18 months of high cognitive ability in the preschool years was the provision of materials and a variety of experiences in the home. These findings illustrate the importance of the cognitive environment provided by parents in the development of children's giftedness.

Individuals who are highly gifted are typically not gifted in many domains, and research on giftedness is increasingly focused on domain-specific developmental trajectories (Matthews, 2009; Matthews, Subotnik, & Horowitz, 2009; Winner, 2009). During the childhood years, the domains in which individuals are gifted usually emerge. Thus, at some point in the childhood years, the child who will become a gifted artist or the child who will become a gifted mathematician begins to show expertise in that domain. Regarding domain-specific giftedness, software genius Bill Gates (1998), the founder of Microsoft and one of the world's richest persons, commented that when you are good at something you may have to resist the urge to think that you will be good at everything. Gates says that because he has been so successful at software development, people expect him to be brilliant about other domains in which he is far from being a genius.

Identifying an individual's domain-specific talent and providing the individual with individually appropriate and optional educational opportunities needs to be accomplished by adolescence at the latest (Keating, 2009). During adolescence, individuals who are talented become less reliant on parental support and increasingly pursue their own interests.

Some children who are gifted become gifted adults, but many gifted children do not become gifted and highly creative adults. In Terman's research on children with superior IQs, the children typically became experts in a well-established domain, such as medicine, law, or business. However, they did not become major creators (Winner, 2000). That is, they did not create a new domain or revolutionize an old domain.

Education of Children Who Are Gifted An increasing number of experts argue that the education of children who are gifted in the United States requires a significant overhaul (Jarvin & others, 2008; Sternberg, 2010a). Underchallenged gifted children can become disruptive, skip classes, and lose interest in achieving. Sometimes these children just disappear into the woodwork,

Margaret (Peg) Cagle with some of the gifted seventh- and eighth-grade math students she teaches at Lawrence Middle School in Chatsworth, California. Cagle especially advocates challenging students who are gifted to take intellectual risks. To encourage collaboration, she often has students work together in groups of four, and frequently tutors students during lunch hour. As 13-year-old Madeline Lewis commented, "If you don't get it one way, she'll explain it another and talk to you about it and show you until you do get it." Cagle says it is important to be passionate about teaching math and open up a world for students that shows them how beautiful learning math can be (Wong Briggs, 2007, p. 6D).

A young Bill Gates, founder of Microsoft and now the world's richest person. Like many highly gifted students, Gates was not especially fond of school. He hacked a computer security system when he was 13 and as a high school student, he was allowed to take some college math classes. He dropped out of Harvard University and began developing a plan for what was to become Microsoft Corporation. *What are some ways that schools can enrich the education of such highly talented students as Gates to make it a more challenging, interesting, and meaningful experience?*

giftedness Possession of above-average intelligence (an IQ of 130 or higher) and/or superior talent for something.

connecting with careers

Sterling Jones, Supervisor of Gifted and Talented Education

Sterling Jones is program supervisor for gifted and talented children in the Detroit Public School System. Jones has been working for more than three decades with children who are gifted. He believes that students' mastery of skills mainly depends on the amount of time devoted to instruction and the length of time allowed for learning. Thus, he believes that many basic strategies for challenging children who are gifted to develop their skills can be applied to a wider range of students than once believed. He has rewritten several pamphlets for use by teachers and parents, including *How to Help Your Child Succeed* and *Gifted and Talented Education for Everyone*.

Jones holds undergraduate and graduate degrees from Wayne State University, and he taught English for a number of years before becoming involved in the program for gifted children. He also has written materials on African Americans, such as *Voices from the Black Experience,* that are used in the Detroit schools.

Sterling Jones with some of the children in the gifted program in the Detroit Public School System.

For more information about what teachers of exceptional children (special education) do, see page 45 in the Careers in Child Development appendix following Chapter 1.

becoming passive and apathetic toward school. It is extremely important for teachers to challenge children who are gifted to reach high expectations (Webb & others, 2007; Winner, 2009).

Ellen Winner (1996, 2006) argues that too often children who are gifted are socially isolated and underchallenged in the classroom. It is not unusual for them to be ostracized and labeled "nerds" or "geeks." A child who is truly gifted often is the only child in the classroom who does not have the opportunity to learn with students of like ability. Many eminent adults report that school was a negative experience for them, that they were bored and sometimes knew more than their teachers (Bloom, 1985). Winner argues that American education will benefit when standards are raised for all children. When some children are still underchallenged, she recommends that they be allowed to attend advanced classes in their domain of exceptional ability. For example, some especially precocious middle school students should be allowed to take college classes in their area of expertise. For example, Bill Gates, founder of Microsoft, took college math classes and hacked a computer security system at 13; Yo-Yo Ma, famous cellist, graduated from high school at 15 and attended Juilliard School of Music in New York City.

A number of individuals work in various capacities in school systems with children who are gifted. To read about the work of Sterling Jones, specialist in gifted and talented education, see *Connecting With Careers.*

CREATIVITY

We brought up the term "creative" on several occasions in our discussion of intelligence and giftedness. What does it mean to be creative? **Creativity** is the ability to think about something in novel and unusual ways and come up with unique solutions to problems.

creativity The ability to think in novel and unusual ways and come up with unique solutions to problems.

Intelligence and creativity are not the same thing (Kaufman & Sternberg, 2010). Most creative people are quite intelligent, but the reverse is not necessarily true. Many highly intelligent people (as measured by high scores on conventional tests of intelligence) are not very creative (Sternberg, 2009f). Many highly intelligent people produce large numbers of products that are not necessarily novel.

Why don't IQ scores predict creativity? Creativity requires divergent thinking (Guilford, 1967). **Divergent thinking** produces many answers to the same question. In contrast, conventional intelligence tests require **convergent thinking.** For example, a typical question on a conventional intelligence test is, "How many quarters will you get in return for 60 dimes?" There is only one correct answer to this question. In contrast, a question such as "What image comes to mind when you hear the phrase 'sitting alone in a dark room'?" has many possible answers; it calls for divergent thinking.

Just as in being gifted, children show creativity in some domains more than others (Rickards, Moger, & Runco, 2009; Sternberg, 2010b, e). For example, a child who shows creativity in mathematics might not be as creative in art. To read about some strategies for helping children become more creative, see the following *Caring Connections*.

divergent thinking Thinking that produces many answers to the same question; characteristic of creativity.

convergent thinking Thinking that produces one correct answer; characteristic of the kind of thinking required on conventional intelligence tests.

brainstorming A technique in which children are encouraged to come up with creative ideas in a group, play off one another's ideas, and say practically whatever comes to mind.

caring *connections*

Guiding Children's Creativity

An important goal of teachers is to help children become more creative (Beghetto & Kaufman, 2010; Hennessey & Amabile, 2010; Sternberg, 2010b, e). What are the best strategies for accomplishing this goal? We examine some of these strategies next.

Encourage Creative Thinking on a Group and Individual Basis

Brainstorming is a technique in which children are encouraged to come up with creative ideas in a group, play off each other's ideas, and say practically whatever comes to mind that seems relevant to a particular issue. Participants are usually told to hold off from criticizing others' ideas at least until the end of the brainstorming session.

Provide Environments That Stimulate Creativity

Some environments nourish creativity, while others inhibit it. Parents and teachers who encourage creativity often rely on children's natural curiosity (Fairweather & Cramond, 2011). They provide exercises and activities that stimulate children to find insightful solutions to problems, rather than ask a lot of questions that require rote answers (Beghetto & Kaufman, 2010; Skiba & others, 2010; Sternberg, 2010e). Teachers also encourage creativity by taking students on field trips to locations where creativity is valued. Howard Gardner (1993) emphasizes that science, discovery, and children's museums offer rich opportunities to stimulate creativity.

What are some good strategies teachers can use to guide children in thinking more creatively?

Don't Overcontrol Students

Teresa Amabile (1993) says that telling children exactly how to do things leaves them feeling that originality is a mistake and exploration is a waste of time. If, instead of dictating which activities they should engage in, you let children select their interests and you support their

(continued)

(continued)

inclinations, you will be less likely to destroy their natural curiosity (Hennessey, 2010). Amabile also emphasizes that when parents and teachers hover over students all of the time, they make students feel that they are constantly being watched while they are working. When children are under constant surveillance, their creative risk taking and adventurous spirit diminish. Children's creativity also is diminished when adults have grandiose expectations for children's performance and expect perfection from them, according to Amabile.

Encourage Internal Motivation

Excessive use of prizes, such as gold stars, money, or toys, can stifle creativity by undermining the intrinsic pleasure students derive from creative activities (Hennessey & Amabile, 2010). Creative children's motivation is the satisfaction generated by the work itself. Competition for prizes and formal evaluations often undermine intrinsic motivation and creativity (Amabile & Hennessey, 1992). However, this should not rule out material rewards altogether.

Guide Children to Help Them Think in Flexible Ways

Creative thinkers approach problems in many different ways, rather than getting locked into rigid patterns of thought. Give children opportunities to exercise this flexibility in their thinking.

Build Children's Confidence

To expand children's creativity, encourage them to believe in their own ability to create something innovative and worthwhile. Building chil-

dren's confidence in their creative skills aligns with Bandura's (2009, 2010a) concept of *self-efficacy,* the belief that one can master a situation and produce positive outcomes.

Guide Children to Be Persistent and Delay Gratification

Most highly successful creative products take years to develop. Most creative individuals work on ideas and projects for months and years without being rewarded for their efforts (Sternberg & Williams, 1996). As we discussed in Chapter 7, children don't become experts at sports, music, or art overnight. It usually takes many years of working at something to become an expert at it; so it is with being a creative thinker who produces a unique, worthwhile product.

Encourage Children to Take Intellectual Risks

Creative individuals take intellectual risks and seek to discover or invent something never before discovered or invented (Sternberg & Williams, 1996). They risk spending a lot of time on an idea or project that may not work. Creative individuals are not afraid of failing or getting something wrong (Sternberg, 2010b, e). They often see failure as an opportunity to learn. They might go down 20 dead-end streets before they come up with an innovative idea.

Which of these strategies specifically encourages divergent thinking?

Review *Connect* Reflect

 Describe the characteristics of mental retardation, giftedness, and creativity.

Review
- What is mental retardation, and what are its causes?
- What makes individuals gifted?
- What makes individuals creative?

Connect
- In this section you learned how mental retardation is assessed and classified. What did you learn in Chapter 2 about the prevalence of Down syndrome in the population and the factors that might cause an infant to be born with Down syndrome?

Reflect *Your Own Personal Journey of Life*
- If you were an elementary school teacher, what would you do to encourage students' creativity?

Intelligence

The Concept of Intelligence   **LG1**   Explain the concept of intelligence.

What Is Intelligence?

- Intelligence consists of the ability to solve problems and to adapt and learn from experiences. A key aspect of intelligence focuses on its individual variations. Traditionally, intelligence has been measured by tests designed to compare people's performance on cognitive tasks.

Intelligence Tests

- Alfred Binet developed the first intelligence test and created the concept of mental age. William Stern developed the concept of IQ for use with the Binet test. Revisions of the Binet test are called the Stanford-Binet. The test scores on the Stanford-Binet approximate a normal distribution. The Wechsler scales, created by David Wechsler, are the other main intelligence assessment tool. These tests provide an overall IQ, scores on a number of subtests, and several composite indexes. When used by a judicious examiner, tests can be valuable tools for determining individual differences in intelligence. Test scores should be only one type of information used to evaluate an individual. IQ scores can produce unfortunate stereotypes and false expectations.

Theories of Multiple Intelligences

- Sternberg's triarchic theory states that there are three main types of intelligence: analytical, creative, and practical. Sternberg created the Sternberg Triarchic Abilities Test to assess these three types of intelligence and has described applications of triarchic theory to children's education. Gardner maintains that there are eight types of intelligence, or frames of mind: verbal skills, mathematical skills, spatial skills, bodily-kinesthetic skills, musical skills, interpersonal skills, intrapersonal skills, and naturalist skills. The Key School applies Gardner's view to educating children by immersing students in activities that closely correlate with Gardner's eight frames of mind. Emotional intelligence is the ability to perceive and express emotion accurately and adaptively, to understand emotion and emotional knowledge, to use feelings to facilitate thought, and to manage emotions in oneself and others. The multiple-intelligences approaches have broadened the definition of intelligence and motivated educators to develop programs that instruct students in different domains. Critics maintain that Gardner's multiple-intelligence classification seems arbitrary. Critics also say that there is insufficient research to support the concept of multiple intelligences.

The Neuroscience of Intelligence

- Interest in discovering links between the brain and intelligence has been stimulated by advances in brain imaging. A moderate correlation has been found between overall brain size and intelligence. Recent research has revealed a link between a distributed neural network in the frontal and parietal lobes and intelligence. Research on a connection between neural processing speed and intelligence has produced inconsistent findings.

The Influence of Heredity and Environment

- Genetic similarity might explain why identical twins show stronger correlations on intelligence tests than fraternal twins do. Some studies indicate that the IQs of adopted children are more similar to the IQs of their biological parents than to those of their adoptive parents. Many studies show that intelligence has a reasonably strong heritability component, but environmental influences also are important. Intelligence test scores have risen considerably around the world in recent decades—called the Flynn effect—and this supports the role of environment in intelligence. Researchers have found that being deprived of formal education lowers IQ scores. Ramey's research revealed the positive effects of educational child care on intelligence.

- Cultures vary in the way they define intelligence. Early intelligence tests favored White, middle-socioeconomic-status, urban individuals. Tests may be biased against certain groups that are not familiar with a standard form of English, with the content tested, or with the testing situation. Tests are likely to reflect the values and experience of the dominant culture. In the United States, children from African American and Latino families score below children from White families on standardized intelligence tests.

The Development of Intelligence Discuss the development of intelligence.

Tests of Infant Intelligence

- A test developed by Gesell was an important early contributor to the developmental testing of infants. Tests designed to assess infant intelligence include the widely used Bayley scales. The Fagan Test of Infant Intelligence, which assesses how effectively infants process information, is increasingly being used. Infant information-processing tasks that involve attention—especially habituation and dishabituation—are related to standardized scores of intelligence in childhood.

Stability and Change in Intelligence Through Adolescence

- Intelligence is not as stable across childhood and adolescence as the original theorists believed. Many children's scores on intelligence tests fluctuate considerably.

The Extremes of Intelligence and Creativity LG3 Describe the characteristics of mental retardation, giftedness, and creativity.

Mental Retardation

- Mental retardation is a condition of limited mental ability in which the individual (1) has a low IQ, usually below 70; (2) has difficulty adapting to everyday life; and (3) has an onset of these characteristics by age 18. Most affected individuals have an IQ in the 55 to 70 range (mild retardation). Mental retardation can have an organic cause (called organic retardation) or be social and cultural in origin (called cultural-familial retardation).

Giftedness

- Individuals who are gifted have above-average intelligence (an IQ of 130 or higher) and/or superior talent for something. Three characteristics of gifted children are precocity, marching to their own drummer, and a passion to master their domain. Giftedness is likely a consequence of both heredity and environment. Developmental changes characterize giftedness, and increasingly the domain-specific aspect of giftedness is emphasized. Concerns exist about the education of children who are gifted.

Creativity

- Creativity is the ability to think about something in novel and unusual ways and come up with unique solutions to problems. Although most creative people are intelligent, individuals with high IQs are not necessarily creative. Creative people tend to be divergent thinkers; traditional intelligence tests measure convergent thinking. Parents and teachers can use a number of strategies to increase children's creative thinking.

key terms

intelligence 235
mental age (MA) 236
intelligence quotient (IQ) 236
normal distribution 236
triarchic theory of
    intelligence 238

emotional intelligence 239
heritability 241
culture-fair tests 244
stereotype threat 246
developmental quotient
    (DQ) 247

Bayley Scales of Infant
    Development 247
mental retardation 249
gifted 251
creativity 252

divergent thinking 253
convergent
    thinking 253
brainstorming 253

key people

chapter 9 · LANGUAGE DEVELOPMENT

chapter outline

A stunning portrayal of a child isolated from the mainstream of language is the case of Helen Keller (1880–1968). At 18 months of age, Helen was an intelligent toddler in the process of learning to say her first words. Then she developed an illness that left her both deaf and blind, suffering the double affliction of sudden darkness and silence. For the next five years, she lived in a world she learned to fear because she could not see or hear.

Even with her fears, Helen spontaneously invented a number of gestures to reflect her wants and needs. For example, when she wanted ice cream, she turned toward the freezer and shivered. When she wanted bread and butter, she imitated the motions of cutting and spreading. But this homemade language system severely limited her ability to communicate with the surrounding community, which did not understand her idiosyncratic gestures.

Alexander Graham Bell, the famous inventor of the telephone, suggested to her parents that they hire a tutor named Anne Sullivan to help Helen overcome her fears. By using sign language, Anne was able to teach Helen to communicate. Anne realized that language learning needs to occur naturally, so she did not force Helen to memorize words out of context as in the drill methods that were in vogue at the time. Sullivan's success depended not only on the child's natural ability to organize language according to form and meaning but also on introducing language in the context of communicating about objects, events, and feelings about others. Helen Keller eventually graduated from Radcliffe with honors, became a very successful educator, and crafted books about her life and experiences. She had this to say about language:

> Whatever the process, the result is wonderful. Gradually from naming an object we advance step by step until we have traversed the vast distance between our first stammered syllable and the sweep of thought in a line of Shakespeare.

Helen Keller.

preview

In this chapter, we will tell the remarkable story of language and how it develops. The questions we will explore include these: What is language? What is the developmental course of language? What does biology contribute to language? How does experience influence language? How are language and cognition linked?

What Is Language? (LG1) Define language and describe its rule systems.

Defining Language

Language's Rule Systems

In 1799, a nude boy was observed running through the woods in France. The boy was captured when he was 11 years old. He was called the Wild Boy of Aveyron and was believed to have lived in the woods alone for six years (Lane, 1976). When found, he made no effort to communicate. He never learned to communicate effectively. Sadly, a modern-day wild child named Genie was discovered in Los Angeles in 1970. Despite intensive intervention, Genie has acquired only a limited form of spoken language. Both cases—the Wild Boy of Aveyron and Genie—raise questions about the biological and environmental determinants of language, topics that we will examine later in the chapter. First, though, we need to define language.

DEFINING LANGUAGE

Language is a form of communication—whether spoken, written, or signed—that is based on a system of symbols. Language consists of the words used by a community and the rules for varying and combining them.

> Words not only affect us temporarily; they change us, they socialize us, and they unsocialize us.
>
> —**DAVID RIESMAN**
> *American Social Scientist, 20th Century*

Think how important language is in our everyday lives. It is difficult to imagine what Helen Keller's life would have been like if she had never learned language. We need language to communicate with others—to speak, listen, read, and write. Our language enables us to describe past events in detail and to plan for the future. Language lets us pass down information from one generation to the next and create a rich cultural heritage.

All human languages have some common characteristics (Berko Gleason, 2009). These include infinite generativity and organizational rules. **Infinite generativity** is the ability to produce an endless number of meaningful sentences using a finite set of words and rules. When we say "rules," we mean that language is orderly and that rules describe the way language works. Let's further explore what these rules involve.

LANGUAGE'S RULE SYSTEMS

When 19th-century American writer Ralph Waldo Emerson said, "The world was built in order and the atoms march in tune," he must have had language in mind. Language is highly ordered and organized (Berko Gleason, 2009; Colombo, McCardle, & Freund, 2009). The organization involves five systems of rules: phonology, morphology, syntax, semantics, and pragmatics.

Phonology Every language is made up of basic sounds. **Phonology** is the sound system of a language, including the sounds that are used and how they may be combined (Menn & Stoel-Gammon, 2009; Stoel-Gammon & Sosa, 2010). For example, English has the sounds *sp*, *ba*, and *ar*, but the sound sequences *zx* and *qp* do

language A form of communication, whether spoken, written, or signed, that is based on a system of symbols.

infinite generativity The ability to produce an endless number of meaningful sentences using a finite set of words and rules.

phonology The sound system of a language, which includes the sounds used and rules about how they may be combined.

not occur. A *phoneme* is the basic unit of sound in a language; it is the smallest unit of sound that affects meaning. A good example of a phoneme in English is /k/, the sound represented by the letter *k* in the word *ski* and the letter *c* in the word *cat*. The /k/ sound is slightly different in these two words, and in some languages such as Arabic these two sounds are separate phonemes. However, this variation is not distinguished in English, and the /k/ sound is therefore a single phoneme.

Morphology **Morphology** is the rule system that governs how words are formed in a language. A *morpheme* is a minimal unit of meaning; it is a word or a part of a word that cannot be broken into smaller meaningful parts. Every word in the English language is made up of one or more morphemes. Some words consist of a single morpheme (for example, *help*), whereas others are made up of more than one morpheme (for example, *helper*, which has two morphemes, *help* and *er*, with the morpheme *-er* meaning "one who"—in this case "one who helps"). Thus, not all morphemes are words by themselves; for example, *-pre*, *-tion*, and *-ing* are morphemes.

Just as the rules that govern phonology describe the sound sequences that can occur in a language, the rules of morphology describe the way meaningful units (morphemes) can be combined in words (Tager-Flusberg, & Zukowski, 2009). Morphemes have many jobs in grammar, such as marking tense (for example, she *walks* versus she *walked*) and number (*she* walks versus *they* walk).

Syntax **Syntax** involves the way words are combined to form acceptable phrases and sentences. The term *syntax* is often used interchangeably with the term *grammar*. If someone says to you, "Bob slugged Tom" or "Bob was slugged by Tom," you know who did the slugging and who was slugged in each case because you have a syntactic understanding of these sentence structures. You also understand that the sentence, "You didn't stay, did you?" is a grammatical sentence but that "You didn't stay, didn't you?" is unacceptable and ambiguous.

If you learn another language, English syntax will not get you very far. For example, in English an adjective usually precedes a noun (as in *blue sky*), whereas in Spanish the adjective usually follows the noun (*cielo azul*). Despite the differences in their syntactic structures, however, the world's languages have much in common (Lidz, 2010; Saffran, 2009). For example, consider the following short sentences:

The cat killed the mouse.
The farmer chased the cat.

In many languages, it is possible to combine these sentences into more complex sentences. For example:

The farmer chased the cat that killed the mouse.
The mouse the cat killed ate the cheese.

However, no language we know of permits sentences like the following one:

The mouse the cat the farmer chased killed ate the cheese.

Language allows us to communicate with others. *What are some important characteristics of language?*

FRANK & ERNEST © Thaves. Distr. by United Features Syndicate, Inc.

morphology The rule system that governs how words are formed in a language.

syntax The ways words are combined to form acceptable phrases and sentences.

Rule System	Description	Examples
Phonology	The sound system of a language. A phoneme is the smallest sound unit in a language.	The word *chat* has three phonemes or sounds: /ch/ /ā/ /t/. An example of phonological rule in the English language is while the phoneme /r/ can follow the phonemes /t/ or /d/ in an English consonant cluster (such as *track* or *drab*), the phoneme /l/ cannot follow these letters.
Morphology	The system of meaningful units involved in word formation.	The smallest sound units that have a meaning are called morphemes, or meaning units. The word *girl* is one morpheme, or meaning unit; it cannot be broken down any further and still have meaning. When the suffix *s* is added, the word becomes *girls* and has two morphemes because the *s* changed the meaning of the word, indicating that there is more than one girl.
Syntax	The system that involves the way words are combined to form acceptable phrases and sentences.	Word order is very important in determining meaning in the English language. For example, the sentence "Sebastian pushed the bike" has a different meaning than "The bike pushed Sebastian."
Semantics	The system that involves the meaning of words and sentences.	Knowing the meaning of individual words—that is, vocabulary. For example, semantics includes knowing the meaning of such words as *orange*, *transportation*, and *intelligent*.
Pragmatics	The system of using appropriate conversation and knowledge of how to effectively use language in context.	An example is using polite language in appropriate situations, such as being mannerly when talking with one's teacher. Taking turns in a conversation involves pragmatics.

FIGURE **9.1**

THE RULE SYSTEMS OF LANGUAGE

Can you make sense of this sentence? If you can, you probably can do it only after wrestling with it for several minutes. You likely could not understand it at all if someone uttered it during a conversation. It appears that language users cannot process subjects and objects arranged in too complex a fashion in a sentence. That is good news for language learners, because it means that all syntactic systems have some common ground. Such findings are also considered important by researchers who are interested in the universal properties of syntax (Tager-Flusberg & Zukowski, 2009).

Semantics **Semantics** refers to the meaning of words and sentences. Every word has a set of semantic features, or required attributes related to meaning. *Girl* and *woman*, for example, share many semantic features but differ semantically in regard to age.

Words have semantic restrictions on how they can be used in sentences (Diesendruck, 2010; Li, 2009). The sentence *The bicycle talked the boy into buying a candy bar* is syntactically correct but semantically incorrect. The sentence violates our semantic knowledge that bicycles don't talk.

Pragmatics A final set of language rules involves **pragmatics,** the appropriate use of language in different contexts. Pragmatics covers a lot of territory. When you take turns speaking in a discussion or use a question to convey a command ("Why is it so noisy in here?" "What is this, Grand Central Station?"), you are demonstrating knowledge of pragmatics. You also apply the pragmatics of English when you use polite language in appropriate situations (for example, when talking to your teacher) or tell stories that are interesting, jokes that are funny, and lies that convince. In each of these cases, you are demonstrating that you understand the rules of your culture for adjusting language to suit the context.

Pragmatic rules can be complex and differ from one culture to another (Bryant, 2009; Siegal & Surian, 2010). If you were to study the Japanese language, you would come face-to-face with countless pragmatic rules about conversing with individuals of various social levels and with various relationships to you. Some of these pragmatic rules concern the ways of saying *thank you*. Indeed, the pragmatics of saying *thank you* are complex even in our own culture. Preschoolers' use of the phrase *thank you* varies with sex, socioeconomic status, and the age of the individual they are addressing.

At this point, we have discussed five important rule systems involved in language. An overview of these rule systems is presented in Figure 9.1.

semantics The meaning of words and sentences.

pragmatics The appropriate use of language in different contexts.

How Language Develops   **LG2** Describe how language develops.

Infancy   Early Childhood   Middle and Late Childhood   Adolescence

According to an ancient historian, a 13th-century emperor of Germany, Frederick II, had a cruel idea. He wanted to know what language children would speak if no one talked to them. He selected several newborns and threatened their caregivers with death if they ever talked to the infants. Frederick never found out what language the children would speak because they all died. As we move forward in the 21st century, we are still curious about infants' development of language, although our experiments and observations are, to say the least, far more humane than the evil Frederick's.

INFANCY

Whatever language they learn, infants all over the world follow a similar path in language development. What are some key milestones in this development?

Babbling and Other Vocalizations   Long before infants speak recognizable words, they produce a number of vocalizations (Sachs, 2009). The functions of these early vocalizations are to practice making sounds, to communicate, and to attract attention. Babies' sounds go through the following sequence during the first year:

1. *Crying*. Babies cry even at birth. Crying can signal distress, but as we will discuss in Chapter 10, different types of cries signal different things.
2. *Cooing*. Babies first coo at about 1 to 2 months. These are gurgling sounds that are made in the back of the throat and usually express pleasure during interaction with the caregiver.
3. *Babbling*. In the middle of the first year babies babble—that is, they produce strings of consonant-vowel combinations, such as *ba, ba, ba, ba*.

Long before infants speak recognizable words, they communicate by producing a number of vocalizations and gestures. *At approximately what ages do infants begin to produce different types of vocalization and gestures?*

When deaf infants are born to deaf parents who use sign language, they babble with their hands and fingers at about the same age that hearing children babble vocally (Bloom, 1998). Such similarities in timing and structure between manual and vocal babbling indicate that a unified language capacity underlies signed and spoken language.

- - - - - - - - →
developmental connection

Emotional Development. Three basic cries that infants display are the basic cry, anger cry, and pain cry. Chapter 10, p. 294
← - - - - - - -

FIGURE **9.2**

FROM UNIVERSAL LINGUIST TO LANGUAGE-SPECIFIC LISTENER. In Patricia Kuhl's research laboratory, babies listen to tape-recorded voices that repeat syllables. When the sounds of the syllables change, the babies quickly learn to look at the bear. Using this technique, Kuhl has demonstrated that babies are universal linguists until about 6 months of age, but in the next six months become language-specific listeners. *Does Kuhl's research give support to the view that either "nature" or "nurture" is the source of language acquisition?*

Gestures

Infants start using gestures, such as showing and pointing, at about 8 to 12 months of age. They may wave bye-bye, nod to mean "yes," show an empty cup to want more milk, and point to a dog to draw attention to it. Some early gestures are symbolic, as when an infant smacks her lips to indicate food or drink. Pointing is considered by language experts to be an important index of the social aspects of language, and it follows this developmental sequence: from pointing without checking on adult gaze to pointing while looking back and forth between an object and the adult (Goldin-Meadow, 2009; Goldin-Meadow & Iverson, 2010; Rowe & Goldin-Meadow, 2009). Lack of pointing is a significant indicator of problems in the infant's communication system. For example, failure to engage in pointing characterizes many autistic children.

A recent study found that parents of high socioeconomic status (SES) were more likely to use gestures when communicating with their 14-month-old infants (Rowe & Goldin-Meadow, 2009). Further, the infants' use of gestures at 14 months of age in high-SES families was linked to a larger vocabulary at 54 months of age.

Recognizing Language Sounds

Long before they begin to learn words, infants can make fine distinctions among the sounds of the language (Sachs, 2009). In Patricia Kuhl's (1993, 2000, 2007, 2009) research, phonemes from languages all over the world are piped through a speaker for infants to hear (see Figure 9.2). A box with a toy bear in it is placed where the infant can see it. A string of identical syllables is played; then the syllables are changed (for example, *ba ba ba ba*, and then *pa pa pa pa*). If the infant turns its head when the syllables change, the box lights up and the bear dances and drums, rewarding the infant for noticing the change.

Kuhl's (2007, 2009) research has demonstrated that from birth to about 6 months of age, infants are "citizens of the world": they recognize when sounds change most of the time, no matter what language the syllables come from. But over the next six months, infants get even better at perceiving the changes in sounds from their "own" language, the one their parents speak, and gradually lose the ability to recognize differences that are not important in their own language.

Infants must fish out individual words from the nonstop stream of sound that makes up ordinary speech (Menn & Stoel-Gammon, 2009). To do so, they must find the boundaries between words, which is very difficult for infants because adults don't pause between words when they speak. Still, infants begin to detect word boundaries by 8 months of age. For example, in one study, 8-month-old infants listened to recorded stories that contained unusual words, such as hornbill and python (Jusczyk & Hohne, 1997). Two weeks later, the researchers tested the infants with two lists of words, one made up of words in the stories, the other of new, unusual words that did not appear in the stories. The infants listened to the familiar words for a second longer, on average, than the new words.

First Words

Infants understand words before they can produce or speak them (Pan & Uccelli, 2009). For example, many infants recognize their name when someone says it as early as 5 months of age. However, the infant's first spoken word, a

What characterizes the infant's early word learning?

milestone eagerly anticipated by every parent, usually doesn't occur until 10 to 15 months of age and at an average of about 13 months. Yet long before babies say their first words, they have been communicating with their parents, often by gesturing and using their own special sounds. The appearance of first words is a continuation of this communication process (Berko Gleason, 2009).

A child's first words include those that name important people (dada), familiar animals (kitty), vehicles (car), toys (ball), food (milk), body parts (eye), clothes (hat), household items (clock), and greeting terms (bye). These were the first words of babies 50 years ago. They are the first words of babies today. Children often express various intentions with their single words, so that "cookie" might mean "That's a cookie" or "I want a cookie."

As indicated earlier, children understand their first words earlier than they speak them. On the average, infants understand about 50 words at about 13 months, but they can't say this many words until about 18 months (Menyuk, Liebergott, & Schultz, 1995). Thus, in infancy *receptive vocabulary* (words the child understands) considerably exceeds *spoken vocabulary* (words the child uses).

The infant's spoken vocabulary rapidly increases once the first word is spoken (Pan & Uccelli, 2009; Waxman, 2009). The average 18-month-old can speak about 50 words, but by the age of 2 years a child can speak about 200 words. This rapid increase in vocabulary that begins at approximately 18 months is called the *vocabulary spurt* (Bloom, Lifter, & Broughton, 1985).

Like the timing of a child's first word, the timing of the vocabulary spurt varies. Figure 9.3 shows the range for these two language milestones in 14 children. On average, these children said their first word at 13 months and had a vocabulary spurt at 19 months. However, the ages for the first word of individual children varied from 10 to 17 months and for their vocabulary spurt from 13 to 25 months.

Cross-linguistic differences occur in word learning. Children learning Mandarin Chinese, Korean, and Japanese acquire more verbs earlier in their development than do children learning English. This cross-linguistic difference reflects the greater use of verbs in these Asian languages.

Children sometimes overextend or underextend the meanings of the words they use (Woodward & Markman, 1998). Overextension is the tendency to apply a word to objects that are inappropriate for the word's meaning. For example, children at first may say "dada" not only for "father" but also for other men, strangers, or boys. Children may overextend word meanings because they don't know the appropriate word or can't recall it. With time, overextensions decrease and eventually disappear. Underextension is the tendency to apply a word too narrowly; it occurs when children fail to use a word to name a relevant event or object. For example, a child might use the word *boy* to describe a 5-year-old neighbor but not apply the word to a male infant or to a 9-year-old male. The most common explanation of underextension is that children have heard a name used in reference to a small, unrepresentative sample.

Two-Word Utterances By the time children are 18 to 24 months of age, they usually utter two-word messages. To convey meaning with just two words, the child relies heavily on gesture, tone, and context. The wealth of meaning children can communicate with a two-word utterance includes the following (Slobin, 1972):

- Identification: "See doggie."
- Location: "Book there."
- Repetition: "More milk."
- Possession: "My candy."
- Attribution: "Big car."
- Agent-action: "Mama walk."
- Question: "Where ball?"

These examples are from children whose first language is English, German, Russian, Finnish, Turkish, or Samoan.

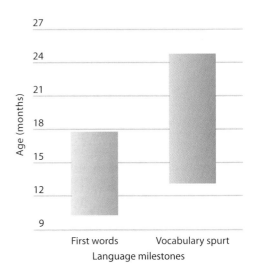

FIGURE 9.3
VARIATION IN LANGUAGE MILESTONES

What is a difference in the way children learn Chinese Mandarin and English?

Around the world, most young children learn to speak in two-word utterances, at about 18 to 24 months of age. *What implications does this have for the biological basis of language?*

Typical Age	Language Milestones
Birth	Crying
2 to 4 months	Cooing begins
5 months	Understands first word
6 months	Babbling begins
7 to 11 months	Change from universal linguist to language-specific listener
8 to 12 months	Uses gestures, such as showing and pointing Comprehension of words appears
13 months	First word spoken
18 months	Vocabulary spurt starts
18 to 24 months	Uses two-word utterances Rapid expansion of understanding of words

FIGURE **9.4**

SOME LANGUAGE MILESTONES IN INFANCY.
Despite great variations in the language input received by infants, around the world they follow a similar path in learning to speak.

telegraphic speech The use of short, precise words without grammatical markers such as articles, auxiliary verbs, and other connectives.

Notice that the two-word utterances omit many parts of speech and are remarkably succinct. In fact, in every language, a child's first combinations of words have this economical quality; they are telegraphic. **Telegraphic speech** is the use of short and precise words without grammatical markers such as articles, auxiliary verbs, and other connectives. Telegraphic speech is not limited to two words. "Mommy give ice cream" and "Mommy give Tommy ice cream" also are examples of telegraphic speech.

We have discussed a number of language milestones in infancy. Figure 9.4 summarizes the ages at which infants typically reach these milestones.

EARLY CHILDHOOD

Toddlers move rather quickly from producing two-word utterances to creating three-, four-, and five-word combinations. Between 2 and 3 years of age they begin the transition from saying simple sentences that express a single proposition to saying complex sentences (Bloom, 1998).

Young children's understanding sometimes goes far beyond their speech. One 3-year-old, laughing with delight as an abrupt summer breeze stirred his hair and tickled his skin, commented, "I got breezed!" Many of the oddities of young children's language sound like mistakes to adult listeners. However, from the children's point of view, they are not mistakes. They represent the way young children perceive and understand their world. As children go through their early childhood years, their grasp of the rule systems that govern language increase.

As young children learn the special features of their own language, there are extensive regularities in how they acquire that particular language (Berko Gleason, 2009). For example, all children learn the prepositions *on* and *in* before other prepositions. Children learning other languages, such as Russian or Chinese, also acquire the particular features of those languages in a consistent order.

However, some children develop language problems, including speech and hearing problems. To read about the work of one individual who helps children who have speech/language and hearing problems, see *Connecting With Careers*.

Understanding Phonology and Morphology   During the preschool years, most children gradually become more sensitive to the sounds of spoken words and become increasingly capable of producing all the sounds of their language (National Research Council, 1999). By the time, children are 3 years of age, they can produce all the vowel sounds and most of the consonant sounds (Menn & Stoel-Gammon, 2009).

Young children can even produce complex consonant clusters such as *str-* and *-mpt-*. They notice rhymes, enjoy poems, make up silly names for things by substituting one sound for another (such as bubblegum, bubblebum, bubbleyum), and clap along with each syllable in a phrase.

By the time children move beyond two-word utterances, they demonstrate a knowledge of morphology rules (Tager-Flusberg & Zukowski, 2009). Children begin using the plural and possessive forms of nouns (such as *dogs* and *dog's*). They put appropriate endings on verbs (such as *-s* when the subject is third-person singular and *-ed* for the past tense). They use prepositions (such as *in* and *on*), articles (such as *a* and *the*), and various forms of the verb *to be* (such as "I was going to the store"). Some of the best evidence for changes in children's use of morphological rules occurs in their overgeneralization of the rules, as when a preschool child says "foots" instead of "feet," or "goed" instead of "went."

In a classic experiment that was designed to study children's knowledge of morphological rules, such as how to make a plural, Jean Berko (1958) presented preschool children and first-grade children with cards such as the one shown in Figure 9.5. Children were asked to look at the card while the experimenter read aloud the words on the card. Then the children were asked to supply the missing word. This might sound easy, but Berko was interested in the children's ability to apply the appropriate morphological rule—in this case, to say "wugs" with the *z* sound that indicates the plural.

connecting with careers

Sharla Peltier, Speech Pathologist

A speech pathologist is a health professional who works with individuals who have a communication disorder. Sharla Peltier is a speech pathologist in Manitoulin, Ontario, Canada. Peltier works with Native American children in the First Nations Schools. She conducts screening for speech/language and hearing problems and assesses infants as young as 6 months of age as well as school-aged children. She works closely with community health nurses to identify hearing problems.

Diagnosing problems is only about half of what Peltier does in her work. She especially enjoys treating speech/language and hearing problems. She conducts parent training sessions to help parents understand and help with their children's language problems. As part of this training, she guides parents in improving their communication skills with their children.

For more information about what speech therapists do, see page 46 in the Careers in Child Development appendix following Chapter 1.

Speech therapist Sharla Peltier, helping a young child improve her language and communication skills.

Although the children's answers were not perfect, they were much better than they could have been by chance. What makes Berko's study impressive is that most of the words were made up for the experiment. Thus, the children could not base their responses on remembering past instances of hearing the words. Since they could make the plurals or past tenses of words they had never heard before, this was proof that they knew the morphological rules.

Changes in Syntax and Semantics   Preschool children also learn and apply rules of syntax (Lidz, 2010; Tager-Flusberg & Zukowski, 2009). They show a growing mastery of complex rules for how words should be ordered.

Consider *wh-* questions, such as "Where is Daddy going?" or "What is that boy doing?" To ask these questions properly, the child must know two important differences between *wh-* questions and affirmative statements (for instance, "Daddy is going to work" and "That boy is waiting on the school bus"). First, a *wh-* word must be added at the beginning of the sentence. Second, the auxiliary verb must be inverted—that is, exchanged with the subject of the sentence. Young children learn quite early where to put the *wh-* word, but they take much longer to learn the auxiliary-inversion rule. Thus, preschool children might ask, "Where Daddy is going?" and "What that boy is doing?"

Gains in semantics also characterize early childhood. Vocabulary development is dramatic (Diesendruck, 2010; Pan & Uccelli, 2009). Some experts have concluded that between 18 months and 6 years of age, young children learn approximately one new word every waking hour (Carey, 1977; Gelman & Kalish, 2006)! By the time they enter first grade, it is estimated that children know about 14,000 words (Clark, 1993). Children who enter elementary school with a small vocabulary are at risk for developing reading problems (Berninger, 2006).

This is a wug.

Now there is another one. There are two of them. There are two _____.

FIGURE **9.5**

STIMULI IN BERKO'S STUDY OF YOUNG CHILDREN'S UNDERSTANDING OF MORPHOLOGICAL RULES. In Jean Berko's (1958) study, young children were presented cards, such as this one with a "wug" on it. Then the children were asked to supply the missing word; in supplying the missing word, they had to say it correctly too. "Wugs" is the correct response here.

How do children's language abilities develop during early childhood?

Why can children learn so many new words so quickly? One possible explanation is **fast mapping,** which involves children's ability to make an initial connection between a word and its referent after only limited exposure to the word (Woodward, Markman, & Fitzimmons, 1994). Researchers have found that exposure to words on multiple occasions over several days results in more successful word learning than the same number of exposures in a single day (Childers & Tomasello, 2002).

Language researchers have proposed that young children may use a number of working hypotheses to accomplish their fast mapping (Pan & Uccelli, 2009). One working hypothesis children use is to give a novel label to a novel object. Parents can be especially helpful in aiding children's learning of novel labels for novel objects. As a mother looks at a picture book with her young child, she knows that the child understands the referent for *car* but not *bus*, so she says, "That's a bus, not a car. A bus is bigger than a car." Another working hypothesis children use is that a word refers to a whole object rather than parts of an object, such as labeling a tiger a tiger instead of tail or paw. Sometimes children's initial mappings are incorrect. In such cases, they benefit from hearing the words mature speakers use to test and revise their word-referent connections (Gershkoff-Stowe & Hahn, 2007).

How parents talk to their children is linked with the children's vocabulary growth and the family's socioeconomic status. To read about how family environment affects children's language development, see *Connecting Through Research.*

Advances in Pragmatics   Changes in pragmatics also characterize young children's language development (Bryant, 2009; Siegal & Surian, 2010). A 6-year-old is simply a much better conversationalist than a 2-year-old is. What are some of the improvements in pragmatics during the preschool years?

Young children begin to engage in extended discourse (Akhtar & Herold, 2008). For example, they learn culturally specific rules of conversation and politeness, and increasingly adapt their speech in different settings. Their developing linguistic skills and improving ability to understand the perspective of others contribute to their use of more competent narratives.

What characterizes advances in pragmatics during early childhood?

fast mapping A process that helps to explain how young children learn the connection between a word and its referent so quickly.

As children get older, they become increasingly able to talk about things that are not here (Grandma's house, for example) and not now (what happened to them yesterday or might happen tomorrow, for example). A preschool child can tell you what she wants for lunch tomorrow, something that would not have been possible at the two-word stage of language development.

At about 4 years of age, children develop a remarkable sensitivity to the needs of others in conversation. One way in which they show such sensitivity is through their use of the articles *the* and *an* (or *a*). When adults tell a story or describe an event, they generally use *an* (or *a*) when they first refer to an animal or an object, and then use *the* when referring to it later. (For example, "Two boys were walking through the jungle when *a* fierce lion appeared. *The* lion lunged at one boy while the other ran for cover.") Even 3-year-olds follow part of this rule; they consistently use the word *the* when referring to previously mentioned things. However, the use of the word *a* when something is initially mentioned develops more slowly. Although 5-year-old children follow this rule on some occasions, they fail to follow it on others.

At around 4 to 5 years of age, children learn to change their speech style to suit the situation. For example, even 4-year-old children speak differently to a 2-year-old than to a same-aged peer; they use shorter sentences with the 2-year-old. They also speak differently to an adult than to a same-aged peer, using more polite and formal language with the adult (Shatz & Gelman, 1973).

How Does Family Environment Affect Young Children's Language Development?

What characteristics of families influence children's language development? Socioeconomic status has been linked with how much parents talk to their children and with young children's vocabulary. Betty Hart and Todd Risley (1995) observed the language environments of children whose parents were professionals and children whose parents were on welfare. Compared with the professional parents, the parents on welfare talked much less to their young children, talked less about past events, and provided less elaboration. As indicated in Figure 9.6, the children of the professional parents had a much larger vocabulary at 36 months of age than the children whose parents were on welfare.

Other research has explored the relationship between how much mothers speak to their infants and the infants' vocabularies. For example, in one study by Janellen Huttenlocher and her colleagues (1991), infants whose mothers spoke to them more often had markedly higher vocabularies. By age 2, vocabulary differences were substantial. However, a study of 1- to 3-year-old children living in low-income families found that the sheer amount of maternal talk was not the best predictor of a child's vocabulary growth (Pan & others, 2005). Rather, it was maternal language and literacy skills and mothers' use of diverse vocabulary that best predicted children's vocabulary development.

A recent study revealed that maternal sensitivity (warm response to the child's bids for attention and anticipation of her child's emotional needs, for example), regardless of socioeconomic status and ethnicity, was positively linked with growth in young children's receptive and expressive language development from 18 to 36 months of age (Pungello & others, 2009). In this study, negative intrusive parenting (physically restraining the child or dominating interaction with the child with unnecessary verbal direction, for example) was related to a slower rate of growth of receptive language.

These research studies and others (NICHD Early Child Care Research Network, 2005) demonstrate the important effect that early speech input and poverty can have on the development of a child's language skills. Children in low-income families are more likely to have less educated parents, receive inadequate nutrition, live in low-income communities, and attend substandard schools than children in middle- and high-income families (Row, Burns, & Griffin, 1998). However, living in a low-income family should not be used as the sole identifier in predicting whether children will have difficulties in language development, such as a low vocabulary and reading problems. If children growing up in low-income families experience effective instruction and support, they can develop effective language skills (Barbarin & Aikens, 2009).

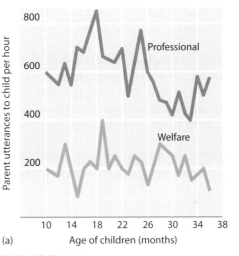

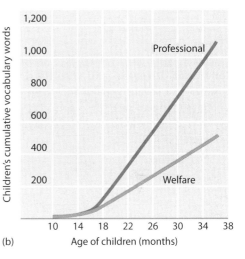

(a) Age of children (months)

(b) Age of children (months)

FIGURE **9.6**

LANGUAGE INPUT IN PROFESSIONAL AND WELFARE FAMILIES AND YOUNG CHILDREN'S VOCABULARY DEVELOPMENT. (*a*) In this study (Hart & Risley, 1995), parents from professional families talked with their young children more than parents from welfare families. (*b*) All of the children learned to talk, but children from professional families developed vocabularies that were twice as large as those from welfare families. Thus, by the time children go to preschool, they already have experienced considerable differences in language input in their families and developed different levels of vocabulary that are linked to their socioeconomic context. *Does this study indicate that poverty caused deficiencies in vocabulary development?*

Early Literacy   Concern about U.S. children's reading and writing skills has led to a careful examination of preschool and kindergarten children's educational experiences, with the hope that a positive orientation toward reading and writing can be developed early in life (Jalongo, 2011; Otto, 2010; Wagner, 2010). What should a literacy program for preschool children be like? Instruction should be built on what children already know about oral language, reading, and writing. Further, early precursors of literacy and academic success include language skills,

developmental connection

Attention. The ability of children to control and sustain their attention is related to school readiness. Chapter 7, p. 207

What are some effective strategies for supporting young children's literacy skills?

phonological and syntactic knowledge, letter identification, and conceptual knowledge about print and its conventions and functions (Christie, Ewz, & Vukelich, 2011). Parents and teachers need to provide a supportive environment to help children develop literacy skills (Beatty & Pratt, 2011). A recent study revealed that children whose mothers had more education had more advanced emergent literacy skills than children whose mothers had less education (Korat, 2009). Another recent study found that literacy experiences (such as how often the child was read to), the quality of the mother's engagement with her child (such as attempts to cognitively stimulate the child) and provision of learning materials (such as age-appropriate learning materials and books) were important home literacy experiences in low-income families that were linked to the children's language development in positive ways (Rodriquez & others, 2009).

The following longitudinal studies indicate the importance of early language skills and children's school readiness:

- Phonological awareness, letter name and sound knowledge, and naming speed in kindergarten were linked to reading success in the first and second grade (Schattschneider & others, 2004).
- Children's early home environment influenced their early language skills, which in turn predicted their readiness for school (Forget-Dobois & others 2009).

So far, our discussion of early literacy has focused on U.S. children. For example, the extent to which phonological awareness is linked to learning to read effectively varies across language to some extent (McBride-Chang, 2004). One study of second-grade students from Beijing, Hong Kong, Korea, and the United States revealed that phonological awareness may be more important for early reading development in English and Korean than it is for Chinese (McBride-Chang & others, 2005). Further, rates of dyslexia differ across countries and are linked with the spelling and phonetic rules that characterize the language (McBride-Chang & others, 2008). English is one of the more difficult languages to learn because of its irregular spellings and pronunciations. In countries where English is spoken, the rate of dyslexia is higher than it is in countries where the alphabet script is more phonetically pronounced.

developmental **connection**

Conditions, Diseases, and Disorders. Dyslexia is a severe impairment in the ability to read and spell; dysgraphia is a severe impairment in handwriting ability. Chapter 16, p. 468

MIDDLE AND LATE CHILDHOOD

Children gain new skills as they enter school that make it possible for them to learn to read and write, or to advance the reading and writing skills they have developed in early childhood. These new skills include increasingly using language to talk about things that are not physically present, learning what a word is, and learning how to recognize and talk about sounds (Berko Gleason, 2005). They have to learn the alphabetic principle, that the letters of the alphabet represent sounds of the language. As children develop during middle and late childhood, changes in their vocabulary and grammar also take place (Vukelich, Christie, & Enz, 2008).

Vocabulary, Grammar, and Metalinguistic Awareness   During middle and late childhood, changes occur in the way children's mental vocabulary is organized. When asked to say the first word that comes to mind when they hear a word, young children typically provide a word that often follows the word in a sentence. For example, when asked to respond to *dog* the young child may say "barks," or to the word *eat* say "lunch." At about 7 years of age, children begin to respond with a word that is the same part of speech as the stimulus word. For example, a child may now respond to the word *dog* with "cat" or "horse."

Children pick up words as pigeons peas.

—JOHN RAY
English Naturalist, 17th Century

Stage	Age range/Grade level	Descripton
0	Birth to first grade	Children master several prerequisites for reading. Many learn the left-to-right progression and order of reading, how to identify letters of the alphabet, and how to write their names. Some learn to read words that appear on signs. As a result of TV shows like *Sesame Street* and attending preschool and kindergarten programs, many young children today develop greater knowledge about reading earlier than in the past.
1	First and second grades	Many children learn to read at this time. In doing so, they acquire the ability to sound out words (that is, translate letters into sounds and blend sounds into words). They also complete their learning of letter names and sounds.
2	Second and third grades	Children become more fluent at retrieving individual words and other reading skills. However, at this stage reading is still not used much for learning. The demands of reading are so taxing for children at this stage that they have few resources left over to process the content.
3	Fourth through eighth grades	In fourth through eighth grade, children become increasingly able to obtain new information from print. In other words, they read to learn. They still have difficulty understanding information presented from multiple perspectives within the same story. When children don't learn to read, a downward spiral unfolds that leads to serious difficulties in many academic subjects.
4	High school	Many students become fully competent readers. They develop the ability to understand material told from many perspectives. This allows them to engage in sometimes more sophisticated discussions of literature, history, economics, and politics.

FIGURE **9.7**

A MODEL OF DEVELOPMENTAL STAGES IN READING

To *eat*, they now might say "drink." This is evidence that at age 7 children have begun to categorize their vocabulary by parts of speech (Berko Gleason, 2003).

The process of categorizing becomes easier as children increase their vocabulary. Children's vocabulary increases from an average of about 14,000 words at 6 years of age to an average of about 40,000 words by 11 years of age.

Children make similar advances in grammar. During the elementary school years, children's improvement in logical reasoning and analytical skills helps them to understand constructions such as the appropriate use of comparatives (shorter, deeper) and subjectives ("If you were president . . ."). During the elementary school years, children become increasingly able to understand and use complex grammar, such as the following sentence: "The boy who kissed his mother wore a hat." They also learn to use language to produce connected discourse. They become able to relate sentences to one another to produce descriptions, definitions, and narratives that make sense. Children must be able to do these things orally before they can be expected to deal with them in written assignments.

These advances in vocabulary and grammar during the elementary school years are accompanied by the development of **metalinguistic awareness,** which is knowledge about language, such as understanding what a preposition is or being able to discuss the sounds of a language. Metalinguistic awareness allows children "to think about their language, understand what words are, and even define them" (Berko Gleason, 2009, p. 4). This awareness improves considerably during the elementary school years (Pan & Uccelli, 2009). Defining words becomes a regular part of classroom discourse, and children increase their knowledge of syntax as they study and talk about the components of sentences such as subjects and verbs (Melzi & Ely, 2009).

Children also make progress in understanding how to use language in culturally appropriate ways—pragmatics (Bryant, 2009). By the time they enter adolescence, most children know the rules for the use of language in everyday contexts—that is, what is appropriate to say and what is inappropriate to say.

Reading One model identifies five stages in the development of reading skills (Chall, 1979) (see Figure 9.7). The age boundaries are approximate and do not apply to every child, but the stages convey a sense of the developmental changes involved in learning to read.

Before learning to read, children learn to use language to talk about things that are not present; they learn what a word is; and they learn how to recognize sounds and talk about them (Berko Gleason, 2003). If they develop a large vocabulary, their

developmental **connection**

Information Processing. Metacognition is cognition about cognition or knowing about knowing. Chapter 7, p. 225

This teacher is helping a student sound out words. Researchers have found that phonics instruction is a key aspect of teaching students to read, especially beginning readers and students with weak reading skills.

metalinguistic awareness Knowledge about language.

path to reading is eased. Children who begin elementary school with a small vocabulary are at risk when it comes to learning to read (Berko Gleason, 2003).

Vocabulary development plays an important role in reading comprehension (Cunningham, 2009). For example, one study revealed that a good vocabulary was linked with reading comprehension in second-grade students (Berninger & Abbott, 2005). Having a good vocabulary helps readers access word meaning effortlessly.

Recent analyses by Rich Mayer (2008) focused on the cognitive processes a child needs to go through in order to read a printed word. In his view, the three processes are (1) being aware of sound units in words, which consists of recognizing phonemes; (2) decoding words, which involves converting printed words into sounds; and (3) accessing word meaning, which consists of finding a mental representation of a word's meaning.

What are the most effective ways to teach children how to read? Education and language experts continue to debate how children should be taught to read. Currently, debate focuses on the phonics approach versus the whole-language approach (Vacca & others, 2009).

The **phonics approach** emphasizes that reading instruction should focus basic rules for translating written symbols into sounds. Early reading instruction should involve simplified materials. Only after children have learned the correspondence rules that relate spoken phonemes to the alphabet letters that represent them should they be given complex reading materials, such as books and poems (Cunningham & Hall, 2009).

By contrast, the **whole-language approach** stresses that reading instruction should parallel children's natural language learning. Reading materials should be whole and meaningful. That is, children should be given material in its complete form, such as stories and poems, so that they learn to understand language's communicative function. Reading should be connected with listening and writing skills. Although there are variations in whole-language programs, most share the premise that reading should be integrated with other skills and subjects, such as science and social studies, and that it should focus on real-world material. Thus, a class might read newspapers, magazines, or books, and then write about and discuss them. In some whole-language classes, beginning readers are taught to recognize whole words or even entire sentences, and to use the context of what they are reading to guess at unfamiliar words.

Which approach is better? Children can benefit from both approaches, but direct instruction in phonics needs to take place, especially in kindergarten and the first grade (Cunningham & Allington, 2010; Tompkins, 2011).

At the beginning of our discussion of reading, we described Mayer's (2008) view that decoding words is a key cognitive process in learning to read. Important in this regard are certain metacognitive skills and increasing automaticity that is characterized by fluency (Allington, 2009; Kuhn, 2009). Metacognition, which we discussed in Chapter 7, is involved in reading in the sense that good readers develop control of their own reading skills and understand how reading works. For example, good readers know that it is important to comprehend the "gist" of what an author is saying. Teachers can help students develop good metacognitive strategies for reading by getting them to monitor their own reading, especially when they run into difficulties in their reading (Boulware-Gooden & others, 2007).

When students process information automatically, they do so with little or no conscious effort. When word recognition occurs rapidly, meaning also often follows in a rapid fashion. Many beginning or poor readers do not recognize words automatically. Their processing capacity is consumed by the demands of word recognition, so they have less capacity to devote to comprehension of groupings of words as phrases or sentences. As their processing of words and passages become more automatic, it is said that their reading becomes more fluent (Kuhn, 2009).

Reading, like other important skills, takes time and effort. In a national assessment, children in the fourth grade had higher scores on a national reading test when

Children most at risk for reading difficulties in the first grade are those who began school with less verbal skill, less phonological awareness, less letter knowledge, and less familiarity with the basic purposes and mechanisms of reading.

—CATHERINE SNOW
Harvard University

phonics approach An approach that emphasizes that reading instruction should focus on phonics and its basic rules for translating written symbols into sounds.

whole-language approach An approach that stresses that reading instruction should parallel children's natural language learning. Reading materials should be whole and meaningful.

they read 11 or more pages daily for school and homework (National Assessment of Educational Progress, 2000) (see Figure 9.8). Teachers who required students to read a great deal on a daily basis had students who were more proficient at reading than teachers who required little reading by their students.

Writing Children's writing emerges out of their early scribbles, which appear at around 2 to 3 years of age. In early childhood, children's motor skills usually develop to the point that they can begin printing letters. Most 4-year-olds can print their first name. Five-year-olds can reproduce letters and copy several short words. They gradually learn to distinguish the distinctive characteristics of letters, such as whether the lines are curved or straight, open or closed. Through the early elementary grades, many children continue to reverse letters such as *b* and *d* and *p* and *q* (Temple & others, 1993). At this age, if other aspects of the child's development are normal, letter reversals do not predict literacy problems.

As they begin to write, children often invent spellings. Usually they base these spellings on the sounds of words they hear (Cunningham & Allington, 2010; Spandel, 2009). Parents and teachers should encourage children's early writing but not be overly concerned about letter formation or spelling.

Like becoming a good reader, becoming a good writer takes many years and lots of practice (Jalongo, 2011). Children should be given many writing opportunities in the elementary and secondary school years (Graham, 2009; Wyse, Andrews, & Hoffman, 2010). As their language and cognitive skills improve with good instruction, so will their writing skills. For example, developing a more sophisticated understanding of syntax and grammar serves as an underpinning for better writing (Irvin, Buehl, & Klemp, 2007).

So do cognitive skills such as organization and logical reasoning (Perin, 2007). Through elementary, middle, and high school, students develop increasingly sophisticated methods of organizing their ideas. In early elementary school, they narrate and describe or write short poems. In late elementary and middle school, they move to projects such as book reports that combine narration with more reflection and analysis. In high school, they become more skilled at forms of exposition that do not depend on narrative structure (Conley, 2008). A recent meta-analysis (use of statistical techniques to combine the results of studies) revealed that the following interventions were the most effective in improving fourth- through twelfth-grade students' writing quality: (1) strategy instruction, (2) summarization, (3) peer assistance, and (4) setting goals (Graham & Perin, 2007).

Major concerns about students' writing competence are increasingly being voiced (Graham, 2009). One study revealed that 70 to 75 percent of U.S. students in grades 4 through 12 are low-achieving writers (Persky, Dane, & Jin, 2003). College instructors report that 50 percent of high school graduates are not prepared for college-level writing (Achieve, Inc., 2005).

As with reading, teachers play a critical role in students' development of writing skills (Ariza & Lapp, 2011; Christie, Enz, & Vukelich, 2011; Graham, 2009). Classroom

Anna Mudd is the 6-year-old author of "The Devl and the Babe Goste." Anna has been writing stories for at least two years. Her story includes poetic images, sophisticated syntax, and vocabulary that reflect advances in language development.

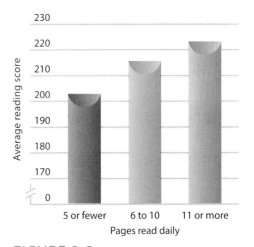

FIGURE **9.8**

THE RELATION OF READING ACHIEVEMENT TO NUMBER OF PAGES READ DAILY. In the analysis of reading in the fourth grade in the National Assessment of Educational Progress (2000), reading more pages daily in school and as part of homework assignments was related to higher scores on a reading test in which scores ranged from 0 to 500.

PEANUTS © United Features Syndicate, Inc.

Beverly Gallagher, a third-grade teacher in Princeton, New Jersey, working with students to stimulate their interest in writing. She created the Imagine the Possibilities program, which brings nationally known poets and authors to her school. She phones each student's parents periodically to describe their child's progress and new interests. She invites students from higher grades to work with small groups in her class so that she can spend more one-on-one time with students. Each of her students keeps a writer's notebook to record thoughts, inspirations, and special words that intrigue them. Students get special opportunities to sit in an author's chair, where they read their writing to the class. (*Source: USA Today*, 2000)

observations made by Michael Pressley and his colleagues (2007) indicate that students become good writers when teachers spend considerable time on writing instruction and are passionate about teaching students to write. Their observations also indicate that classrooms with students who receive high scores on writing assessments have walls that overflow with examples of effective writing, whereas it is much harder to find such examples on the walls of classrooms that have many students who receive low scores on writing assessments.

Bilingualism and Second-Language Learning   Are there sensitive periods in learning a second language? That is, if individuals want to learn a second language, how important is the age at which they begin to learn it? For many years, it was claimed that if individuals did not learn a second language prior to puberty, they would never reach native-language-learners' proficiency in the second language (Johnson & Newport, 1991). However, recent research indicates a more complex conclusion: Sensitive periods likely vary across different language systems (Thomas & Johnson, 2008). Thus, for late language learners, such as adolescents and adults, new vocabulary is easier to learn than new sounds or new grammar (Neville, 2006). For example, children's ability to pronounce words with a nativelike accent in a second language typically decreases with age, with an especially sharp drop occurring after the age of about 10 to 12. Also, adults tend to learn a second language faster than children, but their final level of second-language attainment is not as high as children's. And the way children and adults learn a second language differs somewhat. Compared with adults, children are less sensitive to feedback, less likely to use explicit strategies, and more likely to learn a second language from a large amount of input (Thomas & Johnson, 2008).

Some aspects of children's ability to learn a second language are transferred more easily to the second language than are others (Paradis, 2010; Pena & Bedore, 2009). A recent research review indicated that in learning to read, phonological awareness is rooted in general cognitive processes and thus transfers easily across languages; however, decoding is more language-specific and needs to be relearned with each language (Bialystok, 2007).

Students in the United States are far behind their counterparts in many developed countries in learning a second language. For example, schools in Russia have 10 grades, called forms, that correspond roughly to the 12 grades in American schools. Children begin school at age 7 in Russia and begin learning English in the third form. Because of this emphasis on teaching English, most Russian citizens under the age of 40 today are able to speak at least some English. The United States is the only technologically advanced Western nation that does not require foreign language study in high school, even for students in rigorous academic programs.

U.S. students may be missing more than the chance to acquire a skill by not learning to speak a second language (Quiocho & Ulanhoff, 2009). Bilingualism—the ability to speak two languages—has a positive effect on children's cognitive development (Gibbons & Ng, 2004). Children who are fluent in two languages perform better than their single-language counterparts on tests of control of attention, concept formation, analytical reasoning, cognitive flexibility, and cognitive complexity (Bialystok, 2001, 2007). They also are more conscious of the structure of spoken and written language and better at noticing errors of grammar and meaning, skills that benefit their reading ability (Bialystok, 1997). However, a research review concluded that bilingual children have lower formal language proficiency (smaller vocabulary, for example) than monolingual children (Bialystok & Craik, 2010).

In the United States, many immigrant children go from being monolingual in their home language to bilingual in that language and in English, only to end up

metaphor *An implied comparison between two unlike things.*

satire The use of irony, derision, or wit to expose folly or wickedness.

Salvador Tamayo, Bilingual Education Teacher

Salvador Tamayo teaches bilingual education in the fifth grade at Indian Knoll Elementary School in West Chicago. In 2000, he received a National Educator Award from the Milken Family Foundation for his work in bilingual education at Turner Elementary School in West Chicago. Tamayo is especially adept at integrating technology into his bilingual education classes. He and his students created several award-winning Web sites about the West Chicago City Museum, the local Latino community, and the history of West Chicago. His students also developed an "I Want to Be an American Citizen" Web site to assist family and community members in preparing for the U.S. Citizenship Test. Tamayo also teaches a bilingual education class at Wheaton College.

For more information about what elementary school teachers do, see page 44 in the Careers in Child Development appendix following Chapter 1.

Salvador Tamayo working with bilingual education students.

monolingual speakers of English. This is called subtractive bilingualism, and it can have negative effects on children if they become ashamed of their home language.

A current controversy related to bilingualism involves the most effective way of teaching children whose primary language is not English and who are enrolled in U.S. schools (Oller & Jarmulowicz, 2010; Gonzales, 2009). To read about the work of one bilingual education teacher, see the *Connecting With Careers* profile of Salvador Tamayo, and for a discussion of the debate about bilingual education, read the *Connecting With Diversity* that follows.

> **developmental connection**
>
> **Cognitive Theory.** According to Piaget, at 11 to 15 years of age a new stage—formal operational thought—emerges that is characterized by thought that is more abstract, idealistic, and logical. Chapter 6, p. 185

ADOLESCENCE

Language development during adolescence includes increased sophistication in the use of words (Berman, 2010). With an increase in abstract thinking, adolescents are much better than children at analyzing the function a word performs in a sentence.

Adolescents also develop more subtle abilities with words. They make strides in understanding **metaphor,** which is an implied comparison between unlike things. For example, individuals "draw a line in the sand" to indicate a nonnegotiable position; a political campaign is said to be "a marathon, not a sprint"; a person's faith is "shattered." And adolescents become better able to understand and to use **satire,** which is the use of irony, derision, or wit to expose folly or wickedness. Caricatures are an example of satire. More advanced logical thinking also allows adolescents, from about 15 to 20 years of age, to understand complex literary works.

Most adolescents are also much better readers and writers than children are. As indicated in Figure 9.7, many adolescents

What are some changes in language development in adolescence?

Bilingual Education

What is the best way to teach children whose primary language is not English? For the last two decades, the preferred strategy has been *bilingual education,* which teaches academic subjects to immigrant children in their native language while slowly teaching English (Herrera & Murry, 2011; Peregoy & Boyle, 2009). Advocates of bilingual education programs argue that if children who do not know English are taught only in English, they will fall behind in academic subjects. How, they ask, can 7-year-olds learn arithmetic or history taught only in English when they do not speak the language?

Some critics of bilingual programs argue that too often it is thought that immigrant children need only one year of bilingual education. However, in general it takes immigrant children approximately three to five years to develop speaking proficiency and seven years to develop reading proficiency in English (Hakuta, Butler, & Witt, 2001). Also, immigrant children vary in their ability to learn English (Lessow-Hurley, 2009; Levine & McClosky, 2009). Children who come from lower socioeconomic backgrounds have more difficulty than those from higher socioeconomic backgrounds (Hakuta, 2001). Thus, especially for immigrant children from lower socioeconomic backgrounds, more years of bilingual education may be needed than they currently are receiving.

Critics who oppose bilingual education argue that as a result of these programs, the children of immigrants are not learning English, which puts them at a permanent disadvantage in U.S. society. California, Arizona, and Massachusetts have significantly reduced the number of bilingual education programs they offer. Some states continue to endorse bilingual education, but the emphasis that test scores be reported separately for English-language learners (students whose main language is not English) in the No Child Left Behind state assessments has shifted attention to literacy in English (Rivera & Collum, 2006; Snow & Yang, 2006).

What have researchers found regarding outcomes of bilingual education programs? Drawing conclusions about the effectiveness of bilingual education programs is difficult because of variations across programs in the number of years they are in effect, type of instruction, qualities of schooling other than bilingual education, teachers, children, and other factors. Further, no effectively conducted experiments that compare bilingual education with English-only education in the United States have been conducted (Snow & Yang, 2006). Some experts have concluded that the quality of instruction is more important in determining outcomes than the language in which it is delivered (Lesaux & Siegel, 2003).

Research supports bilingual education in that (1) children have difficulty learning a subject when it is taught in a language they do not understand; and (2) when both languages are integrated in the classroom, children learn the second language more readily and participate more actively (Gonzales, Yawkey, & Minaya-Rowe, 2006; Hakuta, 2005). However, many of the research results report only modest rather than strong support for bilingual education, and some supporters of bilingual education now acknowledge that English-only instruction can produce positive outcomes for English-language learners (Lesaux & Siegel, 2003).

You learned that immigrant children who come from lower-socioeconomic-status (SES) backgrounds typically have a more difficult time learning English. What did you learn about SES and vocabulary development in the Connecting Through Research *interlude earlier in this chapter? What research questions are suggested by comparing these findings?*

---

increase their understanding of material told from different perspectives, which allows them to engage in more sophisticated discussions of various topics. In terms of writing, they are better at organizing ideas before they write, at distinguishing between general and specific points as they write, at stringing together sentences that make sense, and at organizing their writing into an introduction, body, and concluding remarks.

Everyday speech changes during adolescence, and "part of being a successful teenager is being able to talk like one" (Berko Gleason, 2005, p. 9). Young adolescents often speak a **dialect** with their peers that is characterized by jargon and slang (Cave, 2002). A dialect is a variety of language that is distinguished by its vocabulary, grammar, or pronunciation. For example, when meeting a friend, instead of saying hello, a young adolescent might say, "Hey, dude, 'sup?" Nicknames that are satirical and derisive ("Stilt," "Refrigerator," "Spaz") also characterize the dialect of young adolescents. Such labels might be used to show that one belongs to the group and to reduce the seriousness of a situation (Cave, 2002).

dialect A variety of language that is distinguished by its vocabulary, grammar, or pronunciation.

Biological and Environmental Influences

LG3 Discuss the biological and environmental contributions to language development.

Biological Influences   Environmental Influences   An Interactionist View of Language

We have described how language develops, but we have not explained what makes this amazing development possible. Everyone who uses language in some way "knows" its rules and has the ability to create an infinite number of words and sentences. Where does this knowledge come from? Is it the product of biology? Or is language learned and influenced by experiences?

BIOLOGICAL INFLUENCES

Some language scholars view the remarkable similarities in how children acquire language all over the world, despite the vast variation in language input they receive, as strong evidence that language has a biological basis. What role did evolution play in the biological foundations of language?

In the wild, chimps communicate through calls, gestures, and expressions, which evolutionary psychologists believe might be the roots of true language.

Evolution and the Brain's Role in Language   The ability to speak and understand language requires a certain vocal apparatus as well as a nervous system with certain capabilities. The nervous system and vocal apparatus of humanity's predecessors changed over hundreds of thousands or millions of years. With advances in the nervous system and vocal structures, Homo sapiens went beyond the grunting and shrieking of other animals to develop speech. Although estimates vary, many experts believe that humans acquired language about 100,000 years ago, which in evolutionary time represents a very recent acquisition. It gave humans an enormous edge over other animals and increased the chances of human survival (Pinker, 1994).

There is evidence that particular regions of the brain are predisposed to be used for language (Bortfeld, Fava, & Boas, 2009; Shafer & Garrido-Nag, 2010; Spocter & others, 2010). Two regions involved in language were first discovered

developmental connection

Language. Much of language is processed in the brain's left hemisphere. Chapter 4, p. 114

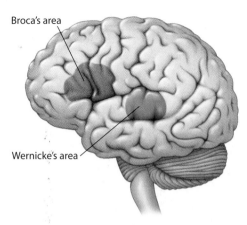

Broca's area

Wernicke's area

FIGURE **9.9**

BROCA'S AREA AND WERNICKE'S AREA.
Broca's area is located in the frontal lobe of the brain's left hemisphere, and it is involved in the control of speech. Individuals with damage to Broca's area have problems saying words correctly. Also shown is Wernicke's area, a portion of the left hemisphere's temporal lobe that is involved in understanding language. Individuals with damage to this area cannot comprehend words; that is, they hear the words but don't know what they mean.

MIT linguist Noam Chomsky. *What is Chomsky's view of language?*

Broca's area An area of the brain's left frontal lobe that is involved in speech production and grammatical processing.

Wernicke's area An area of the brain's left hemisphere that is involved in language comprehension.

aphasia A disorder resulting from brain damage to Broca's area or Wernicke's area that involves a loss or impairment of the ability to use or comprehend words.

language acquisition device (LAD) Chomsky's term that describes a biological endowment that enables the child to detect the features and rules of language, including phonology, syntax, and semantics.

in studies of brain-damaged individuals: **Broca's area,** an area in the left frontal lobe of the brain involved in speech production and grammatical processing, and **Wernicke's area,** a region of the brain's left hemisphere involved in language comprehension (see Figure 9.9). Damage to either of these areas produces types of **aphasia,** which is a loss or impairment of language processing. Individuals with damage to Broca's area have difficulty producing words correctly; individuals with damage to Wernicke's area have poor comprehension and often produce fluent but incomprehensible speech.

Chomsky's Language Acquisition Device (LAD)   Linguist Noam Chomsky (1957) proposed that humans are biologically prewired to learn language at a certain time and in a certain way. He said that children are born into the world with a **language acquisition device (LAD),** a biological endowment that enables the child to detect certain features and rules of language, including phonology, syntax, and semantics. Children are prepared by nature with the ability to detect the sounds of language, for example, and follow rules such as how to form plurals and ask questions.

Chomsky's LAD is a theoretical construct, not a physical part of the brain. Is there evidence for the existence of a LAD? Supporters of the LAD concept cite the uniformity of language milestones across languages and cultures, evidence that children create language even in the absence of well-formed input, and biological substrates of language. But as we will see, critics argue that even if infants have something like a LAD, it cannot explain the whole story of language acquisition.

ENVIRONMENTAL INFLUENCES

Decades ago, behaviorists opposed Chomsky's hypothesis and argued that language represents nothing more than chains of responses acquired through reinforcement (Skinner, 1957). A baby happens to babble "Ma-ma"; Mama rewards the baby with hugs and smiles; the baby says "Mama" more and more. Bit by bit, said the behaviorists, the baby's language is built up. According to behaviorists, language is a complex, learned skill, much like playing the piano or dancing.

The behaviorial view of language learning has several problems. First, it does not explain how people create novel sentences—sentences that people have never heard or spoken before. Second, children learn the syntax of their native language even if they are not reinforced for doing so. Social psychologist Roger Brown (1973) spent long hours observing parents and their young children. He found that parents did not directly or explicitly reward or correct the syntax of most children's utterances. That is, parents did not say "good," "correct," "right," "wrong," and so on. Also, parents did not offer direct corrections such as "You should say two shoes, not two shoe." However, as we will see shortly, many parents do expand on their young children's grammatically incorrect utterances and recast many of those that have grammatical errors (Clark, 2009).

The behavioral view is no longer considered a viable explanation of how children acquire language. But a great deal of research describes ways in which children's environmental experiences influence their language skills (Berko Gleason & Ratner, 2009). Many language experts argue that a child's experiences, the particular language to be learned, and the context in which learning takes place can strongly influence language acquisition (Goldfield & Snow, 2009).

Language is not learned in a social vacuum. Most children are bathed in language from a very early age (Sachs, 2009). The Wild Boy of Aveyron, who never learned to communicate effectively, had lived in social isolation for years. The support and involvement of caregivers and teachers greatly facilitate a child's language learning (Otto, 2010; Wagner, 2010). For example, one study found that when mothers immediately smiled and touched their 8-month-old infants after they babbled, the infants subsequently made more complex speechlike sounds than when mothers responded to their infants in a random manner (Goldstein, King, & West, 2003) (see Figure 9.10).

Michael Tomasello (2008, 2009) stresses that young children are intensely interested in their social world and that early in their development they can understand the intentions of other people. His interaction view of language emphasizes that children learn language in specific contexts. For example, when a toddler and a father are jointly focused on a book, the father might say, "See the birdie." In this case, even a toddler understands that the father intends to name something and knows to look in the direction of the pointing. Through this kind of joint attention, early in their development children are able to use their social skills to acquire language (Meltzoff, 2009; Tomasello, 2009).

One intriguing component of the young child's linguistic environment is **child-directed speech,** language spoken in a higher pitch than normal with simple words and sentences (Clark, 2009). It is hard to use child-directed speech when not in the presence of a baby. As soon as you start talking to a baby, though, you shift into child-directed speech. Much of this is automatic and something most parents are not aware they are doing. As mentioned previously in this chapter, even 4-year-olds speak in simpler ways to 2-year-olds than to their 4-year-old friends. Child-directed speech has the important function of capturing the infant's attention and maintaining communication (Jaswal & Fernald, 2007).

Adults often use strategies other than child-directed speech to enhance the child's acquisition of language, including recasting, expanding, and labeling:

- **Recasting** is rephrasing something the child has said, perhaps turning it into a question or restating the child's immature utterance in the form of a fully grammatical sentence. For example, if the child says, "The dog was barking," the adult can respond by asking, "When was the dog barking?" Effective recasting lets the child indicate an interest and then elaborates on that interest.

- **Expanding** is restating, in a linguistically sophisticated form, what a child has said. For example, a child says, "Doggie eat," and the parent replies, "Yes, the doggie is eating."

- **Labeling** is identifying the names of objects. Young children are forever being asked to identify the names of objects. Roger Brown (1958) called this "the original word game" and claimed that much of a child's early vocabulary is motivated by this adult pressure to identify the words associated with objects.

Parents use these strategies naturally and in meaningful conversations. Parents do not (and should not) use any deliberate method to teach their children to talk, even for children who are slow in learning language. Children usually benefit when parents guide their children's discovery of language rather than overloading them with language; "following in order to lead" helps a child learn language. If children are not ready to take in some information, they are likely to tell you (perhaps by turning away). Thus, giving the child more information is not always better.

Infants, toddlers, and young children benefit when adults read books to and with them (shared reading) (DeLoache & Ganea, 2009). Storybook reading especially benefits children when parents extend the meaning of the text by discussing the text with children and encouraging them to ask and answer questions (Barbarin & Aikens, 2009; Whitehurst & Lonigan, 1998).

In one study, a majority of U.S. mothers in low-income families reported that they were reading to their infants and toddlers with some regularity (Raikes & others, 2006).

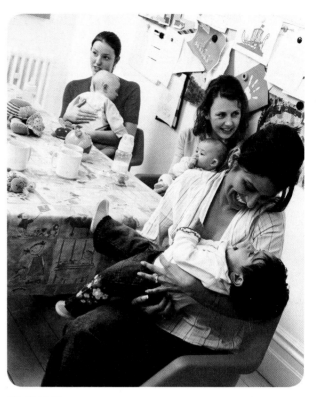

FIGURE **9.10**

SOCIAL INTERACTION AND BABBLING. One study focused on two groups of mothers and their 8-month-old infants (Goldstein, King, & West, 2003). One group of mothers was instructed to smile and touch their infants immediately after the babies cooed and babbled; the other group was also told to smile and touch their infants but in a random manner, unconnected to sounds the infants made. The infants whose mothers immediately responded in positive ways to their babbling subsequently made more complex, speechlike sounds, such as "*da*" and "*gu*."

> The linguistics problems children
> have to solve are always embedded
> in personal and interpersonal contexts.
>
> —**Lois Bloom**
> *Contemporary Psychologist, Columbia University*

child-directed speech Language spoken in a higher pitch than normal, with simple words and sentences.

recasting Rephrasing a statement that a child has said, perhaps turning it into a question, or restating a child's immature utterance in the form of a fully grammatical utterance.

expanding Restating, in a linguistically sophisticated form, what a child has said.

labeling Identifying the names of objects.

How might peers' language skills influence a child's language development?

In this study, non-Latino White, more highly educated mothers who were parenting a first-born child were more likely to read books to their infants and toddlers than were African American and Latino mothers who were parenting later-born children. Reading daily to children at 14 to 24 months of age was positively related to the children's language and cognitive development at 36 months of age. To read further about ways that parents can facilitate children's language development, see *Caring Connections*.

Our discussion of environmental influences on language development has mainly focused on parents. However, children interact with many other people who can influence their language development, including teachers and peers. A recent study of more than 1,800 4-year-olds focused on ways in which peers might influence children's language development (Mashburn & others, 2009). In this study, peers' expressive language abilities were positively linked with young children's receptive and expressive language development.

AN INTERACTIONIST VIEW OF LANGUAGE

If language acquisition depended only on biology, then Genie and the Wild Boy of Aveyron (discussed earlier in the chapter) should have talked without difficulty. A child's experiences influence language acquisition. But we have seen that language does have strong biological foundations (Shafer & Garrido-Nag, 2010). No matter how much you converse with a dog, it won't learn to talk. In contrast, children are biologically prepared to learn language. Children all over the world acquire language milestones at about the same time and in about the same order. However, there are cultural variations in the type of support given to children's language development. For example, caregivers in the Kaluli culture prompt young children to use a loud voice and particular morphemes that direct the speech act performed (calling out) and to refer to names, kinship relations, and places where there has been a shared past experience that indicates a closeness to the person being addressed (Ochs & Schieffelin, 2008; Schieffelin, 2005).

An interactionist view emphasizes that both biology and experience contribute to language development (Bohannon & Bonvillian, 2009; Mueller & Hoff, 2010). This interaction of biology and experience can be seen in the variations in the acquisition of language. Children vary in their ability to acquire language, and this variation cannot be readily explained by differences in environmental input alone. For children who are slow in developing language skills, however, opportunities to talk and be talked with are important. Children whose parents provide them with a rich verbal environment show many positive benefits. Parents who pay attention to what their children are trying to say, who expand their children's utterances, who read to them, and who label things in the environment are providing valuable, if unintentional, benefits (Berko Gleason, 2009).

American psychologist Jerome Bruner (1983, 1996) proposed that the sociocultural context is extremely important in understanding children's language development. His view has some similarities with the ideas of Lev Vygotsky that were described in Chapter 2 and Chapter 6. Bruner stresses the role of parents and teachers in constructing what he called a language acquisition support system (LASS).

Today, most language acquisition researchers maintain that children from a wide variety of cultural contexts acquire their native language without explicit teaching. In some cases, they do so even without encouragement. However, caregivers greatly facilitate a child's language learning (Berko Gleason, 2009; Goldfield & Snow, 2009).

developmental connection

Cognitive Theory. In Vygotsky's theory, children's thinking is shaped by the cultural context in which they live. Chapter 2, p. 70; Chapter 6, p. 201

caring *connections*

How Parents Can Facilitate Infants' and Toddlers' Language Development

In *Growing Up with Language,* linguist Naomi Baron (1992) provided ideas to help parents facilitate their child's language development. A summary of her ideas follows:

Infants

- *Be an active conversational partner.* Initiate conversation with the infant. If the infant is in an all-day child-care program, ensure that the baby receives adequate language stimulation from adults.
- *Talk as if the infant understands what you are saying.* Parents can generate self-fulfilling prophecies by addressing their young children as if they understand what is being said. The process may take four to five years, but children's language comprehension gradually rises to match the language model presented to them.
- *Use a language style with which you feel comfortable.* Don't worry about how you sound to other adults when you talk with your child. Your affect is more important than the content when talking with an infant. Use any type of talk with which you feel comfortable.

Toddlers

- *Continue to be an active conversational partner.* Engaging toddlers in conversation, even one-sided conversation, is the most important thing a parent can do to nourish a child linguistically.
- *Remember to listen.* Since toddlers' speech is often slow and laborious, parents are often tempted to supply words and thoughts for them. Be patient and let toddlers express themselves, no matter how painstaking the process is or how great a hurry you are in.
- *Use a language style with which you are comfortable, but consider ways of expanding your child's language abilities and horizons.* For example, using long sentences need not be problematic. Use rhymes. Ask questions that encourage answers other than "Yes" and "No." Actively repeat, expand, and recast the child's utterances. Introduce new topics. And use humor in your conversation.
- *Adjust to your child's idiosyncrasies instead of working against them.* Many toddlers have difficulty pronouncing words and making themselves understood. Whenever possible, make toddlers feel that they are being understood.
- *Avoid sexual stereotypes.* Don't let the toddler's sex (or your own) determine your amount or style of conversation. Many American mothers are more linguistically supportive of girls than of boys, and many fathers talk less with their children than mothers do. Cognitively

It is a good idea for parents to begin talking to their babies at the start. The best language teaching occurs when the talking is begun before the infant becomes capable of intelligible speech. *What are some other guidelines for parents to follow in helping their infants and toddlers develop their language?*

enriching initiatives from both mothers and fathers benefit both boys and girls.

- *Resist making normative comparisons.* Be aware of the ages at which your child reaches specific milestones (such as the first word, first 50 words), but do not measure this development rigidly against that of other children. Such social comparisons can bring about unnecessary anxiety.

Based on what you read earlier in this section of the chapter, would parents be wise to combine these strategies here with deliberate methods to teach their children to talk?

Review *Connect* Reflect

LG3 Discuss the biological and environmental contributions to language development.

Review

- What are the biological foundations of language?
- What are the behavioral and environmental aspects of language?
- How does an interactionist view describe language?

Connect

- In this section, you learned about two areas in the left hemisphere of the brain that are involved in speech production and recognition. Related to this, what did you learn in Chapter 2 about hemisphere specialization in infants?

Reflect *Your Own Personal Journey of Life*

- If and when you become a parent, how should you respond to your child's grammatical mistakes when conversing with the child? Will you allow the mistakes to continue and assume that your young child will grow out of them, or will you closely monitor your young child's grammar and correct mistakes whenever you hear them? Explain.

Language and Cognition   Evaluate how language and cognition are linked.

As a teenager, Wendy Verougstraete felt that she was on the road to becoming a professional author. "You are looking at a professional author," she said. "My books will be filled with drama, action, and excitement. And everyone will want to read them. I am going to write books, page after page, stack after stack."

Overhearing her remarks, you might have been impressed not only by Wendy's optimism and determination, but also by her expressive verbal skills. In fact, at a young age Wendy showed a flair for writing and telling stories. Wendy has a rich vocabulary, creates lyrics for love songs, and enjoys telling stories. You probably would not be able to immediately guess that she has an IQ of only 49 and cannot tie her shoes, cross the street by herself, read or print words beyond the first-grade level, and do even simple arithmetic.

Wendy Verougstraete has Williams syndrome, a genetic birth disorder that was first described in 1961 and affects about 1 in 20,000 births (Mervis & Becerra, 2007; Morris, 2010). Williams syndrome stems from a genetic deletion on chromosome 7 (Haas & others, 2009; Palomares, Landau, & Egeth, 2009). The most noticeable features of the syndrome include a unique combination of expressive verbal skills with an extremely low IQ and limited visuospatial skills and motor control (O'Hearn & Luna, 2009). Children with Williams syndrome are natural-born storytellers who provide highly expressive narratives (Martens & others, 2009; Mervis & John, 2010; Palomoares, Landau, & Egeth, 2009). Figure 9.11 shows the great disparity in the verbal and motor skills of one person with Williams syndrome. Individuals with Williams syndrome often have good musical skills and interpersonal skills (Lincoln & others, 2007). One study indicated that children with Williams syndrome in the United States and Japan were more sociable than normally developing children in their respective countries, reflecting a genetic predisposition for sociability in children with Williams syndrome (Zitzer-Comfort & others, 2007). However, normally developing U.S. children were as sociable as Japanese children with Williams syndrome, reflecting different cultural expectations in the two countries. The syndrome also includes a number of physical characteristics as well, such as heart defects and a pixielike facial appearance. Despite having excellent verbal skills and competent interpersonal skills, most individuals with Williams syndrome cannot live

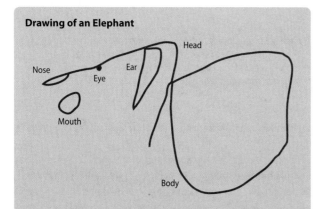

Drawing of an Elephant

Verbal Description of an Elephant

And what an elephant is, it is one of the animals. And what the elephant does, it lives in the jungle. It can also live in the zoo. And what it has, it has long gray ears, fan ears, ears that can blow in the wind. It has a long trunk that can pick up grass, or pick up hay.... If they're in a bad mood it can be terrible.... If the elephant gets mad it could stomp; it could charge. Sometimes elephants can charge. They have big long tusks. They can damage a car.... It could be dangerous. When they're in a pinch, when they're in a bad mood it can be terrible. You don't want an elephant as a pet. You want a cat or a dog or a bird.....

FIGURE **9.11**
DISPARITY IN THE VERBAL AND MOTOR SKILLS OF AN INDIVIDUAL WITH WILLIAMS SYNDROME

independent lives (American Academy of Pediatrics, 2001). For example, Wendy Verougstraete lives in a group home for adults who are mentally retarded.

The verbal abilities of individuals with Williams syndrome are very distinct from those shown by individuals with Down syndrome, a type of mental retardation that we discussed in Chapters 2 and 8 (Brock, 2007). On vocabulary tests, children with Williams syndrome show a liking for unusual words. When asked to name as many animals as they can think of in one minute, Williams children come up with creatures like ibex, chihuahua, saber-toothed tiger, weasel, crane, and newt. Children with Down syndrome give simple examples like dog, cat, and mouse. When children with Williams syndrome tell stories, their voices come alive with drama and emotion, punctuating the dialogue with audience attention-grabbers like "gadzooks" or "lo and behold!" By contrast, children with Down syndrome tell very simple stories with little emotion.

Aside from being an interesting genetic disorder, Williams syndrome offers insights into the normal development of thinking and language (Thomas & others, 2010). In our society, verbal ability is generally associated with high intelligence. But Williams syndrome raises the possibility that thinking and language might not be so closely related. Williams disorder is due to a defective gene that seems to protect expressive verbal ability but not reading and many other cognitive skills (Haas & others, 2009). Thus, cases like Wendy Verougstraete's cast some doubt on the general categorization of intelligence as verbal ability and prompt the question, "What is the relationship between thinking and language?"

Two basic and separate issues characterize connections between language and cognition. The first is whether cognition is necessary for language. Although some researchers have noted that certain aspects of language development typically follow mastery of selected cognitive skills in both normally developing children and children with mental retardation, it is not clear that language development depends on any specific aspect of cognitive abilities (Lenneberg, 1967). Some experts argue that it is more likely that language and cognitive development occur in parallel but dissociated fashions (Cromer, 1987). Thus, according to research and experts' judgments, cognition is not necessary for language development.

The second issue is whether language is necessary for (or important to) cognition. This issue is addressed by studies of deaf children. On a variety of thinking and problem-solving skills, deaf children perform at the same level as children of the same age who have no hearing problems. Some of the deaf children in these studies do not even have command of written or sign language (Furth, 1973). Thus, based on studies of deaf children, language is not necessary for cognitive development.

There is, however, evidence of links between the cognitive and language worlds of children (Oates & Grayson, 2004). Piaget's concept of object permanence has been the focus of some research that connects cognitive and language development. Piaget emphasized that children come to learn about the world first and then they learn to label what they know. Infants may need a concept of object permanence before they start to use words for disappearance, such as "all gone" (Gopnik & Meltzoff, 1997).

A recent study examined whether four aspects of information processing skills—memory, representational competence, processing speed, and attention—were related to infants' and young children's language development (Rose, Feldman, & Jankowski, 2009). In this study, memory and representational competence assessed at 12 months of age predicted language at 36 months of age independently of birth status, 12-month language, and 12-month scores on the Bayley Developmental Scales. The dimensions of memory that best predicted language development were recognition and recall but not short-term memory; the dimensions of representation competence that best predicted language development were cross-modal transfer (matching touch to vision) and object permanence. Other research has found that joint attention in infancy is linked to vocabulary development in childhood (Colombo & others, 2009a, b).

reach your **learning goals**

Language Development

What Is Language?

LG1 Define language and describe its rule systems.

- Defining Language

- Language's Rule Systems

- Language is a form of communication, whether spoken, written, or signed, that is based on a system of symbols. Language consists of all the words used by a community and the rules for varying and combining them. Infinite generativity is the ability to produce an endless number of meaningful sentences using a finite set of words and rules.

- The five main five rule systems of language are phonology, morphology, syntax, semantics, and pragmatics. Phonology is the sound system of a language, including the sounds used and the particular sound sequences that may occur in the language. Morphology refers to how words are formed. Syntax is the way words are combined to form acceptable phrases and sentences. Semantics involves the meaning of words and sentences. Pragmatics is the appropriate use of language in different contexts.

How Language Develops

LG2 Describe how language develops.

- Infancy

- Early Childhood

- Middle and Late Childhood

- Among the milestones in infant language development are crying (birth), cooing (1 to 2 months), babbling (6 months), making the transition from universal linguist to language-specific listener (6 to 12 months), using gestures (8 to 12 months), recognition of their name (as early as 5 months), first word spoken (10 to 15 months), vocabulary spurt (18 months), rapid expansion of understanding words (18 to 24 months), and two-word utterances (18 to 24 months).

- Advances in phonology, morphology, syntax, semantics, and pragmatics continue in early childhood. The transition to complex sentences begins at 2 or 3 years and continues through the elementary school years. Currently, there is considerable interest in the early literacy of children.

- In middle and late childhood, children become more analytical and logical in their approach to words and grammar. Chall's model proposes five stages in reading, ranging from birth/first grade to high school. Current debate involving how to teach children to read focuses on the phonics approach versus the whole-language approach. Researchers have found strong evidence that the phonics approach should be used in teaching children to read, especially in kindergarten and the first grade and with struggling readers, but that children also benefit from the whole-language approach. Children's writing emerges out of scribbling. Advances in children's language and cognitive development provide the underpinnings for improved writing. Strategy instruction is especially effective in improving children's writing. Bilingual education aims to teach academic subjects to immigrant children in their native languages, while gradually adding English instruction. Researchers have found that bilingualism does not interfere with performance in either language. Success in learning a second language is greater in childhood than in adolescence.

Adolescence

- In adolescence, language changes include more effective use of words; improvements in the ability to understand metaphor, satire, and adult literary works; and improvements in writing. Young adolescents often speak a dialect with their peers, using jargon and slang.

Biological and Environmental Influences Discuss the biological and environmental contributions to language development.

Biological Influences

- In evolution, language clearly gave humans an enormous edge over other animals and increased their chance of survival. A substantial portion of language processing occurs in the brain's left hemisphere, with Broca's area and Wernicke's area being important left-hemisphere locations. Chomsky argues that children are born with the ability to detect basic features and rules of language. In other words, they are biologically equipped to learn language with a prewired language acquisition device (LAD).

Environmental Influences

- The behavioral view of language acquisition—that children acquire language as a result of reinforcement—is no longer supported. Adults help children acquire language through child-directed speech, recasting, expanding, and labeling. Environmental influences are demonstrated by differences in the language development of children as a consequence of being exposed to different language environments in the home. Parents should talk extensively with an infant, especially about what the baby is attending to.

An Interactionist View of Language

- An interactionist view emphasizes the contributions of both biology and experience in language. One interactionist view is that both Chomsky's LAD and Bruner's LASS are involved in language acquisition.

Language and Cognition Evaluate how language and cognition are linked.

- Children with Williams syndrome have a unique combination of expressive verbal skills with an extremely low IQ and limited visuospatial skills and motor control. Study of these children offers insights into the normal development of thinking and language. Two basic and separate issues are these: (1) Is cognition necessary for language? (2) Is language necessary for cognition? At an extreme, the answer likely is no to these questions, but there is evidence of linkages between language and cognition. A recent study revealed that infants' information-processing skills were linked to the growth of language development in early childhood.

key terms

language 260
infinite generativity 260
phonology 260
morphology 261
syntax 261
semantics 262
pragmatics 262

telegraphic speech 266
fast mapping 268
metalinguistic
  awareness 271
phonics approach 272
whole-language
  approach 272

metaphor 275
satire 275
dialect 276
Broca's area 278
Wernicke's area 278
aphasia 278

language acquisition
  device (LAD) 278
child-directed speech 279
recasting 279
expanding 279
labeling 279

key people

Helen Keller 259
Patricia Kuhl 264
Jean Berko 266

Betty Hart and Todd Risley 269
Janellen Huttenlocher 269

Noam Chomsky 278
Roger Brown 279

Jerome Bruner 280
Naomi Baron 281

I am what I hope and give.

—ERIK ERIKSON
European-Born American Psychotherapist, 20th Century

Socioemotional Development

As children develop, they need the meeting eyes of love. They split the universe into two halves: "me" and "not me." They juggle the need to curb their own will with becoming what they can will freely. They also want to fly but discover that first they have to learn to stand and walk and climb and dance. As they become adolescents, they try on one face after another, looking for a face of their own. In Section 4, you will read four chapters: "Emotional Development" (Chapter 10), "The Self and Identity" (Chapter 11), "Gender" (Chapter 12), and "Moral Development" (Chapter 13).

chapter 10 EMOTIONAL DEVELOPMENT

Today an increasing number of fathers are staying home to care for their children (Lamb, 2010; O'Brien & Moss, 2010). Consider 17-month-old Darius. On weekdays, Darius' father, a writer, cares for him during the day while his mother works full-time as a landscape architect. Darius' father is doing a great job of caring for him. Darius' father keeps Darius nearby while he is writing and spends lots of time talking to him and playing with him. From their interactions, it is clear that they genuinely enjoy each other's company.

Last month, Darius began spending one day a week at a child-care center. His parents carefully selected the center after observing a number of centers and interviewing teachers and center directors. His parents placed him in the center one day a week because they wanted Darius to get some experience with peers and to give his father some time out from his caregiving.

Darius' father looks to the future and imagines the Little League games Darius will play in and the many other activities he can enjoy with Darius. Remembering how little time his own father spent with him, he is dedicated to making sure that Darius has an involved, nurturing experience with his father.

When Darius' mother comes home in the evening, she spends considerable time with him. Darius has a secure attachment with both his mother and his father.

Many fathers are spending more time with their infants today than in the past.

preview

For many years, emotion was neglected in the study of children's development. Today, emotion is increasingly important in conceptualizations of development. Even infants show different emotional styles, display varying temperaments, and begin to form emotional bonds with their caregivers. In this chapter, we will study the roles of temperament and attachment in development. But first we will examine emotion itself, exploring the functions of emotions in children's lives and the development of emotion from infancy through middle and late childhood.

Exploring Emotion **LG1** Discuss basic aspects of emotion.

What Are Emotions? · A Functionalist View of Emotions · Emotional Competence

Imagine your life without emotion. Emotion is the color and music of life, as well as the tie that binds people together. How do psychologists define and classify emotions, and why are they important to development?

WHAT ARE EMOTIONS?

> Blossoms are scattered
> by the wind
> And the wind cares nothing, but
> The Blossoms of the heart,
> No wind can touch.
>
> —YOUSHIDA KENKO
> *Buddhist Monk, 14th Century*

For our purposes, we will define **emotion** as feeling, or affect, that occurs when people are in a state or an interaction that is important to them, especially one that influences their well-being. In many instances emotions involve people's communication with the world. Although emotion consists of more than communication, in infancy the communication aspect is at the forefront of emotion (Campos, 2009).

Psychologists classify the broad range of emotions in many ways, but almost all classifications designate an emotion as either positive or negative (Izard, 2009). Positive emotions include enthusiasm, joy, and love. Negative emotions include anxiety, anger, guilt, and sadness.

Emotions are influenced by biological foundations and experience (Kagan, 2010). In evolutionary theory, evolution endowed human beings with a biological foundation for emotion. The biological foundation of emotion involves the development of the nervous system. Emotions are linked with early-developing regions of the human nervous system, including structures of the limbic system and the brain stem (de Haan & Matheson, 2009; Thompson, Easterbrooks, & Walker, 2003). The capacity of infants to show distress, excitement, and rage reflects the early emergence of these biologically rooted emotional brain systems. Significant advances in emotional responding occur during infancy and childhood as a result of changes in neurobiological systems (including the frontal regions of the cerebral cortex) that can exert control over the more primitive limbic system (Bell, Greene, & Wolfe, 2010; Payne & Bachevalier, 2009; Perlman & Pelphrey, 2010). As children develop, maturation of the cerebral cortex allows a decrease in unpredictable mood swings and an increase in the self-regulation of emotion. However, such mood swings increase during adolescence, likely as a result of the earlier development of the amygdala (which is extensively involved in emotional processing) and the protracted development of the frontal cortex (which is heavily involved in reasoning and self-regulation (Paus, 2009).

Cultural variations reveal the role of experience in emotion. For example, display rules—when, where, and how emotions should be expressed—are not culturally universal (Novin & others, 2009; Shiraev & Levy, 2010). For example, researchers have found that East Asian infants display less frequent and less intense positive and negative emotions than non-Latino White infants (Camras & others, 1998).

developmental **connection**

Brain Development. The prefrontal cortex is not as well developed in adolescence as it is in adults. For adolescents, it is as if their brain doesn't have the brakes to slow down their emotions. Chapter 4, p. 119

emotion Feeling, or affect, that occurs when people are engaged in an interaction that is important to them, especially one that influences their well-being.

Throughout childhood, East Asian parents encourage their children to show emotional reserve rather than emotional expressivity (Cole & Tan, 2007). Further, Japanese parents try to prevent their children from experiencing negative emotions, whereas non-Latino White mothers are more likely to respond after their children become distressed and then help them cope (Cole & Tan, 2007).

Caregivers play a role in the infant's neurobiological regulation of emotions (Stern, 2010; Thompson, 2010). For example, by soothing the infant when the infant cries and shows distress, caregivers help infants to modulate their emotion and reduce the level of stress hormones (Gunnar & Quevado, 2007).

In sum, biological evolution has endowed human beings to be emotional, but culture and relationships with others provide diversity in emotional experiences. As we see next, this emphasis on the role of relationships in emotion is at the core of the functionalist view of emotion.

How do Japanese mothers handle their infants' and children's emotional development differently from non-Latino White mothers?

A FUNCTIONALIST VIEW OF EMOTIONS

Many developmentalists today view emotions as the result of individuals' attempts to adapt to specific contextual demands (Saarni & others, 2006). Thus, a child's emotional responses cannot be separated from the situations in which they are evoked. In many instances, emotions are elicited in interpersonal contexts. For example, emotional expressions serve the important functions of signaling to others how one feels, regulating one's own behavior, and playing pivotal roles in social exchange.

One implication of the functionalist view is that emotions are *relational rather than strictly internal, intrapsychic phenomena* (Kopp, 2011; Thompson, 2010). Consider just some of the roles of emotion in parent-child relationships. The beginnings of an emotional bond between parents and an infant are based on affectively toned interchanges, as when an infant cries and the caregiver sensitively responds. By the end of the first year, a parent's facial expression—either smiling or fearful—influences whether an infant will explore an unfamiliar environment. Well-functioning families often include humor in their interactions, sometimes making each other laugh and creating a light mood state to defuse conflict. When a positive mood has been induced in a child, the child is more likely to comply with a parent's directions.

A second implication of the functionalist view is that emotions are *linked with an individual's goals in a variety of ways* (Saarni & others, 2006). Regardless of what the goal is, an individual who overcomes an obstacle to attain a goal experiences happiness. By contrast, a person who must relinquish a goal as unattainable experiences sadness. And a person who faces difficult obstacles in pursuing a goal often experiences frustration, which can become anger when the obstacles are perceived as unfair or intentionally put in the way to hinder the individual's goal attainment.

The specific nature of the goal can affect the experience of a given emotion. For example, the avoidance of threat is linked with fear, the desire to atone is related to guilt, and the wish to avoid the scrutiny of others is associated with shame.

What are some implications of the functional view in explaining this 7-month-old girl's emotional expression?

EMOTIONAL COMPETENCE

In Chapter 8, we briefly described the concept of emotional intelligence. Here we will examine a closely related concept, emotional competence, that focuses on the adaptive nature of emotional experience. Carolyn Saarni (1999; Saarni & others, 2006) argues that becoming emotionally competent involves developing a number of skills in social contexts. Figure 10.1 describes these skills and provides examples of each one.

As children acquire these emotional competence skills in a variety of contexts, they are more likely to effectively manage their emotions, become resilient in the face of stressful circumstances, and develop more positive relationships.

developmental **connection**

Intelligence. Emotional intelligence involves perceiving and expressing emotions accurately, understanding emotion and emotional knowledge, using feelings to facilitate thought, and managing emotions effectively. Chapter 8, p. 239

FIGURE 10.1

EMOTIONAL COMPETENCE SKILLS

Skill	Example
Awareness of one's emotional states	Being able to differentiate whether sad or anxious
Detecting others' emotions	Understanding when another person is sad rather than afraid
Using the vocabulary of emotion terms in socially and culturally appropriate ways	Appropriately describing a social situation in one culture's when a person is feeling distress
Empathic and sympathetic sensitivity to others' emotional experiences	Being sensitive to others when they are feeling distressed
Recognizing that inner emotional states do not have to correspond to outer expressions	Recognizing that one can feel very angry yet manage one's emotional expression so that it appears more neutral
Adaptively coping with negative emotions by using self-regulatory strategies that reduce the intensity or duration of such emotional states	Reducing anger by walking away from an aversive situation and engaging in an activity that takes one's mind off of the aversive situation
Awareness that the expression of emotions plays a major role in a relationship	Knowing that expressing anger toward a friend on a regular basis is likely to harm the friendship
Viewing oneself overall as feeling the way one wants to feel	Feeling like one can cope effectively with the stress in one's life and feeling that one is doing this successfully

Review *Connect* Reflect

LG1 Discuss basic aspects of emotion.

Review

- How is emotion defined?
- What characterizes functionalism in emotion?
- What constitutes emotional competence, according to Saarni?

Connect

- How are the competence skills listed in Figure 10.1 related to the four aspects of emotional intelligence described in Chapter 8?

Reflect Your Own Personal Journey of Life

- Think back to your childhood and adolescent years. How would you describe your emotional competence as a child and adolescent, based on the descriptions in Figure 10.1?

Development of Emotion **LG2** Describe the development of emotion.

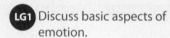

Infancy   Early Childhood   Middle and Late Childhood

Does an older child's emotional life differ from a younger child's? Does a young child's emotional life differ from an infant's? Does an infant even have an emotional life? In this section, we will sketch an overview of the changes in emotion from infancy through middle childhood, looking not only at changes in emotional experience but also at the development of emotional competence.

INFANCY

What are some early developmental changes in emotions? What functions do infants' cries serve? When do infants begin to smile?

Early Emotions A leading expert on infant emotional development, Michael Lewis (2007, 2008) distinguishes between primary emotions and self-conscious emotions. **Primary emotions** are emotions that are present in humans and other animals; these emotions appear in the first six months of the human infant's development. Primary emotions include surprise, interest, joy, anger, sadness, fear, and disgust (see Figure 10.2 for infants' facial expressions of some of these early emotions). In Lewis' classification, **self-conscious emotions** require self-awareness that involves consciousness and a sense of "me." Self-conscious emotions include jealousy, empathy, embarrassment, pride, shame, and guilt. Lewis argues that these self-conscious emotions occur for the first time at some point in the second half of the first year through the second year. Some experts on emotion call self-conscious emotions such as embarrassment, shame, guilt, and pride *other-conscious emotions* because they involve the emotional reactions of others when they are generated (Saarni & others, 2006). For example, approval from parents is linked to toddlers beginning to show pride when they successfully complete a task.

Leading researchers such as Joseph Campos (2009) and Michael Lewis (2008) debate how early in the infant and toddler years the emotions that we have described first appear and their sequence. As an indication of the controversy regarding when certain emotions first are displayed by infants, consider jealousy. Some researchers argue that jealousy does not emerge until approximately 18 months of age (Lewis, 2007), whereas others emphasize that it is displayed much earlier (Draghi-Lorenz, Reddy, & Costall, 2001). Consider a research study in which 6-month-old infants observed their mothers giving attention either to a life-like baby doll (hugging or gently rocking it, for example) or to a book (Hart & Carrington, 2002). When mothers directed their attention to the doll, the infants were more likely to display negative emotions, such as anger and sadness, which may have indicated their jealousy (see Figure 10.3). However, their expressions of anger and sadness may have reflected frustration in not being able to have the novel doll to play with.

Debate about the onset of an emotion such as jealousy illustrates the complexity and difficulty of indexing early emotions. That said, some experts on infant socioemotional development, such as Jerome Kagan (2010), conclude that the structural immaturity of the infant brain make it unlikely that emotions requiring thought—such as guilt, pride, despair, shame, empathy, and jealousy—can be experienced in the first year. Thus, both Kagan (2010) and Campos (2009) argue that so-called "self-conscious" emotions don't occur until after the first year, which increasingly reflects the view of most developmental psychologists. Thus, in regard to the photograph in Figure 10.3, it is unlikely that the 6-month old infant is experiencing jealousy.

Emotional Expression and Social Relationships

Emotional expressions are involved in infants' first relationships. The ability of infants to communicate emotions permits coordinated interactions with their caregivers and the beginning of an emotional bond between them (Thompson, 2010; Thompson & Newton, 2009). Not only do parents change their emotional expressions in response to infants' emotional expressions, but infants also modify their emotional expressions in response to their parents' emotional expressions. In other words, these interactions are mutually regulated (Bridgett & others, 2009). Because of this coordination, the interactions are described

Joy

Sadness

Fear

Surprise

FIGURE 10.2

EXPRESSION OF DIFFERENT EMOTIONS IN INFANTS

FIGURE 10.3

IS THIS THE EARLY EXPRESSION OF JEALOUSY? In the study by Hart and Carrington (2002), the researchers concluded that the 6-month old infants who observed their mothers giving attention to a baby doll may indicate the early appearance of jealousy because of the negative emotions—such as anger and sadness—they displayed. However, experts on emotional development, such as Joseph Campos (2009) and Jerome Kagan (2010) argue that emotions such as jealousy don't appear during the first year. *Why do they conclude that jealousy does not occur in the first year?*

primary emotions Emotions that are present in humans and other animals, and emerge early in life; examples are joy, anger, sadness, fear, and disgust.

self-conscious emotions Emotions that require self-awareness, especially consciousness and a sense of "me"; examples include jealousy, empathy, and embarrassment.

What are some different types of cries?

as *reciprocal,* or *synchronous,* when all is going well. Sensitive, responsive parents help their infants grow emotionally, whether the infants respond in distressed or happy ways (Thompson & Newton, 2009).

Crying and smiling are two emotional expressions that infants display when interacting with parents. These are babies' first forms of emotional communication.

Crying   Crying is the most important mechanism newborns have for communicating with their world. The first cry verifies that the baby's lungs have filled with air. Cries also may provide information about the health of the newborn's central nervous system. Newborns even tend to respond with cries and negative facial expressions when they hear other newborns cry (Dondi, Simion, & Caltran, 1999).

Babies have at least three types of cries:

- **Basic cry:** A rhythmic pattern that usually consists of a cry, followed by a briefer silence, then a shorter whistle that is somewhat higher in pitch than the main cry, then another brief rest before the next cry. Some infancy experts argue that hunger is one of the conditions that incite the basic cry.
- **Anger cry:** A variation of the basic cry in which more excess air is forced through the vocal cords.
- **Pain cry:** A sudden long, initial loud cry followed by breath holding; no preliminary moaning is present. The pain cry is stimulated by a high-intensity stimulus.

Most adults can determine whether an infant's cries signify anger or pain (Zeskind, Klein, & Marshall, 1992). Parents can distinguish the cries of their own baby better than those of another baby.

Smiling   Smiling is critical as a means of developing a new social skill and is a key social signal (Campos, 2009). Two types of smiling can be distinguished in infants:

- **Reflexive smile:** A smile that does not occur in response to external stimuli and appears during the first month after birth, usually during sleep.
- **Social smile:** A smile that occurs in response to an external stimulus, typically a face in the case of the young infant. Social smiling occurs as early as 4 to 6 weeks of age in response to a caregiver's voice (Campos, 2005).

Daniel Messinger (2008) recently described the developmental course of infant smiling. From two to six months after birth, infants' social smiling increases considerably, both in self-initiated smiles and smiles in response to others' smiles. At 6 to 12 months of age, smiles that couple what is called the Duchenne marker (eye constriction) and mouth opening occur in the midst of highly enjoyable interactions and play with parents (see Figure 10.4). In the second year, smiling continues to occur in such positive circumstances with parents, and in many cases an increase in smiling occurs when interacting with peers. Also in the second year, toddlers become increasingly aware of the social meaning of smiles, especially in their relationship with parents.

Infants also engage in *anticipatory smiling,* in which they communicate preexisting positive emotion by smiling at an object and then turning their smile toward an adult. A recent study revealed that anticipatory smiling at 9 months of age was linked to parents' rating of the child's social competence at 2½ years of age (Parlade & others, 2009).

Fear   One of a baby's earliest emotions is fear, which typically first appears at about 6 months of age and peaks at about 18 months. However, abused and neglected

He who binds himself to joy
Does the winged life destroy;
But he who kisses the joy as it flies;
Lives in eternity's sun rise.

—**WILLIAM BLAKE**
English Poet, 19th Century

basic cry A rhythmic pattern usually consisting of a cry, a briefer silence, a shorter inspiratory whistle that is higher pitched than the main cry, and then a brief rest before the next cry.

anger cry A cry similar to the basic cry but with more excess air forced through the vocal cords.

pain cry A sudden appearance of loud crying without preliminary moaning, and a long initial cry followed by an extended period of breath holding.

reflexive smile A smile that does not occur in response to external stimuli. It happens during the month after birth, usually during sleep.

social smile A smile in response to an external stimulus, which, early in development, typically is a face.

infants can show fear as early as 3 months (Campos, 2005). Researchers have found that infant fear is linked to guilt, empathy, and low aggression at 6 to 7 years of age (Rothbart, 2007).

The most frequent expression of an infant's fear involves **stranger anxiety,** in which an infant shows a fear and wariness of strangers. Stranger anxiety usually emerges gradually. It first appears at about 6 months of age in the form of wary reactions. By age 9 months, the fear of strangers is often more intense, and it continues to escalate through the infant's first birthday (Scher & Harel, 2008).

Not all infants show distress when they encounter a stranger. Besides individual variations, whether an infant shows stranger anxiety also depends on the social context and the characteristics of the stranger (Kagan, 2008).

Infants show less stranger anxiety when they are in familiar settings. For example, in one study, 10-month-olds showed little stranger anxiety when they met a stranger in their own home but much greater fear when they encountered a stranger in a research laboratory (Sroufe, Waters, & Matas, 1974). Also, infants show less stranger anxiety when they are sitting on their mothers' laps than when they are placed in an infant seat several feet away from their mothers (Bohlin & Hagekull, 1993). Thus, it appears that when infants feel secure, they are less likely to show stranger anxiety.

Who the stranger is and how the stranger behaves also influence stranger anxiety in infants. Infants are less fearful of child strangers than adult strangers. They also are less fearful of friendly, outgoing, smiling strangers than of passive, unsmiling strangers (Bretherton, Stolberg, & Kreye, 1981).

In addition to stranger anxiety, infants experience fear of being separated from their caregivers (Scher & Harel, 2008). The result is **separation protest**—crying when the caregiver leaves. Separation protest tends to peak at about 15 months among U.S. infants (Kagan, 2008). In fact, one study found that separation protest peaked at about 13 to 15 months in four different cultures (Kagan, Kearsley, & Zelazo, 1978). As indicated in Figure 10.5, the percentage of infants who engaged in separation protest varied across cultures, but the infants reached a peak of protest at about the same age—just before the middle of the second year of life.

Emotional Regulation and Coping   During the first year of life, the infant gradually develops an ability to inhibit, or minimize, the intensity and duration of emotional reactions (Eisenberg, Spinrad, & Smith, 2004). From early in infancy, babies put their thumbs in their mouths to soothe themselves. But at first, infants mainly depend on caregivers to help them soothe their emotions, as when a caregiver rocks an infant to sleep, sings lullabies to the infant, gently strokes the infant, and so on.

The caregivers' actions influence the infant's neurobiological regulation of emotions (Saarni & others, 2006). By soothing the infant, caregivers help infants to modulate their emotion and reduce the level of stress hormones (de Haan & Gunnar, 2009). Many developmentalists stress that it is a good strategy for a caregiver to soothe an infant before the infant gets into an intense, agitated, uncontrolled state (Thompson, 1994).

In the second year of life, when they become aroused, infants sometimes redirect their attention or distract themselves in order to reduce their arousal (Grolnick, Bridges, & Connell, 1996). By 2 years of age, toddlers can use language to define their feeling states and the context that is upsetting them (Kopp & Neufeld, 2002). A toddler might say, "Feel bad. Dog scare." This type of communication may help caregivers to assist the child in regulating emotion.

Contexts can influence emotional regulation (Thompson, 2010). Infants are often affected by fatigue, hunger, time of day, which people are around them, and where they are. Infants must learn to adapt to different contexts that require emotional regulation. Further, new demands appear as the infant becomes older and

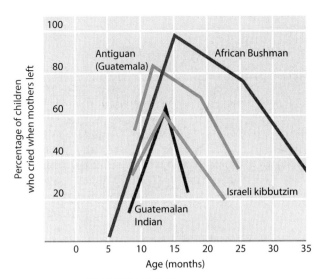

FIGURE **10.5**

SEPARATION PROTEST IN FOUR CULTURES.
Note that separation protest peaked at about the same time in all four cultures in this study (13 to 15 months of age) (Kagan, Kearsley, & Zelazo, 1978). However, a higher percentage (100 percent) of infants in an African Bushman culture engaged in separation protest compared to only about 60 percent of infants in Guatemalan Indian and Israeli kibbutzim cultures. *What might explain the fact that separation protest peaks at about the same time in these cultures?*

stranger anxiety An infant's fear of and wariness toward strangers; it tends to appear in the second half of the first year of life.

separation protest Occurs when infants experience a fear of being separated from a caregiver, which results in crying when the caregiver leaves.

Should a baby be given attention and soothed, or does this spoil the infant? Should the infant's age, the type of cry, and the circumstances be considered?

parents modify their expectations. For example, a parent may take it in stride if a 6-month-old infant screams in a grocery store but may react very differently if a 2-year-old starts screaming.

To soothe or not to soothe—should a crying baby be given attention and soothed, or does this spoil the infant? Many years ago, the behaviorist John Watson (1928) argued that parents spend too much time responding to infant crying. As a consequence, he said, parents reward crying and increase its incidence. Some researchers have found that a caregiver's quick, soothing response to crying increased crying (Gewirtz, 1977). However, infancy experts Mary Ainsworth (1979) and John Bowlby (1989) stress that you can't respond too much to infant crying in the first year of life. They argue that a quick, comforting response to the infant's cries is an important ingredient in the development of a strong bond between the infant and caregiver. In one of Ainsworth's studies, infants whose mothers responded quickly when they cried at 3 months of age cried less later in the first year of life (Bell & Ainsworth, 1972).

Controversy still characterizes the question of whether or how parents should respond to an infant's cries (Lewis & Ramsay, 1999). However, developmentalists increasingly argue that an infant cannot be spoiled in the first year of life, which suggests that parents should soothe a crying infant. This reaction should help infants develop a sense of trust and secure attachment to the caregiver.

EARLY CHILDHOOD

The young child's growing awareness of self is linked to the ability to feel an expanding range of emotions. Young children, like adults, experience many emotions during the course of a day. At times, they also try to make sense of other people's emotional reactions and to control their own emotions. Parents and peers play important roles in children's emotional development.

Expressing Emotions Recall from our discussion of emotional development in infancy that there is controversy about how early in their development infants experience what Michael Lewis (2007) called *self-conscious emotions.* To experience self-conscious emotions such as pride, shame, embarrassment, and guilt, children must be able to refer to themselves and be aware of themselves as distinct from others (Lewis, 2007). Self-conscious emotions do not appear to develop until self-awareness appears at around 18 months of age.

During the early childhood years, emotions such as pride and guilt become more common. They are especially influenced by parents' responses to children's behavior. For example, a young child may experience shame when a parent says, "You should feel bad about biting your sister."

A child expressing the emotion of shame, which occurs when a child evaluates his or her actions as not living up to standards. A child experiencing shame wishes to hide or disappear. *Why is shame called a self-conscious emotion?*

Understanding Emotions Among the most important changes in emotional development in early childhood is an increased understanding of emotion (Carpendale & Lewis, 2011; Hughes & Ensor, 2010). During early childhood, young children increasingly understand that certain situations are likely to evoke particular emotions, that facial expressions indicate specific emotions, that emotions affect behavior, and that emotions can be used to influence others' emotions (Cole & others, 2009). A recent meta-analysis revealed that emotion knowledge (such as understanding emotional cues—for example, when a young child understands that a peer feels sad about being left out of a game) was positively related to 3- to 5-year-olds' social competence (such as offering an empathic response to the child left out of a game) and negatively related to their internalizing (high level of anxiety, for example) and externalizing problems (high level of aggressive behavior, for example) (Trentacosta & Fine, 2009). A recent study also found that young children's understanding of emotions was linked to their prosocial behavior (Ensor, Spencer, & Hughes, 2010).

Between 2 and 4 years of age, children considerably increase the number of terms they use to describe emotions. During this time, they are also learning about the causes and consequences of feelings (Denham, Bassett, & Wyatt, 2007).

When they are 4 to 5 years of age, children show an increased ability to reflect on emotions. They also begin to understand that the same event can elicit different feelings in different people. Moreover, they show a growing awareness that they need to manage their emotions to meet social standards. And, by 5 years of age, most children can accurately identity emotions that are produced by challenging circumstances and describe strategies they might call on to cope with everyday stress (Cole & others, 2009).

Regulating Emotions   Emotional regulation especially plays a key role in children's ability to manage the demands and conflicts they face in interacting with others (Cole & others, 2009; Eisenberg, 2010; Lewis, Todd, & Xu, 2011). Let's explore the roles that parents and peers play in children's emotional regulation.

Parenting and Children's Emotional Development   Parents can play an important role in helping young children regulate their emotions (Grusec, 2011; Grusec & Davidor, 2010). Depending on how they talk with their children about emotion, parents can be described as taking an *emotion-coaching* or an *emotion-dismissing* approach (Gottman, 2009). The distinction between these approaches is most evident in the way the parent deals with the child's negative emotions (anger, frustration, sadness, and so on). *Emotion-coaching parents* monitor their children's emotions, view their children's negative emotions as opportunities for teaching, assist them in labeling emotions, and coach them in how to deal effectively with emotions. In contrast, *emotion-dismissing parents* view their role as to deny, ignore, or change negative emotions. Emotion-coaching parents interact with their children in a less rejecting manner, use more scaffolding and praise, and are more nurturant than are emotion-dismissing parents (Gottman & DeClaire, 1997). Moreover, the children of emotion-coaching parents are better at soothing themselves when they get upset, more effective in regulating their negative affect, focus their attention better, and have fewer behavior problems than the children of emotion-dismissing parents. A recent study revealed that having emotion-dismissing parents was linked with children's poor emotional regulation (Lunkenheimer, Shields, & Cortina, 2007).

A problem that parents face is that young children typically don't want to talk about difficult emotional topics, such as being distressed or engaging in negative behaviors. Among the strategies young children use to avoid these conversations is to not talk at all, change the topic, push away, or run away. In a recent study, Ross Thompson and his colleagues (2009) found that young children were more likely to openly discuss difficult emotional circumstances when they were securely attached to their mother and when their mother conversed with them in a way that validated and accepted the child's views.

Regulation of Emotion and Peer Relations   Emotions play a strong role in determining the success of a child's peer relationships (Howes, 2009). Specifically, the ability to modulate one's emotions is an important skill that benefits children in their relationships with peers. Moody and emotionally negative children are more likely to experience rejection by their peers, whereas emotionally positive children are more popular (Stocker & Dunn, 1990). Emotional regulation typically increases as children mature. A recent study revealed that 4-year-olds recognized and generated strategies for controlling their anger more than did 3-year-olds (Cole & others, 2009).

MIDDLE AND LATE CHILDHOOD

During middle and late childhood, many children show marked improvement in understanding and managing their emotions (Cunningham, Kliewer, & Garner, 2009). However, in some instances, as when they experience stressful circumstances, their coping abilities can be challenged.

developmental **connection**

Peers. The combination of being rejected by peers and being aggressive often forecasts problems. Chapter 15, p. 434

What are some developmental changes in emotion in middle and late childhood?

Developmental Changes in Emotion   Here are some important developmental changes in emotions during middle and late childhood (Denham, Bassett, & Wyatt, 2007; Kuebli, 1994; Thompson, 2009a):

- *Improved emotional understanding.* Children in elementary school develop an increased ability to understand complex emotions such as pride and shame. These emotions become less tied to the reactions of other people; they become more self-generated and integrated with a sense of personal responsibility.

- *Increased understanding that more than one emotion can be experienced in a particular situation.* A third-grader, for example, may realize that achieving something might involve both anxiety and joy.

- *Increased tendency to be aware of the events leading to emotional reactions.* A fourth-grader may become aware that her sadness today is influenced by her friend moving to another town last week.

- *Ability to suppress or conceal negative emotional reactions.* A fifth-grader has learned to tone down his anger better than he used to when one of his classmates irritates him.

- *The use of self-initiated strategies for redirecting feelings.* During the elementary school years, children become more reflective about their emotional lives and increasingly use strategies to control their emotions. They become more effective at cognitively managing their emotions, such as by soothing themselves after an upset.

- *A capacity for genuine empathy.* For example, a fourth-grader feels sympathy for a distressed person and experiences vicariously the sadness the distressed person is feeling.

Coping with Stress   An important aspect of children's lives is learning how to cope with stress (Findlay, Coplan, & Bowker, 2009; Swearer, Givens, & Frerichs, 2010). As children get older, they are able to more accurately appraise a stressful situation and determine how much control they have over it. Older children gen-

What are some effective strategies to help children cope with traumatic events such as Hurricane Katrina in August 2005?

erate more coping alternatives to stressful conditions and use more cognitive coping strategies (Saarni & others, 2006). For example, older children are better than younger children at intentionally shifting their thoughts to a topic that is less stressful. Older children are also better at reframing, or changing their perceptions of a stressful situation. For example, younger children may be very disappointed that their teacher did not say hello to them when they arrived at school. Older children may reframe this type of situation and think, "She may have been busy with other things and just forgot to say hello."

By 10 years of age, most children are able to use cognitive strategies to cope with stress (Saarni & others, 2006). However, in families that have not been supportive and are characterized by turmoil or trauma, children may be so overwhelmed by stress that they do not use such strategies (Field & others, 2008).

Disasters can especially harm children's development and produce adjustment problems. Among the outcomes for children who experience disasters are acute stress reactions, depression, panic disorder, and post-traumatic stress disorder

(Kar, 2009). Proportions of children developing these problems following a disaster depend on factors such as the nature and severity of the disaster, as well as the support available to the children. The terrorist attacks on the World Trade Center in New York City and the Pentagon in Washington, DC, on September 11, 2001, and hurricanes Katrina and Rita in September 2005, raised special concerns about how to help children cope with such stressful events (Osofsky, 2007).

Recommendations for parents, teachers, and other adults caring for children who are involved in disasters and terrorist attacks include the following (Gurwitch & others, 2001, pp. 4–11):

- Reassure children (numerous times, if necessary) of their safety and security.
- Allow children to retell events, and be patient in listening to them.
- Encourage children to talk about any disturbing or confusing feelings, reassuring them that such feelings are normal after a stressful event.
- Protect children from reexposure to frightening situations and reminders of the trauma—for example, by limiting discussion of the event in front of the children.
- Help children make sense of what happened, keeping in mind that children may misunderstand what took place. For example, young children "may blame themselves, believe things happened that did not happen, believe that terrorists are in the school, etc. Gently help children develop a realistic understanding of the event" (p. 10).

Review Connect Reflect

 LG2 Describe the development of emotion.

Review

- How does emotion develop in infancy?
- What characterizes emotional development in early childhood?
- What changes take place in emotion during middle and late childhood?

Connect

- In this section, you learned about how children develop the ability to recognize and react appropriately to the emotions of others. How is this ability related to children's theory of mind (discussed in Chapter 7)?

Reflect *Your Own Personal Journey of Life*

- Imagine that you are the parent of an 8-month-old baby and you are having difficulty getting any sleep because the baby wakes up in the middle of the night crying. How would you deal with this situation?

Temperament   **LG3**   Characterize variations in temperament and their significance.

| Describing and Classifying Temperament | Biological Foundations and Experience | Goodness of Fit and Parenting |

Do you get upset often? Does it take much to get you angry, or to make you laugh? Even at birth, babies seem to have different emotional styles. One infant is cheerful and happy much of the time; another baby seems to cry constantly. These tendencies reflect **temperament,** which involves individual differences in behavioral styles, emotions, and characteristic ways of responding. With regard to its link to emotion, temperament refers to individual differences in how quickly the emotion is shown, how strong it is, how long it lasts, and how quickly it fades away (Campos, 2009).

temperament Involves individual differences in behavioral styles, emotions, and characteristic ways of responding.

"Oh, he's cute, all right, but he's got the temperament of a car alarm."
© Barbara Smaller/The New Yorker Collection/www.cartoonbank.com

DESCRIBING AND CLASSIFYING TEMPERAMENT

How would you describe your temperament or the temperament of a friend? Researchers have described and classified the temperament of individuals in different ways. Here we will examine three of those ways.

Chess and Thomas' Classification   Psychiatrists Alexander Chess and Stella Thomas (Chess & Thomas, 1977; Thomas & Chess, 1991) identified three basic types, or clusters, of temperament:

- An **easy child** is generally in a positive mood, quickly establishes regular routines in infancy, and adapts easily to new experiences.
- A **difficult child** reacts negatively and cries frequently, engages in irregular daily routines, and is slow to accept change.
- A **slow-to-warm-up child** has a low activity level, is somewhat negative, and displays a low intensity of mood.

In their longitudinal investigation, Chess and Thomas found that 40 percent of the children they studied could be classified as easy, 10 percent as difficult, and 15 percent as slow to warm up. Notice that 35 percent did not fit any of the three patterns. Researchers have found that these three basic clusters of temperament are moderately stable across the childhood years. A recent study revealed that young children with a difficult temperament showed more problems when they experienced low-quality child care and fewer problems when they experienced high-quality child care than did young children with an easy temperament (Pluess & Belsky, 2009).

Kagan's Behavioral Inhibition   Another way of classifying temperament focuses on the differences between a shy, subdued, timid child and a sociable, extraverted, bold child (Asendorph, 2008). Jerome Kagan (2002, 2008, 2010) regards shyness with strangers (peers or adults) as one feature of a broad temperament category called *inhibition to the unfamiliar.* Inhibited children

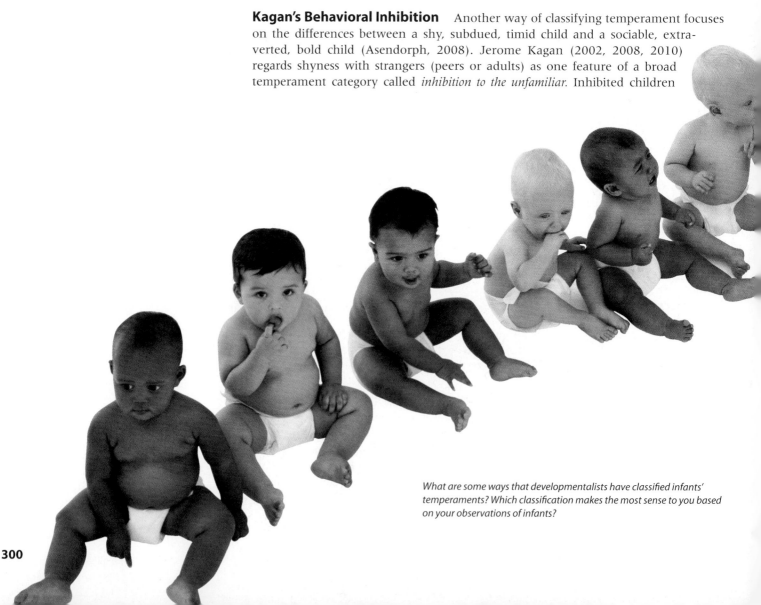

What are some ways that developmentalists have classified infants' temperaments? Which classification makes the most sense to you based on your observations of infants?

react to many aspects of unfamiliarity with initial avoidance, distress, or subdued affect, beginning at about 7 to 9 months of age.

Kagan has found that inhibition shows considerable stability from infancy through early childhood. One study classified toddlers into extremely inhibited, extremely uninhibited, and intermediate groups (Pfeifer & others, 2002). Follow-up assessments occurred at 4 and 7 years of age. Continuity was demonstrated for both inhibition and lack of inhibition, although a substantial number of the inhibited children moved into the intermediate groups at 7 years of age.

Rothbart and Bates' Classification   New classifications of temperament continue to be forged. Mary Rothbart and John Bates (2006) argue that three broad dimensions best represent what researchers have found to characterize the structure of temperament: extraversion/surgency, negative affectivity, and effortful control (self-regulation):

- *Extraversion/surgency* includes "positive anticipation, impulsivity, activity level, and sensation seeking" (Rothbart, 2004, p. 495). Kagan's uninhibited children fit into this category.

- *Negative affectivity* includes "fear, frustration, sadness, and discomfort" (Rothbart, 2004, p. 495). These children are easily distressed; they may fret and cry often. Kagan's inhibited children fit this category. Negative emotional reactivity or irritability reflect the core of Chess and Thomas' category of the difficult child (Bates & Pettit, 2007).

- *Effortful control (self-regulation)* includes "attentional focusing and shifting, inhibitory control, perceptual sensitivity, and low-intensity pleasure" (Rothbart, 2004, p. 495). Infants who are high on effortful control show an ability to keep their arousal from getting too high and have strategies for soothing themselves. By contrast, children low on effortful control are often unable to control their arousal; they become easily agitated and intensely emotional (Rothbart & Sheese, 2007). A recent study of school-age children in the United States and China revealed that in both cultures low effortful control was linked to externalizing problems, such as lying, cheating, being disobedient, and being overly aggressive (Zhou, Lengua, & Wang, 2009).

In Rothbart's (2004, p. 497) view, "early theoretical models of temperament stressed the way we are moved by our positive and negative emotions or level of arousal, with our actions driven by these tendencies." The more recent emphasis on effortful control, however, advocates that individuals can engage in a more cognitive, flexible approach to stressful circumstances.

easy child A temperament style in which the child is generally in a positive mood, quickly establishes regular routines, and adapts easily to new experiences.

difficult child A temperament style in which the child tends to react negatively and cry frequently, engages in irregular daily routines, and is slow to accept new experiences.

slow-to-warm-up child A temperament style in which the child has a low activity level, is somewhat negative, and displays a low intensity of mood.

An important point about temperament classifications such as those devised by Chess and Thomas and by Rothbart and Bates is that children should not be pigeonholed as having only one temperament dimension, such as "difficult" or "negative affectivity." A good strategy when attempting to classify a child's temperament is to think of temperament as consisting of multiple dimensions (Bates, 2008). For example, a child might be extraverted, show little emotional negativity, and have good self-regulation. Another child might be introverted, show little emotional negativity, and have a low level of self-regulation.

Rothbart and Maria Gartstein (2008, p. 323) recently described the following developmental changes in temperament during infancy. During early infancy, smiling and laughter are emerging as part of the positive affectivity dimension of temperament. Also, by 2 months of age, infants show anger and frustration when their actions don't produce an interesting outcome. During this time, infants often are susceptible to distress and overstimulation. From 4 to 12 months of age fear and irritability become more differentiated, with inhibition (fear) increasingly linked to new and unpredictable experiences. Not all temperament characteristics are in place by the first birthday. Positive emotionality becomes more stable later in infancy, and the characteristics of extraversion/surgency can be determined in the toddler period. Improved attention skills in the toddler and preschool years are related to an increase in effortful control, which serves as a foundation for improved self-regulation.

The developmental changes just described reflect normative capabilities of children, not individual differences in children. The development of these capabilities, such as effortful control, allows individual differences to emerge (Bates, 2008). For example, although maturation of the brain's prefrontal lobes must occur for any child's attention to improve and the child to achieve effortful control, some children develop effortful control and others do not. And it is these individual differences in children that are at the heart of what temperament is (Bates, 2008).

BIOLOGICAL FOUNDATIONS AND EXPERIENCE

How does a child acquire a certain temperament? Kagan (2002, 2010) argues that children inherit a physiology that biases them to have a particular type of temperament. However, through experience they may learn to modify their temperament to some degree. For example, children may inherit a physiology that biases them to be fearful and inhibited, but they can learn to reduce their fear and inhibition to some degree.

Biological Influences   Physiological characteristics have been linked with different temperaments (Nigg & others, 2010; Schmidt & Jetha, 2009). In particular, an inhibited temperament is associated with a unique physiological pattern that includes high and stable heart rate, high level of the hormone cortisol, and high activity in the right frontal lobe of the brain (Kagan, 2003, 2008, 2010). This pattern may be tied to the excitability of the amygdala, a structure of the brain that plays an important role in fear and inhibition (Kagan, 2003, 2008). An inhibited temperament or negative affectivity may also be linked to low levels of the neurotransmitter serotonin, which may increase an individual's vulnerability to fear and frustration (Pauli-Pott & others, 2009).

What is heredity's role in the biological foundations of temperament? Twin and adoption studies suggest that heredity has a moderate influence on differences in temperament within a group of people (Goldsmith, 2011; Plomin & others, 2009). The contemporary view is that temperament is a biologically based but evolving aspect of behavior; it evolves as the child's experiences are incorporated into a network of self-perceptions and behavioral preferences that characterize the child's personality (Thompson & Goodvin, 2005).

Developmental Connections   Do young adults show the same behavioral style and characteristic emotional responses as they did when they were infants or young children? Activity level is an important dimension of temperament. Are

developmental **connection**

Research Methods. Twin and adoption studies have been used to sort out hereditary and environmental influences on development. Chapter 2, p. 69

children's activity levels linked to their personality in early adulthood? In one longitudinal study, children who were highly active at age 4 were likely to be very outgoing at age 23, which reflects continuity (Franz, 1996). From adolescence into early adulthood, most individuals show fewer emotional mood swings, become more responsible, and engage in less risk-taking behavior, which reflects discontinuity (Caspi, 1998).

Is temperament in childhood linked with adjustment in adulthood? Here is what we know based on the few longitudinal studies that have been conducted on this topic (Caspi, 1998). In one longitudinal study, children who had an easy temperament at 3 to 5 years of age were likely to be well adjusted as young adults (Chess & Thomas, 1977). In contrast, many children who had a difficult temperament at 3 to 5 years of age were not well adjusted as young adults. Also, other researchers have found that boys with a difficult temperament in childhood are less likely as adults to continue their formal education, whereas girls with a difficult temperament in childhood are more likely to experience marital conflict as adults (Wachs, 2000).

Inhibition is another temperament characteristic that has been studied extensively (Kagan, 2002, 2010). Researchers have found that individuals with an inhibited temperament in childhood are less likely as adults to be assertive or to experience social support, and more likely to delay entering a stable job track (Wachs, 2000). A recent study revealed that infants classified as highly reactive (vigorous motor activity and frequent crying) to unfamiliar stimuli were likely to avoid unfamiliar events in infancy and often were subdued, cautious, and wary of new situations in adolescence (Kagan & others, 2007). By contrast, low-reactive infants were likely to approach unfamiliar events in infancy and to be emotionally spontaneous and sociable in adolescence.

Yet another aspect of temperament involves emotionality and the ability to control one's emotions. In one longitudinal study, when 3-year-old children showed good control of their emotions and were resilient in the face of stress, they were likely to continue to handle emotions effectively as adults (Block, 1993). By contrast, when 3-year-olds had low emotional control and were not very resilient, they were likely to show problems in these areas as young adults.

In sum, these studies reveal some continuity between certain aspects of temperament in childhood and adjustment in early adulthood. However, keep in mind that these connections between childhood temperament and adult adjustment are based on only a small number of studies; more research is needed to verify these linkages.

Developmental Contexts   What accounts for the continuities and discontinuities between a child's temperament and an adult's personality? Physiological and hereditary factors likely are involved in continuity (Kagan, 2008, 2010). Theodore Wachs (1994, 2000) proposed ways that linkages between temperament in childhood and personality in adulthood might vary depending on the contexts in individuals' experience. Figure 10.6 summarizes how one characteristic might develop in different ways, depending on the context.

Gender may be an important factor shaping the context that influences the fate of temperament (Blakemore, Berenbaum, & Liben, 2009). Parents might react differently to an infant's temperament depending on whether the baby is a boy or a girl. For example, in one study, mothers were more responsive to the crying of irritable girls than to the crying of irritable boys (Crockenberg, 1986).

Similarly, the reaction to an infant's temperament may depend in part on culture (Gartstein & others, 2009; Kagan, 2010). For example, an active temperament might be valued in some cultures (such as the United States) but not in other cultures (such as China). Indeed, children's temperaments can vary across cultures (Putnam, Sanson, & Rothbart, 2002). Behavioral inhibition is more highly valued in China than in North America, and researchers have found that Chinese children are more inhibited than Canadian infants (Chen & others, 1998).

developmental **connection**

Culture and Ethnicity. Cross-cultural studies seek to determine culture-universal and culture-specific aspects of development. Chapter 1, p. 11

	Child A	Child B
Intervening Context		
Caregivers	Caregivers (parents) who are sensitive and accepting, and let child set his or her own pace.	Caregivers who use inappropriate "low-level control" and attempt to force the child into new situations.
Physical Environment	Presence of "stimulus shelters" or "defensible spaces" that the children can retreat to when there is too much stimulation.	Child continually encounters noisy, chaotic environments that allow no escape from stimulation.
Peers	Peer groups with other inhibited children with common interests, so the child feels accepted.	Peer groups consist of athletic extroverts, so the child feels rejected.
Schools	School is "undermanned," so inhibited children are more likely to be tolerated and feel they can make a contribution.	School is "overmanned," so inhibited children are less likely to be tolerated and more likely to feel undervalued.
Personality Outcomes		
	As an adult, individual is closer to extraversion (outgoing, sociable) and is emotionally stable.	As an adult, individual is closer to introversion and has more emotional problems.

FIGURE **10.6**

TEMPERAMENT IN CHILDHOOD, PERSONALITY IN ADULTHOOD, AND INTERVENING CONTEXTS. Varying experiences with caregivers, the physical environment, peers, and schools may modify links between temperament in childhood and personality in adulthood. The example given here is for inhibition.

In short, many aspects of a child's environment can encourage or discourage the persistence of temperament characteristics. One useful way of thinking about these relationships applies the concept of goodness of fit, which we examine next.

GOODNESS OF FIT AND PARENTING

Goodness of fit refers to the match between a child's temperament and the environmental demands the child must cope with. Suppose Jason is an active toddler who is made to sit still for long periods of time and Jack is a slow-to-warm-up toddler who is abruptly pushed into new situations on a regular basis. Both Jason and Jack face a lack of fit between their temperament and environmental demands. Lack of fit can produce adjustment problems (Rothbart & Bates, 2006).

Some temperament characteristics pose more parenting challenges than others, at least in modern Western societies (Rothbart & Gartstein, 2008). When children are prone to distress, as exhibited by frequent crying and irritability, their parents may eventually respond by ignoring the child's distress or trying to force the child to "behave." In one research study, though, extra support and training for mothers of distress-prone infants improved the quality of mother-infant interaction (van den Boom, 1989). The training led the mothers to alter their demands on the child, improving the fit between the child and the environment.

Many parents don't become believers in temperament's importance until the birth of their second child. They viewed their first child's behavior as a result of how they treated the child. But then they find that some strategies that worked with their first child are not as effective with the second child. Some problems experienced with the first child (such as those involved in feeding, sleeping, and coping with strangers) do not exist with the second child, but new problems arise. Such experiences strongly suggest that children differ from each other very early in life, and that these differences have important implications for parent-child interaction (Kwak & others, 1999; Putnam, Sanson, & Rothbart, 2002).

To read further about some positive strategies for parenting that take into account the child's temperament, see *Caring Connections*.

goodness of fit The match between a child's temperament and the environmental demands the child must cope with.

caring *connections*

Parenting and the Child's Temperament

What are the implications of temperamental variations for parenting? Although answers to this question necessarily are speculative, these conclusions regarding the best parenting strategies to use in relation to children's temperaments were reached by temperament experts Ann Sanson and Mary Rothbart (1995):

- ***Attention to and respect for individuality.*** One implication is that it is difficult to generate general prescriptions for "good parenting." A goal might be accomplished in one way with one child and in another way with another child, depending on the child's temperament. Parents need to be sensitive and flexible to the infant's signals and needs.

- ***Structuring the child's environment.*** Crowded, noisy environments can pose greater problems for some children (such as a "difficult child") than for others (such as an "easy child"). We might also expect that a fearful, withdrawing child would benefit from slower entry into new contexts.

- ***The "difficult child" and packaged parenting programs.*** Programs for parents often focus on dealing with children who have "difficult" temperaments, such as children who are irritable, display anger often, and don't follow directions well. Acknowledging that some children are harder than others to parent is often helpful, and advice on how to handle particular difficult characteristics can be useful. However, whether a particular characteristic is difficult depends on its fit with the environment. To label a child "difficult" has the danger of becoming a self-fulfilling prophecy. If a child is identified as difficult, people may treat the child in a way that actually elicits difficult behavior. One recent study found that having access to experiences that encourage coping and build self-regulatory skills was beneficial to children with a difficult temperament (Bradley & Corwyn, 2008).

What are some good strategies for parents to adopt when responding to their infant's temperament?

Too often, we pigeonhole children into categories without examining the context (Rothbart & Bates, 2006; Wachs, 2000). Nonetheless, caregivers need to take children's temperaments into account. Research does not yet allow for many highly specific recommendations, but in general, caregivers should (1) be sensitive to the individual characteristics of the child, (2) be flexible in responding to these characteristics, and (3) avoid applying negative labels to the child.

How does the advice to "structure the child's environment" reflect what you learned about the concept of "goodness of fit"?

Review *Connect* Reflect

 Characterize variations in temperament and their significance.

Review

- How can temperament be described and classified?
- How is temperament influenced by biological foundations and experience?
- What is goodness of fit? What are some positive parenting strategies for dealing with a child's temperament?

Connect

- In this section, you learned that twin and adoption studies suggest that heredity has a moderate influence on differences in temperament. In Chapter 2, what did you learn were the issues that complicate the interpretation of twin studies?

Reflect *Your Own Personal Journey of Life*

- Consider your own temperament. We described a number of temperament categories. Which one best describes your temperament? Has your temperament changed as you have gotten older? If your temperament has changed, what factors contributed to the changes?

Social Orientation/Understanding, Attachment, and Child Care

 LG4 Explain the early development of social orientation/ understanding, attachment, and child care.

So far, we have discussed how emotions and emotional competence change as children develop. We have also examined the role of emotional style; in effect, we have seen how emotions set the tone of our experiences in life. But emotions also write the lyrics because they are at the core of our interest in the social world and our relationships with others.

SOCIAL ORIENTATION/UNDERSTANDING

As socioemotional beings, infants show a strong interest in their social world and are motivated to orient to it and understand it. In earlier chapters, we described many of the biological and cognitive foundations that contribute to the infant's development of social orientation and understanding. We will call attention to relevant biological and cognitive factors as we explore social orientation; locomotion; intention, goal-directed behavior, and cooperation; and social referencing. Discussing biological, cognitive, and social processes together reminds us of an important aspect of development that was pointed out in Chapter 1: These processes are intricately intertwined (Diamond, 2009; Diamond, Casey, & Munakata, 2010).

Social Orientation From early in their development, infants are captivated by their social world. As we discussed in our coverage of infant perception in Chapter 5, young infants stare intently at faces and are attuned to the sounds of human voices, especially their caregiver's (Ramsay-Rennels & Langlois, 2007). Later, they become adept at interpreting the meaning of facial expressions.

Face-to-face play often begins to characterize caregiver-infant interactions when the infant is about 2 to 3 months of age. The focused social interaction of face-to-face play may include vocalizations, touch, and gestures (Leppanen & others, 2007). Such play is part of many mothers' motivation to create a positive emotional state in their infants (Thompson, 2009a, b).

In part because of such positive social interchanges between caregivers and infants, by 2 to 3 months of age infants respond to people differently from the way they respond to objects, showing more positive emotion toward people than inanimate objects, such as puppets (Legerstee, 1997). At this age, most infants expect people to react positively when the infants initiate a behavior, such as a smile or a vocalization. This finding has been discovered using a method called the *still-face paradigm*, in which the caregiver alternates between engaging in face-to-face interaction with the infant and remaining still and unresponsive (Conradt & Ablow, 2010; Johnson, 2010). As early as 2 to 3 months of age, infants show more withdrawal, negative emotions, and self-directed behavior when their caregivers are still and unresponsive (Adamson & Frick, 2003). The frequency of face-to-face play decreases after 7 months of age as infants become more mobile (Thompson, 2006). A recent meta-analysis revealed that infants' higher positive affect and lower negative affect as displayed during the still-face paradigm were linked to secure attachment at 1 year of age (Mesman, van IJzendoorn, & Bakersman-Kranenburg, 2009).

Infants also learn about their social world through contexts other than face-to-face play with a caregiver (Stern, 2010; Tronick, 2010). Even though infants as young as 6 months of age show an interest in each other, their interaction with peers increases considerably in the last half of the second year. Between 18 and 24 months of age, children markedly increase their imitative and reciprocal play,

A mother and her baby engaging in face-to-face play. *At what age does face-to-face play usually begin, and when does it typically start decreasing in frequency?*

developmental connection

Dynamic Systems Theory. Dynamic systems theory is increasingly recognized as an important theory in understanding children's development. Chapter 5, pp. 143–144 such as imitating nonverbal actions like jumping and running (Eckerman & Whitehead, 1999). One study involved presenting 1- and 2-year-olds with a simple cooperative task that consisted of pulling a lever to get an attractive toy (Brownell, Ramani, & Zerwas, 2006) (see Figure 10.7). Any coordinated actions of the 1-year-olds appeared to be mostly coincidental rather than cooperative, whereas the 2-year-olds' behavior was characterized more as active cooperation to reach a goal. As increasing numbers of U.S. infants experience child care outside the home, they are spending more time in social play with other peers (Field, 2007). Later in the chapter, we will further discuss child care.

Locomotion Recall from earlier in the chapter how important independence is for infants, especially in the second year of life. As infants develop the ability to crawl, walk, and run, they are able to explore and expand their social world. These newly developed self-produced loco-motor skills allow the infant to independently initiate social interchanges on a more frequent basis (Thompson, 2006). Remember from Chapter 5 that the development of these gross motor skills is the result of a number of factors including the development of the nervous system, the goal the infant is motivated to reach, and environmental support for the skill (Adolph & Joh, 2009).

The infant's and toddler's push for independence also is likely paced by the development of locomotor skills (Campos, 2009). Locomotion is also important for its motivational implications (Thompson, 2008). Once infants have the ability to move in goal-directed pursuits, the reward from these pursuits leads to further efforts to explore and develop skills.

Intention, Goal-Directed Behavior, and Cooperation Perceiving people as engaging in intentional and goal-directed behavior is an important social cognitive accomplishment, and this initially occurs toward the end of the first year (Laible & Thompson, 2007). Joint attention and gaze following help the infant to understand that other people have intentions (Meltzoff & Brooks, 2009). Recall from Chapter 7 that *joint attention* occurs when the caregiver and infant focus on the same object or event. We indicated that emerging aspects of joint attention occur at about 7 to 8 months, but at about 10 to 11 months of age joint attention intensifies and infants begin to follow the caregiver's gaze. By their first birthday, infants have begun to direct the caregiver's attention to objects that capture their interest (Heimann & others, 2006).

Social Referencing Another important social cognitive accomplishment in infancy is developing the ability to "read" the emotions of other people (Kim, Walden, & Knieps, 2010). **Social referencing** is the term used to describe "reading" emotional cues in others to help determine how to act in a particular situation. The development of social referencing helps infants to interpret ambiguous situations more accurately, as when they encounter a stranger and need to know whether to fear the person (Thompson, 2006). By the end of the first year, a mother's facial expression—either smiling or fearful—influences whether an infant will explore an unfamiliar environment.

FIGURE **10.7**

THE COOPERATION TASK. The cooperation on task consisted of two handles on a box, atop which was an animated musical toy, surreptitiously activated by remote control when both handles were pulled. The handles were placed far enough apart that one child could not pull both handles. The experimenter demonstrated the task, saying, "Watch! If you pull the handles, the doggie will sing" (Brownell, Ramani, & Zerwas, 2006).

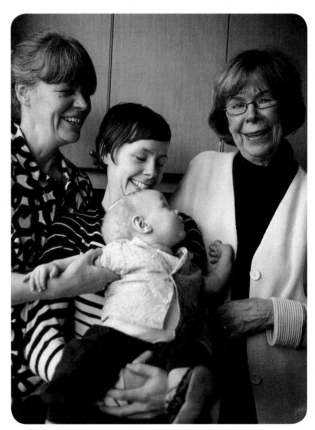

What is social referencing? What are some developmental changes in social referencing?

social referencing "Reading" emotional cues in others to help determine how to act in a particular situation.

FIGURE **10.8**

CONTACT TIME WITH WIRE AND CLOTH SURROGATE MOTHERS. Regardless of whether the infant monkeys were fed by a wire or a cloth mother, they overwhelmingly preferred to spend contact time with the cloth mother. *How do these results compare with what Freud's theory and Erikson's theory would predict about human infants?*

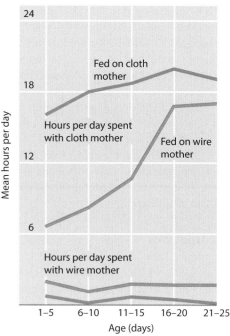

Infants become better at social referencing in the second year of life. At this age, they tend to "check" with their mother before they act; they look at her to see if she is happy, angry, or fearful. For example, in one study, 14- to 22-month-old infants were more likely to look at their mother's face as a source of information for how to act in a situation than were 6- to 9-month-old infants (Walden, 1991).

Infants' Social Sophistication and Insight   In sum, researchers are discovering that infants are more socially sophisticated and insightful at younger ages than was previously envisioned (Hamlin, Hallinan, & Woodward, 2008; Thompson, 2010; Tronick, 2010). This sophistication and insight is reflected in infants' perceptions of others' actions as intentionally motivated and goal-directed (Brune & Woodward, 2007) and their motivation to share and participate in that intentionality by their first birthday (Tomasello, Carpenter, & Liszkowski, 2007). The more advanced social cognitive skills of infants could be expected to influence their understanding and awareness of attachment to a caregiver.

ATTACHMENT

What is attachment? **Attachment** is a close emotional bond between two people. Interest in attachment has especially focused on infants and their caregivers.

Theories of Attachment   There is no shortage of theories about why infants become attached to a caregiver. Three theorists discussed in Chapter 1—Freud, Erikson, and Bowlby—proposed influential views.

Freud reasoned that infants become attached to the person or object that provides oral satisfaction. For most infants, this is the mother, since she is most likely to feed the infant. Is feeding as important as Freud thought? A classic study by Harry Harlow (1958) reveals that the answer is no (see Figure 10.8).

Harlow removed infant monkeys from their mothers at birth; for six months they were reared by surrogate (substitute) "mothers." One surrogate mother was made of wire, the other of cloth. Half of the infant monkeys were fed by the wire mother, half by the cloth mother. Periodically, the amount of time the infant monkeys spent with either the wire or the cloth mother was computed. Regardless of which mother fed them, the infant monkeys spent far more time with the cloth

attachment A close emotional bond between two people.

308   CHAPTER 10   Emotional Development

mother. Even if the wire mother but not the cloth mother provided nourishment, the infant monkeys spent more time with the cloth mother. And when Harlow frightened the monkeys, those "raised" by the cloth mother ran to the mother and clung to it; those raised by the wire mother did not. Whether the mother provided comfort seemed to determine whether the monkeys associated the mother with security. This study clearly demonstrated that feeding is not the crucial element in the attachment process, and that contact comfort is important.

Physical comfort also plays a role in Erik Erikson's (1968) view of the infant's development. Recall Erikson's proposal that the first year of life represents the stage of trust versus mistrust. Physical comfort and sensitive care, according to Erikson (1968), are key to establishing a basic trust in infants. The infant's sense of trust, in turn, is the foundation for attachment and sets the stage for a lifelong expectation that the world will be a good and pleasant place to be.

The ethological perspective of British psychiatrist John Bowlby (1969, 1989) also stresses the importance of attachment in the first year of life and the responsiveness of the caregiver. Bowlby points out that both infants and their primary caregivers are biologically predisposed to form attachments. He argues that the newborn is biologically equipped to elicit attachment behavior. The baby cries, clings, coos, and smiles. Later, the infant crawls, walks, and follows the mother. The immediate result is to keep the primary caregiver nearby; the long-term effect is to increase the infant's chances of survival.

Attachment does not emerge suddenly but rather develops in a series of phases, moving from a baby's general preference for human beings to a partnership with primary caregivers. Following are four such phases based on Bowlby's conceptualization of attachment (Schaffer, 1996):

- *Phase 1: From birth to 2 months.* Infants instinctively orient to human figures. Strangers, siblings, and parents are equally likely to elicit smiling or crying from the infant.

- *Phase 2: From 2 to 7 months.* Attachment becomes focused on one figure, usually the primary caregiver, as the baby gradually learns to distinguish familiar from unfamiliar people.

- *Phase 3: From 7 to 24 months.* Specific attachments develop. With increased locomotor skills, babies actively seek contact with regular caregivers, such as the mother or father.

- *Phase 4: From 24 months on.* Children become aware of others' feelings, goals, and plans and begin to take these into account in directing their own actions. Researchers' recent findings that infants are more socially sophisticated and insightful than previously envisioned suggests that some of the characteristics of Bowlby's phase 4, such as understanding the goals and intentions of the attachment figure, appear to be developing in phase 3 as attachment security is taking shape (Thompson, 2008).

In Bowlby's model, what are the four phases of attachment?

Bowlby argued that infants develop an *internal working model* of attachment: a simple mental model of the caregiver, their relationship, and the self as deserving of nurturant care. The infant's internal working model of attachment with the caregiver influences the infant's and later the child's subsequent responses to other people (Bretherton & Munholland, 2008; Posada, 2008). The internal model of attachment also has played a pivotal role in the discovery of links between attachment and subsequent emotion understanding, conscience development, and self-concept (Thompson, 2006).

In sum, attachment emerges from the social cognitive advances that allow infants to develop expectations for the caregiver's behavior and to determine the affective quality of their relationship (Thompson, 2006). These social cognitive advances include recognizing the caregiver's face, voice, and other features, as well as developing an internal working model of expecting the caregiver to provide pleasure in social interaction and relief from distress.

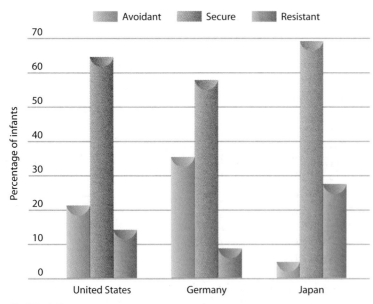

FIGURE **10.9**

CROSS-CULTURAL COMPARISON OF ATTACHMENT. In one study, infant attachment in three countries—the United States, Germany, and Japan—was measured in the Ainsworth Strange Situation (van IJzendoorn & Kroonenberg, 1988). The dominant attachment pattern in all three countries was secure attachment. However, German infants were more avoidant and Japanese infants were less avoidant and more resistant than U.S. infants. *What are some explanations for differences in how German, Japanese, and U.S. infants respond to the Strange Situation?*

Strange Situation Ainsworth's observational measure of infant attachment to a caregiver, which requires the infant to move through a series of introductions, separations, and reunions with the caregiver and an adult stranger in a prescribed order.

securely attached babies Babies who use the caregiver as a secure base from which to explore the environment.

insecure avoidant babies Babies who show insecurity by avoiding the mother.

insecure resistant babies Babies who might cling to the caregiver, then resist her by fighting against the closeness, perhaps by kicking or pushing away.

insecure disorganized babies Babies who show insecurity by being disorganized and disoriented.

Individual Differences in Attachment Although attachment to a caregiver intensifies midway through the first year, isn't it likely that the quality of babies' attachment experiences varies? Mary Ainsworth (1979) thought so. Ainsworth created the **Strange Situation,** an observational measure of infant attachment in which the infant experiences a series of introductions, separations, and reunions with the caregiver and an adult stranger in a prescribed order. In using the Strange Situation, researchers hope that their observations will provide information about the infant's motivation to be near the caregiver and the degree to which the caregiver's presence provides the infant with security and confidence.

Based on how babies respond in the Strange Situation, they are described as being securely attached or insecurely attached (in one of three ways) to the caregiver:

- **Securely attached babies** use the caregiver as a secure base from which to explore the environment. When they are in the presence of their caregiver, securely attached infants explore the room and examine toys that have been placed in it. When the caregiver departs, securely attached infants might protest mildly, and when the caregiver returns these infants reestablish positive interaction with her, perhaps by smiling or climbing onto her lap. Subsequently, they often resume playing with the toys in the room.

- **Insecure avoidant babies** show insecurity by avoiding the mother. In the Strange Situation, these babies engage in little interaction with the caregiver, are not distressed when she leaves the room, usually do not reestablish contact with her on her return, and may even turn their back on her. If contact is established, the infant usually leans away or looks away.

- **Insecure resistant babies** often cling to the caregiver and then resist her by fighting against the closeness, perhaps by kicking or pushing away. In the Strange Situation, these babies often cling anxiously to the caregiver and don't explore the playroom. When the caregiver leaves, they often cry loudly and push away if she tries to comfort them on her return.

- **Insecure disorganized babies** are disorganized and disoriented. In the Strange Situation, these babies might appear dazed, confused, and fearful. To be classified as disorganized, babies must show strong patterns of avoidance and resistance or display certain specified behaviors, such as extreme fearfulness around the caregiver.

Evaluating the Strange Situation Does the Strange Situation capture important differences among infants? As a measure of attachment, it may be culturally biased. For example, German and Japanese babies often show patterns of attachment different from those of American infants. As illustrated in Figure 10.9, German infants are more likely to show an avoidant attachment pattern and Japanese infants are less likely to display this pattern than U.S. infants (van IJzendoorn & Kroonenberg, 1988). The avoidant pattern in German babies likely occurs because their caregivers encourage them to be independent (Grossmann & others, 1985). Also as shown in Figure 10.9, Japanese babies are more likely than American babies to be categorized as resistant. This may have more to do with the Strange Situation as a measure of attachment than with attachment insecurity itself. Japanese mothers rarely let anyone unfamiliar with their babies care for them. Thus, the Strange Situation might create considerably more stress for Japanese infants than for American infants, who are more accustomed to separation from their mothers (Miyake, Chen, & Campos,

1985). Even though there are cultural variations in attachment classification, the most frequent classification in every culture studied so far is secure attachment (Thompson, 2006; van IJzendoorn & Kroonenberg, 1988).

Some critics stress that behavior in the Strange Situation—like other laboratory assessments—might not indicate what infants would do in a natural environment. But researchers have found that infants' behaviors in the Strange Situation are closely related to how they behave at home in response to separation and reunion with their mothers (Pederson & Moran, 1996). Thus, many infant researchers conclude that the Strange Situation continues to show merit as a measure of infant attachment.

Interpreting Differences in Attachment   Do individual differences in attachment matter? Ainsworth observes that secure attachment in the first year of life provides an important foundation for psychological development later in life. The securely attached infant moves freely away from the mother but keeps track of where she is through periodic glances. The securely attached infant responds positively to being picked up by others and, when put back down, freely moves away to play. An insecurely attached infant, by contrast, avoids the mother or is ambivalent toward her, fears strangers, and is upset by minor, everyday separations.

If early attachment to a caregiver is important, it should relate to a child's social behavior later in development. For some children, early attachments seem to foreshadow later functioning. In the extensive longitudinal study conducted by Alan Sroufe and his colleagues (2005), early secure attachment (assessed by the Strange Situation at 12 and 18 months) was linked with positive emotional health, high self-esteem, self-confidence, and socially competent interaction with peers, teachers, camp counselors, and romantic partners through adolescence. Another study revealed that being classified as insecure resistant in infancy was a negative predictor of cognitive development in elementary school (O'Connor & McCartney, 2007). Yet another study found that attachment security at 24 and 36 months was linked to the child's enhanced social problem-solving skills at 54 months (Raikes & Thompson, 2009). And a recent meta-analysis found that disorganized attachment was more strongly linked to externalizing problems (aggression, hostility, opposition problems, for example) than were avoidant and resistant attachment (Fearon & others, 2010).

For some children, though, there is little continuity (Thompson, 2006). Not all research reveals the power of infant attachment to predict subsequent development. In one longitudinal study, attachment classification in infancy did not predict attachment classification at 18 years of age (Lewis, Feiring, & Rosenthal, 2000). In this study, the best predictor of an insecure attachment classification at 18 was the occurrence of parental divorce in the intervening years. Consistently positive caregiving over a number of years is likely an important factor in connecting early attachment with the child's functioning later in development. Indeed, researchers have found that early secure attachment *and* subsequent experiences, especially maternal care and life stresses, are linked with children's later behavior and adjustment (Thompson, 2006).

Some developmentalists conclude that too much emphasis has been placed on the attachment bond in infancy (Newcombe, 2007). Jerome Kagan (1987, 2002), for example, points out that infants are highly resilient and adaptive; he argues that they are evolutionarily equipped to stay on a positive developmental course, even in the face of wide variations in parenting. Kagan and others stress that genetic characteristics and temperament play more important roles in a child's social competence than the attachment theorists, such as Bowlby and Ainsworth, are willing to acknowledge (Bakermans-Kranenburg & others, 2007). For example, if some infants inherit a low tolerance for stress, this—rather than an insecure attachment bond—may be responsible for an inability to get along with peers. A recent study found links between disorganized attachment in infancy, a specific gene, and level of maternal responsiveness. In this study, a disorganized attachment style developed in infancy only when infants had the short version of the serotonin transporter

developmental **connection**

Nature vs. Nurture. What is involved in gene-environment (G × E) interaction? Chapter 2, pp. 71–72

In the Hausa culture, siblings and grandmothers provide a significant amount of care for infants. *How might this practice affect attachment?*

gene—5-HTTLPR (Spangler & others, 2009). Infants were not characterized by this attachment style when they had the long version of the gene (Spangler & others, 2009). Further, this gene-environment interaction only occurred when mothers showed a low level of responsiveness toward their infants.

Another criticism of attachment theory is that it ignores the diversity of socializing agents and contexts that exists in an infant's world. A culture's value system can influence the nature of attachment (Cole & Tan, 2007; Shiraev & Levy, 2010). Mothers' expectations for infants to be independent are high in northern Germany, whereas Japanese mothers are more strongly motivated to keep their infants close to them (Grossmann & others, 1985; Rothbaum & Trommsdorff, 2007). Not surprisingly, northern German infants tend to show less distress than Japanese infants when separated from their mothers. Also, in some cultures, infants show attachments to many people. Among the Hausa (who live in Nigeria), both grandmothers and siblings provide a significant amount of care for infants (Harkness & Super, 1995). Infants in agricultural societies tend to form attachments to older siblings, who are assigned a major responsibility for younger siblings' care. Researchers recognize the importance of competent, nurturant caregivers in an infant's development (Thompson & others, 2009). At issue, though, is whether or not secure attachment, especially to a single caregiver, is critical (Lamb, 2010; Thompson, 2006).

Despite such criticisms, there is ample evidence that security of attachment is important to development (Sroufe, Coffino, & Carlson, 2010; Thompson & Newton, 2009). Secure attachment in infancy is important because it reflects a positive parent-infant relationship and provides a foundation that supports healthy socioemotional development in the years that follow.

Caregiving Styles and Attachment   Is the style of caregiving linked with the quality of the infant's attachment? Securely attached babies have caregivers who are sensitive to their signals and are consistently available to respond to their infants' needs (Bigelow & others, 2010). These caregivers often let their babies have an active part in determining the onset and pacing of interaction in the first year of life. A recent study revealed that maternal sensitive responding was linked to infant attachment security (Finger & others, 2009). Another study found that maternal sensitivity in parenting was related to secure attachment in infants in two different cultures: the United States and Colombia (Carbonell & others, 2002). Although maternal sensitivity is positively linked to the development of secure attachment in infancy, it is important to note that the link is not especially strong (Campos, 2009).

How do the caregivers of insecurely attached babies interact with them? Caregivers of avoidant babies tend to be unavailable or rejecting (Cassidy, 2008). They often don't respond to their babies' signals and have little physical contact with them. When they do interact with their babies, they may behave in an angry and irritable way. Caregivers of resistant babies tend to be inconsistent; sometimes they respond to their babies' needs, and sometimes they don't. In general, they tend not to be very affectionate with their babies and show little synchrony when interacting with them. Caregivers of disorganized babies often neglect or physically abuse them (Lyons-Ruth & Jacobvitz, 2008). In some cases, these caregivers are depressed (Thompson, 2008).

Developmental Social Neuroscience and Attachment   In Chapter 1, we described the emerging field of developmental social neuroscience that examines connections between socioemotional processes, development, and the brain (Beauchamp & Anderson, 2010; Parsons & others, 2010). Attachment is one of the main areas in which theory and research on developmental social neuroscience has focused. These connections of attachment and the brain involve the neuroanatomy of the brain, neurotransmitters, and hormones.

Theory and research on the role of the brain's regions in mother-infant attachment is just emerging (De Haan & Gunnar, 2009; Parsons & others, 2010). A recent theoretical view proposed that the prefrontal cortex likely has an important role in maternal attachment behavior, as do the subcortical (areas of the brain lower than the cortex) regions of the amygdala (which is strongly involved in emotion) and the hypothalamus (Gonzalez, Atkinson, & Fleming, 2009). An ongoing fMRI longitudinal study is exploring the possibility that different attachment patterns can be distinguished by different patterns of brain activity (Strathearn, 2007).

Research on the role of hormones and neurotransmitters in attachment has emphasized the importance of two neuropeptide hormones—oxytocin and vasopressin—in the formation of the maternal-infant bond (Bales & Carter, 2009). Oxytocin, a mammalian hormone that also acts as a neurotransmitter in the brain, is released during breastfeeding and by contact and warmth (Campbell, 2010). Oxytocin is especially thought to be a likely candidate in the formation of infant-mother attachment (Bales & Carter, 2009).

The influence of these neuropeptides on the neurotransmitter dopamine in the nucleus accumbens (a collection of neurons in the forebrain that are involved in pleasure) likely is important in motivating approach to the attachment object (de Haan & Gunnar, 2009). Figure 10.10 shows the regions of the brain we have described that are likely to be important in infant-mother attachment.

FATHERS AND MOTHERS AS CAREGIVERS

Much of our discussion of attachment has focused on mothers as caregivers. Do mothers and fathers differ in their caregiving roles?

On average, mothers spend considerably more time in caregiving with infants and children than do fathers (Blakemore, Berenbaum, & Liben, 2009). Mothers especially are more likely to engage in the managerial role with their children, coordinating their activities, making sure their health care needs are fulfilled, and so on (Parke & Buriel, 2006).

However, an increasing number of U.S. fathers stay home full-time with their children (Wong & Rochlen, 2008). As indicated in Figure 10.11, there was a 300-plus percent increase in stay-at-home fathers in the United States from 1996 to 2006. A large portion of full-time fathers have career-focused wives who provide the main family income. A recent study revealed that the stay-at-home fathers were as satisfied with their marriage as traditional parents, although they indicated that they missed their daily life in the workplace (Rochlen & others, 2007). In this study, the stay-at-home fathers reported that they tended to be ostracized when they took their children to playgrounds and often were excluded from parent groups.

Can fathers take care of infants as competently as mothers can? Observations of fathers and their infants suggest that fathers have the ability to act as sensitively and responsively as mothers with their infants (Parke & Buriel, 2006; Parke & others, 2008). Consider the Aka pygmy culture in Africa where fathers spend as much time interacting with their infants as do their mothers (Hewlett, 1991, 2000; Hewlett & MacFarlan, 2010). Remember, however, that although fathers can be active, nurturant, involved caregivers with their infants as Aka pygmy fathers do, in many cultures men have not chosen to follow this pattern (Lamb, 2005).

Do fathers behave differently from mothers with their infants? Maternal interactions usually center on child-care activities—feeding, changing diapers, and bathing. Paternal interactions are more likely to include play (Parke, 2002; Parke & Buriel, 2006). Fathers engage in more rough-and-tumble play. They bounce infants,

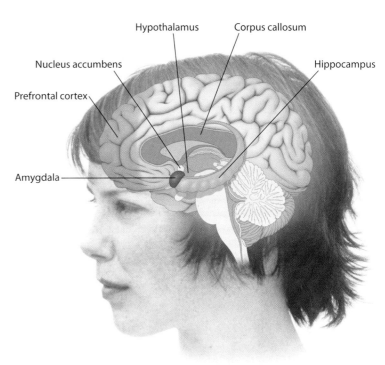

FIGURE 10.10

REGIONS OF THE BRAIN PROPOSED AS LIKELY IMPORTANT IN INFANT-MOTHER ATTACHMENT. This illustration shows the brain's left hemisphere. The corpus collosum is the large bundle of axons that connect the brain's two hemispheres.

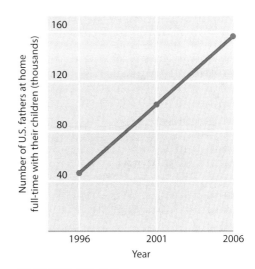

FIGURE 10.11

THE INCREASE IN THE NUMBER OF U.S. FATHERS STAYING AT HOME FULL-TIME WITH THEIR CHILDREN

An Aka pygmy father with his infant son. In the Aka culture, fathers were observed to be holding or nearby their infants 47 percent of the time (Hewlett, 1991).

How do most fathers and mothers interact differently with infants?

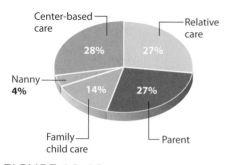

Center-based care 28%
Relative care 27%
Nanny 4%
Family child care 14%
Parent 27%

FIGURE 10.12

PRIMARY CARE ARRANGEMENTS IN THE UNITED STATES FOR CHILDREN UNDER 5 YEARS OF AGE WITH EMPLOYED MOTHERS

throw them up in the air, tickle them, and so on (Lamb, 1986, 2000). Mothers do play with infants, but their play is less physical and arousing than that of fathers.

In one study, fathers were interviewed about their caregiving responsibilities when their children were 6, 15, 24, and 36 months of age (NICHD Early Child Care Research Network, 2000). Some of the fathers were videotaped while playing with their children at 6 and 36 months. Fathers were more involved in caregiving—bathing, feeding, dressing the child, taking the child to child care, and so on—when they worked fewer hours and mothers worked more hours, when mothers and fathers were younger, when mothers reported greater marital intimacy, and when the children were boys.

Do children benefit when fathers are positively involved in their caregiving? One study of more than 7,000 children who were assessed from infancy to adulthood revealed that those whose fathers were extensively involved in their lives (such as engaging in various activities with them and showing a strong interest in their education) were more successful in school (Flouri & Buchanan, 2004).

CHILD CARE

Many U.S. children today experience multiple caregivers. Most do not have a parent staying home to care for them; instead, the children have some type of care provided by others—"child care." Many parents worry that child care will reduce their infants' emotional attachment to them, retard infants' cognitive development, fail to teach them how to control anger, and allow them to be unduly influenced by their peers. How extensive is the use of child care? Are the worries of these parents justified?

Parental Leave Today far more young children are in child care than at any other time in history. About 2 million children in the United States currently receive formal, licensed child care, and uncounted millions of children are cared for by unlicensed babysitters. In part, these numbers reflect the fact that U.S. adults cannot receive paid leave from their jobs to care for their young children. However, as described in *Connecting With Diversity*, many countries provide extensive parental leave policies.

Variations in Child Care Because the United States does not have a policy of paid leave for child care, child care in the United States has become a major national concern (Belsky, 2009; Phillips & Lowenstein, 2011; Thompson, 2009c). Many factors influence the effects of child care, including the age of the child, the type of child care, and the quality of the program.

The type of child care varies extensively. Child care is provided in large centers with elaborate facilities and in private homes. Some child-care centers are commercial operations; others are nonprofit centers run by churches, civic groups, and employers. Some child-care providers are professionals; others are untrained adults who want to earn extra money. Figure 10.12 presents the primary care arrangement for children under 5 years of age with employed mothers (Clarke-Stewart & Miner, 2008).

In the United States, approximately 15 percent of children 5 years of age and younger attend more than one child-care arrangement. A recent study of 2- and 3-year-old children revealed that an increase in the number of child-care arrangements the children experienced was linked to an increase in behavioral problems and a decrease in prosocial behavior (Morrissey, 2009).

Use of different types of child care varies by ethnicity (Howes & Wishard Guerra, 2009). For example, Latino families are far less likely than non-Latino White and African American families to have children in child-care centers—11 percent, 20 percent, and 21 percent, respectively, in one study (Smith, 2002). Despite indicating a

Child-Care Policies Around the World

Child-care policies around the world vary (O'Brien & Moss, 2010; Tolani & Brooks-Gunn, 2008). Europe led the way in creating new standards of parental leave: The European Union (EU) mandated a paid 14-week maternity leave in 1992. In most European countries today, working parents on leave receive from 70 to 100 percent of their prior wage, and paid leave averages about 16 weeks (Tolani & Brooks-Gunn, 2008). The United States currently allows up to 12 weeks of unpaid leave for caring for a newborn.

Most countries restrict eligible benefits to women employed for a minimum time prior to childbirth. In Denmark, even unemployed mothers are eligible for extended parental leave related to childbirth. In Germany, child-rearing leave is available to almost all parents. The Nordic countries (Denmark, Norway, and Sweden) have extensive gender-equity family leave policies for childbirth that emphasize the contributions of both women and men (O'Brien & Moss, 2010; Tolani & Brooks-Gunn, 2008). For example, in Sweden, parents can take an 18-month job-protected parental leave with benefits allowed to be shared by parents and applied to full-time or part-time work.

In light of the data you saw in Figure 10.11, why might it be helpful if U.S. leave policies were more like those in Scandinavian countries?

How are child-care policies in many European countries, such as Sweden, different from those in the United States?

preference for center-based care, African American and Latino families often rely on family-based care, especially by grandmothers. However, there has been a substantial increase in the use of center-based care by African American mothers.

Child-care quality makes a difference. What constitutes a high-quality child-care program for infants? In high-quality child care (Clarke-Stewart & Miner, 2008, p. 273),

> caregivers encourage the children to be actively engaged in a variety of activities, have frequent, positive interactions that include smiling, touching, holding, and speaking at the child's eye level, respond properly to the child's questions or requests, and encourage children to talk about their experiences, feelings, and ideas.

High-quality child care also involves providing children with a safe environment, access to age-appropriate toys and participation in age-appropriate activities, and a low caregiver-to-child ratio that allows caregivers to spend considerable time with children on an individual basis.

Children are more likely to experience poor-quality child care if they come from families with few resources (psychological, social, and economic) (Cabrera, Hutchens, & Peters, 2006). Many researchers have examined the role of poverty in quality of child care (Lucas & others, 2008). One study found that extensive child care was harmful to low-income children only when the care was of low quality (Votruba-Drzal, Coley, & Chase-Lansdale, 2004). Even if the child was in child care more than 45 hours a week, high-quality care was linked with fewer internalizing problems

connecting with careers

Wanda Mitchell, Child-Care Director

Wanda Mitchell is the Center Director at the Hattie Daniels Day Care Center in Wilson, North Carolina. Her responsibilities include directing the operation of the center, which involves creating and maintaining an environment in which young children can learn effectively, and for ensuring that the center meets state licensing requirements. Wanda obtained her undergraduate degree from North Carolina A & T University, majoring in Child Development. Prior to her current position, she had been an education coordinator for Head Start and an instructor at Wilson Technical Community College. Describing her work, Wanda says, "I really enjoy working in my field. This is my passion. After graduating from college, my goal was to advance in my field."

For more information about what early education educators do, see page 45 in the Careers in Child Development appendix following Chapter 1.

Wanda Mitchell, child-care director, working with some of the children at her center.

> We have all the knowledge necessary to provide absolutely first-rate child care in the United States. What is missing is the commitment and the will.
>
> —**EDWARD ZIGLER**
> *Contemporary Developmental Psychologist,*
> *Yale University*

(anxiety, for example) and externalizing problems (aggressive and destructive behaviors, for example). A recent study revealed that children from low-income families benefited in terms of school readiness and language development when their parents selected higher-quality child care (McCartney & others, 2007).

To read about one individual who provides quality child care to individuals from impoverished backgrounds, see the *Connecting With Careers* profile of Rashmi Nakhre. Do children in low-income families get quality care at day care? For the answer to that question, as well as other information on the effects of child care on children's development, see *Connecting Through Research*.

What are some strategies parents can follow in regard to child care? Child-care expert Kathleen McCartney (2003, p. 4) offered this advice:

- *Recognize that the quality of your parenting is a key factor in your child's development.*
- *Make decisions that will improve the likelihood you will be good parents.* "For some this will mean working full-time"—for personal fulfillment, income, or both. "For others, this will mean working part-time or not working outside the home."
- *Monitor your child's development.* "Parents should observe for themselves whether their children seems to be having behavior problems." They need to talk with child-care providers and their pediatrician about their child's behavior.
- *Take some time to find the best child care available.* Observe different child-care facilities and be certain that you like what you see. Quality child care costs money, and not all parents can afford the child care they want. However, state subsidies and programs like Head Start are available for families in need.

connecting through research

How Does the Quality and Quantity of Child Care Affect Children?

In 1991, the National Institute of Child Health and Human Development (NICHD) began a comprehensive, longitudinal study of child-care experiences. Data were collected on a diverse sample of almost 1,400 children and their families at 10 locations across the United States over a period of seven years. Researchers used multiple methods (trained observers, interviews, questionnaires, and testing) and measured many facets of children's development, including physical health, cognitive development, and socioemotional development. Following are some of the results of what is now referred to as the NICHD Study of Early Child Care and Youth Development or NICHD SECCYD (NICHD Early Child Care Network, 2001, 2002, 2003, 2004, 2005, 2006).

- *Patterns of use.* Many families placed their infants in child care very soon after the child's birth, and there was considerable instability in the child-care arrangements. By 4 months of age, nearly three-fourths of the infants had entered some form of nonmaternal child care. Almost half of the infants were cared for by a relative when they first entered care; only 12 percent were enrolled in child-care centers. Socioeconomic factors were linked to the amount and type of care. For example, mothers with higher incomes and families that were more dependent on the mother's income placed their infants in child care at an earlier age. Mothers who believed that maternal employment has positive effects on children were more likely than other mothers to place their infant in nonmaternal care for more hours. Low-income families were more likely than more affluent families to use child care, but infants from low-income families who were in child care averaged as many hours as other income groups. In the preschool years, mothers who were single, those with more education, and families with higher incomes used more hours of center care than other families. Minority families and mothers with less education used more hours of care by relatives.

- *Quality of care.* Evaluations of quality of care were based on such characteristics as group size, child-adult ratio, physical environment, caregiver characteristics (such as formal education, specialized training, and child-care experience), and caregiver behavior (such as sensitivity to children). An alarming conclusion is that a majority of the child care in the first three years of life was of unacceptably low quality. Positive caregiving by nonparents in child-care settings was infrequent—only 12 percent of the children studied experienced positive nonparental child care (such as positive talk, lack of detachment or flat affect, and language stimulation)! Further, infants from low-income families experienced lower-quality child care than infants from higher-income families. When quality of caregivers' care was high, children performed better on cognitive and language tasks, were more cooperative with their mothers during play, showed more positive and skilled interaction with peers, and

What are some important findings from the National Longitudinal Study of Child Care conducted by the National Institute of Child Health and Human Development?

had fewer behavior problems. Caregiver training and good child-staff ratios were linked with higher cognitive and social competence when children were 54 months of age.

Higher-quality child care was also related to higher-quality mother-child interaction among the families that used nonmaternal care. Further, poor-quality care was related to an increase of insecure attachment to the mother among infants who were 15 months of age, but only when the mother was low in sensitivity and responsiveness. However, child-care quality was not linked to attachment security at 36 months of age.

- *Amount of child care.* The quantity of child care predicted some child outcomes. When children spent extensive amounts of time in child care beginning in infancy, they experienced less sensitive interactions with their mother, showed more behavior problems, and had higher rates of illness. Many of these comparisons involved children

(continued)

(continued)

in child care for less than 30 hours a week versus those in child care for more than 45 hours a week. In general, though, when children spent 30 hours or more per week in child care, their development was less than optimal (Ramey, 2005).

- *Family and parenting influences.* The influence of families and parenting was not weakened by extensive child care. Parents played a significant role in helping children to regulate their emotions. Especially important parenting influences were sensitivity to children's needs, involvement with children, and provision of cognitive stimulation. Indeed, parental sensitivity has been the most consistent predictor of a secure attachment, with child-care experiences being relevant in many cases only when mothers engage in insen-

sitive parenting (Friedman, Melhuish, & Hill, 2009). An important final point about the extensive NICHD SECC research is that findings have consistently shown that family factors are considerably stronger and more consistent predictors of a wide variety of child outcomes than are child-care experiences (quality, quantity, type).

This study reinforces the conclusions of other researchers cited earlier in this section of the chapter—it is not the *quantity* so much as the *quality* of child care a child receives that is important. What is also significant to note is the emphasis on the positive effect families and parents can have on children's child-care experiences.

Review *Connect* Reflect

 LG4 Explain the early development of social orientation/understanding, attachment, and child care.

Review

- What characterizes the early development of social orientation and social understanding?
- How does attachment develop in infancy?
- How do mothers and fathers interact with infants?
- What is the nature of child care?

Connect

- In this section, you learned that maternal sensitive responding was linked (if not strongly) to security of infant attachment.

What did you learn about maternal sensitivity and children's language development in the *Connecting Through Research* interlude in Chapter 9?

Reflect *Your Own Personal Journey of Life*

- Imagine that a friend of yours is getting ready to put her baby in child care. What advice would you give to her? Do you think she should stay home with the baby? Why or why not? What type of child care would you recommend?

Emotional Development

Exploring Emotion

LG1 Discuss basic aspects of emotion.

What Are Emotions?

- Emotion is feeling, or affect, that occurs when people are engaged in interactions that are important to them, especially those that influence their well-being. Emotions can be classified as positive or negative. Darwin described the evolutionary basis of emotions, and today psychologists stress that emotions, especially facial expressions of emotions, have a biological foundation. Facial expressions of emotion are similar across cultures, but display rules are not culturally universal. Biological evolution endowed humans to be emotional, but culture and relationships with others provide diversity in emotional experiences.

A Functionalist View of Emotions

- The functionalist view of emotion emphasizes the importance of contexts and relationships in emotion. For example, when parents induce a positive mood in their child, the child is more likely to follow the parents' directions. In this view, goals are involved in emotions in a variety of ways, and the goal's specific nature can affect the individual's experience of a given emotion.

Emotional Competence

- Saarni argues that becoming emotionally competent involves developing a number of skills such as being aware of one's emotional states, discerning others' emotions, adaptively coping with negative emotions, and understanding the role of emotions in relationships.

Development of Emotion

LG2 Describe the development of emotion.

Infancy

- Infants display a number of emotions early in their development, although researchers debate the onset and sequence of these emotions. Lewis distinguishes between primary emotions and self-conscious emotions. Primary emotions include joy, anger, and fear, while self-conscious emotions include pride, shame, and guilt. Crying is the most important mechanism newborns have for communicating with their world. Babies have at least three types of cries—basic, anger, and pain cries. Social smiling in response to a caregiver's voice occurs as early as 4 to 6 weeks of age. Two fears that infants develop are stranger anxiety and separation from a caregiver (which is reflected in separation protest). Controversy swirls about whether babies should be soothed when they cry, although increasingly experts recommend immediately responding in a caring way during the first year. Infants gradually develop an ability to inhibit the duration and intensity of their emotional reactions.

Early Childhood

- Advances in young children's emotions involve expressing emotions, understanding emotions, and regulating emotions. Young children's range of emotions expands during early childhood as they increasingly experience self-conscious emotions such as pride, shame, and guilt. Between 2 and 4 years old, children use an increasing number of terms to describe emotion and learn more about the causes and consequences of feelings. At 4 to 5 years of age, children show an increased ability to reflect on emotions and understand that a single event can elicit different emotions in different people. They also show a growing awareness of the need to manage emotions to meet social standards. Emotion-coaching parents have children who engage in more effective self-regulation of their emotions than do emotion-dismissing parents. Young children in a secure attachment relationship with their mother are more willing to engage in conversation about difficult emotional circumstances. Emotional regulation plays an important role in successful peer relations.

| Middle and Late Childhood | • In middle and late childhood, children show a growing awareness about controlling and managing emotions to meet social standards. Also in this age period, they show improved emotional understanding, markedly improve their ability to suppress or conceal negative emotions, use self-initiated strategies for redirecting feelings, have an increased tendency to take into fuller account the events that lead to emotional reactions, and develop a capacity for genuine empathy. |

Temperament

 LG3 Characterize variations in temperament and their significance.

| Describing and Classifying Temperament | • Temperament involves individual differences in behavioral styles, emotions, and characteristic ways of responding. Developmentalists are especially interested in the temperament of infants. Chess and Thomas classified infants as (1) easy, (2) difficult, or (3) slow to warm up. Kagan argues that inhibition to the unfamiliar is an important temperament category. Rothbart and Bates' view of temperament emphasizes the following classification: (1) extraversion/surgency, (2) negative affectivity, and (3) effortful control (self-regulation). |

| Biological Foundations and Experience | • Physiological characteristics are associated with different temperaments, and a moderate influence of heredity has been found in twin and adoption studies of the heritability of temperament. Children inherit a physiology that biases them to have a particular type of temperament, but through experience they learn to modify their temperament style to some degree. Very active young children are likely to become outgoing adults. In some cases, a difficult temperament is linked with adjustment problems in early adulthood. The link between childhood temperament and adult personality depends in part on context, which helps shape the reaction to a child and thus the child's experiences. For example, the reaction to a child's temperament depends in part on the child's gender and on the culture. |

| Goodness of Fit and Parenting | • Goodness of fit refers to the match between a child's temperament and the environmental demands the child must cope with. Goodness of fit can be an important aspect of a child's adjustment. Although research evidence is sketchy at this point, some general recommendations are that caregivers should (1) be sensitive to the individual characteristics of the child, (2) be flexible in responding to these characteristics, and (3) avoid negative labeling of the child. |

Social Orientation/Understanding, Attachment, and Child Care

LG4 Explain the early development of social orientation/understanding, attachment, and child care.

| Social Orientation/ Understanding | • Infants show a strong interest in their social world and are motivated to understand it. Infants orient to their social world early in their development. Face-to-face play with a caregiver begins to occur at 2 to 3 months of age. Newly developed self-produced locomotion skills significantly expand the infant's ability to initiate social interchanges and explore their social world more independently. Perceiving people as engaging in intentional and goal-directed behavior is an important social cognitive accomplishment, and this occurs toward the end of the first year. Social referencing increases in the second year of life. |

| Attachment | • Attachment is a close emotional bond between two people. In infancy, contact comfort and trust are important in the development of attachment. Bowlby's ethological theory stresses that the caregiver and the infant are biologically predisposed to form an attachment. Attachment develops in four phases during infancy. Securely attached babies use the caregiver, usually the mother, as a secure base from which to explore the environment. Three types of insecure attachment are avoidant, resistant, and disorganized. Ainsworth created the Strange Situation, an observational measure of attachment. Ainsworth points out that secure attachment in the first year of life provides an important foundation for psychological development later in life. The strength of the link between early attachment and later development has varied somewhat across studies. Some critics argue that attachment |

theorists have not given adequate attention to genetics and temperament. Other critics stress that they have not adequately taken into account the diversity of social agents and contexts. Cultural variations in attachment have been found, but in all cultures studied to date, secure attachment is the most common classification. Caregivers of secure babies are sensitive to the babies' signals and are consistently available to meet their needs. Caregivers of avoidant babies tend to be unavailable or rejecting. Caregivers of resistant babies tend to be inconsistently available to their babies and usually are not very affectionate. Caregivers of disorganized babies often neglect or physically abuse their babies. Increased interest has been directed toward the role of the brain in the development of attachment. The hormone oxytocin is a key candidate for influencing the development of maternal-infant attachment.

Fathers and Mothers as Caregivers

- In recent years fathers have increased the amount of time they interact with infants, but mothers still spend considerably more time in caregiving with infants than do fathers. The mother's primary role when interacting with the infant is caregiving; the father's is playful interaction.

Child Care

- More U.S. children are in child care now than at any earlier point in history. The quality of child care is uneven, and child care remains a controversial topic. Quality child care can be achieved and seems to have few adverse effects on children. In the NICHD child-care study, infants from low-income families were more likely to receive the lowest quality of care. Also, higher quality of child care was linked with fewer childhood problems.

key terms

emotion 290	reflexive smile 294	difficult child 300	securely attached babies 310
primary emotions 293	social smile 294	slow-to-warm-up child 300	insecure avoidant babies 310
self-conscious emotions 293	stranger anxiety 295	goodness of fit 304	insecure resistant babies 310
basic cry 294	separation protest 295	social referencing 307	insecure disorganized babies 310
anger cry 294	temperament 299	attachment 308	
pain cry 294	easy child 300	Strange Situation 310	

key people

Joseph Campos 293	Mary Ainsworth 310	Jerome Kagan 300	Alan Sroufe 311
Carolyn Saarni 291	John Bowlby 309	Mary Rothbart 301	Kathleen McCartney 316
Michael Lewis 293	Daniel Messinger 294	Theodore Wachs 303	
John Watson 296	Alexander Chess and	Harry Harlow 308	
Ross Thompson 297	Stella Thomas 300	Erik Erikson 309	

chapter 11 THE SELF AND IDENTITY

Maxine Hong Kingston's vivid portrayals of her Chinese ancestry and the struggles of Chinese immigrants have made her one of the world's leading Asian American writers. Kingston's parents were Chinese immigrants. Born in California in 1940, she spent many hours working with her parents and five brothers and sisters in the family's laundry. As a youth, Kingston was profoundly influenced by her parents' struggle to adapt to American culture and by their descriptions of their Chinese heritage.

Growing up as she did, Kingston felt the pull of two very different cultures. She was especially intrigued by stories about Chinese women who were perceived as either privileged or degraded.

Her first book was *The Woman Warrior: Memoirs of a Girlhood Among Ghosts* (Kingston, 1976). In *The Woman Warrior,* Kingston described her aunt, who gave birth to an illegitimate child. Because having a child outside of wedlock was taboo and perceived as a threat to the community's stability, the entire Chinese village condemned her, pushing her to kill herself and her child. From then on, even mentioning her name was forbidden. Kingston says she likes to guide people to find meaning in their lives, especially by exploring their cultural backgrounds.

Maxine Hong Kingston as a young girl and as an adult.

preview

Maxine Hong Kingston's life and writings reflect important aspects of each of our lives as we grew up: our efforts to understand ourselves and to develop an identity that reflects our cultural heritage. This chapter is about the self and identity. As we examine these topics, reflect on how well you understood yourself at different points in your life as you were growing up, and think about how you acquired the stamp of your identity.

Self-Understanding and Understanding Others

LG1 Discuss the development of self-understanding and understanding others.

- Self-Understanding
- Understanding Others

Recent research studies have revealed that young children are more psychologically aware of themselves and others than used to be thought (Thompson, 2009, 2010). This psychological awareness reflects young children's expanding psychological sophistication.

SELF-UNDERSTANDING

Self-understanding is a child's cognitive representation of the self—the substance and content of the child's self-conceptions. For example, an 11-year-old boy understands that he is a student, a boy, a football player, a family member, a video game lover, and a rock music fan. A 13-year-old girl understands that she is a middle school student, in the midst of puberty, a girl, a cheerleader, a student council member, and a movie fan. A child's self-understanding is based, in part, on the various roles and membership categories that define who children are (Harter, 2006). Though not the whole of personal identity, self-understanding provides its rational underpinnings.

> When I say "I,"
> I mean something
> absolutely unique,
> not to be confused
> with any other.
>
> —UGO BETTI
> *Italian Playwright,
> 20th Century*

Developmental Changes Children are not just given a self by their parents or culture; rather, they construct selves. As children develop, their self-understanding changes.

Infancy According to leading expert Ross Thompson (2007), studying the self in infancy is difficult mainly because infants cannot tell us how they experience themselves. Infants cannot verbally express their views of the self. They also cannot understand complex instructions from researchers.

A rudimentary form of self-recognition—being attentive and positive toward one's image in a mirror—appears as early as 3 months of age (Mascolo & Fischer, 2007; Pipp, Fischer, & Jennings, 1987). However, a central, more complete index of self-recognition—the ability to recognize one's physical features—does not emerge until the second year (Thompson, 2006).

One ingenious strategy to test infants' visual self-recognition is the use of a mirror technique, in which an infant's mother first puts a dot of rouge on the infant's nose. Then an observer watches to see how often the infant touches its nose. Next, the infant is placed in front of a mirror, and observers detect whether nose touching increases. Why does this matter? The idea is that increased nose touching indicates that the infant recognizes the self in the mirror and is trying to touch or rub off the rouge because the rouge violates the infant's view of the self. Increased touching indicates that the infant realizes that it is the self in the mirror but that something is not right since the real self does not have a dot of rouge on it.

self-understanding A child's cognitive representation of the self—the substance and content of a child's self-conceptions.

Figure 11.1 displays the results of two investigations that used the mirror technique. The researchers found that before they were 1 year old, infants did not recognize themselves in the mirror (Amsterdam, 1968; Lewis & Brooks-Gunn, 1979). Signs of self-recognition began to appear among some infants when they were 15 to 18 months old. By the time they were 2 years old, most children recognized themselves in the mirror. In sum, infants begin to develop a self-understanding called *self-recognition* at approximately 18 months of age (Hart & Karmel, 1996; Lewis & others, 1989).

In one study, biweekly assessments from 15 to 23 months of age were conducted (Courage, Edison, & Howe, 2004). Self-recognition gradually emerged over this time, first appearing in the form of mirror recognition, followed by use of the personal pronoun and then by recognizing a photo of themselves. These aspects of self-recognition are often referred to as the first indications of toddlers' understanding of the mental state of "me," "that they are objects in their own mental representation of the world" (Lewis, 2005, p. 363).

Mirrors are not familiar to infants in all cultures (Rogoff, 2003). Thus, physical self-recognition may be a more important marker of self-recognition in Western than non-Western cultures (Thompson & Virmani, 2010). Supporting this cultural variation view, one study revealed that 18- to 20-month old toddlers from urban middle SES German families were more likely to recognize their mirror images than were toddlers from rural Cameroon farming families.

Late in the second year and early in the third year, toddlers show other emerging forms of self-awareness that reflect a sense of "me" (Laible & Thompson, 2007). For example, they refer to themselves by saying "Me big"; they label internal experiences such as emotions; they monitor themselves, as when a toddler says, "Do it myself"; and they say that things are theirs (Bullock & Lutkenhaus, 1990; Fasig, 2000). A recent study revealed that it is not until the second year that infants develop a conscious awareness of their own bodies (Brownell & others, 2009). This developmental change in body awareness marks the beginning of children's representation of their own three-dimensional body shape and appearance, providing an early step in the development of their self-image and identity (Brownell, 2009).

Early Childhood Because children can communicate verbally, research on self-understanding in childhood is not limited to visual self-recognition, as it is during infancy. Mainly through interviews, researchers have probed many aspects of children's self-understanding (Carpendale & Lewis, 2011; Hughes & Ensor, 2010). Here are five main characteristics of self-understanding in young children:

- *Confusion of self, mind, and body.* Young children generally confuse self, mind, and body. Most young children conceive of the self as part of the body, which usually means the head. For them, the self can be described along many material dimensions, such as size, shape, and color.
- *Concrete descriptions.* Preschool children mainly think of themselves and define themselves in concrete terms. A young child might say, "I know my ABC's," "I can count," and "I live in a big house" (Harter, 2006). Although young children mainly describe themselves in terms of concrete, observable features and action tendencies, at about 4 to 5 years of age, as they hear others use psychological trait and emotion terms, they begin to include these in their own self-descriptions (Thompson, 2006). Thus, in a self-description, a 4-year-old might say, "I'm not scared. I'm always happy."
- *Physical descriptions.* Young children also distinguish themselves from others through many physical and material attributes. Says 4-year-old Sandra, "I'm different from Jennifer because I have brown hair and she has blond hair." Says 4-year-old Ralph, "I am different from Hank because I am taller, and I am different from my sister because I have a bicycle."
- *Active descriptions.* The *active dimension* is a central component of the self in early childhood. For example, preschool children often describe themselves in terms of activities such as play.

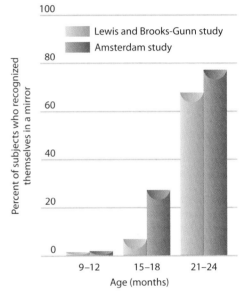

FIGURE **11.1**

THE DEVELOPMENT OF SELF-RECOGNITION IN INFANCY. The graph shows the findings of two studies in which infants less than 1 year of age did not recognize themselves in the mirror. A slight increase in the percentage of infant self-recognition occurred around 15 to 18 months of age. By 2 years of age, a majority of children recognized themselves. *Why do researchers study whether infants recognize themselves in a mirror?*

The living self has one purpose only: to come into its own fullness of being, as a tree comes into full blossom, or a bird into spring beauty, or a tiger into lustre.

—D. H. LAWRENCE
English Author, 20th Century

What characterizes young children's self-understanding?

- *Unrealistic positive overestimations.* Self-evaluations during early childhood are often unrealistically positive and represent an overestimation of personal attributes (Harter, 2006). These unrealistic positive overestimations of the self occur because young children (1) have difficulty in differentiating their desired and actual competence, (2) cannot yet generate an ideal self that is distinguished from a real self, and (3) rarely engage in *social comparison*—exploring how they compare with others. Perhaps as adults we should all be so optimistic about our abilities! (Thompson, 2008)

Middle and Late Childhood   Children's self-evaluation becomes more complex during middle and late childhood. Five key changes characterize the increased complexity:

- *Psychological characteristics and traits.* In middle and late childhood, especially from 8 to 11 years of age, children increasingly describe themselves with psychological characteristics and traits in contrast to the more concrete self-descriptions of younger children. Older children are more likely to describe themselves as *popular, nice, helpful, mean, smart,* and *dumb* (Harter, 2006).

- *Social descriptions.* In middle and late childhood, children begin to include *social aspects* such as references to social groups in their self-descriptions (Harter, 2006; Livesly & Bromley, 1973). For example, children might describe themselves as Girl Scouts, as Catholics, or as someone who has two close friends.

- *Social comparison.* Children's self-understanding in middle and late childhood includes increasing reference to social comparison (Harter, 2006). At this point in development, children are more likely to distinguish themselves from others in comparative rather than in absolute terms. That is, elementary-school-age children are likely to think about what they can do *in comparison with others.* In one study in which children were given feedback about the performance of other children their age on a difficult task, children younger than 7 made virtually no reference to the information about other children's performances (Ruble, 1983). However, many children older than 7 included socially comparative information in their self-descriptions.

- *Real self and ideal self.* In middle and late childhood, children begin to distinguish between their real and ideal selves (Harter, 2006). This involves differentiating their actual competencies from those they aspire to have and think are the most important.

- *Realistic.* In middle and late childhood, children's self-evaluations become more realistic (Harter, 2006). This may occur because of increased social comparison and perspective taking.

Adolescence   The development of self-understanding in adolescence is complex and involves a number of aspects of the self (Harter, 2006). The tendency to compare themselves with others continues to increase during the adolescent years. However, when asked whether they engage in social comparison, most adolescents deny it because they are aware that it is somewhat socially undesirable to do so. Let's examine other ways in which the adolescent's self-understanding differs from the child's:

- *Abstract and idealistic.* Remember from our discussion of Piaget's theory of cognitive development in Chapter 6 that many adolescents begin to think in more *abstract* and *idealistic* ways. When asked to describe themselves, adolescents are more likely than children to use abstract and idealistic labels. Consider 14-year-old Laurie's abstract description of herself: "I am a human being. I am indecisive. I don't know who I am." Also consider her idealistic description of herself: "I am a naturally sensitive person who really cares

developmental connection

Cognitive Theory. In Piaget's fourth stage of cognitive development, thought becomes more abstract, idealistic, and logical. Chapter 6, p. 185

about people's feelings. I think I'm pretty good looking." Not all adolescents describe themselves in idealistic ways, but most adolescents distinguish between the real self and the ideal self.

- *Self-consciousness.* Adolescents are more likely than children to be *self-conscious* about and *preoccupied* with their self-understanding. This self-consciousness and self-preoccupation reflect adolescent egocentrism, which we discussed in Chapter 6.

- *Contradictions within the self.* As adolescents begin to differentiate their concept of the self into multiple roles in different relationship contexts, they sense potential contradictions between their differentiated selves (Harter, 2006). An adolescent might use this self-description: "I'm moody *and* understanding, ugly *and* attractive, bored *and* inquisitive, caring *and* uncaring, and introverted *and* fun-loving" (Harter, 1986). These contradictions characterize the self-descriptions of young adolescents more than older adolescents.

- *The fluctuating self.* The adolescent's self-understanding fluctuates across situations and across time (Harter, 2006). The adolescent's self continues to be characterized by instability until the adolescent constructs a more unified theory of self, usually not until late adolescence or emerging adulthood.

- *Real and ideal selves.* The adolescent's emerging ability to construct ideal selves in addition to actual ones can be perplexing and agonizing to the adolescent. In one view, an important aspect of the ideal or imagined self is the **possible self**—what individuals might become, what they would like to become, and what they are afraid of becoming (Markus & Nurius, 1986). Thus, adolescents' possible selves include what adolescents hope to be as well as what they dread they will become. The attributes of future positive selves (getting into a good college, being admired, having a successful career) can direct future positive states. The attributes of future negative selves (being unemployed, being lonely, not getting into a good college) can identify what is to be avoided.

- *Self-integration.* In late adolescence and emerging adulthood, self-understanding becomes more *integrative,* with the disparate parts of the self more systematically pieced together (Harter, 2006). Older adolescents are more likely to detect inconsistencies in their earlier self-descriptions as they attempt to construct a general theory of self and an integrated sense of identity.

How does self-understanding change in adolescence?

> Know thyself, for once we know ourselves, we may learn how to care for ourselves, but otherwise we never shall.
>
> **—SOCRATES**
> *Greek Philosopher, 5th Century* B.C.

UNDERSTANDING OTHERS

Young children are more sophisticated at understanding not only themselves, but others, than used to be thought (Carpendale & Lewis, 2011; Hughes & Ensor, 2010; Nichols, Svetlova, & Brownell, 2009). The term **social cognition** refers to the processes involved in understanding the world around us, especially how we think and reason about other people. Developmental psychologists are increasingly studying how children develop this understanding of others.

In Chapter 10, "Emotional Development," we described the development of social understanding in infancy. Recall that perceiving people as engaging in intentional and goal-directed behavior is an important social cognitive accomplishment, and this occurs toward the end of the first year. Social referencing, which involves "reading" emotional cues in others to help determine how to act in a particular situation, increases in the second year of life. Here we will describe further changes in social understanding that occur during the childhood years.

What characterizes adolescents' possible selves?

possible self What an individual might become, would like to become, and is afraid of becoming.

social cognition The processes involved in understanding the world around us, especially how we think and reason about other people.

Early Childhood   Children also make advances in their understanding of others in early childhood (Gelman, Heyman, & Legare, 2007). As we saw in Chapter 7, "Information

developmental **connection**

Attention. Joint attention and gaze following help the infant to understand that other people have intentions. Chapter 10, p. 307

developmental **connection**

Eclectic Theoretical Orientation. Developmental psychologists are increasingly focusing on connections across major domains of development, such as cognitive and socioemotional development. Chapter 1, p. 30

Young children are more psychologically aware of themselves and others than used to be thought. Some children are better than others at understanding people's feelings and desires—and, to some degree, these individual differences are influenced by conversations caregivers have with young children about feelings and desires.

developmental **connection**

Cognitive Theory. *Theory of mind* refers to awareness of one's own mental processes and the mental processes of others. Chapter 7, p. 225

perspective taking The ability to assume others' perspectives and understand their thoughts or feelings.

Processing," young children's theory of mind includes understanding that other people have emotions and desires. And at about 4 to 5 years, children not only start describing themselves in terms of psychological traits but also begin to perceive others in terms of psychological traits. Thus, a 4-year-old might say, "My teacher is nice."

Something important for children to develop is an understanding that people don't always give accurate reports of their beliefs (Gee & Heyman, 2007). Researchers have found that even 4-year-olds understand that people may make untrue statements to obtain what they want or to avoid trouble (Lee & others, 2002). For example, one recent study revealed that 4- and 5-year-olds were increasingly skeptical of another child's claim to be sick when the children were informed that the child was motivated to avoid having to go to camp (Gee & Heyman, 2007).

Although in some ways children can be fairly sophisticated in determining what sources to doubt, they also show signs of gullibility. In one study, preschoolers were introduced to a new fantasy character called the "Candy Witch" who could visit the houses of children, after Halloween, who were interested in trading their candy for a toy. Preschoolers sometimes believed that the Candy Witch was real after hearing about her only a few times. Children's level of belief in other fantasy beings, such as Santa Claus, was highly related to their belief in the Candy Witch, suggesting that perhaps an understanding of different kinds of fantasy beings is connected (Woolley, Boerger, & Markman, 2004).

Even though children do sometimes believe things that are false, it may be adaptive to believe most things that people say, given that it is impossible to learn everything about the world through firsthand experience (Harris & Koenig, 2006). If we made decisions based only on our own perceptions, for instance, we might think the world is flat, perhaps with a dome-shaped roof. By being able to talk with others who are more knowledgeable than we are, we can learn that the world is indeed spherical. Figuring out what information to trust and what information to discount is an important aspect of developing an effective understanding of others.

Another important aspect of understanding others involves understanding joint commitments. A recent study revealed that 3-year-olds, but not 2-year-olds, recognized when an adult is committed and when they themselves are committed to joint activity that involves obligation to a partner.

Both the extensive theory of mind research (discussed in Chapter 7) and the recent research on young children's social understanding underscore that young children are not as *egocentric* as Piaget envisioned (Sokol & others, 2010). A leading expert on children's socioemotional development, Ross Thompson (2009), recently described his amazement that Piaget's concept of egocentrism has become so ingrained in people's thinking about young children, given the fact that the current research on social awareness in infancy and early childhood is so dissonant with Piaget's egocentrism concept.

Individual differences characterize young children's social understanding (Laible & Thompson, 2007). Some young children are better than others at understanding what people are feeling and what they desire, for example. To some degree, these individual differences are linked to conversations caregivers have with young children about other people's feelings and desires, and children's opportunities to observe others talking about people's feelings and desires. For example, a mother might say to a 3-year-old, "You should think about Raphael's feelings next time before you hit him."

Middle and Late Childhood In middle and late childhood, children show an increase in **perspective taking,** the ability to assume other people's perspectives and understand their thoughts and feelings. In Robert Selman's view (1980), at about 6 to 8 years of age children begin to understand that others may have differing perspectives because some people have more access to information. Then, he says, in the next several years, children become aware that each individual is aware of the other's perspective and that putting one's self in the other's place is a way of judging the other person's intentions, purposes, and actions.

Perspective taking is thought to be especially important in determining whether children develop prosocial or antisocial attitudes and behavior. In terms of prosocial behavior, taking another's perspective improves children's likelihood of understanding and sympathizing with others who are distressed or in need (Eisenberg, Fabes, & Spinrad, 2006). In terms of antisocial behavior, some researchers have found that children who have low levels of perspective-taking skills engage in more antisocial behavior than children who have higher levels (Chandler, 1973).

In middle and late childhood, children also become more skeptical of others' claims. Earlier we indicated that even 4-year-old children show some skepticism of others' claims. In middle and late childhood, children become increasingly skeptical of some sources of information about psychological traits. For example, in one study, 10- to 11-year-olds were more likely to reject other children's self-reports that they were *smart* and *honest* than were 6- to 7-year-olds (Heyman & Legare, 2005). The more psychologically sophisticated 10- to 11-year-olds also showed a better understanding than the 6- to 7-year-olds that others' self-reports may involve socially desirable tendencies.

Elementary-school-aged children also begin to understand other motivations. For example, they understand that a desire to win a prize may tarnish someone's judgment (Mills & Keil, 2005).

What are some changes in children's understanding of others in middle and late childhood?

Review Connect Reflect

LG1 Discuss the development of self-understanding and understanding others.

Review

- What is self-understanding? How does self-understanding change from infancy through adolescence?
- How does the understanding of others develop?

Connect

- In this section, you learned that in middle and late childhood, children show an increase in perspective taking. Which disorder (discussed in Chapter 7) involves children to have difficulty understanding others' beliefs and emotions?

Reflect *Your Own Personal Journey of Life*

- If a psychologist had interviewed you at 10 and at 16 years of age, how would your self-understanding have differed?

Self-Esteem and Self-Concept **LG2** Explain self-esteem and self-concept.

| What Are Self-Esteem and Self-Concept? | Assessment | Developmental Changes | Variations in Self-Esteem |

Self-conception involves more than self-understanding. Not only do children try to define and describe attributes of the self (self-understanding), but they also evaluate these attributes. These evaluations create self-esteem and self-concept, and they have far-reaching implications for children's development.

WHAT ARE SELF-ESTEEM AND SELF-CONCEPT?

Sometimes the terms *self-esteem* and *self-concept* are used interchangeably, or they are not precisely defined (Harter, 2006). Here we use **self-esteem** to refer to a person's self-worth or self-image, a global evaluation of the self. For example, a child might

self-esteem The global evaluative dimension of the self; also called self-worth or self-image.

FIGURE **11.2**
EVALUATING SELF-ESTEEM

These items are from a widely used measure of self-esteem, the Rosenberg Scale of Self-Esteem. The items deal with your general feelings about yourself. Place a check mark in the column that best describes your feelings about yourself:
1 = strongly agree, 2 = agree, 3 = disagree, 4 = strongly disagree.

	1	2	3	4
1. I feel that I am a person of worth, at least on an equal plane with others.				
2. I feel that I have a number of good qualities.				
3. All in all, I am inclined to feel that I am a failure.				
4. I am able to do things as well as most other people.				
5. I feel I do not have much to be proud of.				
6. I take a positive attitude toward myself.				
7. On the whole, I am satisfied with myself.				
8. I wish I could have more respect for myself.				
9. I certainly feel useless at times.				
10. At times I think I am no good at all.				

To obtain your self-esteem score, reverse your scores for items 3, 5, 8, 9, and 10. (That is, on item 3 if you gave yourself a 1, instead give yourself a 4.) Add those scores to your scores for items 1, 2, 4, 6, and 7 for your overall self-esteem score. Scores can range from 10 to 40. If you scored below 20, consider contacting the counseling center at your college or university for help in improving your self-esteem.

perceive that she is not merely a person but a good person. (To evaluate your self-esteem, see Figure 11.2.) We use the term **self-concept** to refer to domain-specific evaluations of the self. Children can make self-evaluations in many domains of their lives—academic, athletic, physical appearance, and so on. In sum, self-esteem refers to global self-evaluations, self-concept to more domain-specific evaluations.

For most children, high self-esteem and a positive self-concept are important aspects of their well-being (Kaplan, 2009). However, for some children, self-esteem reflects perceptions that do not always match reality (Krueger, Vohs, & Baumeister, 2008). A child's self-esteem might reflect a belief about whether he or she is intelligent and attractive, for example, but that belief is not necessarily accurate. Thus, high self-esteem may refer to accurate, justified perceptions of one's worth as a person and one's successes and accomplishments, but it can also refer to an arrogant, grandiose, unwarranted sense of superiority over others. In the same manner, low self-esteem may reflect either an accurate perception of one's shortcomings or a distorted, even pathological insecurity and inferiority.

ASSESSMENT

Measuring self-esteem and self-concept hasn't always been easy (Dusek & McIntyre, 2003). An example of a useful measure developed to assess self-evaluations by children is Susan Harter's (1985) Self-Perception Profile for Children. It taps general self-worth plus self-concept for five specific domains: scholastic competence, athletic competence, social acceptance, physical appearance, and behavioral conduct.

The Self-Perception Profile for Children is designed to be used with third-grade through sixth-grade children. Harter also developed a separate scale for adolescents, the Self-Perception Profile for Adolescents (Harter, 1989). It assesses global self-worth and the five domains tested for children plus three additional domains—close friendship, romantic appeal, and job competence.

self-concept Domain-specific self-evaluations.

Harter's measures can separate self-evaluations in different domains of one's life. How are these specific self-evaluations related to self-esteem in general? Even children have both a general level of self-esteem and varying levels of self-conceptions in particular domains of their lives (Harter, 1998; Ward, 2004). For example, a child might have a moderately high level of general self-esteem but have varying self-conceptions in specific areas: high in athletic competence, high in social acceptance, high in physical appearance, high in behavioral conduct, but low in scholastic competence.

Self-esteem appears to have an especially strong tie with self-perception in one domain in particular: physical appearance. Researchers have found that among adolescents, global self-esteem is correlated more strongly with perceived physical appearance than with scholastic competence, social acceptance, behavioral conduct, or athletic competence (Harter, 1999, 2006; Maeda, 1999) (see Figure 11.3). Notice in Figure 11.3 that the link between perceived physical appearance and self-esteem has been made in many countries. This association between physical appearance and self-esteem is not confined to adolescence; it holds from early childhood through middle age (Harter, 1999, 2006).

DEVELOPMENTAL CHANGES

Researchers disagree about the extent to which self-esteem varies with age. One study found that self-esteem is high in childhood, declines in adolescence, and increases in adulthood until late adulthood, when it declines again (Robins & others, 2002) (see Figure 11.4). Some researchers argue that although there may be a decrease in self-esteem during adolescence, the drop is actually very slight and not nearly as pronounced as it is presented in the media (Harter, 2002; Hyde, 2007). One study revealed that self-esteem increased during emerging adulthood (18 to 25 years of age) (Galambos, Barker, & Krahn, 2006).

Notice in Figure 11.4 that the self-esteem of males was higher than that of females through most of the life span. During adolescence, the self-esteem of girls declined more than that of boys. Another study revealed that male adolescents had higher self-esteem than did female adolescents. One explanation for this gender difference holds that the drop in self-esteem is driven by a negative body image and that girls have more negative body images during pubertal change than boys do. Another explanation emphasizes the greater interest that adolescent girls take in social relationships and society's failure to reward that interest (Impett, & others, 2008). But also note in Figure 11.4 that despite the drop in self-esteem among adolescent girls, their average self-esteem score (3.3) was still higher than the neutral point on the scale (3.0). How do adolescents rate different aspects of their self-images, such as their psychological self, social self, coping self, familial self, and sexual self? To find out, see *Connecting Through Research*.

Domain	Harter's U.S. samples	Other countries
Physical Appearance	.65	.62
Scholastic Competence	.48	.41
Social Acceptance	.46	.40
Behavioral Conduct	.45	.45
Athletic Competence	.33	.30

FIGURE **11.3**

CORRELATIONS BETWEEN GLOBAL SELF-ESTEEM AND SELF-EVALUATIONS OF DOMAINS OF COMPETENCE. *Note:* The correlations shown are the average correlations computed across a number of studies. The other countries in this evaluation were England, Ireland, Australia, Canada, Germany, Italy, Greece, the Netherlands, and Japan. Recall from Chapter 1 that correlation coefficients can range from −1.00 to +1.00. The correlations between physical appearance and global self-esteem (.65 and .62) are moderately high.

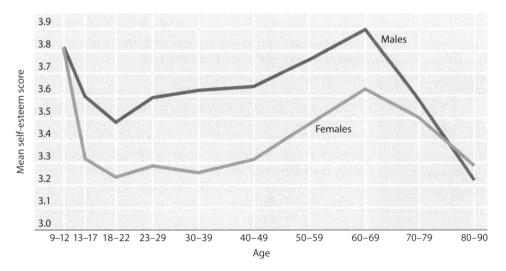

FIGURE **11.4**

SELF-ESTEEM ACROSS THE LIFE SPAN. One large-scale study asked more than 300,000 individuals to rate the extent to which they have high self-esteem on a 5-point scale, 5 being "Strongly Agree" and 1 being "Strongly Disagree." Self-esteem dropped in adolescence and late adulthood. Self-esteem of females was lower than self-esteem of males through most of the life span.

How Do Adolescents Rate Their Self-Images Across Five Different Areas?

One study examined the self-images of 675 adolescents (289 males and 386 females) ranging from 13 to 19 years of age in Naples, Italy (Bacchini & Magliulo, 2003). Self-image was assessed using the Offer Self-Image Questionnaire, which consists of 130 items grouped into 11 scales that define five different aspects of self-image:

- The psychological self (made up of scales that assess impulse control, emotional tone, and body image)
- The social self (consists of scales that evaluate social relationships, morals, and vocational and educational aspirations)
- The coping self (composed of scales to measure mastery of the world, psychological problems, and adjustment)
- The familial self (made up of only one scale that evaluates how adolescents feel about their parents)
- The sexual self (composed of only one scale that examines adolescents' feelings and attitudes about sexual matters)

The adolescents had positive self-images, with scores higher than a neutral score (3.5) on all 11 scales. For example, the adolescents' average body self-image score was 4.2. The aspect of their lives in which adolescents had the most positive self-image involved their educational and vocational aspirations (average score of 4.8). The lowest self-image score was for impulse control (average score of 3.9). These results support the view that adolescents have a more positive perception of themselves than is commonly believed.

Gender differences were found on a number of the self-image scales, with boys consistently having more positive self-images than did girls. Keep in mind, though, that as we indicated earlier, even though girls reported lower self-images than boys, their self-images still were mainly in the positive range.

VARIATIONS IN SELF-ESTEEM

Variations in self-esteem have been linked with many aspects of children's development. However, much of the research is *correlational* rather than *experimental*. Recall from Chapter 1 that correlation does not equal causation. Thus, if a correlational study finds an association between children's low self-esteem and low academic achievement, low academic achievement could cause the low self-esteem as much as low self-esteem might cause low academic achievement (Bowles, 1999). In fact, there are only moderate correlations between school performance and self-esteem, and these correlations do not suggest that high self-esteem produces better school performance (Baumeister & others, 2003). Efforts to increase students' self-esteem have not always led to improved school performance (Davies & Brember, 1999).

Children with high self-esteem show greater initiative, but this can produce positive or negative outcomes (Baumeister & others, 2003). High-self-esteem children are prone to both prosocial and antisocial actions (Bushman & others, 2009). For example, they are more likely than children with low self-esteem to defend victims against bullies, but they are also more likely to be bullies themselves.

Researchers have also found strong links between self-esteem and happiness (Baumeister & others, 2003). For example, the two were strongly related in an international study of 13,000 college students from 49 universities in 31 countries (Diener & Diener, 1995). It seems likely that high self-esteem increases happiness (Baumeister & others, 2003).

Many studies have found that individuals with low self-esteem report that they feel more depressed than individuals with high self-esteem (Orth & others, 2009). Low self-esteem has also been linked to suicide attempts and to anorexia nervosa (Osvath, Voros, & Fekete, 2004). A recent study found that low

What are some issues involved in understanding children's self-esteem in school?

caring *connections*

Increasing Children's Self-Esteem

A current concern is that too many of today's children and adolescents grow up receiving empty praise and as a consequence develop inflated self-esteem (Graham, 2005; Stipek, 2005). Too often they are given praise for performance that is mediocre or even poor. They may have difficulty handling competition and criticism. The title of a book, *Dumbing Down Our Kids: Why American Children Feel Good About Themselves But Can't Read, Write, or Add* (Sykes, 1995) vividly captures the theme that the academic problems of many U.S. children, adolescents, and college students stem from unmerited praise aimed at propping up their self-esteem. But it is possible to raise children's self-esteem by (1) identifying the domains of competence important to the child, (2) providing emotional support and social approval, (3) praising achievement, and (4) encouraging coping.

Harter (1999) argues that intervention must occur at the level of the causes of self-esteem if the individual's self-esteem is to improve significantly. Children have the highest self-esteem when they perform competently in domains that are important to them. Therefore, children should be encouraged to identify and to value areas in which they are competent.

Emotional support and social approval also powerfully influence children's self-esteem. Some children with low self-esteem come from conflicted families or experienced abuse or neglect—situations in which emotional support was unavailable. For some children, formal programs such as Big Brothers and Big Sisters can provide alternative sources of emotional support and social approval; for others, support

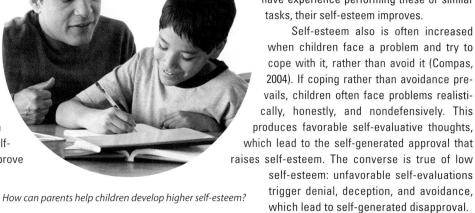

How can parents help children develop higher self-esteem?

can come informally through the encouragement of a teacher, a coach, or another significant adult. Peer approval becomes increasingly important during adolescence, but adult as well as peer support continues to be an important influence on self-esteem through adolescence.

Achievement also can improve children's self-esteem. The straightforward teaching of real skills to children often results in increased achievement and enhanced self-esteem. When children know what tasks are necessary to achieve goals and have experience performing these or similar tasks, their self-esteem improves.

Self-esteem also is often increased when children face a problem and try to cope with it, rather than avoid it (Compas, 2004). If coping rather than avoidance prevails, children often face problems realistically, honestly, and nondefensively. This produces favorable self-evaluative thoughts, which lead to the self-generated approval that raises self-esteem. The converse is true of low self-esteem: unfavorable self-evaluations trigger denial, deception, and avoidance, which lead to self-generated disapproval.

Dumbing Down Our Kids suggests that the academic problems of many U.S. children, adolescents, and college students stem from unmerited praise aimed at propping up their self-esteem. What did you learn earlier in the "Variations in Self-Esteem" section of this chapter about self-esteem and school performance?

self-esteem in childhood was linked with depression in adolescence and early adulthood (Orth & others, 2008).

Are a parent's characteristics and behavior linked to a child's self-esteem? In the most extensive investigation of parent-child relationships and self-esteem, the following attributes of parenting were associated with boys' high self-esteem (Coopersmith, 1967): expression of affection; concern about the child's problems; harmony in the home; participation in joint family activities; availability to give competent, organized help when needed; setting clear and fair rules; abiding by these rules; and allowing the children freedom within well-defined limits. Remember that these findings are correlational, and so we cannot say that these parenting attributes cause children's high self-esteem. Such factors as parental acceptance and allowing children freedom within well-defined limits probably are important determinants of children's self-esteem, but we still must say that they are related to, rather than that they cause, children's self-esteem, based on the available research data. To explore ways that children's low self-esteem might be increased, see *Caring Connections*.

Review *Connect* Reflect

LG2 Explain self-esteem and self-concept.

Review

- What are self-esteem and self-concept?
- What are two measures for assessing self-esteem and self-concept?
- How is self-esteem linked with age?
- What are some variations in self-esteem, and how are they linked to children's development? What role do parent-child relationships play in self-esteem?

Connect

- Discussed in the "Regulation of Emotion" section of Chapter 10, which parenting approach might help accomplish the fourth strategy for increasing children's self-esteem mentioned in the *Caring Connections* on page 333?

Reflect *Your Own Personal Journey of Life*

- Review the characteristics of self-understanding in adolescence. Which of these characteristics do you associate most closely with your self-understanding as an adolescent?

Identity **LG3** Describe identity and its development.

| What Is Identity? | Erikson's View | Developmental Changes | Social Contexts |

Who am I? What am I all about? What am I going to do with my life? What is different about me? How can I make it on my own? These questions reflect the search for an identity. By far the most comprehensive and provocative theory of identity development is Erik Erikson's. In this section, we examine his views on identity. We also discuss contemporary research on how identity develops and how social contexts influence that development.

WHAT IS IDENTITY?

Identity is a self-portrait composed of many pieces, including these:

- The career and work path the person wants to follow (vocational/career identity)
- Whether the person is conservative, liberal, or middle-of-the-road (political identity)
- The person's spiritual beliefs (religious identity)
- Whether the person is single, married, divorced, and so on (relationship identity)
- The extent to which the person is motivated to achieve and is intellectually oriented (achievement, intellectual identity)
- Whether the person is heterosexual, homosexual, bisexual, or transgendered (sexual identity)
- Which part of the world or country a person is from and how intensely the person identifies with his or her cultural heritage (cultural/ethnic identity)
- The kind of things a person likes to do, which can include sports, music, hobbies, and so on (interests)
- The individual's personality characteristics, such as being introverted or extraverted, anxious or calm, friendly or hostile, and so on (personality)
- The individual's body image (physical identity)

We put these pieces together to form a sense of ourselves continuing through time within a social world. Synthesizing the identity components can be a long and

What are some important dimensions of identity?

drawn-out process, with many negations and affirmations of various roles and faces. Identity development takes place in bits and pieces. Decisions are not made once and for all, but have to be made again and again. Identity development does not happen neatly, nor does it happen cataclysmically (Coté, 2009).

ERIKSON'S VIEW

Questions about identity surface as common, virtually universal, concerns during adolescence. It was Erik Erikson (1950, 1968) who first understood how central such questions are to understanding adolescent development. That identity is now believed to be a key aspect of adolescent development is a result of Erikson's masterful thinking and analysis. Recall that his fifth developmental stage, which individuals experience during adolescence, is **identity versus identity confusion.** During this time, said Erikson, adolescents are faced with deciding who they are, what they are all about, and where they are going in life.

These questions about identity occur throughout life, but they become especially important for adolescents. Erikson points out that adolescents face an overwhelming number of choices. As they gradually come to realize that they will be responsible for themselves and their own lives, adolescents try to determine what those lives are going to be.

The search for an identity during adolescence is aided by a **psychosocial moratorium,** which is Erikson's term for the gap between childhood security and adult autonomy. During this period, society leaves adolescents relatively free of responsibilities and able to try out different identities. Adolescents in effect search their culture's identity files, experimenting with different roles and personalities. They may want to pursue one career one month (lawyer, for example) and another career the next month (doctor, actor, teacher, social worker, or astronaut, for example). They may dress neatly one day, sloppily the next. This experimentation is a deliberate effort on the part of adolescents to find out where they fit in the world.

Youth who successfully cope with these conflicting identities emerge with a new sense of self that is both refreshing and acceptable. Adolescents who do not successfully resolve this identity crisis suffer what Erikson calls *identity confusion*. The confusion takes one of two courses: individuals withdraw, isolating themselves from peers and family, or they immerse themselves in the world of peers and lose their identity in the crowd.

There are hundreds of roles for adolescents to try out, and probably just as many ways to pursue each role. Erikson stresses that, by late adolescence, vocational roles are central to identity development, especially in a highly technological society like the United States. Youth who have been well trained to enter a workforce that offers the potential of reasonably high self-esteem will experience the least stress during this phase of identity development.

A current concern about the development of identity in adolescence and emerging adulthood was voiced recently by William Damon (2008) in his book, *The Path to Purpose*. Damon acknowledges that successful identity development is a long-term process of extended exploration and reflection, and in some instances it can involve postponing decisions for a number of years. However, Damon feels that too many of today's youth aren't moving toward any identity resolution. In Damon's (2008, pp. 5, 7) words,

> Their delay is characterized more by indecision than by motivated reflection, more by confusion than by pursuit of clear goals, more by ambivalence than by determination. Directionless shift is not a constructive moratorium in either a developmental or a societal sense. Without a sense of direction, opportunities are lost, and doubt and self-absorption can set in. Maladaptive habits are established and adaptive ones not built. . . What is too often missing is . . . the kind of wholehearted dedication to an activity or interest that stems from serious purpose, a purpose that can give meaning and direction to life.

In Damon's (2008, p. 47) view, too many youth are left to their own devices in dealing with some of life's biggest questions: "What is my calling? What can I

"Who are you?" said the caterpillar. Alice replied rather shyly, "I—I hardly know, sir, just at present—at least I know who I was when I got up this morning, but I must have changed several times since then."

—LEWIS CARROLL
English Writer, 19th Century

Erik Erikson.

identity versus identity confusion Erikson's fifth developmental stage, which individuals experience during the adolescent years. At this time, adolescents examine who they are, what they are all about, and where they are going in life.

psychosocial moratorium Erikson's term for the gap between childhood security and adult autonomy that adolescents experience as part of their identity exploration.

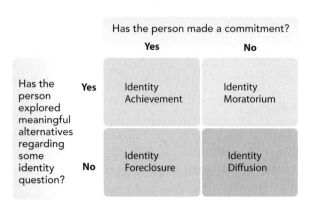

Has the person made a commitment?

	Yes	No
Yes	Identity Achievement	Identity Moratorium
No	Identity Foreclosure	Identity Diffusion

Has the person explored meaningful alternatives regarding some identity question?

FIGURE **11.5**

MARCIA'S FOUR STATUSES OF IDENTITY

crisis A period of identity development during which the adolescent is choosing among meaningful alternatives.

commitment Personal investment in identity.

identity diffusion Marcia's term for the status of individuals who have not yet experienced a crisis (that is, they have not yet explored meaningful alternatives) or made any commitments.

identity foreclosure Marcia's term for the status of individuals who have made a commitment but have not experienced a crisis.

identity moratorium Marcia's term for the status of individuals who are in the midst of a crisis but whose commitments either are absent or are only vaguely defined.

identity achievement Marcia's term for the status of individuals who have undergone a crisis and made a commitment.

contribute to the world? What am I here for?" Damon acknowledges that adults can't make youths' decisions for them, but he emphasizes that it is very important for parents, teachers, mentors, and other adults to provide guidance, feedback, and contexts that will improve the likelihood that youth will develop a positive identity. Youth need a cultural climate that inspires rather than demoralizes them and supports their chances of reaching their aspirations.

DEVELOPMENTAL CHANGES

Although questions about identity are particularly likely to emerge during adolescence, identity formation neither begins nor ends during these years (Coté, 2009; Juang & Syed, 2010). It begins with the appearance of attachment, the development of the sense of self, and the emergence of independence in infancy; the process reaches its final phase with a life review and integration in old age. What is important about identity development in adolescence, especially late adolescence, is that for the first time, physical development, cognitive development, and socioemotional development advance to the point at which the individual can begin to sort through and synthesize childhood identities and identifications to construct a viable path toward adult maturity.

Some decisions made during adolescence might seem trivial: whom to date, whether or not to break up, which major to study, whether to study or play, whether or not to be politically active, and so on. Over the years of adolescence, however, such decisions begin to form the core of what the individual is all about as a human being—what is called his or her identity.

Identity Statuses How do individual adolescents go about the process of forming an identity? Eriksonian researcher James Marcia (1980, 1994) proposes that Erikson's theory of identity development contains four statuses of identity, or ways of resolving the identity crisis: identity diffusion, identity foreclosure, identity moratorium, and identity achievement. What determines an individual's identity status? Marcia classifies individuals based on the existence or extent of their crisis or commitment (see Figure 11.5). **Crisis** is defined as a period of identity development during which the individual is exploring alternatives. Most researchers use the term *exploration* rather than crisis. **Commitment** is personal investment in identity.

The four statuses of identity are as follows:

- **Identity diffusion** is the status of individuals who have not yet experienced a crisis or made any commitments. Not only are they undecided about occupational and ideological choices, they are also likely to show little interest in such matters.

- **Identity foreclosure** is the status of individuals who have made a commitment but not experienced a crisis. This occurs most often when parents hand down commitments to their adolescents, usually in an authoritarian way, before adolescents have had a chance to explore different approaches, ideologies, and vocations on their own.

- **Identity moratorium** is the status of individuals who are in the midst of a crisis but whose commitments are either absent or are only vaguely defined.

- **Identity achievement** is the status of individuals who have undergone a crisis and made a commitment.

To evaluate your identity in different areas of development, see Figure 11.6. Let's explore some examples of Marcia's identity statuses. Thirteen-year-old Mia has neither begun to explore her identity in any meaningful way nor made an identity commitment; she is identity diffused. Eighteen-year-old Oliver's parents want him to be a medical doctor, so he is planning on majoring in premedicine in college and has not explored other options; he is identity foreclosed. Nineteen-year-old Sasha is

Think deeply about your exploration and commitment in the areas listed here. For each area, check whether your identity status is diffused, foreclosed, moratorium, or achieved.

Identity Component	Identity Status			
	Diffused	Foreclosed	Moratorium	Achieved
Vocational (career)				
Political				
Religious				
Relationships				
Achievement				
Sexual				
Gender				
Ethnic/Cultural				
Interests				
Personality				
Physical				

FIGURE **11.6**

EXPLORING YOUR IDENTITY. If you checked diffused or foreclosed for any areas, take some time to think about what you need to do to move into a moratorium identity status in those areas.

not quite sure what life paths she wants to follow, but she recently went to the counseling center at her college to find out about different careers; she is in identity moratorium status. Twenty-one-year-old Marcelo extensively explored several career options in college, eventually getting his degree in science education, and is looking forward to his first year of teaching high school students; his status is identity achieved. These examples focused on the career dimension, but remember that identity has a number of dimensions.

In Marcia's terms, young adolescents are primarily in the identity statuses of diffusion, foreclosure, or moratorium. To move to the status of identity achievement, young adolescents need three things (Marcia, 1987, 1996): (1) they must be confident that they have parental support, (2) they must have an established sense of industry, and (3) they must be able to adopt a self-reflective stance toward the future.

The identity status approach has been sharply criticized by some researchers and theoreticians (Coté, 2009). They maintain that the identity status approach distorts and trivializes Erikson's notions of crisis and commitment. For example, Erikson's idea of commitment loses the meaning of investing oneself in certain lifelong projects and is interpreted simply as having made a firm decision or not. Others argue that the identity status approach is a valuable contribution to understanding identity (Marcia, 2002; Waterman, 1992).

Emerging Adulthood and Beyond A consensus is developing that the key changes in identity are more likely to take place in emerging adulthood (18 to 25 years of age) or later than in adolescence (Coté, 2009; Kroger, 2007; Kroger, Martinussen, & Marcia, 2010; Luyckx & others, 2008). For example, Alan Waterman (1985, 1992) has found that from the years preceding high school through the last few years of college, the number of individuals who are identity achieved increases, whereas the number who are identity diffused decreases. College upperclassmen are more likely to be identity achieved than college freshmen or high school students. Many young adolescents, on the other hand, are identity diffused. These developmental changes are especially true for vocational choice. In terms of religious beliefs and political ideology, fewer college students reach the identity-achieved status; a substantial number are characterized by foreclosure and diffusion. Thus, the timing of identity development may depend on the particular dimension involved.

As long as one keeps
searching, the answers come.

—JOAN BAEZ

American Folk Singer, 20th Century

developmental **connection**

Attachment. Even while adolescents seek autonomy, attachment to parents is important; secure attachment in adolescence is linked to a number of positive outcomes. Chapter 14, p. 402

individuality Consists of two dimensions: self-assertion, the ability to have and communicate a point of view; and separateness, the use of communication patterns to express how one is different from others.

connectedness Consists of two dimensions: mutuality, sensitivity to and respect for others' views; and permeability, openness to others' views.

ethnic identity An enduring aspect of the self that includes a sense of membership in an ethnic group, along with the attitudes and feelings related to that membership.

Why might college produce some key changes in identity? Increased complexity in the reasoning skills of college students combined with a wide range of new experiences that highlight contrasts between home and college and between themselves and others stimulates them to reach a higher level of integrating various dimensions of their identity (Phinney, 2008).

A recent meta-analysis of 124 studies revealed that identity moratorium status rose steadily to 19 years of age and then declined; identity achievement rose across late adolescence and early adulthood; and foreclosure and diffusion statuses declined across the high school years but fluctuated in late adolescence and early adulthood (Kroger, Martinussen, & Marcia, 2010). A large portion of individuals were not identity achieved by early adulthood.

Resolution of the identity issue during adolescence and emerging adulthood does not mean that identity will be stable through the remainder of life. Many individuals who develop positive identities follow what are called "MAMA" cycles; that is, their identity status changes from *moratorium* to *achievement* to *moratorium* to *achievement* (Marcia, 1994). These cycles may be repeated throughout life (Francis, Fraser, & Marcia, 1989). Marcia (2002) points out that the first identity is just that—it is not, and should not be expected to be, the final product.

SOCIAL CONTEXTS

Social contexts play important roles in identity. Let's examine how family, culture, and ethnicity are linked to identity development.

Family Influences   Parents are important figures in the adolescent's development of identity (Schacter & Ventura, 2008). It is during adolescence that the search for balance between the need for autonomy and the need for connectedness becomes especially important to identity. Developmentalist Catherine Cooper and her colleagues (Carlson, Cooper, & Hsu, 1990; Cooper & Grotevant, 1989; Grotevant & Cooper, 1985, 1998) found that the presence of a family atmosphere that promotes both individuality and connectedness are important to the adolescent's identity development:

- **Individuality** consists of two dimensions: self-assertion—the ability to have and communicate a point of view, and separateness—the use of communication patterns to express how one is different from others.

- **Connectedness** also consists of two dimensions: mutuality, which involves sensitivity to and respect for others' views, and permeability, which involves openness to others' views.

In general, Cooper's research indicates that identity formation is enhanced by family relationships that are both individuated, which encourages adolescents to develop their own point of view, and connected, which provides a secure base from which to explore the widening social worlds of adolescence. When connectedness is strong and individuation weak, adolescents often have an identity-foreclosure status. When connectedness is weak, adolescents often reveal identity confusion.

How is an adolescent's identity development influenced by parents?

Culture and Ethnicity   "I feel that I have had to translate a whole Eastern culture and bring it to the West," Maxine Hong Kingston told one interviewer, "then bring the two cultures together seamlessly . . ." (Alegre & Welsch, 2003). For Kingston, this melding is "how one makes the Asian American culture." Her efforts illustrate one way of developing an **ethnic identity,** which is an enduring aspect of the self that includes a sense of membership in an ethnic group, along with the attitudes and feelings related to that membership (Phinney, 1996).

Throughout the world, ethnic minority groups have struggled to maintain their ethnic identities while blending in with the dominant culture (Erikson, 1968). Erikson saw this struggle for a separate identity within the larger culture as the driving force in the founding of churches, empires, and revolutions throughout history.

Many aspects of sociocultural contexts may influence ethnic identity (Phinney, 2008; Syed & Azmitia, 2010; Swanson, 2010). Ethnic identity tends to be stronger among members of minority groups than among members of mainstream groups. For example, in one study, the exploration of ethnic identity was higher among ethnic minority college students than among White non-Latino college students (Phinney & Alipuria, 1990).

Time is another aspect of the sociocultural context that influences ethnic identity. The indicators of identity often differ for each succeeding generation of immigrants (Phinney, 2003; Phinney & Ong, 2007). First-generation immigrants are likely to be secure in their identities and unlikely to change much; they may or may not develop a new identity. The degree to which they begin to feel "American" appears to be related to whether or not they learn English, develop social networks beyond their ethnic group, and become culturally competent in their new country. Second-generation immigrants are more likely to think of themselves as "American," possibly because citizenship is granted at birth. Maxine Hong Kingston noted, "I have been in America all of my life; Chinese is a foreign culture to me" (Alegre & Welsch, 2003). For second-generation immigrants, ethnic identity is likely to be linked to retention of their ethnic language and social networks. In the third and later generations, the issues become more complex. Broad social factors may affect the extent to which members of this generation retain their ethnic identities. For example, media images may encourage members of an ethnic group to identify with their group or retain parts of its culture. Discrimination may force people to see themselves as cut off from the majority group and encourage them to seek support from their own ethnic culture.

Researchers are also increasingly finding that a positive ethnic identity is related to positive outcomes for ethnic minority adolescents (Umana-Taylor & others, 2008; Umana-Taylor, Updegraff, & Gonzales-Backen, 2010). One study indicated that Navajo adolescents' positive ethnic heritage was linked to higher self-esteem, school connectedness, and social functioning (Jones & Galliher, 2007). And a recent longitudinal study of Latino adolescents found that ethnic identity resolution predicted proactive coping with discrimination over time (Umana-Taylor & others, 2008). Further, a recent study found that

---

developmental **connection**

Culture and Ethnicity. Historical, economic, and social experiences produce differences between various ethnic groups and the majority non-Latino White group in the United States. Chapter 17, pp. 496–497

Michelle Chin, age 16: "Parents do not understand that teenagers need to find out who they are, which means a lot of experimenting, a lot of mood swings, a lot of emotions and awkwardness. Like any teenager, I am facing an identity crisis. I am still trying to figure out whether I am a Chinese American or an American with Asian eyes."

Researcher Margaret Beale Spencer, shown here talking with adolescents, stresses that adolescence is often a critical juncture in the identity development of ethnic minority individuals. Most ethnic minority individuals consciously confront their ethnicity for the first time in adolescence.

exploration was an important aspect of establishing a secure sense of one's ethnic identity, which in turn was linked to a positive attitude toward one's own group and other groups (Whitehead & others, 2009). Yet another recent study of Latino youth indicated that growth in identity exploration was linked with a positive increase in self-esteem (Umana-Taylor, Gonzales-Backen, & Guimond, 2009).

To read about one individual who guides Latino adolescents in developing a positive identity, see the *Connecting With Careers* profile of Armando Ronquillo.

Jean Phinney (2006) recently described how ethnic identity may change in emerging adulthood, especially highlighting how certain experiences of ethnic minority individuals may shorten or lengthen emerging adulthood. For ethnic minority individuals who must take on family responsibilities and cannot go to college, identity formation may occur earlier. By contrast, especially for ethnic minority individuals who go to college, identity formation may take longer because of the complexity of exploring and understanding a bicultural identity. The cognitive challenges of higher education likely stimulate ethnic minority individuals to reflect on their identity and examine changes in the way they want to identify themselves. This increased reflection may focus on integrating parts of one's ethnic minority culture with elements of the mainstream non-Latino White culture. For example, some emerging adults have to come to grips with resolving a conflict between family loyalty and interdependence emphasized

connecting with careers

Armando Ronquillo, High School Counselor

Armando Ronquillo is a high school counselor and admissions advisor at Pueblo High School in a low-income area of Tucson, Arizona. More than 85 percent of the students have a Latino background. Ronquillo was named the top high school counselor in the state of Arizona for the year 2000.

Ronquillo especially works with Latino students to guide them in developing a positive identity. He talks with them about their Latino background and what it's like to have a bicultural identity—preserving important aspects of their Latino heritage while also pursuing the elements of success in the contemporary culture of the United States.

He believes that helping Latino youth to stay in school and getting them to think about the lifelong opportunities provided by a college education will benefit their identity development. Ronquillo also works with parents to help them understand that sending their child to college is doable and affordable.

Armando Ronquillo, counseling a Latina high school student about college.

For more information about what school counselors do, see page 45 in the Careers in Child Development appendix following Chapter 1.

The Contexts of Ethnic Identity Development

The environmental contexts of ethnic minority youth influence their identity development (Juang & Syed, 2010; Swanson, 2010). In the United States, many ethnic minority youth live in low-SES urban settings where support for developing a positive identity is lacking. Many of these youth live in pockets of poverty; are exposed to drugs, gangs, and criminal activities; and interact with youth and adults who have dropped out of school or are unemployed. In such settings, support organizations and programs for youth can make an important contribution to identity development.

A recent study by Niobe Way and her colleagues (2008) underscored the importance of local social contexts and prevailing images in the development of positive or negative ethnic identity. In two public high schools in the same neighborhood in New York City, Puerto Rican adolescents were highest in the social hierarchy, Chinese American adolescents the lowest—a different arrangement from many contexts in the wider society. There were virtually no changes in ethnic attitudes across the four years of the study, indicating that the adolescents had essentially accepted their place in the school hierar-

chy and were not actively exploring their ethnic identity. In Erikson's terminology, these adolescents may have foreclosed on their identity too early. The hope is that individuals with a negative ethnic identity will reexamine their identity as they go to college and/or enter the work world, where they may find less negative stereotypes of their ethnic group. A positive note in the study by Way and others (2008) was the finding that the Chinese American adolescents who had more positive connections to their ethnic group, possibly because they rejected the negative images they had encountered, were better adjusted than their counterparts who did not have positive connections to their ethnic group.

Individuals with a negative ethnic identity are likely to reexamine their identity as they go to college and/or enter the work world. What did you read earlier in this section of the chapter about why identity formation might take longer for ethnic minorities?

in their ethnic minority culture and the values of independence and self-assertion emphasized by the mainstream non-Latino White culture (Arnett, 2006). One recent study of Mexican American and Asian American college students found that they identified both with the American mainstream culture and their culture of origin (Devos, 2006). To read further about ethnic identity development in adolescence, see *Connecting With Diversity*.

Review *Connect* Reflect

 Describe identity and its development.

Review

- What is identity?
- What is Erikson's view of identity?
- How do individuals develop their identity? What identity statuses can be used to classify individuals?
- How do the social contexts of family, culture, and ethnicity influence identity?

Connect

- Identity vs. identity confusion is the fifth stage of Erikson's theory of development. What crisis should a child have resolved in

the fourth stage to be able to successfully move on to confront the identity vs. identity confusion crisis?

Reflect *Your Own Personal Journey of Life*

- How did your identity change as you developed through adolescence? How does your current identity differ from your identity as an adolescent? To guide your self-evaluation of your identity changes, revisit Figure 11.6 and reflect on what are likely some of the key aspects of your identity.

The Self and Identity

Self-Understanding and Understanding Others

 Discuss the development of self-understanding and understanding others.

- Self-Understanding

- Understanding Others

- Self-understanding is a child's cognitive representation of the self—the substance and content of the child's self-conceptions. It provides the rational underpinnings for personal identity. Infants develop a rudimentary form of self-recognition as early as 3 months of age and a more complete form of self-understanding at approximately 18 months of age. Self-understanding in early childhood is characterized by confusion of self, mind, and body; concrete, physical, and active descriptions; and unrealistic positive overestimations. Self-understanding in middle and late childhood involves an increase in the use of psychological characteristics and traits, social descriptions, and social comparison; distinction between the real and ideal self; and an increase in realistic self-evaluations. Adolescents tend to engage in more social comparison, to develop abstract and idealistic conceptions of themselves, and to become self-conscious about their self-understanding. Their self-understanding often fluctuates, and they construct multiple selves, including possible selves.

- Young children display more sophisticated self-understanding and understanding of others than was previously thought. Even 4-year-olds understand that people make statements that aren't true to obtain what they want or to avoid trouble. Children increase their perspective taking in middle and late childhood, and they become even more skeptical of others' claims.

Self-Esteem and Self-Concept

 Explain self-esteem and self-concept.

- What Are Self-Esteem and Self-Concept?

- Assessment

- Developmental Changes

- Variations in Self-Esteem

- Self-esteem, also referred to as self-worth or self-image, is the global, evaluative dimension of the self. Self-concept refers to domain-specific evaluations of the self.

- Harter's Self-Perception Profile for Children is used with third-grade through sixth-grade children to assess general self-worth and self-concept in five skill domains. Harter's Self-Perception Profile for Adolescents assesses global self-worth in five skill domains, plus additional domains dealing with friendship, romance, and job competence.

- Some researchers have found that self-esteem drops in adolescence, more so for girls than boys, but there is controversy about how extensively self-esteem varies with age.

- Researchers have found only moderate correlations between self-esteem and school performance. Individuals with high self-esteem have greater initiative than those with low self-esteem, and this can produce positive or negative outcomes. Self-esteem is related to perceived physical appearance and happiness. Low self-esteem is linked with depression, suicide attempts, and anorexia nervosa. In Coopersmith's study, children's self-esteem was associated with parental acceptance and allowing children freedom within well-defined limits.

Identity

LG3 Describe identity and its development.

- What Is Identity?

- Erikson's View

- Developmental Changes

- Social Contexts

- Identity development is complex and takes place in bits and pieces. At a bare minimum, identity involves commitment to a vocational direction, an ideological stance, and a sexual orientation. Synthesizing identity components can be a long, drawn-out process.

- Erikson argues that identity versus identity confusion is the fifth stage of the human life span, which individuals experience during adolescence. This stage involves entering a psychosocial moratorium between the security of childhood and the autonomy of adulthood. Personality and role experimentation are important aspects of identity development. In technological societies like those in North America, the vocational role is especially important.

- Identity development begins during infancy and continues through old age. James Marcia proposed four identity statuses—identity diffusion, foreclosure, moratorium, and achievement—that are based on crisis (exploration) and commitment. Some experts argue the main changes in identity occur in emerging adulthood rather than adolescence. Individuals often follow *moratorium-achievement-moratorium-achievement* (MAMA) cycles in their lives.

- Parents are important figures in adolescents' identity development. Both individuality and connectedness in family relations are related to identity development. Throughout the world, ethnic minority groups have struggled to maintain their identities while blending into the majority culture. A positive ethnic identity is linked to positive outcomes for ethnic minority adolescents.

key terms

self-understanding 324
possible self 327
social cognition 327
perspective taking 328
self-esteem 329

self-concept 330
identity versus identity
   confusion 335
psychosocial
    moratorium 335

crisis 336
commitment 336
identity diffusion 336
identity foreclosure 336
identity moratorium 336

identity achievement 336
individuality 338
connectedness 339
ethnic identity 339

key people

Ross Thompson 324
Susan Harter 330
Erik Erikson 335

William Damon 335
James Marcia 336

Alan Waterman 337
Catherine Cooper 338

Jean Phinney 340
Niobe Way 341

chapter **12** GENDER

Gender and emotion researcher Stephanie Shields (1998) analyzed how the movie *Jerry Maguire* reflects the role of gender in emotions and relationships. In brief, the movie is a "buddy" picture in which sports agent Jerry Maguire (played by Tom Cruise) is paired with two buddies: the too-short Arizona Cardinals wide receiver Rod Tidwell (played by Cuba Gooding, Jr.) and 6-year-old Ray, son of Jerry's love interest, accountant Dorothy Boyd (played by Renee Zellweger). Through his buddies, the thinking-but-not-feeling Jerry discovers the right path by connecting to Ray's emotional honesty and Rod's devotion to his family.

How are gender, emotion, and caring portrayed in the movie Jerry Maguire?

Images of nurturing and nurtured males are woven throughout the movie. In discovering a caring relationship with Ray, Jerry makes his first genuine move toward emotional maturity. The boy is the guide to the man. Chad, Ray's babysitter, provides another good example of appropriate caring by a male.

Males are shown crying in the movie. Jerry sheds tears while writing his mission statement, thinking about Dorothy's possible move to another city (which also means he would lose Ray), and witnessing the success of his lone client (Rod). Rod is brought to tears when he speaks of his family. Historically, weeping, more than any other form of emotional expression, has been associated with feminine emotion. However, it has increasingly taken on a more prominent role in the male's emotional makeup.

The movie *Jerry Maguire* reflects changes in gender roles as an increasing number of males show an interest in improving their social relationships and achieving emotional maturity. However, as we will see later in this chapter, experts on gender argue that overall females are more competent in their social relationships than males, and that large numbers of males still have a lot of room for improvement in dealing with their emotions.

preview

We begin this chapter by examining what gender involves, then turn our attention to various influences on gender development—biological, social, and cognitive. Next, we explore gender stereotypes, similarities, and differences. Our final discussion focuses on how gender roles are classified.

What Is Gender? Summarize what gender involves.

> To be meek, patient, tactful, modest, honorable, brave, is not to be either manly or womanly, but is to be humane.
>
> —JANE HARRISON
> *English Writer, 20th Century*

Gender refers to the characteristics of people as males and females. **Gender identity** involves a sense of one's own gender, including knowledge, understanding, and acceptance of being male or female (Blakemore, Berenbaum, & Liben, 2009; Egan & Perry, 2001). **Gender roles** are sets of expectations that prescribe how females or males should think, act, and feel. During the preschool years, most children increasingly act in ways that match their culture's gender roles. **Gender typing** refers to acquisition of a traditional masculine or feminine role. For example, fighting is more characteristic of a traditional masculine role and crying is more characteristic of a traditional feminine role.

One aspect of gender identity involves knowing whether you are a boy or a girl. Until recently, it was thought that this aspect of gender identity emerged at about 2½ years. However, a recent longitudinal study that explored the acquisition of gender labels in infancy and their implications for gender-typed play revealed that gender identity likely emerges before 2 years of age (Zosuls & others, 2009). In this study, infants began using gender labels on average at 19 months of age, with girls beginning to use gender labels earlier than boys. This gender difference became present at 17 months of age and increased at 21 months of age. Use of gender labels was linked to gender-typed play, indicating that knowledge of gender categories may affect gender typing earlier than 2 years of age.

A recent study revealed that sex-typed behavior (boys playing with cars and girls with jewelry, for example) increased during the preschool years and children that who engaged in the most sex-typed behavior during the preschool years were still doing so at 8 years of age (Golombok & others, 2008).

At what age do children, know whether they are male or female?

Review Connect Reflect

 Summarize what gender involves.

Review

- What is gender? What are some components of gender?

Connect

- In Chapter 1, what did you learn about gender and research that you should keep in mind as you read more about research in the area of gender and development in the following sections of this chapter?

Reflect *Your Own Personal Journey of Life*

- As you begin this chapter, think about the role of gender in your life as you were growing up. What are some examples of how your behavior as a child reflected a masculine or feminine role?

Influences on Gender Development

LG2 Discuss the main biological, social, and cognitive influences on gender.

- Biological Influences
- Social Influences
- Cognitive Influences

How is gender influenced by biology? By children's social experiences? By cognitive factors?

BIOLOGICAL INFLUENCES

It was not until the 1920s that researchers confirmed the existence of human sex chromosomes, the genetic material that determines our sex. Humans normally have 46 chromosomes, arranged in pairs. A 23rd pair with two X-shaped chromosomes produces a female. A 23rd pair with an X chromosome and a Y chromosome produces a male.

Hormones In Chapter 4, we discussed the two classes of hormones that have the most influence on gender: estrogens and androgens. Estrogens and androgens occur in both females and males, but in very different concentrations.

Estrogens primarily influence the development of female physical sex characteristics and help regulate the menstrual cycle. Estrogens are a general class of hormones. An example of an important estrogen is estradiol. In females, estrogens are produced mainly by the ovaries.

Androgens primarily promote the development of male genitals and secondary sex characteristics. One important androgen is testosterone. Androgens are produced by the adrenal glands in males and females, and by the testes in males.

In the first few weeks of gestation, female and male embryos look alike. Male sex organs start to differ from female sex organs when a gene on the Y chromosome directs a small piece of tissue in the embryo to turn into testes. Once the tissue has turned into testes, they begin to secrete testosterone. Because females have no Y chromosome, the tissue turns into ovaries. To explore biological influences on gender, researchers have studied individuals who are exposed to unusual levels of sex hormones early in development (Blakemore, Berenbaum, & Liben, 2009). Here are four examples of problems that may occur as a result (Lippa, 2005, pp. 122–124, 136–137):

- *Congenital adrenal hyperplasia (CAH).* Some girls have this condition, which is caused by a genetic defect. Their adrenal glands enlarge, resulting in abnormally high levels of androgens. Although CAH girls are XX females, they vary in how much their genitals look like male or female genitals. Their genitals may be surgically altered to look more like those of a typical female. Although CAH girls usually grow up to think of themselves as girls and women, they are less content with being a female and show a stronger interest in being a male than non-CAH girls (Berenbaum & Bailey, 2003; Ehrhardt & Baker, 1974; Hall & others, 2004). They like sports and enjoy playing with boys and boys' toys. CAH girls usually don't like typical girl activities such as playing with dolls and wearing makeup.
- *Androgen-insensitive males.* Because of a genetic error, a small number of XY males don't have androgen cells in their bodies. Their bodies look female, they develop a female gender identity, and they usually are sexually attracted to males.
- *Pelvic field defect.* A small number of newborns have a disorder called pelvic field defect, which in boys involves a missing penis. These XY boys have normal amounts of testosterone prenatally but usually have been castrated just

developmental **connection**

Biological Processes. Hormones are powerful chemical substances secreted by the endocrine glands and carried through the body by the bloodstream. Chapter 4, pp. 110–111

gender The characteristics of people as males and females.

gender identity The sense of being male or female, which most children acquire by the time they are 3 years old.

gender role A set of expectations that prescribes how females or males should think, act, and feel.

gender typing Acquisition of a traditional masculine or feminine role.

estrogens Hormones, the most important of which is estradiol, that influence the development of female physical sex characteristics and help regulate the menstrual cycle.

androgens Hormones, the most important of which is testosterone, that promote the development of male genitals and secondary sex characteristics.

developmental connection

Theories. Evolutionary psychology emphasizes the importance of adaptation, reproduction, and "survival of the fittest" in shaping behavior. Chapter 2, p. 53

"How is it gendered?"
© Edward Koren/The New Yorker Collection/
www.cartoonbank.com

social role theory A theory stating that gender differences result from the contrasting roles of women and men—social hierarchy and division of labor strongly influence gender differences in power, assertiveness, and nurture.

psychoanalytic theory of gender A theory that stems from Freud's view that preschool children develop erotic feelings toward the opposite-sex parent. Eventually these feelings cause anxiety, so that at 5 or 6 years of age, children renounce these feelings and identify with the same-sex parent, unconsciously adopting the same-sex parent's characteristics.

social cognitive theory of gender This theory emphasizes that children's gender development occurs through observation and imitation of gender behavior, and through rewards and punishments they experience for gender-appropriate and gender-inappropriate behavior.

after being born and raised as females. One study revealed that despite the efforts by parents to rear them as girls, most of the XY children insisted that they were boys (Reiner & Gearhart, 2004). Apparently, normal exposure to androgens prenatally had a stronger influence on their gender identity than being castrated and raised as girls.

- In another intriguing case, one of two identical twin boys lost his penis due to a botched circumcision. The twin who lost his penis was surgically reassigned to be a girl and reared as a girl. Bruce (the real name of the boy) became "Brenda." Early indications were that the sex reassignment had positive outcomes (Money, 1975), but later it was concluded that "Brenda" had not adjusted well as a girl (Diamond & Sigmundson, 1997). As a young adult, Brenda became Bruce once again and lived as a man with a wife and adopted children (Colapinto, 2000). Tragically in 2004, when Bruce was 38 years old, he committed suicide.

Although sex hormones alone do not determine behavior, researchers have found links between sex hormone levels and certain behaviors. The most established effects of testosterone on humans involve aggressive behavior and sexual behavior (Hyde, 2007b). Levels of testosterone are correlated with sexual behavior in boys during puberty (Udry & others, 1985). And a recent study revealed that higher fetal testosterone levels measured from amniotic fluid were linked to increased male-typical play, such as increased aggression, in 6- to 10-year-old boys and girls (Auyeung & others, 2009).

The Evolutionary Psychology View In Chapter 2 we described the approach of evolutionary psychology, which emphasizes that adaptation during the evolution of humans produced psychological differences between males and females (Buss, 1995, 2008). Evolutionary psychologists argue that primarily because of their differing roles in reproduction, males and females faced different pressures in primeval environments when the human species was evolving. In particular, because having multiple sexual liaisons improves the likelihood that males will pass on their genes, natural selection favored males who adopted short-term mating strategies. These males competed with other males to acquire more resources in order to access females. Therefore, say evolutionary psychologists, males evolved dispositions that favor violence, competition, and risk taking.

In contrast, according to evolutionary psychologists, females' contributions to the gene pool were enhanced by securing resources for their offspring, which was promoted by obtaining long-term mates who could support a family. As a consequence, natural selection favored females who devoted effort to parenting and chose mates who could provide their offspring with resources and protection. Females developed preferences for successful, ambitious men who could provide these resources (Geher & Miller, 2007).

Critics of evolutionary psychology argue that its hypotheses are backed by speculations about prehistory, not evidence, and that in any event people are not locked into behavior that was adaptive in the evolutionary past. Critics also claim that the evolutionary view pays little attention to cultural and individual variations in gender differences (Matlin, 2008).

SOCIAL INFLUENCES

Many social scientists do not locate the cause of psychological gender differences in biological dispositions. Rather, they argue that these differences are due to social experiences. Three theories that reflect this view have been influential.

Alice Eagly (2001, 2009; Eagly & Fischer, 2009; Eagly & Sczesny, 2009) proposed **social role theory,** which states that gender differences result from the contrasting roles of women and men. In most cultures around the world, women have less power and status than men do and they control fewer resources (UNICEF,

Theory	Processes	Outcome
Psychoanalytic theory	Sexual attraction to opposite-sex parent at 3 to 5 years of age; anxiety about sexual attraction and subsequent identification with same-sex parent at 5 to 6 years of age	Gender behavior similar to that of same-sex parent
Social cognitive theory	Rewards and punishments of gender-appropriate and -inappropriate behavior by adults and peers; observation and imitation of models' masculine and feminine behavior	Gender behavior

FIGURE **12.1**

PARENTS INFLUENCE THEIR CHILDREN'S GENDER DEVELOPMENT BY ACTION AND EXAMPLE

2009, 2010). Compared with men, women perform more domestic work, spend fewer hours in paid employment, receive lower pay, and are more thinly represented in the highest levels of organizations. In Eagly's view, as women adapted to roles with less power and less status in society, they showed more cooperative, less dominant profiles than men. Thus, the social hierarchy and division of labor are important causes of gender differences in power, assertiveness, and nurture (Eagly, 2009).

The **psychoanalytic theory of gender** stems from Sigmund Freud's view that the preschool child develops erotic feelings toward the opposite-sex parent. Eventually, these feelings arouse anxiety, so that at 5 or 6 years of age, the child renounces these feelings and identifies with the same-sex parent, unconsciously adopting the same-sex parent's characteristics. However, developmentalists do not believe gender development proceeds as Freud proposed (Callan, 2001).

The social cognitive approach discussed in Chapter 1 provides an alternative explanation of how children develop gender-typed behavior (see Figure 12.1). According to the **social cognitive theory of gender,** children's gender development occurs through observation and imitation, and through the rewards and punishments children experience for gender-appropriate and gender-inappropriate behavior (Bussey & Bandura, 1999).

developmental **connection**

Social Cognitive Theory. Social cognitive theory holds that behavior, environment, and person/cognitive factors are the key aspects of development. Chapter 1, pp. 27–28

Parents, by action and example, influence their children's and adolescents' gender development (Blakemore, Berenbaum, & Liben, 2009). As soon as the label *girl* or *boy* is assigned, virtually everyone, from parents to siblings to strangers, begins treating the infant in gender-specific ways (see Figure 12.2). Parents often use rewards and punishments to teach their daughters to be feminine ("Karen, you are such a good mommy with your dolls") and their sons to be masculine ("C'mon now, Keith, big boys don't cry").

Mothers and fathers often interact differently with their children and adolescents. Mothers are more involved with their children and adolescents than are fathers, although fathers increase the time they spend in parenting when they have sons and are less likely to become divorced when they have sons (Diekmann & Schmidheiny, 2004; Galambos, Berenbaum, & McHale, 2009). Mothers' interactions with their children and adolescents often center on caregiving and teaching activities, while fathers' interactions often involve leisure activities (Galambos, Berenbaum, & McHale, 2009).

FIGURE **12.2**

EXPECTATIONS FOR BOYS AND GIRLS.
First imagine that this is a photograph of a baby girl. *What expectations would you have for her?* Then imagine that this is a photograph of a baby boy. *What expectations would you have for him?*

How do mothers and fathers interact differently with their children and adolescents?

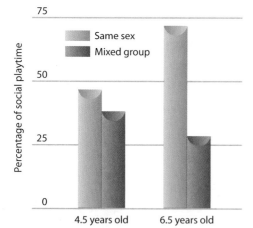

Mothers and fathers often interact differently with sons and daughters, and these gendered interactions that begin in infancy usually continue through childhood and adolescence. In reviewing research on this topic, Phyllis Bronstein (2006) recently provided these conclusions:

- *Mothers' socialization strategies.* In many cultures mothers socialize their daughters to be more obedient and responsible than their sons. They also place more restrictions on daughters' autonomy.
- *Fathers' socialization strategies.* Fathers show more attention to sons than daughters, engage in more activities with sons, and put forth more effort to promote sons' intellectual development.

Thus, according to Bronstein (2006, pp. 269–270), "Despite an increased awareness in the United States and other Western cultures of the detrimental effects of gender stereotyping, many parents continue to foster behaviors and perceptions that are consonant with traditional gender role norms."

Children also learn about gender from observing other adults in the neighborhood and in the media (Fagot, Rodgers, & Leinbach, 2000). As children get older, the reactions of peers become increasingly important. Peers extensively reward and punish gender behavior (Leaper & Friedman, 2007). For example, when children play in ways that the culture says are sex-appropriate, they tend to be rewarded by their peers. Those who engage in activities that are considered inappropriate tend to be criticized or abandoned by their peers.

Children show a clear preference for being with and liking same-sex peers, and this tendency usually becomes stronger during the middle and late childhood years (Maccoby, 2002) (see Figure 12.3). What kind of socialization takes place in these same-sex play groups? In one study, researchers observed preschoolers over a period of six months (Martin & Fabes, 2001). The more time boys spent interacting with other boys, the more their activity level, rough-and-tumble play, and sex-typed choice of toys and games increased, and the less time boys spent near adults. By contrast, the more time preschool girls spent interacting with other girls, the more their activity level and aggression decreased, and the more their girl-type play activities and time spent near adults increased. After watching elementary school children repeatedly play in same-sex groups, two researchers characterized the playground as "gender school" (Luria & Herzog, 1985).

COGNITIVE INFLUENCES

Observation, imitation, rewards, and punishment—these are the mechanisms by which gender develops according to social cognitive theory. Interactions between the child and the social environment are the main keys to gender development in this view. Some critics argue that this explanation pays too little attention to the child's own mind and understanding, and portrays the child as passively acquiring gender roles (Martin, Ruble, & Szkrybalo, 2002).

FIGURE **12.3**

DEVELOPMENTAL CHANGES IN PERCENTAGE OF TIME SPENT IN SAME-SEX AND MIXED-GROUP SETTINGS. Observations of children show that they are more likely to play in same-sex than mixed-sex groups. This tendency increases between 4 and 6 years of age.

gender schema theory According to this theory, gender typing emerges as children gradually develop schemas of what is gender-appropriate and gender-inappropriate in their culture.

One influential cognitive theory is **gender schema theory,** which states that gender-typing emerges as children gradually develop gender schemas of what is gender-appropriate and gender-inappropriate in their culture (Blakemore, Berenbaum,

How Do Young Children Use Gender Schemas to Make Judgments About Occupations?

In one study, researchers interviewed children 3 to 7 years old about 10 traditionally masculine occupations (airplane pilot, car mechanic) and feminine occupations (clothes designer, secretary), using questions such as the following (Levy, Sadovsky, & Troseth, 2000):

- *Example of a traditionally masculine occupation item:* An airplane pilot is a person who "flies airplanes for people." Who do you think would do the best job as an airplane pilot, a man or a woman?
- *Example of a traditionally feminine occupation item:* A clothes designer is a person "who draws up and makes clothes for people." Who do you think would do the best job as a clothes designer, a man or a woman?

As indicated in Figure 12.4, the children had well-developed gender schemas, in this case reflected in stereotypes of occupations. They "viewed men as more competent than women in masculine occupations, and rated women as more competent than men in feminine occupations" (p. 993). Also, "girls' ratings of women's competence at feminine occupations were substantially higher than their ratings of men's competence at masculine occupations. Conversely, boys' ratings of men's competence at masculine occupations were considerably greater than their ratings of women's competence at feminine occupations" (p. 1002). These findings demonstrate that most children as young as 3 to 4 years of age tend to have strong gender schemas regarding the perceived competencies of men and women in gender-typed occupations.

The researchers also asked the children to select from a list of emotions how they would feel if they grew up to have each of the 10 occupations. Girls said they would be happy with the femi-nine occupations and angry or disgusted with the masculine occupations. As expected, boys reversed their choices, saying they would be happy if they grew up to have the masculine occupations but angry and disgusted with the feminine occupations. However, the boys' emotions were more intense (more angry and disgusted) in desiring to avoid the feminine occupations than girls in wanting to avoid the masculine occupations. This finding supports other research that indicates gender roles tend to constrict boys more than girls (Hyde, 2007a; Matlin, 2008).

It is important to note that the children in this study were at the height of gender stereotyping, a topic that will be discussed shortly. Most older children, adolescents, and adults become more flexible about occupational roles (Hyde, 2007a; Leaper & Friedman, 2007).

	Boy	Girl
"Masculine Occupations"		
Percentage who judged men more competent	87	70
Percentage who judged women more competent	13	30
"Feminine Occupations"		
Percentage who judged men more competent	35	8
Percentage who judged women more competent	64	92

FIGURE **12.4**

CHILDREN'S JUDGMENTS ABOUT THE COMPETENCE OF MEN AND WOMEN IN GENDER-STEREOTYPED OCCUPATIONS

& Liben, 2009; Zosuls, Lurye, & Ruble, 2008). A *schema* is a cognitive structure, a network of associations that guide an individual's perceptions. A *gender schema* organizes the world in terms of female and male. Children are internally motivated to perceive the world and to act in accordance with their developing schemas. Bit by bit, children pick up what is gender-appropriate and gender-inappropriate in their culture, and develop gender schemas that shape how they perceive the world and what they remember (Blakemore, Berenbaum, & Liben, 2009). Children are motivated to act in ways that conform with these gender schemas. Thus, gender schemas fuel gender-typing.

How do young children use gender schemas to make judgments about occupations? To find out, see *Connecting Through Research*.

In sum, cognitive factors contribute to the way children think and act as males and females. Through biological, social, and cognitive processes, children develop their gender attitudes and behaviors (Blakemore, Berenbaum, & Liben, 2009; Lippa, 2005).

Gender Stereotypes, Similarities, and Differences

 LG3 Describe gender stereotypes, similarities, and differences.

Gender Stereotyping   Gender Similarities and Differences

How pervasive is gender stereotyping? What are the real differences between boys and girls?

GENDER STEREOTYPING

Gender stereotypes are general impressions and beliefs about females and males. For example, men are powerful; women are weak. Men make good mechanics; women make good nurses. Men are good with numbers; women are good with words. Women are emotional; men are not. All of these are stereotypes. They are generalizations about a group that reflect widely held beliefs (Matlin, 2008).

Traditional Masculinity and Femininity A classic study in the early 1970s assessed which traits and behaviors college students believed were characteristic of females and which they believed were characteristic of males (Broverman & others, 1972). The traits associated with males were labeled *instrumental:* They included characteristics such as being independent, aggressive, and power oriented. The traits associated with females were labeled *expressive:* They included characteristics such as being warm and sensitive.

> If you are going to generalize about women, you will find yourself up to here in exceptions.
>
> —**Dolores Hitchens**
> *American Mystery Writer, 20th Century*

Thus, the instrumental traits associated with males suited them for the traditional masculine role of going out into the world as the breadwinner. The expressive traits associated with females paralleled the traditional feminine role of being the sensitive, nurturing caregiver in the home. These roles and traits, however, are not just different; they also are unequal in terms of social status and power. The traditional feminine characteristics are childlike, suitable for someone who is dependent upon and subordinate to others. The traditional masculine characteristics equip a person to deal competently with the wider world and to wield authority.

Stereotyping and Culture How widespread is gender stereotyping? In a far-ranging study of college students in 30 countries, stereotyping of females and males was pervasive (Williams & Best, 1982). Males were widely believed to be dominant, independent, aggressive, achievement oriented, and enduring. Females were widely believed to be nurturant, affiliative, less esteemed, and more helpful in times of distress.

gender stereotypes Broad categories that reflect impressions and widely held beliefs about what behavior is appropriate for females and males.

Of course, in the decades since this study was conducted, traditional gender stereotypes and gender roles have been challenged in many societies, and social inequalities between men and women have diminished. Do gender stereotypes change when the relationship between men and women changes? In a subsequent study, women and men who lived in relatively wealthy, industrialized countries perceived themselves as more similar than did women and men who lived in less-developed countries (Williams & Best, 1989). In the more-developed countries, the women were more likely to attend college and to be gainfully employed. Thus, as sexual equality increases, gender stereotypes may diminish.

However, recent research continues to find that gender stereotyping is pervasive (Best, 2010; Blakemore, Berenbaum, & Liben, 2009; Zosuls, Lurye, & Ruble, 2008). For example, a recent study found extensive differences in the stereotyping of females' and males' emotions (Durik & others, 2006). Females were stereotyped as expressing more fear, guilt, love, sadness, shame, surprise, and sympathy than their male counterparts. Males were stereotyped as expressing more anger and pride than their female counterparts. Researchers also have found that boys' gender stereotypes are more rigid than girls' (Blakemore, Berenbaum, & Liben, 2009).

Developmental Changes in Gender Stereotyping   Earlier we described how young children stereotype occupations as being "masculine" or "feminine." When do children begin to engage in gender stereotyping? One study examined the extent to which children and their mothers engage in gender stereotyping (Gelman, Taylor, & Nguyen, 2004). The researchers videotaped mothers and their 2-, 4-, and 6-year-old sons and daughters as they discussed a picture book with stereotyped (a boy playing football, for example) and nonstereotyped (a female race car driver, for example) gender activities. Children engaged in more gender stereotyping than did their mothers. However, mothers expressed gender concepts to their children by referencing categories of gender ("Why do you think only *men* can be firefighters?" for example), labeling gender ("That looks like a daddy," for example), and contrasting males and females ("Is that a girl job or a boy job?" for example). Gender stereotyping by children was present even in the 2-year-olds, but increased considerably by 4 years of age. This study demonstrated that even when adults don't explicitly engage in gender stereotyping when talking with children, they provide children with information about gender by categorizing gender, labeling gender, and contrasting males and females. Children use these cues to construct an understanding of gender and to guide their behavior (Leaper & Bigler, 2004).

Gender stereotyping continues to change during middle and late childhood and adolescence (Blakemore, Berenbaum, & Liben, 2009). By the time children enter elementary school, they have considerable knowledge about which activities are linked with being male or female. Until about 7 to 8 years of age, gender stereotyping is extensive because young children don't recognize individual variations in masculinity and femininity. By 5 years of age, both boys and girls stereotype boys as powerful and in more negative terms, such as mean, and girls in more positive terms, such as nice (Miller & Ruble, 2005). Across the elementary school years, children become more flexible in their gender attitudes (Trautner & others, 2005).

A recent study of 3- to 10-year old U.S. children revealed that girls and older children used a higher percentage of gender stereotypes (Miller & others, 2009). In this study, appearance stereotypes were more prevalent on the part of girls while activity (sports, for example) and trait (aggressive, for example) stereotyping was more commonly engaged in by boys.

What are some developmental changes in children's gender stereotyping?

GENDER SIMILARITIES AND DIFFERENCES

What is the reality behind gender stereotypes? Let's examine some of the differences between the sexes, keeping in mind that (1) the differences are averages and do not apply to all females or all males; (2) even when gender differences occur, there often is considerable overlap between males and females; and (3) the differences may be due primarily to biological factors, sociocultural factors, or both.

Physical Similarities and Differences   We could devote pages to describing physical differences between the average man and woman. For example, women have about twice the body fat of men, with most of it concentrated around their breasts and hips. In males, fat is more likely to go to the abdomen. On the average, males grow to be 10 percent taller than females. Androgens (the "male" hormones) promote the growth of long bones; estrogens (the "female" hormones) stop such growth at puberty.

Many physical differences between men and women are tied to health. From conception on, females have a longer life expectancy than males, and females are less likely than males to develop physical or mental disorders. Females are more resistant to infection, and their blood vessels are more elastic than males'. Males have higher levels of stress hormones, which cause faster clotting and higher blood pressure.

Does gender matter when it comes to brain structure and activity? Human brains are much more alike than different, whether the brain belongs to a male or a female (Hyde, 2007b). However, researchers have found some brain differences between females and males. Among the differences that have been discovered are the following:

- Female brains are smaller than male brains, but female brains have more folds; the larger folds (called *convolutions*) allow more surface brain tissue within the skulls of females than males (Luders & others, 2004).
- One part of the hypothalamus involved in sexual behavior tends to be larger in men than in women (Swaab & others, 2001).
- Portions of the corpus callosum—the band of tissues through which the brain's two hemispheres communicate—may be larger in females than in males, although some studies have found this not to be the case (Bishop & Wahlsten, 1997; Driesen & Raz, 1995; LeVay, 1994).
- An area of the parietal lobe that functions in visuospatial skills tends to be larger in males than in females (Frederikse & others, 2000).
- The areas of the brain involved in emotional expression tend to show more metabolic activity in females than in males (Gur & others, 1995).

Although some differences in brain structure and function have been found, many of these differences are either small or inconsistently supported by research. Also, when sex differences in the brain have been revealed, in many cases they have not been directly linked to psychological differences (Blakemore, Berenbaum, & Liben, 2009). Although research on sex differences in the brain is still in its infancy, it is likely that there are far more similarities than differences in the brains of females and males. A further point is worth noting: Anatomical sex differences in the brain may be due to the biological origins of these differences, behavioral experiences (which underscores the brain's continuing plasticity), or a combination of these factors.

Cognitive Similarities and Differences   No gender differences in general intelligence have been revealed, but gender differences have been found in some cognitive areas (Blakemore, Berenbaum, & Liben, 2009). Research has shown that girls and women generally have slightly better verbal skills than boys and men, although in some areas of verbal skill the differences are substantial (Blakemore, Berenbaum, & Liben, 2009). For example, in recent national assessments, girls were significantly better than boys in reading and writing (National Assessment of Educational Progress, 2005, 2007).

Are there gender differences in math aptitude? A recent very large-scale study of more than 7 million U.S. students in grades 2 through 11 revealed no differences in math scores for boys and girls (Hyde & others, 2008).

---

developmental connection

Brain Development. The human brain has two hemispheres (left and right). To some extent the type of information processed by neurons depends on whether they are in the left or right hemisphere of the brain. Chapter 4, p. 114

"So according to the stereotype, you can put two and two together, but I can read the handwriting on the wall."

One area of math that has been examined for possible gender differences is visuospatial skills, which include being able to rotate objects mentally and determine what they would look like when rotated. These types of skills are important in courses such as plane and solid geometry and geography. A recent research review revealed that boys have better visuospatial skills than girls (Halpern & others, 2007). For example, despite equal participation in the National Geography Bee, in most years all 10 finalists are boys (Liben, 1995). However, some experts argue that the gender difference in visuospatial skills is small (Hyde, 2007b) (See Figure 12.5).

With regard to school achievement, females earn better grades and complete high school at a higher rate than boys (Halpern, 2006). Males are more likely than females to be assigned to special/remedial education classes. Females are more likely to be engaged with academic material, be attentive in class, put forth more academic effort, and participate more in class than boys are (DeZolt & Hull, 2001).

Thus, we can conclude that females show greater overall academic interest and achievement than males in the United States. However, despite these positive characteristics of girls, the increasing evidence that there is similarity in the math and science skills of girls and boys, and the legislative efforts to attain gender equality in recent years, gender differences in science, technology, and math careers continue to favor males (Watt, 2008; Watt & Eccles, 2008). Toward the end of high school, girls are less likely to be taking high-level math courses and less likely to plan to enter the so-called "STEM" fields of science, technology, engineering, and math. Thus, the middle school and high school years are especially important in shaping girls' career plans in these areas.

Might same-sex education be better for children than co-ed education? The research evidence related to this question is mixed (Blakemore, Berenbaum, & Liben, 2009). Some research indicates that same-sex education has positive outcomes for girls' achievement, whereas other research does not show any improvements in achievement for girls or boys in same-sex education (Mael, 1998; Warrington & Younger, 2003). A recent study did reveal that girls who took a physics class in an all-girls school had a more positive physics-related self-concept than girls who took a physics class in a co-ed school.

Socioemotional Similarities and Differences Four areas of socioemotional development in which gender similarities and differences have been studied extensively are aggression, relationship communication, emotion, and prosocial behavior.

Aggression One of the most consistent gender differences is that boys are more physically aggressive than girls (Brendgen, 2009). The difference occurs in all cultures and appears very early in children's development. The physical aggression difference is especially pronounced when children are provoked. Both biological and environmental factors have been proposed to account for gender differences in aggression. Biological factors include heredity and hormones. Environmental factors include cultural expectations, adult and peer models, and social agents that reward aggression in boys and punish aggression in girls.

Although boys are consistently more physically aggressive than girls, might girls show at least as much verbal aggression (such as yelling) as boys? When verbal aggression is examined, gender differences often disappear; sometimes, though, verbal aggression is more pronounced in girls than boys (Eagly & Steffen, 1986).

Recently, increased interest has been shown in *relational aggression*, which involves harming someone by manipulating a relationship (Crick & others, 2009; Salmivalli & Peets, 2009). Relational aggression includes such behaviors as trying to make others dislike a certain individual by spreading malicious

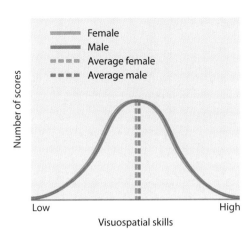

FIGURE **12.5**

VISUOSPATIAL SKILLS OF MALES AND FEMALES. Notice that, although an average male's visuospatial skills are higher than an average female's, scores for the two sexes almost entirely overlap. Not all males have better visuospatial skills than all females—the overlap indicates that, although the average male score is higher, many females outperform most males on such tasks.

developmental **connection**

Culture and Ethnicity. East Asian children and adolescents consistently outperform their U.S. counterparts in math achievement. Chapter 16, pp. 479–480

What are some gender differences in aggression?

rumors about the person (Underwood, 2004). Relational aggression increases in middle and late childhood (Dishion & Piehler, 2009). Mixed findings have characterized research on whether girls show more relational aggression than boys, but one consistency in findings is that relational aggression comprises a greater percentage of girls' overall aggression than is the case for boys (Putallaz & others, 2007). And a recent research review revealed that girls engage in more relational aggression than boys in adolescence but not in childhood (Smith, Rose, & Schwartz-Mette, 2010). A recent study found links between parenting and children's relational aggression (Kuppens & others, 2009). In this study, parents' psychological control (nonphysical attempts to control the child, such as guilt induction) was linked to a higher incidence of relational aggression in their children.

Relationship Communication   Are males and females so dramatically different that "men are from Mars" and "women are from Venus," as was proposed in a popular trade book (Gray, 1992)? Perhaps the gender differences that fascinate people most involve how males and females communicate with each other.

In relationship communication, sociolinguist Deborah Tannen (1990) distinguishes between rapport talk and report talk:

- **Rapport talk** is the language of conversation and a way of establishing connections and negotiating relationships. Girls enjoy rapport talk and conversation that is relationship oriented more than boys do.
- **Report talk** is talk that gives information. Public speaking is an example of report talk. Males hold center stage through report talk with verbal performances such as storytelling, joking, and lecturing with information.

Tannen says that boys and girls grow up in different worlds of talk—parents, siblings, peers, teachers, and others talk to boys and girls differently. The play of boys and girls is also different. Boys tend to play in large groups that are hierarchically structured, and their groups usually have a leader who tells the others what to do and how to do it. Boys' games have winners and losers and often are the subject of arguments. And boys often boast of their skill and argue about who is best at what. In contrast, girls are more likely to play in small groups or pairs, and at the center of a girl's world is often a best friend. In girls' friendships and peer groups, intimacy is pervasive. Turn-taking is more characteristic of girls' games than of boys' games. And much of the time, girls simply like to sit and talk with each other, concerned more about being liked by others than jockeying for status in some obvious way.

In sum, Tannen concludes that females are more relationship oriented than males—and that this relationship orientation should be prized as a skill in our culture more than it currently is. Note, however, that some researchers criticize Tannen's ideas as being overly simplified and suggest that communication between males and females is more complex than Tannen indicates (Edwards & Hamilton, 2004). Further, some researchers have found similarities in males' and females' relationship communication strategies (Hyde, 2007a, b). In one study, in their talk men and women described and responded to relationship problems in ways that were more similar than different (MacGeorge, 2004).

The need for further modification of Tannen's view is suggested by a recent *meta-analytic* review of gender differences in talkativeness (general communicative competence), affiliative speech (language used to establish or maintain connections with others, such as showing support or expanding on a person's prior remarks), and self-assertive speech (language used to influence others, such as directive statements or disagreements) (Leaper & Smith, 2004). This review confirms the criticism that Tannen overemphasizes the size of the gender differences in communication. Gender differences did occur, with girls slightly more talkative and engaging in more affiliative speech than boys, and boys being

What have researchers found about gender similarities and differences in children's and adolescents' talkativeness, affiliative speech, and self-assertive speech?

rapport talk The language of conversation and a way of establishing connections and negotiating relationships; more characteristic of females than of males.

report talk Talk that conveys information; more characteristic of males than females.

more likely to use self-assertive speech. But the gender differences were small. Perhaps the most important message from this review is that gender differences in communication often depended on the context. For example, the gender difference in talkativeness (girls being more competent in communicating) occurred more in large groups than in dyads. Age also was linked to gender communication. For example, the gender difference in affiliative speech was largest in adolescence, which may be due to adolescent girls' increased participation in socioemotional behavior traditionally prescribed for females.

What gender differences characterize children's prosocial behavior?

Emotion and Its Regulation   Are there gender differences in processing of emotions? Girls are more likely to express their emotions openly and intensely than are boys, especially in displaying sadness and fear (Blakemore, Berenbaum, & Liben, 2009). Girls also are better at reading others' emotions and more likely to show empathy than boys are (Blakemore, Berenbaum, & Liben, 2009). Males usually show less self-regulation of emotion than females, and this lower level of self-control can translate into behavioral problems (Eisenberg, Spinrad, & Smith, 2004).

Prosocial Behavior   Are there gender differences in prosocial behavior? Females view themselves as more prosocial and empathic than males (Eisenberg & others, 2009). Across childhood and adolescence, females engage in more prosocial behavior (Hastings, Utendale, & Sullivan, 2007). The biggest gender difference occurs for kind and considerate behavior, with a smaller difference in sharing.

Gender Controversy   Controversy continues about the extent of gender differences and what might cause them (Blakemore, Berenbaum, & Liben, 2009). As we saw earlier, evolutionary psychologists such as David Buss (2008) argue that gender differences are extensive and caused by the adaptive problems they have faced across their evolutionary history. Alice Eagly (2001, 2009) also concludes that gender differences are substantial, but she reaches a very different conclusion about their cause. She emphasizes that gender differences are due to social conditions that have resulted in women having less power and controlling fewer resources than men.

By contrast, Janet Shibley Hyde (2007b) concludes that gender differences have been greatly exaggerated, especially fueled by popular books such as John Gray's (1992) *Men Are from Mars, Women Are from Venus* and Deborah Tannen's (1990) *You Just Don't Understand.* She argues that the research indicates females and males are similar on most psychological factors. In a research review, Hyde (2005) summarized the results of 44 meta-analyses of gender differences and similarities. A *meta-analysis* is a statistical analysis that combines the results of many different studies. In most areas, gender differences either were nonexistent or small, including math ability and communication. Gender differences in physical aggression were moderate. The largest difference occurred on motor skills (favoring males), followed by sexuality (males masturbate more and are more likely to endorse sex in a casual, uncommitted relationship) and physical aggression (males are more physically aggressive than are females).

Hyde's summary of meta-analyses is still not likely to quiet the controversy about gender differences and similarities, but further research should continue to provide a basis for more accurate judgments about this controversy.

At this point, we have discussed many aspects of gender stereotypes, similarities, differences, and controversies in children's development. The following *Caring Connections* provides some recommendations for parents and teachers with regard to children's gender development.

> **developmental connection**
>
> **Moral Development.** Prosocial behavior involves behavior intended to benefit other people. Chapter 13, pp. 382–383

caring *connections*

Guiding Children's Gender Development

Boys

1. ***Encourage boys to be sensitive in relationships and engage in more prosocial behavior.*** An important socialization task is to help boys become more interested in having positive close relationships and become more caring. Fathers can play an especially important role for boys in this regard by being a model of a male who is sensitive and caring.
2. ***Encourage boys to be less physically aggressive.*** Too often, boys are encouraged to be tough and physically aggressive. A positive strategy is to encourage them to be self-assertive but not physically aggressive.
3. ***Encourage boys to handle their emotions more effectively.*** This involves helping boys not only to regulate their emotions, as in controlling their anger, but also to learn to express their anxieties and concerns rather than keeping them bottled up.
4. ***Work with boys to improve their school performance.*** Girls get better grades, put forth more academic effort, and are less likely than boys to be assigned to special/remedial classes. Parents and teachers can help boys by emphasizing the importance of school and expecting better academic effort.

Girls

1. ***Encourage girls to be proud of their relationship skills and caring.*** The strong interest that girls show in relationships and caring should be supported by parents and teachers.
2. ***Encourage girls to develop their self-competencies.*** While guiding girls to retain their relationship strengths, adults can help girls to develop their ambition and achievement.
3. ***Encourage girls to be more self-assertive.*** Girls tend to be more passive than boys and can benefit from being encouraged to be more self-assertive.
4. ***Encourage girls' achievement.*** This can involve encouraging girls to have higher academic expectations and exposing them to a wider range of career options.

Boys and Girls

1. ***Help children to reduce gender stereotyping and discrimination.*** Don't engage in gender stereotyping and discrimination yourself; otherwise, you will be providing a model of gender stereotyping and discrimination for children.

The second piece of advice for guiding boys' gender development is to encourage them to be less physically aggressive. In the beginning of the chapter, what did you learn about hormones and boys' aggression?

Review *Connect* Reflect

 LG3 Describe gender stereotypes, similarities, and differences.

Review

- What are gender stereotypes? How extensive is gender stereotyping?
- What are some gender similarities and differences in the areas of biological, cognitive, and socioemotional development?

Connect

- In this section, you learned about the ways in which parents may purposefully or unwittingly engage in the gender stereotyping of their children. In Chapter 10, you learned that parents have to deal with being gender stereotyped too. For instance, according to one study, what did some stay-at-home fathers report?

Reflect *Your Own Personal Journey of Life*

- How is your gender behavior and thinking similar to or different from your mother's and grandmothers' if you are a female? How is your gender behavior and thinking different from your father's and grandfathers' if you are a male?

Gender-Role Classification

LG4 Identify how gender roles can be classified.

- What Is Gender-Role Classification?
- Masculinity in Childhood and Adolescence
- Gender Role Transcendence
- Gender in Context

Not long ago, it was accepted that boys should grow up to be masculine and girls to be feminine, that boys are made of "snips and snails and puppy dogs' tails" and girls are made of "sugar and spice and everything nice." Let's further explore gender classifications of boys and girls as "masculine" and "feminine."

WHAT IS GENDER-ROLE CLASSIFICATION?

In the past, a well-adjusted boy was expected to be independent, aggressive, and powerful. A well-adjusted girl was expected to be dependent, non-aggressive, and uninterested in power. The masculine characteristics were valued more highly by society than the feminine ones.

In the 1970s, as both females and males became dissatisfied with the burdens imposed by their stereotypic roles, alternatives to femininity and masculinity were proposed. Instead of describing masculinity and femininity as a continuum in which more of one means less of the other, it was proposed that individuals could have both masculine and feminine traits. This thinking led to the development of the concept of **androgyny,** the presence of masculine and feminine characteristics in the same person (Bem, 1977; Spence & Helmreich, 1978). The androgynous boy might be assertive (masculine) and nurturant (feminine). The androgynous girl might be powerful (masculine) and sensitive to others' feelings (feminine). In one study, it was confirmed that societal changes are encouraging females to be more assertive (Spence & Buckner, 2000).

Measures have been developed to assess androgyny. One of the most widely used measures is the Bem Sex-Role Inventory. To find out whether your gender-role classification is masculine, feminine, or androgynous, see Figure 12.6.

Gender experts such as Sandra Bem argue that androgynous individuals are more flexible, competent, and mentally healthy than their masculine or feminine counterparts. To some degree, though, deciding which gender-role classification is best depends on the context involved (Woodhill & Samuels, 2004). For example, in close relationships, feminine and androgynous orientations might be more desirable because of the expressive nature of such relationships. However, masculine and androgynous orientations might be more desirable in traditional academic and work settings because of the achievement demands in these contexts. For example, one study found that masculine and androgynous individuals had higher expectations for being able to control the outcomes of their academic efforts than feminine or undifferentiated (neither masculine nor feminine) individuals (Choi, 2004).

MASCULINITY IN CHILDHOOD AND ADOLESCENCE

Concern about the ways boys traditionally have been brought up to behave has been called a "national crisis of boyhood" by William Pollack (1999) in his book *Real Boys.* Pollack says that although there has been considerable talk about the "sensitive male," little has been done to change what he calls the "boy code." He says that this code tells boys they should show little if any emotion as they are growing up. Too often boys are socialized to not show their feelings and to act

Examples of masculine items

- Defends open beliefs
- Forceful
- Willing to take risks
- Dominant
- Aggressive

Examples of feminine items

- Does not use harsh language
- Affectionate
- Loves children
- Understanding
- Gentle

Scoring: The items are scored on independent dimensions of masculinity and femininity as well as androgyny and undifferentiate classifications.

FIGURE **12.6**

THE BEM SEX-ROLE INVENTORY. These items are from the Bem Sex-Role Inventory (BSRI). When taking the BSRI, an individual is asked to indicate on a 7-point scale how well each of the 60 characteristics describes herself or himself. The scale ranges from 1 (never or almost never true) to 7 (always or almost always true). The items are scored on independent dimensions of masculinity and femininity. Individuals who score high on the masculine items and low on the feminine items are categorized as masculine; those who score high on the feminine items and low on the masculine items are categorized as feminine; and those who score high on both the masculine and feminine items are categorized as androgynous.

androgyny The presence of masculine and feminine characteristics in the same person.

tough, says Pollack. Boys learn the boy code in many different contexts—sandboxes, playgrounds, schoolrooms, camps, hangouts—and are taught the code by parents, peers, coaches, teachers, and other adults. Pollack, as well as many others, argues that boys would benefit from being socialized to express their anxieties and concerns rather than keep them bottled up, as well as being guided in how to better regulate their aggression.

There also is a special concern about boys who adopt a strong masculine role in adolescence, because this is associated with problem behaviors. Joseph Pleck (1995) points out that what defines traditional masculinity in many Western cultures includes behaviors that do not have social approval but nonetheless validate the adolescent boy's masculinity. In the male adolescent culture, male adolescents perceive that they will be thought of as more masculine if they engage in premarital sex, drink alcohol, take drugs, and participate in illegal delinquent activities.

GENDER-ROLE TRANSCENDENCE

Some critics of androgyny say that there has been too much talk about gender and that androgyny is less of a panacea than originally envisioned. An alternative is *gender-role transcendence*, the view that when an individual's competence is at issue, it should be conceptualized on a personal basis rather than on the basis of masculinity, femininity, or androgyny (Pleck, 1983). That is, we should think about ourselves as people first, not as being masculine, feminine, or androgynous. Parents should rear their children to be competent boys and girls, not masculine, feminine, or androgynous, say the gender-role critics. They stress that such gender-role classification leads to too much stereotyping.

GENDER IN CONTEXT

The concept of gender-role classification involves categorization of a person in terms of personality traits. However, it may be helpful to think of personality in terms of person-situation interaction rather than traits alone. Thus, in our discussion of gender-role classification, we described how some gender roles might be more appropriate than others, depending on the context, or setting, involved.

To see the importance of considering gender in context, let's examine helping behavior and emotion. The stereotype is that females are better than males at helping. However, the difference depends on the situation. Females are more likely than males to volunteer their time to help children with personal problems and to engage in caregiving behavior (Taylor, 2002). However, in situations in which males feel a sense of competence, especially circumstances that involve danger, males are more likely than females to help (Eagly & Crowley, 1986). For example, a male is more likely than a female to stop and help a person who is stranded by the roadside with a flat tire.

"She is emotional; he is not"—that is the master emotional stereotype. However, like differences in helping behavior, emotional differences in males and females depend on the particular emotion involved and the context in which it is displayed (Shields, 1998). Males are more likely to show anger toward strangers, especially male strangers, when they feel they have been challenged. Males also are more likely to turn their anger into aggressive action. Emotional differences between females and males often show up in contexts that highlight social roles and relationships. For example, females are more likely than males to discuss emotions in terms of relationships, and they are more likely to express fear and sadness.

The importance of considering gender in context is nowhere more apparent than when examining what is culturally prescribed behavior for females and males in various countries around the world (Best, 2010; Lamb & Bougher, 2009; Shiraev & Levy, 2010). To read further about cross-cultural variations in gender, see *Connecting With Diversity*.

developmental **connection**

Theories. Bronfenbrenner's ecological theory emphasizes the importance of contexts; in his theory, the macrosystem includes cross-cultural comparisons. Chapter 1, p. 29

Gender Roles Across Cultures

In recent decades, roles assumed by males and females in the United States have become increasingly similar—that is, more androgynous. In many countries, though, gender roles have remained more gender-specific (UNICEF, 2010). For example, in a number of Middle Eastern countries, the division of labor between males and females is dramatic: males are socialized to work in the public sphere, females in the private world of home and child rearing; a man's duty is to provide for his family, the woman's to care for her family and household. Any deviations from this traditional gender-role orientation receive severe disapproval.

Access to education for girls has improved somewhat around the world, but girls' education still lags behind boys' education. For example, according to a UNICEF (2003) analysis of education around the world, by age 18, girls have received, on average, 4.4 years less education than boys have. This lack of education reduces their chances of developing their potential. Noticeable exceptions to lower participation and completion rates in education for girls occur in Western nations, Japan, and the Philippines (Brown & Larson, 2002). In most countries, more men than women gain advanced training or advanced degrees (Fussell & Greene, 2002).

Although most countries still have gender gaps that favor males, evidence of increasing gender equality is appearing (Brown & Larson,

Although access to education for girls has improved, boys still receive approximately 4.4 years more education around the world than girls do. Shown here is a private school for boys in Africa.

2002). For example, among upper-socioeconomic-status families in India and Japan, fathers are assuming more child-rearing responsibilities (Stevenson & Zusho, 2002; Verma & Saraswathi, 2002). Rates of employment and career opportunities for women are expanding in many countries. Control over adolescent girls' social relationships, especially sexual and romantic relationships, is decreasing in some countries.

Cultural and ethnic backgrounds also influence how boys and girls are socialized in the United States (Chuang & Tamis-LeMonda, 2009; Pinto & Coltrane, 2009; Updegraff, Delgado, & Wheeler, 2009). One study revealed that Latino and Latina adolescents were socialized differently as they were growing up (Raffaelli & Ontai, 2004). Latinas experienced far greater restrictions than Latinos in curfews, interacting with members of the other sex, getting a driver's license, getting a job, and participating in after-school activities.

The last study mentioned above focused on adolescents. In Chapter 4, what did you learn about differences in adolescent girls' perceptions of their bodies?

Review *Connect* Reflect

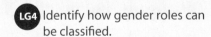 Identify how gender roles can be classified.

Review

- What is gender-role classification?
- What are some risks of masculinity in childhood and adolescence?
- What is gender-role transcendence?
- How can gender be conceptualized in terms of context?

Connect

- In this section, you learned about risks related to masculinity in childhood and

adolescence. How might early or late maturation (discussed in Chapter 4) affect these risks?

Reflect *Your Own personal Journey of Life*

- If and when you have a child, how sensitive will you likely be in rearing the child to be masculine, feminine, or androgynous? Explain.

Gender

What Is Gender?

 Summarize what gender involves.

- Gender refers to the characteristics of people as males and females. Among the components of gender are gender identity, gender roles, and gender stereotyping. Recent research indicates that knowing whether you are a boy or a girl emerges by 2 years of age.

Influences on Gender Development

 Discuss the main biological, social, and cognitive influences on gender.

Biological Influences

- The 23rd pair of chromosomes determines our sex. Ordinarily, females have two X chromosomes, and males have one X and one Y. Males and females also produce different concentrations of the hormones known as androgens and estrogens. Early hormonal production is linked with later gender development. In the evolutionary psychology view, evolutionary adaptations produced psychological sex differences that are especially present in sexual behavior and mating strategies. Chromosomes determine anatomical sex differences, but culture and society strongly influence gender.

Social Influences

- In social role theory, gender differences result from men's and women's contrasting roles; in most cultures, women have less power and status than men and control fewer resources. This gender hierarchy and sexual division of labor are important causes of sex-differentiated behavior. Psychoanalytic theory of gender emphasizes sexual attraction to the same-sex parent, anxiety about this attraction, and subsequent adoption of the same-sex parent's gender characteristics. Social cognitive theory emphasizes rewards and punishments for gender-appropriate and gender-inappropriate behavior. Parents and other adults also might assign gender roles to children and reward or punish behavior along gender lines. Peers are especially adept at rewarding gender-appropriate behavior.

Cognitive Influences

- Gender schema theories emphasize the role of cognition in gender development. In gender schema theory, gender typing emerges gradually as children develop gender schemas of what their culture considers to be gender-appropriate and gender-inappropriate.

Gender Stereotypes, Similarities, and Differences

 Describe gender stereotypes, similarities, and differences.

Gender Stereotyping

- Gender stereotypes are general impressions and beliefs about males and females. Gender stereotypes are widespread. Gender stereotyping changes developmentally; it is present even at 2 years of age but increases considerably in early childhood. In middle and late childhood, children become more flexible in their gender attitudes, but gender stereotyping may increase again in early adolescence. By late adolescence, gender attitudes are often more flexible.

Gender Similarities and Differences

- Physical and biological differences between males and females are substantial. Women have about twice the body fat of men, are less likely to develop physical or mental disorders, and have a longer life expectancy. Boys and girls show similar achievement in math, although boys have slightly better visuospatial skills. Girls perform better in writing and reading. Some experts, such as Hyde, argue that cognitive differences between males and females have been exaggerated. Males are more physically aggressive than females, while females are more likely to show stronger affiliative interests in adolescence, express their emotions openly and intensely, have better emotional control, and engage in more prosocial behavior. There is considerable controversy about how similar or different females and males are in a number of areas.

Gender-Role Classification

 Identify how gender roles can be classified.

What Is Gender-Role Classification?

Masculinity in Childhood and Adolescence

Gender-Role Transcendence

Gender in Context

- In the past, the well-adjusted male was supposed to show masculine traits; the well-adjusted female, feminine traits. During the 1970s, alternatives to traditional gender roles were introduced. It was proposed that competent individuals could show both masculine and feminine traits. This thinking led to the development of the concept of androgyny, the presence of masculine and feminine traits in one individual. Gender-role measures often categorize individuals as masculine, feminine, androgynous, or undifferentiated. Most androgynous individuals are flexible and mentally healthy, although the particular context and the individual's culture also determine the adaptiveness of a gender-role orientation.

- A special concern is that boys raised in a traditional manner are socialized to conceal their emotions. Researchers have found that problem behaviors often characterize highly masculine adolescents.

- One alternative to androgyny is gender-role transcendence, a theory which states that there has been too much emphasis on gender and that a better strategy is to think about competence in terms of people rather than gender.

- In thinking about gender, it is important to keep in mind the context in which gender behavior is displayed. In many countries, traditional gender roles remain dominant.

key terms

gender 346
gender identity 346
gender role 346
gender typing 346
estrogens 347

androgens 347
social role theory 348
psychoanalytic theory of gender 349

social cognitive theory of gender 349
gender schema theory 350
gender stereotypes 352

rapport talk 356
report talk 356
androgyny 359

key people

Alice Eagly 348
Sigmund Freud 349
Phyllis Bronstein 350

Eleanor Maccoby 350
Janet Shibley Hyde 355
Deborah Tannen 356

David Buss 357
Sandra Bem 359

William Pollack 359
Joseph Pleck 360

chapter 13 MORAL DEVELOPMENT

The mayor of the city says that this young woman is "everywhere." She recently persuaded the city's school committee to consider ending the practice of locking tardy students out of their classrooms. She also swayed a neighborhood group to support her proposal for a winter jobs program. According to one city councilman, "People are just impressed with the power of her arguments and the sophistication of the argument" (Silva, 2005, pp. B1, B4). She is Jewel E. Cash, and she is just 16 years old.

A junior at Boston Latin Academy, Jewel was raised in one of Boston's housing projects by her mother, a single parent. Today she belongs to the Boston Student Advisory Council, mentors children, volunteers at a women's shelter, manages and dances in two troupes, and volunteers with a neighborhood watch group—among other activities. Jewel told an interviewer from the *Boston Globe,* "I see a problem and I say, 'How can I make a difference?' . . . I can't take on the world, even though I can try. . . . I'm moving forward but I want to make sure I'm bringing people with me" (Silva, 2005, pp. B1, B4). Jewel is far from typical, but her motivation to help others illustrates the positive side of moral development.

Jewel Cash, seated next to her mother, participating in a crime-watch meeting at a community center. She is an exemplar of positive teenage community involvement.

preview

Most people have strong opinions not only about moral and immoral behavior but also about how moral behavior should be fostered in children. We will begin our coverage of moral development by exploring its main domains and then examine some important contexts that influence moral development. Next, we discuss children's prosocial and antisocial behavior. The chapter concludes with an overview of children's religious and spiritual development.

Domains of Moral Development **LG1** Discuss theory and research on the domains of moral development.

| What Is Moral Development? | Moral Thought | Moral Behavior | Moral Feeling | Moral Personality |

What is moral development? What are its main domains?

WHAT IS MORAL DEVELOPMENT?

Moral development involves changes in thoughts, feelings, and behaviors regarding standards of right and wrong. Moral development has an *intrapersonal* dimension, which regulates a person's activities when she or he is not engaged in social interaction, and an *interpersonal* dimension, which regulates social interactions and arbitrates conflict (Walker, 2006). To understand moral development, we need to consider four basic questions:

> First, how do individuals *reason* or *think* about moral decisions?
> Second, how do individuals actually *behave* in moral circumstances?
> Third, how do individuals *feel* about moral matters?
> Fourth, what characterizes an individual's moral *personality*?

As we consider these four domains in the following sections, keep in mind that thoughts, behaviors, feelings, and personality often are interrelated. For example, if the focus is on an individual's behavior, it is still important to evaluate the person's reasoning. Also, emotions can distort moral reasoning. And moral personality encompasses thoughts, behavior, and feelings.

> It is one of
> the beautiful
> compensations of
> this life that no one
> can sincerely try to
> help another without
> helping himself.
>
> —**CHARLES DUDLEY WARNER**
> *American Essayist, 19th Century*

MORAL THOUGHT

How do individuals think about what is right and wrong? Are children able to evaluate moral questions in the same way that adults can? Piaget had some answers to these questions. So did Lawrence Kohlberg.

Piaget's Theory Interest in how children think about moral issues was stimulated by Piaget (1932), who extensively observed and interviewed children from the ages of 4 through 12. Piaget watched children play marbles to learn how they used and thought about the game's rules. He also asked children about ethical issues—theft, lies, punishment, and justice, for example. Piaget concluded that children go through two distinct stages, separated by a transition period, in how they think about morality.

- From 4 to 7 years of age, children display **heteronomous morality,** the first stage of moral development in Piaget's theory. Children think of justice and rules as unchangeable properties of the world, removed from the control of people.

- From 7 to 10 years of age, children are in a transition showing some features of the first stage of moral reasoning and some stages of the second stage, autonomous morality.

---

developmental connection

Cognitive Theory. In which of Piaget's cognitive stages is a 5-year-old heteronomous thinker likely to be? Chapter 6, p. 182

---

moral development Changes in thoughts, feelings, and behaviors regarding standards of right and wrong.

heteronomous morality The first stage of moral development in Piaget's theory, occurring from 4 to 7 years of age. Justice and rules are conceived of as unchangeable properties of the world, removed from the control of people.

- From about 10 years of age and older, children show **autonomous morality,** Piaget's second stage of moral development. They become aware that rules and laws are created by people, and in judging an action, they consider the actor's intentions as well as the consequences.

Because young children are heteronomous moralists, they judge the rightness or goodness of behavior by considering its consequences, not the intentions of the actor. For example, to the heteronomous moralist, breaking twelve cups accidentally is worse than breaking one cup intentionally. As children develop into moral autonomists, intentions assume paramount importance.

The heteronomous thinker also believes that rules are unchangeable and are handed down by all-powerful authorities. When Piaget suggested to young children that they use new rules in a game of marbles, they resisted. By contrast, older children—moral autonomists—accept change and recognize that rules are merely convenient conventions, subject to change.

The heteronomous thinker also believes in **immanent justice,** the concept that if a rule is broken, punishment will be meted out immediately. The young child believes that a violation is connected automatically to its punishment. Thus, young children often look around worriedly after doing something wrong, expecting inevitable punishment. Immanent justice also implies that if something unfortunate happens to someone, the person must have transgressed earlier. Older children, who are moral autonomists, recognize that punishment occurs only if someone witnesses the wrongdoing and that, even then, punishment is not inevitable. They also realize that bad things can happen to innocent people.

How do these changes in moral reasoning occur? Piaget argued that, as children develop, they become more sophisticated in thinking about social matters, especially about the possibilities and conditions of cooperation. Piaget reasoned that this social understanding comes about through the mutual give-and-take of peer relations. In the peer group, where others have power and status similar to the child's, plans are negotiated and coordinated, and disagreements are reasoned about and eventually settled. Parent-child relations, in which parents have the power and children do not, are less likely to advance moral reasoning, because rules are often handed down in an authoritarian way.

Kohlberg's Theory A second major perspective on moral development was proposed by Lawrence Kohlberg (1958, 1986). Piaget's cognitive stages of development serve as the underpinnings for Kohlberg's theory, but Kohlberg suggested that there are six stages of moral development. These stages, he argued, are universal. Development from one stage to another, said Kohlberg, is fostered by opportunities to take the perspective of others and to experience conflict between one's current stage of moral thinking and the reasoning of someone at a higher stage.

Kohlberg arrived at his view after 20 years of using a unique interview with children. In the interview, children are presented with a series of stories in which characters face moral dilemmas. The following is the most popular Kohlberg dilemma:

> In Europe a woman was near death from a special kind of cancer. There was one drug that the doctors thought might save her. It was a form of radium that a druggist in the same town had recently discovered. The drug was expensive to make, but the druggist was charging ten times what the drug cost him to make. He paid $200 for the radium and charged $2,000 for a small dose of the drug. The sick woman's husband, Heinz, went to everyone he knew to borrow the money, but he could only get together $1,000, which is half of what it cost. He told the druggist that his wife was dying and asked him to sell it cheaper or let him pay later. But the druggist said, "No, I discovered the drug, and I am going to make money from it." So Heinz got desperate and broke into the man's store to steal the drug for his wife. (Kohlberg, 1969, p. 379)

This story is one of 11 that Kohlberg devised to investigate the nature of moral thought. After reading the story, the interviewee answers a series of questions about the moral dilemma. Should Heinz have stolen the drug? Was stealing it right or

How is this child's moral thinking likely to be different about stealing a cookie depending on whether he is in Piaget's heteronomous or autonomous stage?

Lawrence Kohlberg.

autonomous morality The second stage of moral development in Piaget's theory, displayed by older children (about 10 years of age and older). The child becomes aware that rules and laws are created by people and that, in judging an action, one should consider the actor's intentions as well as the consequences.

immanent justice Piaget's concept of the childhood expectation that if a rule is broken, punishment will be meted out immediately.

LEVEL 1	LEVEL 2	LEVEL 3
Preconventional Level	**Conventional Level**	**Postconventional Level**
Stage 1 Punishment and Obedience Orientation *Children obey because adults tell them to obey. People base their moral decisions on fear of punishment.*	**Stage 3** Mutual Interpersonal Expectations, Relationships, and Interpersonal Conformity *Individuals value trust, caring, and loyalty to others as a basis for moral judgments.*	**Stage 5** Social Contract or Utility and Individual Rights *Individuals reason that values, rights, and principles undergird or transcend the law.*
Stage 2 Individualism, Purpose, and Exchange *Individuals pursue their own interests but let others do the same. What is right involves equal exchange.*	**Stage 4** Social System Morality *Moral judgments are based on understanding and the social order, law, justice, and duty.*	**Stage 6** Universal Ethical Principles *The person has developed moral judgments that are based on universal human rights. When faced with a dilemma between law and conscience, a personal, individualized conscience is followed.*

FIGURE **13.1**
KOHLBERG'S THREE LEVELS AND SIX STAGES OF MORAL DEVELOPMENT

wrong? Why? Is it a husband's duty to steal the drug for his wife if he can get it no other way? Would a good husband steal? Did the druggist have the right to charge that much when there was no law setting a limit on the price? Why or why not?

The Kohlberg Stages   Based on the answers interviewees gave for this and other moral dilemmas, Kohlberg described three levels of moral thinking, each of which is characterized by two stages (see Figure 13.1). A key concept in understanding progression through the levels and stages is that the person's morality gradually becomes more internal or mature. That is, their reasons for moral decisions or values begin to go beyond the external or superficial reasons they gave when they were younger. Let's further examine Kohlberg's stages.

Kohlberg's Level 1: Preconventional Reasoning   **Preconventional reasoning** is the lowest level of reasoning in Kohlberg's theory and consists of two stages: punishment and obedience orientation (stage 1) and individualism, instrumental purpose, and exchange (stage 2).

- Stage 1. *Punishment and obedience orientation* is the first Kohlberg stage of moral development. At this stage, moral thinking is often tied to punishment. For example, children and adolescents obey adults because adults tell them to obey.
- Stage 2. *Individualism, instrumental purpose, and exchange* is the second stage of Kohlberg's theory. At this stage, individuals pursue their own interests but also let others do the same. Thus, what is right involves an equal exchange. People are nice to others so that others will be nice to them in return.

Kohlberg's Level 2: Conventional Reasoning   **Conventional reasoning** is the second, or intermediate, level in Kohlberg's theory of moral development. Individuals abide by certain standards (internal), but they are the standards of others (external), such as parents or the laws of society. The conventional reasoning level consists of two stages: mutual interpersonal expectations, relationships, and interpersonal conformity (stage 3) and social systems morality (stage 4).

- Stage 3. *Mutual interpersonal expectations, relationships, and interpersonal conformity* is Kohlberg's third stage of moral development. At this stage, individuals value trust, caring, and loyalty to others as a basis of moral judgments. Children and adolescents often adopt their parents' moral standards at this stage, seeking to be thought of by their parents as a "good girl" or a "good boy."
- Stage 4. *Social systems morality* is the fourth stage in Kohlberg's theory of moral development. At this stage, moral judgments are based on understanding the

preconventional reasoning The lowest level in Kohlberg's theory. At this level, morality is often focused on reward and punishment. The two stages in preconventional reasoning are punishment and obedience orientation (stage 1) and individualism, instrumental purpose, and exchange (stage 2).

conventional reasoning The second, or intermediate, level in Kohlberg's theory of moral development. At this level, individuals abide by certain standards (internal), but they are the standards of others such as parents or the laws of society (external). The conventional level consists of two stages: mutual interpersonal expectations, relationships, and interpersonal conformity (stage 3) and social systems morality (stage 4).

social order, law, justice, and duty. For example, adolescents may say that, for a community to work effectively, it needs to be protected by laws that are adhered to by its members.

Kohlberg's Level 3: Postconventional Reasoning

Postconventional reasoning is the third and highest level in Kohlberg's theory. At this level, morality is more internal. The postconventional level of morality consists of two stages: social contract or utility and individual rights (stage 5) and universal ethical principles (stage 6).

- Stage 5. *Social contract or utility and individual rights* is the fifth Kohlberg stage. At this stage, individuals reason that values, rights, and principles undergird or transcend the law. A person evaluates the validity of actual laws and examines social systems in terms of the degree to which they preserve and protect fundamental human rights and values.

- Stage 6. *Universal ethical principles* is the sixth and highest stage in Kohlberg's theory of moral development. At this stage, the person has developed a moral standard based on universal human rights. When faced with a conflict between law and conscience, the person will follow conscience, even though the decision might involve personal risk.

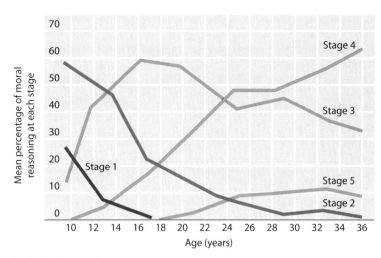

FIGURE **13.2**

AGE AND THE PERCENTAGE OF INDIVIDUALS AT EACH KOHLBERG STAGE. In one longitudinal study of males from 10 to 36 years of age, at age 10 most moral reasoning was at stage 2 (Colby & others, 1983). At 16 to 18 years of age, stage 3 became the most frequent type of moral reasoning, and it was not until the mid-twenties that stage 4 became the most frequent. Stage 5 did not appear until 20 to 22 years of age and it never characterized more than 10 percent of the individuals. In this study, the moral stages appeared somewhat later than Kohlberg envisioned, and stage 6 was absent.

Kohlberg observed that these levels and stages occur in a sequence and are age related: Before age 9, most children use stage 1, preconventional reasoning based on external rewards and punishments, when they consider moral choices. By early adolescence, their moral reasoning is increasingly based on the application of standards set by others. Most adolescents reason at stage 3, with some signs of stages 2 and 4. By early adulthood, a small number of individuals reason in postconventional ways.

What evidence supports this model of moral development? A 20-year longitudinal investigation found that use of stages 1 and 2 decreased with age (Colby & others, 1983) (see Figure 13.2). Stage 4, which did not appear at all in the moral reasoning of 10-year-olds, was reflected in the moral thinking of 62 percent of the 36-year-olds. Stage 5 did not appear until age 20 to 22 and never characterized more than 10 percent of the individuals.

Thus, the moral stages appeared somewhat later than Kohlberg initially envisioned, and reasoning at the higher stages, especially stage 6, was rare. Although stage 6 has been removed from the Kohlberg moral judgment scoring manual, it still is considered to be theoretically important in the Kohlberg scheme of moral development.

Why did Piaget and Kohlberg think peer relations are so important in moral development?

Influences on the Kohlberg Stages

What factors influence movement through Kohlberg's stages? Although moral reasoning at each stage presupposes a certain level of cognitive development, Kohlberg argued that advances in children's cognitive development did not ensure development of moral reasoning. Instead, moral reasoning also reflects children's experiences in dealing with moral questions and moral conflict.

Several investigators have tried to advance individuals' levels of moral development by having a person present arguments that reflect moral thinking one stage above

postconventional reasoning The third and highest level in Kohlberg's theory of moral development. At this level, morality is more internal. The postconventional level consists of two stages: social contract or utility and individual rights (stage 5) and universal ethical principles (stage 6).

the individuals' established levels. This approach applies the concepts of equilibrium and conflict that Piaget used to explain cognitive development. By presenting arguments slightly beyond the children's level of moral reasoning, the researchers created a disequilibrium that motivated the children to restructure their moral thought. The upshot of studies using this approach is that virtually any plus-stage discussion, for any length of time, seems to promote more advanced moral reasoning (Walker, 1982).

Kohlberg emphasized that peer interaction and perspective taking are critical aspects of the social stimulation that challenges children to change their moral reasoning. Whereas adults characteristically impose rules and regulations on children, the give-and-take among peers gives children an opportunity to take the perspective of another person and to generate rules democratically. Kohlberg stressed that in principle, encounters with any peers can produce perspective-taking opportunities that may advance a child's moral reasoning. A recent research review of cross-cultural studies involving Kohlberg's theory revealed strong support for a link between perspective-taking skills and more advanced moral judgments (Gibbs & others, 2007).

Kohlberg's Critics   Kohlberg's theory has provoked debate, research, and criticism (Gibbs, 2010; Narvaez & Lapsley, 2009). First, let's examine the extent of the link between moral thought and moral behavior.

Moral Thought and Moral Behavior   Kohlberg's theory has been criticized for placing too much emphasis on moral thought and not enough emphasis on moral behavior (Walker, 2004). Moral reasons can sometimes be a shelter for immoral behavior. Corrupt CEOs and politicians endorse the loftiest of moral virtues in public until their own behavior is exposed. Whatever the latest public scandal, you will probably find that the culprits displayed virtuous thoughts but engaged in immoral behavior. No one wants a nation of cheaters and thieves who can reason at the postconventional level. The cheaters and thieves may know what is right yet still do what is wrong. Heinous actions can be cloaked in a mantle of moral virtue.

Culture and Moral Reasoning   Kohlberg emphasized that his stages of moral reasoning are universal, but some critics claim his theory is culturally biased (Miller, 2007). Both Kohlberg and his critics may be partially correct.

One review of 45 studies in 27 cultures around the world, mostly non-European, provided support for the universality of Kohlberg's first four stages (Snarey, 1987). Individuals in diverse cultures developed through these four stages in sequence as Kohlberg predicted. A more recent research study revealed support for the qualitative shift from stage 2 to stage 3 across cultures (Gibbs & others, 2007).

Stages 5 and 6, however, have not been found in all cultures (Gibbs & others, 2007; Snarey, 1987). Furthermore, Kohlberg's scoring system does not recognize the higher-level moral reasoning of certain cultures—thus, moral reasoning is more culture-specific than Kohlberg envisioned (Snarey, 1987).

In particular, researchers have heard moral judgments based on the principles of communal equity and collective happiness in Israel, the unity and sacredness of all life forms in India, and collective moral responsibility in New Guinea (Snarey, 1987). These examples of moral reasoning would not be scored at the highest level in Kohlberg's system because they are not based on principles of justice. Similar results occurred in a study that assessed the moral development of 20 adolescent male Buddhist monks in Nepal (Huebner & Garrod, 1993). Justice, a basic theme in Kohlberg's theory, was not of paramount importance in the monks' moral views, and their concerns about the prevention of suffering and the role of compassion are not captured by Kohlberg's theory.

In the view of John Gibbs (2010), most young adolescents around the world use the moral judgment of mutuality (stage 3) that makes intimate friendships possible. And by late adolescence, many individuals

developmental **connection**

Research Methods. Cross-cultural studies provide information about the degree to which children's development is universal, or similar, across cultures or is culture-specific. Chapter 17, p. 486

This 14-year-old boy in Nepal is thought to be the sixth holiest Buddhist in the world. In one study of 20 adolescent male Buddhist monks in Nepal, the issue of justice, a basic theme in Kohlberg's theory, was not a central focus in the monks' moral views (Huebner & Garrad, 1993). Also, the monks' concerns about prevention of suffering and the importance of compassion are not captured in Kohlberg's theory.

Moral Reasoning in the United States and India

Cultural meaning systems vary around the world, and these systems shape children's morality (Gibbs, 2010; Shiraev & Levy, 2010). Consider a comparison of American and Indian Hindu Brahman children (Shweder, Mahapatra, & Miller, 1987). Like people in many other non-Western societies, Indians view moral rules as part of the natural world order. This means that Indians do not distinguish between physical, moral, and social regulation, as Americans do. For example, in India, violations of food taboos and marital restrictions can be just as serious as acts intended to cause harm to others. In India, social rules are seen as inevitable, much like the law of gravity.

According to William Damon (1988), in places where culturally specific practices take on profound moral and religious significance, as in India, the moral development of children focuses extensively on their adherence to custom and convention. In contrast, Western moral doctrine tends to elevate abstract principles, such as justice and welfare, to a higher moral status than customs or conventions. As in India, socialization practices in many Third World countries actively instill in children a great respect for their culture's traditional codes and practices.

How would you revise Kohlberg's stages of moral development to better accommodate other cultures? Or can you?

How might Asian Indian children and American children reason differently about moral issues?

---

also are beginning to grasp the importance of agreed-upon standards and institutions for the common good (stage 4). A main exception, though, is the delayed moral judgment of adolescents who regularly engage in delinquency.

In sum, although Kohlberg's approach does capture much of the moral reasoning voiced in various cultures around the world, his approach misses or misconstrues some important moral concepts in particular cultures (Gibbs, 2010). To read further about cultural variations in moral reasoning, see *Connecting With Diversity*.

Families and Moral Development   Kohlberg argued that family processes are essentially unimportant in children's moral development. As noted earlier, he argued that parent-child relationships usually provide children with little opportunity for give-and-take or perspective taking. Rather, Kohlberg said that such opportunities are more likely to be provided by children's peer relations.

Did Kohlberg underestimate the contribution of family relationships to moral development? A number of developmentalists stress that parents' moral values influence children's developing moral thoughts (Gibbs, 2010). Nonetheless, most developmentalists agree with Kohlberg, and Piaget, that peers play an important role in the development of moral reasoning.

Gender and the Care Perspective   The most publicized criticism of Kohlberg's theory has come from Carol Gilligan (1982, 1992, 1996), who argues that Kohlberg's theory reflects a gender bias. According to Gilligan, Kohlberg's theory is based on a male norm that puts abstract principles above relationships and concern for others and

Carol Gilligan. *What is Gilligan's view of moral development?*

developmental **connection**

Gender. Janet Shibley Hyde concluded that many views and studies of gender exaggerate differences. Chapter 12, p. 357

sees the individual as standing alone and independently making moral decisions. It puts justice at the heart of morality. In contrast to Kohlberg's **justice perspective,** which focuses on the rights of the individual, Gilligan argues for a **care perspective,** a moral perspective that views people in terms of their connectedness with others and emphasizes interpersonal communication, relationships with others, and concern for others. According to Gilligan, Kohlberg greatly underplayed the care perspective, perhaps because he was a male, because most of his research was with males rather than females, and because he used male responses as a model for his theory.

A meta-analysis (a statistical analysis that combines the results of many different studies) casts doubt on Gilligan's claim of substantial gender differences in moral judgment (Jaffee & Hyde, 2000). In this study, overall, only a small sex difference in care-based reasoning favored females, but this sex difference was greater in adolescence than childhood. When differences occurred, they were better explained by the nature of the dilemma than by gender (for example, both males and females tended to use care-based reasoning to deal with interpersonal dilemmas and justice reasoning to handle societal dilemmas). In sum, experts now conclude that there is no evidence to support Gilligan's claim that Kohlberg downplayed females' moral thinking (Hyde, 2007; Walker, 2006).

Social Conventional Reasoning Some theorists and researchers argue that Kohlberg did not adequately distinguish between moral reasoning and social conventional reasoning (Smetana, 2006; Turiel, 2006). **Social conventional reasoning** focuses on conventional rules that have been established by social consensus in order to control behavior and maintain the social system. The rules themselves are arbitrary, such as using a fork at meals and raising your hand in class before speaking.

In contrast, moral reasoning focuses on ethical issues and rules of morality. Unlike conventional rules, moral rules are not arbitrary. They are obligatory, widely accepted, and somewhat impersonal (Turiel, 2006). Rules pertaining to lying, cheating, stealing, and physically harming another person are moral rules because violation of these rules affronts ethical standards that exist apart from social consensus and convention. Moral judgments involve concepts of justice, whereas social conventional judgments are concepts of social organization.

Recently, a distinction also has been made between moral and conventional issues, which are viewed as legitimately subject to adult social regulation, and personal issues, which are more likely subject to the child's or adolescent's independent decision making and personal discretion (Lagattuta, Nucci, & Bosacki, 2010; Smetana, 2006). Personal issues include control over one's body, privacy, and choice of friends and activities. Thus, some actions belong to a *personal* domain, not governed by moral strictures or social norms.

How does social conventional reasoning differ from moral reasoning? What are some examples of social conventional reasoning?

MORAL BEHAVIOR

What are the basic processes responsible for moral behavior? What is the nature of self-control and resistance to temptation? How does social cognitive theory view moral development?

Basic Processes The processes of reinforcement, punishment, and imitation have been invoked to explain how individuals learn certain responses and why their responses differ from one another (Grusec, 2006). When individuals are reinforced for behavior that is consistent with laws and social conventions, they are likely to repeat that behavior. When provided with models who behave morally, individuals are likely to adopt their actions. Finally, when individuals are punished for immoral behaviors, those behaviors can be eliminated, but at the expense of sanctioning punishment by its very use and of causing emotional side effects for the individual.

justice perspective A moral perspective that focuses on the rights of the individual; individuals independently make moral decisions.

care perspective The moral perspective of Carol Gilligan, in which people are assessed in terms of their connectedness with others and the quality of their interpersonal communication, relationships with others, and concern for others.

social conventional reasoning Focuses on conventional rules established by social consensus, as opposed to moral reasoning that stresses ethical issues.

These general conclusions come with some important qualifiers. The effectiveness of reward and punishment depends on the consistency and timing with which they are administered. For example, it is generally more effective to reward moral behavior soon after the event occurs than to do so later. The effectiveness of modeling depends on the characteristics of the model and the cognitive skills of the observer. For example, if a parent models giving a donation to a charity, her child must be old enough to understand this behavior in order for these actions to have an impact on the child's moral development.

Behavior is situationally dependent. Thus, individuals do not consistently display moral behavior in different situations. How consistent is moral behavior? In a classic investigation of moral behavior, one of the most extensive ever conducted, Hugh Hartshorne and Mark May (1928–1930) observed the moral responses of 11,000 children who were given the opportunity to lie, cheat, and steal in a variety of circumstances—at home, at school, at social events, and in athletics. A completely honest or a completely dishonest child was difficult to find. Situation-specific behavior was the rule. Children were more likely to cheat when their friends put pressure on them to do so and when the chance of being caught was slim. However, other analyses suggest that although moral behavior is influenced by situational determinants, some children are more likely than others to cheat, lie, and steal (Burton, 1984).

Social Cognitive Theory   The **social cognitive theory of morality** emphasizes a distinction between an individual's moral competence (the ability to perform moral behaviors) and moral performance (performing those behaviors in specific situations) (Mischel & Mischel, 1975). *Moral competencies* include what individuals are capable of doing, what they know, their skills, their awareness of moral rules and regulations, and their cognitive ability to construct behaviors. Moral competence is the outgrowth of cognitive-sensory processes. *Moral performance*, or behavior, however, is determined by motivation and the rewards and incentives to act in a specific moral way.

Albert Bandura (1991, 2002) also stresses that moral development is best understood by considering a combination of social and cognitive factors, especially those involving self-control. He proposes that in developing a moral self, individuals adopt standards of right and wrong that serve as guides and deterrents for conduct. In this self-regulatory process, people monitor their conduct and the conditions under which it occurs, judge it in relation to moral standards, and regulate their actions by the consequences they apply to themselves. They do things that provide them satisfaction and a sense of self-worth. They refrain from behaving in ways that violate their moral standards because such conduct will bring self-condemnation. Self-sanctions keep conduct in line with internal standards (Bandura, 2002). Thus, in Bandura's view, self-regulation rather than abstract reasoning is the key to positive moral development.

MORAL FEELING

Think about how you feel when you do something you sense is wrong. Does it affect you emotionally? Maybe you get a twinge of guilt. And when you give someone a gift, you might feel joy. What role do emotions play in moral development, and how do these emotions develop?

Psychoanalytic Theory   According to Sigmund Freud, guilt and the desire to avoid feeling guilty are the foundation of moral behavior. In Freud's theory, the *superego* is the moral branch of personality. According to Freud, children fear losing their parents' love and being punished for their unacceptable sexual attraction to the opposite-sex parent. To reduce anxiety, avoid punishment, and maintain parental affection, children identify with the same-sex parent. Through this identification, children *internalize* the parents' standards of right and wrong, which reflect societal prohibitions, and hence develop the superego. In the psychoanalytic account of moral development, children conform to societal standards to avoid guilt. In this way, self-control replaces parental control.

developmental **connection**

Social Cognitive Theory. What are the main themes of Bandura's social cognitive theory? Chapter 1, pp. 27–28

social cognitive theory of morality The theory that distinguishes between moral competence—the ability to produce moral behaviors—and moral performance—use of those behaviors in specific situations.

What characterizes a child's conscience?

Freud's claims regarding the formation of the ego ideal and conscience cannot be verified. However, researchers can examine the extent to which children feel guilty when they misbehave. Grazyna Kochanska and her colleagues (Kochanska & Askan, 2007; Kochanska & others, 2002, 2005, 2008) have conducted a number of studies that explore children's conscience development. In a recent research review of children's conscience, she concluded that young children are aware of right and wrong, have the capacity to show empathy toward others, experience guilt, indicate discomfort following a transgression, and are sensitive to violating rules (Kochanska & Aksan, 2007). In one study, Kochanska and her colleagues (2002) observed 106 preschool children in laboratory situations in which they were led to believe that they had damaged valuable objects. In these mishaps, the behavioral indicators of guilt that were coded by observers included avoiding gaze (looking away or down), body tension (squirming, backing away, hanging head down, covering face with hands), and distress (looking uncomfortable, crying). Girls expressed more guilt than boys did. Children with a more fearful temperament expressed more guilt. Children of mothers who used power-oriented discipline (such as spanking, slapping, and yelling) displayed less guilt.

Empathy Positive feelings, such as empathy, contribute to the child's moral development (Eisenberg & others, 2009). Feeling **empathy** means reacting to another's feelings with an emotional response that is similar to the other's feelings. To empathize is not just to sympathize; it is to put oneself in another's place emotionally.

Although empathy is an emotional state, it has a cognitive component—the ability to discern another's inner psychological states, or what we have previously called *perspective taking* (Eisenberg & others, 2009). Infants have the capacity for some purely empathic responses, but for effective moral action, children must learn to identify a wide range of emotional states in others and to anticipate what kinds of action will improve another person's emotional state.

What are the milestones in children's development of empathy? According to an analysis by child developmentalist William Damon (1988), changes in empathy take place in early infancy, at 1 to 2 years of age, in early childhood, and at 10 to 12 years of age.

Global empathy is the young infant's empathic response in which clear boundaries between the feelings and needs of the self and those of another have not yet been established. For example, one 11-month-old infant fought off her own tears, sucked her thumb, and buried her head in her mother's lap after she had seen another child fall and hurt himself. Not all infants cry every time someone else is hurt, though. Many times, an infant will stare at another's pain with curiosity. Although global empathy is observed in some infants, it does not consistently characterize all infants' behavior.

When they are 1 to 2 years of age, infants may feel genuine concern for the distress of other people, but only when they reach early childhood can they respond appropriately to another person's distress. This ability depends on children's new awareness that people have different reactions to situations. By late childhood, they may begin to feel empathy for the unfortunate.

At about 10 to 12 years of age, individuals develop an empathy for people who live in unfortunate circumstances (Damon, 1988). Children's concerns are no longer limited to the feelings of specific persons in situations they

developmental **connection**

Identity. In Robert Selman's view, perspective taking is a key aspect of whether children develop prosocial or antisocial attitudes and behavior. Chapter 11, pp. 328–329

empathy Reacting to another's feelings with an emotional response that is similar to the other's feelings.

What characterizes empathy in adolescence?

Age Period	Nature of Empathy
Early infancy	Characterized by global empathy, the young infant's empathic response does not distinguish between feelings and needs of self and others.
1 to 2 years of age	Undifferentiated feelings of discomfort at another's distress grow into more genuine feelings of concern, but infants cannot translate realization of other's unhappy feelings into effective action.
Early childhood	Children become aware that every person's perspective is unique and that someone else may have a different reaction to a situation. This awareness allows the child to respond more appropriately to another person's distress.
10 to 12 years of age	Children develop an emergent orientation of empathy for people who live in unfortunate circumstances—the poor, the handicapped, and the socially outcast. In adolescence, this newfound sensitivity may give a humanitarian flavor to the individual's ideological and political views.

FIGURE 13.3

DAMON'S DESCRIPTION OF DEVELOPMENTAL CHANGES IN EMPATHY

directly observe. Instead, 10- to 12-year-olds expand their concerns to the general problems of people in unfortunate circumstances—those who are poor, handicapped, social outcasts, and so forth. This newfound sensitivity may lead older children to behave altruistically, and later may give a humanitarian flavor to adolescents' development of ideological and political views.

Although every adolescent may be capable of responding with empathy, not everyone does so. Adolescents' empathic behavior varies considerably. For example, in older children and adolescents, empathic dysfunctions can contribute to antisocial behavior. Some delinquents convicted of violent crimes show a lack of feeling for their victims' distress. A 13-year-old boy convicted of violently mugging a number of older adults, when asked about the pain he had caused one blind woman, said, "What do I care? I'm not her" (Damon, 1988). To read further about Damon's description of the developmental changes in empathy from infancy through adolescence, see Figure 13.3.

The Contemporary Perspective on the Role of Emotion in Moral Development We have seen that classical psychoanalytic theory emphasizes the power of unconscious guilt in moral development but that other theorists, such as Damon, emphasize the role of empathy. Today, many child developmentalists conclude that both positive feelings—such as empathy, sympathy, admiration, and self-esteem—and negative feelings—such as anger, outrage, shame, and guilt—contribute to children's moral development (Damon, 1988; Eisenberg & others 2006, 2009; Thompson, 2009a, b). When strongly experienced, these emotions influence children to act in accord with standards of right and wrong (Prinz, 2009).

MORAL PERSONALITY

So far we have examined three key dimensions of moral development: thoughts, behavior, and feelings. Recently, there has been a surge of interest in a fourth dimension: personality (Lapsley & Narvaez, 2006; Walker & Frimer, 2009). Three aspects of moral personality that have recently been emphasized are (1) moral identity, (2) moral character, and (3) moral exemplars.

Moral Identity A central aspect of the recent interest in the role of personality in moral development focuses on **moral identity.** Individuals have a moral identity when moral notions and commitments are central to their life (Blasi, 2005). In this view, behaving in a manner that violates this moral commitment places the integrity of the self at risk (Narvaez & Lapsley, 2009).

Moral Character In James Rest's (1995) view, *moral character* involves having the strength of your convictions, persisting, and overcoming distractions and obstacles. If individuals don't have moral character, they may wilt under pressure or fatigue, fail to follow through, or become distracted and discouraged, and fail to behave

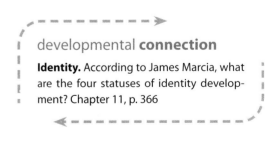

developmental **connection**

Identity. According to James Marcia, what are the four statuses of identity development? Chapter 11, p. 366

moral identity The aspect of personality that is present when individuals have moral notions and commitments that are central to their lives.

Rosa Parks (*left photo,* sitting in the front of a bus after the U.S. Supreme Court ruled that segregation was illegal on her city's bus system) and Andrei Sakharov (*right photo*) are moral exemplars. Parks (1913–2005), an African American seamstress in Montgomery, Alabama, became famous for her quiet, revolutionary act of not giving up her bus seat to a non-Latino White man in 1955. Her heroic act is cited by many historians as the beginning of the modern civil rights movement in the United States. Across the next four decades, Parks continued to work for progress in civil rights. Sakharov (1921–1989) was a Soviet physicist who spent several decades designing nuclear weapons for the Soviet Union and came to be known as the father of the Soviet hydrogen bomb. However, later in his life he became one of the Soviet Union's most outspoken critics and worked relentlessly to promote human rights and democracy.

morally. Moral character presupposes that the person has set moral goals and that achieving those goals involves the commitment to act in accord with those goals.

Lawrence Walker (2002; Walker & Pitts, 1998) has studied moral character by examining people's conceptions of moral excellence. Among the moral virtues people emphasize are "honesty, truthfulness, and trustworthiness, as well as those of care, compassion, thoughtfulness, and considerateness. Other salient traits revolve around virtues of dependability, loyalty, and conscientiousness" (Walker, 2002, p. 74).

Moral Exemplars   **Moral exemplars** are people who have lived exemplary lives. Moral exemplars have a moral personality, identity, character, and set of virtues that reflect moral excellence and commitment.

In one study, three different exemplars of morality were examined—brave, caring, and just (Walker & Hennig, 2004). Different personality profiles emerged for the three exemplars. The brave exemplar was characterized by being dominant and extraverted, the caring exemplar by being nurturant and agreeable, and the just exemplar by being conscientious and open to experience. However, a number of traits characterized all three moral exemplars, considered by the researchers to reflect a possible core of moral functioning. This core included being honest and dependable.

So far, we have examined four key domains of moral development—thoughts, behaviors, feelings, and personality. We noted that both Piaget and Kohlberg stressed that peer relations exert an important influence on moral development.

moral exemplars People who have lived extraordinary lives. Emphasizes the development of personality, identity, character, and virtue to a level that reflects moral excellence and commitment.

Review *Connect* Reflect

 Discuss theory and research on the domains of moral development.

Review

- What is moral development?
- What are Piaget's and Kohlberg's theories of moral development? What are some criticisms of Kohlberg's theory? What is social conventional reasoning?
- What processes are involved in moral behavior? What is the social cognitive theory of moral development?
- How are moral feelings related to moral development?
- What characterizes moral personality?

Connect

- In this section, you learned that, according to Piaget, children from 7 to 10 years of

age are in a transition period between the heteronomous morality and autonomous morality stages of development. In which stage of cognitive development (as discussed on Chapter 1) would these children be in, according to Piaget?

Reflect *Your Own Personal Journey of Life*

- Which of the four approaches—cognitive, psychoanalytic, behavioral/social cognitive, and personality—do you think best describes the way you developed morally? Explain.

Contexts of Moral Development

LG2 Explain how parenting and schools influence moral development.

Parenting | Schools

What other contexts play a role in moral development? In particular, what are the roles of parents and schools?

PARENTING

Both Piaget and Kohlberg held that parents do not provide unique or essential inputs to children's moral development. Parents, in their view, are responsible for providing role-taking opportunities and cognitive conflict, but peers play the primary role in moral development. Research reveals that both parents and peers contribute to children's moral maturity (Malti & Buchmann, 2010; Walker, Hennig, & Krettenauer, 2000).

In Ross Thompson's (2006, 2010) view, young children are moral apprentices, striving to understand what is moral. They can be assisted in this quest by adult mentors in the home who communicate lessons about morality in everyday experiences (Thompson, McGinley, & Meyer, 2006). Among the most important aspects of the relationship between parents and children that contribute to children's moral development are relational quality, parental discipline, and proactive strategies.

Relational Quality Parent-child relationships introduce children to the mutual obligations of close relationships (Laible & Thompson, 2007; Thompson, 2009b, 2010). Parents' obligations include engaging in positive caregiving and guiding children to become competent human beings. Children's obligations include responding appropriately to parents' initiatives and maintaining a positive relationship with parents. A recent study revealed that an early mutually responsive orientation between parents and their infant and a decrease in parents' use of power assertion in disciplining a young child were linked to an increase in the child's internalization and self-regulation (Kochanska & others, 2008). Thus, warmth and responsibility in the mutual obligations of parent-child relationships are important foundations for positive moral growth in children.

In terms of relationship quality, secure attachment may play an important role in children's moral development (Thompson, 2009b). A secure attachment can place the child on a positive path for internalizing parents' socializing goals and family values (Waters & others, 1990). In one study, secure attachment in infancy was linked to early conscience development (Laible & Thompson, 2000).

Parental Discipline Discipline techniques used by parents can be classified as love withdrawal, power assertion, and induction (Hoffman, 1970, 1988):

- **Love withdrawal** is a discipline technique in which a parent withholds attention or love from the child, as when the parent refuses to talk to the child or states a dislike for the child. For example, the parent might say, "I'm going to leave you if you do that again" or "I don't like you when you do that."
- **Power assertion** is a discipline technique in which a parent attempts to gain control over the child or the child's resources. Examples include spanking, threatening, or removing privileges.
- **Induction** is a discipline technique in which a parent uses reasoning and explains how the child's actions are likely to affect other people. Examples of induction include, "Don't hit him. He was only trying to help" and "Why are you yelling at her? She didn't mean to trip you."

In contrast to love withdrawal and power assertion, induction is more likely to produce a moderate level of arousal in children, a level that permits them to attend

> Both theory and empirical data support the conclusion that parents play an important role in children's moral development.
>
> —**NANCY EISENBERG**
> *Contemporary Psychologist,*
> *Arizona State University*

love withdrawal A discipline technique in which a parent withholds attention or love from the child in an effort to control the child's behavior.

power assertion A discipline technique in which a parent attempts to gain control over the child or the child's resources.

induction A discipline technique in which a parent uses reasoning and explains how the child's actions are likely to affect others.

How are parents' discipline techniques linked to children's moral development? What are some proactive strategies parents can use to avert potential misbehavior by children before it happens?

to the cognitive rationale parents offer. Furthermore, induction focuses the child's attention on the action's consequences for others, not on the child's own shortcomings. Thus, child developmentalists recommend induction over power assertion and love withdrawal in disciplining children.

Proactive Strategies An important parenting strategy is to proactively avert potential misbehavior by children before it takes place (Thompson, 2009b; Thompson, McGinley, & Meyer, 2006). With younger children, being proactive means using diversion, such as distracting their attention or moving them to alternative activities. With older children, being proactive may involve talking with them about values that the parents deem important. Transmitting these values can help older children and adolescents to resist the temptations that inevitably emerge in contexts such as peer relations and the media that can be outside the scope of direct parental monitoring.

To read further about strategies parents can adopt to promote their children's moral development, see *Caring Connections*.

SCHOOLS

No matter how parents treat their children at home, they may feel that they have little control over a great deal of their children's moral education. Children spend extensive time away from their parents at school, and the time spent in that environment can influence children's moral development (Lapsley, 2008; Narvaez & Lapsley, 2009).

The Hidden Curriculum More than 60 years ago, educator John Dewey (1933) recognized that even when schools do not have specific programs in moral education, they provide moral education through a "hidden curriculum." The **hidden curriculum** is conveyed by the moral atmosphere that is a part of every school. The moral atmosphere is created by school and classroom rules, the moral orientation of teachers and school administrators, and text materials. Teachers serve as models of ethical or unethical behavior. Classroom rules and peer relations at school transmit attitudes about cheating, lying, stealing, and consideration of others. And through its rules and regulations, the school administration infuses the school with a value system.

Character Education Yet another approach to moral education is **character education,** a direct education approach that involves teaching students a basic "moral literacy" to prevent them from engaging in immoral behavior and doing harm to themselves or others (Narvaez & Lapsley, 2009). The argument is that behaviors such as lying, stealing, and cheating are wrong, and students should be taught this throughout their education (Berkowitz, Battistich, & Bier, 2008).

Every school should have an explicit moral code that is clearly communicated to students. Any violations of the code should be met with sanctions. Instruction in specified moral concepts, such as cheating, can take the form of example and definition, class discussions and role playing, or rewarding students for proper behavior. More recently, an emphasis on the importance of encouraging students to develop a care perspective has been accepted as a relevant aspect of character education (Noddings, 2008). Rather than just instructing adolescents in refraining from engaging in morally deviant behavior, a care perspective advocates educating students in the importance of engaging in prosocial behaviors, such as considering others' feelings, being sensitive to others, and helping others in a semester-long course to discuss a number of moral issues. The hope is that students will develop more advanced notions of concepts such as cooperation, trust, responsibility, and community (Enright & others, 2008). Currently, 40 of 50 states have mandates to include character education in children's education (Nucci & Narvaez, 2008).

Values Clarification One approach to providing moral education is **values clarification,** which means helping people to clarify what their lives are for and what is worth working for. Unlike character education, which tells students what

hidden curriculum The pervasive moral atmosphere that characterizes each school.

character education A direct moral education approach that involves teaching students a basic "moral literacy" to prevent them from engaging in immoral behavior or doing harm to themselves or others.

values clarification Helping people clarify their sense of their purpose in life and what is worth working for. Students are encouraged to define their own values and understand others' values.

caring *connections*

Parenting Recommendations for Raising a Moral Child

A research review (Eisenberg & Valiente, 2002, p. 134) concluded that, in general, children who behave morally tend to have parents who:

- "are warm and supportive rather than punitive;
- use inductive discipline;
- provide opportunities for the children to learn about others' perspectives and feelings;
- involve children in family decision making and in the process of thinking about moral decisions;
- model moral behaviors and thinking themselves, and provide opportunities for their children to do so;
- provide information about what behaviors are expected and why; and
- foster an internal rather than an external sense of morality."

Parents who show this configuration of behaviors likely foster concern and caring about others in their children, and create a positive parent-child relationship.

In addition, parenting recommendations based on Ross Thompson's (2006, 2010; Thompson, McGinley, & Meyer, 2006) analysis of parent-child relations suggest that children's moral development is likely to benefit when there are mutual parent-child obligations involving warmth and responsibility, and when parents use proactive strategies.

One of the strategies above suggests modeling moral behaviors and thinking. According to the research cited in the Moral Exemplars *section of this chapter, what two traits were common to moral exemplars?*

What are some good strategies parents can adopt to foster their child's moral development?

---

their values should be, values clarification encourages students to define their own values and understand the values of others (Williams & others, 2003).

Advocates of values clarification say it is value-free. However, critics argue that its content offends community standards and that the values-clarification exercises fail to stress right behavior.

Cognitive Moral Education Another approach to moral education, **cognitive moral education,** is based on the belief that students should learn to value such things as democracy and justice as their moral reasoning develops. Kohlberg's theory has served as the foundation for a number of cognitive moral education programs. In a typical program, high school students meet in a semester-long course to discuss a number of moral issues. The instructor acts as a facilitator rather than as a director of the class. The hope is that students will develop more advanced notions of concepts such as cooperation, trust, responsibility, and community (Power & Higgins-D'Alessandro, 2008).

Service Learning At the beginning of the chapter you read about 16-year-old Jewell Cash, who is strongly motivated to make a positive difference in her community.

cognitive moral education Education based on the belief that students should learn to value things like democracy and justice as their moral reasoning develops; Kohlberg's theory has been the basis for many of the cognitive moral education approaches.

More than just about anything else, 12-year-old Katie Bell (*at bottom*) wanted a playground in her New Jersey town. She knew that other kids also wanted one so she put together a group, which generated fund-raising ideas for the playground. They presented their ideas to the town council. Her group got more youth involved. They helped raise money by selling candy and sandwiches door-to-door. Katie says, "We learned to work as a community. This will be an important place for people to go and have picnics and make new friends." Katie's advice: "You won't get anywhere if you don't try."

Jewell Cash has a sense of social responsibility that an increasing number of educational programs seek to promote in students through **service learning,** a form of education that promotes social responsibility through service to the community. In service learning, adolescents engage in activities such as tutoring, helping older adults, working in a hospital, assisting at a child-care center, or cleaning up a vacant lot to make a play area.

An important goal of service learning is to help adolescents become less self-centered and more strongly motivated to help others (Dallago & others, 2010; Hart, Matsuba, & Atkins, 2008). Service learning takes education out into the community. Adolescent volunteers tend to be extraverted, be committed to others, and have a high level of self-understanding (Eisenberg & others, 2009). Also, a recent study revealed that adolescent girls participated in service learning more than adolescent boys (Webster & Worrell, 2008).

Researchers have found that service learning benefits adolescents in a number of ways (Hart, Matsuba, & Atkins, 2008). Improvements in adolescent development attributed to service learning include higher grades in school, increased goal-setting, higher self-esteem, an improved sense of being able to make a difference for others, and an increased likelihood that they will serve as volunteers in the future. A study of more than 4,000 high school students revealed that those who worked directly with individuals in need were better adjusted academically, while those who worked for organizations had better civic outcomes (Schmidt, Shumow, & Kackar, 2007). And, in a recent study, 74 percent of African American and 70 percent of Latino adolescents said that service learning programs could have a "fairly or very big effect" on keeping students from dropping out of school (Bridgeland, DiIulio, & Wulsin, 2008).

One analysis revealed that 26 percent of U.S. public high schools require students to participate in service learning (Metz & Youniss, 2005). The benefits of service learning, both for the volunteer and the recipient, suggest that more adolescents should be required to participate in such programs (Enfield & Collins, 2008; Nelson & Eckstein, 2008).

Cheating A moral education concern is whether students cheat and how to handle the cheating if teachers discover it (Anderman & Anderman, 2010). Academic cheating can take many forms, including plagiarism, using "cheat sheets" during an exam, copying from a neighbor during a test, purchasing papers, and falsifying lab results. A 2008 survey of almost 30,000 high school students revealed that 64 percent of the students said they had cheated on a test in school during the past year and 36 percent of the students reported that they had plagiarized information from the Internet for an assignment in the past year (Josephson Institute of Ethics, 2008).

Why do students cheat? Among the reasons students give for cheating include pressure to get high grades, compressed schedules, poor teaching, and lack of interest

Nina Vasan (*center*) founded ACS Teens, a nationwide group of adolescent volunteers who support the efforts of the American Cancer Society (ACS). Nina's organization has raised hundreds of thousands of dollars for cancer research, helped change state tobacco laws, and conducted a number of cancer control programs. She created a national letter-writing campaign to obtain volunteers, established a Web site and set up an e-mail network, started a newsletter, and arranged monthly phone calls to communicate ideas and plan projects.

In Nina's words.

> . . . I realized that teenagers like myself could make a big difference in the fight against cancer. I knew that the best way to help was to start a teen organization. . . . To be a beneficial part of the human race, it is essential and fundamental to give back to the community and others. (Vasan, 2002, p. 1)

Nina Vasan's work on behalf of cancer involved pursuing a purpose. She says that the success of her work involving cancer far outweighs the many honors she has been awarded (Damon, 2008).

(Stephens, 2008). In terms of poor teaching, "students are more likely to cheat when they perceive their teacher to be incompetent, unfair, and uncaring" (Stephens, 2008, p. 140).

The contexts affects whether or not students cheat (Vandehey, Diekhoff, & LaBeff, 2007). For example, students are more likely to cheat when they are not being closely monitored during a test, when they know their peers are cheating, when they know whether another student has been caught cheating, and when student scores are made public (Anderman & Anderman, 2010).

Among the strategies for decreasing academic cheating are preventive measures such as making sure students are aware of what constitutes cheating and what the consequences will be if they cheat; closely monitoring students' behavior while they are taking tests; and emphasizing the importance of being a moral, responsible individual who engages in academic integrity. In promoting academic integrity, many colleges have instituted an honor code policy that emphasizes self-responsibility, fairness, trust, and scholarship. However, few secondary schools have developed honor code policies. The Center for Academic Integrity (www.academicintegrity.org/) has made extensive materials available to help schools develop academic integrity policies.

Why do students cheat? What are some strategies teachers can adopt to prevent cheating?

An Integrative Approach   Darcia Narvaez (2006) emphasizes an *integrative approach* to moral education that encompasses both the reflective moral thinking and commitment to justice advocated in Kohlberg's approach, and the process of developing a particular moral character emphasized in the character education approach. She highlights the Child Development Project as an excellent example of an integrative moral education approach. In the Child Development Project, students are given multiple opportunities to discuss other students' experiences, which encourages empathy and perspective taking, and they participate in exercises that encourage them to reflect on their own behaviors in terms of values such as fairness and social responsibility (Solomon & others, 2002). Adults coach students in ethical decision making and guide them in becoming more caring individuals. Students experience a caring community, not only in the classroom, but also in after-school activities and through parental involvement in the program. Research evaluations of the Child Development Project indicate that it is related to an improved sense of community, an increase in prosocial behavior, better interpersonal understanding, and enhanced social problem solving (Battistich, 2008).

service learning A form of education that promotes social responsibility and service to the community.

Review *Connect* Reflect

 Explain how parenting and schools influence moral development.

Review

- How does parental discipline affect moral development? What are some effective parenting strategies for advancing children's moral development?
- What is the hidden curriculum? What are some contemporary approaches to moral education?

Connect

- In this section, you learned that secure attachment in infancy was linked to early development of conscience. What characterizes secure attachment (discussed in Chapter 10)?

Reflect *Your Own Personal Journey of Life*

- What type of discipline did your parents use with you? What effect do you think this approach has had on your moral development?

Prosocial Behavior   Antisocial Behavior

Service learning encourages positive moral behavior. This behavior is not just moral behavior but behavior that is intended to benefit other people, and psychologists call it *prosocial behavior* (Eisenberg & others, 2009). Jewel Cash, whose story was introduced at the beginning of the chapter, is an exemplary model of someone committed to prosocial behavior. Of course, people have always engaged in antisocial behavior as well. In this section, we will take a closer look at prosocial and antisocial behavior, focusing on how each type of behavior develops.

PROSOCIAL BEHAVIOR

Caring about the welfare and rights of others, feeling concern and empathy for them, and acting in a way that benefits others are all components of prosocial behavior. The purest forms of prosocial behavior are motivated by **altruism,** an unselfish interest in helping another person (Eisenberg & others, 2009). As we see next, learning to share is an important aspect of prosocial behavior.

William Damon (1988) described a developmental sequence by which sharing develops in children. Most sharing during the first three years of life is done for nonempathic reasons, such as for the fun of the social play ritual or out of imitation. Then, at about 4 years of age, a combination of empathic awareness and adult encouragement produces a sense of obligation on the part of the child to share with others. Most 4-year-olds are not selfless saints, however. Children believe they have an obligation to share but do not necessarily think they should be as generous to others as they are to themselves. Neither do their actions always support their beliefs, especially when they covet an object. What is important developmentally is that the child has developed a belief that sharing is an obligatory part of a social relationship and involves a question of right and wrong. These early ideas about sharing set the stage for giant strides that children make in the years that follow.

By the start of the elementary school years, children begin to express more complicated notions of what is fair. Throughout history, varied definitions of fairness have been used as the basis for distributing goods and resolving conflicts. These definitions involve the principles of equality, merit, and benevolence: *Equality* means that everyone is treated the same; *merit* means giving extra rewards for hard work, a talented performance, or other laudatory behavior; *benevolence* means giving special consideration to individuals in a disadvantaged condition.

How does children's sharing change from the preschool to the elementary school years?

Equality is the first of these principles used regularly by elementary school children. It is common to hear 6-year-old children use the word *fair* as synonymous with *equal* or *same*. By the middle to late elementary school years, children also believe that equity means special treatment for those who deserve it—a belief that applies the principles of merit and benevolence.

Parental advice and prodding certainly foster standards of sharing, but the give-and-take of peer requests and arguments provide the most immediate stimulation of sharing. Parents can set examples that children carry into their interactions and communication with peers, but parents are not present during all of their children's peer exchanges. The day-to-day construction of fairness standards is done by children in collaboration and negotiation with each other.

How does prosocial behavior change through childhood and adolescence? Prosocial behavior occurs more often in adolescence than in childhood, although

altruism An unselfish interest in helping another person.

examples of caring for others and comforting someone in distress occur even during the preschool years (Eisenberg, Spinrad, & Sadovsky, 2006).

Also, keep in mind the gender differences in prosocial behavior described in Chapter 12. Recall that females view themselves as more prosocial and empathic, and they also engage in more prosocial behavior than males (Eisenberg & others, 2009).

Two other aspects of prosocial behavior are forgiveness and gratitude. **Forgiveness** is an aspect of prosocial behavior that occurs when the injured person releases the injurer from possible behavioral retaliation. In one investigation, individuals from the fourth grade through college and adulthood were asked questions about forgiveness (Enright, Santos, & Al-Mabuk, 1989). The individuals were especially swayed by peer pressure in their willingness to forgive others.

Gratitude is a feeling of thankfulness and appreciation, especially in response to someone doing something kind or helpful. A recent study of young adolescents revealed that gratitude was linked to a number of positive aspects of development, including satisfaction with one's family, optimism, and prosocial behavior (Froh, Yurkewicz, & Kashdan, 2009).

ANTISOCIAL BEHAVIOR

Most children and adolescents at one time or another act out or do things that are destructive or troublesome for themselves or others. If these behaviors occur often, psychiatrists diagnose them as conduct disorders. If these behaviors result in illegal acts by juveniles, society labels them *delinquents*. Both problems are much more common in males than in females.

Conduct Disorder   **Conduct disorder** refers to age-inappropriate actions and attitudes that violate family expectations, society's norms, and the personal or property rights of others. Children with conduct problems show a wide range of rule-violating behaviors, from swearing and temper tantrums to severe vandalism, theft, and assault (Farrington, 2009; Sterzer & others, 2005). Conduct disorder is much more common among boys than girls (McCabe & others, 2004).

What are some characteristics of conduct disorder?

An estimated 5 percent of children show serious conduct problems. These children are often described as showing an *externalizing*, or *undercontrolled*, pattern of behavior. Children who show this pattern often are impulsive, overactive, and aggressive and engage in delinquent actions.

Conduct problems in children are best explained by a confluence of causes, or risk factors, operating over time (Dodge & Pettit, 2003; Thio, 2010). These include possible genetic inheritance of a difficult temperament, ineffective parenting, and living in a neighborhood where violence is the norm.

Despite considerable efforts to help children with conduct problems, there is a lack of consensus on what works (Mash & Wolfe, 2007). Sometimes recommended is a multisystem treatment carried out with all family members, school personnel, juvenile justice staff, and other individuals in the child's life.

Juvenile Delinquency   What is a juvenile delinquent? What are the antecedents of delinquency? What types of interventions have been used to prevent or reduce delinquency?

What Is Juvenile Delinquency?   The term **juvenile delinquency** refers to a broad range of behaviors, from socially unacceptable behavior (such as acting out in school) to status offenses (such as running away) to criminal acts (such as burglary). For legal purposes, a distinction is made between index offenses and status offenses:

- **Index offenses** are criminal acts, whether they are committed by juveniles or adults. They include acts such as robbery, aggravated assault, rape, and homicide.

forgiveness An aspect of prosocial behavior that occurs when an injured person releases the injurer from possible behavioral retaliation.

gratitude A feeling of thankfulness and appreciation, especially in response to someone doing something kind or helpful.

conduct disorder Age-inappropriate actions and attitudes that violate family expectations, society's norms, and the personal or property rights of others.

juvenile delinquency Refers to a great variety of behaviors by an adolescent, ranging from unacceptable behavior to breaking the law.

index offenses Criminal acts, such as robbery, rape, and homicide, whether they are committed by juveniles or adults.

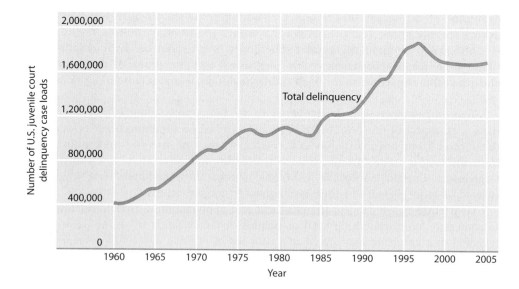

- **Status offenses,** such as running away, truancy, underage drinking, sexual promiscuity, and uncontrollability, are less serious acts. They are performed by youth under a specified age, which classifies them as juvenile offenses.

One issue in juvenile justice is whether an adolescent who commits a crime should be tried as an adult (Steinberg, 2009). Some psychologists have proposed that individuals 12 and under should not be evaluated under adult criminal laws and that those 17 and older should be (Steinberg & Cauffman, 2001; Steinberg, 2009). They also recommend that individuals 13 to 16 years of age be given some type of individualized assessment in terms of whether to be tried in a juvenile court or an adult criminal court. This framework argues strongly against court placement based solely on the nature of an offense and takes into account the offender's developmental maturity. The Society for Adolescent Medicine has argued that the death penalty should not be used with adolescents (Morreale, 2004).

Juvenile court delinquency caseloads in the United States increased dramatically from 1960 to 1996 but have decreased slightly since 1996 (see Figure 13.4) (Puzzanchera & Sickmund, 2008). Note that this figure reflects only adolescents who have been arrested and assigned to juvenile court delinquency caseloads and does not include those who were arrested and not assigned to the delinquency caseloads, nor does the figure include youth who committed offenses but were not apprehended.

Males are more likely to engage in delinquency than are females (Thio, 2010). However, U.S. government statistics revealed that the percentage of delinquency caseloads involving females increased from 19 percent in 1985 to 27 percent in 2005 (Puzzanchera & Sickmund, 2008).

As adolescents reach adulthood, do their rates of delinquency and crime change? Recent analyses indicate that theft, property damage, and physical aggression decrease from 18 to 26 years of age (Schulenberg & Zarrett, 2006). The peak for property damage is 16 to 18 years of age for males, and 15 to 17 years of age for females. However, the peak for violence is 18 to 19 years of age for males and 19 to 21 years of age for females (Farrington, 2009).

A distinction is made between early-onset (before age 11) and late-onset (11 and older) antisocial behavior. Early-onset antisocial behavior is associated with more negative developmental outcomes than late-onset antisocial behavior (Schulenberg & Zarrett, 2006). Early-onset antisocial behavior is more likely to persist into emerging adulthood and is associated with increased problems involving mental health and relationships.

status offenses Juvenile offenses, performed by youth under a specified age, that are not as serious as index offenses. These offenses may include acts such as underage drinking, truancy, and sexual promiscuity.

Antecedents of Juvenile Delinquency   Predictors of delinquency include conflict with authority, minor covert acts that are followed by property damage and other more serious acts, minor aggression followed by fighting and violence, identity (negative identity), self-control (low degree), cognitive distortions (egocentric bias), age (early initiation), sex (male), expectations for education (low expectations, little commitment), school achievement (low achievement in early grades), peer influence (heavy influence, low resistance), socioeconomic status (low), parental role (lack of monitoring, low support, and ineffective discipline), siblings (having an older sibling who is a delinquent), and neighborhood quality (urban, high crime, high mobility).

In the Pittsburgh Youth Study, a longitudinal study involving more than 1,500 inner-city boys, three developmental pathways to delinquency were identified (Loeber & Farrington, 2001; Loeber & others, 1998, 2008; Stouthamer-Loeber & others, 2002, 2004):

- *Authority conflict.* Youth on this pathway showed stubbornness prior to age 12, then moved on to defiance and avoidance of authority.
- *Covert.* This pathway included minor covert acts, such as lying, followed by property damage and moderately serious delinquency, then serious delinquency.
- *Overt.* This pathway included minor aggression followed by fighting and violence.

Family support systems are also associated with delinquency (Farrington, 2009; Hyde, Shaw, & Moilanen, 2010). Parental monitoring of adolescents is especially important in determining whether an adolescent becomes a delinquent (Laird & others, 2008). For example, a recent study of families living in high-risk neighborhoods revealed that parents' lack of knowledge of their young adolescents' whereabouts was linked to whether the adolescents engaged in delinquency later in adolescence (Lahey & others, 2008). Family discord and inconsistent and inappropriate discipline are also associated with delinquency (Capaldi & Shortt, 2003). And another recent study revealed that harsh discipline at 8 to 10 years of age was linked with persistence of criminal activity after age 21 (Farrington, Ttofi, & Coid, 2009).

Rare are the studies that actually demonstrate in an experimental design that changing parenting practices in childhood can lead to a lower incidence of juvenile delinquency in adolescence. However, one recent study by Marion Forgatch and her colleagues (2009) randomly assigned divorced mothers of sons to an experimental group (mothers received extensive parenting training) or a control group (mothers received no parenting training) when their sons were in the first through third grades. The parenting training consisted of 14 parent group meetings that focused primarily on improving parenting practices (skill encouragement, limit setting, monitoring, problem solving, and positive involvement). Best practices for emotion regulation, managing interparental conflict, and talking with children about divorce also were included in the sessions. Improved parenting practices and reduced contact with deviant peers were linked with lower rates of delinquency in the experimentral group than in the control group at a 9-year follow-up assessment.

An increasing number of studies have found that siblings can have a strong influence on delinquency (Bank, Burraston, & Snyder, 2004). In one study, high levels of hostile sibling relationships and older sibling delinquency were linked with younger sibling delinquency in both brother pairs and sister pairs (Slomkowski & others, 2001).

Having delinquent peers increases the risk of becoming delinquent. For example, a recent study revealed that peer rejection and having deviant friends at 7 to 13 years of age were linked with increased delinquency at 14 to 15 years of age (Vitaro, Pedersen, & Brendgen, 2007). Also, another study found that associating with deviant peers was related to a higher incidence of delinquency in African American adolescents (Bowman, Prelow, & Weaver, 2007).

developmental **connection**

Parenting. A neglectful parenting style is linked with a low level of self-control in children. Chapter 14, p. 405

Rodney Hammond, Health Psychologist

In describing his college experiences, Rodney Hammond recalls, "When I started as an undergraduate at the University of Illinois at Champaign-Urbana, I hadn't decided on my major. But to help finance my education, I took a part-time job in a child development research program sponsored by the psychology department. There, I observed inner-city children in settings designed to enhance their learning. I saw firsthand the contribution psychology can make, and I knew I wanted to be a psychologist" (American Psychological Association, 2003, p. 26).

Rodney Hammond went on to obtain a doctorate in school and community psychology with a focus on children's development.

For a number of years, he trained clinical psychologists at Wright State University in Ohio and directed a program to reduce violence in ethnic minority youth. There, he and his associates taught at-risk youth how to use social skills to effectively manage conflict and to recognize situations that could lead to violence. Today, Hammond is Director of Violence Prevention at the Centers for Disease Control and Prevention in Atlanta. Hammond says that if you are interested in people and problem solving, psychology is a wonderful way to put these together. (Source: American Psychological Association, 2003, pp. 26–27.)

Rodney Hammond.

Although delinquency is less exclusively a lower-SES phenomenon than it was in the past, some characteristics of lower-SES culture can promote delinquency. The norms of many low-SES peer groups and gangs are antisocial, or counterproductive, to the goals and norms of society at large. Getting into and staying out of trouble are prominent features of life for some adolescents in low-income neighborhoods. Adolescents from low-income backgrounds may sense that they can gain attention and status by performing antisocial actions. Being "tough" and "masculine" are high-status traits for low-SES boys, and these traits are often measured by the adolescent's success in performing and getting away with delinquent acts.

The nature of a community can contribute to delinquency (Loeber, Burke, & Pardini, 2009). A community with a high crime rate allows adolescents to observe many models who engage in criminal activities and might be rewarded for their criminal accomplishments. Such communities often are characterized by poverty, unemployment, and feelings of alienation. Poor-quality schools, lack of funding for education, and the absence of organized neighborhood activities are other community factors that might be related to delinquency.

Cognitive factors such as low self-control, low intelligence, and lack of sustained attention also are implicated in delinquency. For example, a recent study revealed that low-IQ habitual delinquents were characterized by low self-control (Koolhof & others, 2007). Another recent study found that at age 16 nondelinquents were more likely to have a higher verbal IQ and engage in sustained attention than delinquents (Loeber & others, 2007). And in a longitudinal study, one of the strongest predictors of reduced likelihood of engaging in serious theft was high school academic achievement (Loeber & others, 2008).

One individual whose goal is to reduce juvenile delinquency and help adolescents cope more effectively with their lives is Rodney Hammond. To read about his work, see *Connecting With Careers*. Next, read *Connecting Through Research* to find out if intervening in the lives of children who show early conduct problems can reduce their delinquency risk in adolescence.

connecting through research

Can Intervention in Childhood Reduce Delinquency in Adolescence?

Fast Track is an intervention that attempts to reduce the incidence of juvenile delinquency and other problems (Conduct Problems Prevention Research Group, 2007, 2010a, b; Dodge & McCourt, 2010; Dodge & Conduct Problems Prevention Research Group, 2007; Lochman & Conduct Problems Prevention Research Group, 2007; Slough, McMahon, & Conduct Problems Prevention Research Group, 2008). Schools in four areas (Durham, North Carolina; Nashville, Tennessee; Seattle, Washington; and rural central Pennsylvania) were identified as high-risk based on neighborhood crime and poverty data. Researchers screened more than 9,000 kindergarten children in the four school systems and randomly assigned 891 of the highest-risk and moderate-risk children to intervention or control conditions. The average age of the children when the intervention began was 6.5 years.

The 10-year intervention consisted of parent behavior management training, child social cognitive skills training, tutoring in reading skills, home visitations, mentoring, and a revised classroom curriculum that was designed to increase socioemotional competence and decrease aggression. Outcomes were assessed in the third, sixth, and ninth grades for conduct disorder (multiple instances of behaviors such as truancy,

running away, fire setting, cruelty to animals, breaking and entering, and excessive fighting across a six-month period); oppositional defiant disorder (an ongoing pattern of disobedient, hostile, and defiant behavior toward authority figures); attention deficit hyperactivity disorder (having one or more of the following characteristics over a period of time: inattention, hyperactivity, and impulsivity); any externalizing disorder (presence of any of the three disorders previously described); and self-reported antisocial behavior (a list of 34 behaviors, such as skipping school, stealing, and attacking someone with an intent to hurt them).

The extensive intervention was successful only for children and adolescents who were identified as the highest risk in kindergarten, lowering their incidence of conduct disorder, attention deficit hyperactivity disorder, any externalized disorder, and antisocial behavior (Dodge & McCourt, 2010). Positive outcomes for the intervention occurred as early as the third grade and continued through the ninth grade. For example, in the ninth grade the intervention reduced the likelihood that the highest-risk kindergarten children would develop conduct disorder by 75 percent, attention deficit hyperactivity disorder by 53 percent, and any externalized disorder by 43 percent.

Review *Connect* Reflect

 Describe the development of prosocial and antisocial behavior.

Review

- How is altruism defined? How does prosocial behavior develop?
- What is juvenile delinquency? What is conduct disorder? What are key factors in the development of juvenile delinquency?

Connect

- In this section, you learned that being "tough" and "masculine" are high-status traits for low-SES boys and that this can lead to delinquent acts. In Chapter 12, what did researcher Joseph Pleck say about boys who adopt a strong masculine role in adolescence?

Reflect *Your Own Personal Journey of Life*

- Did you commit acts of delinquency as an adolescent? Most adolescents commit one or more acts of juvenile delinquency without becoming habitual juvenile delinquents. Reflect on your experiences of either committing juvenile offences or not committing them, then review the discussion of factors that are likely causes of juvenile delinquency and apply them to your development.

Religious and Spiritual Development

 Summarize the nature of children's and adolescents' religious and spiritual development.

Childhood   Adolescence

Earlier in the chapter, we described the many positive benefits of service learning. A number of studies have found that that adolescents who are involved in religious institutions are more likely to engage in service learning than their

> Religion enlightens, terrifies, subdues; it gives faith, inflicts remorse, inspires resolutions, and inflames devotion.
>
> —HENRY NEWMAN
> *English Churchman and Writer, 19th Century*

counterparts who don't participate in religious institutions (Oser, Scarlett, & Bucher, 2006).

Researchers have found that adolescent girls are more religious than are adolescent boys (King & Roeser, 2009). One study of 13- to 17-year-olds revealed that girls are more likely to attend religious services frequently, perceive that religion shapes their daily lives, participate in religious youth groups, pray more alone, and feel closer to God (Smith & Denton, 2005).

CHILDHOOD

How do parents influence children's religious thought and behavior? Societies use many methods—such as Sunday schools, parochial education, and parental teaching—to ensure that people will carry on a religious tradition. In a recent national study, 63 percent of parents with children at home said they pray or read Scripture with their children, and 60 percent reported that they send their children to religious education programs (Pew Research Center, 2008). Does this religious socialization work? In many cases it does, and children usually adopt the religious beliefs of their parents (Paloutzian, 2000).

ADOLESCENCE

Religious issues are important to many adolescents and emerging adults (King & Roeser, 2009; Lerner, Roeser, & Phelps, 2009). However, in the 21st century, a downturn in religious interest among adolescents has occurred. In a national study of American college freshmen in 2007, 78 percent said they had attended religious services frequently or occasionally during their senior year in high school, down from a high of 85 percent in 1997 (Pryor & others, 2007). Further, in 2007, more than twice as many first-year college students (19 percent) reported that they didn't have a religious preference as in 1978 (8 percent).

A recent developmental study revealed that religiousness declined among adolescents between age 14 and age 20 in the United States (Koenig, McGue, & Iacono, 2008) (see Figure 13.5). In this study, religiousness was assessed with items such as frequency of prayer, frequency of discussing religious teachings, frequency of deciding moral actions for religious reasons, and the overall importance of religion in everyday life. As indicated in Figure 13.5, a greater change in religiousness occurred from 14 to 18 years of age than from 20 to 25 years of age. Also, reported frequency of attending religious services was highest at 14 years of age, declining from 14 to 18 years of age and increasing at 20 years of age. More change occurred in attending religious services than in religiousness.

Analysis of the World Values Survey of 18- to 24-year-olds revealed that emerging adults in less-developed countries were more likely to be religious than their counterparts in more-developed countries (Lippman & Keith, 2006). For example, emerging adults' reports of religion being very important in their lives ranged from a low of 0 percent in Japan to 93 percent in Nigeria, and belief in God ranged from a low of 40 percent in Sweden to a high of 100 percent in Pakistan.

It is important, however, to consider the quality of the parent-adolescent relationship (Ream & Savin-Williams, 2003). Adolescents who have a positive relationship with their parents or are securely attached to them are likely to adopt the religious orientation of their parents (Dudley, 1999). Adolescents who have a negative relationship with their parents or are insecurely attached to them may turn away from religion or seek religion-based attachments that are missing in their family system (Streib, 1999).

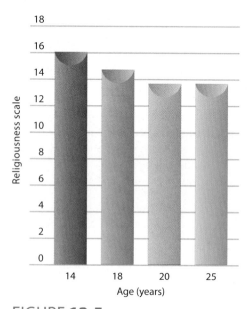

FIGURE **13.5**

DEVELOPMENTAL CHANGES IN RELIGIOUSNESS FROM 14 TO 25 YEARS OF AGE. *Note:* The religiousness scale ranged from 0 to 32, with higher scores indicating stronger religiousness.

Religion and Cognitive Development Adolescence and emerging adulthood can be especially important junctures in religious development (Good & Willoughby, 2008; Lerner, Roeser, & Phelps, 2009). Even if children have been indoctrinated into a religion by their parents, because of advances in their cognitive development adolescents and emerging adults may question what their own religious beliefs truly are.

Many of the cognitive changes thought to influence religious development involve Piaget's stages of cognitive development discussed in Chapter 6. More so than in childhood, adolescents think abstractly, idealistically, and logically. The increase in abstract thinking lets adolescents consider various ideas about religious and spiritual concepts. For example, an adolescent might ask how a loving God can possibly exist given the extensive suffering of many people in the world (Good & Willoughby, 2008). Adolescents' increasingly idealistic thinking provides a foundation for questioning whether religion provides the best route to a better, more ideal world. And adolescents' increased logical reasoning gives them the ability to develop hypotheses and systematically sort through different answers to spiritual questions (Good & Willoughby, 2008).

Religion and Identity Development   During adolescence and emerging adulthood, especially emerging adulthood, identity development becomes a central focus (Coté, 2009; Erikson, 1968). Adolescents and emerging adults are looking for answers to questions like these: "Who am I?" "What am I all about as a person?" "What kind of life do I want to lead?" As part of their search for identity, adolescents and emerging adults begin to grapple in more sophisticated, logical ways with questions such as "Why am I on this planet?" "Is there really a God or higher spiritual being, or have I just been believing what my parents and the church imprinted in my mind?" "What are my own religious views?" A recent analysis of the link between identity and spirituality concluded that adolescence and adulthood can serve as gateways to developing a spiritual identity that "transcends, but not necessarily excludes, the assigned religious identity in childhood" (Templeton & Eccles, 2006, p. 261).

The Positive Role of Religion in Adolescents' Lives
Researchers have found that various aspects of religion are linked with positive outcomes for adolescents (King & Roeser, 2009; Lerner, Roeser, & Phelps, 2009). Religion also plays a role in adolescents' health and influences whether they engage in problem behaviors (King & Roeser, 2009). For example, in a recent national random sample of more than 2,000 11- to 18-year-olds, those who were higher in religiosity were less likely to smoke, drink alcohol, use marijuana, be truant from school, engage in delinquent activities, and be depressed than their low-religiosity counterparts (Sinha, Cnaan, & Gelles, 2007).

Adolescents participating in a church choir. *What are some positive aspects of religion in adolescents' lives?*

Review *Connect* Reflect

 LG4 Summarize the nature of children's and adolescents' religious and spiritual development.

Review

- How does religious and spiritual interest and understanding develop in childhood?
- What characterizes religious and spiritual development in adolescence?

Connect

- In this section, you learned that many of the cognitive changes thought to influence adolescents' religious development reflect Piaget's stages of cognitive development. What is the adolescent stage of Piaget's theory called, and what else characterizes it?

Reflect *Your Own Personal Journey of Life*

- Reflect on your religious/spiritual upbringing. How have your religious/spiritual views changed or stayed the same as you developed through childhood and adolescence? Have your religious/spiritual views changed since adolescence? Explain.

Moral Development

Domains of Moral Development

 Discuss theory and research on the four domains of moral development.

What Is Moral Development?

Moral Thought

- Moral development involves changes in thoughts, feelings, and behaviors regarding right and wrong. Moral development includes intrapersonal and interpersonal dimensions.

- Piaget distinguished between the heteronomous morality of younger children and the autonomous morality of older children. Kohlberg developed a provocative theory of moral reasoning. He argued that development of moral reasoning consists of three levels—preconventional, conventional, and postconventional—and six stages (two at each level). Kohlberg reasoned that these stages were age related. Influences on the Kohlberg stages include cognitive development, dealing with moral questions and moral conflict, peer relations, and perspective taking. Criticisms of Kohlberg's theory have been made, especially by Gilligan, who advocates a stronger care perspective. Other criticisms focus on the inadequacy of moral reasoning to predict moral behavior, account for the influences of culture and family, and assess moral reasoning. A distinction can be made between moral reasoning and social conventional reasoning, which concerns social consensus and conventions designed to control behavior and maintain the social system.

Moral Behavior

- The processes of reinforcement, punishment, and imitation have been used to explain the acquisition of moral behavior, but they provide only a partial explanation. Situational variability is stressed by behaviorists. Social cognitive theory emphasizes a distinction between moral competence and moral performance.

Moral Feeling

- In Freud's theory, the superego is the moral branch of personality. According to Freud, guilt is the foundation of children's moral behavior. Empathy is an important aspect of moral feelings, and it changes developmentally. In the contemporary perspective, both positive and negative feelings contribute to moral development.

Moral Personality

- Recently, there has been a surge of interest in studying moral personality. This interest has focused on moral identity, moral character, and moral exemplars. Blasi points out that individuals have a moral identity when notions and commitment are central to the individual's life. Moral character involves having strong convictions, persisting, overcoming distractions and obstacles; and having virtues such as honesty, truthfulness, loyalty, and compassion. Moral exemplars have a moral character, identity, personality, and a set of virtues reflecting excellence and commitment; they are honest and dependable.

Contexts of Moral Development

 Explain how parenting and schools influence moral development.

Parenting

- Warmth and responsibility in mutual obligations of parent-child relationships provide important foundations for the child's positive moral growth. Love withdrawal, power assertion, and induction are discipline techniques. Induction is most likely to be linked with positive moral development. Moral development can be advanced by parenting strategies such as being warm and supportive rather than punitive; using inductive discipline; providing opportunities to learn about others' perspectives and feelings; involving children in family decision making; modeling moral behaviors; and averting misbehavior before it takes place.

Schools

- The hidden curriculum, initially described by Dewey, is the moral atmosphere of each school. Contemporary approaches to moral education include character education, values clarification, cognitive moral education, service learning, and integrative ethical education. Cheating is a moral education concern that can take many forms. Various aspects of the school situation influence whether students will cheat or not.

Prosocial and Antisocial Behavior

 LG3 Describe the development of prosocial and antisocial behavior.

Prosocial Behavior

- An important aspect of prosocial behavior is altruism, an unselfish interest in helping others. Damon described a sequence by which children develop their understanding of fairness and come to share more consistently. Peers play a key role in this development. Forgiveness and gratitude are two additional aspects of prosocial behavior.

Antisocial Behavior

- Conduct disorder is a psychiatric diagnostic category used to describe multiple delinquent-type behaviors occurring over a six-month period. Juvenile delinquency consists of a broad range of behaviors, from socially undesirable behavior to status offenses. For legal purposes, a distinction is made between index and status offenses. Predictors of juvenile delinquency include authority conflict, minor covert acts such as lying, overt acts of aggression, a negative identity, cognitive distortions, low self-control, early initiation of delinquency, being a male, low expectations for education and school grades, low parental monitoring, low parental support and ineffective discipline, having an older delinquent sibling, heavy peer influence and low resistance to peers, low socioeconomic status, and living in a high-crime, urban area. Effective juvenile delinquency prevention and intervention programs have been identified.

Religious and Spiritual Development

LG4 Summarize the nature of children's and adolescents' religious and spiritual development.

Childhood

- Many children and adolescents show an interest in religion. Many children adopt their parents' religious beliefs.

Adolescence

- The 21st century has shown a downturn in adolescents' religious interest. Emerging adults from less-developed countries are more likely to be religious than those from more-developed countries. Cognitive changes in adolescence—such as increases in abstract, idealistic, and logical thinking—increase the likelihood that adolescents will seek a better understanding of religion and spirituality. As part of their search for identity, many adolescents and emerging adults begin to grapple with more complex aspects of religion. When adolescents have a positive relationship with their parents or are securely attached to them, they often adopt their parents' religious beliefs. Various aspects of religion are linked with positive outcomes in adolescent development.

key terms

moral development 366
heteronomous morality
   (Piaget) 366
autonomous morality 367
immanent justice 367
preconventional
   reasoning 368
conventional reasoning 368
postconventional
   reasoning 369

justice perspective 372
care perspective 372
social conventional
   reasoning 372
social cognitive theory
   of morality 373
empathy 374
moral identity 375
moral exemplars 376
love withdrawal 377

power assertion 377
induction 377
hidden curriculum 378
character education 378
values clarification 378
cognitive moral
   education 379
service learning 380
altruism 382
forgiveness 383

gratitude 383
conduct disorder 383
juvenile delinquency 383
index offenses 383
status offenses 384

key people

Jean Piaget 366
Lawrence
   Kohlberg 367
Carol Gilligan 371

Hugh Hartshorne and
   Mark May 373
Albert Bandura 373
Sigmund Freud 373

Grazyna Kochanska 374
William Damon 374
James Rest 375
Lawrence Walker 376

Ross Thompson 377
John Dewey 378
Darcia Narvaez 381
Marion Forgatch 385

It is not enough for parents to understand children. They must also accord children the privilege of understanding them.

—MILTON SAPIRSTEIN
American Psychiatrist and Writer, 20th Century

Social Contexts of Development

Parents cradle children's lives, but children's growth is also shaped by successive choirs of siblings, peers, friends, and teachers. Children's small worlds widen as they discover new refuges and new people. In the end, there are but two lasting bequests that parents can leave children: one being roots, the other wings. In this section, we will study four chapters: "Families" (Chapter 14), "Peers" (Chapter 15), "Schools and Achievement" (Chapter 16), and "Culture and Diversity" (Chapter 17).

chapter 14 FAMILIES

When Shelley Peterman Schwarz (2004) and her husband, David, had been married four years, they decided to have children. They had two children, Jamie and Andrew. When the children were 3 and 5 years old, Shelley was diagnosed with multiple sclerosis. Two years later, she had to quit her job as a teacher of hearing-impaired children because of her worsening condition.

By the time the children were 7 and 9 years old, it was more difficult for Shelley to prepare meals for the family by herself, so David began taking over that responsibility. They also enlisted the children's help in preparing meals.

Despite her multiple sclerosis, Shelley participated in parenting classes and workshops at her children's school. She even initiated a "Mothers-of-10-Year-Olds" support group. But parenting with multiple sclerosis had its frustrations for Shelley. In her words,

Shelley Peterman Schwarz (*left*) with her family.

> attending school functions, teacher's conferences, and athletic events often presented problems because the facilities weren't always easily wheelchair accessible. I felt guilty if I didn't at least "try" to attend. I didn't want my children to think I didn't care enough to try. . . .
>
> When Jamie was 19 and Andrew was 17, I started to relax a little. I could see how capable and independent they were becoming. My having a disability hadn't ruined their lives. In fact, in some ways, they are better off because of it. They learned to trust themselves and to face personal challenges head-on. When the time came for them to leave the nest and head off to college, I knew they were ready.
>
> As for me, I now understand that having a disability wasn't the worst thing in the world that could happen to a parent. What would be a tragedy is letting your disability cripple your ability to stay in your children's lives. Parenting is so much more than driving car pools, attending gymnastic meets, or baking cookies for an open house. It's loving, caring, listening, guiding, and supporting your child. It's consoling a child crying because her friends thought her haircut was ugly. It's counseling a child worried because his 12-year-old friend is drinking. It's helping a child understand relationships and what it's like to "be in love." (Schwarz, 2004, p. 5)

preview

This chapter is about the many aspects of children's development in families. We will explore how families work, ways to parent children, relationships among siblings, and the changing family in a changing social world. Along the way, we will examine topics such as child maltreatment, working parents, children in divorced families, stepfamilies, and many others.

Family Processes **LG1** Discuss family processes.

- Interactions in the Family System
- Multiple Developmental Trajectories
- Sociocultural and Historical Changes
- Cognition and Emotion in Family Processes
- Domain-Specific Socialization

---►

developmental **connection**

Theories. An important contribution of Bronfenbrenner's ecological theory is its focus on a range of social contexts that influence the child's development. Chapter 1, p. 29

◄---

There's no vocabulary for love within a family, love that's lived in but not looked at, love within the light of which all else is seen, the love within which all other love finds speech. That love is silent.

—**T. S. Eliot**
American-Born English Poet, 20th Century

---►

developmental **connection**

Attention. Joint attention can play an important role in interchanges between a caregiver and an infant. Chapter 7, p. 205

◄---

scaffolding Adjusting the level of parental guidance to fit the child's efforts, allowing children to be more skillful than they would be if they relied only on their own abilities.

reciprocal socialization The bidirectional process by which children socialize parents just as parents socialize them.

As we examine the family and other social contexts of development, it will be helpful to keep in mind Urie Bronfenbrenner's (2000, 2004) ecological theory, which we discussed in Chapter 1. Recall that Bronfenbrenner analyzes the social contexts of development in terms of five environmental systems:

- The microsystem or the setting in which the individual lives, such as a family, the world of peers, schools, work, and so on
- The mesosystem, which consists of links between microsystems, such as the connection between family processes and peer relations
- The exosystem, which consists of influences from another setting that the individual does not experience directly, such as how parents' experiences at work might affect their parenting at home
  - The macrosystem or the culture in which the individual lives, such as a nation or an ethnic group
    - The chronosystem or sociohistorical circumstances, such as increased numbers of working mothers, divorced parents, and stepparent families in the United States in the last 30 to 40 years

Let's begin our examination of the family at the level of the microsystem.

INTERACTIONS IN THE FAMILY SYSTEM

Every family is a *system*—a complex whole made up of interrelated and interacting parts. The relationships never go in just one direction. For example, the interaction of mothers and their infants is sometimes symbolized as a dance in which successive actions of the partners are closely coordinated. This coordinated dance can assume the form of *mutual synchrony,* which means that each person's behavior depends on the partner's previous behavior. Or the interaction can be *reciprocal* in a precise sense, which means that the actions of the partners can be matched, as when one partner imitates the other or when there is mutual smiling (Cohn & Tronick, 1988). An important example of early synchronized interaction is mutual gaze or eye contact.

Another example of synchronization occurs in **scaffolding,** which means adjusting the level of guidance to fit the child's performance, as we discussed in Chapter 6 (Bibok, Carpendale, & Muller, 2009; Robinson, Burns, & Davis, 2009). The parent responds to the child's behavior with scaffolding, which in turn affects the child's behavior. Scaffolding can be used to support children's efforts at any age. A recent study of Hmong families living in the United States revealed that maternal scaffolding, especially in the form of cognitive support, of young children's problem solving the summer before kindergarten predicted the children's reasoning skills in kindergarten (Stright, Herr, & Neitzel, 2009).

The game peek-a-boo, in which parents initially cover their babies, then remove the covering, and finally register "surprise" at the babies' reappearance, reflects the concept of scaffolding. As infants become more skilled at peek-a-boo, infants gradually do some of the covering and uncovering. Parents try to time their actions in such a way that the infant takes turns with the parent.

In addition to peek-a-boo, patty-cake and so-big are other caregiver games that exemplify scaffolding and turn-taking sequences. In one investigation, infants who had more extensive scaffolding experiences with their parents, especially in the form of turn taking, were more likely to engage in turn taking as they interacted with their peers (Vandell & Wilson, 1988). Engaging in turn taking and games like peek-a-boo reflect the development of joint attention by the caregiver and infant, which we discussed in Chapter 7, "Information Processing" (Tomasello, 2009).

The mutual influence that parents and children exert on each other goes beyond specific interactions in games such as peek-a-boo; it extends to the whole process of socialization. Socialization between parents and children is not a one-way process. Parents do socialize children, but socialization in families is reciprocal (Dunn, 2010; Gauvain & Parke, 2010). **Reciprocal socialization** is socialization that is bidirectional; children socialize parents just as parents socialize children.

Of course, while parents are interacting with their children, they are also interacting with each other. To understand these interactions and relationships, it helps to think of the family as a constellation of subsystems defined in terms of generation, gender, and role. Each family member participates in several subsystems—some *dyadic* (involving two people) and some *polyadic* (involving more than two people). The father and child represent one dyadic subsystem, the mother and father another; the mother-father-child represent one polyadic subsystem, the mother and two siblings another (Parke & others, 2008).

These subsystems interact and influence one another (Cox & others, 2008; Feldman & Masalha, 2010; Fosco & Grych, 2010). Thus, as Figure 14.1 illustrates, marital relations, parenting, and infant/child behavior can have both direct and indirect effects on one another (Belsky, 1981). The link between marital relationships and parenting has received increased attention. The most consistent findings are that compared with unhappily married parents, happily married parents are more sensitive, responsive, warm, and affectionate toward their children (Grych, 2002).

Researchers have found that promoting marital satisfaction often leads to good parenting. The marital relationship provides an important support for parenting (Cox & others, 2008). When parents report more intimacy and better communication in their marriage, they are more affectionate to their children (Grych, 2002). Thus, marriage-enhancement programs may end up improving parenting and helping children. Programs that focus on parenting skills might also benefit from including attention to the participants' marriages.

COGNITION AND EMOTION IN FAMILY PROCESSES

Both cognition and emotion are increasingly thought to be central to understanding how family processes work (Gauvain & Parke, 2010). The role of cognition in family socialization takes many forms, including parents' cognitions, beliefs, and values about their parental role, as well as how parents perceive, organize, and understand their children's behaviors and beliefs. For example, one study found a link between mothers' beliefs and their preschool children's social problem-solving skills (Rubin, Mills, & Rose-Krasnor, 1989). Mothers who placed a higher value on skills such as making friends, sharing with others, and leading or influencing other children had

How does the game of peek-a-boo reflect the concept of scaffolding?

Children socialize parents just as parents socialize children.

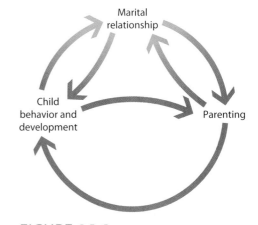

FIGURE **14.1**

INTERACTION BETWEEN CHILDREN AND THEIR PARENTS: DIRECT AND INDIRECT EFFECTS

How is parents' sensitivity to children's emotions linked to children's ability to manage their emotions?

- - - - - - - - →

developmental **connection**

Parenting. Emotion-coaching parents use more scaffolding and praise when interacting with their children than do emotion-dismissing parents. Chapter 10, p. 297

← - - - - - - - -

multiple developmental trajectories Concept that adults follow one trajectory and children and adolescents another one; understanding how these trajectories mesh is important.

children who were more assertive, prosocial, and competent problem solvers than mothers who valued these skills less.

Children's social competence is also linked to the emotional lives of their parents (Denham, Bassett, & Wyatt, 2007). For example, one study found that parents who expressed positive emotions had children who were high in competence (Boyum & Parke, 1995). Through interaction with parents, children learn to express their emotions in appropriate ways.

Researchers are also finding that parental sensitivity to children's emotions is related to children's ability to manage their emotions in positive ways (Gauvain & Parke, 2010; Thompson, 2009). Recall from Chapter 10, "Emotional Development," the distinction that was made between emotion-coaching and emotion-dismissing parents (Gottman, 2002). *Emotion-coaching parents* monitor their children's emotions, view their children's negative emotions as opportunities for teaching, assist them in labeling emotions, and coach them in how to deal effectively with emotions. In contrast, *emotion-dismissing parents* view their role as to deny, ignore, or change negative emotions.

MULTIPLE DEVELOPMENTAL TRAJECTORIES

The concept of **multiple developmental trajectories** refers to the fact that adults follow one trajectory and children and adolescents another one (Parke & Buriel, 2006; Parke & others, 2008). How adult and child/adolescent developmental trajectories mesh is important for understanding the timing of entry into various family tasks. Adult developmental trajectories include timing of entry into marriage, cohabitation, or parenthood; child developmental trajectories include timing of child care and entry into middle school. The timing of some family tasks and changes are planned, such as reentry into the workforce or delaying parenthood, whereas others are not, such as job loss or divorce (Parke & Buriel, 2006).

Consider the developmental period of adolescence. Most adolescents' parents either are in middle adulthood or are rapidly approaching this period of life. However, in the last two decades, the timing of parenthood in the United States has undergone some dramatic shifts (Popenoe & Whitehead, 2008). Parenthood is taking place earlier for some, and later for others, than in previous decades. First, the number of adolescent pregnancies in the United States increased considerably in the 1970s and 1980s. Although the adolescent pregnancy rate has decreased since then, the U.S. adolescent pregnancy rate remains one of the highest in the developed world. Second, the number of women who postpone childbearing until their thirties and early forties simultaneously has increased (Popenoe & Whitehead, 2008).

There are many contrasts between becoming a parent in adolescence and becoming a parent 15 to 30 years later. Delayed childbearing allows for considerable progress in occupational and educational domains. For both males and females, education usually has been completed, and career development is well established.

The marital relationship varies with the timing of parenthood onset. In one investigation, couples who began childbearing in their early twenties were compared with those who began in their early thirties (Walter, 1986). The late-starting couples had more egalitarian relationships, with men more often participating in child care and household tasks.

Is parent-child interaction different for families in which parents delay having children until their thirties or forties? Investigators have found that older fathers are warmer, communicate better, encourage more achievement, place fewer demands on their children, are more lax in enforcing rules, and show less rejection with their children than younger fathers. However, older fathers also are less likely to engage in physical play or sports with their children (MacDonald, 1987). These findings suggest that sociohistorical changes are resulting in different developmental trajectories for many families, trajectories that involve changes in the way marital partners and parents and children interact.

DOMAIN-SPECIFIC SOCIALIZATION

When discussion turns to how parents socialize children, it has been common to describe the socialization process and child outcomes in general terms, such as "Parents who are warm, sensitive, and involved with their children have children who are socially competent." In such broad descriptions, too often the complexity and specificity of parental socialization and child outcomes become lost.

Recently, interest in the domain-specificity of socializing children has increased. Joan Grusec and Marilyn Davidov (2010) proposed a domain-specific view of parenting that emphasizes how parents often operate in different domains characterized by different types of relationships. The five domains are described below:

- *Protection.* Many species, including *homo sapiens*, have evolved so that their young maintain proximity to a caregiver, especially when they are in stressful or dangerous circumstances. In this domain, effective parenting involves responding in such a manner that the child develops a sense of security and perceives being comforted. Child outcomes of appropriate parental protection include the ability to respond appropriately to danger and to engage in self-regulation of distress.

- *Reciprocity.* This domain is not involved when the child is distressed but rather when the parent and child are interacting on an equal basis as partners, as in the context of play. Child outcomes in the reciprocity domain include the development of cooperativeness and the desire to comply with parental requests.

- *Control.* In the control domain, interactions between parents and children typically involve conflict because parents want one thing and children another. The control domain is often activated when the children misbehave. In such circumstances, parents can use their power advantage to discourage the misbehavior through various means such as reasoning, social isolation, and physical punishment. Child outcomes in the control domain include the development of moral and principled behavior.

- *Guided Learning.* In this domain, parents guide children's learning of skills through the use of effective strategies and feedback. In the guided learning domain, parents function as teachers and their children as students. Children's outcomes in the guided learning domain include acquiring knowledge and skills.

- *Group Participation.* In this domain, socialization involves increasing children's participation in cultural practices. Child outcomes include conformity to cultural group practices and values that provide the child with a sense of social identity.

SOCIOCULTURAL AND HISTORICAL CHANGES

Family development does not occur in a social vacuum. Important sociocultural and historical influences affect family processes, which reflect Bronfenbrenner's concepts of the macrosystem and chronosystem (Bronfenbrenner & Morris, 2006; Gauvain & Parke, 2010). Both great upheavals such as war, famine, or massive immigration and subtle transitions in ways of life may stimulate changes in families (Tamis-LeMonda & McFadden, 2010). One example is the effect on U.S. families of the Great Depression of the 1930s. During its height, the Depression produced economic deprivation, adult discontent, and widespread unemployment. It also increased marital conflict, inconsistent child rearing, and unhealthy lifestyles—heavy drinking, demoralized attitudes, and health impairments—especially in fathers (Elder & Shanahan, 2006).

Subtle changes in a culture have significant influences on the family (Bornstein & Lansford, 2010; Gauvain & Parke, 2010). Such changes include increased longevity of older adults, movement to urban and suburban areas, technological advances, and a general dissatisfaction and restlessness (Mead, 1978).

In the first part of the 20th century, individuals who survived infancy were usually hardy and still closely linked to the family, often helping to maintain the family's existence. Today, individuals live longer, which means that middle-aged children are often pressed into a caregiving role for their parents, or the elderly parents may be placed in a nursing home (Holden & Hatcher, 2006). Older parents may have lost some of their socializing role in the family during the 20th century as many of their children moved great distances away. However, in the 21st century, an increasing number of grandparents are raising their grandchildren (Matzek & Cooney, 2009).

Many of the family moves in the last 75 years have been away from farms and small towns to urban and suburban settings. In the small towns and farms, individuals were surrounded by lifelong neighbors, relatives, and friends. Today, neighborhood and extended-family support systems are not nearly as prevalent. Families now move all over the country, often uprooting children from a school and peer group they have known for a considerable length of time. And it is not unusual for this type of move to occur every several years, as one or both parents are transferred from job to job.

The media and technology also play a major role in the changing family (Murray & Murray, 2008). Many children who watch television find that parents are too busy working to share this experience with them. Children increasingly experience a world in which their parents are not participants. Instead of interacting in neighborhood peer groups, children come home after school and watch television play video games, or use the Internet for entertainment.

Another change in families has been an increase in general dissatisfaction and restlessness. The result of such restlessness and the tendency to divorce and remarry has been a hodgepodge of family structures, with far greater numbers of divorced and remarried families than ever before in history (Lansford, 2009).

Many of the changes we have described in this section apply not only to U.S. families but also to families in many countries around the world. Later in this chapter, we discuss aspects of the changing social world of the child and the family in greater detail.

developmental **connection**

Media. Recent research indicates that the average U.S. child and adolescent spends almost 6 hours a day using media as compared with approximately 2½ hours of time spent with parents. Chapter 17, p. 500

Review *Connect* Reflect

LG1 Discuss family processes.

Review

- How can the family be viewed as a system? What is reciprocal socialization?
- How are cognition and emotion involved in family processes?
- What characterizes multiple developmental trajectories?
- What are five domain-specific socialization practices?
- What are some sociocultural and historical changes that have influenced the family?

Connect

- In this section, scaffolding was mentioned as an example of synchronization. Which concept of Vygotsky's is scaffolding also linked to in Chapter 6?

Reflect *Your Own Personal Journey of Life*

- Reflect on your own family as you were growing up for several moments and give some examples of the family processes discussed in this section as you experienced them in your own family.

Parenting

LG2 Explain how parenting is linked to children's and adolescents' development.

- Adapting Parenting to Developmental Changes in Children
- Parenting Styles and Discipline
- Intergenerational Relationships
- Parents as Managers of Children's Lives
- Parent-Adolescent Relationships

Parenting calls on a number of interpersonal skills and makes intense emotional demands, yet there is little in the way of formal education for this task. Most parents learn parenting practices from their own parents. Some of these practices they accept, and others they discard. Husbands and wives may bring different views of parenting to the marriage.

Unfortunately, when parents' methods are passed on from one generation to the next, both desirable and undesirable practices are perpetuated. What have developmentalists learned about parenting? How should parents adapt their practices to developmental changes in their children? How important is it for parents to be effective managers of their children's lives? And how do various parenting styles and methods of discipline influence children's development?

ADAPTING PARENTING TO DEVELOPMENTAL CHANGES IN CHILDREN

Children change as they grow from infancy to early childhood and on through middle and late childhood and adolescence. The 5-year-old and the 2-year-old have different needs and abilities. A competent parent adapts to the child's developmental changes (Maccoby, 1984). As we see next, though, considerable adaptation also is required in making the transition to parenting.

The Transition to Parenting Whether people become parents through pregnancy, adoption, or stepparenting, they face disequilibrium and must adapt. Parents want to develop a strong attachment with their infant, but they still want to maintain strong attachments to their spouse and friends, and possibly continue their careers. Parents ask themselves how this new being will change their lives. A baby places new restrictions on partners; no longer will they be able to rush out to a movie on a moment's notice, and money may not be readily available for vacations and other luxuries. Dual-career parents ask, "Will it harm the baby to place her in child care? Will we be able to find responsible babysitters?"

In a longitudinal investigation of couples from late pregnancy until 3½ years after the baby was born, couples enjoyed more positive marital relations before the baby was born than after (Cowan & Cowan, 2000, 2009; Cowan & others, 2005). Still, almost one-third showed an increase in marital satisfaction. Some couples said that the baby had both brought them closer together and moved them farther apart; being parents enhanced their sense of themselves and gave them a new, more stable identity as a couple. Babies opened men up to a concern with intimate relationships, and the demands of juggling work and family roles stimulated women to manage family tasks more efficiently and pay attention to their own personal growth.

The Bringing Home Baby project is a workshop for new parents that emphasizes strengthening the relationship with their partner, understanding and becoming acquainted with their baby, resolving conflict, and developing parenting skills. Evaluations of the project revealed that parents who participated improved their ability to work together as parents, fathers

What characterizes the transition to parenting?

were more involved with their baby and sensitive to the baby's behavior, mothers had a lower incidence of postpartum depression symptoms, and their baby showed better overall development than participants in a control group (Gottman Relationship Institutes, 2009; Gottman, Gottman, & Shapiro, 2009; Shapiro & Gottman, 2005).

Infancy and Early Childhood During the first year, parent-child interaction moves from a heavy focus on routine caregiving—feeding, changing diapers, bathing, and soothing—to later include more noncaregiving activities, such as play and visual-vocal exchanges (Bornstein, 2002). During the child's second and third years, parents often handle disciplinary matters by physical manipulation: They carry the child away from a mischievous activity to the place they want the child to go to; they put fragile and dangerous objects out of reach; they sometimes spank. As the child grows older, however, parents increasingly turn to reasoning, moral exhortation, and giving or withholding special privileges. As children move toward the elementary school years, parents show them less physical affection.

Parent-child interactions during early childhood focus on such matters as modesty, bedtime regularities, control of temper, fighting with siblings and peers, eating behavior and manners, autonomy in dressing, and attention seeking (Edwards & Liu, 2002). Although some of these issues—fighting with siblings, for example—are carried forward into the elementary school years, many new issues appear by the age of 7. These include whether children should be made to perform chores and, if so, whether they should be paid for them, how to help children learn to entertain themselves rather than relying on parents for everything, and how to monitor children's lives outside the family in school and peer settings.

Middle and Late Childhood As children move into the middle and late childhood years, parents spend less time with them. In one study, parents spent less than half as much time with their children aged 5 to 12 in caregiving, instruction, reading, talking, and playing as when the children were younger (Hill & Stafford, 1980). Although parents spend less time with their children in middle and late childhood than in early childhood, parents continue to be extremely important in their children's lives. In a recent analysis of the contributions of parents during middle and late childhood, the following conclusion was reached: "Parents serve as gatekeepers and provide scaffolding as children assume more responsibility for themselves and . . . regulate their own lives" (Huston & Ripke, 2006, p. 422).

Parents especially play an important role in supporting and stimulating children's academic achievement in middle and late childhood (Huston & Ripke, 2006). The value parents place on education can determine whether children do well in school. Parents not only influence children's in-school achievement, but they also make decisions about children's out-of-school activities (Barber, Stone, & Eccles, 2010; Mahoney, Parente, & Zigler, 2010). Whether children participate in sports, music, and other activities is heavily influenced by the extent to which parents sign up children for such activities and encourage their participation (Simpkins & others, 2006).

Elementary school children tend to receive less physical discipline than they did as preschoolers. Instead of spanking or coercive holding, their parents are more likely to use deprivation of privileges, appeals to the child's self-esteem, comments designed to increase the child's sense of guilt, and statements that the child is responsible for his or her actions.

During middle and late childhood, some control is transferred from parent to child. The process is gradual, and it produces *coregulation* rather than control by either the child or the parent alone. Parents continue to exercise general supervision and control, and children are allowed to engage in moment-to-moment self-regulation. The major shift to autonomy does not occur until about the age of 12 or later. A key developmental task as children move toward autonomy is learning to relate to adults outside the family on a regular basis—adults such as teachers who interact with the child much differently from parents.

In sum, considerable adaptation in parenting is required as children develop. Later in the chapter, we will further examine adaptations in parenting when discussing family influences on adolescents' development.

PARENTS AS MANAGERS OF CHILDREN'S LIVES

Parents can play important roles as managers of children's opportunities, as monitors of their lives, and as social initiators and arrangers (Parke & Buriel, 2006; Gauvain & Parke, 2010). An important developmental task of childhood and adolescence is to develop the ability to make competent decisions in an increasingly independent manner. To help children and adolescents reach their full potential, an important parental role is to be an effective manager, one who finds information, makes contacts, helps structure choices, and provides guidance (Gauvain & Parke, 2010). Parents who fulfill this important managerial role help children and adolescents to avoid pitfalls and to work their way through a myriad of choices and decisions (Furstenberg & others, 1999). Mothers are more likely than fathers to engage in a managerial role in parenting.

From infancy through adolescence, parents can serve important roles in managing their children's experiences and opportunities. In infancy, this might involve taking a child to a doctor and arranging for child care; in early childhood, it might involve a decision about which preschool the child should attend; in middle and late childhood, it might include directing the child to take a bath, to match their clothes and wear clean clothes, and to put away toys; in adolescence, it could involve participating in a parent-teacher conference and subsequently managing the adolescent's homework activity.

A key aspect of the managerial role of parenting is effective monitoring of the adolescent (Smetana, 2008; Smetana & others, 2009). This is especially important as children move into the adolescent years. Monitoring includes supervising adolescents' choice of social settings, activities, and friends, as well as their academic efforts. Also, as we saw in Chapter 13, "Moral Development," a lack of adequate parental monitoring is the parental factor most related to juvenile delinquency.

To read about one individual who helps parents become more effective in managing their children's lives, see *Connecting With Careers*.

What factors are involved in whether adolescents will voluntarily disclose information to their parents?

Researchers also have found that family management practices are related positively to students' grades and self-responsibility, and negatively to school-related problems (Eccles, 2007; Taylor & Lopez, 2005). Among the most important family management practices in this regard are maintaining a structured and organized family environment, such as establishing routines for homework, chores, bedtime, and so on, and effectively monitoring the child's behavior.

PARENTING STYLES AND DISCIPLINE

Good parenting takes time and effort. You can't do it in a minute here and a minute there. You can't do it with CDs. Of course, it's not just the quantity of time parents spend with children that is important for children's development—the quality of the parenting is clearly important (Bornstein & Lansford, 2010; Chen, 2009a, b). To understand variations in parenting, let's consider the styles parents use when they interact with their children, how they discipline their children, and coparenting.

Baumrind's Parenting Styles   Diana Baumrind (1971) points out that parents should be neither punitive nor aloof. Rather, they should develop rules for their children and be affectionate with them. She has described four types of parenting styles:

authoritarian parenting A restrictive, punitive style in which the parent exhorts the child to follow the parent's directions and to respect their work and effort. Firm limits and controls are placed on the child, and little verbal exchange is allowed. This style is associated with children's social incompetence, including a lack of initiative and weak communication skills.

authoritative parenting This style encourages children to be independent but still places limits and controls on their actions. Extensive verbal give-and-take is allowed, and parents are warm and nurturant toward the child. This style is associated with children's social competence, including being achievement-oriented and self-reliant.

neglectful parenting A style in which the parent is very uninvolved in the child's life. It is associated with children's social incompetence, especially a lack of self-control and poor self-esteem.

indulgent parenting A style in which parents are highly involved with their children but place few demands or controls on them. This is associated with children's social incompetence, especially a lack of self-control and a lack of respect for others.

- **Authoritarian parenting** is a restrictive, punitive style in which parents exhort the child to follow their directions and respect their work and effort. The authoritarian parent places firm limits and controls on the child and allows little verbal exchange. For example, an authoritarian parent might say, "You do it my way or else." Authoritarian parents also might spank the child frequently, enforce rules rigidly but not explain them, and show rage toward the child. Children of authoritarian parents are often unhappy, fearful, and anxious about comparing themselves with others, fail to initiate activity, and have weak communication skills. Sons of authoritarian parents may behave aggressively (Hart & others, 2003).

- **Authoritative parenting** encourages children to be independent but still places limits and controls on their actions. Extensive verbal give-and-take is allowed, and parents are warm and nurturant toward the child. An authoritative parent might put his arm around the child in a comforting way and say, "You know you should not have done that. Let's talk about how you can handle the situation better next time." Authoritative parents show pleasure and support in response to children's constructive behavior. They also expect mature, independent, and age-appropriate behavior by children. Children

Calvin and Hobbes   by Bill Watterson

whose parents are authoritative are often cheerful, self-controlled and self-reliant, and achievement oriented; they tend to maintain friendly relations with peers, cooperate with adults, and cope well with stress.

- **Neglectful parenting** is a style in which the parent is very uninvolved in the child's life. Children whose parents are neglectful develop the sense that other aspects of the parents' lives are more important than they are. These children tend to be socially incompetent. Many have poor self-control and don't handle independence well. They frequently have low self-esteem, are immature, and may be alienated from the family. In adolescence, they may show patterns of truancy and delinquency.

- **Indulgent parenting** is a style in which parents are highly involved with their children but place few demands or controls on them. Such parents let their children do what they want. The result is that the children never learn to control their own behavior and always expect to get their way. Some parents deliberately rear their children in this way because they believe the combination of warm involvement and few restraints will produce a creative, confident child. However, children whose parents are indulgent rarely learn respect for others and have difficulty controlling their behavior. They might be domineering, egocentric, noncompliant, and have difficulties in peer relations.

These four classifications of parenting involve combinations of acceptance and responsiveness on the one hand and demand and control on the other (Maccoby & Martin, 1983). How these dimensions combine to produce authoritarian, authoritative, neglectful, and indulgent parenting is shown in Figure 14.2.

Parenting Styles in Context   Do the benefits of authoritative parenting transcend the boundaries of ethnicity, socioeconomic status (SES), and household composition? Although occasional exceptions have been found, evidence linking authoritative parenting with competence on the part of the child occurs in research across a wide range of ethnic groups, social strata, cultures, and family structures (Steinberg & Silk, 2002).

Nonetheless, researchers have found that in some ethnic groups, aspects of the authoritarian style may be associated with more positive child outcomes than Baumrind predicts (Parke & Buriel, 2006). Elements of the authoritarian style may take on different meanings and have different effects depending on the context.

For example, Asian American parents often continue aspects of traditional Asian child-rearing practices that have sometimes been described as authoritarian. The parents exert considerable control over their children's lives. However, Ruth Chao (2001, 2005, 2007; Chao & Tseng, 2002) argues that the style of parenting used by many Asian American parents is distinct from the domineering control of the authoritarian style. Instead, Chao argues that the control reflects concern and involvement in their children's lives and is best conceptualized as a type of training. The high academic achievement of Asian American children may be a consequence of their "training" parents (Stevenson & Zusho, 2002).

An emphasis on requiring respect and obedience is also associated with the authoritarian style, but in Latino child rearing this focus may be positive rather than punitive. Rather than suppressing the child's development, it may encourage the development of a self and an identity that are embedded in the family and require respect and obedience (Harwood & others, 2002).

Even physical punishment, another characteristic of the authoritarian style, may have varying effects in different contexts. African American parents are more likely than non-Latino White parents to use physical punishment (Deater-Deckard & Dodge, 1997). The use of physical punishment has been linked with increased

	Accepting, responsive	Rejecting, unresponsive
Demanding, controlling	Authoritative	Authoritarian
Undemanding, uncontrolling	Indulgent	Neglectful

FIGURE **14.2**

CLASSIFICATION OF PARENTING STYLES. The four types of parenting styles (authoritative, authoritarian, indulgent, and neglectful) involve the dimensions of acceptance and responsiveness, on the one hand, and demand and control on the other. For example, authoritative parenting involves being both accepting/responsive and demanding/controlling.

According to Ruth Chao, what type of parenting style do many Asian American parents use?

externalized child problems (such as acting out and high levels of aggression) in non-Latino White families but not in African American families. One explanation of this finding points to the need for African American parents to enforce rules in the dangerous environments in which they are more likely to live (Harrison-Hale, McLoyd, & Smedley, 2004).

Further Thoughts on Parenting Styles   Several caveats about parenting styles are in order. First, the parenting styles do not capture the important themes of reciprocal socialization and synchrony (Laursen & Collins, 2009). Keep in mind that children socialize parents, just as parents socialize children (Parke & Gauvain, 2010). Second, many parents use a combination of techniques rather than a single technique, although one technique may be dominant. Although consistent parenting is usually recommended, the wise parent may sense the importance of being more permissive in certain situations, more authoritarian in others, and yet more authoritative in others. Also, some critics argue that the concept of parenting style is too broad and that more research needs to be conducted to "unpack" parenting styles by studying various components of the styles (Maccoby, 2007). For example, is parental monitoring more important than warmth in predicting child and adolescent outcomes?

Punishment   For centuries, corporal (physical) punishment, such as spanking, has been considered a necessary and even desirable method of disciplining children. Use of corporal punishment is legal in every state in America. A national survey of U.S. parents with 3- and 4-year-old children found that 26 percent of parents reported spanking their children frequently, and 67 percent of the parents reported yelling at their children frequently (Regalado & others, 2004). A cross-cultural comparison found that individuals in the United States and Canada were among those with the most favorable attitudes toward corporal punishment and were the most likely to remember it being used by their parents (Curran & others, 2001) (see Figure 14.3).

An increasing number of studies have examined the outcomes of physically punishing children, although those that have been conducted are correlational. Clearly, it would be highly unethical to randomly assign parents to either spank or not spank their children in an experimental study. Recall that cause and effect cannot be determined in a correlational study. In one correlational study, spanking by parents was linked with children's antisocial behavior, including cheating, telling lies, being mean to others, bullying, getting into fights, and being disobedient (Strauss, Sugarman, & Giles-Sims, 1997).

A research review concluded that corporal punishment by parents is associated with higher levels of immediate compliance and aggression by the children (Gershoff, 2002). The review also found that corporal punishment is linked to lower levels of moral internalization and mental health (Gershoff, 2002). A study in six countries revealed that mothers' use of physical punishment was linked to highest rates of aggression in their children (Gershoff & others, 2010). A recent study also discovered that a history of harsh physical discipline was related to adolescent depression and externalized problems, such as juvenile delinquency (Bender & others, 2007).

What are some reasons to avoid spanking or similar punishments? The reasons include:

- When adults punish a child by yelling, screaming, or spanking, they are presenting children with out-of-control models for handling stressful situations. Children may imitate this aggressive, out-of-control behavior.

- Punishment can instill fear, rage, or avoidance. For example, spanking the child may cause the child to avoid being around the parent and to fear the parent.

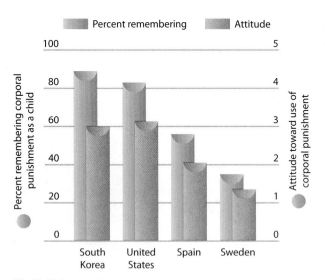

FIGURE **14.3**

CORPORAL PUNISHMENT IN DIFFERENT COUNTRIES. A 5-point scale was used to assess attitudes toward corporal punishment with scores closer to 1 indicating an attitude against its use and scores closer to 5 suggesting an attitude favoring its use. *Why are studies of corporal punishment correlational studies, and how does that affect their interpretation?*

Do Marital Conflict and Individual Hostility Predict the Use of Physical Punishment in Parenting?

A longitudinal study assessed couples across the transition to parenting to investigate possible links between marital conflict, individual adult hostility, and the use of physical punishment with young children (Kanoy & others, 2003). Before the birth of the first child, the level of marital conflict was observed in a marital problem-solving discussion; answers to questionnaires regarding individual characteristics were also obtained. Thus, these characteristics of the couples were not influenced by characteristics of the child. When the children were 2 and 5 years old, the couples were interviewed about the frequency and intensity of their physical pun-

ishment of the children. At both ages, the parents' level of marital conflict was again observed in a marital problem-solving discussion.

The researchers found that both hostility and marital conflict were linked with the use of physical punishment. Individuals with high rates of hostility on the prenatal measures used more frequent and more severe physical punishment with their children. The same was evident for marital conflict—when marital conflict was high, both mothers and fathers were more likely to use physical punishment in disciplining their young children.

- Punishment tells children what not to do rather than what to do. Children should be given feedback, such as "Why don't you try this?"
- Punishment can be abusive. Parents might unintentionally become so emotional when they are punishing the child that they become abusive (Durrant, 2008; Knox, 2010).

Most child psychologists recommend handling misbehavior by reasoning with the child, especially explaining the consequences of the child's actions for others. *Time out*, in which the child is removed from a setting that offers positive reinforcement, can also be effective. For example, when the child has misbehaved, a parent might take away TV viewing for a specified time.

A final point about the use of punishment with children is that debate about its effects on children's development continues (Grusec, 2009; Thompson, 2009). Some experts (including Diana Baumrind) argue that much of the evidence for the negative effects of physical punishment has been based on studies in which parents acted in an abusive manner (Baumrind, Larzelere, & Cowan, 2002). She concludes from her research that when parents used punishment in a calm, reasoned manner (which she says characterized most of the authoritative parents in her studies), children's development benefitted. Thus, she emphasizes that physical punishment does not need to present children with an out-of-control adult who is yelling and screaming, as well as spanking. A research review of 26 studies concluded that only severe or predominant use of spanking, not mild spanking, compared unfavorably with alternative practices for disciplining children (Larzelere & Kuhn, 2005).

Indeed, there are few longitudinal studies of punishment and few studies that distinguish adequately between moderate and heavy use of punishment. Thus, in the view of some experts, available research evidence makes it difficult to tell whether the effects of physical punishment are harmful to children's development, even though such a view might be distasteful to some individuals (Grusec, 2009). One thing that is clear regarding research on punishment of children is that if physical punishment is used, it needs to be mild, infrequent, age-appropriate, and used in the context of a positive parent-child relationship (Grusec, 2011). And also clear is that when physical punishment involves abuse, it can be very harmful to children's development (Cicchetti, 2011; Cicchetti & Toth, 2011).

Earlier in this chapter, we described the family as a system and discussed possible links between marital relationships and parenting practices (Cox & others, 2004). Do marital conflict and individual hostility predict the use of physical punishment in parenting? To find out, read *Connecting Through Research*.

Darla Botkin, Marriage and Family Therapist

Darla Botkin is a marriage and family therapist who teaches, conducts research, and engages in marriage and family therapy. She is on the faculty of the University of Kentucky. Botkin obtained a bachelor's degree in elementary education with a concentration in special education and then went on to receive a master's degree in early childhood education. She spent the next six years working with children and their families in a variety of settings, including child care, elementary school, and Head Start. These experiences led Botkin to recognize the interdependence of the developmental settings that children and their parents experience (such as home, school, and work). She returned to graduate school and obtained a Ph.D. in family studies from the University of Tennessee. She then became a faculty member in the Family Studies program at the University of Kentucky. Completing further coursework and clinical training in marriage and family therapy, she became certified as a marriage and family therapist.

Botkin's current interests include working with young children in family therapy, addressing gender and ethnic issues in family therapy, and exploring the role of spirituality in family wellness.

Darla Botkin (*left*), conducting a family therapy session.

For more information about what marriage and family therapists do, see page 47 in the Careers in Child Development appendix following Chapter 1.

What characterizes coparenting?

coparenting Support parents provide for each other in jointly raising children.

Coparenting   The relationship between marital conflict and the use of punishment highlights the importance of **coparenting,** which is the support that parents provide one another in jointly raising a child. Poor coordination between parents, undermining of the other parent, lack of cooperation and warmth, and disconnection by one parent are conditions that place children at risk for problems (Feinberg & Kan, 2008; Pruett & Pruett, 2009; Talbot, Baker, & McHale, 2009). For example, a recent study revealed that coparenting influenced young children's effortful control above and beyond maternal and paternal parenting by themselves (Karreman & others, 2008).

Parents who do not spend enough time with their children or who have problems in child rearing can benefit from counseling and therapy. To read about the work of marriage and family counselor Darla Botkin, see *Connecting With Careers.*

Child Maltreatment   Unfortunately, punishment sometimes leads to the abuse of infants and children (Corso & Fertig, 2010; Kennedy, 2009; Macmillan, 2010). In 2006, approximately 905,000 U.S. children were found to be victims of child abuse (U.S. Department of Health and Human Services, 2008). Eighty-four percent of these children were abused by a parent or parents. Laws in many states now require physicians and teachers to report suspected cases of child abuse, yet many cases go unreported, especially those involving battered infants.

Whereas the public and many professionals use the term *child abuse* to refer to both abuse and neglect, developmentalists increasingly use the term *child* maltreatment (Cicchetti, 2011; Cicchetti & Toth, 2011). This term does not have quite the emotional impact of the term *abuse* and acknowledges that maltreatment includes diverse conditions.

Types of Child Maltreatment   The four main types of child maltreatment are physical abuse, child neglect, sexual abuse, and emotional abuse (National Clearinghouse on Child Abuse and Neglect, 2004):

- *Physical abuse* is characterized by the infliction of physical injury as result of punching, beating, kicking, biting, burning, shaking, or otherwise harming a child. The parent or other person may not have intended to hurt the child; the injury may have resulted from excessive physical punishment (Milot & others, 2010).

- *Child neglect* is characterized by failure to provide for the child's basic needs (Newton & Vandeven, 2010; Thompson, 2010). Neglect can be physical (abandonment, for example), educational (allowing chronic truancy, for example), or emotional (marked inattention to the child's needs, for example). Child neglect is by far the most common form of child maltreatment. In every country where relevant data have been collected, neglect occurs up to three times as often as abuse (Benoit, Coolbear, & Crawford, 2008).

- *Sexual abuse* includes fondling a child's genitals, intercourse, incest, rape, sodomy, exhibitionism, and commercial exploitation through prostitution or the production of pornographic materials (Bahali & others, 2010; Leventhal, Murphy, & Asnes, 2010).

- *Emotional abuse (psychological/verbal abuse/mental injury)* includes acts or omissions by parents or other caregivers that have caused, or could cause, serious behavioral, cognitive, or emotional problems (van Harmelen & others, 2010; Wekerle & others, 2009).

Although any of these forms of child maltreatment may be found separately, they often occur in combination. Emotional abuse is almost always present when other forms are identified.

The Context of Abuse   No single factor causes child maltreatment (Cicchetti, 2011; Cicchetti & others, 2009). A combination of factors, including the culture, family, and developmental characteristics of the child, likely contribute to child maltreatment (Appleton & Stanley, 2009; Prinz & others, 2009).

The extensive violence that takes place in the American culture, including TV violence, is reflected in the occurrence of violence in the family (Durrant, 2008). The family itself is obviously a key part of the context of abuse (Kennedy, 2009; Shin, Hong, & Hazen, 2010). The interactions of all family members need to be considered, regardless of who performs the violent acts against the child. For example, even though the father may be the one who physically abuses the child, the behavior of the mother, the child, and siblings also should be evaluated.

Were abusive parents abused by their own parents? About one-third of parents who were abused themselves when they were young go on to abuse their own children (Cicchetti & Toth, 2006). Thus, some, but not a majority, of parents are involved in an intergenerational transmission of abuse.

Developmental Consequences of Abuse   Among the consequences of child maltreatment in childhood and adolescence are poor emotional regulation, attachment problems, problems in peer relations, difficulty in adapting to school, and other psychological problems such as depression and delinquency. As shown in Figure 14.4, maltreated young children in foster care were more likely to show abnormal stress hormone levels than middle-SES young children living with their birth family (Gunnar & Fisher, 2006). In this study, the abnormal stress hormone levels were mainly present in the foster children who were neglected, best described as "institutional neglect" (Fisher, 2005). Abuse also may have this effect on young children (Gunnar & Fisher, 2006). Adolescents who experienced abuse or neglect as children are more

> Child maltreatment involves grossly inadequate and destructive aspects of parenting.
>
> —**DANTE CICCHETTI**
> *Contemporary Developmental Psychologist, University of Minnesota*

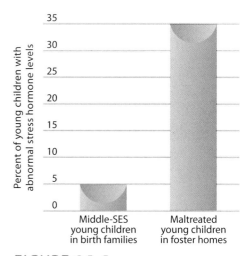

FIGURE 14.4

ABNORMAL STRESS HORMONE LEVELS IN YOUNG CHILDREN IN DIFFERENT TYPES OF REARING CONDITIONS

likely than adolescents who were not maltreated as children to engage in violent romantic relationships, delinquency, sexual risk taking, and substance abuse (Shin, Hong, & Hazen, 2010; Wekerle & others, 2009).

Later, during the adult years, individuals who were maltreated as children often have difficulty establishing and maintaining healthy intimate relationships (Dozier, Stovall-McClough, & Albus, 2009). As adults, maltreated children are also at higher risk for violent behavior toward other adults—especially dating partners and marital partners—as well as for substance abuse, anxiety, and depression (Kennedy, 2009). A recent study also revealed that adults who experienced child maltreatment were at increased risk for financial and employment-related difficulties (Zielinski, 2009).

What can be done to prevent or reduce the incidence of child maltreatment? In one study of maltreating mothers and their 1-year-olds, two treatments were effective in reducing child maltreatment: (1) home visitation that emphasized improved parenting, coping with stress, and increasing support for the mother; and (2) parent-infant psychotherapy that focused on improving maternal-infant attachment (Cicchetti, Toth, & Rogosch, 2005).

PARENT-ADOLESCENT RELATIONSHIPS

Even the best parents may find their relationship with their child strained during adolescence. Important aspects of parent-adolescent relationships include autonomy/attachment and conflict.

Autonomy and Attachment   With most adolescents, parents are likely to find themselves engaged in a delicate balancing act, weighing competing needs for autonomy and control, for independence and connection.

The Push for Autonomy   The typical adolescent's push for autonomy and responsibility puzzles and angers many parents. Most parents anticipate that their teenager will have some difficulty adjusting to the changes that adolescence brings, but few parents imagine and predict just how strong an adolescent's desires will be to spend time with peers or how intensely adolescents will want to show that it is they—not their parents—who are responsible for their successes and failures.

Adolescents' ability to attain autonomy and gain control over their behavior is acquired through appropriate adult reactions to their desire for control (Laursen & Collins, 2009; McElhaney & others, 2009). At the onset of adolescence, the average individual does not have the knowledge to make appropriate or mature decisions in all areas of life. As the adolescent pushes for autonomy, the wise adult relinquishes control in those areas where the adolescent can make reasonable decisions, but continues to guide the adolescent to make reasonable decisions in areas in which the adolescent's knowledge is more limited. Gradually, adolescents acquire the ability to make mature decisions on their own.

What are strategies that parents can use to guide adolescents in effectively handling their increased motivation for autonomy?

Gender differences characterize autonomy-granting in adolescence. Boys are given more independence than girls. In one study, this was especially true in U.S. families with a traditional gender-role orientation (Bumpus, Crouter, & McHale, 2001). Also, Latino parents protect and monitor their daughters more closely than is the case for non-Latino White parents (Allen & others, 2008; Updegraff & others, 2010).

developmental **connection**

Attachment. Securely attached infants use the caregiver as a secure base from which to explore the environment. Chapter 10, p. 310

The Role of Attachment   Recall from Chapter 10 that one of the most widely discussed aspects of socioemotional development in infancy is secure attachment to caregivers. In the past decade, researchers have explored whether secure attachment also might be an important concept in adolescents' relationships with their parents (Laursen & Collins, 2009). For example, Joseph Allen and his colleagues (2009) found that adolescents who were securely attached at 14 years of age were more likely to report that they were in an exclusive relationship, comfortable with intimacy in relationships, and achieving increased financial independence at 21 years of age.

Balancing Freedom and Control   We have seen that parents play very important roles in adolescent development (Laursen & Collins, 2009). Although adolescents are moving toward independence, they still need to stay connected with families (McElhaney & others, 2009). For example, the National Longitudinal Study on Adolescent Health surveyed more than 12,000 adolescents and found that those who did not eat dinner with a parent five or more days a week had dramatically higher rates of smoking, drinking, marijuana use, getting into fights, and initiation of sexual activity (Council of Economic Advisors, 2000).

Parent-Adolescent Conflict   Although parent-adolescent conflict increases in early adolescence, it does not reach the tumultuous proportions G. Stanley Hall envisioned at the beginning of the 20th century (Laursen & Collins, 2009). Rather, much of the conflict involves the everyday events of family life, such as keeping a bedroom clean, dressing neatly, getting home by a certain time, and not talking forever on the phone. The conflicts rarely involve major dilemmas such as drugs or delinquency.

Conflict with parents often escalates during early adolescence, remains somewhat stable during the high school years, and then lessens as the adolescent reaches 17 to 20 years of age. Parent-adolescent relationships become more positive if adolescents go away to college than if they attend college while living at home (Sullivan & Sullivan, 1980).

The everyday conflicts that characterize parent-adolescent relationships may actually serve a positive developmental function. These minor disputes and negotiations facilitate the adolescent's transition from being dependent on parents to becoming an autonomous individual. Recognizing that conflict and negotiation can serve a positive developmental function can tone down parental hostility.

The old model of parent-adolescent relationships suggested that as adolescents mature they detach themselves from parents and move into a world of autonomy apart from parents. The old model also suggested that parent-adolescent conflict is intense and stressful throughout adolescence. The new model emphasizes that parents serve as important attachment figures and support systems while adolescents explore a wider, more complex social world. The new model also emphasizes that, in most families, parent-adolescent conflict is moderate rather than severe and that the everyday negotiations and minor disputes not only are normal but also can serve the positive developmental function of helping the adolescent make the transition from childhood dependency to adult independence (see Figure 14.5).

Still, a high degree of conflict characterizes some parent-adolescent relationships. And this prolonged, intense conflict is associated with various adolescent

> When I was a boy of 14, my father was so ignorant I could hardly stand to have the man around. But when I got to be 21, I was astonished at how much he had learnt in 7 years.
>
> —**MARK TWAIN**
> *American Writer and Humorist, 19th Century*

Conflict with parents increases in early adolescence. *What is the nature of this conflict in a majority of American families?*

Old Model		New Model
Autonomy, detachment from parents; parent and peer worlds are isolated Intense, stressful conflict throughout adolescence; parent-adolescent relationships are filled with storm and stress on virtually a daily basis		Attachment and autonomy; parents are important support systems and attachment figures; adolescent-parent and adolescent-peer worlds have some important connections Moderate parent-adolescent conflict is common and can serve a positive developmental function; conflict greater in early adolescence

FIGURE 14.5

OLD AND NEW MODELS OF PARENT-ADOLESCENT RELATIONSHIPS

Stacey Christensen, age 16: "I am lucky enough to have open communication with my parents. Whenever I am in need or just need to talk, my parents are there for me. My advice to parents is to let your teens grow at their own pace, be open with them so that you can be there for them. We need guidance; our parents need to help but not be too overwhelming."

> The generations of living things pass in a short time, and like runners hand on the torch of life.
>
> —LUCRETIUS
> *Roman Poet, 1st Century BC*

problems: movement out of the home, juvenile delinquency, school dropout, pregnancy and early marriage, membership in religious cults, and drug abuse (Brook & others, 1990). In a recent study of Latino families, higher levels of conflict with either the mother or the father were linked to higher levels of adolescent boys' and girls' internalizing (depression, for example) and externalizing (delinquency, for example) behaviors (Crean, 2008). In this study, conflict with the mother was especially detrimental for Latina girls.

INTERGENERATIONAL RELATIONSHIPS

Connections between generations play important roles in development through the life span (Silverstein, 2009; Szinovacz, 2009). With each new generation, personality characteristics, attitudes, and values are replicated or changed (Pratt & others, 2008). As older family members die, their biological, intellectual, emotional, and personal legacies are carried on in the next generation. Their children become the oldest generation and their grandchildren the second generation. In many families, females' relationships across generations are closer and more intimate than are males' relationships (Etaugh & Bridges, 2010).

The following studies provide evidence of the importance of intergenerational relationships in children's development:

- Supportive family environments and parenting in childhood (assessed when the children were 3 to 15 years of age) were linked with more positive relationships (in terms of contact, closeness, conflict, and reciprocal assistance) between the children and their middle-aged parents when the children were 26 years of age (Belsky & others, 2001).
- Adult children of divorce who were classified as securely attached were less likely to divorce in the early years of their marriage than their insecurely attached counterparts (Crowell, Treboux, & Brockmeyer, 2009).
  - Parents who smoked early and often, and persisted in becoming regular smokers, were more likely to have adolescents who became smokers (Chassin & others, 2008).
  - Evidence was found for the intergenerational transmission of conduct disorder (multiple delinquent activities) across three generations, with the connection stronger for males than females (D'Onofrio & others, 2007).

Review Connect Reflect

 LG2 Explain how parenting is linked to children's and adolescents' development.

Review

- In what ways do parents need to adapt their behavior to developmental changes in their children?
- How can parents be effective managers of children's lives?
- What are the main parenting styles and variations in discipline?
- What are some important aspects of parenting adolescents?
- How do intergenerational relationships influence children's development?

Connect

- In this section, we learned about Baumrind's four parenting styles. In Chapter 13, we learned about three types of discipline techniques. Which techniques are more likely to be used by parents from each parenting style?

Reflect *Your Own Personal Journey of Life*

- What was the nature of your relationship with your parents during middle school and high school? Has your relationship with your parents changed since then? Does it involve less conflict today? What do you think are the most important characteristics of a competent parent of adolescents?

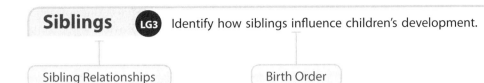
What are sibling relationships like? How extensively does birth order influence behavior?

SIBLING RELATIONSHIPS

Approximately 80 percent of American children have one or more siblings—that is, sisters and brothers (Dunn, 2007). If you grew up with siblings, you probably have a rich memory of aggressive, hostile interchanges. Siblings in the presence of each other when they are 2 to 4 years of age, on average, have a conflict once every 10 minutes. The conflicts go down somewhat from 5 to 7 years of age (Kramer, 2006). One recent study revealed that an increase in sibling conflict was linked to an increase in children's depressive symptoms, whereas an increase in sibling intimacy was related to an increase in children's peer competence (Kim & others, 2007). A recent review concluded that sibling relationships in adolescence are not as close, are not as intense, and are more egalitarian than in childhood (East, 2009).

What do parents do when they encounter siblings in the midst of a verbal or physical confrontation? One study revealed that they do one of three things: (1) intervene and try to help them resolve the conflict, (2) admonish or threaten them, or (3) do nothing at all (Kramer & Perozynski, 1999). Of interest is that in families with two siblings 2 to 5 years of age, the most frequent parental reaction is to do nothing at all.

Laurie Kramer (2006), who had conducted a number of research studies on siblings, says that not intervening and letting sibling conflict escalate is not a good strategy. She developed a program titled "More Fun with Sisters and Brothers" that teaches 4- to 8-year-old siblings social skills for developing positive interactions (Kramer & Radey, 1997). Among the social skills taught in the program are how to appropriately initiate play, how to accept and refuse invitations to play, how to understand another person's perspective, how to deal with angry feelings, and how to manage conflict. A recent study of 5- to 10-year-old siblings and their parents found that training parents to mediate sibling disputes increased children's understanding of conflicts and reduced sibling conflict (Smith & Ross, 2007).

As intense as it can be, however, conflict is only one of the many dimensions of sibling relations (Howe & Recchia, 2008; Steelman & Koch, 2009). Sibling relations include helping, sharing, teaching, fighting, and playing, and siblings can act as emotional supports, rivals, and communication partners (East, 2009).

Judy Dunn (2007), a leading expert on sibling relationships, recently described three important characteristics of sibling relationships:

• *Emotional quality of the relationship.* Both intensive positive and negative emotions are often expressed by siblings toward each other. Many children and adolescents have mixed feelings toward their siblings.

What are some characteristics of sibling relationships?

- *Familiarity and intimacy of the relationship.* Siblings typically know each other very well, and this intimacy suggests that they can either provide support or tease and undermine each other, depending on the situation.
- *Variation in sibling relationships.* Some siblings describe their relationships more positively than others. Thus, there is considerable variation in sibling relationships. We previously indicated that many siblings have mixed feelings about each other, but some children and adolescents mainly describe their sibling in warm, affectionate ways, whereas others primarily talk about how irritating and mean a sibling is.

Negative aspects of sibling relationships, such as high conflict, are linked to negative outcomes for adolescents. The negative outcomes can develop not only through conflict but also through direct modeling of a sibling's behavior, as when a younger sibling has an older sibling who has poor study habits and engages in delinquent behavior. By contrast, close and supportive sibling relationships can buffer the negative effects of stressful circumstances in an adolescent's life (East, 2009).

BIRTH ORDER

Whether a child has older or younger siblings has been linked to development of certain personality characteristics. For example, a recent review concluded that "firstborns are the most intelligent, achieving, and conscientious, while later-borns are the most rebellious, liberal, and agreeable" (Paulhus, 2008, p. 210). Compared with later-born children, firstborn children have also been described as more adult oriented, helpful, conforming, and self-controlled. However, when such birth order differences are reported, they often are small.

What accounts for differences related to birth order? Proposed explanations usually point to variations in interactions with parents and siblings associated with being in a particular position in the family. This is especially true in the case of the firstborn child (Teti, 2001). The oldest child is the only one who does not have to share parental love and affection with other siblings—until another sibling comes along. An infant requires more attention than an older child; this means that the firstborn sibling receives less attention after the newborn arrives. Does this result in conflict between parents and the firstborn? In one research study, mothers became more negative, coercive, and restraining and played less with the firstborn following the birth of a second child (Dunn & Kendrick, 1982).

What is the only child like? The popular conception is that the only child is a "spoiled brat," with such undesirable characteristics as dependency, lack of self-control, and self-centered behavior. But researchers present a more positive portrayal of the only child. Only children often are achievement oriented and display a desirable personality, especially in comparison with later-borns and children from large families (Falbo & Poston, 1993; Jiao, Ji, & Jing, 1996).

So far, our discussion suggests that birth order might be a strong predictor of behavior. However, an increasing number of family researchers stress that when all of the factors that influence behavior are considered, birth order itself shows limited ability to predict behavior.

Think about some of the other important factors in children's lives that influence their behavior beyond birth order. They include heredity, models of competency or incompetency that parents present to children on a daily basis, peer influences, school influences, socioeconomic factors, sociohistorical factors, and cultural variations. When someone says firstborns are always like this but lastborns are always like that, the person is making overly simplistic statements that do not adequately take into account the complexity of influences on a child's development.

The one-child family is becoming much more common in China because of the strong motivation to limit the population growth in the People's Republic of China. The effects of this policy have not been fully examined. *In general, what have researchers found the only child to be like?*

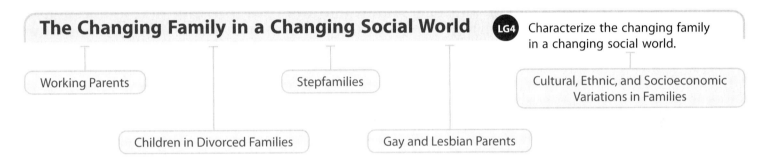

The Changing Family in a Changing Social World

LG4 Characterize the changing family in a changing social world.

Working Parents

Stepfamilies

Cultural, Ethnic, and Socioeconomic Variations in Families

Children in Divorced Families

Gay and Lesbian Parents

U.S. children are growing up in a greater variety of family contexts than ever before. As we discussed in Chapter 10, "Emotional Development," children are experiencing many sorts of caregiving—not only from stay-at-home mothers but also from stay-at-home fathers, from various types of child-care programs, and from after-school programs. The structure of American families also varies. As shown in Figure 14.6, the United States has a higher percentage of single-parent families than other countries with similar levels of economic and technological development. And many U.S. children are being raised in stepfamilies formed after a divorce and by gay or lesbian parents. How are these and other variations in family life affecting children?

WORKING PARENTS

The increased number of mothers in the labor force represents one source of change in families and society in the United States (Burchinal & Clarke-Stewart, 2007).

developmental connection

Environment. Research consistently shows that family factors are considerably better at predicting children's developmental outcomes than are child care experiences. Chapter 10, pp. 317–318

FIGURE **14.6**

SINGLE-PARENT FAMILIES IN DIFFERENT COUNTRIES

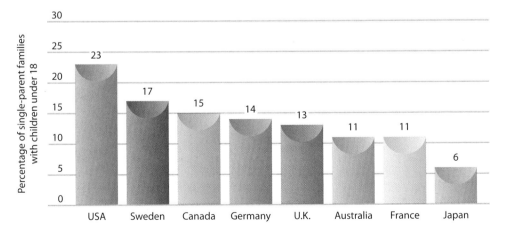

How does work affect parenting?

Many mothers spend the greatest part of their day away from their children, even their infants. More than one of every two mothers with a child under the age of 5 is in the labor force; more than two of every three with a child from 6 to 17 years of age is. How have these changes influenced children's development?

Work can produce positive and negative effects on parenting (Han, 2009). Recent research indicates that what matters for children's development is the nature of parents' work rather than whether parents works outside the home (Clarke-Stewart, 2006; Han, 2009). Ann Crouter (2006) recently described how parents bring their experiences at work into their homes. She concluded that parents who have poor working conditions, such as long hours, overtime work, stressful work, and lack of autonomy on the job, are likely to be more irritable at home and engage in less effective parenting than their counterparts who enjoy better working conditions. A consistent finding is the children (especially girls) of working mothers engage in less gender stereotyping and have more egalitarian views of gender (Goldberg & Lucas-Thompson, 2008).

CHILDREN IN DIVORCED FAMILIES

Divorce rates changed rather dramatically in the United States and many countries around the world during the late 20th century (Amato & Dorius, 2010). The U.S. divorce rate increased dramatically in the 1960s and 1970s but has declined since the 1980s. However, the divorce rate in the United States is still much higher than in most other countries.

It is estimated that 40 percent of children born to married parents in the United States will experience their parents' divorce (Hetherington & Stanley-Hagan, 2002). Let's examine some important questions about children in divorced families:

• *Are children better adjusted in intact, never-divorced families than in divorced families?* Most researchers agree that children from divorced families show poorer adjustment than their counterparts in nondivorced families (Amato & Dorius, 2010; Hetherington, 2006; Lansford, 2009; Wallerstein, 2008) (see Figure 14.7). Those who have experienced multiple divorces are at greater risk. Children in divorced families are more likely than children in nondivorced families to have academic problems, to show externalized problems (such as acting out and delinquency) and internalized problems (such as anxiety and depression), to be less socially responsible, to have less competent intimate relationships, to drop out of school, to become sexually active at an early age, to take drugs, to associate with antisocial peers, to have low self-esteem, and to be less securely attached as young adults (Lansford, 2009). A recent study revealed that adolescent girls with divorced parents were especially vulnerable to developing depressive symptoms (Oldehinkel & others, 2008). Another study found that experiencing a divorce in childhood was associated with insecure attachment in early adulthood (Brockmeyer, Treboux, & Crowell, 2005). Yet another study revealed that when individuals experienced the divorce of their parents in childhood and adolescence, it was linked to having unstable romantic and marital relationships and low levels of education in adulthood (Amato, 2006). Nonetheless, keep in mind that a majority of children (75 percent) in divorced families do not have significant adjustment problems.

• *Should parents stay together for the sake of the children?* Whether parents should stay in an unhappy or conflicted marriage for the sake of their children is one of the most commonly asked questions about divorce (Deutsch & Pruett, 2009; Hetherington, 2006; Ziol-Guest, 2009). If the stresses and disruptions in family relationships associated with an unhappy, conflictual marriage that

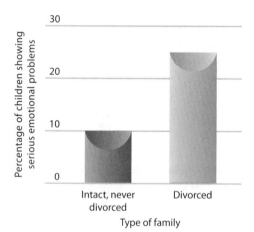

FIGURE **14.7**

DIVORCE AND CHILDREN'S EMOTIONAL PROBLEMS. In Hetherington's research, 25 percent of children from divorced families showed serious emotional problems compared with only 10 percent of children from intact, never-divorced families. However, keep in mind that a substantial majority (75 percent) of the children from divorced families did not show serious emotional problems.

erode the well-being of children are reduced by the move to a divorced, single-parent family, divorce can be advantageous. However, if the diminished resources and increased risks associated with divorce also are accompanied by inept parenting and sustained or increased conflict, not only between the divorced couple but also among the parents, children, and siblings, the best choice for the children would be for an unhappy marriage to be retained (Hetherington & Stanley-Hagan, 2002). It is difficult to determine how these "ifs" will play out when parents either remain together in an acrimonious marriage or become divorced.

Note that marital conflict may have negative consequences for children in the context of marriage or divorce (Cummings & Merrilees, 2009; Yu & others, 2010). A longitudinal study revealed that conflict in nondivorced families was associated with emotional problems in children (Amato, 2006). Indeed, many of the problems children from divorced homes experience begin during the predivorce period, a time when parents are often in active conflict with each other. Thus, when children from divorced homes show problems, the problems may be due not only to the divorce, but also to the marital conflict that led to it (Thompson, 2008).

E. Mark Cummings and his colleagues (Cummings, El-Sheikh, & Kouros, 2009; Cummings & Kouros, 2008; Cummings & Merrilees, 2009) have proposed *emotion security theory*, which has its roots in attachment theory and states that children appraise marital conflict in terms of their sense of security and safety in the family. They make a distinction between marital conflict that is negative for children (such as hostile emotional displays and destructive conflict tactics) and marital conflict that can be positive for children (such as marital disagreement that involves a calm discussion of each person's perspective and working together to reach a solution).

What concerns are involved in whether parents should stay together for the sake of the children and adolescents or become divorced?

- *How much do family processes matter in divorced families?* Family processes matter a great deal (Lansford, 2009; Pruett & Barker, 2009a, b; Ziol-Guest, 2009). When divorced parents' relationship with each other is harmonious, and when they use authoritative parenting, the adjustment of children improves (Hetherington, 2005, 2006). A number of researchers have shown that a disequilibrium, which includes diminished parenting skills, occurs in the year following the divorce—but by two years after the divorce, restabilization has occurred and parenting skills have improved (Hetherington, 1989).

- *What factors influence an individual child's vulnerability to suffering negative consequences as a result of living in a divorced family?* Among the factors influencing the child's risk and vulnerability are the child's adjustment prior to the divorce, as well as the child's personality and temperament, gender, and custody situation (Hetherington, 2005, 2006). Children whose parents later divorce show poorer adjustment before the breakup (Amato & Booth, 1996; Lansford, 2009). Children who are socially mature and responsible, who show few behavioral problems, and who have an easy temperament are better able to cope with their parents' divorce. Children with a difficult temperament often have problems in coping with their parents' divorce (Hetherington, 2005).

Earlier studies reported gender differences in response to divorce, with divorce being more negative for girls than boys in mother-custody families. However, more recent studies have shown that gender differences are less pronounced and consistent than was previously believed. Some of the inconsistency may be due to the increase in father custody, joint custody, and increased involvement of noncustodial fathers, especially in their sons' lives (Ziol-Guest, 2009). One analysis of studies found that children in joint-custody

caring *connections*

Communicating with Children About Divorce

Ellen Galinsky and Judy David (1988) developed a number of guidelines for communicating with children about divorce.

Explain the Separation

As soon as daily activities in the home make it obvious that one parent is leaving, tell the children. If possible, both parents should be present when children are told about the separation to come. The reasons for the separation are very difficult for young children to understand. No matter what parents tell children, children can find reasons to argue against the separation. It is extremely important for parents to tell the children who will take care of them and to describe the specific arrangements for seeing the other parent.

Explain That the Separation Is Not the Child's Fault

Young children often believe their parents' separation or divorce is their own fault. Therefore, it is important to tell children that they are not the cause of the separation. Parents need to repeat this a number of times.

Explain That It May Take Time to Feel Better

Tell young children that it's normal to not feel good about what is happening and that many other children feel this way when their parents become separated. It is also okay for divorced parents to share some of their emotions with children, by saying something like "I'm having a hard time since the separation just like you, but I know it's going to get better after a while." Such statements are best kept brief and should not criticize the other parent.

Keep the Door Open for Further Discussion

Tell your children to come to you anytime they want to talk about the separation. It is healthy for children to express their pent-up emotions in discussions with their parents and to learn that the parents are willing to listen to their feelings and fears.

Provide as Much Continuity as Possible

The less children's worlds are disrupted by the separation, the easier their transition to a single-parent family will be. This means maintaining the rules already in place as much as possible. Children need parents who care enough to not only give them warmth and nurturance but also set reasonable limits.

Provide Support for Your Children and Yourself

After a divorce or separation, parents are as important to children as before the divorce or separation. Divorced parents need to provide children with as much support as possible. Parents function best when other people are available to give them support as adults and as parents. Divorced parents can find people who provide practical help and with whom they can talk about their problems.

How does the third piece of advice above correspond to what you learned in Chapter 10 about emotion-coaching?

families were better adjusted than children in sole-custody families (Bauserman, 2002). Some studies have shown that boys adjust better in father-custody families, girls in mother-custody families, whereas other studies have not (Maccoby & Mnookin, 1992; Santrock & Warshak, 1979).

- *What role does socioeconomic status play in the lives of children in divorced families?* Custodial mothers experience the loss of about one-fourth to one-half of their predivorce income, in comparison with a loss of only one-tenth by custodial fathers (Emery, 1994). This income loss for divorced mothers is accompanied by increased workloads, high rates of job instability, and residential moves to less desirable neighborhoods with inferior schools (Lansford, 2009).

In sum, many factors are involved in determining how divorce influences a child's development (Amato & Dorius, 2010; Lansford, 2009; Pruett & Barker, 2009a, b). To read about some strategies for helping children cope with the divorce of their parents, see *Caring Connections*.

STEPFAMILIES

Not only has divorce become commonplace in the United States, so has getting remarried (Hetherington, 2006). It takes time for parents to marry, have children, get divorced, and then remarry. Consequently, there are far more elementary and secondary school children than infant or preschool children living in stepfamilies.

The number of remarriages involving children has grown steadily in recent years. Also, divorces occur at a 10 percent higher rate in remarriages than in first marriages (Cherlin & Furstenberg, 1994). About half of all children whose parents divorce will have a stepparent within four years of the separation.

Remarried parents face some unique tasks. The couple must define and strengthen their marriage and at the same time renegotiate the biological parent-child relationships and establish stepparent-stepchild and stepsibling relationships (Ganong, Coleman, & Hans, 2006). The complex histories and multiple relationships make adjustment difficult in a stepfamily (Goldscheider & Sassler, 2006). Only one-third of stepfamily couples stay remarried.

How does living in a stepfamily influence a child's development?

In some cases, the stepfamily may have been preceded by the death of a spouse. However, by far the largest number of stepfamilies are preceded by divorce rather than death (Pasley & Moorefield, 2004). Three common types of stepfamily structure are (1) stepfather, (2) stepmother, and (3) blended or complex. In stepfather families, the mother typically had custody of the children and remarried, introducing a stepfather into her children's lives. In stepmother families, the father usually had custody and remarried, introducing a stepmother into his children's lives. In a blended or complex stepfamily, both parents bring children from previous marriages to live in the newly formed stepfamily.

In E. Mavis Hetherington's (2006) most recent longitudinal analyses, children and adolescents who had been in a simple stepfamily (stepfather or stepmother) for a number of years were adjusting better than in the early years of the remarried family and were functioning well in comparison with children and adolescents in conflicted nondivorced families and children and adolescents in complex (blended) stepfamilies. More than 75 percent of the adolescents in long-established simple stepfamilies described their relationships with their stepparents as "close" or "very close." Hetherington (2006) concluded that in long-established simple stepfamilies adolescents seem to eventually benefit from the presence of a stepparent and the resources provided by the stepparent.

Children often have better relationships with their custodial parents (mothers in stepfather families, fathers in stepmother families) than with stepparents (Santrock, Sitterle, & Warshak, 1988). Also, children in simple families (stepmother, stepfather) often show better adjustment than their counterparts in complex (blended) families (Anderson & others, 1999; Hetherington & Kelly, 2002).

As in divorced families, children in stepfamilies show more adjustment problems than children in nondivorced families (Hetherington, 2006). The adjustment problems are similar to those found among children of divorced parents—academic problems and lower self-esteem, for example (Anderson & others, 1999). However, it is important to recognize that a majority of children in stepfamilies do not have problems. In one analysis, 25 percent of children from stepfamilies showed adjustment problems compared with 10 percent in intact, never-divorced families (Hetherington & Kelly, 2002).

Adolescence is an especially difficult time for the formation of a stepfamily (Anderson & others, 1999). Becoming part of a stepfamily may exacerbate normal adolescent concerns about identity, sexuality, and autonomy.

GAY AND LESBIAN PARENTS

Increasingly, gay and lesbian couples are creating families that include children (Patterson, 2009; Patterson & Farr, 2010; Patterson & Wainright, 2010) (see Figure 14.8).

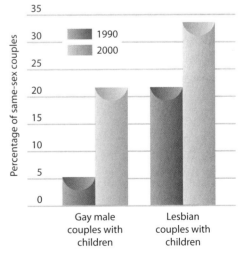

FIGURE **14.8**

PERCENTAGE OF GAY MALE AND LESBIAN COUPLES WITH CHILDREN: 1990 AND 2000.
Why do you think more lesbian couples have children than gay male couples?

What are the research findings regarding the development and psychological well-being of children raised by gay and lesbian couples?

Approximately 33 percent of lesbian couples and 22 percent of gay couples are parents (Patterson, 2004). There may be more than 1 million gay and lesbian parents in the United States today.

Like heterosexual couples, gay and lesbian parents vary greatly. They may be single or they may have same-gender partners. Many lesbian mothers and gay fathers are noncustodial parents because they lost custody of their children to heterosexual spouses after a divorce.

Most children of gay and lesbian parents were born in a heterosexual relationship that ended in a divorce: In most cases, it was probably a relationship in which one or both parents only later identified themselves as gay or lesbian. In other cases, lesbians and gay men became parents as a result of donor insemination and surrogates, or through adoption.

Parenthood by lesbian and gay couples is controversial. Opponents claim that being raised by gay or lesbian parents harms the child's development. But researchers have found few differences in children growing up with lesbian mothers or gay fathers and children growing up with heterosexual parents (Golombok & Tasker, 2010; Patterson & Wainright, 2010). For example, children growing up in gay or lesbian families are just as popular with their peers, and there are no differences in the adjustment and mental health of children living in these families as compared with children in heterosexual families (Hyde, 2007). Also, the overwhelming majority of children growing up in a gay or lesbian family have a heterosexual orientation (Tasker & Golombok, 1997).

CULTURAL, ETHNIC, AND SOCIOECONOMIC VARIATIONS IN FAMILIES

Parenting can be influenced by culture, ethnicity, and socioeconomic status. In Bronfenbrenner's theory (introduced in Chapter 1), these influences are described as part of the macrosystem.

Cross-Cultural Studies Different cultures often give different answers to such basic questions as what the father's role in the family should be, what support systems are available to families, and how children should be disciplined (Hewlett & McFarlen, 2010; Shiraev & Levy, 2010). There are important cross-cultural variations in parenting (Bornstein & Lansford, 2010). In some countries, authoritarian parenting is widespread. For example, in the Arab world, many families today are very authoritarian, dominated by the father's rule, and children are taught strict codes of conduct and family loyalty (Booth, 2002). In one study, Chinese mothers of preschool children reported that they used more physical coercion, more encouragement of modesty, more shaming and love withdrawal, less warmth, and less democratic participation than U.S. mothers of preschool children (Wu & others, 2002).

What type of parenting is most frequent? In one study of parenting behavior in 186 cultures around the world, the most common pattern was a warm and controlling style, one that was neither permissive nor restrictive (Rohner & Rohner, 1981). The investigators commented that the majority of cultures have discovered, over many centuries, that children's healthy social development is most effectively promoted by love and at least moderate parental control.

Cultural change is coming to families in many countries around the world (Larson, Wilson, & Rickman, 2009). There are trends toward greater family mobility, migration to urban areas, separation as some family members work in cities or countries far from their homes, smaller families, fewer extended-family households, and increases in maternal employment (Brown & Larson, 2002). These trends can change the resources that are available to children. For example, when several generations no longer live near each other, children may lose support and guidance from grandparents, aunts, and uncles. Also, smaller families may produce more openness and communication between parents and children.

Ethnicity   Families within different ethnic groups in the United States differ in their typical size, structure, composition, reliance on kinships networks, and levels of income and education (Fuligni, Hughes, & Way, 2009; Galindo & Durham, 2009; Livas-Dlott & others, 2010). Large and extended families are more common among minority groups than among the White majority. For example, 19 percent of Latino families have three or more children, as compared with 14 percent of African American and 10 percent of White families. African American and Latino children interact more with grandparents, aunts, uncles, cousins, and more-distant relatives than do White children.

Single-parent families are more common among African Americans and Latinos than among White Americans (Harris & Graham, 2007). In comparison with two-parent households, single parents often have more limited resources of time, money, and energy (Ryan, Fauth, & Brooks-Gunn, 2006). Ethnic minority parents also are less educated and more likely to live in low-income circumstances than their White counterparts. Still, many impoverished ethnic minority families manage to find ways to raise competent children (McLoyd & others, 2009).

Some aspects of home life can help protect ethnic minority children from injustice. The family can filter out destructive racist messages, and parents can present alternative frames of reference to counter those presented by the majority. For example, TV shows may tell a 10-year-old boy that he will grow up to be either a star athlete or a bum; his parents can show him that his life holds many possibilities other than these. The extended family also can serve as an important buffer to stress (McAdoo, 2006).

Of course, individual families vary, and how ethnic minority families deal with stress depends on many factors (McLoyd & others, 2009; Tamis-Lemonda & McFadden, 2010). Whether the parents are native-born or immigrants, how long the family has been in this country, their socioeoncomic status, and their national origin all make a difference (Fuligni, Hughes, & Way, 2009; Parke & Gauvain, 2010). The characteristics of the family's social context also influence its adaptation. What are the attitudes toward the family's ethnic group within its neighborhood or city? Can the family's children attend good schools? Are there community groups that welcome people from the family's ethnic group? Do members of the family's ethnic group form community groups of their own? To read further about ethnic minority parenting, see *Connecting With Diversity*.

Socioeconomic Status   Low-income families have less access to resources than higher-income families (Brandon, 2009; McLoyd & others, 2009; Tamis-Lemonda & McFadden, 2010). The differential in access to resources includes nutrition, health care, protection from danger, and enriching educational and socialization opportunities, such as tutoring and lessons in various activities. These differences are compounded in low-income families characterized by long-term poverty (McLoyd & others, 2009; Philipsen, Johnson, & Brooks-Gunn, 2009).

In America and most Western cultures, differences also have been found in child rearing among different socioeconomic-status (SES) groups (Hoff, Laursen, & Tardif, 2002, p. 246):

- "Lower-SES parents (1) are more concerned that their children conform to society's expectations, (2) create a home atmosphere in which it is clear that parents have authority over children," (3) use physical punishment more in disciplining their children, and (4) are more directive and less conversational with their children.

- "Higher-SES parents (1) are more concerned with developing children's initiative" and delay of gratification, "(2) create a home atmosphere in which

developmental **connection**

Culture and Ethnicity. Many families that have immigrated to the United States in recent decades, such as Mexican Americans and Asian Americans, come from collectivist cultures in which family obligation is strong. Chapter 17, p. 494

What are some characteristics of families in different ethnic groups?

developmental **connection**

Socioeconomic Status. Living in poverty has many psychological effects on both parents and children. Chapter 17, p. 489

Acculturation and Ethnic Minority Parenting

Ethnic minority children and their parents "are expected to transcend their own cultural background and to incorporate aspects of the dominant culture" into children's development. They undergo varying degrees of **acculturation,** which refers to cultural changes that occur when one culture comes in contact with another. Asian American parents, for example, may feel pressed to modify the traditional training style of parental control discussed earlier as they encounter the more permissive parenting typical of the dominant culture.

The level of family acculturation can affect parenting style by influencing expectations for children's development, parent-child interactions, and the role of the extended family (Fuligni, Hughes, & Way, 2009). For example, in one study, the level of acculturation and maternal education were the strongest predictors of maternal-infant interaction patterns in Latino families (Perez-Febles, 1992).

The family's level of acculturation also influences important decisions about child care and early childhood education. For example, "an African American mother might prefer to leave her children with extended family while she is at work because the kinship network is seen as a natural way to cope with maternal absence. This well-intentioned, culturally appropriate decision might, however, put the child at an educational and social disadvantage relative to other children of similar age who have the benefit of important preschool experiences that may ease the transition into early school years." Less acculturated and more acculturated family members may disagree about the appropriateness of various caregiving practices, possibly creating conflict or confusion.

The opportunities for acculturation that young children experience depend mainly on their parents and extended family. If parents send the children to a child-care center, school, church, or other community setting, the children are likely to learn about the values and behaviors of the dominant culture, and they may be expected to adapt to that culture's norms. Thus, Latino children raised in a traditional family in which

How is acculturation involved in ethnic minority parenting?

the family's well-being is considered more important than the individual's interests may attend a preschool in which children are rewarded for asserting themselves. Chinese American children, whose traditional parents value behavioral inhibition (as discussed in Chapter 10), may be rewarded outside the home for being active and emotionally expressive. Over time, the differences in the level of acculturation experienced by children and by their parents and extended family may grow. (Source: Garcia Coll & Pachter, 2002, pp. 7–8)

In this interlude you learned that preschools may encourage behavior that is at odds with some ethnic groups' parenting styles. Is this common worldwide? Which type of parenting is most frequently found worldwide?

---

children are more nearly equal participants and in which rules are discussed as opposed to being laid down" in an authoritarian manner, (3) are less likely to use physical punishment, and (4) "are less directive and more conversational" with their children.

Parents in different socioeconomic groups also tend to think differently about education (Huston & Ripke, 2006). Middle- and upper-income parents more often think of education as something that should be mutually encouraged by parents and teachers. By contrast, low-income parents are more likely to view education as the teacher's job. Thus, increased school-family linkages especially can benefit students from low-income families. In Chapter 17, "Culture and Diversity," we will have much more to say about socioeconomic variations in families, especially the negative ramifications of poverty for children's development, as well as other aspects of culture and its role in parenting and children's development.

acculturation Cultural changes that occur when one culture comes in contact with another culture.

Review

- How are children influenced by working parents?
- How does divorce affect children's development?
- How does living in a stepfamily influence children's development?
- How do lesbian mothers and gay fathers influence children's development?
- How do culture, ethnicity, and socioeconomic status of families influence children's development?

Connect

- In this section, you learned that low-income families have less access to nutrition, health care, protection from danger, and enriching educational and socialization opportunities. In Chapter 4, what did you learn regarding the specific health outcomes for children living in poverty?

Reflect *Your Own Personal Journey of Life*

- Now that you have studied many aspects of families in this chapter, imagine that you have decided to write a book on some aspect of your own family. What aspect of your family would you focus on? What would be the title of your book? What would be the major theme of the book?

reach your **learning goals**

Families

Family Processes

LG1 Discuss family processes.

Interactions in the Family System

Cognition and Emotion in Family Processes

Multiple Developmental Trajectories

Domain-Specific Socialization

Sociocultural and Historical Changes

- The family is a system of interrelated and interacting individuals with different subsystems—some dyadic, some polyadic. The subsystems have both direct and indirect effects on one another. Positive marital relations can have a positive influence on parenting. Reciprocal socialization is the bidirectional process by which children socialize parents just as parents socialize them.

- Cognition and emotion are central to understanding how family processes work. The role of cognition includes parents' cognitions, beliefs, and values about their parental role, as well as the way they perceive, organize, and understand their children's behaviors and beliefs. The role of emotion includes the regulation of emotion in children, understanding emotion in children, and emotion in carrying out the parenting role. Children learn to express and manage emotions appropriately through interaction with emotion-coaching parents and have fewer behavior problems than children of emotion-dismissing parents.

- Adults follow one developmental trajectory and children and adolescents another one. How these trajectories mesh is important for understanding the effects of timing of entry into various family tasks.

- Increasingly a domain-specific approach to socialization is being emphasized. One recent proposal focuses on five domains, each linked to specific child outcomes. The five domains are: protection, reciprocity, control, guided learning, and group participation.

- Changes in families may be due to great upheavals, such as war, or more subtle changes, such as technological advances and greater mobility of families. Increased restlessness and dissatisfaction in families has resulted in more divorced and remarried families than at any other point in history.

Parenting

 LG2 Explain how parenting is linked to children's and adolescents' development.

Adapting Parenting to Developmental Changes in Children

- The transition to parenthood requires considerable adaptation and adjustment on the part of parents. Discipline with younger children is often handled by physical manipulation, such as carrying a 2-year-old away from mischief. As children grow older, parents increasingly turn to reasoning or withholding privileges in disciplining children. Parents spend less time with children in middle and late childhood, a time when parents play an especially important role in their children's academic achievement. Control is more coregulatory in middle and late childhood.

Parents as Managers of Children's Lives

- A recent trend is to conceptualize parents as managers of children's lives. Parents play important roles as managers of children's opportunities, effectively monitoring children's relationships and acting as social initiators and arrangers. Parental monitoring is linked to lower levels of juvenile delinquency, and effective parental management is related to children's higher academic achievement.

Parenting Styles and Discipline

- Authoritarian, authoritative, neglectful, and indulgent are the four main categories of parenting styles. Authoritative parenting is associated with socially competent child behavior more than the other styles. However, ethnic variations in parenting styles indicate that in African American and Asian American families, some aspects of control may benefit children. Latino parents often emphasize connectedness with the family and respect and obedience in their child rearing. There are a number of reasons not to use physical punishment in disciplining children, and in Sweden physical punishment of children has been outlawed. Intense punishment presents the child with an out-of-control model. Punishment can instill fear, rage, or avoidance in children. Punishment tells children what not to do rather than what to do. Punishment can be abusive. Coparenting has positive outcomes for children. Child maltreatment is a multifaceted problem. Understanding child maltreatment requires information about the cultural context and family influences. Child maltreatment places the child at risk for a number of developmental problems.

Parent-Adolescent Relationships

- Many parents have a difficult time handling the adolescent's push for autonomy. Secure attachment to parents increases the likelihood that the adolescent will be socially competent. Conflict with parents often increases in early adolescence, but this conflict is generally moderate rather than severe. The increase in conflict probably serves the positive developmental functions of facilitating adolescent autonomy and identity. A subset of adolescents experience high parent-adolescent conflict, and this is linked with negative outcomes for adolescents.

Intergenerational Relationships

- Connections between parents play important roles in development through the life span. An increasing number of studies indicate that intergenerational relationships influence children's development. Marital interaction, a supportive family environment, divorce, and conduct disorder in the child's family of origin are among the factors that are linked to the child's development.

Siblings

 LG3 Identify how siblings influence children's development.

Sibling Relationships

- Three important aspects of sibling relationships involve (1) emotional quality of the relationship, (2) familiarity and intimacy of the relationship, and (3) variation. Sibling relationships include not only conflict and fighting but also helping, teaching, sharing, and playing—and siblings can function as rivals, emotional supports, and communication partners.

Birth Order

- Birth order is related in certain ways to child characteristics. Firstborn children are more self-controlled, conforming, have more guilt and anxiety, argue and excel academically and professionally compared with later-born children. However, some critics argue that the influence of birth order has been overestimated as a predictor of child behavior.

The Changing Family in a Changing Social World

 LG4 Characterize the changing family in a changing social world.

- **Working Parents**

  - In general, having both parents employed full-time outside the home has not been shown to have negative effects on children. However, depending on the circumstances, work can produce positive or negative effects on parenting. If parents experience poor work conditions, they frequently become inattentive to their children, who show more behavioral problems and do more poorly at school. There is a positive link between participation in extracurricular activities and academic achievement, psychological adjustment, and positive interaction with parents.

- **Children in Divorced Families**

  - Children in divorced families show more adjustment problems than their counterparts in nondivorced families. Whether parents should stay in an unhappy or conflicted marriage for the sake of the children is difficult to determine. Children show better adjustment in divorced families when parents' relationships with each other are harmonious and authoritative parenting is used. Factors to be considered in the adjustment of children in divorced families are adjustment prior to the divorce, personality and temperament, developmental status, gender, and custody. Income loss for divorced mothers may be linked with a number of stresses that can affect the child's adjustment.

- **Stepfamilies**

  - As in divorced families, children in stepfamilies have more problems than their counterparts in nondivorced families. Restabilization often takes longer in stepfamilies than in divorced families. Children often have better relationships with their biological parents than with their stepparents and show more problems in complex, blended families than simple ones. Adolescence is an especially difficult time to experience the remarriage of parents.

- **Gay and Lesbian Parents**

  - Approximately 33 percent of lesbians and 22 percent of gay men are parents. There is considerable diversity among lesbian mothers, gay fathers, and their children. Researchers have found few differences between children growing up with gay or lesbian parents and children growing up with heterosexual parents.

- **Cultural, Ethnic, and Socioeconomic Variations in Families**

  - Cultures vary on a number of issues regarding families. African American and Latino children are more likely than White American children to live in single-parent families, larger families, and families with extended connections. Higher-SES families tend to avoid using physical discipline, strive to create a home atmosphere in which rules are discussed, and are concerned with developing children's initiative and delay of gratification. Lower-SES families are more likely to use physical punishment in disciplining their children, are more directive and less conversational, and want their children to conform to society's expectations.

key terms

scaffolding 396
reciprocal
    socialization 397

multiple developmental
    trajectories 398
authoritarian parenting 404

authoritative parenting 404
neglectful parenting 405
indulgent parenting 405

coparenting 408
acculturation 422

key people

Urie Bronfenbrenner 396
Joan Grusec and
    Marilyn Davidov 399

Diana Baumrind 404
Ruth Chao 405
Joseph Allen 410

Laurie Kramer 413
Judy Dunn 413
Ann Crouter 416

E. Mavis Hetherington 419
Reed Larson 420

chapter 15 PEERS

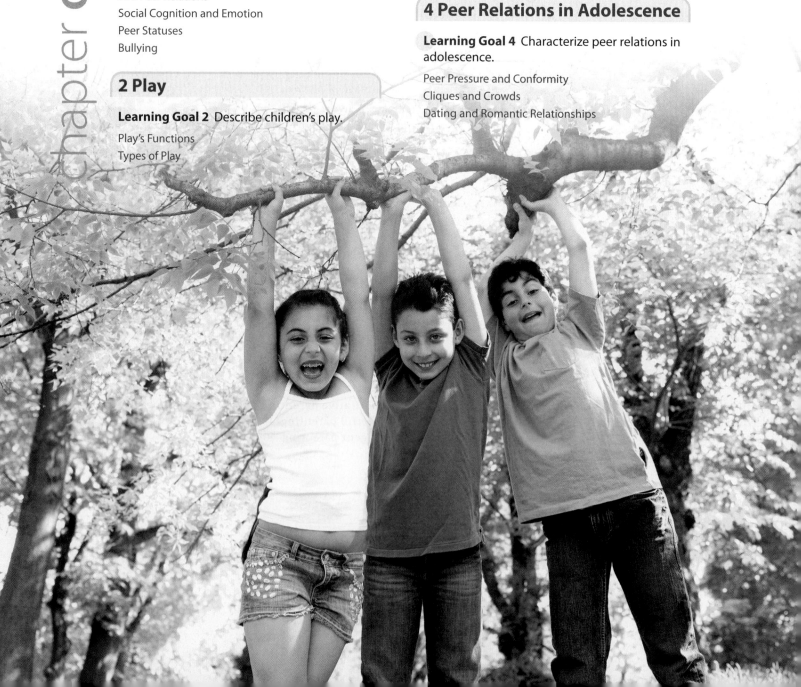

Lynn Brown and Carol Gilligan (1992) conducted in-depth interviews of one hundred 10- to 13-year-old girls who were making the transition to adolescence. They listened to what these girls were saying.

A number of the girls talked about how many girls say nice things to be polite but often don't really mean them. The girls know the benefits of being perceived as the perfect, happy girl. Judy spoke about her interest in romantic relationships. Although she and her girlfriends were only 13, they wanted to be romantic, and she talked about her lengthy private conversations with her girlfriends about boys. Noura said that she learned how very painful it is to be the person everyone doesn't like.

Cliques figured largely in these girls' lives. They provided emotional support for girls who were striving to be perfect but knew they were not. Victoria commented that sometimes girls like her, who weren't very popular, nonetheless were accepted into a "club" with three other girls. Now when she was sad or depressed she could count on the "club" for support. Though they were "leftovers" and did not get into the most popular cliques, these four girls knew they were liked.

Through these interviews, we see the girls' curiosity about the social world they lived in. They kept track of what was happening to their peers and friends. The girls spoke at length about the pleasure they derived from the intimacy and fun of human connection, about the potential for hurt in relationships, and about the importance of friends.

preview

This chapter is about peers, who clearly are very important in the lives of the adolescent girls just described. They also are very important in the lives of children. We begin this chapter by examining a number of ideas about children's peer relations, including their functions and variations. Then we turn to children's play and the roles of friends in children's development. We conclude by discussing peer relationships in adolescence.

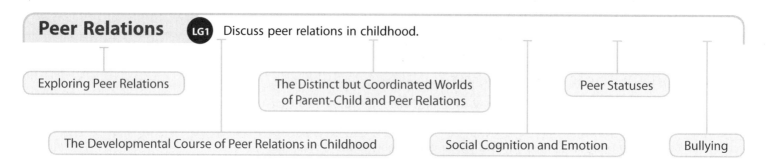

Peer Relations   (LG1)   Discuss peer relations in childhood.

- Exploring Peer Relations
- The Distinct but Coordinated Worlds of Parent-Child and Peer Relations
- Peer Statuses
- The Developmental Course of Peer Relations in Childhood
- Social Cognition and Emotion
- Bullying

As children grow up, they spend increasing amounts of time with their peers. What are some key aspects of peer relations?

EXPLORING PEER RELATIONS

> You are troubled at seeing him spend his early years in doing nothing. What! Is it nothing to be happy? Is it nothing to skip, to play, to run about all day long? Never in his life will he be so busy as now.
>
> —JEAN-JACQUES ROUSSEAU
> *Swiss-Born French Philosopher,*
> *18th Century*

Peers are children who share the same age or maturity level. They fill a unique role in the child's development. One of their most important functions is to provide a source of information and comparison about the world outside the family. Children receive feedback about their abilities from their peer group. They evaluate what they do in terms of whether it is better than, as good as, or worse than what other children do. It is hard to do this at home because siblings are usually older or younger.

Are Peers Necessary for Development?   Good peer relations may be necessary for normal social development (Brown & Larson, 2009). Social isolation, or the inability to "plug in" to a social network, is linked with different problems and disorders ranging from delinquency and problem drinking to depression (Conduct Problems Prevention Research Group, 2010; Dodge & others, 2010).

Positive and Negative Peer Relations   Peer influences can be both positive and negative (Asher & McDonald, 2009; Bukowski, Motzoi, & Meyer, 2009; Chung-Hall & Chen, 2010; Knecht & others, 2010). Both Jean Piaget (1932) and Harry Stack Sullivan (1953) were influential theorists who stressed that it is through peer interaction that children and adolescents learn important aspects of relationships. They also learn to be keen observers of peers' interests and perspectives in order to smoothly integrate themselves into ongoing peer activities. In addition, Sullivan argued that adolescents learn to be skilled and sensitive partners in intimate relationships by forging close friendships with selected peers. These intimacy skills are carried forward to help form the foundation of later dating and marital relationships, according to Sullivan.

We discussed yet another function of peers in Chapter 13: According to Piaget and Lawrence Kohlberg, through the give-and-take of peer relations, children develop their social understanding and moral reasoning. Children explore the principles of fairness and justice by working through disagreements with peers.

peers Children who share the same age or maturity level.

Consider the results of these longitudinal studies that illustrate the potential long-term benefits of peer relations in childhood:

- Competence in peer relations during middle and late childhood was linked to work success and satisfaction in romantic relationships in early adulthood (Collins & van Dulmen, 2006).
- Popularity with peers and a low level of aggression at age 8 foreshadowed a higher occupational status at age 48 (Huesmann & others, 2006).

In contrast, some theorists have emphasized the negative influences of peers on children's and adolescents' development. Being rejected or overlooked by peers leads some children and adolescents to feel lonely or hostile. Further, such rejection and neglect by peers are related to an individual's subsequent mental health and criminal problems. Some theorists have also described the peer culture as a negative influence that undermines parental values and control. Further, peer relations are linked to adolescents' patterns of drug use, delinquency, and depression. Consider the results of these studies:

- Time spent hanging out with antisocial peers in adolescence was a stronger predictor of substance abuse than time spent with parents (Nation & Heflinger, 2006).
- Deviant peer affiliation was related to adolescents' depressive symptoms (Connell & Dishion, 2006).

As you read further about peers, keep in mind that findings about the influence of peers vary according to the way peer experience is measured, the outcomes specified, and the developmental trajectories traversed (Hartup & Laursen, 1999). "Peers" and "peer group" are global concepts. A "peer group" of an adolescent might refer to a neighborhood crowd, reference crowd, church crowd, sports team, friendship group, and friend (Brown, 1999).

Peer Contexts Peer interaction is influenced by contexts, which can include the type of peer the child or adolescent interacts with—such an acquaintance, a crowd, a clique, a friend, or a romantic partner—and the situation or location—such as a school, neighborhood, community center, dance, religious setting, sporting event, and so on, as well as the culture in which when the child or adolescent lives (Brown & Larson, 2009; Rubin, Cheah, & Menzer, 2010). As they interact with peers in these various contexts, children and adolescents likely encounter different messages and different opportunities to engage in adaptive and maladaptive behavior that can influence their development (Prinstein & Dodge, 2008).

In terms of contexts, peers play an important role in the development of individuals in all cultures. However, as indicated in *Connecting With Diversity*, cultures vary in the significance of the socializing role of peers.

Individual Difference Factors Individual differences among peers also are important to consider in understanding peer relations. Among the wide range of individual differences that can affect peer relations are personality traits such as how shy or outgoing children are. For example, a very shy child is more likely than a gregarious child to be neglected by peers and have anxiety about introducing himself or herself to new peers. One individual difference factor that impairs peer relations is the trait of negative emotionality, which involves a relatively low threshold for experiencing anger, fear, anxiety, and irritation. For example, one recent study revealed that adolescents characterized by negative emotionality tended to engage in negative interpersonal behavior when interacting with a friend or a romantic partner (Hatton & others, 2008).

THE DEVELOPMENTAL COURSE OF PEER RELATIONS IN CHILDHOOD

Some researchers argue that the quality of peer interaction in infancy provides valuable information about socioemotional development (Hughes & Dunn, 2007; Williams,

In what ways can peer relations be positive and negative?

Cross-Cultural Comparisons of Peer Relations

In some countries, adults restrict adolescents' access to peers. For example, in many areas of rural India and in Arab countries, opportunities for peer relations in adolescence are severely restricted, especially for girls (Brown & Larson, 2002). If girls attend school in these regions of the world, it is usually in sex-segregated schools. In these countries, interaction with the other sex or opportunities for romantic relationships are restricted (Booth, 2002).

In a cross-cultural analysis, the peer group was more important to U.S. adolescents than to Japanese adolescents (Rothbaum & others, 2000). Japanese adolescents spend less time outside the home, have less recreational leisure time, and engage in fewer extracurricular activities with peers than U.S. adolescents (White, 1993). Also, U.S. adolescents are more likely to put pressure on their

Street youth in Rio de Janeiro.

peers to resist parental influence than Japanese adolescents are (Rothbaum & others, 2000).

In some cultures, children are placed in peer groups for much greater lengths of time at an earlier age than they are in the United States. For example, in the Murian culture of eastern India, both male and female children live in a dormitory from the age of 6 until they get married (Barnouw, 1975). The dormitory is a religious haven where members are devoted to work and spiritual harmony. Children work for their parents, and the parents arrange the children's marriages.

In some cultural settings, peers even assume responsibilities usually handled by parents. For example, street youth in South America rely on networks of peers to help them negotiate survival in urban environments (Welti, 2002).

In Chapter 1, you learned that cross-cultural studies compare aspects of two or more cultures, and the comparison provides information about the degree to which development is similar—or universal—across cultures or is culture-specific. From the results of this cross-cultural study, what can you say about peer pressure?

Ontai, & Mastergeorge, 2010). For example, in one investigation, positive affect in infant peer relations was related to easy access to peer play groups and to peer popularity in early childhood (Howes, 1985). As increasing numbers of children attend child care, peer interaction in infancy takes on a more important developmental role.

Around the age of 3, children already prefer to spend time with same-sex rather than opposite-sex playmates, and this preference increases in early childhood. During these same years the frequency of peer interaction, both positive and negative, picks up considerably (Hartup, 1983). Although aggressive interaction and rough-and-tumble play increase, the proportion of aggressive exchanges, compared with friendly exchanges, decreases. Many preschool children spend considerable time in peer interaction just conversing with playmates about such matters as "negotiating roles and rules in play, arguing, and agreeing" (Rubin, Bukowski, & Parker, 2006).

In early childhood, children distinguish between friends and nonfriends (Howes, 2009). For most young children, a friend is someone to play with. Young preschool children are more likely than older children to have friends who are of a different gender or ethnicity (Howes, 2009).

As children enter the elementary school years, reciprocity becomes especially important in peer interchanges. Children play games, function in groups, and cultivate friendships. The amount of time children spend in peer interaction also rises during middle and late childhood and adolescence. Researchers estimate that the percentage of time spent in social interaction with peers increases from approximately

10 percent at 2 years of age to more than 30 percent in middle and late childhood (Rubin, Bukowski, & Parker, 2006). Other changes in peer relations as children move through middle and late childhood involve an increase in the size of their peer group and peer interaction that is supervised less closely by adults (Rubin, Bukowski, & Parker, 2006).

Peer interactions take varied forms—cooperative and competitive, boisterous and quiet, joyous and humiliating. There is increasing evidence that gender plays an important role in these interactions (Blakemore, Berenbaum, & Liben, 2009). Gender influences not only the composition of children's groups but also their size and the types of interactions within them (Maccoby, 2002). From about 5 years of age onward, boys tend to associate in large clusters more than girls do; girls are more likely than boys to play in groups of two or three. As discussed in Chapter 12, "Gender," boys' groups and girls' groups also tend to favor different types of activities. Boys' groups are more likely to engage in rough-and-tumble play, competition, conflict, ego displays, risk taking, and dominance seeking. By contrast, girls' groups are more likely to engage in collaborative discourse (Leman, Ahmed, & Ozarow, 2005).

THE DISTINCT BUT COORDINATED WORLDS OF PARENT-CHILD AND PEER RELATIONS

Parents may influence their children's peer relations in many ways, both direct and indirect (Booth-LaForce & Kerns, 2009; Ross & Howe, 2009; Updegraff & others, 2010). Parents affect their children's peer relations through their interactions with their children, how they manage their children's lives, and the opportunities they provide their children. A recent study revealed that warmth, advice giving, and provision of opportunities by mothers and fathers were linked to children's social competence (high prosocial behavior, low aggression), and subsequently to social acceptance (being well-liked by peers and teachers) one year later (McDowell & Parke, 2009).

Basic lifestyle decisions by parents—their choices of neighborhoods, churches, schools, and their own friends—largely determine the pool from which their children select possible friends. These choices in turn affect which children their children meet, their purpose in interacting, and eventually which children become their friends.

What are some developmental changes in peer relations?

What are some ways that parents influence their children's peer relations?

developmental **connection**

Attachment. Securely attached infants use the caregiver as a secure base from which to explore their environment. Chapter 10, p. 310

developmental **connection**

Social Cognitive Theory. Social cognition refers to the processes involved in understanding the world around us, especially how we think and reason about others. Chapter 11, p. 327

perspective taking The ability to perceive another person's point of view.

Researchers also have found that children's peer relations are linked to attachment security and parents' marital quality (Booth-Laforce & Kerns, 2009; Ross & Howe, 2009). Early attachments to caregivers provide a connection to children's peer relations not only by creating a secure base from which children can explore social relationships beyond the family but also by conveying a working model of relationships (Hartup, 2009).

Do these results indicate that children's peer relations always are wedded to parent-child relationships? Although parent-child relationships influence children's subsequent peer relations, children also learn other modes of relating through their relationships with peers. For example, rough-and-tumble play occurs mainly with other children, not in parent-child interaction. In times of stress, children often turn to parents rather than peers for support. In parent-child relationships, children learn how to relate to authority figures. With their peers, children are likely to interact on a much more equal basis and to learn a mode of relating based on mutual influence.

SOCIAL COGNITION AND EMOTION

Mariana expects all her playmates to let her play with their toys whenever she asks. When Josh isn't picked for a team on the playground, he thinks his friends have turned against him. These are examples of social cognitions, which involve thoughts about social matters (Dodge, 2010; Prinstein & others, 2009). How might children's social cognitions contribute to their peer relations? Possibilities include their perspective-taking ability, social information-processing skills, and emotional regulation.

Perspective Taking   As children enter the elementary school years, both their peer interaction and their perspective-taking ability increase. As we discussed in Chapter 13, "Moral Development," **perspective taking** involves perceiving another's point of view. Researchers have documented a link between perspective-taking skills and the quality of peer relations, especially in the elementary school years (LeMare & Rubin, 1987).

Perspective taking is important in part because it helps children communicate effectively. In one investigation, the communication exchanges among peers at kindergarten, first-, third-, and fifth-grade levels were evaluated (Krauss & Glucksberg, 1969). Children were asked to instruct a peer in how to stack a set of blocks. The peer sat behind a screen with blocks similar to those the other child was stacking (see Figure 15.1). The kindergarten children made numerous errors in telling the peer how to duplicate the novel block stack. The older children, especially the fifth-graders, were much more efficient in communicating to a peer how to stack the blocks. They were far superior at perspective taking and figuring out how to talk to a peer so that the peer could understand them. During the elementary school years, children also become more efficient at understanding complex messages, so the listening skills of the peer in this experiment probably helped the communicating peer as well.

FIGURE **15.1**

THE DEVELOPMENT OF COMMUNICATION SKILLS. This is an experimental arrangement of speaker and listener in the investigation of the development of communication skills.

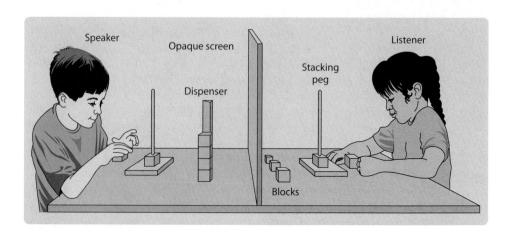

Social Information-Processing Skills How children process information about peer relationships also influences those relationships (Dodge, 2010; Fontaine & Dodge, 2009; Pettit & others, 2010). For example, suppose Andrew accidentally trips and knocks Alex's soft drink out of his hand. Alex misinterprets the encounter as hostile, which leads him to retaliate aggressively against Andrew. Through repeated encounters of this kind, other peers come to perceive Alex as habitually acting inappropriately.

Peer relations researcher Kenneth Dodge (1993) argues that children go through five steps in processing information about their social world: decoding social cues, interpreting, searching for a response, selecting an optimal response, and enacting it. Dodge has found that aggressive boys are more likely to perceive another child's actions as hostile when the child's intention is ambiguous—and when aggressive boys search for clues to determine a peer's intention, they respond more rapidly, less efficiently, and less reflectively than nonaggressive children.

Emotional Regulation Not only does cognition play an important role in peer relations, so does emotion. For example, the ability to regulate emotion is linked to successful peer relations (Rubin, Bukowski, & Parker, 2006). Moody and emotionally negative individuals experience greater rejection by peers, whereas emotionally positive individuals are more popular (Saarni & others, 2006). Children who have effective self-regulatory skills can modulate their emotional expressiveness in contexts that evoke intense emotions, as when a peer says something negative (Orobio de Castro & others, 2005).

PEER STATUSES

Which types of children are likely to be popular with their peers, and which ones tend to be disliked? Developmentalists address this and similar questions by examining *sociometric status*, a term that describes the extent to which children are liked or disliked by their peer group (Cillessen, 2009; LaFontana & Cillessen, 2009). Sociometric status is typically assessed by asking children to rate how much they like or dislike each of their classmates. Or it may be assessed by asking children to name the children they like the most and those they like the least.

Developmentalists have distinguished five peer statuses (Wentzel & Asher, 1995):

- **Popular children** are frequently nominated as a best friend and are rarely disliked by their peers.
- **Average children** receive an average number of both positive and negative nominations from their peers.
- **Neglected children** are infrequently nominated as a best friend but are not disliked by their peers.
- **Rejected children** are rarely nominated as someone's best friend and are actively disliked by their peers.
- **Controversial children** are frequently nominated both as someone's best friend and as being disliked.

Popular children have a number of social skills that contribute to their being well liked. Researchers have found that popular children give out reinforcements, listen carefully, maintain open lines of communication with peers, are happy, control their negative emotions, act like themselves, show enthusiasm and concern for others, and are self-confident without being conceited (Hartup, 1983; Rubin, Bukowski, & Parker, 2006).

Neglected children engage in low rates of interaction with their peers and are often described as shy by peers. Rejected children often have more serious adjustment problems than those who are neglected (Dishion & Piehler, 2009; Prinstein & others, 2009). One study evaluated 112 fifth-grade boys over a period of seven years until the end of high school (Kupersmidt & Coie, 1990). The best predictor of

How do aggressive boys process information about their social world?

popular children Children who are frequently identified as a best friend and are rarely disliked by their peers.

average children Children who receive an average number of both positive and negative nominations from their peers.

neglected children Children who are infrequently identified as a best friend but are not disliked by their peers.

rejected children Children who are infrequently identified as a best friend and are actively disliked by their peers.

controversial children Children who are frequently identified both as someone's best friend and as being disliked.

What are some statuses that children have with their peers?

whether rejected children would engage in delinquent behavior or drop out of school later during adolescence was aggression toward peers in elementary school. A recent study revealed that over the course of elementary school, during periods of peer rejection children were less likely to engage in classroom participation, but during times when they were not rejected, they participated more in class (Ladd, Herald-Brown, & Reiser, 2008).

Peer Rejection and Aggression   The combination of being rejected by peers and being aggressive especially forecasts problems (Dishion & Piehler, 2009; Prinstein & others, 2009). For example, one study found that when third-grade boys were highly aggressive and rejected by their peers, they showed markedly higher levels of delinquency as adolescents and young adults than other boys did (Miller-Johnson, Coie, & Malone, 2003).

An analysis by John Coie (2004, pp. 252–253) provided three reasons why aggressive peer-rejected boys have problems in social relationships:

- First, the rejected, aggressive boys are more impulsive and have problems sustaining attention. As a result, they are more likely to be disruptive of ongoing activities in the classroom and in focused group play.

- Second, rejected, aggressive boys are more emotionally reactive. They are aroused to anger more easily and probably have more difficulty calming down once aroused. Because of this they are more prone to become angry at peers and to attack them verbally and physically.

- Third, rejected children have fewer social skills for making friends and maintaining positive relationships with peers.

Not all rejected children are aggressive (Erath & others, 2009; Vaillancourt & Hymel, 2006). Although aggression and its related characteristics of impulsiveness and disruptiveness underlie rejection about half the time, approximately 10 to 20 percent of rejected children are shy.

> Peer rejection contributes to subsequent problems of adaptation, including antisocial behavior.
>
> —JOHN COIE
> *Contemporary Psychologist,*
> *Duke University*

What are the antecedents of peer rejection? According to Gerald Patterson, Tom Dishion, and their colleagues (Patterson, DeBaryshe, & Ramsey, 1989; Patterson, Reid, & Dishion, 1992; Shaw & others, 2006), poor parenting skills are at the root of children being rejected by their peers. These researchers especially argue that inadequate monitoring and harsh punishment, in some instances being reactions to a child's difficult temperament, produce a child with aggressive, antisocial tendencies. The child carries these tendencies to the world of peers, where the child is rejected by better-adjusted peers who have a more positive temperament (such as "easy" or "effortful control") and have experienced more positive parenting (such as authoritative parenting).

Not all rejected children are aggressive (Rubin, Cheah, & Menzer, 2010). Although aggression and its related characteristics of impulsiveness and disruptiveness underlie rejection about half the time, approximately 10 to 20 percent of rejected children are shy.

How can rejected children be trained to interact more effectively with their peers? Rejected children may be taught to more accurately assess whether the intentions of their peers are negative. They may be asked to engage in role playing or to discuss hypothetical situations involving negative encounters with peers, such as times when a peer cuts into a line ahead of them. In some programs, children are shown videotapes of appropriate peer interaction and asked to draw lessons from what they have seen (Ladd, Buhs, & Troop, 2004).

Despite the positive outcomes of some programs that attempt to improve the social skills of adolescents, researchers have often found it difficult to improve the social skills of adolescents who are actively disliked and rejected. Many of these adolescents are rejected because they are aggressive or impulsive and lack the self-control to keep these behaviors in check. Still, some intervention programs have been successful in reducing the aggressive and impulsive behaviors of these adolescents (Ladd, Buhs, & Troop, 2004).

Social-skills training programs have generally been more successful with children 10 years of age or younger than with adolescents (Malik & Furman, 1993). Peer reputations become more fixed as cliques and peer groups become more salient in adolescence. Once an adolescent gains a negative reputation among peers as being "mean," "weird," or a "loner," the peer group's attitude is often slow to change, even after the adolescent's problem behavior has been corrected. Thus, researchers have found that skill interventions may need to be supplemented by efforts to change the minds of peers.

BULLYING

Significant numbers of students are victimized by bullies (Espelage, Holt, & Poteat, 2010; Faris, 2009; Salmivalli & Peets, 2009; Vernberg & Biggs, 2010). In a national survey of more than 15,000 sixth- through tenth-grade students, nearly one of every three students said that they had experienced occasional or frequent involvement as a victim or perpetrator in bullying (Nansel & others, 2001) (see Figure 15.2). In this study, bullying was defined as verbal or physical behavior intended to disturb someone less powerful. A recent study revealed that bullying decreased as students went from the beginning of sixth grade (20 percent were bullied extensively) through the end of eighth grade (6 percent were bullied extensively) (Nylund & others, 2007). Boys are more likely to be bullies than girls, but gender differences regarding victims of boys is less clear (Salmivalli & Peets, 2009).

Who is likely to be bullied? In the study just described, boys and younger middle school students were most likely to be affected (Nansel & others, 2001). Children who said they were bullied reported more loneliness and difficulty in making friends, while those who did the bullying were more likely to have low grades and to smoke and drink alcohol. Researchers have found that anxious, socially withdrawn, and aggressive children are often the victims of bullying (Hanish & Guerra, 2004). Anxious and socially withdrawn children may be victimized because they are nonthreatening and unlikely to retaliate if bullied, whereas aggressive children may be the targets of bullying because their behavior is irritating to bullies (Rubin, Bukowski, & Parker, 2006).

Social contexts also influence bullying (Schwartz & others, 2010; Veenstra & others, 2010). Recent research indicates that 70 to 80 percent of victims and their bullies are in the same school classroom (Salmivalli & Peets, 2009). Classmates are often aware of bullying incidents and in many cases witness bullying. The larger social context of the peer group plays an important role in bullying (Salmivalli & Peets, 2009). In many cases, bullies torment victims to gain higher status in the peer group, and bullies need others to witness their power displays. Many bullies are not rejected by the peer group. In one study, bullies were only rejected by peers for whom they were a potential threat (Veenstra & others, 2010). In another study, bullies often affiliated with each other or in some cases maintained their position in the popular peer group (Witvliet & others, 2010).

What are the outcomes of bullying? A recent study indicated that bullies and their victims in adolescence were more likely to experience depression and engage in suicide ideation and attempt suicide than their counterparts who were not involved in bullying (Brunstein Klomek & others, 2007). Recently, bullying has been linked to suicides. In one case, an 8-year-old jumped out of a two-story building in Houston, in another case, a 13-year-old hanged himself in Houston, and in yet another case in Massachusetts, teenagers harassed a girl so mercilessly that she killed herself (Meyers, 2010). Another study revealed that bullies, victims, or those who were both bullies and victims had more health problems (such as headaches, dizziness,

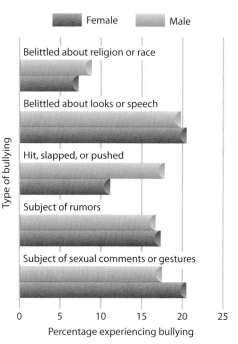

FIGURE **15.2**

BULLYING BEHAVIORS AMONG U.S. YOUTH.
This graph shows the type of bullying most often experienced by U.S. youth (Nansel & others, 2001). The percentages reflect the extent to which bullied students said that they had experienced a particular type of bullying. In terms of gender, note that when they were bullied, boys were more likely to be hit, slapped, or pushed than girls were.

developmental **connection**

Media. Cyberbullying (peer bullying and harassment on the Internet) is an increasing concern. Chapter 17, p. 504

What Are the Perspective Taking and Moral Motivation of Bullies, Bully-Victims, Victims, and Prosocial Children?

A recent study explored the roles that perspective taking and moral motivation play in the lives of bullies, bully-victims, victims, and prosocial children (Gasser & Keller, 2009):

- *Bullies* are highly aggressive toward other children but are not victims of bullying.
- *Bully-victims* are not only highly aggressive toward other children but also are the recipients of other children's bullying.
- *Victims* are passive, non-aggressive respondents to bullying.
- *Prosocial children* engage in positive behaviors such as sharing, helping, comforting, and empathizing.

Teacher and peer ratings in 34 classrooms were used to classify 212 boys and girls 7 to 8 years old into the aforementioned four categories. On a 5-point scale (from never to several times a week), teachers rated (1) how often the child bullied others, and (2) how often the child was bullied. The ratings focused on three types of bullying and being victimized: physical, verbal, and exclusion. On a four-point scale (from not applicable to very clearly applicable), teachers also rated children's prosocial behavior on three items: "willingly shares with others," "comforts others if necessary," and "empathizes with others." Peer ratings were used to identify which children in the classroom acted as bullies, were victimized by bullies, and engaged in prosocial behavior. Combining the teacher and peer ratings after eliminating those that did not agree on which children were bullies, victims, or prosocial children,

the final sample consisted of 49 bullies, 80 bully-victims, 33 victims, and 50 prosocial children.

Children's perspective-taking skills were assessed using theory-of-mind tasks, and moral motivation was examined by interviewing children about aspects of right and wrong in stories about children's transgressions. In one theory-of-mind task, children were tested to see if they understood that people may have false beliefs about another individual. In another theory-of-mind task, children were assessed to determine whether they understood that people sometimes hide their emotions by showing an emotion different from their true feelings. A moral interview also was conducted in which children were told four moral transgression stories (with content about being unwilling to share with a classmate, stealing sweets from a classmate, hiding a victim's shoes, and verbally bullying a victim) and then asked to judge whether the acts were right or wrong and how the participants in the stories likely felt.

In Chapter 13, we discussed moral thought and moral behavior and noted that cheaters and thieves may know what is right while still doing what is wrong. To ensure that child bullies, who show this same pattern of thought and behavior, don't grow up to be adults who continue to reason this way and to engage in delinquent behavior, it is necessary to implement effective intervention techniques, as described later in this section.

---

sleep problems, and anxiety) than their counterparts who were not involved in bullying (Srabstein & others, 2006). And a recent meta-analysis of 33 studies revealed that peer victimization had a small but significant link with lower academic achievement (Nakamoto & Schwartz, 2010).

What kind of perspective taking and moral motivation skills do bullies, bully-victims, and prosocial children tend to exhibit? To find out, see *Connecting Through Research*.

Extensive interest is developing in preventing and treating bullying and victimization (Biggs & Vernberg, 2010; Guerra & Williams, 2010; Singh, Orpinas, & Horne, 2010). Two reviews of research studies indicated mixed results for school-based intervention (Merrell & others, 2008; Vreeman & Carroll, 2007). School-based interventions vary greatly, ranging from involving the whole school in an antibullying campaign to providing individualized social skills training. Two of the most promising bullying intervention programs are described below.

- *Olweus Bullying Prevention.* Created by Dan Olweus, this program focuses on 6- to 15-year-olds, with the goal of decreasing opportunities and rewards for bullying. School staff are instructed in ways to improve peer relations and make schools safer. When properly implemented, the program reduces bullying by 30 to 70 percent

What are some strategies to reduce bullying?

(Ericson, 2001; Olweus, 2003). Information on how to implement the program can be obtained from the Center for the Prevention of Violence at the University of Colorado (www.colorado.edu/espv/blueprints).

- *Steps to Respect.* This bullying program consists of three steps: (1) establishing a school-wide approach, such as creating antibullying policies and specifying consequences for bullying; (2) training staff and parents to deal with bullying; and (3) teaching students to recognize—not tolerate—and handle bullying. In this third step, teachers provide skills training, such as how to be assertive, and information about bullying to students in grades 3 through 6. The skills training by teachers occurs over a 12- to 14-week period. A recent assessment found that Steps to Respect was successful in reducing bullying and argumentativeness in third- through fifth-grade students (Frey & others, 2005, 2009). In this study, two-year declines in playground bullying and victimization occurred. For more information about Steps to Respect, visit www.cfchildren.org.

Review *Connect* Reflect

LG1 Discuss peer relations in childhood.

Review

- What are some key aspects of peer relations?
- What is the developmental course of peer relations in childhood?
- In what ways are the worlds of parents and peers distinct but coordinated?
- How is social cognition involved in peer relations? How is emotion involved in peer relations?
- What are five peer statuses of children?
- What is the nature of bullying?

Connect

- Earlier in this chapter and in Chapter 13, you learned that most developmentalists agree that peers play an important role in children's development of moral reasoning. Of the five peer status groups you learned about in this section, in which group do you think children would have the least opportunity to fully develop their moral reasoning capacities? Why?

Reflect *Your Own Personal Journey of Life*

- Think back to your middle school/junior high and high school years. What kind of relationship did you have with your parents? Were you securely attached or insecurely attached to them? How do you think your relationship with your parents affected your friendships and peer relations?

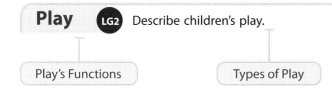

Play **LG2** Describe children's play.

Play's Functions   Types of Play

Much of the time when children, especially young children, are interacting with their peers, they are playing. **Play** is a pleasurable activity that is engaged in for its own sake, and social play is just one type of play.

PLAY'S FUNCTIONS

Play makes important contributions to young children's cognitive and socioemotional development (Bergen & Fromberg, 2009; Coplan & Arbeau, 2009). Theorists have focused on different aspects of play and highlighted a long list of functions.

According to Freud and Erikson, play helps the child master anxieties and conflicts. Because tensions are relieved in play, the child can cope more effectively with

play A pleasurable activity that is engaged in for its own sake.

life's problems. Play permits the child to work off excess physical energy and to release pent-up tensions. Therapists use **play therapy** both to allow the child to work off frustrations and to analyze the child's conflicts and ways of coping with them (Sanders, 2008). Children may feel less threatened and be more likely to express their true feelings in the context of play.

Play also is an important context for cognitive development (Coplan & Arbeau, 2009). Both Piaget and Vygotsky concluded that play is the child's work. Piaget (1962) maintained that play advances children's cognitive development. At the same time, he said that children's cognitive development *constrains* the way they play. Play permits children to practice their competencies and acquired skills in a relaxed, pleasurable way. Piaget thought that cognitive structures needed to be exercised and that play provided the perfect setting for this exercise.

Vygotsky (1962) also considered play to be an excellent setting for cognitive development. He was especially interested in the symbolic and make-believe aspects of play, as when a child substitutes a stick for a horse and rides the stick as if it were a horse. For young children, the imaginary situation is real. Parents should encourage such imaginary play, because it advances the child's cognitive development, especially creative thought.

Daniel Berlyne (1960) described play as exciting and pleasurable in itself because it satisfies our exploratory drive. This drive involves curiosity and a desire for information about something new or unusual. Play encourages exploratory behavior by offering children the possibilities of novelty, complexity, uncertainty, surprise, and incongruity.

More recently, play has been described as an important context for the development of language and communication skills (Coplan & Arbeau, 2009) through discussions and negotiations regarding roles and rules in play. These types of social interactions during play can benefit young children's literacy skills (Coplan & Arbeau, 2009). And as we will discuss in Chapter 16, "Schools and Achievement," play is a central focus of the child-centered kindergarten and thought to be an essential aspect of early childhood education (Feeney & others, 2010).

An increasing concern is that the large number of hours children spend with electronic media, such as television and computers, takes time away from play (Bergen & Fromberg, 2009). An important priority for parents should be to include ample time for play in their children's lives.

TYPES OF PLAY

The contemporary perspective on play emphasizes both the cognitive and the social aspects of play (Bergen & Fromberg, 2009). Among the most widely studied types of children's play today are sensorimotor and practice play, pretense/symbolic play, social play, constructive play, and games (Bergen, 1988).

Sensorimotor and Practice Play **Sensorimotor play** is behavior that allows infants to derive pleasure from exercising their sensorimotor schemes. The development of sensorimotor play follows Piaget's description of sensorimotor thought,

developmental **connection**

Cognitive Theory. Vygotsky emphasized that children mainly develop their ways of thinking and understanding through social interaction. Chapter 6, p. 195

developmental **connection**

Social Cognitive Theory. The child-centered kindergarten emphasizes the education of the whole child, not just his or her cognitive development, because play is extremely important in the child's development. Chapter 16, p. 456

play therapy Therapy that allows the child to work off frustrations and is a medium through which the therapist can analyze the child's conflicts and ways of coping with them. Children may feel less threatened and be more likely to express their true feelings in the context of play.

sensorimotor play Behavior that allows infants to derive pleasure from exercising their existing sensorimotor schemes.

practice play Play that involves repetition of behavior when new skills are being learned or when physical or mental mastery and coordination of skills are required for games or sports. Practice play can be engaged in throughout life.

pretense/symbolic play Play that occurs when a child transforms the physical environment into a symbol.

social play Play that involves interactions with peers.

which we discussed in Chapter 6. Infants initially engage in exploratory and playful visual and motor transactions during the second quarter of the first year of life. At 9 months of age, infants begin to select novel objects for exploration and play, especially those that are responsive, such as toys that make noise or bounce. At 12 months of age, infants enjoy making things work and exploring cause and effect.

Practice play involves repeating behavior when new skills are being learned or when physical or mental mastery and coordination of skills are required for games or sports. Sensorimotor play, which often involves practice play, is primarily confined to infancy, whereas practice play can be engaged in throughout life. During the preschool years, children often engage in play that involves practicing various skills. Although practice play declines during the elementary school years, practice play activities such as running, jumping, sliding, twirling, and throwing balls or other objects are frequently observed on the playgrounds at elementary schools.

A preschool "superhero" at play.

Pretense/Symbolic Play
Pretense/symbolic play occurs when the child transforms the physical environment into a symbol. Between 9 and 30 months of age, children increase their use of objects in symbolic play (Lillard, 2007). They learn to transform objects, substituting them for other objects and acting toward them as if they were those other objects (Smith, 2007). For example, a preschool child treats a table as if it were a car and says, "I'm fixing the car," as he grabs a leg of the table.

Many experts on play view the preschool years as the "golden age" of symbolic/pretense play that is dramatic or sociodramatic in nature (Fein, 1986; Rubin, Bukowski, & Parker, 2006). This type of make-believe play often appears at about 18 months of age and reaches a peak at 4 to 5 years of age, then gradually declines. Some child psychologists conclude that pretend play is an important aspect of young children's development and often reflects advances in their cognitive development, especially their capacity for symbolic understanding. For example, Catherine Garvey (2000) and Angeline Lillard (2007) emphasize that hidden in young children's pretend play narratives are remarkable capacities for role-taking, balancing of social roles, metacognition (thinking about thinking), testing of the reality-pretense distinction, and numerous nonegocentric capacities that reveal the remarkable cognitive skills of young children. In one recent analysis, a major accomplishment in early childhood is the development of children's ability to share their pretend play with peers (Coplan & Arbeau, 2009).

Social Play
Social play is play that involves interaction with peers. Social play increases dramatically during the preschool years and includes varied interchanges such as turn taking, conversations about numerous topics, social games and routines, and physical play (Sumaroka & Bornstein, 2008). Social play often evokes a high degree of pleasure on the part of the participants (Sumaroka & Bornstein, 2008).

In the elementary school years, children, such as those playing hopscotch here on a school playground, increasingly play games.

Constructive Play
Constructive Play combines sensorimotor/practice play with symbolic representation of ideas. Constructive play occurs when children engage in the self-regulated creation of a product or a solution. Constructive play increases in the preschool years as symbolic play increases and sensorimotor play decreases. During the preschool years, some practice play is replaced by constructive play. For example, instead of moving their fingers around and around in finger paint (practice play), children are more likely to draw the outline of a house or a person in the paint (constructive play). Constructive play is also a frequent form of play in the elementary school years, both within and outside the classroom. Constructive play is one of the few playlike activities allowed in work-centered classrooms. For example, if children create a skit about a social studies topic, they are engaging in constructive play.

constructive play Play that combines sensorimotor/practice play with symbolic representation of ideas. Constructive play occurs when children engage in self-regulated creation or construction of a product or a solution.

games Activities engaged in for pleasure that include rules and often competition with one or more individuals.

Games
Games are activities that are engaged in for pleasure and are governed by rules. Often they involve competition between two or more individuals. Preschool

children may begin to participate in social game play that involves simple rules of reciprocity and turn taking. However, games take on a much more prominent role in the lives of elementary school children. In one study, the highest incidence of game playing occurred between 10 and 12 years of age (Eiferman, 1971). After age 12, games decline in popularity (Bergen, 1988).

In sum, play ranges from an infant's simple exercise of a new sensorimotor talent to a preschool child's riding a tricycle to an older child's participation in organized games. It is also important to note that children's play can involve a combination of the play categories we have described. For example, social play can be sensorimotor (rough-and-tumble), symbolic, and constructive.

Review *Connect* Reflect

LG2 Describe children's play.

Review

- What are the functions of play?
- What are the different types of play?

Connect

- Pretense/symbolic play takes place during what Piaget called the symbolic function substage of the preoperational stage. According to Piaget, what are two important limitations of children's thought during this substage?

Reflect *Your Own Personal Journey of Life*

- Do you think most young children's lives today are too structured? If and when you become a parent, how will you manage your children's development to provide enough time for play?

Friendship **LG3** Explain friendship.

| Friendship's Functions | Similarity and Intimacy | Gender and Friendship | Mixed-Age Friendships |

Children play with varying acquaintances. They interact with some children they barely know, and with others they know well, for hours every day. It is to the latter type—friends—that we now turn.

FRIENDSHIP'S FUNCTIONS

Friendships serve six functions (Gottman & Parker, 1987):

1. *Companionship*. Friendship provides children with a familiar partner, someone who is willing to spend time with them and join in collaborative activities.
2. *Stimulation*. Friendship provides children with interesting information, excitement, and amusement.
3. *Physical support*. Friendship provides resources and assistance.
4. *Ego support*. Friendship provides the expectation of support, encouragement, and feedback that helps children to maintain an impression of themselves as competent, attractive, and worthwhile individuals.
5. *Social comparison*. Friendship provides information about where children stand vis-à-vis others and whether children are doing okay.
6. *Intimacy/affection*. Friendship provides children with a warm, close, trusting relationship with another individual, a relationship that involves self-disclosure.

Although having friends can be a developmental advantage, not all friendships are alike (Brendgen & others, 2010; Erath & others, 2010; Rubin, Fredstrom, & Bowker, 2008). People differ in the company they keep—that is, who their friends are.

What are some characteristics of children's friendships?

What changes take place in friendship during the adolescent years?

Developmental advantages occur when children have friends who are socially skilled, supportive, and oriented toward academic achievement (Crosnoe & others, 2008). However, it is not developmentally advantageous to have coercive, conflict-ridden, and poor-quality friendships (Laursen & Pursell, 2009; Vitaro, Boivin, & Bukowski, 2009).

Not only does the quality of friendships have important influences on adolescents, but the friend's character, interests, and attitudes also matter (Brown, 2004). For example, researchers have found that delinquent adolescents often have delinquent friends, and they reinforce each other's delinquent behavior (Dishion, Andrews, & Crosby, 1995). By the same token, having friends who are involved in school activities, sports, or religion is likely to have a positive influence on the adolescent.

The importance of friendship was underscored in a two-year longitudinal study (Wentzel, Barry, & Caldwell, 2004). Sixth-grade students who did not have a friend engaged in less prosocial behavior (cooperation, sharing, helping others), had lower grades, and were more emotionally distressed (depression, low well-being) than their counterparts who had one or more friends. Two years later, in the eighth grade, the students who did not have a friend in the sixth grade continued to be more emotionally distressed. Why are friendships so significant?

Harry Stack Sullivan (1953) was the most influential theorist to discuss the importance of friendships. In contrast with other psychoanalytic theorists' narrow emphasis on the importance of parent-child relationships, Sullivan contended that friends also played important roles in shaping children's and adolescents' well-being and development.

According to Sullivan, all people have a number of basic social needs, including tenderness (secure attachment), playful companionship, social acceptance, intimacy,

developmental **connection**

Gender. Recent research indicates that relational aggression occurs more often in girls than boys in adolescence but not in childhood. Chapter 12, pp. 355–356

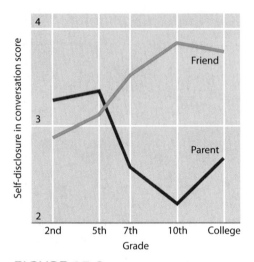

FIGURE **15.3**

DEVELOPMENTAL CHANGES IN SELF-DISCLOSING CONVERSATIONS. Self-disclosing conversations with friends increased dramatically in adolescence while declining in an equally dramatic fashion with parents. However, self-disclosing conversations with parents began to pick up somewhat during the college years. The measure of self-disclosure involved a 5-point rating scale completed by the children and youth, with a higher score representing greater self-disclosure. The data shown represent the means for each age group.

intimacy in friendship Self-disclosure or the sharing of private thoughts.

and sexual relations. Whether or not these needs are fulfilled largely determines our emotional well-being. For example, if the need for playful companionship goes unmet, then we become bored and depressed; if the need for social acceptance is not met, we suffer a lowered sense of self-worth. Sullivan stressed that the need for intimacy intensifies during early adolescence, motivating teenagers to seek out close friends.

Gossip about peers often dominates the conversation of friends in adolescence (Buhrmester & Chong, 2009). Much of the gossip is characterized by negative comments about others, such as talking about how someone got drunk last weekend, how unattractive someone looked at school yesterday, and how someone could have the nerve to say what they did. In some cases, the negative gossip takes the form of *relational aggression*, which involves spreading disparaging rumors to harm someone (discussed in Chapter 12, "Gender"). However, not all gossip among friends is negative. Some gossip can involve collaborative construction that contributes to developing perspectives on intimacy and close relationships. Friends also can show their trust by disclosing risky opinions. The talk-featured, gossip aspect of friendship is more common in girls than boys.

Research findings support many of Sullivan's ideas. For example, adolescents report disclosing intimate and personal information to their friends more often than do younger children (Buhrmester, 1990; Buhrmester & Furman, 1987) (see Figure 15.3). Adolescents also say they depend more on friends than on parents to satisfy their needs for companionship, reassurance of worth, and intimacy (Furman & Buhrmester, 1992).

Friendship relationships are often important sources of support (Berndt, 1999). Sullivan described how adolescent friends support one another's sense of personal worth. When close friends disclose their mutual insecurities and fears about themselves, they discover that they are not "abnormal" and that they have nothing to be ashamed of. Friends also act as important confidants who help children and adolescents work through upsetting problems (such as difficulties with parents or the breakup of romance) by providing both emotional support and informational advice.

To read about appropriate and inappropriate strategies for making friends, see *Caring Connections.*

SIMILARITY AND INTIMACY

What characteristics do children and adolescents look for in their friends? The answers change somewhat as children grow up, but one characteristic of friends is found throughout the childhood and adolescent years: Friends are generally similar—in terms of age, sex, ethnicity, and many other factors (Giordano, 2009). Friends often have similar attitudes toward school, similar educational aspirations, and closely aligned achievement orientations. Friends like the same music, wear the same kinds of clothes, and prefer the same leisure activities (Berndt, 1982). Differences may lead to conflicts that weaken the friendship. For example, if two friends have differing attitudes toward school, one may repeatedly want to play basketball or go to the mall while the other insists on completing homework, and the two may drift apart.

Priorities change as the child reaches adolescence (Brown & Larson, 2009). The most consistent finding in the last two decades of research on adolescent friendships is that intimacy is an important feature of friendship (Berndt & Perry, 1990). In most research studies, **intimacy in friendship** is defined narrowly as self-disclosure or sharing of private thoughts; private or personal knowledge about a friend has been used as an index of intimacy. When young adolescents are asked what they want from a friend or how they can tell someone is their best friend, they frequently say that a best friend will share problems with them, understand them, and listen when they talk about their own thoughts or feelings. When young children talk about their friendships, they rarely comment about intimate self-disclosure or mutual understanding. In one investigation, friendship intimacy was more prominent in 13- to 16-year-olds than in 10- to 13-year-olds (Buhrmester, 1990).

Making Friends

Here are some strategies that adults can recommend to children and adolescents for making friends (Wentzel, 1997):

- **Initiate interaction.** Learn about a friend: Ask for his or her name, age, favorite activities. Use these prosocial overtures: introduce yourself, start a conversation, and invite him or her to do things.
- **Be nice.** Show kindness, be considerate, and compliment the other person.
- **Engage in prosocial behavior.** Be honest and trustworthy: tell the truth, keep promises. Be generous, share, and be cooperative.
- **Show respect for yourself and others.** Have good manners, be polite and courteous, and listen to what others have to say. Have a positive attitude and personality.
- **Provide social support.** Show you care.

What are some appropriate and inappropriate strategies for making friends?

And here are some inappropriate strategies for making friends that adults can recommend that children and adolescents avoid using (Wentzel, 1997):

- **Be psychologically aggressive.** Show disrespect and have bad manners. Use others, be uncooperative, don't share, ignore others, gossip, and spread rumors.
- **Present yourself negatively.** Be self-centered, snobby, conceited, and jealous; show off, care only about yourself. Be mean, have a bad attitude, be angry, throw temper tantrums, and start trouble.
- **Behave antisocially.** Be physically aggressive, yell at others, pick on them, make fun of them, be dishonest, tell secrets, and break promises.

Based on what you read earlier in this chapter, what might you recommend to an adolescent about approaching someone as a potential friend?

GENDER AND FRIENDSHIP

Are the friendships of girls different from the friendships of boys? An increasing number of studies indicate that they are different (Rose & Smith, 2009). For example, the influence of friendship, both positive and negative, may be stronger for girls. Also, issues of control and intimacy likely play a more powerful role in girls' friendships. For example, in a recent study girls reported that intimacy was more important in their friendships, whereas boys indicated that doing things together, such as engaging in common activities like sports or playing computer games, was more important in their friendships (McDougall & Hymel, 2007).

Let's further examine gender differences in the intimacy aspect of friendship. When asked to describe their best friends, girls refer to intimate conversations and faithfulness more than boys do (Rose & Smith, 2009). For example, girls are more likely to describe their best friend as "sensitive just like me" or "trustworthy just like me" (Duck, 1975). When conflict is present, girls place a higher priority on relationship goals such as being patient until the relationship improves, whereas boys are more likely to seek control over a friend (Rose & Asher, 1999; Blakemore, Berenbaum, & Ruble, 2009). Although girls' friendships in adolescence are more likely to focus on intimacy, boys' friendships tend to emphasize power and excitement (Rose & Smith, 2009). Boys may discourage one another from openly disclosing their problems because self-disclosure is not viewed as masculine (Maccoby, 1996). Boys make themselves vulnerable to being called "wimps" if they can't handle their own problems and insecurities. These gender differences are generally assumed to reflect a greater orientation toward interpersonal relationships among girls than boys.

As indicated in the *Caring Connections*, friendship often provides social support. A recent study of third- through ninth-graders, though, revealed that one aspect of girls' social support in friendship may have costs as well as benefits (Rose, Carlson, & Waller, 2007). In the study, girls' co-rumination (as reflected in excessively discussing problems) predicted not only an increase in positive friendship quality but also an increase in further co-rumination as well as an increase in depressive and anxiety symptoms. One implication of the research is that some girls who are vulnerable to developing internalized problems may go undetected because they have supportive friendships (Rose & Smith, 2009).

The study just described indicates that the characteristics of an adolescents' friends can influence whether the friends have a positive or negative influence on the adolescent. Consider a recent study which revealed that the grade-point averages of friends were an important positive attribute (Cook, Deng, & Morgano, 2007). Friends' grade-point averages consistently predicted positive school achievement and also were linked to lower levels of negative behavior in areas such as drug abuse and acting out. Another recent study found that taking math courses in high school, especially for girls, was strongly linked to the achievement levels of their best friends (Crosnoe & others, 2008). And as we saw in Chapter 13, having delinquent peers and friends greatly increases the risk of becoming delinquent (Dishion, Piehler, & Myers, 2008).

MIXED-AGE FRIENDSHIPS

Although most adolescents develop friendships with individuals who are close to their own age, some adolescents become best friends with younger or older individuals. A common fear, especially among parents, is that adolescents who have older friends will be encouraged to engage in delinquent behavior or early sexual behavior. Researchers have found that adolescents who interact with older youth do engage in these behaviors more frequently, but it is not known whether the older youth guide younger adolescents toward deviant behavior or whether the younger adolescents were already prone to deviant behavior before they developed the friendship with the older youth (Billy, Rodgers, & Udry, 1984). A recent study also revealed that over time, from the sixth through tenth grades, girls were more likely to have older male friends, which places some girls on a developmental trajectory for engaging in problem behavior (Poulin & Pedersen, 2007).

What are some gender differences in peer relations and friendships in adolescence?

Review *Connect* Reflect

 LG3 Explain friendship.

Review

- What are six functions of friendship? What is Sullivan's view of friendship?
- What roles do similarity and intimacy play in friendship?
- How does gender influence friendship?
- What is the developmental outcome of mixed-age friendship?

Connect

- Relational aggression was discussed here and in Chapter 12. In one of the studies in Chapter 12, what connection was made between parents and the relational aggression of their children?

Reflect *Your Own Personal Journey of Life*

- Examine the list of six functions of friendships at the beginning of this section. Rank the six functions from most (1) to least (6) important to you as you were developing in three different time frames: early childhood, middle and late childhood, and adolescence.

Peer Relations in Adolescence

LG4 Characterize peer relations in adolescence.

| Peer Pressure and Conformity | Cliques and Crowds | Dating and Romantic Relationships |

We already have discussed a number of changes in adolescents' peer relations, including the increasing importance of friendships. Peer relations play such a powerful role in the lives of adolescents that we further consider additional aspects in this section.

Peer relations undergo important changes in adolescence. In childhood, the focus of peer relations is on being liked by classmates and being included in games or lunchroom conversations. Being overlooked or, worse yet, being rejected can have damaging effects on children's development that sometimes are carried forward to adolescence. Beginning in early adolescence, teenagers typically prefer to have a smaller number of friendships that are more intense and intimate than those of young children. Cliques are formed and shape the social lives of adolescents as they begin to "hang out" together. And romantic relationships become a more central aspect of adolescents' lives.

PEER PRESSURE AND CONFORMITY

Young adolescents conform more to peer standards than children do. Around the eighth and ninth grades, conformity to peers—especially to their antisocial standards—peaks (Berndt, 1979; Brown & Larson, 2009). At this point, adolescents are most likely to go along with a peer to steal hubcaps off a car, draw graffiti on a wall, or steal cosmetics from a store counter. A recent study revealed that 14 to 18 years of age is an especially important time for developing the ability to stand up for what one believes and resist peer pressure to do otherwise (Steinberg & Monahan, 2007). Another study found that U.S. adolescents are more likely than Japanese adolescents to put pressure on their peers to resist parental influence (Rothbaum & others, 2000).

Which adolescents are most likely to conform to peers? Mitchell Prinstein and his colleagues (Cohen & Prinstein, 2006; Prinstein, 2007; Prinstein & Dodge, 2008) have recently conducted research and analysis addressing this question. They conclude that adolescents who are uncertain about their social identity, which can appear in the form of low self-esteem and high social anxiety, are most likely to conform to peers. This uncertainty often increases during times of transition, such as school and family transitions. Also, peers are more likely to conform when they are in the presence of someone they perceive to have higher status than they do.

> I didn't belong as a kid, and that always bothered me. If only I'd known that one day my differentness would be an asset, then my early life would have been much easier.
>
> —**BETTE MIDLER**
> *Contemporary American Actress*

CLIQUES AND CROWDS

Cliques and crowds assume more important roles in adolescence than in childhood (Brown & Larson, 2009). **Cliques** are small groups that range from 2 to about 12 individuals and average about 5 or 6 individuals. The clique members are usually of the same sex and about the same age. Cliques can form because adolescents engage in similar activities, such as being in a club or on a sports team. Some cliques also form because of friendship. Several adolescents may form a clique because they have spent time with each other and enjoy each other's company. Not necessarily friends, they often develop a friendship if they stay in the clique. What do adolescents do in cliques? They share ideas, hang out together, and often develop an in-group identity in which they believe that their clique is better than other cliques.

Some cliques also form because of friendship. In the high school years, friendship cliques become more heterosexual with many high school seniors averaging two opposite-sex and four same-sex friendships (Buhrmester & Chong, 2009). High

What characterizes adolescent cliques? How are they different from crowds?

cliques Small groups that range from 2 to about 12 individuals and average about 5 or 6 individuals. Cliques can form because of friendship or because individuals engage in similar activities, and members usually are of the same sex and about the same age.

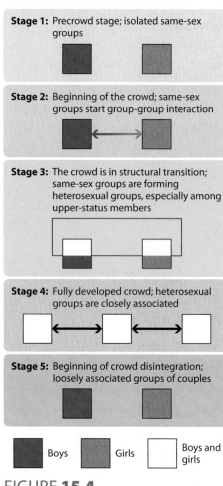

Stage 1: Precrowd stage; isolated same-sex groups

Stage 2: Beginning of the crowd; same-sex groups start group-group interaction

Stage 3: The crowd is in structural transition; same-sex groups are forming heterosexual groups, especially among upper-status members

Stage 4: Fully developed crowd; heterosexual groups are closely associated

Stage 5: Beginning of crowd disintegration; loosely associated groups of couples

■ Boys ■ Girls ☐ Boys and girls

FIGURE **15.4**
DUNPHY'S PROGRESSION OF PEER GROUP RELATIONS IN ADOLESCENCE

crowds The crowd is a larger group structure than a clique. Adolescents usually are members of a crowd based on reputation and may or may not spend much time together. Many crowds are defined by the activities in which adolescents engage.

school seniors average two opposite-sex and four same-sex friendships compared with none or one opposite-sex and five or more same-sex friendships in sixth-graders. These mixed-sex friendships can provide adolescents with access to potential romantic partners.

Dexter Dunphy (1963) documented this increase in mixed-sex groups in a well-known observational study. Figure 15.4 outlines his view of how these mixed-sex groups develop. In late childhood, boys and girls participate in small, same-sex cliques. As they move into the early adolescent years, the same-sex cliques begin to interact with each other. Gradually, the leaders and high-status members form further cliques based on mixed-sex relationships. Eventually, the newly created mixed-sex cliques replace the same-sex cliques. The mixed-sex cliques interact with each other in large crowd activities, too—at dances and athletic events, for example. In late adolescence, the crowd begins to dissolve as couples develop more serious relationships and make long-range plans that may include engagement and marriage.

Crowds are a larger group structure than cliques. Adolescents are usually members of a crowd based on reputation and may or may not spend much time together. Crowds are less personal than cliques. Many crowds are defined by the activities adolescents engage in (such as "jocks," who are good at sports, or "druggies," who take drugs). Reputation-based crowds often appear for the first time in early adolescence and usually become less prominent in late adolescence (Collins & Steinberg, 2006).

In one study, crowd membership was associated with adolescent self-esteem (Brown & Lohr, 1987). The crowds included jocks (athletically oriented), populars (well-known students who led social activities), normals (middle-of-the-road students who made up the masses), druggies or toughs (known for illicit drug use or other delinquent activities), and nobodies (low in social skills or intellectual abilities). The self-esteem of the jocks and the populars was highest, whereas that of the nobodies was lowest. One group of adolescents not in a crowd had self-esteem equivalent to that of the jocks and the populars; this group was the independents, who indicated that crowd membership was not important to them. Keep in mind that these data are correlational; self-esteem could increase an adolescent's probability of becoming a crowd member, just as crowd membership could increase the adolescent's self-esteem.

DATING AND ROMANTIC RELATIONSHIPS

Adolescents spend considerable time either dating or thinking about dating (Collins, Welsh, & Furman, 2009; Connolly & McIsaac, 2009). Dating can be a form of recreation, a source of status, or a setting for learning about close relationships, as well as a way of finding a mate.

Types of Dating and Developmental Changes A number of dating variations and developmental changes characterize dating and romantic relationships. First, we examine heterosexual romantic relationships and then turn to romantic relationships among sexual minority youth (gay and lesbian adolescents).

Heterosexual Romantic Relationships Three stages characterize the development of romantic relationships in adolescence (Connolly & McIsaac, 2009):

1. *Entry into romantic attractions and affiliations at about 11 to 13 years of age.* This initial stage is triggered by puberty. From 11 to 13, adolescents become intensely interested in romance, and the topic dominates many conversations with same-sex friends. Developing a crush on someone is common, and the crush often is shared with a same-sex friend. Young adolescents may or may not interact with the individual who is the object of their infatuation. When dating occurs, it usually takes place in a group setting.

2. *Exploring romantic relationships at approximately 14 to 16 years of age.* At this point in adolescence, two types of romantic involvement occur: (1) *Casual dating* emerges between individuals who are mutually attracted. These dating experiences are often short-lived, last a few months at best, and usually only endure for a few

weeks. (2) *Dating in groups* is common and reflects embeddedness in the peer context. Friends often act as a third-party facilitator of a potential dating relationship by communicating their friend's romantic interest and confirming whether this attraction is reciprocated.

3. *Consolidating dyadic romantic bonds at about 17 to 19 years of age.* At the end of the high school years, more serious romantic relationships develop. This is characterized by strong emotional bonds more closely resembling those in adult romantic relationships. These bonds often are more stable and enduring than earlier bonds, typically lasting one year or more.

What are some developmental changes in romantic relationships in adolescence?

Two variations on these stages in the development of romantic relationships in adolescence involve early and late bloomers (Connolly & McIssac, 2009). *Early bloomers* include 15 to 20 percent of 11- to 13-year-olds who say that they currently are in a romantic relationship and 35 percent who indicate that they have had some prior experience in romantic relationships. *Late bloomers* comprise approximately 10 percent of 17- to 19-year-olds who say that they have had no experience with romantic relationships and another 15 percent who report that they have not engaged in any romantic relationships that lasted more than 4 months.

In their early romantic relationships, today's adolescents are not motivated to fulfill attachment or even sexual needs. Rather, early romantic relationships serve as a context for adolescents to explore how attractive they are, how to interact romantically, and how all of these aspects look to the peer group. Only after adolescents acquire some basic competencies in interacting with romantic partners does the fulfillment of attachment and sexual needs become a central function of these relationships (Furman & Wehner, 1998).

Adolescents often find comfort in numbers during their early exploration of romantic relationships (Connolly & McIsaac, 2009). They may begin hanging out together in heterosexual groups. Sometimes they just hang out at someone's house or get organized enough to ask an adult to drive them to a mall or a movie. A special concern in early dating and "going with" someone is the associated risk for adolescent pregnancy and problems at home and school.

Romantic Relationships in Sexual Minority Youth   Most research on romantic relationships in adolescence has focused on heterosexual relationships. Recently, researchers have begun to study romantic relationships in gay, lesbian, and bisexual youth (Diamond & Savin-Williams, 2009).

The average age of the initial same-sex activity for females ranges from 14 to 18 years of age and for males from 13 to 15 (Diamond & Savin-Williams, 2009). The most common initial same-sex partner is a close friend. More lesbian adolescent girls have sexual encounters with boys before same-sex activity, whereas gay adolescent boys are more likely to show the opposite sequence (Savin-Williams, 2006).

Most sexual minority youth have same-sex sexual experience, but relatively few have same-sex romantic relationships because of limited opportunities and the social disapproval such relationships may generate from families or heterosexual peers (Diamond & Savin-Willliams, 2009). The importance of romance to sexual minority youth was underscored in a study that found that they rated the breakup of a current romance as their second most stressful problem, second only to disclosure of their sexual orientation to their parents (D'Augelli, 1991).

The romantic possibilities of sexual minority youth are complex (Diamond & Savin-Williams, 2009). To adequately address the relational interests of sexual minority youth, we can't generalize from heterosexual youth and simply switch

What characterizes romantic relationships in sexual minority youth?

the labels. Instead, we need to consider the full range of variation in sexual minority youths' sexual desires and romantic relationships for same- and other-sex partners.

Dating and Adjustment   Researchers have linked dating and romantic relationships with various measures of how well adjusted adolescents are (Connolly & McIsaac, 2009). For example, a recent study of 200 tenth-graders revealed that the more romantic experiences they had, the more likely they were to report higher levels of social acceptance, friendship competence, and romantic competence; however, having more romantic experience also was linked to a higher level of substance use, delinquency, and sexual behavior (Furman, Low, & Ho, 2009). Another recent study of adolescent girls revealed that a higher frequency of dating was linked to having depressive symptoms and emotionally unavailable parents (Steinberg & Davila, 2008). Yet another recent study of adolescent girls found that those who engaged in co-rumination (excessive discussion of problems with friends) were more likely to be involved in a romantic relationship, and together co-rumination and romantic involvement predicted an increase in depressive symptoms (Starr & Davila, 2009).

Dating and romantic relationships at an early age can be especially problematic (Connolly & McIsaac, 2009). Researchers have found that early dating and "going with" someone are linked with adolescent pregnancy and problems at home and school (Florsheim, Moore, & Edgington, 2003).

What are some ethnic variations in dating during adolescence?

Sociocultural Contexts and Dating   The sociocultural context exerts a powerful influence on adolescents' dating patterns (Crissey, 2009). This influence may be seen in differences in dating patterns among ethnic groups within the United States. For example, one study found that Asian American adolescents were less likely to have been involved in a romantic relationship in the past 18 months than African American or Latino adolescents (Carver, Joyner, & Udry, 2003).

Values, religious beliefs, and traditions often dictate the age at which dating begins, how much freedom in dating is allowed, whether dates must be chaperoned by adults or parents, and the roles of males and females in dating. For example, Latino and Asian American cultures have more conservative standards regarding adolescent dating than does the Anglo-American culture. Dating may become a source of conflict within a family if the parents have immigrated from cultures in which dating begins at a late age, little freedom in dating is allowed, dates are chaperoned, and dating by adolescent girls is especially restricted. When immigrant adolescents choose to adopt the ways of the dominant U.S. culture (such as unchaperoned dating), they often clash with parents and extended-family members who hold more traditional values.

Review Connect Reflect

 Characterize peer relations in adolescence.

Review

- How are peer pressure and conformity shown in adolescence?
- How are cliques and crowds involved in adolescent development?
- What characterizes adolescents' dating and romantic relationships?

Connect

- In the *Connecting With Diversity* interlude in this chapter, you learned about the Murian culture of eastern India. Based on the information in this last section, how

do you think Murian immigrants in the United States might react to their adolescents' dating?

Reflect *Your Own Personal Journey of Life*

- What were your peer relationships like during adolescence? What peer groups were you involved in? How did they influence your development? If you could change anything about the way you experienced peer relations in adolescence, what would it be?

Peers

Peer Relations

LG1 Discuss peer relations in childhood.

Exploring Peer Relations

- Peers are children who share the same age or maturity level. Peers provide a means of social comparison and a source of information about the world outside the family. Good peer relations may be necessary for normal social development. The inability to "plug in" to a social network is associated with a number of problems. Peer relations can be both positive and negative. Piaget and Sullivan stressed that peer relations provide the context for learning important aspects of relationships, such as observing others' interests and perspectives and exploring fairness and justice by working through disagreements. Peer relations vary according to the way peer experience is measured, the outcomes specified, and the developmental trajectories traversed. Contexts and individual differences influence peer relations.

The Developmental Course of Peer Relations in Childhood

- Some researchers argue that the quality of social interaction with peers in infancy provides valuable information about socioemotional development. As increasing numbers of infants attend child care, infant peer relations have increased. The frequency of peer interaction, both positive and negative, increases during the preschool years. Children spend even more time with peers in the elementary and secondary school years, and their preference for same-sex groups increases. Boys' groups are larger than girls', and they participate in more organized games than girls. Girls engage in more collaborative discourse in peer groups than boys do.

The Distinct but Coordinated Worlds of Parent-Child and Peer Relations

- Healthy family relations usually promote healthy peer relations. Parents can model or coach their children in ways of relating to peers. Parents' choices of neighborhoods, churches, schools, and their own friends influence the pool from which their children might select possible friends. Rough-and-tumble play occurs mainly in peer relations rather than in parent-child relations. In times of stress, children usually turn to parents rather than peers. Peer relations have a more equal basis than parent-child relations.

Social Cognition and Emotion

- Perspective taking and social information-processing skills are important dimensions of social cognition in peer relations. Perspective taking helps children communicate effectively. Self-regulation of emotion is associated with positive peer relations.

Peer Statuses

- Popular children are frequently identified as a best friend by other children and are rarely disliked by their peers. Average children receive an average number of both positive and negative nominations from their peers. Neglected children are infrequently identified as a best friend but are not disliked by their peers. Rejected children are infrequently identified as a best friend and are disliked by their peers. Rejected children often have more serious adjustment problems than neglected children do. Controversial children are frequently identified both as one's best friend and as being disliked by peers.

Bullying

- Bullying is physical or verbal behavior meant to disturb a less powerful individual. Significant numbers of students are bullied, and this is linked to adjustment problems for the victim, the bully, or the individual who is both a bully and a victim.

Play

LG2 Describe children's play.

Play's Functions

- The functions of play include affiliation with peers, tension release, advances in cognitive development, and exploration.

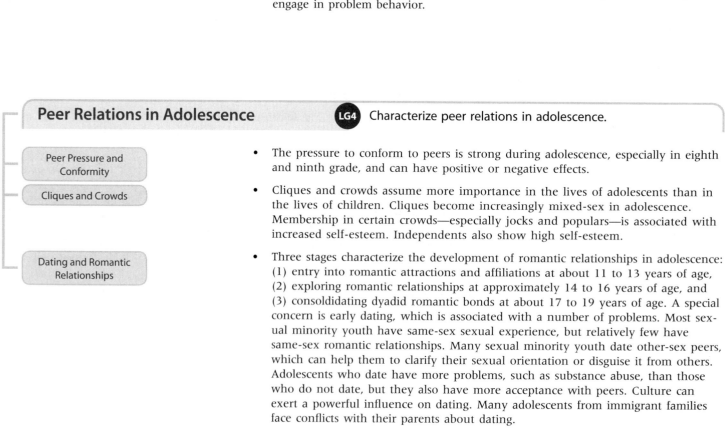

Types of Play

- The contemporary perspective emphasizes both social and cognitive aspects of play. The most widely studied types of play include sensorimotor and practice play, pretense/symbolic play, social play, constructive play, and games.

Friendship   **LG3** Explain friendship.

Friendship's Functions

- The functions of friendship include companionship, stimulation, physical support, ego support, social comparison, and intimacy/affection. Sullivan pointed out that whether or not these functions of friendship are fulfilled largely determines our emotional well-being. Sullivan argued that there is a dramatic increase in the psychological importance and intimacy of close friends in early adolescence. Research findings support his view.

Similarity and Intimacy

- Similarity and intimacy are two of the most common characteristics of friendships. Friends often have similar attitudes toward school, similar educational aspirations, and so on. Intimacy in friendship is much more common among adolescents than children.

Gender and Friendship

- An increasing number of studies indicate that the friendships of girls differ from the friendships of boys. The influence of friendship, both positive and negative, may be stronger for girls. Intimacy plays a powerful role in girls' friendships, and power, excitement, and control play important roles in boys' friendships.

Mixed-Age Friendships

- Children and adolescents who become friends with older individuals engage in more deviant behaviors than do their counterparts with same-age friends. Girls in grades 6 through 10, who often have older male friends, may be more likely to engage in problem behavior.

Peer Relations in Adolescence   **LG4** Characterize peer relations in adolescence.

Peer Pressure and Conformity

- The pressure to conform to peers is strong during adolescence, especially in eighth and ninth grade, and can have positive or negative effects.

Cliques and Crowds

- Cliques and crowds assume more importance in the lives of adolescents than in the lives of children. Cliques become increasingly mixed-sex in adolescence. Membership in certain crowds—especially jocks and populars—is associated with increased self-esteem. Independents also show high self-esteem.

Dating and Romantic Relationships

- Three stages characterize the development of romantic relationships in adolescence: (1) entry into romantic attractions and affiliations at about 11 to 13 years of age, (2) exploring romantic relationships at approximately 14 to 16 years of age, and (3) consolidating dyadic romantic bonds at about 17 to 19 years of age. A special concern is early dating, which is associated with a number of problems. Most sexual minority youth have same-sex sexual experience, but relatively few have same-sex romantic relationships. Many sexual minority youth date other-sex peers, which can help them to clarify their sexual orientation or disguise it from others. Adolescents who date have more problems, such as substance abuse, than those who do not date, but they also have more acceptance with peers. Culture can exert a powerful influence on dating. Many adolescents from immigrant families face conflicts with their parents about dating.

key terms

peers 428
perspective taking 432
popular children 433
average children 433
neglected children 433

rejected children 433
controversial children 433
play 437
play therapy 438
sensorimotor play 438

practice play 439
pretense/symbolic play 439
social play 439
constructive play 439
games 439

intimacy in friendship 442
cliques 445
crowds 446

key people

Kenneth Dodge 433
Erik Erikson 437
Sigmund Freud 437

Jean Piaget 438
Lev Vygotsky 438
Daniel Berlyne 438

Catherine Garvey and
  Angeline Lillard 439
Harry Stack Sullivan 441

Mitchell Prinstein 445
Dexter Dunphy 446

The Reggio Emilia approach is an educational program for young children that was developed in the northern Italian city of Reggio Emilia. Children of single parents and children with disabilities have priority in admission; other children are admitted according to a scale of needs. Parents pay on a sliding scale based on income.

The children are encouraged to learn by investigating and exploring topics that interest them. A wide range of stimulating media and materials is available for children to use as they learn—music, movement, drawing, painting, sculpting, collages, puppets and disguises, and photography, for example (Strong-Wilson & Ellis, 2007).

In this program, children often explore topics in a group, which fosters a sense of community, respect for diversity, and a collaborative approach to problem solving (Hyson, Copple, & Jones, 2006). Two co-teachers are present to serve as guides for children. The Reggio Emilia teachers view a project as an adventure, which can start from an adult's suggestion, from a child's idea, or from an event, such as a snowfall or something else unexpected. Every project is based on what the children say and do. The teachers allow children enough time to think and craft a project.

At the core of the Reggio Emilia approach is the image of children who are competent and have rights, especially the right to outstanding care

A Reggio Emilia classroom in which young children explore topics that interest them.

and education. Parent participation is considered essential, and cooperation is a major theme in the schools. Many early childhood education experts believe the Reggio Emilia approach provides a supportive, stimulating context in which children are motivated to explore their world in a competent and confident manner (New, 2005, 2007).

preview

This chapter is about becoming educated and achieving. We will explore topics such as contemporary approaches to student learning, school transitions, the roles that socioeconomic status and ethnicity play in schools, educational issues involving children with disabilities, and motivation to achieve goals.

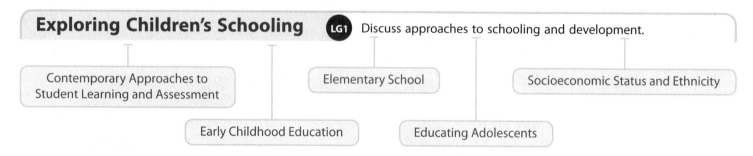

Exploring Children's Schooling **LG1** Discuss approaches to schooling and development.

- Contemporary Approaches to Student Learning and Assessment
- Elementary School
- Socioeconomic Status and Ethnicity
- Early Childhood Education
- Educating Adolescents

developmental connection

Cognitive Theory. Piaget's and Vygotsky's theories can be applied to children's education. Chapter 6, pp. 187–188; Chapter 6, pp. 192–193

> The whole art of teaching is the art of awakening the natural curiosity of young minds.
>
> —**Anatole France**
> *French Novelist, 20th Century*

We have discussed many aspects of schools throughout this book, especially in Section 3, "Cognition and Language." Recall our coverage of applications of Piaget's and Vygotsky's theories to education in Chapter 6, strategies for encouraging children's critical thinking in schools in Chapter 7, applications of Gardner's and Sternberg's theories of intelligence to education in Chapter 8, and bilingual education in Chapter 9. Here we take a closer look at contemporary approaches to student learning in U.S. schools, variations in schooling from early childhood education through high school, and the influence of socioeconomic status and ethnicity on children's education.

For most children, entering the first grade signals new obligations. They form new relationships and develop new standards by which to judge themselves. School provides children with a rich source of new ideas to shape their sense of self. They will spend many years in schools as members of small societies in which there are tasks to be accomplished, people to be socialized and to be socialized by, and rules that define and limit behavior, feelings, and attitudes. By the time students graduate from high school, they will have spent 12,000 hours in the classroom.

Is this classroom more likely constructivist or direct instruction? Explain.

constructivist approach A learner-centered approach that emphasizes the importance of individuals actively constructing their knowledge and understanding, with guidance from the teacher.

CONTEMPORARY APPROACHES TO STUDENT LEARNING AND ASSESSMENT

Controversy swirls about the best ways to teach children and how to hold schools and teachers accountable for whether children are learning (Armstrong, Henson, & Savage, 2009; Johnson & others, 2011; Parkay & Stanford, 2010).

Constructivist and Direct Instruction Approaches The **constructivist approach** is a learner-centered approach that emphasizes the importance of individuals actively constructing their knowledge and understanding with guidance from the teacher. In the constructivist view, teachers should not attempt to simply pour information into children's minds. Rather, children should be encouraged to explore their world, discover knowledge, reflect, and think critically, with careful monitoring and meaningful guidance from the teacher (Abruscato & DeRosa, 2010; Eby, Herrell, & Jordan, 2011). The constructivists believe that for too long in American education children have been required to sit still, be passive learners, and rotely memorize irrelevant as well as relevant information.

Today, constructivism may include an emphasis on collaboration—children working with each other in their efforts to know and understand (Holzman, 2009). A teacher with a constructivist instructional philosophy would not have children memorize information rotely but would give them opportunities to meaningfully construct the knowledge and understand the material while guiding their learning (Maxim, 2010; McCombs, 2010).

By contrast, the **direct instruction approach** is a structured, teacher-centered approach that is characterized by teacher direction and control, high teacher expectations for students' progress, maximum time spent by students on academic tasks, and efforts by the teacher to keep negative affect to a minimum. An important goal in the direct instruction approach is maximizing student learning time.

Advocates of the constructivist approach argue that the direct instruction approach turns children into passive learners and does not adequately challenge them to think in critical and creative ways (Abruscato & DeRosa, 2010; Eby, Herrell, & Jordan, 2011). The direct instruction enthusiasts say that the constructivist approaches do not give enough attention to the content of a discipline, such as history or science. They also believe that the constructivist approaches are too relativistic and vague.

Some experts in educational psychology believe that many effective teachers use both a constructivist *and* a direct instruction approach rather than relying on either exclusively (Bransford & others, 2006). Further, some circumstances may call more for a constructivist approach and others for a direction instruction approach. For example, experts increasingly recommend an explicit, intellectually engaging direct instruction approach when teaching students with a reading or a writing disability (Berninger, 2006).

Accountability   Since the 1990s, the U.S. public and governments at every level have demanded increased accountability from schools. One result was the spread of state-mandated testing to measure what students had or had not learned (Gronlund & Waugh, 2009; Popham, 2011). Many states identified objectives for students in their state and created tests to measure whether students were meeting those objectives. This approach became national policy in 2002 when the No Child Left Behind (NCLB) legislation was signed into law.

Advocates argue that statewide standardized testing will have a number of positive effects. These include improved student performance; more time teaching the subjects that are tested; high expectations for all students; identification of poorly performing schools, teachers, and administrators; and improved confidence in schools as test scores rise.

Critics argue that the NCLB legislation is doing more harm than good (Noddings, 2007). One criticism stresses that using a single test as the sole indicator of students' progress and competence presents a very narrow view of students' skills (Lewis, 2007). This criticism is similar to the one leveled at IQ tests, which we described in Chapter 8. To assess student progress and achievement, many psychologists and educators emphasize that a number of measures should be used, including tests, quizzes, projects, portfolios, classroom observations, and so on. Also, the tests used as part of NCLB don't measure creativity, motivation, persistence, flexible thinking, and social skills (Stiggins, 2008). Critics point out that teachers end up spending far too much class time "teaching to the test" by drilling students and having them memorize isolated facts at the expense of teaching that focuses on thinking skills, which students need for success in life (Pressley, 2007). Also, there is concern that in the era of No Child Left Behind students who are gifted are being neglected in the effort to raise the achievement level of students who are not doing well (Clark, 2008).

Consider also the following: Each state is allowed to have different criteria for what constitutes passing or failing grades on tests designated for NCLB inclusion. An analysis of NCLB data indicated that almost every fourth-grade student in Mississippi knows how to read but only half of Massachusetts' students do (Birman

> Education is the transmission of civilization.
>
> —**Ariel and Will Durant**
> *American Authors and Philosophers, 20th Century*

direct instruction approach A teacher-centered approach characterized by teacher direction and control, mastery of academic material, high expectations for students' progress, and maximum time spent on learning tasks.

What are some of the most important purposes of standardized tests?

& others, 2007). Clearly, Mississippi's standards for passing the reading test are far below those of Massachusetts. In the recent analysis of state-by-state comparisons, many states have taken the safe route and kept the minimum scores low. Thus, while one of NCLB's goals was to raise standards for achievement in U.S. schools, apparently allowing states to set their own standards has lowered overall achievement.

Despite such criticisms, the U.S. Department of Education is committed to implementing No Child Left Behind, and schools are making accommodations to meet the requirements of this law. Indeed, most educators support the importance of high expectations and high standards of excellence for students and teachers. At issue, however, is whether the tests and procedures mandated by NCLB are the best route to achieving these high standards (Nitko & Brookhart, 2011; Popham, 2011).

Let's now explore what schools are like at different developmental levels of students. We will begin with early childhood education.

EARLY CHILDHOOD EDUCATION

To the teachers in a Reggio Emilia program (described at the beginning of this chapter), preschool children are active learners, exploring the world with their peers, constructing their knowledge of the world in collaboration with their community, aided but not directed by their teachers. In many ways, the Reggio Emilia approach applies ideas consistent with the views of Piaget and Vygotsky discussed in Chapter 6, "Cognitive Developmental Approaches." Our exploration of early childhood education focuses on variations in programs, educational strategies for young children who are disadvantaged, and some controversies in early childhood education.

Variations in Early Childhood Education   Attending preschool is rapidly becoming the norm for U.S. children. There are many variations in the way young children are educated (Follari, 2011; Hendrick & Weissman, 2010; Morrison, 2011; Shonkoff, 2010). The foundation of early childhood education has been the child-centered kindergarten.

The Child-Centered Kindergarten   Nurturing is a key aspect of the **child-centered kindergarten,** which emphasizes the education of the whole child and concern for his or her physical, cognitive, and socioemotional development (Marion, 2010). Instruction is organized around children's needs, interests, and learning styles. Emphasis is placed on the process of learning, rather than what is learned (Feeney & others, 2010; Hendrick & Weissman, 2010). The child-centered kindergarten honors three principles: Each child follows a unique developmental pattern; young children learn best through firsthand experiences with people and materials; and play is extremely important in the child's total development. Experimenting, exploring, discovering, trying out, restructuring, speaking, and listening are frequent activities in excellent kindergarten programs. Such programs are closely attuned to the developmental status of 4- and 5-year-old children.

The Montessori Approach   Montessori schools are patterned after the educational philosophy of Maria Montessori (1870–1952), an Italian physician-turned-educator who crafted a revolutionary approach to young children's education at the beginning of the twentieth century. The **Montessori approach** is a philosophy of education in which children are given considerable freedom and spontaneity in choosing activities. They are allowed to move from one activity to another as they desire. The teacher acts as a facilitator rather than a director. The teacher shows the child how to perform intellectual activities, demonstrates interesting ways to explore curriculum materials, and offers help when the child requests it (Drake, 2008; Lillard, 2008). "By encouraging children to make decisions from an early age, Montessori programs seek to develop self-regulated problem solvers who can make choices and

developmental connection

Cognitive Theory. Both Piaget and Vygotsky believed that play is an excellent setting for young children's cognitive development. Chapter 15, p. 438

child-centered kindergarten Education that involves the whole child by considering both the child's physical, cognitive, and socioemotional development and the child's needs, interests, and learning styles.

Montessori approach An educational philosophy in which children are given considerable freedom and spontaneity in choosing activities and are allowed to move from one activity to another as they desire.

manage their time effectively" (Hyson, Copple, & Jones, 2006, p. 14). The number of Montessori schools in the United States has expanded dramatically in recent years, from one school in 1959 to 355 schools in 1970 to more than 4,000 today.

Some developmentalists favor the Montessori approach, but others conclude that it neglects children's socioemotional development. For example, although Montessori fosters independence and the development of cognitive skills, it deemphasizes verbal interaction between the teacher and child and between the children themselves. Montessori's critics also argue that it restricts imaginative play and that its heavy reliance on self-corrective materials may not adequately allow for creativity or accommodate a variety of learning styles.

Developmentally Appropriate and Inappropriate Education   Many educators and psychologists conclude that preschool and young elementary school children learn best through active, hands-on teaching methods such as games and dramatic play. They know that children develop at varying rates and that schools need to allow for these individual differences. They also argue that schools should focus on facilitating children's socioemotional development as well as their cognitive development. Educators refer to this type of schooling as **developmentally appropriate practice** (DAP), which is based on knowledge of the typical development of children within an age span (age-appropriateness), as well as the uniqueness of the child (individual-appropriateness) (Bredekamp, 2011; Kostelnik, Soderman, & Whirem, 2011). In contrast, developmentally inappropriate practice for young children relies on abstract paper-and-pencil activities presented to large groups. Desired outcomes for DAP include thinking critically, working cooperatively, solving problems, developing self-regulatory skills, and enjoying learning. The emphasis in DAP is on the process of learning rather than its content (Barbarin & Miller, 2009; Ritchie, Maxwell, & Bredekamp, 2009). Figure 16.1 provides the National Association for the Education of Young Children's (NAEYC) recent update of developmentally appropriate education in a number of areas (NAEYC, 2009).

Many but not all studies show significant positive benefits for developmentally appropriate education (Hyson, 2007). Among the reasons it is difficult to generalize about research on developmentally appropriate education is that individual programs often vary, and developmentally appropriate education is an evolving concept. Recent changes in the concept have focused more attention on sociocultural factors, the teacher's active involvement and implementation of systematic intentions, as well as the degree to which academic skills should be emphasized and how they should be taught.

Education for Young Children Who Are Disadvantaged
For many years, U.S. children from low-income families did not receive any education before entering the first grade. Often, they began first grade already several steps behind their classmates in their readiness to learn. In the summer of 1965, the federal government began an effort to break the cycle of poverty and poor education for young children in the United States through **Project Head Start.** It is a compensatory program designed to provide children from low-income families the opportunity to acquire the skills and experiences important for success in school (Zigler & Styfco, 2010). After almost half a century, Head Start continues to be the largest federally funded program for U.S. children, with almost 1 million children enrolled annually (Hagen & Lamb-Parker, 2008). In 2007, 3 percent of Head Start children were 5 years old, 51 percent were 4 years old, 36 percent were 3 years old, and 10 percent were under three years of age (Administration for Children and Families, 2008).

Larry Page and Sergey Brin, founders of the highly successful Internet search engine, Google, recently said that their early years at Montessori schools were a major factor in their success (International Montessori Council, 2006). During an interview with Barbara Walters, they said they learned how to be self-directed and self-starters at Montessori (ABC News, 2005). They commented that Montessori experiences encouraged them to think for themselves and allowed them the freedom to develop their own interests.

developmentally appropriate practice Education that focuses on the typical developmental patterns of children (age-appropriateness) and the uniqueness of each child (individual-appropriateness). Such practice contrasts with developmentally inappropriate practice, which relies on abstract paper-and-pencil activities presented to large groups of young children.

Project Head Start Compensatory education designed to provide children from low-income families the opportunity to acquire the skills and experiences important for school success.

Core Considerations in Developmentally Appropriate Practice

1 Knowledge to Consider in Making Decisions

In all aspects of working with children, early childhood practitioners need to consider these three areas of knowledge: 1) What is known about child development and learning, especially age-related characteristics; 2) What is known about each child as an individual; and 3) What is known about the social and cultural contexts in which children live.

2 Challenging and Achieveable Goals

Keeping in mind desired goals and what is known about the children as a group and individually, teachers plan experiences to promote children's learning and development.

Principles of Child Development and Learning that Inform Practice

1 All the domains of development and learning—physical, cognitive, and social—are important, and they are linked.

2 Many aspects of children's learning and development follow well-documented sequences, with later abilities, skills, and knowledge building on those already acquired.

3 Development and learning proceed at varying rates from child to child, and at uneven rates across different areas of a child's individual functioning.

4 Development and learning result from the interaction of biology and experience.

5 Early experiences have strong effects—both cumulative and delayed—on children's development and learning; optimal periods exist for certain types of development and learning.

6 Development proceeds toward greater complexity, self-regulation, and symbolic or representational capacities.

7 Children develop best when they have secure, consistent relationships with responsive adults and opportunities for positive peer relations.

8 Development and learning occur in and are influenced by multiple social and cultural contexts.

9 Always mentally active in seeking to understand the world around them, children learn in a variety of ways; a wide range of teaching strategies can be effective in guiding children's learning.

10 Play is an important context for developing self-regulation and for promoting language, cognition, and competence.

11 Development and learning advance when children are challenged to achieve at a level just beyond their current mastery and when they are given opportunities to practice newly acquired skills.

12 Children's experiences shape their motivation and approaches to learning, such as persistence, initiative, and flexibility; in turn, these characteristics influence their learning and development.

Guidelines for Developmentally Appropriate Practice

1 Creating a Caring Community of Learners

Each member of the community should be valued by the others; relationships are an important context through which children learn; practitioners ensure that members of the community feel psychologically safe.

2 Teaching to Enhance Development and Learning

The teacher takes responsibility for stimulating, directing, and supporting children's learning by providing the experiences that each child needs.

3 Planning Curriculum to Achieve Important Goals

The curriculum is planned to help children achieve goals that are developmentally appropriate and educationally significant.

4 Assessing Children's Development and Learning

In developmentally appropriate practice, assessments are linked to the program's goals for children.

5 Establishing Reciprocal Relationships with Families

A positive partnership between teachers and families benefits children's learning and development.

FIGURE **16.1**

RECOMMENDATIONS BY NAEYC FOR DEVELOPMENTALLY APPROPRIATE PRACTICE IN EARLY CHILDHOOD PROGRAMS SERVING CHILDREN FROM BIRTH THROUGH AGE 8. Source: Adapted from: NAEYC (2009). Developmentally appropriate practice in early childhood programs serving children from birth through age 8.

Early Head Start was established in 1995 to serve children from birth to 3 years of age. In 2007, half of all new funds appropriated for Head Start programs were used for the expansion of Early Head Start. Researchers have found positive effects for Early Head Start (Hoffman & Ewen, 2007).

Head Start programs are not all created equal. One estimate is that 40 percent of the 1,400 Head Start programs are of questionable quality (Zigler & Styfco, 1994). More attention needs to be given to developing consistently high-quality Head Start programs (Chambers, Cheung, & Slavin, 2006). One individual who is strongly motivated to make Head Start a valuable learning experience for young children from disadvantaged backgrounds is Yolanda Garcia. To read about her work, see *Connecting With Careers*.

Evaluations support the positive influence of quality early childhood programs on both the cognitive and social worlds of disadvantaged young children (Ryan, Fauth, & Brooks-Gunn, 2006). A recent national evaluation of Head Start revealed

Yolanda Garcia, Director of Children's Services/Head Start

Yolanda Garcia has been the Director of the Children's Services Department for the Santa Clara, California, County Office of Education since 1980. As director, she is responsible for managing child development programs for 2,500 3- to 5-year-old children in 127 classrooms. Her training includes two master's degrees, one in public policy and child welfare from the University of Chicago and another in education administration from San Jose State University.

Garcia has served on many national advisory committees that have resulted in improvements in the staffing of Head Start programs. Most notably, she served on the Head Start Quality Committee that recommended the development of Early Head Start and revised performance standards for Head Start programs. Garcia currently is a member of the American Academy of Science Committee on the Integration of Science and Early Childhood Education.

Yolanda Garcia, Director of Children's Services/Head Start, working with a Head Start child in Santa Clara, California.

that the program had a positive influence on the language and cognitive development of the 3- and 4-year-olds (Puma & others, 2010). However, by the end of the first grade, there were few lasting outcomes, except for a larger vocabulary for those who went to Head Start as 4-year-olds and better oral comprehension for those who went to Head Start as three-year-olds. Another recent study found that when young children initially began Head Start, they were well below their more academically advantages peers in literacy and math (Hindman & others, 2010). However, by the end of the first grade, the Head Start children were on par with national averages in literacy and math.

One high-quality early childhood education program (although not a Head Start program) is the Perry Preschool program in Ypsilanti, Michigan, a two-year preschool program that includes weekly home visits from program personnel. In analyses of the long-term effects of the program, adults who had been in the Perry Preschool program were compared with a control group of adults from the same background who had not received the enriched early childhood education (Schweinhart & others, 2005; Weikert, 1993). Those who had been in the Perry Preschool program had fewer teen pregnancies and higher high school graduation rates, and at age 40 more were in the workforce, owned their own homes, and had a savings account, and fewer had been arrested.

Controversies in Early Childhood Education Two current controversies in early childhood education involve (1) what the curriculum for early childhood education should be (Hyson, 2007), and (2) whether preschool education should be universal in the United States (Zigler, Gilliam, & Jones, 2006).

Curriculum Controversy A current curriculum controversy in early childhood involves on one side those who advocate a child-centered, constructivist approach much like that emphasized by the NAEYC along the lines of developmentally appropriate practice. On the other side are those who endorse an academic, direct instruction approach.

What are two controversies in early childhood education?

In reality, many high-quality early childhood education programs include both academic and constructivist approaches. Many education experts such as Lilian Katz (1999), though, worry about academic approaches that place too much pressure on young children to achieve and don't provide any opportunities to actively construct knowledge. Competent early childhood programs also should focus on both cognitive development and socioemotional development, not exclusively on cognitive development (Kagan & Scott-Little, 2004).

Universal Preschool Education Another early childhood education controversy focuses on whether preschool education should be instituted for all 4-year-old children in the United States. Edward Zigler and his colleagues (2006) recently argued that the United States should have universal preschool education. They emphasize that quality preschools prepare children for success in school. Zigler and his colleagues (2006) cite research that shows quality preschool programs increase the likelihood that once children go to elementary and secondary school they will be less likely to be retained in a grade or to drop out of school. They also point to analyses indicating that universal preschool would bring considerable cost savings on the order of billions of dollars because of a diminished need for remedial and justice services (Karoly & Bigelow, 2005).

Critics of universal preschool education argue that the gains attributed to preschool and kindergarten education are often overstated. They especially stress that research has not proven that nondisadvantaged children improve as a result of attending a preschool. Thus, the critics say it is more important to improve preschool education for young children who are disadvantaged than to mandate preschool education for all 4-year-old children. Some critics, especially homeschooling advocates, emphasize that young children should be educated by their parents, not by schools. Thus, controversy continues to surround the issue of universal preschool education.

In Japan and many developing countries, some of the goals of early childhood education are quite different from those of American programs. To read about the differences, see *Connecting With Diversity*.

ELEMENTARY SCHOOL

For many children, entering the first grade signals a change from being a "home-child" to being a "school-child"—a situation in which new roles and obligations are experienced. Children take up the new role of being a student, interact with peers and teachers, develop new relationships, adopt new reference groups, and discover new standards by which to judge themselves. School provides children with a rich source of new ideas to shape their sense of self.

Too often early schooling proceeds mainly on the basis of negative feedback. For example, children's self-esteem in the latter part of elementary school is lower than it is in the earlier part, and older children rate themselves as less smart, less good, and less hard-working than do younger ones (Blumenfeld & others, 1981; Eccles, 2003).

EDUCATING ADOLESCENTS

What is the transition from elementary to middle or junior high school like? What are the characteristics of effective schools for young adolescents? How can adolescents be encouraged to stay in school?

The Transition to Middle or Junior High School The first year of middle school or junior high school can be difficult for many students (Anderman & Anderman, 2010; Anderman & Mueller, 2010). For example, in one study of the transition from sixth grade in an elementary school to seventh grade in a junior

As children make the transition to elementary school, they interact and develop relationships with new and significant others. School provides them with a rich source of new ideas to shape their sense of self.

Early Childhood Education in Japan and Developing Countries

As in America, there is diversity in Japanese early childhood education. Some Japanese kindergartens have specific aims, such as early musical training or the practice of Montessori strategies. In large cities, some kindergartens are attached to universities that have elementary and secondary schools. In most Japanese preschools, however, little emphasis is put on academic instruction.

In one study, 300 Japanese and 210 American preschool teachers, child development specialists, and parents were asked about various aspects of early childhood education (Tobin, Wu, & Davidson, 1989). Only 2 percent of the Japanese respondents listed "to give children a good start academically" as one of their top three reasons for a society to have preschools. In contrast, over half the American respondents chose this as one of their top three choices. Japanese schools do not teach reading, writing, and mathematics but rather skills like persistence, concentration, and the ability to function as a member of a group. The vast majority of young Japanese children are taught to read at home by their parents.

In the comparison of Japanese and American parents, more than 60 percent of the Japanese parents said that the purpose of preschool is to give children experience being a member of the group, as compared with about 20 percent of the U.S. parents (Tobin, Wu, & Davidson, 1989) (see Figure 16.2). Lessons in living and working together grow naturally out of the Japanese culture. In many Japanese kindergartens, children wear the same uniforms, including caps in different colors to indicate the classrooms to which they belong. They have identical sets of equipment, kept in identical drawers and shelves. This is not intended to turn the young children into robots, as some Americans have observed, but to impress on them that other people, just like themselves, have needs and desires that are equally important (Hendry, 1995).

Japan is a highly advanced industrialized country. What about developing countries— how do they compare to the United States in educating young children? The wide range of programs and emphasis on the education of the whole child—physically, cognitively, and socioemotionally—that characterize U.S. early childhood education do not exist in many developing countries (Roopnarine & Metindogan, 2006). Economic pressures and parents' belief that education should be academically rigorous have produced teacher-centered rather than child-centered early childhood education programs in most developing countries. Among the countries in which this type of early childhood education has been observed are Jamaica, rural China, Thailand, Kenya, and Turkey. In these countries, young children are usually given few choices and are educated in highly structured settings. Emphasis is on learning academic skills through rote memorization and recitation (Lin, Johnson, & Johnson, 2003). Programs in Mexico, Singapore, Korea, and Hong Kong have been observed to be closer to those in the United States in their emphasis on curriculum flexibility and play-based methods (Cisneros-Cohernour, Moreno, & Cisneros, 2000).

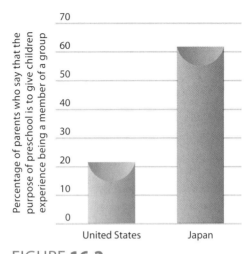

FIGURE 16.2

COMPARISON OF JAPANESE AND U.S. PARENTS' VIEWS ON THE PURPOSE OF PRESCHOOL

y-axis: Percentage of parents who say that the purpose of preschool is to give children experience being a member of a group (0–70)

x-axis: United States, Japan

What characterizes early childhood education in Japan?

A kindergarten class in Kingston, Jamaica. *What characterizes kindergarten in many developing countries like Jamaica?*

The transition from elementary to middle or junior high school occurs at the same time as a number of other developmental changes. *What are some of these other developmental changes?*

high school, adolescents' perceptions of the quality of their school life plunged during the seventh grade (Hirsch & Rapkin, 1987). Compared with their earlier feelings as sixth-graders, the seventh-graders were less satisfied with school, were less committed to school, and liked their teachers less. The drop in school satisfaction occurred regardless of how academically successful the students were. The transition to middle or junior high school is less stressful when students have positive relationships with friends and go through the transition in team-oriented schools in which 20 to 30 students take the same classes together (Hawkins & Berndt, 1985).

The transition to middle or junior high school takes place at a time when many changes—in the individual, in the family, and in school—are occurring simultaneously (Anderman & Mueller, 2010; Eccles & Roeser, 2010). These changes include puberty and related concerns about body image; the emergence of at least some aspects of formal operational thought, including accompanying changes in social cognition; increased responsibility and decreased dependency on parents; change to a larger, more impersonal school structure; change from one teacher to many teachers and from a small, homogeneous set of peers to a larger, more heterogeneous set of peers; and an increased focus on achievement and performance. Moreover, when students make the transition to middle or junior high school, they experience the **top-dog phenomenon** of moving from being the oldest, biggest, and most powerful students in elementary school to being the youngest, smallest, and least powerful students in middle or junior high school.

There can also be positive aspects to the transition to middle or junior high school. Students are more likely to feel grown up, have more subjects from which to select, have more opportunities to spend time with peers and locate compatible friends, and enjoy increased independence from direct parental monitoring. They also may be more challenged intellectually by academic work.

Effective Schools for Young Adolescents Critics argue that middle and junior high schools should offer activities that reflect a wide range of individual differences in biological and psychological development among young adolescents. In 1989 the Carnegie Corporation issued an extremely negative evaluation of our nation's middle schools. It concluded that most young adolescents attended massive, impersonal schools; were taught from irrelevant curricula; trusted few adults in school; and lacked access to health care and counseling. It recommended that the nation should develop smaller "communities" or "houses" to lessen the impersonal nature of large middle schools, have lower student-to-counselor ratios (10 to 1 instead of several hundred to 1), involve parents and community leaders in schools, develop new curricula, have teachers team teach in more flexibly designed curriculum blocks that integrate several disciplines, boost students' health and fitness with more in-school programs, and help students who need public health care to get it. Twenty years later, experts are still finding that middle schools throughout the nation need a major redesign if they are to be effective in educating adolescents (Eccles & Roeser, 2009; Elmore, 2009).

top-dog phenomenon The circumstance of moving from the top position in elementary school to the lowest position in middle or junior high school.

High School Just as there are concerns about U.S. middle school education, so are there concerns about U.S. high school education (Smith, 2009). Critics stress that in many high schools expectations for success and standards for learning are

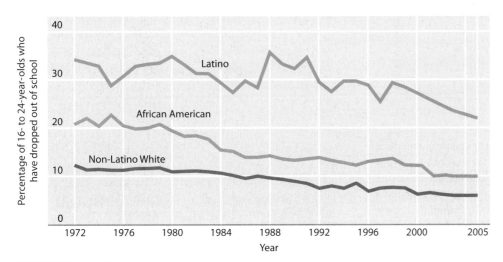

FIGURE **16.3**

TRENDS IN HIGH SCHOOL DROPOUT RATES. From 1972 through 2006, the school dropout rate for Latinos remained very high (22.1 percent of 16- to 24-year-olds in 2006). The African American dropout rate was still higher (10.7 percent) than the White non-Latino rate (5.8 percent) in 2004. (*Source:* National Center for Education Statistics, 2008a).

too low. Critics also argue that too often high schools foster passivity and that schools should create a variety of pathways for students to achieve an identity. Many students graduate from high school with inadequate reading, writing, and mathematical skills—including many who go on to college and have to enroll in remediation classes there. Other students drop out of high school and do not have skills that will allow them to obtain decent jobs, much less to be informed citizens.

In the last half of the 20th century and the first several years of the 21st century, U.S. high school dropout rates declined (National Center for Education Statistics, 2008) (see Figure 16.3). In the 1940s, more than half of U.S. 16- to 24-year-olds had dropped out of school; by 2006, this figure had decreased to 9.3 percent. The dropout rate of Latino adolescents remains high, although it is decreasing in the 21st century (from 28 percent in 2000 to 22.1 percent in 2006). The highest dropout rate in the United States, though, likely occurs for Native American youth—less than 50 percent finish high school.

Students drop out of school for many reasons (Jimerson, 2009). In one study, almost 50 percent of the dropouts cited school-related reasons for leaving school, such as not liking school or being expelled or suspended (Rumberger, 1995). Twenty percent of the dropouts (but 40 percent of the Latino students) cited economic reasons for leaving school. One-third of the female students dropped out for personal reasons such as pregnancy or marriage.

According to one review, the most effective programs to discourage dropping out of high school provide early reading programs, tutoring, counseling, and mentoring (Lehr & others, 2003). They also emphasize the creation of caring environments and relationships, use block scheduling, and offer community-service opportunities.

Early detection of children's school-related difficulties, and getting children engaged with school in positive ways, are important strategies for reducing the dropout rate. Recently the Bill and Melinda Gates Foundation (2006, 2008) has funded efforts to reduce the dropout rate in schools where dropout rates are high. One strategy that is being emphasized in the Gates' funding is keeping students who are at risk for dropping out of school with the same teachers through their high school years. The hope is that the teachers will get to know these students much

Students in the technology training center at Wellpint Elementary/High School located on the Spokane Indian Reservation in Washington. An important educational goal is to increase the high school graduation rate of Native American adolescents.

"I Have a Dream"

"I Have a Dream" (IHAD) is an innovative, comprehensive, long-term dropout prevention program administered by the national "I Have a Dream" Foundation in New York. Since the national IHAD Foundation was created in 1986, it has grown to comprise more than 180 projects in 64 cities and 27 states, serving more than 12,000 children ("I Have a Dream" Foundation, 2010). Local IHAD projects around the country "adopt" entire grades (usually the third or fourth) from public elementary schools, or corresponding age cohorts from public housing developments. These children—"Dreamers"—are then provided with a program of academic, social, cultural, and recreational activities throughout their elementary, middle school, and high school years. An important part of this program is that it is personal rather than institutional: IHAD sponsors and staff develop close long-term relationships with the children. When participants complete high school, IHAD provides the tuition assistance necessary for them to attend a state or local college or vocational school.

The IHAD program was created in 1981, when philanthropist Eugene Lang made an impromptu offer of college tuition to a class of graduating sixth-graders at P.S. 121 in East Harlem. Evaluations of IHAD programs have found dramatic improvements in grades, test scores, and school attendance, as well as a reduction of behavioral problems of Dreamers. In a recent analysis of the "I Have a Dream" program in Houston, 91 percent of the participants received passing grades in

These adolescents participate in the "I Have a Dream" (IHAD) program, a comprehensive, long-term dropout prevention program that has been very successful.

reading/English, 83 percent said they liked school, 98 percent said getting good grades is important to them, 100 percent said they plan to graduate from high school, and 94 percent reported that they plan to go to college ("I Have a Dream" Foundation, 2008).

How does participation in extracurricular activities influence development in adolescence and emerging adulthood?

better, their relationship with the students will improve, and they will be able to monitor and guide the students toward graduating from high school. To read about one program that attempts to reduce the school dropout rate, see *Caring Connections.*

Extracurricular Activities Adolescents in U.S. schools usually can choose from a wide array of extracurricular activities in addition to their academic courses. These adult-sanctioned activities typically occur in the after-school hours and can be sponsored either by the school or the community. They include such diverse activities as sports, academic clubs, band, drama, and math clubs. Researchers have found that participation in extracurricular activities is linked to higher grades, increased school engagement, reduced likelihood of dropping out of school, improved probability of going to college, higher self-esteem, and lower rates of depression, delinquency, and substance abuse (Barber, Stone, & Eccles, 2010; Mahoney, Parente, & Zigler, 2010). Adolescents benefit from a breadth of extracurricular activities more than focusing on a single extracurricular activity.

Of course, the quality of the extracurricular activities matters (Mahoney & others, 2009; Parente & Mahoney, 2009). High-quality extracurricular activities that are likely to promote positive adolescent development include competent and supportive adult mentors, opportunities for increasing school connectedness, challenging and meaningful activities, and opportunities for improving skills.

SOCIOECONOMIC STATUS AND ETHNICITY

Children from low-income, ethnic minority backgrounds have more difficulties in school than do their middle-socioeconomic-status, White counterparts (Hutson, 2008). Why? Critics argue that schools are not doing a good job of educating low-income or ethnic minority students (Banks, 2010; Entwisle, Alexander, & Olson, 2010). Let's further explore the roles of socioeconomic status and ethnicity in schools.

developmental connection

Socioeconomic Status. Socioeconomic differences are a proxy for material, human, and social capital within and beyond the family (Huston & Ripke, 2006). Chapter 17, p. 488

Educating Students from Low-Income Backgrounds Many children living in poverty face problems that present barriers to their learning (McLoyd & others, 2009; Rowley, Kurtz-Costas, & Cooper, 2011; Tamis-LeMonda & McFadden, 2010). They might have parents who don't set high educational standards for them, who are incapable of reading to them, or who don't have enough money to pay for educational materials and experiences, such as books and trips to zoos and museums. They might be malnourished or live in areas where crime and violence are a way of life. A recent study revealed that the longer children experienced poverty, the more detrimental the poverty was to their cognitive development (Najman & others, 2009).

The schools that children from impoverished backgrounds attend often have fewer resources than schools in higher-income neighborhoods (Tamis-LeMonda & McFadden, 2010). In low-income areas, schools are more likely to be staffed by young teachers with less experience than schools in higher-income neighborhoods (Liu & Hernandez, 2008). Schools in low-income areas also are more likely to encourage rote learning, whereas schools in higher-income areas are more likely to work with children to improve their thinking skills (Koppelman & Goodhart, 2011; Spring, 2010). In sum, far too many schools in low-income neighborhoods provide students with environments that are not conducive to effective learning (Huston & Bentley, 2010; Rowley, Kurtz-Costas, & Cooper, 2011).

Jill Nakamura, teaching in her first-grade classroom. Jill teaches in a school located in a high-poverty area. She visits students at home early in the school year in an effort to connect with them and develop a partnership with their parents. "She holds a daily afternoon reading club for students reading below grade level . . . In one school year (2004), she raised the percent of students reading at or above grade level from 29 percent to 76 percent" (Wong Briggs, 2004, p. 6D).

Ethnicity in Schools More than one-third of all African American and almost one-third of all Latino students attend schools in the 47 largest city school districts in the United States, compared with only 5 percent of all White and 22 percent of all Asian American students. Many of these inner-city schools are still segregated, are grossly underfunded, and do not provide adequate opportunities for children to learn effectively. Thus, the effects of SES and the effects of ethnicity are often intertwined (Banks, 2010; Bennett, 2011; Healey, 2009).

Even outside of inner-city schools, school segregation remains a factor in U.S. education (Koppelman, 2011; Spring, 2010). Almost one-third of all African American and Latino students attend schools in which 90 percent or more of the students are from minority groups (Banks, 2008).

The school experiences of students from different ethnic groups vary considerably (Ceballo, Huerta, & Ngo, 2010). African American and Latino students are much less likely than non-Latino White or Asian American students to be enrolled in academic, college preparatory programs and are much more likely to be enrolled

What are some features of a jigsaw classroom?

in remedial and special education programs. Asian American students are far more likely than other ethnic minority groups to take advanced math and science courses in high school. African American students are twice as likely as Latinos, Native Americans, or Whites to be suspended from school.

Following are some strategies for improving interaction among ethnically diverse students:

- *Turn the class into a jigsaw classroom.* When Eliot Aronson was a professor at the University of Texas at Austin, the school system contacted him for ideas on how to reduce the increasing racial tension in classrooms. Aronson (1986) developed the concept of "jigsaw classroom," in which students from different cultural backgrounds are placed in a cooperative group in which they have to construct different parts of a project to reach a common goal. Aronson used the term jigsaw because he saw the technique as much like a group of students cooperating to put different pieces together to complete a jigsaw puzzle. How might this work? Team sports, drama productions, and music performances are examples of contexts in which students participate cooperatively to reach a common goal; however, the jigsaw technique also lends itself to group science projects, history reports, and other learning experiences with a variety of subject matter.

- *Encourage students to have positive personal contact with diverse other students.* Mere contact does not do the job of improving relationships with diverse others. For example, busing ethnic minority students to predominantly White schools, or vice versa, has not reduced prejudice or improved interethnic relations. What matters is what happens after children get to school. Especially beneficial in improving interethnic relations is sharing one's worries, successes, failures, coping strategies, interests, and other personal information with people of other ethnicities. When this happens, people tend to look at others as individuals rather than as members of a homogeneous group.

- *Reduce bias.* Teachers can reduce bias by displaying images of children from diverse ethnic and cultural groups, selecting play materials and classroom activities that encourage cultural understanding, helping students resist stereotyping, and working with parents to reduce children's exposure to bias and prejudice at home.

- *View the school and community as a team.* James Comer (1988, 2004, 2006, 2010) advocates a community-wide, team-oriented approach as the best way to educate children. Three important aspects of the Comer Project for Change are (1) a governance and management team that develops a comprehensive school plan, assessment strategy, and staff development plan; (2) a mental health or school support team; and (3) a program for parents. Comer believes that the entire school community should have a cooperative rather than an adversarial attitude. The Comer program is currently operating in more than 600 schools in 26 states. Read further about James Comer's work in the *Connecting With Careers* profile.

- Be *a competent cultural mediator.* Teachers can play a powerful role as cultural mediators by being sensitive to biased content in curriculum materials and classroom interactions, learning more about different ethnic groups, being sensitive to children's ethnic attitudes, viewing students of color positively, and thinking of positive ways to get parents of color more involved as partners with teachers in educating children (Manning & Baruth, 2009; Taylor & Whittaker, 2009).

connecting with careers

James Comer, Child Psychiatrist

James Comer grew up in a low-income neighborhood in East Chicago, Indiana, and credits his parents with leaving no doubt about the importance of education. He obtained a BA degree from Indiana University. He went on to obtain a medical degree from Howard University College of Medicine, a Master of Public Health degree from the University of Michigan School of Public Health, and psychiatry training at the Yale University School of Medicine's Child Study Center. He currently is the Maurice Falk professor of Child Psychiatry at the Yale University Child Study Center and an associate dean at the Yale University Medical School. During his years at Yale, Comer has concentrated his career on promoting a focus on child development as a way of improving schools. His efforts in support of healthy development of young people are known internationally.

Comer is, perhaps, best known for the founding of the School Development Program in 1968, which promotes the collaboration of parents, educators, and the surrounding community to improve social, emotional, and academic outcomes for children.

James Comer (*left*) is shown with some of the inner-city children who attend a school that became a better learning environment because of Comer's intervention.

For more information about what psychiatrists do, see page 45 in the Careers in Child Development appendix following Chapter 1.

Review *Connect* Reflect

 LG1 Discuss approaches to schooling and development.

Review

- What are some contemporary approaches to student learning?
- What are some variations in early childhood education?
- What are some characteristics of elementary education?
- How are U.S. adolescents educated, and what are the challenges in educating adolescents?
- How do socioeconomic status and ethnicity affect children's education?

Connect

- In this section, you learned about socioeconomic status (SES) and education.

In Chapter 14, what did you learn about SES and how parents think about education? How does that tie into the importance of programs like IHAD and those sponsored by the Bill and Melinda Gates Foundation?

Reflect *Your Own Personal Journey of Life*

- How would you characterize the approach of the schools that you attended as a child and as an adolescent? Do you think your schools were effective? Explain.

LG2 Characterize children with disabilities and their education.

The Scope of Disabilities   Educational Issues

Disability	Percentage of All Children in Public Schools
Learning disabilities	5.6
Speech and language impairments	3.0
Mental retardation	1.1
Emotional disturbance	0.9

FIGURE 16.4

U.S. CHILDREN WITH A DISABILITY WHO RECEIVE SPECIAL EDUCATION SERVICES. Figures are for the 2006–2007 school year and represent the four categories with the highest number and percentage of children. Both learning disability and attention deficit hyperactivity disorder are combined in the learning disabilities category (National Center for Education Statistics, 2008b).

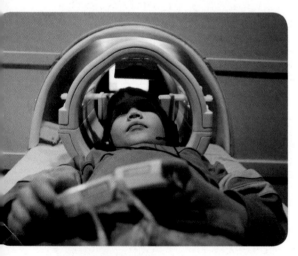

FIGURE 16.5

BRAIN SCANS AND LEARNING DISABILITIES. An increasing number of studies are using MRI brain scans to examine the brain pathways involved in learning disabilities. Shown here is 9-year-old Patrick Price, who has dyslexia. Patrick is going through an MRI scanner disguised by drapes to look like a child-friendly castle. Inside the scanner, children must lie virtually motionless as words and symbols flash on a screen, and they are asked to identify them by clicking different buttons.

What are some of the disabilities that children have? What characterizes the education of children with disabilities?

THE SCOPE OF DISABILITIES

Approximately 14 percent of all children from 3 to 21 years of age in the United States receive special education or related services (National Center for Education Statistics, 2008). Figure 16.4 shows the four largest groups of students with a disability who were served by federal programs in the 2006–2007 school year (National Center for Education Statistics, 2008). As indicated in Figure 16.4, students with a learning disability were by far the largest group of students with a disability to be given special education, followed by children with speech or language impairments, mental retardation, and emotional disturbance.

Learning Disabilities   The U.S. government created a definition of learning disabilities in 1997 and then reauthorized the definition with a few minor changes in 2004. Following is a description of the government's definition of what determined whether a child should be classified as having a learning disability. A child with a **learning disability** has difficulty in learning that involves understanding or using spoken or written language, and the difficulty can appear in listening, thinking, reading, writing, and spelling. A learning disability also may involve difficulty in doing mathematics. To be classified as a learning disability, the learning problem is not primarily the result of visual, hearing, or motor disabilities; mental retardation; emotional disorders; or due to environmental, cultural, or economic disadvantage.

About three times as many boys as girls are classified as having a learning disability. Among the explanations for this gender difference are a greater biological vulnerability among boys and *referral bias.* That is, boys are more likely to be referred by teachers for treatment because of troublesome behavior.

Approximately 80 percent of children with a learning disability have a reading problem (Shaywitz, Gruen, & Shaywitz, 2007). Three types of learning disabilities are dyslexia, dysgraphia, and discalculia:

- **Dyslexia** is a category reserved for individuals who have a severe impairment in their ability to read and spell (Ise & Schulte-Korne, 2010; Reid & others, 2009).

- **Dysgraphia** is a learning disability that involves difficulty in handwriting (Rosenblum, Aloni, & Josman, 2010). Children with dysgraphia may write very slowly, their writing products may be virtually illegible, and they may make numerous spelling errors because of their inability to match up sounds and letters.

- **Dyscalculia,** also known as developmental arithmetic disorder, is a learning disability that involves difficulty in math computation (Rubinsten & Henik, 2009; Rykhlevskaia & others, 2010).

The precise causes of learning disabilities have not yet been determined (Hallahan, Kauffman, & Pullen, 2009; Rosenberg, Westling, & McLeskey, 2011). Researchers have used brain-imaging techniques, such as magnetic resonance imaging, to reveal any regions of the brain that might be involved in learning disabilities (Shaywitz, Lyon, & Shaywitz, 2006) (see Figure 16.5). This research indicates that it is unlikely learning disabilities reside in a single, specific brain location. More likely, learning disabilities are due to problems in integrating information from multiple brain regions or subtle abnormalities in brain structures and functions.

Interventions with children who have a learning disability often focus on improving reading ability (Bursuck & Damer, 2011). Intensive instruction over a period of time by a competent teacher can help many children (Berninger, 2006; Waber, 2010).

Attention Deficit Hyperactivity Disorder (ADHD) **Attention deficit hyperactivity disorder (ADHD)** is a disability in which children consistently show one or more of the following characteristics over a period of time: (1) inattention, (2) hyperactivity, and (3) impulsivity. Children who are inattentive have so much difficulty focusing on any one thing that they may get bored with a task after only a few minutes—or even seconds. Children who are hyperactive show high levels of physical activity, seeming to be almost constantly in motion. Children who are impulsive have difficulty curbing their reactions; they do not do a good job of thinking before they act. Depending on the characteristics that children with ADHD display, they can be diagnosed as (1) ADHD with predominantly inattention, (2) ADHD with predominantly hyperactivity/impulsivity, or (3) ADHD with both inattention and hyperactivity/impulsivity.

The number of children diagnosed and treated for ADHD has increased substantially in recent decades. The disorder occurs as much as four to nine times more frequently in boys than in girls. There is controversy, however, about the increased diagnosis of ADHD (Stolzer, 2009). Some experts attribute the increase mainly to heightened awareness of the disorder; others are concerned that many children are being incorrectly diagnosed (Parens & Johnston, 2009).

Definitive causes of ADHD have not been found. However, a number of causes have been proposed (Faraone & Mick, 2010; Stolzer, 2009). Some children likely inherit a tendency to develop ADHD from their parents (Durston, 2010; Pennington & others, 2009). Other children likely develop ADHD because of damage to their brain during prenatal or postnatal development (Linblad & Hjern, 2010). Among early possible contributors to ADHD are cigarette and alcohol exposure during prenatal development and low birth weight (Knopik, 2009).

As with learning disabilities, the development of brain-imaging techniques is leading to a better understanding of ADHD (Hoeksema & others, 2010). A recent study revealed that peak thickness of the cerebral cortex occurred three years later (10.5 years) in children with ADHD than in children without ADHD (peak at 7.5 years) (Shaw & others, 2007). The delay was more prominent in the prefrontal regions of the brain that are especially important in attention and planning (see Figure 16.6). Researchers also are exploring the roles that various neurotransmitters, such as serotonin and dopamine might play in ADHD (Levy, 2009; Rondou, Haegeman, & van Craenenbroeck, 2010; Zhou & others, 2010).

Stimulant medication such as Ritalin or Adderall (which has fewer side effects than Ritalin) is effective in improving the attention of many children with ADHD, but it usually does not improve their attention to the same level as children who do not have ADHD (Brams, Mao, & Doyle, 2009; Stray, Ellertsen, & Stray, 2010). A recent meta-analysis concluded that behavior management treatments are effective in reducing the effects of ADHD (Fabiano & others, 2009). Researchers have often found that a combination of medication (such as Ritalin) and behavior management tends to improve the behavior of children with ADHD better than medication alone or behavior management alone, although this is not true in all cases (Parens & Johnston, 2009).

Emotional and Behavioral Disorders Most children have minor emotional difficulties at some point during their school years. A small percentage have problems

developmental **connection**

Attention. Attention, which involves the focusing of mental resources, improves cognitive processing on many tasks. Chapter 7, p. 204

Many children with ADHD show impulsive behavior, such as this child who is getting ready to hurl a paper airplane at other children. *How would you handle this situation if you were a teacher and this were to happen in your classroom?*

learning disabilities Disabilities involving understanding or using spoken or written language. The difficulty can appear in listening, thinking, reading, writing, spelling, or mathematics. To be classified as a learning disability, the problem must not be primarily the result of visual, hearing, or motor disabilities; mental retardation; emotional disorders; or environmental, cultural, or economic disadvantage.

dyslexia A category of learning disabilities involving a severe impairment in the ability to read and spell.

dysgraphia A learning disability that involves difficulty in handwriting.

dyscalculia Also known as developmental arithmetic disorder; a learning disability that involves difficulty in math computation.

attention deficit hyperactivity disorder (ADHD) A disability in which children consistently show one or more of the following characteristics: (1) inattention, (2) hyperactivity, and (3) impulsivity.

Prefrontal cortex   Prefrontal cortex

☐ Greater than 2 years delay
■ 0 to 2 years delay

FIGURE 16.6

REGIONS OF THE BRAIN IN WHICH CHILDREN WITH ADHD HAD A DELAYED PEAK IN THE THICKNESS OF THE CEREBRAL CORTEX.
Note: The greatest delays occurred in the prefrontal cortex.

What characterizes autism spectrum disorders?

FIGURE 16.7

A SCENE FROM THE DVD ANIMATIONS USED IN A STUDY BY BARON-COHEN AND OTHERS (2007). *What did they do to improve autistic children's ability to read facial expressions?*
© Crown copyright MMVI, www.thetransporters.com, courtesy of Changing Media Development

so serious and persistent that they are classified as having an emotional or a behavioral disorder (Gargiulo, 2009; Kauffman & Landrum, 2009).

Emotional and behavioral disorders consist of serious, persistent problems that involve relationships, aggression, depression, and fears associated with personal or school matters, as well as other inappropriate socioemotional characteristics. Approximately 8 percent of children who have a disability and require an individualized education plan fall into this classification. Boys are three times as likely as girls to have these disorders.

Autism Spectrum Disorders   **Autism spectrum disorders (ASD),** also called pervasive developmental disorders, range from the severe disorder labeled autistic disorder to the milder disorder called Asperger syndrome. Autism spectrum disorders are characterized by problems in social interaction, problems in verbal and nonverbal communication, and repetitive behaviors (Boutot & Myles, 2011; Hall, 2008). Children with these disorders may also show atypical responses to sensory experiences (National Institute of Mental Health, 2008). Autism spectrum disorders often can be detected in children as young as 1 to 3 years of age.

Recent estimates of autism spectrum disorders indicate that they are increasing in occurrence or are increasingly being detected and labeled (Neal, 2009). Once thought to affect only 1 in 2,500 individuals, today's estimates suggest that they occur in about 1 in 150 individuals (Centers for Disease Control and Prevention, 2009).

Autistic disorder is a severe developmental autism spectrum disorder that has its onset in the first three years of life and includes deficiencies in social relationships, abnormalities in communication, and restricted, repetitive, and stereotyped patterns of behavior.

Asperger syndrome is a relatively mild autism spectrum disorder in which the child has relatively good verbal ability, milder nonverbal language problems, and a restricted range of interests and relationships (Bennett & others, 2008). Children with Asperger syndrome often engage in obsessive, repetitive routines and preoccupations with a particular subject. For example, a child may be obsessed with baseball scores or railroad timetables.

What causes the autism spectrum disorders? The current consensus is that autism is a brain dysfunction with abnormalities in brain structure and neurotransmitters (Anderson & others, 2009; Gilbert & others, 2009). Genetic factors likely play a role in the development of the autism spectrum disorders (El-Fishawy & State, 2010; Shen & others, 2010). A recent study revealed that mutations—missing or duplicated pieces of DNA—on chromosome 16 can raise a child's risk of developing autism 100-fold (Weiss & others, 2008). There is no evidence that family socialization causes autism. Mental retardation is present in some children with autism; others show average or above-average intelligence (Hoekstra & others, 2010).

Boys are four times as likely to have autism spectrum disorders as girls are (Gong & others, 2009). Expanding on autism's male linkage, Simon Baron-Cohen (2008) recently argued that autism reflects an extreme male brain, especially indicative of males' lesser ability to show empathy and read facial expressions and gestures. In an attempt to improve these skills in 4- to 8-year-old autistic boys, Baron-Cohen and his colleagues (2007) produced a number of animations on a DVD that place faces with different emotions on toy trains and tractor characters in a boy's bedroom (see Figure 16.7). (See www.thetransporters.com for a look at a number of the facial expression animations in addition to the one shown in Figure 16.7.) After the autistic children watched the animations 15 minutes every weekday for one month, their ability to recognize real faces in a different context equaled that of children without autism.

Children with autism benefit from a well-structured classroom, individualized instruction, and small-group instruction. Behavior modification techniques are sometimes effective in helping autistic children learn (Boutot & Myles, 2011; Hall, 2008; Kasari & Lawton, 2010). A recent research review concluded that when these behavior modifications are intensely provided and used early in the autistic child's life, they are more effective (Howlin, Magiati, & Charman, 2009).

EDUCATIONAL ISSUES

Until the 1970s most U.S. public schools either refused enrollment to children with disabilities or inadequately served them. This changed in 1975, when Public Law 94-142, the Education for All Handicapped Children Act, required that all students with disabilities be given a free, appropriate public education. In 1990, Public Law 94-142 was recast as the Individuals with Disabilities Education Act (IDEA). IDEA was amended in 1997 and then reauthorized in 2004 and renamed the Individuals with Disabilities Education Improvement Act.

IDEA spells out broad mandates for services to children with disabilities of all kinds (Friend, 2011; Gargiulo, 2009). These services include evaluation and eligibility determination, appropriate education and an individualized education program (IEP), and education in the least restrictive environment (LRE).

An **individualized education program (IEP)** is a written statement that spells out a program that is specifically tailored for the student with a disability. The **least restrictive environment (LRE)** is a setting that is as similar as possible to a classroom in which children who do not have a disability are educated. This provision of the IDEA has given a legal basis to efforts to educate children with a disability in regular classrooms. The term **inclusion** describes educating a child with special educational needs full-time in the regular classroom (Hick & Thomas, 2009; Valle & Connor, 2011). Figure 16.8 indicates that in a recent school year slightly more than 50 percent of U.S. students with a disability spent more than 80 percent of their school day in a general classroom.

Many legal changes regarding children with disabilities have had extremely positive effects (Carter, Prater, & Dyches, 2009; Rosenberg, Westling, & McLeskey,

Increasingly, children with disabilities are being taught in the regular classroom, as is this child with mild mental retardation.

emotional and behavioral disorders Serious, persistent problems that involve relationships, aggression, depression, fears associated with personal or school matters, as well as other inappropriate socioemotional characteristics.

autism spectrum disorders (ASDs) Also called pervasive developmental disorders, they range from the severe disorder labeled autistic disorder to the milder disorder called Asperger syndrome. Children with these disorders are characterized by problems in social interaction, verbal and nonverbal communication, and repetitive behaviors.

autistic disorder A severe developmental autism spectrum disorder that has its onset in the first three years of life and includes deficiencies in social relationships; abnormalities in communication; and restricted, repetitive, and stereotyped patterns of behavior.

Asperger syndrome A relatively mild autism spectrum disorder in which the child has relatively good verbal skills, milder nonverbal language problems, and a restricted range of interests and relationships.

individualized education program (IEP) A written statement that spells out a program tailored to the needs of a child with a disability.

least restrictive environment (LRE) The concept that a child with a disability must be educated in a setting that is similar to classrooms in which children without a disability are educated.

inclusion Educating a child with special educational needs full-time in the regular classroom.

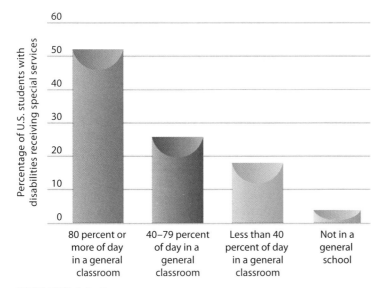

FIGURE **16.8**

PERCENTAGE OF U.S. STUDENTS WITH DISABILITIES 6 TO 21 YEARS OF AGE RECEIVING SPECIAL SERVICES IN THE GENERAL CLASSROOM.
Note: Data for 2004–2005 School Year; National Center for Education Statistics, 2007.

2011). Compared with several decades ago, far more children today are receiving competent, specialized services. For many children, inclusion in the regular classroom, with modifications or supplemental services, is appropriate. However, some leading experts on special education argue that in some cases the effort to educate children with disabilities in the regular classroom has become too extreme. For example, James Kauffman and his colleagues (Kauffman, McGee, & Brigham, 2004) state that inclusion too often has meant making accommodations in the regular classroom that do not always benefit children with disabilities. They advocate a more individualized approach that does not always involve full inclusion but allows options such as special education outside the regular classroom. Kauffman and his colleagues (2004, p. 620) acknowledge that children with disabilities "*do* need the services of specially trained professionals" and "*do* sometimes need altered curricula or adaptations to make their learning possible." However, "we sell students with disabilities short when we pretend that they are not different from typical students. We make the same error when we pretend that they must *not* be expected to put forth extra effort if they are to learn to do some things—or learn to do something in a different way." Like general education, special education should challenge students with disabilities "to become all they can be."

Review *Connect* Reflect

 LG2 Characterize children with disabilities and their education.

Review

- Who are children with disabilities? What characterizes children with learning disabilities? How would you describe children with attention deficit hyperactivity disorder? What are emotional and behavioral disorders? What are autism spectrum disorders, what are they caused by, and how are they characterized?
- What are some issues involved in educating children with disabilities?

Connect

- In this section, you learned that exposure to cigarette smoke during prenatal development may be linked to ADHD. In Chapter 3, what were agents that can potentially cause a birth defect or negatively alter cognitive and behavioral outcomes called?

Reflect *Your Own Personal Journey of Life*

- Think about your own schooling and how children with learning disabilities or ADHD either were or were not diagnosed. Were you aware of such individuals in your classes? Were they helped by specialists? You may know one or more individuals with a learning disability or ADHD. Ask them about their educational experiences and whether they think schools could have done a better job of helping them.

Achievement **LG3** Explain the development of achievement in children.

Extrinsic and Intrinsic Motivation   Cognitive Processes   Ethnicity and Culture

In any classroom, no matter who the teacher is or what approach is used, some children achieve more than others. Why? The reasons for variations in achievement include motivation, expectations, goals, and other characteristics of the child as well as sociocultural contexts.

EXTRINSIC AND INTRINSIC MOTIVATION

extrinsic motivation Response to external incentives such as rewards and punishments.

intrinsic motivation Internal motivational factors such as self-determination, curiosity, challenge, and effort.

Extrinsic motivation involves external incentives such as rewards and punishments. **Intrinsic motivation** is based on internal factors such as self-determination, curiosity, challenge, and effort. Cognitive approaches stress the importance of intrinsic motivation in achievement. Some students study hard because they want to make good grades or avoid parental disapproval (extrinsic motivation). Other students work hard because they are internally motivated to achieve high standards in their work (intrinsic motivation).

Current evidence strongly favors establishing a classroom climate in which students are intrinsically motivated to learn (Eccles & Roeser, 2009). For example, a study of third- through eighth-grade students found that intrinsic motivation was positively linked with grades and standardized test scores, whereas extrinsic motivation was negatively related to achievement outcomes (Lepper, Corpus, & Iyengar, 2005). A longitudinal study revealed that parental intrinsic/extrinsic motivational practices were linked to children's motivation (Gottfried & others, 2009). In this study, children had higher intrinsic motivation in math and science from 9 to 17 years of age when their parents engaged in task-intrinsic practices (encouraging children's pleasure and engagement in learning) than when their parents engaged in task-extrinsic practices (providing external rewards and consequences contingent on children's performance).

Students are more motivated to learn when they are given choices, become absorbed in challenges that match their skills, and receive rewards that have informational value but are not used for control. Praise also can enhance students' intrinsic motivation. To see why these things are so, let's first explore three perspectives on intrinsic motivation: (1) self-determination and personal choice, (2) interest, and (3) cognitive engagement and self-responsibility. Then we'll discuss how external rewards can either enhance or undermine intrinsic motivation. Finally, we will offer some concluding thoughts about intrinsic and extrinsic motivation.

Self-Determination and Personal Choice One view of intrinsic motivation emphasizes self-determination (Deci & Ryan, 2000; Ryan & Deci, 2009). In this view, students want to believe that they are doing something because of their own will, not because of external success or rewards (Vansteenkiste & others, 2009). The architects of self-determination theory, Richard Ryan and Edward Deci (2009) refer to teachers who create circumstances for students to engage in self-determination as *autonomy-supportive teachers*.

Researchers have found that students' internal motivation and intrinsic interest in school tasks increase when students have some choice and are given opportunities to take personal responsibility for their learning (Anderman & Anderman, 2010).

Cognitive Engagement and Self-Responsibility Another variation on intrinsic motivation emphasizes the importance of creating learning environments that encourage students to become cognitively engaged and to take responsibility for their learning

These students were given an opportunity to write and perform their own play. These kinds of self-determining opportunities can enhance students' motivation to achieve.

Calvin and Hobbes   by Bill Watterson

The student:

- Says "I can't"
- Doesn't pay attention to teacher's instructions
- Doesn't ask for help, even when it is needed
- Does nothing (for example, stares out the window)
- Guesses or answers randomly without really trying
- Doesn't show pride in successes
- Appears bored, uninterested
- Is unresponsive to teacher's exhortations to try
- Is easily discouraged
- Doesn't volunteer answers to teacher's questions
- Maneuvers to get out of or to avoid work (for example, has to go to the nurse's office)

FIGURE 16.9

BEHAVIORS THAT SUGGEST A HELPLESS ORIENTATION

mastery motivation An orientation in which one is task oriented, focusing on learning strategies and the achievement process rather than ability or the outcome.

helpless orientation An orientation in which one seems trapped by the experience of difficulty and attributes one's difficulty to a lack of ability.

performance orientation An orientation in which one focuses on winning rather than achievement outcomes, and happiness is thought to result from winning.

(Blumenfeld, Kempler, & Krajcik, 2006). The goal is to get students to become motivated to expend the effort to persist and master ideas rather than simply doing enough work to just get by and make passing grades. Especially important in encouraging students to become cognitively engaged and responsible for their learning is to embed subject matter content and skills learning within meaningful contexts, especially real-world situations that mesh with students' interests (Eccles & Roeser, 2009).

Some Final Thoughts About Intrinsic and Extrinsic Motivation   It is important for parents and teachers to encourage students to become intrinsically motivated and to create learning environments that promote students' cognitive engagement and self-responsibility for learning (Blumenfeld, Marx, & Harris, 2006). That said, the real world is not just one of intrinsic motivation, and too often intrinsic and extrinsic motivation have been pitted against each other as polar opposites. In many aspects of students' lives, both intrinsic and extrinsic motivation are at work (Cameron & Pierce, 2008; Schunk, 2008). Keep in mind, though, that many psychologists recommend that extrinsic motivation by itself is not a good strategy.

COGNITIVE PROCESSES

Our discussion of extrinsic and intrinsic motivation sets the stage for introducing other cognitive processes involved in motivating students to learn. As we explore these additional cognitive processes, notice how intrinsic and extrinsic motivation continue to be important. The processes are (1) mastery motivation and mindset; (2) self-efficacy; (3) expectations; and (4) goal setting, planning, and self-monitoring, and (5) purpose.

Mastery Motivation and Mindset   Becoming cognitively engaged and self-motivated to improve are reflected in adolescents with a mastery motivation. These children also have a growth mindset—a belief that they can produce positive outcomes if they put forth the effort.

Mastery Motivation   Developmental psychologists Valanne Henderson and Carol Dweck (1990) have found that children often show two distinct responses to difficult or challenging circumstances. Children who display **mastery motivation** are task oriented; they concentrate on learning strategies and the process of achievement rather than their ability or the outcome. Those with a **helpless orientation** seem trapped by the experience of difficulty, and they attribute their difficulty to lack of ability. They frequently say such things as "I'm not very good at this," even though they might earlier have demonstrated their ability through many successes. And, once they view their behavior as failure, they often feel anxious, and their performance worsens even further. Figure 16.9 describes some behaviors that might reflect helplessness (Stipek, 2002).

In contrast, mastery-oriented children often instruct themselves to pay attention, to think carefully, and to remember strategies that have worked for them in previous situations. They frequently report feeling challenged and excited by difficult tasks, rather than being threatened by them (Anderman & Mueller, 2010; Dweck, Mangels, & Good, 2004).

Another issue in motivation involves whether to adopt a mastery or a performance orientation. Children with a **performance orientation** are focused on winning, rather than on achievement outcome, and believe that happiness results from winning. Does this mean that mastery-oriented children do not like to win and that performance-oriented children are not motivated to experience the self-efficacy that comes from being able to take credit for one's accomplishments? No. A matter of emphasis or degree is involved, though. For mastery-oriented individuals, winning isn't everything; for performance-oriented individuals, skill development and self-efficacy take a back seat to winning. One recent study of seventh-grade students found that girls were more likely than boys to have mastery rather than performance goals in their approach to math achievement (Kenny-Benson & others, 2006).

A final point needs to be made about mastery and performance goals: They are not always mutually exclusive. Students can be both mastery and performance oriented, and researchers have found that mastery goals combined with performance goals often enhance students' success (Schunk, Pintrich, & Meece, 2008).

Mindset Carol Dweck's (2006, 2007) most recent analysis of motivation for achievement stresses the importance of children developing a **mindset,** which she defines as the cognitive view individuals develop for themselves. She concludes that individuals have one of two mindsets: (1) *fixed mindset,* in which they believe that their qualities are carved in stone and cannot change; or (2) *growth mindset,* in which they believe their qualities can change and improve through their effort. A fixed mindset is similar to a helpless orientation; a growth mindset is much like having mastery motivation (Dweck, 2007).

In her recent book *Mindset,* Dweck (2006) argued that individuals' mindsets influence whether they will be optimistic or pessimistic, shape their goals and how hard they will strive to reach those goals, and affect many aspects of their lives, including achievement and success in school and sports. Dweck says that mindsets begin to be shaped as children interact with parents, teachers, and coaches, who themselves have either a fixed mindset or a growth mindset. She described the growth mindset of Patricia Miranda:

> [She] was a chubby, unathletic school kid who wanted to wrestle. After a bad beating on the mat, she was told, "You're a joke." First she cried, then she felt: "That really set my resolve. . . I had to keep going and had to know if effort and focus and belief and training could somehow legitimize me as a wrestler." Where did she get this resolve?
>
> Miranda was raised in a life devoid of challenge. But when her mother died of an aneurysm at age forty, ten-year-old Miranda . . . [thought] "If you only go through life doing stuff that's easy, shame on you." So when wrestling presented a challenge, she was ready to take it on. Her effort paid off. At twenty-four, Miranda was having the last laugh. She won a spot on the U.S. Olympic team and came home from Athens with a bronze medal. And what was next? Yale Law School. People urged her to stay where she was already on top, but Miranda felt it was more exciting to start at the bottom again and see what she could grow into this time. (Dweck, 2006, pp. 22–23)

Related to her emphasis on encouraging students to develop a growth mindset, Dweck and her colleagues (Blackwell & Dweck, 2008; Blackwell, Trzesniewski, & Dweck, 2007; Dweck & Master, 2009) have recently incorporated information about the brain's plasticity into their effort to improve students' motivation to achieve and succeed. In one study, they assigned two groups of students to eight sessions of either (1) study skills instruction or (2) study skills instruction plus information about the importance of developing a growth mindset (called incremental theory in the research) (Blackwell & others, 2007). One of the exercises in the growth mindset group was titled, "You Can Grow Your Brain," which emphasized that the brain is like a muscle that can change and grow as it gets exercise and develops new connections. Students were informed that the more you challenge your brain to learn, the more your brain cells grow. Both groups had a pattern of declining math scores prior to the intervention. Following the intervention, the group who only received the study skills instruction continued to decline, but the group that received the combination of study skills instruction plus the growth mindset information reversed the downward trend and improved their math achievement.

In other work, Dweck has been creating a computer-based workshop, "Brainology," to teach students that their intelligence can change (Blackwell & Dweck, 2008). Students experience six modules about how the brain works and how they can make their brains improve. After being tested in 20 New York City schools recently, students strongly endorsed the value of the computer-based brain modules. Said one student, "I will try harder because I know that the more you try the more your brain knows." (Dweck & Master, 2009, p. 137).

Patricia Miranda (*in blue*) winning the bronze medal in the 2004 Olympics. *What characterizes her growth mindset and how is it different from someone with a fixed mindset?*

mindset Dweck's concept that refers to the cognitive view individuals develop for themselves; individuals have either a fixed or growth mindset.

SELF-EFFICACY

----►

developmental **connection**

Cognitive Theory. Social cognitive theory holds that behavior, environment, and person/cognitive factors are the key influences on development. Chapter 1, pp. 27–28

◄----

They can because they
think they can.

—VIRGIL

Roman Poet, 1st Century BC

A student and teacher at Langston Hughes Elementary School in Chicago, a school whose teachers have high expectations for students. *How do teachers' expectations influence students' achievement?*

self-efficacy The belief that one can master a situation and produce favorable outcomes.

Like having a growth mindset, **self-efficacy**—the belief that one can master a situation and produce favorable outcomes—is an important cognitive view for children to develop. Albert Bandura (1997, 2000, 2004, 2008, 2009, 2010), whose social cognitive theory we described in Chapter 1, argues that self-efficacy is a critical factor in whether or not children achieve. Self-efficacy has much in common with mastery motivation. Self-efficacy is the belief that "I can"; helplessness is the belief that "I cannot" (Stipek, 2002). Children with high self-efficacy agree with statements such as "I know that I will be able to learn the material in this class" and "I expect to be able to do well at this activity."

Dale Schunk (2008) has applied the concept of self-efficacy to many aspects of students' achievement. In his view, self-efficacy influences a student's choice of activities. Students with low self-efficacy for learning might avoid many learning tasks, especially those that are challenging. In contrast, their high-self-efficacy counterparts eagerly work at learning tasks. High-self-efficacy students are more likely to expend effort and persist longer at a learning task than low-self-efficacy students. High-self-efficacy students are more likely to have confidence in exploring challenging career options (Betz, 2004).

Expectations Children's motivation, and likely their performance, are influenced by the expectations that their parents, teachers, and other adults have for their achievement. Children benefit when both parents and teachers have high expectations for them and provide the necessary support for them to meet those expectations. An especially important factor in the lower achievement of students from low-income families is lack of adequate resources, such as an up-to-date computer in the home (or even any computer at all) to support students' learning (Schunk, Pintrich, & Meece, 2008).

Teachers' expectations influence students' motivation and performance (Eccles & Roeser, 2009). "When teachers hold high generalized expectations for student achievement and students perceive these expectations, students achieve more, experience a greater sense of self-esteem and competence as learners, and resist involvement in problem behaviors both during childhood and adolescence" (Wigfield & others, 2006, p. 976). In a recent observational study of twelve classrooms, teachers with high expectations spent more time providing a framework for students' learning, asked higher-level questions, and were more effective in managing students' behavior than teachers with average and low expectations (Rubie-Davies, 2007).

In thinking about teachers' expectations, it also is important to examine these expectations in concert with parents' expectations. For example, a recent study revealed that mothers' and teachers' high expectations had a positive effect on urban youths' achievement outcomes, and further that mothers' high achievement expectations for their youth had a buffering effect in the face of low teacher expectations (Benner & Mistry, 2007). Interestingly, in another recent study, teachers' positive expectations for students' achievement tended to protect students from the negative influence of low parental expectations (Wood, Kaplan, & McLoyd, 2007).

Teachers often have more positive expectations for high-ability than for low-ability students, and these expectations are likely to influence their behavior toward them. For example, teachers require high-ability students to work harder, wait longer for them to respond to questions, respond to them with more information and in a more elaborate fashion, criticize them less often, praise them more often, are more friendly to them, call on them more often, seat them closer to the teachers' desks, and are more likely to give them the benefit of the doubt on close calls in grading than they are for students with low ability (Brophy, 2004). An important strategy for teachers is to monitor their expectations and be sure to have positive expectations for students with low abilities. Fortunately, researchers have found that with support teachers can adapt and raise their expectations for students with low abilities (National Research Council, 2004).

Goal Setting, Planning, and Self-Monitoring

Goal setting, planning, and self-monitoring are important aspects of children's and adolescents' achievement (Eccles & Roeser, 2009; Urdan, 2010). Researchers have found that self-efficacy and achievement improve when individuals set goals that are specific, proximal, and challenging (Bandura, 1997). An example of a nonspecific, fuzzy goal is "I want to be successful." A more concrete, specific goal is "I want to make the honor roll at the end of this semester."

Individuals can set both long-term (distal) and short-term (proximal) goals. It is okay to set some long-term goals, such as "I want to graduate from high school" or "I want to go to college," but it also is important to create short-term goals, which are steps along the way. "Getting an A on the next math test" is an example of a short-term, proximal goal. So is "Doing all of my homework by 4 P.M. Sunday."

Another good strategy is to set challenging goals. A challenging goal is a commitment to self-improvement. Strong interest and involvement in activities is sparked by challenges. Goals that are easy to reach generate little interest or effort. However, goals should be optimally matched to the adolescent's skill level. If goals are unrealistically high, the result will be repeated failures that lower self-efficacy.

It is not enough to simply set goals. It also is important to plan how to reach the goals (Urdan, 2010). Being a good planner means managing time effectively, setting priorities, and being organized.

Researchers have found that high-achieving individuals often are self-regulatory learners (Schunk, Pintrich, & Meece, 2008). For example, high-achieving students self-monitor their learning more and systematically evaluate their progress toward a goal more than low-achieving students do. When parents and teachers encourage students to self-monitor their learning, they give them the message that they are responsible for their own behavior and that learning requires their active, dedicated participation (Zimmerman, Bonner, & Kovach, 1996).

Purpose

In Chapter 11, "The Self and Identity," we discussed William Damon's (2008) ideas on the importance of purpose in identity development. Here we explore how purpose is a missing ingredient in many adolescents' and emerging adults' achievement.

For Damon, *purpose* is an intention to accomplish something meaningful to oneself and to contribute something to the world beyond the self. Finding purpose involves answering questions such as "*Why* am I doing this? *Why* does it matter? *Why* is it important for me and the world beyond me? *Why* do I strive to accomplish this end?" (Damon, 2008, pp. 33–34).

In interviews with 12- to 22-year-olds, Damon found that only about 20 percent had a clear vision of where they wanted to go in life, what they wanted to achieve, and why. The largest percentage—about 60 percent—had engaged in some potentially purposeful activities, such as service learning or fruitful discussions with a career counselor, but they still did not have a real commitment or any reasonable plans for reaching their goals. And slightly more than 20 percent expressed no aspirations and in some instances said they didn't see any reason to have aspirations.

Damon concludes that most teachers and parents communicate the importance of goals such as studying hard and getting good grades, but rarely discuss what the goals might

Life is a gift . . . Accept it.
Life is an adventure . . . Dare it.
Life is a mystery . . . Unfold it.
Life is a struggle . . . Face it.
Life is a puzzle . . . Solve it.
Life is an opportunity . . . Take it.
Life is a mission . . . Fulfill it.
Life is a goal . . . Achieve it.

—AUTHOR UNKNOWN

developmental connection

Identity. William Damon (2008) concludes that too many of today's youth aren't moving toward any identity resolution. Chapter 11, pp. 335–336

Hari Prabhakar (*in rear*) at a screening camp in India that he created as part of his Tribal India Health Foundation. Hari Prabhakar reflects William Damon's concept of finding a path to purpose. Hari's ambition is to become an international health expert. Hari graduated from Johns Hopkins University in 2006 with a double major in public health and writing. A top student (3.9 GPA), he took the initiative to pursue a number of activities outside the classroom, in the health field. As he made the transition from high school to college, Hari created the Tribal India Health Foundation (www.tihf.org), which provides assistance in bringing low-cost health care to rural areas in India. Juggling his roles as a student and as the foundation's director, Hari spent about 15 hours a week leading Tribal India Health throughout his four undergraduate years. In describing his work, Hari said (Johns Hopkins University, 2006):

I have found it very challenging to coordinate the international operation. . . . It takes a lot of work, and there's not a lot of free time. But it's worth it when I visit our patients and see how they and the community are getting better.

(*Sources:* Johns Hopkins University (2006); Prabhakar (2007)).

lead to—the purpose for studying hard and getting good grades. Damon emphasizes that too often students focus only on short-term goals without exploring the big, long-term picture of what they want to do in life. The following interview questions that Damon (2008, p. 135) has used in his research are good springboards for getting students to reflect on their purpose:

What's most important to you in your life?

Why do you care about those things?

Do you have any long-term goals?

Why are these goals important to you?

What does it mean to have a good life?

What does it mean to be a good person?

If you were looking back on your life now, how would you like to be remembered?

ETHNICITY AND CULTURE

How do ethnicity and culture influence children's achievement? Of course, diversity exists within every group in terms of achievement. But Americans have been especially concerned about two questions related to ethnicity and culture. First, does their ethnicity deter ethnic minority children from high achievement in school? And second, is there something about American culture that accounts for the poor performance of U.S. children in math and science?

Ethnicity Sandra Graham (1986, 1990) has conducted a number of studies that reveal stronger differences in achievement related to socioeconomic status than ethnicity. She is struck by how consistently middle-income African American students, like their White middle-income counterparts, have high achievement expectations and understand that failure is usually due to a lack of effort.

A special challenge for many ethnic minority students is dealing with negative stereotypes and discrimination. Many ethnic minority students living in poverty must also deal with conflict between the values of their neighborhood and those of the majority culture, a lack of high-achieving role models, and as discussed earlier, poor schools (McLoyd & others, 2009). Even students who are motivated to learn and achieve may find it difficult to perform effectively in such contexts.

Cross-Cultural Comparisons In the past three decades, the poor performance of American children in math and science has become well publicized. In a recent large-scale comparison of math and science achievement among fourth-grade students in 2007, the average U.S. fourth-grade math score was higher than 23 of the 35 countries and lower than 8 countries (all in Asia and Europe) (TIMMS, 2008). Fourth-graders from Hong Kong had the highest math scores. The average fourth-grade U.S. math score had improved slightly (11 points) from the same assessment in 1995, but some Asian countries had improved their scores considerably more—the Hong Kong score was 50 points higher and the Slovenia score 40 points higher in 2007 than in 1995, for example.

In 2007, the fourth-grade U.S. science score was higher than those in 25 countries and lower than those in 4 countries (all in Asia). However, the average U.S. fourth-grade science score decreased 3 points from 1995 to 2007 while the science scores for some countries increased dramatically—63 points in Singapore, 56 points in Latvia, and 55 points in Iran, for example. Why do American students fare so poorly in mathematics? To learn about one researcher's conclusions on the subject, read *Connecting Through Research*.

developmental **connection**

Culture and Ethnicity. Ethnicity refers to characteristics rooted in cultural heritage, including nationality, race, religion, and language. Chapter 1, p. 11

UCLA educational psychologist Sandra Graham is shown talking with adolescent boys about motivation. She has conducted a number of studies which reveal that middle-socioeconomic-status African American students—like their White counterparts—have high achievement expectations and attribute success to internal factors such as effort rather than external factors such as luck.

connecting through research

How Do Different Cultures Compare In Their Attitudes and Behaviors Regarding Learning Math and Math Instruction?

Harold Stevenson conducted research on children's learning for five decades. The research explored the reasons for the poor performance of American students. Stevenson and his colleagues (Stevenson, 1995; Stevenson & others, 1990) completed five cross-cultural comparisons of students in the United States, China, Taiwan, and Japan. In these studies, Asian students consistently outperformed American students. And, the longer the students were in school, the wider the gap became between Asian and American students—the lowest difference was in the first grade, the highest in the eleventh grade (the highest grade studied).

To learn more about the reasons for these large cross-cultural differences, Stevenson and his colleagues spent thousands of hours observing in classrooms, as well as interviewing and surveying teachers, students, and parents. They found that the Asian teachers spent more of their time teaching math than did the American teachers. For example, more than one-fourth of total classroom time in the first grade was spent on math instruction in Japan, compared with only one-tenth of the time in the U.S. first-grade classrooms. Also, the Asian stu-

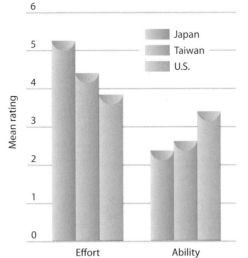

FIGURE **16.10**

MOTHERS' BELIEFS ABOUT THE FACTORS RESPONSIBLE FOR CHILDREN'S MATH ACHIEVEMENT IN THREE COUNTRIES. In one study, mothers in Japan and Taiwan were more likely to believe that their children's math achievement was due to effort rather than innate ability, while U.S. mothers were more likely to believe their children's math achievement was due to innate ability (Stevenson, Lee, & Stigler, 1986). If parents believe that their children's math achievement is due to innate ability and their children are not doing well in math, the implication is that they are less Likely to think their children will benefit from putting forth more effort.

dents were in school an average of 240 days a year, compared with 178 days in the United States.

In addition, differences were found between the Asian and American parents. The American parents had much lower expectations for their children's education and achievement than did the Asian parents. Also, the American parents were more likely to state that their children's math achievement was due to innate ability; the Asian parents were more likely to say that their children's math achievement was the consequence of effort and training (see Figure 16.10). The Asian students were more likely to do math homework than were the American students, and the Asian parents were far more likely to help their children with their math homework than were the American parents (Chen & Stevenson, 1989).

As you'll recall from Chapter 14, Asian and Asian American parenting approaches have been characterized by some as an authoritarian style and by others as a "training" style. Those who endorse the training view note that it reflects the parents' concern and involvement in their children's lives and that the high academic achievement of their children may result from this training.

Asian grade schools intersperse studying with frequent periods of activities. This approach helps children maintain their attention and likely makes learning more enjoyable. Shown here are Japanese fourth-graders making wearable masks. *What are some differences in the way children in many Asian countries are taught compared with children in the United States?*

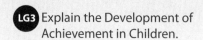
Review

- What are intrinsic and extrinsic motivation? How are they related to achievement?
- What role do mastery motivation and mindset play in children's achievement?
- What is self-efficacy, and how is it related to achievement? How are expectations involved in children's achievement? Why are goal setting, planning, and self-monitoring important in achievement? What is purpose and how is it involved in achieving?
- How do cultural, ethnic, and socioeconomic variations influence achievement?

Connect

- In this section, you learned about the importance of purpose in adolescents' and emerging adults' achievement. In Chapter 11, what did Damon identify as some of the possible negative outcomes of not having purpose?

Reflect *Your Own Personal Journey of Life*

- Think about several of your own past schoolmates who showed low motivation in school. Why do you think they behaved that way? What teaching strategies might have helped them?

reach your **learning goals**

Schools and Achievement

Exploring Children's Schooling   **LG1**   Discuss approaches to schooling and development.

Contemporary Approaches to Student Learning and Assessment

- Contemporary approaches to student learning include direct instruction, which is a teacher-centered approach, and constructivist instruction, which is learner-centered. Some experts recommend that both a constructivist and direct instruction approach be used, depending on circumstances. Increased concern by the public and government in the United States has produced extensive state-mandated testing, which has both strengths and weaknesses and is controversial. The most visible example of the increased state-mandated testing is the No Child Left Behind federal legislation.

Early Childhood Education

- The child-centered kindergarten emphasizes the education of the whole child, paying particular attention to individual variation, the process of learning, and the importance of play in development. The Montessori approach is an increasingly popular early childhood education choice. Developmentally appropriate practice focuses on the typical patterns of children (age-appropriateness) and the uniqueness of each child (individual-appropriateness). Such practice contrasts with developmentally inappropriate practice, which relies on pencil-and-paper activities. The U.S. government has tried to break the poverty cycle with programs such as Head Start. Model programs have been shown to have positive effects on children who live in poverty. Controversy surrounds early childhood education curricula. On the one side are the child-centered, constructivist advocates, on the other are those who advocate an instructivist, academic approach. Another controversy focuses on whether universal preschool education should be implemented.

Elementary School

- Children take up the new role of student, interact, develop new relationships, and discover rich sources of new ideas in elementary school. A special concern is that early elementary school education proceeds too much on the basis of negative feedback to children.

- The transition to middle or junior high school coincides with many social, familial, and individual changes in the adolescent's life, and this transition is often stressful. One source of stress is the move from the top-dog to the lowest position in school. Some critics argue that a major redesign of U.S. middle schools is needed. Critics say that U.S. high schools foster passivity and do not develop students' academic skills adequately. A number of strategies have been proposed for improving U.S. high schools, including higher expectations and better support. The overall high school dropout rate declined considerably in the last half of the twentieth century, but the dropout rates of Latino and Native American youth remain very high. Participation in extracurricular activities is associated with positive academic and psychological outcomes. Adolescents benefit from participating in a variety of high-quality extracurricular activities.

- Children living in poverty face problems at home and at school that present barriers to learning. Neighborhoods are dangerous, and fear may be a way of life. Many schools' buildings are crumbling with age. Teachers are likely to encourage rote learning, and parents often don't set high educational standards. The school experiences of children from different ethnic groups vary considerably. Teachers often have low expectations for children of color. A number of strategies can be adopted to improve relationships with diverse others.

Children with Disabilities

LG2 Characterize children with disabilities and their education.

- Approximately 14 percent of U.S. children from 3 to 21 years of age receive special education or related services. A child with a learning disability has difficulty in learning that involves understanding or using spoken or written language, and the difficulty can appear in listening, thinking, reading, writing, and spelling. A learning disability also may involve difficulty in doing mathematics. To be classified as a learning disability, the learning problem is not primarily the result of visual, hearing, or motor disabilities; mental retardation; emotional disorders; or due to environmental, cultural, or economic disadvantage. Dyslexia is a category of learning disabilities that involves a severe impairment in the ability to read and spell. Dysgraphia is a learning disability that involves difficulty in expressing thoughts in writing. Dyscalculia is a learning disability that involves difficulties in math computation.

  Attention deficit hyperactivity disorder (ADHD) is a disability in which individuals consistently show problems in one or more of these areas: (1) inattention, (2) hyperactivity, and (3) impulsivity. ADHD has been increasingly diagnosed. Emotional and behavioral disorders consist of serious, persistent problems that involve relationships, aggression, depression, fears associated with personal or school matters, as well as other inappropriate socioemotional characteristics. Autism spectrum disorders (ASD), also called pervasive developmental disorders, range from autistic disorder, a severe developmental disorder, to Asperger syndrome, a relatively mild autism spectrum disorder. The current consensus is that autism is a brain dysfunction with abnormalities in brain structure and neurotransmitters. Children with autism spectrum disorders are characterized by problems in social interaction, verbal and nonverbal communication, and repetitive behaviors.

- In 1975, Public Law 94-142, the Education for All Handicapped Children Act, required that all children with disabilities be given a free, appropriate public education. This law was renamed the Individuals with Disabilities Education Act (IDEA) in 1990 and updated in 2004. IDEA includes requirements that children with disabilities receive an individualized education program (IEP), which is a written plan that spells out a program tailored to the child, and that they be educated in the least restrictive environment (LRE), which is a setting that is as similar as possible to the one in which children without disabilities are educated. Inclusion means educating children with disabilities full-time in the regular classroom.

Achievement

LG3 Explain the development of achievement in children.

Extrinsic and Intrinsic Motivation

- Extrinsic motivation involves external incentives such as rewards and punishment. Intrinsic motivation is based on internal factors such as self-determination, curiosity, challenge, and effort. One view is that giving students some choice and providing opportunities for personal responsibility increase intrinsic motivation. It is important for teachers to create learning environments that encourage students to become cognitively engaged and to develop a responsibility for their learning. Overall, the overwhelming conclusion is that it is a wise strategy to create learning environments that encourage students to become intrinsically motivated. In many real-world situations, both intrinsic and extrinsic motivation are involved, although too often intrinsic and extrinsic motivation have been pitted against each other as polar opposites.

Cognitive Processes

- A mastery orientation is preferred over helpless or performance orientations in achievement situations. Mindset is the cognitive view that individuals develop regarding their own potential. Dweck argues that a key aspect of adolescents' development is to guide them in developing a growth mindset. Self-efficacy is the belief that one can master a situation and produce positive outcomes. Bandura points out that self-efficacy is a critical factor in whether students will achieve. Schunk argues that self-efficacy influences a student's choice of tasks, with low-efficacy students avoiding many learning tasks. Students' expectations for success influence their motivation. Children benefit when their parents, teachers, and other adults have high expectations for their achievement. Setting specific, proximal (short-term), and challenging goals benefits students' self-efficacy and achievement. Being a good planner means managing time effectively, setting priorities, and being organized. Self-monitoring is a key aspect of self-regulation and benefits student learning. Recently, Damon has proposed that purpose is an especially important aspect of achievement that has been missing from many adolescents' lives. Purpose is the intention to accomplish something meaningful in one's life and to contribute something to the world beyond oneself. Finding purpose involves answering a number of questions.

Ethnicity and Culture

- In most investigations, socioeconomic status predicts achievement better than ethnicity. U.S. children receive lower scores on math and science achievement tests than those of children in Asian countries such as China and Japan.

key terms

key people

chapter 17 CULTURE AND DIVERSITY

Sonya, a 16-year-old Japanese American girl, was upset over her family's reaction to her White American boyfriend. "Her parents refused to meet him and on several occasions threatened to disown her" (Sue & Morishima, 1982, p. 142). Her older brothers also reacted angrily to Sonya's dating a White American, warning that they were going to beat him up. Her parents were also disturbed that Sonya's grades, above average in middle school, were beginning to drop.

Generational issues contributed to the conflict between Sonya and her family (Nagata, 1989). Her parents had experienced strong sanctions against dating Whites when they were growing up and were legally prevented from marrying anyone but a Japanese. As Sonya's older brothers were growing up, they valued ethnic pride and solidarity. The brothers saw her dating a White as "selling out" her own ethnic group. Sonya and the other members of her family obviously had different cultural values.

Michael, a 17-year-old Chinese American high school student, was referred to a therapist by the school counselor because he was depressed and had suicidal tendencies (Huang & Ying, 1989). Michael was failing several classes and frequently was absent from school. Michael's parents, successful professionals, expected Michael to excel in school and go on to become a doctor. They were angered by Michael's school failures, especially since he was the firstborn son, who in Chinese families is expected to achieve the highest standards.

The therapist encouraged the parents to put less academic pressure on Michael and to have more realistic expectations for Michael (who had no interest in becoming a doctor). Michael's school attendance changed, and his parents noticed his improved attitude toward school. Michael's case illustrates how expectations that Asian American youth will be "whiz kids" can become destructive.

preview

Culture had a strong influence on the conflicts Sonya and Michael experienced within their families and on their behavior outside of the family—in Sonya's case, dating; in Michael's case, school. Of course, a family's cultural background does not always produce conflict between children and other family members, but these two cases underscore the importance of culture in children's development. In this chapter, we will explore many aspects of culture, including cross-cultural comparisons of children's development, the harmful effects of poverty, the role of ethnicity, and the benefits and dangers that technology can bring to children's lives.

Culture and Children's Development **LG1** Discuss the role of culture in children's development.

> The Relevance of Culture to the Study of Children

> Cross-Cultural Comparisons

In Chapter 1, we defined **culture** as the behavior, patterns, beliefs, and all other products of a particular group of people that are passed on from generation to generation. The products result from the interaction between groups of people and their environment over many years. Here we examine the role of culture in children's development.

THE RELEVANCE OF CULTURE TO THE STUDY OF CHILDREN

A key aspect of the relevance of culture to the study of children is that culture is reflected in attitudes that people have and the way they interact with children. For example, culture is manifested in parents' beliefs, values, and goals for their children, and these in turn influence the contexts in which children develop (Kim & others, 2009).

Despite all the differences among cultures, research by American psychologist Donald Campbell and his colleagues (Brewer & Campbell, 1976) revealed that people in all cultures tend to believe that what happens in their culture is "natural" and "correct" and that what happens in other cultures is "unnatural" and "incorrect"; to perceive their cultural customs as universally valid—that is, they believe that what is good for them is good for everyone; and to behave in ways that favor their cultural group and feel hostile toward other cultural groups. In other words, people in all cultures tend to be *ethnocentric*—favoring their own group over others.

The future will bring extensive contact between people from varied cultural and ethnic backgrounds (Bornstein & Cote, 2010; Chen & Wang, 2010). If the study of child development is to be a relevant discipline in the remainder of the 21st century, increased attention will need to be given to culture and ethnicity. Global interdependence is no longer a matter of belief or choice. It is an inescapable reality. Children and their parents are not just citizens of the United States, or Canada, or some other country. They are citizens of the world—a world that, through advances in transportation and technology, has become increasingly interactive. By better understanding the behavior and values of cultures around the world, we may be able to interact more effectively with each other and make this planet a more hospitable, peaceful place in which to live (Kim & others, 2009).

---

developmental **connection**

Theories. In Bronfenbrenner's ecological theory, the macrosystem is the environmental system that involves the influence of culture on children's development. Chapter 1, p. 29

> Our most basic common link is that we all inhabit this planet. We all breathe the same air. We all cherish our children's future.
>
> —**JOHN F. KENNEDY**
> *United States President, 20th Century*

culture The behavior, patterns, beliefs, and all other products of a particular group of people that are passed on from generation to generation.

CROSS-CULTURAL COMPARISONS

As we described in Chapter 1, **cross-cultural studies** compare a culture with one or more other cultures, provide information about other cultures, and examine the role of culture in children's development. This comparison provides information about the degree to which children's development is similar, or universal, across cultures, or the degree to which it is culture-specific (Schlegal, 2009; Shiraev & Levy, 2010). In terms of gender, for example, the experiences of male and female children and adolescents continue to be worlds apart in some cultures (Larson, Wilson, & Rickman, 2009). In many countries, males have far greater access to educational opportunities, more freedom to pursue a variety of careers, and fewer restrictions on sexual activity than females (UNICEF, 2009, 2010).

In Chapter 16, "Schools and Achievement," we discussed the higher math and science achievement of Asian children in comparison with U.S. children. A recent study revealed that from the beginning of the seventh grade through the end of the eighth grade, U.S. adolescents valued academics less and their motivational behavior also decreased (Wang & Pomerantz, 2009). By contrast, the value placed on academics by Chinese adolescents did not change across this time frame, and their motivational behavior was sustained.

In cross-cultural research, the search for basic traits has focused on the dichotomy between individualism and collectivism (Triandis, 2007):

- **Individualism** involves giving priority to personal goals rather than to group goals; it emphasizes values that serve the self, such as feeling good, seeking personal distinction and recognition for achievement, and asserting independence.
- **Collectivism** emphasizes values that serve the group by subordinating personal goals to preserve group integrity, interdependence of the members, and harmonious relationships.

Figure 17.1 summarizes some of the main characteristics of individualistic and collectivistic cultures. Many Western cultures, such as the United States, Canada, Great Britain, and the Netherlands, are described as individualistic; many Eastern cultures, such as China, Japan, India, and Thailand, are described as collectivistic. So is Mexican culture.

Researchers have found that self-conceptions are related to culture. In one study, American and Chinese college students completed 20 sentences beginning with "I am _____" (Trafimow, Triandis, & Goto, 1991). As indicated in Figure 17.2, the American college students were much more likely to describe themselves with personal traits ("I am assertive"), whereas the Chinese students were more likely to identify themselves by their group affiliations ("I am a member of the math club"). A recent study also revealed the lack of a group orientation in the United States (Mejia-Arauz & others, 2007). The study focused on the interaction of 6- to 10-year-old children from three different cultures while they worked on a task. The children were observed in a group of three (triad). Triads of children whose families had immigrated to the United States from indigenous regions of Mexico, and whose mothers averaged only seven years of schooling, were more likely to coordinate their work on the task as an ensemble; in contrast, the triads of European-heritage children who had more extensive schooling more frequently engaged dyadically (in twos) or individually. Mexican-heritage U.S. triads whose mothers had extensive schooling showed an intermediate pattern or more closely resembled the European-heritage children.

Human beings have always lived in groups, whether large or small, and have always needed one another for survival. Critics of the Western notion of psychology argue that the Western emphasis on individualism may undermine the basic need of our species for relatedness (Shiraev & Levy, 2010). Some social scientists conclude that many problems in Western cultures are intensified by their emphasis on individualism. Compared with collectivist cultures, individualistic cultures have higher

- - - - - - - - - - ➤

developmental connection

Culture and Ethnicity. In the research of Harold Stevenson and his colleagues, the longer students were in school, the wider the gap was between Asian and U.S. students in math achievement. Chapter 16, p. 479

◄ - - - - - - - - - -

Cross-cultural studies involve the comparison of a culture with one or more other cultures. Shown here is a 14-year-old !Kung girl who has added flowers to her beadwork during the brief rainy season in the Kalahari desert in Botswana, Africa. Delinquency and violence occur much less frequently in the peaceful !Kung culture than in most other cultures around the world.

cross-cultural studies Research that compares a culture with one or more other cultures, provides information about other cultures, and examines the role of culture in children's development.

individualism Giving priority to personal goals rather than to group goals; emphasizing values that serve the self, such as feeling good, striving for personal distinction and recognition for achievement, and asserting independence.

collectivism Emphasizing values that serve the group by subordinating personal goals to preserve group integrity, interdependence of members, and harmonious relationships.

Individualistic	Collectivistic
Focuses on individual	Focuses on groups
Self is determined by personal traits independent of groups; self is stable across contexts	Self is defined by in-group terms; self can change with context
Private self is more important	Public self is most important
Personal achievement, competition, power are important	Achievement is for the benefit of the in-group; cooperation is stressed
Cognitive dissonance is frequent	Cognitive dissonance is infrequent
Emotions (such as anger) are self-focused	Emotions (such as anger) are often relationship based
People who are the most liked are self-assured	People who are the most liked are modest, self-effacing
Values: pleasure, achievement, competition, freedom	Values: security, obedience, in-group harmony, personalized relationships
Many casual relationships	Few, close relationships
Save own face	Save own and other's face
Independent behaviors: swimming, sleeping alone in room, privacy	Interdependent behaviors: co-bathing, co-sleeping
Relatively rare mother-child physical contact	Frequent mother-child physical contact (such as hugging, holding)

FIGURE **17.1**
CHARACTERISTICS OF INDIVIDUALISTIC AND COLLECTIVISTIC CULTURES

rates of suicide, drug abuse, crime, teenage pregnancy, divorce, child abuse, and mental disorders.

A recent analysis proposed four values that reflect the beliefs of parents in individualistic cultures about what is required for children's effective development of autonomy: (1) personal choice; (2) intrinsic motivation; (3) self-esteem; and (4) self-maximization, which consists of achieving one's full potential (Tamis-LeMonda & others, 2008). The analysis also proposed that three values reflect the beliefs of parents in collectivistic cultures: (1) connectectness to the family and other close relationships; (2) orientation to the larger group; and (3) respect and obedience.

Critics of the concepts of individualistic and collectivistic cultures argue that these terms are too broad and simplistic, especially in an era of increasing globalization (Greenfield, 2009; Rothbaum & Trommsdorff, 2007). Regardless of their cultural background, people need both a positive sense of self and connectedness to others to develop fully as human beings. The analysis by Catherine Tamis-LeMonda and her colleagues (2008) emphasizes that in many families, children are not reared in environments that uniformly endorse individualistic or collectivistic values, thoughts, and actions. Rather, in many families, children are

> expected to be quiet, assertive, respectful, curious, humble, self-assured, independent, dependent, affectionate, or reserved depending on the situation, people present, children's age, and social-political and economic circles.

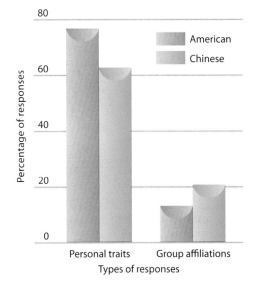

FIGURE **17.2**
AMERICAN AND CHINESE SELF-CONCEPTIONS.
College students from the United States and China completed 20 "I am _____" sentences. Both groups filled in personal traits more than group affiliations. However, the U.S. college students more often filled in the blank with personal traits, the Chinese with group affiliations.

Review

- What is the relevance of culture to the study of children?
- What are cross-cultural comparisons? What characterizes individualistic and collectivistic cultures? What are some criticisms of the concepts of individualistic and collectivistic cultures?

Connect

- Give examples of individualistic and collectivistic behaviors or beliefs that you read about in previous chapters.

Reflect *Your Own Personal Journey of Life*

- What was the achievement orientation in your family as you grew up? How did the cultural background of your parents influence this orientation?

Socioeconomic Status and Poverty

 LG2 Describe how socioeconomic status and poverty affect children's lives.

What Is Socioeconomic Status?

Socioeconomic Variations in Families, Neighborhoods, and Schools

Poverty

Many subcultures exist within countries. For example, Sonya's family, discussed in the opening of the chapter, had beliefs and patterns different from those of Michael's family. Some, but not all, subcultures are tied to ethnicity or socioeconomic characteristics or both. For example, the values and attitudes of children growing up in an urban ghetto or rural Appalachia may differ from those of children growing up in a wealthy suburb. In any event, children growing up in these different contexts are likely to have different socioeconomic statuses, and this inequality may influence their development.

WHAT IS SOCIOECONOMIC STATUS?

In Chapter 1, "Introduction," we defined **socioeconomic status (SES)** as the grouping of people with similar occupational, educational, and economic characteristics. Socioeconomic status implies certain inequalities. Generally, members of a society have (1) occupations that vary in prestige, and some individuals have more access than others to higher-status occupations; (2) different levels of educational attainment, and some individuals have more access than others to better education; (3) different economic resources; and (4) different levels of power to influence a community's institutions. These differences in the ability to control resources and to participate in society's rewards produce unequal opportunities (Entwisle, Alexander, & Olson, 2010; McLoyd & others, 2009). Socioeconomic differences are a "proxy for material, human, and social capital within and beyond the family" (Huston & Ripke, 2006, p. 425).

The number of significantly different socioeconomic statuses depends on the community's size and complexity. Most research on socioeconomic status delineates two categories, low and middle, but some research delineates as many as six categories. Sometimes low socioeconomic status is described as low-income, working class, or blue-collar; sometimes the middle category is described as middle-income, managerial, or white-collar. Examples of low-SES occupations are factory worker, manual laborer, and maintenance worker. Examples of middle-SES occupations include skilled worker, manager, and professional (doctor, lawyer, teacher, accountant, and so on).

socioeconomic status (SES) A grouping of people with similar occupational, educational, and economic characteristics.

SOCIOECONOMIC VARIATIONS IN FAMILIES, NEIGHBORHOODS, AND SCHOOLS

The families, neighborhoods, and schools of children have socioeconomic characteristics. A parent's SES is likely linked to the neighborhoods and schools in which children live and the schools they attend (Leventhal, Dupere, & Brooks-Gunn, 2009). Such variations in neighborhood settings can influence children's adjustment (Conger & Conger, 2008). For example, a recent study revealed that neighborhood disadvantage (involving such characteristics as low neighborhood income and high unemployment), was linked to less consistent, less stimulating, and more punitive parenting, and ultimately to negative child outcomes (low verbal ability and behavioral problems) (Kohen & others, 2008). Schools in low-income areas not only have fewer resources than those in higher-income areas but also tend to have more students with lower achievement test scores, lower rates of graduation, and smaller percentages of students going to college (Eccles & Roeser, 2009; Entwisle, Alexander, & Olson, 2010).

Let's further examine socioeconomic differences in family life. In Chapter 14, "Families," we described socioeconomic differences in child rearing (Hoff, Laursen, & Tardif, 2002). Recall that lower-SES parents are more concerned that their children conform to society's expectations, tend to have an authoritarian parenting style, rely on physical punishment more in disciplining their children, and are more directive and less conversational with their children. By contrast, higher-SES parents tend to be more concerned with developing children's initiative, strive to create a home atmosphere in which children are more nearly equal participants, are less likely to use physical punishment, and are less directive and more conversational with their children.

Like their parents, children from low-SES backgrounds are at high risk for experiencing mental health problems (McLoyd & others, 2009). Problems such as depression, low self-confidence, peer conflict, and juvenile delinquency are more prevalent among children living in low-SES families than among economically advantaged children (Healey, 2009).

Of course, children from low-SES backgrounds vary considerably in intellectual and psychological functioning. For example, a sizable portion of children from low-SES backgrounds perform well in school; some perform better than many middle-SES students. One study found that high educational aspirations among low-income parents were linked to more positive educational outcomes in youth (Schoon, Parsons, & Sacker, 2004). When children from low-SES backgrounds are achieving well in school, it is not unusual to find a parent or parents making special sacrifices to provide the living conditions and support that contribute to school success.

So far we have focused on the challenges faced by many children and adolescents from low-income families. However, research by Souniya Luthar and her colleagues (Ansary & Luthar, 2009; Luthar, 2006; Luthar & Goldstein, 2008) suggests that adolescents from affluent families also face challenges. In her research, adolescents from affluent families are vulnerable to high rates of substance abuse. Also, in the affluent families she has studied, males tend to have more adjustment difficulties than females, with affluent female adolescents more likely than male adolescents to attain superior levels of academic success.

(*Top*) Children playing in Nueva Era, a low-income area on the outskirts of Nuevo Laredo, Mexico. (*Bottom*) Two boys who live in a poverty section of the South Bronx in New York City. *How might socioeconomic status affect the lives of children like these?*

POVERTY

When sixth-graders in a poverty-stricken area of St. Louis were asked to describe a perfect day, one boy said he would erase the world, then he would sit and think (Children's Defense Fund, 1992). Asked if he wouldn't rather go outside and play, the boy responded, "Are you kidding—out *there*?"

The world is a dangerous and unwelcoming place for too many of America's children, especially those whose families, neighborhoods, and schools are in low-income contexts (Leventhal, Dupere, & Brooks-Gunn, 2009). Some children are

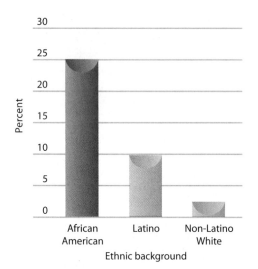

developmental **connection**

Socioeconomic Status. Reducing the poverty level and improving the lives of children living in poverty are important goals of U.S. social policy. Chapter 1, pp. 13–14

Note: A distressed neighborhood is defined by high levels (at least one standard deviation above the mean) of (1) poverty; (2) female-headed families; (3) high school dropouts; (4) unemployment; and (5) reliance on welfare.

FIGURE **17.3**

PERCENTAGES OF YOUTH UNDER 18 WHO ARE LIVING IN DISTRESSED NEIGHBORHOODS

resilient and cope with the challenges of poverty without any major setbacks, but too many struggle unsuccessfully (Entwisle, Alexander, & Olson, 2010). Each child of poverty who reaches adulthood unhealthy, unskilled, or alienated keeps our nation from being as competent and productive as it could be (Children's Defense Fund, 2009, 2010).

In 2006, 17 percent of children under 18 years of age were living in families with incomes below the poverty line (Federal Interagency Forum on Child and Family Statistics, 2008). This is an increase from 2001 (16.2 percent) but down from a peak of 22.7 percent in 1993. The U.S. figure of 17 percent of children living in poverty is much higher than those from other industrialized nations. For example, Canada has a child poverty rate of 9 percent and Sweden has a rate of 2 percent. Especially problematic is poverty that persists in children's lives over a number of years (Hutson, 2008). For example, a recent study also revealed that the more years children spent living in poverty, the higher their physiological indices of stress (Evans & Kim, 2007).

Poverty in the United States is demarcated along family structure and ethnic lines (Federal Interagency Forum on Child and Family Statistics, 2008). In 2006, 42 percent of female-headed families lived in poverty compared with only 8 percent of married-couple families. In 2006, 33 percent of African American families and 27 percent of Latino families lived in poverty, compared with only 10 percent of non-Latino White families. Compared with White children, ethnic minority children are more likely to experience persistent poverty over many years and live in isolated poor neighborhoods where social supports are minimal and threats to positive development abound (Jarrett, 1995) (see Figure 17.3).

Psychological Ramifications of Poverty   Living in poverty has many psychological effects on both adults and children (Leon-Guerrero, 2009). First, the poor are often powerless. In occupations, they rarely are the decision makers. Rules are handed down to them in an authoritarian manner. Second, the poor are often vulnerable to disaster. They are not likely to be given notice before they are laid off from work and usually do not have financial resources to fall back on when problems arise. Third, their range of alternatives is often restricted. Only a limited number of jobs are open to them. Even when alternatives are available, the poor

How are the environments that economically more advantaged children and adolescents live in different from the environments that children and adolescents live in that are characterized by poverty?

might not know about them or be prepared to make a wise decision, because of inadequate education and inability to read well. Fourth, being poor means having less prestige. This lack of prestige is transmitted to children early in their lives. The child living in poverty observes that many other children wear nicer clothes and live in more attractive houses.

Although positive times occur in the lives of children growing up in poverty, many of their negative experiences are worse than those of their middle-SES counterparts (McLoyd & others, 2009). These adversities involve physical punishment and lack of structure at home, violence in the neighborhood, and domestic violence in their buildings. A research review concluded that compared with their economically more advantaged counterparts, poor children experience widespread environmental inequities that include the following (Evans, 2004, p. 77):

- Exposure "to more family turmoil, violence, separation from their families, instability, and chaotic households" (Emery & Laumann-Billings, 1998)
- "Less social support, and their parents are less responsive and more authoritarian" (Bo, 1994)
- "Read to relatively infrequently, watch more TV, and have less access to books and computers" (Bradley & others, 2001)
- Schools and child-care facilities that are inferior and parents who "are less involved in their children's school activities" (Benveniste, Carnoy, & Rothstein, 2003)
- Air and water that are more polluted and homes that "are more crowded, more noisy, and of lower quality" (Myers, Baer, & Choi, 1996)
- More dangerous and physically deteriorating neighborhoods with less adequate municipal services (Brody & others, 2001)

Do children living in poverty face higher levels of these risks? To find out, see *Connecting Through Research*.

Because of advances in their cognitive growth, adolescents living in poverty likely are more aware of their social disadvantage and the associated stigma than are children (McLoyd & others, 2009). Combined with the increased sensitivity to peers in adolescence, such awareness may cause them to try to hide their poverty status as much as possible from others.

A special concern is the high percentage of single mothers in poverty. More than one-third of single mothers are in poverty, compared with only one-tenth of single fathers. Vonnie McLoyd (1998) concluded that because poor, single mothers are more distressed than their middle-SES counterparts are, they often show low support, nurturance, and involvement with their children. Among the reasons for the high poverty rate of single mothers are women's lower incomes, infrequent awarding of alimony payments, and poorly enforced child support by fathers.

Vonnie McLoyd (*right*) has conducted a number of important investigations of the roles of poverty, ethnicity, and unemployment in children's and adolescents' development. She has found that economic stressors often diminish children's and adolescents' belief in the utility of education and their achievement strivings.

Countering Poverty's Effects One trend in antipoverty programs is to conduct two-generation interventions (McLoyd, 1998). That is, the programs provide services for children (such as educational child care or preschool education) as well as services for parents (such as adult education, literacy training, and job-skill training). Evaluations suggest that two-generation programs have more positive effects on parents than they do on children (St. Pierre, Layzer, & Barnes, 1996). Also, when the two-generation programs do show benefits for children, these are more likely to be health benefits than cognitive gains. Some studies have shown that poverty interventions are more effective with young children than with older children and adolescents (Duncan & Magnuson, 2008; McLoyd & others, 2009). However, a downward trajectory is not inevitable for older children and youth living in poverty, and the success of poverty interventions likely depends on the quality and type of intervention (Huston & Bentley, 2010).

What Risks Are Experienced by Children Living in Poverty?

In Chapter 1, we briefly described the results of one study that explored multiple risks in the lives of children from poverty and middle-income backgrounds (Evans & English, 2002). Here we provide more details about this study. Six multiple risks were examined in 287 8- to 10-year-old non-Latino White children living in rural areas of upstate New York: family turmoil, child separation (a close family member being away from home often), exposure to violence, crowding, high noise levels, and inferior housing quality. Family turmoil, child separation, and exposure to violence were assessed by maternal reports of the life events their children had experienced. Crowding was determined by the number of people per room, and noise level was measured by the decibel level in the home. Housing quality (based on structural quality, cleanliness, clutter, resources for children, safety hazards, and climatic conditions) was rated by observers who visited the homes. Each of the six factors was defined as presenting a risk or no risk. Thus, the multiple stressor exposure for children could range from 0 to 6. Families were defined as poor if the household lived at or below the federally defined poverty line.

Children in poor families experienced greater risks than their middle-income counterparts. As shown in Figure 17.4, a higher percentage of children in poor families were exposed to each of the six risk factors (family turmoil, child separation, exposure to violence, crowding, noise level, and poor quality of housing).

Were there differences in the children's adjustment that might reflect these differences in exposure to risk factors? The researchers assessed the children's levels of psychological stress through reports

Risk factor (stressor)	Poor children exposed (%)	Middle-income children exposed (%)
Family turmoil	45	12
Child separation	45	14
Exposure to violence	73	49
Crowding	16	7
Excessive noise	32	21
Poor housing quality	24	3

FIGURE 17.4

PERCENTAGE OF POOR AND MIDDLE-INCOME CHILDREN EXPOSED TO EACH OF SIX STRESSORS

by the children and their mothers. Problems in self-regulation of behavior were determined by whether children chose immediate rather than delayed gratification on a task. Resting blood pressure and overnight neuroendocrine hormones were measured to indicate children's levels of psychophysiological stress.

The researchers found that in comparison with children from middle-income backgrounds, poor children had higher levels of psychological stress, more problems in self-regulation of behavior, and elevated psychophysiological stress. Analysis indicated that cumulative exposure to stressors may contribute to difficulties in socioemotional development for children living in poverty.

In a recent experimental study, Aletha Huston and her colleagues (2006; Gupta, Thornton, & Huston, 2007) evaluated the effects of New Hope, a program designed to increase parental employment and reduce family poverty, on adolescent development. They randomly assigned families with 6- to 10-year-old children living in poverty to the New Hope program and a control group. New Hope offered benefits to poor adults who were employed at least 30 hours a week: wage supplements ensuring that net income increased as parents earned more; work supports in the form of subsidized child care (for any child under age 13); and health insurance. Management services were provided to New Hope participants to assist them with job searches and other needs. The New Hope program was available to the experimental group families for three years (until the children were 9 to 13 years old). Five years after the program began and two years after it had ended, the program's effects on the children were examined when they were 11 to 16 years old. Compared with adolescents in the control group, New Hope adolescents were more competent at reading, had better school performance, were less likely to be in special education classes, had more positive social skills, and were more likely to be in formal after-school arrangements. New Hope parents reported better psychological well-being and a greater sense of self-efficacy in managing their adolescents than control parents did. To read about another program that benefitted youth living in poverty, see *Caring Connections*.

caring *connections*

The Quantum Opportunities Program

A downward trajectory is not inevitable for youth living in poverty (Carnegie Council on Adolescent Development, 1995). One potential positive path out of poverty for such youth is to become involved with a caring mentor. The Quantum Opportunities program, funded by the Ford Foundation, was a four-year, year-round mentoring effort (Carnegie Council on Adolescent Development, 1995). The students involved in this program were entering the ninth grade at a high school with high rates of poverty, were members of ethnic minority groups, and came from families that received public assistance. Each day for four years, mentors provided sustained support, guidance, and concrete assistance to their students.

The Quantum program required students to participate in (1) academic-related activities outside school hours, including reading, writing, math, science, and social studies, peer tutoring, and computer skills training; (2) community service projects, including tutoring elementary school students, cleaning up the neighborhood, and volunteering in hospitals, nursing homes, and libraries; and (3) cultural enrichment and personal development activities, including life skills training, college preparation, and job planning. In exchange for their commitment to the program, students were offered financial incentives that encouraged participation, completion, and long-range planning. A stipend of $1.33 was given to students for each hour they participated in these activities. For every 100 hours of education, ser-

Children participating in the Quantum Opportunities program at the Carver Center in Washington, DC.

vice, or development activities, students received a bonus of $100. The average cost per participant was $10,600 for the four years, which is one-half the cost of one year in prison.

An evaluation of the Quantum project compared the mentored students with a nonmentored control group. Sixty-three percent of the mentored students graduated from high school, but only 42 percent of the control group did; 42 percent of the mentored students were enrolled in college, but only 16 percent of the control group were. Furthermore, control-group students were twice as likely as the mentored students to receive food stamps or welfare, and they had more arrests. Such programs clearly have the potential to overcome the intergenerational transmission of poverty and its negative outcomes. While the original Quantum Opportunities program no longer exists, the Eisenhower Foundation (2010) recently began replicating the Quantum program in Alabama, South Carolina, New Hampshire, Virginia, Mississsipi, Oregon, Maryland, and Washington, DC.

These research results confirm what we learned in Chapter 16: the most effective programs to discourage dropping out of high school provide tutoring and mentoring, emphasize the creation of caring environments and relationships, and offer community-service opportunities. This research also reinforces the philosophy that goal-setting (such as planning for college and/or a career) is an integral part of achievement.

Review *Connect* Reflect

 Describe how socioeconomic status and poverty affect children's lives.

Review

- What is socioeconomic status?
- What are some socioeconomic variations in families, neighborhoods, and schools?
- What characterizes children living in poverty?

Connect

- In this section, you learned about antipoverty programs that take a two-generation approach to intervention.

How is this similar to efforts to improve the health of children living in poverty (discussed in Chapter 4)?

Reflect *Your Own Personal Journey of Life*

- What would you label the socioeconomic status of your family as you grew up? How do you think the SES status of your family influenced your development?

Immigration   Ethnicity and Socioeconomic Status   Differences and Diversity   Prejudice and Discrimination

Immigrant children from 12 countries participating in a U.S. citizenship ceremony in Queens, New York, on June 11, 2009. *What are some characteristics of immigrant children in the United States?*

Nowhere are cultural changes in the United States more dramatic than in the increasing ethnic diversity of America's children. Recall from Chapter 1 that **ethnicity** refers to characteristics rooted in cultural heritage, including nationality, race, religion, and language. Ninety-three languages are spoken in Los Angeles alone! With increased diversity have come conflict and concerns about the future.

IMMIGRATION

Relatively high rates of minority immigration have contributed to the increasing proportion of ethnic minorities in the U.S. population (Grigorenko & Takanishi, 2010; Tamis-LeMonda & McFadden, 2010). And this growth of ethnic minorities is expected to continue throughout the rest of the 21st century. Asian Americans are expected to be the fastest-growing ethnic group of adolescents, with a growth rate of almost 600 percent by 2100. Latino adolescents are projected to increase almost 400 percent by 2100. Figure 17.5 shows the actual numbers of adolescents in different ethnic groups in the year 2000, as well as the numbers projected through 2100. Notice that by 2100, Latino adolescents are expected to outnumber non-Latino White adolescents.

Immigrants often experience special stressors (Liu & others, 2009). These include language barriers, separations from support networks, changes in SES, and the struggle both to preserve ethnic identity and to adapt to the majority culture (Grigorenko & Takanishi, 2010; Healey, 2009; Ho & Birman, 2010).

Recent research increasingly shows links between acculturation and adolescent problems (Gonzales & others, 2006, 2007, 2008). For example, more-acculturated Latino youth in the United States experience higher rates of conduct problems, substance abuse, depression, and risky sexual behavior than their less-acculturated counterparts (Gonzales & others, 2006, 2007, 2008). Conflict between parents and adolescents that results from the cultural shifts that have taken place in immigrant families is likely responsible for the link between acculturation and adolescent problems (Gonzales & others, 2008). The conflict is often greatest when adolescents have acculturated more quickly than their parents.

Many of the families that have immigrated in recent decades to the United States, such as Mexican Americans and Asian Americans, come from collectivist cultures that emphasize family obligations and duties (Chen & Wang, 2010; De Castro Ribas, 2010). This family obligation and duty may take the form of adolescents assisting parents in their occupations and contributing to the family's welfare (Fuligni, Hughes, & Way, 2009). This type of support often occurs in service and manual labor jobs, such as those in construction, gardening, cleaning, and restaurants.

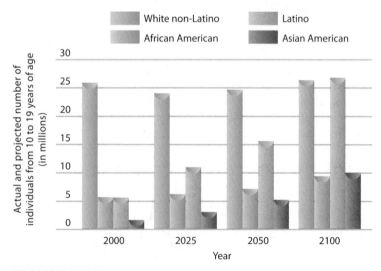

FIGURE **17.5**

ACTUAL AND PROJECTED NUMBER OF U.S. ADOLESCENTS AGED 10 TO 19, 2000 TO 2100. In 2000, there were more than 25 million White non-Latino adolescents 10 to 19 years of age in the United States, whereas the numbers for ethnic minority groups were substantially lower. However, projections for 2025 through 2100 reveal dramatic increases in the number of Latino and Asian American adolescents to the point at which in 2100 it is projected that there will be more Latino than non-Latino White adolescents in the United States and more Asian American than African American adolescents.

ethnicity A dimension of culture based on cultural heritage, nationality, race, religion, and language.

Carola Suárez-Orozco, Immigration Studies Researcher and Professor

Carola Suárez-Orozco currently is Chair and Professor of Applied Psychology and Co-director of Immigration Studies at New York University. She formerly was Co-director of the Harvard University Immigration Projects. Carola obtained her undergraduate degree (in development studies) and doctoral degree (in clinical psychology) at the University of California at Berkeley.

Suárez-Orozco has worked both in clinical and public school settings in California and Massachusetts. While at Harvard, she conducted a five-year longitudinal study of the adaptation of immigrant adolescents (coming from Central America, China, and the Dominican Republic) to schools and society. She especially advocates more research involving the role of cultural and psychological factors in the adaptation of immigrant and ethnic minority youth (Suárez-Orozco, 2007).

Carola Suárez-Orozco, with her husband, Marcelo, who also studies the adaptation of immigrants.

For more information about what researchers and professors do, see page 44 in the Careers in Child Development appendix following Chapter 1.

Asian American and Latino families place a greater emphasis on family duty and obligation than do non-Latino White families (Ceballo, Huerta, & Ngo, 2010; German & others, 2009). In one study of 18- to 25-year-olds, greater numbers of Asian Americans than non-Latino Whites said family interdependence was important to them (Tseng, 2004). Asian American and Latino adolescents believe that they should spend more time taking care of their siblings, helping around the house, assisting their parents at work, and being with their family than do adolescents with a European heritage (Fuligni, Hughes, & Way, 2009)

Of course, individual families vary, and how ethnic minority families deal with stress depends on many factors (Grigorenko & Takanishi, 2010; Hall, 2010). Whether the parents are native-born or immigrants, how long the family has been in this country, their socioeconomic status, and their national origin all make a difference (Fuligni, Hughes, & Way, 2009). The characteristics of the family's social context also influence its adaptation. What are the attitudes toward the family's ethnic group within its neighborhood or city? Can the family's children attend good schools? Are there community groups that welcome people from the family's ethnic group? Do members of the family's ethnic group form community groups of their own? To read about the work of one individual who studies immigrant adolescents, see *Connecting With Careers*.

Latino immigrants in the Rio Grande Valley, Texas. *What are some characteristics of the families who have recently immigrated to the United States?*

ETHNICITY AND SOCIOECONOMIC STATUS

Too often the research on ethnic minority children has failed to tease apart the influences of ethnicity and socioeconomic status (SES). Ethnicity and SES can interact in ways that exaggerate the negative influence of ethnicity because ethnic

developmental **connection**

Identity. Many aspects of sociocultural contexts influence children's and adolescents' ethnic identity. Chapter 11, p. 339

minority individuals are overrepresented in the lower socioeconomic levels of American society (McLoyd & others, 2009). Ethnicity has often defined who will enjoy the privileges of citizenship and to what degree and in what ways. In many instances, an individual's ethnic background has determined whether the individual will be alienated or disadvantaged.

In some cases, researchers have given ethnic explanations of child development that were largely based on socioeconomic status rather than ethnicity. For example, decades of research on group differences in self-esteem failed to consider the socioeconomic status of African American and White American children (Hare & Castenell, 1985). When the self-esteem of African American children from low-income backgrounds is compared with that of White American children from middle-class backgrounds, the differences are often large but not informative because of the confounding of ethnicity and SES (Scott-Jones, 1995).

A recent longitudinal study illustrated the importance of separating SES from ethnicity in determining the educational and occupational aspirations of individuals from 14 to 26 years of age (Mello, 2009). SES successfully predicted educational and occupational expectations across ethnic groups. In this study, after controlling for SES, African American youth reported the highest educational expectations, followed by Latino and Asian American/Pacific Islander, non-Latino White, and American Indian/Alaska Native youth. African/American and Asian American/Pacific Islander youth had the highest occupational expectations, followed by Latino, American Indian/Alaska Native, and non-Latino White youth. The ethnic group patterns were consistent across the adolescent and emerging adult years.

Even ethnic minority children from middle-SES backgrounds do not entirely escape the problems of minority status (Cushner, McClelland, & Safford, 2009). Middle-SES ethnic minority children still encounter much of the prejudice, discrimination, and bias associated with being a member of an ethnic minority group.

Although not all ethnic minority families are poor, poverty contributes to the stressful life experiences of many ethnic minority children (Grigorenko & Takanishi, 2010; Hall, 2010; Kao & Turney, 2010). Vonnie McLoyd and her colleagues (McLoyd, 1998; McLoyd, Aikens, & Burton, 2006; McLoyd & others, 2009) conclude that ethnic minority children experience a disproportionate share of the adverse effects of poverty and unemployment in America today. Thus, many ethnic minority children experience a double disadvantage: (1) prejudice, discrimination, and bias because of their ethnic minority status; and (2) the stressful effects of poverty.

> Consider the flowers of a garden: Though differing in kind, color, form, and shape, yet, in as much as they are refreshed by the waters of one spring, revived by the breath of one wind, invigorated by the rays of one sun, this diversity increases their charm and adds to their beauty.... How unpleasing to the eye if all the flowers and plants, the leaves and blossoms, the fruits, the branches, and the trees of that garden were all of the same shape and color! Diversity of hues, form, and shape enriches and adorns the garden and heightens its effect.
>
> —ABDU'L BAHA
> *Persian Baha'i Religious Leader,*
> *19th/20th Century*

DIFFERENCES AND DIVERSITY

Historical, economic, and social experiences produce differences between various ethnic minority groups, and between ethnic minority groups and the majority White group (Fuligni, Hughes, & Way, 2009; Tamis-LeMonda & McFadden, 2010). Individuals living in a particular ethnic or cultural group adapt to the values, attitudes, and stresses of that culture. Recognizing and respecting these differences is an important aspect of getting along with others in a diverse, multicultural world. Children, like all of us, need to take the perspective of individuals from ethnic and cultural groups that are different from their own and think, "If I were in their shoes, what kind of experiences might I have had?" "How would I feel if I were a member of their ethnic or cultural group?" "How would I think and behave if I had grown up in their world?" Such perspective taking often increases empathy and understanding of individuals from ethnic and cultural groups different from one's own.

For too long, differences between any ethnic minority group and Whites were conceptualized as deficits or inferior characteristics on the part of the ethnic minority group. Indeed, research on ethnic minority groups often focused only on a group's negative, stressful aspects. For example, research on African American adolescent girls invariably examined topics such as poverty, unwed motherhood, and dropping out of school; research on the psychological strengths of African American adolescent girls was sorely needed. The self-esteem, achievement, motivation, and self-control of children from different ethnic minority groups deserve considerable study.

The current, long-overdue emphasis of research on ethnic groups underscores the strengths of various minority groups (Umana-Taylor, 2009). For example, the extended-family support system that characterizes many ethnic minority groups is now recognized as an important factor in coping. And researchers are finding that African American males are better than Anglo-American males at detecting and using nonverbal cues such as body language in communication, at communicating with people from different cultures, and at solving unexpected problems (Evans & Whitfield, 1988).

As we noted in Chapter 1, there is considerable diversity within each ethnic group (Cushner, McClelland, & Safford, 2009). Ethnic minority groups have different social, historical, and economic backgrounds (Rowley, Kurtz-Costes, & Cooper, 2010; Shwalb & others, 2010). For example, Mexican, Cuban, and Puerto Rican immigrants are Latinos, but they had different reasons for migrating, came from varying socioeconomic backgrounds in their native countries, and experience different rates and types of employment in the United States. The U.S. federal government now recognizes the existence of 511 different Native American tribes, each having a unique ancestral background with differing values and characteristics. Asian Americans include Chinese, Japanese, Filipinos, Koreans, and Southeast Asians, each group having a distinct ancestry and language. The diversity of Asian Americans is reflected in their educational attainment: Some achieve a high level of education; many others have little education (Lee & Wong, 2009). For example, 90 percent of Korean American males graduate from high school, but only 71 percent of Vietnamese American males do.

Diversity also exists within each of these groups (Suyemoto, 2009). No group is homogeneous. Sometimes, well-meaning individuals fail to recognize the diversity within an ethnic group (Sue, 1990). For example, a sixth-grade teacher had two Mexican American adolescents in her class. She asked them to be prepared to demonstrate to the class on the following Monday how they danced at home. The first boy got up in front of the class and began dancing in a typical American fashion. The teacher said, "No, I want you to dance like you and your family do at home, like you do when you have Mexican American celebrations." The boy informed the teacher that his family did not dance that way. The second boy demonstrated a Mexican folk dance to the class. Failing to recognize diversity within ethnic groups reinforces stereotypes and encourages prejudice.

PREJUDICE AND DISCRIMINATION

Prejudice is an unjustified negative attitude toward an individual because of the individual's membership in a group. The group toward which the prejudice is directed can be made up of people of a particular ethnic group, sex, age, religion, or other detectable difference (Alvarez, 2009; Paluck & Green, 2009). Our concern here is prejudice against members of ethnic minority groups.

Research studies provide insight into the discrimination experienced by ethnic minority adolescents (Rivas-Drake, Hughes, & Way, 2009). A recent study revealed that adolescents' perceived racial discrimination is linked to negative views that the broader society has about African Americans (Seaton, Yip, & Sellers, 2009). In another study, discrimination against seventh- to tenth-grade African American students was related to lower levels of psychological functioning, including perceived stress, symptoms of depression, and lower perceived well-being; more positive attitudes toward African Americans were associated with more positive psychological functioning in adolescents (Sellers & others, 2006). Figure 17.6 shows the percentage of African American adolescents who reported experiencing different

Jason Leonard, age 15: "I want America to know that most of us black teens are not troubled people from broken homes and headed to jail. . . . In my relationships with my parents, we show respect for each other and we have values in our house. We have traditions we celebrate together, including Christmas and Kwanzaa."

Type of Racial Hassle	Percent of Adolescents Who Reported the Racial Hassle in the Past Year
Being accused of something or treated suspiciously	71.0
Being treated as if you were "stupid," being "talked down to"	70.7
Others reacting to you as if they were afraid or intimidated	70.1
Being observed or followed while in public places	68.1
Being treated rudely or disrespectfully	56.4
Being ignored, overlooked, not given service	56.4
Others expecting your work to be inferior	54.1
Being insulted, called a name, or harassed	52.2

FIGURE **17.6**

AFRICAN-AMERICAN ADOLESCENTS' REPORTS OF RACIAL HASSLES IN THE PAST YEAR

prejudice An unjustified negative attitude toward an individual because of her or his membership in a group.

The United States and Canada: Nations with Many Cultures

The United States has been and continues to be a great receiver of ethnic groups. It has embraced new ingredients from many cultures (Fuligni, Hughes, & Way, 2009). The cultures often collide and cross-pollinate, mixing their ideologies and identities. Some of the culture of origin is retained, some of it is lost, and some of it is mixed with the American culture.

Other nations have also experienced the immigration of varied ethnic groups. Possibly we can learn more about the potential benefits, problems, and varied responses by examining their experiences. Canada is a prominent example. Canada comprises a mixture of cultures that are loosely organized along the lines of economic power. The Canadian cultures include the following (Siegel & Wiener, 1993):

• Native peoples, or First Nations, who were Canada's original inhabitants;

• Descendants of French settlers who came to Canada during the 17th and 18th centuries;

• Descendants of British settlers who came to Canada during and after the 17th century, or from the United States after the American Revolution in the latter part of the 18th century;

• Descendants of immigrants from Asia, mainly China, who settled on the west coast of Canada in the latter part of the 19th and early 20th centuries;

• Descendants of 19th-century immigrants from various European countries, who settled in central Canada and the prairie provinces;

• Twentieth-century and current immigrants from countries in economic and political turmoil (in Latin America, the Caribbean, Asia, Africa, the Indian subcontinent, the former Soviet Union, and the Middle East), who have settled in many parts of Canada

Canada has two official languages: English and French. Primarily French-speaking individuals reside mainly in the province of Quebec; primarily English-speaking individuals reside mainly in other Canadian provinces. In addition to its English- and French-speaking populations, Canada has a large multicultural community. In three large Canadian cities—Toronto, Montreal, and Vancouver—more than 50 percent of the children and adolescents come from homes in which neither English nor French is the native language (Siegel & Wiener, 1993).

(*Left*) A Canadian Inuit family in Baker Lake, Canada; (*Right*) Chinese girls in Toronto. *What are some characteristics of Canada's Chinese population?*

Canada has two official languages, based on their two largest ethnic populations. If the United States were to base its official languages on the largest ethnic populations they expect to have in 2100, what might they be? (See Figure 17.5.)

types of racial hassles in the past year. Also, in a study of Latino youth, discrimination was negatively linked—and social and parental support were positively related—to their academic success (DeGarmo & Martinez, 2006).

Progress has been made in ethnic minority relations, but discrimination and prejudice still exist, and equality has not been achieved. Much remains to be accomplished (Rowley, Kurtz-Costes, & Cooper, 2010). To read further about diversity and ethnicity, see *Connecting With Diversity*.

Review Connect Reflect

 LG3 Explain how ethnicity is linked to children's development.

Review

- How does immigration influence children's development?
- How are ethnicity and socioeconomic status related?
- What is important to know about differences and diversity?
- How do prejudice and discrimination affect children's development?

Connect

- In this section, we learned that taking the perspective of individuals from ethnic and cultural groups that are different from their own can help children (and adults) to better respect and get along with others in a diverse, multicultural world. What did you learn in Chapter 15 about perspective taking and elementary school children's communication skills?

Reflect: *Your Own Personal Journey of Life*

- No matter how well intentioned children are, their life circumstances likely have given them some prejudices. If and when you become a parent, how would you attempt to reduce your children's prejudices?

Technology

LG4 Summarize the influence of technology on children's development.

| Media Use | Television and Electronic Media | Computers and the Internet |

A major change in children's and adolescents' lives involves the dramatic increase in the use of media and technology by children and adolescents (Strasberger, 2009; Uhls & Greenfield, 2009). "Unlike their parents, they have never known anything but a world dominated by technology. Even their social lives revolve around the Web, iPods, and cell phones" (Jayson, 2006, p. 1D).

More than likely, the technology revolution is affecting children and adolescents in both positive and negative ways. Technology can provide expansive knowledge and can be used in a constructive way to enhance children's and adolescents' education (Egbert, 2009; Forcier & Descy, 2008). However, the possible downside of technology was captured in a recent book, *The Dumbest Generation: How the Digital Age Stupefies Young Americans and Jeopardizes Our Future (Or, Don't Trust Anyone Under 30)*, written by Emory University English Professor Mark Bauerlein (2008). Among the book's themes are that many of today's youth are more interested in information retrieval than information formation, don't read books and aren't motivated to read them, can't spell without spellcheck, and have become encapsulated in a world of cell phones, iPods, text messaging, YouTube, MySpace, *Grand Theft Auto* (the video game's introduction in 2008 had first-week sales of $500 million, dwarfing other movie and video sales), and other technology contexts. In terms of retaining general information and historical facts, Bauerlein may be correct. And in terms of some skills, such as adolescents' reading and writing, there is considerable cause for concern, with U.S. employers spending 1.3 billion dollars a year to teach writing skills to employees (Begley & Interlandi, 2008). However, in terms of cognitive skills such as thinking and reasoning, Bauerlein likely is wrong given that IQ scores have been rising significantly since the 1930s (Flynn, 2007). Further, there is no research evidence that being immersed in a technological world of iPods and YouTube impairs thinking skills (Begley & Interlandi, 2008).

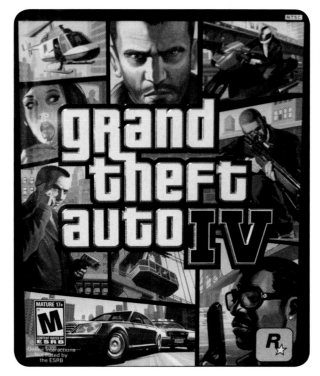

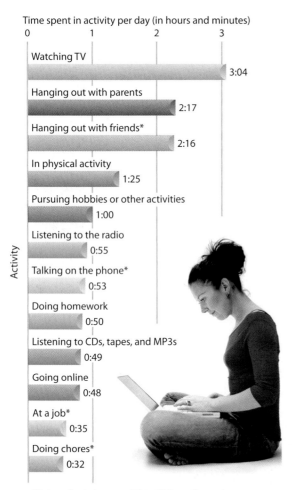

Time spent in activity per day (in hours and minutes)

Activity

Watching TV — 3:04

Hanging out with parents — 2:17

Hanging out with friends* — 2:16

In physical activity — 1:25

Pursuing hobbies or other activities — 1:00

Listening to the radio — 0:55

Talking on the phone* — 0:53

Doing homework — 0:50

Listening to CDs, tapes, and MP3s — 0:49

Going online — 0:48

At a job* — 0:35

Doing chores* — 0:32

*Data collected among 7th to 12th graders only.
All other results are among all 8- to 18-year-olds

FIGURE 17.7

AMOUNT OF TIME U.S. 8- TO 18-YEAR-OLDS SPEND PER DAY IN DIFFERENT ACTIVITIES

"Mrs. Horton, could you stop by school today?"
Copyright © 1981 Martha F. Campbell. Used by permission of Martha F. Campbell.

A major trend in the use of technology is the dramatic increase in media multitasking (Roberts, Henriksen, & Foehr, 2009). It is not unusual for children and youth to simultaneously watch TV while text messaging their friends, for example. In some cases, media multitasking—such as text messaging, listening to an iPod, and updating a YouTube site—is engaged in at the same time as doing homework. It is hard to imagine how that can be a good thing for doing homework efficiently, although there is little research on such media multitasking. As indicated in Chapter 7, "Information Processing," if a key task is complex and challenging, multitasking considerably reduces attention to the task.

MEDIA USE

If the amount of time spent in an activity is any indication of its importance, then there is no doubt that the mass media play important roles in the lives of U.S. children and adolescents (Roberts, Henriksen, & Foehr, 2009). A national study that surveyed more than 2,000 children and adolescents from 8 through 18 years of age confirmed that they use media heavily (Rideout, Roberts, & Foehr, 2005). The average child and adolescent in the study spent almost 6 hours a day using media compared with approximately 2¼ hours interacting with parents, about 1¼ hours in physical activity, and 50 minutes in homework (see Figure 17.7). As shown in the figure, the children and adolescents spent the most time watching TV (just over 3 hours a day). A recent estimate indicates that when media multitasking is taken into account, 8- through 18-year-olds use media an average of 8 hours per day rather than just 6 hours per day (Roberts & Foehr, 2008).

TELEVISION AND ELECTRONIC MEDIA

Few developments during the second half of the 20th century had a greater impact on children than television (Strasberger, 2009). Many children spend more time in front of the television set than they do with their parents. Although it is only one of the many mass media that affect children's behavior, television is the most influential. The persuasive capabilities of television are staggering. The 20,000 hours of television watched by the time the average American adolescent graduates from high school are greater than the number of hours spent in the classroom.

Television can have positive or negative effects on children's development. Television can have a positive influence on children's development by presenting motivating educational programs, bringing information about the world beyond their immediate environment, and providing models of prosocial behavior (Bryant, 2007). However, television can have a negative influence on children by making them passive learners, distracting them from doing homework, teaching them stereotypes, providing them with violent models of aggression, and presenting them with unrealistic views of the world (Murray, 2007). Further, researchers have found that a high level of TV viewing is linked to a greater incidence of obesity in youth (Escobar-Chaves & Anderson, 2008).

Television, Violent Video Games, and Aggression What role does televised violence play in aggression among children and adolescents? Does television merely stimulate a child to go out and buy a Star Wars ray gun, or can it trigger an attack on a playmate? When children grow up, can television violence increase the likelihood that they will violently attack someone?

In one longitudinal investigation, the amount of violence viewed on television at age 8 was significantly related to the seriousness of criminal acts performed as an adult (Huesmann & others, 2003). In another investigation, long-term exposure to television violence was significantly related to the likelihood of aggression in 1,565 boys 12 to 17 years old (Belson, 1978). Boys who watched the most aggression on television were the most likely to commit a violent crime, swear, be aggressive in sports, threaten violence toward another boy, write slogans on walls, or break windows. A recent study revealed that when 2- to 5-year-old boys regularly watched violent TV shows they were at risk for engaging in antisocial behavior at 7 to 10 years of age; no link was found for girls (Christakis & Zimmerman, 2007). These investigations are correlational, so we can't conclude from them that television violence causes children to be more aggressive, only that watching television violence is associated with aggressive behavior.

In one experiment, children were randomly assigned to one of two groups: One group watched television shows taken directly from violent Saturday-morning cartoons on 11 different days; the second group watched television cartoon shows with all of the violence removed (Steur, Applefield, & Smith, 1971). The children were then observed during play at their preschool. The preschool children who saw the TV cartoon shows with violence kicked, choked, and pushed their playmates more than the preschool children who watched nonviolent TV cartoon shows did. Because children were randomly assigned to the two conditions (TV cartoons with violence versus with no violence), we can conclude that exposure to TV violence caused the increased aggression in children in this investigation.

A recent study revealed a link between media violence exposure and both physical aggression and relational aggression in third- to fifth-grade students (Gentile, Mathieson, & Crick, 2010). In this study, the link with relational aggression was stronger for girls than boys.

Some critics have argued that research results do not warrant the conclusion that TV violence causes aggression (Freedman, 1984). However, many experts insist that TV violence can cause aggressive or antisocial behavior in children (Comstock & Scharrer, 2006; Strasberger, 2009). Of course, television violence is not the only cause of aggression. There is no one cause of any social behavior. Aggression, like all other social behaviors, has multiple determinants. The link between TV violence and aggression in children is influenced by children's aggressive tendencies and by their attitudes toward violence and their exposure to it.

A recent 7-month classroom-based intervention was successful in reducing the amount of time elementary school children watched violent TV and in decreasing their identification with TV superheroes (Rosenkoetter, Rosenkoetter, & Acock, 2009). The classroom-based intervention consisted of 28 lessons of 20 to 30 minutes each that focused on the many ways that television distorts violence.

Violent video games, especially those that are highly realistic, also raise concerns about their effects on children and adolescents (Anderson, Gentile, & Buckley, 2007; Escobar-Chaves & Anderson, 2008). One difference between television and violent video games is that the games can engage children and adolescents so intensely that they experience an altered state of consciousness in "which rational thought is suspended and highly arousing aggressive scripts are increasingly likely to be learned" (Roberts, Henriksen, & Foehr, 2004, p. 498). Another difference involves the direct rewards ("winning points") that game players receive for their behavior. Research indicates that children and adolescents who extensively play violent electronic games are more aggressive, less sensitive to real-life violence, and more likely to engage in delinquent acts than are their counterparts who spend less time playing the games or do not play them at all (Anderson, Gentile, & Buckley, 2007; Barlett & Anderson, 2009; Barlett, Anderson, & Swing, 2009). Are there any positive outcomes when children play violent video games? Some evidence points to video games improving children's visuospatial skills (Schmidt & Vandewater, 2008).

Prosocial Behavior Television and electronic media also can teach children that it is better to behave in positive, prosocial ways than in

How is television violence linked to children's aggression?

How might playing violent video games be linked to adolescent aggression?

developmental **connection**

Moral Development. Prosocial behavior is behavior that is intended to help other people. Chapter 13, p. 382

negative, antisocial ways (Bryant, 2007). Aimee Leifer (1973) demonstrated that television is associated with prosocial behavior in young children. She selected a number of episodes from the television show *Sesame Street* that reflected positive social interchanges. She was especially interested in situations that taught children how to use their social skills. For example, in one interchange, two men were fighting over the amount of space available to them. They gradually began to cooperate and to share the space. Children who watched these episodes copied these behaviors, and in later social situations they applied the prosocial lessons they had learned. More recent research has documented that electronic media programs designed to promote prosocial behavior are effective in increasing children's altruism, cooperation, and tolerance of others (Wilson, 2008).

When children and adolescents play prosocial video games (depicting scenes involving behaviors intended to help others), does their prosocial behavior increase? Douglas Gentile and his colleagues (2009) conducted three studies that indicated the answer to this question is "yes." In one study, Singaporean middle-school students who played prosocial video games behaved in more prosocial ways. In a longitudinal study of Japanese children and adolescents, playing prosocial video games predicted later increases in prosocial behavior. In an experimental study, U.S. college students who were randomly assigned to play prosocial video games subsequently behaved more prosocially toward another student. Thus, it is not video games by themselves that have negative outcomes for children and adolescents, but rather the content of the video games.

Electronic Media, Learning, and Achievement   The effects of electronic media on children depend on the child's age and the type of media. A recent research review reached the following conclusions about infants and young children (Kirkorian, Wartella, & Anderson, 2008):

What have researchers found about TV watching by infants?

- *Infancy.* Learning from electronic media is difficult for infants and toddlers, and they learn much more easily from direct experiences with people.

- *Early childhood.* At about 3 years of age, children can learn from electronic media with educational material if the media use effective strategies, such as repeating concepts a number of times, using images and sounds that capture young children's attention, and speaking with the voices of children rather than adults. However, the vast majority of media young children experience is entertainment rather than education oriented.

The American Academy of Pediatrics (2001) has recommended that children under 2 years of age should not watch television because it likely reduces direct interactions with parents. One study found that the more hours 1- and 3-year-olds watched TV per day, the more likely they were to have attention problems at 7 years of age (Christakis & others, 2004), and a recent study also revealed that daily TV exposure at 18 months was linked to increased inattention/hyperactivity at 30 months of age (Cheng & others, 2010). A recent study of 2- to 48-month-olds indicated that each hour of audible TV was linked to a reduction in child vocalizations (Christakis & others, 2009) and another study revealed that 8- to 16-month-olds who viewed baby DVDs/videos had poor language development (Zimmerman, Christakis, & Meltzoff, 2007). Further, in a recent study of 18-month-olds, those who were language-delayed preferred watching videos characterized as "realistic animations" and "baby education" (Okuma & Tanimura, 2009).

Several important cognitive shifts take place between early childhood and middle and late childhood, and these shifts influence the effects of electronic media. Children bring varied cognitive skills and abilities to their television viewing. Preschool children often focus on the most striking perceptual features of a

TV program and are likely to have difficulty distinguishing reality from fantasy in the portrayals. As children enter elementary school, they are better able to link scenes together and draw causal conclusions from narratives. Judgments about what is reality and what is fantasy also become more accurate as children grow up.

How does television influence children's attention, creativity, and mental ability? Overall, media use has not been found to cause attention deficit hyperactivity disorder, but a small link has been identified between heavy television viewing and nonclinical reduced attention levels in children (Schmidt & Vandewater, 2008). In general, television has not been shown to influence children's creativity but is negatively related to their mental ability (Comstock & Scharrer, 2006). Exposure to aural and printed media does more than television to enhance children's verbal skills, especially their expressive language (Williams, 1986).

The more children watch TV, the lower their school achievement (Comstock & Scharrer, 2006). Why might TV watching be negatively linked to children's achievement? Three possibilities involve interference, displacement, and self-defeating tastes/preferences (Comstock & Scharrer, 2006). In terms of interference, having a television on while doing homework can distract children while they are doing cognitive tasks. In terms of displacement, television can take away time and attention from engaging in achievement-related tasks, such as homework, reading, writing, and mathematics. Researchers have found that children's reading achievement is negatively linked with the amount of time they watch TV (Comstock & Scharrer, 2006). In terms of self-defeating tastes and preferences, television attracts children to entertainment, sports, commercials, and other activities that capture their interest more than school achievement. Children who are heavy TV watchers tend to view books as dull and boring (Comstock & Scharrer, 2006).

However, some types of television content—such as educational programming for young children—may enhance achievement. In one longitudinal study, viewing educational programs, such as *Sesame Street* and *Mr. Rogers' Neighborhood,* as preschoolers was related to a number of positive outcomes through high school, including higher grades, reading of more books, and enhanced creativity (Anderson & others, 2001) (see Figure 17.8). Newer technologies, especially interactive television, hold promise for motivating children to learn and become more exploratory in solving problems.

COMPUTERS AND THE INTERNET

Culture involves change, and nowhere is that change greater than in the technological revolution today's children and adolescents are experiencing with increased use of computers and the Internet. Today's children and adolescents are using computers to communicate the way their parents used pens, postage stamps, and telephones.

The Internet The **Internet** is the core of computer-mediated communication. The Internet system is worldwide and connects thousands of computer networks, providing an incredible array of information children and adolescents can access.

Youth throughout the world are increasingly using the Internet, despite substantial variation in use in different countries around the world and in different socioeconomic groups (Brookshear, 2009; Reed, 2009; Subrahmanyam & Greenfield, 2008). In 2005, 75 percent of U.S. 8- to 18-year-olds lived in a home with an Internet connection, and almost one-third had a computer in their bedroom and 20 percent had an Internet connection there (Rideout, Roberts, & Foehr, 2005). Among 15- to 17-year-olds, one-third use the Internet for six hours a week or more, 24 percent use it for three to five hours a week, and 20 percent use it for one hour a week or less (Woodard, 2000). In a typical day, about half of 8- to 18-year-olds go online from home, and their most frequent online recreational

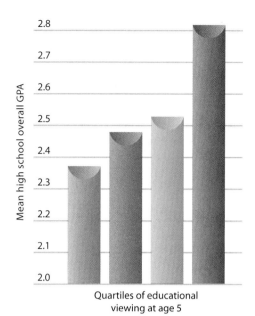

FIGURE **17.8**

EDUCATIONAL TV VIEWING IN EARLY CHILDHOOD AND HIGH SCHOOL GRADE-POINT AVERAGE FOR BOYS. When boys watched more educational television (especially *Sesame Street*) as preschoolers, they had higher grade-point averages in high school. The graph displays the boys' early TV viewing patterns in quartiles and the means of their grade-point averages. The bar on the left is for the lowest 25 percent of boys who viewed educational TV programs, the next bar the next 25 percent, and so on, with the bar on the right for the 25 percent of the boys who watched the most educational TV shows as preschoolers.

Internet Worldwide computer-mediated communication system that provides a vast array of information.

developmental **connection**

Media Influence. Significant numbers of children are victimized by bullies, and bullying has a number of negative outcomes for children. Chapter 15, p. 435

activities are playing games and communicating via instant messaging (Rideout, Roberts, & Foehr, 2005).

Special concerns have emerged about children's and adolescents' access to information on the Internet, which has been largely unregulated. Youth can access adult sexual material, instructions for making bombs, and other information that is inappropriate for them. Another concern is peer bullying and harassment on the Internet (called *cyber-bullying*). A recent survey found that peer bullying and harassment both online and offline were the most frequent threats that minors encountered (Palfrey & others, 2009).

In one study, about half of parents said that being online is more positive than watching TV for adolescents (Tarpley, 2001). However, an analysis of content suggests they might be wise to be more concerned about children's and adolescents' use of the Internet. One study found that 12 percent of adolescents have visited a Web site where they can obtain information about how to buy a gun (Donnerstein, 2002). A national study revealed that 42 percent of U.S. 10- to 17-year-olds had been exposed to Internet pornography in the past year, with 66 percent of the exposure being unwanted (Wolak, Mitchell, & Finkelhor, 2007). And a recent study revealed that the use of most Internet activities did not differ for early-, on-time, and late-maturing adolescent boys (Skoog, Stattin, & Kerr, 2009). However, in this study early-maturing adolescent boys were more likely to download and view pornographic material from the Internet than were their counterparts who matured on time or late (Skoog, Stattin, & Kerr, 2009).

The Digitally Mediated Social Environment   The digitally mediated social environment of adolescents and emerging adults includes e-mail, chat rooms, instant messaging, blogs, social networking sites such as Facebook, videosharing and photosharing, multiplayer online computer games, and virtual worlds (Subrahmanyam & Greenfield, 2008; Uhls & Greenfield, 2009). Most of these digitally mediated social interactions began on computers but more recently have also shifted to cell phones, especially smart phones (Roberts, Henriksen, & Foehr, 2009).

The Internet continues to serve as the main focus of digitally mediated social interaction. Chat-room conversations are mainly public and often involve multiple participants and simultaneous conversations; in many cases, the participants are strangers (Subrahmanyam & Greenfield, 2008). Adolescents and emerging adults usually use instant messaging on their computers and cell phones to communicate with friends from school. Gossip is a frequent component of such communication.

One recent study examined the content of 583 participants in online teen chat rooms (Subrahmanyam, Smahel, & Greenfield, 2006). More than 50 percent of the participants provided identity information, usually their gender. Younger participants (self-described as 10 to 13 years of age) were the most self-disclosing about their identity, older ones the least (self-described as 18 to 24 years of age). Sexual themes comprised 5 percent of the utterances (one sexual comment per minute) and bad/obscene language occurred in 3 percent of the utterances. Females discussed sex in more implicit ways, males in a more explicit manner. Older participants discussed sex more explicitly than younger participants.

A recent study examined the sequence of electronic communication technologies that college students in a midwestern University used in managing their social networks (Yang & Brown, 2009). In this study, female college students followed a consistent sequence as their relationships developed, typically beginning by contacting new acquaintances on Facebook, then moving on to instant messaging, after which they might "exchange cell phone numbers, text each other, talk over their cell phone, and finally schedule a time to meet, if everything went well" (Yang & Brown, 2009, p. 2). Male college students were less likely to follow this sequence as consistently, although they did follow it more when communicating with females than males, suggesting that females may maintain more control over communication patterns.

What characterizes the online social environment of adolescents?

Recent research has found that approximately one in three adolescents self-disclose better online than in person; in this research, boys report that they feel more comfortable self-disclosing online than do girls (Schouten, Valkenburg, & Peter, 2007; Valkenburg & Peter, 2009). In contrast, girls are more likely to feel comfortable self-disclosing in person than are boys. Thus, boys' self-disclosure may benefit from online communication with friends (Valkenburg & Peter, 2009). A recent study revealed that adolescents who were better adjusted at 13 to 14 years of age were more likely to use social networking sites at 20 to 22 years of age (Mikami & others, 2010). In this study, young adolescents' friendship quality and behavioral adjustment predicted similar qualities of interaction and problem behavior on social networking sites in emerging adulthood.

Clearly, the Internet is a technology that should be monitored and regulated by the parents of adolescents (Pujazon-Zazik & Park, 2010; Uhls & Greenfield, 2009). Consider Bonita Williams, who began to worry about how obsessed her 15-year-old daughter, Jade, had become with MySpace (Kornblum, 2006). She became even more concerned when she discovered that Jade was posting suggestive photos of herself and giving our her cell phone number to people in different parts of the United States. She grounded her daughter, blocked MySpace at home, and moved Jade's computer out of her bedroom and into the family room. A recent study revealed that parents' high estimates of online dangers were not matched by their low rates of setting limits and monitoring their adolescents' online activities (Rosen, Cheever, & Carrier, 2008). Also in this study, adolescents who perceived their parents as having an indulgent parenting style (high in warmth and involvement but low in strictness and supervision) reported engaging in the most risky online behavior, such as meeting someone in person with whom they had initially communicated online.

Review Connect Reflect

 LG4 Summarize the influence of technology on children's development.

Review

- What role do mass media play in the lives of children and adolescents?
- How do television and electronic media influence children's development?
- What roles do computers and the Internet play in children's development?

Connect

- In this section, you learned about cyberbullying. In Chapter 15, what did you learn about the outcomes of bullying for those who are bullied?

Reflect *Your Own Personal Journey of Life*

- How much television did you watch as a child? What effect do you believe TV viewing has had on your development?

Culture and Diversity

Culture and Children's Development

> The Relevance of Culture to the Study of Children

> Cross-Cultural Comparisons

 LG1 Discuss the role of culture in children's development.

- Culture refers to the behavior patterns, beliefs, and all other products of a particular group of people that are passed on from generation to generation. If the study of children is to be a relevant discipline in the 21st century, increased attention must be paid to culture. In future years, children will be citizens of the world, and the more we understand the values of other cultures and others' cultural behaviors, the more effectively we will be able to interact.

- Cross-cultural comparisons compare one culture with one or more other cultures, which provides information about the degree to which characteristics are universal or culture-specific. The social contexts in which children develop—gender, family, and school—display important differences from one culture to another. One analysis of cross-cultural comparisons suggests that children raised in individualistic cultures are taught different values and self-concepts from those raised in collectivistic cultures. However, critics argue that categorization of cultures as individualist or collectivist is too broad and simplistic, and that in many families, parents expect their children to think and act in ways that reflect both individualistic and collectivistic values.

Socioeconomic Status and Poverty

> What Is Socioeconomic Status?

> Socioeconomic Variations in Families, Neighborhoods, and Schools

> Poverty

 LG2 Describe how socioeconomic status and poverty affect children's lives.

- Socioeconomic status (SES) is the grouping of people who share similar occupational, educational, and economic characteristics. SES implies inequalities.

- The families, neighborhoods, and schools of children have SES characteristics that are related to the child's development. Parents from low-SES families are more likely to value conformity and to use physical punishment to a greater extent than their middle-SES counterparts. High-SES children live in more attractive homes and in safer neighborhoods than low-SES children. Low-SES children are more apt to experience problems such as depression, low self-esteem, and delinquency. When low-SES children do well in school, it often is because parents have made sacrifices to improve conditions and provide support that contributes to school success.

- Poverty is defined by economic hardship. The poor often face not only economic hardship but also social and psychological difficulties. Poor children are exposed to more family violence, have less access to books and computers, attend inferior child care and schools, and receive less social support. When poverty is persistent and long-lasting, it has particularly adverse effects on children's development.

Ethnicity

> Immigration

LG3 Explain how ethnicity is linked to children's development.

- Ethnicity is based on cultural heritage, nationality characteristics, race, religion, and language. The immigration of families to the United States brings about a number of challenges for helping children adapt to their new culture. Immigrant children often experience language barriers, changes in SES, and separation from support networks in addition to struggling to preserve their ethnic identity while adapting to the majority culture. Parents and children may be at different stages of acculturation, leading to intergenerational conflict.

| Ethnicity and Socioeconomic Status | • Too often researchers have not teased apart the influences of ethnicity and socioeconomic status when studying ethnic minority children. Many ethnic minority children experience prejudice and discrimination, along with the difficulties caused by poverty. Although not all ethnic minority families are poor, poverty contributes to the stress of many ethnic minority families and to differences between ethnic minority groups and the White majority. |

• Recognizing and respecting differences in ethnicity is an important aspect of getting along with others in a diverse, multicultural world. Too often differences have been described as deficits on the part of ethnic minority individuals. Ethnic minority groups are not homogeneous. Failure to recognize this diversity results in stereotyping.

Differences and Diversity

Prejudice and Discrimination

• Prejudice is an unjustified negative attitude toward an individual because of the individual's membership in a group. Despite progress in the treatment of minority groups, children who are members of these groups often face prejudice and discrimination.

Technology

LG4 Summarize the influence of technology on children's development.

Media Use

• In terms of exposure, the average U.S. 8- to 18-year-old spends almost 6 hours a day using electronic media, with the most time spent watching television (if media multitasking is taken into account, they use electronic media 8 hours per day). Both children and adolescents are rapidly increasing the time they spend online. Adolescents also use the print media more than children do. There are large individual variations in adolescent media use.

Television and Electronic Media

• One negative aspect of television is that it involves passive learning. Special concerns involve the ways ethnic minorities, sex, and aggression are portrayed on television. TV violence is not the only cause of adolescents' aggression, but most experts agree that it can induce aggression and antisocial behavior. On the other hand, prosocial behavior on TV is associated with increased positive behavior by children. There also is concern about adolescents playing violent video games; however, playing prosocial video games is linked with an increase in prosocial behavior. Children's cognitive skills and abilities influence their TV viewing experiences. TV viewing is negatively related to children's mental ability and achievement. However, educational TV programming can enhance achievement.

Computers and the Internet

• Today's children and adolescents are experiencing a technology revolution through the widespread use of computers, the Internet, and sophisticated cell phones. The social environment of adolescents has increasingly become digitally mediated. The Internet continues to serve as the main focus of digitally mediated social interaction for adolescents but increasingly involves a variety of digital devices, including cell phones (especially smart phones). Adolescents' online time can have positive or negative outcomes. Large numbers of adolescents and college students engage in social networking on Facebook. A special concern is the difficulty parents face in monitoring the information their children are accessing.

key **terms**

culture 485
cross-cultural studies 486
individualism 486

collectivism 486
socioeconomic status
  (SES) 488

ethnicity 494
prejudice 497
Internet 503

key **people**

Donald Campbell 485
Catherine Tamis-LeMonda 487

Souniya Luthar 489
Vonnie McLoyd 491

Aletha Huston 492
Aimee Leifer 502

507

Social Contexts of Development

glossary

A

accommodation Piagetian concept of adjusting schemes to fit new information and experiences.

acculturation Cultural changes that occur when one culture comes in contact with another culture.

active (niche-picking) genotype-environment correlations Correlations that exist when children seek out environments they find compatible and stimulating.

adolescence The developmental period of transition from childhood to early adulthood, entered at approximately 10 to 12 years of age and ending at 18 or 19 years of age.

adolescent egocentrism The heightened self-consciousness of adolescents, which is reflected in adolescents' beliefs that others are as interested in them as they are in themselves, and in adolescents' sense of personal uniqueness and invulnerability.

adoption study A study in which investigators seek to discover whether, in behavior and psychological characteristics, adopted children are more like their adoptive parents, who provided a home environment, or more like their biological parents, who contributed their heredity. Another form of the adoption study is one that compares adoptive and biological siblings.

affordances Opportunities for interaction offered by objects that are necessary to perform activities.

afterbirth The third stage of birth, when the placenta, umbilical cord, and other membranes are detached and expelled.

altruism An unselfish interest in helping another person.

amnion Prenatal life-support system that is a bag or envelope that contains a clear fluid in which the developing embryo floats.

amygdala The seat of emotions in the brain.

androgens Hormones, the most important of which is testosterone, that promote the development of male genitals and secondary sex characteristics.

androgyny The presence of masculine and feminine characteristics in the same person.

anger cry A cry similar to the basic cry but with more excess air forced through the vocal cords.

animism A facet of preoperational thought: the belief that inanimate objects have lifelike qualities and are capable of action.

A-not-B error Also called A–$\overline{\text{B}}$ error, this occurs when infants make the mistake of selecting the familiar hiding place (A) rather than the new hiding place ($\overline{\text{B}}$) as they progress into substage 4 in Piaget's sensorimotor stage.

Apgar Scale A widely used method to assess the health of newborns at one and five minutes after birth. The Apgar Scale evaluates infants' heart rate, respiratory effort, muscle tone, body color, and reflex irritability.

aphasia A disorder resulting from brain damage to Broca's area or Wernicke's area that involves a loss or impairment of the ability to use or comprehend words.

Asperger syndrome A relatively mild autism spectrum disorder in which the child has relatively good verbal skills, milder nonverbal language problems, and a restricted range of interests and relationships.

assimilation Piagetian concept of the incorporation of new information into existing knowledge.

attachment A close emotional bond between two people.

attention Concentrating and focusing mental resources.

attention deficit hyperactivity disorder (ADHD) A disability in which children consistently show one or more of the following characteristics: (1) inattention, (2) hyperactivity, and (3) impulsivity.

authoritarian parenting A restrictive, punitive style in which the parent exhorts the child to follow the parent's directions and to respect their work and effort. Firm limits and controls are placed on the child, and little verbal exchange is allowed. This style is associated with children's social incompetence, including a lack of initiative and weak communication skills.

authoritative parenting This style encourages children to be independent but still places limits and controls on their actions. Extensive verbal give-and-take is allowed, and parents are warm and nurturant toward the child. This style is associated with children's social competence, including being achievement oriented and self-reliant.

autism spectrum disorders (ASDs) Also called pervasive developmental disorders, they range from the severe disorder labeled

autistic disorder to the milder disorder called Asperger syndrome. Children with these disorders are characterized by problems in social interaction, verbal and nonverbal communication, and repetitive behaviors.

autistic disorder A severe developmental autism spectrum disorder that has its onset in the first three years of life and includes deficiencies in social relationships; abnormalities in communication; and restricted, repetitive, and stereotyped patterns of behavior.

automaticity The ability to process information with little or no effort.

autonomous morality The second stage of moral development in Piaget's theory, displayed by older children (about 10 years of age and older). The child becomes aware that rules and laws are created by people and that, in judging an action, one should consider the actor's intentions as well as the consequences.

average children Children who receive an average number of both positive and negative nominations from their peers.

B

basic cry A rhythmic pattern usually consisting of a cry, a briefer silence, a shorter inspiratory whistle that is higher pitched than the main cry, and then a brief rest before the next cry.

Bayley Scales of Infant Development Initially created by Nancy Bayley, these scales are widely used in assessing infant development. The current version has five scales: cognitive, language, motor, socioemotional, and adaptive.

behavior genetics The field that seeks to discover the influence of heredity and environment on individuals differences in human traits and development.

biological processes Changes in an individual's body.

blastocyst The inner layer of cells that develops during the germinal period. These cells later develop into the embryo.

bonding The formation of a close connection, especially a physical bond, between parents and their newborn in the period shortly after birth.

brainstorming A technique in which children are encouraged to come up with creative ideas in a group, play off one another's ideas, and say practically whatever comes to mind.

Brazelton Neonatal Behavioral Assessment Scale (NBAS) A measure that is used in the first month of life to assess the newborn's neurological development, reflexes, and reactions to people and objects.

breech position The baby's position in the uterus that causes the buttocks to be the first part to emerge from the vagina.

Broca's area An area of the brain's left frontal lobe that is involved in speech production and grammatical processing.

Bronfenbrenner's ecological theory An environmental systems theory that focuses on five environmental systems: microsystem, mesosystem, exosystem, macrosystem, and chronosystem.

C

care perspective The moral perspective of Carol Gilligan, in which people are assessed in terms of their connectedness with others and the quality of their interpersonal communication, relationships with others, and concern for others.

case study An in-depth look at a single individual.

centration Focusing attention on one characteristic to the exclusion of all others.

cephalocaudal pattern The sequence in which the fastest growth occurs at the top of the body—the head—with physical growth in size, weight, and feature differentiation gradually working from top to bottom.

cesarean delivery Removal of the baby from the mother's uterus through an incision made in her abdomen.

character education A direct moral education approach that involves teaching students a basic "moral literacy" to prevent them from engaging in immoral behavior or doing harm to themselves or others.

child-centered kindergarten Education that involves the whole child by considering both the child's physical, cognitive, and socioemotional development and the child's needs, interests, and learning styles.

child-directed speech Language spoken in a higher pitch than normal, with simple words and sentences.

chromosomes Threadlike structures that come in 23 pairs, with one member of each pair coming from each parent. Chromosomes contain the genetic substance DNA.

cliques Small groups that range from 2 to about 12 individuals and average about 5 or 6 individuals. Cliques can form because of friendship or because individuals engage in similar activities, and members usually are of the same sex and about the same age.

cognitive moral education Education based on the belief that students should learn to value things like democracy and justice as their moral reasoning develops; Kohlberg's theory has been the basis for many of the cognitive moral education approaches.

cognitive processes Changes in an individual's thinking, intelligence, and language.

collectivism Emphasizing values that serve the group by subordinating personal goals to preserve group integrity, interdependence of members, and harmonious relationships.

commitment Personal investment in identity.

concrete operational stage Piaget's third stage, which lasts from approximately 7 to 11 years of age, when children can perform concrete operations, and logical reasoning replaces intuitive reasoning as long as the reasoning can be applied to specific or concrete examples.

conduct disorder Age-inappropriate actions and attitudes that violate family expectations, society's norms, and the personal or property rights of others.

connectedness Consists of two dimensions: mutuality, sensitivity to and respect for others' views; and permeability, openness to others' views.

conservation The idea that altering an object's or substance's appearance does not change its basic properties.

constructive play Play that combines sensorimotor/practice play with symbolic representation of ideas. Constructive play occurs when children engage in self-regulated creation or construction of a product or a solution.

constructivist approach A learner-centered approach that emphasizes the importance of individuals actively constructing their knowledge and understanding, with guidance from the teacher.

context The settings, influenced by historical, economic, social, and cultural factors, in which development occurs.

continuity-discontinuity issue Question about whether development involves gradual, cumulative change (continuity) or distinct stages (discontinuity).

controversial children Children who are frequently identified both as someone's best friend and as being disliked.

conventional reasoning The second, or intermediate, level in Kohlberg's theory of moral development. At this level, individuals abide by certain standards (internal), but they are the standards of others such as parents or the laws of society (external). The conventional level consists of two stages: mutual interpersonal expectations,

relationships, and interpersonal conformity (stage 3) and social systems morality (stage 4).

convergent thinking Thinking that produces one correct answer; characteristic of the kind of thinking required on conventional intelligence tests.

coparenting Support parents provide for each other in jointly raising children.

core knowledge approach States that infants are born with domain-specific innate knowledge systems, such as those involving space, number sense, object permanence, and language.

corpus callosum Brain area where fibers connect the brain's left and right hemispheres.

correlation coefficient A number based on statistical analysis that is used to describe the degree of association between two variables.

correlational research Research in which the goal is to describe the strength of the relationship between two or more events or characteristics.

creativity The ability to think in novel and unusual ways and come up with unique solutions to problems.

crisis A period of identity development during which the adolescent is choosing among meaningful alternatives.

critical thinking Thinking reflectively and productively, and evaluating the evidence.

cross-cultural studies Comparisons of one culture with one or more other cultures. These provide information about the degree to which children's development is similar, or universal, across cultures, and to the degree to which it is culture-specific.

cross-sectional approach A research strategy in which individuals of different ages are compared at the same point in time.

crowds The crowd is a larger group structure than a clique. Adolescents usually are members of a crowd based on reputation and may or may not spend much time together. Many crowds are defined by the activities in which adolescents engage.

culture-fair tests Intelligence tests that aim to avoid cultural bias.

culture The behavior patterns, beliefs, and all other products of a particular group of people that are passed on from generation to generation.

D

descriptive research Research that involves observing and recording behavior.

development The pattern of movement or change that begins at conception and continues through the life span.

developmental quotient (DQ) An overall developmental score that combines subscores on motor, language, adaptive, and personal-social domains in the Gesell assessment of infants.

developmentally appropriate practice Education that focuses on the typical developmental patterns of children (age-appropriateness) and the uniqueness of each child (individual-appropriateness). Such practice contrasts with developmentally inappropriate practice, which relies on abstract paper-and-pencil activities presented to large groups of young children.

dialect A variety of language that is distinguished by its vocabulary, grammar, or pronunciation.

difficult child A temperament style in which the child tends to react negatively and cry frequently, engages in irregular daily routines, and is slow to accept new experiences.

direct instruction approach A teacher-centered approach characterized by teacher direction and control, mastery of academic material, high expectations for students' progress, and maximum time spent on learning tasks.

dishabituation The recovery of a habituated response after a change in stimulation.

divergent thinking Thinking that produces many answers to the same question; characteristic of creativity.

divided attention Concentrating on more than one activity at the same time.

DNA A complex molecule that contains genetic information.

doula A caregiver who provides continuous physical, emotional, and educational support for the mother before, during, and after childbirth.

Down syndrome A chromosomally transmitted form of mental retardation, caused by the presence of an extra copy of chromosome 21.

dual-process model States that decision-making is influenced by two systems, one analytical and one experiential, that compete with each other. In this model, it is the experiential system—monitoring and managing actual experiences—that benefits adolescent decision making.

dynamic systems theory A theory, proposed by Esther Thelen, that seeks to explain how motor behaviors are assembled for perceiving and acting.

dyscalculia Also known as developmental arithmetic disorder; a learning disability that involves difficulty in math computation.

dysgraphia A learning disability that involves difficulty in handwriting.

dyslexia A category of learning disabilities involving a severe impairment in the ability to read and spell.

E

early childhood The developmental period that extends from the end of infancy to about 5 or 6 years of age, sometimes called the preschool years.

early-later experience issue Controversy regarding the degree to which early experiences (especially during infancy) or later experiences are the key determinants of children's development.

easy child A temperament style in which the child is generally in a positive mood, quickly establishes regular routines, and adapts easily to new experiences.

eclectic theoretical orientation An orientation that does not follow any one theoretical approach but rather selects from each theory whatever is considered its best aspects.

ecological view The view, proposed by the Gibsons, that people directly perceive information in the world around them. Perception brings people in contact with the environment in order to interact with it and adapt to it.

egocentrism An important feature of preoperational thought: the inability to distinguish between one's own and someone else's perspective.

embryonic period The period of prenatal development that occurs two to eight weeks after conception. During the embryonic period, the rate of cell differentiation intensifies, support systems for the cells form, and organs appear.

emotion Feeling, or affect, that occurs when people are engaged in an interaction that is important to them, especially one that influences their well-being.

emotional and behavioral disorders Serious, persistent problems that involve relationships, aggression, depression, fears associated with personal or school matters, as well as other inappropriate socioemotional characteristics.

emotional intelligence The ability to perceive and express emotion accurately and adaptively, to understand emotion and emotional knowledge, to use feelings to facilitate thought, and to manage emotions in oneself and others.

empathy Reacting to another's feelings with an emotional response that is similar to the other's feelings.

encoding The mechanism by which information gets into memory.

epigenetic view Emphasizes that development is the result of an ongoing, bidirectional interchange between heredity and environment.

equilibration A mechanism that Piaget proposed to explain how children shift from one stage of thought to the next. The shift occurs as children experience cognitive conflict, or disequilibrium, in trying to understand the world. Eventually, they resolve the conflict and reach a balance, or equilibrium, of thought.

Erikson's theory Description of eight stages of human development. Each stage consists of a unique developmental task that confronts individuals with a crisis that must be resolved.

estradiol An estrogen that is a key hormone in girls' pubertal development.

estrogens The main class of female sex hormones, the most important of which is estradiol, that influence the development of female physical sex characteristics and help regulate the menstrual cycle.

ethnic gloss Use of an ethnic label such as *African American* or *Latino* in a superficial way that portrays an ethnic group as being more homogeneous than it really is.

ethnic identity An enduring aspect of the self that includes a sense of membership in an ethnic group, along with the attitudes and feelings related to that membership.

ethnicity A dimension of culture based on cultural heritage, nationality, race, religion, and language.

ethology Stresses that behavior is strongly influenced by biology, is tied to evolution, and is characterized by critical or sensitive periods.

evocative genotype-environment correlations Correlations that exist when the child's genotype elicits certain types of physical and social environments.

evolutionary psychology Branch of psychology that emphasizes the importance of adaptation, reproduction, and "survival of the fittest" in shaping behavior.

executive attention Involves action planning, allocating attention to goals, error detection and compensation, monitoring progress on tasks, and dealing with novel or difficult circumstances.

expanding Restating, in a linguistically sophisticated form, what a child has said.

experiment A carefully regulated procedure in which one or more of the factors believed to influence the behavior being studied are manipulated while all other factors are held constant.

explicit memory Conscious memory of facts and experiences.

extrinsic motivation Response to external incentives such as rewards and punishments.

F

fast mapping A process that helps to explain how young children learn the connection between a word and its referent so quickly.

fertilization A stage in reproduction whereby an egg and a sperm fuse to create a single cell, called a zygote.

fetal alcohol spectrum disorders (FASD) A cluster of abnormalities and problems that appear in the offspring of mothers who drink alcohol heavily during pregnancy.

fetal period The period from two months after conception until birth, lasting about seven months in typical pregnancies.

fine motor skills Motor skills that involve more finely tuned movements, such as finger dexterity.

forgiveness An aspect of prosocial behavior that occurs when an injured person releases the injurer from possible behavioral retaliation.

formal operational stage Piaget's fourth and final stage, which occurs between the ages of 11 and 15, when individuals move beyond concrete experiences and think in more abstract and logical ways.

fragile X syndrome A genetic disorder involving an abnormality in the X chromosome, which becomes constricted and often breaks.

fuzzy trace theory States that memory is best understood by considering two types of memory representations: (1) verbatim memory trace; and (2) fuzzy trace, or gist. According to this theory, older children's better memory is attributed to the fuzzy traces created by extracting the gist of information.

G

games Activities engaged in for pleasure that include rules and often competition with one or more individuals.

gender The characteristics of people as males and females.

gender identity The sense of being male or female, which most children acquire by the time they are 3 years old.

gender role A set of expectations that prescribes how females or males should think, act, and feel.

gender schema theory According to this theory, gender typing emerges as children gradually develop schemas of what is gender-appropriate and gender-inappropriate in their culture.

gender stereotypes Broad categories that reflect impressions and widely held beliefs about what behavior is appropriate for females and males.

gender typing Acquisition of a traditional masculine or feminine role.

gene × environment (G × E) interaction The interaction of a specific measured variation in the DNA and a specific measured aspect of the environment.

genes Units of hereditary information composed of DNA. Genes direct cells to reproduce themselves and manufacture the proteins that maintain life.

genotype A person's genetic heritage; the actual genetic material.

germinal period The period of prenatal development that takes place in the first two weeks after conception. It includes the creation of the zygote, continued cell division, and the attachment of the zygote to the uterine wall.

giftedness Possession of above-average intelligence (an IQ of 130 or higher) and/or superior talent for something.

goodness of fit The match between a child's temperament and the environmental demands the child must cope with.

grasping reflex A neonatal reflex that occurs when something touches the infant's palms. The infant responds by grasping tightly.

gratitude A feeling of thankfulness and appreciation, especially in response to someone doing something kind or helpful.

gross motor skills Motor skills that involve large-muscle activities, such as moving one's arms and walking.

H

habituation Decreased responsiveness to a stimulus after repeated presentations of the stimulus.

helpless orientation An orientation in which one seems trapped by the experience of difficulty and attributes one's difficulty to a lack of ability.

heritability The fraction of the variance in a population that is attributed to genetics.

heteronomous morality The first stage of moral development in Piaget's theory, occurring from 4 to 7 years of age. Justice and rules are conceived of as unchangeable properties of the world, removed from the control of people.

hidden curriculum The pervasive moral atmosphere that characterizes each school.

horizontal décalage Piaget's concept that similar abilities do not appear at the same time within a stage of development.

hormones Powerful chemical substances secreted by the endocrine glands and carried through the body by the bloodstream.

hypotheses Specific assumptions and predictions that can be tested to determine their accuracy.

hypothetical-deductive reasoning Piaget's formal operational concept that adolescents have the cognitive ability to develop hypotheses about ways to solve problems and can systematically deduce which is the best path to follow in solving the problem.

I

identity achievement Marcia's term for the status of individuals who have undergone a crisis and made a commitment.

identity diffusion Marcia's term for the status of individuals who have not yet experienced a crisis (that is, they have not yet explored meaningful alternatives) or made any commitments.

identity foreclosure Marcia's term for the status of individuals who have made a commitment but have not experienced a crisis.

identity moratorium Marcia's term for the status of individuals who are in the midst of a crisis but whose commitments either are absent or are only vaguely defined.

identity versus identity confusion Erikson's fifth developmental stage, which individuals experience during the adolescent years. At this time, adolescents examine who they are, what they are all about, and where they are going in life.

imaginary audience The aspect of adolescent egocentrism that involves attention-getting behavior motivated by a desire to be noticed, visible, and "onstage."

immanent justice Piaget's concept of the childhood expectation that if a rule is broken, punishment will be meted out immediately.

implicit memory Memory without conscious recollection; memory of skills and routine procedures that are performed automatically.

inclusion Educating a child with special educational needs full-time in the regular classroom.

index offenses Criminal acts, such as robbery, rape, and homicide, whether they are committed by juveniles or adults.

individualism Giving priority to personal goals rather than to group goals; emphasizing values that serve the self, such as feeling good, striving for personal distinction and recognition for achievement, and asserting independence.

individuality Consists of two dimensions: self-assertion, the ability to have and communicate a point of view; and separateness, the use of communication patterns to express how one is different from others.

individualized education program (IEP) A written statement that spells out a program tailored to the needs of a child with a disability.

induction A discipline technique in which a parent uses reasoning and explains how the child's actions are likely to affect others.

indulgent parenting A style in which parents are highly involved with their children but place few demands or controls on them. This is associated with children's social incompetence, especially a lack of self-control and a lack of respect for others.

infancy The developmental period that extends from birth to about 18 to 24 months.

infinite generativity The ability to produce an endless number of meaningful sentences using a finite set of words and rules.

information-processing approach An approach that focuses on the ways children process information about their world—how they manipulate information, monitor it, and create strategies to deal with it.

information-processing theory Emphasizes that individuals manipulate information, monitor it, and strategize about it. Central to this theory are the processes of memory and thinking.

innate goodness view The idea, presented by Swiss-born French philosopher Jean-Jacques Rousseau, that children are inherently good.

insecure avoidant babies Babies who show insecurity by avoiding the mother.

insecure disorganized babies Babies who show insecurity by being disorganized and disoriented.

insecure resistant babies Babies who might cling to the caregiver, then resist her by fighting against the closeness, perhaps by kicking or pushing away.

intelligence The ability to solve problems and to adapt to and learn from experiences.

intelligence quotient (IQ) An individual's mental age divided by chronological age and multiplied by 100; devised in 1912 by William Stern.

intermodal perception The ability to relate and integrate information about two or more sensory modalities, such as vision and hearing.

Internet Worldwide computer-mediated communication system that provides a vast array of information.

intimacy in friendship Self-disclosure or the sharing of private thoughts.

intrinsic motivation Internal motivational factors such as self-determination, curiosity, challenge, and effort.

intuitive thought substage The second substage of preoperational thought, occurring between approximately 4 and 7 years of age, when children begin to use primitive reasoning.

J

joint attention Individuals focusing on the same object or event; requires the ability to track another's behavior, one person directing another's attention, and reciprocal interaction.

justice perspective A moral perspective that focuses on the rights of the individual; individuals independently make moral decisions.

juvenile delinquency Refers to a great variety of behaviors by an adolescent, ranging from unacceptable behavior to breaking the law.

K

kangaroo care Treatment for preterm infants that involves skin-to-skin contact.

Klinefelter syndrome A chromosomal disorder in which males have an extra X chromosome, making them XXY instead of XY.

kwashiorkor Severe malnutrition caused by a protein-deficient diet, causing the feet and abdomen to swell with water.

L

labeling Identifying the names of objects.

laboratory A controlled setting from which many of the complex factors of the "real world" have been removed.

language A form of communication, whether spoken, written, or signed, that is based on a system of symbols.

language acquisition device (LAD) Chomsky's term that describes a biological endowment that enables the child to detect the features and rules of language, including phonology, syntax, and semantics.

lateralization Specialization of function in one hemisphere of the cerebral cortex or the other.

learning disabilities Disabilities involving understanding or using spoken or written language. The difficulty can appear in listening, thinking, reading, writing, spelling, or mathematics. To be classified as a learning disability, the problem must not be primarily the result of visual, hearing, or motor disabilities; mental retardation; emotional disorders; or environmental, cultural, or economic disadvantage.

least restrictive environment (LRE) The concept that a child with a disability must be educated in a setting that is similar to classrooms in which children without a disability are educated.

longitudinal approach A research strategy in which the same individuals are studied over a period of time, usually several years.

long-term memory A relatively permanent and unlimited type of memory.

love withdrawal A discipline technique in which a parent withholds attention or love from the child in an effort to control the child's behavior.

low birth weight infant Infant that weighs less than 5½ pounds at birth.

M

marasmus Severe malnutrition caused by an insufficient protein-calorie intake, resulting in a shrunken, elderly appearance.

mastery motivation An orientation in which one is task oriented, focusing on learning strategies and the achievement process rather than ability or the outcome.

meiosis A specialized form of cell division that forms eggs and sperm (or gametes).

memory Retention of information over time.

menarche A girl's first menstruation.

mental age (MA) An individual's level of mental development relative to others.

mental retardation A condition of limited mental ability in which the individual (1) has a low IQ, usually below 70 on a traditional intelligence test; (2) has difficulty adapting to everyday life; and (3) has an onset of these characteristics by age 18.

metacognition Cognition about cognition, or "knowing about knowing."

metalinguistic awareness Knowledge about language.

metamemory Knowledge about memory.

metaphor An implied comparison between two unlike things.

middle and late childhood The developmental period that extends from about 6 to 11 years of age, sometimes called the elementary school years.

mindfulness Being alert, mentally present, and cognitively flexible while going through life's everyday activities and tasks.

mindset Dweck's concept that refers to the cognitive view individuals develop for themselves; individuals have either a fixed or growth mindset.

mitosis Cellular reproduction in which the cell's nucleus duplicates itself with two new cells being formed, each containing the same DNA as the parent cell, arranged in the same 23 pairs of chromosomes.

Montessori approach An educational philosophy in which children are given considerable freedom and spontaneity in choosing activities and are allowed to move from one activity to another as they desire.

moral development   Changes in thoughts, feelings, and behaviors regarding standards of right and wrong.

moral exemplars   People who have lived extraordinary lives. Emphasizes the development of personality, identity, character, and virtue to a level that reflects moral excellence and commitment.

moral identity   The aspect of personality that is present when individuals have moral notions and commitments that are central to their lives.

Moro reflex   A neonatal startle response that occurs in reaction to a sudden, intense noise or movement. When startled, the newborn arches its back, throws its head back, and flings out its arms and legs. Then the newborn rapidly closes its arms and legs to the center of the body.

morphology   The rule system that governs how words are formed in a language.

multiple developmental trajectories Concept that adults follow one trajectory and children and adolescents another one; understanding how these trajectories mesh is important.

myelination   The process of encasing axons with a myelin sheath that increases the speed of processing information.

N

natural childbirth   This method attempts to reduce the mother's pain by decreasing her fear through education about childbirth and relaxation techniques during delivery.

naturalistic observation   Behavioral observation that takes place in real-world settings.

nature-nurture issue   Debate about whether development is primarily influenced by nature or nurture. The "nature" proponents claim biological inheritance is the most important influence on development; the "nurture" proponents claim that environmental experiences are the most important.

neglected children   Children who are infrequently identified as a best friend but are not disliked by their peers.

neglectful parenting   A style in which the parent is very uninvolved in the child's life. It is associated with children's social incompetence, especially a lack of self-control and poor self-esteem.

Neonatal Intensive Care Unit Network Neurobehavioral Scale (NNNS)   An "offspring" of the NBAS, the NNNS provides an assessment of the "at-risk" newborn's behavior, neurological and stress responses, and regulatory capacities.

neo-Piagetians   Developmentalists who have elaborated on Piaget's theory, believing that children's cognitive development is more specific in many respects than Piaget thought and giving more emphasis to how children use memory, attention, and strategies to process information.

neurons   Nerve cells, which handle information processing at the cellular level in the brain.

nonshared environmental experiences   The child's own unique experiences, both within the family and outside the family, that are not shared by another sibling. Thus, experiences occurring within the family can be part of the "nonshared environment."

normal distribution   A symmetrical distribution with a majority of the cases falling in the middle of the possible range of scores and few scores appearing toward the extremes of the range.

O

object permanence   The Piagetian term for one of an infant's most important accomplishments: understanding that objects and events continue to exist even when they cannot directly be seen, heard, or touched.

operations   Internalized actions that allow children to do mentally what before they had done only physically. Operations also are reversible mental actions.

organization   Piaget's concept of grouping isolated behaviors into a higher-order, more smoothly functioning cognitive system; the grouping or arranging of items into categories.

organogenesis   Organ formation that takes place during the first two months of prenatal development.

original sin view   Advocated during the Middle Ages, the belief that children were born into the world as evil beings and were basically bad.

P

pain cry   A sudden appearance of loud crying without preliminary moaning, and a long initial cry followed by an extended period of breath holding.

passive genotype-environment correlations Correlations that exist when the natural parents, who are genetically related to the child, provide a rearing environment for the child.

peers   Children who share the same age or maturity level.

perception   The interpretation of sensation.

performance orientation   An orientation in which one focuses on winning rather than achievement outcomes, and happiness is thought to result from winning.

personal fable   The part of adolescent egocentrism that involves an adolescent's sense of uniqueness and invincibility.

perspective taking   The ability to assume others' perspectives and understand their thoughts or feelings.

phenotype   The way an individual's genotype is expressed in observed and measurable characteristics.

phenylketonuria (PKU)   A genetic disorder in which an individual cannot properly metabolize an amino acid. PKU is now easily detected but, if left untreated, results in mental retardation and hyperactivity.

phonics approach   An approach that emphasizes that reading instruction should focus on phonics and its basic rules for translating written symbols into sounds.

phonology   The sound system of a language, which includes the sounds used and rules about how they may be combined.

Piaget's theory   Theory stating that children actively construct their understanding of the world and go through four stages of cognitive development.

placenta   A life-support system that consists of a disk-shaped group of tissues in which small blood vessels from the mother and offspring intertwine.

play   A pleasurable activity that is engaged in for its own sake.

play therapy   Therapy that allows the child to work off frustrations and is a medium through which the therapist can analyze the child's conflicts and ways of coping with them. Children may feel less threatened and be more likely to express their true feelings in the context of play.

popular children   Children who are frequently identified as a best friend and are rarely disliked by their peers.

possible self   What an individual might become, would like to become, and is afraid of becoming.

postconventional reasoning   The third and highest level in Kohlberg's theory of moral development. At this level, morality is more internal. The postconventional level consists of two stages: social contract or utility and individual rights (stage 5) and universal ethical principles (stage 6).

postpartum depression   Characteristic of women who have such strong feelings of sadness, anxiety, or despair that they have trouble coping with daily tasks during the postpartum period.

postpartum period   The period after childbirth when the mother adjusts, both physically and psychologically, to the process of childbirth. This period lasts about six weeks or until her body has completed its adjustment and returned to a near prepregnant state.

power assertion A discipline technique in which a parent attempts to gain control over the child or the child's resources.

practice play Play that involves repetition of behavior when new skills are being learned or when physical or mental mastery and coordination of skills are required for games or sports. Practice play can be engaged in throughout life.

pragmatics The appropriate use of language in different contexts.

precocious puberty Very early onset and rapid progression of puberty.

preconventional reasoning The lowest level in Kohlberg's theory. At this level, morality is often focused on reward and punishment. The two stages in preconventional reasoning are punishment and obedience orientation (stage 1) and individualism, instrumental purpose, and exchange (stage 2).

prefrontal cortex The highest level of the frontal lobes that is involved in reasoning, decision making, and self-control.

prejudice An unjustified negative attitude toward an individual because of her or his membership in a group.

prenatal period The time from conception to birth.

preoperational stage The second Piagetian developmental stage, which lasts from about 2 to 7 years of age, when children begin to represent the world with words, images, and drawings.

prepared childbirth Developed by French obstetrician Ferdinand Lamaze, this childbirth strategy is similar to natural childbirth but includes a special breathing technique to control pushing in the final stages of labor and a more detailed anatomy and physiology course.

pretense/symbolic play Play that occurs when a child transforms the physical environment into a symbol.

preterm infants Those born before the completion of 37 weeks of gestation (the time between fertilization and birth).

primary emotions Emotions that are present in humans and other animals, and emerge early in life; examples are joy, anger, sadness, fear, and disgust.

Project Head Start Compensatory education designed to provide children from low-income families the opportunity to acquire the skills and experiences important for school success.

proximodistal pattern The sequence in which growth starts at the center of the body and moves toward the extremities.

psychoanalytic theories Theories that describe development as primarily unconscious and heavily colored by emotion. Behavior is merely a surface characteristic, and the symbolic workings of the mind have to be analyzed to understand behavior. Early experiences with parents are emphasized.

psychoanalytic theory of gender A theory that stems from Freud's view that preschool children develop erotic feelings toward the opposite-sex parent. Eventually these feeling cause anxiety, so that at 5 or 6 years of age, children renounce these feelings and identify with the same-sex parent, unconsciously adopting the same-sex parent's characteristics.

psychosocial moratorium Erikson's term for the gap between childhood security and adult autonomy that adolescents experience as part of their identity exploration.

puberty A period of rapid physical maturation involving hormonal and bodily changes that take place primarily in early adolescence.

R

rapport talk The language of conversation and a way of establishing connections and negotiating relationships; more characteristic of females than of males.

recasting Rephrasing a statement that a child has said, perhaps turning it into a question, or restating a child's immature utterance in the form of a fully grammatical utterance.

reciprocal socialization The bidirectional process by which children socialize parents just as parents socialize them.

reflexes Built-in reactions to stimuli.

reflexive smile A smile that does not occur in response to external stimuli. It happens during the month after birth, usually during sleep.

rejected children Children who are infrequently identified as a best friend and are actively disliked by their peers.

report talk Talk that conveys information; more characteristic of males than females.

rooting reflex A newborn's built-in reaction that occurs when the infant's cheek is stroked or the side of the mouth is touched. In response, the infant turns its head toward the side that was touched, in an apparent effort to find something to suck.

S

satire The use of irony, derision, or wit to expose folly or wickedness.

scaffolding Adjusting the level of parental guidance to fit the child's efforts, allowing children to be more skillful than they would be if they relied only on their own abilities.

schema theory States that when people reconstruct information, they fit it into information that already exists in their minds.

schemas Mental frameworks that organize concepts and information.

schemes In Piaget's theory, actions or mental representations that organize knowledge.

scientific method An approach that can be used to obtain accurate information by carrying out four steps: (1) conceptualize the problem, (2) collect data, (3) draw conclusions, and (4) revise research conclusions and theory.

securely attached babies Babies who use the caregiver as a secure base from which to explore the environment.

selective attention Focusing on a specific aspect of experience that is relevant while ignoring others that are irrelevant.

self-concept Domain-specific self-evaluations.

self-conscious emotions Emotions that require self-awareness, especially consciousness and a sense of "me"; examples include jealousy, empathy, and embarrassment.

self-efficacy The belief that one can master a situation and produce favorable outcomes.

self-esteem The global evaluative dimension of the self; also called self-worth or self-image.

self-understanding A child's cognitive representation of the self—the substance and content of a child's self-conceptions.

semantics The meaning of words and sentences.

sensation Reaction that occurs when information contacts sensory receptors—the eyes, ears, tongue, nostrils, and skin.

sensorimotor play Behavior that allows infants to derive pleasure from exercising their existing sensorimotor schemes.

sensorimotor stage The first of Piaget's stages, which lasts from birth to about 2 years of age; infants construct an understanding of the world by coordinating sensory experiences (such as seeing and hearing) with motoric actions.

separation protest Occurs when infants experience a fear of being separated from a caregiver, which results in crying when the caregiver leaves.

seriation The concrete operation that involves ordering stimuli along a quantitative dimension (such as length).

service learning A form of education that promotes social responsibility and service to the community.

shape constancy Recognition that an object remains the same even though its orientation to the viewer changes.

shared environmental experiences Siblings' common environmental experiences, such as their parents' personalities and intellectual orientation, the family's socioeconomic status, and the neighborhood in which they live.

short-term memory Limited-capacity memory system in which information is usually retained for up to 30 seconds, assuming there is no rehearsal of the information. Using rehearsal, individuals can keep the information in short-term memory longer.

sickle-cell anemia A genetic disorder that affects the red blood cells and occurs most often in people of African descent.

size constancy Recognition that an object remains the same even though the retinal image of the object changes.

slow-to-warm-up child A temperament style in which the child has a low activity level, is somewhat negative, and displays a low intensity of mood.

small for date infants Also called small for gestational age infants, these infants have birth weights that are below normal when the length of pregnancy is considered. Small for date infants may be preterm or full term.

social cognition The processes involved in understanding the world around us, especially how we think and reason about other people.

social cognitive theory The view of psychologists who emphasize behavior, environment, and cognition as the key factors in development.

social cognitive theory of gender This theory emphasizes that children's gender development occurs through observation and imitation of gender behavior, and through rewards and punishments they experience for gender-appropriate and gender-inappropriate behavior.

social cognitive theory of morality The theory that distinguishes between moral competence—the ability to produce moral behaviors—and moral performance—use of those behaviors in specific situations.

social constructivist approach An emphasis on the social contexts of learning and the construction of knowledge through social interaction. Vygotsky's theory reflects this approach.

social conventional reasoning Focuses on conventional rules established by social consensus, as opposed to moral reasoning that stresses ethical issues.

social play Play that involves interactions with peers.

social policy A government's course of action designed to promote the welfare of its citizens.

social referencing "Reading" emotional cues in others to help determine how to act in a particular situation.

social role theory A theory stating that gender differences result from the contrasting roles of women and men—social hierarchy and division of labor strongly influence gender differences in power, assertiveness, and nurture.

social smile A smile in response to an external stimulus, which, early in development, typically is a face.

socioeconomic status (SES) A grouping of people with similar occupational, educational, and economic characteristics.

socioemotional processes Changes in an individual's relationships with other people, emotions, and personality.

standardized test A test with uniform procedures for administration and scoring. Many standardized tests allow a person's performance to be compared with the performance of other individuals.

status offenses Juvenile offenses, performed by youth under a specified age, that are not as serious as index offenses. These offenses may include acts such as underage drinking, truancy, and sexual promiscuity.

stereotype threat Anxiexy that one's behavior might confirm a stereotype about one's group.

Strange Situation Ainsworth's observational measure of infant attachment to a caregiver, which requires the infant to move through a series of introductions, separations, and reunions with the caregiver and an adult stranger in a prescribed order.

stranger anxiety An infant's fear of and wariness toward strangers; it tends to appear in the second half of the first year of life.

strategy construction Creation of new procedures for processing information.

sucking reflex A newborn's built-in reaction of automatically sucking an object placed in its mouth. The sucking reflex enables the infant to get nourishment before it has associated a nipple with food.

sudden infant death syndrome (SIDS) A condition that occurs when an infant stops breathing, usually during the night, and suddenly dies without an apparent cause.

sustained attention The ability to maintain attention to a selected stimulus for a prolonged period of time. Sustained attention is also called *focused attention* and *vigilance.*

symbolic function substage The first substage of preoperational thought, occurring roughly between the ages of 2 and 4. In this substage, the young child gains the ability to represent mentally an object that is not present.

syntax The ways words are combined to form acceptable phrases and sentences.

T

tabula rasa view The idea, proposed by John Locke, that children are like a "blank tablet."

telegraphic speech The use of short, precise words without grammatical markers such as articles, auxiliary verbs, and other connectives.

temperament Involves individual differences in behavioral styles, emotions, and characteristic ways of responding.

teratogen From the Greek word *tera*, meaning "monster." Any agent that causes a birth defect. The field of study that investigates the causes of birth defects is called teratology.

testosterone An androgen that is a key hormone in boys' pubertal development.

theory An interrelated, coherent set of ideas that helps to explain and make predictions.

theory of mind Awareness of one's own mental processes and the mental processes of others.

thinking Manipulating and transforming information in memory, usually to form concepts, reason, think critically, and solve problems.

top-dog phenomenon The circumstance of moving from the top position in elementary school to the lowest position in middle or junior high school.

transitivity Principle that says if a relation holds between a first object and a second object, and holds between the second object and a third object, then it holds between the first object and the third object. Piaget argued that an understanding of transitivity is characteristic of concrete operational thought.

triarchic theory of intelligence Sternberg's theory that intelligence comes in three forms: analytical, creative, and practical.

trophoblast The outer layer of cells that develops in the germinal period. These cells provide nutrition and support for the embryo.

Turner syndrome A chromosome disorder in females in which either an X chromosome is missing, making the person XO instead of XX, or the second X chromosome is partially deleted.

twin study A study in which the behavioral similarity of identical twins is compared with the behavioral similarity of fraternal twins.

U

umbilical cord A life-support system that contains two arteries and one vein and connects the baby to the placenta.

V

values clarification Helping people clarify their sense of their purpose in life and what is worth working for. Students are encouraged to define their own values and understand others' values.

visual preference method A method developed by Fantz to determine whether infants can distinguish one stimulus from another by measuring the length of time they attend to different stimuli.

Vygotsky's theory A sociocultural cognitive theory that emphasizes how culture and social interaction guide cognitive development.

W

Wernicke's area An area of the brain's left hemisphere that is involved in language comprehension.

whole-language approach An approach that stresses that reading instruction should parallel children's natural language learning. Reading materials should be whole and meaningful.

working memory A mental "workbench" where individuals manipulate and assemble information when making decisions, solving problems, and comprehending written and spoken language.

X

XYY syndrome A chromosomal disorder in which males have an extra Y chromosome.

Z

zone of proximal development (ZPD) Vygotsky's term for tasks that are too difficult for children to master alone but can be mastered with assistance from adults or more-skilled children.

zygote A single cell formed through fertilization.

references

A

Abasi, M., & others. (2009). The effect of hypnosis on pain relief during labor and childbirth in Iranian pregnant women. *International Journal of Clinical and Experimental Hypnosis, 57,* 174–183.

ABC News. (2005, December 12). Larry Page and Sergey Brin. Retrieved from http://abcnews.go.com?Entertainment/12/8/05.

Abruscato, J. A., & DeRosa, D. A. (2010). *Teaching children science: A discovery approach* (7th ed.). Boston: Allyn & Bacon.

Achieve, Inc. (2005). *An action agenda for improving America's high schools.* Washington, DC: Author.

Accornero, V. H., Anthony, J. C., Morrow, C. E., Xue, L., & Bandstra, E. S. (2006). Prenatal cocaine exposure: An examination of childhood externalizing and internalizing behavior problems at age 7 years. *Epidemiology, Psychiatry, and Society, 15,* 20–29.

Ackerman, J. P., Riggins, T., & Black, M. M. (2010). A review of the effects of prenatal cocaine exposure among school-aged children. *Pediatrics, 125,* 554–565.

Adams, S. M., Good, M. W., & Defranco, G. M. (2009). Sudden infant death syndrome. *American Family Physician, 79,* 870–874.

Adamson, L., & Frick, J. (2003). The still face: A history of a shared experimental paradigm. *Infancy, 4,* 451–473.

Administration for Children and Families. (2008). *Statistical fact sheet, fiscal year 2008.* Washington, DC: Author.

Adolph, K. E. (1997). Learning in the development of infant locomotion. *Monographs of the Society for Research in Child Development, 62* (3, Serial No. 251).

Adolph, K. E. (2010). Perceptual learning. Retrieved January 10, 2010, from http://www.psych.nyu.edu/adolph/research1.php

Adolph, K. E., & Berger, S. E. (2005). Physical and motor development. In M. H. Bornstein & M. E. Lamb (Eds.), *Developmental psychology* (5th ed.). Mahwah, NJ: Erlbaum.

Adolph, K. E., Berger, S. E., & Leo, A. (2010, in press). Developmental continuity? Crawling, cruising, and walking. *Developmental Science.*

Adolph, K. E., Eppler, M. A., & Joh, A. S. (2010, in press). Infants' perception of affordances of slopes under low and high friction conditions. *Journal of Experimental Psychology: Human Perception & Performance.*

Adolph, K. E., & Joh, A. S. (2009). Multiple learning mechanisms in the development of action. In A. Woodward & A. Needham (Eds.), *Learning and the infant mind.* New York: Oxford University Press.

Adolph, K. E., Karasik, L. B., & Tamis-LeMonda, C. S. (2010). Moving between cultures: Cross-cultural research on motor development. In M. Bornstein (Ed.), *Handbook of cross-cultural developmental science, Vol. 1: Domains of development across cultures.* New York: Psychology Press.

Adolph, K. E., Vereijken, B., & Shrout, P. E. (2003). What changes in infant walking and why. *Child Development, 74,* 475–497.

Agency for Healthcare Research and Quality. (2007). *Evidence report/Technology assessment Number 153: Breastfeeding and maternal and health outcomes in developed countries.* Rockville, MD: U.S. Department of Health and Human Services.

Agras, W. S., Hammer, L. D., McNicholas, F., & Kraemer, H. C. (2004). Risk factors for childhood overweight: A prospective study from birth to 9.5 years. *Journal of Pediatrics, 145,* 20–25.

Ainsworth, M. D. S. (1979). Infant-mother attachment. *American Psychologist, 34,* 932–937.

Akbari, A., & others. (2010, in press). Parity and breastfeeding are preventive measures against breast cancer in Iranian women. *Breast Cancer.*

Akhtar, N., & Herold, K. (2008). Pragmatic development. In M. M. Haith & J. B. Benson (Eds.), *Encyclopedia of infant and early childhood development.* Oxford, UK: Elsevier.

Alberts, E., Elkind, D., & Ginsberg. S. (2007). The personal fable and risk taking in early adolescence. *Journal of Youth and Adolescence, 36,* 71–76.

Alegre, M., & Welsch, D. (2003). *Maxine Hong Kingston after the fire.* Retrieved January 26, 2003, from www.powers.com/authors

Allen, E. G., Freeman, S. B., Druschel, C., Hobbs, C. A., O'Leary, L. A., Romitti, P. A., Royle, M. H., Torfs, C. P., & Sherman, S. L. (2009). Maternal age and risk for trisomy 21 assessed by the origin of chromosome nondisjunction: A report from the Atlanta and National Down Syndrome Projects. *Human Genetics, 125,* 41–52.

Allen, J. P., & others. (2009, April). *Portrait of the secure teen as an adult.* Paper presented at the meeting of the Society for Research in Child Development, Denver.

Allen, M., Svetaz, M. V., Hardeman, R., & Resnick, M. D. (2008, February). *What research tells us about parenting practices and their relationship to youth sexual behavior.* Campaign to Prevent Teen and Unplanned Pregnancy. Retrieved December 2, 2008, from www.TheNationalCampaign.org

Allington, R. L. (2009). *What really matters in fluency.* Boston: Allyn & Bacon.

Alloway, T. P., Gathercole, S. E., & Elliott, J. (2010, in press). Examining the link between working memory behavior and academic attainment in children with ADHD. *Developmental Medicine and Child Neurology.*

Allstate Foundation. (2005). *Teen driving: Chronic—A report on the state of teen driving.* Northbrook, IL: Author.

Alm, B., Lagercrantz, H., & Wennergren, G. (2006). Stop SIDS—sleeping solitary supine, sucking smoother, stopping smoking substitutes. *Acta Paediatrica, 95,* 260–262.

Als, H., & Butler, S. C. (2008). Screening, newborn, and maternal well-being. In M. M. Haith & J. B. Benson (Eds.), *Encyclopedia of infancy and early childhood.* Oxford, UK: Elsevier.

Altarac, M., & Saroha, E. (2007). Lifetime prevalence of learning disability among U.S. children. *Pediatrics, 119, Suppl 1,* S77–S83.

Alvarez, A. (2009). Racism: "It isn't fair." In N. Tewari & A. Alvarez (Eds.), *Asian American psychology.* Clifton, NJ: Psychology Press.

Alvarez, A., & del Rio, P. (2007). Inside and outside the zone of proximal development: An eco-functional reading of Vygotsky. In H. Daniels, J. Wertsch, & M. Cole (Eds.), *The Cambridge companion to Vygotsky.* New York: Cambridge University Press.

Amabile, T. M. (1993). Commentary. In D. Goleman, P. Kaufman, & M. Ray. *The creative spirit.* New York: Plume.

Amabile, T. M., & Hennessey, B. A. (1992). The motivation for creativity in children. In A. K. Boggiano & T. S. Pittman (Eds.), *Achievement and motivation.* New York: Cambridge University Press.

Amato, P. R. (2006). Marital discord, divorce, and children's well-being: Results from a 20-year longitudinal study of two generations. In A. Clarke-Stewart & J. Dunn (Eds.), *Families count.* New York: Cambridge University Press.

Amato, P. R., & Booth, A. (1996). A prospective study of divorce and parent-child relationships. *Journal of Marriage and the Family, 58,* 356–365.

Amato, P. R., & Dorius, C. (2010). Fathers, children, and divorce. In M. E. Lamb (Ed.), *The role of the father in child development* (5th ed.). New York: Wiley.

Amed, S., Daneman, D., Mahmud, F. H., & Hamilton, J. (2010). Type 2 diabetes in children and adolescents. *Expert Review of Cardiovascular Therapy, 8,* 393–406.

American Academy of Pediatrics. (2001). Committee on Public Education: Children, adolescents, and television. *Pediatrics, 107,* 423–426.

American Academy of Pediatrics. (2001). Health care supervision for children with Williams syndrome. *Pediatrics, 107,* 1192–1204.

American Academy of Pediatrics Council on Sports Medicine and Fitness, McCambridge, T. M., & Stricker, P. R. (2008). Strength training by children and adolescents. *Pediatrics, 121*, 835–840.

American Academy of Pediatrics Task Force on Infant Positioning and SIDS. (2000). Changing concepts of sudden infant death syndrome. *Pediatrics, 105*, 650–656.

American Academy of Pediatrics (AAP) Work Group on Breastfeeding. (1997). Breastfeeding and the use of human milk. *Pediatrics, 100*, 1035–1039.

American Association on Mental Retardation, Ad Hoc Committee on Terminology and Classification. (1992). *Mental retardation* (9th ed.). Washington, DC: Author.

American Psychological Association. (2003). *Psychology: Scientific problem solvers*. Washington, DC: Author.

Amos, D., & Johnson, S. P. (2006). Learning by selection: Visual search and object perception in young infants. *Developmental Psychology, 42*, 1236–1245.

Amos, D., & Johnson, S. P. (2010, in press). Building object knowledge from perceptual input. To appear in B. Hood & L. Santos (Eds.), *The origins of object knowledge*. New York: Oxford University Press.

Amsterdam, B. K. (1968). *Mirror behavior in children under two years of age*. Unpublished doctoral dissertation, University of North Carolina, Chapel Hill.

Anastasi, A., & Urbina, S. (1997). *Psychological testing* (7th ed.). Upper Saddle River, NJ: Prentice Hall.

Anderman, E. M., & Anderman, L. H. (2010). *Classroom motivation*. Upper Saddle River, NJ: Prentice Hall.

Anderman, E. M., & Mueller, C. E. (2010). Middle school transitions and adolescent development: Disentangling psychological, social, and biological effects. In J. Meece & J. Eccles (Eds.), *Handbook of research on schools, schooling, and human development*. Clifton, NJ: Psychology Press.

Anderson, B. M., & others. (2009). Examination of association of genes in the serotonin system to autism. *Neurogenetics, 10*(3), 209–216.

Anderson, C. A., Gentile, D. A., & Buckley, K. E. (2007). *Violent video game effects on children and adolescents*. New York: Oxford University Press.

Anderson, D. R., Huston, A. C., Schmitt, K., Linebarger, D. L., & Wright, J. C. (2001). Early childhood viewing and adolescent behavior: The recontact study. *Monographs of the Society for Research in Child Development, 66*(1), Serial No. 264.

Anderson, D. R., Lorch, E. P., Field, D. E., Collins, P. A., & Nathan, J. G. (1985, April). *Television viewing at home: Age trends in visual attention and time with TV*. Paper presented at the biennial meeting of the Society of Research in Child Development, Toronto.

Anderson, E., Greene, S. M., Hetherington, E. M., & Clingempeel, W. G. (1999). The dynamics of parental remarriage. In E. M. Hetherington (Ed.), *Coping with divorce, single parenting, and remarriage*. Mahwah, NJ: Erlbaum.

Andersson, U. (2010, in press). The contribution of working memory capacity to foreign language comprehension in children. *Memory*.

Ang, S. Y., & Lee, K. (2010). Exploring developmental differences in visual short-term memory and working memory. *Developmental Psychology, 46*, 279–285.

Ansary, N. S., & Luthar, S. S. (2009). Distress and academic achievement among adolescents of affluence: A study of externalizing and internalizing problem behaviors and school performance. *Development and Psychopathology, 21*, 319–341.

Appleton, J. V., & Stanley, N. (2009). Editorial: Childhood outcomes. *Child Abuse Review, 18*, 1–5.

Ara, I., Vicente-Rodriguez, G., Jimenez-Ramirez, J., Dorado, C., Serrano-Sanchez, J. A., & Calbet, J. A. (2004). Regular participation in sports is associated with enhanced physical fitness and lower body mass in prepubertal boys. *International Journal of Obesity and Related Metabolic Disorders, 28*, 1585–1593.

Arendas, K., Qui, Q., & Gruslin, A. (2008). Obesity in pregnancy: Pre-conceptual to postpartum consequences. *Journal of Obstetrics and Gynecology Canada, 30*, 477–488.

Ariés, P. (1962). *Centuries of childhood* (R. Baldrick, Trans.). New York: Knopf.

Ariza, E. N. W., & Lapp, S. I. (2011). *Literacy, language, and culture*. Boston: Allyn & Bacon.

Armstrong, D. G., Henson, K. T., & Savage, T. V. (2009). *Teaching today* (8th ed.). Boston: Allyn & Bacon.

Arnett, J. (1990). Contraceptive use, sensation seeking, and adolescent egocentrism. *Journal of Youth and Adolescence, 19*, 171–180.

Arnett, J. J. (2006). Emerging adulthood: Understanding the new way of coming of age. In J. J. Arnett & J. L. Tanner (Eds.), *Emerging adults in America*. Washington, DC: American Psychological Association.

Aronson, E. (1986, August). *Teaching students things they think they already know about: The case of prejudice and desegregation*. Paper presented at the meeting of the American Psychological Association, Washington, DC.

Aronson, J. (2002). Stereotype threat: Contending and coping with unnerving expectations. In J. Aronson (Ed.), *Improving academic achievement*. San Diego: Academic Press.

Arterberry, M. E. (2008). Perceptual development. In M. E. Haith & J. B. Benson (Eds.), *Encyclopedia of infant and early childhood development*. Oxford, UK: Elsevier.

Asendorph, J. B. (2008). Shyness. In M. M. Haith & J. B. Benson (Eds.), *Encyclopedia of infant and early childhood development*. Oxford, UK: Elsevier.

Asher, S. R., & McDonald, K. L. (2009). The behavioral basis of acceptance, rejection, and perceived popularity. In K. H. Rubin, W. M. Bukowski, & B. Laursen (Eds.), *Handbook of peer interactions, relationships, and groups*. New York: Guilford.

Ashmead, D. H., Wall, R. S., Ebinger, K. A., Hill, M. M., Yang, X., and Eaton, S. (1998). Spatial hearing in children with visual disabilities. *Perception, 27*, 105–122.

Asian, A., Zellner, M., & Bauml, K. H. (2010, in press). Working memory capacity predicts listwise directed forgetting in adults and children. *Memory*.

Aslin, R. N. (2009). The role of learning in cognitive development. In A. Woodward & A. Needham (Eds.), *Learning and the infant mind*. New York: Oxford University Press.

Aslin, R. N., Jusczyk, P. W., & Pisoni, D. B. (1998). Speech and auditory processing during infancy: Constraints on and precursors to language. In W. Damon (Ed.), *Handbook of child psychology* (5th ed., Vol. 2). New York: Wiley.

Aslin, R. N., & Lathrop, A. L. (2008). Visual perception. In M. M. Haith & J. B. Benson (Eds.), *Encyclopedia of infant and early childhood development*. Oxford, UK: Elsevier.

Audesirk, G., Audesirk, T., & Byers, B. E. (2011). *Biology* (9th ed.). Upper Saddle River, NJ: Benjamin Cummings.

Auyeung, B., Baron-Cohen, S., Ashwin, E., Knickmeyer, R., Taylor, K., Hackett, G., & Hines, M. (2009). Fetal testosterone predicts sexually differentiated childhood behavior in girls and boys. *Psychological Science, 20*, 144–148.

Avent, N. D., Plummer, Z. E., Madgett, T. E., Maddocks, D. G., & Soothill, P. W. (2008). Post-genomic studies and their application to non-invasive prenatal diagnosis. *Seminars in Fetal and Neonatal Medicine, 13*, 91–98.

B

Babble, E. R. (2011). *The basics of social research* (5th ed.). Boston: Cengage.

Bacchini, D., & Magliulo, F. (2003). Self-image and perceived self-efficacy during adolescence. *Journal of Youth and Adolescence. 32*, 337–349.

Badaly, D. & Adolph, K. E. (2008). Beyond the average: Walking infants take steps longer than their leg length. *Infant Behavior and Development, 31*, 554–558.

Baddeley, A. D. (1990). *Human memory: Theory and practice*. Boston: Allyn & Bacon.

Baddeley, A. D. (2001). *Is working memory still working?* Paper presented at the meeting of the American Psychological Association, San Francisco.

Baddeley, A. D. (2007). *Working memory, thought, and action*. New York: Oxford University Press.

Baddock, S. A., Galland, B. C., Taylor, B. J., & Bolton, D. P. (2007). Sleep arrangements and behavior of bed-sharing families in the home setting. *Pediatrics, 119*, e200–e2007.

Bahali, K., Akcan, R., Tahiroglu, A. Y., & Avci, A. (2010, in press). Child sexual abuse: Seven years into practice. *Journal of Forensic Science.*

Bahrick, L. E., & Hollich, G. (2008). Intermodal perception. In M. M. Haith & J. B. Benson (Eds.), *Encyclopedia of infant and early childhood development.* Oxford, UK: Elsevier.

Baillargeon, R. (1995). The object concept revisited: New directions in the investigation of infants' physical knowledge, In C. E. Granrud (Ed.), *Visual perception and cognition in infancy.* Hillsdale, NJ: Erlbaum.

Baillargeon, R. (2004). The acquisition of physical knowledge in infancy: A summary in eight lessons. In U. Goswami (Ed.), *Blackwell handbook of childhood cognitive development.* Malden, MA: Blackwell.

Baillargeon, R. (2008). Innate ideas revisited: For a principle of persistence in infants' physical reasoning. *Perspectives on Psychological Science, 3,* 2–13.

Baillargeon, R., & Devoe, S. J. (1991). Object permanence in young children: Further evidence. *Child Development, 62,* 1227–1246.

Baillargeon, R., Li, J., Gernter, Y., & Wu, D. (2011). How do infants reason about physical events? *Wiley-Blackwell handbook of childhood cognitive development* (2nd ed.). New York: Wiley-Blackwell.

Baillargeon, R., Li, J., Ng, W., & Yuan, S. (2009). A new account of infants' physical reasoning. In A. Woodward & A. Needham (Eds.), *Learning and the infant mind* (pp. 66–116). New York: Oxford University Press.

Bajanowski, T., & others. (2007). Nicotine and cotinine in infants dying from sudden infant death syndrome. *International Journal of Legal Medicine, 122*(1), 23–28.

Bakeman, R., & Brown, J. V. (1980). Early interaction: Consequences for social and mental development at three years. *Child Development, 51,* 437–447.

Bakermans-Kranenburg, M. J., Breddels-Van Bardewijk, F., Juffer, M. K., Velderman, M. H., & van IJzendoorn, M. H. (2007). Insecure mothers with temperamentally reactive infants. In F. Juffer, M. J. Bakermans-Kranenburg, & M. H. van IJzendoorn (Eds.), *Promoting positive parenting.* Mahwah, NJ: Erlbaum.

Balaji, P., Dhillon, P., & Russell, I. F. (2009). Low-dose epidural top up for emergency cesarean delivery: a randomized comparison of levobpivacaine versus lildocaine/epinephrine/fentanyl. *International Journal of Obstetric Anethesia, 18,* 335–341.

Balas, B. (2010). Using innate visual biases to guide face learning in natural scenes: A computational investigation. *Developmental Science, 13,* 469–478.

Balchin, I., & Steer, P. J. (2007). Race, prematurity, and immaturity. *Early Human Development, 83,* 749–754.

Bales, K. L., & Carter, C. S. (2009). Neuroendocrine mechanisms of social bonds and child-parent attachment, from the child's perspective. In M. De Haan & M. R. Gunnar (Eds.), *Handbook of developmental social neuroscience.* New York: Guilford.

Balsano, A. B., Theokas, C., & Bobek, D. L. (2009). A shared commitment to youth: The integration of theory, research practice, and social policy. In R. M. Lerner & L. Steinberg (Eds.), *Handbook of adolescent psychology* (3rd ed.). New York: Wiley.

Baltes, P. B., & Smith, J. (2008). The fascination of wisdom: Its nature, ontogeny, and function. *Perspectives in Psychological Sciences, 3,* 56–64.

Bandura, A. (1991). Social cognitive theory of moral thought and action. In W. M. Kurtines & J. L. Gewirtz (Eds.), *Handbook of moral behavior and development* (Vol. 1). Hillsdale, NJ: Erlbaum.

Bandura, A. (1997). *Self-efficacy.* New York: W. H. Freeman.

Bandura, A. (1998, August). *Swimming against the mainstream: Accentuating the positive aspects of humanity.* Paper presented at the meeting of the American Psychological Association, San Francisco.

Bandura, A. (2000). Self-efficacy. In A. Kazdin (Ed.), *Encyclopedia of psychology.* Washington, DC, and New York: American Psychological Association and Oxford University Press.

Bandura, A. (2001). Social cognitive theory. *Annual Review of Psychology* (Vol. 52). Palo Alto, CA: Annual Reviews.

Bandura, A. (2002). Selective moral disengagement in the exercise of moral agency. *Journal of Moral Education, 31,* 101–119.

Bandura, A. (2004, May). *Toward a psychology of human agency.* Paper presented at the meeting of the American Psychological Society, Chicago.

Bandura, A. (2007). Social cognitive theory. In W. Donsbach (Ed.), *International encyclopedia of communication.* Thousand Oaks, CA: Sage.

Bandura, A. (2008). Reconstrual of "free will" from the agentic perspective of social cognitive theory. In J. Baer, J. C. Kaufman, & R. F. Baumeister (Eds.), *Are we free? Psychology and free will.* Oxford, UK: Oxford University Press.

Bandura, A. (2009). Social and policy impact of social cognitive theory. In M. Mark, S. Donaldson & B. Campell (Eds.), *Social psychology and program/policy evaluation.* New York: Guilford.

Bandura, A. (2010a). Self-efficacy. In D. Matsumoto (Ed.), *Cambridge dictionary of psychology.* New York: Cambridge University Press.

Bandura, A. (2010b). Vicarious learning. In D. Matsumoto (Ed.), *Cambridge dictionary of psychology.* New York: Cambridge University Press.

Bangdiwala, S. I., & others. (2010). NIH consensus development conference draft statement on vaginal birth after cesarean: New insights. *NIH Consensus Statements and Scientific Statements, 27*(3).

Bank, L., Burraston, B., & Snyder, J. (2004). Sibling conflict and ineffective parenting as predictors of adolescent boys' antisocial behavior and peer difficulties: Additive and interactive effects. *Journal of Research on Adolescence, 14,* 99–125.

Banks, J. A. (Ed.) (2010). *The Routledge international companion to multicultural education.* New York: Routledge.

Banks, M. S. (2005). The benefits and costs of combining information between and within the senses. In J. J. Reiser, J. J. Lockman, & C. A. Nelson (Eds.), *The role of action in learning and development.* Mahwah, NJ: Erlbaum.

Banta, S. (2010). The experiences and perspectives of Japanese substitute caregivers and maltreated children: A cultural-developmental approach to child welfare practice. *Social Work, 55,* 127–137.

Barabasz, A., & Perez, N. (2007). Salient findings: Hypnotizability as core construct and the clinical utility of hypnosis. *International Journal of Clinical Hypnosis, 55,* 372–379.

Barbarin, O. A., & Aikens, N. (2009). Supporting parental practices in the language and literacy development of young children. In O. A. Barbarin & H. Wasik (Eds.), *Handbook of child development and early education.* New York: Guilford.

Barbarin, O. A., & Miller, K. M. (2009). Developmental science and early education: An introduction. In O. A. Barbarin & B. H. Wasik (Eds.), *Handbook of child development and early education.* New York: Oxford University.

Barber, B., Stone, M., & Eccles, J. (2010). Protect, prepare, support, and engage: The roles of school-based extracurricular activities in students' development. In J. Meece & J. Eccles (Eds.), *Handbook of research on schools, schooling, and human development.* New York: Routledge.

Barbu-Roth, M., Anderson, D. I., Despres, A., Provasi, J., Cabrol, D., & Campos, J. J. (2009). Neonatal stepping in relation to terrestrial optical flow. *Child Development, 80,* 8–14.

Barlett, C. P., & Anderson, C. A. (2009). Violent video games and public policy. In T. Bevc & H. Zapf (Eds.), *Wie wir spielen, was wir werden: Computerspiele in unserer Gesellschaft.* Konstanz: UVK Verlagsgesellschaft. (German version)

Barlett, C. P., Anderson, C. A., & Swing, E. L. (2009). Video game effects confirmed, suspected and speculative: A review of the evidence. *Simulation & Gaming, 40,* 377–403.

Barnett, W. S., & others. (2006). *Educational effectiveness of the Tools of the Mind curriculum: A randomized trial.* New Brunswick, NJ: National Institute of Early Education Research, Rutgers University.

Barnouw, V. (1975). *An introduction to anthropology: Vol. 2. Ethnology.* Homewood, IL: Dorsey Press.

Baron, N. S. (1992). *Growing up with language.* Reading, MA: Addison-Wesley.

Baron-Cohen, S. (2008). Autism, hypersystemizing, and truth. *Quarterly Journal of Experimental Psychology, 61,* 64–75.

Baron-Cohen, S. (2009). Autism: The empathizing-systematizing (E-S) theory. *Annals of the New York Academy of Sciences, 1156,* 68–80.

Baron-Cohen, S. (2011). The empathizing-systematizing (E-S) theory of autism: A cognitive developmental account. In U. Goswami (Ed.), *Wiley-Blackwell handbook of childhood cognitive development* (2nd ed.). New York: Wiley-Blackwell.

Baron-Cohen, S., Golan, O., Chapman, E., & Granader, Y. (2007). Transported to a world of emotions. *The Psychologist, 20,* 76–77.

Barrett, D. E., Radke-Yarrow, M., & Klein, R. E. (1982). Chronic malnutrition and child behavior: Effects of calorie supplementation on social and emotional functioning at school age. *Developmental Psychology, 18,* 541–556.

Barrett, T. M., Traupman, E., & Needham, A. (2008). Infants' visual anticipation of object structure in grasp planning. *Infant Behavior and Development, 31,* 1–9.

Barta, E., & Drugan, A. (2010). Glucose transfer from mother to fetus: A theoretical study. *Journal of Theoretical Biology, 263,* 295–302.

Bartle, C. (2007). Developing a service for children with iron deficiency anemia. *Nursing Standard, 21,* 44–49.

Bartsch, K., & Wellman, H. M. (1995). *Children talk about the mind.* Oxford, UK: Oxford University Press.

Bates, J. E. (2008). Unpublished review of J. W. Santrock, *Children* (11th ed.). New York: McGraw-Hill.

Bates, J. E. & Pettit, G. S. (2007). Temperament, parenting, and socialization. In J. E. Grusec & P. D. Hastings (Eds.), *Handbook of socialization.* New York: Guilford.

Battistich, V. A. (2008). The Child Development Project: Creating caring school communities. In L. Nucci & D. Narváez (Eds.), *Handbook of moral and character education.* Clifton, NJ: Psychology Press.

Bauer, P. J. (2006). Event memory. In W. Damon & R. Lerner (Eds.), *Handbook of child psychology* (6th ed.). New York: Wiley.

Bauer, P. J. (2007). *Remembering the times of our lives.* Mahwah. NJ: Erlbaum.

Bauer, P. J. (2009). Learning and memory: Like a horse and carriage. In A. Netdham & A. Woodward (Eds.), *Learning and the infant mind.* New York: Oxford University Press.

Bauer, P. J., Larkina, M., & Deocampo, J. (2011). Early memory development. In U. Goswami (Ed.), *Wiley-Blackwell handbook of childhood cognitive development* (2nd ed.). New York: Wiley-Blackwell.

Bauer, P. J., Wenner, J. A., Dropik, P. I., & Wewerka, S. S. (2000). Parameters of remembering and forgetting in the transition from infancy to early childhood. *Monographs of the Society for Research in Child Development, 65* (4, Serial No. 263).

Bauerlein. M. (2008). *The dumbest generation: How the digital age stupefies young Americans and jeopardizes our future (Or, don't trust anyone under 30).* New York: Tarcher.

Baumeister, R. F., Campbell, J. D., Krueger, J. L., & Vohs, K. D. (2003). Does high self-esteem cause better performance, interpersonal success, happiness, or healthier lifestyles? *Psychological Science in the Public Interest, 4*(1), 1–44.

Baumrind, D. (1971). Current patterns of parental authority. *Developmental Psychology Monographs, 4* (1, Pt. 2).

Baumrind, D. (1999, November). Unpublished review of J. W. Santrock's *Child development* (9th ed.). New York: McGraw-Hill.

Baumrind, D., Larzelere, R. E., & Cowan, P. A. (2002). Ordinary physical punishment: Is it harmful? Comment on Gershoff. *Psychological Bulletin, 128,* 590–595.

Bauserman, R. (2002). Child adjustment in joint-custody versus sole-custody arrangements: A meta-analytic review. *Journal of Family Psychology, 16,* 91–102.

Bayley, N. (1969). *Manual for the Bayley Scales of Infant Development.* New York: Psychological Corporation.

Bayley, N. (2006). *Bayley Scales of Infant and Toddler Development* (3rd ed.). San Antonio: Harcourt Assessment.

Bayraktar, M. R. Ozerol, I. H., Gucluer, N., & Celik, O. (2010). Prevalence and antibiotic susceptibility: Mycoplasma hominis and Ureaplasma urealyticum in pregnant women. *International Journal of Infectious Diseases, 14,* e90–e95.

Baysinger, C. L. (2010). Imaging during pregnancy. *Anesthesia and Analgesia, 110,* 863–867.

Bearman, S. K., Presnall, K., Martinez, E., & Stice, E. (2006). The skinny on body dissatisfaction: A longitudinal study of adolescent girls and boys. *Journal of Youth and Adolescence, 35,* 217–229.

Beatty, J. J., & Pratt, L. (2011). *Early literacy in preschool and kindergarten* (3rd ed.). Boston: Allyn & Bacon.

Beauchamp, M. H., & Anderson, V. (2010). SOCIAL: An integrative framework for the development of social skills. *Psychological Bulletin, 136,* 39–64.

Bechtold, A. G., Bushnell, E. W., & Salapatck, P. (1979, April.) *Infants' visual localization of visual and auditory targets.* Paper presented at the meeting of the Society for Research in Child Development, San Francisco.

Beck, C. T. (2006). Postpartum depression: It isn't just the blues. *American Journal of Nursing, 106,* 40–50.

Beeghly, M., Martin, B., Rose-Jacobs, R., Cahral, H., Heeren, T., Augustyn, M., Bellinger, D., & Frank, D. A. (2006). Prenatal cocaine exposure and children's language functioning at 6 and 9.5 years: Moderating effects of child age, birthweight, and gender. *Journal of Pediatric Psychology, 31,* 98–115.

Beets, M. W., & Foley, J. T. (2008). Association of father involvement and neighborhood quality with kindergarteners' physical activity: A multilevel structural equation model. *American Journal of Health Promotion, 22,* 195–203.

Beghetto, R. A., & Kaufman, J. C. (Eds.). (2010). *Nurturing creativity in the classroom.* New York: Cambridge University Press.

Begley, S., & Interlandi, J. (2008, June 2). The dumbest generation? Don't be dumb. *Newsweek.* Retrieved on July 22, 2008, from www.newsweek.com/id/138536/

Begum, E. A., & others. (2008). Cerebral oxygenation responses during kangaroo care in low birth weight infants. *BMC Pediatrics, 8,* 51.

Beilock, S. L, Rydell, R. J., & McConnell, A. R. (2007). Stereotype threat and working memory: Mechanisms, alleviation, and spillover. *Journal of Experimental Psychology: General, 136,* 256–276.

Bell, K. N., & Oakley, G. P. (2009). Update on prevention of folic acid-preventable spina bifida and anencephaly. *Birth Defects Research Part A: Clinical and Molecular Terotology, 85,* 102–107.

Bell, M. A., & Fox, N. A. (1992). The relations between frontal brain activity and cognitive development during infancy. *Child Development, 63,* 1142–1163.

Bell, M. A., Greene, D. R., & Wolfe, C. D. (2010). Psychobiological mechanisms of cognition-emotion integration in early development. In S. D. Calkins & M. A. Bell (Eds.), *Child development at the intersection of emotion and cognition.* Washington, DC: American Psychological Association.

Bell, M. A., & Morasch, K. C. (2007). Individual differences in the development of working memory during infancy. In L. M. Oakes & P. J. Bauer (Eds.), *Short- and long-term memory in early childhood: Taking the first steps toward remembering.* New York: Guilford.

Bell, M. A., & Wolfe, C. D. (2007). The use of the electroencephalogram in research on cognitive development. In L. A. Schmidt & S. J. Segalowitz (Eds.), *Developmental psychophysiology: Theory, systems, and methods.* New York: Cambridge.

Bell, S. M., & Ainsworth, M. D. S. (1972). Infant crying and maternal responsiveness. *Child Development, 43,* 1171–1190.

Bellinger, D. C. (2008). Very low lead exposures and children's neurodevelopment. *Current Opinion in Pediatrics, 20,* 172–177.

Belsky, J. (1981). Early human experience: A family perspective. *Developmental Psychology, 17,* 3–23.

Belsky, J. (2009). Classroom composition, childcare history, and social development: Are childcare effects disappearing or spreading? *Social Development, 18,* 230–238.

Belsky, J., Jaffe, S., Hsieh, K., & Silva, P. (2001). Child-rearing antecedents of intergenerational relations in young adulthood: A prospective study. *Developmental Psychology, 37,* 801–813.

Belson, W. (1978). *Television violence and the adolescent boy.* London: Saxon House.

Bem, S. L. (1977). On the utility of alternative procedures for assessing psychological androgyny. *Journal of Consulting and Clinical Psychology, 45,* 196–205.

Bender, H. L., Allen, J. P., McElhaney, K. B., Antonishak, J., Moore, C. M., Kello, H. O., & Davis, S. M. (2007). Use of harsh physical discipline and developmental outcomes in adolescence. *Development and Psychopathology, 19,* 227–242.

Bendersky, M., & Sullivan, M. W. (2007). Basic methods in infant research. In A. Slater & M. Lewis (Eds.), *Infant development* (2nd ed.). New York: Oxford University Press.

Benn, P. A., & Chapman, A. R. (2010). Ethical challenges in providing noninvasive prenatal diagnosis. *Current Opinion in Obstetrics and Gynecology, 22,* 128–134.

Benner, A. D., & Mistry, R. S. (2007). Congruence of mother and teacher educational expectations and low-income youth's academic competence. *Journal of Educational Psychology, 99,* 140–153.

Bennett, C. I. (2011). *Comprehensive multicultural education.* Boston: Allyn & Bacon.

Bennett, T., & others. (2008). Differentiating autism and Asperger syndrome on the basis of language delay or impairment. *Journal of Autism and Developmental Disorders, 38,* 616–625.

Benoit, D., Coolbear, J., & Crawford, A. (2008). Abuse, neglect, and maltreatment of infants. In M. M. Haith & J. B. Benson (Eds.), *Encyclopedia of infant and early childhood development.* Oxford, UK: Elsevier.

Benson, J. M., & Therrell, B. L. (2010). History and current status of newborn screening for hemoglobinopathies. *Seminars in Perinatology, 34,* 134–144.

Benson, L., Baer, H. J., & Kaelber, D. C. (2009). Trends in the diagnosis of overweight and obesity in children and adolescents: 1999–2007. *Pediatrics, 123,* e153–e158.

Benveniste, L., Carnoy, M., & Rothstein, R. (2003). *All else equal.* New York: Routledge-Farmer.

Berenbaum, S. A., & Bailey, J. M. (2003). Effects on gender identity of prenatal androgens and genital appearance: Evidence from girls with congenital adrenal hyperplasia. *Journal of Clinical Endocrinology and Metabolism, 88,* 1102–1106.

Bergen, D. (1988). Stages of play development. In D. Bergen (Ed.), *Play as a medium for learning and development.* Portsmouth, NH: Heinemann.

Bergen, D., & Fromberg, D. P. (2009). Play and social interaction in middle childhood. *Phi Delta Kappan, 90,* 426–430.

Berghella, V., Baxter, J. K., & Chauhan, S. P. (2008). Evidence-based labor and delivery management. *American Journal of Obstetrics and Gynecology, 199,* 445–454.

Berk, L. E. (1994). Why children talk to themselves. *Scientific American, 271*(5), 78–83.

Berk, L. E., & Spuhl, S. T. (1995). Maternal interaction, private speech, and task performance in preschool children. *Early Childhood Research Quarterly, 10,* 145–169.

Berko, J. (1958). The child's learning of English morphology. *Word, 14,* 15–177.

Berko Gleason, J. (2003). Unpublished review of J. W. Santrock's *Life-span development,* 9th ed. (New York: McGraw-Hill).

Berko Gleason, J. (2005). The development of language: An overview and a preview. In J. Berko Gleason (Ed.), *The development of language* (6th ed.). Boston: Allyn & Bacon.

Berko Gleason, J. (2009). The development of language. An overview. In J. Berko Gleason & N. B. Rather (Eds.), *The development of language* (7th ed.). Boston: Allyn & Bacon.

Berko Gleason, J., & Ratner, N. B. (Eds.). (2009). *The development of language* (7th ed.). Boston: Allyn & Bacon.

Berkowitz, M. W., Battistich, V. A., & Bier, M. (2008). What works in character education: What is known and what needs to be known. In L. Nucci & D Narvaez (Eds.), *Handbook of moral and character education.* New York: Psychology Press.

Berlin, C. M., Paul, I. M., & Vesell, E. S. (2009). Safety issues of maternal drug therapy during breastfeeding. *Clinical Pharmacology and Therapeutics, 85,* 20–22.

Berman, R. A. (2010). Developing linguistic knowledge and language use across adolescence. In E. Hoff & M. Shatz (Eds.), *Blackwell handbook of language development.* New York: Wiley.

Bernard, K., & Dozier, M. (2008). Adoption and foster placement. In M. M. Haith & J. B. Benson (Eds.), *Encyclopedia of infant and early childhood development.* Oxford, UK: Elsevier.

Berndt, T. J. (1979). Developmental changes in conformity to peers and parents. *Developmental Psychology, 15,* 608–616.

Berndt, T. J. (1982). The features and effects of friendships in early adolescence. *Child Development, 53,* 1447–1460.

Berndt, T. J. (1999). Friends' influence on children's adjustment. In W. A. Collins & B. Laursen (Eds.), *Relationships as developmental contexts.* Mahwah, NJ: Erlbaum.

Berndt, T. J., & Perry, T. B. (1990). Distinctive features and effects of early adolescent friendships. In R. Montemayor (Ed.), *Advances in adolescent research.* Greenwich, CT: JAI Press.

Berninger, V. W. (2006). Learning disabilities. In W. Damon & R. Lerner (Eds.), *Handbook of child psychology* (6th ed.). New York: Wiley.

Berninger, V. W., & Abbott, R. (2005, April). *Paths leading to reading comprehension in at-risk and normally developing second-grade readers.* Paper presented at the meeting of the Society for Research in Child Development, Atlanta.

Bertenthal, B. I. (2008). Perception and action. In M. M. Haith & J. B. Benson (Eds.), *Infant and early childhood development.* Oxford, UK: Elsevier.

Bertenthal, B. I., Longo, M. R., & Kenny, S. (2007). Phenomenal permanence and the development of predictive tracking in infancy. *Child Development, 78,* 350–363.

Bertoglio, K., & Hendren, R. L. (2009). New developments in autism. *Psychiatric Clinics of North America, 32,* 1–14.

Best, D. L. (2010). Gender. In M. H. Bornstein (Ed.), *Handbook of cultural developmental science.* New York: Psychology Press.

Betz, N. E. (2004). Contributions of self-efficacy theory to career counseling: A personal perspective. *Career Development Quarterly, 52,* 340–353.

Bialystok, E. (1997). Effects of bilingualism and biliteracy on children's emerging concepts of print. *Developmental Psychology, 33,* 429–440.

Bialystok, E. (2001). *Bilingualism in development: Language, literacy, and cognition.* New York: Cambridge University Press.

Bialystok, E. (2007). Acquisition of literacy in preschool children: A framework for research. *Language Learning, 57,* 45–77.

Bialystok, E., & Craik, F.I.M. (2010). Cognitive and linguistic processing in the bilingual mind. *Current Directions in Psychological Science, 19,* 19–23.

Bibok, M. B., Carpendale, J. I. M., & Muller, U. (2009). Parental scaffolding and the development of executive function. *New Directions in Child and Adolescent Development, 123,* 17–34.

Bigelow, A. E., & others. (2010). Maternal sensitivity throughout infancy: Continuity and relation to attachment security. *Infant Behavior and Development, 33,* 50–60.

Biggs, B. K., & Vernberg, E. M. (2010). Preventing and treating bullying and victimization: Best practices and future directions. In E. M. Vernberg & B. K. Biggs (Eds.), *Preventing and treating bullying and victimization.* New York: Oxford University Press.

Bill and Melinda Gates Foundation. (2006). *The silent epidemic: Perspectives on high school dropouts.* Seattle: Author.

Bill and Melinda Gates Foundation. (2008). *Report gives voice to dropouts.* Retrieved July 5, 2008, from www.gatesfoundation.org/UnitedStates/Education/TransformingHighSchools/Related.

Billy, J. O. G., Rodgers, J. L., & Udry, J. R. (1984). Adolescent sexual behavior and friendship choice. *Social Forces, 62,* 653–678.

Binder, T., & Vavrinkova, B. (2008). Prospective randomized comparative study of the effect of buprenorphine, methadone, and heroin on the course of pregnancy, birthweight of newborns, early postpartum adaptation, and the course of neonatal abstinence syndrome (NAS). *Neuoroendocrinology Letters, 29,* 80–86.

Birman, B. F., & others. (2007). *State and local implementation of the "No Child Left Behind Act." Volume II—Teacher quality under "NCLB": Interim report.* Jessup, MD: U.S. Department of Education.

Bishop, K. M., & Wahlsten, D. (1997). Sex differences in the human corpus callosum: Myth or reality? *Neuroscience and Biobehavioral Reviews, 21,* 581–601.

Bjorklund, D. (2005). *Children's thinking* (4th ed.). Belmont, CA: Wadsworth.

Bjorklund, D. F. (2007). *Why youth is not wasted on the young.* Malden, MA: Blackwell.

Bjorklund, D. F., Dukes, C., & Brown, R. D. (2009). The development of memory strategies in infancy and childhood. In M. Courage & N. Cowan (Eds.) *The development of memory in infancy and childhood.* New York: Psychology Press.

Bjorklund, D. F., & Pellegrini, A. D. (2002). *The origins of human nature.* New York: Oxford University Press.

Bjorklund, D. F., & Rosenbaum, K. (2000). Middle childhood: Cognitive development. In A. Kazdin (Ed.), *Encyclopedia of psychology.* Washington, DC & New York: American Psychological Association and Oxford University Press.

Black, M. M., & Hurley, K. M. (2007). Helping children develop healthy eating habits. In Tremblay, R. E., Barr, R. G., Peters, R., & Boivin, M. (Eds.), *Encyclopedia on early childhood development* (Rev. Ed.). Retrieved March 11, 2008 at www.child-encyclopedia.com/en-ca/child-eating-behaviour/acording-to-experts.html

Black, M. M., Hurley, K. M., Oberlander, S. E., Hager, E. R., McGill, A. E., White, N. T., & Quigg, A. M. (2009). Participants' comments on changes in the revised special supplemental nutrition program for women, infants, and children food packages: the Maryland food preference study. *Journal of the American Dietetic Association, 109,* 116–123.

Black, M. M., & Lozoff, B. (2008). Nutrition and diet. In M. M. Haith & J. B. Benson (Eds.), *Encyclopedia of infant and early childhood development.* Oxford, UK: Elsevier.

Blackwell, L. S., & Dweck, C. S. (2008). *The motivational impact of a computer-based program that teaches how the brain changes with learning.* Unpublished manuscript, Department of Psychology, Stanford University, Palo Alto, CA.

Blackwell, L. S., Trzesniewski, K. H., & Dweck, C. S. (2007). Implicit theories of intelligence predict achievement across an adolescent tradition: A longitudinal study and an intervention. *Child Development, 78,* 246–263.

Blaga, O. M., Shaddy, D. J., Anderson, C. J., Kannass, K. N., Little, T. D., & Colombo, J. (2009). Structure and continuity of intellectual development in early childhood. *Intelligence, 37,* 106–113.

Blake, J. S. (2011). *Nutrition and you.* Upper Saddle River, NJ: Pearson.

Blakemore, J. E. O., Berenbaum, S. A. & Liben, I., S. (2009). *Gender development.* Clifton, NJ: Psychology Press.

Blakemore, S. J. (2010). The developing social brain: Implications for education. *Neuron, 65,* 744–747.

Blasi, A. (2005). Moral character: A psychological approach. In D. K. Lapsley & F. C. Power (Eds.), *Character psychology and character education.* Notre Dame, IN: University of Notre Dame Press.

Blass, E. (2008). Suckling. In M. M. Haith & J. B. Benson (Eds.), *Encyclopedia of infant and early childhood development.* Oxford, UK: Elsevier.

Block, J. (1993). Studying personality the long way. In D. Funder, R. D. Parke, C. Tomlinson-Keasey, & K. Widaman (Eds.), *Studying lives through time.* Washington, DC: American Psychological Association.

Blood-Siegfried, J., & Rende, E. K. (2010). The long-term effects of prenatal nicotine exposure on neurologic development. *Journal of Midwifery and Women's Health, 55,* 143–152.

Bloom, B. (1985). *Developing talent in young people.* New York: Ballantine.

Bloom, L. (1998). Language acquisition in its developmental context. In W. Damon (Ed.), *Handbook of child psychology* (5th ed., Vol. 2). New York: Wiley.

Bloom, L., Lifter, K., & Broughton, J. (1985). The convergence of early cognition and language in the second year of life. Problems in conceptualization and measurement. In M. Barrett (Ed.), *Single word speech.* London: Wiley.

Blumenfeld, P. C., Kempler, T. M., & Krajcik, J. S. (2006). Motivation and cognitive engagement in learning environments. In R. K. Sawyer (Ed.), *The Cambridge handbook of the learning sciences.* New York: Cambridge University Press.

Blumenfeld, P. C., Marx, R. W., & Harris, C. J. (2006). Learning environments. In W. Damon & R. Lerner (Eds.), *Handbook of child psychology* (6th ed.). New York: Wiley.

Blumenfeld, P. C., Pintrich, P. R., Wessles, K., & Meece, J. (1981, April). *Age and sex differences in the impact of classroom experiences on self-perceptions.* Paper presented at the biennial meeting of the Society of Research in Child Development, Boston.

Bo, L. (1994). The sociocultural environment as a source of support. In F. Nestmann & K. Hurrelmann (Eds.), *Social networks and social support in childhood and adolescence.* New York: Walter de Gruyter.

Bodrova, E., & Leong, D. J. (2007). *Tools of the mind* (2nd ed.). Geneva, Switzerland: International Bureau of Education, UNESCO.

Bohannon, J. N., & Bonvillian, J. D. (2009). Theoretical approaches to language acquisition. In J. Berko Gleason & N. B. Ratner (Eds.), *The development of language.* Boston: Allyn & Bacon.

Bohlin, G., & Hagekull, B. (1993). Stranger wariness and sociability in the early years. *Infant Behavior and Development, 16,* 53–67.

Boks, M. P., Derks, E. M., Dolan, C. V., Kahn, R. S., & Ophoff, R. A. (2010). "Forward genetics" as a method to maximize power and cost-efficiency in studies of human complex traits. *Behavior Genetics,* published online March 16, 2010.

Bolling, C. F., & Daniels, S. R. (2008). Obesity. In M. M. Haith & J. B. Benson (Eds.), *Encyclopedia of infant and early childhood development.* Oxford UK: Elsevier.

Bolte, G., Fromme, H., & the GME Study Group. (2009). Socioeconomic determinants of children's environmental tobacco smoke exposure and family's home smoking policy. *European Journal of Public Health, 19,* 52–58.

Bonney, C. R., & Sternberg, R. J. (2010, in press). Teaching and learning to think critically. In R. E. Mayer & P. A. Alexander (Eds.), *Handbook of research on learning and instruction.* New York: Routledge.

Booth, A. (2006). Object function and categorization in infancy: Two mechanisms of facilitation. *Infancy,10,* 145–169.

Booth, A. E., & Ware, E. A. (2010). Categories, concepts, and causality: A reply to Samuelson and Perone. *Cognitive Development, 25,* 154–157.

Booth, M. (2002). Arab adolescents facing the future: Enduring ideals and pressures to change. In B. B. Brown, R. W. Larson, & T. S. Saraswathi (Eds.), *The world's youth.* New York: Cambridge University Press.

Booth-LaForce, C., & Kerns, K. A. (2009). Child-parent attachment relationships, peer relationships, and peer-group functioning. In K. H. Rubin, W. M. Bukowksi, & B. Laursen (Eds.), *Handbook of peer interactions, relationships, and groups.* New York: Guilford.

Bornstein, M. H. (1975). Qualities of color vision in infancy. *Journal of Experimental Child Psychology, 19,* 401–409.

Bornstein, M. H. (2002). Parenting infants. In M. H. Bornstein (Ed.), *Handbook of parenting* (2nd ed., Vol. 1). Mahwah, NJ: Erlbaum.

Bornstein, M. H., & Cote, L. R. (2010). Immigration and acculturation. In M. H. Bornstein (Ed.), *Handbook of cultural developmental science.* New York: Routledge.

Bornstein, M. H., & Lansford, J. E. (2010). Parenting. In M. H. Bornstein (Ed.), *Handbook of cultural developmental science.* New York: Psychology Press.

Bortfeld, H., Fava, E., & Boas, D. A. (2009). Identifying cortical lateralization of speech processing in infants using near-infrared spectroscopy. *Developmental Neuropsychology, 34,* 52–65.

Bouchard, T. J., Lykken, D. T., McGue, M., Segal, N. L., & Tellegen, A. (1990). Source of human psychological differences: The Minnesota Study of Twins Reared Apart. *Science, 250,* 223–228.

Boukydis, C. F., & Lester, B. M. (2008). Mother-infant consultation during drug treatment: research and innovative clinical practice. *Harm Reduction Journal, 5,* 6.

Boulware-Gooden, R., Carreker, S., Thornill, A., & Joshi, R. M. (2007). Instruction of metacognitive strategies enhances reading comprehension and vocabulary achievement of third-grade students. *Reading Teacher, 61,* 70–77.

Boutot, E. A., & Myles, B. S. (2011). *Autism spectrum disorders.* Upper Saddle River, NJ: Merrill.

Bower, T. G. R. (1966). Slant perception and shape constancy in infants. *Science, 151,* 832–834.

Bowlby, J. (1969). *Attachment and loss* (Vol. 1). London: Hogarth Press.

Bowlby, J. (1989). *Secure and insecure attachment.* New York: Basic Books.

Bowles, T. (1999). Focusing on time orientation to explain adolescent self concept and academic achievement: Part II. Testing a model. *Journal of Applied Health Behaviour, I,* 1–8.

Bowman, M. A., Prelow, H. M., & Weaver, S. R. (2007). Parenting behaviors, association with deviant peers, and delinquency in African American adolescents: A mediated-moderation model. *Journal of Youth and Adolescence, 36,* 517–527.

Boyer, K., & Diamond, A. (1992). Development of memory for temporal order in infants and young children. In A. Diamond (Ed.), *Development and neural bases of higher cognitive function.* New York Academy of Sciences.

Boyle, J., & Cropley, M. (2004). Children's sleep: Problems and solutions. *Journal of Family Health Care, 14,* 61–63.

Boyum, L., & Parke, R. D. (1995). Family emotional expressiveness and children's social competence. *Journal of Marriage and the Family, 57,* 593–608.

Bradley, R. H., & Corwyn, R. F. (2008). Infant temperament, parenting, and externalizing behavior in first grade: A test of the differential susceptibility hypothesis. *Journal of Child Psychology and Psychiatry, 49,* 124–131.

Bradley, R. H., Corwyn, R. F., McAdoo, H., & Coll, C. (2001). The home environments of children in the United States: Part I. Variations by age, ethnicity, and poverty status. *Child Development, 72,* 1844–1867.

Brainerd, C. J., & Gordon, L. L. (1994). Development of verbatim and gist memory for numbers. *Developmental Psychology, 30,* 163–177.

Brainerd, C. J., & Reyna, V. F. (2004). Fuzzy-trace theory and memory development. *Developmental Review, 24,* 396–439.

Brams, H., Mao, A. R., & Doyle, R. L. (2009). Onset of efficacy of long-lasting psychostimulants in pediatric attention-deficit/hyperactivity disorder. *Postgraduate Medicine, 120,* 69–88.

Brandon, P. D. (2009). Poverty, childhood, and adolescence. In D. Carr (Ed.), *Encyclopedia of the life course and human development.* Boston: Gale Cengage.

Brans, R. G., & others. (2010). Brain plasticity and intellectual ability are influenced by shared genes. *Journal of Neuroscience, 30,* 5519–5524.

Bransford, J., & others. (2006). Learning theories in education. In P. A. Alexander & P. H. Winne (Eds.), *Handbook of educational psychology* (2nd ed.). Mahwah, NJ: Erlbaum.

Brazelton, T. B. (1956). Sucking in infancy. *Pediatrics, 17,* 400–404.

Brazelton, T. B. (2004). Preface: The Neonatal Intensive Care Unit Network Neurobehavioral Scale. *Pediatrics, 113, Suppl,* S632–S633.

Bredekamp, S. (2011). *Effective practices in early childhood education.* Upper Saddle River, NJ: Merrill.

Bremner, G. (2007). Perception and knowledge of the world. In A. Slater & M. Lewis (Eds.), *Introduction to infant development* (2nd ed.). Malden, MA: Blackwell.

Bremner, J. G., Slater, A. M., Johnson, S. P., Mason, U. C., Spring, J., & Bremner, M. E. (2010 in press). Development of the other-race effect in infancy: Evidence toward universality?. *Child Development.*

Brendgen, M., Lamarche, V., Wanner, B., & Vitaro, F. (2010). Links between friendship relations and early adolescents' trajectories of depressed mood. *Developmental Psychology, 46*(2), 491–501.

Brendgen, R. M. (2009). Aggression, Childhood and adolescence. In D. Carr (Ed.), *Encyclopedia of the life course and human development.* Boston: Gale Cengage.

Brent, R. L. (2009). Saving lives and changing family histories: Appropriate counseling of pregnant women and men and women of reproductive age concerning the risk of diagnostic radiation exposure during and before pregnancy. *American Journal of Obstetrics and Gynecology, 200,* 4–24.

Bretherton, I., & Munholland, K. A. (2008). Internal working models in attachment relationships: Elaborating a central construct in attachment theory. In J. Cassidy & P. R. Shaver (Eds.), *Handbook of attachment* (2nd ed.). New York: Guilford.

Bretherton, I., Stolberg, U., & Kreye, M. (1981). Engaging strangers in proximal interaction: Infants' social initiative. *Developmental Psychology, 17,* 746–755.

Brewer, M. B., & Campbell, D. T. (1976). *Ethnocentrism and intergroup attitudes.* New York: Wiley.

Bridgeland, J. M., Dilulio, J. J., & Wulsin, S. C. (2008). *Engaged for success.* Washington, DC: Civic Enterprises.

Bridgett, D. J., & others. (2009). Maternal and contextual influences and the effect of temperament development during infancy on parenting in toddlerhood. *Infant Behavior and Development, 32,* 103–116.

Bril, B. (1999). Dires sur l'enfant selon les cultures. Etat des lieux et perspectives. In B. Bril, P. R. Dasen, C. Sabatier, & B. Krewer (Eds.), *Propos sur l'enfant et l'adolescent. Quels enfants pour quelles cultures?* Paris: L'Harmattan.

Britton, J. R., Britton, H. L., & Gronwaldt, V. (2006). Breastfeeding, sensitivity, and attachment. *Pediatrics, 118,* e1436–e1443.

Brock, J. (2007). Language abilities in Williams syndrome: A critical review. *Developmental Psychopathology, 19,* 97–127.

Brockmeyer, S., Treboux, D., & Crowell, J. A. (2005, April). *Parental divorce and adult children's attachment status and marital relationships.* Paper presented at the meeting of the Society for Research in Child Development, Atlanta.

Brody, G. H., & others. (2001). The influence of neighborhood disadvantage, collective socialization, and parenting on African American children's affiliation with deviant peers. *Child Development, 72,* 1231–1246.

Brody, N. (2000). Intelligence. In A. Kazdin (Ed.), *Encyclopedia of psychology.* Washington, DC, & New York: American Psychological Association and Oxford University Press.

Brody, N. (2007). Does education influence intelligence? In P. C. Kyllonen, R. D. Roberts, & L. Stankov (Eds.), *Extending intelligence.* Mahwah, NJ: Erlbaum.

Brodzinsky, D. M., & Pinderhughes, E. (2002). Parenting and child development in adoptive families. In M. H. Bornstein (Ed.), *Handbook of parenting* (Vol. 1). Mahwah, NJ: Erlbaum.

Bronfenbrenner, U. (1986). Ecology of the family as a context for human development: Research perspectives. *Developmental Psychology, 22,* 723–742.

Bronfenbrenner, U. (2000). Ecological theory. In A. Kazdin (Ed.), *Encyclopedia of psychology.* Washington, DC, & New York: American Psychological Association and Oxford University Press.

Bronfenbrenner, U. (2004). *Making human beings human.* Thousand Oaks, CA: Sage.

Bronfenbrenner, U., & Morris, P. (1998). The ecology of developmental processes. In W. Damon (Ed.), *Handbook of child psychology* (5th ed., Vol. 1). New York: Wiley.

Bronfenbrenner, U., & Morris, P. A. (2006). The ecology of developmental processes. In W. Damon & R. Lerner (Eds.), *Handbook of child psychology* (6th ed.). New York: Wiley.

Bronstein, P. (2006). The family environment: Where gender role socialization begins. In J. Worell & C. D. Goodheart (Eds.), *Handbook of girls' and women's psychological health.* New York: Oxford University Press.

Brook, J. S., Brook, D. W., Gordon, A. S., Whiteman, M., & Cohen, P. (1990). The psychological etiology of adolescent drug use: A family interactional approach. *Genetic, Social, and General Psychology Monographs, 116,* 110–267.

Brooker, R. (2011). *Biology* (2nd ed.). New York: McGraw-Hill.

Brooks, J. G., & Brooks, M. G. (1993). *The case for constructivist classrooms.* Alexandria, VA: Association for Supervision and Curriculum.

Brooks, J. G., & Brooks, M. G. (2001). *The case for constructivist classrooms.* (2nd ed.). Upper Saddle River, NJ: Erlbaum.

Brooks. R., & Meltzoff. A. N. (2005). The development of gaze following and its relation to language. *Developmental Science, 8,* 535–543.

Brooks-Gunn, J. (2003). Do you believe in magic?: What we can expect from early childhood programs. *Social Policy Report, Society for Research in Child Development, XVII* (1), 1–13.

Brooks-Gunn, J., Johnson, A., & Leventhal, T. (2010). Disorder, turbulence, and resources in children's homes and neighborhoods. In G. W.

Evans & T. D. Wachs (Eds.), *Chaos and its influence on children's development: An ecological perspective.* Washington, DC: American Psychological Association.

Brooks-Gunn, J., & Warren, M. P. (1989). The psychological significance of secondary sexual characteristics in 9- to 11-year-old girls. *Child Development, 59,* 161–169.

Brookshear, J. G. (2009). *Computer science* (10th ed.). Upper Saddle River, NJ: Addison-Wesley.

Brophy, J. (2004). *Motivating students to learn* (2nd ed.). Mahwah, NJ: Erlbaum.

Broverman, I., Vogel, S., Broverman, D., Clarkson, F., & Rosenkranz, P. (1972). Sex-role stereotypes: A current appraisal. *Journal of Social Issues, 28,* 59–78.

Brown, A. L., & Day, J. D. (1983). Macrorules for summarizing texts: The development of expertise. *Journal of Verbal Learning and Verbal Behavior, 22,* 1–14.

Brown, B. B. (1999). Measuring the peer environment of American adolescents. In S. L. Friedman & T. D. Wachs (Eds.), *Measuring environment across the life span.* Washington, DC: American Psychological Association.

Brown, B. B. (2004). Adolescents' relationships with peers. In R. Lerner & L. Steinberg (Eds.), *Handbook of adolescent psychology* (2nd ed.). New York: Wiley.

Brown, B. B., & Larson, J. (2009). Peer relationships in adolescence. In R. L. Lerner & L. Steinberg (Eds.), *Handbook of adolescent psychology* (3rd ed.). New York: Wiley.

Brown, B. B., & Larson, R. W. (2002). The kaleidoscope of adolescence: Experiences of the world's youth at the beginning of the 21st century. In B. B. Brown, R. W. Larson, & T. S. Saraswathi (Eds.), *The world's youth.* New York: Cambridge University Press.

Brown, B. B., & Lohr, M. J. (1987). Peer-group affiliation and adolescent self-esteem: An integration of ego-identity and symbolic-interaction theories. *Journal of Personality and Social Psychology, 52,* 47–55.

Brown, L. M., & Gilligan, C. (1992). *Meeting at the crossroads: Women's and girls' development.* Cambridge, MA: Harvard University Press.

Brown, R. (1958). *Words and things.* Glencoe, IL: Free Press.

Brown, R. (1973). *A first language: The early stage.* Cambridge, MA: Harvard University Press.

Brown, W. H., Pfeiffer, K. A., Mclver, K. L., Dowda, M., Addy, C. L., & Pate, R. R. (2009). Social and environmental factors associated with preschoolers' nonsedentary physical activity. *Child Development, 80,* 45–58.

Brownell, C. (2009). *Brownell—Early social development lab.* Retrieved on November 9, 2009, from www.pitt.edu/~toddlers/ESDL/brownell.html

Brownell, C., Nichols, S., Svetlova, M., Zerwas, S. & Ramani, G. (2009). The head bone's connected to the neck bone: When do toddlers represent their own body topography? *Child Development, 81*(3), 797–810.

Brownell, C. A., Ramani, G. B., & Zerwas, S. (2006). Becoming a social partner with peers: Cooperation and social understanding in one-and two-year-olds. *Child Development, 77,* 803–821.

Bruck, M., & Ceci, S. J. (1999). The suggestibility of children's memory. *Annual Review of Psychology, 50,* 419–439.

Bruck, M., Ceci, S. J., & Hembrooke, H. (1998). Reliability and credibility of young children's reports: From research to policy and practice. *American Psychologist, 53*(2), 136–151.

Bruck, M., Ceci, S. J., & Principe, G. F. (2006). The child and the law. In W. Damon & R. Lerner (Eds.), *Handbook of child psychology* (6th ed.). New York: Wiley.

Bruine de Bruin, W., Parker, A., & Fischhoff, B. (2007). Can teens predict significant life events? *Journal of Adolescent Health, 41,* 208–210.

Brune, C. W., & Woodward, A. L. (2007). Social cognition and social responsiveness in 10-month-old infants. *Journal of Cognition and Development, 2,* 3–27.

Bruner, J. S. (1983). *Child talk.* New York: W. W. Norton.

Bruner, J. S. (1996). *The culture of education.* Cambridge, MA: Harvard University Press.

Brunstein Klomek, A., Marrocco, F., Kleinman, M., Schofeld, I. S., & Gould, M. S. (2007). Bullying, depression, and suicidality in adolescents. *Journal of the American Academy of Child and Adolescent Psychiatry, 46,* 40–49.

Bryant, J. (Ed.). (2007). *The children's television community.* Mahway, NJ: Erlbaum.

Bryant. J. B. (2009). Language in social contexts: Communication competence in the preschool years. In J. Berko Gleason & N. Ratner (Eds.), *The development of language* (7th ed.). Boston: Allyn & Bacon.

Buhimschi, C. S., & Weiner, C. P. (2009). Medications in pregnancy and lactation: part.1. Teratology. *Obstetrics and Gynecology, 113,* 166–188.

Buhrmester, D. (1990). Friendship, interpersonal competence, and adjustment in preadolescence and adolescence. *Child Development, 61,* 1101–1111.

Buhrmester, D., & Chong, C. M. (2009). Friendship in adolescence. In H. Reis & S. Sprecher (Eds.), *Encyclopedia of human relationships.* Thousand Oaks, CA: Sage.

Buhrmester, D., & Furman, W. (1987). The development of companionship and intimacy. *Child Development, 58,* 1101–1113.

Bukowski, R., & others. (2008, January). *Folic acid and preterm birth.* Paper presented at the meeting of the Society for Maternal-Fetal Medicine, Dallas.

Bukowski, W. M., Motzoi, C., & Meyer, F. (2009). Friendship as process, function, and outcome. In K. H. Rubin, W. M. Bukowski, & B. Laursen (Eds.), *Handbook of peer interactions, relationships, and groups.* New York: Guilford.

Bullock, M., & Lutkenhaus, P. (1990). Who am I? Self-understanding in toddlers. *Merrill-Palmer Quarterly, 36,* 217–238.

Bumpus, M. F., Crouter, A. C., & McHale, S. M. (2001). Parental autonomy granting during adolescence: Exploring gender differences in context. *Developmental Psychology, 37,* 161–173.

Burchinal, M. R., & Clarke-Stewart, K. A. (2007). Maternal employment and child cognitive outcomes: The importance of analytic approach. *Developmental Psychology, 43*(5), 1140–1155.

Burns, C., Dunn, A., Brady, M., Starr, N. B., & Blosser, C. (2009). *Pediatric primary care.* Oxford, UK: Elsevier.

Bursuck, W. D., & Damer, M. (2011). *Teaching reading to students who are at-risk or have disabilities* (2nd ed.). Upper Saddle River, NJ: Merrill.

Burt, S. A., McGue, M., & Iacono, W. G. (2010). Environmental contributions to the stability of antisocial behavior over time: Are they shared or non-shared? *Journal of Abnormal Child Psychology, 38,* 327–337.

Burton, R. V. (1984). A paradox in theories and research in moral development. In W. M. Kurtines & J. L. Gewirtz (Eds.), *Morality, moral behavior, and moral development.* New York: Wiley.

Bushman, B. J., Baumeister, R., Thomaes, S., Ryu, E., Begeer, S., & West, S. (2009). Looking again, and harder, for a link between low self-esteem and aggression. *Journal of Personality, 77,* 427–446.

Bushnell, I. W. R. (2003). Newborn face recognition. In O. Pascalis & A. Slater (Eds.), *The development of face processing in infancy and early childhood.* New York: NOVA Science.

Buss, D. M. (1995). Psychological sex differences: Origins through sexual selection. *American Psychologist, 50,* 164–168.

Buss, D. M. (2004). *Evolutionary psychology* (2nd ed.). Boston: Allyn & Bacon.

Buss, D. M. (2008). *Evolutionary psychology* (3rd ed.). Boston: Allyn & Bacon.

Bussey, K. & Bandura A. (1999). Social cognitive theory of gender development and differentiation. *Psychological Review, 106,* 676–713.

Bustamante-Aragones, A., Gonzalez-Gonzalez, C., de Abla, M. R., Ainse, E, & Ramos, C. (2010). Noninvasive prenatal diagnosis using ccffDNA in maternal blood: State of the art. *Expert Review of Molecular Diagnostics, 10,* 197–205.

Butcher, K., Sallis, J. F., Mayer, J. A., & Woodruff, S. (2008). Correlates of physical activity guideline compliance for adolescents in 100 cities. *Journal of Adolescent Health, 42,* 360–368.

Byrd-Williams, C. E., & others. (2008). Cardiorespiratory fitness predicts change in adiposity in overweight Hispanic boys. *Obesity, 16*(5), 1072–1077.

C

Cabrera, N., Hutchens, R., & Peters, H. E. (Eds.) (2006). *From welfare to childcare.* Mahwah, NJ: Erlbaum.

Cairns, R. B., & Cairns, B. D. (2006). The making of developmental psychology. In W. Damon & R. Lerner (Eds.), *Handbook of child psychology* (6th ed.). New York: Wiley.

Caley, L., Syms, C., Robinson, L., Cederbaum, J., Henry, M., & Shipkey, N. (2008). What human service professionals know and want to know about fetal alcohol syndrome. *Canadian Journal of Clinical Pharmacology, 15,* e117–e123.

Calkins, S. D., & Bell, M. A. (Eds.) (2010). *Child development at the intersection of emotion and cognition.* Washington, DC: American Psychological Association.

Callan, J. E. (2001). Gender development: Psychoanalytic perspectives. In J. Worrel (Ed.), *Encyclopedia of women and gender.* San Diego: Academic Press.

Cameron, J., & Pierce, D. (2008). Intrinsic versus extrinsic motivation. In N. J. Salkind (Ed.), *Encyclopedia of educational psychology.* Thousand Oaks, CA: Sage.

Campbell, A. (2010, in press). Oxytocin and human social behavior. *Personality and Social Psychology Review.*

Campbell, F. A. (2007). The malleability of the cognitive development of children of low-income African American families: Intellectual test performance over twenty-one years. In P. C. Kyllonen, R. D. Roberts, & L. Stankov (Eds.), *Extending intelligence.* Mahwah, NJ: Erlbaum.

Campbell, F. A., Pungello, E. P., Miller-Johnson, S., Burchinal, M., & Ramey, C. T. (2001). The development of cognitive and academic abilities: Growth curves from an early childhood educational experiment. *Developmental Psychology, 37,* 231–243.

Campbell, L., Campbell, B., & Dickinson, D. (2004). *Teaching and learning through multiple intelligences* (3rd ed.), Boston: Allyn & Bacon.

Campos, J. J. (2005). Unpublished review of J. W. Santrock's *Life-span development* (11th ed.). (New York: McGraw-Hill).

Campos, J. J. (2009). Unpublished review of J. W. Santrock's *Life-span development* (13th ed.). New York: McGraw-Hill.

Campos, J. J., Langer, A., & Krowitz, A. (1970). Cardiac responses on the visual cliff in prelocomotor human infants. *Science, 170,* 196–197.

Camras, L. A., & others. (1998). Production of emotional facial expressions in European American, Japanese, and Chinese infants. *Developmental Psychology, 34,* 616–628.

Canfield, R. L., & Jusko, T. A. (2008). Lead poisoning. In M. M. Haith & J. B. Benson (Eds.), *Encyclopedia of infant and early childhood development.* Oxford, UK: Elsevier.

Capaldi, D. M., & Shortt, J. W. (2003). Understanding conduct problems in adolescence from a lifespan perspective. In G. R. Adams & M. D. Berzonsky (Eds.), *Blackwell handbook of adolescence.* Malden, MA: Blackwell.

Carbonell, O. A., Alzte, G., Bustamante, M. R., & Quiceno, J. (2002). Maternal caregiving and infant security in two cultures. *Developmental Psychology, 38,* 67–78.

Cardelle-Elawar, M. (1992). Effects of teaching metacognitive skills to students with low mathematics ability. *Teaching and Teacher Education, 8*(2), 109–121.

Carey, D. P. (2007). Is bigger really better? The search for brain size and intelligence in the twenty-first century. In S. Della Sala (Ed.), *Tall tales about the mind and brain: Separating fact from fiction.* Oxford: Oxford University Press.

Carey, S. (1977). The child as word learner. In M. Halle, J. Bresman, & G. Miller (Eds.), *Linguistic theory and psychological reality.* Cambridge, MA: MIT Press.

Carlsen, K. H., & Carlsen, K. C. (2008). Respiratory effects of tobacco smoking on infants and young children. *Pediatric Respiratory Reviews, 9,* 11–20.

Carlson, C., Cooper, C., & Hsu, J. (1990, March). *Predicting school achievement in early adolescence: The role of family process.* Paper presented at the meeting of the Society for Research in Adolescence, Atlanta.

Carnegie Council on Adolescent Development. (1995). *Great transitions.* New York: Carnegie Foundation.

Carnethon, M. R., Gulati, M., & Greenland, P. (2005). Prevalence of cardiovascular disease correlates of low cardiorespiratory fitness in adolescents and adults. *Journal of the American Medical Association, 294,* 2981–2988.

Carpendale, J. I., & Chandler, M. J. (1996). On the distinction between false belief understanding and subscribing to an interpretive theory of mind. *Child Development, 67,* 1686–1706.

Carpendale, J. I. M., & Lewis, C. (2010). The development of social understanding: A relational perspective. In R. M. Lerner, W. F. Overton, A. M. Freund, & M. E. Lamb (Eds.), *Handbook of life-span development,* New York: Wiley.

Carpendale, J. I. M., Muller, U., & Bibok, M. B. (2008). Piaget's theory of cognitive development. In N. J. Salkind (Ed.), *Encyclopedia of educational psychology.* Thousand Oaks, CA: Sage.

Carpenter, J., Nagell, K., & Tomasello, M. (1998). Social cognition, joint attention, and communicative competence from 9 to 15 months of age. *Monographs of the Society for Research in Child Development, 70* (1, Serial No. 279).

Carpenter, M. (2011). Social cognition and social motivations in infancy. In U. Goswami (Ed.), *Wiley-Blackwell handbook of childhood cognitive development* (2nd ed.). New York: Wiley-Blackwell.

Carroll, J. (1993). *Human cognitive abilities.* Cambridge: Cambridge University Press.

Carskadson, M. A. (Ed.). (2002). *Adolescent sleep patterns.* New York: Cambridge University Press.

Carskadon, M. A. (2004). Sleep difficulties in young people. *Adolescent Medicine, 158,* 597–598.

Carskadon, M. A. (2005). Sleep and circadian rhythms in children and adolescents: Relevance for athletic performance of young people. *Clinical Sports Medicine, 24,* 319–328.

Carskadon, M. A. (2006, March). *Too little, too late: Sleep bioregulatory across adolescence.* Paper presented at the meeting of the Society for Research on Adolescence, San Francisco.

Carter, N., Prater, M. A., & Dyches, T. T. (2009). *What every teacher should know about: Adaptations and accommodations for students with mild to moderate disabilities.* Upper Saddle River, NJ: Prentice Hall.

Cartwright, R., Agargun, M. Y., Kirkby, J., & Friedman, J. K. (2006). Relation of dreams to waking concerns. *Psychiatry Research, 141,* 261–270.

Carvalho Bos, S., & others. (2009). Sleep and behavioral/emotional problems in children: A population-based study. *Sleep Medicine, 10,* 66–74.

Carver, K., Joyner, K., & Udry, J. R. (2003). National estimates of romantic relationships. *Annual Review of Psychology* (Vol. 60). Palo Alto. CA: Annual Reviews.

Case, R. (1987). Neo-Piagetian theory: Retrospect and prospect. *International Journal of Psychology, 22,* 773–791.

Case, R. (1999). Conceptual development in the child and the field: A personal view of the Piagetian legacy. In E. K. Skolnick, K. Nelson, S. A. Gelman, & P. H. Miller (Eds.), *Conceptual development.* Mahwah, NJ: Erlbaum.

Case, R., Kurland, D. M., & Goldberg, J. (1982). Operational efficiency and the growth of short-term memory span. *Journal of Experimental Child Psychology, 33,* 386–404.

Casey, P. H. (2008). Growth of low birth weight preterm children. *Seminars in Perinatology, 32,* 20–27.

Cashon, C. (2010). Development of specialized face perception during infancy: An information-processing perspective. In L. Oakes, C. Cashon, M. Casasola, & D. Rakison (Eds.), *Infant perception and cognition.* New York: Oxford University Press.

Caspers, K. M., Paraiso, S., Yucuis, R., Troutman, B., Arndt, S., & Philibert, R. (2009). Association between the serotonin transporter polymorphism (5-HTTLPR) and adult unresolved attachment. *Developmental Psychology, 45,* 64–76.

Caspi, A. (1998). Personality development across the life course. In W. Damon (Ed.), *Handbook of child psychology* (Vol. 3). New York: Wiley.

Caspi, A., (2003). Influence of life stress on depression: Moderation by a polymorphism in the 5-HTT gene. *Science, 301,* 386–389.

Caspi, A., Hariri, A. R., Holmes, A., Uher, R., & Moffitt, T. E. (2010). Genetic sensitivity to the environment: The case of serotonin transporter gene and its implications for studying complex diseases and traits. *American Journal of Psychiatry, 167*(5), 509–527.

Castle, J., & others. (2010). Parents' evaluation of adoption success: A follow-up study of intercountry and domestic adoptions. *American Journal of Orthopsychiatry, 79,* 522–531.

Caughey, A. B., Hopkins, L. M., & Norton, M. E. (2006). Chorionic villus sampling compared with amniocentesis and the difference in the rate of pregnancy loss. *Obstetrics and Gynecology, 108,* 612–616.

Cavanagh, S. E. (2009). Puberty. In D. Carr (Ed.), *Encyclopedia of the life course and human development.* Boston: Gale Cengage.

Cave, R. K. (2002, August). *Early adolescent language: A content analysis of child development and educational psychology textbooks.* Unpublished doctoral dissertation. University of Nevada–Reno, Reno, NV.

Ceballo, R., Huerta, M., & Ngo, Q. E. (2010). Schooling experience of Latino students. In J. Meece & J. Eccles (Eds.), *Handbook of research on schools, schooling, and human development.* New York: Routledge.

Center for Science in the Public Interest. (2008, August). *Kids' meals: Obesity on the menu.* Washington, DC: Author.

Centers for Disease Control and Prevention. (2006, December). *Assisted reproductive success rates.* Atlanta: Author

Centers for Disease Control and Prevention. (2009). *Autism and developmental disabilities monitoring (ADDM) network.* Atlanta: Author.

Centers for Disease Control and Prevention. (2009). *Body mass index for children and teens.* Atlanta: Centers for Disease Control and Prevention.

Cerda, M., Sagdeo, A., Johnson, J., & Galea, S. (2010). Genetic and environmental influences on psychiatric comorbidity: A systematic review. *Journal of Affective Disorders.* (Available online December 11, 2009.)

Ceci, S. J., & Gilstrap, L. L. (2000). Determinants of intelligence: Schooling and intelligence. In A. Kazdin (Ed.), *Encyclopedia of psychology.* Washington, DC, & New York: American Psychological Association and Oxford University Press.

Ceci, S. J., Papierno, P. B., & Kulkovsky, S. (2007). Representational constraints on children's suggestibility. *Psychological Science, 18,* 503–509.

Cetin, I., & Alvino, G. (2009). Intrauterine growth restriction: Implications for placental metabolism and transport: A review. *Placenta, 30,* Suppl A, S77–S82.

Chall, J. S. (1979). The great debate: Ten years later with a modest proposal for reading stages. In L. B. Resnick & P. A. Weaver (Eds.), *Theory and practice of early reading.* Hillsdale. NJ: Erlbaum.

Chambers, B., Cheung, A. C. K., & Slavin, R. F. (2006). Effective preschool programs for children at risk of school failure: A best-evidence synthesis. In B. Spodek & O. N. Saracho (Eds.), *Handbook of research on the education of young children.* Mahwah, NJ: Erlbaum.

Chan, C. (2008). Childhood obesity and adverse health effects in Hong Kong. *Obesity Reviews, 9,* Suppl 1, S87–S90.

Chance, P. (2009). *Learning and behavior* (6th ed.). Boston: Cengage.

Chandler, M. (1973). Egocentrism and antisocial behavior: The assessment and training of social perspective-taking skills. *Developmental Psychology, 9,* 326–332.

Chang, J. S. (2009). Parental smoking and childhood leukemia. *Methods in Molecular Biology, 472,* 103–137.

Chang, M. Y., Chen, C. H., & Huang, K. F. (2006). A comparison of massage effects on labor pain using the McGill Pain Questionnaire. *Journal of Nursing Research, 14,* 190–197.

Chao, R. (2001). Extending research on the consequences of parenting style for Chinese Americans and European Americans. *Child Development, 72,* 1832–1843.

Chao, R., & Tseng, V. (2002). Parenting of Asians. In M. H. Bornstein (Ed.), *Handbook of parenting.* Mahwah, NJ: Erlbaum.

Chao, R. K. (2005, April). *The importance of Guan in describing control of immigrant Chinese.* Paper pesented at a meeting of the Society for Research in Child Development, Atlanta.

Chao, R. K. (2007, March). *Research with Asian Americans: Looking back and moving forward.* Paper presented at a meeting of the Society for Research in Child Development, Boston.

Chassin, L., & others. (2008). Multiple trajectories of cigarette smoking and the intergenerational transmission of smoking: A multigenerational, longitudinal study of a midwestern community sample. *Health Psychology, 27,* 819–828.

Chen, C., & Stevenson, H. W. (1989). Homework: A cross-cultural examination. *Child Development, 60,* 551–561.

Chen, X., & others. (2009). Interactions of IL-12A and IL-12B polymorphisms on the risk of cervical cancer in Chinese women. *Clinical Cancer Research, 15,* 400–405.

Chen, X., Hastings, P. D., Rubin, K. H., Chen, H., Cen, G., & Stewart, S. L. (1998). Childrearing attitudes and behavioral inhibition in Chinese and Canadian toddlers: A cross-cultural study. *Developmental Psychology, 34,* 677–686.

Chen, X., & Wang, L. (2010). China. In M. H. Bornstein (Ed.), *Handbook of cultural developmental science.* New York: Psychology Press.

Chen, X. K., Wen, S. W., Yang, Q., & Walker, M. C. (2007). Adequacy of prenatal care and neonatal mortality in infants born to mothers with and without antenatal high-risk conditions. *Australian and New Zealand Journal of Obstetrics and Gynecology, 47,* 122–127.

Chen, Z-Y. (2009a). Parenting style. In D. Carr (Ed.), *Encyclopedia of the life course and human development.* Boston: Gale Cengage.

Chen, Z-Y. (2009b). Parent-child relationships, childhood, and adolescence. In D. Carr (Ed.), *Encyclopedia of the life course and human development.* Boston: Gale Cengage.

Cheng, S., Maeda, T., Yoichi, S., Yamagata, Z., Tomiwa, K., & Japan Children's Study Group. (2010). Early television exposure and children's behavioral and social outcomes at age 30 months. *Journal of Epidemiology,* Suppl 2, S482–S489.

Cheok, M. H., Pottier, N., Kager, L., & Evans, W. E. (2009). Pharmacokinetics in acute lymphoblastic leukemia. *Seminars in Hematology, 46,* 39–51.

Cherlin, A. J., & Furstenberg, F. F. (1994). Stepfamilies in the United States: A reconsideration. In J. Blake & J. Hagen (Eds.), *Annual review of sociology.* Palo Alto, CA: Annual Reviews.

Chess, S., & Thomas, A. (1977). Temperamental individuality from childhood to adolescence. *Journal of Child Psychiatry, 16,* 218–226.

Chi, M. T. (1978). Knowledge structures and memory development. In R. S. Siegler (Ed.), *Children's thinking: What develops?* Hillsdale, NJ: Erlbaum.

Childers, J. B., & Tomasello, M. (2002). Two-year-olds learn novel nouns, verbs and conventional actions from massed or distributed exposures. *Developmental Psychology, 38,* 967–978.

Children's Defense Fund. (1992). *The state of America's children, 1992.* Washington, DC: Author.

Children's Defense Fund. (2009). *Children's welfare and mental health.* Retrieved July 2, 2009, from www.childrensdefense.org

Children's Defense Fund. (2010). *Children's health.* Retrieved January 5, 2010, from www.childrensdefense.org/helping-americas-children/

Choi, N. (2004). Sex role group differences in specific, academic, and general self-efficacy. *Journal of Psychology, 138,* 149–159.

Chomsky, N. (1957). *Syntactic structures.* The Hague: Mouton.

Christakis, D. A., & others. (2009). Audible television and decreased adult words, infant vocalizations, and conversational turns. *Archives of Pediatrics & Adolescent Medicine, 163,* 554–558.

Christakis, D. A., & Zimmerman, F. J. (2007). Violent television viewing during preschool is associated with antisocial behavior during school age. *Pediatrics, 120,* 993–999.

Christakis, D. A., Zimmerman, F. J., DiGiuseppe, D. L., & McCarty, C. A. (2004). Early television exposure and subsequent attentional problems in children *Pediatrics, 113,* 708–713.

Christensen, L. B., Johnson, R. B., & Turner, L. A. (2011). *Research methods, design, & analysis* (11th ed.). Upper Saddle River, NJ: Pearson.

Christie, J., Enz, B. J., & Vukelich, C. (2011). *Teaching language and literacy* (4th ed.). Boston: Allyn & Bacon.

Chuang, S. S., & Tamis-Lemonda, C. (2009). Gender roles in immigrant families: Parenting views, practices, and child development. *Sex Roles, 60,* 451–455.

Chung-Hall, J., & Chen, X. (2010, in press). Aggressive and prosocial peer group functioning: Effects on children's social, school, and psychological adjustment. *Social Development.*

Cicchetti, D. (2011). Developmental psychopathology. In R. M. Lerner, W. F. Overton, A. M. Freund, & M. E. Lamb (Eds.), *Handbook of life-span development*. New York: Wiley.

Cicchetti, D., & Toth, S. L. (2006). Developmental psychopathology and preventive intervention. In W. Damon & R. Lerner (Eds.), *Handbook of child psychology*. (6th ed.). New York: Wiley.

Cicchetti, D., & Toth, S. L. (2011). Child maltreatment: The research imperative and the exploration of results to clinical contexts. In B. Lester & J. D. Sparrow (Eds.), *Nurturing children and families*. New York: Wiley.

Cicchetti, D., Toth, S. L., Nilsen, W. J., & Manly, J. T. (2009). What do we know and why does it matter? The dissemination of evidence-based interventions for child maltreatment. In H. R. Schaffer & K. Durkin (Eds.), *Blackwell Handbook of Developmental Psychology in Action*. Oxford: Blackwell.

Cicchetti, D., Toth, S. L., & Rogosch, F. A. (2005). *A prevention program for child maltreatment*. Unpublished manuscript, University of Rochester, Rochester, NY.

Cignini, P., & others. (2010). The role of ultrasonography in the diagnosis of fetal isolated complete agenesis of the corpus callosum: A long-term prospective study. (Available online March 16, 2010.)

Cillessen, A. H. N. (2009). Sociometric methods. In K. H. Rubin, W. M. Bukowski, & B. Laursen (Eds.), *Handbook of peer interactions, relationships, and groups*. New York: Guilford.

Cisneros-Cohernour, E. J., Moreno, R. P., & Cisneros, A. A. (2000). Curriculum reform in Mexico: Kindergarten teachers' challenges and dilemmas. Proceedings of the Lilian Katz Symposium. In D. Rothenberg (Ed.), *Issues in early childhood education: Curriculum reform, teacher education, and dissemination of information*. Urbana-Champaign: University of Illinois.

Clark, B. (2008). *Growing up gifted* (7th ed.). Upper Saddle River, NJ: Prentice Hall.

Clark, E. (1993). *The lexicon in acquisition*. New York: Cambridge University Press.

Clark, E. V. (2009). What shapes children's language? Child-directed speech and the process of acquisition. In V. C. M. Gathercole (Ed.), *Routes to language: Essays in honor of Melissa Bowerman*. New York: Psychology Press.

Clarke-Stewart, K. A. (2006). What have we learned: Proof that families matter, policies for families and children, prospects for future research. In A. Clarke-Stewart & J. Dunn (Eds.), *Families count*. New York: Cambridge University.

Clarke-Stewart, K. A., & Miner, J. L. (2008). Effects of child and day care. In M. M. Haith & J. B. Benson (Eds.), *Encyclopedia of infant and early childhood development*. Oxford, UK: Elsevier.

Clay, R. (2001, February). Fulfilling an unmet need. *Monitor on Psychology*, No. 2.

Clearfield, M. W., Diedrich, F. J., Smith, L. B., & Thelen, E. (2006). Young infants reach correctly in A-not-B tasks: On the development of stability and perseveration. *Infant Behavior and Development, 29,* 435–444.

Clearfield, M. W., Dineva, E., Smith, L. B., Diedrich, F. J., & Thelen, E. (2009). Cue salience and infant perseverative reaching: Tests of the dynamic field theory. *Developmental Science, 12,* 26–40.

Clifton, R. K., Morrongiello, B. A., Kulig, J. W., & Dowd, J. M. (1981). Developmental changes in auditory localization in infancy. In R. N. Aslin, J. R. Alberts, & M. R. Petersen (Eds.), *Development of perception* (Vol. 1). Orlando, FL: Academic Press.

Clifton, R. K., Muir, D. W., Ashmead, D. H., & Clarkson, M. G. (1993). Is visually guided reaching in early infancy a myth? *Child Development, 64,* 1099–1110.

Cluett, E. R., & Burns, E. (2009). Immersion in water in labour and birth. *Cochrane Database of Systematic Reviews,* CD000111.

Coatsworth, J. D., & Conroy, D. E. (2009). The effects of autonomy-supportive coaching, need satisfaction, and self-perceptions on initiative and identity in youth swimmers. *Developmental Psychology, 45,* 320–328.

Cohen, G. L., & Prinstein, M. J. (2006). Peer contagion of aggression and health-risk behavior among adolescent males: An experimental investigation of effects on public conduct and private attitudes. *Child Development, 77,* 967–983.

Cohen, L. B. (2002, April). *Can infants really add and subtract?* Paper presented at the meeting of the International Conference on Infant Studies, Toronto.

Cohen, L. B. (2009). Commentary on Part I: Unresolved issues in infant categorization. In D. H. Rakison & L. M. Oakes (Eds.), *Early category and concept development*. New York: Oxford University Press.

Cohen, N. J., Lojkasek, M., Zadch, Z. Y., Pugliese, M., & Kiefer. H. (2008). Children adopted in China: A prospective study of their growth and development. *Journal of Child Psychology and Psychiatry, 49,* 458–468.

Cohn, J. F., & Tronick, E. Z. (1988). Mother-infant face-to-face interaction. Influence is bidirectional and unrelated to periodic cycles in either partner's behavior. *Developmental Psychology, 24,* 396–397.

Coie, J. (2004). The impact of negative social experiences on the development of antisocial behavior. In J. B. Kupersmidt & K. A. Dodge (Eds.), Children's peer relations: From development to intervention. Washington, DC: American Psychological Association.

Colapinto, J. (2000). *As nature made him*. New York: Simon & Schuster.

Colby, A., Kohlberg, L., Gibbs, J., & Lieberman, M. (1983). A longitudinal study of moral judgment. *Monographs of the Society for Research in Child Development, 48* (21, Serial No. 201).

Cole, M. (2006). Culture and cognitive development in phylogenetic, historical, and ontogenetic perspective. In W. Damon & R. Lerner (Eds.). *Handbook of child psychology* (6th ed.). New York: Wiley.

Cole, M., & Cagigas, X. E. (2010). Cognition. In M. Bornstein (Ed.), *Handbook of cultural developmental science*. New York: Psychology Press.

Cole, P. M., Dennis, T. A., Smith-Simon, K. E., & Cohen, L. H. (2009). Preschoolers' emotion regulation strategy understanding: Relations with emotion socialization and child self-regulation. *Social Development, 18*(2), 324–352.

Cole, P. M., & Tan, P. Z. (2007). Emotion socialization from a cultural perspective. In J. E. Grusec & P. D. Hastings (Eds.), *Handbook of socialization*. New York: Guilford.

Coleman-Phox, Odouli, R., & Li, D. K. (2008). Use of a fan during sleep and the risk of sudden infant death syndrome. *Archives of Pediatric and Adolescent Medicine, 162,* 963–968.

Coles, C. D., Lynch, M. E., Kable, J. A., Johnson, K. C., & Goldstein, F. C. (2010). Verbal and nonverbal memory in adults prenatally exposed to alcohol. *Alcoholism, Clinical and Experimental Research, 34*(5), 897–906.

Collins, W. A., & Steinberg, L. (2006). Adolescent development in interpersonal context. In W. Damon & R. Lerner (Eds.), *Handbook of child psychology* (6th ed.). New York: Wiley.

Collins, W. A., & van Dulmen, M. (2006). The significance of middle childhood peer competence for work and relationships in early adulthood. In A. C. Huston & M. N. Ripke (Eds.), *Developmental contexts in middle childhood*. New York: Cambridge University Press.

Collins, W. A., Welsh, D. P., & Furman, W. (2009). Adolescent romantic relationships. *Annual Review of Psychology* (Vol. 60). Palo Alto, CA: Annual Reviews.

Colom, R., & others. (2009). Gray matter correlates of fluid, crystallized, and spatial intelligence. *Intelligence, 37,* 124–135.

Colom, R., Jung, R. E., & Haier, R. J. (2007). General intelligence and memory span: Evidence for a common neuro-anatomic framework. *Cognitive Neuropsychology, 24*(8), 867–878.

Colombo, J., McCardle, P., & Freund, L. (Eds.). (2009). *Infant pathways to language*. New York: Psychology Press.

Colombo, J., Shaddy, D. J., Blaga, O. M., Anderson, C. J., Kannass, K. N., & Richman, W. A. (2009a). Attentional predictors of vocabulary from infancy. In J. Colombo, P. McCardle, & L. Freund (Eds.), *Infant pathways to language*. New York: Psychology Press.

Colombo, J., Shaddy, D. J., Blaga, O. M., Anderson, C. J., Kannass, K. N., & Richman, W. A. (2009b). Early attentional predictors of vocabulary in childhood. In J. Colombo, P. McCardle, & L. Freund (Eds.), *Infant pathways to language*. New York: Psychology Press.

Colombo, J., Shaddy, D. J., Anderson, C. J., Gibson, L. J., Blaga, O. M., & Kannass, K. N. (2010). What habituates in infant visual habituation? A psychophysiological analysis. *Infancy, 15,* 107–124.

Colombo, J., Shaddy, D. J., Blaga, O. M., Anderson, C. J., & Kannass, K. N. (2009). High cognitive ability in infancy and early childhood. In F. D. Horowitz, R. F. Subotnik, & D. J. Matthews (Eds.), *The development of giftedness and talent across the life span.* Washington, DC: American Psychological Association.

Colombo, J., Shaddy, D. J., Richman, W. A., Maikranz, J. M., & Blaga, O. M. (2004). The developmental course of attention in infancy and preschool cognitive outcome. *Infancy, 4,* 1–38.

Comer, J. (1988). Educating poor minority children. *Scientific American, 259,* 42–48.

Comer, J. (2004). *Leave no child behind.* New Haven, CT: Yale University Press.

Comer, J. (2006). Child development: The under-weighted aspect of intelligence. In P. C. Kyllonen, R. D. Roberts, & L. Stankov (Eds.), *Extending intelligence.* Mahwah, NJ: Erlbaum.

Comer, J. (2010). Comer School Development Program. In J. Meece & J. Eccles (Eds.), *Handbook of research on schools, schooling, and human development.* New York: Routledge.

Commoner, B. (2002). Unraveling the DNA myth: The spurious foundation of genetic engineering. *Harper's Magazine, 304,* 39–47.

Compas, B. E. (2004). Processes of risk and resilience during adolescence: Linking contexts and individuals. In R. Lerner & L. Steinberg (Eds.), *Handbook of adolescent psychology.* New York: Wiley.

Comstock, G., & Scharrer, E. (2006). Media and popular culture. In W. Damon & R. Lerner (Eds.), *Handbook of child psychology* (6th ed.). New York: Wiley.

Conduct Problems Prevention Research Group. (2007). The Fast Track randomized controlled trial to prevent externalizing psychiatric disorders: Findings from grades 3 to 9. *Journal of the American Academy of Child and Adolescent Psychiatry, 46,* 1250–1262.

Conduct Problems Prevention Research Group. (2010a, in press). The effects of the Fast Track preventive intervention on the development of conduct disorder across childhood. *Child Development.*

Conduct Problems Prevention Research Group. (2010b, in press). The difficulty of maintaining positive intervention effect: A look at disruptive behavior, deviant peer relations, and social skills during the middle school years. *Journal of Early Adolescence.*

Confer, J. C., & others. (2010). Evolutionary psychology. *American Psychologist, 65,* 110–126.

Conger, R., & Conger, K. J. (2008). Understanding the processes through which economic hardship influences rural families and children. In D. R. Crane & T. B. Heaton (Eds.), *Handbook of families and poverty.* Thousand Oaks, CA: Sage.

Conley, M. W. (2008). *Content area literacy: learners in context.* Boston: Allyn & Bacon.

Connell, A. M., & Dishion, T. J. (2006). The contribution of peers to monthly variation in adolescent depressed mood: A short-term longitudinal study with time-varying predictors. *Developmental Psychopathology, 18,* 139–154.

Connolly, J. A., & McIsaac, C. (2009). Romantic relationships in adolescence. In R. M. Lerner & L. Steinberg (Eds.), *Handbook of adolescent psychology* (3rd ed.). New York: Wiley.

Conradt, E., & Ablow, J. (2010, in press). Infant physiological response to the still-face paradigm: Contributions of maternal sensitivity and infants' early regulatory behavior. *Infant Behavior and Development.*

Constanzo, M., & others. (2010). The genetic landscape of a cell. *Science, 327,* 425–431.

Cook, M., & Birch, R. (1984). Infant perception of the shapes of tilted plane forms. *Infant Behavior and Development, 7,* 389–402.

Cook, T. D., Deng, Y., & Morgano, E. (2007). Friendship influences during early adolescence: The special role of friends' grade point average. *Journal of Research on Adolescence, 17,* 325–356.

Coonrod, D. V. & others. (2008). The clinical context of preconception care: Immunizations as part of preconception care. *American Journal of Gynecology, 199*(6), *Suppl 2,* S290–S295.

Cooper, C. R., & Grotevant, H. D. (1989, April). *Individuality and connectedness in the family and adolescent's self and relational competence.* Paper presented at the meeting of the Society for Research in Child Development, Kansas City.

Coopersmith, S. (1967). *The antecedents of self-esteem.* San Francisco: W. H. Freeman.

Coplan, R. J., & Arbeau, K. A. (2009). Peer interactions and play in early childhood. In K. H. Rubin, W. M. Bukowski, & B. Laursen (Eds.), *Handbook of peer interactions, relationships, and groups.* New York: Guilford.

Corbetta, D., & Snapp-Childs, W. (2009). Seeing and touching: The role of sensory-motor experience on the development of reaching. *Infant Behavior and Development, 32,* 44–58.

Cordier, S. (2008). Evidence for a role of paternal exposure in developmental toxicity. *Basic and Clinical Pharmacology and Toxicology, 102,* 176–181.

Corso, P. S., & Fertig, A. R. (2010). The economic impact of child maltreatment in the United States: Are the estimates credible? *Child Abuse and Neglect, 34*(5), 296–304.

Cosmides, L. (2011). Evolutionary psychology. *Annual Review of Psychology* (Vol. 62). Palo Alto, CA: Annual Reviews.

Cote, J. E. (2009). Identity formation and self development in adolescence. In R. M. Lerner & L. Steinberg (Eds.), *Handbook of adolescent psychology* (3rd ed.). New York: Wiley.

Council of Economic Advisors. (2000). *Teens and their parents in the 21st century: An examination of trends in teen behavior and the role of parent involvement.* Washington, DC: Author.

Courage, M. L., Edison, S. C., & Howe, M. L. (2004). Variability in the early development of visual self-recognition. *Infant Behavior and Development, 27,* 509–532.

Courage, M. L., Howe, M. L., & Squires, S. E. (2004). Individual differences in 3.5-month-olds' visual attention: What do they predict at 1 year? *Infant Behavior and Development, 127,* 19–30.

Courage, M. L., & Richards, J. E. (2008). Attention. In M. M. Haith & J. B. Benson (Eds.), *Encyclopedia of infant and early childhood development.* Oxford, UK: Elsevier.

Cowan, N., & Alloway, T. (2009). The development of working memory in childhood. In M. Courage & N. Cowan (Eds.), *The development of memory in infancy and childhood.* New York: Psychology Press.

Cowan, P. & Cowan, C. (2000) *When partners become parents: The big life change for couples.* Mahwah, NJ: Erlbaum.

Cowan, P., Cowan, C., Ablow, J., Johnson, V. K., & Measelle, J. (2005). *The family context of parenting in children's adaptation to elementary school.* Mahwah, NJ: Erlbaum.

Cowan, P. A., & Cowan, C. P. (2009). How working with couples fosters children's development. In M. S. Schulz, P. K., Kerig, M. K. Pruett, & R. D. Parke (Eds.), *Feathering the nest.* Washington, DC: American Psychological Association.

Cox, M. J., Burchinal, M., Taylor, L. C., Frosch, B., Goldman, B., & Kanoy, K. (2004). The transition to parenting: Continuity and change in early parenting behavior and attitudes. In R. D. Conger, F. O. Lorenz, & K. A. S. Wickrama (Eds.), *Continuity and change in family relations.* Mahwah, NJ: Erlbaum.

Cox, M. J., Neilbron, N., Mills-Koonce, W. R., Pressel, A., Oppenheimer, C. W., & Szwedo, D. E. (2008). Marital relationship. In M. M. Haith & J. B. Benson (Eds.), *Encyclopedia of infant and early childhood development.* Oxford, UK: Elsevier.

Cozzi, B., & others. (2010). Ontogenesis and migration of metallothionein I/II-containing glial cells in the human telencephalon during the second trimester. *Brain Research, 1327,* 16–23.

Crawford, D., & others. (2010, in press). The longitudinal influence of home and neighborhood environments on children's body mass index and physical activity over 5 years: The CLAN study. *International Journal of Obesity.*

Crean, H. F. (2008). Conflict in the Latino parent-youth dyad: The role of emotional support from the opposite parent. *Journal of Family Psychology, 22,* 484–493.

Creswell, J. W. (2008). *Educational research* (3rd ed.). Upper Saddle River, NJ: Prentice Hall.

Crick, N. R., Murray-Close, D., Marks, P. E. L., & Mohajeri-Nelson, N. (2009). Aggression and peer relationships in school-age children: Relational and physical aggression in group and dyadic contexts. In K. H. Rubin, W. M. Bukowski, & B. Laursen (Eds.), *Handbook of peer interactions, relationships, and groups.* New York: Guilford.

Crissey, S. R. (2009). Dating and romantic relationships, childhood and adolescence. In D. Carr (Ed.), *Encyclopedia of the life course and human development.* Boston: Gale Cengage.

Crockenberg, S. B. (1986). Are temperamental differences in babies associated with predictable differences in caregiving? In J. V. Lerner & R. M. Lerner (Eds.), *Temperament and social interaction during infancy and childhood*. San Francisco: Jossey-Bass.

Cromer, R. (1987). Receptive language in the mentally retarded: Processes and diagnostic distinctions. In R. Schielebusch & L. Lloyd (Eds.), *Language perspectives: Acquisition, retardation, and intervention*. Baltimore: University Park Press.

Crosnoe, R., Riegle-Crumb, C., Field, S., Frank, K., & Muller, C. (2008). Peer group contexts of girls' and boys' academic experiences. *Child Development, 79,* 139–155.

Croucher, E. (2010). Comments on shaken baby syndrome. *Nursing for Women's Health, 14,* 9–10.

Crouter, A. C. (2006). Mothers and fathers at work. In A. Clarke-Stewart & J. Dunn (Eds.), *Families count*. New York: Cambridge University Press.

Crowell, J. A., Treboux, D., & Brockmeyer, S. (2009). Parental divorce and adult children's attachment representations and marital status. *Attachment and human development, 11,* 87–101.

Crowley, K., Callahan, M. A., Tenenbaum, H. R., & Allen, E. (2001). Parents explain more to boys than to girls during shared scientific thinking. *Psychological Science, 12,* 258–261.

Cummings, E. M., El-Sheikh, M., & Kouros, C. D. (2009). Children and violence: The role of children's regulation in the marital aggression-child adjustment link. *Clinical Child and Family Psychology Review, 12*(1), 3–15.

Cummings, E. M., & Kouros, C. D. (2008). Stress and coping. In M. M. Haith & J. B. Benson (Eds.), *Encyclopedia of infant and early childhood development, Vol. 3* (pp. 267–281). San Diego: Academic Press.

Cummings, E. M., & Merrilees, C. E. (2009). Identifying the dynamic processes underlying links between marital conflict and child adjustment. In M. S. Schulz, P. K. Kerig, M. K. Pruett, & R. D. Parke (Eds.), *Feathering the nest*. Washington, DC: American Psychological Association.

Cunningham, J. N., Kliewer, W., & Garner, P. W. (2009). Emotion socialization, child emotion understanding and regulation, and adjustment in urban African American families: Differential associations across child gender. *Development and Psychopathology, 21,* 261–283.

Cunningham, P. M. (2009). *What really matters in vocabulary*. Boston: Allyn & Bacon.

Cunningham, P. M., & Allington, R. L. (2010). *Classrooms that work: They can all read and write* (5th ed.). Boston: Allyn & Bacon.

Cunningham, P. M., & Hall, D. P. (2009). *Making words first grade*. Boston: Allyn & Bacon.

Curran, K., DuCette, J., Eisenstein, J., & Hyman, I. A. (2001, August). *Statistical analysis of the cross-cultural data: The third year*. Paper presented at the meeting of the American Psychological Association, San Francisco, CA.

Cushner, K. H., McClelland, A., & Safford, P. (2009). *Human diversity in education* (6th ed.). New York: McGraw-Hill.

D

da Fonseca, E. B., Bittar, R. E., Damiao, R., & Zugiab, M. (2009). Prematurity prevention: The role of progesterone. *Current Opinion in Obstetrics and Gynecology, 21,* 142–147.

Dahl, R. E. (2004). Adolescent brain development: A period of vulnerabilities and opportunities. *Annals of the New York Academy of Sciences, 1021,* 1–22.

Daley, A. J., Macarthur, C., & Winter, H. (2007). The role of exercise in treating postpartum depression: A review of the literature. *Journal of Midwifery & Women's Health, 52,* 56–62.

Dallago, L., Christini, F. Perkins, D. D., Nation, M., & Santinello, M. (2010). The Adolescents, Life Context, and School Project: Youth voice and civic presentation. *Journal of Prevention and Intervention in the Community, 38,* 41–54.

Dalton, T. C., & Bergenn, V. W. (2007). *Early experience, the brain, and consciousness*. Mahwah, NJ: Erlbaum.

Daltro, P., & others. (2010). Congenital chest malformations: A multimodality approach with emphasis on fetal MRI imaging. *Radiographics, 30,* 385–395.

Damon, W. (1988). *The moral child*. New York: Free Press.

Damon, W. (2008). *The path to purpose*. New York: The Free Press.

Daniels, H. (2007). Pedagogy. In H. Daniels, J. Wertsch, & M. Cole (Eds.), *The Cambridge companion to Vygotsky*. New York: Cambridge University Press.

Daniels, H. (2011). Vygotsky and psychology. In U. Goswami (Ed.), *Wiley-Blackwell handbook of childhood cognitive development* (2nd ed.). New York: Wiley-Blackwell.

Darrah, J., Senthilselvan, A., & Magill-Evans, J. (2009). Trajectories of serial motor scores of typically developing children: Implications for clinical decision making. *Infant Behavior and Development, 32,* 72–78.

Darwin, C. (1859). *On the origin of species*. London: John Murray.

Dasen, P. R. (1977). Are cognitive processes universal? A contribution to cross-cultural Piagetian Psychology. In N. Warran (Ed.), *Studies in cross-cultural psychology* (Vol. 1). London: Academic Press.

D'Augelli, A. R. (1991). Gay men in college: Identity processes and adaptations. *Journal of College Student Development, 32,* 140–146.

Davidson, J. (2000). Giftedness. In A. Kazdin (Ed.), *Encyclopedia of psychology*. Washington, DC, & New York: American Psychological Association and Oxford University Press.

Davies, J., & Brember, I. (1999). Reading and mathematics attainments and self-esteem in years 2 and 6: An eight-year cross-sectional study. *Educational Studies, 25,* 145–157.

Davis, B. E., Moon, R. Y., Sachs, H. C., & Ottolini, M. C. (1998). Effects of sleep position on infant motor development. *Pediatrics, 102,* 1135–1140.

Davis, C. F., Lazariu, V., & Sekhobo, J. P. (2010, in press). Smoking cessation in the WIC program. *Maternal and Child Health Journal*.

Davis, C. L., & others. (2007). Effects of aerobic exercise on overweight children's cognitive functioning: A randomized controlled trial. *Research Quarterly for Exercise and Sport, 78,* 510–519.

Davis, L., & Keyser, J. (1997). *Becoming the parent you want to be*. New York: Broadway Books.

Davis, O. S. P, Arden, R., & Plomin, R. (2008). *g* in middle childhood: moderate genetic and shared environmental influence diverse measures of general cognitive ability at 7, 9, and 10 years in large population sample of twins. *Intelligence, 36,* 68–80.

Day, N. L., Goldschmidt, L., & Thomas, C. A. (2006). Prenatal marijuana exposure contributes to the prediction of marijuana use at age 14. *Addiction, 101,* 1313–1322.

Day, R. H., & McKenzie, B. E. (1973). Perceptual shape constancy in early infancy. *Perception, 2,* 315–320.

Deary, I. J., Penke, L., & Johnson, W. (2010). The neuroscience of human intelligence differences. *Nature Review: Neuroscience, 11,* 201–211.

Deary, I. J., Strand, S., Smith, P., & Fernandes, C. (2007). Intelligence and educational achievement. *Intelligence, 35,* 13–21.

Deater-Deckard, K., & Dodge K. (1997). Externalizing behavior problems and discipline revisited: Non-linear effects and variation by culture, context and gender. *Psychological Inquiry, 8,* 161–175.

DeCasper, A. J., & Spence, M. J. (1986). Prenatal maternal speech influences newborn's perception of speech sounds. *Infant Behavior and Development, 9,* 133–150.

De Castro Ribas, R. (2010). Central and South America. In M. H. Bornstein (Ed.), *Handbook of cultural developmental science*. New York: Psychology Press.

Deci, E. L., & Ryan, R. M. (2000). The "what" and "why" of goal pursuits: Human needs and the self-determination of behavior. *Psychological Inquiry, 11,* 227–268.

Deeley, Q., & Murphy, D. (2009). Pathophysiology of autism: Evidence from brain imaging. *British Journal of Hospital Medicine, 70,* 138–142.

DeGarmo, D. S., & Martinez, C. R. (2006). A culturally informed model of academic well-being for Latino youth: The importance of discriminatory experiences and social support. *Family Relations, 55,* 267–278.

de Haan, M., & Gunnar, M. R. (Eds.). (2009). *Handbook of developmental social neuroscience*. New York: Guilford.

de Haan, M., & Matheson, A. (2009). The development and neural bases of processing emotion in faces and voices. In M. De Haan & M. R. Gunnar (Eds.), *Handbook of developmental social neuroscience.* New York: Guilford.

de Hevia, M. D. & Spelke, E. S. (2010, in press). Number-space mapping in human infants. *Psychological Science.*

DeLeon, C. W., & Karraker, K. H. (2007). Intrinsic and extrinsic factors associated with night waking in 9-month-old infants. *Infant Behavior and Development, 30,* 596–605.

DeLoache, J. S. (1989). The development of representation in young children. In H. W. Reese (Ed.), *Advances in child development and behavior.* New York: Academic Press.

DeLoache, J. S. (2004). Early development of the understanding and use of symbolic artifacts. In U. Goswami (Ed.), *Blackwell handbook of childhood cognitive development.* Malden, MA: Blackwell.

DeLoache, J. S. (2011). Early development and use of symbolic artifacts. In U. Goswami (Ed.), *Wiley-Blackwell handbook of childhood cognitive development* (2nd ed.). New York: Wiley-Blackwell.

DeLoache, J. S., & Ganea, P. A. (2009). Symbol-based learning in infancy. In A. Woodward & A. Needham (Eds.), *Learning and the infant mind.* New York: Oxford University Press.

DeLoache, J. S., Simcock, G., & Macari, S. (2007). Planes, trains, and automobiles—and tea sets: Extremely intense interests in very young children. *Developmental Psychology, 43,* 1579–1586.

Demetriou, A. (2001, April). *Towards a comprehensive theory of intellectual development: Integrating psychometric and post-Piagetian theories.* Paper presented at the meeting of the Society for Research in Child Development Minneapolis.

Dempster, F. N. (1981). Memory span: Sources of individual and developmental differences. *Psychological Bulletin, 80,* 63–100.

Denham, S. A., Bassett., H. H., & Wyatt, T. (2007). The socialization of emotional competence. In J. E. Grusec & P. D. Hastings (Eds.), *Handbook of socialization.* New York: Guilford.

de Onis, M., de Onis, M., Onyango, A. W., Borghi, E., Garza, C., & Yang, H. (2006). Comparison of the World Health Organization (WHO) child growth standards and the National Center for Health Statistics/WHO international growth reference: Implications for child health programs. *Public Health Nutrition, 9,* 942–947.

Denmark, F. L., Russo, N. F., Frieze, I. H., & Eschuzur, J. (1988). Guidelines for avoiding sexism in psychological research: A report of the ad hoc committee on nonsexist research. *American Psychologist, 43,* 582–585.

Depp, C., Vahia, I. V., & Jeste, D. (2010). Successful aging: Focusing on cognitive and emotional health. *Annual Review of Clinical Psychology,* Vol. 6. Palo Alto, CA: Annual Reviews.

Deutsch, R. & Pruett, M. K. (2009). Child adjustment and high conflict divorce. In R. M. Galatzer-Levy and L. Kraus (Eds.), *The scientific basis of custody decisions* (2nd ed.). New York: Wiley.

Devos, T. (2006). Implicit bicultural identity among Mexican American and Asian American college students. *Cultural Diversity and Ethnic Minority Psychology, 12,* 381–402.

Dewey, J. (1933). *How we think.* Lexington, MA: D. C. Heath.

DeZolt, D. M., & Hull, S. H. (2001). Classroom and school climate. In J. Worell (Ed.), *Encyclopedia of women and gender.* San Diego: Academic Press.

Diamond, A. D. (1985). Development of the ability to use recall to guide action as indicated by infants' performance on AB. *Child Development, 56,* 868–883.

Diamond, A. (2009). The interplay of biology and the environment broadly defined. *Developmental Psychology, 45,* 1–8.

Diamond, A., Barnett, W. S., Thomas, J., & Munro, S. (2007). Preschool program improves cognitive control. *Science, 318,* 1387–1388.

Diamond, A., Casey, B. J., & Munakata, Y. (2011). *Developmental cognitive neuroscience.* New York: Oxford University Press.

Diamond, L. M., & Savin-Williams, R. C. (2009). Adolescent sexuality. In R. M. Lerner & L. Steinberg (Eds.), *Handbook of adolescent psychology* (3rd ed.). New York: Wiley.

Diamond, M., & Sigmundson, H. K. (1997). Sex reassignment at birth: Long-term review and clinical implications. *Archives of Pediatric and Adolescent Medicine, 151,* 298–304.

Diego, M. A., Field, T., & Hernandez-Reif, M. (2008). Temperature increases in preterm infants during massage therapy. *Infant Behavior and Development, 31,* 149–152.

Diego, M. A., Field, T., Hernandez-Reif, M. Schanberg, S., Kuh, C., & Gonzales-Quintero, V. H. (2009). Prenatal depression restricts fetal growth. *Early Human Development, 85,* 65–70.

Diekmann, A., & Schmidheiny, K. (2004). Do parents of girls have a higher risk of divorce? An eighteen-country study. *Journal of Marriage and the Family, 66,* 651–660.

Diener, E., & Diener, M. (1995). Cross-cultural correlates of life satisfaction and self-esteem. *Journal of Personality and Social Psychology, 68,* 653–663.

Diesendruck, G. (2010). Mechanisms of word learning. In E. Hoff & M. Shatz (Eds.), *Blackwell handbook of language development* (2nd ed.). New York: Wiley.

Dietz, L. J., Jennings, K. D., Kelley, S. A., & Marshal, M. (2009). Maternal depression, paternal psychopathology, and toddlers' behavior problems. *Journal of Clinical Child and Adolescent Psychology, 38,* 48–61.

Dishion, T. J., Andrews, D. W., & Crosby, L. (1995). Antisocial boys and their friends in adolescence: Relationship characteristics, quality,

and interactional process. *Child Development, 66,* 139–151.

Dishion, T. J., & Piehler, T. F. (2009). Deviant by design: Peer contagion in development, interventions, and schools. In K. H. Rubin, W. M. Bukowski, & B. Laursen (Eds.), *Handbook of peer interactions, relationships, and groups.* New York: Guilford.

Dishion, T. J., Piehler, T. F., & Myers, M. W. (2008). Dynamics and ecology of adolescent peer influence. In M. J. Prinstein & K. A. Dodge (Eds.), *Understanding peer influence in children and adolescents.* New York: Guilford.

Divall, S. A., & Radovick, S. (2008). Pubertal development and menarche. *Annals of the New York Academy of Sciences, 1135,* 19–28.

Dodge, K. A. (1993). Social cognitive mechanisms in the development of conduct disorder and depression. *Annual Review of Psychology, 44,* 559–584.

Dodge, K. A. (2010, in press). Social information processing models of aggressive behavior. In M. Mikulincer & P. R. Shaver (Eds.), *Understanding and reducing aggression, violence, and their consequences.* Washington, DC: American Psychological Association.

Dodge, K. A., & Conduct Problems Prevention Research Group. (2007, March). *The impact of Fast Track on adolescent conduct disorder.* Paper presented at the meeting of the Society for Research in Child Development, Boston.

Dodge, K. A., Malone, P. S., Lansford, J. E., Miller, S., Pettit, G. S., & Bates, J. E. (2010, in press). A dynamic cascade model of the development of substance-use onset. *Monographs of the Society for Research in Child Development.*

Dodge, K. A., & McCourt, S. N. (2010). Translating models of antisocial behavioral development into efficacious intervention policy to prevent adolescence violence. *Developmental Psychobiology, 52,* 277–285.

Dodge, K. A., & Pettit, G. S. (2003). A biopsychosocial model of the development of chronic conduct problems in adolescence. *Developmental Psychology, 39,* 349–371.

Doherty, M. (2009). *Theory of mind.* Philadelphia: Psychology Press.

Donatelle, R. J. (2011). *Health* (9th ed.). Upper Saddle River, NJ: Pearson.

Dondi, M., Simion, F., & Caltran, G. (1999). Can newborns discriminate between their own cry and the cry of another newborn infant? *Developmental Psychology, 35*(2), 418–426.

Donegan, S., Maluccio, J. A., Myers, C. K., Menon, P., Ruel, M. T., & Habicht, J. P. (2010, in press). Two food-assisted maternal and child health nutrition programs help mitigate the impact of economic hardship on child stunting in Haiti. *Journal of Nutrition.*

Donnerstein, E. (2002). The Internet. In V. C. Strasburger & B. J. Wilson (Eds.), *Children, adolescents, and the media.* Newbury Park, CA: Sage.

D'Onofrio, B. M., & others. (2007). Intergenerational transmission of childhood conduct problems: A children of twins study. *Archives of General Psychiatry, 64,* 820–829.

Doty, R. L., & Shah, M. (2008). Taste and smell. In M. M. Haith & J. B. Benson (Eds.), *Encyclopedia of infant and early childhood development.* Oxford, UK: Elsevier.

Dowda, M., & others. (2009). Policies and characteristics of the preschool environment and physical activity of young children. *Pediatrics, 123,* e261–e266.

Dozier, M., Stovall-McClough, K. C., & Albus, K. E. (2009). Attachment and psychopathology in adulthood. In J. Cassidy & P. R. Shaver (Eds.), *Handbook of attachment* (2nd ed.). New York: Guilford.

Draghi-Lorenz, Reddy, V., & Costall, A. (2001). Rethinking the development of "nonbasic" emotions: A critical review of existing theories. *Developmental Review, 21,* 263–304.

Drake, M. (2008). Developing resilient children after 100 years of Montessori education. *Montessori Life, 20*(2), 28–31.

Driesen, N. R., & Raz, N. (1995). The influence of sex, age, and handedness on corpus callosum morphology: A meta-analysis. *Psychobiology, 23,* 240–247.

Drummond, R. J., & Jones, K. D. (2010). *Assessment procedures* (7th ed.). Upper Saddle River, NJ: Pearson.

Duck, S. W. (1975). Personality similarity and friendship choices by adolescents. *European Journal of Social Psychology, 5,* 351–365.

Duczkowska, A., & others. (2010). Magnetic resonance imaging in the evaluation of fetal spinal canal contents. *Brain Development.* (Available online February 24, 2010.)

Dudley, R. L. (1999). Youth religious commitment over time: Longitudinal study of retention. *Review of Religious Research, 41,* 110–121.

Duncan, G., & Magnuson, K. (2008). Can society profit from investing in early education programs? In A. Tarlov (Ed.), *Nurturing the national treasure: Childhood education and development before kindergarten.* New York: Palgrave Macmillan.

Duncan, G. J., Ziol-Guest, K. M., & Kalil, A. (2010). Early-childhood poverty and adult attainment, behavior, and health. *Child Development, 81,* 306–325.

Dunn, J. (2007). Siblings and socialization. In J. E. Grusec & P. D. Hastings (Eds.), *Handbook of socialization.* New York: Guilford.

Dunn, J. (2010). Commentary and challenges to Grusec and Davidov's domain-specific approach. *Child Development, 81,* 710–714.

Dunn, J., & Kendrick, C. (1982). *Siblings.* Cambridge, MA: Harvard University Press.

Dunphy, D. C. (1963). The social structure of urban adolescent peer groups. *Society, 26,* 230–246.

Durik, A. M., Hyde, J. S., Marks, A. C., Roy, A. L., Anaya, D., & Schultz, G. (2006). Ethnicity and stereotypes of emotions. *Sex Roles, 54*(7–8), 429–445.

Durrant, J. E. (2008). Physical punishment, culture, and rights: Current issues for professionals. *Journal of Developmental and Behavioral Pediatrics, 29,* 55–66.

Durston, S. (2010, in press). Imaging genetics in ADHD. *Neuroimage.*

Durston, S., & others. (2006). A shift from diffuse to focal cortical activity with development. *Developmental Science, 9,* 1–8.

Dusek, J. B., & McIntyre, J. G. (2003). Self-concept and self-esteem development. In G. Adams & M. Berzonsky (Eds.), *Blackwell handbook of adolescence.* Malden, MA: Blackwell.

Dweck, C. S. (2006). *Mindset.* New York: Random House.

Dweck, C. S. (2007). Boosting achievement with messages that motivate. *Education Canada, 47,* 6–10.

Dweck, C. S., Mangels, J. A., & Good, C. (2004). Motivational effects on attention, cognition, and performance. In D. Yun Dai & R. J. Sternberg (Eds.), *Motivation, emotion, and cognition.* Mahwah, NJ: Erlbaum.

Dweck, C. S., & Master, A. (2009). Self-theories and motivation: Students' beliefs about intelligence. In K. R. Wentzel & A. Wigfield (Eds.), *Handbook of motivation at school.* New York: Routledge.

Dwyer, T., & Ponsonby, A. L. (2009). Sudden infant death syndrome and prone sleeping position. *Annals of Epidemiology, 19,* 245–249.

Dyck, M., & Piek, J. (2010). How to distinguish normal from disordered children with poor language or motor skills. *International Journal of Language and Communication Disorders, 45,* 336–344.

E

Eagly, A. H. (2001). Social role theory of sex differences and similarities. In J. Worrell (Ed.), *Encyclopedia of women and gender.* San Diego: Academic Press.

Eagly, A. H. (2009). Gender roles. In J. Levine & M. Hogg (Eds.), *Encyclopedia of group processes and intergroup relations.* Thousand Oaks, CA: Sage.

Eagly, A. H., & Crowley, M. (1986). Gender and helping behavior: A meta-analytic review of the social psychological literature. *Psychological Bulletin, 100,* 283–308.

Eagly, A. H., & Fischer, A. (2009). Gender inequalities in power in organizations. In B. van Knippenberg & D. Tjosvold (Eds.), *Power and interdependence in organizations.* New York: Cambridge University Press.

Eagly, A. H., & Sczesny, S. (2009). Stereotypes about women, men, and leaders: Have times changed? In M. Barreto, M. Ryan, & M. Schmitt (Eds.), *Barriers to diversity: The glass ceiling after 20 years.* Washington, DC: APA Books.

Eagly, A. H., & Steffen, V. J. (1986). Gender and aggressive behavior: A meta-analytic review of the social psychological literature. *Psychological Bulletin, 100,* 309–330.

East, P. (2009). Adolescent relationships with siblings. In R. M. Lerner & L. Steinberg (Eds.), *Handbook of adolescent psychology* (3rd ed.). New York: Wiley.

Eaton, D. K., & others. (2006, June 9). Youth risk behavior surveillance—United States, 2005. *MMWR Surveillance Summary, 55*(5), 1–108.

Eby, J. W., Herrell, A. L., & Jordan, M. L. (2011). *Teaching in elementary school: A reflective approach* (6th Ed.). Boston: Allyn & Bacon.

Eaton, W. O. (2008). Milestones: Physical. In M. M. Haith & J. B. Benson (Eds.), *Encyclopedia of infant and early childhood development.* Oxford, UK: Elsevier.

Eccles, J. (2003). Education: Junior and high school. In G. Adams & M. Berzonsky (Eds.), *Blackwell handbook of adolescence.* Malden, MA: Blackwell.

Eccles, J. S., & Roeser, R. W. (2009). Schools, academic motivation, and stage-environment fit. In R. M. Lerner & L. Steinberg (Eds.), *Handbook of adolescent psychology* (3rd ed.). New York: Wiley.

Eccles, J., & Roeser, R. W. (2010). Schools, academic motivation, and stage-environment fit. In J. Meece & J. Eccles (Eds.), *Handbook of research on schools, schooling, and human development.* New York: Routledge.

Eccles, J. S. (2007). Families, schools, and developing achievement-related motivations and engagement. In J. E. Grusec & P. D. Hastings (Eds.), *Handbook of socialization.* New York: Guilford.

Eckenrode, J., & others. (2010). Long-term effects of prenatal and infancy nurse home visitation on the life course of youths: 19-year follow-up of a randomized trial. *Archives of Pediatric and Adolescent Medicine, 164,* 9–15.

Eckerman, C. & Whitehead, H. (1999). How toddler peers generate coordinated action: A cross-cultural exploration. *Early Education & Development, 10,* 241–266.

Eden, T. (2010, in press). Etiology of childhood leukemia. *Cancer Treatment Reviews.*

Edwards, C. P., & Liu, W. (2002). Parenting toddlers. In M. H. Bornstein (Ed.), *Handbook of parenting* (2nd ed., Vol. 1). Mahwah, NJ: Erlbaum.

Edwards, R., & Hamilton, M. A. (2004). You need to understand my gender role: An empirical test of Tannen's model of gender and communication. *Sex Roles, 50,* 491–504.

Edwardson, C. L., & Gorely, T. (2010). Activity-related parenting practices and children's objectively measured physical activity. *Pediatric Exercise Science, 22,* 105–113.

Efklides, A. (2009). The role of metacognitive experiences in the learning process. *Psicothema, 21,* 76–82.

Egan, S. K., & Perry, D. G. (2001). Gender identity: A multidimensional analysis with implications for psychosocial adjustment. *Developmental Psychology, 37,* 451–463.

Egbert, J. L. (2009). *Supporting learning with technology.* Boston: Allyn & Bacon.

Ehrhardt, A. A., & Baker, S. W. (1974). Fetal androgens, human central nervous system differentiation, and behavior sex differences. In R. C. Friedman, R. M. Richart, & R. L. Vande Wiele (Eds.), *Sex differences in behavior.* New York: Wiley.

Eiferman, R. R. (1971). Social play in childhood. In R. Herron & B. Sutton-Smith (Eds.), *Child's play*. New York: Wiley.

Eisenberg, N. (2010). Emotion regulation in children. *Annual Review of Clinical Psychology* (Vol. 6). Palo Alto, CA: Annual Reviews.

Eisenberg, N., Fabes, R. A., & Spinrad, T. L. (2006). Prosocial development. In W. Damon & R. Lerner (Eds.), *Handbook of child psychology* (6th ed.). New York: Wiley.

Eisenberg, N., Morris, A. S., McDaniel, B., & Spinrad, T. L. (2009). Moral cognitions and prosocial responding in adolescence. In R. M. Lerner & L. Steinberg (Eds.), *Handbook of adolescent psychology* (3rd ed.). New York: Wiley.

Eisenberg, N., Spinrad, T., & Sadovsky, A. (2006). Empathy-related responding in children. In M. Killen & J. Smetana (Eds.), *Handbook of moral development*. Mahwah, NJ: Erlbaum.

Eisenberg, N., Spinrad, T. L., & Smith, C. L. (2004). Emotion-related regulation: Its conceptualization, relations to social functioning, and socialization. In P. Philippot & R. S. Feldman (Eds.), *The regulation of emotion*. Mahway, NJ: Erlbaum.

Eisenberg, N., & Valiente, C. (2002). Parenting and children's prosocial and moral development. In M. H. Bornstein (Ed.), *Handbook of parenting* (2nd ed.). Mahwah, NJ: Erlbaum.

Eisenhower Foundation. (2010). *Quantum Opportunities Program*. Retrieved January 5, 2010, from www.eisenhowerfoundation.org/qop.php

Ekeblad, S. (2010). Islet cell tumors. *Advances in Experimental Medicine and Biology, 654*, 771–789.

Elder, G. H., & Shanahan, M. J. (2006). The life course and human development. In W. Damon & R. Lerner (Eds.), *Handbook of child psychology* (6th ed.). New York: Wiley.

El-Fishawy, P., & State, M. W. (2010). The genetics of autism: Key issues, recent findings, and clinical implications. *Psychiatric Clinics of North America, 33*, 83–105.

Elkind, D. (1976). *Child development and education. A Piagetian perspective*. New York: Oxford University Press.

Elkind, D. (1978). Understanding the young adolescent. *Adolescence, 13*, 127–134.

Elmore, R. F. (2009). Schooling adolescents. In R. M. Lerner & L. Steinberg (Eds.), *Handbook of adolescent psychology* (3rd ed.). New York: Wiley.

Emery, R. E. (1994). *Renegotiating family relationships*. New York: Guilford Press.

Emery, R. E., & Laumann-Billings, L. (1998). An overview of the nature, causes, and consequences of abusive family relationships. *American Psychologist, 53*, 121–135.

Enfield, A., & Collins, D. (2008). The relationship of service-learning social justice multicultural competence, and civic engagement. *Journal of College Student Development, 49*, 95–109.

Enright, M. S., Schaefer, L. V., Schaefer, P., & Schaefer, K. A. (2008). Building a just adolescent community. *Montessori Life, 20*, 36–42.

Enright, R. D., Santos, M. J. D., & Al-Mabuk, R. (1989). The adolescent as forgiver. *Journal of Adolescence, 12*, 95–110.

Ensor, R., Spencer, D., & Hughes, C. (2010, in press). "You feel sad?" Emotional understanding mediates effects of verbal ability and mother-child mutuality on prosocial behaviors: Findings from 2 to 4 years. *Social Development*.

Entringer, S., Kumsta, R., Hellhammer, D. H., Wadhwa, P. D., & Wust, S. (2009). Prenatal exposure to maternal psychosocial stress and HPA axis regulation in young adults. *Hormones and Behavior, 123*, 886–893.

Entwisle, D., Alexander, K., & Olson, L. (2010). The long reach of socioeconomic status in education. In J. Meece & J. Eccles (Eds.), *Handbook of research on schools, schooling, and human development*. New York: Routledge.

Erath, S. A., Flanagan, K. S., Bierman, K. L., & Tu, K. M. (2010). Friendships moderate psychosocial maladjustment in socially anxious early adolescents. *Journal of Applied Developmental Psychology, 31*, 15–26.

Erath, S. A. Pettit, G. S., Dodge, K. A., & Bates, J. E. (2009). Who dislikes whom, and for whom does it matter: Predicting aggression in middle childhood. *Social Development, 18*, 577–596.

Ericson, N. (2001, June). *Addressing the problem of juvenile bullying*. Washington, DC: Office of Juvenile Justice and Delinquency Prevention, Office of Justice Programs, U.S. Department of Justice.

Ericsson, K. A., N. Charness, P. J. Feltovich, & R. R. Hoffman. (Eds.). (2006). *The Cambridge handbook of expertise and expert performance*. New York: Cambridge University Press.

Ericsson, K. A., Krampe, R., & Tesch-Romer, C. (1993). The role of deliberate practice in the acquisition of expert performance. *Psychological Review, 100*, 363–406.

Erikson, E. H. (1950). *Childhood and society*. New York: W. W. Norton.

Erikson, E. H. (1968). *Identity: Youth and crisis*. New York: W. W. Norton.

Eriksson, U. J. (2009). Congenital malformations in diabetic pregnancy. *Seminar in Fetal and Neonatal Medicine, 14*, 85–93.

Ernst, M., & Mueller, S. C. (2008). The adolescent brain: Insights from functional neuroimaging research. *Developmental Neuroscience, 68*, 729–743.

Escobar-Chaves, S. L., & Anderson, C. A. (2008). Media and risky behavior. *Future of Children, 18*(1), 147–180.

Espelage, D., Holt, M., & Poteat, P. (2010). The school context, bullying, and victimization. In J. Meece & J. Eccles (Eds.), *Handbook of research on schools, schooling, and human development*. New York: Routledge.

Espirito Santo, J. L., Portuguez, M. W., & Nunes, M. L. (2009). Cognitive and behavioral status of low birth weight preterm children raised in a developing country at preschool age. *Journal of Pediatrics, 85*, 35–41.

Etaugh, C. A., & Bridges, J. S. (2010). *Women's lives* (2nd ed.). Boston: Allyn & Bacon.

Evans, B. J., & Whitfield, J. R. (Eds.). (1988). *Black males in the United States: An annotated bibliography from 1967 to 1987*. Washington, DC: American Psychological Association.

Evans, G. W. (2004). The environment of childhood poverty. *American Psychologist, 59*, 77–92.

Evans, G. W., & English, K. (2002). The environment of poverty: Multiple stressor exposure, psychophysiological stress, and socioemotional adjustment. *Child Development, 73*, 1238–1248.

Evans, G. W., & Kim, P. (2007). Childhood poverty and health: Cumulative risk exposure and stress dysregulation. *Psychological Science, 18*, 953–957.

F

Fabiano, G. A., Pelham, W. E., Coles, E. K., Gnagy, E. M., Chronis-Tuscano, A., & O'Connor, B. C. (2009). A meta-analysis of behavioral treatments for attention deficit/ hyperactivity disorder. *Clinical Psychology Review, 29*(2), 129–140.

Fagan, J. F. (1992). Intelligence: A theoretical viewpoint. *Current Directions in Psychological Science, 1*, 82–86.

Fagan, J. F., Holland, C. R., & Wheeler, K. (2007). The prediction, from infancy, of adult IQ and achievement. *Intelligence, 35*, 225–231.

Fagot, B. J., Rodgers, C. S., & Leinbach, M. D. (2000). Theories of gender socialization. In T. Eckes & H. M. Trautner (Eds.), *The developmental social psychology of gender*. Mahwah, NJ: Erlbaum.

Fahey, T. D., Insel, P. M., & Roth, W. T. (2011). *Fit and well*. (9th ed.). New York: McGraw-Hill.

Fair, D., & Schlaggar, B. L. (2008). Brain development. In M. M. Haith & J. B. Benson (Eds.), *Encyclopedia of infant and early childhood development*. London, UK: Elsevier.

Fairweather, E., & Cramond, B. (2011). Infusing creative and critical thinking into the classroom. In R. A. Beghetto & J. C. Kaufman (Eds.), *Nurturing creativity in the classroom*. New York: Cambridge University Press.

Faissner, A., & others. (2010). Contributions of astrocytes to synapse formation and maturation— potential functions of the perisynaptic extracellular matrix. *Brain Research Reviews*. (Available online January 21, 2010.)

Falbo, T., & Poston, D. L. (1993). The academic, personality, and physical outcomes of only children in China. *Child Development, 64*, 18–35.

Fanconi, M., & Lips, U. (2010, in press). Shaken baby syndrome in Switzerland: Results of a prospective follow-up study, 2002–2007. *European Journal of Pediatrics*.

Fantz, R. L. (1963). Pattern vision in newborn infants. *Science, 140*, 296–297.

Faraone, S. V., & Mick, E. (2010). Molecular genetics of attention deficit hyperactivity disorder. *Psychiatric Clinics of North America, 33*, 159–180.

Faris, R. (2009). Bullying and peer victimization. In D. Carr (Ed.), *Encyclopedia of the life course and human development*. Boston: Gale Cengage.

Farrington, D. P. (2009). Conduct disorder, aggression, and delinquency. In R. M. Lerner & L. Steinberg (Eds.), *Handbook of adolescent psychology* (3rd ed.). New York: Wiley.

Farrington, D. P., Ttofi, M. M., & Coid, J. W. (2009). Development of adolescence-limited, late-onset, and persistent offenders from 8 to 48. *Aggressive Behavior, 35,* 150–163.

Fasig, L. (2000). Toddlers' understanding of ownership: Implications for self-concept development. *Social Development, 9,* 370–382.

Fearon, R. P., & others. (2010). The significance of insecure attachment and disorganization in the development of children's externalizing behavior: A meta-analytic study. *Child Development, 81,* 435–456.

Federal Interagency Forum on Child and Family Statistics. (2008). *America's children in brief: Key national indicators of well-being, 2008.* Retrieved July 31, 2008, from http://www .childstats.gov/

Feeney, S., Moravcik, E., Nolte, S., & Christensen, D. (2010). *California version of who am I in the lives of children* (8th ed.). Upper Saddle River, NJ: Prentice Hall.

Fein, G. G. (1986). Pretend play. In D. Görlitz & J. E. Wohlwill (Eds.), *Curiosity, imagination, and play.* Hillsdale, NJ: Erlbaum.

Feinberg, M. E., & Kan, M. L. (2008). Establishing family foundations: Intervention effects on coparenting, parent/infant well-being, and parent-child relations. *Journal of Family Psychology, 22,* 253–263.

Feldman, H. D. (2001, April). *Contemporary developmental theories and the concept of talent.* Paper presented at the meeting of the Society for Research in Child Development, Minneapolis.

Feldman, R., & Masalha, S. (2010). Parent-child and triadic antecedents of children's social competence: Cultural specificity, shared process. *Developmental Psychology, 46,* 455–467.

Feng, Y., Caiping, M., Li, C., Can, R., Feichao, X., Li, Z., & Zhice, X. (2010). Fetal and offspring arrhythmia following exposure to nicotine during pregnancy. *Journal of Applied Toxicology, 30,* 53–58.

Ferguson, D. M., Harwood, L. J., & Shannon, F. T. (1987). Breastfeeding and subsequent social adjustment in 6- to 8-year-old children. *Journal of Child Psychology and Psychiatry, 28,* 378–386.

Fidler, D. J. (2008). Down syndrome. In M. M. Haith & J. B. Benson (Eds.), *Encyclopedia of infancy and early childhood development.* Oxford, UK: Elsevier.

Field, A., Cartwright-Hatton, S., Reynolds, S., & Creswell, C. (Eds.). (2008). *Child anxiety theory and treatment.* New York: Psychology Press.

Field, T. (2010). Postpartum depression effects on early interactions, parenting, and safety practices: A review. *Infant Behavior and Development, 33,* 1–6.

Field, T., Diego, M., & Hernandez-Reif, M. (2008). *International Journal of Neuroscience, 118,* 277–289.

Field, T., Diego, M., & Hernandez-Reif, M. (2010). Preterm infant massage therapy research: A review. *Infant Behavior and Development, 33,* 115–124.

Field, T., Figueiredo, B., Hernandez-Reif, M., Deeds, O., & Ascencio, A. (2008). Massage therapy reduces pain in pregnant women, alleviates prenatal depression in both parents and improves their relationships. *Journal of Bodywork and Movement Therapies, 12,* 146–150.

Field, T. M. (2001). Massage therapy facilitates weight gain in preterm infants. *Current Directions in Psychological Science, 10,* 51–55.

Field, T. M. (2007). *The amazing infant.* Malden, MA: Blackwell.

Field, T. M., & others. (1997). Brief report: Autistic children's attentiveness and responsivity improve after touch therapy. *Journal of Autism and Developmental Disorders, 27,* 333–338.

Field, T. M., & others. (1998). Children with asthma have improved pulmonary functions after massage therapy. *Journal of Pediatrics, 132,* 854–858.

Field, T. M., Grizzle, N., Scafidi, F., & Schanberg, S. (1996). Massage and relaxation therapies' effects on depressed adolescent mothers. *Adolescence, 31,* 903–911.

Field, T. M., Hernandez-Reif, M., Diego, M., Feijo, L., Vera, Y., & Gil, K. (2004). Massage therapy by parents improves early growth and development. *Infant Behavior & Development, 27,* 435–442.

Field, T. M., Hernandez-Reif, M., Feije, L., & Freedman, J. (2006). Prenatal, perinatal, and neonatal stimulation, *Infant Behavior & Development, 29,* 24–31.

Field, T. M., Hernandez-Reif, M., Taylor, S., Quintino, O., & Burman, I. (1997). Labor pain is reduced by massage therapy. *Journal of Psychosomatic Obstetrics and Gynecology, 18,* 286–291.

Field, T. M., Quintino, O., Hernandez-Reif, M., & Koslosky, G. (1998). Adolescents with attention deficit hyperactivity disorder benefit from massage therapy. *Adolescence, 33,* 103–108.

Findlay, L. C., Coplan, R. J., & Bowker, A. (2009). Keeping it all inside: Shyness, internalizing coping strategies and socio-emotional adjustment in middle childhood. *International Journal of Behavioural Development, 33*(1), 47–54.

Finger, B., Hans, S. L., Bernstein, V. J., & Cox, S. M. (2009). Parent relationship quality and infant-mother attachment. *Attachment and Human Development, 11,* 285–306.

Fischhoff, B., Bruine de Bruin, W., Parker, A. M., Millstein, S. G., & Halpern-Felsher, B. L. (2010). Adolescents' perceived risk of dying. *Journal of Adolescent Health, 46,* 265–269.

Fisher, C. B. (2009). *Decoding the ethics code* (2nd ed.). Thousand Oaks, CA: Sage.

Fisher, P. A. (2005, April). *Translational research on underlying mechanisms of risk among foster children: Implications for prevention science.* Paper presented at the meeting of the Society for Research in Child Development, Washington, DC.

Fivush, R. (2009). Sociocultural perspectives in autobiographical memory. In M. Courage & N. Cowan (Eds.), *The development of memory in infancy and childhood.* New York: Psychology Press.

Flavell, J. H. (2004). Theory-of-mind development: Retrospect and prospect. *Merrill-Palmer Quarterly, 50,* 274–290.

Flavell, J. H., Friedrichs, A., & Hoyt, J. (1970). Developmental changes in memorization processes. *Cognitive Psychology, 1,* 324–340.

Flavell, J. H., Green, F. L., & Flavell, E. R. (1993). Children's understanding of the stream of consciousness. *Child Development, 64,* 95–120.

Flavell, J. H., Green, F. L., and Flavell, E. R. (1998). The mind has a mind of its own developing knowledge about mental uncontrollability. *Cognitive Development, 13,* 127–138.

Flavell, J. H., & Miller, P. H. (1998). Social cognition. In W. Damon (Ed.), *Handbook of child psychology* (5th ed.). New York: Wiley.

Flavell, J. H., Miller, P. H., & Miller, S. (2002). *Cognitive development* (4th ed.). Upper Saddle River, NJ: Prentice Hall.

Flavell, J., Mumme, D., Green, F., and Flavell E. (1992). Young children's understanding of different types of beliefs. *Child Development, 63,* 960–977.

Flegal, W. A. (2007). Blood group genotyping in Germany. *Transfusion, 47* (Suppl. I), S47–S53.

Flint, M. S., Baum, A., Chambers, W. H., & Jenkins, F. J. (2007). Induction of DNA damage, alteration of DNA repair, and transcriptional activation by stress hormones. *Psychoneuroendocrinology, 32,* 470–479.

Flom, R., & Pick, A. D. (2003). Verbal encouragement and joint attention in 18-month-old infants. *Infant Behavior and Development, 26,* 121–134.

Flom, R., & Pick, A. D. (2007). Increasing specificity and the development of joint visual attention. In R. Flom, K. Lee, & D. Muir (Eds.), *Gaze-following.* Mahwah. NJ: Erlbaum.

Florence, N. (2010). *Multiculturalism 101.* New York: McGraw-Hill.

Florsheim, P., Moore, D., & Edgington, C. (2003). Romantic relationships among adolescent parents. In P. C. Florsheim (Ed.), *Adolescent romantic relations and sexual behavior.* Oxford, UK: Routledge.

Flouri, E., & Buchanan, A. (2004). Early father's and mother's involvement and child's later educational outcomes. *British Journal of Educational Psychology, 74,* 141–153.

Flynn, J. R. (1999). Searching for justice: The discovery of IQ gains over time. *American Psychologist, 54,* 5–20.

Flynn, J. R. (2007a). The history of the American mind in the 20th century: A scenario to explain gains over time and a case for the irrelevance of *g*. In P. C. Kyllonen, R. D. Roberts, & L. Stankov (Eds.), *Extending intelligence.* Mahwah, NJ: Erlbaum.

Flynn, J. R. (2007b). *What is intelligence? Beyond the Flynn effect.* New York: Cambridge University Press.

Fogelholm, M. (2008). How physical activity can work. *International Journal of Pediatric Obesity, 3, Suppl,* S10–S14.

Follari, L. (2011). *Foundations and best practices in early childhood education* (2nd ed.). Upper Saddle River, NJ: Merrill.

Fonseca, E. B., Celik, E., Parra, M., Singh, M., Nicolaides, K. H., & Fetal Medicine Foundation Second Trimester Screening Group. (2007). Progesterone and the risk of preterm birth among women with a short cervix. *New England Journal of Medicine, 357,* 462–469.

Fontaine, R. G., & Dodge, K. A. (2009). Social information processing and aggressive behavior: A transactional perspective. In A. J. Sameroff (Ed.), *The transactional model of development: How children and contexts shape each other* (pp. 117–135). Washington, DC: American Psychological Association.

Fontenot, H. B. (2007). Transition and adaptation to adoptive motherhood. *Journal of Obstetrics, Gynecologic, and Neonatal Nursing, 36,* 175–182.

Food & Nutrition Service. (2009). *The new look of the women, infants, and children (WIC) program.* Retrieved January 21, 2009 from www.health.state.ny.us/prevention/nutrition/wic/the_new_look_of_wic.htm

Forcier, R. C., & Descy, D. E. (2008). *Computer as an educational tool* (5th ed.). Boston: Allyn & Bacon.

Forgatch, M. S., Patterson, G. R., Degarmo, D. S., & Beldavs, Z. G. (2009). Testing the Oregon delinquency model with 9-year follow-up of the Oregon Divorce Study. *Development and Psychopathology, 21,* 637–660.

Forget-Dubois, N., Dionne, G., Lemelin, J-P., Perusse, D., Tremblay, R. E., & Boivin, M. (2009). Early child language mediates the relation between home environment and school readiness. *Child Development, 80,* 736–749.

Forster, B., Eardley, A. F., & Eimer, M. (2007). Altered tactile spatial attention in the early blind. *Brain Research, 113,* 149–154.

Fosco, G. M., & Grych, J. H. (2010). Adolescent triangulation into parental conflicts: Longitudinal implications for appraisals and adolescent-parent relations. *Journal of Marriage and the Family, 72,* 254–266.

Fox, M. K., Pac, S., Devaney, B., & Jankowski, L. (2004). Feeding infants and toddlers study: What foods are infants and toddlers eating? *American Journal, 104, Suppl,* S22–S30.

Fox, S. E., Levitt, P., & Nelson, C. A. (2010). How the timing and quality of early experiences influence the development of brain architecture. *Child Development, 81,* 28–40.

Franchak, J. M., Kretch, K. S., Soska, K. C., Babcock, J. S., & Adolph, K. E. (2010, in press). Head-mounted eye-tracking of infants' natural interactions: A new method. *Proceedings of the 2010 Symposium on Eye Tracking Research & Application.*

Francis, D. D., Szegda, K., Campbell, G., Martin, W. D., & Insel, T. R. (2003). Epigenetic sources of behavioural differences in mice. *Nature Neuroscience, 6,* 445–446.

Francis, J., Fraser, G., & Marcia, J. E. (1989). *Cognitive and experimental factors in moratorium-achievement (MAMA) cycles.* Unpublished manuscript, Department of Psychology, Simon Fraser University, Burnaby, British Columbia.

Frank, M. C., Vul, E., & Johnson, S. P. (2009). Development of infants' attention to faces during the first year. *Cognition, 110,* 160–170.

Franklin, A., Bevis, L., Ling, Y., & Hulbert, A. (2010). Biological components of color preference in infancy. *Developmental Science, 13,* 346–354.

Franz, C. E. (1996). The implications of preschool tempo and motoric activity level for personality decades later. Reported in A. Caspi (1998), Personality development across the life course. In W. Damon (Ed.), *Handbook of child psychology* (Vol. 3, p. 337). New York: Wiley.

Fraser-Abder, P. (2010). *Teaching budding scientists.* Boston: Allyn & Bacon.

Frederikse, M., Lu, A., Aylward, E., Barta, P., Sharma, T., & Pearlson, G. (2000). Sex differences in inferior lobule volume in schizophrenia. *American Journal of Psychiatry, 157,* 422–427.

Freedman, J. L. (1984). Effects of television violence on aggressiveness. *Psychological Bulletin, 96,* 227–246.

Freeman, K. E., & Gehl, K. S. (1995, March). *Beginnings, middles, and ends: 24-month-olds' understanding of analogy.* Paper presented at the meeting of the Society for Research in Child Development, Indianapolis.

Freeman, S. (2011). *Biological Science with Mastering Biology* (4th ed.). Upper Saddle River, NJ: Benjamin Cummings.

Frey, K., Hirschstein, M. K., Edstrom, L. V., & Snell, J. (2009). Observed reductions in school bullying, nonbullying aggression, and destructive bystander behavior: A longitudinal evaluation, *Journal of Educational Psychology, 101,* 466–481.

Frey, K. S., Hirschstein, M. K., Snell, J. L., Edstrom, L. V. S., & Broderick, C. J. (2005). Reducing playground bullying and supporting beliefs: An experimental trial of the Steps to Respect program. *Developmental Psychology, 41,* 479–790.

Friedman, S. L., Melhuish, E. & Hill, C. (2009). Childcare research at the dawn of a new millennium: An update. In G. Bremner & T.

Wachs (Eds.), *Wiley-Blackwell handbook of infant development* (2nd ed.). Oxford, UK: Wiley-Blackwell.

Friend, M. (2011). *Special education* (3rd ed.). Upper Saddle River, NJ: Merrill.

Freud, S. (1917). *A general introduction to psychoanalysis.* New York: Washington Square Press.

Frisbie, W. P., Hummer, R. A., & McKinnon, S. (2009). Infant and child mortality. In D. Carr (Ed.), *Encyclopedia of the life course and human development.* Boston: Gale Cengage.

Frisco, M. L. (2009). Obesity, childhood and adolescence. In D. Carr (Ed.), *Encyclopedia of the life course and human development.* Boston: Gale Cengage.

Froh, J. J., Yurkewicz, C., & Kashdan, T. B. (2009). Gratitude and subjective well-being in early adolescence: Examining gender differences. *Journal of Adolescence, 32*(3), 633–650.

Fry, B. G. (2009). Mining genomes to identify toxins. *Annual Review of Genomics and Human Genetics* (Vol. 10). Palo Alto, CA: Annual Reviews.

Frye, D. (1999). Development of intention: The relation of executive function to theory of mind. In P. D. Zelazo, J. W. Astington, & D. R. Olson (Eds.), *Developing theories of intention: Social understanding and self-control.* Mahwah, NJ: Erlbaum.

Frye, D. (2004). Unpublished review of Santrock, J. W., *Child development* (11th ed.). New York: McGraw-Hill.

Fu, L. Y., Colson, E. R., Corwin, M .J., & Moon, R. Y. (2008). Infant sleep location: Associated maternal and infant characteristics with sudden infant death syndrome prevention recommendations. *Journal of Pediatrics,* 503–508.

Fuligni, A. J., Hughes, D. L., & Way, N. (2009). Ethnicity and immigration. In R. M. Lerner & L. Steinberg (Eds.), *Handbook of adolescent psychology* (3rd ed.). New York: Wiley.

Furman, W., & Buhrmester, D. (1992). Age and sex differences in perceptions of networks of personal relationships. *Child Development, 63,* 103–115.

Furman, W., Low, S., & Ho, M. J. (2009). Romantic experience and psychosocial adjustment in middle adolescence. *Journal of Clinical Child and Adolescent Psychology, 38,* 75–90.

Furman, W., & Wehner, E. A. (1998). Adolescent romantic relationships: A developmental perspective. In S. Shulman & W. A. Collins (Eds.), *New directions for child development: Adolescent romantic relationships.* San Francisco: Jossey-Bass.

Furstenberg, F. F., Cook, T. D., Eccles, J., Elder, G. H., & Sameroff, A. (1999). *Managing to make it: Urban families and adolescent success.* Chicago: The University of Chicago Press.

Furth, H. G. (1973). *Deafness and learning: A psychosocial approach.* Belmont, CA: Wadsworth.

Furth, H. G., & Wachs, H. (1975). *Thinking goes to school.* New York: Oxford University Press.

Fussell, E., & Greene, M. E. (2002). Demographic trends affecting youth around the world. In B. B. Brown, R. W. Larson, & T. S. Saraswathi (Eds.), *The world's youth*. New York: Cambridge University Press.

G

Galambos, N. L., Barker, E. T., & Krahn, H. J. (2006). Depression, self-esteem, and anger in emerging adulthood: Seven-year trajectories. *Developmental Psychology, 42*, 350–365.

Galambos, N. L., Berenbaum, S. A., & McHale, S. M. (2009). Gender development in adolescence. In R. M. Lerner & L. Steinberg (Eds.), *Handbook of adolescent psychology*. New York: Wiley.

Galindo, C., & Durham, R. E. (2009). Immigration, childhood, and adolescence. In D. Carr (Ed.), *Encyclopedia of the life course and human development*. Boston: Gale Cengage.

Galinsky, E., & David, J. (1988). *The preschool years: Family strategies that work—from experts and parents*. New York: Times Books.

Galloway, J. C., & Thelen, E. (2004). Feet first: Object exploration in young infants. *Infant Behavior & Development, 27*, 107–112.

Ganong, L., Coleman, M., & Hans, J. (2006). Divorce as prelude to stepfamily living and the consequences of re-divorce. In M. A. Fine & J. H. Harvey (Eds.), *Handbook of divorce and relationship dissolution*. Mahwah, NJ: Erlbaum.

Gao, L. L., Chan, S. W., & Mao, Q. (2009). Depression, perceived stress, and social support among first-time Chinese mothers and fathers in the postpartum period. *Research in Nursing and Health, 32*, 50–58.

Garcia Coll, C., & Pachter, L. M. (2002). Ethnic and minority parenting. In M. H. Bornstein (Ed.), *Handbook of parenting* (2nd ed., Vol. 4). Mahwah, NJ: Erlbaum.

Gardner, D. S., Hosking, J., Metcalf, B. S., An, J., Voss, L. D., & Wilkin, T. J. (2009). Contribution of early weight gain to childhood overweight and metabolic health: A longitudinal study (EarlyBird 36). *Pediatrics, 123*, e67–e73.

Gardner, H. (1983). *Frames of mind*. New York: Basic Books.

Gardner, H. (1993). *Multiple intelligences*. New York: Basic Books.

Gardner, H. (2002). Learning from extraordinary minds. In M. Ferrari (Ed.), *The pursuit of excellence through education*. Mahwah, NJ: Erlbaum.

Gargiulo, R. M. (2009). *Special education in contemporary society*. Thousand Oaks, CA: Sage.

Garofalo, R. (2010). Cytokines in human milk. *Journal of Pediatrics, 156, Supp 2*, S36–S40.

Gartstein, M. A., Peleg, Y., Young, B. N., & Slobodskaya, H. R. (2009). Infant temperament in Russia, United States of America, and Israel: Differences and similarities between Russian-speaking families. *Child Psychiatry and Human Development, 40*(2), 241–256.

Garvey, C. (2000). *Play* (Enlarged Ed.). Cambridge, MA: Harvard University Press.

Gasser, L., & Keller, M. (2009). Are the competent morally good? Perspective taking and moral motivation of children involved in bullying. *Social Development, 18*(4), 798–816.

Gates, W. (1998, July 20). Charity begins when I'm ready (interview). *Fortune*.

Gathwala, G., Singh, B., & Balhara, B. (2008). KMC facilitates baby attachment in low birth weight infants. *Indian Journal of Pediatrics, 75*, 43–47.

Gaudernack, L. C., Forbord, S., & Hole, E. (2006). Acupuncture administered after spontaneous rupture of membranes at term significantly reduces the length of birth and use of oxytocin. *Acta Obstetricia et Gynecologica Scandinavica, 85*, 1348–1353.

Gaudreau, P., Amiot, C. E., & Vallerand, R. J. (2009). Trajectories of affective states in adolescent hockey players: Turning point and motivational antecedents. *Developmental Psychology, 45*, 307–319.

Gauvain, M. (2008). Vygotsky's sociocultural theory. In M. M. Haith & J. B. Benson (Eds.). *Encyclopedia of infant and early childhood development*. Oxford, UK: Elsevier.

Gauvain, M., & Parke, R. D. (2010). Socialization. In M. H. Bornstein (Ed.), *Handbook of cultural developmental science*. New York: Psychology Press.

Ge, X., & Natsuaki, M. N. (2010). In search of explanations for early pubertal timing effects on developmental psychopathology. *Current Directions in Psychological Science, 18*, 327–331.

Gee, C. L., & Heyman, G. D. (2007). Children's evaluations of other people's self-descriptions. *Social Development, 16*(4), 800–818.

Geher, G., & Miller, G. (Eds.) (2007). *Mating intelligence*. Mahwah, NJ: Erlbaum.

Gelman, R. (1969). Conservation acquisition: A problem of learning to attend to relevant attributes. *Journal of Experimental Child Psychology, 7*, 67–87.

Gelman, R., & Williams, E. M. (1998). Enabling constraints for cognitive development and learning. In W. Damon (Ed.), *Handbook of child psychology* (5th ed., Vol. 4). New York: Wiley.

Gelman, S. A. (2009). Learning from others: Children's construction of concepts. *Annual Review of Psychology* (Vol. 60). Palo Alto, CA: Annual Reviews.

Gelman, S. A., Heyman, G. D., & Legare, C. H. (2007). Developmental changes in the coherence of essentialist beliefs about psychological characteristics. *Child Development, 78*, 757–774.

Gelman, S. A., & Kalish, C. W. (2006). Conceptual development. In W. Damon & R. Lerner (Eds.), *Handbook of child psychology* (6th ed.). New York: Wiley.

Gelman, S. A., & Opfer, J. E. (2004). Development of the animate-inanimate distinction. In U. Goswami (Ed.), *Blackwell handbook of childhood cognitive development*. Malden, MA: Blackwell.

Gelman, S. A., Taylor, M. G., & Nguyen, S. P. (2004). Mother-child conversations about gender. *Monographs of the Society for Research in Child Development, 69* (1, Serial No. 275).

Gennetian, L. A., & Miller, C. (2002). Children and welfare reform: A view from an experimental welfare reform program in Minnesota. *Child Development, 73*, 601–620.

Gentile, D. A., & others. (2009). The effects of prosocial video games on prosocial behaviors: International evidence from correlational, experimental, and longitudinal studies. *Personality and Social Psychology Bulletin, 35*(6), 752–763.

Gentile, D. A., Mathieson, L. C., & Crick, N. R. (2010, in press). Media violence associations with the form and function of aggression among elementary school children. *Social Development*.

Genuis, S. J. (2009). Nowhere to hide: Chemical intoxicants in the unborn child. *Reproductive Toxicology, 28*, 115–116.

Gerards, F. A., Twisk, J. W., Fetter, W. P., Wijnaendts, L. C., & van Vugt, J. M. (2008). Predicting pulmonary hypoplasia with 2- or 3-dimensional ultrasonography in complicated pregnancies. *American Journal of Gynecology and Obstetrics, 198*, e1–e6.

German, M., Gonzales, N., Bonds, D., Dumka, L., & Millsap, R. (2009). Familism Values as a protective factor for Mexican-origin adolescents exposed to deviant peers. *Journal of Early Adolescence, 29*(1), 16–42.

Gershkoff-Stowe, L., & Hahn, E. R. (2007). Fast mapping skills in the developing lexicon. *Journal of Speech, Language, and Hearing, 50*, 682–697.

Gershoff, E. T. (2002). Corporal punishment by parents and associated child behaviors and experiences: A meta-analysis and theoretical review. *Psychological Bulletin, 128*, 539–579.

Gershoff, E. T., & others. (2010). Parent discipline practices in an international sample: Associations with child behaviors and moderation by perceived normativeness. *Child Development, 81*, 487–502.

Gesell, A. L. (1928). *Infancy and human growth*. New York: Macmillan.

Gesell, A. L. (1934). *Infancy and human growth*. New York: MacMillan.

Gewirtz, J. (1977). Maternal responding and the conditioning of infant crying: Directions of influence within the attachment-acquisition process. In B. C. Etzel, J. M. LeBlanc, & D. M. Baer (Eds.), *New developments in behavioral research*. Hillsdale, NJ: Erlbaum.

Ghetti, S., & Alexander, K. W. (2004). "If it happened, I would remember it": Strategic use of event memorability in the rejection of false autobiographical events. *Child Development, 75*, 542–561.

Ghosh, S., Feingold, E., Chakaborty, S., & Dey, S. K. (2010). Telomere length is associated with types of chromosome 21 nondisjunction: A new insight into the maternal age effect on Down syndrome birth. *Human Genetics*. (Available online January 10, 2010.)

Giavecchio, L. (2001, April). *Sustained attention and receptive language in preschool Head Start story time.* Paper presented at the meeting of the Society for Research in Child Development, Minneapolis.

Gibbons, J., & Ng, S. H. (2004). Acting bilingual and thinking bilingual. *Journal of Language and Social Psychology, 23*, 4–6.

Gibbons, R. D., Hedeker, D., & DuToit, S. (2010). Advances in analysis of longitudinal data. *Annual Review of Clinical Psychology* (Vol. 6). Palo Alto, CA: Annual Reviews.

Gibbs, J. C. (2010). *Moral development and reality.* (2nd ed.). Boston: Allyn & Bacon.

Gibbs, J. C., Basinger, K. S., Grime, R. L., & Snarey, J. R. (2007). Moral judgment development across cultures: Revisiting Kohlberg's universality claims. *Developmental Review, 27*, 443–500.

Gibbs, J. T., & Huang, L. N. (1989). A conceptual framework for assessing and treating minority youth. In J. T. Gibbs & L. N. Huang (Eds.), *Children of color.* San Francisco: Jossey-Bass.

Gibson, E. J. (1969). *Principles of perceptual learning and development* New York: Appleton-Century-Crofts.

Gibson, E. J. (1989). Exploratory behavior in the development of perceiving, acting, and the acquiring of knowledge. *Annual Review of Psychology, 39*. Palo Alto, CA: Annual Reviews.

Gibson, E. J. (2001). *Perceiving the affordances.* Mahwah, NJ: Erlbaum.

Gibson, E. J., & Walk, R. D. (1960). The "visual cliff." *Scientific American, 202*, 64–71.

Gibson, J. J. (1966). *The senses considered as perceptual systems.* Boston: Houghton Mifflin.

Gibson, J. J. (1979). *The ecological approach to visual perception.* Boston: Houghton Mifflin.

Gibson, L. Y., Byrne, S. M., Blair, E., Davis, E. A., Jacoby, P., & Zubrick, S. R. (2008). Clustering of psychological symptoms in overweight children. *Australian and New Zealand Journal of Psychiatry, 42*, 118–125.

Giedd, J. N., & others. (2009). Anatomical brain magnetic imaging of typically developing children and adolescents. *Journal of the American Academy of Child and Adolescent Psychiatry, 48*, 465–470.

Gilbert, S. J., Meusese, J. D., Towgood, K. J., Frith, C. D., & Burgess, P. W. (2009). Abnormal functional specialization within medial prefrontal cortex in high-functioning autism: A multi-voxel similarity analysis. *Brain, 132*(4), 869–878.

Gill, S. V., Adolph, K. E., & Vereijken, B. (2009). Change in action: how infants learn to walk down slopes. *Developmental Science, 12*, 888–902.

Gilligan, C. (1982). *In a different voice.* Cambridge, MA: Harvard University Press.

Gilligan, C. (1992, May). *Joining the resistance: Girls' development in adolescence.* Paper presented at the symposium on development and vulnerability in close relationships, Montreal, Quebec.

Gilligan, C. (1996). The centrality of relationships in psychological development: A puzzle, some evidence, and a theory. In G. G. Noam & K. W. Fischer (Eds.), *Development and vulnerability in close relationships.* Hillsdale, NJ: Erlbaum.

Giordano, P. C. (2009). Friendship, childhood and adolescence. In D. Carr (Ed.), *Encyclopedia of the life course and human development.* Boston: Gale Cengage.

Glascher, J., & others. (2009). Lesion mapping of cognitive abilities linked to intelligence. *Neuron, 61*, 681–691.

Glascher, J., & others. (2010). Distributed neural system for general intelligence revealed by lesion mapping. *Proceedings of the National Academy of Sciences USA, 107*, 4705–4709.

Glessner, J. T., & others. (2009). Autism genome-wide copy number variation reveals ubiquitin and neuronal genes. *Nature, 459*, 569–573.

Glover, M. B., Mullineaux, P. Y., Deater-Deckard, K., & Petrill, S. A. (2010). Parents' feelings toward their adoptive and non-adoptive children. *Infant and Child Development, 19*(3), 238–251.

Gluck, M. E., Venti, C. A., Lindsay, R. S., Knowler, W. C., Salbe, A. D., & Krakoff, J. (2009). Maternal influence, not diabetic intraturine environment, predicts children's energy intake. *Obesity, 17*, 772–777.

Gobet, F., & Charness, N. (2006). In K. A. Ericsson, N. Charness, P. J. Feltovich, & R. R. Hoffman (Eds.), *The Cambridge handbook of expertise and expert performance.* New York: Cambridge University Press.

Gogtay, N., & Thompson, P. M. (2010). Mapping gray matter development: Implications for typical development and vulnerability to psychopathology. *Brain and Cognition, 72*, 6–15.

Goldbeck, L., Gagsteiger, F., Minderman, I., Strobele, S., & Izat, Y. (2008). Cognitive development of singletons conceived by intracytoplasmic sperm injection or in vitro fertilization at age 5 and 10 years. *Journal of Pediatric Psychology, 34*, 774–781.

Goldberg, W. A., & Lucas-Thompson, R. (2008). Maternal and paternal employment, effects of. In M. M. Haith & J. B. Benson (Eds.), *Encyclopedia of infant and early childhood development.* Oxford, UK: Elsevier.

Goldenberg, R. L., & Culhane, J. F. (2007). Low birth weight in the United States. *American Journal of Clinical Nutrition, 85, Suppl*, S584–S590.

Goldenberg R. L., & Nagahawatte, N. T. (2008). Poverty, mental health, and adverse pregnancy outcomes. *Annals of the New York Academy of Sciences, 1136*, 80–85.

Goldfield. B. A., & Snow, C. A. (2009). Individual differences in language development. In J. Berko Gleason & N. Ratner (Eds.), *The development of language* (7th ed.). Boston: Allyn & Bacon.

Goldin-Meadow, S. (2009). Using the hands to study how children learn language. In J. Colombo, P. McCardle & L. Freund (Eds.), *Infant pathways to language.* New York: Psychology Press.

Goldin-Meadow, S., & Iverson, J. (2010, in press). Gesturing across the lifespan. In R. M. Lerner (Ed.), *Handbook of life-span development.* New York: Wiley.

Goldman, N. Giel, D. A., Lin, Y. H., & Weinstein, M. (2010). The serotonin transporter polymorphism (5-HTTLPR): Allelic variation and links with depressive symptoms. *Depression and Anxiety, 27*, 260–269.

Goldscheider, F., & Sassler, S. (2006). Creating stepfamilies: Integrating children into the study of union formation. *Journal of Marriage and the Family, 68*, 275–291.

Goldschmidt, L., Richardson, G. A., Willford, J., & Day, N. L. (2008). Prenatal marijuana exposure and intelligence test performance at age 6. *Journal of the American Academy of Child and Adolescent Psychiatry, 47*, 254–263.

Goldsmith, H. H. (2011). Human development: Biological and genetic processes. *Annual Review of Psychology* (Vol. 62). Palo Alto, CA: Annual Reviews.

Goldstein, E. B. (2011). *Cognitive psychology.* Boston: Cengage.

Goldstein, M. H., King, A. P., & West, M. J. (2003). Social interaction shapes babbling: Testing parallels between birdsong and speech. Proceedings of the National Academy of Sciences, *100*(13), 8030–8035.

Goleman, D. (1995). *Emotional intelligence.* New York: Basic Books.

Goleman, D., Kaufman, P., & Ray, M. (1993). *The creative spirit.* New York: Plume.

Golombok, S., MacCallum, F., & Goodman, E. (2001). The "test-tube" generation: Parent-child relationships and the psychological well-being of in vitro fertilization children at adolescence. *Child Development, 72*, 599–608.

Golombok, S., Rust, J., Zervoulis, K., Croudace, T., Golding, J., & Hines, M. (2008). Developmental trajectories of sex-typed behavior in boys and girls: A longitudinal general population study of children aged 2.5–8 years. *Child Development, 79*, 1583–1593.

Golombok, S., & Tasker, F. (2010). Gay fathers. In M. E. Lamb (Ed.), *The role of the father in child development* (5th ed.). New York: Wiley.

Gomez-Raposo, C., & others. (2010). Male breast cancer. *Cancer Treatment Reviews.* (in press.)

Gong, X., & others. (2009). An investigation of ribosomal protein L10 gene in autism spectrum disorders. *BMC Medical Genetics, 10*, 7.

Gonzalez, A., Atkinson, L., & Fleming, A. S. (2009). Attachment and the comparative psychobiology of mothering. In M. De Haan & M. R. Gunnar (Eds.), *Handbook of developmental social neuroscience.* New York: Guilford.

González, J. M. (Ed.). (2009). *Encyclopedia of bilingual education.* Thousand Oaks, CA: Sage.

Gonzales, N. A., Deardorff, J., Formoso, D., Barr, A., & Barrera, M. (2006). Family mediators of the relation between acculturation and adolescent mental health. *Family Relations, 55,* 318–330.

Gonzales, N. A., Dumka, L. E., Muaricio, A. M., & German, M. (2007). Building bridges: Strategies to promote academic and psychological resilience for adolescents of Mexican origin. In J. E. Lansford, K. Deater Deckhard, & M. H. Bornstein (Eds.), *Immigrant families in contemporary society.* New York: Guilford.

Gonzales, N. A., & others. (2008). Mexican American adolescents' cultural orientation, externalizing behavior and academic engagement: The role of traditional cultural values. *American Journal of Community Psychology, 41,* 151–164.

Gonazalez, V., Yawkey, T. D., & Minaya-Rowe, L. (2006). *English-as-a-second-language (ESL) teaching and learning.* Boston: Allyn & Bacon.

Good, M., & Willoughby, T. (2008). Adolescence as a sensitive period for spiritual development. *Child Development Perspectives, 2,* 32–37.

Goodnow, J. (2010). Culture. In M. H. Bornstein (Ed.), *Handbook of cultural developmental science.* New York: Psychology Press.

Goodwin, J. L., Vasquez, M. M., Silva, G. E., & Quan, S. F. (2010, in press). Incidence and remission of sleep-disordered breathing and related symptoms in 6- to 17-year old children—the Tucson Children's Assessment of Sleep Apnea Study. *Journal of Pediatrics.*

Gopnik, A., & Meltzoff, A. (1997). *Words, thoughts, and theories.* Cambridge, MA: MIT Press.

Gottfried, A. E., Marcoulides, G. A., Gottfried, A. W., & Oliver, P. H. (2009). A latent curve model of motivational practices and developmental decline in math and science academic intrinsic motivation. *Journal of Educational Psychology, 101,* 729–739.

Gottlieb, G. (2007). Probabilistic epigenesis. *Developmental Science, 10,* 1–11.

Gottleib, G., Wahlsten, D., & Lickliter, R. (2006). The significance of biology for human development: A developmental psychobiological systems view. In W. Damon & R. Lerner (Eds.), *Handbook of child psychology* (6th ed.). New York: Wiley.

Gottman, J., Gottman, J., & Shapiro, A. (2009). A new couples approach to interventions for the transition to parenthood. In M. S. Schulz, P. K. Kerig, M. K. Pruett, & R. D. Parke (Eds.), *Feathering the nest.* Washington, DC: American Psychological Association.

Gottman, J. M. (2002). *Four parenting styles: The emotion-coaching parent.* Seattle: Talaris Research Institute.

Gottman, J. M. (2009). *Research on parenting.* Retrieved January 30, 2009, from www .gottman.com/parenting/research

Gottman, J. M., & DeClaire, J. (1997). *The heart of parenting: Raising an emotionally intelligent child.* New York: Simon & Schuster.

Gottman, J. M., & Parker, J. G. (Eds.). (1987). *Conversations of friends.* New York: Cambridge University Press.

Gottman Relationship Institute. (2009). *Research on parenting.* Retrieved on December 9, 2009 from www.gottman.com/parenting/research

Gould, S. J. (1981). *The mismeasure of man.* New York: W. W. Norton.

Grabe, S., & Hyde, J. S. (2006). Ethnicity and body dissatisfaction among women in the United States: A meta-analysis. *Psychological Bulletin, 132,* 622–640.

Graber, J. A. (2008). Pubertal and neuroendocrine development and risk for depressive disorders. In N.B. Allen, & L. Sheeber (Eds.), *Adolescent emotional development and the emergence of depressive disorders.* New York: Cambridge University Press.

Graham, G. M., Holt/Hale, S., & Parker, M. A. (2010). *Children moving.* New York: McGraw-Hill.

Graham, S. (1986, August). *Can attribution theory tell us something about motivation in blacks?* Paper presented at the meeting of the American Psychological Association, Washington, DC.

Graham, S. (1990). Motivation in Afro-Americans. In G. L. Berry & J. K. Asamen (Eds.), *Black students: Psychosocial issues and academic achievement.* Newbury Park, CA: Sage.

Graham, S. (2005, February 16). Commentary in *USA TODAY,* p. 2D.

Graham, S. (2009). Teaching writing. P-Hogan (Ed.), *Cambridge encyclopedia of language sciences.* Cambridge, UK: Cambridge University Press.

Graham, S., & Perin. D. (2007). A meta-analysis of writing instruction for adolescent students. *Journal of Educational Psychology, 99,* 445–476.

Grant, J. P. (1997). *The state of the world's children.* New York: UNICEF and Oxford University Press.

Graven, S. (2006). Sleep and brain development. *Clinical Perinatology, 33,* 693–706.

Gray, J. (1992). *Men are from Mars, women are from Venus.* New York: HarperCollins.

Graziano, A. M., & Raulin, M. L. (2010). *Research methods* (7th ed.). Boston: Allyn & Bacon.

Gredler, M. E. (2009). Hiding in plain sight: The stages of mastery/self-regulation in Vygotsky's cultural-history theory. *Educational Psychologist, 44,* 1–19.

Greenfield, P. M. (1966). On culture and conservation. In J. S. Bruner, R. P. Oliver, & P. M. Greenfield (Eds.), *Studies in cognitive growth.* New York: Wiley.

Greenfield, P. M. (2003, February). Commentary. *Monitor on Psychology, 3*(2), 58.

Greenfield, P. M. (2009). Linking social change and developmental change: Shifting pathways of human development. *Developmental Psychology, 43,* 401–418.

Greer, F. R., Sicherer, S. H., Burks, A. W., & Committee on Nutrition and Section on Allergy and Immunology. (2008). Effects of early nutritional interventions on the development of atopic disease in infants and children: The role of maternal dietary restriction, breast feeding, timing of introduction of complementary foods, and hydrolyzed formulas. *Pediatrics, 121,* 183–191.

Greve, W., & Bjorklund, D. F. (2009). The nestor effect: Extending evolutionary developmental psychology to a lifespan perspective. *Developmental Review, 29,* 163–179.

Griffiths, L. J., Hawkins, S. S., Cole, T. J., & Dezateux, C. (2010). Risk factors for rapid weight gain in preschool children: findings from a UK-wide prospective study. *International Journal of Obesity, 34,* 624–632.

Grigorenko, E. (2000). Heritability and intelligence. In R. J. Sternberg (Ed.), *Handbook of intelligence.* New York: Cambridge U. Press.

Grigorenko, E. L., & Takanishi, R. (2010). *Immigration, diversity, and education.* New York: Routledge.

Grolnick, W. S., Bridges, L. J., & Connell, J. P. (1996). Emotion regulation in two-year-olds: Strategies and emotional expression in four contexts. *Child Development, 67,* 928–941.

Gronlund, N. E., & Waugh, C. K. (2009). *Assessment of student achievement* (9th ed.). Upper Saddle River, NJ: Prentice Hall.

Grosse, S. D. (2010). Late-treated phenylketonuria and partial reversibility of intellectual impairment. *Child Development, 81,* 200–211.

Grossmann, K., Grossmann, K. E., Spangler, G., Suess, G., & Unzner, L. (1985). Maternal sensitivity and newborns' orientation responses as related to quality of attachment in northern Germany. In I. Bretherton & E. Waters (Eds.), Growing points of attachment theory and research. *Monographs of the Society for Research in Child Development, 50* (1–2, Serial No. 209).

Grotevant, H. D., & others. (2006). Antisocial behavior of adoptees and nonadoptees: Prediction from early history and adolescent relationships. *Journal of Research on Adolescence, 16,* 105–131.

Grotevant, H. D., & Cooper, C. R. (1985). Patterns of interaction in family relationships and the deyelopment of identity exploration in adolescence. *Child Development, 56,* 415–428.

Grotevant, H. D., & Cooper, C. R. (1998). Individuality and connectedness in adolescent development: Review and prospects for research on identity, relationship, and context. In E. Skoe & A. von der Lippe (Eds.), *Personality development in adolescence: A cross-national and life-span perspective.* London: Routledge.

Gruenfeld, E. (2010). Thinking creatively is thinking critically. *New Directions for Youth Development, 125,* 71–83.

Grusec, J. E. (2006). Development of moral behavior and a conscience from a socialization perspective. In M. Killen & J. G. Smetana (Eds.), *Handbook of moral development.* Mahwah, NJ: Erlbaum.

Grusec, J. E. (2009). Unpublished review of J. W. Santrock's *Child Development*, 13th ed. (New York: McGraw-Hill.)

Grusec, J. E. (2011). Socialization processes in the family: Social and emotional development. *Annual Review of Psychology* (Vol. 62). Palo Alto, CA: Annual Reviews.

Grusec, J. E., & Davidov, M. (2010). Integrating different perspectives on socialization theory and research: A domain-specific approach. *Child Development, 81,* 687–709.

Grych, J. H. (2002). Marital relationships and parenting. In M. H. Bornstein (Ed.), *Handbook of parenting.* Mahwah, NJ: Erlbaum.

Guerra, N. G., & Williams, K. R. (2010). Implementing bullying prevention in diverse settings: Geographic, economic, and cultural influences. In E. M. Vernberg & B. K. Biggs (Eds.), *Preventing and treating bullying and victimization.* New York: Oxford University Press.

Guilford, J. P. (1967). *The structure of intellect.* New York: McGraw-Hill.

Gumbo, F. Z., & others. (2010). Rising mother-to-child HIV transmission in a resource-limited breastfeeding population. *Tropical Doctor, 40,* 70–73.

Gunderson, E. P., & others. (2008). Association of fewer hours of sleep at 6 months postpartum with substantial weight retention at 1 year postpartum. *American Journal of Epidemiology, 167,* 178–187.

Gunnar, M. R., Fisher, P. A., & Early Experience, Stress, and Prevention Network. (2006). Bringing basic research on early experience and stress neurobiology to bear on preventive interventions for neglected and maltreated children. *Development and Psychopathology, 18,* 651–677.

Gunnar, M. R., Malone, S., & Fisch, R. O. (1987). The psychobiology of stress and coping in the human neonate: Studies of the adrenocortical activity in response to stress in the first week of life. In T. Field, P. McCabe, & N. Scheiderman (Eds.). *Stress and coping.* Hillsdale, NJ: Erlbaum.

Gunnar, M. R., & Quevado, K. (2007). The neurobiology of stress and development. *Annual Review of Psychology* (Vol. 58). Palo Alto, CA: Annual Reviews.

Guo, G., & Tillman, K. H. (2009). Trajectories of depressive symptoms, dopamine D2 and D4 receptors, family socioeconomic status, and social support in adolescence and young adulthood. *Psychiatric Genetics, 19,* 14–26.

Gupta, A., Thornton, J. W., & Huston, A. C. (2007). Working families should not be poor—the New Hope project. In D. R. Crane & T. B. Heaton (Eds.), *Handbook of families and poverty.* Thousand Oaks, CA: Sage.

Gur, R. C., & others. (1995). Sex differences in regional cerebral glucose metabolism during a resting state. *Science, 267,* 528–531.

Gurwitch, R. H., Silovksy, J. F., Schultz, S., Kees, M., & Burlingame, S. (2001). *Reactions and guidelines for children following trauma/disaster.*

Norman, OK: Department of Pediatrics, University of Oklahoma Health Sciences Center.

Gustafsson, J-E. (2007). Schooling and intelligence: Effects of track of study on level and profile of cognitive abilities. In P. C. Kyllonen, R. D. Roberts, & L. Stankov (Eds.), *Extending intelligence.* Mahwah, NJ: Erlbaum.

Gutman, L. M. (2008). Risk and resilience. In M. M. Haith & J. B. Benson (Eds.). *Encyclopedia of infancy and early childhood.*

Guzzetta, A., & others. (2008). Language organization in left perinatal stroke. *Neuropediatrics, 39,* 157–163.

H

Haas, B. W., Mills, D., Yam, A., Hoeft, F., Bellugi, U., & Reiss, A. (2009). Genetic influences on sociability: Heightened amygdala reactivity and event-related responses to positive stimuli in Williams syndrome. *Journal of Neuroscience, 29,* 1132–1139.

Haga, M. (2008). The relationship between physical fitness and motor competence in children. *Child: Child Care and Health Development, 34,* 329–334.

Hagen, J. W., & Lamb-Parker, F. G. (2008). Head Start. In M. M. Haith & J. B. Benson (Eds.), *Encyclopedia of infant and early childhood development.* Oxford, UK: Elsevier.

Hahn, D. B., Payne, W. A., & Lucas, E. B. (2011). *Focus on health* (10th ed.). New York: McGraw-Hill.

Haier, R. J. (2009). Neuro-intelligence, neuro-metrics, and the next phase of brain imaging studies. *Intelligence, 37,* 121–123.

Hakuta, K. (2001, April 5). *Key policy milestones and directions in the education of English language learners.* Paper prepared for the Rockefeller Foundation Symposium, Leveraging change: An emerging framework for educational equity, Washington, DC.

Hakuta, K. (2005, April). *Bilingualism at the intersection of research and public policy.* Paper presented at the meeting of the Society for Research in Child Development, Atlanta.

Hakuta, K., Butler, Y. G., & Witt, D. (2001). *How long does it take English learners to attain proficiency?* Berkeley, CA: The University of California Linguistic Minority Research Institute Policy Report 2000–1.

Halford, G. S. (2008). Cognitive developmental theories. In M. M. Haith & J. B. Benson (Eds.). *Encyclopedia of infant and early childhood development.* Oxford, UK: Elsevier.

Halford, G. S., & Andrews, G. S. (2011). Information processing models of cognitive development. In U. Goswami (Ed.), *Wiley-Blackwell handbook of childhood cognitive development* (2nd ed.). New York: Wiley-Blackwell.

Hall, C. M., & others. (2004). Behavioral and physical masculinization are related to genotype in girls with congenital adrenal hyperplasia. *Journal of Clinical Endocrinology and Metabolism, 89,* 419–424.

Hall, G. N. (2010). *Multicultural psychology* (2nd ed.). Upper Saddle River, NJ: Prentice Hall.

Hall, G. S. (1904). *Adolescence* (Vols. 1 & 2). Englewood Cliffs, NJ: Prentice Hall.

Hall, L. (2008). *Autism spectrum disorders: From theory to practice.* Upper Saddle River, NJ: Prentice Hall.

Hallahan, D. P., Kaufmann, J. M., & Pullen, P. C. (2009). *Exceptional learners* (11th ed.). Boston: Allyn & Bacon.

Halpern, D. F. (2006). Girls and academic success: Changing patterns of academic achievement. In J. Worell & C. D. Goodheart (Eds.), *Handbook of girls' and women's psychological health.* New York: Oxford University Press.

Halpern, D. F., Benbow, C. P., Geary, D. C., Gur, R. C. & Hyde, J. S. (2007). The science of sex differences in science and mathematics. *Psychological Science in the Public Interest, 8,* 1–51.

Hamilton, A. C., Martin, R. C., & Burton, P. C. (2010, in press). Converging functional magnetic imaging evidence for a role of the left inferior front lobe in semantic retention during language comprehension. *Cognitive Neuropsychology.*

Hamlin, J. K., Hallinan, E. V., & Woodward, A. L. (2008). Do as I do: 7-month-old infants selectively reproduce others' goals. *Developmental Science, 11*(4) 487–494.

Han, J. J., Leichtman, M. D., & Wang, Q. (1998). Autobiographical memory in Korean, Chinese, and American children. *Developmental Psychology, 34,* 701–713.

Han, W-J. (2009). Maternal employment. In D. Carr (Ed.). *Encyclopedia of the life course and human development.* Boston: Gale Cengage.

Hancox, R. J., Milne, B. J., & Poulton, R. (2004). Association between child and adolescent television viewing and adult health: A longitudinal birth cohort study. *Lancet, 364,* 257–262.

Hanish, L., D., & Guerra, N. G. (2004). Aggressive victims, passive victims, and bullies: Developmental continuity or developmental change? *Merrill-Palmer Quarterly, 50,* 17–38.

Hannan, M. A., Faraji, B., Tanguma, J., Longoria, N., & Rodriguez, R. C. (2009). Maternal milk concentration of zinc, iron, selenium, and iodine and its relationship to dietary intake. *Biological Trace Element Research, 127,* 6–15.

Hansen, M. L., Gunn, P. W., & Kaelber, D. C. (2007). Underdiagnosis of hypertension in children and adolescents. *Journal of the American Medical Association, 298,* 874–879.

Hansen, M., Janssen, I., Schiff, A., Zee, P. C., & Dubocovich, M. L. (2005). The impact of school daily schedule on adolescent sleep. *Pediatrics, 115,* 1555–1561.

Hare, B. R., & Castenell, L. A. (1985). No place to run, no place to hide: Comparative status and future prospects of Black boys. In M. B. Spencer, G. K. Brookins, & W. R. Allen (Eds.), *Beginnings: The social and affective development of Black children.* Hillsdale, NJ: Erlbaum.

Harkness, S., & Super, B. M. (1995). Culture and parenting. In M. H. Bornstein (Ed.), *Handbook of parenting* (Vol. 3). Hillsdale, NJ: Erlbaum.

Harlow, H. F. (1958). The nature of love. *American Psychologist, 13,* 673–685.

Harris, G., Thomas, A., & Booth, D. A. (1990). Development of salt taste in infancy. *Developmental Psychology, 26,* 534–538.

Harris, J. R. (1998). *The nurture assumption: Why children turn out the way they do: Parents matter less than you think and peers matter more.* New York: Free Press.

Harris, J. R. (2009). *The nurture assumption* (rev. ed.). New York: The Free Press.

Harris, P. L. (2000). *The work of the imagination.* Oxford University Press.

Harris, P. L. (2006). Social cognition. In W. Damon & R. Lerner (Eds.), *Handbook of child psychology* (6th ed.). New York: Wiley.

Harris, P. L., & Koenig, M. A. (2006). Trust in testimony: How children learn about science and religion. *Child Development, 77,* 505–524.

Harris, R. J., Schoen, L. M., & Hensley, D. L., (1992). A cross-cultural study of story memory. *Journal of Cross-Cultural Psychology, 23,* 133–147.

Harris, Y. R., & Graham, J. A. (2007). *The African American child.* New York: Springer.

Harrison-Hale, A. O., McLoyd, V. C., & Smedley, B. (2004). Racial and ethnic status: Risk and protective processes among African-American families. In K. L. Maton, C. J. Schellenbach, B. J. Leadbetter, & A. L. Solarz (Eds.), *Investing in children, families, and communities.* Washington, DC: American Psychological Association.

Hart, B., & Risley, T. R. (1995). *Meaningful differences.* Baltimore, MD: Paul Brookes.

Hart, D., Burock, D., London, B., & Atkins, R. (2003). Prosocial development, antisocial development, and moral development. In A. M. Slater & G. Bremner (Eds.), *An introduction to developmental psychology.* Malden. MA: Blackwell.

Hart, D., & Karmel, M. P. (1996). Self-awareness and self-knowledge in humans, great apes, and monkeys. In A. Russon, K. Bard, & S. Parker (Eds.), *Reaching into thought.* New York: Cambridge University Press.

Hart, D., Matsuba, M. K., & Atkins, R. (2008). The moral and civic effects of learning to serve. In L. Nucci & D. Narváez (Eds.), *Handbook of moral and character education.* New York: Psychology Press.

Hart, S., & Carrington, H. (2002). Jealousy in 6-month-old infants. *Infancy, 3,* 395–402.

Harter, S. (1985). *Self-Perception Profile for Children.* Denver: University of Denver. Department of Psychology.

Harter, S. (1986). Processes underlying the construction, maintenance, and enhancement of the self-concept of children. In. J. Suls & A. Greenwald (Eds.), *Psychological perspectives on the self* (Vol. 3). Hillsdale, NJ: Erlbaum.

Harter, S. (1989). *Self-Perception Profile for Adolescents.* Denver: University of Denver. Department of Psychology.

Harter, S. (1998). The development of self-representations. In W. Damon (Ed.), *Handbook of child psychology* (5th ed., Vol. 3). New York: Wiley.

Harter, S. (1999). *The construction of the self.* New York: Guilford.

Harter, S. (2002). Unpublished review of J. W. Santrock's *Child development* (10th ed.). (New York: McGraw-Hill).

Harter, S. (2006). The self. In W. Damon & R. Lerner (Eds.), *Handbook of child psychology* (6th ed.), New York: Wiley.

Hartshorne, H., & May, M. S. (1928–1930). *Moral studies in the nature of character: Studies in deceit* (Vol. 1); *Studies in self-control* (Vol. 2). *Studies in the organization of character* (Vol. 3). New York: Macmillan.

Hartup, W. W. (1983). The peer system. In P. H. Mussen (Ed.), *Handbook of child psychology* (4th ed., Vol. 4). New York: Wiley.

Hartup, W. W. (2009). Critical issues and theoretical viewpoints. In K. H. Rubin, W. M. Bukowski, & B. Laursen (Eds.), *Handbook of peer interactions, relationships, and groups.* New York: Guilford.

Hartup, W. W., & Laursen, B. (1999). Relationships as developmental contexts: Retrospective themes and contemporary issues. In W. Andrew Collins & B. Laursen (Eds.), *Relationships as developmental contexts.* Mahwah, NJ: Erlbaum.

Hartwig, S., & others. (2010). Genomic characterization of Wilms' tumor suppressor 1 targets in nephron progenitor cells during kidney development. *Development, 137,* 1189–1203.

Harwood, R., Leyendecker, B., Carlson, V., Asencio, M., & Miller, A. (2002). Parenting among Latino families in the U.S. In M. H. Bornstein (Ed.), *Handbook of parenting* (2nd ed.). Mahwah, NJ: Erlbaum.

Hastings, P. D., Utendale, W. T., & Sullivan, C. (2007). The socialization of prosocial development. In J. E. Grusec & P. D. Hastings (Eds.), *Handbook of socialization.* New York: Guilford.

Hatton, H., Donnellan, M. B., Maysn, K., Feldman, B. J., Larsen-Riffe, D., & Conger, R. D. (2008). Family and individual difference predictors of trait aspects of negative interpersonal behaviors during emerging adulthood. *Journal of Family Psychology, 22,* 448–455.

Hauck, F. R., Signore, C., Fein, S. B., & Raju, T. N. (2008). Infant sleeping arrangements and practices during the first year of life. *Pediatrics, 122, Suppl 2,* S113–S120.

Hawkins, J. A., & Berndt, T. J. (1985, April). *Adjustment following the transition to junior high school.* Paper presented at the biennial meeting of the Society for Research in Child Development, Toronto.

Healey, J. F. (2009). *Race, ethnicity and class* (5th ed.). Thousand Oaks, CA: Sage.

Health Management Resources. (2001). *Child health and fitness* Boston: Author.

Hegaard, H. K., Hedegaard, M., Damm, P., Ottesen, B., Petersson, K., & Henriksen, T. B. (2008). Leisure time physical activity is associated with a reduced risk of preterm delivery. *American Journal of Obstetrics and Gynecology, 198,* e1–e5.

Heiman, G. W. (2011). *Basic statistics for the behavioral sciences* (6th ed.). Boston: Cengage.

Heimann, M., Strid, K., Smith, L., Tjus, T., Ulvund, S. E., & Melzoff, A. N. (2006). Exploring the relation between memory, gestural communication, and the emergence of language in infancy: A longitudinal study. *Infant and Child Development, 15,* 233–249.

Heinig, M. J., Ishii, K. D., Banuelos, J. L., Campbell, E., O'Laughlin, C., & Becerra, L. E. (2009). Sources and acceptance of infant-feeding advice among low-income women. *Journal of Human Lactation,, 25,* 163–172.

Helgeson, V. (2009) *Psychology of gender* (3rd ed.). Upper Saddle River, NJ: Prentice Hall.

Henderson, V. L., & Dweck, C. S. (1990). Motivation and achievement. In S. S. Feldman & G. R. Elliott (Eds.), *At the threshold: The developing adolescent.* Cambridge, MA: Harvard University Press.

Hendrick, J., & Weissman, P. (2010). *The whole child: Developmental education for the early years* (9th ed.). Upper Saddle River, NJ: Prentice Hall.

Hendry, J. (1995). *Understanding Japanese society.* London: Routledge.

Hennessey, B. A. (2010). Intrinsic motivation and creativity: Have we come full circle? In R. A. Beghetto & J. C. Kaufman (Eds.), *Nurturing creativity in the classroom.* New York: Cambridge University Press.

Hennessey, B. A., & Amabile, T. M. (2010). Creativity. *Annual Review of Psychology* (Vol. 61). Palo Alto, CA: Annual Reviews.

Henriksen, T. B., & others. (2004). Alcohol consumption at the time of conception and spontaneous abortion. *American Journal of Epidemiology, 160,* 661–667.

Herman-Giddens, M. E. (2007). The decline in the age of menarche in the United States: Should we be concerned? *Journal of Adolescent Health, 40,* 201–203.

Herrera, S. G., & Murry, K. G. (2011). *Mastering ESL and bilingual methods* (2nd ed.). Boston: Allyn & Bacon.

Herrmann, M., King, K., & Weitzman, M. (2008). Prenatal tobacco smoke and postnatal secondhand smoke exposure and child neurodevelopment. *Current Opinion in Pediatrics, 20,* 184–190.

Hernandez-Reif, M., Diego, M., & Field, T. (2007). Preterm infants show reduced stress behaviors and activity after 5 days of massage therapy. *Infant Behavior and Development, 30,* 557–561.

Hesketh, K. D., & Campbell, K. J. (2010). Interventions to prevent obesity in 0–5 year olds: An updated systematic review of the literature. *Obesity, 18, Suppl 1,* S27–S35.

Hetherington, E. M. (1989). Coping with family transitions: Winners, losers, and survivors. *Child Development, 60,* 1–14.

Hetherington, E. M. (1993). An overview of the Virginia Longitudinal Study of Divorce and Remarriage with a focus on early adolescence. *Journal of Family Psychology, 7,* 39–56.

Hetherington, E. M. (2005). Divorce and the adjustment of children. *Pediatrics in Review, 26,* 163–169.

Hetherington, E. M. (2006). The influence of conflict, marital problem solving, and parenting on children's adjustment in nondivorced, divorced, and remarried families. In A. Clarke-Stewart & J. Dunn (eds.), *Families count.* New York: Oxford University Press.

Hetherington, E. M., & Kelly, J. (2002). *For better or for worse: Divorce reconsidered.* New York: Norton.

Hetherington, E. M., & Stanley-Hagan, M. (2002). Parenting in divorced and remarried families. In M. H. Bornstein (Ed.), *Handbook of parenting* (2nd ed., Vol. 3). Mahwah, NJ: Erlbaum.

Heuwinkel, M. K. (1996). New ways of learning: Five new ways of teaching. *Childhood Education, 72,* 27–31.

Hewitt-Taylor, J. (2010). Supporting children with complex health needs. *Nursing Standards, 24,* 50–56.

Hewlett, B. S. (1991). *Intimate fathers: The nature and context of Aka Pygmy.* Ann Arbor: University of Michigan Press.

Hewlett, B. S. (2000). Culture, history and sex: Anthropological perspectives on father involvement. *Marriage and Family Review, 29,* 324–340.

Hewlett, B. S., & MacFarlan, S. J. (2010). Fathers' roles in hunter-gatherer and other small-scale cultures. In M. E. Lamb (Ed.), *The role of the father in child development* (5th ed.). New York: Wiley.

Heyman, G. D., & Legare, C. H. (2005). Children's evaluation of source of information about traits. *Developmental Psychology, 41,* 636–647.

Hick, P., & Thomas, G. (Eds.). (2009). *Inclusion and diversity in education.* Thousand Oaks, CA: Sage.

Highfield, R. (2008, April 30). *Harvard's baby brain research lab.* Retrieved on January 24, 2009, from www.telegraph.co.uk/scienceandtechnology/science/sciencenews/3341166/

Hill, C. R., & Stafford, E. P. (1980). Parental care of children: Time diary estimate of quantity, predictability, and variety. *Journal of Human Resources, 15,* 219–239.

Hill, M. A. (2007). Early human development. *Clinical Obstetrics and Gynecology, 50,* 2–9.

Hillman, C. H., Buck, S. M., Themanson, J. R., Pontifex, M. B., & Castelli, D. M. (2009). Aerobic fitness and cognitive development: Event-related brain potential and task performance indices of executive control in preadolescent children. *Developmental Psychology, 45,* 114–129.

Hindman, A. H., Skibbek, L. E., Miller, A., & Zimmerman, M. (2010). Ecological contexts and early learning: Contributions of child, family, and classroom factors during Head Start to literacy and mathematics growth through first grade. *Early Childhood Research Quarterly, 25,* 235–250.

Hirsch, B. J., & Rapkin, B. D. (1987). The transition to junior high school: A longitudinal study of self-esteem, psychological symptomatology, school life, and social support. *Child Development, 58,* 1235–1243.

Ho, J., & Birman, D. (2010). Acculturation gaps in Vietnamese immigrant families: Impact on family relationships. *International Journal of Intercultural Relations, 34,* 22–23.

Hockenberry, M., & Wilson, D. (2009). *Wong's essentials of pediatric nursing.* Oxford, UK: Elsevier.

Hoeksema, E., & others. (2010, in press). Enhanced neural activity in frontal and cerebellar circuits after cognitive training in children with attention deficit hyperactivity disorder. *Human Brain Mapping.*

Hoekstra, R. A., Happe, F., Baron-Cohen, S, & Ronald, A. (2010, in press). Limited genetic covariance between autistic traits and intelligence: Findings from a longitudinal twin study. *American Journal of Medical Genetics, B. Neuropsychiatric Genetics.*

Hoff, E., Laursen, B., & Tardif, T. (2002). Socioeconomic status and parenting. In M. H. Bornstein (Ed.), *Handbook of parenting* (2nd ed.). Mahwah, NJ: Erlbaum.

Hoffman, E., & Ewen, D. (2007). Supporting families, nurturing young children. *CLASP Policy Brief No. 9,* 1–11.

Hoffman, M. L. (1970). Moral development. In P. H. Mussen (Ed.), *Manual of child psychology* (3rd ed., Vol. 2). New York: Wiley.

Hoffman, M. L. (1988). Moral development. In M. H. Bornstein & E. Lamb (Eds.), *Developmental psychology: An advanced textbook* (2nd ed.). Hillsdale, NJ: Erlbaum.

Holden, K., & Hatcher, C. (2006). Economic status of the aged. In R. H. Binstock and L. K. George (Eds.), *Handbook of aging and the social sciences.* San Diego: Academic Press.

Hollich, G. J., Newman, R. S., & Jusczyk, P. W. (2005). Infants' use of synchronized visual information to separate streams of speech. *Child Development, 76,* 598–613.

Hollier, L., & Wendel, G. (2008). Third trimester antiviral prophylaxis for preventing maternal genital herpes simplex virus (HSV) recurrences and neonatal infection. *Cochrane Database of Systematic Reviews, 1,* CD004946.

Hollis-Sawyer, L. A., & Sawyer, T. P. (2008). Potential stereotype threat and face validity effects on cognitive-based test performance in the classroom. *Educational Psychology, 28,* 291–304.

Holzman, L. (2009). *Vygotsky at work and play.* Oxford, UK: Routledge.

Hommel, B., Li, K. Z. H., & Li, S-C (2004). Visual search across the life span. *Developmental Psychology, 40,* 545–558.

Honzik, M. P., MacFarlane, I. W., & Allen, L. (1948). The stability of mental test performance between two and eighteen years. *Journal of Experimental Education, 17,* 309–324.

Hood, B. M. (1995). Gravity rules for 2- to-4 year-olds? *Cognitive Development, 10,* 577–598.

Hooper, S. R., & others. (2008). Executive functions in young males with fragile X syndrome in comparison to mental age-matched controls: baseline findings from a longitudinal study. *Neuropsychology, 22,* 36–47.

Hopkins, B. (1991). Facilitating early motor development: An intracultural study of West Indian mothers and their infants living in Britain. In J. K. Nugent, B. M. Lester, & T. B. Brazelton (Eds.), *The cultural context of infancy, Vol. 2: Multicultural and interdisciplinary approaches to parent-infant relations.* Norwood, NJ: Ablex.

Hopkins, B., & Westra, T. (1988). Maternal handling and motor development: An intracultural study. *Genetic Psychology Monographs, 14,* 377–420.

Hopkins, B., & Westra, T. (1990). Motor development, maternal expectations, and the role of handling. *Infant Behavior and Development, 13,* 117–122.

Horn, J. (2007). Spearman, *g,* expertise, and the nature of human cognitive capacity. In P. C. Kyllonen, R. D. Roberts, & L. Stankov (Eds.), *Extending intelligence.* Mahwah, NJ: Erlbaum.

Horne, R. S., Franco, P., Adamson, T. M., Groswasser, J., & Kahn, A. (2002). Effects of body position on sleep and arousal characteristics in infants. *Early Human Development, 69,* 25–33.

Hornickel, J., Skoe, E., & Kraus, N. (2008). Subcortical laterality of speech encoding. *Audiology and Neuro-Otology, 14,* 198–207.

Horowitz, F. D. (2009). Introduction: A developmental understanding of giftedness and talent. In F. D. Horowitz, R. F. Subotnik, & D. J. Matthews (Eds.), *The development of giftedness and talent across the life span.* Washington, DC: American Psychological Association.

Horton, R. (2006). The coming decade for global action on child health. *Lancet, 367,* 3–5.

The Hospital for Sick Children, Dipchard, A., Friedman, J., Gupta, S., Bismilla, Z., & Lam, C. (2010). *The Hospital for Sick Children's handbook of pediatrics* (11th ed.). London: Elsevier.

Howe, M. J. A., Davidson, J. W., Moore, D. G., & Sloboda, J. A. (1995). Are there early childhood signs of musical ability? *Psychology of Music, 23,* 162–176.

Howe, M. L., Courage, M. L., & Rooksby, M. (2009). The genesis and development of autobiographical memory. In M. Courage & N. Cowan (Eds.), *The development of memory in infancy and childhood.* New York: Psychology Press.

Howe, N., & Recchia, H. E. (2008). Siblings and sibling rivalry. In M. M. Haith & J. B. Benson (Eds.), *Encyclopedia of infant and early childhood development.* Oxford, UK: Elsevier.

Howell, D. C. (2010). *Statistical methods for psychology* (7th ed.). Boston: Cengage.

Howes, C. (1985, April). *Predicting preschool sociometric status from toddler peer interaction.* Paper presented at the meeting of the Society for Research in Child Development, Toronto.

Howes, C. (2009). Friendship in early childhood. In K. H. Rubin, W. M., Bukowski, & B. Laursen (Eds.), *Handbook of peer interactions, relationships, and groups.* New York: Guilford.

Howes, C. (2009). The impact of child care on young children (0–2). In R. E. Tremblay, R deV Peters, M. Boivan, & R. G. Barr (Eds.), *Encyclopedia on early childhood development.* Montreal: Centre of Excellence for Early Childhood Development.

Howes, C., & Wishard Guerra, A. G. (2009). Networks of attachment relationships in low-income children of Mexican heritage: Infancy through preschool. *Social Development, 18*(4), 896–914.

Howlin, P., Magiati, I., & Charman, T. (2009). Systematic review of early intensive behavioral interventions with autism. *American Journal on Intellectual and Developmental Disabilities, 114,* 23–41.

Hoyert, D. L., Mathews, T. J., Menacker, F., Strobino, D. M., & Guyer, B. (2006). Annual summary of vital statistics: 2004. *Pediatrics, 117,* 168–183.

Huang, L. N., and Ying, Y. (1989). Chinese American children and adolescents. In J. T. Gibbs and L. N. Huang (Eds.), *Children of color.* San Francisco: Jossey-Bass.

Huda, S. S., Brodie, L. E., & Sattar, N. (2010). Obesity in pregnancy: Prevalence and metabolic consequences. *Seminars in pregnancy: Prevalence and metabolic consequences, 15,* 70–76.

Huebner, A. M., & Garrod, A. C. (1993). Moral reasoning among Tibetan monks: A study of Buddhist adolescents and young adults in Nepal. *Journal of Cross-Cultural Psychology, 24,* 167–185.

Huesmann, L. R., Dubow, E. F., Eron, L. D., & Boxer, P. (2006). Middle childhood family-contextual and personal factors as predictors of adult outcomes. In A. C. Huston & M. N. Ripke (Eds.), *Developmental contexts in middle childhood.* New York: Cambridge University Press.

Huesmann, L. R., Moise-Titus, Podolski, C., & Eron, L. D. (2003). Longitudinal Relations between children's exposure to TV violence and their aggressive and violent behavior in young adulthood, 1977–1992. *Developmental Psychology, 39,* 201–221.

Hughes, C., & Dunn, J. (2007). Children's relationships with other children. In C. A. Brownell & C. B. Kopp (Eds.), *Socioemotional development in the toddler years.* New York: Guilford.

Hughes, C., & Ensor, R. (2010). Do early social cognition and executive function predict individual differences in preschoolers' prosocial and antisocial behavior? In B. Sokol, U. Muller, J. Carpendale, A. Young, & G. Larocci (Eds.),

Self and social regulation. New York: Oxford University Press.

Hurt, H., Brodsky, N. L., Roth, H., Malmud, F., & Glannetta, J. M. (2005). School performance of children with gestational cocaine exposure. *Neurotoxicology and Teratology, 27,* 203–211.

Huston, A. C., & Bentley, A. C. (2010). Human development in societal context. *Annual Review of Psychology* (Vol. 61). Palo Alto, CA: Annual Reviews.

Huston, A. C., Epps, S. R., Shim, M. S., Duncan, G. J., Crosby, D. A., & Ripke, M. N. (2006). Effects of a family poverty intervention program last from middle childhood to adolescence. In A. C. Huston, & M. N. Ripke (Eds.). *Developmental contexts of middle childhood.* New York: Cambridge University Press.

Huston, A. C., & Ripke, M. N. (2006). Experiences in middle childhood and children's development: A summary and integration of research. In A. C. Huston & M. N. Ripke (Eds.), *Developmental contexts in middle childhood.* New York: Cambridge University Press.

Hutson, R. A. (2008). Poverty. In N. J. Salkind (Ed.), *Encyclopedia of educational psychology.* Thousand Oaks, CA: Sage.

Huttenlocher, J., Haight, W., Bruk, A., Seltzer, M., & Lyons, T. (1991). Early vocabulary growth: Relation to language input and gender. *Developmental Psychology, 27,* 236–248.

Huttenlocher, P. R., & Dabholkar, A. S. (1997). Regional differences in synaptogenesis in human cerebral cortex. *Journal of Comparative Neurology, 37*(2), 167–178.

Hyde, D. C. & Spelke, E. S. (2009). All numbers are not equal: An electrophysiological investigation of small and large number representations. *Journal of Cognitive Neuroscience, 21,* 1039–1053.

Hyde, J. S. (2005). The gender similarities hypothesis. *American Psychologist, 60,* 581–592.

Hyde, J. S. (2007a). *Half the human experience* (7th ed.). Boston: Houghton Mifflin.

Hyde, J. S. (2007b). New directions in the study of gender similarities and differences. *Current Directions in Psychological Science, 16,* 259–263.

Hyde, J. S., Lindberg, S. M., Linn, M. C., Ellis, A. B., & Williams, C. C. (2008). Gender similarities characterize math performance. *Science, 321,* 494–495.

Hyde, L. W., Shaw, D. S., & Moilanen, K. L. (2010). Developmental precursors of moral disengagement and the role of moral disengagement in the development of antisocial behavior. *Journal of Abnormal Child Psychology, 38,* 197–209.

Hyson, M. (2007). Curriculum. In R. New & M. Cochran (Eds.), *Early childhood education: An international encyclopedia of early childhood education.* New York: Greenwood.

Hyson, M. C., Copple, C., & Jones, J. (2006). Early childhood development and education. In W. Damon & R. Lerner (Eds.), *Handbook of child psychology* (6th ed.). New York: Wiley.

I

"I Have a Dream" Foundation. (2008). *About us.* Retrieved July 5, 2008, from http://www.ihad.org

"I Have a Dream" Foundation. (2010). *About us.* Retrieved June 6, 2010, from http://www.ihad.org

Ige, F., & Shelton, D. (2004). Reducing risk of sudden infant death syndrome (SIDS) in African-American communities. *Journal of Pediatrics Nursing, 19,* 290–292.

Imada, T., Zhang, Y., Cheour, M., Taulu, S., Ahonen, A., & Kuhl, P. K. (2007). Infant speech perception activates Boca's area: A developmental magnetoencephalography study. *Neuroreport, 17,* 957–962.

Impett, E. A., Schoolder, D., Tolman, L., Sorsoli, L., & Henson, J. M. (2008). Girls' relationship authenticity and self-esteem across adolescence. *Developmental Psychology, 44,* 722–733.

Insel, P. M., & Roth, W. T. (2010). *Core concepts in health* (11th ed.). New York: McGraw-Hill.

International Montessori Council. (2006). Larry Page and Sergey Brin, founders of Google.com, credit their Montessori education for much of their success on prime-time television. Retrieved June 24, 2010, from www.Montessori.org/enews/barbara_walters.html

Ip, S., Chung, M., Raman, G., Trikalinos, T. A., & Lau, J. (2009). A summary of the Agency for Healthcare Research and Quality's evidence report on breastfeeding in developed countries. *Breastfeeding Medicine, 4, Suppl 1,* S17–S30.

Irvin, J. L., Buehl, D. R., & Klemp, R. M. (2007). *Reading and the high school student* (2nd ed.). Boston: Allyn & Bacon.

Irvine, S. H., & Berry, J. W. (Eds.). (2010). *Human abilities in cultural contexts.* New York: Cambridge University Press.

Ise, E., & Schulte-Korne, G. (2010, in press). Spelling deficits in dyslexia: Evaluation of an orthographic spelling training. *Annals of Dyslexia.*

Isen, J., & Baker, L. A. (2008). Genetic disorders: Sex-linked. In M. M. Haith & J. B. Benson (Eds.), *Encyclopedia of infancy and early childhood development.* Oxford, UK: Elsevier.

Isen, J. D., Baker, L. A., Raine, A., & Bezdjian, S. (2009). Genetic and environmental influences on the Junior Temperament and Character Inventory in a preadolescent twin sample. *Behavior Genetics, 39,* 36–47.

Iturria-Medina, Y., & others (2010, in press). Brain hemispheric structural efficiency and interconnectivity rightward asymmetry in human and nonhuman primates. *Cerebral Cortex.*

Izard, C. E. (2009). Emotion theory and research: Highlights, unanswered questions, and emerging issues. *Annual Review of Psychology* (Vol. 60). Palo Alto, CA: Annual Reviews.

Izard, V., Dehaene-Lambertz, G., & Dehaene, S. (2008). Distinct cerebral pathways for object identity and number in human infants. *PLoS Biology, 6,* e11.

Izard, V., & Spelke, E. S. (2010, in press). Development of sensitivity of geometry in visual forms. *Human Evolution*.

J

Jackson, S. L. (2008). *Research methods*. Belmont, CA: Wadsworth.

Jackson-Newsom, J., & Shelton, T. L. (2010). Psychobiological models of adolescent risk: Implications for prevention and risk. *Developmental Psychobiology, 52*, 295–297.

Jaeggi, S. M., Berman, M. G., & Jonides, J. (2009). Training attentional processes. *Trends in Cognitive Science, 37*, 644–654.

Jaffee, S., & Hyde, J. S. (2000). Gender differences in moral orientation: A meta-analysis. *Psychological Bulletin, 126*, 703–726.

Jago, R., Froberg, K., Cooper, A. R., Eiberg, S., & Andersen, L. B. (2010). Three-year changes in fitness and adiposity are independently associated with cardiovascular risk factors among Danish children. *Journal of Physical Activity and Health, 7*, 37–44.

Jalongo, M. R. (2011). *Early childhood language arts* (5th ed.). Boston: Allyn & Bacon.

James, A. H., Brancazio, L. R., & Price, T. (2008). Aspirin and reproductive outcomes. *Obstetrical and Gynecological Survey, 63*, 49–57.

James, D. C., & Dobson, B. (2005). Position of the American Dietetic Association: Promoting and supporting breastfeeding. *Journal of the American Dietetic Association, 105*, 810–818.

Jamieson, P. E., & Romer, D. (2008). Unrealistic fatalism in U.S. youth ages 14–22: Prevalence and characteristics. *Journal of Adolescent Health, 42*, 154–160.

Jansen, J., de Weerth, C., & Riksen-Walraven, J. M. (2008). Breastfeeding and the mother-infant relationship—A review. *Developmental Review, 28*, 503–521.

Jarrett, R. L. (1995). Growing up poor: The family experiences of socially mobile youth in low-income African-American neighborhoods. *Journal of Adolescent Research, 10*, 111–135.

Jarvin, L., Newman, T., Randi, J., Sternberg, R. J., & Grigorenko, E. L. (2008). Matching instruction and assessment. In J. A. Plucker & C. M. Callahan (Eds.), *Critical issues and practices in gifted education* (pp. 345–365). Waco, TX: Prufrock.

Jaswal, V. K., & Fernald, A. (2007). Learning to communicate. In A. Slater & M. Lewis (Eds.), *Introduction to infant development* (2nd ed.). New York: Oxford University Press.

Jayson, S. (2006, June 29). The 'millenials' come of age. *USA TODAY*, pp. 1–2D.

Jencks, C. (1979). *Who gets ahead? The determinants of economic success in America*. New York: Basic Books.

Jenkins, J. M., & Astington, J. W. (1996). Cognitive factors and family structure associated with theory of mind development in young children. *Developmental Psychology, 32*, 70–78.

Jensen, A. R. (2008). Book review. *Intelligence, 36*, 96–97.

Ji, B. T., & others. (1997). Paternal cigarette smoking and the risk of childhood cancer among offspring of nonsmoking mothers. *Journal of the National Cancer Institute, 89*, 238–244.

Jiao, S., Ji, G., & Jing, Q. (1996). Cognitive development of Chinese urban only children and children with siblings. *Child Development, 67*, 387–395.

Jimerson, S. R. (2009). High school dropout. In D. Carr (Ed.), *Encyclopedia of the life course and human development*. Boston: Gale Cengage.

Johns Hopkins University. (2006). *Research: Tribal connections*. Retrieved on January 31, 2008 from http://www.krieger.jhu.edu/research/spotlight/prabhakar.html

Johnson, G. B., & Losos, J. (2010). *The living world* (6th ed.). New York: McGraw-Hill.

Johnson, J. A., Musial, D. L., Hall, G. E., & Gollnick, D. M. (2011). *Foundations of American education in a changing world* (15th ed.). Upper Saddle River, NJ: Merrill.

Johnson, J. S., & Newport, E. L. (1991). Critical period effects on universal properties of language: The status of subjacency in the acquisition of a second language. *Cognition, 39*, 215–258.

Johnson, M. H. (2010). Understanding the social world: A developmental neuroscience approach. In S. D. Calkins & M. A. Bell (Eds.), *Child development at the intersection of emotion and cognition*. Washington, DC: American Psychological Association.

Johnson, M. H., Grossmann, T. and Cohen-Kadosh, K. (2009). Mapping functional brain development: Building a social brain through Interactive Specialization. *Developmental Psychology, 45*, 151–159.

Johnson, S. P. (2004). Development of perceptual completion in infancy. *Psychological Science, 15*, 769–775.

Johnson, S. P. (2009). Development origins of object perception. In A. Woodward & A. Needham (Eds.), *Learning and the infant mind*. New York: Oxford University Press.

Johnson, S. P. (2010a, in press). Perceptual completion in infancy. In S. P. Johnson (Ed.), *Neoconstructivism: The new science of cognitive development*. New York: Oxford University Press.

Johnson, S. P. (2010b, in press). A constructivist view of object perception in infancy. To appear in L. M. Oakes, C. H. Cashon, M. Casasola, & D. H Rakison (Eds.), *Early perceptual and cognitive development*. New York: Oxford University Press.

Johnson, S. P., Bremner, J. G., Slater, A., & Mason, U. (2000). The role of good form in young infants' perception of partly occluded objects. *Journal of Experimental Child Psychology, 76*, 1–25.

Johnson, W., te Nijenhuis, J., & Bouchard, T. J. (2008). Still just l g: Consistent results from five test batteries. *Intelligence, 36*, 81–95.

John-Steiner, V. (2007). Vygotsky on thinking and speaking. In H. Daniels, J. Wertsch, & M. Cole (Eds.), *The Cambridge companion to Vygotsky*. New York: Cambridge University Press.

Johnston, M. (2008, April 30). Commentary in R. Highfield *Harvard's baby brain research lab*. Retrieved on January 24, 2008, from www.telegraph.co.uk/scienceandtechnology/science/sciencenews/3341166/

Johnston, C. C., & others. (2009). Enhanced kangaroo care for heel lance in preterm neonates: A crossover trial. *Journal of Perinatology, 29*, 51–56.

Jones, H. W. (2007). Iatrogenic multiple births: A 2003 checkup: *Fertility and Sterility, 87*, 453–455.

Jones, M. C. (1965). Psychological correlates of somatic development. *Child Development, 36*, 899–911.

Jones, M. D., & Galliher, R. V. (2007). Navajo ethnic identity: Predictors of psychosocial outcomes in Navajo adolescents. *Journal of Research on Adolescence, 17*, 683–696.

Jordan, S. J., & others. (2008). Serious ovarian, fallopian tube, and primary peritoneal cancers: A comprehensive epidemiological analysis. *International Journal of Cancer, 122*, 1598–1603.

Joseph, J. (2006). *The missing gene*. New York: Algora.

Josephson Institute of Ethics. (2008). *The ethics of American youth 2008*. Los Angeles: Josephson Institute.

Juang, L., & Syed, M. (2010, in press). Family cultural socialization practices and ethnic identity in college-going emerging adults. *Journal of Adolescence*.

Juffer, F., & van IJzendoorn, M. H. (2005). Behavior problems and mental health referrals of international adoptees: A meta-analysis. *Journal of the American Medical Association, 293*, 2501–2513.

Juffer, F., & van IJzendoorn, M. H. (2007). Adoptees do not lack self-esteem: A meta-analysis of studies on self-esteem of transracial, international, and domestic adoptees, *Psychological Bulletin, 133*, 1067–1083.

Jusczyk, P. W., & Hohne, E. A. (1997). Infants' memory for spoken words. *Science, 277*, 1984–1986.

Jylhava, J., & others. (2009). Genetics of C-reactive protein and complement factor H have an epistatic effect on carotid artery compliance: The Cardiovascular Risk in Young Finns Study. *Clinical and Experimental Immunology, 155*, 53–58.

K

Kaatsch, P. (2010, in press). Epidemiology of childhood cancer. *Cancer Treatment Reviews*.

Kagan, J. (1987). Perspectives on infancy. In J. D. Osofsky (Ed.), *Handbook on infant development* (2nd ed.). New York: Wiley.

Kagan, J. (1992). Yesterday's promises, tomorrow's promises. *Developmental Psychology, 28*, 990–997.

Kagan, J. (2000). Temperament. In A. Kazdin (Ed.), *Encyclopedia of psychology*.

Kagan, J. (2002). Behavioral inhibition as a temperamental category. In R. J. Davidson, K. R. Scherer, & H. H. Goldsmith (Eds.), *Handbook of affective sciences.* New York: Oxford University Press.

Kagan, J. (2003). Biology, context, and development. *Annual Review of Psychology* (Vol. 54). Palo Alto, CA: Annual Reviews.

Kagan, J. (2008). Fear and wariness. In M. M. Haith & J. B. Benson (Eds.), *Encyclopedia of infant and early childhood development.* Oxford, UK: Elsevier.

Kagan, J. (2010). Emotions and temperament. In M. H. Bornstein (Ed.), *Handbook of cultural developmental science.* New York: Psychology Press.

Kagan, J., Kearsley, R. B., & Zelazo, P. R. (1978). *Infancy: Its place in human development.* Cambridge, MA: Harvard University Press.

Kagan, J., & Snidman, N. (1991). Infant predictors of inhibited and uninhibited behavioral profiles. *Psychological Science, 2,* 40–44.

Kagan, J., Snidman, N., Kahn, V., & Towsley, S. (2007). The preservation of two infant temperaments into adolescence. *Monographs of the Society for Research in Child Development, 72*(2), 1–75.

Kagan, S. L., & Scott-Little, C. (2004). Early learning standards. *Phi Delta Kappan, 82,* 388–395.

Kail, R. V. (2007). Longitudinal evidence that increases in processing speed and working memory enhance children's reasoning. *Psychological Science, 18,* 312–313.

Kalder, M., Knoblauch, K., Hrgovic, I., & Munstedt, K. (2010). Use of complementary and alternative medicine during pregnancy and delivery. *Archives of Gynecology and Obstetrics.* (Available online February 23, 2010.)

Kamii, C. (1985). *Young children reinvent arithmetic: Implications of Piaget's theory.* New York: Teachers College Press.

Kamii, C. (1989). *Young children continue to reinvent arithmetic.* New York: Teachers College Press.

Kandler, C., Riemann, R., & Kampfe, N. (2009). Genetic and personality mediation between measures of personality and family environment in twins reared together. *Behavior Genetics, 39,* 24–35.

Kanoy, K., Ulku-Steiner, B., Cox, M., & Burchinal, M. (2003). Marital relationship and individual psychological characteristics that predict physical punishment of children. *Journal of Family Psychology, 17,* 20–28.

Kao, G., & Turney, K. (2010). Adolescents and schooling: Differences by race, ethnicity, and immigrant status. In D. P. Swanson, M. C. Edwards, & M. B. Spencer (Eds.), *Adolescence: Development in a global era.* San Diego: Academic Press.

Kaplan, H. B. (2009). Self-esteem. In D. Carr (Ed.), *Encyclopedia of the life course and human development.* Boston: Gale Cengage.

Kar, B. R., Rao, S. L, & Chandramouli, B. A. (2008). Cognitive development in children with chronic energy malnutrition. *Behavioral and Brain Functions, 4,* 31.

Kar, N. (2009). Psychological impact of disasters on children: Review of assessment and interventions. *World Journal of Pediatrics, 5,* 5–11.

Karama, S., & others. (2009). Positive association between cognitive ability and cortical thickness in a representative sample of healthy 6- to 18-year-olds. *Intelligence, 37,* 145–155.

Karoly, L. A. & Bigelow, J. A. (2005). *The economics of investing in universal preschool education in California.* Santa Monica, CA: The RAND Corporation.

Karpov, Y. V. (2006). *The neo-Vygotskian approach to child development.* New York: Cambridge University Press.

Karreman, A., van Tuijl, C., van Aken, M. A. G., & Dekovic, M. (2008). Parenting, coparenting, and effortful control in preschoolers. *Journal of Family Psychology, 22,* 30–40.

Kasari, C., & Lawton, K. (2010). New directions in behavioral treatment of autism spectrum disorders. *Current Opinion in Neurology, 23,* 137–143.

Katz, L. (1999). Curriculum disputes in early childhood education. *ERIC Clearinghouse on Elementary and Early Childhood Education,* Document EDO-PS-99-13.

Kauffman, J. M., & Landrum, T. J. (2009). *Characteristics of emotional and behavioral disorders of children and youth* (9th ed.). Boston: Allyn & Bacon.

Kauffman, J. M., McGee, K., & Brigham, M. (2004). Enabling or disabling? Observations on changes in special education. *Phi Delta Kappan, 85,* 613–620.

Kaufman, J. C., & Sternberg, R. J. (Eds.) (2010). *Cambridge handbook of creativity.* New York: Cambridge University Press.

Kavsek, M. (2009). The perception of subjective contours and neon color spreading figures in young infants. *Attention, Perception, and Psychophysics, 71,* 412–420.

Keating, D. P. (1990). Adolescent thinking. In S. S. Feldman & G. R. Elliott (Eds.), *At the threshold: The developing adolescent.* Cambridge, MA: Harvard University Press.

Keating, D. P. (2009). Developmental science and giftedness: An integrated life-span framework. In F. D. Horowitz, R. F. Subotnik, & D. J. Matthews (Eds.), *The development of giftedness and talent across the life span.* Washington, DC: American Psychological Association.

Keen, R. (2005). Unpublished review of Santrock, *Topical Life-Span Development,* 3rd ed. New York: McGraw-Hill

Keers, R., & others. (2010). Interaction between serotonin transporter gene variants and life events predicts response to antidepressants in the GENDEP project. *Pharmacogenomics.* (Available online March 9, 2010.)

Kellman, P. J., & Arterberry, M. E. (2006). Infant visual perception. In W. Damon & R. Lerner (Eds.), *Handbook of child psychology* (6th ed.). New York: Wiley.

Kellman, P. J., & Banks, M. S. (1998). Infant visual perception. In W. Damon (Eds.), *Handbook of child psychology* (5th ed., Vol. 2). New York: Wiley.

Kellogg, R. T. (2007). *Fundamentals of cognitive psychology.* Thousand Oaks, CA: Sage.

Kellow, J. T., & Jones, B. D. (2008). The effects of stereotypes on the achievement gap: Reexamining the academic performance of African American high school students. *Journal of Black Psychology, 34,* 94–120.

Kelly, D. J., & others. (2007). Cross-race preferences for same-race faces extend beyond the African versus Caucasian contrast in 3-month-old infants. *Infancy, 11,* 87–95.

Kelly, D., J., Liu, S., Lee, K., Quinn, P. C., Pascalls, O., Slater, A. M., & Ge, L. (2009). Development of the other-race effect in infancy: Evidence toward universality? *Journal of Experimental Child Psychology, 104*(1), 105–114.

Kelly, J. P., Borchert., J., & Teller, D. Y. (1997). The development of chromatic and achromatic sensitivity in infancy as tested with the sweep VEP. *Vision Research, 37,* 2057–2072.

Kennedy, M. A. (2009). Child abuse. In D. Carr (Ed.), *Encyclopedia of the life course and human development.* Boston: Gale Cengage.

Kennell, J. H. (2006). Randomized controlled trial of skin-to-skin contact from birth versus conventional incubator for physiological stabilization in 1200 g to 2199 g newborns. *Acta Paediatrica (Sweden), 95,* 15–16.

Kennell, J. H., & McGrath, S. K. (1999). Commentary: Practical and humanistic lessons from the third world for perinatal caregivers everywhere. *Birth, 26,* 9–10.

Kenney-Benson, G. A., Pomerantz, E. M., Ryan, A. M., & Patrick, H. (2006). Sex differences in math performance: The role of children's approach to schoolwork. *Developmental Psychology, 42,* 11–26.

Kessen, W., Haith, M. M., & Salapatek, P. (1970). Human infancy. In P. H. Mussen (Ed.), *Manual of child psychology* (3rd ed., Vol. 1). New York: Wiley.

Keyes, M. A., Sharma, A., Elkins, I. J., Iacono, W. G., & McGue, M. (2008). The mental health of U.S. adolescents adopted in infancy. *Archives of Pediatric and Adolescent Medicine, 162,* 419–425.

Kiess, H. O., & Green, B. A. (2010). *Statistical concepts for the behavioral sciences* (4th ed.). Boston: Allyn & Bacon.

Kim, G., Walden, T. A., & Knieps, L. J. (2010). Impact and characteristics of positive and fearful emotional messages during infant social referencing. *Infant Behavior and Development, 33,* 189–195.

Kim, H., & Johnson, S. P. (2010, in press). Infant perception. To appear in B. Goldstein (Ed.), *Encyclopedia of perception.* Thousand Oaks, CA: Sage.

Kim, J., & others. (2006). Trends in overweight from 1980 through 2001 among preschool-aged children enrolled in a health maintenance organization. *Obesity, 14*, 1107–1112.

Kim, J-K., McHale, S. M., Crouter, A. C., & Osgood, D. W. (2007). Longitudinal linkages between sibling relationships and adjustment from middle childhood through adolescence. *Developmental Psychology, 43*, 960–973.

Kim, S. Y., Su, J., Yancura, L., & Yee, B. (2009). Asian American and Pacific Islander families. In N. Tewari & A. Aluarez (Eds.), *Asian American Psychology*. New York Psychology Press.

Kimber, L., McNabb, M., McCourt, C., Haines, A., & Brocklehurst, P. (2008). Massage or music for pain relief in labor: A pilot randomized placebo controlled trial. *European Journal of Pain, 12*, 961–969.

King, P. E., & Roeser, R. W. (2009). Religion and spirituality in adolescent development. In R. M. Lerner & L. Steinberg (Eds.), *Handbook of adolescent psychology* (3rd ed.). New York: Wiley.

Kingston, M. H. (1976). *The woman warrior: Memoirs of a girlhood among ghosts*. New York: Vintage Books.

Kini, S., Morrell, D., Thong, K. J., Kopakaki, A., Hillier, S., & Irvine, D. S. (2010). Lack of impact of semen quality on fertilization in assisted conception. *Scottish Medicine, 55*, 20–23.

Kinney, H. C., Richerson, G. B., Dymecki, S. M., Darnall, R. A., & Nattie, E. E. (2009). The brainstem and serotonin in sudden infant death syndrome. *Annual Review of Pathology, 4*, 517–550.

Kirkorian, H. L., Wartella, E. A., & Anderson, D. A. (2008). Media and young children's learning. *Future of Children, 18*(1), 39–61.

Kisilevsky, B. S. & others (2009). Fetal sensitivity to properties of maternal speech and language. *Infant Behavior and Development, 32*, 59–71.

Kisilevsky, B. S., & Hains, S. M. J. (2010, in press). Onset and maturation of fetal heart rate response to the mother's voice over late gestation. *Developmental Science*.

Kisilevsky, S., Hains, S. M., Jacquet, A. Y., Granier-Deferre, C., & Lecanuet, J. P. (2004). Maturation of fetal responses to music. *Developmental Science, 7*, 550–559.

Kitayama, S. (2011). Psychology and culture: Cross-country or regional comparisons. *Annual Review of Psychology* (Vol. 62). Palo Alto, CA: Annual Reviews.

Kitsantas, P., & Gaffney, K. F. (2010). Racial/ ethnic disparities in infant mortality. *Journal of Perinatal Medicine, 38*, 87–94.

Klaczynski, P. (2001). The influence of analytic and heuristic processing on adolescent reasoning and decision making. *Child Development, 72*, 844–861.

Klaus, M., & Kennell, H. H. (1976). *Maternal-infant bonding*. St. Louis: Mosbv.

Kliegman, R. M., Behrman, R. E., Jenson, H. B., & Stanton, B. F. (2007). *Nelson textbook of pediatrics* (18th ed.). London: Elsevier.

Klima, C., Norr, K., Conderheld, S., & Handler, A. (2009). Introduction of Centering Pregnancy in a public health clinic. *Journal of Midwifery and Women's Health, 54*, 27–34.

Klingenberg, C. P., & others. (2010). Prenatal alcohol exposure alters the patterns of facial asymmetry. *Alcohol*. (Available online January 7, 2010.)

Klug, W. S., Cummings, M. R., Spencer, C., & Palladino, M. A. (2010). *Essentials of genetics* (7th ed.). Upper Saddle River, NJ: Benjamin Cummings.

Knecht, A., Snijders, T. A. B., Baervedlt, C., Steglich, C. E. G., & Raub, W. (2010, in press). Friendship and delinquency: Selection and influence processes in early adolescence. *Social Development*.

Knopik, V. S. (2009). Maternal smoking during pregnancy and child outcomes: Real or spurious effect? *Developmental Neuropsychology, 34*, 1–36.

Kohen, D. E., Leventhal, T., Dahinten, V. S., & McIntosh, C. N. (2008). Neighborhood disadvantage: Pathways of effects for young children. *Child Development, 79*, 156–169.

Kopp, C. B. (2011). Socio-emotional development in the early years: Socialization and consciousness. *Annual Review of Psychology* (Vol. 62). Palo Alto, CA: Annual Reviews.

Kopp, C. B., & Neufeld, S. J. (2002). Emotional development in infancy. In R. Davidson & K. Scherer (Eds.), *Handbook of affective sciences*. New York: Oxford University Press.

Koppelman, K. (2011). *Perspectives on human differences*. Boston: Allyn & Bacon.

Koppelman, K., & Goodhart, L. (2011). *Understanding human differences* (3rd ed.). Boston: Allyn & Bacon.

Korat, O. (2009). The effect of maternal teaching talk on children's emergent literacy as a function of type of activity and maternal education level. *Journal of Applied Developmental Psychology, 30*, 34–42.

Kornblum, J. (2006, March 9). How to monitor the kids? *USA Today, 1D*, p. 1.

Kostelnik, M. J., Soderman, A. K., & Whiren, A. P. (2011). *Developmentally appropriate curricula* (5th ed.). Upper Saddle River, NJ: Merrill.

Koutures, C. G., & Gregory, A. J. (2010). Injuries in youth soccer. *Pediatrics, 125*, 410–414.

Knopik, V. S. (2009). Maternal smoking during pregnancy and child outcomes: Real or spurious? *Developmental Neuropsychology, 34*, 1–36.

Knox, M. (2010). On hitting children: A review of corporal punishment in the United States. *Journal of Pediatric Health Care, 24*, 103–107.

Kochanska, G., & Aksan, N. (2007). Conscience in childhood: Past, present, and future. *Merrill-Palmer Quarterly, 50*, 299–310.

Kochanska, G., Aksan, N., Prisco, T. R., & Adams, E. E. (2008). Mother-child and father-child mutually responsive orientation in the first two years and children's outcomes at preschool age: Mechanisms of influence. *Child Development, 79*, 30–44.

Kochanska, G., Forman, D. R., Aksan, N., & Dunbar, S. B. (2005). Pathways to conscience: Early mother-child mutually responsive orientation and children's moral emotion, conduct, and cognition. *Journal of Child Psychology and Psychiatry, 46*, 19–34.

Kochanska, G., Gross, J. N., Lin, M., & Nichols, K. E. (2002). Guilt in young children: Development, determinants, and relations with a broader set of standards. *Child Development, 73*, 461–482.

Koenig, L. B., McGue, M., & Iacono, W. G. (2008). Stability and change in religiousness during emerging adulthood. *Developmental Psychology. 44*, 523–543.

Koerner, M. V., & Barlow, D. P. (2010). Genomic imprinting—an epigenetic regulatory model. *Current Opinion in Genetics & Development, 202*(2), 164–170.

Kohlberg, L. (1958). *The development of modes of moral thinking and choice in the years 10 to 16*. Unpublished doctoral dissertation, University of Chicago.

Kohlberg, L. (1969). Stage and sequence: The cognitive-developmental approach to socialization. In D. A. Goslin (Ed.), *Handbook of socialization theory and research*. Chicago: Rand McNally.

Kohlberg, L. (1986). A current statement on some theoretical issues. In S. Modgil & C. Modgil (Eds.), *Lawrence Kohlberg*. Philadelphia: Falmer.

Koolhof, R. Loeber, R., Wei, E. H., Pardini, D., & D'Escury, A. C. (2007). Inhibition deficits of serious delinquent boys of low intelligence. *Criminal Behavior and Mental Health, 17*, 274–292.

Kopp, C. P. (2011). Socio-emotional development in the early years: Socialization and consciousness. *Annual Review of Psychology* (Vol. 62). Palo Alto, CA: Annual Reviews.

Kotovsky, L., & Baillargeon, R. Calibration-based reasoning about collision events in 11-month-old infants. *Cognition, 51*, 107–129.

Kramer, L. (2006, July 10). Commentary in "How your siblings make you who you are" by J. Kluger. *Time*, pp. 46–55.

Kramer, L., & Perozynski, L. (1999). Parental beliefs about managing sibling conflict. *Developmental Psychology, 35*, 489–499.

Kramer, L., & Radey, C. (1997). Improving sibling relationships among young children: A social skills training model. *Family Relations, 46*, 237–246.

Kramer, M. (2003). Commentary: Breastfeeding and child health, growth, and survival. *International Journal of Epidemiology, 32*, 96–98.

Krauss, R. A., & Glucksberg, S. (1969). The development of communication: Competence as a function of age. *Child Development, 40*, 255–266.

Kreimler, S., & others. (2010, in press). Effect of school-based physical activity program (KISS) on fitness and adiposity in primary school children: Cluster randomized controlled trial. *British Medical Journal.*

Kreutzer, L. C., & Flavell, J. H. (1975). An interview study of children's knowledge about memory. *Monographs of the Society for Research in Child Development, 40*(1), Serial No. 159.

Krimer, L. S., & Goldman-Rakic, P. S. (2001). Prefrontal microcircuits. *Journal of Neuroscience, 21,* 3788–3796.

Kroger, J. (2007). *Identity development: Adolescence through adulthood* (2nd ed.). Thousand Oaks, CA: Sage.

Kroger, J., Martinussen, M., & Marcia, J. E. (2010, in press). Identity change during adolescence and young adulthood: A meta-analysis. *Journal of Adolescence.*

Kronenberg, G., & others. (2010). Impact of actin filament stabilization on adult hippocampal and olfactory bulb neurogenesis. *Journal of Neuoroscience, 30,* 3419–3431.

Krueger, J. I., Vohs, K. D., & Baumeister, R. F. (2008). Is the allure of self-esteem a mirage after all? *American Psychologist, 63,* 64.

Kuebli, J. (1994, March). Young children's understanding of everyday emotions. *Young Children,* pp. 36–48.

Kuhl, P. K. (1993). Infant speech perception: A window on psycholinguistic development. *International Journal of Psycholinguistics, 9,* 33–56.

Kuhl, P. K. (2000). A new view of language acquisition. *Proceedings of the National Academy of Science, 97*(22), 11850–11857.

Kuhl, P. K. (2007). Is speech learning 'gated' by the social brain? *Developmental Science, 10,* 110–120.

Kuhl, P. K. (2009). Linking infant speech perception to language acquisition: Phonetic learning predicts language growth. In J. Colombo, P. McCardle, & L. Freund (Eds.), *Infant pathways to language.* New York: Psychology Press.

Kuhn, D. (1998). Afterword to Volume 2: Cognition, perception, and language. In W. Damon (Ed.), *Handbook of child psychology* (5th ed., Vol. 2). New York: Wiley.

Kuhn, D. (2008). Formal operations from a twenty-first century perspective. *Human Development, 51,* 48–55.

Kuhn, D. (2009). Adolescent thinking. In R. M. Lerner & L. Steinberg (Eds.), *Handbook of adolescent psychology* (3rd ed.). New York: Wiley.

Kuhn, D. (2011). What is scientific thinking and how does it develop? In U. Goswami (Ed.), *Wiley-Blackwell handbook of childhood cognitive development* (2nd ed.). New York: Wiley-Blackwell.

Kuhn, D., Cheney, R., & Weinstock, M. (2000). The development of epistemological understanding. *Cognitive Development, 15,* 309–328.

Kuhn, D., Iordanou, K., Pease, M., & Wirkala, C. (2008). Beyond control variables: What needs to develop to achieve skilled scientific knowledge? *Cognitive Development, 23,* 435–451.

Kuhn, D., Schauble, L., & Garcia-Mila, M. (1992). Cross-domain development of scientific reasoning. *Cognition and Instruction, 9,* 285–327.

Kuhn, M. R. (2009). *The hows and whys of fluency instruction.* Boston: Allyn & Bacon.

Kulkofsky, S., & Klemfuss, J. Z. (2008). What the stories children tell can tell about their memory: Narrative skill and young children's suggestibility. *Developmental Psychology, 44,* 1442–1456.

Kupersmidt, J. B., & Coie, J. D. (1990). Pre-adolescent peer status, aggression, and school adjustment as predictors of externalizing problems in adolescence. *Child Development, 61,* 1350–1363.

Kuppens, S., Grietens, H. Onghena, P., & Michiels, D. (2009). Relations between parental psychological control and childhood relational aggression: Reciprocal in nature? *Journal of Clinical Child and Adolescent Psychology, 38,* 117–131.

Kuriyama, S., & Mayor, R. (2009). A role for Syndecan-4 in neural induction ERK-and PKC-dependent pathways. *Development, 136,* 575–584.

Kwak, H. K., Kim, M., Cho, B. H., & Ham, Y. M. (1999, April). *The relationship between children's temperament, maternal control strategies, and children's compliance.* Paper presented at the meeting of the Society for Research in Child Development, Albuquerque.

L

Ladd, G., Buhs, E., & Troop, W. (2004). School adjustment and social skills training. In P. K. Smith & C. H. Hart (Eds.), *Blackwell handbook of childhood social development.* Malden, MA: Blackwell.

Ladd, G. W., Herald-Brown, S. L., & Reiser, M. (2008). Does chronic peer rejection predict the development of children's classroom participation during the grade school years? *Child Development, 79,* 1001–1015.

LaFontana, K. M., & Cillessen, A.H.N. (2009). Developmental changes in the priority of perceived status in childhood and adolescence. *Social Development, 19*(1), 130–147.

Lagattuta, K. H., Nucci, L., & Bosacki, S. L. (2010). Bridging theory of mind and the personal domain: Children's reasoning about resistance to parental control. *Child Development, 81,* 616–635.

Lahey, B. B., Van Hulle, C. A., D'Onofrio, B. M., Roders, J. L., & Waldman, I. D. (2008). Is parental knowledge of their offspring's whereabouts and peer associations spuriously associated with offspring delinquency? *Journal of Abnormal Child Psychology, 36,* 807–823.

Laible, D. J., & Thompson, R. A. (2000). Mother-child discourse, attachment security, shared positive affect, and early conscience development. *Child Development, 71,* 1424–1440.

Laible, D., & Thompson, R. A. (2007). Early socialization: A relationship perspective. In J. E. Grusec & P. D. Hastings (eds.), *Handbook of socialization.* New York: Guilford.

Laird, R. D. Criss, M. M., Pettit, G. S., Dodge, K. A., & Bates, J. E. (2008). Parents' monitoring

knowledge attenuates the link between antisocial friends and adolescent delinquent behavior. *Journal of Abnormal Child Psychology, 36,* 299–310.

Lajunen, H. R., Keski-Rahkonen, A., Pulkkinen, L., Rose, R. J., Rissanen, A., & Kaprio, J. (2007). Are computer and cell phone use associated with body mass index and overweight? A population study among twin adolescents. *BMC Public Health, 26,* 24.

Lamb, M. E. (1986). *The father's role: Applied perspectives.* New York: Wiley.

Lamb, M. E. (1994). Infant care practices and the application of knowledge. In C. B. Fisher & R. M. Lerner (Eds.), *Applied developmental psychology.* New York: McGraw-Hill.

Lamb, M. E. (2000). The history of research on father involvement: An overview. *Marriage and Family Review, 29,* 23–42.

Lamb, M. E. (2005). Attachments, social networks, and developmental contexts. *Human Development, 43,* 108–112.

Lamb, M. E. (2010). How do fathers influence children's development? In M. E. Lamb (Ed.), *The role of the father in child development* (5th ed.). New York: Wiley.

Lamb, M. E., Bornstein, M. H., & Teti, D. M. (2002). *Development in infancy* (4th ed.). Mahwah, NJ: Erlbaum.

Lamb, M. E., & Bougher, L. D. (2009). How does migration affect mothers' and fathers' roles within their families? Reflections on some general research. *Sex Roles, 60,* 611–614.

Lamb, M. E., & Sternberg, K. J. (1992). Socio-cultural perspectives in nonparental childcare. In M. E. Lamb, K. J. Sternberg, C. Hwang, & A. G. Broberg (Eds.), *Child care in context.* Hillsdale, NJ: Erlbaum.

Lamb, M. M., & others. (2010). Early-life predictors of higher body mass index in healthy children. *Annals of Nutrition & Metabolism, 56,* 16–22.

Lampl, M. (2008). Physical growth. In M. M. Hath & J. B. Benson (Eds.), *Encyclopedia of infant and early childhood development.* Oxford, UK: Elsevier.

Landa, S. (2000, Fall). If you can't make waves, make ripples. *Intelligence Connections Newsletter of the ASCD, X*(1), 6–8.

Landau, B., Smith, L., & Jones, S. (1998). Object perception and object naming in early development. *Trends in Cognitive Science, 2,* 19–24.

Lane, H. (1976). *The wild boy of Aveyron.* Cambridge, MA: Harvard University Press.

Langer, E. J. (2005). *On becoming an artist.* New York: Ballantine.

Lansford, J. E. (2009). Parental divorce and children's adjustment. *Perspectives on Psychological Science, 4,* 140–152.

Laopaiboon, M., & others. (2009). Music during caesarean section under regional anaesthesia for improving maternal and infant outcomes. *Cochrane Database of Systematic Reviews,* CD006914.

Lapsley, D. (2008). Moral self-identity as the aim of education. In L. Nucci & D. Narvaez (Eds.), *Handbook of moral and character education.* Clifton, NJ: Psychology Press.

Lapsley, D. K., & Narváez, D. (2006). Character education. In W. Damon & R. Lerner (Eds.), *Handbook of child psychology* (6th ed.). New York: Wiley.

Larson, R., Wilson, S., & Rickman, A. (2009). Globalization, societal change, and adolescence across the world. In R. M. Lerner & L. Steinberg (Eds.), *Handbook of adolescent psychology* (3rd ed.). New York: Wiley.

Larzelere, R. E., & Kuhn, B. R. (2005). Comparing child outcomes of physical punishment and alternative disciplinary tactics: a meta-analysis. *Clinical Child and Family Psychology Review, 8*, 1–37.

Laursen, B., & Collins, W. A. (2009). Parent-child relationships during adolescence. In R. M. Lerner & L. Steinberg (Eds.), *Handbook of adolescent psychology* (3rd ed.). New York: Wiley.

Laursen, B., & Pursell, G. (2009). Conflict in peer relationships. In K. H. Rubin, W. M. Bukowski, & B. Laursen (Eds.), *Handbook of peer interaction, relationships, and groups.* New York: Guilford.

Lawrence, J. M., Contreras, R., Chen, W., & Sacks, D. A. (2008). Trends in the prevalence of preexisting diabetes and gestational diabetes mellitus among a racially/ethnically diverse population of pregnant women, 1999–2005. *Diabetes Care, 31*, 899–904.

Lawrence, R. A. (2008). Breastfeeding. In M. M. Haith & J. B. Benson (Eds.), *Encyclopedia of infant and early childhood development.* Oxford, UK: Elsevier.

Lazic, T., & others. (2010). Effects of nicotine on pulmonary surfactant proteins A and D in ovine lung epithelia. *Pediatric Pulmonology, 45*, 255–262.

Leach, P. (1990). *Your baby and child: From birth to age five.* New York: Knopf.

Leaper, C., & Bigler, R. S (2004). Commentary. Gender language and sexist thought. *Monographs of the Society for Research in Child Development, 69* (1, Serial No. 275), 128–142.

Leaper, C., & Friedman, C. K. (2007). The socialization of gender. In J. E. Grusec & P. D. Hastings (Eds.), *Handbook of socialization.* New York: Guilford.

Leaper, C., & Smith, T. E. (2004). A meta-analytic review of gender variations in children's language use: Talkativeness, affiliative speech, and assertive speech. *Developmental Psychology, 40*, 993–1027.

Lebel, C., Rasmussen, C., Wyper, K., Andrew, G., & Beaulieu, C. (2010). Brain microstructure is related to math ability in children with fetal alcohol spectrum disorder. *Alcoholism, Clinical and Experimental Research, 34*, 354–363.

Lee, E., Mitchell-Herzfeld, S. D., Lowenfels, A. A., Greene, R., Dorabawila, V., & DuMont, K. A. (2009). Reducing low birth weight through home visitation: A randomized controlled trial. *American Journal of Preventive Medicine, 36*, 154–160.

Lee, H. C., El-Sayed, Y. Y., & Gould, J. B. (2008). Population trends in cesarean delivery for breech presentation in the United States, 1997–2003. *American Journal of Obstetrics and Gynecology, 199*, e1–e8.

Lee, K., Cameron, C. A., Doucette, J., & Talwar, V. (2002). Phantoms and fabrications: Young children's detection of implausible lies. *Child Development, 73*, 1688–1702.

Lee, K. C., Shults, R. A., Greenspan, A. I., Haileyesus, T., & Dellinger, A. M. (2008). Child passenger restraint use and emergency department-reported injuries: A special study using the National Electronic Injury Surveillance System—All Injury Program, 2004. *Journal of Safety Research, 39*, 25–31.

Lee, S. J., & Wong, A. N. (2009). The model minority and the perceptual foreigner: Stereotypes of Asian Americans. In N. Tewari & A. Alvaraez (Eds.), *Asian American psychology.* Clifton, NJ: Psychology Press.

Leedy, P. D., & Ormrod, J. E. (2010). *Practical research* (9th ed.). Upper Saddle River, NJ: Prentice Hall.

Legerstee, M. (1997). Contingency effects of people and objects on subsequent cognitive functioning in 3-month-old infants. *Social Development, 6*, 307–321.

Lehr, C. A., Hanson, A., Sinclair, M. F., & Christensen, S. I. (2003). Moving beyond dropout prevention towards school completion. *School Psychology Review, 32*, 342–364.

Lehrer, R., & Schauble, L. (2006). Scientific thinking and scientific literacy. In W. Damon & R. Lerner (Eds.), *Handbook of child psychology* (6th ed.). New York: Wiley.

Leifer, A. D. (1973). *Television and the development of social behavior.* Paper presented at the meeting of the International Society for the Study of Behavioral Development. Ann Arbor, Michigan.

Leman, P. J., Ahmed, S., & Ozarow, L. (2005). Gender, gender relations, and the social dynamics of children's conversations. *Developmental Psychology, 41*, 64–74.

LeMare, L. J., & Rubin, K. H. (1987). Perspective taking and peer interaction: Structural and developmental analyses. *Child Development, 58*, 306–315.

Lempers, J. D., Flavell, E. R., & Flavell, J. H. (1977). The development in very young children of tacit knowledge concerning visual perception. *Genetic Psychology Monographs, 95*, 3–53.

Lenneberg, E. (1967). *The biological foundation of language.* New York: Wiley.

Lennon, E. M., Gardner, J. M., Karmel, B. Z., & Flory, M. J. (2008). Bayley Scales of Infant Development. In M. M. Haith & J. B. Benson (Eds.), *Encyclopedia of Infant and early childhood development.* Oxford, UK: Elsevier.

Lenoir, C. P., Mallet, E., & Calenda, E. (2000). Siblings of sudden infant death syndrome and near miss in about 30 families: Is there a genetic link? *Medical Hypotheses, 54*, 408–411.

Lenzi, T. A., & Johnson, T. R. B. (2008). Screening. prenatal. In M. M. Haith & J. B. Benson (Eds.), *Encyclopedia of infant and early childhood development.* Oxford, UK: Elsevier.

Leon-Guerrero, A. (2009). *Social problems* (2nd ed.). Thousand Oaks, CA: Sage.

Leonardi-Bee, J. A., Smyth, A. R., Britton, J., & Coleman. T. (2008). Environmental tobacco smoke on fetal health: Systematic review and analysis. *Archives of Disease in Childhood. Fetal and Neonatal Edition, 93*, F351–F361.

Leppanen, J. M., Moulson, M., Vogel-Farley, V. K., & Nelson, C. A. (2007). An ERP study of emotional face processing in the adult and infant brain. *Child Development, 78*, 232–245.

Lepper, M. R., Corpus, J. H., & Iyengar, S. S. (2005). Intrinsic and extrinsic orientations in the classroom: Age differences and academic correlates. *Journal of Educational Psychology, 97*, 184–196.

Lerner, R. M., Boyd, M., & Du, D. (2009). Adolescent development. In I. B. Weiner & C. B. Craighead (Eds.), *Encyclopedia of Psychology* (4th ed.). Hoboken, NJ: Wiley.

Lerner, R. M., Roeser, R. W., & Phelps, E. (Eds.). (2009). *Positive youth development and spirituality: From theory to research.* West Conshohocken, PA: Templeton Foundation Press.

Lesaux, N. K., & Siegel, L. S. (2003). The development of reading in children who speak English as a second language. *Developmental Psychology, 39*, 1005–1019.

Lessow-Hurley, J. (2009). *The foundation of dual language instruction* (5th ed.). Boston: Allyn & Bacon.

Lester, B. M., Tronick, E. Z., & Brazelton, T. B. (2004). The Neonatal Intensive Care Unit Network Neurobehavioral Scale procedures. *Pediatrics, 113, Suppl,* S641–S667.

Lester, B. M., & others. (2002). The maternal lifestyle study: Effects of substance exposure during pregnancy on neurodevelopmental outcome in 1-month-old infants. *Pediatrics, 110,* 1182–1192.

Leung, E., Tasker, S. L., Atkinson, L, Vaillancourt, T., Schulkin, J., & Schmidt, L. A. (2010). Perceived maternal stress during pregnancy and its relation to infant stress reactivity at 2 days and 10 months of postnatal life. *Clinical Pediatrics, 49*, 158–165.

LeVay, S. (1994). The sexual brain. Cambridge, MA: MIT Press.

Levene, M. I., & Chervenak, F. A. (2009). *Fetal and neonatal neurology and neurosurgery* (4th ed.). London: Elsevier.

Leventhal, J., Dupere, V., & Brooks-Gunn, J. (2009). Neighborhood influences on adolescent development. In R. M. Lerner & L. Steinberg (Eds.), *Handbook of adolescent psychology* (3rd ed.). New York: Wiley.

Leventhal, J. M., Murphy, J. L., & Asnes, A. G. (2010). Evaluations of child sexual abuse: Recognition of overt and latent family concerns. *Child Abuse and Neglect, 34*(5), 289–295.

Levine, L. N., & McCloskey, M. L. (2009). *Teaching learners of English in mainstream classrooms (K-8).* Boston: Allyn & Bacon.

Levine, T. P., & others. (2008). Effects of prenatal cocaine exposure on special education in school-aged children. *Pediatrics, 122,* e83–e91.

Levy, F. (2009). Dopamine versus noradrenaline: Inverted-U effects and ADHD theories. *Australian and New Zealand Journal of Psychiatry, 43,* 101–108.

Levy, G. D., Sadovsky, A. L., & Troseth, G. L. (2000). Aspects of young children's perceptions of gender-typed occupations. *Sex Roles, 42,* 993–1006.

Lewis, A. C. (2007). Looking beyond NCLB. *Phi Delta Kappan, 88,* 483–484.

Lewis, M. (2005). Selfhood. In B. Hopkins (Ed.), *The Cambridge encyclopedia of child development.* Cambridge, UK: Cambridge University Press.

Lewis, M. (2007). Early emotional development. In A. Slater & M. Lewis (eds.), *Introduction to infant development.* Malden, MA: Blackwell.

Lewis, M. (2008). The emergence of human emotions. In M. Lewis, J. M. Haviland Jones, & L. Feldman Barrett (Eds.), *Handbook of emotions* (3rd ed.). New York: Guilford.

Lewis, M., & Brooks-Gunn, J. (1979). *Social cognition and the acquisition of the self.* New York: Plenum.

Lewis, M., Feiring, C. & Rosenthal, S. (2000). Attachment over time. *Child Development, 71,* 707–20.

Lewis, M., & Ramsay, D. S. (1999). Effect of maternal soothing on infant stress response. *Child Development, 70,* 11–20.

Lewis, M., Sullivan, M. W., Sanger, C., & Weiss, M. (1989). Self-development and self-conscious emotions. *Child Development, 60,* 146–156.

Lewis, M. D., Todd, R., & Xu, X. (2011). The development of emotion regulation: A neuro-psychological perspective. In R. M. Lerner, W. F. Overton, A. M. Freund, & M. E. Lamb (Eds.), *Handbook of life-span development.* New York: Wiley.

Lewis, R. (2010). *Human genetics* (9th ed.). New York: McGraw-Hill.

Li, C., Goran, M. I., Kaur, H., Nollen, N., & Ahluwalia, J. S. (2007). Developmental trajectories of overweight during childhood: Role of early life factors. *Obesity, 15,* 760–761.

Li, D. K., Willinger, M., Petitti, D. B., Odulil, R. K., Liu, L., & Hoffman, H. J. (2006). Use of a dummy (pacifier) during sleep and risk of sudden infant death syndrome (SIDS): Population based case-control study. *British Medical Journal, 332,* 18–22.

Li, L., Law, C., Lo Conte, R., & Power, C. (2009). Intergenerational influences on childhood body mass index: The effect of parental body mass index trajectories. *American Journal of Clinical Nutrition, 89,* 551–557.

Li, P. (2009). What's in a lexical system? Discovering meaning through an interactive eye. In V. C. M. Gathercole (Ed.), *Routes to language: Essays in honor of Melissa Bowerman.* New York: Psychology Press.

Liben, L. S. (1995). Psychology meets geography: Exploring the gender gap on the national geography bee. *Psychological Science Agenda, 8,* 8–9.

Lidral, A. C., & Murray, J. C. (2005). Genetic approaches to identify disease genes for birth defects with cleft lip/palate as a model. *Birth Defects Research, 70,* 893–901.

Lidz, J. (2010). The abstract nature of syntactic representations: Consequences for a theory of learning. In E. Hoff & M. Shatz (Eds.), *Blackwell handbook of language development.* New York: Wiley.

Lie, E., & Newcombe, N. (1999) Elementary school children's explicit and implicit memory for faces of preschool classmates. *Developmental Psychology, 35,* 102–112.

Lieberman, E., Davidson, K., Lee-Parritz, A., & Shearer, E. (2005). Changes in fetal position during labor and their association with epidural analgesia. *Obstetrics and Gynecology, 105,* 974–982.

Liegeois, F., Connelly, A., Baldeweg, T., & Vargha-Khadem, F. (2008). Speaking with a single cerebral hemisphere: IMRI language organization after hemispherectomy in childhood. *Brain and Language, 106,* 195–203.

Lillard, A. (2007). Pretend play in toddlers. In C. A. Brownell & C. B. Kopp (Eds.), *Socioemotional development in the toddler years.* New York: Guilford.

Lillard, A. (2008). How important are Montessori materials? *Montessori Life, 20*(4), 20–25.

Lima, J. J., Blake, K. V., Tantisira K. G., & Weiss, S. T. (2009). Pharmacogenetics of asthma. *Current Opinion in Pulmonary Medicine, 15,* 57–62.

Lin, M., Johnson, J. E., & Johnson, K. M. (2003). Dramatic play in Montessori kindergartens in Taiwan and Mainland China. Unpublished manuscript. Department of Curriculum and Instruction, Pennsylvania State University, University Park, PA.

Lincoln, A. J., Searcy, Y. M., Jones, W., & Lord, C. (2007). Social interaction behaviors discriminate young children with autism and Williams syndrome. *Journal of the American Academy of Child and Adolescent Psychiatry, 46,* 323–331.

Lindblad, F., & Hjern, A. (2010). ADHD after fetal exposure to maternal smoking. *Nicotine and Tobacco Research, 12,* 408–415.

Lippa, R. A. (2005). *Gender, nature, and nurture* (2nd ed.). Mahwah, NJ: Erlbaum.

Lippman, L. A., & Keith, J. D. (2006). The demographics of spirituality among youth: International perspectives. In E. Roehlkepartain, P. E. King, L. Wagener, & P. L. Benson (Eds.), *The handbook of spirituality in childhood and adolescence.* Thousand Oaks, CA: Sage.

Lipton, J., & Spelke, E. (2004). Discrimination of large and small numerosities by human infants. *Infancy, 5,* 271–290.

Liszkowski, U. (2007, March). *A new look at infant pointing.* Paper presented at the meeting of the Society for Research in Child Development, Boston.

Liu, C. H., Murakami, J., Eap, S., & Nagayama Hall, G. C. (2009). Who are Asian Americans? An overview of history, immigration, and communities. In N. Tewari & A. Alvarez (Eds.), *Asian American psychology.* Clifton, NJ: Psychology Press.

Liu, J., & others. (2010). Neonatal neurobehavior predicts medical and behavioral outcome. *Pediatrics, 125*(1), e90–e98.

Liu, T., Shi, I, Zhang, Q., Zhao, D., & Yang, J. (2007). Neural mechanisms of auditory sensory processing in children with high intelligence. *Neuroreport, 18*(15), 1571–1575.

Liu, W. M., & Hernandez, J. (2008). Social class and classism. In N. J. Salkind (Eds.), *Encyclopedia of educational psychology.* Thousand Oaks, CA: Sage.

Livas-Dlott, A. Fuller, B., Stein, G. L., Bridges, M., Figueroa, A. M., & Mireles, L. (2010). Commands, competence, and *Carino:* Maternal socialization processes in Mexican American families. *Developmental Psychology, 46,* 566–578.

Lively, W., & Bromley, D. (1973). *Person perception in childhood and adolescence.* New York: Wiley.

Locascio, G., Mahone, E. M., Eason, S., & Cutting, L. (2010, in press). Executive dysfunction among children with reading comprehension deficits. *Journal of Learning Disabilities.*

Lochman, J., & Conduct Problems Prevention Research Group. (2007, March). *Fast Track intervention outcomes in the middle school years.* Paper presented at the meeting of Society for Research Child Development.

Loeber, R., Burke, J., & Pardini, D. (2009). The etiology and development of antisocial and delinquent behavior. *Annual Review of Psychology* (Vol. 60). Palo Alto, CA: Annual Reviews.

Loeber, R., DeLamatre, M., Keenan, K., & Zhang, Q. (1998). A prospective replicatioan of developmental pathways in disruptive and delinquent behavior. In R. Cairns, L. Bergman, & J. Kagan (Eds.), *Methods and models for studying the individual.* Thousand Oaks, CA: Sage.

Loeber, R., & Farrington, D. P. (Eds.). (2001). *Child delinquents: Development, intervention and service needs.* Thousand Oaks, CA: Sage.

Loeber, R., Farrington, D. P., Stouthamer-Loeber, M., & White, H. R. (2008). *Violence and serious theft: Development and predictions from childhood to adulthood.* New York: Routledge.

Loeber, R., Pardini, D. A., Stouthamer-Loeber, M., & Raine, A. (2007). Do cognitive, physiological, and psychosocial risk and promotive factors predict desistance from delinquency in males? *Development and Psychopathology, 19,* 867–887.

Loehlin, J. C. (2010). Is there an active gene-environment correlation in adolescent drinking behavior? *Behavior Genetics.* (Available online March 9, 2010.)

Loehlin, J. C., Horn, J. M., & Ernst, J. L. (2007). Genetic and environmental influences on adult life outcomes: Evidence from the Texas adoption project. *Behavior Genetics, 37,* 463–476.

Logsdon, M. C., Wisner, K., & Hanusa, B. H. (2009). Does maternal role functioning improve with antidepressant treatment in women with postpartum depression? *Journal of Women's Health, 18*, 85–90.

Loprinzi, P. D., & Trost, S. G. (2010). Parental influences on physical activity behavior in preschool children. *Preventive Medicine, 50*, 129–133.

Lorenz, K. Z. (1965). *Evolution and the modification of behavior.* Chicago: University of Chicago Press.

Lowdermilk, D. L., Perry, S. E., & Cashion, M. C. (2010). *Maternity Nursing* (8th ed.). New York: Elsevier.

Lozoff, B., & others. (2007). Preschool-aged children with iron deficiency anemia show altered affect and behavior. *Journal of Nutrition, 137*, 683–689.

Lu, L. H., & others. (2009). Effects of prenatal methamphetamine exposure on verbal memory revealed with functional magnetic resonance imaging. *Journal of Developmental and Behavioral Pediatrics, 30*, 185–192.

Lu, M. C., & Lu, J. S. (2008). Prenatal care. In M. M. Haith & J. B. Benson (Eds.), *Encyclopedia of infancy and early childhood development.* Oxford, UK: Elsevier.

Lubinski, D. (2000). Measures of intelligence: Intelligence tests. In A. Kazdin (Ed.), *Encyclopedia of psychology.* Washington, DC, & New York: American Psychological Association and Oxford University Press.

Lucas, P. J., McIntosh, K., Petticrew, M., Roberts, H., & Shiell, A. (2008). Financial benefits for child health and well-being in low income or socially disadvantaged families in developed world countries. *Cochrane Database of Systematic Reviews, 16.* CD006358.

Lucurto, C. (1990). The malleability of IQ as judged from adoption studies. *Intelligence, 14*, 275–292.

Luders, E., & others. (2004). Gender differences in cortical complexity. *Nature Neuroscience, 7*, 799–800.

Luders, E., Narr, K. L., Thompson, P. M., & Toga, A. W. (2009). Neuroanatomical correlates of intelligence. *Intelligence, 37*, 156–163.

Ludington-Hoe, S. M., Lewis, T., Morgan, K., Cong, X., Anderson, L., & Reese, S. (2006). Breast and infant temperatures with twins during kangaroo care. *Journal of Obstetric, Gynecologic, and Neonatal Nursing, 35*, 223–231.

Lumpkin, A. (2011). *Introduction to physical education, exercise science, and sports studies* (8th Ed.). New York: McGraw-Hill.

Lunkenheimer, E. S., Shields, A. M., & Cortina, K. S. (2007). Parental coaching and dismissing of children's emotions in family interaction. *Social Development, 16*, 232–248.

Luo, Y., Kaufman, L., & Baillargeon, R. (2009). Young infants' reasoning about events involving inert and self-propelled objects. *Cognitive Psychology, 58*, 441–486.

Luria, A., & Herzog, E. (1985, April). *Gender segregation across and within settings.* Paper presented at the biennial meeting of the Society for Research in Child Development, Toronto.

Luthar, S. S. (2006). Resilience in development: A synthesis of research across five decades. In D. Cicchetti & D. J. Cohen (Eds.), *Developmental psychopathology: Vol 3. Risk, disorder, and adaptation* (2nd ed.). Hoboken, NJ: Wiley.

Luthar. S. S., & Goldstein. A. S. (2008). Substance use and related behaviors among suburban late adolescents: The importance of perceived parent containment. *Development and Psychopathology, 20*, 591–614.

Luyckx, K., Schwartz, S. J., Berzonsky, M. D., Soenens, B., Vansteenkiste, M., Smits, I., & Goossens, L. (2008). Capturing ruminative exploration: Extending the four-dimensional model of identity formation in late adolescence. *Journal of Research in Personality, 42*, 58–62.

Lykken, D. (2001). *Happiness: What studies on twins show us about nature, nurture, and the happiness set point.* New York: Golden Books.

Lynn, R. (1996). Racial and ethnic differences in intelligence in the U.S. on the Differential Ability Scale. *Personality and Individual Differences. 26*, 271–273.

Lynn, R. (2009). What caused the Flynn effect? Secular increases in the development quotients of infants. *Intelligence, 37*, 16–24.

Lyon, T. D., & Flavell, J. H. (1993). Young children's understanding of forgetting over time. *Child Development, 64*, 789–800.

Lyons-Ruth, R., & Jacobvitz, D. (2008). Attachment disorganization: Genetic factors, parenting contexts, and developmental transformation from infancy to adulthood. In J. Cassidy & P. R. Shaver (Eds.), *Handbook of attachment* (2nd ed.). New York: Guilford.

M

Mader, S. S. (2011). *Inquiry into life* (13th ed.). New York: McGraw-Hill.

Maccoby, E. E. (1984). Middle childhood in the context of the family. In W. A. Collins (Ed.), *Development during middle childhood.* Washington, DC: National Academy Press.

Maccoby, E. E. (1996). Peer conflict and intra-family conflict: Are there conceptual bridges? *Merrill-Palmer Quarterly, 42*, 165–176.

Maccoby, E. E. (2002). Gender and group process: A developmental perspective. *Current Directions in Psychological Science, 11*, 54–57.

Maccoby, E. E. (2007). Historical overview of socialization research and theory. In J. E. Grusec & P. D. Hastings (Eds.), *Handbook of socialization.* New York: Guilford.

Maccoby, E. E., & Martin, J. A. (1983). Socialization in the context of the family: Parent-child interaction. In P. H. Mussen (Ed.), *Handbook of child psychology* (4th ed., Vol. 4). New York: Wiley.

Maccoby, E. E., & Mnookin, R. H. (1992). *Dividing the child: Social and legal dilemmas of custody.* Cambridge, MA: Harvard University Press.

MacDonald, K. (1987). Parent-child physical play with rejected, neglected, and popular boys. *Developmental Psychology, 23*, 705–711.

MacFarlane, J. A. (1975). Olfaction in the development of social preferences in the human neonate. In *Parent-infant interaction.* Ciba Foundation Symposium No. 33. Amsterdam: Elsevier.

MacGeorge, E. L. (2004). The myth of gender cultures: Similarities outweigh differences in men's and women's provisions of and responses to supportive communication. *Sex Roles, 50*, 143–175.

Macmillan, H. L. (2010). Commentary: Child maltreatment and physical health: A call to action. *Journal of Pediatric Psychology, 35*(5), 533–535.

Maeda, K. (1999). *The Self-Perception Profile for children administered to a Japanese sample.* Unpublished data, Ibaraki Prefectural University of Health Sciences, Ibaraki, Japan.

Mael, F. A. (1998). Single-sex and coeducational schooling: Relationships to socioemotional and academic development. *Review of Educational Research, 68*(2), 101–129.

Maffulli, N., Longo, U. G., Gougoulias, N., Loppini, M., & Denaro, V. (2010). Long-term health outcomes of youth sports injuries. *British Journal of Sports Medicine, 44*, 21–25.

Magnusson, S. J., & Palinscar, A. S. (2005). Teaching to promote the development of scientific knowledge and reasoning about light at the elementary school level. In *How people learn.* Washington, DC: National Academies Press.

Mahoney, J., Parente, M. E., & Zigler, E. (2010). After-school program engagement and in-school competence: Program quality, content, and staffing. In J. Meece & J. Eccles (Eds.), *Handbook of research on schools, and human development.* New York: Routledge.

Mahoney, J. L., Vandell, D. L., Simpkins, S., & Zarrett, N. (2009). Adolescent out-of-school activities. In R. M. Lerner & L. Steinberg (Eds.), *Handbook of adolescent psychology* (3rd ed.). New York: Wiley.

Malamitsi-Puchner, A., & Boutsikou, T. (2006). Adolescent pregnancy and perinatal outcome. *Pediatric Endocrinology Reviews, 3, Suppl 1*, 170–171.

Malik, N. M., & Furman, W. (1993). Practitioner review: Problems in children's peer relations: What can the clinician do? *Journal of Child Psychology and Psychiatry, 34*, 1303–1326.

Malizia, B. A., Hacker, M. R., & Penzias, A. S. (2009). Cumulative live-birth rates after in vitro fertilization. *New England Journal of Medicine, 360*, 236–243.

Malti, T., & Buchmann, M. (2010). Socialization and individual antecedents of adolescents' and young adults' moral motivation. *Journal of Youth and Adolescence, 39*, 138–149.

Mamtani, M., Patel, A., & Kulkarni, H. (2008). Association of the pattern of transition between arousal states in neonates with the cord blood lead level. *Early Human Development, 55*, 109–112.

Mandler, J. (2000). Unpublished review of J. W. Santrock's *Life-Span Development*, 8th ed. (New York: McGraw-Hill).

Mandler, J. M. (2004). *The foundations of mind.* New York: Oxford University Press.

Mandler, J. M. (2009). Conceptual categorization. In D. H. Rakison & L. M. Oakes (Eds.), *Early category and concept development.* New York: Oxford University Press.

Mandler, J. M. (2010). Jean Mandler. Retrieved May 26, 2010 from http://www.cogsci.ucsd .edu/~jean/

Mandler, J. M., & McDonough, L. (1993). Concept formation in infancy. *Cognitive Development, 8*, 291–318.

Manning, M. L., & Baruth, L. G. (2009). *Multicultural education of children and adolescents* (5th ed.). Boston: Allyn & Bacon.

Marcdante, K., Kliegman, R. M., & Behrman, R. E. (2011). *Nelson's essentials of pediatrics* (6th ed.)

Marcia, J. E. (1980). Ego identity development. In J. Adelson (Ed.), *Handbook of adolescent psychology.* New York: Wiley.

Marcia, J. E. (1987). The identity status approach to the study of ego identity development. In T. Honess & K. Yardley (Eds.), *Self and identity: Perspectives across the lifespan.* London: Routledge & Kegan Paul.

Marcia, J. E. (1994). The empirical study of ego identity. In H. A. Bosma, T.L.G. Graafsma, H. D. Grotevant, & D. J. DeLevita (Eds.), *Identity and development.* Newbury Park, CA: Sage.

Marcia, J. E. (1996). Unpublished review of J. W. Santrock's *Adolescence*, 7th ed. (Dubuque, IA: Brown & Benchmark).

Marcia, J. E. (2002). Identity and psychosocial development in adulthood. *Identity, 2*, 7–28.

Marinucci, L., & others. (2009). Patterns of some extracellular matrix gene expression are similar in cells from cleft lip-palate patients and in human palatal fibroblasts to diazepam in culture. *Toxicology, 257*, 10–16.

Marion, M. C. (2010). *Introduction to early childhood education.* Upper Saddle River, NJ: Prentice Hall.

Markus, H. R., & Nurius, P. (1986). Possible selves. *American Psychologist, 41*, 954–969.

Marret, S., & others. (2010). Prenatal low-dose aspirin and neurobehavioral outcomes of children born very preterm. *Pediatrics, 125*, e29–e34.

Martens, M. A., Wilson, S. J., Dudgeon, P., & Reutens, D. C. (2009). Approachability and the amygdala: Insights from Williams syndrome. *Neuropsychologia, 47*(12), 2446–2453.

Martin, C., & Ruble, D. N. (2010). Gender-role development. *Annual Review of Psychology* (Vol. 61). Palo Alto, CA: Annual Reviews.

Martin, C. L., & Fabes, R. A. (2001). The stability and consequences of young children's same-sex peer interactions. *Development Psychology, 37*, 431–446.

Martin, C. L., & Ruble, D. N., & Szkrybalo, J. (2002). Cognitive theories of early gender development. *Psychological Bulletin, 128*, 903–933.

Martin, J. A., Hamilton, B. E., Menacker, F., Sutton, P. D., & Matthews, T. J. (2005, November 15). Preliminary births for 2004: Infant and maternal health. *Health E-Stats.* Atlanta: National Center for Health Statistics.

Martin, R., Sexton, C., Franklin, T., & Gerlovich, J. (2005). *Teaching science for all children* (4th ed.). Boston: Allyn & Bacon.

Martinez, M. E. (2009). *Learning and cognition.* Upper Saddle River, NJ: Allyn & Bacon.

Mascolo, M. F., & Fischer, K. (2007). The co-development of self and socio-moral emotions during the toddler years. In C. A. Brownell & C. B. Kopp (Eds.), *Transitions in early development,* New York: Guilford.

Mash, E. J., & Wolfe, D. A. (2007). *Abnormal child psychology* (3rd ed.). Belmont, CA: Wadsworth.

Mashburn, A. J., Justice, L. M., Downer, J. T., & Pianta, R. C. (2009). Peer effects on children's language achievement during pre-kindergarten. *Child Development, 80*, 686–702.

Masten, A. S. (2006). Developmental psychopathology: Pathways to the future. *International Journal of Behavioral Development, 31*, 46–53.

Masten, A. S. (2009a). Ordinary Magic: Lessons from research on resilience in human development. *Education Canada, 49*(3): 28–32.

Masten, A. S. (2009b). Resilience in children and youth: A practical guide. *Schools for All Encyclopedia.* Vancouver: Health Canada and the Health and Learning Knowledge Centre of the Canadian Council.

Masten, A. S., Burt, K., & Coatsworth, J. D. (2006). Competence and psychopathology in development. In D. Cicchetti & D. Cohen (eds.), *Developmental psychopathology (Vol. 3): Risk, disorder and psychopathology* (2nd ed.) New York: Wiley.

Masten, A. S., Cutuli, J. J., Herbers, J. E., & Gabrielle-Reed, M. J. (2009b). Resilience in development. In Snyder, C. R., & Lopez, S. J. (Eds.), *The handbook of positive psychology* (2nd ed.) (pp. 117–131). New York: Oxford University Press.

Masten, A. S., Long, J. D., Kuo, S. I-C., McCormick, C. M., & Desjardins, C. D. (2009a). Developmental models of strategic intervention. *European Journal of Developmental Science, 3*, 282–291.

Matlin, M. W. (2008). *The psychology of women* (6th ed.). Belmont, CA: Wadsworth.

Matsumoto, D., & Juang, L. (2008). *Culture and psychology* (4th ed.). Belmont, CA: Wadsworth.

Matthews, D. J. (2009). Developmental transitions in giftedness and talent: Childhood into adolescence. In F. D. Horowitz, R. F. Subotnik, & D. J. Matthews (Eds.), *The development of giftedness and talent across the life span.* Washington, DC: American Psychological Association.

Matthews, D. J., Subotnik, R. F., & Horowitz, F. D. (2009). A developmental perspective on giftedness and talent: Implications for research, policy, and practice. In F. D. Horowitz, R. F. Subotnik, & D. J. Matthews (Eds.), *The development of giftedness and talent across the life span.* Washington, DC: American Psychological Association.

Matthews, G., Zeidner, M., & Roberts, R. D. (2006). Models of personality and affect for education: A review and synthesis. In P. A. Alexander & P. H. Wynne (Eds.), *Handbook of educational psychology* (2nd ed.). Mahwah, NJ: Erlbaum.

Mattson, S., & Smith, J. E. (2011). *Core curriculum for maternal-newborn nursing* (4th ed.). New York: Elsevier.

Matzek, A. E., & Cooney, T. M. (2009). Spousal perceptions of marital stress and support among grandparent caregivers: Variations by life stage. *International Journal of Aging and Human Development, 68*, 109–126.

Maxim, G. W. (2010). *Dynamic social studies for constructive classrooms* (9th ed.). Boston: Allyn & Bacon.

Mayer, K. D., & Zhang, L. (2009). Short-and long-term effects of cocaine abuse during pregnancy on heart development. *Therapeutic Advances in Cardiovascular Disease, 3*, 7–16.

Mayer, R. E. (2008). *Learning and instruction* (2nd ed.). Upper Saddle River, NJ: Prentice Hall.

Mayo Clinic. (2009). *Pregnancy week by week.* Retrieved October 1, 2009, from www .mayoclinic.com/health/pregnancy-nutrition/ PR00109

Mbugua Gitau, G., Liversedge, H., Goffey, D., Hawton, A., Liversedge, N., & Taylor, M. (2009). The influence of maternal age on the outcomes of pregnancy complicated by bleeding at less than 12 weeks. *Acta Obstetricia et Gynecologica Scandinavica, 88*, 116–118.

McAdoo, H. P. (2006). *Black families* (4th ed.). Thousand Oaks, CA: Sage.

McBride-Chang, C. (2004). *Children's Literacy Development* (Texts in Developmental Psychology Series). London: Edward Arnold/Oxford Press.

McBride-Chang, C., & others. (2005). Changing models across cultures: Associations of phonological and morphological awareness to reading in Beijing, Hong Kong, Korea, and America. *Journal of Experimental Child Psychology, 92*, 140–160.

McBride-Chang, C., Lam, F., Lam, C., Doo, S., Wong, S. W., L., & Chow, Y. Y. Y. (2008). Word recognition and cognitive profiles of Chinese preschool children at-risk for dyslexia through language delay or familial history of dyslexia. *Journal of Child Psychology and Psychiatry, 49*, 211–218.

McCabe, K. M., Rodgers, C., Yeh, M., & Hough, R. (2004). Gender differences in childhood onset conduct disorder. *Development and Psychopathology, 16*, 179–192.

McCall, R. B., Appelbaum, M. I., & Hogarty, P. S. (1973). Developmental changes in mental performance. *Monographs of the Society for Research in Child Development, 38* (Serial No. 150).

McCartney, K. (2003, July 16). Interview with Kathleen McCartney in A. Bucuvalas, Child care and behavior, *HGSE News*, pp. 1–4. Cambridge, MA: Harvard Graduate School of Education.

McCartney, K., Dearing, E., Taylor, B. A., & Bub, K. L. (2007). Quality child care supports the achievement of low-income children: Direct and indirect pathways through caregiving and the home environment. *Journal of Applied Developmental Psychology, 28,* 411–426.

McCombs, B. (2010). Learner-centered practices: providing the context for positive learner development, motivation, and achievement. In J. Meece & J. Eccles (Eds.), *Handbook of schools, schooling, and human development*. New York: Routledge.

McDonald, S., & others. (2009). Preterm birth and low birth weight among in vitro fertilization singletons: A systematic review and meta-analyses. *European Journal of Obstetrics, Gynecology, and Reproductive Biology, 146,* 138–148.

McDonald, S. D., & others. (2010). Preterm birth and low birth weight among in vitro fertilization twins: A systematic review and meta-analyses. *European Journal of Obstetrics, Gynecology, and Reproductive Biology, 148,* 105–113.

McDougall, P., & Hymel, S. (2007). Same-gender versus cross-gender friendship conceptions. *Merrill-Palmer Quarterly, 53,* 347–380.

McDowell, D. J., & Parke, R. D. (2009). Parental correlates of children's peer relations: An empirical test of a tripartite model. *Developmental Psychology, 45,* 224–235.

McElhaney, K. B., Allen, J. P., Stephenson, J. C., & Hare, A. L. (2009). Attachment and autonomy during adolescence. In R. M. Lerner & L. Steinberg (Eds.), *Handbook of adolescent psychology* (3rd ed.). New York: Wiley.

McElwain, N. L. (2009). Attachment theory. In D. Carr (Ed.), *Encyclopedia of the life course and human development*. Boston: Gale Cengage.

McGarry, J., Kim, H., Sheng, X., Egger, M., & Baksh, L. (2009). Postpartum depression and help-seeking behavior. *Journal of Midwifery and Women's Health, 54,* 50–56.

McGarvey, C., McDonnell, M., Hamilton, K., O'Regan, M., & Matthews, T. (2006). An 8-year study of risk factors for SIDS: Bed-sharing versus non-bed-sharing. *Archives of Disease in Childhood, 91,* 318–323.

McGuigan, M. R., Tatasciore, M., Newton, R. U., & Pettigrew, S. (2009). Eight weeks of resistance training can significantly alter body composition in children who are overweight or obese. *Journal of Strength and Conditioning Research, 23,* 80–85.

McGuire, W., Dyson, L., & Renfrew, M. (2010). Maternal obesity: consequences for children, challenges for clinicians and carers. *Seminars in Fetal and Neonatal Medicine, 15,* 108–112.

McLoyd, V. C. (1998). Children in poverty. In I. E. Siegel & K. A. Renninger (Eds.), *Handbook of child psychology* (5th ed., Vol. 4). New York: Wiley.

McLoyd, V. C., Aikens, N. L., & Burton, L. M. (2006). Childhood poverty, policy, and practice. In W. Damon & R. Lerner (Eds.), *Handbook of child psychology* (6th ed.). New York: Wiley.

McLoyd, V. C., Kaplan, R., Purtell, K. M., Bagley, E., Hardaway, C. R., & Smalls, C. (2009). Poverty and social disadvantage in adolescence. In R. M. Lerner & L. Steinberg (Eds.), *Handbook of adolescent psychology* (3rd ed.). New York: Wiley.

McMillan, J. H., & Wergin, J. F. (2010). *Understanding and evaluating educational research* (4th ed.). Upper Saddle River, NJ: Pearson.

McMullen, S. L., Lipke, B., & LeMura, C. (2009). Sudden infant death syndrome prevention: A model program for NICUs. *Neonatal Network, 28,* 7–12.

McNamara, F., & Sullivan, C. E. (2000). Obstructive sleep apnea in infants. *Journal of Pediatrics, 136,* 318–323.

Mead, M. (1978, Dec. 30–Jan. 5). The American family: An endangered species. *TV Guide,* pp. 21–24.

Meaney, M. J. (2010). Epigenetics and the biological definition of gene X environment interactions. *Child Development, 81,* 41–79.

Meece, J. L., & Schaefer, V. A. (2010). Introduction. In J. Meece & J. Eccles (Eds.), *Handbook of research on schools, schooling, and human development*. New York: Routledge.

Meerlo, P., Sgoifo, A., & Suchecki, D. (2008). Restricted and disrupted sleep: Effects on autonomic function, neuroendocrine stress systems, and stress responsivity. *Sleep Medicine Review, 12,* 197–210.

Mejia-Arauz, R., Rogoff, B., Dexter, A., & Najafi, B. (2007). Cultural variation in children's social organization. *Child Development, 78,* 1001–1014.

Melgar-Quinonez, H. R., & Kaiser, L. L. (2004). Relationship of child-feeding practices to overweight in low-income Mexican-American preschool-aged children. *Journal of the American Dietetic Association, 104,* 1110–1119.

Melinder, A., & others. (2010). Children's eyewitness memory: A comparison of two interviewing strategies as realized by forensic professionals. *Journal of Experimental Child Psychology, 105,* 156–177.

Mello, Z. R. (2009). Racial/ethnic group and socioeconomic status variation in educational and occupational expectations from adolescence to adulthood. *Journal of Applied Developmental Psychology, 30,* 494–504.

Meltzoff, A. N. (2008). Unpublished review of Santrock, J. W., *Life-span development* (12th ed.). New York: McGraw-Hill.

Meltzoff, A. N. (2009). Roots of social cognition: The like-me framework. In D. Cicchetti & M. R. Gunnar (Eds.), *Minnesota symposia on child psychology: Meeting the challenge of translational research in child psychology*. Hoboken, NJ: Wiley.

Meltzoff, A. N. (2011). Social cognition and the origins of imitation, empathy, and theory of mind. In U. Goswami (Ed.), *Wiley-Blackwell handbook of childhood cognitive development* (2nd ed.). New York: Wiley-Blackwell.

Meltzoff, A. N., & Brooks, R. (2006). Eyes wide shut: The importance of eyes in infant gaze following and understanding of other minds. In R. Flom, K. Lee, & D. Muir (Eds.), *Gaze-following*. Mahwah, NJ: Erlbaum.

Meltzoff, A. N., & Brooks, R. (2009). Social cognition and language: The role of gaze in word learning. In J. Colombo, P. McCardle, & L. Freund (Eds.), *Infant pathways to language*. Clifton, NJ: Psychology Press.

Melzi, G., & Ely, R. (2009). Language development in the school years. In J. B. Gleason & N. Ratner (Eds.), *The development of language* (7th ed.). Boston: Allyn & Bacon.

Menias, C. O., Elsayes, K. M., Peterson, C. M., Huete, A., Gratz, B. I., & Bhalla, S. (2007). CT of pregnancy-related complications. *Emergency Radiology, 13,* 299–306.

Menn, L., & Stoel-Gammon, C. (2009). Phonological development: Learning sounds and sound patterns. In J. Berko Gleason & N. B. Ratner (Ed.). *The development of language* (6th ed.). Boston: Allyn & Bacon.

Menyuk, P., Liebergott, J., & Schultz, M. (1995). *Early language development in full-term and premature infants*. Hillsdale, NJ: Erlbaum.

Meredith, N. V. (1978). Research between 1960 and 1970 on the standing height of young children in different parts of the world. In H. W. Reece & L. P. Lipsitt (Eds.), *Advances in child development and behavior* (Vol. 12). New York: Academic Press.

Merrell, K. W., Gueldner, B. A., Ross, S. W., & Isava, D. M. (2008). How effective are school bullying intervention program? A meta-analysis of intervention research. *School Psychology Quarterly, 23,* 26–42.

Merrick, J., Morad, M., Halperin, J., & Kandel, I. (2005). Physical fitness and adolescence. *International Journal of Adolescent Medicine, 17,* 89–91.

Mervis, C. B., & Becerra, A. M. (2007). Language and communicative development in Williams syndrome. *Mental Retardation and Developmental Disabilities Research Review, 13,* 3–15.

Mervis, C. B., & John, A. E. (2010). Cognitive and behavioral characteristics of children with Williams syndrome: Implications for intervention approaches. *American Journal of Medical Genetics. Part C, Seminars in Medical Genetics, 154C,* 229–248.

Mesman, J., van IJzendoorn, M. H., & Bakersman-Kranenburg, M. J. (2009). The many faces of the still-face paradigm: A review and meta-analysis. *Developmental Review, 29,* 120–162.

Messinger, D. (2008). Smiling. In M. M. Haith & J. B. Benson (Eds.), *Encyclopedia of infant and early childhood development*. Oxford, UK: Elsevier.

Metz, E. C., & Youniss, J. (2005). Longitudinal gains in civic development through school-based required service. *Political Psychology, 26,* 413–437.

Meyer, S. L., Weible, C. M., & Woeber, K. (2010). Perceptions and practice of waterbirth: A survey of Georgia midwives. *Journal of Midwifery and Women's Health, 55,* 55–59.

Meyers, J. (2010, April 1). Suicides open eyes to bullying. *Dallas Morning News*, pp. 1A–2A.

Miano, S., & others. (2009). Development of NREM sleep instability-continuity (cyclic alternating pattern in healthy term infants aged 1 to 4 months. *Sleep, 32,* 83–90.

Mihov, K. M., Denzler, M., & Forster, J. (2010). Hemispheric specialization and creative thinking: A meta-analytic review of lateralization of creativity. *Brain and Cognition, 72,* 442–448.

Mikami, A. Y., Szwedo, D. E., Allen, J. P., Evans, M. A., & Hare, A. L. (2010). Adolescent peer relationships and behavior problems predict young adults' communication on social networking websites. *Developmental Psychology, 46,* 46–56.

Mikkelsson, L., Kaprio, J., Kautiainen, H., Kujala, U., Mikkelsson, M., & Nupponen, H. (2006). School fitness tests as predictors of adult health-related fitness. *American Journal of Human Biology, 18,* 342–349.

Miller, C. F., Lurye, L. E., Zusuls, K. M., & Ruble, D. N. (2009). Accessibility of gender stereotype domains: Developmental and gender differences in children. *Sex Roles, 60,* 870–881.

Miller, C. F., & Ruble, D. N. (2005). *Developmental changes in the accessibility of gender stereotypes.* Unpublished manuscript. Department of Psychology, New York University.

Miller, J. (2007). Cultural psychology of moral development. In S. Kitayama & D. Cohen (Eds.), *Handbook of cultural psychology.* New York: Guilford.

Miller, P. H. (2011). Piaget's theory: Past, present, and future. In U. Goswami (Ed.), *Wiley-Blackwell handbook of childhood cognitive development* (2nd ed.). New York: Wiley-Blackwell.

Miller-Johnson, S., Coie, J., & Malone, P. S. (2003, April). *Do aggression and peer rejection in childhood predict early adult outcomes?* Paper presented at the biennial meeting of the Society for Research in Child Development, Tampa, FL.

Miller-Jones, D. (1989). Culture and testing. *American Psychologist. 44,* 360–366.

Mills, B., Reyna, V., & Estrada, S. (2008). Explaining contradictory relations between risk perception and risk taking. *Psychological Science, 19,* 429–433.

Mills, C. M., & Keil. F. C. (2005). The development of cynicism. *Psychological Science. 16,* 385–390.

Mills, D., & Mills, C. (2000). *Hungarian kindergarten curriculum translation.* London: Mills Production.

Milot, T., Ethier, L. S., St-Laurent, D., & Provost, M. A. (2010). The role of trauma symptoms in the development of behavioral problems in maltreated preschoolers. *Child Abuse and Neglect, 34(4),* 225–234.

Minde, K., & Zelkowitz, P. (2008). Premature babies. In M. M. Haith & J. B. Benson (Eds.), *Encyclopedia of infancy and early childhood development.* Oxford, UK: Elsevier.

Mindell, J. A., Sadeh, A., Kohyama, J., & How, T. H. (2010a, in press). Parental behaviors and sleep outcomes in infants and toddlers: A cross-cultural comparison. *Sleep Medicine.*

Mindell, J. A., Sadeh, A., Wiegand, B., How, T. H., & Goh, D. Y. (2010b). Cross-cultural differences in infant and toddler sleep. *Sleep Medicine, 11,* 274–280.

Minnesota Family Investment Program (2009). *Longitudinal study of early MFIP recipients.* Retrieved on January 12, 2009, from www.dhs .state.mn.us/main/

Mischel, W., & Mischel, H. (1975, April). *A cognitive social-learning analysis of moral development.* Paper presented at the meeting of the Society for Research in Child Development, Denver.

Mitchell, E. A. (2007). Recommendations for sudden infant death syndrome prevention: A discussion document. *Archives of Disease in Childhood, 92,* 155–159.

Mitchell, E. A. (2009). What is the mechanism of SIDS? Clues from epidemiology. *Developmental Psychobiology, 51,* 215–222.

Mitchell, E. A., Stewart, A. W., Crampton, P., & Salarnod, C. (2000). Deprivation and sudden infant death syndrome. *Social Science and Medicine, 51,* 147–150.

Mitchell, M. L., & Jolley, J. M. (2010). *Research design explained* (7th ed.). Boston: Cengage.

Miyake, K, Chen, S., & Campos, J. (1985). Infants' temperament, mothers' mode of interaction and attachment in Japan: An interim report. H. I. Bretherton & F. Waters (Eds.), Growing points of attachment theory and research, *Monographs of the Society for Research in Child Development, 50*(1–2, Serial No. 109), 276–297.

Moise, K. J. (2005). Fetal RhD typing with free DNA I maternal plasma. *American Journal of Obstetrics and Gynecology, 192,* 663–665.

Moleti, C. A. (2009). Trends and controversies in labor induction. *MCN The American Journal of Maternal and Child Nursing, 34,* 40–47.

Money, J. (1975). Ablato penis: Normal male infant sex-reassigned as a girl. *Archives of Sexual Behavior, 4,* 65–71.

Moore, D. (2001). *The dependent gene.* New York: W. H. Freeman.

Moore, M. K., & Meltzoff, A. N. (2008). Factors affecting infants' manual search for occluded objects and the genesis of object permanence. *Infant Behavior and Development, 31,* 168–180.

Moorthy, A., & others. (2009). Nevirapine resistance and breast-milk HIV transmission: effects of single and extended-dose nevirapine prophylaxis in sub-type C HIV-infected infants. *PLoS ONE, 4,* e4096.

Moran, S., & Gardner, H. (2006). Extraordinary achievements. In W. Damon & R. Lerner (Eds.), *Handbook of child psychology* (6th ed.), New York: Wiley.

Morelli, G. A., Rogoff, B., Oppenheim, D., & Goldsmith, D. (1992). Cultural variation in infants' sleeping arrangements: Questions of independence. *Developmental Psychology, 28,* 604–613.

Morra, S., Gobbo, C. Marini, Z., & Sheese, R. (2007). *Cognitive development: Neo-Piagetian perspectives.* Mahwah, NJ: Erlbaum.

Morreale, M. C. (2004). Executing juvenile offenders: A fundamental failure of society. *Journal of Adolescent Health, 35,* 341.

Morris, C. A. (2010). Introduction: Williams syndrome. *American Journal of Medical Genetics. Part C, Seminars in Medical Genetics, 154C,* 203–208.

Morrissey, T. W. (2009). Multiple child-care arrangements and young children's behavioral outcomes. *Child Development, 80,* 59–76.

Morrison, G. S. (2011). *Fundamentals of early childhood education* (6th ed.). Upper Saddle River, NJ: Merrill.

Moschonis, G., Grammatikaki, E., & Manios, Y. (2008). Perinatal predictors of overweight at infancy and preschool childhood: the GENESIS study. *International Journal of Obesity, 32,* 39–47.

Moseley, L., & Gradisar, M. (2009). Evaluation of a school-based intervention for adolescent sleep problems. *Sleep, 32,* 334–341.

Most, O. L., Kim, J. H., Arsian, A. A., & Klauser, C. (2009). Maternal and neonatal outcomes in early glucose tolerance testing in an obstetric population in New York City. *Journal of Perinatal Medicine, 37,* 114–117.

Moulson, M. C., & Nelson, C. A. (2008). Neurological development. In M. M. Haith & J. B. Benson (Eds.), *Encyclopedia of infancy and early childhood.* Oxford. UK: Elsevier.

Moya, J., Bearer, C. F., & Etzel, R. A. (2004). Children's behavior and physiology and how it affects exposure to environmental contaminants. *Pediatrics, 113, Suppl 4,* 996–1006.

Mueller, A. S. (2009). Body image, childhood and adolescence. In D. Carr (Ed.), *Encyclopedia of the life course and human development.* Boston: Gale Cengage.

Mueller, V. C., & Hoff, E. (2010). Input and the acquisition of language: Three questions. In E. Hoff & M. Shatz (Eds.), *Blackwell handbook of language development* (2nd ed.). New York: Wiley.

Murphy, M. M., & Mazzocco, M. M. (2008). Mathematics learning disabilities in girls with fragile X or Turner syndrome during late elementary school. *Journal of Learning Disabilities, 41,* 29–46.

Murray, J. P. (2007). TV violence: Research and controversy. In N. Pecora, J. P. Murray, & E. A. Wartella (Eds.), *Children and television.* Mahwah, NJ: Erlbaum.

Murray, J. P., & Murray, A. D. (2008). Television: Uses and effects. In M. M. Haith & J. B. Benson (Eds.), *Encyclopedia of infant and early childhood development.* Oxford, UK: Elsevier.

Murray, S. S., & McKinney, E. L. (2010). *Foundations of maternal-newborn and women's health* (5th ed.). New York: Elsevier.

Mustelin, L., Silventoinen, K., Pietilainen, K., Rissanen, A., & Kaprio, J. (2009). Physical activity reduces the influence of genetic effects on BMI and waist circumference: A study of young adult twins. *International Journal of Obesity, 33,* 29–36.

Myers, D. (2008, June 2). Commentary in S. Begley & J. Interlandi, The dumbest generation? Don't be dumb. Retrieved on July 22, 2008, at www.newsweek.com/id/138536/

Myers, D., Baer, W., & Choi, S. (1996). The changing problem of overcrowded housing. *Journal of the American Planning Association, 62,* 66–84.

Myers, D. G. (2010). *Psychology* (9th ed.). New York: Worth.

Myerson, J., Rank, M. R., Raines, F. Q., & Schnitzler, M. A. (1998). Race and general cognitive ability: The myth of diminishing returns in education. *Psychological Science, 9,* 139–142.

N

NAEYC (National Association for the Education of Young Children). (2009). Developmentally appropriate practice in early childhood programs serving children from birth through age 8. Washington, DC: Author.

Nagata, D. K. (1989). Japanese American children and adolescents. In J. T. Gibbs & L. N. Huang (Eds.), *Children of color.* San Francisco: Jossey-Bass.

Nagel, H. T., Kneght, A. C, Kloosterman, M. D., Wildschut, H. I., Leschot, N. J., & Vandenbussche, F. P. (2007). Prenatal diagnosis in the Netherlands, 1991-2000: Number of invasive procedures, indications, abnormal results, and terminations of pregnancies. *Prenatal Diagnosis, 27,* 251–257.

Najman, J. M., Hayatbakhsh, M. R., Heron, M. A., Bor, W., O'Callaghan, M. J., & Williams, G. M. (2009). The impact of episodic and chronic poverty on child cognitive development. *Journal of Pediatrics, 154,* 284–289.

Nakamoto, J., & Schwartz, D. (2010). Is peer victimization associated with academic achievement? A meta-analytic review. *Social Development, 19,* 221–242.

Nansel, T. R., Overpeck, M., Pilla, R., Ruan, W., Simons-Morton, B., & Scheidt, P. (2001). Bullying behaviors among U.S. youth. *Journal of the American Medical Association, 285,* 2094–2100.

Nardi, P. M. (2006). *Doing survey research* (2nd ed.). Boston: Allyn & Bacon.

Narendran, S., Nagarathna, R., Narendran, V., Gunasheela, S., & Nagendra, H. R. (2005). Efficacy of yoga on pregnancy outcomes. *Journal of Alternative and Complementary Medicine, 11,* 234–244.

Narváez, D. (2006). Integrative moral education. In M. Killen & J. Smetana (Eds.), *Handbook of moral development.* Mahwah, NJ: Erlbaum.

Narváez, D., & Lapsley, D. (Eds.). (2009). *Moral personality, identity, and character: An interdisciplinary future.* New York: Cambridge University Press.

Nation, M., & Heflinger, C. A. (2006). Risk factors for serious alcohol and drug use: The role of psychosocial variables in predicting the frequency of substance abuse among adolescents. *American Journal of Alcohol Abuse, 32,* 415–433.

National Assessment of Educational Progress. (2000). *Reading achievement.* Washington, DC: National Center for Education Statistics.

National Assessment of Educational Progress. (2005). *The nation's report card: 2005.* Washington, DC: U.S. Department of Education.

National Assessment of Educational Progress. (2007). *The nation's report card: 2007.* Washington, DC: U.S. Department of Education.

National Association for Sport and Physical Education. (2002). *Active start: A statement of physical activity guidelines for children birth to five years.* Reston, VA: National Association for Sport and Physical Education.

National Autism Association. (2010). *All about autism.* Retrieved January 5, 2009 from www.nationalautismassociation.org/definitions.php

National Cancer Institute (2009a). *Cancer trends progress report.* Retrieved on January 15, 2009, at http://progressreport.cancer.gov/highlights.asp

National Center for Education Statistics. (2008). *School dropout rates.* Washington, DC: U.S. Department of Education.

National Center for Health Statistics. (2000). *Health United States, 1999.* Atlanta: Centers for Disease Control and Prevention.

National Center for Health Statistics. (2008). *Health United States, 2008.* Atlanta: Centers for Disease Control and Prevention.

National Center for Health Statistics. (2009, January 7). *Public Release Statement: Preterm births rise 36 percent since early 1980s.* Atlanta: Centers for Disease Control and Prevention.

National Center on Shaken Baby Syndrome. (2010). *Shaken baby syndrome.* Retrieved April 22, 2010, from www.dontshake.org/

National Clearinghouse on Child Abuse and Neglect. (2004). *What is child abuse and neglect?* Washington, DC: U.S. Department of Health and Human Services.

National Institute of Mental Health. (2008). *Autism spectrum disorders (pervasive developmental disorders).* Retrieved January 6, 2008, from http://www.nimh.nih.gov/Publicat/autism.clm

National Institute of Neurological Disorders and Stroke. (2009). *Brain basics: Understanding sleep.* Retrieved May 5, 2009 from www.ninds.nih.gov/disorders/brain_basics/understanding_sleep.htm

National Institutes of Health (2008). *Clinical trial.gov.* Retrieved April 22, 2008 from http://clinicaltrials.gov/ct2/show/

National Research Council. (1999). *Starting out right: A guide to promoting children's reading success.* Washington, DC: National Academy Press.

National Research Council. (2004). *Engaging schools: Fostering high school students' motivation to learn.* Washington, DC: National Academic Press.

National Sleep Foundation (2006). *Sleep in America Poll: Children and sleep.* Washington, DC: National Sleep Foundation.

National Sleep Foundation (2007). *Sleep in America poll 2007.* Washington, DC: Author.

National Sleep Foundation (2010). *Children's sleep habits.* Retrieved on April 22, 2010 at www.sleepfoundation.org

National Vital Statistics Report (2004 March 7). Deaths: Leading causes for 2002. Atlantic: Centers for Disease Control and Prevention.

Neal, A. R. (2009). Autism. In D. Carr (Ed.), *Encyclopedia of the life course and human development.* Boston: Gale Cengage.

Needham, A. (2009). Learning in infants' object perception, object-directed action, and tool use. In A. Woodward & A. Needham (Eds.), *Learning and the infant mind.* New York: Oxford University Press.

Needham, A. Barrett, T., & Peterman, K. (2002) A pick-me-up for infants' exploratory skills: Early simulated experiences reaching for objects using "sticky mittens" enhances young infants' object exploration skills. *Infant Behavior and Development, 25,* 279–295.

Neisser, U., & others. (1996). Intelligence: Knowns and unknowns. *American Psychologist, 51,* 77–101.

Nelson, C. A. (2003). Neural development and lifelong plasticity. In R. M. Lerner, F. Jacobs, & D. Wertlieb (Eds.), *Handbook of applied developmental science.* Thousand Oaks, CA: Sage.

Nelson, C. A. (2007). A developmental cognitive neuroscience approach to the study of atypical development: A model system involving infants of diabetic mothers. In D. Coch, G. Dawson, & K. W. Fischer (eds.), *Human behavior, learning, and the developing brain.* New York: Guilford.

Nelson, C. A. (2011). Brain development and behavior. In A. M. Rudolph, C. Rudolph, L. First, G. Lister, & A. A. Gersohon (Eds.), *Rudolph's pediatrics* (22nd ed.). New York: McGraw-Hill.

Nelson, J. A., & Eckstein, D. (2008). A service-learning model for at-risk adolescents. *Education and Treatment of Children, 31,* 223–237.

Nelson, K. (1999). Levels and modes of representation: Issues for the theory of conceptual change and development. In E. K. Skolnick, K. Nelson, S. A. Gelman, & P. H. Miller (Eds.), *Conceptual development.* Mahwah, NJ: Erlbaum.

Neubauer, A. C., & Fink, A. (2009). Intelligence and neural efficiency: Measures of brain activation versus measures of functional connectivity in the brain. *Intelligence, 37,* 223–229.

Neukrug, E. S., & Fawcett, R. C. (2010). *Essentials of testing and assessment* (2nd ed.). Boston: Cengage.

Neville, H. J. (2006). Different profiles of plasticity within human cognition. In Y. Munakata & M. H. Johnson (Eds.), *Attention and Performance XXI: Processes of change in brain and cognitive development.* Oxford, UK: Oxford University Press.

Nevsimalova, S. (2009). Narcolepsy in childhood. *Sleep Medicine Reviews, 13,* 169–180.

New, R. (2005). The Reggio Emilia approach: Provocations and partnerships with U. S. early childhood educators. In J. I. Roopnarine & J. E.

Johnson (Eds.), *Approaches to early childhood education* (4th ed.). Columbus, OH: Merrill/Prentice Hall.

New, R. (2007). Reggio Emilia as cultural activity. *Theory into Practice, 46*(1), 5–13.

Newcombe, N. (2007). The development of implicit and explicit memory. In N. Cowan & M. Courage (Eds.), *The development of memory in childhood*. Philadelphia: Psychology Press.

Newcombe, N. S. (2007). Developmental psychology meets the mommy wars. *Journal of Applied Developmental Psychology, 28*, 553–555.

Newell, K., Scully, D. M., McDonald, P. V., & Baillargeon, R. (1989). Task constraints and infant grip configurations. *Developmental Psychobiology, 22*, 817–832.

Newton, A. W., & Vandeven, A. M. (2006). Unexplained infant death: A review of sudden infant death syndrome, sudden unexplained infant death, and child maltreatment fatalities including shaken baby syndrome. *Current Opinions in Pediatrics, 18*, 196–200.

Newton, A. W., & Vandeven, A. M. (2010). Child abuse and neglect: A worldwide concern. *Current Opinion in Pediatrics, 22*, 226–233.

NICHD. (2010). *SIDS facts*. Retrieved on April 22, 2010 at www.nichd.nih/gov/sids

NICHD Early Child Care Research Network. (2000). Factors associated with fathers' caregiving activities and sensitivity with young children. *Developmental Psychology, 14*, 200–219.

NICHD Early Child Care Research Network. (2001). Nonmaternal care and family factors in early development: An overview of the NICHD study of Early Child Care. *Journal of Applied Developmental Psychology, 22*, 457–492.

NICHD Early Child Care Research Network. (2002). Structure?Process?Outcome: Direct and indirect effects of child care quality on young children's development. *Psychological Science, 13*, 199–206.

NICHD Early Child Care Research Network. (2003). Does amount of time spent in child care predict socioemotional adjustment during the transition to kindergarten? *Child Development, 74*, 976–1005.

NICHD Early Child Care Research Network. (2004). Type of child care and children's development at 54 months. *Early Childhood Research Quarterly, 19*, 203–230.

NICHD Early Child Care Research Network. (2005). *Child care and development*. New York: Guilford.

NICHD Early Child Care Research Network. (2005). Duration and developmental timing of poverty and children's cognitive and social development from birth through third grade. *Child Development, 76*, 795–810.

NICHD Early Child Care Research Network. (2005). Predicting individual differences in attention, memory, and planning in first-graders from experiences at home, child care, and school. *Developmental Psychology, 41*, 99–114.

NICHD Early Child Care Research Network. (2006). Infant-mother attachment classification:

Risk and protection in relation to changing maternal caregiving quality. *Developmental Psychology, 42*, 38–58.

NICHD Early Child Care Research Network. (2009). Family-peer linkages: The mediational role of attentional processes. *Social Development, 18*(4), 875–895.

NICHD Early Child Care Research Network. (2010). Testing a series of causal propositions relating time spent in child care to children's externalizing behavior. *Developmental Psychology, 46*(1), 1–17.

Nichols, S., Svetlova, M. & Brownell, C. (2010). Toddlers' understanding of peers' emotions. *Journal of Genetic Psychology, 171*(1), 35–53.

Nielsen, L. S., Danielson, K. V., & Sorensen, T. J. (2010, in press). Short sleep duration as a possible cause of obesity: Critical analysis of epidemiological evidence. *Obesity Reviews*.

Nieto, S. (2010). Multicultural education in the United States: Historical realities, ongoing challenges, and transformative possibilities. In J. A. Banks (Ed.), *The Routledge international companion to multicultural education*. New York: Routledge.

Nigg, J. T., Martel, M. M., Nikolas, M., & Casey, B. J. (2010). Intersection of emotion and cognition in developmental psychopathology. In S. D. Calkins & M. A. Bell (Eds.), *Child development at the intersection of emotion and cognition*. Washington, DC: American Psychological Association.

Nippold, M. A. (2009). School-age children talk about chess: Does knowledge drive syntactic complexity? *Journal of Speech, Language, and Hearing Research, 52*, 856–871.

Nisbett, R. (2003). *The geography of thought*. New York: Free Press.

Nitko, A. J., & Brookhart, S. M. (2011). *Educational assessment of students* (6th ed.). Boston: Allyn & Bacon.

Nixon, G. M., & others. (2008). Short sleep duration in middle childhood: Risk factors and consequences. *Sleep, 31*, 71–78.

Noddings, N. (2007). *When school reform goes wrong*. New York: Teachers College Press.

Noddings, S. N. (2008). Caring and moral education. In L. Nucci & D. Narvaez (Eds.), *Handbook of moral and character education*. Clifton, NJ: Psychology Press.

Noland, H., Price, J. H., Dake, J., & Telijohann, S. K. (2009). Adolescents' sleep behaviors and perceptions of sleep. *Journal of School Health, 79*, 224–230.

Nolen-Hoeksema, S. (2011). *Abnormal psychology* (5th ed.). New York: McGraw-Hill.

Norgard, B., Puho, E., Czeilel, A. E., Skriver, M. V., & Sorensen, H. T. (2006). Aspirin use during early pregnancy and the risk of congenital abnormalities. *American Journal of Obstetrics & Gynecology, 192*, 922–923.

Norman, J. E., & others. (2009). Progesterone for the prevention of preterm birth in twin pregnancy (STOPPIT): A randomized, double-

blind, placebo-controlled study and meta-analysis. *Lancet, 373*, 2034–2040.

Nottleman, E. D., & others. (1987). Gonadal and adrenal hormone correlates of adjustment in early adolescence. In R. M. Lerner & T. T. Foch (Eds.), *Biological-psychological interactions in early adolescence* Hillsdale, NJ: Erlbaum.

Novin, S., Banderjee, R., Dadkhah, A., Rieffe, C. (2009). Self-reported use of emotional display rules in the Netherlands and Iran: Evidence for sociocultural influence. *Social Development, 18*, 397–411.

Nucci, L., & Narvaez, D. (2008). Introduction and overview. In L. Nucci & D. Narvaez (Eds.), *Handbook of moral and character education*. Clifton, NJ: Psychology Press.

Nylund, K., Bellmore, A., Nishina, A., & Graham, S. (2007). Subtypes, severity, and structural stability of peer victimization: What does latent class analysis say? *Child Development, 78*, 1706–1722.

Nyqvist, K. H., & others. (2010). Towards universal Kangaroo Mother Care: Recommendations and report from the First European conference and Seventh International Workshop on Kangaroo Mother Care. *Acta Pediatrica, 99*(6), 820–826.

O

Oakes, L. M., & Rakison, D. H. (2009). Issues in the early development of concepts and categories: An introduction. In D. H. Rakison & L. M. Oakes (Eds.), *Early category and concept development*. New York: Oxford University Press.

Oates, J., & Abraham, S. (2010). *Llewellyn-Jones fundamentals of obstetrics and gynecology* (9th ed.). New York: Elsevier.

Oates, J., & Grayson, A. (2004). *Cognitive and language development in children*. Malden, MA: Blackwell.

Obenauer, S., & Maestre, L. A. (2008). Fetal MRI of lung hypoplasia: Imaging findings. *Clinical Imaging, 32*, 48–50.

Oberlander, T. F., Bonaguro, R. J., Misri, S., Papsdorf, M., Ross, C. J., & Simpson, E. M. (2008). Infant serotonin transporter (SLC6A4) promoter genotype is associated with adverse neonatal outcomes after prenatal exposure to serotonin reuptake inhibitor medications. *Molecular Psychiatry, 13*, 65–73.

O'Brien, J. M., & Lewis, D. F. (2009). Progestins for the prevention of spontaneous preterm birth: Review and implications of recent studies. *Journal of Reproductive Medicine, 54*, 73–87.

O'Brien, M., & Moss, P. (2010). Fathers, work, and family policies in Europe. In M. E. Lamb (Ed.), *The role of the father in child development* (5th ed.). New York: Wiley.

Ochs, E., & Schieffelin, B. (2008). Language socialization and language acquisition. In P. A. Duff & N. H. Hornberger (Eds.), *Encyclopedia of language and education*. New York: Springer.

O'Connor, A. B., & Roy, C. (2008). Electric power plant emissions and public health. *American Journal of Nursing, 108*, 62–70.

O'Connor, E., & McCartney, K. (2007). Attachment and cognitive skills: An investigation of mediating mechanisms. *Journal of Applied Developmental Psychology, 28,* 458–476.

Ogbu, J., & Stern, P. (2001). Caste status and intellectual ability. In R. J. Sternberg & E. L. Grigorento (Eds.), *Environmental effects on cognitive abilities.* Mahwah, NJ: Erlbaum.

Ogden, C. L., Carroll, M. D., & Flegal, K. M. (2008). High body mass index for age among U.S. children and adolescents, 2003-2006. *Journal of the American Medical Association, 299,* 2401–2405.

O'Hearn, K., & Luna, B. (2009). Mathematical skills in Williams syndrome: Insight into the importance of underlying representations. *Developmental Disabilities Research Reviews, 15,* 11–20.

Okuma, K., & Tanimura, M. (2009). A preliminary study on the relationship between characteristics of TV content and delayed speech development in young children. *Infant Behavior and Development, 32,* 312–321.

Oladokun, R. E., Brown, B. J., & Osinusi, K. (2010, in press). Infant-feeding pattern of HIV-positive women in a prevention of mother-to-child transmissions (PMTCT) program. *AIDS Care.*

Oldehinkel, A. J., Ormel, J., Veenstra, R., De Winter, A., & Verhulst, F. C. (2008). Parental divorce and offspring depressive symptoms: Dutch developmental trends during early adolescence. *Journal of Marriage and the Family, 70,* 284–293.

Oliver, S. R., & others. (2010, in press). Increased oxidative stress and altered substrated metabolism in obese children. *International Journal of Pediatric Obesity.*

Oller, D. K., & Jarmulowicz, L. (2010). Language and literacy in bilingual children in the early school years. In E. Hoff & M. Shatz (Eds.), *Blackwell handbook of language development.* New York:

Olson, B. H., Haider, S. J., Vangjel, L., Bolton, T. A., & Gold, J. G. (2010a). A quasi-experimental evaluation of a breastfeeding support program for low-income women in Michigan. *Maternal and Child Health Journal, 14*(1), 86–93.

Olson, B. H., Horodynski, M. A., Brophy-Herb, H., & Iwanski, K. C. (2010b). Health professionals' perspectives on the infant feeding practices of low-income mothers. *Maternal and Child Health Journal, 14*(1), 75–85.

Olweus, D. (2003). Prevalence estimation of school bullying with the Olweus bully/victim questionnaire. *Aggressive Behavior, 29*(3), 239–269.

Oostdam, N., van Poppel, M. N., Eekohff, E. M., Wouters, M. G., & Van Mechelen, W. (2009). Design of FitFor2 study: The effects of an exercise program on insulin sensitivity and plasma glucose levels in pregnant women at high risk for gestational diabetes. *BMC Pregnancy and Childbirth, 9,* 1.

Opfer, J. E., & Gelman, S. A. (2011). Development of the animate-inanimate distinction. In U. Goswami (Ed.), *Wiley-Blackwell handbook of childhood cognitive development* (2nd ed.). New York: Wiley-Blackwell.

Ornstein, P., Coffman, J. L., & Grammer, J. K., (2007, April). *Teachers' memory-relevant conversations and children's memory performance.* Paper presented at the biennial meeting of the Society for Research in Child Development, Boston.

Ornstein, P. A., Coffman, J. L., & Grammer, J. K. (2009). Learning to remember. In O. A. Barbarin & B. H. Wasik (Eds.), *Handbook of child development and early education.* New York: Guilford.

Ornstein, P. A., Coffman, J. L., Grammer, J. K., San Souci, P. P., & McCall, L. E. (2010, in press). Linking the classroom context and the development of children's memory skills. In J. Meece & J. Eccles (Eds.), *The handbook of research on schools, schooling, and human development.* New York: Routledge.

Orobio de Castro, B., Merk, W., Koops, W., Veerman, J. W., & Bosch, J. D. (2005). Emotions in social information processing and their relations with reactive and proactive aggression in referred aggressive boys. *Journal of Clinical Child and Adolescent Psychology, 34,* 105–116.

Orth, U., Robins, R. W., & Roberts. B. W. (2008). Low self-esteem prospectively predicts depression in adolescence and young adulthood. *Journal of Personality and Social Psychology, 95,* 695–708.

Orth, U., Robins, R. W., Trzesniewski, K. H., Maes, J., & Schmitt, M. (2009). Low self-esteem is a risk factor for depressive symptoms from young adulthood to old age. *Journal of Abnormal Psychology, 118*(3), 472–478

Osborne, J. (2010). Arguing to learn in science: The role of collaborative, critical discourse. *Science, 328,* 463–468.

Oser, F. K., Scarlett, W. G., & Bucher, A. (2006). Religious and spiritual development throughout the life span. In W. Damon & R. Lerner (Eds.), *Handbook of child psychology* (4th ed.). New York: Wiley.

Osofsky, J. D. (Ed.). (2007). *Young children and trauma.* New York: Guilford.

Ostchega, Y., Carroll, M., Prineas, R. J., McDowell, M. A., Louis, T., & Tilert, T. (2009). Trends of elevated blood pressure among children and adolescents: Data from the National Health and Nutrition Examination Survey 1988–2006. *American Journal of Hypertension, 22,* 59–67.

Ostfeld, B. M., Esposito, L., Perl, H., & Hegyi, T. (2010). Concurrent risks in sudden infant death syndrome. *Pediatrics, 125,* 447–453.

Otto, B. W. (2010). *Language development in early childhood* (3rd ed.). Upper Saddle River, NJ: Prentice Hall.

Osvath, P., Voros, V., & Fekete, S. (2004). Life events and psychopathology in a group of suicide attempters. *Psychopathology, 37,* 36–40.

P

Palfrey, J., Sacco, D., Boyd, D., & DeBonis, L. (2009). *Enhancing child safety and online technologies.* Cambridge, MA: Berkman Center for Internet & Society.

Palomares, M., Landau, B., & Egeth, H. (2009). Orientation perception in Williams syndrome: Discrimination and integration. *Brain and Cognition, 70,* 21–30.

Paloutzian, R. F. (2000). *Invitation to the psychology of religion* (3rd ed.). Needham Heights, MA: Allyn & Bacon.

Paluck, E. L., & Green, D. P. (2009). Prejudice reduction: What works? A review and assessment of research and practice. *Annual Review of Psychology* (Vol. 60). Palo Alto, CA: Annual Reviews.

Pan, B. A., Rowe, M. L., Singer, J. D., & Snow, C. E. (2005). Maternal correlates of growth in toddler vocabulary production in low-income families. *Child Development, 76,* 763–782.

Pan. B. A., & Uccelli, P. (2009). Semantic development. In J. Berko Gleason & N. Ratner (Eds.), *The development of language* (7th ed.). Boston: Allyn & Bacon.

Panigrahy, A., Borzaga, M., & Blumi, S. (2010). Basic principles and concepts underlying recent advances in magnetic resonance imaging of the developing brain. *Seminars in Perinatology, 34,* 3–19.

Paradis, J. (2010). Second-language acquisition in childhood. In E. Hoff & M. Shatz (Eds.), *Blackwell handbook of language development.* New York: Wiley.

Parens, E., & Johnston, J. (2009). Facts, values, and attention-deficit hyperactivity disorder (ADHD): An update on the controversies. *Child and Adolescent Psychiatry and Mentol Health, 3,* 1.

Parente, M. E., & Mahoney, J. L. (2009). Activity participation in childhood and adolescence. In D. Carr (Ed.), *Encyclopedia of the life course and human development.* Boston: Gale Cengage.

Parkay, F. W., & Stanford, B. H. (2010). *Becoming a teacher* (8th ed.). Upper Saddle River, NJ: Prentice Hall.

Parke, R. D. (2002). Fathering. In M. H. Bornstein (Ed.), *Handbook of parenting* (2nd ed.). Mahwah, NJ: Erlbaum.

Parke, R. D., & Buriel, R. (2006). Socialization in the family: Ethnic and ecological perspectives. In W. Damon & R. Lerner (Eds.), *Handbook of child psychology* (6th ed.). New York: Wiley.

Parke, R. D., Leidy, M. S., Schofield, T. J., Miller, M. A., & Morris, K. L. (2008). Socialization. In M. M. Haith & J. B. Benson (Eds.), *Encyclopedia of infant and early childhood development.* Oxford, UK: Elsevier.

Parlade, M. V., Messinger, D. S., Delgado, C. D., Kaiser, M. Y., Van Hecke, A. V., & Mundy, P. C. (2009). Anticipatory smiling: Linking early affective communication and social outcome. *Infant Behavior and Development, 32,* 33–43.

Parsons, C. E., Young, K. S., Murray, L., Stein, A., & Kringelbach, M. L. (2010, in press). The functional neuroanatomy of the evolving parent-infant relationship. *Progress in Neurobiology.*

Pascalis, O., & Kelly, D. J. (2008). Face processing. In M. M. Haith & J. B. Benson (Eds.), *Encyclopedia of infant and early childhood development*. Oxford, UK: Elsevier.

Pasley, K., & Moorefield, B. S. (2004). Stepfamilies. In M. Coleman & L. Ganong (Eds.), *Handbook of contemporary families*. Thousand Oaks, CA: Sage.

Pate, R. R., Pfeiffer, K. A., Trost, S. G., Ziegler, P., & Dowda, M. (2004). Physical activity among children attending preschools. *Pediatrics, 114,* 1258–1263.

Patterson, C. J. (2004). What difference does a civil union make? Changing public policies and the experience of same-sex couples. Comment on Solomon, Rothblum, & Balsam (2004). *Journal of Family Psychology, 18,* 287–289.

Patterson, C. J. (2009). Lesbian and gay parents and their children: A social science perspective. *Nebraska Symposium on Motivation, 54,* 142–182.

Patterson, C. J., & Farr, R. H. (2010, in press). Children of gay and lesbian parents: Reflections on the research-policy interface. In H. R. Schaffer & Durkin, K. (Eds.), *Blackwell handbook of developmental psychology in action.* London: Blackwell.

Patterson, C. J., & Wainright, J. L. (2010, in press). Adolescents with same-sex parents: Findings from the National Longitudinal Study of Adolescent Health. In D. Brodzinsky, A. Pertman, & D. Kunz (Eds.), *Lesbian and gay adoption: A new American reality.* New York: Oxford University Press.

Patterson, G. R., DeBaryshe, B. D., & Ramsey, E. (1989). A developmental perspective on antisocial behavior, *American Psychologist, 44*(20), 329–335.

Patterson, G. R., Reid, J. B., & Dishion, T. J. (1992). *Antisocial boys: Vol. 4. A social interactional approach.* Eugene, OR: Castalia.

Paulhus, D. L. (2008). Birth order. In M. M. Haith & J. B. Benson (Eds.), *Encyclopedia of infant and early childhood development.* Oxford, UK: Elsevier.

Pauli-Pott, U., Friedl, S., Hinney, A., & Hebebrand, J. (2009). Serotonin transporter gene polymorphism (5-HTTLPR), environmental conditions, and developing negative emotionality and fear in early childhood. *Journal of Neural Transmission 116*(4), 503–512.

Paus, T. (2009). Brain development. In R. M. Lerner & L. Steinberg (Eds.), *Handbook of adolescent psychology* (3rd ed.). New York: Wiley.

Paus, T., & others. (2007). Morphological properties of the action-observation cortical network in adolescents with low and high resistance to peer influence. *Social Neuroscience, 3,* 303–316.

Pavlov, I. P. (1927). In G. V. Anrep (Trans.), *Conditioned reflexes.* London: Oxford University Press.

Paz-Alonso, P. M., Larson, R. P., Castelli, P., Alley, D., & Gooman, G. S. (2009). Memory development: Emotion, stress, and trauma. In M. Courage & N. Cowan (Eds.), *The development of memory in infancy and childhood.* New York: Psychology Press.

Payne, C., & Bachevalier, J. (2009). Neuro-anatomy and the developing brain. In M. De Haan & M. R. Gunnar (Eds.), *Handbook of developmental social neuroscience.* New York: Guilford.

Pederson, D. R., & Moran, G. (1996). Expressions of the attachment relationship outside of the Strange Situation. *Child Development, 67,* 915–927.

Pedersen, L. H., Henriksen, T. B., Vestergaard, M., Olsen, J., & Bech, B. H. (2009). Selective serotonin reuptake inhibitors in pregnancy and congenital malformations: population based cohort study. *British Medical Journal, 339,* 3569.

Pedroso, F. S. (2008). Reflexes. In M. H. Haith & J. B. Benson (Eds.), *Infant and early childhood development.* Oxford, UK: Elsevier.

Pei, J. R., Rinaldi, C. M., Rasmussen, C., Massey, V., & Massey, D. (2008). Memory patterns of acquisition and retention of verbal and nonverbal information in children with fetal alcohol spectrum disorders. *Canadian Journal of Clinical Pharmacology, 15,* e44–e56.

Pelayo, R., Owens, J., Mindell, J., & Sheldon, S. (2006). Bed sharing with unimpaired parents is not an important risk for sudden infant death syndrome: Letter to the editor, *Pediatrics, 117,* 993–994.

Pellicano, E. (2010). Individual differences in executive function and central coherence predict developmental changes in theory of mind in autism. *Developmental Psychology, 46,* 530–544.

Pena, E., & Bedore, J. A. (2009). Bilingualism. In R. G. Schwartz (Ed.), *Handbook of child language disorders.* Clifton, NJ: Psychology Press.

Penagarikano, O., Mulle, J. G., & Warren, S. T. (2007). The pathophysiology of fragile X syndrome. *Annual Review of Genomics and Human Genetics* (Vol. 8). Palo Alto, CA: Annual Reviews.

Pennington, B. F., & others. (2009). Gene × environment interactions in reading disability and attentions deficit/hyperactivity disorder. *Developmental Psychology, 45,* 77–89.

Peregoy, S. F., & Boyle, O. F. (2009). *Reading, writing, and learning in ESL* (5th ed.). Boston: Allyn & Bacon.

Perez-Febles, A. M. (1992). *Acculturation and interactional styles of Latina mothers and their infants.* Unpublished honors thesis, Brown University, Providence, RI.

Perin, D. (2007). Best practices in teaching writing to adolescents. In S. Graham, C. A. MacArthur, & J. Fitzgerald (Eds.), *Best practices in writing instruction.* New York: Guilford.

Perlman, S. B., & Pelphrey, K. A. (2010, in press). Regulatory brain development: Balancing emotion and cognition. *Social Neuroscience.*

Perner, J., Stummer, S., Sprung, M., & Doherty, M. (2002). Theory of mind finds its Piagetian perspective: Why alternative naming comes with understanding belief. *Cognitive Development, 17,* 1451–1472.

Perry, S. E., Hockenberry, M. J., Lowdermilk, D. L., & Wilson, D. W. (2010). *Maternal-child nursing care* (4th ed.). New York: Elsevier.

Persky, H. R., Dane, M. C., & Jin, Y. (2003). *The nation's report card: Writing 2002.* U.S. Department of Education.

Peskin, H. (1967). Pubertal onset and ego functioning. *Journal of Abnormal Psychology, 72,* 1–15.

Petersen, A. C. (1979, January). Can puberty come any faster? *Psychology Today,* pp. 45–56.

Petersen, M. B., Wang, Q., & Willems, P. J. (2008). Sex-linked deafness. *Clinical Genetics, 73,* 14–23.

Peterson, C. C. (2005). Mind and body: Concepts of human cognition, physiology and false belief in children with autism or typical development. *Journal of Autism and Developmental Disorders, 35,* 487–497.

Peterson, C. C., Garnett, M., Kelly, A., & Attwood, T. (2009). Everyday social and conversation applications of theory-of-mind understanding by children with autism-spectrum disorders or typical development. *European Child and Adolescent Psychiatry, 18,* 105–115.

Petrill, S. A., & Deater-Deckard, K. (2004). The heritability of general cognitive ability: A within-family adoption design. *Intelligence, 32,* 403–409.

Pettit, G. S., Lansford, J. E., Malone, P. S., Dodge, K. A., & Bates, J. E. (2010, in press). Domain specificity in relationship history, social-information processing, and violent behavior in early adulthood. *Journal of Personality and Social Psychology.*

Pew Research Center. (2008). *Pew forum on religion and public life: U.S. Religious Landscape Survey.* Washington, DC: Author.

Pfeifer, M., Goldsmith, H. H., Davidson, R. J., & Rickman, M. (2002). Continuity and change in inhibited and uninhibited children. *Child Development, 73,* 1474–1485.

Pfluger, M., Winkler, Hummel, S., & Ziegler, A. G. (2010). Early infant diet in children at risk for type 1 diabetes. *Hormone and Metabolic Research, 42,* 143–148.

Philipsen, N. M., Johnson, A. D., & Brooks-Gunn, J. (2009). Poverty, effects on social and emotional development. *International Encyclopedia of Education.* Oxford, UK: Elsevier.

Phillips, D. A., & Lowenstein, A. (2011). Early care, education, and child development. *Annual Review of Psychology* (Vol. 62). Palo Alto, CA: Annual Reviews.

Phinney, J. S. (1996). When we talk about American ethnic groups, what do we mean? *American Psychologist, 51,* 918–927.

Phinney, J. S. (2003). Identity and acculturation. In K. M. Chun, P. B. Organista, & G. Marin (Eds.), *Acculturation.* Washington. DC: American Psychological Association.

Phinney, J. S. (2006). Ethnic identity exploration in emerging adulthood. In J. J. Arnett & J. L. Tanner (Eds.), *Emerging adults in America.* Washington, DC: American Psychological Association.

Phinney, J. S. (2008). Bridging identities and disciplines: Advances and challenges in understanding multiple identities. In M. Azmitia,

M. Syed, & K. Radmacher (Eds.), *The intersections of personal and social identities. New Directions for Child and Adolescent Development, 120,* 81–95.

Phinney, J. S., & Alipuria, L. L. (1990). Ethnic identity in college students from four ethnic groups. *Journal of Adolescence, 13,* 171–183.

Phinney, J. S., & Ong, A. D. (2007). Conceptualization and measurement of ethnic identity: Current status and future directions. *Journal of Counseling Psychology, 54,* 271–281.

Piaget, J. (1932). *The moral judgment of the child.* New York: Harcourt Brace Jovanovich.

Piaget, J. (1952). *The origins of intelligence in children.* (M. Cook, Trans.). New York International Universities Press.

Piaget, J. (1954). *The construction of reality in the child.* New York: Basic Books.

Piaget, J. (1962). *Play, dreams, and imitation in childhood.* New York: W. W. Norton.

Piaget, J., & Inhelder, B. (1969). *The child's conception of space* (F. J. Langdon & J. L. Lunger, Trans.). New York: W. W. Norton.

Pickrell, J., & Loftus, E. F. (2001). *Creating false memories.* Paper presented at the American Psychological Society, Toronto.

Pinette, M., Wax, J. & Wilson, E. (2004). The risks of underwater birth. *American Journal of Obstetrics & Gynecology, 190,* 1211–1215.

Ping, H., & Hagopian, W. (2006). Environmental factors in the development of type 1 diabetes. *Review in Endocrine and Metabolic Disorders,7,* 149–162.

Pinker, S. (1994). *The language instinct.* New York: HarperCollins.

Pinkhardt, E. H., & others. (2009). Intensified testing for attention deficit hyperactivity disorder (ADHD) in girls should reduce depression and smoking in adult females and the prevalence of ADHD in the long term. *Medical Hypotheses, 72,* 409–412.

Pinto, K. M., & Coltrane, S. (2009). Divisions of labor in Mexican origin and Anglo families: Structure and culture. *Sex Roles, 60,* 482–495.

Pipp, S. L., Fischer, K. W., & Jennings, S. L. (1987). The acquisition of self and mother knowledge in infancy. *Developmental Psychology, 23,* 86–96.

Pleck, J. H. (1983). The theory of male sex role identity: Its rise and fall, 1936–present. In M. Levin (Ed.), *In the shadow of the past: Psychology portrays the sexes.* New York: Columbia University Press.

Pleck, J. H. (1995). The gender-role strain paradigm. In R. F. Levant & W. S. Pollack (Eds.), *A new psychology of men.* New York: Basic Books.

Plomin, R. (2004). Genetics and developmental psychology. *Merrill-Palmer Quarterly, 50,* 341–352.

Plomin, R., DeFries, J. C., & Fulker, D. W. (2007). *Nature and nurture during infancy and early childhood* (2nd ed.). New York: Cambridge University Press.

Plomin, R., DeFries, J. C., McClearn, G. E., & McGuffin, P. (2009). *Behavioral genetics* (5th ed.). New York: W. H. Freeman.

Pluess, M., & Belsky, J. (2009). Differential susceptibility to rearing experience: the case of child care. *Journal of Child Psychology and Psychiatry, 50*(4), 396–404.

Pollack, S., & others. (2010). Neuro-developmental effects of early deprivation in postinstitutionalized children, *Child Development, 81,* 224–236.

Pollack, W. (1999). *Real boys.* New York: Owl Books.

Poole, D. A., & Lindsay, D. S. (1996). *Effects of parents' suggestions, interviewing techniques, and age on young children's event reports.* Presented at the NATO Advanced Study Institute, Port de Bourgenay, France.

Popenoe, D., & Whitehead, B. D. (2008). *2008 update to the state of our unions.* Piscataway, NJ: The National Marriage Project, Rutgers University.

Popham, W. J. (2011). *Classroom assessment* (6th ed.). Boston: Allyn & Bacon.

Posada, G. (2008). Attachment. In M. M. Haith & J. B. Benson (Eds.), *Encyclopedia of infant and early childhood development.* Oxford, UK: Elsevier.

Posner, M. I., & Rothbart, M. K. (2007). *Educating the human brain.* Washington, DC: American Psychological Association.

Pott, W., Albayrak, O., Hebebrand, J., & Pauli-Pott, U. (2009). Treating childhood obesity: Family background variables and the child's success in a weight-controlled intervention. *International Journal of Eating Disorders, 42,* 284–289.

Poulin, F., & Pedersen, S. (2007). Developmental changes in gender composition of friendship networks in adolescent girls and boys. *Developmental Psychology, 43,* 1484–1496.

Power, F. C., & Higgins-D'Alessandro, A. (2008). The Just Community Approach to moral education and moral atmosphere of the school. In L. Nucci & D. Narvaez (Eds.), *Handbook of moral and character education.* Clifton, NJ: Psychology Press.

Prabhakar, H. (2007). Hopkins Interactive Guest Blog: *The public health experience at Johns Hopkins.* Retrieved on January 31, 2008 from http://hopkins.typepad.com/guest/2007/03/the_public_heal.html

Prakash, A., Powell, A. J., & Geva, T. (2010). Multimodality noninvasive imaging for assessment of congenital heart disease. *Circulation and Cardiovascular Imaging, 3,* 112–125.

Pratt, C., & Bryant, P. E. (1990). Young children understand that looking leads to knowing (so long as they are looking in a single barrel). *Child Development, 61,* 973–982.

Pratt, M. W., Norris, J. E., Hebblethwaite, S., & Arnold, M. L. (2008). Intergenerational transmission of values: Family generativity and adolescents' narratives of parent and grandparent value teaching. *Journal of Personality, 76,* 171–198.

Pressley, M. (2003). Psychology of literacy and literacy instruction. In I. B. Weiner (Ed.). *Handbook of psychology* (Vol. 7). New York: Wiley.

Pressley, M. (2007). Achieving best practices. In L. B. Gambrell, L. M. Morrow, & M. Pressley (Eds.), *Best practices in literacy instruction.* New York: Guilford.

Pressley, M. (2007). An interview with Michael Pressley by Terri Flowerday and Michael Shaughnessy. *Educational Psychology Review, 19,* 1–12.

Pressley, M., Allington, R., Wharton-McDonald, R., Block, C. C., & Morrow, L. M. (2001). *Learning to read: Lessons from exemplary first grades.* New York: Guilford.

Pressley, M., Cariligia-Bull, T., Deane, S., & Schneider, W. (1987). Short-term memory, verbal competence, and age as predictors of imagery instructional effectiveness. *Journal of Experimental Child Psychology, 43,* 194–211.

Pressley, M., Dolezal, S. E., Raphael, L. M., Welsh, L. M. Bogner, K., & Roehrig, A. D. (2003). *Motivating primary-grades teachers.* New York: Guilford.

Pressley, M., & Harris, K. (2006). Cognitive strategies instruction. In P. A. Alexander & P. H. Winne (Eds.), *Handbook of educational psychology* (2nd ed.). Mahwah, NJ: Erlbaum.

Pressley, M., & Hilden, K. (2006). Cognitive strategies. In W. Damon & R. Lerner (Eds.), *Handbook of child psychology* (6th ed.). New York: Wiley.

Pressley, M., Mohan, L., Fingeret, L., Reffitt, K., & Raphael Bogaert, L. R. (2007). Writing instruction in engaging and effective elementary settings. In S. Graham, C. A. MacArthur, & J. Fitzgerald (Eds.), *Best practices in writing instruction.* New York: Guilford.

Pressley, M., Mohan, L., Raphael, L. M., & Fingeret, L. (2007). How does Bennett Woods Elementary School produce such high reading and writing achievement? *Journal of Educational Psychology, 99,* 221–240.

Pressley, M., Raphael, L. Gallagher, D., & Dibella, J. (2004). Providence-St. Mel School: How a school that works for African-American students works. *Journal of Educational Psychology, 96,* 216–235.

Presson, J. C., & Jenner, J. V. (2008). *Biology.* New York: McGraw-Hill.

Prinstein, M. J. (2007). Moderators of peer contagion: A longitudinal examination of depression socialization between adolescents and their best friends. *Journal of Clinical Child and Adolescent Psychology, 36,* 159–170.

Prinstein, M. J., & Dodge, K. A. (2008). Current issues in peer influence. In M. J. Prinstein & K. A. Dodge (Eds.), *Understanding peer influence in children and adolescents.* New York: Guilford.

Prinstein, M. J., Rancourt, D., Guerry, J. D., & Browne, C. B. (2009). Peer reputations and psychological adjustment. In K. H. Rubin, W. M. Bukowksi, & B. Laursen (Eds.), *Handbook of peer interactions, relationships, and groups.* New York: Guilford.

Prinz, J. (2009). *The emotional construction of morals.* New York: Oxford University Press.

Prinz, R. J., Sanders, M. R., Shapiro, C. J., Witaker, D. J., Lutzker, J. R. (2009). Population-based prevention of child maltreatment: The U.S. Triple P System Population Trial. *Prevention Science, 10*(1), 1–12.

Provenzo, E. F. (2002). *Teaching, learning, and schooling in American culture: A critical perspective.* Boston: Allyn & Bacon.

Pruett, K. D., & Pruett, M. K. (2009). *Parenting partnership.* New York: Perseus.

Pruett, M. K., & Barker, R. (2009a). Children of divorce: New trends and ongoing dilemmas. In James Bray (Ed.), *Family handbook of psychology.* Washington, DC: American Psychological Association.

Pruett, M. K., & Barker, R. (2009b). Influencing co-parenting effectiveness after divorce: What works and how it works. In M. Schulz, P. Kerig, M. K. Pruett, & R. Parke (Eds.), *Feathering the nest: Couple relationships, couples interventions and children's development.* Washington DC: American Psychological Association.

Pryor, J. H., Hurtado, S., Sharkness, J., & Korn, W. S. (2007). *The American freshman: National norms for fall 2007.* Los Angeles: Higher Education Research Institute, UCLA.

Pujazon-Zazik, M., & Park, M. J. (2010). To tweet, or not to tweet: Gender differences and potential positive and negative health outcomes of adolescents' social Internet use. *American Journal of Men's Health, 4,* 77–85.

Pujol, J., & others. (2004). Delayed myelination in children with developmental delay detected by volumetric MRI. *Neuroimage, 22,* 897–903.

Puma, M., & others. (2010). *Head Start impact study. Final report.* Washington, DC: Administration for Children & Families.

Pungello, E. P., Iruka, I. U., Dotterer, A. M., Mills-Koonce, R., & Reznick, J. S. (2009). The effects of socioeconomic status, race, and parenting on language development in early childhood. *Developmental Psychology, 45,* 544–557.

Putallaz, M., Grimes, C. L., Foster, K. J., Kupersmidt, J. B., Coie, J. D., & Dearing, K. (2007). Overt and relational aggression and victimization: Multiple perspectives within the school setting. *Journal of School Psychology, 45,* 523–547.

Putnam, S. P., Sanson, A. V., & Rothbart, M. K. (2002). Child temperament and parenting. In M. H. Bornstein (Ed.), *Handbook of parenting* (2nd ed.), Mahwah, NJ: Erlbaum.

Puzzanchera, C., & Sickmund, M. (2008, July). *Juvenile court statistics 2005.* Pittsburgh: National Center for Juvenile Justice.

Q

Quadrelli, R., Quadrelli, A., Mechoso, B., Laufer, M., Jaumandreu, C., & Vaglio, A. (2007). Parental decisions to abort or continue a pregnancy following prenatal diagnosis of chromosomal abnormalities in a setting where termination of pregnancy is not legally available. *Prenatal Diagnosis, 27,* 228–232.

Quinn, P. C. (2009a). Concepts are not just for objects: Categorization of spatial relation information by infants. In D. H. Rakison & L. M. Oakes (Eds.), *Early category and concept development.* New York: Oxford University Press.

Quinn, P. C. (2009b). Born to categorize. In U. Goswami (Ed.), *Blackwell handbook of childhood cognitive development* (2nd ed.). Oxford, UK: Blackwell Publishers.

Quinn, P. C. (2011). Born to categorize. In U. Goswami (Ed.), *Wiley-Blackwell handbook of childhood cognitive development* (2nd ed.). New York: Wiley-Blackwell.

Quinn, P. C., & Eimas, P. D. (1996). Perceptual cues that permit categorical differentiation of animal species by infants. *Journal of Experimental Child Psychology, 63,* 189–211.

Quinn, P. C. Lee, K., Pascalls, O., & Slater, A. M. (2009). Perceptual development: Face perception. In E. B. Goldstein (Ed.), *Encyclopedia of perception.* Thousand Oaks, CA: Sage.

Quiocho, A. L., & Ulanoff, S. H. (2009). *Differentiated literacy instruction for English language learners.* Boston: Allyn & Bacon.

R

Raffaelli, M., & Ontai, L. L. (2004). Gender socialization in Latino/a families: Results from two retrospective studies. *Sex Roles, 50,* 287–299.

Raghuveer, G. (2010, in press). Lifetime cardiovascular risk of childhood obesity. *American Journal of Clinical Nutrition.*

Raikes, H., & others. (2006). Mother-child bookreading in low-income families: Correlates and outcomes during the first three years of life. *Child Development, 77,* 924–953.

Raikes, H. A., & Thompson, R. A. (2009). Attachment security and parenting quality predict children's problem-solving, attributions, and loneliness with peers. *Attachment and Human Development, 10,* 319–344.

Rajendran, G., & Mitchell, P. (2007). Cognitive theories of autism. *Developmental Review, 27,* 224–260.

Ram, K. T., & others. (2008). Duration of lactation is associated with lower prevalence of the metabolic syndrome in midlife—SWAN, the study of women's health across the nation. *American Journal of Obstetrics and Gynecology, 198,* e1–e6.

Ramey, C. T., & Campbell, F. A. (1984). Preventive education for high-risk children: Cognitive consequences of the Carolina Abecedarian Project. *American Journal of Mental Deficiency, 88,* 515–523.

Ramey, C. T., & Ramey, S. L. (1998). Early prevention and early experience. *American Psychologist, 53,* 109–120.

Ramey, C. T., Ramey, S. L., & Lanzi, R. G. (2001). Intelligence and experience. In R. J. Sternberg & E. L. Grigorenko (Eds.), *Environmental effects on cognitive abilities.* Mahwah, NJ: Erlbaum.

Ramey, C. T., Ramey, S. L., & Lanzi, R. G. (2006). Children's health and education. In W. Damon & R. Lerner (Eds.), *Handbook of child psychology* (6th ed.). New York: Wiley.

Ramey, S. L. (2005). Human developmental science serving children and families: Contributions of the NICHD study of early child care. In NICHD Early Child Care Network (Eds.), *Child care and development.* New York: Guilford.

Ramon, R., & others. (2009). Fish consumption during pregnancy, prenatal mercury exposure, and anthropometric measures at birth in a prospective mother-infant study in Spain. *American Journal of Clinical Nutrition, 90,* 1047–1055.

Ramphal, C. (1962). *A study of three current problems in education.* Unpublished doctoral dissertation, University of Natal, India.

Ramsey-Rennels, J. L., & Langlois, J. H. (2007). How infants perceive and process faces. In A. Slater & M. Lewis (Eds.), *Introduction to infant development* (2nd ed.), Malden, MA: Blackwell.

Rasmussen, M. M., Clemmensen, D. (2010). Folic acid supplementation in pregnant women. *Danish Medical Bulletin, 57,* A4134.

Raven, P. H. (2011). *Biology* (9th ed.). New York: McGraw-Hill.

Ream, G. L., & Savin-Williams, R. (2003). Religious development in adolescence. In G. Adams & M. Berzonksy (Eds.), *Blackwell handbook of adolescence.* Malden, MA: Blackwell.

Reeb, B. C., Fox, N. A., Nelson, C. A., & Zeanah, C. H. (2009). The effects of early institutionalization on social behavior and underlying neural correlates. In M. de Haan & M. Gunnar (Eds.), *Handbook of social developmental neuroscience.* Maldon, MA: Blackwell.

Reed, D. (2009). *Balanced introduction to computer science* (2nd ed.). Upper Saddle River, NJ: Prentice Hall.

Reed, S. K. (2010). *Cognition* (8th ed.). Boston: Cengage.

Regalado, M., Sareen, H., Inkelas, M., Wissow, L. S., & Halfon, N. (2004). Parents' discipline of young children: Results from the National Survey of Early Childhood Health. *Pediatrics, 113,* 1952–1958.

Regev, R. H., & others. (2003). Excess mortality and morbidity among small-for-gestational-age premature infants: A population based study. *Journal of Pediatrics, 143,* 186–191.

Reid, G., Fawcett, A., Manis, F., & Siegel, L. (2009). *The SAGE handbook of dyslexia.* Thousand Oaks, CA: Sage.

Reid, P. T., & Zalk, S. R. (2001). Academic environments: Gender and ethnicity in U.S. higher education. In J. Worell (Ed.), *Encyclopedia of women and gender.* San Diego: Academic Press.

Reiner, W. G., & Gearhart, J. P. (2004). Discordant sexual identity in some genetic males with cloacal exstrophy assigned to female sex at birth. *New England Journal of Medicine, 350,* 333–341.

Reis, M., & Kallen, B. (2010). Delivery outcome after maternal use of antidepressant drugs in pregnancy: an update using Swedish data. *Psychological Medicine.* (Available online January 5, 2010.)

Renner, P., Grofer Klinger, L., & Klinger, M. R. (2006). Exogenous and endogenous attention orienting in autism spectrum disorders. *Child Neuropsychology, 12,* 361–382.

Repacholi, B. M., & Gopnik, A. (1997). Early reasoning about desires: Evidence from 14- and 18-month-olds. *Developmental Psychology, 33,* 12–21.

Rest, J. R. (1995). *Concern for the social–psychological development of youth and educational strategies: Report for the Kaufmann Foundation.* Minneapolis: University of Minnesota, Department of Educational Psychology.

Reyna, V. F., & Brainerd, C. J. (1995). Fuzzy-trace theory: An interim synthesis. *Learning and Individual Differences, 7,* 1–75.

Reyna, V. F., & Farley, F. (2006). Risk and rationality in adolescent decision-making: Implications for theory, practice, and public policy. *Psychological Science in the Public Interest, 7,* 1–44.

Reyna, V. F., & Rivers, S. E. (2008). Current theories of risk and rational decision making. *Developmental Review, 28,* 1–11.

Reynolds, F. (2010). The effects of maternal labour analgesia on the fetus. *Best Practices & Research. Clinical Obstetrics & Gynaecology.* (Available online December 11, 2009.)

Reznick, J. S. (2009). Working memory in infant and toddlers. In M. Courage & N. Cowan (Eds.), *The development of memory in infancy and childhood.* New York: Psychology Press.

Richardson, G. A., Goldschmidt, L., & Willford, J. (2008). The effects of prenatal cocaine use on infant development. *Neurotoxicology and Teratology, 30,* 96–106.

Richter, L. (2004). Poverty, underdevelopment, and infant mental health. *Journal of Pediatric and Child Health, 39,* 243–248.

Rickards, T., Moger, S., & Runco, M. (2009). *The Routledge companion to creativity.* Oxford, UK: Routledge.

Rideout, V., Roberts, D. F., & Foehr, U. G. (2005). *Generation M: Media in the lives of 8- to 18-year-olds.* San Francisco: Kaiser Family Foundation.

Rinehart, S. D., Stahl, S. A., & Erickson, L. G. (1986). Some effects of summarization training on reading and studying. *Reading Research Quarterly, 21,* 422–438.

Rink, J. E. (2009). *Designing the physical education curriculum.* New York: McGraw-Hill.

Risch, N., & others. (2009). Interaction between the serotonin transporter gene (5-HTTLPR), stressful life events, and risk of depression: A meta-analysis. *Journal of the American Medical Association, 301,* 2462–2471.

Ritchie, S., Maxwell, K. L., & Bredekamp, S. (2009). Rethinking early schooling: Using developmental science to transform young children's early school experiences. In O. A. Barbarin & B. H. Wasik (Eds.), *Handbook of child development and early education.* New York: Oxford University Press.

Rivas-Drake, D., Hughes, D., & Way, N. (2009). Public ethnic regard and perceived socioeconomic stratification: Associations with well-being among Dominican and Black American youth. *Journal of Early Adolescence, 29,* 122–141.

Rivera, C., & Collum, E. (Eds.). (2006). *State assessment policy and practice for English Language Learners.* Mahwah, NJ: Erlbaum.

Rizzo, M. S. (1999, May 8). Genetic counseling combines science with a human touch. *Kansas City Star,* p. 3.

Roberts, D. F., & Foehr, U. G. (2008). Trends in media use. *Future of Children, 18*(1), 11–37.

Roberts, D. F., Henriksen, L., & Foehr, U. G. (2004). Adolescents and the media. In R. Lerner & L. Steinberg (Eds.), *Handbook of adolescent psychology* (2nd ed.). New York: Wiley.

Roberts, D. F., Henriksen, L., & Foehr, U. G. (2009). Adolescence, adolescents, and the media. In R. M. Lerner & L. Steinberg (Eds.), *Handbook of adolescent psychology* (3rd ed.). New York: Wiley.

Robins, R. W., Trzesniewski, K. H., Tracy, J. L., Gosling, S. D., & Potter, J. (2002). Global self-esteem across the life span. *Psychology and Aging, 17,* 423–434.

Robinson, J. B., Burns, B. M., & Davis, D. W. (2009). Maternal scaffolding and attention regulation in children living in poverty. *Journal of Applied Developmental Psychology, 30,* 82–91.

Rochlen, A. B., Suizzo, M. A., Scaringi, V., Bredow, A., & McKelley, R. A. (2007, August). *A paper qualitative study of stay-at-home fathers.* Presented at the meeting of the American Psychological Association, San Francisco.

Rode, J. C., & others. (2008). An examination of the structural, discriminant, nomological, incremental predictive validity of the MSCEIT. *Intelligence, 36,* 350–366.

Rode, L., & others. (2009). Systematic review of progesterone for the prevention of preterm birth in singleton pregnancies. *Acta Obstetrica et Gynecologica Scandinavica, 88,* 1180–1189.

Rode, S. S., Chang, P., Fisch, R. O., & Sroufe, L. A. (1981). Attachment patterns of infants separated at birth. *Developmental Psychology, 17,* 188–191.

Rodriquez, E. T., & others. (2009). The formative role of home literacy experiences across the first three years of life in children from low-income families. *Journal of Applied Developmental Psychology, 30*(6), 677–694.

Roemmich, J. N., & Lambiase, M., Slavy, S. J., & Horvath, P. J. (2009). Protective effect of interval exercise on psychophysical stress reactivity in children. *Psychophysiology, 46,* 852–861.

Rogaev, E. L., Grigorenko, A. P., Faskhutdinova, G., Kittler, E. L., & Moliaka, Y. K. (2009). Genotype analysis identifies the cause of the "royal disease" *Science, 326,* 817.

Rogoff, B. (1990). *Apprenticeship in thinking.* New York: Oxford University Press.

Rogoff, B. (2003). *The cultural nature of human development.* New York: Oxford University Press.

Rogoff, B., Moore, L., Najafi, B., Dexter, A., Correa-Chavez, M., & Solis, J. (2007). Children's development of cultural repertoires through participation in everyday routines and practices. In J. E. Grusec & P. D. Hastings (Eds.), *Handbook of socialization.* New York: Guilford.

Rohner, R. P., & Rohner, E. C. (1981). Parental acceptance-rejection and parental control: Cross-cultural codes. *Ethnology, 20,* 245–260.

Rojas, A., Khoo, A, Tejedo, J. R., Bedoya, F. J., Soria, B., & Martin, F. (2010). Islet cell development. *Advances in Experimental Medicine and Biology, 654,* 59–75.

Rondou, P., Haegeman, G., & Van Craenenbroeck, K. (2010, in press). The dopamine D4 receptor: Biochemical and signaling properties. *Cellular and Molecular Life Sciences.*

Roopnarine, J. L., & Metindogan, A., (2006). Early childhood education research in cross-national perspective. In B. Spodek & O. N. Saracho (Eds.). *Handbook of research on the education of young children.* Mahwah, NJ: Erlbaum.

Rose, A. J., & Asher, S. R. (1999). Children's goals and strategies in response to conflicts within a friendship. *Developmental Psychology, 35,* 69–79.

Rose, A. J., Carlson, W., & Waller, E. M. (2007). Prospective associations of co-rumination with friendship and emotional adjustment: Considering the socioemotional trade-offs of co-rumination. *Developmental Psychology, 43,* 1019–1031.

Rose, A. J., & Smith, R. L. (2009). Sex differences in peer relationships. In K. H. Rubin, W. M. Bukowski, & B. Laursen (Eds.), *Handbook of peer interactions, relationships, and groups.* New York: Guilford.

Rose, S. A., Feldman, J. F., & Wallace, I. F. (1992). Infant information processing in relation to six-year cognitive outcomes. *Child Development, 63,* 1126–1141.

Rose, S. A., Feldman, J. F., & Jankowski, J. J. (2009). A cognitive approach to the development of early language. *Child Development, 80,* 134–150.

Rosen, L. D., Cheever, N. A., & Carrier, L. M. (2008). The association of parenting style and child age with parental limit setting and adolescent MySpace behavior. *Journal of Applied Developmental Psychology, 29,* 459–471.

Rosenberg, M. S., Westling, D. L., & McLeskey, J. (2011). *Special education for today's teachers* (2nd ed.). Upper Saddle River, NJ: Merrill.

Rosenblith, J. F. (1992). *In the beginning* (2nd ed.). Newbury Park, CA: Sage.

Rosenblum, S., Aloni, T., & Josman, N. (2010). Relationships between handwriting performance and organizational abilities among children with and without dysgraphia: A preliminary study. *Research in Developmental Disabilities, 31,* 502–509.

Rosenheck, R. (2008). Fast food consumption and increased caloric intake: A systematic review of a trajectory towards weight gain and obesity risk. *Obesity Reviews, 9*(6), 535–547.

Rosenkoetter, L. I., Rosenkoetter, S. E., & Acock, A. C. (2009). Television violence: An intervention to reduce its impact on children. *Journal of Applied Developmental Psychology, 30,* 381–397.

Rosenstein, D., & Oster, H. (1988). Differential facial responses to four basic tastes in newborns. *Child Development, 59,* 1555–1568.

Rosnow, R. L., & Rosenthal, R. (1996). *Beginning behavioral research* (2nd ed.). Upper Saddle River, NJ: Prentice Hall.

Ross, H., & Howe, N. (2009). Family influences on children's peer relationships. In K. H. Rubin, W. M. Bukowksi, & B. Laursen (Eds.), *Handbook of peer interactions, relationships, and groups.* New York: Guilford.

Ross, J. L., & others. (2008). Cognitive and motor development during childhood in boys with Klinefelter syndrome. *American Journal of Medical Genetics A, 146A,* 708–719.

Rothbart, M. K. (2004). Temperament and the pursuit of an integrated developmental psychology. *Merrill-Palmer Quarterly, 50,* 492–505.

Rothbart, M. K. (2007). Temperament, development, and personality. *Current Directions in Psychological Science, 16,* 207–212.

Rothbart, M. K., & Bates, J. E. (2006). Temperament. In W. Damon & R. Lerner (Eds.), *Handbook of child psychology* (6th ed.). New York: Wiley.

Rothbart, M. K., & Gartstein, M. A. (2008). Temperament. In M. M. Haith & J. B. Benson (Eds.), *Encyclopedia of infant and early childhood development.* Oxford, UK: Elsevier.

Rothbart, M. K., & Sheese, B. E. (2007). Temperament and emotion regulation. In J. J. Gross (Ed.), *Handbook of emotion regulation.* New York: Guilford Press.

Rothbaum, F., Poll, M., Azuma, H., Miyake, K., & Weisz, J. (2000). The development of close relationships in Japan and the United States: Paths of symbiotic harmony and generative tension. *Child Development, 71,* 1121–1142.

Rothbaum, F., & Trommsdorff, G. (2007). Do roots and wings complement or oppose one another?: The socialization of relatedness and autonomy in cultural context. In J. E. Grusec & P. D. Hastings (Eds.), *Handbook of Socialization.* New York: Guilford.

Rovee-Collier, C. (1987). Learning and memory in children. In J. D. Osofsky (Ed.), *Handbook of infant development* (2nd ed.). New York: Wiley.

Rovee-Collier, C. (2004). Infant learning and memory. In U. Goswami (Ed.), *Blackwell handbook of childhood cognitive development.* Malden, MA: Blackwell.

Rovee-Collier, C. (2007). The development of infant memory. In N. Cowan & M. Courage (eds.), *The development of memory in childhood.* Philadelphia: Psychology Press.

Rovee-Collier, C., & Cuevas, K. (2009). The development of infant memory. In M. Courage & N. Cowan (Eds.), *The development of memory in infancy and childhood.* New York: Psychology Press.

Rovers, M. M., de Kok, I. M., & Schilder, A. G. (2006). Risk factors for otitis media: An international perspective. *International Journal of Otorhinolaryngology, 70,* 1251–1256.

Row, C., Burns, S., & Griffin, P. (Eds.). (1998). *Preventing reading difficulties in young children.* Washington, DC: National Academy Press.

Rowe, M. L., & Goldin-Meadow, S. (2009). Differences in early gesture explain SES disparities in child vocabulary size at school entry. *Science, 323,* 951–953.

Rowley, S., Kurtz-Costes, B., & Cooper, S. M. (2010). The role of schooling in ethnic minority achievement and attainment. In J. Meece & J. Eccles (Eds.), *Handbook of research on schools, schooling, and human development.* New York: Routledge.

Roza, S. J., & others. (2010). Maternal folic acid supplement use in early pregnancy and child behavioural problems: The Generation R study. *British Journal of Nutrition, 103,* 445–452.

Ruano, D., & others. (2010). Functional gene group analysis reveals a role of synaptic heterotrimeric G proteins in cognitive ability. *American Journal of Human Genetics, 86,* 113–125.

Rubie-Davies, C. M. (2007). Classroom interactions: exploring the practices of high- and low-expectation teachers. *British Journal of Educational Psychology, 77,* 289–306.

Rubin, K. H., Bukowski, W., & Parker, J. (2006). Peer interactions, relationships, and groups. In W. Damon & R. Lerner (Eds.), *Handbook of child psychology* (6th ed.). New York: Wiley.

Rubin, K. H., Cheah, C., & Menzer, M. M. (2010). Peers. In M. H. Bornstein (Ed.), *Handbook of cultural developmental science.* New York: Psychology Press.

Rubin, K. H., Fredstrom, B., & Bowker, J. (2008). Future directions in . . . friendship in childhood and early adolescence. *Social Development, 17,* 1085–1096.

Rubin, K. H., Mills, R. S. L., & Rose-Krasnor, L. (1989). Maternal beliefs and children's competence. In B. Schneider, G. Attili, J. Nadel, & R. Weissberg (Eds.), *Social competence in developmental perspective.* Amsterdam: Kluwer Academic.

Rubinsten, O., & Henik, A. (2009). Developmental dyscalculia: Heterogeneity might not mean different mechanisms. *Trends in Cognitive Science, 13,* 92–99.

Ruble, D. (1983). The development of social comparison processes and their role in achievement-related self-socialization. In E. Higgins, D. Ruble, & W. Hartup (Eds.), *Social cognitive development: A social-cultural perspective,* New York: Cambridge University Press.

Rueda, M. R., Posner, M. I., & Rothbart, M. K. (2005). The development of executive attention: Contributions to the emergence of self-regulation. *Developmental Neuropsychology, 28,* 573–594.

Ruel, M. T. (2010). The Oriente study: Program and policy impacts. *Journal of Nutrition, 140,* 415–418.

Ruel, M. T., & others. (2008). Age-based preventive targeting of food assistance and behavior change and communication for reduction of childhood undernutrition in Haiti: A cluster randomized trial. *Lancet, 371,* 588–595.

Ruffman, T., Slade, L., & Crowe, E. (2002). The relation between children's and mothers' mental state language and theory-of-mind understanding. *Child Development, 73,* 734–751.

Rumberger, R. W. (1995). Dropping out of middle school: The influence of race, sex, and family background. *American Educational Research Journal, 3,* 583–625.

Runquist, J. (2007). Persevering through postpartum fatigue. *Journal of Obstetric, Gynecologic, and Neonatal Nursing, 36,* 28–37.

Ryan, R. M., & Deci, E. L. (2009). Promoting self-determined school engagement: Motivation, learning, and well-being. In K. Wentzel, & A. Wigfield (Eds.), *Handbook of motivation at school.* New York: Routledge.

Ryan, R. M., Fauth, R. C., & Brooks-Gunn, J. (2006). Childhood poverty: Implications for school readiness and early childhood education. In B. Spodek & O. N. Saracho (Eds.), *Handbook of research on the education of young children.* Mahwah, NJ: Erlbaum.

Rykhlevskaia, E., Uddin, L. Q., Kondos, L., & Menon, V. (2010, in press). Neuoroanatomical correlates of developmental dyscalculia: Combined evidence from morphometry and tractography. *Frontiers in Human Neuroscience.*

S

Saarni, C. (1999). *The development of emotional competence.* New York: Guilford.

Saarni, C., Campos, J., Camras, L. A., & Witherington, D. (2006). Emotional development. In W. Damon & R. Lerner (Eds.), *Handbook of child psychology* (6th ed.). New York: Wiley.

Sabbagh, M. A., Xu, F., Carlson, S. M., Moses, L. J., & Lee, K. (2006). The development of executive functioning and theory of mind: A comparison of Chinese and U.S. preschoolers. *Psychological Science, 17,* 74–81.

Sachs, J. (2009). Communication development in infancy. In J. Berko Gleason & N. B. Ratner (Eds.), *The development of language* (7th ed.). Boston: Allyn & Bacon.

Sackett, P. R., Hardison, C. M., & Cullen, M. J. (2005). On interpreting research on stereotype threat and test performance. *American Psychologist, 60,* 271–272.

Sadeh, A. (2008). Sleep. In M. M. Haith & J. B. Benson (Eds.), *Encyclopedia of infant and early childhood development.* Oxford, UK: Elsevier.

Saffran, J. R. (2009). Acquiring grammatical patterns: Constraints on learning. In J. Colombo,

P. McCardle, & L. Freund (Eds.), *Infant pathways to language*. Clifton, NJ: Psychology Press.

Saffran, J. R., Werker, J. F., & Warner, L. A. (2006). The infant's auditory world: Hearing, speech, and the beginnings of language. In W. Damon & R. Lerner (Eds.), *Handbook of child psychology* (6th ed.). New York: Wiley.

Saifer, S. (2007, August 29). *Tools of the Mind—A Vygotskian-inspired early childhood curriculum.* Paper presented at the 17th Annual Conference of the European Early Childhood Education Research Association, Prague.

Salazar-Martinez, E., Allen, B., Fernandez-Ortega, C., Torres-Mejia, G., Galal, O., & Lazcano-Ponce, E. (2006). Overweight and obesity status among adolescents from Mexico and Egypt. *Archives of Medical Research, 37,* 535–542.

Salmivalli, C., & Peets, K. (2009). Bullies, victims, and bully-victim relationships in middle childhood and adolescence. In K. H. Rubin, W. M. Bukowski, & B. Laursen (Eds.), *Handbook of peer interactions, relationships, and groups.* New York: Guilford.

Salovey, P., & Mayer, J. D. (1990). Emotional intelligence. *Imagination, Cognition, and Personality, 9,* 185–211.

Sameroff, A. (2010). A unified theory of development: A dialectic integration of nature and nurture. *Child Development, 81,* 6–22.

Sanders, E. (2008). Medical art and play therapy with accident survivors. In C. A. Malchiodi (Ed.), *Creative interventions with traumatized children.* New York: Guilford.

Sandler, I., Wolchik, S., & Schoenfelder, E. (2011). Evidence-based family-focused prevention programs for children. *Annual Review of Psychology* (Vol. 62). Palo Alto, CA: Annual Reviews.

Sanson, A., & Rothbart, M. K. (1995). Child temperament and parenting. In M. H. Bornstein (Ed.), *Handbook of parenting* (Vol. 4). Hillsdale, NJ: Erlbaum.

Santrock, J. W., Sitterle, K. A., & Warshak, R. A. (1988). Parent-child relationships in stepfather families. In P. Bronstein & C. P. Cowan (Eds.), *Fatherhood today: Men's changing roles in the family.* New York: Wiley.

Santrock, J. W., & Warshak, R. A. (1979). Father custody and social development in boys and girls. *Journal of Social Issues, 35,* 112–125.

Savin-Williams, R. C. (2006). *The new gay teenager.* Cambridge, MA: Harvard University Press.

Scarr, S. (1984, May). Interview. *Psychology Today.* pp. 59–63.

Scarr, S. (1993). Biological and cultural diversity: The legacy of Darwin for development. *Child Development, 64,* 1333–1353.

Scarr, S., & Weinberg, R. A. (1983). The Minnesota adoption studies: Genetic differences and malleability. *Child Development, 54,* 182–259.

Schacter, D. L. (2001). *The seven sins of memory.* Boston: Houghton Mifflin.

Schacter, E. P., & Ventura, J. J. (2008). Identity agents: Parents as active and reflective participants in their children's identity formation. *Journal of Research on Adolescence, 18,* 449–476.

Schaffer, H. R. (1996). *Social development.* Cambridge, MA: Blackwell.

Schaie, K. W. (2009). "When does age-related cognitive decline begin?" Salthouse again reifies the "cross-sectional fallacy." *Neurobiology of Aging, 30*(4), 528–529.

Schaie, K. W. (2010, in press). Adult intellectual abilities. *Corsini encyclopedia of psychology.* New York: Wiley.

Schaie, K. W., (2011). *Developmental influences on adult intellectual development.* New York: Oxford University Press.

Schattschneider, C., Fletcher, J. M., Francis, D. L. Carlson, C. D., & Foorman, B. R. (2004). Kindergarten prediction of reading skills: A longitudinal comparative analysis. *Journal of Educational Psychology, 96,* 265–282.

Schauble, L. (1996). The development of scientific reasoning in knowledge-rich contexts. *Developmental Psychology, 32,* 102–119.

Scheibe, S., & Carstensen, L. L. (2010). Emotional aging: Recent findings and future trends. *Journal of Gerontology: Psychological Sciences, 65B,* 135–144.

Scher, A., & Harel, J. (2008). Separation and stranger anxiety. In M. M. Haith & J. B. Benson (Eds.), *Encyclopedia of infant and early childhood development.* Oxford, UK: Elsevier.

Schieffelin, B. (2005). *The give and take of everyday life.* Tucson, AZ: Fenestra.

Schiff, W. J. (2011). *Nutrition for healthy living* (2nd ed.). New York: McGraw-Hill.

Schlegal, A. (2009). Cross-cultural issues in the study of adolescent development. In R. M. Lerner & L. Steinberg (Eds.), *Handbook of adolescent psychology* (3rd ed.). New York: Wiley.

Schlegel, M. (2000). All work and play. *Monitor on Psychology, 31*(11), 50–51.

Schmidt, J., Shumow, L., & Kacker, H. (2007). Adolescents' participation in service activities and its impact on academic, behavioral, and civic outcomes. *Journal of Youth and Adolescence. 36,* 127–140.

Schmidt, L. A., & Jetha, M. K. (2009). Temperament and affect vulnerability: Behavioral, electrocortical, and neuroimaging perspectives. In M. de Haan & M. R. Gunnar (Eds.), *Handbook of developmental social neuroscience.* New York: Guilford.

Schmidt, M. E., & Vandewater, E. A. (2008). Media and attention, cognition, and school achievement. *Future of Children, 18*(1), 64–85.

Schneider, W. (2004). Memory development in childhood. In P. Smith & C. Han (Eds.), *Blackwell handbook of childhood cognitive development.* Malden, MA: Blackwell.

Schneider, W. (2011). Memory development in childhood. In U. Goswami (Ed.), *Wiley-Blackwell handbook of childhood cognitive development* (2nd ed.). New York: Wiley-Blackwell.

Schneider, W., & Pressley, M. (1997). *Memory development between two and twenty.* Mahwah, NJ: Erlbaum.

Schoon, I., Parsons, S., & Sacker, A. (2004). Socioeconomic adversity, educational resilience, and subsequent levels of adult adaptation. *Journal of Adolescent Research, 19,* 383–404.

Schouten, A. P., Valkenburg, P. M., & Peter, J. (2007). Precursors and underlying processes of adolescents' online self-disclosure: Developing and testing an "Internet-attribute-perception" model. *Media Psychology, 10,* 292–314.

Schulenberg, J. E., & Zarrett, N. R. (2006). Mental health during emerging adulthood: Continuities and discontinuities in course, content, and meaning. In J. J. Arnett & J. Tanner (Eds.), *Advances in emerging adulthood.* Washington, DC: American Psychological Association.

Schultz, M. S., Kerig, P. K., Pruett, M. K., & Parke, R. D. (Eds.). (2009) *Feathering the nest.* Washington, DC: American Psychological Association.

Schunk, D. H. (2008). *Learning theories* (5th ed.). Upper Saddle River, NJ: Prentice Hall.

Schunk, D. H., Pintrich, P. R., & Meece, J. L. (2008). *Motivation in education: Theory, research, and applications* (3rd ed.). Upper Saddle River, NJ: Prentice Hall.

Schwartz, D., Kelly, B. M., Duong, M., & Badaly, D. (2010). Contextual perspective on intervention and prevention efforts for bully/victim problems. In E. M. Vernberg & B. K. Biggs (Eds.), *Preventing and treating bullying and victimization.* New York: Oxford University Press.

Schwarz, S. P. (2004). A mother's story. Available at http://www.makinglifeeasier.com

Schweinhart, L. J., Montie, J., Xiang, Z., Barnett, W. S., Belfield, C. R., & Nores, M. (2005). *Lifetime effects: The High/Scope Perry Preschool Study Through Age 40.* Ypsilanti, MI: High/Scope Press.

Science Daily. (2008, January 15). Human gene count tumbles again (p. 1).

Scott-Jones, D. (1995, March). *Incorporating ethnicity and socioeconomic status in research with children.* Paper presented at the meeting of the Society for Research in Child Development, Indianapolis.

Scourfield, J., Van den Bree, M., Martin, N., & McGuffin, P. (2004). Conduct problems in children and adolescents: A twin study. *Archives of General Psychiatry, 61,* 489–496.

Seabrook, J. A., & Avison, W. R. (2010). Genotype-environment interaction and sociology: Contributions and complexities. *Social Science & Medicine, 70*(9), 1277–1284.

Seaton, E. K., Yip, T., & Sellers, R. M. (2009). A longitudinal examination of racial identity and racial discrimination among African American adolescents. *Child Development, 80,* 406–417.

Sekhobo, J. P., Edmunds, L. S., Reynolds, D. K., & Dalenius, K., & Sharma, A. (2010). Trends in the prevalence of obesity and overweight among children enrolled in the New York State WIC program, 2002–2007. *Public Health Reports, 125,* 218–224.

Sellers, R. M., Linder, N. C., Martin., P. P., & Lewis, R. L. (2006). Racial identity matters: The relationship between racial discrimination and psychological functioning in African American adolescents. *Journal of Research on Adolescence, 16*(2), 187–216.

Sellner, J., & others. (2009). A case of maternal herpes simplex virus encephalitis during pregnancy. *Nature Clinical Practice: Neurology, 5,* 51–56.

Selman, R. L. (1980). *The growth of interpersonal understanding.* New York: Academic Press.

Semmler, C., Ashcroft, J., van Jaarsveld, C. H., Carnell, S., & Wardle, J. (2009). Development of overweight in children in relation to parental weight and socioeconomic status. *Obesity, 17.* 814–820.

Serpell, R. (1974). Aspects of intelligence in a developing country. *African Social Research, 17,* 576–596.

Serpell, R. (1982). Measures of perception, skills, and intelligence. In W. W. Hartup (Ed.), *Review of child development research* (Vol. 6). Chicago: University of Chicago Press.

Serpell, R. (2000). Culture and intelligence. In A. Kazdin (Ed.), *Encyclopedia of psychology.* Washington, DC, & New York: American Psychological Association and Oxford University Press.

Shafer, V. L., & Garrido-Nag, K. (2010). The neurodevelopmental bases of language. In E. Hoff & M. Shatz (Eds.), *Blackwell handbook of language development* (2nd ed.). New York:

Shamah, T., & Villalpando, S. (2006). The role of enriched foods in infant and child nutrition. *British Journal of Nutrition, 96, Suppl,* S73–S77.

Shapira, N. (2008). Prenatal nutrition: A critical window of opportunity for mother and child. *Women's Health, 4,* 639–656.

Shapiro, A. F., & Gottman, J. M. (2005). Effects on marriage of a psycho-education intervention with couples undergoing the transition to parenthood: Evaluation at 1-year post-intervention. *Journal of Family Communication, 5,* 1–24.

Sharma, A. R., McGue, M. K., & Benson, P. L. (1996). The emotional and behavioral adjustment of adopted adolescents: Part I: Age at adoption. *Children and Youth Services Review, 18,* 101–114.

Shatz, M., & Gelman, R. (1973). The development of communication skills: Modifications in the speech of young children as a function of the listener. *Monographs of the Society for Research in Child Development, 38* (152).

Shaw, D. S., Dishion, T. J., Supplee, L., & Gardner, F., & Arnds, K. (2006). Randomized trial of family-centered approach to the prevention of early conduct problems: Two-year effects of the family check-up in early childhood. *Journal of Consulting and Clinical Psychology, 74,* 1–9.

Shaw, P., & others. (2007). Attention-deficit/hyperactivity disorder is characterized by a delay in cortical maturation. *Proceedings of the National Academy of Sciences, 104*(49), 19649–19654.

Shayer, M., & Adhami, M. (2010, in press). Realizing the cognitive potential of children 5–7 with a mathematics focus: Post-test and long-term effects of a 2-year intervention. *British Journal of Educational Psychology.*

Shaywitz, B. A., Lyon, G. R., & Shaywitz, S. E. (2006). The role of functional magnetic resonance imaging in understanding reading and dyslexia. *Developmental Neuropsychology, 30,* 613–632.

Shaywitz, S. E., Gruen, J. R., & Shaywitz, B. A. (2007). Management of dyslexia, its rationale, and underlying neurobiology. *Pediatric Clinics of North America, 54,* 609–623.

Shea, A. K., & Steiner, M. (2008). Cigarette smoking during pregnancy. *Nicotine and Tobacco Research, 10,* 267–278.

Shema, L, Ore, L., Ben-Shachar, M., Haj, M., & Linn, S. (2007). The association between breastfeeding and breast cancer occurrence among Jewish women: A case control study. *Journal of Cancer Research and Clinical Oncology, 133,* 903.

Shen, J. (2009). Evaluation of environmental and personal susceptibility characteristics that modify genetic risks. *Methods in Molecular Biology, 471,* 163–177.

Shen, Y., & others. (2010). Clinical genetic testing for patients with autism spectrum disorders. *Pediatrics, 125,* e727–e735.

Sheridan, M., & Nelson, C. A. (2008). Neurobiology of fetal and infant development: Implications of mental health. In C. H. Zeanh (Ed.), *Handbook of infant mental health* (3rd ed.). New York: Guilford.

Shields, S. A. (1998, August). *What Jerry Maguire can tell us about gender and emotion.* Paper presented at the meeting of the International Society for Research on Emotions, Wurzburg, Germany.

Shin, S. H., Hong, H. G., & Hazen, A. L. (2010, in press). Childhood sexual abuse and Sadolescence substance use: A latent class analysis. *Drug and Alcohol Dependence, 109*(1), 226–235.

Shiraev, E., & Levy, D. (2010). *Cross-cultural psychology: Critical thinking and critical applications* (4th ed.). Boston: Allen & Bacon.

Shonkoff, J. P. (2010). Building a new biodevelopmental framework to guide the future of early childhood policy. *Child Development, 81,* 357–367.

Shookhoff, J. M., & Ian Gallicano, G. (2010, in press). A new perspective on neural tube defects: Folic and microRNA misexpression. *Genesis.*

Shoup, J. A., Gattshall, M., Dandamudi, P., & Estabrooks, P. (2008). Physical activity, quality of life, and weight status in overweight children. *Quality of Life Research, 17*(3), 407–412.

Shwalb, D. W., & others. (2010). East and Southeast Asia: Japan, South Korea, Vietnam, and Indonesia. In M. H. Bornstein (Ed.), *Handbook of cultural developmental science.* New York: Psychology Press.

Shweder, R., Mahapatra, M., & Miller, J. (1987). Culture and moral development. In J.

Kagan & S. Lamb (Eds.), *The emergence of morality in young children.* Chicago: University of Chicago Press.

Siegel, L. S., & Wiener, J. (1993, Spring). Canadian special education policies: Children with disabilities in a bilingual and multicultural society. *Social Policy Report, Society for Research in Child Development, 7,* 1–16.

Siegler, R. S. (1976). Three aspects of cognitive development. *Cognitive Psychology, 8,* 481–520.

Siegler, R. S. (2006). Microgenetic analysis of learning. In W. Damon & R. Lerner (Eds.), *Handbook of child psychology* (6th ed.). New York: Wiley.

Siegler, R. S., & Alibali, M. W. (2005). *Children's thinking* (4th ed.). Upper Saddle River, NJ: Prentice Hall.

Silberg, J. L., Maes, H., & Eaves, L. J. (2010). Genetic and environmental influences on the transmission of parental depression to children's depression and conduct disturbance: an extended Children of Twins study. *Journal of Child Psychology and Psychiatry.* (Available online February 16, 2010.)

Siegal, M., & Surian, L. (2010). Conversational understanding in young children. In E. Hoff & M. Shatz (Eds.), *Blackwell handbook of language development.* New York: Wiley.

Silva, C. (2005, October 31). When teen dynamo talks, city listens. *Boston Globe,* pp. 81–84.

Silverstein, M. (2009). Caregiving. In D. Carr (Ed.), *Encyclopedia of the life course and human development.* Boston: Gale Cengage.

Simoncelli, M., Martin, B., & Berard, A. (2010). Antidepressant use during pregnancy: A critical systematic review of the literature. *Current Drug Safety, 5,* 153–170.

Simkin, P., & Bolding, A. (2004). Update on nonpharmacological approaches to relieve labor pain and prevent suffering. *Journal of Midwifery and Women's Health, 49,* 489–504.

Simpkins, S. D., Fredricks, J. A., Davis-Kean, P. E., & Eccles, J. S. (2006). Healthy mind, healthy habits: The influence of activity involvement in middle childhood. In A. C. Huston & M. N. Ripke (Eds.), *Developmental contexts in middle childhood.* Mahwah, NJ: Erlbaum.

Singh, A. A., Orpinas, P., & Horne, A. M. (2010). Empowering schools to prevent bullying: A holistic approach. In E. M. Vernberg & B. K. Biggs (Eds.), *Preventing and treating bullying and victimization.* New York: Oxford University Press.

Sinha, J. W., Cnaan, R. A., & Gelles, R. J. (2007). Adolescent risk behaviors and religion: Findings from a national study. *Journal of Adolescence, 30,* 231–249.

Sivell, S. & others. (2008). How risk is perceived, constructed, and interpreted by clients in clinical genetics, and the effects on decision making: A review. *Journal of Genetic Counseling, 17,* 30–63.

Skiba, T., Tan, M., Sternberg, R. J., & Grigorenko, E. L. (2010, in press). Roads not taken, new roads to take: Looking for creativity in the classroom. In J. Kaufman & R. Beghetto (Eds.), *Creativity in classrooms.* New York: Springer.

Skinner, B. F. (1938). *The behavior of organisms: An experimental analysis.* New York: Appleton-Century-Crofts.

Skinner, B. F. (1957). *Verbal behavior.* New York: Appleton-Century-Crofts.

Skoog, T., Stattin, H., & Kerr, M. (2009). The role of pubertal timing in what adolescent boys do online. *Journal of Research on Adolescence, 19,* 1–7.

Slater, A., Field, T., & Hernandez-Reif, M. (2007). The development of the senses. In A. Slater & M. Lewis (Eds.), *Introduction to infant development* (2nd ed.). New York: Oxford University Press.

Slater, A., Morison, V., & Somers, M. (1988). Orientation discrimination and cortical function in the human newborn. *Perception, 17,* 597–602.

Slater, A. M., Riddell, P., Quinn, P. C., Pascalls, O., Lee, K., & Kelly, D. J. (2010). Visual perception. In G. Bremner & T. Wachs (Eds.), *Blackwell handbook of infant development,* (2nd ed.). Oxford, UK: Blackwell.

Slawta, J. N., & Deneui, D. (2010, in press). Be a fit kid: Nutrition and physical activity for the fourth grade. *Health Promotion Practices.*

Slobin, D. (1972, July). Children and language: They learn the same way around the world. *Psychology Today,* 71–76.

Slomkowski, C., Rende, R., Conger, K. J., Simmons, R. L., & Conger, R. D. (2001). Sisters, brothers, and delinquency: Social influence during early and middle adolescence. *Child Development, 72,* 271–283.

Slough, N. M., McMahon, R. J., & Conduct Problems Prevention Research Group. (2008). Preventing serious conduct problems in school-age youth: The Fast Track Program. *Cognitive and Behavioral Practice, 15,* 3–17.

Smaldone, A., Honig, J. C., & Byrne, M. W. (2007). Sleepless in America: Inadequate sleep and relationships to health and well-being of our nation's children. *Pediatrics, 119, Suppl,* S29–S37.

Smetana, J. (2006). Social domain theory. In M. Killen & J. G. Smetana (Eds.), *Handbook of moral development.* Mahwah, NJ: Erlbaum.

Smetana, J. G. (2008). "It's 10 o'clock: Do you know where your children are?": Recent advances in understanding parental monitoring and adolescents' information management. *Child Development Perspectives, 2*(1), 19–25.

Smetana, J. G., Villalobos, M., Tasopoulos-Chan, M., Gettman, D. C., & Campione-Barr, N. (2009). Early and middle adolescents' disclosure to parents about activities in different domains. *Journal of Adolescence, 32,* 693–713.

Smith, C., & Denton, M. L. (2005). *Soul searching: The religious and spiritual lives of American teenagers.* New York: Oxford University Press.

Smith, J., & Ross, H. (2007). Training parents to mediate sibling disputes affects children's negotiation and conflict understanding. *Child Development, 78,* 790–805.

Smith, J. B. (2009). High school organization. In D. Carr (Ed.), *Encyclopedia of the life course and human development.* Boston: Gale Cengage.

Smith, K. (2002). *Who's minding the kids? Child care arrangements: Spring 1977.* Current Population Reports, P70–86. Washington, DC: U.S. Census Bureau.

Smith, L. E., & Howard, K. S. (2008). Continuity of paternal social support and depressive symptoms among new mothers. *Journal of Family Psychology, 22,* 763–773.

Smith, L. M., & others. (2001). Brain proton magnetic resonance spectroscopy and imaging in children exposed to cocaine in utero. *Pediatrics, 107,* 227.

Smith, P. K. (2007). Pretend play and children's cognitive and literacy development: Sources of evidence and some lessons from the past. In K. A. Roskos & J. F. Christie (Eds.), *Play and literacy in early childhood.* Mahway, NJ: Erlbaum.

Smith, R. P. (2009). *Netter's obstetrics and gynecology* (2nd ed.). London: Elsevier.

Smith, R. A., & Davis, S. F. (2010). *The psychologist as detective* (5th ed.). Upper Saddle River, NJ: Prentice Hall.

Smith, R. L., Rose, A.. J., & Schwartz-Mette, R. A. (2010). Relational andovert aggression in childhood and adolescence: Clarifying mean-level gender differences and associations with peer acceptance. *Social Development, 19,* 243–269.

Snarey, J. (1987, June). A question of morality. *Psychology Today,* pp. 6–8.

Snijders, B. E., & others. (2007). Breast-feeding duration and infant atopic manifestations, by maternal allergic status, in the first two years of life (KOALA study). *Journal of Pediatrics, 151,* 347–351.

Snow, C. E., & Yang, J. Y. (2006). Becoming bilingual, biliterate, and bicultural. In W. Damon & R. Lerner (Eds.), *Handbook of child psychology* (6th ed.). New York: Wiley.

Snowdon, A. W., Hussein, A., High, L., Millar-Polgar, J., Patriack, L., & Ahmed, E. (2008). The effectiveness of a multimedia intervention on parents' knowledge and use of vehicle safety systems for children. *Journal of Pediatric Nursing, 23,* 126–139.

Snyder, K. A., & Torrence, C. M. (2008). Habituation and novelty. In M. M. Haith & J. B. Benson (Eds.), *Encyclopedia of infant and early childhood development.* Oxford, UK: Elsevier.

Sokol, B. W., Snjezana, H., & Muller, U. (2010). Social understanding and self-regulation: From perspective-taking to theory of mind. In B. Sokol, U. Muller, J. Carpendale, A. Young, & G. larocci (Eds.), *Self-and social cognition.* New York: Oxford University Press.

Solomon, D., Watson, M. S., & Battistich, V. A. (2002). Teaching and school effects on moral/prosocial development. In V. Richardson (Ed.), *Handbook for research on teaching.* Washington, DC: American Educational Research Association.

Sophian, C. (1985). Perseveration and infants' search: A comparison of two- and three-location tasks. *Developmental Psychology, 21,* 187–194.

Sorte, J., Daeschel, l., & Amador, C. (2011). Nutrition, health, and wellness. Upper Saddle River, NJ: Merrill.

Soska, K. C., Adolph, K. E., & Johnson, S. P. (2010). Systems in development: Motor skills acquisition facilitates 3D object completion. *Developmental Psychology, 46,* 129–138.

Spandel, V. (2009). *Creating young writers* (4th ed.). Boston: Allyn & Bacon.

Spangler, G., Johann, M., Ronai, Z., & Zimmermann, P. (2009). Genetic and environmental influence on attachment disorganization. *Journal of Child Psychology and Psychiatry, 50,* 952–961.

Sparling, P., & Redican, K. (2011). *MP iHealth.* New York: McGraw-Hill.

Spelke, E. S. (1979). Perceiving bimodally specified events in infancy. *Developmental Psychology, 5,* 626–636.

Spelke, E. S. (1991). Physical knowledge in infancy: Reflections on Piaget's theory. In S. Carey & R. Gelman (Eds.), *The epigenesis of mind: Essays on biology and cognition.* Hillsdale, NJ: Erlbaum.

Spelke, E. S. (2000). Core knowledge. *American Psychologist, 55,* 1233–1243.

Spelke, E. S., Breinlinger, K., Macomber, J., & Jacobson, K. (1992). Origins of knowledge. *Psychological Review, 99,* 605–632.

Spelke, E. S., & Hespos. S. J. (2001). Continuity, competence, and the object concept. In E. Dupoux (Ed.), *Language, brain, and behavior.* Cambridge, MA: Bradford/MIT Press.

Spelke, E. S., & Kinzler, K. D. (2007). Core knowledge. *Development Science, 10,* 89–96.

Spelke, E. S. & Kinzler, K. D. (2009). Innateness, learning and rationality. *Cognitive Development Perspectives, 3*(2), 96–98.

Spelke, E. S., & Owsley, C. J. (1979). Intermodal exploration and knowledge in infancy. *Infant Behavior and Development, 2,* 13–28.

Spence, J. T., & Buckner, C. E. (2000). Instrumental and expressive traits, trait stereotypes, and sexist attitudes: What do they signify? *Psychology of Women Quarterly, 24,* 44–62.

Spence, J. T., & Helmreich, R. (1978). *Masculinity and femininity: Their psychological dimensions.* Austin: University of Texas Press.

Spencer, J. P., Blumberg, M. S., McMurray, B., Robinson, S. R., Samuelson, L. K., & Tomlin, J. B. (2009). *Short arms and talking eggs: Why we should no longer abide the nativist-empiricist debate. Child Development Perspectives, 3,* 79–87.

Spocter, M. A., & others. (2010, in press). Wernicke's area homologue in chimpanzees (Pan troglodytes) and its relation to the appearance of human language. *Proceedings: Biological Sciences.*

Spring, J. (2010). *Deculturalization and the struggle for equality* (6th ed.). New York: McGraw-Hill.

Srabstein, J. C., McCarter, R. J., Shao, C., & Huang, Z. J. (2006). Morbidities associated with bullying behaviors in adolescents: School-based study of American adolescents. *International Journal of Adolescent Medicine and Health, 18,* 587–596.

Sroufe, L. A., Coffino, B., & Carlson, E. A. (2010). Conceptualizing the role of early experience: Lessons from the Minnesota longitudinal study. *Developmental Review, 30,* 36–51.

Sroufe, L. A., Egeland, B., Carlson, E., & Collins, W. A. (2005). The place of early attachment in developmental context. In K. E. Grossman, K. Grossman, & E. Waters (Eds.), *The power of longitudinal attachment research: From infancy and childhood to adulthood.* New York: Guilford.

Sroufe, L. A., Waters, E., & Matas, L. (1974). Contextual determinants of infant affectional response. In M. Lewis & L. Rosenblum (Eds.), *Origins of fear.* New York: Wiley.

St. Pierre, R., Layzer, J., & Barnes, H. (1996). *Regenerating two-generation programs.* Cambridge, MA: Abt Associates.

Stager, L. (2009–2010). Supporting women during labor and birth. *Midwifery Today with International Midwife, 23,* 12–15.

Stangor, C. (2011). *Research methods for the behavioral sciences* (4th ed.). Boston: Cengage.

Stanulla, M., & Schrappe, M. (2009). Treatment of childhood acute lymphoblastic leukemia. *Seminars in Hematology, 46,* 52–63.

Starr, C. (2011). *Biology* (8th ed.). Boston: Cengage.

Starr, L. R., & Davila, J. (2009). Clarifying co-rumination: Associations with internalizing symptoms and romantic involvement among adolescent girls. *Journal of Adolescence, 32,* 19–37.

Staudinger, U. M., & Gluck, J. (2011). Psychological wisdom research. *Annual Review of Psychology* (Vol. 62). Palo Alto, CA: Annual Reviews.

Steel, A. J., & Sutcliffe, A. (2010). Long-term health implications for children conceived by IVF/ ICSI. *Human Fertility, 12,* 21–27.

Steele, C. M., & Aronson, J. A. (2004). Stereotype threat does not live by Steele and Aronson (1995) alone. *American Psychologist, 59,* 47–48.

Steelman, L. C., & Koch, P. R. (2009). Sibling relationships, childhood, and adolescence. In D. Carr (Ed.), *Encyclopedia of the life course and human development.* Boston: Gale Cengage.

Steinberg, L. D. (2008). A social neuroscience perspective on adolescent risk-taking *Developmental Review, 28,* 78–106.

Steinberg, L. D. (2009). Adolescent development and juvenile justice. *Annual review of Clinical Psychology* (Vol. 5). Palo Alto. CA: Annual Reviews.

Steinberg, L. D., & Cauffman, E. (2001). Adolescents as adults in court. *SRCD Social Policy Report, 15*(4), 1–13.

Steinberg, L. D., & Monahan, K. (2007). Age differences in resistance to peer influence. *Developmental Psychology, 43,* 1531–1543.

Steinberg, L. D., & Silk, J. S. (2002). Parenting adolescents. In M. Bornstein (Ed.), *Handbook of parenting* (2nd ed., Vol. 1). Mahwah, NJ: Erlbaum.

Steinberg, S. J., & Davila, J. (2008). Romantic functioning and depressive symptoms among early adolescent girls: The moderating role of parental emotional availability. *Journal of Clinical Child and Adolescent Psychology, 37,* 350–362.

Steiner, J. E. (1979). Human facial expressions in response to taste and smell stimulation. In H. Reese & L. Lipsitt (Eds.), *Advances in child development and behavior* (Vol. 13). New York: Academic Press.

Steinhausen, H. C., & Blattmann, B., & Pfund, F. (2007). Developmental outcome in children with intrauterine exposure to substances. *European Addiction Research, 13,* 94–100.

Steming, C. (2008). Centering Pregnancy: Group prenatal care. *Creative Nursing, 14,* 182–183.

Stephens, J. M. (2008). Cheating. In N. J. Salkind (Ed.), *Encyclopedia of educational psychology.* Thousand Oaks, CA: Sage.

Stern, D. N. (2010). A new look at parent-infant interaction: Infant arousal dynamics. In B. M. Lester & J. D. Sparrow (Eds.), *Nurturing children and families: Building on the legacy of T. Berry Brazelton.* New York: Wiley.

Sternberg, R. J. (1986). *Intelligence applied.* Fort Worth, TX: Harcourt Brace.

Sternberg, R. J. (Ed.). (1998). *Wisdom.* New York: Cambridge University Press.

Sternberg, R. J. (2004). Individual differences in cognitive development. In P. Smith & C. Hart (Eds.), *Blackwell handbook of cognitive development.* Malden, MA: Blackwell.

Sternberg, R. J. (2008). The triarchic theory of successful intelligence. In N. Salkind (Ed.), *Encyclopedia of educational psychology.* Thousand Oaks, CA: Sage.

Sternberg, R. J. (2009a). *Cognitive psychology* (5th ed.). Belmont, CA: Wadsworth.

Sternberg, R. J. (2009b). Intelligence. In *The Chicago companion to the child.* Chicago: University of Chicago Press.

Sternberg, R. J. (2009c). Leadership and giftedness. In B. MacFarlane & T. Stambaugh (Eds.), *Leading change in gifted education* (pp. 513–526). Waco, TX: Prufrock.

Sternberg, R. J. (2009d). The triarchic theory of successful intelligence. In B. Kerr (Ed.), *Encyclopedia of giftedness, creativity, and talent.* Thousand Oaks, CA: Sage.

Sternberg, R. J. (2009e). Wisdom. In S. J. Lopez (Ed.), *Encyclopedia of positive psychology* (Vol. 2) New York: Wiley-Blackwell.

Sternberg, R. J. (2009f). Wisdom, intelligence, and creativity synthesized. *The School Administrator, 66*(2), 10–14.

Sternberg, R. J. (2010a, in press). Human intelligence. In V. S. Ramachandran (Ed.), *Encyclopedia of human behavior* (2nd ed.). New York: Elsevier.

Sternberg, R. J. (2010b, in press). The triarchic theory of successful intelligence. In B. Kerr (Ed.), *Encyclopedia of giftedness, creativity, and talent.* Thousand Oaks, CA: Sage Publications, Inc.

Sternberg, R. J. (2010c, in press). Componential models of creativity. In M. Runco & S. Spritzker (Eds.), *Encyclopedia of creativity.* New York: Elsevier.

Sternberg, R. J. (2010d, in press). Intelligence. In B. McGaw, P. Peterson, & E. Baker (Eds.), *International encyclopedia of education* (3rd ed.). New York: Elsevier.

Sternberg, R. J. (2010e, in press). Teaching for creativity. In R. A. Beghetto & J. C. Kaufman (Eds.), *Nurturing creativity in the classroom.* New York: Cambridge University Press.

Sternberg, R. J., & Grigorenko, E. L. (2008). Ability testing across cultures. In L. A. Suzuki & J. G. Ponterotto (Eds.), *Handbook of multicultural assessment* (3rd ed.). San Francisco: Jossey-Bass.

Sternberg, R. J., Jarvin, L., & Rezmtskaya, A. (2009). Teaching for wisdom through history: Infusing wise thinking skills in the school curriculum. In M. Ferrari (Ed.), *Teaching for wisdom.* Amsterdam: Springer.

Sternberg, R. J., & others. (2001). The relationship between academic and practical intelligence: A case study in Kenya. *Intelligence. 29,* 401–418.

Sternberg, R. J., & Williams. W. M. (1996). *How to develop student creativity.* Alexandria, VA: ASCD.

Sterzer, P., Stadler, C., Krebs, A., Kleinschmidt, A., & Poustka, F. (2005). Abnormal neural responses to emotional visual stimuli in adolescents with conduct disorder. *Biological Psychiatry, 57,* 7–15.

Steur, F. B., Applefield, J. M., & Smith, R. (1971). Televised aggression and the inter-personal aggression of preschool children. *Journal of Experimental Child Psychology, 11,* 442–447.

Stevenson, H. W. (1995). Mathematics achievement of American students: First in the world by the year 2000? In C. A. Nelson (Ed.), *Basic and applied perspectives on learning, cognition, and development.* Minneapolis: University of Minnesota Press.

Stevenson, H. W., Lee, S., Chen, C., Stigler, J. W., Hsu, C., & Kitamura, S. (1990). Contexts of achievement. *Monograph of the Society for Research in Child Development, 55* (Serial No. 221).

Stevenson, H. W., & Zusho, A. (2002). Adolescence in China and Japan: Adapting to a changing environment. In B. B. Brown, R. W. Larson, & T. S. Saraswathi (Eds.), *The world's youth.* New York: Cambridge University Press.

Stiggins, R. (2008). *Introduction to student-involved assessment for learning* (5th ed.). Upper Saddle River. NJ: Prentice Hall.

Stipek, D. J. (2002). *Motivation to learn* (4th ed.). Boston: Allyn & Bacon.

Stipek, D. (2005, February 16). Commentary in *USA TODAY,* p.1D.

Stocker, C., & Dunn, J. (1990). Sibling relationships in childhood: Links with friendships and peer relationships. *British Journal of Developmental Psychology, 8,* 227–244.

Stoel-Gammon, C., & Sosa, A. V. (2010). Phonological development. In E. Hoff & M. Shatz (Eds.), *Blackwell handbook of language development* (2nd ed.). New York: Wiley.

Stolzer, J. M. (2009). Attention deficit/hyperactivity disorder. In D. Carr (Ed.), *Encyclopedia of the life course and human development.* Boston: Gale Cengage.

Stone, M. R., Rowlands, A. V., Middlebrooks, A. R., Jawis, M. N., & Eston, R. G. (2009). The pattern of physical activity in relation to health outcomes in boys. *International Journal of Pediatric Obesity.*

Stouthamer-Loeber, M., Loeber, R., Wei, E., Farrington, D. P., & Wikstrom, P. H. (2002). Risk and promotive effects in the explanation of persistent serious delinquency in boys. *Journal of Consulting and Clinical Psychology, 70,* 111–123.

Stouthamer-Loeber, M., Wei, E., Loeber, R., & Masten, A. (2004). Desistance from serious delinquency in the transition to adulthood. *Development and Psychopathology, 16,* 897–918.

Strasberger, V. C. (2009). Why do adolescent health researchers ignore the impact of the media? *Journal of Adolescent Health, 44,* 203–205.

Strathearn, L. (2007). Exploring the neurobiology of attachment. In L. C. Mayes, P. Fonagy, & M. Target (Eds.), *Developmental science and psychoanalysis.* London: Karnac Press.

Strauss, M. A., Sugarman, D. B., & Giles-Sims, J. (1997). Spanking by parents and subsequent anti-social behavior in children. *Archives of Pediatrics and Adolescent Medicine, 151,* 761–767.

Stray, L. L., Ellertsen, B., & Stray, T. (2010, in press). Motor function and methylphenidate effect in children with attention deficit hyperactivity disorder. *Acta Pediatrica.*

Streib, H. (1999). Off-road religion? A narrative approach to fundamentalist and occult orientations of adolescents. *Journal of Adolescence, 22,* 255–267.

Strenze, T. (2007). Intelligence and socioeconomic success: A meta-analytic review of longitudinal research. *Intelligence, 35,* 401–426.

Streri, A. (1993). *Seeing, reaching, touching: The relations between vision and touch in infancy.* London: Harvester Wheatshaft.

Stright, A. D., Herr, M. Y., & Neitzel, C. (2009). Maternal scaffolding of children's problem solving and children's adjustment in kindergarten: Hmong families in the United States. *Journal of Educational Psychology, 101,* 207–218.

Strong-Wilson, T., & Ellis, J. (2007). Children and place: Reggio Emilia's environment as a third teacher. *Theory Into Practice, 46,* 5–13.

Stroobant, N., Buijs, D., & Vingerhoets, G. (2009). Variation in brain lateralization during various language tasks: A functional transcranial Doppler study. *Behavioral Brain Research, 199,* 190–196.

Stuebe, A. (2009). The risks of not breastfeeding for mothers and infants. *Reviews in Obstetrics and Gynecology, 2,* 222–231.

Stuebe, A. M., & Schwartz, E. G. (2010). The risks and benefits of infant feeding practices for women and their children. *Journal of Perinatology, 30,* 155–162.

Sturm, R. (2005). Childhood obesity—what we can learn from existing data on societal trends. *Prevention of Chronic Diseases, 2,* A12.

Suarez-Orozco, C. (2007, March). *Immigrant family educational advantages and challenges.* Paper presented at the meeting of the Society for Research in Child Development, Boston.

Suarez-Orosco, M., & Suarez-Orozco, C. (2010). Globalization, immigration, and schooling. In J. A. Banks (Ed.), *The Routledge international companion to multicultural education.* New York: Routledge.

Subrahmanyam, K., & Greenfield, P. (2008). Online communication and adolescent relationships. *Future of Children, 18*(1), 119–146.

Subrahmanyam, K., Smahel, D., & Greenfield, P. (2006). Connecting developmental constructions on the Internet: Identity presentation and sexual exploration in online chat rooms. *Developmental Psychology, 42,* 395–406.

Sue, S. (1990, August). *Ethnicity and culture in psychological research and practice.* Paper presented at the meeting of the American Psychological Association, Boston.

Sue, S., & Morishima, J. K. (1982). *The mental health of Asian Americans: Contemporary issues in identifying and treating mental problems.* San Francisco: Jossey-Bass.

Sugita, Y. (2004). Experience in early infancy is indispensable for color perception. *Current Biology, 14,* 1267–1271.

Sullivan, E. L., & others. (2010). Chronic consumption of a high-fat diet during pregnancy causes perturbations in the serotonergic system and increased anxiety-like behavior in nonhuman primate offspring. *Journal of Neuroscience, 30,* 3826–3830.

Sullivan, H. S. (1953). *The interpersonal theory of psychiatry.* New York: W. W. Norton.

Sullivan, K., & Sullivan, A. (1980). Adolescent-parent separation. *Developmental Psychology, 16,* 93–99.

Sumaroka, M., & Bornstein, M. H. (2008). Play. In M. M. Haith & J. B. Benson (Eds.), *Encyclopedia of infant and early childhood development.* Oxford, UK: Elsevier.

Sunstein. C. S. (2008). Adolescent risk-taking and social meaning: A commentary. *Developmental Review, 28,* 145–152.

Super, C., & Harkness, S. (1997). The cultural structuring of child development. In J. W. Berry, Y. H. Poortinga, & J. Pandey (Eds.), *Handbook of cross-cultural psychology: Theory and method* (Vol. 2). Boston: Allyn & Bacon.

Susman, E. J., & Dorn, L. D. (2009). Puberty: Its role in development. In R. M. Lerner & L. Steinberg (Eds.), *Handbook of adolescent psychology* (3rd ed.). New York: Wiley.

Susman, M. R., Amor, D. J., Muggli, E., Jaques, A. M., & Halliday, J. (2010). Using population-based data to predict the impact of introducing noninvasive prenatal diagnosis for Down syndrome. *Genetics in Medicine, 12*(5), 298–303.

Suyemoto. K. L. (2009). Multiracial Asian Americans. In N. Tewari & A. Alvarez (Eds.), *Asian American psychology.* New York: Psychology Press.

Sveistrup, H., Schneiberg, S., McKinley, P. A., McGadyen, B. J., & Levin, M. F. (2008). Head, arm, and trunk coordination during reaching in children. *Experimental Brain Research, 188*(2), 237–247.

Swaab, D. F., Chung, W. C., Kruijver, F. P., Hofman, M. A., & Ishunina, T. A. (2001). Structural and functional sex differences in the human hypothalamus. *Hormones and Behavior, 40,* 93–98.

Swamy, G. K., Ostbye, T., & Skjaerven, R. (2008). Association of preterm birth with long-term survival, reproduction, and next generation preterm birth. *Journal of the American Medical Association, 299,* 1429–1436.

Swanson, D. P. (2010). Adolescent psychosocial processes: Identity, stress, and competence. In D. P. Swanson, M. C. Edwards, & M. B. Spencer (Eds.), *Adolescence: Development in a global era.* San Diego: Academic Press.

Swanson, H. L. (1999). What develops in working memory? A life-span perspective. *Developmental Psychology, 35,* 986–1000.

Swearer, S. M., Givens, J. E., & Frerichs, L. J. (2010). Cognitive-behavioral interventions for depression and anxiety. In G. G. Peacock, R. A. Ervin, E. J. Daly, & K. W. Merrell (Eds.), *Handbook of school psychology.* New York: Guilford.

Sweeting, H. N. (2008). Gendered dimensions of obesity in childhood and adolescence. *Nutrition Journal, 14,* 1.

Syed, M., & Azmitia, M. (2010). Narrative and ethnic identity exploration: A longitudinal account of emerging adults' ethnicity-related experiences. *Developmental Psychology, 46,* 208–219.

Sykes, C. J. (1995). *Dumbing down our kids: Why America's children feel good about themselves but can't read, write, or add.* New York: St. Martin's Press.

Szinovacz, M. E. (2009). Grandparenthood. In D. Carr (Ed.), *Encyclopedia of the life course and human development.* Boston: Gale Cengage.

T

Taddio, A. (2008). Circumcision. In M. M. Haith & J. B. Benson (Eds.), *Encyclopedia of infant and early childhood development.* Oxford, UK: Elsevier.

Tager-Flusberg, H., & Zukowski, A. (2009). Putting words together: Morphology and syntax in the preschool years. In J. Berko Gleason & N. B. Ratner (Eds.), *The development of language* (7th ed.). Boston: Allyn & Bacon.

Tagore, T. (2009). Why music matters. *Midwifery Today with International Midwife, 23,* 33–34, 67–68.

Taige, N. M., & others. (2007). Antenatal maternal stress and long-term effects on child neurodevelopment: How and why? *Journal of Child Psychology and Psychiatry, 48,* 245–261.

Talbot, J., Baker, J. K., & McHalo, J. P. (2009). Sharing the love: Prebirth adult attachment status and coparenting adjustment during infancy. The transition to parenthood. *Parenting: Science & Practice, 9,* 56–77.

Tamis-LeMonda, C. S., Way, N., Hughes, D., Yoshikawa, H., Kallman, R. K., & Niwa, E. Y. (2008). Parents' goals for children: The dynamic coexistence of individualism and collectivism in cultures and individuals. *Social Development, 17,* 183–209.

Tamis-Lemonda, C. S., & McFadden, K. E. (2010). The United States of America. In M. H. Bornstein (Ed.), *Handbook of cultural developmental science.* New York: Psychology Press.

Tang, Y. & Posner, M. I. (2009). Attention training and attention state training. *Trends in Cognitive Science, 13,* 222–227.

Tannen, D. (1990). *You just don't understand!* New York: Ballantine.

Tappan, M. B. (1998). Sociocultural psychology and caring psychology: Exploring Vygotsky's "hidden curriculum." *Educational Psychologist, 33,* 23–33.

Tarpley, T. (2001). Children, the Internet, and other new technologies. In D. Singer & J. Singer (Eds.), *Handbook of children and the media.* Thousand Oaks, CA: Sage.

Tasker, F. L., and Golombok, S. (1997). *Growing up in a lesbian family: Effects on child development.* New York: Guilford.

Taylor, L. S., & Whittaker, C. R. (2009). *Bridging multiple worlds* (2nd ed.). Boston: Allyn & Bacon.

Taylor, R. D., & Lopez, E. I. (2005). Family management practice, school achievement, and problem behavior in African American adolescents: Mediating processes. *Applied Developmental Psychology, 26,* 39–49.

Taylor, S. E. (2002). *The tending instinct.* New York: Times Books.

Teichert, M., & others. (2010). Isotretinoin and compliance with the Dutch pregnancy prevention program: A retrospective cohort study in females of reproductive age using pharmacy dispensing data. *Drug Safety, 33*(4), 315–326.

Temple, C., Nathan, R., Temple, F., & Burris, N. A. (1993). *The beginnings of writing* (3rd ed.). Boston: Allyn & Bacon.

Templeton, J. L., & Eccles, J. S. (2006). The relation between spiritual development and identity processes. In E. Roehlkepartain, P. E. King, L. Wagener, & P. L. Benson (Eds.), *The handbook of spirituality in childhood and adolescence.* Thousand Oaks, CA: Sage.

Tenenbaum, H. R., Callahan, M., Alba-Speyer, C., & Sandoval, L. (2002). Parent-child science conversations in Mexican-descent families: Educational background, activity, and past experience as moderators. *Hispanic Journal of Behavioral Sciences, 24,* 225–248.

Terman, L. (1925). *Genetic studies of genius. Vol. 1: Mental and physical traits of a thousand gifted children.* Stanford, CA: Stanford University Press.

Teti, D. (2001). Retrospect and prospect in the psychological study of sibling relationships. In J. P. McHale & W. S. Grolnick (Eds.), *Retrospect and prospect in the psychological study of families.* Mahwah, NJ: Erlbaum.

Tharp, R. G. (1994). Intergroup differences among Native Americans in socialization and child cognition: An erthogenetic analysis. In P. M. Greenfield & R. Cocking (Eds.), *Cross-cultural roots of minority child development.* Mahwah, NJ: Erlbaum.

Tharp, R. G., & Gallimore, R. (1988). *Rousing minds to life: Teaching, learning, and schooling in social context.* New York: Cambridge University Press.

Thelen, E., Corbetta, D., Kamm, K., Spencer, J. P., Schneider, K., & Zernicke, R. F. (1993). The transition to reaching: Mapping intention and intrinsic dynamics. *Child Development. 64,* 1058–1098.

Thelen, E., & Smith, L. B. (1998). Dynamic systems theory. In W. Damon (Ed.), *Handbook of child psychology* (5th ed., Vol. 1.). New York: Wiley.

Thelen, E., & Smith, L. B. (2006). Dynamic development of action and thought. In W. Damon & R. Lerner (Eds.), *Handbook of child psychology* (6th ed.). New York: Wiley.

Theokas, C. (2009). Youth sports participation—A view of the issues: Introduction to the special section. *Developmental Psychology, 45,* 303–306.

Therrell, B. L., & others. (2010). Newborn Screening System Performance Evaluation Assessment (PEAS). *Seminars in Perinatology, 34,* 105–120.

Thio, A. (2010). *Deviant behavior* (10th ed.). Boston: Allyn & Bacon.

Thomas, A., & Chess, S. (1991). Temperament in adolescence and its functional significance. In R. M. Lerner, A. C. Petersen, & J. Brooks-Gunn (Eds.), *Encyclopedia of adolescence* (Vol. 2). New York: Garland.

Thomas, M. S., & others. (2010). The development of metaphorical language comprehension in typical development and in Williams syndrome. *Journal of Experimental Child Psychology, 106,* 99–114.

Thomas, M. S. C., & Johnson, M. H. (2008). New advances in understanding sensitive periods in brain development. *Current Directions in Psychological Science, 17,* 1–5.

Thompson, D. R., & others. (2007). Childhood overweight and cardiovascular disease risk factors: The National Heart, Lung, and Blood Institute Growth and Health Study. *Journal of Pediatrics, 150,* 18–25.

Thompson, J., Manore, M., & Vaughan, L. (2011). *Science of nutrition* (2nd ed.). Upper Saddle River, NJ: Pearson.

Thompson, P. M., Giedd, J. N., Woods, R. P., MacDonald, D., Evans, A. C., & Toga, A. W. (2000). Growth patterns in the developing brain detected by using continuum mechanical tensor maps. *Nature, 404,* 190–193.

Thompson, R. (2010). Maltreatment and mental health care: Focusing on child neglect. *Psychiatric Services, 61,* 96.

Thompson, R. A. (1994). Emotion regulation: A theme in search of a definition. *Monographs of the Society for Research in Child Development, 59* (Serial No. 240), 2–3.

Thompson, R. A. (2006). The development of the person. In W. Damon & R. Lerner (Eds.), *Handbook of child psychology* (6th ed.). New York: Wiley.

Thompson, R. A. (2007). Unpublished review of J. W. Santrock's *Children* (10th ed.). (New York: McGraw-Hill).

Thompson, R. A. (2008). Unpublished review of J. W. Santrock's *Life-Span Development* (2nd ed.). (New York: McGraw-Hill).

Thompson, R. A. (2009a). Emotional development. In R. A. Schweder (Ed.), *The Chicago companion to the child.* Chicago: University of Chicago Press.

Thompson, R. A. (2009b). Early foundations: Conscience and the development of moral character. In D. Narváez & D. Lapsley (Eds.), *Moral personality, identity, and character: Prospects for a new field of study.* New York: Cambridge University Press.

Thompson, R. A. (2009c). Making the most of small effects. *Social Development, 18,* 247–251.

Thompson, R. A. (2010). Feeling and understanding through the prism of relationships. In S. D. Calkins & M. A. Bell (Eds.), *Child development at the intersection of emotion and cognition.* Washington, DC: American Psychological Association.

Thompson, R. A., Easterbrooks, M. A., & Walker, L. (2003). Social and emotional development in infancy. In I. B. Weiner (Ed.), *Handbook of psychology* (Vol. 6). New York: Wiley.

Thompson, R. A., & Goodvin, R. (2005). The individual child: Temperament, emotion, self and personality. In M. J. Bornstein & M. E. Lamb (Eds.) *Developmental psychology* (5th ed.). Mahwah, NJ: Erlbaum.

Thompson, R. A., McGinley, M., & Meyer, S. (2006). Understanding values in relationships. In M. Killen & J. G. Smetana (Eds.), *Handbook of moral development.* Mahwah, NJ: Erlbaum.

Thompson, R. A., Meyer, S., Virmani, E., Waters, S., Raikes, H. A., & Jochem, R. (2009, April). *Parent-child relationships, conversation, and developing emotion regulation.* Paper presented at the meeting of the Society for Research in Child Development, Denver.

Thompson, R. A., & Newton, E. (2009). Infant-caregiver communication. In H. T. Reis & S. Sprecher (Eds.). *Encyclopedia of human relationships.* Thousand Oaks, CA: Sage.

Thompson, R. A., & Virmani, E. A. (2010). Creating persons: Culture, self, and personality development. In M. H. Bornstein (Ed.), *Handbook of cultural developmental science.* New York: Psychology Press.

Thoni, A., & Moroder, L. (2004). Waterbirth: A safe and natural delivery method. Experience after 1355 waterbirths in Italy. *Midwifery Today, 70,* 44–48.

Thorley, V. (2009). Guidelines to improve maternity practices and support breast feeding are readily available. *Southern Medical Journal, 102,* 222–223.

TIMMS. (2008). *Trends in international mathematics and science study.* Washington, DC: National Center for Education Statistics.

Tobin, J. J., Wu, D. Y. H., & Davidson, D. H. (1989). *Preschool in three cultures.* New Haven, CT: Yale University Press.

Tolani, N., & Brooks-Gunn, J. (2008). Family support, international trends. In M. M. Haith & J. B. Benson (Eds.), *Encyclopedia of infant and early childhood development.* Oxford, UK: Elsevier.

Tomasello, M. (2008). *Origins of human communication.* Cambridge, MA: MIT Press.

Tomasello, M. (2009). *Why we cooperate.* Cambridge, MA: MIT Press.

Tomasello, M., Carpenter, M., & Liszkowski, U. (2007). A new look at infant pointing. *Child Development, 78,* 705–722.

Tompkins, G. E. (2011). *Literacy in the early grades.* (3rd ed.). Boston: Allyn & Bacon.

Tong, S., Baghurst, P., Vimpani, G., & McMichael, A. (2007). Socioeconomic position, maternal IQ, home environment, and cognitive development. *Journal of Pediatrics, 151,* 284–288.

Torchinsky, A., & Toder, V. (2010). Mechanisms of the embryo's response to embryopathic stressors: A focus on p53. *Journal of Reproductive Immunology, 85*(1), 76–80.

Trafimow, D., Triandis, H. C., & Goto, S. G. (1991). Some tests of the distinction between the private and collective self. *Journal of Personality and Social Psychology, 60,* 649–655.

Trautner, H. M., Ruble, D. N., Cyphers, L., Kirsten, B., Behrendt, R., & Hartmann, P. (2005). Rigidity and flexibility of gender stereotypes in children: Developmental or differential? *Infant and Child Development, 14,* 365–381.

Trehub, S. E., Schneider, B. A., Thorpe, L. A., & Judge, P. (1991). Observational measures of auditory sensitivity in early infancy. *Developmental Psychology, 27,* 40–49.

Trentacosta, C. J., & Fine, S. E. (2009). Emotion knowledge, social competence, and behavior problems in childhood and adolescence: A meta-analytic review. *Social Development, 19*(1), 1–29.

Triandis, H. C. (2007). Culture and psychology: A history of their relationship. In S. Kitayama & D. Cohen (Eds.), *Handbook of cultural psychology.* New York: Guilford.

Triche, E. W., & Hossain, N. (2007). Environmental factors implicated in the causation of adverse pregnancy outcome. *Seminars in Perinatology, 31,* 240–242.

Trimble, J. E. (1988, August). *The enculturation of contemporary psychology.* Paper presented at the meeting of the American Psychological Association. New Orleans.

Tronick, E. (2010). Infants and mothers: Self- and mutual regulation and meaning making. In B. M. Lester & J. D. Sparrow (Eds.), *Nurturing children and families: Building on the legacy of T. Berry Brazelton.* New York: Wiley.

Trost, S. G., Fees, B., & Dzewaltowski, D. (2008). Feasibility and efficacy of "move and learn" physical activity curriculum in preschool children. *Journal of Physical Activity and Health, 5,* 88–103.

Tseng, V. (2004). Family interdependence and academic adjustment in college: Youth from immigrant and U.S.-born families. *Child Development, 75,* 966–983.

Turiel, E. (2006). The development of morality. In W. Damon & R. Lerner (Eds.), *Handbook of child psychology* (6th ed.). New York: Wiley.

Turrigiano, G. (2010). Synaptic homeostasis. *Annual Review of Neuroscience* (Vol. 33). Palo Alto, CA: Annual Reviews.

U

Udry, J. R., & others. (1985). Serum androgenic hormones motivate sexual behavior in adolescent boys. *Fertility and Sterility, 43,* 90–94.

Uhls, Y. T., & Greenfield, P. M. (2009). Adolescents and electronic communication. Retrieved June 25, 2010, from http://www .education.com/reference/article/adolescents-online-social-networking/

Ulvund, S. E., & Smith, L. (1996). The predictive validity of nonverbal communicative skills in infants with perinatal hazards. *Infant Behavior and Development, 19,* 441–449.

Umana-Taylor, A. J. (2009). Research with Latino early adolescents. *Journal of Early Adolescence, 29,* 5–15.

Umana-Taylor, A. J., Gonzales-Backen, M. A., & Guimond, A. B. (2009). Latino adolescents' ethnic identity: Is there a developmental progression and does growth in ethnic identity predict growth in self-esteem? *Child Development, 80,* 391–405.

Umana-Taylor, A. J., Updegraff, K. A., & Gonzales-Backen, M. A. (2010, in press). Mexican-origin adolescent mothers' stressors and psychological functioning: Examining ethnic identity affirmation and familism as moderators. *Journal of Youth and Adolescence.*

Umana-Taylor, A. J., Vargas-Changes, D., Garcia, C. D., & Gonzales-Backen, M. (2008). A longitudinal examination of Latino adolescents' ethnic identity, coping with discrimination, and self-esteem. *Journal of Early Adolescence, 28,* 16–50.

Underwood, M. (2004). Sticks and stones and social exclusion: Aggression among boys and girls. In P. K. Smith & C. H. Hart (Eds.), *Blackwell handbook of childhood social development.* Malden, MA: Blackwell.

UNICEF. (2003). *The state of the world's children: 2003.* Geneva, Switzerland: Author.

UNICEF (2004). T*he state of the worlds' children 2004.* Geneva: SWIT: UNICEF.

UNICEF (2006). *The state of the world's children 2006.* Geneva, SWIT: UNICEF.

UNICEF (2007). *The state of the world's children 2007.* Geneva, SWIT: UNICEF.

UNICEF (2009). *The state of the world's children 2009.* Geneva, SWIT: UNICEF.

UNICEF (2010). *The state of the world's children 2010.* Geneva, SWIT: UNICEF.

United Nations. (2002). *Improving the quality of life of girls.* Geneva: UNICEF.

Updegraff, K. A., Delgado, M. Y., & Wheeler, L. A. (2009). Exploring mothers' and fathers' relationships with sons versus daughters: Links to adolescent adjustment in Mexican immigrant families. *Sex Roles, 60,* 559–574.

Updegraff, K. A., Kim, J-Y, Killoren, S. E., & Thayer, S. M. (2010). Mexican American parents' involvement in adolescents' peer relationships: Exploring the role of culture and adolescents' peer experiences. *Journal of Research on Adolescence, 20,* 65–87.

Urbano, M. T., & Tait, D. M. (2004). Can the irradiated uterus sustain a pregnancy? *Clinical Oncology, 16,* 24–28.

Urbina, E. M. (2008). Removing the mask: The danger of hidden hypertension. *Journal of Pediatrics, 152,* 455–456.

Urdan, T. (2010). Classroom goal structures, motivation, and learning. In J. Meece & J. Eccles (Eds.), *Handbook of research on schools, schooling, and motivation.* New York: Routledge.

U.S. Department of Energy. (2001). *The human genome project.* Washington, DC: U.S. Department of Energy.

U.S. Department of Health and Human Services. (2008). *Child maltreatment 2006.* Washington, DC: Government Printing Office. Retrieved April 1, 2008, from www.acf.hhs.gov/programs/cb/pubs/cm06/index.htm

U.S. Department of Health and Human Services. (2009). *Folic acid.* Retrieved January 19, 2009, from http://www.cdc.gov/ncbddd/folicacid/

USA Today. (2000, October 10). All-USA first teacher team. Retrieved November 15, 2004, from http://www.usatoday.com/life/teacher/teach/htm.

V

Vacca, J. A., Vacca, R. T., Gove, M. K., Burkey, L. C., Lenhart, L. A., & McKeon, C. A. (2009). *Reading and learning to read* (7th ed.). Boston: Allyn & Bacon.

Vaillancourt, T. & Hymel, S. (2006). Aggression and social status: The moderating roles of sex and peer-valued characteristics. *Aggressive Behavior, 32*(4), 396–408.

Valkenburg, P. M., & Peter, J. (2009). Social consequences of the Internet for adolescents. *Current Directions in Psychological Science, 18,* 1–5.

Valle, J., & Connor, J. (2011). *Rethinking disability.* New York: McGraw-Hill.

Vandehey, M., Diekhoff, G., & LaBeff, E. (2007). College cheating: A 20-year follow-up and the addition of an honor code. *Journal of College Development, 48,* 468–480.

Vandell, D. L., & Wilson, K. S. (1988). Infants' interactions with mother, sibling, and peer: Contrasts and relations between interaction systems. *Child Development, 48,* 176–186.

van den Broek, P. (2010). Using texts in science education: cognitive processes and knowledge representation. *Science, 328,* 453–456.

van den Boom, D. C. (1989). Neonatal irritability and the development of attachment. In G. A. Kohnstamm, J. E. Bates, & M. K. Rothbart (Eds.), *Temperament in childhood.* New York: Wiley.

van den Dries, L., Juffer, F., van IJzendoorn, M. H., & Bakersman-Kranenburg, M. J. (2010). Infants' physical and cognitive development after international adoption from foster care or institutions in China. *Journal of Developmental and Behavioral Pediatrics, 31,* 144–150.

Van Dyck, P. C. (2007). Final commentary on the special volume of articles from the National Survey of Children's Health. *Pediatrics, 119, Suppl,* S122–S123.

van Harmelen, A. L., & others (2010). Child abuse and negative explicit and automatic self-associations: The cognitive scars of emotional maltreatment. *Behavior Research and Therapy, 48*(6), 486–494.

van Hof, P., van der Kamp, J., & Savelsbergh, G. J. (2008). The relation between infants' perception of catchableness and the control of catching. *Developmental Psychology, 44,* 182–194.

van IJzendoorn, M. H., & Kroonenberg, P. M. (1988). Cross-cultural patterns of attachment: A meta-analysis of the Strange Situation. *Child Development, 59,* 147–156.

van Spronsen, F. J., & Enns, G. M. (2010). Future treatment strategies in phenylketonuria. *Molecular Genetics and Metabolism, 99, Suppl 1,* S90–S95.

Vansteenkiste, M., Sierens, E., Soenens, B., Luyckx, K., & Lens, W. (2009). Motivational profiles from a self-determination perspective: The quality of motivation matters. *Journal of Educational Psychology, 101*(3), 671–688.

Vasdev, G. (2008). *Obstetric anesthesia.* Oxford, UK: Elsevier.

Veenstra, R., Lindenberg, S., Munniksma, A., & Dijkstra, J. K. (2010). The complex relationship between bullying, victimization, acceptance, and rejection: Giving special attention to status, affection, and sex differences. *Child Development, 81*(2), 480–486.

Velagaleti, R. S., & O'Donnell, C. J. (2010). Genomics of heart failure. *Heart Failure Clinics, 6,* 115–124.

Venners, S. A., & others. (2005). Paternal smoking and pregnancy loss: A prospective study using a biomarker of pregnancy. *American Journal of Epidemiology, 159,* 993–1001.

Ventura, A. K., Gromis, J. C., & Lohse, B. (2010, in press). Feeding practices and styles used by a diverse sample of low-income parents of preschool-age children. *Journal of Nutrition Education and Behavior.*

Verhaak, C. M., Linsten, A. M., Evers, A. W., & Braat, D. D. (2010). Who is at risk of emotional problems and how do you know? Screening of women going for IVF treatment. *Human Reproduction.* (Available online March 13, 2010.)

Verma, S., & Saraswathi, T. S. (2002). Adolescence in India: Street urchins or Silicon Valley millionaires? In B. B. Brown, R. W. Larson, & T. S. Saraswathi (Eds.), *The world's youth.* New York: Cambridge University Press.

Vermeersch, H., T'Sjoen, G., Kaufman, J. M., & Vincke, J. (2008). The role of testosterone in aggressive and non-aggressive risk-taking in boys. *Hormones and Behavior, 53,* 463–471.

Vernberg, E. M., & Biggs, B. K. (2010). Preventing and treating bullying and victimization: An evidence-based approach. In E. M. Vernberg, & B. K. Biggs (Eds.), *Preventing and treating bullying and victimization.* New York: Oxford University Press.

Victoria, C. G., de Onis, M., Hallal, P. C., Blossner, M., & Shrimpton, R. (2010). Worldwide timing of growth faltering: Revisiting implications for intervention. *Pediatrics, 125,* e473–e480.

Viet, C. T., & Schmidt, B. L. (2010). Understanding oral cancer in the genome era. *Head and Neck.* (Available online February 24, 2010.)

Viikari, J., Niinikoski, H., Raitakari, O. T., & Simell, O. (2009). The initiatives and outcomes for cardiovascular risks that can be achieved through pediatric counseling. *Current Opinion in Lipidology, 20,* 17–23.

Villegas, R., & others. (2008). Duration of breast-feeding and the incidence of type 2 diabetes mellitus in the Shanghai Women's Health Study. *Diabetologia, 51,* 258–266.

Vimaleswaran, K. S., & Loos, R. J. (2010). Progress in the genetics of common obesity and type 2 diabetes. *Expert Reviews in Molecular Medicine, 12,* e7.

Vitaro, F., Boivin, M., & Bukowski, W. M. (2009). The role of friendship in child and adolescent psychosocial development. In K. H. Rubin, W. M. Bukowski, & B. Laursen (Eds.), *Handbook of peer interaction, relationships, and groups.* New York: Guilford.

Vitaro, F., Pedersen, S., & Brendgen, M. (2007). Children's disruptiveness, peer rejection, friends' deviancy, and delinquent behaviors: A process-oriented approach. *Development and Psychopathology, 19,* 433–453.

Von Hofsten, C. (2008). Motor and physical development manual. In M. M Haith & J. B. Benson (Eds.), *Encyclopedia of infant and early childhood development.* Oxford, UK: Elsevier.

Votruba-Drzal, E., Coley, R. L., & Chase-Lansdale, P. L. (2004). Child care and low-income children's development: Direct and moderated effects. *Child Development, 75,* 296–312.

Vreeman, R. C., & Carroll, A. E. (2007). A systematic review of school-based interventions to prevent bullying. *Archives of Pediatric and Adolescent Medicine, 161,* 78–88.

Vukelich, C., Christie, J., & Enz, B. J. (2008). *Helping children learn language and literacy.* Boston: Allyn & Bacon.

Vygotsky, L. S. (1962). *Thought and language.* Cambridge, MA: MIT Press.

W

Waber, D. P. (2010). *Rethinking learning disabilities.* New York: Guilford University Press.

Wachs, T. D. (1994). Fit, context and the transition between temperament and personality. In C. Halverson, G. Kohnstamm, & R. Martin (Eds.), *The developing structure of personality from infancy to adulthood.* Hillsdale, NJ: Erlbaum.

Wachs, T. D. (2000). *Necessary but not sufficient.* Washington, DC: American Psychological Association.

Wadsworth, S. J., Olson, R. K., & Defries, J. C. (2010, in press). Differential genetic etiology of reading difficulties as a function of IQ: An update. *Behavior Genetics.*

Wagner, D. A. (2010). Literacy. In M. H. Bornstein (Ed.), *Handbook of cultural developmental science.* New York: Psychology Press.

Wagner, R. K., & Sternberg, R. J. (1986). Tacit knowledge and intelligent functioning in the everyday world. In R. J. Sternberg & R. K. Wagner (Eds.), *Practical intelligence.* New York: Cambridge University Press.

Waiter, G. D., & others. (2009). Exploring possible neural mechanisms of intelligence differences using processing speed and working memory tasks. *Intelligence, 37,* 199–206.

Walden, T. (1991). Infant social referencing. In J. Garber & K. Dodge (Eds.), *The development of emotional regulation and dysregulation.* New York: Cambridge University Press.

Walker, A. (2010). Breast milk as the gold standard for protective nutrients. *Journal of Pediatrics, 156, Supp 2,* S3–S7.

Walker, L. (1982). The sequentiality of Kohlberg's stages of moral development. *Child Development, 53,* 1130–1136.

Walker, L. (2006). Gender and morality. In M. Killen & J. G. Smetana (Eds.), *Handbook of moral development.* Mahwah, NJ: Erlbaum.

Walker, L. J. (2002). Moral exemplarity. In W. Damon (Ed.), *Bringing in a new era of character education.* Stanford, CA: Hoover Press.

Walker, L. J. (2004). Progress and prospects in the psychology of moral development. *Merrill-Palmer Quarterly, 50,* 546–557.

Walker, L. J., & Frimer, J. A. (2009). Moral personality exemplified. In D. Narváez & D. K. Lapsley (Eds.), *Moral personality, identity, and* *character: Prospects for a new field of study.* New York: Cambridge University Press.

Walker, L. J., & Hennig, K. H. (2004). Differing conceptions of moral exemplars: Just, brave, and caring. *Journal of Personality and Social Psychology, 86,* 629–647.

Walker, L. J., Hennig, K. H., & Krettenauer, T. (2000). Parent and peer contexts for children's moral development. *Child Development, 71,* 1033–1048.

Walker, L. J., & Pitts, R. C. (1998). Naturalistic conceptions of moral maturity. *Developmental Psychology, 34,* 403–419.

Walker, P., & others. (2010). Preverbal infants' sensitivity to synaesthetic cross-modality correspondences. *Psychological Science, 21,* 21–25.

Walker, S. (2006). Unpublished review of Santrock, J. W., *Topical life-span development* (3rd ed.). New York: McGraw-Hill.

Wallerstein, J. S. (2008). Divorce. In M. M. Haith & J. B. Benson (Eds.), *Encyclopedia of infant and early childhood development.* Oxford, UK: Elsevier.

Walsh, T. J., Pera, R. R., & Turek, P. J. (2010). The genetics of male infertility. *Seminars in Reproductive Medicine, 27,* 124–136.

Walter, C. A. (1986). *The timing of motherhood.* Lexington, MA: D. C. Heath.

Wang, Q., & Pomerantz, E. M. (2009). The motivational landscape of early adolescence in the United States and China: A longitudinal study. *Child Development, 80*(4), 1272–1287.

Ward, L. M. (2004). Wading through stereotypes: Positive and negative associations between media use and black adolescents' conceptions of self. *Developmental Psychology, 40,* 284–294.

Wardlaw, G. M., & Hampl, J. (2007). *Nelson's essentials of pediatric* (7th ed.). New York: McGraw-Hill.

Wardlaw, G. M., & Smith, A. M. (2008). *Contemporary nutrition* (7th ed.). New York: McGraw-Hill.

Wardlaw, G. M., & Smith, A. M. (2011). *Contemporary nutrition* (8th ed.). New York: McGraw-Hill.

Wardle, J., Carnell, S., Haworth, C. M., & Plomin, R. (2008). Evidence for a strong genetic influence on childhood adiposity despite the force of the obesogenic environment. *American Journal of Clinical Nutrition, 87,* 398–404.

Warniment, C., Tsang, K., & Galazka, S. S. (2010). Lead poisoning in children. *American Family Physician, 81,* 751–757.

Warrington, M., & Younger, M. (2003). "We decided to give it a twirl": Single-sex teaching in English comprehensive schools. *Gender and Education, 15,* 339–350.

Warshak, R. A. (2007, January). Personal communication, Department of Psychology, University of Texas at Dallas, Richardson.

Waterman, A. S. (1985). Identity in the context of adolescent psychology. In A. S.

Waterman (Ed.), *Identity in adolescence: Processes and contents* San Francisco: Jossey-Bass.

Waterman, A. S. (1992). Identity as an aspect of optimal psychological functioning. In G. R. Adams, T. P. Gullotta, & R. Montemayor (Eds.), *Adolescent identity formation.* Newbury Park, CA: Sage.

Waters, E., Kondo-Ikemura, K., Posada, G., & Richters, J. E. (1990). Learning to love: Mechanisms and milestones. In M. Gunnar & L. A. Sroufe (Eds.), *Minnesota symposia on child psychology* (Vol. 23). Mahwah, NJ: Erlbaum.

Watson, J. B. (1928). *Psychological care of infant and child.* New York: W. W. Norton.

Watson, J. B., & Rayner, R. (1920). Conditioned emotional reactions. *Journal of Experimental Psychology, 3,* 1–14.

Watt, H. M. G. (2008). Gender and occupational outcomes: An introduction. In H. M. G. Watt & J. S. Eccles (Eds.), *Gender and occupational outcomes.* Washington, DC: American Psychological Association.

Watt, H. M. G., & Eccles, J. S. (Eds.) (2008). *Gender and occupational outcomes.* Washington, DC: American Psychological Association.

Waxman, S. (2009). How infants discover distinct word types and map them to distinctive meaning. In J. Colombo, P. McCardle, & L. Freund (Eds.), *Infant pathways to language.* Clifton, NJ: Psychology Press.

Way, N., Santos, C., Niwa, E. Y., & Kim-Gervy, C. (2008). To be or not to be: An exploration of ethnic identity development in context. In M. Asmitia, M. Syed, & K. Radmacher (Eds.), The intersections of personal and social identities. *New Directions for Child and Adolescent Development, 120,* 61–79.

Webb, J. T., Gore, J. L., Mend, E. R., & DeVries, A. R. (2007). *A parent's guide to gifted children.* Scottsdale, AZ: Great Potential Press.

Webster, N. S., & Worrell, F. C. (2008). Academically-talented adolescents' attitudes toward service in the community. *Gifted Child Quarterly, 52,* 170–179.

Weikert, D. P. (1993). *Long-term positive effects in the Perry Preschool Head Start Program.* Unpublished data, High Scope Foundation, Ypsilanti, MI.

Weiner, C. P., & Buhimschi, C. (2009). *Drugs for pregnant and lactating women* (2nd ed.). London: Elsevier.

Weinstein, R. S. (2004). *Reaching higher: The power of expectations in schooling* (paperback ed.). Cambridge, MA: Harvard University Press.

Weiss, L. A., & others. (2008). Association between microdeletion and microduplication at 16p 11.2 and autism. *New England Journal of Medicine, 358,* 667–675.

Wekerle, C., & others. (2009). The contribution of childhood emotional abuse to teen dating violence among child protective services-involved youth. *Child Abuse and Neglect, 33*(1), 45–58.

Wellman, H. M. (2011). Developing a theory of mind. In U. Goswami (Ed.), *The Blackwell handbook of childhood cognitive development* (2nd Ed.). New York: Wiley.

Wellman, H. M., Cross, D., & Watson, J. (2001). Meta-analysis of theory-of-mind development: The truth about false belief. *Child Development, 72,* 655–684.

Wellman, H. M. & Woolley, J. D. (1990). From simple desires to ordinary beliefs: The early development of everyday psychology. *Cognition, 35,* 245–275.

Wells, J. C., Hallal, P. C., Reichert, F. F., Menezes, A. M. Araujo, C. L., & Victora, C. G. (2008). Sleep patterns and television viewing in relation to obesity and blood pressure: Evidence from an adolescent Brazilian cohort. *International Journal of Obesity, 32*(7), 1042–1049.

Welsh, J. A., Nix, R. L., Blair, C., Bierman, K. L., & Nelson, K. E. (2010). The development of cognitive skills and gains in academic school readiness for children from low-income families. *Journal of Educational Psychology, 102,* 43–53.

Welti, C. (2002). Adolescents in Latin America: Facing the future with skepticism. In B. B. Brown, R. W. Larson, & T. S. Saraswathi (Eds.), *The world's youth.* New York: Cambridge University Press.

Weng, X., Odouli, R., & Li, D. K. (2008). Maternal caffeine consumption during pregnancy and the risk of miscarriage: A prospective cohort study. *American Journal of Obstetrics and Gynecology, 198,* 279.e1–279.e8.

Wentzel, K. (1997). Student motivation in middle school: The role of perceived pedagogical caring. *Journal of Educational Psychology, 89,* 411–419.

Wentzel, K. R., & Asher, S. R. (1995). The academic lives of neglected, rejected, popular, and controversial children. *Child Development, 66,* 754–763.

Wentzel, K. R., Barry, C. M., & Caldwell, K. A. (2004). Friendships in middle school: Influences on motivation and school adjustment. *Journal of Educational Psychology, 96,* 195–203.

Wermter, A. K., & others. (2010). From nature versus nurture, via nature and nurture, to gene X environment interaction in mental disorders. *European Journal of Child and Adolescent Psychiatry, 19,* 199–210.

Wertsch, J. V. (2007). Mediation. In H. Daniels, J. Wertsch, & M. Cole (eds.), *The Cambridge companion to Vygotsky.* New York: Cambridge University Press.

Westling, E., Andrews, J. A., Hampson, S. E., & Peterson, M. (2008). Pubertal timing and substance use: The effects of gender, parental monitoring, and deviant peers. *Journal of Adolescent Health, 42,* 555–563.

Weston, M. J. (2010). Magnetic resonance imaging in fetal medicine: A pictorial review of current and developing indications. *Postgraduate Medicine Journal, 86,* 42–51.

Wheeden, A., Scafidi, F. A., Field, T., Ironson, G., Valdeon, C. & Bandstra, E. (1993). Massage effects on cocaine-exposed preterm neonates. *Journal of Developmental and Behavioral Pediatrics, 14,* 318–322.

Whitehead, K. A., Ainsworth, A. T., Wittig, M. A., & Gadino, B. (2009). Implications of ethnic identity exploration and ethnic identity affirmation and belonging for intergroup attitudes among adolescents. *Journal of Research on Adolescence, 19,* 123–135.

Whitehurst, G., & Lonigan, C. (1998). Child development and emergent literacy. *Child Development, 69*(3), 848–872.

Whittle, S., & others. (2008). Prefrontal and amygdala volumes are related to adolescents' affective behaviors during parent-adolescent interactions. *Proceedings of the National Academy of Sciences USA, 105,* 3652–3657.

White, M. (1993). *The material child: Coming of age in Japan and America.* New York: Free Press.

WIC New York. (2009). *The new look of the women, infants, and children (WIC) program.* Retrieved January 21, 2009 from www.health .state.ny.us/prevention/nutrition/wic/the_new_ look_of_wic.htm

Wick, P., & others. (2010). Barrier capacity of the human placenta for nanosized materials. *Environmental Health Perspectives, 118,* 432–436.

Wickham, S. (2009). *Midwifery: Best practice.* London: Elsevier.

Wider, C., Foroud, T., & Wszolek, Z. K. (2010). Clinical implications of gene discovery in Parkinson's disease and parkinsonism. *Movement Disorders, 25, Suppl 1,* S15–S20.

Wiesner, M., & Ittel, A. (2002). Relations of pubertal timing and depressive symptoms to substance use in early adolescence. *Journal of Early Adolescence, 22,* 5–23.

Wigfield, A., Eccles, J. S., Schiefele, U., Roeser, R., & Davis-Kean, P. (2006). Development of achievement motivation. In W. Damon & R. Lerner (Eds.), *Handbook of child psychology* (6th ed.). New York: Wiley.

Wilcox, J. (2009–2010). The easiest birth yet. *Midwifery Today with International Midwife, 23,* 63–64.

Williams, C. R. (1986). *The impact of television: A natural experiment in three communities.* New York: Academic Press.

Williams, S. T., Ontai, L. L., & Mastergeorge, A. M. (2010). The development of peer interaction in infancy: Exploring the dyadic process. *Social Development, 19,* 348–368.

Wilson, B. J. (2008). Media and children's aggression, fear, and altruism. *Future of Children, 18*(1), 87–118.

Wilson, D. R. (2010). Breastfeeding: A women's issue. *Beginnings, 30,* 6–9.

Willey, J., Sherwood, L., & Woolverton, C. (2011). *Prescott's microbiology* (8th ed.). New York: McGraw-Hill.

Williams, D. D., Yancher, S. C., Jensen, L. C., & Lewis, C. (2003). Character education in a public high school: A multi-year inquiry into unified studies. *Journal of Moral Education, 32,* 3–33.

Williams, J. E., & Best, D. L. (1982). *Measuring sex stereotypes: A thirty-nation study.* Newbury Park, CA: Sage.

Williams, J. E., & Best, D. L. (1989). *Sex and psyche: Self-concept viewed cross-culturally.* Newbury Park, CA: Sage.

Williamson, R. A., Jaswal, V. K., & Meltzoff, A. N. (2010). Learning the rules: Observation and imitation as a sorting strategy by 36-month-old children. *Developmental Psychology, 46,* 57–65.

Windle, W. F. (1940). *Physiology of the human fetus.* Philadelphia: W. B. Saunders.

Winn, I. J. (2004). The high cost of uncritical teaching. *Phi Delta Kappan, 85,* 496–497.

Winner, E. (1996). *Gifted children: Myths and realities.* New York: Basic Books.

Winner, E. (2000). The origins and ends of giftedness. *American Psychologist, 55,* 159–169.

Winner, E. (2006). Development in the arts: Drawing and music. In W. Damon & R. Lerner (Eds.), *Handbook of child psychology* (6th ed.), New York: Wiley.

Winner, E. (2009). Toward broadening our understanding of giftedness: The spatial domain. In F. D. Horowitz, R. F. Subotnik, & D. J. Matthews (Eds.), *The development of giftedness and talent across the life span.* Washington, DC: American Psychological Association.

Winsler, A., Carlton, M. P., & Barry, M. J. (2000). Age-related changes in preschool children's systematic use of private speech in a natural setting. *Journal of Child Language, 27,* 665–687.

Wisborg, K., Ingerslev, H. J., & Henriksen, T. B. (2010). In vitro fertilization and preterm delivery, low birth weight, and admission to the neonatal intensive care unit: A prospective follow-up study. *Fertility and Sterility.* (Available online February 24, 2010.)

Witelson, S. F., Kigar, D. L., & Harvey, T. (1999). The exceptional brain of Albert Einstein. *The Lancet, 353,* 2149–2153.

Witkin, H. A., & others. (1976). Criminality in XYY and XXY men. *Science, 193,* 547–555.

Wittig, S. L., & Spatz, D. L. (2008). Induced lactation: Gaining a better understanding. *MCN. The Journal of Maternal Child Nursing, 33,* 76–81.

Wittmeier, K. D., Mollar, R. C., & Kriellaars, D. J. (2008). Physical activity intensity and risk of overweight and adiposity in children. *Obesity, 16,* 415–420.

Witvliet, M., & others. (2010). Peer group affiliation in children: The role of perceived popularity, likeability, and behavioral similarity in bullying. *Social Development, 19,* 285–303.

Wolak, J., Mitchell, K., & Finkelhor, D. (2007). Unwanted and wanted exposure to online pornography in a national sample of youth Internet users. *Pediatrics, 119,* 247–257.

Wolmetz, M., Poeppel, D., & Rapp, B. (2010, in press). What does the right hemisphere know about phoneme categories? *Journal of Cognitive Neuroscience.*

Women's Sports Foundation. (2001). *The 10 commandments for parents and coaches in youth sports.* Eisenhower Park, NY: Women's Sports Foundation.

Wong, Y. J., & Rochlen, A. B. (2008). *The new psychology of men: The emotional side.* Greenwood Publishing Group.

Wong Briggs, T. W. (2004, October 14). *USA Today's 2004 all-USA team. USA Today,* p. 6D.

Wong Briggs, T. (2005, October 13). *USA Today's 2005 all-USA teacher team. USA Today,* p. 6D.

Wong Briggs, T. (2007, October 18). An early start for learning. *USA Today,* p. 6 D.

Wood, D., Kaplan, R., & McLoyd, V. C. (2007). Gender differences in educational expectations of urban, low-income African American youth: The role of parents and school. *Journal of Youth and Adolescence, 36,* 417–427.

Woodard, E. (2000). *Media in the home 2000: The Fifth Annual Survey of Parents and Children.* Philadelphia: Annenberg Public Policy Center.

Woodhill, B. M., & Samuels, C. A. (2004). Desirable and undesirable androgyny: A prescription for the twenty-first century. *Journal of Gender Studies, 13,* 15–28.

Woodward, A., Markman, E., & Fitzsimmons, C. (1994). Rapid word learning in 13- and 18-month-olds. *Developmental Psychology, 30,* 553–566.

Woodward, A., & Needham, A. (Eds.). (2009). *Learning and the infant mind.* New York: Oxford University Press.

Woodward, A. L., & Markman, E. M. (1998). Early word learning. In D. Kuhn & R. S. Siegler (Eds.), *Handbook of child psychology* (5th ed., Vol. 2). New York: Wiley.

Woolley, J. D., Boerger, E. A., & Markman, A. B. (2004). A visit from the Candy Witch: Factors influencing young children's belief in a novel fantastical being. *Developmental Science, 7,* 456–468.

Wright, R. O., & Christiani, D. (2010). Gene-environment interaction and children's health and development. *Current Opinion in Pediatrics, 22*(2), 197–201.

Wu, P., Robinson, C. C., Yang, C., Hart, C. H., Olsen, S. F., & Porter, C. L. (2002). Similarities and differences in mothers' parenting of preschoolers in China and the United States. *International Journal of Behavioural Development, 6,* 481–491.

Wynn, K. (1992). Addition and subtraction by human infants. *Nature, 358,* 749–750.

Wyse, D., Andrews, R., & Hoffman, J. (Eds.) (2010). *The Routledge international handbook of English, language, and literacy teaching.* New York: Routledge.

X

Xu, F., Spelke, E., & Goddard, S. (2005). Number sense in human infants. *Developmental Science, 8,* 88–101.

Xue, F., Holzman, C., Rahbar, M. H., Trosko, K., & Fischer, L. (2007). Maternal fish consumption, mercury levels, and risk of preterm delivery. *Environmental Health Perspectives, 115,* 42–47.

Y

Yang, C., & Brown, B. (2009, April). *From Facebook to cell calls: Layers of electronic intimacy in college students' peer relations.* Paper presented at the meeting of the Society for Research in Child Development, Denver.

Yang, S., & Sternberg, R. J. (1997). Taiwanese Chinese people's conceptions of intelligence. *Intelligence, 25,* 21–36.

Yazdy, M. M., Liu, S., Mitchell, A. A., & Werler, N. M. (2010). Maternal dietary glycemic intake and the risk of neural tube defects. *American Journal of Epidemiology, 171,* 407–414.

Yolton, K., & others (2010). Associations between secondhand smoke exposure and sleep patterns in children. *Pediatrics, 125,* e261–e268.

Yonkers, K. A., & others. (2009). The management of depression during pregnancy: A report from the American Psychiatric Association and the American College of Obstetricians and Gynecologists. *Obstetrics and Gynecology, 114,* 703–713.

Young, K. T. (1990). American conceptions of infant development from 1955 to 1984: What the experts are telling parents. *Child Development, 61,* 17–28.

Yu, T., Pettit, G. S., Lansford, J. E., Dodge, K., & Bates, J. E. (2010). The interactive effects of marital conflict and divorce on parent-adult children's relationships. *Journal of Marriage and the Family, 72,* 282–292.

Z

Zaghloul, N. A., & Katsanis, N. (2010). Functional modules, mutational load, and human genetic disease. *Trends in Genetics, 26*(4), 168–176.

Zaitoun, I., Downs, K. M., Rosa, G. J., & Khatib, H. (2010). Upregulation of imprinted genes in mice: An insight into the intensity of gene expression and the evolution of genomic imprinting. *Epigenetics, 5,* 149–158.

Zelazo, P. D., & Muller, U. (2004). Executive function in typical and atypical development. In U. Goswami (Ed.), *Blackwell handbook of cognitive development.* Malden, MA: Blackwell.

Zeskind, P. S., Klein, L., & Marshall, T. R. (1992). Adults' perceptions of experimental modifications of durations of pauses and expiratory sounds in infant crying. *Developmental Psychology, 28,* 1153–1162.

Zhang, L., Zhang, X. H., Liang, M. Y., & Ren, M. H. (2010). Prenatal cytogenetic diagnosis study of 2782 cases of high-risk pregnant women. *China Medicine (English), 123,* 423–430.

Zhang, L.-F., & Sternberg, R. J. (2011, in press). Learning in a cross-cultural perspective. In T. Husén & T. N. Postlethwaite (Eds.) *International Encyclopedia of Education* (3rd ed., Learning and Cognition). Oxford: Elsevier.

Zhou, M., & others. (2010). Forebrain overexpression of CK1delta leads to down-regulation of dopamine receptors and altered locomotor activity reminiscent of ADHD. *Proceedings of the National Academy of Sciences, 107,* 4401–4406.

Zhou, Q., Lengua, L. J., & Wang, Y. (2009). The relations of temperament reactivity and effortful control to children's adjustment problems in the United States and China. *Developmental Psychology, 45,* 724–739.

Zielinski, D. S. (2009). Child maltreatment and adult socioeconomic well-being. *Child Abuse and Neglect, 33,* 666–678.

Zigler, E., Gilliam, W. S., & Jones, S. M. (2006). *A vision for universal preschool education.* New York: Cambridge University Press.

Zigler, E. F., & Styfco, S. J. (1994). Head Start: Criticisms in a constructive context. *American Psychologist, 49,* 127–132.

Zigler, E. F., & Styfco, S. J. (2010). *The hidden history of Head Start.* New York: Oxford University Press.

Zimmerman, B. J., Bonner, S., & Kovach, R. (1996). *Developing self-regulated learners.* Washington, DC: American Psychological Association.

Zimmerman, F. J., Christakis, D. A., & Meltzoff, A. N. (2007). Associations between media viewing and language development in children under age 2 years. *Journal of Pediatrics, 151,* 364–368.

Ziol-Guest, K. M. (2009). Child custody and support. In D. Carr (Ed.), *Encyclopedia of the life course and human development.* Boston: Cengage.

Zitzer-Comfort, C., Doyle, T. F., Masataka, N., Korenberg, J., & Bellugi, U. (2007). Nature and nurture: Williams syndrome across cultures. *Developmental Science, 10,* 755–762.

Zosuls, K. M., Lurye, L. E., & Ruble, D. N. (2008). Gender: Awareness, identity, and stereotyping. In M. M. Haith & J. B. Benson (Eds.), *Encyclopedia of infant and early childhood development.* Oxford, UK: Elsevier.

Zosuls, K. M., Ruble, D. N., Tamis-LeMonda, C. S., Shrout, P. E., Bornstein, M. H., & Greulich, F. K. (2009). The acquisition of gender labels in infancy: Implications for gender-typed play. *Developmental Psychology, 45,* 688–701.

credits

PHOTO CREDITS

Chapter 1

p.3: © Geri Lavrov/Flickr/Getty Images; p.4: Image Source/Getty Images; p.5 (top to bottom): © Seanna O'Sullivan/Corbis Sygma; WBBM-TV/AFP/Getty Images; © AP Wide World Photos; Photograph of Alice Walker, Alice Walker Papers, Manuscript, Archives and Rare Book Library, Emory University; p.6: © Erich Lessing/Art Resource, NY Painting by A.I.G. Velasquez, Infants Margarita Teresa in white garb, Kunsthistorisches Museum, Vienna, Austria; p.7: Archives of the History of American Psychology; p.9: Courtesy of Luis Vargas; p.10 (top): National Association for the Education of Young Children, Robert Maust/Photo Agora; p.10 (bottom): Courtesy of Marian Wright Edelman and The Children's Defense Fund; p.11 (top): Photo by Debbie Egan-Chin/NY Daily News Archive via Getty Images; p.11 (bottom): © AFP/Getty Images; p.12:Naser Siddique/UNICEF Bangladesh; p.17 (left to right): Brand X Pictures/PunchStock; © Digital Vision; Laurence Mouton/Photoalto/PictureQuest; © Stockbyte; SW Productions; p.19: Rubberball/PictureQuest; p.20: © Michael Newman/PhotoEdit; p.21: © Bettmann/Corbis; p.22: © Bettmann/Corbis; p.23: L to R: Royalty-free/Corbis, Royalty-free Corbis, © Veer; Royalty-free/Corbis; p.24 (left to right): © Stockbyte/Getty Images; © BananaStock/PunchStock; mage100/Corbis; © RF/Corbis; p.25 (top): © Yves de Braine/Black Star/Stock Photo; p.25 (bottom): A.R. Lauria/Dr. Michael Cole, Laboratory of Human Cognition, University of California, San Diego; p.26: Creatas Images/Jupiter Images; p.27 (top left): Courtesy of Professor Benjamin Harris; p. 27 (top right): © AP Wide World Photos; p.27 (bottom): Courtesy Albert Bandura, Stanford University; p.28: Time & Life Pictures/Getty Images; p.30: Courtesy of Urie Bronfenbrenner; p.31: © AP Wide World Photos; p.33 (top): © Bettmann/Corbis; p.33 (bottom): © Sovereign/Phototake; p.34: © Digital Vision/PunchStock; p.37: © McGraw-Hill Companies, Inc., photographer John Thoeming; p.39: Courtesy of Dr. Pamela Reid; p.40 (left): © Bay Hippisley/ImageState/agefotostock; p.40 (right): ERproductions Ltd./Getty Images; p.47: Courtesy of Katherine Duchen-Smith

Chapter 2

p.49: MedicalRF.com/Getty Images; p.50: Image Source/Getty Images; p.51: © Enrico Ferorelli Enterprises; p.53(top): © Frans Lemmens/Corbis; p.53 (bottom): © 1996 PhotoDisc, Inc./Getty Images; p.54: © David Wilkie; p.56: © AP Wide World Photos; p.57 (top): © Science Source/Photo Researchers; p.57 (bottom): © Custom Medical Stock Photo; p.59: © James Shaffer/PhotoEdit; p.61: © Andrew Eccles/JBGPHOTO.COM; p.62: Courtesy of Holly Ishmael; p.63 (top): © Jacques Pavlousky/Sygma/Corbis; p.63 (bottom): © Larry Berman; p.64: © Newscom; p.66: © Newscom; p.67: Photodisc/Getty Images; p.69: Jack Hollingsworth/Getty Images; p.70: GREG WOOD/AFP/Getty Images

Chapter 3

p.76: © Lennart Nilsson/Albert Bonniers Forlag AB/*A Child is Born,* Dell Publishing Company; p.77:

© John Santrock; p.81 (all): © Lennart Nilsson/Albert Bonniers Forlag AB/A Child is Born, Dell Publishing Company; p.82 (top): © AP Wide World Photos; p.82 (bottom): © Lennart Nilsson/Albert Bonniers Forlag AB/A Child is Born, Dell Publishing Company; p.84: Courtesy of Ann Streissguth; p.85 (top): Monkey Business Images Ltd/PhotoLibrary; p.85 (bottom): © John Chiasson; p.86: © R.I.A. Novosti.Gamma/H.P.P./Eyedea; p.87: © Betty Press/Woodfin Camp @ Associates; p.88: Barbara Penoyar/Getty Images; p.89: Ryan Pyle/Ryan Pyle/Corbis; p.90: © Stephen Maturen; p.91 (top): © Jonathan Nourok/Getty Images; p.91 (bottom): © Viviane Moos/CORBIS; p.92: © RF/Corbis; p.93 (top): Paul Schreck, Photographer, Wellspan Health System; p.93 (bottom): © Dr. Holly Beckwith; p.94: ERproductions Ltd/Getty Images; p.95: altrendo images/Getty Images; p.96: © AP Wide World Photos; p.98 (top): © Marc Asnin/CORBIS SABA; p.98 (bottom): Courtesy of Tiffany Field; p.101: © Tony Schanuel; p.101 (bottom): Howard Grey/Getty Images; p.102: Kaz Mori/The Image Bank/Getty Images

Chapter 4

p.105: Daniel Pangbourne/Digital Vision/Getty Images; p.108: DK Stock/Robert Glenn/Getty Images; p.109: Chris Windsor/Digital Vision/Getty Images; p.112 (top): © Ingram Publishing/Alamy; p.112 (bottom): © image100/Corbis; p.114: (top) © A. Glauberman/Photo Researchers; p.114 (bottom): ER Productions/Getty Images; p.115: Benjamin Benschneider/The Seattle Times; p.116 (left): Courtesy of Dr. Harry T. Chugani, Children's Hospital of Michigan; p.116 (bottom middle): © David Grugin Productions, Inc. Reprinted by permission.; p.116 (bottom right): Image courtesy of Dana Boatman, Ph.D., Department of Neurology, John Hopkins University, reprinted with permission from *The Secret Life of the Brain,* Joseph Henry Press; p.117: © Photo Researchers; p. 119: © Royalty-Free/CORBIS; p.122: Jamie Grill/Getty Images; p.123: © Tom Grill/Getty Images; p.124: © Jim LoScalzo; p.126: © AP Wide World Photos; p.127: Mark Steinmetz /The McGraw-Hill Companies, Inc.; p.128: Blend Images/Getty Images; p.130 (top): © Wendy Stone/Corbis; p.130 (bottom): © Dave Bartruff/Corbis; p.131: © Bob Daemmrich/The Image Works; p.132: ©Syracuse Newspapers/D Blume /The Image Works; p.133: Courtesy Dr. T. Berry Brazelton and Brazelton Touchpoints Center; p.134 (top): Jules Frazier/Getty Images; p.134 (bottom): © Image Source/PunchStock; p.135: Courtesy of Barbara Deloin; p.136–137 (top): RubberBall Productions/Getty Images; p.136 (bottom): Dallas Morning News, photographer Vernon Bryant

Chapter 5

p.141: Image Source/Getty Images; p.142 (all): © Reuters New Media Inc./Corbis; p.143: Courtesy of Esther Thelan; p.144 (top): BananaStock/PictureQuest; p.144 (bottom): © Petit Format/Photo Researchers; p.145: Laurence Mouton/PhotoAlto/Getty Images; p.146: © Fabio Cardosa/zefa/Corbis; p.147: Courtesy Dr. Karen Adolph, New York University; p.148 (left to right): Barbara Penoyar/

Getty Images; Digital Vision/Getty Images; © Image Source/Alamy; Titus/Getty Images; © Digital Vision; BananaStock/PictureQuest; Corbis/PictureQuest; © Brand X Pictures/PunchStock; p.149 (left): © Michael Greenlar/The Image Works; p.149 (right): © Frank Baily Studios; p.150 (top): Charlie Edwards/Getty Images; p.150 (bottom): © Photodisc/Getty Images RF; p.151: © Getty Images; p.152 (top): © Newstockimages/SuperStock; p.152 (bottom): Courtesy Amy Needham, Duke University; p.153: © Digital Vision/Getty Images; p.154: © Mika/zefa/Corbis; p.155: Adapted from "The Origin of Form and Perception" by R.L. Fantz ©; p.156: Photo from Karen Adolph's laboratory at New York University; p.158: Kevin Peterson/Getty images/ Simulation by Vischeck; p.160 (top): © Mark Richards / PhotoEdit; p.160 (bottom): © Dr. Bruce Hood, University of Bristol, England; p.161 (left): © Jill Braaten; p. 161 (right): © Dr. Melanie Spence, University of Texas; p.162 (top): © Jean Guichard/Sygma/Corbis; p.162 (bottom): © David Young-Wolff/PhotoEdit; p.163 (top): From D. Rosenstein and H. Oster "Differential Facial Responses to Four Basic Tastes in Newborns," *Child Development,* Vol. 59, 1988. © Society for Research in Child Development, Inc.; p.163 (bottom): altrendo images/Getty Images; p.164: Anthony Cain/Flickr/Getty Images

Chapter 6

p.169: © Beau Lark/Fancy/PhotoLibrary; p.170: Lifesize/Getty Images; p.172: © Digital Vision/PhotoLibrary; p.173: Plush Studios/Brand X Pictures/Jupiterimages; p.174 (left to right): © Stockbyte/Getty Images; © BananaStock/PunchStock; mage100/Corbis; © RF/Corbis; p.175: © Punchstock; p.176: © Doug Goodman/Photo Researchers; p.178: © Joe McNally; p.180: © BananaStock/PictureQuest; p.183: © Michael Newman/PhotoEdit; p.185: © David Young-Wolff/Photo Edit; p.186: Image Source/ JupiterImages; p.187: © RF/Corbis; p.189 (top): © Archives Jean Piaget, Universite De Geneve, Switzerland; p.189 (bottom): Olivier Asselin/Alamy; p.191: Jose Luis Pelaez Inc./Blend Images/Getty Images; p.192 (top): Courtesy Barbara Rogoff; p.192 (bottom): © James Wertsch/Washington University at St. Louis; p. 193: © BananaStock/PunchStock; p.194: Images courtesy of E. Bodrova and D.J. Leong, from *Tools of the Mind,* 2007; p.195 (left): A.R. Lauria/Dr. Michael Cole, Laboratory of Human Cognition, University of California, San Diego; p.195 (right): © Bettmann/Corbis

Chapter 7

p.199: Peter Dazeley/Getty Images; p.200: Courtesy of Laura Bickford; p.202 (top): BananaStock/agefotostock; p.202 (bottom): Digital Vision/Getty Images; p.204: Photodisc Collection/Getty Images; p.205 (top right): © Radius Images/Corbis; p.205 (bottom right): © Stockbyte/Getty Images; p.205 (figure 7.1): Photos from Meltzoff, A.N., & Brooks, R.(2007). Intersubjectivity before language: Three windows on preverbal sharing. In S. Braten (Ed.), *On being moved: From mirror neurons to empathy* (pp. 149–174). Philadelphia, PA: John Benjamins; p.206: © BananaStock/PunchStock; p.207: © Yellow

573

Dog Productions/Getty; p.210 (top right): Brand X Pictures/PunchStock; p.210 (bottom left): Courtesy of Dr. Carolyn Rovee-Collier; p.211: © AP Wide World Photos; p.215 (top): Disneyland: PCL/Alamay; Bugs Bunny: © Visions of America, LLC/Alamay; p.215 (bottom): © 2005 JAMESKAMP.com; p.217: From Jean Mandler, University of California, San Diego. Reprinted by permission of Oxford University Press, Inc.; p.218 (top): © John Santrock; p.219: Courtesy of Helen Hadani; p.220: © Dale Sparks; p.221: Courtesy of Judy DeLoache; p.222: © BananaStock/PunchStock; p.223: Scott Houston / Corbis; p.225: © John Flavell; p.227: © Robin Nelson/PhotoEdit

Chapter 8

p.233: Blend Images/Getty Images; p.236: © Bettmann/Corbis; p.238: Courtesy of Robert Sternberg; p.239: Alistair Berg/Digital Vision/Getty Images; p.240: ER Productions/Getty Images; p.242: © Owen Franken/Corbis; p.244 (top): © David Austin/Stock Boston, Inc.; p.244 (bottom): © Ben Simmons/The Stock Market/Corbis; p.246: © Image Source/Alamy; p.247: Courtesy of John Santrock; p.248: Bayley Scales of Infant and Toddler Development-Third Edition (Bayley-III). Copyright © 2006 by NCS Pearson, Inc. Reproduced with permission. All rights reserved.; p.250 (top): © Stockbyte/Veer; p.250 (bottom): © Koichi Kamoshida/Newsmakers/Getty Images; p.251 (top): © 2007, USA TODAY. Reprinted with permission; p.251 (bottom): © Doug Wilson/Corbis; p.252: Courtesy of Sterling C. Jones; p.253: Purestock/Getty Images

Chapter 9

p.258: Jack Hollingsworth/Getty Images; p.259: Library of Contress, #LC-USZ61-326; p.261: © Photodisc/Getty Images; p.263: © Don Hammond/Design Pics/Corbis RF; p.264 (top): © 2003 University of Washington, Institute for Learning and Brain Sciences (I-LABS); p.264 (bottom): Kate Powers/Taxi/Getty Images; p.265 (top): © Yang Liu/Corbis; p.265 (bottom): © ABPL Image Library/Animals Animals/Earth Scenes; p.267: Courtesy of Sharla Peltier; p.268 (top): © Image Source/Getty Images; p.268 (bottom): Matsunaga Takuya/Aflo/Getty Images; p.270: Jose Luis Pelaez Inc/Blend Images/Jupiterimages; p.271: © Gideon Mendel/Corbis; p.272: © Comstock/PunchStock; p.274: © Jim Graham; p.275 (top): Courtesy of Salvador Tamayo; p.275 (bottom): © Punchstock/Digital Vision; p.277: © Digital Vision/PunchStock; p.278: © AFP/Getty Images; p.279: © Digital Vision/Getty Images; p.280: © Michael Newman/PhotoEdit; p.281: © John Carter /Photo Researchers

Chapter 10

p.287: Ariel Skelley/Blend Images/Getty Images; p.288: © Photodisc/Getty Images; p.289: Nancy R. Cohen/Getty Images; p.291 (top): Jose Luis Pelaez Inc./Getty Images; p.291 (bottom): Sharon Dominick/Getty Images; p.293 (top clockwise): © BananaStock/PictureQuest; The McGraw-Hill Companies, Inc./Jill Braaten, photographer; David Sacks/Getty Images; © Getty Images; p.293 (bottom): Photo by Kenny Braun and courtesy of Dr. Sybil L. Hart, Texas Tech University; p.294: Karen Moskowitz/Getty Images; p.296 (top): Photodisc Collection/Getty Images; p.296 (bottom): James Woodson/Digital Vision/Getty Images; p.298 (top): MacGregor & Gordon/Getty Images; p.298 (bottom): Michael Rieger/FEMA; p.300: Tom Merton/Getty Images; p.305: MIXA/Getty Images; p.306: © Digital Vision/Getty Images; p.307 (top):

Courtesy Celia A. Brownell, University of Pittsburgh; p.307 (bottom): © Dan Lepp/Etsa/Corbis; p.308: © Martin Rogers/Stock Boston; p.309: RF/Corbis; p.312: © Penny Tweedie/Stone/Getty Images; p.313: ER Productions/Getty Images; p.314 (top): Courtesy of Dr. Barry Hewlett; p.314 (bottom): Polka Dot Images/PhotoLibrary; p.315: © Peter Forsberg/Alamy; p.316: Courtesy of Wanda Mitchell; p.317: © BananaStock/PunchStock

Chapter 11

p.322: © David Malan/Getty Images; p.323 (top): Courtesy of Maxine Hong Kingston; p.323 (bottom): © AP Wide World Photos; p.325: Digital Vision/Getty Images; p.326: © Kevin Dodge/Corbis; p.327 (top): © RF/Corbis; p.327 (bottom): Stockbyte/PictureQuest; p.328: © RF/Corbis; p.329: Image Source/PunchStock; p.332: Inti St Clair/Getty Images; p.333: © Masterfile; p.334: © Digital Vision/Getty Images; p.335: © Bettmann/Corbis; p.338: © BananaStock/JupiterImages; p.339 (top): JUPITERIMAGES/Thinkstock/Alamy; p.339 (bottom): © USA Today Library, Photo by Robert Deutsch; p.340 (top): Courtesy of Margaret Beale Spencer; p.340 (bottom): Courtesy of Armando Ronquillo

Chapter 12

p.344: © Jennie Hart/Alamy; p.345: © Shooting Star; p.346: © Rubberball/Getty Images; p.349 (left): © Getty Images; p.349 (right): © Digital Vision; p.350 (top): altrendo images/Getty Images; p.350 (bottom): © Cindy Charles/PhotoEdit; p.353 (top): © Peter Dazeley/zefa/Corbis; p.353 (bottom): © Turbo/zefa/Corbis; p.355: © RF/Corbis; p.356: © Rob Melnychuk/Brand X/Corbis RF; p.357: Somos Images/Corbis; p.361: © Owen Franken/Corbis

Chapter 13

p.364: © Simon Jarratt/Corbis; p.365: © Copyright 2005, Globe Newspaper Company, Matthew J. Lee photographer. Republished with permission.; p.367 (top): © Tom Grill/Corbis; p.369: Randy Faris / Corbis; p.370: © Raghu-Rai/Magnum Photos; p.371 (top): © David Frazier Photo Library; p.371 (bottom): Photo by Joyce Ravid and Courtesy of Dr. Carol Gilligan; p.372: © Jim Craigmyle/Corbis; p.374 (top): © Martin Harvey/Corbis; p.374 (bottom): © ThinkStock/Corbis; p.376 (left): © Bettmann/Corbis; p.376 (right): © Alain Nogues/Corbis Sygma; p.378: Rubberball/Getty Images; p.379: Stockbyte/PunchStock; p.380 (top): © Ronald Cortes; p.380 (bottom): Courtesy of Nina Vasan; p.381: Eric Audras/PhotoAlto Agency RF Collections/Getty Images; p.382: © Photodisc/Getty Images; p.383: © Stockdisc/PunchStock; p.384: Comstock Images/Alamy; p.386: Courtesy of Rodney Hammond; p.389: Digital Vision/Getty Images

Chapter 14

p.393: Monkey Business Images /PhotoLibrary; p.394: Blend Images/Jasper Cole/Getty Images; p.395: Courtesy of Shelley Peterson Schwarz, URL: www.meetinglifechallenges.com Email: help@MeetingLifesChallenges.com; p.397 (top): Jamie Grill/Getty Images; p.397 (bottom): Photodisc/Getty Images; p.398: © Image Source/PunchStock; p.401: © BananaStock/PictureQuest; p.403 (top): Courtesy of Janis Keyser; p.403 (bottom): Ryan McVay/Getty Images; p.405 (top): © Purestock; p.405 (bottom): © Digital Archive Japan/PunchStock; p.408 (top): Courtesy of Darla Botkin; p.408 (bottom): © BananaStock/PunchStock, p.410: © BananaStock/PunchStock, p.411 (top): © BananaStock/

PunchStock; p.411 (Fig. 14.5): © BananaStock/PunchStock; p.412: © Pat Vasquez-Cunningham 1999; p.413 (all): RubberBall Productions/Getty Images; p.414: Image Source/Getty Images; p.416: Eric Audras/Photoalto/PictureQuest; p.417: © Image Source/PunchStock; p.419: Todd Wright/Blend Images/Getty Images; p.420: © 2009 Jupiterimages Corporation; p.421: © Big Cheese Photo/PunchStock; p.422: © Spencer Grant/Photo Edit

Chapter 15

p.426: Blend Images/Jasper Cole/Getty Images; p.429: Getty Images/SW Productions; p.430: Tom Stoddart/Getty Images; p.431 (top): © Image Source/PunchStock; p.431 (bottom): © BananaStock/PunchStock; p.433: © Pixland/PunchStock; p.434: © BananaStock; p.436: SW Productions/Getty Images; p.438: The McGraw-Hill Companies, Inc/Ken Karp photographer; p.439 (top): Jean-Pierre Pieuchot/Stockbyte/Getty Images; p.439 (bottom): Laurence Mouton/Photoalto/PictureQuest; p.441(left): © Purestock/PunchStock; p.441 (right): ©BananaStock/Punchstock; p.443: Image Source/Corbis; p:444: (top) Kevin Dodge / Corbis (bottom) Michael A. Keller / Zefa / Corbis; p.445: © Punchstock/Brand X Pictures; p.447 (top): © Digital Vision/Getty Images; p.447 (bottom): Pinto/Zefa/ Corbis; p.448: Jenny Acheson/Getty Images

Chapter 16

p.452: © Superstock/PhotoLibrary; p.453: Ruby Washington/The New York Times/Redux Pictures; p.454: © Michael Newman/PhotoEdit; p.455: Tony Cordoza/Alamy; p.456: Image Source/Alamy; p.457: Michael Grecco/Hulton Archive/Getty Images; p.459 (top): Courtesy of Yolanda Garcia; p.459 (bottom): © Newscom; p.460: Blend Images/Getty Images; p.461 (left): © Karen Kasmauski/Corbis; p.461 (right): © SOS Children's Villages (www.sos-usa.org); p.462: © Creatas/PunchStock; p.463: © Ed Kashi/Corbis; p.464 (top): © Ray A. Llanos; p.464 (bottom): © Patrik Giardino/CORBIS; p.465: © 2004, USA Today. Reprinted with permission.; p.466: Blend Images/Alamy; p.467: © Chris Volpe Photography; p.468 © AP Wide World Photos; p.469: © JupiterImages; p.470 (top): © Robin Nelson / PhotoEdit; p.470 (bottom): Crown copyright MMVI, www.thetransporters.com, courtesy Changing Media Development; p.471: © Richard Hutchings/Photo Researchers; p.473: © Elizabeth Crews/The Image Works; p.475: © AP Wide World Photos; p.476: © Ralf-Finn Hestoft/Corbis; p.477: Courtesy of Hari Prabhakar; p.478: Courtesy of Sandra Graham; p.479: © Eiji Miyazawa/Stock Photo

Chapter 17

p.483: © Dave Nagel/Getty Images; p.486: © Marjorie Shostak/Anthro Photos; p.489 (top): © Janet Jarman/Corbis; p.489 (bottom): © Joseph Sohm/Visions of America/Corbis; p.490: Awakening Arts Corporation/Getty Images; p.491: Courtesy of Vonnie McLoyd; p.493: Courtesy Eisenhower Foundation, Washington, DC; p.494: Mario Tama/Getty Images; p.495 (top): Courtesy of Carola Suarez-Orozco and photographer Kris Snibble/Harvard News Office; p.495 (bottom): © Alison Wright/Corbis; p.497: © USA Today Library, photo by H. Darr Beiser; p.498 (left): Wayne R Bilenduke/Getty Images; p.498 (right): © LWA/Taxi/Getty Images; p.499: © McGraw-Hill Companies, Inc., photographer Suzie Ross; p.500: © iStockphoto.com/Dan Wilton; p.501 (top): © BananaStock/PunchStock p.501 (bottom): imagebroker.net/PhotoLibrary; p.502: © Davo Blair/Alamy; p.505: Digital Vision/Alamy

TEXT/LINE ART CREDITS

Prologue

SO 1.1 From the book *100 Ways to Build Self-Esteem and Teach Values.* Copyright © 1994, 2003 by Diana Loomans. Reprinted with permission of HJ Kramer/New World Library, Novato CA. www.newworldlibrary.com.

Chapter 1

Fig 1.3 From *The State of the World's Children*, 2004, Geneva, Switzerland: UNICEF, Fig. 5, p. 27. Reprinted by permission of UNICEF. **Fig 1.5** From Santrock, *Life-Span Development*, 11th ed., Fig. 1.4. Copyright © 2008 The McGraw-Hill Companies. Reprinted by permission of The McGraw-Hill Companies, Inc. **Fig 1.13** From "Bronfenbrenner's Ecological Theory of Development," C.B. Kopp & J.B. Krakow, 1982, *Child Development in the Social Context*, p. 648. Reprinted by permission of Pearson Education, Inc. **Fig 1.14** From Santrock, *Children*, 8th ed., Fig. 2.9. Copyright © 2005 The McGraw-Hill Companies. Reprinted by permission of The McGraw-Hill Companies, Inc. **Fig 1.15** Psychological Science by Crowley et al. Copyright © 2001 by Sage Publications Inc. Journals. Reproduced with permission of Sage Publications Inc. Journals via Copyright Clearance Center. **Fig 1.17** From *Adolescence*, 12ed, by John Santrock. Copyright © 2008 The McGraw-Hill Companies, Inc. **Fig 1.18** From Santrock, *Children*, 7th ed., Fig. 2.11. Copyright © 2003 The McGraw-Hill Companies. Reprinted by permission of The McGraw-Hill Companies, Inc.

Chapter 2

Fig 2.1 Bonner, John T., THE EVOLUTION OF CULTURE IN ANIMALS. © 1980 Princeton University Press. Reprinted by permission of Princeton University Press. **Fig 2.2** From Santrock, *Life-Span Development*, 11th ed., Fig. 3.3. Copyright © 2008 The McGraw-Hill Companies. Reprinted by permission of The McGraw-Hill Companies, Inc. **Fig 2.5** From Santrock, *Life-Span Development*, 11th ed., Fig. 3.7. Copyright © 2008 The McGraw-Hill Companies. Reprinted by permission of The McGraw-Hill Companies, Inc. **Fig 2.9** From Golombok et al., 2001, "The 'Test-Tube' Generation," *Child Development*, 72, 599–608. Reprinted with permission of the Society for Research in Child Development. **Fig 2.10** From Santrock, *Children*, 7th ed., Fig. 3.14. Copyright © 2003 The McGraw-Hill Companies. Reprinted by permission of The McGraw-Hill Companies, Inc. **Fig 2.11** From Santrock, *Life-Span Development*, 12ed. Copyright © 2009 The McGraw-Hill Companies. Reprinted by permission of The McGraw-Hill Companies, Inc.

Chapter 3

Fig 3.1 From Charles Carroll and Dean Miller, *Health: The Science of Human Adaptation*, 5th ed. Copyright © 1991 The McGraw-Hill Companies. Reprinted by permission of The McGraw-Hill Companies, Inc. **Fig 3.5** Reprinted from K.L. Moore, *The Developing Human: Clinically Oriented Embryology*, 4th ed., with permission from Elsevier. **Fig 3.6** Virginia Apgar, "The Apgar Scale" from "A Proposal for a New Method of Evaluation of a Newborn Infant," *Anesthesia and Analgesia* (32), pp. 260–267. © 1975. Reprinted by permission. **Fig 3.9** Reprinted from *Infant Behavior and Development*, 30, "Preterm Infants Show Reduced Stress Behaviors and Activity After Five Days of Massage Therapy," pp. 557–561. Copyright © 2007 with permission from Elsevier.

Chapter 4

Fig 4.1 From Santrock, *Children*, 7th ed., Fig. 3.14. Copyright © 2003 The McGraw-Hill Companies. Reprinted by permission of The McGraw-Hill Companies, Inc. **Fig 4.2** From Santrock, *Adolescence*, 8th ed., Fig. 3.4. Copyright © 2001 The McGraw-Hill Companies. Reprinted with permission of The McGraw-Hill Companies, Inc. **Fig 4.3** Reproduced from "Standards from Birth to Maturity for Height, Weight, Height Velocity: British Children" by J.M. Tanner, R.H. Whitehouse, and M. Takaishi, *Archives of Diseases in Childhood*, vol. 41, issue 200. Copyright © 1966 with permission from BMJ Publishing Group Ltd. **Fig 4.4** Originally appeared in J.M. Tanner, "Growing Up," *Scientific American*, September 1973. Reprinted by permission of Nelson H. Prentiss. **Fig 4.6** From Santrock, *Children*, 9th ed., Fig. 6.6. Copyright © 2003 The McGraw-Hill Companies. Reprinted by permission of The McGraw-Hill Companies, Inc. **Fig 4.7** From Santrock, *Child Development*, 9th ed. Copyright © 2001 The McGraw-Hill Companies. Reprinted by permission of The McGraw-Hill Companies, Inc. **Fig 4.13** From Santrock, *Psychology*, 7th ed., p. 128. Copyright © 2003 The McGraw-Hill Companies. Reprinted by permission of The McGraw-Hill Companies, Inc. **Fig 4.15** From Santrock, *Essentials of Life-Span Development*, Fig 9.3. Copyright © 2008 The McGraw-Hill Companies. Reprinted by permission of The McGraw-Hill Companies, Inc. **Fig 4.16** From Santrock, *Children*, 10th ed., Fig. 5.10. Copyright © 2008 The McGraw-Hill Companies. Reprinted by permission of The McGraw-Hill Companies, Inc. **Fig 4.18** From Santrock, *Children*, 10th ed., Fig. 5.11. Copyright © 2008 The McGraw-Hill Companies. Reprinted by permission of The McGraw-Hill Companies, Inc. **Fig 4.21** From Santrock, *Children*, 10th ed., Fig. 14.10. Copyright © 2008 The McGraw-Hill Companies. Reprinted by permission of The McGraw-Hill Companies, Inc.

Chapter 5

Fig 5.3 Reprinted from *Journal of Pediatrics*, 71, W.K. Frankenburg & J.B. Dodds, "The Denver Development Screening Test," pp. 181–191, © 1967, with permission from Elsevier. http://www.sciencedirect.com/science/journal **p. 151** Reprinted with the permission of the Women's Sports Foundation. **Fig 5.5(a)** Adapted from Alexander Semenoick, in R.L. Fantz, "The Origin of Form Perception," *Scientific American*, 1961. **Fig 5.6** From Slater, et al., 1988, "Orientation Discrimination and Cortical Function in the Human Newborn," *Perception*, 17, 597–602 (Figure 1 and Table 1). Reprinted with permission of Pion Limited, London. **Fig 5.9** Bennett I. Bertenthal, Matthew R. Longo, and Sarah Kenny, "Phenomenal Permanence and the Development of Predictive Tracking in Infancy" from *Child Development*, 78, p. 354, © 2007 by John Wiley & Sons. Reprinted with permission. www.interscience.wiley.com

Chapter 6

p. 171 Reprinted from *The Origins of Intelligence* by J. Piaget by permission of International Universities Press, Inc. Copyright 1952 by International Universities Press Inc. and Taylor & Francis Books UK. **Fig 6.1** Text from Santrock, *Topical Life-Span*, 2ed., Fig. 6.1. Copyright © 2005 The McGraw-Hill Companies. Reprinted by permission of The McGraw-Hill Companies, Inc. **Fig 6.2** From Santrock, *Life-Span Development*, 11ed., Fig. 6.1. Copyright © 2008 The McGraw-Hill Companies. Reprinted by permission of The McGraw-Hill Companies, Inc. **Fig 6.4** From R. Baillargeon & J. Devoe, "Object Permanence in Young Children: Further Evidence," *Child Development*, 62, pp. 1227–1246. Reprinted with permission of the Society for Research in Child Development. **Fig 6.6** From Santrock, *Children*, 7th ed., Fig. 10.1. Copyright © 2003 The McGraw-Hill Companies. Reprinted by permission of The McGraw-Hill Companies, Inc. **Fig 6.7** Reprinted courtesy of D. Wolf and J. Nove. **Fig 6.8 line art** From Santrock, *Children*, 7ed., Fig. 10.4. Copyright © 2003 The McGraw-Hill Companies. Reprinted by permission of The McGraw-Hill Companies, Inc. **Fig 6.9** From Santrock, *Children*, 7th ed., Fig. 10.5. Copyright © 2003 The McGraw-Hill Companies. Reprinted by permission of The McGraw-Hill Companies, Inc. **Fig 6.10** From Santrock, *Children*, 7th ed., Fig. 13.1. Copyright © 2003 The McGraw-Hill Companies. Reprinted by permission of The McGraw-Hill Companies, Inc. **Fig 6.12** Leong & Bodrova, *Tools of the Mind,* Figure 7.8, p. 87, © 1996. Reproduced by permission of Pearson Education, Inc.

Chapter 7

Fig 7.2 From Santrock, *Child Development*, 10th ed., Fig. 8.1. Copyright © 2004 The McGraw-Hill Companies. Reprinted by permission of The McGraw-Hill Companies, Inc. **Fig 7.3** From Santrock, *Topical Life-Span*, 2ed., Fig. 7.8. Copyright © 2005 The McGraw-Hill Companies. Reprinted by permission of The McGraw-Hill Companies, Inc. **Fig 7.4** *Children's Thinking: What Develops?* (Duro) by R.S. Siegler (ed). Copyright © 1978 by Taylor & Francis Group LLC—Books Reproduced with permission of Taylor & Francis Group LLC—Books via Copyright Clearance Center. **Fig 7.6** From *Learning and the Infant Mind* by A. Woodward and A. Needham (eds.), p. 12. Copyright © 2009 Oxford University Press. By permission of Oxford University Press, Inc. www.oup.com. **Fig 7.7** From Santrock, *Psychology*, 7th ed., Fig. 8.15. Copyright © 2005 The McGraw-Hill Companies. Reprinted by permission of The McGraw-Hill Companies, Inc. **Fig 7.12** From Deloache, Simcock, & Macasi (2007), *Developmental Psychology* vol. 43, p. 1583. Copyright © 2007 by the American Psychological Association. **Fig 7.13** From Robert S. Siegler, *Four Rules for Solving the Balance Scale Task*. Copyright © Robert S. Siegler. Reprinted by permission. **Fig 7.15** The Sally and Anne False-Belief Task from *Autism: Explaining the Enigma* by U. Frith, p. 83. Copyright © 1989 by Wiley-Blackwell. Reprinted with permission.

Chapter 8

p. 234 Excerpts from Shiffy Landa, "If you can't make waves, make ripples," *Intelligence Connections: Newsletter of the ASCD*, Vol. X, No. 1 (Fall 2000), p. 6–8. Reprinted by permission of Thomas R. Hoerr, Ph.D., Head of School, New City School, St. Louis. www.newcityschool.org. **Fig 8.1** From Santrock, *Psychology*, 7ed., Fig. 10.1. Copyright © 2003 The McGraw-Hill Companies. Reprinted by permission of The McGraw-Hill Companies, Inc. **Fig 8.8** From Santrock, *Psychology*, 7ed., Fig. 10.6. Copyright © 2003 The McGraw-Hill Companies. Reprinted by permission of The McGraw-Hill Companies, Inc.

Chapter 9

Fig 9.1 "The Rule Systems of Language," from S.L. Haight, *Language Overview*. Reprinted by permission.

Fig 9.3 From Santrock, *Children*, 7ed., Fig. 7.6. Copyright © 2003 The McGraw-Hill Companies. Reprinted by permission of The McGraw-Hill Companies, Inc. **Fig 9.4** From Santrock, *Children*, 7ed., Fig. 7.7. Copyright © 2003 The McGraw-Hill Companies. Reprinted by permission of The McGraw-Hill Companies, Inc. **Fig 9.5** From Jean Berko, 1958, "The Child's Learning of English Morphology," in *Word*, Vol. 14, p. 154. Used with permission. **Fig 9.6** From B. Hart and T. R. Risley, *Meaningful Differences in the Everyday Experiences of Young American Children*, copyright © 1995, Figures 2 and 3, pp. 47 and 60. Baltimore: Paul H. Brookes Publishing Co., Inc. Reprinted by permission. **Fig 9.7** *Theory and Practice of Early Reading* by J.S. Chall. Copyright © 1980 by Taylor & Francis Group LLC—Books. Reproduced with permission of Taylor & Francis Group LLC—Books via Copyright Clearance Center. **p. 273** The devl and the babe ghoste from Gleason, *The Development of Language*, Table 10.11, p. 336, © 1993. Reproduced by permission of Pearson Education, Inc. **Fig 9.11** Copyright © Dr. Ursula Bellugi, The Salk Institute for Biological Studies, La Jolla, CA. Used with permission.

Chapter 10

Fig 10.1 From *The Development of Emotional Competence* by C. Saarni, p. 5. Copyright © 1999 by Guilford Publications, Inc. Reprinted by permission. **Fig 10.5** Reprinted by permission of the publisher from *Infancy: Its Place in Human Development* by Jerome Kagan, R.B. Kearsley, and P.R. Zelazo, p. 107, Cambridge, Mass.: Harvard University Press. Copyright © 1978 by the President and Fellows of Harvard College. **Fig 10.6** From Santrock, *Topical Life-Span Development*, Fig. 10.3. Copyright © 2002 The McGraw-Hill Companies. Reprinted by permission of The McGraw-Hill Companies, Inc. **Fig 10.9** From "Cross-Cultural Pattern of Attachment: A Meta-Analysis of the Strange Situation" by M.H. van Ijzendoorn and P.M. Kroonenberg. *Child Development*, 59, pp. 147–156. Copyright © 1988 by Blackwell Publishing Ltd. Reprinted with permission of Blackwell Publishing Ltd. **Fig 10.10** From *Topical Life-Span Development*, 5th Edition, by John Santrock. Copyright © 2010 The McGraw-Hill Companies. Reprinted by permission of The McGraw-Hill Companies, Inc. **Fig 10.11** Data from U.S. Census Bureau, 2006. **Fig 10.12** A.K. Clarke-Stewart and J.L. Miner, "Child and day care, effects of." From M.M. Haith and J.B. Benson (Eds.), *Encyclopedia of Infant and Early Childhood Development*, Vol. 1, Fig. 2, p. 269. Copyright © 2008 by Elsevier. Reprinted with permission.

Chapter 11

Fig 11.1(b) From M. Lewis & J. Brooks-Gunn, "The Development of Self-Recognition in Infancy" from *Social Cognition and the Acquisition of the Self* by M. Lewis and J. Brooks-Gunn, p. 64. Reprinted with kind permission of Springer Science and Business Media. **Fig 11.3** From *The Construction of the Self* by Susan Harter. Copyright © 1999 by Guilford Press. Reprinted by permission. **Fig 11.4** From Santrock, *Children*, 8th ed., Fig. 17.2. Copyright © 2005 The McGraw-Hill Companies. Reprinted by permission of The McGraw-Hill Companies, Inc. **Fig 11.5** From Santrock, *Children*, 8th ed., Fig. 17.3. Copyright © 2005 The McGraw-Hill Companies. Reprinted by permission of The McGraw-Hill Companies, Inc. **Fig 11.6** From Santrock, *Children*, 7th ed., p. 542. Copyright © 2003 The McGraw-Hill Companies. Reprinted by permission of The McGraw-Hill Companies, Inc.

Chapter 12

Fig 12.5 From Santrock, *Topical Life-Span Development*, 3rd ed, Fig. 12.4. Copyright © 2007 The McGraw-Hill Companies. Reprinted by permission of The McGraw-Hill Companies, Inc. **Fig 12.6** Reproduced by special permission of the Publisher, Mind Garden, Inc., www.mindgarden.com from the *Bem Sex Role Inventory* by Sandra Bem. Copyright 1978, 1981 by Consulting Psychologists Press, Inc. Further reproduction is prohibited without the Publisher's written consent.

Chapter 13

Fig 13.1 From R.S. Selman, "Social-Cognitive Understanding," in Thomas Lickona (Ed.) *Moral Development and Behavior*, 1976. Reprinted by permission of Thomas Lickona. **Fig 13.2** From Colby, et al., 1983, "A Longitudinal Study of Moral Judgment," *Monographs for the Society for Research in Child Development*, Serial #201. Reprinted with permission of the Society for Research in Child Development. **Fig 13.4** From *Adolescence*, 13ed, by John Santrock. Copyright © 2010 The McGraw-Hill Companies. Reprinted by permission of The McGraw-Hill Companies, Inc.

Chapter 14

p. 395 Reprinted by permission of Shelley Peterman Schwarz. **p. 422** *Handbook of Parenting*, 2ed by Garcia Coll and Patcher. Copyright © 2002 by Taylor & Francis Group LLC—Books. Reproduced with permission of Taylor & Francis Group LLC—Books via Copyright Clearance Center. **Fig 14.3** From Santrock, *Life-Span Development*, 11th ed, Fig. 9.6. Copyright © 2008 The McGraw-Hill Companies. Reprinted by permission of The McGraw-Hill Companies, Inc. **Fig 14.4** From p. 666 of "Bringing basic research on early experience and stress neurobiology to bear on preventative interventions for neglected and maltreated children" by M.R. Gunnar and P.A. Fisher, and the Early Experience, Stress, and Prevention Network

(2006). From *Development and Psychopathology*, 18, pp. 651–677. Reprinted with the permission of Cambridge University Press. **Fig 14.5** Text from Santrock, *Child Development*, 9th ed. Copyright © 2001 The McGraw-Hill Companies. Reprinted by permission of The McGraw-Hill Companies, Inc. **Fig 14.8** From Santrock, *Life-Span Development*, 11th ed, Fig. 15.9. Copyright © 2008 The McGraw-Hill Companies. Reprinted by permission of The McGraw-Hill Companies, Inc.

Chapter 15

Fig 15.4 From Dexter C. Dunphy, "The Social Structure of Urban Adolescent Peer Groups," *Sociometry*, Vol. 26, 1963. American Sociological Association, Washington, DC.

Chapter 16

Fig 16.1 From the NAEYC position statement. Reprinted with permission from the National Association for the Education of Young Children (NAEYC). www.naeyc.org **Fig 16.2** From Santrock, *Life-Span Development*, 11th ed, Fig. 18.9. Copyright © 2008 The McGraw-Hill Companies. Reprinted by permission of The McGraw-Hill Companies, Inc. **Fig 16.3** From Santrock, *Adolescence*, 12th ed, Fig. 10.2. Copyright © 2008 The McGraw-Hill Companies. Reprinted by permission of The McGraw-Hill Companies, Inc. **Fig 16.4** From Santrock, *Life-Span Development*, 11th ed, Fig. 10.3. Copyright © 2008 The McGraw-Hill Companies. Reprinted by permission of The McGraw-Hill Companies, Inc. **Fig 16.6** From Shaw et al. (2007). "Attention deficit/hyperactivity disorders is characterized by a delay in cortical maturation," PNAS, Dec. 4, 2007, Vol. 104. P. 19650 gif 2. Copyright © 2007 National Academy of Sciences, USA. Reprinted by permission. **Fig 16.9** From Santrock, *Adolescence*, 12th ed, Fig. 16.6. Copyright © 2008 The McGraw-Hill Companies. Reprinted by permission of The McGraw-Hill Companies, Inc.

Chapter 17

Fig 17.1 From Harry C. Triandis, *Making Basic Texts in Psychology More Culture-Inclusive and Culture-Sensitive*. Used by permission of the author. **Fig 17.5** From Santrock, *Topical Life-Span Development*, 4th ed, Fig. 15.2. Copyright © 2008 The McGraw-Hill Companies. Reprinted by permission of The McGraw-Hill Companies, Inc. **Fig 17.6** From Santrock, *Adolescence*, 12th ed, Fig. 12.3. Copyright © 2008 The McGraw-Hill Companies. Reprinted by permission of The McGraw-Hill Companies, Inc. **Fig 17.7** From Santrock, *Topical Life-Span Development*, 4th ed, Fig. 15.8. Copyright © 2008 The McGraw-Hill Companies. Reprinted by permission of The McGraw-Hill Companies, Inc.

name index

Bruine de Bruin, W., 186
Brune, C. W., 308
Bruner, J. S., 280, 285
Brunstein Klomek, A., 435
Bryant, J., 500, 502
Bryant, J. B., 262, 268, 271
Bryant, P. E., 225
Buchanan, A., 314
Buchmann, M., 377
Buckley, K. E., 501
Buckner, C. E., 359
Buehl, D. R., 273
Buhimschi, C., 83, 84
Buhimschi, C. S., 129
Buhrmester, D., 442, 445
Buhs, E., 434, 435
Buijs, D., 115
Bukowski, R., 88
Bukowski, W., 430, 431, 433, 435, 439
Bukowski, W. M., 428, 441
Bullock, M., 325
Bumpus, M.F., 410
Burchinal, M. R., 415
Burger, S. E., 143
Buriel, R., 313, 398, 403, 405
Burke, J., 386
Burns, B. M., 396
Burns, C., 108, 127
Burns, E., 93
Burns, S., 269
Burraston, B., 385
Bursuck, W. D., 469
Burt, K., 13
Burt, S. A., 70
Burton, L. M., 496
Burton, P. C., 115
Burton, R. V., 373
Burton, Sir Richard, 48
Bushman, B. J., 332
Bushnell, E. W., 162
Bushnell, I. W. R., 157
Buss, D. M., 53, 348, 357
Bussey, K., 349
Bustamante-Aragones, A., 64
Butcher, K., 137
Butler, S. C., 94
Butler, Y. G., 276
Byers, B. E., 52
Byrd-Williams, C. E., 134
Byrne, M. W., 123

C

Cabrera, N., 315
Cagigas, X. E., 11
Cagle, M., 251
Cairns, B. D., 7
Cairns, R. B., 7
Caldwell, K. A., 441
Calenda, E., 122
Caley, L., 84
Calkins, S. D., 15
Callan, J. E., 349
Caltran, G., 294
Cameron, J., 474
Campbell, A., 313
Campbell, B., 238
Campbell, D. T., 485

Campbell, F. A., 242, 243
Campbell, K. J., 127
Campbell, L., 238
Campos, J., 310–311
Campos, J. J., 159–160, 290, 293, 294, 295, 299, 307, 312
Camras, L. A., 290–291
Canfield, R. L., 125
Capaldi, D. M., 385
Carbonell, O. A., 312
Cardelle-Elawar, M., 225
Carey, D. P., 240
Carey, S., 267
Carlsen, K. C., 125
Carlsen, K. H., 125
Carlson, C., 338
Carlson, E. A., 312
Carlson, W., 444
Carlton, M. P., 191
Carnegie Council on Adolescent Development, 493
Carnethon, M. R., 137
Carnoy, M., 491
Carpendale, J. I., 226
Carpendale, J. I. M., 188, 296, 325, 327, 396
Carpenter, J., 206
Carpenter, M., 189, 308
Carrier, L. M., 505
Carrington, H., 293
Carroll, A. E., 436
Carroll, J., 240
Carroll, L., 335
Carroll, M. D., 133
Carskadon, M. A., 123–124
Carstensen, L. L., 19
Carter, C. S., 313
Carter, N., 471
Cartwright, R., 121
Carvalho Bos, S., 123
Carver, K., 448
Case, R., 189, 213
Casey, B. J., 15, 113, 115, 116, 118, 119, 180, 189, 217, 306
Casey, P. H., 97
Cash, J. E., 365, 380, 382
Cashion, M. C., 89, 92
Cashon, C., 157
Caspers, K. M., 72
Caspi, A., 71, 72, 303
Castenell, L. A., 496
Castle, J., 67
Cauffman, E., 384
Caughey, A. B., 64
Cavanagh, S. E., 113
Cave, R. K., 276
Ceballo, R., 40, 465, 495
Ceci, S. J., 215, 242
Center for Science in the Public Interest, 133
Centers for Disease Control and Prevention, 64, 127, 470
Cerda, M., 70
Cetin, I., 79
Chall, J. S., 271, 284
Chambers, B., 458
Chan, C., 133
Chan, S. W., 102
Chance, P., 26
Chandler, M., 329

Chandler, M. J., 226
Chandramouli, B. A., 131
Chang, J. S., 125, 126
Chang, M. Y., 94
Chao, R., 405
Chapman, A. R., 64
Charman, T., 471
Charness, N., 210
Chase-Lansdale, P. L., 315
Chassin, L., 412
Chauhan, S. P., 92
Cheah, C., 429, 434
Cheever, N. A., 505
Chen, C., 479
Chen, C. H., 94
Chen, S., 310–311
Chen, X., 59, 303, 428, 485, 494
Chen, X. K., 97
Chen, Z-Y., 404
Cheney, R., 226
Cheng, S., 502
Cheok, M. H., 72
Cherlin, A. J., 419
Chervenak, F. A., 82, 88
Chess, S., 300, 302, 303, 320
Cheung, A. C. K., 458
Chi, M. T., 210
Childers, J. B., 268
Children's Defense Fund, 489, 490
Chin, M., 339
Choi, N., 359
Choi, S., 491
Chomsky, N., 278, 285
Chong, C. M., 442, 445
Christakis, D. A., 501, 502
Christensen, L. B., 31
Christensen, Stacey, 412
Christiani, D., 71
Christie, J., 270, 273
Chuang, S. S., 361
Chung-Hall, J., 428
Cicchetti, D., 407, 409, 410
Cignini, P., 63
Cillessen, A. H. N., 433
Cisneros, A. A., 461
Cisneros-Cohernour, E. J., 461
Clark, B., 455
Clark, E., 267
Clark, E. V., 278, 279
Clarke-Stewart, K. A., 314, 315, 415, 416
Clay, R., 101
Clearfield, M. W., 143, 178
Clemmensen, D., 82, 87–88
Clifton, R. K., 152, 162
Cluett, E. R., 93
Cnaan, R. A., 389
Coatsworth, J. D., 13, 150
Coffino, B., 312
Coffman, J. L., 214
Cohen, G. L., 445
Cohen, L. B., 179, 216
Cohen, N. J., 65
Cohn, J. F., 396
Coid, J. W., 385
Coie, J., 434
Coie, J. D., 433
Colapinto, J., 348
Colby, A., 369

Du, D., 120
Duck, S. W., 443
Duczkowska, A., 63
Dudley, R. L., 388
Dukes, C., 222
Duncan, G., 491
Duncan, G. J., 72
Dunn, J., 297, 397, 413, 414, 429
Dunphy, D. C., 446
Dupere, V., 489
Durant, A., 455
Durant, W., 455
Durham, R. E., 421
Durik, A. M., 353
Durrant, J. E., 407, 409
Durston, S., 119, 206, 469
Dusek, J. B., 330
DuToit, S., 36
Dweck, C. S., 474, 475
Dwyer, T., 122
Dyches, T. T., 471
Dyck, M., 209
Dyson, L., 82, 128
Dzewaltowski, D., 136

E

Eagly, A. H., 348, 349, 355, 357, 360
Eardley, A. F., 142
East, P., 413, 414
Easterbrooks, M. A., 290
Eaton, D. K., 137
Eaton, W. O., 147
Eaves, L. J., 69
Eby, J. W., 454, 455
Eccles, J., 402, 460, 462, 464
Eccles, J. S., 355, 389, 404, 462, 473, 474, 476, 477, 489
Eckenrode, J., 89
Eckerman, C., 307
Eckstein, D., 380
Edelman, M. W., 10
Edgington, C., 448
Edison, S. C., 325
Edwards, C. P., 402
Edwards, R., 356
Edwardson, C. L., 136
Efklides, A., 225
Egan, S. K., 346
Egbert, J. L., 499
Egeth, H., 282
Ehrhardt, A. A., 347
Eiferman, R. R., 440
Eimas, P. D., 217
Eimer, M., 142
Einstein, A., 20, 240–241
Eisenberg, N., 295, 297, 329, 357, 374, 375, 379, 380, 382, 383
Eisenhower Foundation, 493
Ekeblad, S., 58
Elder, G. H., 400
El-Fishawy, P., 470
Eliot, T. S., 396
Elkind, D., 182, 186, 187
Ellertsen, B., 469
Elliott, J., 209
Ellis, J., 453
Elmore, R. F., 462

El-Sayed, Y. Y., 94
El-Sheikh, M., 417
Ely, R., 271
Emerson, R. W., 260
Emery, R. E., 418, 491
Enfield, A., 380
English, K., 13, 492
Enns, G. M., 60
Enright, M. S., 378
Enright, R. D., 383
Ensor, R., 296, 325, 327
Entringer, S., 88
Entwisle, D., 465, 488, 489
Enz, B. J., 270, 273
Eppler, M. A., 164
Erath, S. A., 434, 440
Erickson, L. G., 222
Ericson, N., 437
Ericsson, K. A., 210, 251
Erikson, E. H., 21–22, 23, 30, 31, 33, 42, 286, 308, 309, 334, 335, 336, 337, 339, 343, 389, 437
Eriksson, U. J., 87
Ernst, J. L., 69
Ernst, M., 119
Escobar-Chaves, S. L., 500, 501
Espelage, D., 435
Espirito Santo, J. L., 97
Estrada, S., 224
Etaugh, C. A., 39, 412
Etzel, R. A., 125
Evans, B. J., 497
Evans, G. W., 13, 490, 491, 492
Ewen, D., 458

F

Fabes, R. A., 329, 350
Fabiano, G. A., 469
Fagan, J. F., 248
Fagot, B. J., 350
Fahey, T. D., 135, 136
Fair, D., 118
Fairweather, E., 253
Faissner, A., 117
Falbo, T., 414
Fanconi, M., 115
Fantz, R. L., 155, 158
Faraone, S. V., 469
Faris, R., 435
Farley, F., 224
Farr, R. H., 419
Farrington, D. P., 383, 384, 385
Fasig, L., 325
Fauth, R. C., 421, 458
Fava, E., 114–115, 277
Fawcett, R. C., 237
Fearon, R. P., 311
Federal Interagency Forum on Child and Family Statistics, 13, 490
Feeney, S., 438, 456
Fees, B., 136
Fein, G. G., 439
Feinberg, M. E., 408
Feiring, C., 311
Fekete, S., 332
Feldman, H. D., 250
Feldman, J. F., 248, 283

Feldman, R., 397
Feng, Y., 85
Ferguson, D. M., 129
Fernald, A., 279
Fertig, A. R., 408
Fidler, D. J., 59
Field, A., 94, 298
Field, T., 98, 101, 157, 159, 178, 205
Field, T. M., 85, 93, 98, 99, 307
Findlay, L. C., 298
Fine, S. E., 296
Finger, B., 19, 312
Fink, A., 240
Finkelhor, D., 504
Fischer, A., 348
Fischer, K., 324
Fischer, K. W., 324
Fischhoff, B., 186
Fisher, C. B., 38
Fisher, P. A., 409
Fitzimmons, C., 268
Fivush, R., 211
Flavell, E. R., 225, 226
Flavell, J., 225
Flavell, J. H., 203, 213, 224, 225, 226, 228
Flegal, K. M., 133
Flegal, W. A., 86
Fleming, A. S., 313
Flint, M. S., 56
Flom, R., 205, 206
Florence, N., 11
Florsheim, P., 448
Flouri, E., 314
Flynn, J. R., 242, 499
Foehr, U. G., 207, 500, 501, 503, 504
Fogelholm, M., 135
Foley, J. T., 136
Follari, L., 456
Fontaine, R. G., 433
Fontenot, H. B., 67
Food and Nutrition Service, 132
Forbord, S., 94
Forcier, R. C., 499
Forgatch, M. S., 385
Forget-Dubois, N., 270
Foroud, T., 61
Forster, B., 142
Forster, J., 115
Fosco, G. M., 397
Fox, M. K., 127
Fox, N. A., 117
Fox, S. E., 115, 116
Fraiberg, S., 145
France, A., 454
Franchak, J. M., 157
Francis, D. D., 56
Francis, J., 338
Frank, M. C., 158
Franklin, A., 158
Franz, C. E., 303
Fraser, G., 338
Fraser-Abder, P., 218
Frederick II, emperor of Germany, 263
Frederikse, M., 354
Fredstrom, B., 440
Freedman, J. L., 501
Freeman, K. E., 221
Freeman, S., 55

Mikami, A. Y., 505
Mikkelsson, L., 137
Miller, C., 14
Miller, C. F., 353
Miller, G., 348
Miller, J., 370, 371
Miller, K. M., 457
Miller, P. H., 189, 213, 226
Miller, S., 213
Miller-Johnson, S., 434
Miller-Jones, D., 244
Mills, B., 224
Mills, C., 206
Mills, D., 206, 329
Mills, R. S. L., 397
Milne, B. J., 135
Milot, T., 409
Minaya-Rowe, L., 276
Minde, K., 96
Mindell, J. A., 121
Miner, J. L., 314, 315
Minnesota Family Investment Program, 14
Miranda, P., 475
Mischel, H., 373
Mischel, W., 373
Mistry, R. S., 476
Mitchell, E. A., 122, 123
Mitchell, K., 504
Mitchell, M. L., 35
Miyake, K., 310–311
Mnookin, R. H., 418
Moger, S., 253
Moilanen, K. L., 385
Moise, K. J., 86
Moleti, C. A., 93, 94
Mollar, R. C., 134, 136
Monahan, K., 445
Money, J., 348
Montessori, M., 456
Moore, D., 56, 448
Moore, M., 201
Moore, N. K., 178
Moorefield, B. S., 419
Moorthy, A., 130
Moran, G., 311
Moran, S., 240
Morasch, K. C., 117
Morelli, G. A., 121
Moreno, R. P., 461
Morgano, E., 444
Morishima, J. K., 484
Morison, V., 156
Moroder, L., 93
Morra, S., 189
Morreale, M. C., 384
Morris, C. A., 282
Morris, D., 52
Morris, P. A., 29, 399
Morris, S., 142
Morrison, G. S., 456
Morrissey, T. W., 314
Moschonis, G., 128
Moseley, L., 123
Moss, M., 289, 315
Most, O. L., 87
Motzoi, C., 428
Moulson, M. C., 82, 115
Moya, J., 125

Mudd, A., 273
Mueller, A. S., 112
Mueller, C. E., 460, 462, 474
Mueller, S. C., 119
Mueller, V. C., 280
Mulle, J. G., 60
Muller, U., 188, 220, 396
Munakata, Y., 15, 113, 115, 116, 118, 119, 180, 189, 217, 306
Munholland, K. A., 309
Murphy, D., 227
Murphy, J. L., 409
Murphy, M. M., 60
Murray, A. D., 400
Murray, J. C., 83
Murray, J. P., 400, 500
Murray, S. S., 89, 128
Murry, K. G., 276
Mustelin, L., 69
Myers, D., 207, 491
Myers, D. G., 72
Myers, M. W., 444
Myerson, J., 245
Myles, B. S., 470, 471

N

NAEYC, 457, 458
Nagahawatte, N. T., 97
Nagata, D. K., 484
Nagel, H. T., 63
Nagell, K., 206
Najman, J. M., 465
Nakamoto, J., 436
Nakamura, J., 465
Nakhre, R., 316
Nansel, T. R., 435
Nardi, P. M., 32
Narendran, S., 96
Narvaez, D., 370, 375, 378, 381
Nation, M., 429
National Assessment of Educational Progress, 273, 354
National Association for Sport and Physical Education, 135, 137
National Autism Association, 227
National Cancer Institute, 125
National Center for Education Statistics, 463, 468, 471
National Center for Health Statistics, 96, 109
National Center on Shaken Baby Syndrome, 115
National Clearinghouse on Child Abuse and Neglect, 409
National Institute of Mental Health, 470
National Institutes of Health, 60
National Institutes of Neurological Disorders and Stroke, 120
National Research Council, 266, 477
National Sleep Foundation, 100, 123
National Vital Statistics Report, 125
Natsuaki, M. N., 113
Neal, A. R., 470
Needham, A., 152, 180
Neisser, U., 241
Neitzel, C., 397
Nelson, C. A., 33, 81, 82, 113, 115, 116, 117, 119, 202, 212
Nelson, J. A., 380

Nelson, K., 180
Neubauer, A. C., 240
Neufeld, S. J., 295
Neukrug, E. S., 237
Neville, H. J., 274
Nevsimalova, S., 123
New, R., 453
Newcombe, N., 212, 311
Newell, K., 152
Newman, H., 388
Newman, R. S., 162
Newport, E. L., 274
Newton, A. W., 122, 409
Newton, E., 293, 294, 312
Ng, S. H., 274
Ngo, Q. E., 40, 465, 495
Nguyen, S. P., 353
NICHD, 122
NICHD Early Child Care Research Network, 207, 269, 314, 317
Nichols, S., 327
Nielsen, L. S., 123
Nieto, S., 10
Nigg, J. T., 302
Nippold, M. A., 210
Nisbett, R., 243
Nitko, A. J., 456
Nixon, G. M., 123
Noddings, N., 455
Noddings, S. N., 378
Noland, H., 123
Nolen-Hoeksema, S., 101
Norgard, B., 84
Norman, J. E., 96
Norton, M. E., 64
Nottleman, E. D., 111
Novin, S., 290
Nucci, L., 372, 378
Nunes, M. L., 97
Nurius, P., 327
Nylund, K., 435
Nyqvist, K. H., 98

O

Oakes, L. M., 216
Oakley, G. P., 82
Oates, J., 92, 283
Obenauer, S., 63
Oberlander, T. F., 95
O'Brien, J. M., 96
O'Brien, P., 289, 315
Ochs, E., 280
O'Connor, A. B., 86
O'Connor, E., 311
O'Donnell, C. J., 61
Odouli, R., 84, 123
Ogbu, J., 245
Ogden, C. L., 133
O'Hearn, K., 282
Okuma, K., 502
Oladokun, R. E., 129, 130
Oldehinkel, A. J., 416
Olds, D., 89
Oliver, S. R., 134
Oller, D. K., 275
Olson, B. H., 132
Olson, L., 465, 488, 489

Raikes, K. T., 279
Rajendran, G.; Mitchell, P., 227
Rakison, D. H., 216
Ram, K. T., 129
Ramani, G. B., 307
Ramey, C. T., 243, 255
Ramey, S. L., 243, 318
Ramon, R., 88
Ramphal, C., 242
Ramsay, D. S., 296
Ramsay-Rennels, J. L., 306
Ramsey, E., 434
Rao, S. L., 131
Rapkin, B. D., 462
Rapp, B., 115
Rasmussen, M. M., 82, 87–88
Ratner, N. B., 278
Raulin, M. L., 20, 35
Raven, P. H., 18, 52
Ray, J., 270
Ray, M., 239
Rayner, R., 27
Raz, N., 354
Ream, G. L., 388
Recchia, H. E., 413
Reddy, V., 293
Redican, K., 9
Reeb, B. C., 116
Reed, D., 503
Reed, S. K., 201
Regalado, M., 406
Regev, R. H., 96
Rehbein, M., 33, 116
Reid, G., 468
Reid, J. B., 434
Reid, P. T., 39
Reiner, W. G., 348
Reis, M., 84
Reiser, M., 434
Rende, E. K., 85
Renfrew, M., 82, 128
Renner, P., 227
Repacholi, B. M., 225
Rest, J. R., 375
Reyna, V., 224
Reyna, V. F., 186, 209, 210, 224
Reynolds, F., 95
Reznick, J. S., 209
Reznitskaya, A., 238
Richards, J. E., 204, 205
Richardson, G. A., 85
Richter, L., 131
Rickards, T., 253
Rickman, A., 11, 420, 486
Rideout, V., 500, 503, 504
Riemann, R., 69
Riesman, D., 260
Riggins, T., 85
Riksen-Walraven, J. M., 129
Rinehart, S. D., 222
Rink, J. E., 135, 150
Ripke, M. N., 402, 422, 465, 488
Risch, N., 72
Risley, T. R., 269
Ritchie, S., 457
Rivas-Drake, D., 497
Rivera, C., 276
Rivers, S. E., 186, 210, 224

Rizzo, M. S., 62
Roberts, D. F., 207, 500, 501, 503, 504
Roberts, R. D., 239
Robins, R. W., 331
Robinson, J. B., 396
Rochlen, A. B., 313
Rode, J. C., 239
Rode, L., 96
Rode, S. S., 102
Rodgers, C. S., 350
Rodgers, J. L., 444
Rodriquez, E. T., 270
Roemmich, J. N., 134–135
Roeser, R. W., 388, 389, 462, 473, 474, 476, 477, 489
Rogaev, E. L., 58
Rogoff, B., 191, 192, 195, 325
Rogosch, F. A., 410
Rohner, E. C., 420
Rohner, R. P., 420
Rojas, A., 79
Romer, D., 186
Rondou, P., 469
Ronquillo, A., 340
Rooksby, M., 212
Roopnarine, J. L., 461
Rose, A. J., 356, 443, 444
Rose, S. A., 248, 283
Rose-Krasnor, L., 397
Rosen, L. D, 505
Rosenbaum, K., 228
Rosenberg, M. S., 468, 471–472
Rosenblatt, R., 24
Rosenblith, J. G., 205
Rosenblum, S., 468
Rosenheck, R., 134
Rosenkoetter, L. L., 501
Rosenkoetter, S. E., 501
Rosenstein, D., 162
Rosenthal, R., 237
Rosenthal, S., 311
Rosnow, R. L., 237
Ross, H., 413, 431, 432
Ross, J. L., 60
Roth, W. T., 106, 135, 136
Rothbart, M. K., 204, 206, 207, 295, 301, 302, 303, 304, 305, 320
Rothbaum, F., 312, 430, 445, 487
Rothstein, R., 491
Rousseau, J-J., 6–7, 172, 428
Rovee-Collier, C., 156, 210, 211
Rovers, M. M., 128
Row, C., 269
Rowe, M. L., 264
Rowley, S., 40, 465, 497, 498
Roy, C., 86
Royal, J., 215
Roza, S. J., 88
Ruano, D., 241
Rubie-Davies, C. M., 476
Rubin, K. H., 397, 429, 430, 431, 432, 433, 434, 435, 439, 440
Rubinstein, O., 468
Ruble, D., 326
Ruble, D. N., 11, 350, 351, 353
Rueda, M. R., 206
Ruel, M. T., 131
Ruffman, T., 226

Rumberger, R. W., 463
Runco, M., 253
Runquist, J., 100
Russell, I. F., 92
Ryan, R. M., 421, 458, 473
Rydell, R. J., 246
Rykhlevskaia, E., 468

S

Saarni, C., 291, 293, 295, 298, 319, 433
Sabbagh, M. A., 227
Sachs, J., 263, 264, 278
Sacker, A., 489
Sackett, P. R., 246
Sadeh, A., 120, 121, 122, 123
Sadovsky, A., 383
Sadovsky, A. L., 351
Safford, P., 496, 497
Saffran, J. R., 161, 261
Saifer, S., 194
Sakharov, A., 376
Salapatek, P., 145, 162
Salazar-Martinez, E., 150
Salmivalli, C., 355, 435
Salovey, P., 239
Sameroff, A., 72
Samuels, C. A., 359
Sanders, E., 438
Sandler, I., 14
Sanford, D., 101
Sanson, A., 305
Sanson, A. V., 303, 304
Santos, M. J. D., 383
Santrock, J. W., 418, 419
Sapirstein, M., 392
Saraswathi, T. S., 361
Saroha, E., 66
Sassler, S., 419
Savage, T. V., 454
Savelsbergh, G. J., 152
Savin-Williams, R., 388
Savin-Williams, R. C., 447
Sawyer, T. P., 246
Scarr, S., 69, 70, 74, 241, 244, 245
Schachter, D. L., 209
Schachter, E. P., 338
Schaefer, V. A., 13
Schaffer, H. R., 309
Schaie, K. W., 16, 19, 29
Scharrer, E., 501, 503
Schattschneider, C., 270
Schauble, L., 219, 220
Scheibe, S., 19
Scher, A., 295
Schieffelin, B., 280
Schiff, W. J., 127, 131
Schilder, A. G., 128
Schlaggar, B. L., 118
Schlegal, A., 486
Schlegel, M., 219
Schmidheiny, K., 349
Schmidt, B. L., 61
Schmidt, J., 380
Schmidt, L. A., 302
Schmidt, M. E., 501, 503
Schneider, W., 214
Schoen, L. M., 211

Wright, R. O., 71
Wszolek, Z. K., 61
Wu, D. Y. H., 461
Wu, P., 420
Wulsin, S. C., 380
Wyatt, T., 297, 298, 398
Wynn, K., 179
Wyse, D., 273

X

Xu, F., 179
Xu, X., 297
Xue, F., 88

Y

Yang, C., 505
Yang, J. Y., 276
Yang, S., 243

Yawkey, T. D., 276
Yazdy, M. M., 82
Ying, Y., 484
Yip, T., 497
Yolton, K., 125
Yonkers, K. A., 84
Young, K. T., 129
Younger, M., 355
Youniss, J., 380
Yu, T., 417
Yurkewicz, C., 383

Z

Zaghloul, N. A., 61
Zaitoun, I., 58
Zalk, S. R., 39
Zarrett, N. R., 384
Zeidner, M., 239
Zelazo, P. D., 220

Zelazo, P. R., 295
Zelkowitz, P., 96
Zellner, M., 209
Zellweger, R., 345
Zerwas, S., 307
Zeskind, P. S., 294
Zhang, L., 64, 85
Zhang, L.-F., 242, 243, 245
Zhou, M., 469
Zhou, Q., 301
Zielinski, D. S., 410
Zigler, E., 14, 402, 459, 460, 464
Zigler, E. F., 457, 458
Zimmerman, B. J., 477
Zimmerman, F. J., 501, 502
Ziol-Guest, K. M., 72, 416, 417
Zitzer-Comfort, C., 282
Zosuls, K. M., 346, 351, 353
Zukowski, A., 261, 262, 266, 267
Zusho, A., 361, 405

subject index

ectoderm of embryo, 79
educable mentally retarded (EMR), 245
education, 454–465. *See also* achievement;
    schools
    in adolescence, 460, 462–465
    bilingual, 276
    of children with disabilities, 468–472
    constructivist approach to, 454–455
    developmentally appropriate, 457, 458
    direct instruction approach to, 455
    for disadvantaged children, 457–459
    in early childhood, 456–460, 461
    electronic media and, 502–503
    extracurricular activities, 464–465
    gender and differences in, 12
    gender differences and, 354–355
    of gifted children, 251–252
    issues for children, 10
    memory teaching strategies, 214
    in middle and late childhood, 460
    moral, 378–381
    Piaget's theory and, 187–188
    poverty and, 465
    state-mandated tests and, 455–456
    Tools of the Mind curriculum, 194
    universal preschool, 460
    Vygotsky's theory and, 192–194
educational and developmental psychologist, 39
educational psychologist, 45
Education for All Handicapped Children
    Act, 471
effortful control, 301
egocentrism
    adolescent, 186
    in Piaget's theory, 180, 181, 186
elaboration (memory strategy), 213–214
electronic media
    aggression and, 500–501
    digitally mediated social environment,
        504–505
    learning and achievement and, 502–503
    prosocial behavior and, 501–502
elementary schools, 460
elementary school teacher, 44, 193
embryo, 79–80
embryonic period, 78–80
emotional abuse, 409
emotional and behavioral disorders, 469–470
emotional competence, 291–292
emotional development, 292–299
    in early childhood, 296–297
    in infancy, 292–296
    in middle and late childhood, 297–299
    parenting and, 297
emotional disorders, education and, 469–470
emotional expression
    in early childhood, 296
    infants' social relationships and, 293–295
emotional intelligence, 239
emotional regulation
    in early childhood, 297
    gender differences in, 357
    in infancy, 295–296
    peer relations and, 297, 433
    temperament and, 303
emotional understanding in children, 296–297
emotion-coaching parents, 398
emotion-dismissing parents, 297, 398

emotions, 290–293. *See also* temperament
    biological foundations of, 290
    cultural variations in, 290–291
    defined, 290
    in family processes, 397–398
    functionalist view of, 291
    moral feeling, 373–375
    in newborns, 293
    other-conscious, 293
    primary, 293
    self-conscious, 293, 296
emotion security theory, 417
empathy, 374–375
empiricists, 163
encoding, 202, 203, 209
endoderm of embryo, 79
environmental hazards, prenatal exposure to, 86
environmental influences. *See also* nature-
        nurture issue
    heredity-environment correlations, 69–70, 71
    on intelligence, 242–243
    on language development, 269, 278–280
    on overweight, 134
    shared and nonshared, 70–71
epigenetic view, 71
equality or equity, moral development and, 382
equilibration in Piaget's theory, 173
Erikson's psychosocial theory
    attachment in, 309
    defined, 21
    Freudian view contrasted with, 21
    life-span stages, 21–22
    strategies based on, 23
estradiol, 110–111
estrogens, 110, 347
ethics in research, 38–39
ethnic gloss, 39–40
ethnic identity, 338, 339–341
ethnicity. *See also* culture; diversity;
        socioeconomic status (SES)
    acculturation and, 422
    achievement and, 478
    bias in research, 39–40
    child care and, 314–315
    dating and, 484
    defined, 10, 11, 494
    differences and diversity within, 496–497
    diversity within, 11
    exercise participation and, 137
    families and parenting and, 421, 422
    identity and, 339–341
    immigration and, 494–495
    intelligence and, 245–246
    parenting styles and, 405–406
    prejudice and discrimination and, 497–498
    in schools, 465–466
    socioeconomic status and, 495–496
    of U.S. adolescents, 2000 to 2100, 494
ethnocentrism of culture, 485
ethological theory, 28, 31, 309
ethology, defined, 29
evocative genotype-environment correlations,
        69, 70
evolution, language development and, 277–278
evolutionary psychology, 52, 53–54, 348
evolutionary theory, 7–8
exceptional children teacher, 45
executive attention, 204, 206

executive function, 227
exemplars, moral, 376
exercise
    in adolescence, 136–137
    in childhood, 135–136, 137
exosystem, 29, 30, 396
expanding (teaching strategy), 279
expectations
    achievement and, 476–477
    culture and, 484
    perceptual development and, 178
    violation of (research method), 177
experiment, defined, 34–35
experimental group, 35
experimental research, 34–35, 36
experts, 210
explicit memory, 210, 211–212
expressive traits, 352
extracurricular activities, 464–465
extraversion/surgency, 301
extremely preterm infants, 96–97
extrinsic motivation, 472–473, 474
eyewitnesses, children as, 214–215

F

face perception, 157–158
false-belief task, 226
families. *See also* fathers; mothers; parenting
    changing social world and, 415–422
    child care and influence of, 318
    cognition and emotion in family processes,
        397–398
    cross-cultural studies, 420–421
    cultural-familial retardation, 250
    divorced, children in, 416–418
    ethnicity and, 421, 422, 495
    gay and lesbian parents, 419–420
    identity influenced by, 338–339
    intergenerational relationships, 412
    language development and, 269
    moral development and, 371
    multiple developmental trajectories in,
        398–399
    siblings, 385, 413–414
    sociocultural and historical changes in,
        399–401
    socioeconomic status and, 421–422
    socioeconomic variations in, 489
    stepfamilies, 418–419
    as systems, 396–397
    working parents and, 415–416
family and consumer science educator, 45
fathers. *See also* families; parenting
    as caregivers, 289, 313–314
    gender development and, 349–350
    postpartum adjustments by, 101–102
    smoking during mother's pregnancy, 89
    socialization strategies of, 350
    stepfathers, 419
fear, 294–295
femininity, traditional, 352
fertilization, 56, 57
fetal alcohol spectrum disorders (FASD), 84–85
fetal MRI, 63
fetal period, 80–81
fetus
    prenatal development, 78–90
    senses in, 160, 162

fine motor skills, 152–153
first habits and primary circular reactions, 174–175
first memories, 210–212
first words, 264–265
fish, mercury in, 88
fixed mindset, 475
Flynn effect, 242
focused attention, 204
folic acid, 87–88
forebrain, 114
forgiveness, 383
formal operational stage, 185–186
    abstract, idealistic, and logical thinking in, 185–186
    adolescent egocentrism in, 186
    described, 24, 25, 174, 185
fragile X syndrome, 59, 60
frames of mind, 238–239
Freudian theory
    of attachment, 308
    criticisms of, 21, 24
    early-later experience issue and, 19
    of gender, 349
    stages of development, 21
friendship, 440–444
    cliques, 445–446
    functions of, 440–442
    gender and, 443–444
    intimacy in, 440, 442, 443
    making friends, 443
    mixed-age, 444
    similarity in, 442
frontal lobes, 114, 117
functionalist view of emotions, 291
functional magnetic resonance imaging (fMRI), 33, 118
fuzzy trace theory, 209–210, 212–213

G

games
    as type of play, 439–440
    video, aggression and, 500–501
gastrointestinal infections, breast versus bottle feeding and, 128
gay couples, 419–420
gender
    aggression and, 355–356
    bias in research, 39
    context of, 360
    defined, 10, 11, 346, 347
    exercise participation and, 137
    friendship and, 443–444
    genetic differences in, 57
    juvenile delinquency and, 384
    moral development and, 371–372
    religiousness and, 388
    sex-linked chromosomal abnormalities, 59–60
    sex-linked genes, 58
    worldwide issues regarding, 12
gender development
    biological influences on, 347–348
    cognitive influences on, 350–352
    evolutionary psychology view of, 348
    guiding, 358
    social influences on, 348–350
gender identity, 346, 347
gender-role classification, 359

gender roles, 346, 347, 361
gender-role transcendence, 360
gender schema theory, 350–351
gender similarities and differences, 353–357
    cognitive, 354–355
    controversy about, 357
    physical, 354
    socioemotional, 355–357
gender stereotypes, 352–353, 360
gender typing, 346, 347
gene-linked abnormalities, 60–61
generativity versus stagnation stage, 22
genes. See also genetics
    cell division and, 56–57
    collaborative action of, 56
    defined, 55
    dominant-recessive principle, 58
    number and functions of, 55–56
    sex-linked, 58
    sources of variability, 57
genetic abnormalities
    chromosomal, 59–60
    dealing with, 61–62
    gene-linked, 60–61
genetic counselor, 46, 62
genetic imprinting, 58
genetic influences. See also nature-nurture issue
    on behavior, 54–55
    heredity-environment correlations, 69–70, 71
    on intelligence, 241–242
    on overweight, 134
genetics. See also genes
    abnormalities, 59–62
    gender differences, 57
    principles of, 58–59
    sources of variability, 57
    teratogen susceptibility and, 83
gene × environment (G × E) interaction, 71–72
genital herpes, prenatal development and, 87
genital stage, 21
genotype-environment correlations, 69–70
genotypes, 56, 57
German measles, prenatal development and, 86
germinal period, 78
gestures in infancy, 264
giftedness, 250–252
gist information, 209–210, 212–213
global empathy, 374–375
goal-directed behavior in infancy, 307
goal setting, achievement and, 477
gonads, 110
goodness of fit, 304
grammar development, 271
grasping reflex, 145
gratitude, 383
gross motor skills, 146–151
    in early childhood, 148–149
    in infancy, 146–148
    in middle and late childhood, 149–151
group participation domain of socialization, 399
growth
    in childhood, 108–109, 118
    in infancy, 108
    patterns of, 107–108
    in puberty, 109, 111
growth mindset, 475
guided learning domain of socialization, 399
guided participation, 192

H

habits, first, 174
habituation, 154, 155–156, 205
health and well-being. See also illness
    breast versus bottle feeding and, 128–131
    issues for children, 9
    poverty and, 126–127
health psychologist, 386
hearing, development of, 160–161
helpless orientation, 474
hemophilia, 61
heredity-environment correlations, 69–70, 71. See also genetic influences; nature-nurture issue
heritability of intelligence, 241–242
heroin, prenatal exposure to, 86
heteronomous morality, 366, 367
heterosexual romantic relationships, 446–447
hidden curriculum, 378
high-amplitude sucking, 156
high school counselor, 340
high school education, 462–464
hippocampus, 114
historical views of childhood, 6–7
HIV/AIDS, 87, 127
horizontal décalage, 184
hormones
    attachment and, 313
    changes after childbirth, 100
    changes during puberty, 110–111
    child maltreatment and, 409
    defined, 110
    gender influenced by, 347–348
Huntington disease, 61, 64
hypnosis during childbirth, 94
hypothalamus, 110, 354
hypothesis, defined, 20
hypothetical-deductive reasoning, 185–186

I

identity, 334–341
    commitment, 336
    components of, 334–335
    crisis or exploration, 336
    Erikson's view of, 22, 23, 335
    gender identity, 346, 347
    moral, 375
    social contexts and, 338–341
    statuses of, 336–337
identity achievement, 336
identity development
    in adolescence, 335–337
    in emerging adulthood, 337–338
    in infancy, 336
    religion and, 388–389
identity diffusion, 336
identity foreclosure, 336
identity moratorium, 336
identity versus identity confusion stage, 22, 23, 335
"I Have a Dream" (IHAD) dropout prevention program, 464
illness
    breast versus bottle feeding and, 128–129
    in childhood, 125–127
    poverty and, 126–127

heredity-environment correlations, 69–70, 71
intelligence and, 241–243
interactionist view of language, 280
nature, defined, 17
nurture, defined, 17
overview, 17–18
perceptual development and, 163–165
sensorimotor stage and, 178–180
shared and nonshared environmental experiences, 70–71
temperament and, 302–304
negative affectivity, 301
neglected children, 433
neglectful parenting, 404, 405
neighborhoods, socioeconomic variations in, 489
Neonatal Intensive Care Unit Network Neurobehavioral Scale (NNNS), 95–96
neonatal nurse, 46
neo-Piagetians, 188, 189–190
neural circuits, 114
neural tube, 82
neural tube defects, 82
neurogenesis, 82
neuronal migration, 82
neurons
blooming and pruning of, 117, 119
defined, 81
development of, 81–82, 116–117
function of, 114–115
neuroscience of intelligence, 240–241
neurotransmitters, 114, 313
newborns. *See also* infancy
assessing, 94–96
bonding by, 102
crying by, 263, 294
emotions in, 293
massage therapy for, 98–99
perceptual sensitivity in, 157, 160–162
preterm and low birth weight, 96–99
reflexes in, 144–145, 174, 175
small for date, 96
New Hope program, 492
niche-picking genotype-environment correlations, 70, 71
nicotine. *See* smoking
No Child Left Behind (NCLB) act, 455–456
noninvasive prenatal diagnosis (NIPD), 64
nonshared environmental experiences, 70–71
normal distribution, 236
number conservation, 183
number sense in infancy, 179
nurse and child-care health consultant, 47
Nurse Family Partnership, 89
nurse-midwife, 46
nutrition
improving, in low-income families, 132
in infancy, 127–128
malnutrition, 129–131
maternal, prenatal development and, 87–88

O

obesity, breast versus bottle feeding and, 128. *See also* overweight
object permanence, 176, 177, 178, 283

observation
laboratory, 31–32
naturalistic, 32
theories of child development and, 36
observational learning, 27
obstetrician/gynecologist, 46
occipital lobes, 114
occluded objects, perception of, 159
occupations, gender and, 12, 351, 353
operant conditioning theory, 27
operations in Piaget's theory, 180
oral stage, 21
organization
memory strategy, 213
in Piaget's theory, 173
organogenesis, 79–80, 83–84
orienting/investigative process, 204–205
orienting response, 156
original sin view, 6
other-conscious emotions, 293
otitis media, breast versus bottle feeding and, 128
ovarian cancer, breast versus bottle feeding and, 129
overt pathway to juvenile delinquency, 385
overweight
breast versus bottle feeding and, 128
in childhood, 132–135
in infancy, 127–128
maternal, 87
oxytocin, 92, 313

P

pain cry, 294
pain sensitivity in infancy, 161
parental leave, 314
parent educator, 403
parenting, 401–412. *See also* caring for children; families; fathers; mothers
adapting to developmental changes in children, 401–403
of adopted children, 67–68
authoritarian, 404, 405–406
authoritative, 404–405
caregiving styles and attachment, 312
child care and influence of, 318
child maltreatment, 408–410
coparenting, 408
cross-cultural studies, 420–421
disability and, 395
discipline, 377–378
domain-specific socialization and, 399
emotional development and, 297
emotion-coaching parents, 297, 398
emotion-dismissing parents, 297, 398
ethnicity and, 421, 422
fathers as caregivers, 289, 313–314
feeding styles, 131–132
by gay and lesbian couples, 419–420
gender development and, 349–350, 358
identity influenced by, 338–339
indulgent, 404, 405
issues for children, 9–10
juvenile delinquency and, 385
language development and, 269, 281
as managing children's lives, 403–404
moral development and, 377–378, 379
mothers as caregivers, 313

multiple developmental trajectories and, 398–399
neglectful, 404, 405
parent-adolescent relations, 388, 410–412
parent-child relations, 377, 431–432
peer relations and, 431–432
proactive strategies, 378
reciprocal socialization in, 396, 397
relational aggression and, 355–356
relational quality of, 377, 388
religiousness and, 388
by remarried parents, 419
scaffolding in, 396–397
self-esteem and, 333
smoking by parents, child health and, 125
socioeconomic status and, 421–422
sports guidelines, 151
styles of, 404–406
temperament and, 304, 305
transition to, 401–402
working parents, 415–416
parietal lobes, 114, 354
passive genotype-environment correlations, 69, 70
paternal factors in prenatal development, 89
pattern perception, 158
pediatrician, 46, 133
pediatric nurse, 46, 135
peer relations
in adolescence, 445–448
aggression and, 434–435
bullying, 435–437
in childhood, 429–431
cliques and crowds, 445–446
contexts of, 429
cross-cultural studies of, 430
dating and romantic, 446–448
emotional regulation and, 297, 433
friendship, 440–444
gossip about peers, 442
individual differences in, 429
moral reasoning and, 370, 371
necessity for development, 428
parent-child relations and, 431–432
peer pressure conformity and, 445
peer statuses, 433–434
perspective taking and, 432
play, 437–440
positive and negative, 429
rejection by peers, 434–435
social information-processing skills and, 433
peers, defined, 428
pelvic field defect, 348
perception, defined, 154
perceptual categorization, 217
perceptual constancy, 158–159
perceptual development, 153–165
cephalocaudal pattern of, 107–108
child's theory of mind and, 225
in early childhood, 160
ecological view of, 154
expectations and, 178
in infancy, 155–160
intermodal perception, 162
nature-nurture issue and, 163–165
in other sensory systems, 160–162
visual perception, 157–160
perceptual-motor coupling, 152, 164–165

performance orientation, 474–475

perinatal nurse, 93

periods of development, 16–17. *See also* stages of development; *specific periods*

personal domain of morality, 372

personal fable, 186

personality, moral development and, 375–376

perspective taking, 328–329, 432, 436

phallic stage, 21

phenotypes, 56, 57

phenylketonuria (PKU), 60, 61

phonics approach, 272

phonology, 260–261, 262, 266

physical abuse, 409

physical activities

exercise, 245–247

sports, 150–151

physical development, 107–113. *See also* brain development

in adolescence (puberty), 109–113

in childhood, 108–109

in infancy, 108

motor development, 143–153

patterns of growth, 107–108

perceptual development, 153–165

prenatal, 78–90

physiological measures, 33

Piaget's theory

adolescent self-understanding and, 326

concrete operational stage in, 24, 25, 174, 182, 183–185

defined, 24

education and, 187–188

evaluating, 178–180, 188–190

formal operational stage in, 24, 25, 174, 185–186

information-processing approach compared to, 203–204

moral development in, 366–367

neo-Piagetians, 188, 189–190

observations of his children and, 171

overview, 24–25, 174

peer relations in, 428–429

preoperational stage in, 24, 25, 174, 180–183

processes of development in, 172–173

sensorimotor stage in, 24, 173–180

Vygotsky's theory compared to, 25, 188, 195

pincer grip, 152

pituitary gland, 110

placenta, 79, 80

planning, achievement and, 477

play, 437–440

defined, 437

functions of, 437–438

types of, 438–440

play therapy, 438

popular children, 433

possible self, 327

postconventional reasoning, 369

postpartum blues, 100–101

postpartum depression, 100, 101

postpartum expert, 101

postpartum period, 99–102

bonding during, 102

defined, 99

emotional and psychological adjustments during, 100–102

physical adjustments during, 100

posture, development of, 146

poverty, 489–493

antipoverty programs, 491–493

education and, 465

illness and, 126–127

low birth weight infants and, 97

malnutrition and, 131

prevalence of, 490

psychological ramifications of, 490–491

risks to children living in, 491, 492

stressors increased with, 13

U.S. trends in, 13

in U.S. versus other nations, 14

power assertion (discipline technique), 377

practical intelligence, 238, 239

practice play, 438, 439

pragmatics, 262, 268

precocious puberty, 110

precocity, 250

preconventional reasoning, 368

prefrontal cortex, 117, 119

pregnancy. *See also* birth; prenatal development

conception, 78

emotional states and stress during, 88–89

maternal age, 88, 97

maternal diet and nutrition, 87–88

maternal diseases, 86–87

postpartum period, 99–102

prenatal care, 89

trimesters of, 81

weight gain during, 128

prejudice, ethnic, 497–498

prenatal care, 89

prenatal development, 78–90

of brain, 81–82

embryonic period, 78–80

fetal period, 80–81

germinal period, 78

hazards to, 83–89

of hearing, 160

normal, 90

trimesters of, 81

prenatal diagnostic tests, 63–64

prenatal period, 16

preoperational stage, 180–183

centration in, 182–183

described, 24, 25, 174, 180

substages, 180–182

prepared childbirth, 92

preschool children. *See* early childhood; infancy

preschools. *See* early childhood education

preschool teacher, 45

pretense/symbolic play, 438, 439

preterm infants, 96–99

primary emotions, 293

principle of persistence, 177

private speech, 191

proactive parenting strategies, 378

problem solving in childhood, 220–222

Project Head Start, 457–459

prosocial behavior

bullying and, 436

gender differences in, 357

moral development and, 382–383

television and electronic media and, 501–502

protection domain of socialization, 399

proximodistal pattern, 108

psychiatrist, 45

psychoactive drugs as teratogens, 84–86

psychoanalytic theories

child development issues and, 31

defined, 21

Erikson's (psychosocial), 21–22, 23

evaluating, 22, 24

of gender, 348, 349

moral feeling and, 373–374

psychosexual (Freud), 21, 24

psychosexual stages, 24

psychosocial moratorium, 335

psychosocial theory. *See* Erikson's psychosocial theory

puberty, 109–113. *See also* adolescence

body image and, 112

defined, 108

determinants of, 109–111

early and late maturation, 112–113

growth spurt in, 109, 111

sexual maturation in, 111–112

punishment. *See also* discipline

corporal, culture and, 406

corporal, ethnicity and, 405–406

corporal, issues for, 406–407

marital conflict and hostility as predictors of, 406

moral development and, 368, 377–378

purpose, achievement and, 477–478

Q

Quantum Opportunities program, 493

R

rapport talk, 356

Raven's Progressive Matrices tests, 244, 245

reaction-time task, 202

reading skills development, 271–273

recasting (teaching strategy), 279

reciprocal socialization, 396, 397

reciprocity domain of socialization, 399

reconstructive memory, 214–215

references for journal articles, 37

reflexes, 144–145, 174, 175

reflexive smile, 294

Reggio Emilia approach, 453

rejected children, 433–434

rejection by peers, 433–435

relational aggression, 355–356

religious development, 387–389

REM sleep, 121

report talk, 356

reproductive technology, 64–65

research

bias minimization, 39–40

correlational, 34

data collection methods, 30–33

descriptive, 34

development of methods for, 7–8

ethics in, 38–39

experimental, 34–35

journal publication of, 37

scientific, defined, 20

scientific method in, 20, 30

social policy decisions and, 13, 14

time span of, 35–36

twin studies in, 51

research designs, 33–36

researcher, 44
resilience, 11, 13
respiratory tract infections, breast versus bottle feeding and, 128
results section of journal articles, 37
Rh-factor, 86
romantic relationships, 446–448
rooting reflex, 144, 145
Rosenberg Scale of Self-Esteem, 330
Rubella, prenatal development and, 86

S

satire, 274, 275
scaffolding, 191, 396–397
schemas, 209, 211, 351
schema theory
    defined, 209
    of gender, 350–351
schemes in Piaget's theory, 172, 175, 176
school counselor, 45
school psychologist, 45
schools. *See also* achievement; education
    accountability from, 455–456
    cheating in, 380–381
    elementary, 460
    ethnicity in, 465–466
    extracurricular activities in, 464–465
    hidden curriculum in, 378
    high, 462–464
    middle or junior high, 460, 462
    moral development and, 378–381
    preschools, 456–460
    socioeconomic status and, 465–466
    socioeconomic variations in, 489
scientific method, 20, 30
scientific thinking in childhood, 218–220
secondary circular reactions substage, 175
second-language learning, 274–275
securely attached babies, 310
selective attention, 204
self-concept
    assessing, 330–331
    defined, 330
self-conscious emotions, 293, 296
self-determination, motivation and, 473
self-efficacy, achievement and, 476–478
self-esteem, 329–333
    assessing, 330–331
    crowd membership and, 446
    defined, 329–330
    developmental changes in, 331
    global, domains of competence and, 331
    increasing children's, 333
    variations in, 332–333
self-image in adolescence, 332
self-modification, 203
self-monitoring, achievement and, 477
Self-Perception Profile for Adolescents, 330–331
Self-Perception Profile for Children, 330–331
self-regulation, 301
self-responsibility, motivation and, 473–474
self-talk in Vygotsky's theory, 191
self-understanding, 324–327
    in adolescence, 326–327
    defined, 324
    in early childhood, 325–326
    in infancy, 324–325
    in middle and late childhood, 326

semantics, 262, 267–268
sensation, defined, 154
sensorimotor play, 438–439
sensorimotor stage, 173–180
    A-not-B error, 176, 178
    described, 24, 173, 174
    evaluating, 176, 178–180
    expectations and, 178
    nature-nurture issue and, 178–180
    object permanence in, 176, 177, 178
    substages, 174–176
sensory development. *See* perceptual development
separation protest, 295
seriation, 184
service learning, 379–380, 387–388
sex-linked chromosomal abnormalities, 59–60
sex-linked genes, 58
sexual abuse, 409
sexual activity, gender and restrictions in, 12
sexual maturation, 111–113
sexual minority youth, romantic relationships in, 447–448
shape constancy, 159
shared environmental experiences, 70–71
shared sleeping, 121–122
short-term memory, 208
siblings, 385, 413–414
sickle-cell anemia, 60–61
similarity in friendship, 442
simple reflexes substage, 174, 175
size constancy, 158–159
sleep, 120–124
    in adolescence, 123–124
    in childhood, 123
    in infancy, 120–123
sleep/wake cycle, 120–121
slow-to-warm-up child, 300, 301
small for date infants, 96
smell sensitivity in infancy, 162
smiling, 294
smoking, 85, 89, 125, 412
social cognition, 327–329
social cognitive theory
    child development issues and, 31
    defined, 27
    evaluating, 28
    evolutionary psychology critiqued in, 54
    of gender, 348, 349–350
    of morality, 373
    observational learning in, 27
    overview and evaluation, 27–28
social constructivist approach, 195
social conventional reasoning, 372
social information-processing skills, peer relations and, 433
socialization
    domain-specific, 399
    parenting styles and, 406
    reciprocal, 396, 397
    strategies of fathers and mothers, 350
social orientation, 306–307
social play, 438, 439
social policy, 13, 14
social referencing, 307–308
social relationships
    emotional expression and, 293–295
    in infancy, 430

social role theory of gender, 348–349
social smile, 294
social sophistication of infants, 307–308
social worker, 45–46
sociocultural cognitive theory. *See* Vygotsky's theory
sociocultural contexts. *See* contexts
socioeconomic status (SES). *See also* poverty
    categories of, 488
    children from low-SES backgrounds, 489
    children in divorced families and, 418
    defined, 10, 11, 488
    ethnicity and, 495–496
    families and, 421–422
    inequalities in, 11
    juvenile delinquency and, 385–386
    language development and, 269
    schools and, 465–466
    variations in, 489
socioemotional processes, 15–16
sociometric status, 433
spatial intelligence, 238, 239
special education teacher, 45
specificity of learning, 147
speech therapist, 46
spina bifida, 61, 64, 82
spiritual and religious development, 387–389
sports, 150–151
stages of birth, 91
stages of development
    Erikson's life-span stages, 21–22
    Freudian theory of, 21, 24
    moral, Kohlberg's, 367–372
    periods of development, 16–17
    Piaget's theory of, 24–25, 173–186
standardized tests, 32–33, 36
Stanford-Binet test, 236–237
startle (Moro) reflex, 144, 145
statuses
    of identity, 336–337
    peer, 433–434
status offenses, 384
stepfamilies, 418–419
stepping reflex, 145
stereotype threat, 246, 247
stranger anxiety, 295
Strange Situation, 310–311
strategy construction, 203
stress
    during childbirth, reducing, 93–94
    coping with, in childhood, 298–299
    maternal, 88
    in preterm infants, reducing, 98–99
subcultures, 488
sucking, high-amplitude, 156
sucking reflex, 144, 145
sudden infant death syndrome (SIDS), 122–123, 128
supervisor of gifted and talented education, 252
surveys, 32, 36
sustained attention, 204–205, 206–207
swimming reflex, 145
symbolic function substage, 180–182
synapses, 114, 117, 118
syntax, 261–262, 267
syphilis, prenatal development and, 87

T

tabula rasa view, 6
taste sensitivity in infancy, 162
Tay-Sachs disease, 61
teachers
  autonomy-supportive, 473
  as cultural mediators, 466
  expectations of, 476–477
teaching. *See* education; schools
technology, 499–505
  aggression and, 500–501
  computers and the Internet, 503–505
  learning and achievement and, 502–503
  media use, 500
  prosocial behavior and, 501–502
  television and electronic media, 500–503
technology revolution, 499–500
telegraphic speech, 266
television
  aggression and, 500–501
  learning and achievement and, 502–503
  prosocial behavior and, 501–502
temperament, 299–305
  biological influences on, 302
  classification of, 300–302
  defined, 299
  development of, 302–304
  goodness of fit and, 304
temporal lobes, 114
teratogens
  defined, 82, 83
  factors influencing effects of, 83–84
  medications, 84
  psychoactive drugs, 84–86
teratology, 83
tertiary circular reactions, novelty, and curiosity
    substage, 175–176
testosterone, 110–111
tests
  academic, state-mandated, 455–456
  intelligence, 236–237, 244–248
  prenatal diagnostic, 63–64
  standardized, 32–33
theories of child development. *See also specific*
    theories
  behavioral, 26–27
  child development issues and, 31
  cognitive, 24–26
  eclectic orientation toward, 30
  ecological, 29–30
  ethological, 28
  overview, 20–21

psychoanalytic, 21–24
  research methods and, 36
  social cognitive, 27–28
theory, defined, 20
theory of mind, child's, 225–227
thinking and thought, 216–224
  abstract, idealistic, and logical, 185–186
  in adolescence, 223–224
  in childhood, 218–222
  child's theory of mind, 225–227
  cognition in family processes, 397–398
  convergent thinking, 252, 253
  critical thinking, 218, 223
  decision making, 223–224, 225
  divergent thinking, 252, 253
  in infancy, 216–218
  intuitive thought substage, 182
  language and, 191–192
  moral reasoning, 366–372
  problem solving, 220–223
  scientific thinking, 218–220
  thinking, defined, 216
time span of research, 35–36
toddlers. *See* infancy
tonic neck reflex, 145
Tools of the Mind curriculum, 194
top-dog phenomenon, 462
touch sensitivity in infancy, 161
toxic wastes, prenatal exposure to, 86
toy designer, 219
tracking, 156–157, 159
transitivity, 185
triarchic theory of intelligence, 238
trimesters, 81
triple screen blood test, 64
trophoblast, 78
trust versus mistrust stage, 22, 23
Turner syndrome, 59, 60
twin studies
  in behavior genetics, 69
  defined, 69
  in vitro fertilization and, 65
  on intelligence, 241
  separated and reared apart, 51
  of sex reassignment, 348
two-word utterances, 265–266

U

ultrasound sonography, 63
umbilical cord, 79, 80
universal preschool education, 460
university professor, 44

V

values clarification, 378–379
vasopression, attachment and, 313
verbal intelligence, 238, 239
verbatim memory trace, 209–210, 212
very preterm infants, 96–97
victims of bullying, 435–437
video games, aggression and, 500–501
vigilance, 204
violation of expectations, 177
visual acuity in infancy, 157
visual perception, 157–160
  in early childhood, 160
  in infancy, 155, 157–160
visual preference method, 154, 155
vocabulary development, 267–268,
    270–271
vocalizations in infancy, 263
Vygotsky's theory
  defined, 25
  evaluating, 195–196
  language and thought in, 191–192
  overview, 25–26
  Piaget's theory compared to, 25,
    188, 195
  scaffolding in, 191
  teaching strategies based on, 192–194
  zone of proximal development in, 190–191,
    192–193

W

walking, learning, 146–147
Wechsler scales, 237
Wernicke's area, 278
whole-language approach, 272
Williams syndrome, 282–283
work, gender and, 12, 351, 353
working memory, 208–209, 216
working parents, 415–416
writing skills development, 273–274

X

X-ray radiation, prenatal exposure to, 86
XYY syndrome, 59, 60

Z

zone of proximal development (ZPD), 190–191,
    192–193
zygote, 56, 57, 78